T0213547

Lecture Notes in Computer Science　　10592

Commenced Publication in 1973
Founding and Former Series Editors:
Gerhard Goos, Juris Hartmanis, and Jan van Leeuwen

More information about this series at http://www.springer.com/series/7410

Tatsuaki Okamoto · Yong Yu
Man Ho Au · Yannan Li (Eds.)

Provable Security

11th International Conference, ProvSec 2017
Xi'an, China, October 23–25, 2017
Proceedings

 Springer

Editors
Tatsuaki Okamoto 🆔
NTT Laboratories
Tokyo
Japan

Yong Yu 🆔
Shaanxi Normal University
Xi'an
China

Man Ho Au 🆔
Hong Kong Polytechnic University
Hong Kong
China

Yannan Li 🆔
University of Wollongong
Wollongong, NSW
Australia

ISSN 0302-9743 ISSN 1611-3349 (electronic)
Lecture Notes in Computer Science
ISBN 978-3-319-68636-3 ISBN 978-3-319-68637-0 (eBook)
https://doi.org/10.1007/978-3-319-68637-0

Library of Congress Control Number: 2017956072

LNCS Sublibrary: SL4 – Security and Cryptology

Printed on acid-free paper

This Springer imprint is published by Springer Nature
The registered company is Springer International Publishing AG
The registered company address is: Gewerbestrasse 11, 6330 Cham, Switzerland

Preface

The 11th International Conference on Provable Security (ProvSec 2017) was held in Xi'an, China, October 23–25, 2017. The conference was organized by Shaanxi Normal University, Xidian University, and Xi'an University of Posts and Telecommunications.

The conference program consisted of two keynote speeches, four invited talks, and 29 contributed papers. We would like to express our special thanks to the distinguished speakers, David Pointcheval from Ecole normale supérieure, Giuseppe Ateniese from Stevens Institute of Technology, Mauro Barni from the University of Siena, Willy Susilo from the University of Wollongong, Joseph Liu from Monash University, and Man Ho Au from Hong Kong Polytechnic University, who gave very enlightening talks.

Out of 76 submissions from 18 countries, 29 papers were selected, presented at the conference, and are included in the proceedings. The accepted papers cover a range of topics in the field of provable security research, including attribute-based cryptography, cloud security, encryption, digital signatures, homomorphic encryption, and blockchain-based cryptography.

The success of this event depended critically on the help and hard work of many people, whose help we gratefully acknowledge. First, we heartily thank the Program Committee and the additional reviewers, listed on the following pages, for their careful and thorough reviews. Most of the papers were reviewed by at least three people, and many by four or five. Significant time was spent discussing the papers. Thanks must also go to the hard-working shepherds for their guidance and helpful advice on improving a number of papers. We also thank the general co-chairs, Bo Yang, Hui Li, and Dong Zheng, for the excellent organization of the conference.

We sincerely thank the authors of all submitted papers. We further thank the authors of accepted papers for revising papers according to the various reviewer suggestions and for returning the source files in good time. The revised versions were not checked by the Program Committee, and thus the authors bear final responsibility for their contents. We would also like to thank the Steering Committee and local Organizing Committee.

We gratefully acknowledge the support of K.C.Wong Education Foundation, Hong Kong. We also want to express our gratitude to our generous sponsors: Springer, Shanghai HeFu Holding(Group) Company Limited, Shaanxi Normal University, Xidian University, Xi'an University of Posts and Telecommunications, National 111 Project for Mobile Internet Security, and State Key Laboratory of Integrated Services Networks. Finally, we would like to express our thanks to Springer again for continuing to support the ProvSec conference and for help in the production of the conference proceedings.

October 2017

Tatsuaki Okamoto
Yong Yu

Organization
ProvSec 2017
The 11th International Conference on Provable Security

Jointly organized by

Shaanxi Normal University
Xidian University
Xi'an University of Posts and Telecommunications

Honorary Co-chairs

Jianfeng Ma   Xidian University, China
Xiaoming Wang   Shaanxi Normal University, China

General Co-chairs

Bo Yang   Shaanxi Normal University, China
Hui Li   Xidian University, China
Dong Zheng   Xi'an University of Posts and Telecommunications, China and
                      Westone Cryptologic Research Center/Morse Laboratory,
                      China

Program Co-chairs

Tatsuaki Okamoto   NTT, Japan
Yong Yu   Shaanxi Normal University, China

Organizing Co-chairs

Zhenqiang Wu   Shaanxi Normal University, China
Qiqi Lai   Shaanxi Normal University, China
Yanwei Zhou   Shaanxi Normal University, China

Publication Co-chairs

Man Ho Au   Hong Kong Polytechnic University, Hong Kong, China
Yannan Li   University of Wollongong, Australia

Publicity Co-chairs

Jianfeng Wang	Xidian University, China
Kaitai Liang	Manchester Metropolitan University, UK
Jianbing Ni	University of Waterloo, Canada

Website Co-chairs

Yanqi Zhao	Shaanxi Normal University, China
Ru Meng	Shaanxi Normal University, China

Registration Co-chairs

Yujie Ding	Shaanxi Normal University, China
Yuanxiao Li	Shaanxi Normal University, China

Program Committee

Janaka Alawatugoda	University of Peradeniya, Sri Lanka
Elena Andreeva	KU Leuven, Belgium
Man Ho Au	Hong Kong Polytechnic University, Hong Kong, China
Colin Boyd	Norwegian University of Science and Technology, Norway
Aniello Castiglione	University of Salerno, Italy
Kefei Chen	Hangzhou Normal University, China
Liqun Chen	University of Surrey, UK
Rongmao Chen	National University of Defense Technology, China
Xiaofeng Chen	Xidian University, China
Céline Chevalier	École normale supérieure, France
Kim-Kwang Raymond Choo	The University of Texas at San Antonio, USA
Bernardo David	Aarhus University, Denmark
Hongzhen Du	Baoji University of Arts and Sciences, China
Christian Esposito	University of Salerno, Italy
Jinguang Han	Nanjing University of Finance and Economics, China
Debiao He	Wuhan University, China
Qiong Huang	South China Agricultural University, China
Xinyi Huang	Fujian Normal University, China
Vincenzo Iovino	University of Luxembourg, Luxembourg
Ryo Kikuchi	NTT, Japan
Junzuo Lai	Jinan University, China
Fagen Li	University of Electronic Science and Technology of China, China
Jin Li	Guangzhou University, China
Shundong Li	Shaanxi Normal University, China
Yannan Li	University of Wollongong, Australia
Xiaodong Lin	University of Ontario Institute of Technology, Canada

Additional Reviewers

Anada, Hiroaki
Aono, Yoshinori
Arita, Seiko
Becerra, Jose
Biwen, Chen
Castiglione, Arcangelo
Chakraborty, Suvradip
Chillotti, Ilaria
Chuah, Chai Wen
Cui, Hui
Cui, Yuzhao
Dai, Feifei
Datta, Pratish
Dowling, Benjamin
Espitau, Thomas
Ferradi, Houda
Flores, Manuela
Galdi, Clemente
Ganesh, Chaya
Genc, Ziya A.
Guo, Hua
Guo, Qingwen
Hu, Zhi

Huang, Jianye
Huang, Yan
Jiang, Yan
Kelarev, Andrei
Lai, Jianchang
Lai, Qiqi
Larangeira, Mario
Li, Hongbo
Li, Huige
Li, Na
Li, Qinyi
Li, Xingxin
Lin, Chengjun
Liu, Dongxi
Liu, Jianghua
Naito, Yusuke
Nguyen, Khoa
Sun, Yang
Takashima, Katsuyuki
Tan, Benjamin Hong
    Meng
Thillard, Adrian
Wang, Fuqun

Wang, Hao
Wang, Huige
Wang, Zheng
Wu, Ge
Xu, Dongqing
Xu, Zhiyan
Xuan Phuong, Tran Viet
Yan, Dingyu
Yang, Xu
Yang, Xuechao
Yoneyama, Kazuki
Zhang, Huang
Zhang, Juanyang
Zhang, Kai
Zhang, Wentao
Zhang, Yaqin
Zhang, Yudi
Zhang, Yuexin
Zhang, Zheng
Zhao, Ling
Zhou, Yanwei
Zhu, Youwen

Contents

Proxy Re-encryption and Functional Encryption

Protocols

Secure Cloud Storage and Computing

Provably Secure Self-Extractable Encryption

Zhi Liang[1,2], Qianhong Wu[1,2]($\boxtimes$), Weiran Liu[1], Jianwei Liu[1,2], and Fu Xiao[3]($\boxtimes$)

[1] School of Electronic and Information Engineering,
Beihang University, Beijing, China
seaeory@126.com, qianhong.wu@buaa.edu.cn, liuweiran900217@gmail.com,
liujianwei@buaa.edu.cn
[2] State Key Laboratory of Cryptology, P.O. Box 5159, Beijing 100878, China
[3] School of Computer, Nanjing University of Posts and Telecommunications,
Nanjing, China
xiaof@njupt.edu.cn

Abstract. There is an increasing demand of data sharing via cloud. Data privacy and secrecy protections are arguably the major challenges in such applications. It is widely suggested to encrypt outsourced data using advanced encryption primitives for flexible sensitive data sharing in cloud. In all existing asymmetric based systems, a subtle issue is that the data owner itself cannot read the encrypted and outsourced data. This raises a problem for the data owner when she needs to access the outsourced data but locally there is no copy in the clear text form. To cope with this problem, we formalize a new framework, referred to as Self-EXtractable Encryption (SEXE). In addition to the normal functionalities of an advanced encryption primitive, SEXE is equipped with a useful self-extractability. With this property, the data owner can always access her encrypted data. We propose a generic SEXE construction from any advanced encryption primitives. Following the proposed generic construction, we instantiate several typical SEXE systems, including Self-EXtractable Identity-Based Encryption (SEXIBE), Self-Extractable Attribute-Based Encryption (SXABE) in Key-Policy setting and in Ciphertext-Policy setting.

Keywords: Cloud storage · Data sharing · Data secrecy · Self-Extractable Encryption

1 Introduction

With the development of communication techniques and the popularity of portable computing devices, people are shifting away from traditional desktops and laptops to cloud storage. Through networks and mobile devices, users are able to seamlessly interact with cloud service providers to enjoy new types of services that were not available before. Cloud storage systems enable users to share their data with peers so that the latter can access their data stored in clouds anywhere and anytime. For instance, users can store their private photos,

© Springer International Publishing AG 2017
T. Okamoto et al. (Eds.): ProvSec 2017, LNCS 10592, pp. 3–23, 2017.
https://doi.org/10.1007/978-3-319-68637-0_1

videos, or other documents on cloud storage providers such as Dropbox, iCloud, so that they can be remotely accessed and shared when necessary.

Most challenging obstacles for the wide usage of cloud storage systems may be the concerns about data privacy and secrecy. Users often hesitate to use cloud storage systems because of the worries of losing control on the outsourced data. Typical method to protect data security is to encrypt them before outsourcing. Encryption is a standard approach to protect the data outsourced to clouds. However, traditional encryption systems cannot enforce fine-grained access control, which brings difficulties for flexible data sharing. To address this problem, advanced encryption primitives, e.g., Identity-Based Encryption [8], Attribute-Based Encryption [35] have been proposed and extensively employed in many cloud storage systems. In these systems, a data owner can specify data attributes for the outsourced data. Each data owner has its own secret key that is associated with key attributes. Access can be done only if the key attributes match the data attributes.

A subtle problem arises when such advanced encryption primitive is used to secure data in cloud. In all existing schemes, there exists a Trusted Keying Authority (TKA) responsible for secret key distribution. The schemes require all data users to be authorized by TKA to get their secret keys. Data owners are not required to be authorized by TKA. They can directly encrypt the data using the public keys. However, after encrypting the data, the data owner herself cannot extract the data hidden in the ciphertext since she does not have any secret keys. In a cloud storage setting, the encrypted files will be outsourced to some cloud server and there is no local copy of the files in the clear, except some meta-data of the file or file identifiers. These meta-data or file identifiers can only used to check the integrity of the files or as clues to retrieve the outsourced files, instead of recovering the encrypted files. Consequently, the outsourced files are no longer accessible to their owners, although the data owners authorized peers can access the files. Clearly, this is undesirable in practice.

At the first glance, this problem may be trivially addressed. One trivial solution is asking the data owner to simultaneously encrypt to herself a copy of the file. However, this would incur significant computation and storage cost if the file is large. Another trivial solution is to let the data owner also specify herself as a data user of the encrypted file. This is difficult in practice. First, advanced encryption primitive is a closed encryption system, i.e., before the data users hold a secret key they must first register to TKA. This implies that each possible data owner has to first register to TKA as an authorized data user, which badly makes the maximal number of data users in such system unnecessarily large. Note that the complexity of most existing systems rely on the scale of the data users. Second, some advanced encryption instantiations, e.g., Identity-Based Encryption (IBE), only allow one receiver in an encryption, which makes it impossible to allow the data owner as an extra receiver.

We investigate how to enable a data owner to access his/her own encrypted data with a cost as low as possible. To achieve this goal, we formalize a new framework, referred to as Self-EXtractable Encryption (SEXE). In addition to the normal functionalities of a regular advanced encryption primitive, SEXE is equipped with a useful self-extractability. Roughly speaking, the data owner can always access her encrypted data in SEXE. We propose a generic SEXE construction from any advanced encryption scheme. The construction only additionally requires a pseudo random function, a symmetric encryption cipher, and some hash functions, all of which are efficient in terms of computation. The desirable self-extractability only incurs a marginal cost, while posing little extra cost on regular receivers. Following the generic construction, we instantiate several typical SEXE schemes, including Self-Extractable Identity-Based Encryption (SEX-IBE), Self-Extractable Attribute-Based Encryption (SXABE) in Key-Policy setting and in Ciphertext-Policy setting.

2 Related Work

Cloud storage follows the area of "database-as-a-service" paradigm, which is a classic data storage topic that has been studied since 2000s. The intended purpose of cloud storage is to enable data owners to outsource their data on the Internet to service providers [20, 21]. The basic idea to protect data privacy and secrecy in cloud storage is to enforce data access control by encrypting the data before outsourcing. Only the authorized data users can have access [2]. Classic schemes employ traditional symmetric key/asymmetric cryptosystems to realize access control [16, 27]. As the number of data users increases, especially for cloud-based data storage systems that potentially allow a vast number of data users, the systems suffer from complicated entity and key managements.

Researches have been devoted to entity and key management problems. In 2001, Boneh and Franklin [8] proposed a new encryption primitive, named Identity-Based Encryption (IBE), the concept of which was first introduced by Shamir [36]. Compared with the traditional asymmetric encryption system, the public keys in IBE can be arbitrary strings, such as social security numbers, email addresses, and phone numbers. Instead of generating the secret key by the data owner itself, a Trusted Key Authority (TKA) is employed in IBE for user authentication and key distribution. Since IBE brings flexibilities for user authentication and entity management, many advanced data access control schemes started to leverage IBE as the basic encryption primitive [12, 19]. Schemes exploiting IBE and various other cryptographic primitives have been proposed to achieve more flexible data sharing functionalities, including cross-domain [38] and emergency sharing [39] for specific data outsourcing applications.

The IBE primitive only allows to assign one receiver in an encryption, which brings difficulties for multi-entity data sharing application scenarios. Briefly speaking, the access policy in IBE is "exact string match", which is a limited data access control mechanism. Although several encryption primitives and schemes, e.g., Hierarchical IBE [15, 24], (Identity-Based) Broadcast Encryption [9, 14], Proxy Re-Encryption [4], were proposed and/or applied to partially support one-to-many data sharing mechanism in cloud storage applications [3], access policies in all of which are somewhat restricted. How to support expressive access policy in encryption primitives remained as an open problem. In 2005, Sahai and

Waters introduced the concept of Attribute-Based Encryption (ABE) [35], in which the access policy can be expressed as a monotonic boolean formula. For example, the access policy for an outsourced data from an university can be "CS AND (Ph.D OR Masters)". The Ph.D or masters in the department of Computer Science can have access to the data. Later, the concept of ABE was extended to be Key-Policy ABE (KP-ABE) [18] (in which the boolean formula is assigned to the secret key) and Ciphertext-Policy ABE (CP-ABE) [6] (in which the boolean formula is assigned to the encrypted data).

With the capability to provide fine-grained access control over encrypted data, ABE is suitable for cloud storage applications. In 2010, Yu *et al.* proposed a KP-ABE based access control scheme for cloud storage [43]. Works [25,42] have also been done to enforce data access control with multi-authority cloud storage systems. To further support search mechanism over encrypted data, Zheng *et al.* [45] and Sun *et al.* [40] respectively proposed two ABE schemes that allow keyword search. Most recently, Zhang *et al.* [44] leverages multiple cryptographic primitives, including CP-ABE [6], Homomorphic Encryption [32], and Oblivious Transfer [11] to construct an outsourced photo sharing and searching scheme.

All above schemes neglect the situation where the data owners, very likely, need to access his/her own encrypted data. We are interested in practical solutions for achieving the desirable self-extractability property.

3   Techniques Preliminaries

3.1   Syntax

We denote $[a, b]$ as the set $\{a, a+1, \cdots, b\}$ containing consecutive integers, and $[a]$ as shorthand for $[1, a]$. The cardinality of a set S is denoted by $|S|$. We write $s \xleftarrow{R} S$ to denote the action of choosing s from a uniform random distribution over the set S, and $s_1, s_2, \cdots, s_n \xleftarrow{R} S$ with $n \in \mathbb{N}$ as shorthand for $s_1 \xleftarrow{R} S, \cdots, s_n \xleftarrow{R} S$. We use $\mathbb{Z}_p^{m \times n}$ to denote the $m \times n$ matrices with entries in $\mathbb{Z}_p$. For a vector $\boldsymbol{v}$ (row vector or column vector), we denote by $\boldsymbol{v}_i$ the i-th element of the vector $\boldsymbol{v}$.

3.2   Pseudo Random Functions

Our construction exploits a classical cryptographic primitive named pseudo random function (PRF), which was introduced by Goldreich, Goldwasser and Micali [17]. A PRF system consists of a keyed function PRF and a key space $\mathcal{K}_{PRF}$ such that for a randomly chosen key $\kappa \in \mathcal{K}_{PRF}$, the outputs of the function $\mathsf{PRF}(\kappa, \chi)$ for any given input $\chi \in \{0, 1\}^*$ look like random numbers [22].

In practice, such PRF is efficient and easy to be implemented. A general approach is to treat the key κ as the password, the given input χ as the salt, and runs classical key derivation technique to produce the output. We recommend following PKCS #5 Version 2.0 Scheme 1, PKCS #5 Version 2.0 Scheme 2, or PKCS #12 Version 1.0 specifications (all of which are standardized in RFC 2898) to implement such PRF.

3.3 Bilinear Groups

Our instantiation demonstrations for self-extractable encryption are based on bilinear groups. Here we review its definition and requirements following the notation of [13]. The bilinear groups can be defined by a group generator $\mathcal{G}$ that takes the security parameter $\lambda \in \mathbb{N}$ as input and outputs a quad-tuple $(p, \mathbb{G}, \mathbb{G}_T, e)$, in which $\mathbb{G}, \mathbb{G}_T$ are two cyclic groups of prime order p, and e is an efficient map $e : \mathbb{G} \times \mathbb{G} \to \mathbb{G}_T$ satisfying the following properties.

- *Bilinearity*: for all $g, h \in \mathbb{G}$ and $a, b \in \mathbb{Z}_p$, we have that $e(g^a, h^b) = e(g, h)^{ab}$.
- *Non-degeneracy*: there exists at least an element $g \in \mathbb{G}$ such that $e(g, g)$ is a generator for the group $\mathbb{G}_T$.

3.4 Access Structures and Linear Secret Sharing Schemes

We next review the formal definitions of access structures and linear secret sharing schemes (LSSS), which will be used in our self-extractable ABE instantiations. Here we follow the definition given by Beimel [5].

Definition 1 *(Access Structure [5]). Consider a set of parties $\mathcal{U}$. A collection $\mathbb{A} \subseteq 2^{\mathcal{U}}$ is monotone if for all B, C, we have that if $B \in \mathbb{A}$ and $B \subseteq C$, then $C \in \mathbb{A}$. An access structure (monotone access structure) on $\mathcal{U}$ is a collection (monotone collection) $\mathbb{A} \subseteq 2^{\mathcal{U}} \setminus \{\emptyset\}$. The sets in $\mathbb{A}$ are called the authorized sets, and the sets not in $\mathbb{A}$ are called the unauthorized sets.*

In most of previous works [6,18,25], the access structure is described with a tree called access tree. Each non-leaf node of the access tree is a threshold gate, while each leaf node is described by an attribute. One data user's access capability matches the access structure if there is a sub-tree containing the root node such that all threshold gates in the sub-tree are satisfied. In recent ABE schemes, the access structure is represented by linear secret sharing schemes (LSSS) [33,37] that can be defined as follows.

Definition 2 *(Linear Secret Sharing Schemes (LSSS) [5,33]). Let p be a prime number and let $\mathcal{U}$ be a set of parties. Let $M \in \mathbb{Z}_p^{l \times n}$ be an $l \times n$ matrix with entries in $\mathbb{Z}_p$. Let $\rho : [l] \to \mathcal{U}$ be a function that labels the row of M with parties in $\mathcal{U}$. A secret sharing scheme Π for access structure $\mathbb{A}$ over a set of parties $\mathcal{U}$ is a linear secret sharing scheme (LSSS) in $\mathbb{Z}_p$ if:*

- *The shares of a secret $s \in \mathbb{Z}_p$ for each party comprise of a vector over $\mathbb{Z}_p$.*
- *For each access structure $\mathbb{A}$, there exists an corresponding matrix $M \in \mathbb{Z}_p^{l \times n}$ and a function $\rho : [l] \to \mathcal{U}$ to represent the access structure. One can compute the shares of s by first constructing a column vector $v = (s, r_2, \cdots, r_n)$, where $r_2, \cdots, r_n \xleftarrow{R} \mathbb{Z}_p$, and then outputting $M \cdot v \in \mathbb{Z}_p^{l \times 1}$ as the vector of l shares. The share $\lambda_i = (Mv)_i$ belongs to the party $\rho(i)$, where $(Mv)_i$ denotes the i-th column element in Mv.*

Lewko and Waters [29] showed that any access structures represented as boolean formulas can be efficiently converted to be an LSSS policy (M, ρ). Later, Liu *et al.* [31] proposed an efficient LSSS matrix generation algorithm from any threshold access trees. Therefore, access tree and LSSS are identical access structure representations both in theory and in practice. In our self-extractable ABE instantiations, we describe the access policy using LSSS.

4   System Overview

4.1   System Model for Cryptography-Based Cloud Storage

We follow the generic cryptography-based cloud storage system model [37,43]. The typical cloud storage system architecture is shown in Fig. 1. There mainly exist four kinds of parties: Trusted Key Authority (TKA), Data Owner, Cloud Storage Server, and Data User.

TKA is responsible for initializing the system and issuing/managing secret keys for data users according to their access capabilities. Data owners share their data to data users via the cloud storage server. To achieve privacy and secrecy of the shared data, data owners encrypt the data with on-demand access policies before uploading. Cloud storage server maintains well-encrypted data and responses to retrieval requests from data users. Each data user requests the secret key associated with its access capability from TKA, retrieves encrypted data from the cloud storage server, and accesses the data that its access capability matches the access policies assigned to.

The basic cloud storage systems can be described using four procedures, namely:

- Setup: performed by TKA to initialize the system.
- KeyGen: performed by TKA to generate secret keys with specified access capabilities for data users.
- Encrypt: performed by data owners to encrypt data with on-demand access policy.
- Access: performed by data users to access data with their secret keys.

The above system model captures basic functionalities for cryptography-based cloud storage systems [37,43]. Such model can be further extended to meet additional mechanisms and security requirements for specific application scenarios, e.g., multi-authority, data user revocation, encrypted search.

Multi-authority [25,34,42]: The basic system architecture has only one single TKA to distribute secret keys. This brings security and efficiency challenges. On one hand, the single TKA has root access capability thus it is easily to be the main target for malicious adversaries. On the other hand, the single TKA would be difficult to maintain since there may be a large number of data users to request their secret keys. It is recommended that the cloud should employ multi-authorities to distribute secret keys [34]. The basic system architecture can cover the multi-authority extension by replacing the single TKA with multiple TKAs.

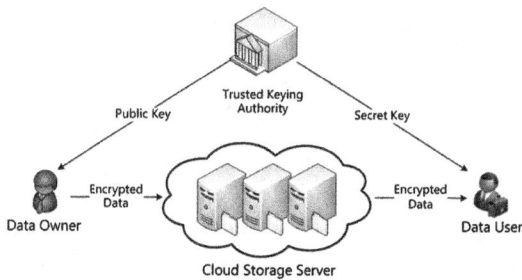

Fig. 1. Typical cloud storage system architecture.

Data User Revocation [26,30]**:** The importance of user revocation have been taken noticed in specific application scenarios, because data users' access capabilities may be changed frequently, or data users themselves may be actively/passively leave the system. One can support user revocation mechanism by introducing revocation-related procedures in the basic system architecture.

Encrypted Search [40,44,45]**:** Data encryption can provide data privacy and secrecy protection, but hinder some useful functions such as searching over the outsourced encrypted data. Researches have been devoted to enable cloud-based data sharing and search as well as preserve data privacy and secrecy. The basic system architecture can be improved to support encrypted search by employing a search server in the cloud, while introducing search-related procedures.

In this paper, we focus on basic functionalities for cryptography-based cloud storage systems. We only consider typical Setup, KeyGen, Encrypt, Decrypt procedures.

4.2   Abstract Access Policy Representation: Predicate

We introduce the notion "Predicate" to better describe access control mechanisms in cryptography-based cloud storage systems. This notion is firstly introduced in data encryption systems by Boneh and Waters [10] and formally defined by Katz, Sahai and Waters [28]. Briefly speaking, a predicate is a function that takes an access policy and an access capability as input, and output $\{0,1\}$. We say that data user's access capability matches the access policy assigned to the encrypted data if the predicate outputs 1, while access is rejected if the predicate outputs 0. Clearly, predicate can describe access control satisfactions and dissatisfactions in a general way.

We follow the definition described by Yamada *et al.* [41] to abstract such access control mechanism as Predicate Encryption (PE). Let $P : \Sigma_k \times \Sigma_e \to \{0,1\}$ be a predicate family, where Σ_k denote the "key attribute" space and Σ_e denote the "data attribute" space. A cryptography-based cloud storage system that represents data user's access capability as Σ_k and access policy as Σ_e can be formally defined with four algorithms Setup, KeyGen, Encrypt, Decrypt:

$(pk, msk) \leftarrow$ Setup(λ). The setup algorithm represents the system setup procedure performed by TKA. It takes the security parameter $\lambda \in \mathbb{N}$ as input, and
outputs a public key pk and a master secret key msk. The public key pk is
treated as the system parameter that is publicly known, while the master secret
key msk is kept secretly by TKA.

$sk_x \leftarrow$ KeyGen(msk, x). The key generation algorithm represents the secret key
generation procedure performed by TKA. The algorithm takes the master secret
key msk and a key attribute $x \in \Sigma_k$ as inputs, where the key attribute x
describes the access capability for the data user. The algorithm outputs a secret
key sk_x associated with the key attribute x if the data user is authorized by
TKA.

$(hdr_y, k) \leftarrow$ Encrypt(pk, y). The encryption algorithm represents the data
encryption procedure run by data owners. It takes as inputs the public key
pk and a data attribute $y \in \Sigma_e$, where the data attribute y describes the access
policy assigned to the data. The algorithm outputs an encryption header hdr_y
associated with the data attribute y, and a symmetric session key k related to
the header hdr_y. The symmetric session key k will be used as the key for a
symmetric encryption scheme to encrypt data of arbitrary length, or be used to
enforce other data service mechanisms, e.g., encrypted search under searchable
symmetric encryption.

$k \leftarrow$ Decrypt(pk, sk_x, hdr_y). The decryption algorithm represents the data access
procedure run by data users. It takes as inputs the public key pk, the data user's
secret key sk_x for the key attribute x, and a header hdr_y associated with the
data attribute y. It recovers the session key k encapsulated in the header hdr_y
if $P(x, y) = 1$, i.e., the access capability matches the access policy. It returns $\bot$
if $P(x, y) = 0$, representing the access failure.

The correctness property requires that for a fixed predicate P, all $\lambda \in \mathbb{N}$, all
$(pk, msk) \leftarrow$ Setup(λ), all $x \in \Sigma_k$, all $sk_x \leftarrow$ KeyGen(msk, x), all $y \in \Sigma_e$, all
$(hdr_y, k) \leftarrow$ Encrypt(pk, y), the following two conditions should be satisfied at
the same time:

- If $P(x, y) = 1$, then $k =$ Decrypt(pk, sk_x, hdr_y).
- If $P(x, y) = 0$, then $\bot =$ Decrypt(pk, sk_x, hdr_y).

4.3   Refined System Model for Self-Extractable Encryption

Our design goal is to help data owners securely share their data with data users
under the existing model. In addition, we allow data owners to retrieve and
extract its own encrypted data from the cloud storage servers without requesting
any secret keys from TKA. To achieve this goal, we explicitly introduce the data
retrieve procedure that is performed by data owners in the original system model.
The refined typical system architecture is shown in Fig. 2.

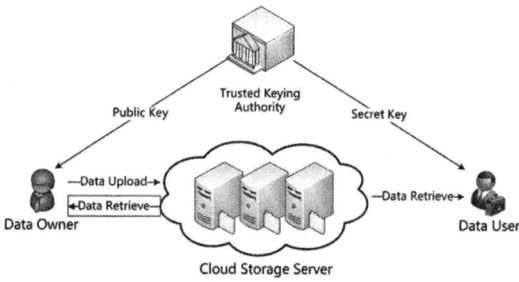

Fig. 2. Self-Extractable Encryption Overview.

Formally, the self-extractable encryption (SEXE) that represents data user's access capability as Σ_k and access policy as Σ_e can be defined with six algorithms: Setup, KeyGen, SelfKeyGen, Encrypt, Decrypt, SelfDecrypt. The system setup algorithm Setup, the secret key generation algorithm KeyGen, and the data decryption algorithm Decrypt are identical with that of in the original system, while the other three algorithms are as follows.

$ek \leftarrow$ SelfKeyGen(pk). The self key generation algorithm is run by each data owner. The algorithm only takes the public key pk as input and outputs an encryptor key ek, which must kept secret by that data owner.

$(hdr_y, k) \leftarrow$ Encrypt(pk, ek, y). The data encryption algorithm is similar with that of in the original system. The difference is that it additionally takes the encryptor key ek as input. The algorithm also outputs a header hdr_y associated with the ciphertext attribute y, and a symmetric session key k.

$k \leftarrow$ SelfDecrypt(pk, ek, hdr_y). The self decryption algorithm is run by each data owner. It takes as inputs the public key pk, the encryptor key ek, and a header hdr_y that was previously generated by itself when outsourcing the data. It recovers the session key k encapsulated in the header hdr_y, or $\perp$ representing the access failure.

SEXE should satisfy the correctness property of the original system. Meanwhile, it should ensure that the data owner can correctly access its own encrypted data. Formally, for all $\lambda \in \mathbb{N}$, all $(pk, msk) \leftarrow$ Setup(λ), all $ek \leftarrow$ SelfKeyGen(pk), and all $(hdr_y, k) \leftarrow$ Encrypt(pk, ek', y),

- If $ek = ek'$, then $k =$ SelfDecrypt(pk, ek, hdr_y).
- If $ek \neq ek'$, then $\perp =$ SelfDecrypt(pk, ek', hdr_y).

4.4 Threat Model

As most existing literatures dealing with the privacy and secrecy in cloud storages [37,43], we assume that TKA is fully trusted. It honestly sets up the system and securely issues secret keys to legal data users. It never reveals any private information to non-entitled parties. All other parties, including data owner, data user, and the cloud storage server, are honest but untrusted. They correctly execute the procedure they need, but may collude to get information that they are not authorized to access. SEXE is said to be secure if no attacker without suitable secret keys can obtain useful information from the encrypted data.

4.5   Design Goal

Our system is designed to achieve self-extractability, compatibility, and efficiency goals.

- **Self-Extractability.** The data owners must correctly access their own encrypted data that were previously uploaded to the cloud storage servers. No local copy of the outsourced files in the clear is required for them, except some meta-data of the file or file identifiers.
- **Compatibility.** Our self-extractable encryption should be compatible with existing schemes. In the functionality aspect, all existing mechanisms supported by the underlying schemes should remain unchange. In the security aspect, SEXE must be secure under the same threat model. In the implementation aspect, the self-extract mechanism can be invoked in a block-box manner, thus easy for the system developers to deploy such functionality.
- **Efficiency.** In some specific application scenarios, some data owners, e.g., mobile clients, may only have limited computation and storage resources. To make SEXE suitable for even such data owners, operations at the data owner's side should be light-weight.

5   Generic SEXE Construction

5.1   Basic Idea

We present a generic SEXE construction that can convert any cryptography-based cloud storage system to have self-extractable property. We first give an overview of our construction. Our basic idea is to parse the header of the underlying encrypted data into two parts, i.e., plaintext-independent part and plaintext-dependent part. In the encryption procedure, a data owner first generates the plaintext-independent part in the original encryption procedure. Then the data owner applies a pseudo random number generator to this part with a long-term key to produce a session key. Finally, the data owner uses the session key to encrypt the digital content. For decryption, data users can access the encrypted data in a regular way, as in the original scheme. However, if necessary, the data owner can also access its own encrypted data as follows. The data owner first extracts the plaintext-independent part of the header. Then it applies the pseudo random number generator to it and obtains the session key with its long-term key. With the recovered session key, the data owner is able to correctly recover the encrypted digital content.

5.2 Our Construction

Let $\overline{\Pi}$ be a secure encryption scheme applied in the cryptography-based cloud storage system with algorithms $\overline{\mathsf{Setup}}$, $\overline{\mathsf{KeyGen}}$, $\overline{\mathsf{Encrypt}}$, $\overline{\mathsf{Decrypt}}$. The access control mechanism of $\overline{\Pi}$ is described using a fixed predicate $P : \Sigma_k \times \Sigma_e \to \{0, 1\}$. Assume that the session key space is $\overline{\mathcal{K}}$. Let $\mathsf{PRF} : \mathcal{K}_{PRF} \times \{0, 1\}^* \to \mathcal{Y}_{PRF}$ be a secure pseudo random function with the key space $\mathcal{K}_{PRF}$ and the output space $\mathcal{Y}_{PRF}$. We can construct an SEXE Π for the same predicate P with the session key space $\mathcal{K} = \mathcal{Y}_{PRF}$ as follows.

$(pk, msk) \leftarrow \mathsf{Setup}(\lambda)$. TKA first runs $(\overline{pk}, \overline{msk}) \leftarrow \overline{\mathsf{Setup}}(\lambda)$. Then, it employs a secure symmetric encryption scheme SymE with the encryption algorithm SymEnc and the decryption algorithm SymDec. TKA outputs the public key $pk = (\overline{pk}, \mathsf{PRF}, \mathsf{SymE})$. It secretly keeps the master secret key $msk = \overline{msk}$.

$sk_x \leftarrow \mathsf{KeyGen}(msk, x)$. TKA simply calls $\overline{sk}_x \leftarrow \overline{\mathsf{KeyGen}}(\overline{msk}, x)$ and returns the secret key $sk_x = \overline{sk}_x$ for the authorized data user who requests its secret key with a key attribute $x \in \Sigma_k$.

$ek \leftarrow \mathsf{SelfKeyGen}(pk)$. Each data owner simply picks a random PRF key $ek \xleftarrow{R} \mathcal{K}_{PRF}$ from the PRF key space $\mathcal{K}_{PRF}$ as the encryptor key. Note that this procedure only involves picking random elements, thus efficient even for resource-limited data owners.

$(hdr_y, k) \leftarrow \mathsf{Encrypt}(pk, ek, y)$. When a data owner wants to share its data via cloud, it encapsulates a session key k in the header under the required data attribute y, and encrypts the data using a secure encryption scheme with k. To generate the header and the session key, the data owner first calls $(\overline{hdr}_y, \overline{k}) \leftarrow \overline{\mathsf{Encrypt}}(\overline{pk}, y)$. Then, it computes the session key by invoking $k \leftarrow \mathsf{PRF}(ek, \overline{hdr}_y)$. Next, the data owner symmetrically encrypts the session key k using $\overline{k}$, i.e., $hdr_k \leftarrow \mathsf{SymEnc}(\overline{k}, k)$. The header associated with the data attribute y and the encryptor key ek is $hdr_y = (\overline{hdr}_y, hdr_k)$.

$k \leftarrow \mathsf{Decrypt}(pk, sk_x, hdr_y)$. If $P(x, y) = 0$, the key attribute x does not satisfy the predicate P for the data attribute y. In this case, the decryption algorithm outputs $\perp$. Otherwise, the secret key $sk_x = \overline{sk}_x$ can be used to recover the session key from the header $hdr_y = (\overline{hdr}_y, hdr_k)$. To do this, the data user runs $\overline{k} \leftarrow \overline{\mathsf{Decrypt}}(\overline{pk}, \overline{sk}_x, \overline{hdr}_y)$ and gets the key $\overline{k}$. Then, it recovers the session key by running $k \leftarrow \mathsf{SymDec}(\overline{k}, hdr_k)$.

$k \leftarrow \mathsf{SelfDecrypt}(pk, ek, hdr_y)$. If the encrypted data is not generated by the data owner with the encryptor key ek, the self decryption algorithm outputs $\perp$. Otherwise, the data owner can use its encryptor key ek to recover the session key k from $hdr_y = (\overline{hdr}_y, hdr_k)$ by calling $k \leftarrow \mathsf{PRF}(ek, \overline{hdr}_y)$.

Our generic SEXE construction satisfies self-extractability, compatibility, and efficiency design goals.

Self-Extractability. If the data is correctly encrypted, the data owner can also use its encryptor key ek to run $k \leftarrow \mathsf{PRF}(ek, \overline{hdr}_y)$ and correctly recovers the session key. With the session key k, the data owner can further symmetrically decrypt the data content, or enforce other data service mechanisms by its own. In this way, we achieve self-extractability property in the SEXE construction.

Compatibility. Our generic SEXE construction is based on the existing schemes. Original algorithms involved in the existing schemes, i.e., Setup, Key-Gen, Encrypt, Decrypt, are essentially the same, except some additional minor operations for generating/recovering session keys. All existing mechanisms supported by the underlying schemes remain unchange. Specifically, if the key attribute x for the secret key sk_x and the data attribute y for the header $hdr_y = (\overline{hdr}_y, hdr_k)$ satisfy $P(x, y) = 1$, then the original encryption system ensures that the key $\overline{k}$ can be correctly recovered by running $\overline{k} \leftarrow \overline{\mathsf{Decrypt}}(\overline{pk}, \overline{sk}_x, \overline{hdr}_y)$. Therefore, the data user can recover the session key $k = \mathsf{SymDec}(\overline{k}, hdr_k)$, where $hdr_k \leftarrow \mathsf{SymEnc}(\overline{k}, k)$.

The security of the original encryption system ensures that data users without necessary access capabilities cannot reveal any useful information from $\overline{hdr}_y$. The security of the symmetric encryption scheme also ensures that hdr_k does not leak useful information about the session key k if $\overline{k}$ cannot be correctly recovered from $\overline{hdr}_y$. Formally, we have the following theorem.

Theorem 1. *Suppose advanced encryption scheme Π used in the cryptography-based cloud storage system with access control mechanism described by the predicate P is secure, the pseudo random function PRF is secure, and the employed symmetric encryption scheme SymE is secure. Then following our generic construction, the resulting SEXE scheme for the same predicate P is also secure.*

The detailed security analysis is shown in Sect. 7.

Performance. Our generic SEXE construction is efficient since only operations for calling pseudo random function PRF and symmetric encryption scheme SymE are additionally required in our proposal. Precisely, operations for algorithms Setup and KeyGen are identical with the underlying encryption system. Encrypt invokes operations for running PRF and $\mathsf{SymEnc}(\overline{k}, k)$, while Decrypt invokes one more operation $\mathsf{SymDec}(\overline{k}, hdr_k)$. The newly required algorithms SelfKeyGen and SelfDecrypt also only involve operations related to PRF. All the added operations are rather efficient.

6   SEXE Instantiations

We now give several instantiations to explicitly show how our generic SEXE construction applies in existing systems. We begin by leveraging our construction into the Boneh-Franklin IBE [8], which is the basic encryption primitive for many cloud-aided communication and storage systems [12,19]. Then, we turn into Key-Policy and Ciphertext-Policy ABE proposed by Rouselakis-Waters [33] that have been deployed in recent cloud storage systems [37,44]. The instantiations imply that our generic transformation is easy to be applied into existing systems for obtaining the corresponding SEXE variations.

6.1   Self-Extractable IBE

We first apply our SEXE transformation into IBE settings to obtain self-extractable IBE (SEXIBE). In IBE, encrypted data and secret keys are associated with arbitrary strings and the secret key can be used to decrypt if and only if the associated strings are equal. To achieve this functionality, we set the key attribute space and the data attribute space to be $\Sigma_k = \Sigma_e = \{0,1\}^*$. The predicate is defined as $P(x, y) = 1$ if $x = y$.

The underlying IBE scheme we choose is the Boneh-Franklin IBE [8], which is the first practical and fully secure IBE scheme that has been widely used in advanced cloud-aided communication and storage systems [12,19]. The SEXIBE construction is described as follows.

$(pk, msk) \leftarrow$ Setup(λ). The setup algorithm generates bilinear groups by running $(p, \mathbb{G}, \mathbb{G}_T, e) \leftarrow \mathcal{G}(\lambda)$. Then, it picks a random generator $g \xleftarrow{R} \mathbb{G}$, a random exponent $s \xleftarrow{R} \mathbb{Z}_p$, and sets $g_s = g^s$. Next, the algorithm employs a cryptographic hash function $\mathsf{H} : \{0,1\}^* \to \mathbb{G}$, a secure pseudo random function $\mathsf{PRF} : \mathcal{K}_{PRF} \times \{0,1\}^* \to \mathcal{Y}_{PRF}$, and a secure symmetric encryption scheme SymE with the encryption algorithm SymEnc and the decryption algorithm SymDec. The public key pk and the master secret key are

$$pk = (g, g_s, \mathsf{H}, \mathsf{PRF}, \mathsf{SymEnc}) \qquad msk = (s)$$

$sk_\mathcal{I} \leftarrow$ KeyGen$(msk, \mathcal{I})$. The secret key $sk_\mathcal{I}$ for an identity $\mathcal{I} \in \mathbb{Z}_p$ is $\mathsf{H}(ID)^s$.

$ek \leftarrow$ SelfKeyGen(pk). The algorithm simply returns a random element $ek \xleftarrow{R} \mathcal{K}_{PRF}$ as the encryptor key.

$(hdr_\mathcal{I}, k) \leftarrow$ Encrypt$(pk, ek, \mathcal{I})$. To encapsulate a session key using an identity $\mathcal{I} \in \mathbb{Z}_p$ and an encryptor key ek, the encryption algorithm generates a random exponent $r \xleftarrow{R} \mathbb{Z}_p$ and outputs the header

$$\begin{aligned} hdr_\mathcal{I} &= (U, hdr_k) = (g^r, hdr_k) \\ &= (g^r, \mathsf{SymEnc}(e(\mathsf{H}(ID), g^s)^r, k))) \end{aligned}$$

where $k \leftarrow \mathsf{PRF}(ek, U)$.

$k \leftarrow$ Decrypt$(pk, sk_\mathcal{I}, hdr_\mathcal{I})$. To recover the session key from $hdr_\mathcal{I} = (U, hdr_k)$ using the secret key $sk_\mathcal{I}$, the decryption algorithm outputs

$$k \leftarrow \mathsf{SymDec}\,(e(sk_\mathcal{I}, U), hdr_k)$$

$k \leftarrow$ SelfDecrypt$(pk, ek, hdr_\mathcal{I})$. To recover the session key from $hdr_\mathcal{I} = (U, hdr_k)$ generated by the data owner with the encryptor key ek, the self decryption algorithm outputs

$$k \leftarrow \mathsf{PRF}(ek, U)$$

Correctness. It is easy to verify that the data owner can correctly recover the session key by running SelfDecrypt since $k \leftarrow \mathsf{PRF}(ek, U)$ is exactly the algorithm for generating k. Also, the data user who has the secret key $sk_{\mathcal{I}}$ can correctly recover the session key encapsulated in $hdr_{\mathcal{I}}$ since

$$e(sk_{\mathcal{I}}, U) = e(\mathsf{H}(ID)^s, g^r) = e(\mathsf{H}(ID), g^s)^r$$

Therefore,

$$\begin{aligned}
&\mathsf{SymDec}\,(e(sk_{\mathcal{I}}, U), hdr_k) \\
&= \mathsf{SymDec}\,(e(\mathsf{H}(ID)^s, g^r), hdr_k) \\
&= \mathsf{SymDec}\,(e(\mathsf{H}(ID), g^s)^r, \mathsf{SymEnc}(e(\mathsf{H}(ID), g^s)^r, k)) \\
&= k
\end{aligned}$$

Security. Boneh and Franklin proved that their IBE scheme is fully secure [8]. Abdalla *et al.* further showed that the the encrypted data in the Boneh-Franklin IBE even does not leak identity information for the potential data receiver [1]. Due to this favorable property (formally called anonymity property), the Boneh-Franklin IBE can be transformed as asymmetric searchable encryption scheme to offer encrypted data keyword search mechanism [7]. Following Theorem 1, we claim that our SEXIBE construction based on the Boneh-Franklin IBE is also fully secure and anonymous.

6.2 Self-Extractable ABE

We next demonstrate how to obtain self-extractable ABE (SEXABE) from existing ABE. ABE allows to share data according to fine-grained access policies. ABE is classified into Key-Policy ABE (KP-ABE) [18] and Ciphertext-Policy ABE (CP-ABE) [6]. Here we roughly describe how we define the predicate P to capture these two kinds of ABE settings.

In KP-ABE, the data owner encrypts the data for a set of attributes S so that users with secret keys for access structure $\mathbb{A}$ such that $S \in \mathbb{A}$ can decrypt. To capture this functionality, we set U as an attribute universe. The key attribute space Σ_k is the collection of access structures over U that can be described by LSSS matrix with bounded polynomial size. The data attribute space is $\Sigma_e = 2^U$. We define the predicate as $P(\mathbb{A}, S) = 1$ if and only if $\mathbb{A} \in \Sigma_k$ accepts $S \in \Sigma_e$.

In contrast, the CP-ABE encrypted data is associated with a set of attributes S and the secret key is assigned to an access structure $\mathbb{A}$. The secret key can be used to decrypt the data if and only if $S \in \mathbb{A}$. Similar to KP-ABE, to achieve this functionality we set U be an attribute universe. The key attribute space is $\Sigma_k = 2^U$ and the data attribute space Σ_k is the collection of access structures over U described by LSSS matrix with bounded polynomial size. The predicate is defined as $P(S, \mathbb{A}) = 1$ if and only if $\mathbb{A} \in \Sigma_e$ accepts $S \in \Sigma_k$.

Our underlying schemes are the Rouselakis-Waters KP-ABE and CP-ABE [33]. Both schemes support exponential number of attributes, achieve selective security, and are equipped with desired properties, e.g., efficient pre-computation [23], proxy re-encryption [37]. Here we show the detailed self-extractable CP-ABE (SEX-CP-ABE) construction based on the Rouselakis-Waters CP-ABE. The self-extractable KP-ABE (SEX-KP-ABE) can be obtained in a similar way [33].

$(pk, msk) \leftarrow \mathsf{Setup}(\lambda)$. The setup algorithm calls the group generator $\mathcal{G}(\lambda)$ and gets the descriptions of the bilinear groups $(p, \mathbb{G}, \mathbb{G}_T, e)$. Then, a secure pseudo random function $\mathsf{PRG} : \mathcal{K}_{PRF} \times \{0,1\}^* \rightarrow \mathcal{Y}_{PRF}$ and a secure symmetric encryption scheme SymE with algorithms SymEnc and SymDec are employed in the system. The setup algorithm picks random elements $g, u, h, w, v \xleftarrow{R} \mathbb{G}$ and a random exponent $\alpha \xleftarrow{R} \mathbb{Z}_p$. It outputs the public key pk and the master secret key msk as

$$pk = (g, u, h, w, v, e(g,g)^\alpha, \mathsf{PRF}, \mathsf{SymEnc}) \qquad msk = (\alpha)$$

$sk_S \leftarrow \mathsf{KeyGen}(msk, S)$. Given a set of attributes $S = \{A_1, A_2, \cdots, A_\tau\}$ where $A_i \in \mathbb{Z}_p$ for $i \in [\tau]$, the key generation algorithms picks $\tau + 1$ random exponents $r, r_1, r_2, \cdots, r_\tau \xleftarrow{R} \mathbb{Z}_p$. Then, it computes $K_0 = g^\alpha w^r$, $K_1 = g^r$, and for every $i \in [\tau]$,

$$K_{i,2} = g^{r_i}, K_{i,3} = \left(u^{A_i} h\right)^{r_i} \cdot v^{-r}$$

The secret key associated with the set of attributes S is $sk_S = (K_0, K_1, \{K_{i,2}, K_{i,3}\}_{i \in \tau})$.

$ek \leftarrow \mathsf{SelfKeyGen}(pp)$. The self key generation algorithm simply returns a random $ek \xleftarrow{R} \mathcal{K}_{PRF}$.

$(hdr_\mathbb{A}, k) \leftarrow \mathsf{Encrypt}(pk, ek, \mathbb{A})$. The encryption algorithm encapsulates a session key for the given access structure $\mathbb{A}$ encoded by the LSSS policy (M, ρ) as follows. It picks random exponents $s, y_2, \cdots, y_n \xleftarrow{R} \mathbb{Z}_p$ and constructs the vector $\boldsymbol{y} = (s, y_2, \cdots, y_n)$. The vector of the shares is computed as $\boldsymbol{\lambda} = (\lambda_1, \cdots, \lambda_l)^\mathrm{T} = M\boldsymbol{y}$. It then picks l random exponents $t_1, \cdots, t_l \xleftarrow{R} \mathbb{Z}_p$ and calculates $C_0 = g^s$, and for every $j \in [l]$,

$$C_{j,1} = w^{\lambda_j} v^{t_j}, C_{j,2} = \left(u^{\rho(j)} h\right)^{-t_j}, C_{j,3} = g^{t_j}$$

The algorithm next generates the session key $k \leftarrow \mathsf{PRF}(ek, C_0 \| C_{1,1} \| C_{1,2} \| C_{1,3} \| \cdots \| C_{l,1} \| C_{l,2} \| C_{l,3})$, and calculates $hdr_k = \mathsf{SymEnc}(e(g,g)^{\alpha s}, k)$. The header output is

$$hdr_\mathbb{A} = (C_0, \{C_{j,1}, C_{j,2}, C_{j,3}\}_{j \in [l]}, hdr_k)$$

$k \leftarrow \mathsf{Decrypt}(pk, sk_S, hdr_\mathbb{A})$. The decryption algorithm first calculates the set of row in M that provides a valid share to attributes in S, i.e., it collects the set $I = \{i : \rho(i) \in S\}$. Then, it computes the constants $\{\omega_i\}_{i \in I}$ such that

$\sum_{i \in I} \omega_i \boldsymbol{M}_i = (1, 0, \cdots, 0)$, where $\boldsymbol{M}_i$ is the i-th row of the matrix M. Next it computes

$$B = \frac{e\left(C_0, K_0\right)}{\prod_{i \in I} \left(e\left(C_{i,1}, K_1\right) e\left(C_{i,2}, K_{j,2}\right) e\left(C_{i,3}, K_{j,3}\right)\right)^{\omega_i}}$$

where j is the index of the attribute $\rho(i)$ in S. The algorithm finally outputs $k \leftarrow \mathsf{SymDec}(B, hdr_k)$.

$k \leftarrow \mathsf{SelfDecrypt}(pp, ek, hdr_\mathbb{A})$. The self decryption algorithm simply outputs

$$k \leftarrow \mathsf{PRF}(ek, C_0 \| C_{1,1} \| C_{1,2} \| C_{1,3} \| \cdots \| C_{l,1} \| C_{l,2} \| C_{l,3})$$

Correctness. Since the way of generating and self decapsulating the session key are exactly the same, i.e., by computing $k \leftarrow \mathsf{PRF}(ek, C_0 \| C_{1,1} \| C_{1,2} \| C_{1,3} \| \cdots \| C_{l,1} \| C_{l,2} \| C_{l,3})$, $\mathsf{SelfDecrypt}$ can correctly recover the session key k. If the attribute set S of the secret key is authorized by the access structure $\mathbb{A}$ encoded by the LSSS policy (M, ρ) assigned in the header $hdr_\mathbb{A}$, we have that $\sum_{i \in I} \omega_i \lambda_i = s$. Therefore,

$$B = \frac{e\left(C_0, K_0\right)}{\prod_{i \in I} \left(e\left(C_{i,1}, K_1\right) e\left(C_{i,2}, K_{j,2}\right) e\left(C_{i,3}, K_{j,3}\right)\right)^{\omega_i}}$$

$$= \frac{e(g,g)^{\alpha s} e(g,w)^{rs}}{\prod_{i \in I} \left(e\left(w^{\lambda_i}, g^r\right)\right)^{\omega_i} = e(g,g)^{\alpha s} e(g,w)^{rs} / e(g,w)^{r \sum_{i \in I} \omega_i \lambda_i}}$$

$$= e(g,g)^{\alpha s} \cdot \frac{e(g,w)^{rs}}{e(g,w)^{rs}} = e(g,g)^{\alpha s}$$

Since $hdr_k = \mathsf{SymEnc}(e(g,g)^{\alpha s}, k)$, we finally have that $\mathsf{SymDec}(B, hdr_k) = \mathsf{SymDec}(e(g,g)^{\alpha s}, C_k) = k$ so that the session key k can be correctly obtained.

Security. The security of our self-extractable CP-ABE is directly followed by the security of the Rouselakis-Waters CP-ABE and Theorem 1.

7   Formal Security Analysis

7.1   Formal Security Model

We use the following security model to formalize the security notions of SEXE. In the security model, we assume there exists an adversary who wishes to extract useful information from a target encrypted data with the header hdr^* associated with a target data attributes x^* of its choice. The adversary assumes to be powerful. Specifically, the adversary can collude with authorized data users, all of which do not have access capabilities to directly access the target data. The adversary can also collude with other data owners with distinct encryptor keys, except the target data owner. We require that even such an adversary cannot obtain any useful information from the target encrypted data with header hdr_y^*. We note that this security notion captures the data privacy and data secrecy, as well as anonymity property.

Formally, the security model of SEXE is defined through a security game played between an adversary $\mathcal{A}$ and a challenger $\mathcal{C}$, both of which take the security parameter $\lambda \in \mathbb{N}$ as inputs.

Setup. The challenger $\mathcal{C}$ runs the setup algorithm to obtain the public key pk and gives it to adversary $\mathcal{A}$.

Phase 1. Adversary $\mathcal{A}$ can adaptively issue the following two kinds of queries to $\mathcal{C}$:

- **Secret Key Query**: Adversary $\mathcal{A}$ submits the key attributes $x \in \Sigma_k$ of its choice to $\mathcal{C}$. If x has not been queried before, challenger $\mathcal{C}$ generates a secret key for x by running $sk_x \leftarrow$ KeyGen(msk, x) and gives it to $\mathcal{A}$. Otherwise, the previously generated secret key sk_x is given to $\mathcal{A}$.
- **Encryptor Key Query**: Adversary $\mathcal{A}$ asks $\mathcal{C}$ for a encryptor key. Challenger $\mathcal{C}$ runs $ek \leftarrow$ SelfKeyGen(pk) and gives the resulting ek to $\mathcal{A}$.

Challenge. When $\mathcal{A}$ decides that **Phase 1** is over, it outputs two challenge data attributes $y_0^*, y_1^* \in \Sigma_e$, which must satisfy that $P(x, y_0^*) = 0$ and $P(x, y_1^*) = 0$ for all the key attributes such that $\mathcal{A}$ queried for the secret key sk_x. The challenger $\mathcal{C}$ first generates its own encryptor key $ek^* \leftarrow$ SelfKeyGen(pp). Then, it flips a random coin $b \xleftarrow{R} \{0, 1\}$ and computes the challenge header/session key by running $(hdr_b^*, k_b^*) \leftarrow$ Encrypt(pk, ek^*, y_b^*). Finally, the challenger $\mathcal{C}$ returns (hdr_b^*, k_b^*) to $\mathcal{A}$.

Phase 2. Adversary $\mathcal{A}$ further adaptively issues secret key queries and encryptor key queries. The submitted key attributes $x \in \Sigma_k$ for the secret key queries should satisfy that $P(x, y_0^*) = 0$ and $P(x, y_1^*) = 0$. The challenger responds the same as in **Phase 1**.

Guess. Finally, adversary $\mathcal{A}$ outputs a guess $b' \in \{0, 1\}$ and wins in the game if $b = b'$.

The probability of such an adversary $\mathcal{A}$ winning the above game in attacking the SEXE with the security parameter λ is defined as

$$Adv_{\mathcal{A}}^{SEXE}(\lambda) = \left| \Pr[b' = b] - \frac{1}{2} \right|$$

We say that the SEXE is secure if $Adv_{\mathcal{A}}^{SEXE}(\lambda)$ is negligible.

7.2 Proof of Theorem 1

Suppose that there is a polynomial time adversary $\mathcal{A}$ that can break the security of our SEXE with non-negligible winning probability. We construct an algorithm

$\mathcal{B}$ that has non-negligible winning probability to break the security of the underlying advanced encryption scheme with the help of algorithm $\mathcal{A}$. Algorithm $\mathcal{B}$ acts as the adversary for the original encryption scheme adversary, and as the challenger for the SEXE. The simulation is run as follows.

Setup. Algorithm $\mathcal{B}$ receives the public key $\overline{pk}$ from the original encryption scheme challenger. It employs a secure symmetric encryption scheme SymE with algorithms SymEnc and SymDec. Algorithm $\mathcal{S}$ gives the public key $pk = (\overline{pk}, \mathsf{PRF}, \mathsf{SymE})$ to $\mathcal{A}$.

Phase 1. Adversary $\mathcal{A}$ adaptively submits key attributes $x \in \Sigma_k$ to algorithm $\mathcal{B}$. Algorithm $\mathcal{B}$ also submits the key attributes to the original encryption scheme, and forwards the secret keys $\overline{sk}_x$ to adversary $\mathcal{A}$. Note that secret keys are the same in both schemes, the secret keys $\overline{sk}_x$ generated by the original encryption scheme challenger can be also used to return the secret key queries issued by adversary $\mathcal{A}$.

When $\mathcal{A}$ issues an encryptor key ek, algorithm $\mathcal{B}$ simply picks a random key $ek \xleftarrow{R} \mathcal{K}_{PRF}$ and returns it to $\mathcal{A}$.

Challenge. When adversary $\mathcal{A}$ decides that **Phase 1** is over, it outputs two data attributes $y_0^*, y_1^* \in \Sigma_e$ on which it wishes to be challenged. Algorithm $\mathcal{B}$ submits y_0^*, y_1^* as the challenge data attributes to the original encryption scheme challenger, which returns a challenge session key $\overline{k}_b^*$ and a challenge header $\overline{hdr}_b^*$ to algorithm $\mathcal{B}$. Algorithm $\mathcal{B}$ randomly picks a challenge encryptor key $ek^* \xleftarrow{R} \mathcal{K}_{PRF}$, and runs $k_b^* \leftarrow \mathsf{PRF}(ek^*, \overline{k}_b^*)$ to generate the challenge session key k_b^*. Then, it encrypts k_b^* using $\overline{k}_b^*$ by calling $hdr_k^* \leftarrow \mathsf{SymEnc}(\overline{k}_b^*, k_b^*)$. The challenge header is $hdr_b^* = (\overline{hdr}_b^*, hdr_k^*)$, and the challenge session key is k_b^*, both of which are returned to adversary $\mathcal{A}$.

Phase 2. Algorithm $\mathcal{B}$ runs as the same in **Phase 1** to respond the secret key queries and encryptor key queries issued by $\mathcal{A}$.

Guess. Eventually, adversary $\mathcal{A}$ outputs a guess $b' \in \{0, 1\}$. Algorithm $\mathcal{B}$ also returns b' as its own guess to the original encryption scheme challenger.

Since the pseudo random function PRF is secure, adversary $\mathcal{A}$ cannot distinguish k_b^* from an actual random number without knowing the challenge encryptor key ek^* chosen randomly by algorithm $\mathcal{B}$, except with negligible probability. Meanwhile, the header component hdr_k^* output by the secure symmetric encryption scheme leaks no information for the value of b, except with negligible probability. Therefore, if adversary $\mathcal{A}$ has non-negligible advantage ϵ to break the security of the SEXE, then algorithm $\mathcal{B}$ can break the security of the underlying encryption scheme with non-negligible probability.

8   Conclusions

We investigated how to enable a data owner to access his/her own encrypted data. We formalized the new SEXE concept which equips advanced encryption scheme with self-extractability property so that the data owner can always access her encrypted data. We proposed a generic SEXE construction from any existing schemes. Following the proposed generic construction, we instantiated self-extractable Identity-Based Encryption and self-extractable Attribute-Based Encryption schemes both in Key-Policy setting and in Ciphertext-Policy setting. These works make it more convenient to securely share sensitive files via clouds.

Acknowledgment. This paper is supported by the National Key Research and Development Program of China through project 2017YFB0802505, the Natural Science Foundation of China through projects 61672083, 61370190, 61532021, 61472429, and 61402029, by the National Cryptography 700 Development Fund through project MMJJ20170106, by the Beijing Natural Science Foundation through project 4132056.

References

1. Abdalla, M., Bellare, M., Catalano, D., Kiltz, E., Kohno, T., Lange, T., Malone-Lee, J., Neven, G., Paillier, P., Shi, H.: Searchable encryption revisited: consistency properties, relation to anonymous IBE, and extensions. In: Shoup, V. (ed.) CRYPTO 2005. LNCS, vol. 3621, pp. 205–222. Springer, Heidelberg (2005). doi:10.1007/11535218_13

2. Anderson, R.: Technical perspective: a chilly sense of security. Commun. ACM **52**(5), 90–90 (2009)

3. Atallah, M.J., Blanton, M., Fazio, N., Frikken, K.B.: Dynamic and efficient key management for access hierarchies. ACM Trans. Inf. Syst. Secur. (TISSEC) **12**(3), 18 (2009)

4. Ateniese, G., Kevin, F., Green, M., Hohenberger, S.: Improved proxy re-encryption schemes with applications to secure distributed storage. ACM Trans. Inf. Syst. Secur. **9**(1), 1–30 (2006)

5. Beimel, A.: Secure schemes for secret sharing and key distribution. Ph.D. thesis, Technion Israel Institute of technology, Faculty of computer science, January 1996

6. Bethencourt, J., Sahai, A., Waters, B.: Ciphertext-policy attribute-based encryption. In: S&P 2007, pp. 321–334. IEEE (2007)

7. Boneh, D., Crescenzo, G., Ostrovsky, R., Persiano, G.: Public key encryption with keyword search. In: Cachin, C., Camenisch, J.L. (eds.) EUROCRYPT 2004. LNCS, vol. 3027, pp. 506–522. Springer, Heidelberg (2004). doi:10.1007/978-3-540-24676-3_30

8. Boneh, D., Franklin, M.: Identity-based encryption from the weil pairing. In: Kilian, J. (ed.) CRYPTO 2001. LNCS, vol. 2139, pp. 213–229. Springer, Heidelberg (2001). doi:10.1007/3-540-44647-8_13

9. Boneh, D., Gentry, C., Waters, B.: Collusion resistant broadcast encryption with short ciphertexts and private keys. In: Shoup, V. (ed.) CRYPTO 2005. LNCS, vol. 3621, pp. 258–275. Springer, Heidelberg (2005). doi:10.1007/11535218_16

10. Boneh, D., Waters, B.: Conjunctive, subset, and range queries on encrypted data. In: Vadhan, S.P. (ed.) TCC 2007. LNCS, vol. 4392, pp. 535–554. Springer, Heidelberg (2007). doi:10.1007/978-3-540-70936-7_29

11. Camenisch, J., Neven, G., Shelat, A.: Simulatable adaptive oblivious transfer. In: Naor, M. (ed.) EUROCRYPT 2007. LNCS, vol. 4515, pp. 573–590. Springer, Heidelberg (2007). doi:10.1007/978-3-540-72540-4_33

12. Chan, A.C.-F., Blake, I.F.: Scalable, server-passive, user-anonymous timed release cryptography. In: ICDCS 2005, pp. 504–513. IEEE (2005)
13. Dan, B., Lynn, B., Shacham, H.: Short signatures from the weil pairing. In: International Conference on the Theory and Application of Cryptology and Information Security, pp. 514–532 (2001)
14. Delerablée, C.: Identity-based broadcast encryption with constant size ciphertexts and private keys. In: Kurosawa, K. (ed.) ASIACRYPT 2007. LNCS, vol. 4833, pp. 200–215. Springer, Heidelberg (2007). doi:10.1007/978-3-540-76900-2_12
15. Gentry, C., Silverberg, A.: Hierarchical ID-based cryptography. In: Zheng, Y. (ed.) ASIACRYPT 2002. LNCS, vol. 2501, pp. 548–566. Springer, Heidelberg (2002). doi:10.1007/3-540-36178-2_34
16. Goh, E.J., Shacham, H., Modadugu, N., Boneh, D.: Sirius: securing remote untrusted storage. In: NDSS 2003, pp. 131–145. Internet Society (2003)
17. Goldreich, O., Goldwasser, S., Micali, S.: How to construct random functions. J. ACM **33**(4), 792–807 (1986)
18. Goyal, V., Pandey, O., Sahai, A., Waters, B.: Attribute-based encryption for fine-grained access control of encrypted data. In: CCS 2006, pp. 89–98. ACM (2006)
19. Guan, Z., Cao, Z., Zhao, X., Chen, R., Chen, Z., Nan, X.: Webibc: identity based cryptography for client side security in web applications. In: ICDCS 2008, pp. 689–696. IEEE (2008)
20. Hacıgümüş, H., Iyer, B., Li, C., Mehrotra, S.: Executing SQL over encrypted data in the database-service-provider model. In: SIGMOD 2002, pp. 216–227. ACM (2002)
21. Hacıgümüş, H., Iyer, B., Mehrotra, S.: Providing database as a service. In: VLDB 2002, pp. 29–38. IEEE (2002)
22. Hohenberger, S., Koppula, V., Waters, B.: Adaptively secure puncturable pseudorandom functions in the standard model. In: Iwata, T., Cheon, J.H. (eds.) ASIACRYPT 2015. LNCS, vol. 9452, pp. 79–102. Springer, Heidelberg (2015). doi:10.1007/978-3-662-48797-6_4
23. Hohenberger, S., Waters, B.: Online/Offline attribute-based encryption. In: Krawczyk, H. (ed.) PKC 2014. LNCS, vol. 8383, pp. 293–310. Springer, Heidelberg (2014). doi:10.1007/978-3-642-54631-0_17
24. Horwitz, J., Lynn, B.: Toward hierarchical identity-based encryption. In: Knudsen, L.R. (ed.) EUROCRYPT 2002. LNCS, vol. 2332, pp. 466–481. Springer, Heidelberg (2002). doi:10.1007/3-540-46035-7_31
25. Hung, T., Li, X., Wan, Z., Wan, M.: Privacy preserving cloud data access with multi-authorities. In: INFOCOM 2013, pp. 2625–2633. IEEE (2013)
26. Hur, J., Noh, D.K.: Attribute-based access control with efficient revocation in data outsourcing systems. IEEE Trans. Parallel Distrib. Syst. **22**(7), 1214–1221 (2011)
27. Kallahalla, M., Riedel, E., Swaminathan, R., Wang, Q., Fu, K.: Plutus: scalable secure file sharing on untrusted storage. In: FAST 2003. USENIX Association (2003)
28. Katz, J., Sahai, A., Waters, B.: Predicate encryption supporting disjunctions, polynomial equations, and inner products. In: Smart, N. (ed.) EUROCRYPT 2008. LNCS, vol. 4965, pp. 146–162. Springer, Heidelberg (2008). doi:10.1007/978-3-540-78967-3_9
29. Lewko, A., Waters, B.: Decentralizing attribute-based encryption. In: Paterson, K.G. (ed.) EUROCRYPT 2011. LNCS, vol. 6632, pp. 568–588. Springer, Heidelberg (2011). doi:10.1007/978-3-642-20465-4_31

30. Li, M., Shucheng, Y., Zheng, Y., Ren, K., Lou, W.: Scalable and secure sharing of personal health records in cloud computing using attribute-based encryption. IEEE Trans. Parallel Distrib. Syst. **24**(1), 131–143 (2013)
31. Liu, Z., Cao, Z., Wong, D.S.: Efficient generation of linear secret sharing scheme matrices from threshold access trees. Cryptology ePrint Archive, Report 2010/374 (2010). http://eprint.iacr.org/2010/374
32. Paillier, P.: Public-key cryptosystems based on composite degree residuosity classes. In: Stern, J. (ed.) EUROCRYPT 1999. LNCS, vol. 1592, pp. 223–238. Springer, Heidelberg (1999). doi:10.1007/3-540-48910-X_16
33. Rouselakis, Y., Waters, B.: Practical constructions and new proof methods for large universe attribute-based encryption. In: CCS 2013, pp. 463–474. ACM (2013)
34. Ruj, S., Stojmenovic, M., Nayak, A.: Decentralized access control with anonymous authentication of data stored in clouds. IEEE Trans. Parallel Distrib. Syst. **25**(2), 384–394 (2014)
35. Sahai, A., Waters, B.: Fuzzy identity-based encryption. In: Cramer, R. (ed.) EUROCRYPT 2005. LNCS, vol. 3494, pp. 457–473. Springer, Heidelberg (2005). doi:10.1007/11426639_27
36. Shamir, A.: Identity-based cryptosystems and signature schemes. In: Blakley, G.R., Chaum, D. (eds.) CRYPTO 1984. LNCS, vol. 196, pp. 47–53. Springer, Heidelberg (1985). doi:10.1007/3-540-39568-7_5
37. Shao, J., Lu, R., Lin, X.: Fine-grained data sharing in cloud computing for mobile devices. In: INFOCOM 2015, pp. 2677–2685. IEEE (2015)
38. Sun, J., Fang, Y.: Cross-domain data sharing in distributed electronic health record systems. IEEE Trans. Parallel Distrib. Syst. **21**(6), 754–764 (2010)
39. Sun, J., Zhu, X., Zhang, C., Fang, Y.: HCPP: cryptography based secure EHR system for patient privacy and emergency healthcare. In: ICDCS 2011, pp. 373–382. IEEE (2011)
40. Sun, W., Yu, S., Lou, W., Hou, Y.T., Li, H.: Protecting your right: attribute-based keyword search with fine-grained owner-enforced search authorization in the cloud. In: INFOCOM 2014, pp. 226–234. IEEE (2014)
41. Yamada, S., Attrapadung, N., Santoso, B., Schuldt, J.C.N., Hanaoka, G., Kunihiro, N.: Verifiable predicate encryption and applications to CCA security and anonymous predicate authentication. In: Fischlin, M., Buchmann, J., Manulis, M. (eds.) PKC 2012. LNCS, vol. 7293, pp. 243–261. Springer, Heidelberg (2012). doi:10.1007/978-3-642-30057-8_15
42. Yang, K., Jia, X., Ren, K., Zhang, B.: Dac-macs: effective data access control for multi-authority cloud storage systems. In: INFOCOM 2010, pp. 2895–2903. IEEE (2013)
43. Yu, S., Wang, C., Ren, K., Lou, W.: Achieving secure, scalable, and fine-grained data access control in cloud computing. In: INFOCOM 2010, pp. 1–9. IEEE (2010)
44. Zhang, L., Jung, T., Liu, C., Ding, X., Li, X.-Y., Liu, Y.: Pop: privacy-preserving outsourced photo sharing and searching for mobile devices. In: 2015 IEEE 35th International Conference on Distributed Computing Systems (ICDCS), pp. 308–317. IEEE (2015)
45. Zheng, Q., Xu, S., Ateniese, G.: Vabks: verifiable attribute-based keyword search over outsourced encrypted data. In: INFOCOM 2014, pp. 522–530. IEEE (2014)

Towards Multi-user Searchable Encryption Supporting Boolean Query and Fast Decryption

Yunling Wang[1], Jianfeng Wang[1,4], Shi-Feng Sun[2], Joseph K. Liu[2],
Willy Susilo[3], and Xiaofeng Chen[1(✉)]

[1] State Key Laboratory of Integrated Service Networks (ISN),
Xidian University, Xi'an, People's Republic of China
{ylwang0304@163.com, jfwang,xfchen}@xidian.edu.cn
[2] Faculty of Information Technology, Monash University, Clayton, Australia
{Shifeng.Sun,joseph.liu}@monash.edu
[3] School of Computing and Information Technology,
Institute of Cybersecurity and Cryptology,
University of Wollongong, Wollongong, Australia
wsusilo@uow.edu.au
[4] State Key Laboratory of Information Security,
Institute of Information Engineering, Chinese Academy of Sciences,
Beijing, People's Republic of China

Abstract. The single-writer/multi-reader searchable encryption (SMSE) allows an arbitrary authorized user to submit a valid search token and get the corresponding encrypted identifiers. In order to achieve fine-grained access control, the identifiers are encrypted by the attribute-based encryption. In this case, the user can decrypt a ciphertext only when the access policy in it matches the user's attribute set. However, the server unable to determine whether the user can decrypt a certain ciphertext without the knowledge of the user's attribute set. As a result, all the ciphertexts based on a search token have to be returned to the user, which causes unnecessary communication and decryption costs. In this paper, we propose a new SMSE scheme, in which the server just needs to return the ones which can be decrypted by the user rather than the whole search results. In order to achieve this goal, we present a server-side match technique with which the server can test whether the user can decrypt a ciphertext without knowing the user's attribute set. Furthermore, the decryption computation is very efficient, irrespective of the structure of access policy. Therefore, both the communication and decryption overheads are dramatically reduced in our scheme.

Keywords: Cloud computing · Searchable encryption · Multi-client · Fast decryption

1 Introduction

Cloud computing [6,7,14] possesses unlimited resources and provides flexible service. A plenty of users prefer to outsource their data to the server as a result of relieving the burden of storing data locally. In this case, the physical access

© Springer International Publishing AG 2017
T. Okamoto et al. (Eds.): ProvSec 2017, LNCS 10592, pp. 24–38, 2017.
https://doi.org/10.1007/978-3-319-68637-0_2

and the administration of the data are also delegated to the server. Thus, the security of the users' data has became a growing concern. Encrypting the data before outsourcing is a positive way to provide data confidentiality. However, it also brings difficulties for the server to search over the ciphertexts. Searchable encryption (SE) [1,8,10,11,17,19,21,24] is proposed to protect the security of data while preserving the search ability over the encrypted data.

In searchable encryption schemes, a data owner encrypts the documents and outsources them to the server, then the server is allowed to search over the ciphertexts based on the user's search token and eventually returns the search results to the user. In single keyword search setting [4,8–10,12,17,18,20], the user is just allowed to submit a search token for a single queried keyword. However, just querying a single keyword is not enough in practice. Then conjunctive keyword search is proposed [1,3,5,11,16,22,26], which enables a user to submit a number of queried keywords and eventually get the corresponding documents which contain all the queried keywords. These conjunctive keyword search schemes are in the single-writer/single-reader setting, where the data owner and the user is the same person. That is, the data owner outsources encrypted documents and then she/he performs search operation. Recently, Sun et al. [19] extended conjunctive keyword search from single-writer/single-reader setting to single-writer/multi-reader (SM) setting, where any authorized user can generate a valid search token and get the corresponding search results. Kermanshahi et al. [13] provided another SM approach by using a threshold secret sharing setting.

In Sun et al.'s SMSE scheme, the authorized users are allocated with different searching and decrypting privileges. On one hand, an authorized user can only generate valid search tokens for the keywords in the authorized keyword set. On the other hand, an authorized user can only decrypt the search results which are delegated to her/him. Specifically, a user submits a search token to the server and then gets all the corresponding search results. Because the search results are encrypted based on the attribute-based encryption (ABE) [2,23], the user can just decrypt the ones in which the access policy is satisfied with the user's attribute set. In this case, the user has to try to decrypt all the search results and obtains the plaintexts or finds out that some ciphertexts don't belong to her/him. As a result, this scheme suffers a waste of both communication and decryption overheads. If we enables the server to have an ability to test whether a ciphertext can be decrypted by a user, the user's attribute set must be leaked to the server. In this way, the access policy as well as the user's attribute set is leaked to the server.

In order to protect the access policy, anonymous ABE [15] is proposed. However, it is very complex for the user to decrypt the ciphertexts. Recently, Zhang et al. [25] proposed a match-then-decrypt anonymous ABE scheme. In their scheme, the user first performs match operation to test whether a ciphertext can be decrypted. If a ciphertext can be decrypted, then the user performs decryption operation to decrypt the ciphertext. However, the match operation is performed on the user side. That is, all the related ciphertexts are also needed to be transmitted and tested by the user. For the sake of unnecessary cost, we propose a server-side match technique for the anonymous ABE scheme, in which the match operation is performed on the server side. During the match operation, both the access policy and the user's attribute set are protected. Then we apply this technique to construct a new SMSE scheme. In our scheme, instead of directly returning all the corresponding search results based on the search token, the server performs match operation and then just returns the search results which can be decrypted by the user. In addition, it is efficient for the user to decrypt the ciphertexts, which is not related to the structure of access policy. Therefore, our scheme is more practical for the communication and computation constrained user.

1.1   Our Contribution

In this paper, we first propose a server-side match technique for the anonymous ABE scheme. With this technique, we then construct a SMSE scheme with fast decryption. Our contributions are two folds:

- We propose a server-side match technique for anonymous ABE scheme. With this technique, the server has an ability to perform a match operation to test whether the access policy in a ciphertext matches a user's attribute set. This match operation neither leakages the knowledge of the access policy nor the user's attribute set to the server. Besides, the match operation for a certain user's attribute set just works over specific ciphertexts rather than the whole ones.
- We propose a new SMSE scheme based on the server-side match technique. In our scheme, the server performs search over the ciphertexts and then finds out the corresponding search results based on the search token. Instead of immediately returning all of the search results, the server tests whether the search results can be decrypted by the user and eventually it just returns the ones which can be decrypted. Furthermore, the decryption for the user is efficient. As a result, both the communication and decryption overheads in our scheme are reduced and thus it can be suitable for lightweight devices.

1.2   Organization

The rest of this paper is organized as follows. Some necessary preliminaries are given in Sect. 2. The proposed server-side match technique and the new SMSE scheme are described detailedly in Sect. 3. Next, we analyze the security of our scheme and compare it with the existing scheme in Sect. 4. Finally, the conclusions will be made in Sect. 5.

2   Preliminaries

2.1   Bilinear Pairings

Suppose $\mathbb{G}$ and $\mathbb{G}_T$ are two cyclic multiplicative groups with prime order p. Let g be a generator of $\mathbb{G}$. A bilinear pairing is a mapping $e : \mathbb{G} \times \mathbb{G} \rightarrow \mathbb{G}_T$ with the following properties:

1. Bilinear: $e(g_1^a, g_2^b) = e(g_1, g_2)^{ab}$ for all $g_1, g_2 \in \mathbb{G}$ and $a, b \in \mathbb{Z}_p$.
2. Non-degenerate: $e(g, g) \neq 1$.
3. Computable: It is efficient to compute $e(g_1, g_2)$ for all $g_1, g_2 \in \mathbb{G}$.

2.2 Intractable Assumption

In this section, we first define some intractable assumptions in the cyclic multiplicative group $\mathbb{G}$ and then we define the strong RSA assumption.

Definition 1. *The Decisional Diffie-Hellman (DDH) assumption holds in $\mathbb{G}$ if for any probabilistic polynomial-time (PPT) algorithm $\mathcal{A}$ there exists a negligible function* $\mathrm{negl}(\cdot)$ *such that*

$$|\Pr[\mathcal{A}(g, g^a, g^b, g^{ab}) = 1] - \Pr[\mathcal{A}(g, g^a, g^b, g^c) = 1]| = \mathrm{negl}(n),$$

where g is randomly selected from $\mathbb{G}$, a, b, c are randomly selected from $\mathbb{Z}_p$ and n is the security parameter.

Definition 2. *The Decisional Bilinear Diffie-Hellman (DBDH) assumption holds in $\mathbb{G}$ if for any PPT algorithm $\mathcal{A}$ there exists a negligible function* $\mathrm{negl}(\cdot)$ *such that*

$$|\Pr[\mathcal{A}(g, g^a, g^b, g^c, e(g, g)^{abc}) = 1] - \Pr[\mathcal{A}(g, g^a, g^b, g^c, g^z) = 1]| = \mathrm{negl}(n),$$

where g is randomly selected from $\mathbb{G}$, a, b, c, z are randomly selected from $\mathbb{Z}_p$ and n is the security parameter.

Definition 3. *The Decision Linear (D-Linear) assumption holds in $\mathbb{G}$ if for any PPT algorithm $\mathcal{A}$ there exists a negligible function* $\mathrm{negl}(\cdot)$ *such that*

$$|\Pr[\mathcal{A}(g, g^{z_1}, g^{z_2}, g^{z_1 z_3}, g^{z_2 z_4}, g^{z_3 + z_4}) = 1] - \Pr[\mathcal{A}(g, g^{z_1}, g^{z_2}, g^{z_1 z_3}, g^{z_2 z_4}, g^z) = 1]| = \mathrm{negl}(n),$$

where g is randomly selected from $\mathbb{G}$, z_1, z_2, z_3, z_4, z are randomly selected from $\mathbb{Z}_p$ and n is the security parameter.

Definition 4 (Strong RSA assumption). *Let p' and q' are primes and p and q are strong primes satisfied $p = 2p' + 1$ and $q = 2q' + 1$. The strong RSA assumption holds if any PPT algorithm $\mathcal{A}$ there exists a negligible function* $\mathrm{negl}(\cdot)$ *such that*

$$|\Pr[\mathcal{A}(n, g) = (z, e)]| = \mathrm{negl}(\cdot),$$

which satisfies $z^e = g \mod n$, where $n = pq$ and g is a random element in $\mathbb{Z}_n^*$.

2.3 Access Policy

In our anonymous CP-ABE scheme, we assume the system attribute set is $\mathcal{U} = \{\tau_1, \tau_2, \cdots, \tau_n\}$ and each attribute has some values $\tau_i = \{\nu_{i,1}, \nu_{i,2}, \cdots, \nu_{i,n_i}\}$. Besides every user owns its attributes $L = \{L_1, L_2, \cdots, L_n\}$. In order to achieve fine-grained control, an access policy set $P = \{P_1, P_2, \cdots, P_n\}$ is embedded in the ciphertext. A user can decrypt the ciphertext only if her/his attributes L satisfy the access policy P in the ciphertext, which is denoted as $L \vDash P$. Otherwise the user cannot decrypt the ciphertext if her/his attributes L don't satisfy the access policy P, which is denoted as $L \nvDash P$. Specifically, we assume the user's attribute set is $L = \{L_1, L_2, \cdots, L_n\} = \{\nu_{1,k_1}, \cdots, \nu_{n,k_n}\}$ and the access policy is $P = \{P_1, \cdots, P_n\} = \{\{\nu_{1,i_1}, \cdots, \nu_{1,i_n}\}, \cdots, \{\nu_{n,i_1}, \cdots, \nu_{n,i_n}\}\}$. The user can decrypt the ciphertext with P when $\nu_{i,k_i} \in P_i$ for all $1 \leq i \leq n$. Otherwise, the user cannot decrypt the ciphertext.

3   SMSE Scheme with Fast Decryption

In this section, we describe our new SMSE scheme with fast decryption. In our scheme, the server first performs search over the ciphertexts based on the search token and then finds out the corresponding search results. Instead of immediately returning the search results to the user, the server tests whether the user can decrypt them and eventually just returns the ones which can be decrypted. This is accomplished based on the server-side match technique, which can be used by the server to test whether the access policy in a ciphertext matches the user's attribute set. It means that the ciphertext can be decrypted by the user if it passes the test.

3.1   Server-Side Match Technique for Anonymous CP-ABE

In this section, we present our server-side match technique for anonymous CP-ABE (smABE). In the traditional anonymous CP-ABE schemes, the server has to return all the corresponding cihertexts to the user. Then the user performs the decryption operation on the whole ciphertexts and gets the corresponding plaintexts or gets the knowledge that she/he cannot decrypt some of them. Our smABE scheme enables the server to test whether the access policy in a ciphertext matches the user's attribute set. If matches, the ciphertext can be decrypted by the user.

- **smABE.Setup**(κ): We denote two cyclic multiplicative groups of prime order p as $\mathbb{G}$ and $\mathbb{G}_T$, and a bilinear map e as $\mathbb{G} \times \mathbb{G} \to \mathbb{G}_T$. We also assume the system attribute set is $\mathcal{U} = \{\tau_1, \tau_2, ..., \tau_n\}$ and each attribute has multiple values, where $\tau_i = \{\nu_{i,1}, \nu_{i,2}, ..., \nu_{i,n_i}\}$. The data owner randomly chooses $g_1, g_2 \xleftarrow{R} \mathbb{G}$ and $y \xleftarrow{R} \mathbb{Z}_p$, then computes $Y \leftarrow e(g_1, g_2)^y$. The system public key is $pk = \langle g_1, g_2, Y \rangle$ and the system master key is $mk = \langle y \rangle$.
- **smABE.KeyGen**(L, pk, mk): This algorithm generates the attribute secrete key $\mathbf{sk}_L$ for a certain user whose attribute set is $L = \{L_1, L_2, ..., L_n\}$. H is a hash function: $\{0,1\}^* \to \mathbb{G}$. First, the data owner randomly chooses $r, \lambda, \hat{\lambda}$ from $\mathbb{Z}_p$ and computes $D_{\Delta,0} \leftarrow g_1^r$, $D_x \leftarrow g_2^r$, $D_0 \leftarrow g_2^\lambda$, $\hat{D}_0 \leftarrow g_1^{\hat{\lambda}}$. Assume $L_i = \nu_{i,k_i}$, the data owner also computes $\hat{D}_{\Delta,0} \leftarrow g_2^y \prod_{i=1}^n H(i||\nu_{i,k_i})^r$, $D_1 \leftarrow g_1^y \prod_{i=1}^n H(0||i||\nu_{i,k_i})^\lambda$ and $\hat{D}_1 \leftarrow g_2^y \prod_{i=1}^n H(1||i||\nu_{i,k_i})^{\hat{\lambda}}$. Then the attribute secrete key is $\mathbf{sk}_L = \langle \mathbf{sk}_{mat}, \mathbf{sk}_{dec} \rangle$, where $\mathbf{sk}_{mat} = \langle D_{\Delta,0}, \hat{D}_{\Delta,0}, D_x \rangle$ and $\mathbf{sk}_{dec} = \{D_0, \hat{D}_0, D_1, \hat{D}_1\}$.

- **smABE.Enc**(M, m, P): The data owner encrypts a message $M \in \mathbb{G}_T$ under the policy of $P = \{P_1, P_2, ..., P_n\}$. In our scheme, every massage M is related to an auxiliary information $m \in \mathbb{Z}_p$. The data owner first generates $s, s', s'' \xleftarrow{R} \mathbb{Z}_p$, and then computes $\tilde{C} \leftarrow MY^s$; $C_\Delta \leftarrow Y^{s'}$; $\hat{C}_0 \leftarrow g_1^{s'}$; $C_1 \leftarrow g_2^{s''}$; $\hat{C}_1 \leftarrow g_1^{s-s''}$; $C_x \leftarrow g_2^{s'm}$. Then the data owner chooses $\{\sigma_{i,\Delta}, \sigma_{i,0}, \sigma_{i,1} \xleftarrow{R} \mathbb{G} | 1 \leq i \leq n\}$ such that $\prod_{i=1}^n \sigma_{i,\Delta} = \prod_{i=1}^n \sigma_{i,0} = \prod_{i=1}^n \sigma_{i,1} = 1_\mathbb{G}$ and computes $[C_{i,t,\Delta}, C_{i,t,0}, \hat{C}_{i,t,0}]$ as follows:
  1. If $v_{i,t} \notin P_i$, $[C_{i,t,\Delta}, C_{i,t,0}, \hat{C}_{i,t,0}] \xleftarrow{R} \mathbb{G}$.
  2. If $v_{i,t} \in P_i$,

$$[C_{i,t,\Delta}, C_{i,t,0}, \hat{C}_{i,t,0}] \leftarrow [\sigma_{i,\Delta} H(i||\nu_{i,t})^{s'}, \sigma_{i,0} H(0||i||\nu_{i,t})^{s''}, \sigma_{i,1} H(1||i||\nu_{i,t})^{s-s''}].$$

Finally, the ciphertext of M is

$$\mathbf{e} = \langle C_\Delta, C_x, \hat{C}_0, \tilde{C}, C_1, \hat{C}_1, \{\{C_{i,t,\Delta}, C_{i,t,0}, \hat{C}_{i,t,0}\}_{1 \leq t \leq n_i}\}_{1 \leq i \leq n}\rangle.$$

- **smABE.Match**$(\mathbf{e}, mt, D_{\Delta,0})$: The server performs this algorithm to test whether a certain user can decrypt the ciphertext $\mathbf{e}$. Here mt and $D_{\Delta,0}$ are given by the user, where $mt = \hat{D}_{\Delta,0} \cdot D_x^m$. This algorithm outputs "yes" if

$$e(C_x \prod_{i=1}^n C_{i,t,\Delta}, D_{\Delta,0}) C_\Delta = e(\hat{C}_0, mt).$$

According to $C_{i,t,\Delta}$, the server finds all the corresponding $C_{i,t,0}$ and $\hat{C}_{i,t,0}$, then computes $C \leftarrow \prod_{i=1}^n C_{i,t,0}$, $\hat{C} \leftarrow \prod_{i=1}^n \hat{C}_{i,t,0}$. Finally, the server sends $\mathbf{e}_{dec} = \langle \tilde{C}, C_1, \hat{C}_1, C, \hat{C} \rangle$ to the user.

- **smABE.Dec**$(\mathbf{e}_{dec}, \mathbf{sk}_{dec})$: The user performs this algorithm to decrypt the ciphertext and gets the M.

$$M \leftarrow \frac{\tilde{C} e(C, D_0) e(\hat{C}, \hat{D}_0)}{e(C_1, D_1) e(\hat{C}_1, \hat{D}_1)}.$$

3.2 Our Construction

In this section, we present our SMSE scheme with fast decryption. Our scheme just returns the search results which can be decrypted by the user. There are five algorithms $\Pi = (\mathbf{SMSE.Setup}, \mathbf{SMSE.KGen}, \mathbf{SMSE.TGen}, \mathbf{SMSE.Search}, \mathbf{SMSE.Retrieve})$ in our scheme. We denote the whole keyword set as $\mathbf{W} = \bigcup_{i=1}^d \mathbf{W}_{id_i}$, where $\mathbf{W}_{id_i}$ represents the keyword set for document d_i; the data owner's database as $\mathrm{DB} = (id_i, \mathbf{W}_{id_i})_{i=1}^d$; the identifiers set containing keyword w as $\mathrm{DB}[w] = \{id : w \in \mathbf{W}_{id}\}$; the decryption key set as K which is used to decrypt the original documents. And we let λ be the security parameter. The details of the proposed scheme are given as follows.

Algorithm 1. Search Index (TSet, XSet) Generated Algorithm

Input: MK, PK, DB, K
Output: TSet, XSet

1: TSet, XSet $\leftarrow \phi$
2: **for** $w \in$ W **do**
3:     $stag_w \leftarrow F(K_S, \tilde{g}_1^{1/w} \mod N)$; $m \leftarrow H(\tilde{g}_1^{1/w} \mod N)$; $c \leftarrow 1$
4:     **for** $id \in \mathrm{DB}[w]$ **do**
5:         $xind \leftarrow F_p(K_I, id)$; $z \leftarrow F_p(K_Z, \tilde{g}_2^{1/w} \mod N || c)$; $l \leftarrow F(stag_w, c)$
6:         $y \leftarrow xind \cdot z^{-1}$;
7:         $\mathbf{e} \leftarrow \mathbf{smABE.Enc}((id||k_{id}), m, P)$
8:         $\mathrm{TSet}[l] = (\mathbf{e}, y)$
9:         $xtag_w \leftarrow g^{F_p(K_X, \tilde{g}_3^{1/w} \mod N) \cdot xind}$; $\mathrm{XSet} \leftarrow \mathrm{XSet} \cup \{xtag_w\}$
10:         $c \leftarrow c + 1$
11:     **end for**
12: **end for**
13: **return** TSet, XSet

- **SMSE.Setup**$(\lambda, \mathrm{DB}, \mathrm{K}, \mathcal{U})$: This algorithm is run by the data owner. On input the security parameter λ, the database DB, the decryption key set K and the system attribute set $\mathcal{U}$, it outputs the system master key MK, system public key PK and the search index (TSet, XSet). Firstly, it chooses two big primes p, q, and computes $N = pq$. It denotes two pseudo-random functions $F : \{0,1\}^\lambda \times \{0,1\}^\lambda \rightarrow \{0,1\}^\lambda$, $F_p : \{0,1\}^\lambda \times \{0,1\}^\lambda \rightarrow \mathbb{Z}_p^*$ and selects random keys K_I, K_Z, K_X for the F_p and K_S for the F. Let $H: \{0,1\}^* \rightarrow \mathbb{Z}_p$ be a hash function. The data owner randomly chooses $g \xleftarrow{R} \mathbb{G}$ and $\tilde{g}_1, \tilde{g}_2, \tilde{g}_3 \xleftarrow{R} \mathbb{Z}_N^*$. Then it outputs the system master key MK $= \langle p, q, K_S, K_I, K_Z, K_X, \tilde{g}_1, \tilde{g}_2, \tilde{g}_3 \rangle$ and system public key PK $= \langle N, g \rangle$. The search index TSet and XSet are generated as in Algorithm 1 and finally they are sent to the server.

- **SMSE.KGen**$(\mathrm{MK}, L, \mathbf{w})$: This algorithm is run by the data owner. Suppose that an authorized user with attribute set L can search over keyword set $\mathbf{w} = \{w_1, w_2, ..., w_n\}$, where the appearance frequency of the keywords satisfies $|w_1| < |w_2| < \cdots < |w_n|$. The attribute private key is computed as $sk_L = \mathbf{smABE.KeyGen}(L, pk, mk) = \langle \mathbf{sk}_{mat}, \mathbf{sk}_{dec} \rangle$ for a user whose attribute set is $L = \{L_1, L_2, ..., L_n\}$. For search keyword set $\mathbf{w}$, the search private key $sk_{\mathbf{w}} = \{sk_{\mathbf{w}}^{(1)}, sk_{\mathbf{w}}^{(2)}, sk_{\mathbf{w}}^{(3)}\}$ is computed as:

$$sk_{\mathbf{w}}^i = (\tilde{g}_i^{1/\prod_{j=1}^n w_j} \mod N), \quad i = \{1, 2, 3\}.$$

Finally, the user's private key $sk = \{K_S, K_Z, K_X, sk_{\mathbf{w}}, sk_L\}$ and $\mathbf{w}$ are all sent to the user.

- **SMSE.TGen**(sk, Q): This algorithm is run by the authorized user. Suppose that an authorized user wants to perform conjunctive keyword search for $\bar{\mathbf{w}} = \{w_1', w_2', \cdots, w_m'\}$, where $m \leq n$ and w_1' is the least frequency keyword among the queried keywords. Then the search token st is generated as follows and finally it is sent to the server.

- $stag \leftarrow F(K_S, (sk_\mathbf{w}^{(1)})^{\prod_{w \in \mathbf{w} \setminus w_1'}{}^w} \bmod N) = F(K_S, \tilde{g}_1^{1/w_1'} \bmod N)$
- For $c = 1, 2, \cdots$ until the server say stop

   For $i = 2, ..., m$
   $$xt[c, i] \leftarrow g^{F_p(K_Z, (sk_\mathbf{w}^{(2)})^{\prod_{w \in \mathbf{w} \setminus w_1'}{}^w} \bmod N || c) \cdot F_p(K_X, (sk_\mathbf{w}^{(3)})^{\prod_{w \in \mathbf{w} \setminus w_i'}{}^w} \bmod N)}$$
   $$= g^{F_p(K_Z, \tilde{g}_2^{1/w_1'} \bmod N || c) \cdot F_p(K_X, \tilde{g}_3^{1/w_i'} \bmod N)};$$
   set $xt[c] = xt[c, 2], \cdots, xt[c, m]$;
- $mt \leftarrow \hat{D}_{\Delta,0} \cdot D_x^{H(\tilde{g}_1^{1/w_1'} \bmod N)}$;
- set $st = (mt, D_{\Delta,0}, stag, xt[1], xt[2], \cdots)$.

- **SMSE.Search**$(st, \text{TSet}, \text{XSet})$. This algorithm is run by the server. On input the search token st and $(\text{TSet}, \text{XSet})$, this algorithm outputs the search result S. In our scheme, the encrypted identifiers in the search result are not only satisfied with the search token, but also can be decrypted by the user. This search operation consists of two steps: *Search Step* and *Match Step*. The details are shown in Algorithm 2.
   - *Search Step*: The server first finds out all the encrypted identifiers which are satisfied with the search token. Specifically, The server uses $stag$ to find out the encrypted identifiers containing w_1', and then justifies whether they contain the other queried keywords $(w_2', \cdots, w_m')$. Finally, this step outputs the encrypted identifiers which contain all the queried keywords.
   - *Match Step*: The server then uses mt and $D_{\Delta,0}$ to test whether the user can decrypt the encrypted identifiers generated in the *Search Step*. Finally, this *Match Step* outputs the ultimate encrypted identifiers which can be decrypted by the user.
- **SMSE.Retrieve**(sk, R). This algorithm is run by the user. On input the private key sk and the search result R, this algorithm outputs the identifiers and the corresponding document keys. Finally the user retrieves the documents and decrypts them.
   - For each $\hat{e} \in R$, parse $\hat{e} = \langle e_{dec} \rangle$ and the user directly decrypts the ciphertext

$$(id \| k_{id}) \leftarrow \text{smABE.Dec}(e_{dec}, sk_{dec}).$$

   - For each id, the user sends it to the server and then gets the corresponding encrypted document. Finally the encrypted document can be decrypted by k_{id}.

Algorithm 2. SMSE.Search(st, TSet, XSet)

Input: st, TSet, XSet
Output: R
1: $S, R \leftarrow \phi$
2: Parse $st = (mt, D_{\Delta,0}, stag, xt[1], xt[2], \cdots)$
3: $c = 1; l \leftarrow F(stag, c)$
4: **while** TSet$[l]$ exist **do**
5:      $(\mathbf{e}, y) \leftarrow$ TSet$[l]$
6:      **if** $xt[c, i]^y \in$ XSet for all i **then**
7:          $S \leftarrow S \cup \{e\}$
8:      **end if**
9:      $c \leftarrow c + 1; l \leftarrow F(stag, c)$
10: **end while**
11: **for** $\mathbf{e} \in S$ **do**
12:     **if** **smABE.Match**($\mathbf{e}, mt, D_{\Delta,0}$) = "yes" **then**
13:         set $\hat{\mathbf{e}} \leftarrow \langle \mathbf{e}_{dec} \rangle; R \leftarrow R \cup \{\hat{\mathbf{e}}\}$
14:     **end if**
15: **end for**
16: **return** R

Remark 1. Based on the RAS assumption, the keywords in our scheme should be mapped to a prime number. This requirement can be achieved by the 'keyword to prime' hash function proposed in [19].

Remark 2. Our scheme can also support the queries in the form of $w_1 \wedge \phi(w_2, ..., w_m)$, where ϕ is an arbitrary boolean formula. The efficiency of such query is the same as that of conjunctive query. Specifically, if a user intends to search a query such as $w_1' \wedge \phi(w_2', ..., w_m')$, she/he should generate the search token st as in conjunctive query setting, then sends the st together with boolean formula ϕ to the server. Upon receiving the search query, the server first finds out the results for w_1', then match each result with other query keywords (for example: $xt[c, i]^y$) to determine whether they are in the XSet. For $1 \leq i \leq m$, if $xt[c, i]^y \in$ XSet, set $v_i = 1$. Otherwise, set $v_i = 0$. Next the server evaluates the query formula. If the result of expression $\phi(v_2, v_3, ..., v_m)$ is equal to 1, the server finally sends the corresponding $\mathbf{e}_{dec}$ to the user. In this case, the search complexity and the security level is the same as conjunctive query.

4   Analysis of Our Proposed Scheme

4.1   Security Analysis

We first describe the security model for our smABE scheme using the following game. A scheme is defined as IND-sCP-CPA security if no PPT adversary can break this game with a non-negligible advantage (Fig. 1).

Init: The adversary $\mathcal{A}$ submits two challenge access policies P_0 and P_1.

Setup: The challenger $\mathcal{C}$ runs the **smABE.Setup** algorithm and gives the public key PK to the $\mathcal{A}$.

Phase 1: $\mathcal{A}$ submits an attribute list L to the $\mathcal{C}$. $\mathcal{C}$ runs **smABE.KeyGen** and returns the secret key sk_L, if $(L \models P_0 \wedge L \models P_1)$ or $(L \nvDash P_0 \wedge L \nvDash P_1)$. $\mathcal{A}$ can repeat this quary polynomial times.

Challenge: $\mathcal{A}$ submits two messages M_0 and M_1 to the $\mathcal{C}$. If any attribute list satisfies both P_0 and P_1, it is required that $M_0 = M_1$. $\mathcal{C}$ randomly chooses a bit $v \in 0, 1$, computes $\mathbf{e}_{P_v} = \mathbf{smABE.Enc}(M_v, m, P_v)$ and sends $\mathbf{e}_{P_v}$ to $\mathcal{A}$.

Phase 2: Repeat the **Phase 1**. $\mathcal{A}$ cannot submit L which satisfies $L \models P_0 \wedge L \models P_1$, if $M_0 \neq M_1$.

Guess: $\mathcal{A}$ outs a guess v' of v. The advantage of $\mathcal{A}$ in this game is defined as

$$\mathbf{Adv}_{\mathrm{smABE}}^{\mathrm{IND-sCP-ABE}} = |\Pr[v' = v] - \tfrac{1}{2}|$$

Fig. 1. The IND-sCP-CPA game

Theorem 1. *Our smABE scheme is IND-sCP-CPA secure under the DBDH assumption and D-linear assumption. The advantage ϵ_{CPA} for a PPT adversary to attack the IND-sCP-CPA game in the random oracle model is negligible.*

Proof. A sequence of hybrid games are used to prove that $\mathcal{A}$ cannot win the original game G with non-negligible probability. It is supposed that the two challenge access policies $P_0 = [P_{0,1}, P_{0,2}, \cdots, P_{0,n}]$ and $P_1 = [P_{1,1}, P_{1,2}, \cdots, P_{1,n}]$ are submitted at the beginning of the game. We first modify game G to game G_0. In game G_0, if $\mathcal{A}$ obtains the secret attribute key sk_L when $(L \nvDash P_0 \wedge L \nvDash P_1)$, the ciphertext component $\tilde{C}$ is randomly chosen in G_T and the rest components are generated as usual. If $\mathcal{A}$ obtains the secret attribute key sk_L when $(L \models P_0 \wedge L \models P_1)$, all components for the ciphertext are generated like in game G. In this case, $G_0 = G_1$. Then we change the components $\{\{C_{i,t,\Delta}, C_{i,t,0}, \hat{C}_{i,t,0}\}_{1 \leq t \leq n_i}\}_{1 \leq i \leq n}$ and define a sequence of other games as follows.

For every attribute value $\nu_{i,t}$ in the universe attribute set, if $(\nu_{i,t} \in P_{0,i} \wedge \nu_{i,t} \in P_{1,i})$ or $(\nu_{i,t} \notin P_{0,i} \wedge \nu_{i,t} \notin P_{1,i})$, the components $\{C_{i,t,\Delta}, C_{i,t,0}, \hat{C}_{i,t,0}\}$ in all games are generated in normal way like in game G. If there exists a $\nu_{i,t}$ such that $(\nu_{i,t} \in P_{0,i} \wedge \nu_{i,t} \notin P_{1,i})$ or $(\nu_{i,t} \notin P_{0,i} \wedge \nu_{i,t} \in P_{1,i})$, the ciphertext components $\{C_{i,t,\Delta}, C_{i,t,0}, \hat{C}_{i,t,0}\}$ generated normally in game G_{l-1} will be replaced in game G_l by a random element in group $\mathbb{G}$. We stop this replace process when there is no such $\nu_{i,t}$ satisfies $(\nu_{i,t} \in P_{0,i} \wedge \nu_{i,t} \notin P_{1,i})$ or $(\nu_{i,t} \notin P_{0,i} \wedge \nu_{i,t} \in P_{1,i})$. In the last game, the advantage of $\mathcal{A}$ is zero because the distribution of the ciphertext components are the same no matter what the random bit ν is. The above games are denoted as $\{G, G_0, G_1, \cdots, G_{l_{max}}\}$. Then we denote the probability for $\mathcal{A}$ to win the original game G as $\Pr[\varepsilon]$ and the probability to win the game G_l is denoted as $\Pr[\varepsilon_l]$. Then the advantage in game G_0 can be represented as ϵ_{CPA}, where $\epsilon_{\mathrm{CPA}} = |\Pr[\varepsilon] - \tfrac{1}{2}| = |\Pr[\varepsilon] - \Pr[\varepsilon_{l_{max}}]|$, which has the following property.

$$\epsilon_{\text{CPA}} \le |\Pr[\varepsilon] - \Pr[\varepsilon_0]| + \sum_{l=1}^{l_{max}} |\Pr[\varepsilon_{l-1}] - \Pr[\varepsilon_l]|.$$

We can prove that ϵ_{CPA} is negligible under the assumption of DBDH and D-linear. From the Lemmas 1 and 2, the inequalities $|\Pr[\varepsilon] - \Pr[\varepsilon_0]| \le \epsilon_{\text{DBDH}}$ and $|\Pr[\varepsilon_{l-1}] - \Pr[\varepsilon_l]| \le \epsilon_{\text{DL}}$ are hold. Here the ϵ_{DBDH} and ϵ_{DL} represent the advantage for a distinguisher to win the DBDH challenge and D-linear challenge. Thus the inequality $\epsilon_{\text{CPA}} \le \epsilon_{\text{DBDH}} + |\mathcal{U}|\epsilon_{\text{DL}}$ holds, where $|\mathcal{U}|$ represents the number of attributes in the system. Under the DBDH and D-linear assumptions, ϵ_{DBDH} and ϵ_{DL} are negligible and thus ϵ_{CPA} is negligible. So we conclude that our proposed scheme smABE is IND-sCP-CPA secure under the DBDH assumption and D-linear assumption.

Lemma 1. *The probability difference for a PPT adversary $\mathcal{A}$ to win the game G and game G_0 is negligible under the DBDH assumption, that is $|\Pr[\varepsilon] - \Pr[\varepsilon_0]| \le \epsilon_{\text{DBDH}}$.*

Lemma 2. *The probability difference for a PPT adversary $\mathcal{A}$ to win the game G_{l-1} and game G_l is negligible under the D-Linear assumption, that is $|\Pr[\varepsilon_{l-1}] - \Pr[\varepsilon_l]| \le \epsilon_{\text{DL}}$ for $1 \le l \le l_{max}$.*

Theorem 2. *Our Multi-user searchable encryption scheme is secure against malicious client who intents to generate a legal search token under the assumption of strong RSA.*

Proof. Suppose that an adversary $\mathcal{A}$ can generate a valid search token for a non-authorized keyword w'. Then there exists an algorithm $\mathcal{B}$ to solve the strong RSA problem based on $\mathcal{A}$ with a non-negligible probability. First, the algorithm $\mathcal{B}$ is given a strong RSA instance (n, h_j), where $h_j \xleftarrow{R} \mathbb{Z}_n^*$. Then $\mathcal{A}$ submits a set of authorized keywords $\mathbf{w} = (w_1, \cdots, w_n)$ to the $\mathcal{B}$. $\mathcal{B}$ computes $g_j = h_j^{\prod_{i=1}^n w_i}$ mod n and sends h_j to $\mathcal{A}$. $\mathcal{A}$ guesses the search token v for a keyword $w' \notin \mathbf{w}$ and sends v to the $\mathcal{B}$. If v is a valid search token, $v = g_j^{1/w'}$ mod n. In this case, v will pass the check by $\mathcal{B}$, that is $v^{w'} = g_j$. Then $\mathcal{B}$ can solve the strong RSA problem as follows. From the construction of our scheme, $gcd(\prod_{i=1}^n w_i, w') = 1$ and $\mathcal{B}$ can find integers a and b such that $a(\prod_{i=1}^n w_i) + bw' = 1$ and then computes $h_j^{1/w'} = v^a h_j^b$. Eventually, $\mathcal{B}$ outputs $(w', h_j^{1/w'})$ which solves the RSA problem. So under the RSA assumption, an adversary cannot generate a valid search token for a non-authorized keyword with a non-negligible probability.

Theorem 3. *Our Multi-user searchable encryption scheme is $\mathcal{L}$-semantically secure against the adaptive attacks under the assumptions that DDH assumption holds in $\mathbb{G}$, F and F_p are secure PRFs and smABE is a CPA secure encryption.*

Proof. This proof is similar as [19]. $\mathcal{L}$ is a leakage function which contains the information captured by the interaction between the user and the server. And a real experiment and an ideal experiment are defined. In the real experiment, $\mathcal{A}$ can see some information generated in our real scheme. While in the ideal experiment, $\mathcal{A}$ can see some information generated in a scheme which is simulated by the leakage function $\mathcal{L}$. In our scheme, there exists two extra components mt and $D_{\Delta,0}$ in search token. However, $\mathcal{A}$ cannot distinguish them from a random element in $\mathbb{G}$. Besides, our leakage function $\mathcal{L}$ contains the information that whether a user can decrypt a certain result. But this is the same in both experiments. Then other information in $\mathcal{L}$ is the same as [19]. So we conclude that there is no simulator can distinguish whether it is in the real experiment or in the ideal experiment.

4.2 Comparison

In this section, we compare our proposed scheme with Sun et al.'s scheme. The ciphertext for a document identifier in our scheme includes special components, which are used to test by the server whether the user's attribute set satisfies the access policy in the ciphertext. In this way, after finding out the search results based on the search token, the server tests and eventually just returns the ones which can be decrypted by the user. As a result, the communication and decryption costs are all reduced.

Specifically, in Sun et al.'s scheme, the document identifiers are encrypted based on ABE. The access policy in a ciphertext is not protected and the user can learn which attribute secret key satisfies the access policy. However, the access policy is also sensitive information and needs to be protected. So in our scheme, the document identifiers are encrypted based on anonymous ABE, in which the user can not learn anything about the access policy. In this way, the ciphertext size for a document identifier is related to the size of the whole attribute set value $\eta = \sum_{i=1}^{n} n_i$. In Sun et al.'s scheme, the ciphertext size is related to the size of access policy $|\mathcal{T}|$ and the number of attributes k in the access policy. In our scheme, the match precess performed in the server side is related to the size of the whole attribute set value $\mu = \prod_{i=1}^{n} n_i$ (at most). However, the communication cost between the server and the user to transmit the search results is reduced. The cost is dramatically saved when a large number of ciphertexts are found out and only a small number can be decrypted. Furthermore, the decryption in our scheme is also very efficient. It just needs 4 paring for every ciphertext which does not depend on the size of access policy.

Table 1 presents the comparison between these two schemes. We denote E as an exponentiation operation in $\mathbb{G}_T$, P as a computation operation of a paring, $|\mathcal{T}|$ as the size of the access policy tree $\mathcal{T}$, k as the number of attributes in the $\mathcal{T}$, h as the number of non-leaf node in $\mathcal{T}$, $|\text{DB}(\bar{\mathbf{w}})|$ as the search results for the queried keywords $\bar{\mathbf{w}}$, $|\mathbb{G}|$ as the bit-length of an element in group $\mathbb{G}$, l as the ratio of the number of search results for the queried keywords to the number of ones which can be decrypted by the user.

Table 1. Comparison between two schemes

Schemes	Sun et al.'s scheme	Our proposed scheme
Access policy protection	No	Yes
Encryption cost	$\|\mathcal{T}\| + \|\mathbb{G}_T\| + (2k+1)\|\mathbb{G}\|$	$2\|\mathbb{G}_T\| + (3\eta + 4)\|\mathbb{G}\|$
Match cost	-	$2\mu P$
Communication cost	$\|DB(\bar{\mathbf{w}})\| \cdot [\|\mathcal{T}\| + \|\mathbb{G}_T\| + (2k+1)\|\mathbb{G}\|]$	$l\|DB(\bar{\mathbf{w}})\| \cdot [\|\mathbb{G}_T\| + 4\|\mathbb{G}\|]$
Decryption cost	$l\|DB(\bar{\mathbf{w}})\| \cdot [(2k+1)P + hE]$	$l\|DB(\bar{\mathbf{w}})\| \cdot 4P$

5 Conclusion

Searchable encryption is a cryptographic primitive which enables the server to search over ciphertexts and to return the corresponding search results to a user. In S/M setting, a data owner outsources the encrypted data and allows any authorized user to perform search and obtain the corresponding search results. In the existing schemes, the search results are ciphertexts which are usually encrypted by ABE and the server sends all the search results to the user. In this case, an authorized user has to try to decrypt all the search results and eventually obtains the plaintexts or finds out that some ciphertexts cannot be decrypted. As a result, this wastes both the communication and decryption overheads. In our scheme, we propose a server-side match technique which can be used by the server to test whether a user can decrypt a ciphertext without knowing the user's attribute set. Based on this technique, we construct a new SMSE scheme with fast decryption, in which the server just needs to return the search results which can be decrypted by a user. Besides, it is very efficient to perform the decryption. Therefore, both the communication and decryption overheads are dramatically reduced in our scheme.

Acknowledgement. This work was supported by the National Natural Science Foundation of China (No. 61572382), China 111 Project (No. B16037), Natural Science Basic Research Plan in Shaanxi Province of China (No. 2016JZ021), China Postdoctoral Science Foundation (No. 2017M613083), and National Key Research and Development Program of China (2017YFB0802202).

References

1. Ballard, L., Kamara, S., Monrose, F.: Achieving efficient conjunctive keyword searches over encrypted data. In: Qing, S., Mao, W., López, J., Wang, G. (eds.) ICICS 2005. LNCS, vol. 3783, pp. 414–426. Springer, Heidelberg (2005). doi:10.1007/11602897_35
2. Bethencourt, J., Sahai, A., Waters, B.: Ciphertext-policy attribute-based encryption. In: 2007 IEEE Symposium on Security and Privacy (S&P 2007), Oakland, California, USA, 20–23 May 2007, pp. 321–334 (2007)
3. Byun, J.W., Lee, D.H., Lim, J.: Efficient conjunctive keyword search on encrypted data storage system. In: Atzeni, A.S., Lioy, A. (eds.) EuroPKI 2006. LNCS, vol. 4043, pp. 184–196. Springer, Heidelberg (2006). doi:10.1007/11774716_15

4. Cash, D., Jaeger, J., Jarecki, S., Jutla, C.S., Krawczyk, H., Rosu, M., Steiner, M.: Dynamic searchable encryption in very-large databases: data structures and implementation. In: 21st Annual Network and Distributed System Security Symposium, NDSS 2014, San Diego, California, USA, 23–26 February 2014 (2014)
5. Cash, D., Jarecki, S., Jutla, C., Krawczyk, H., Roşu, M.-C., Steiner, M.: Highly-scalable searchable symmetric encryption with support for boolean queries. In: Canetti, R., Garay, J.A. (eds.) CRYPTO 2013. LNCS, vol. 8042, pp. 353–373. Springer, Heidelberg (2013). doi:10.1007/978-3-642-40041-4_20
6. Chen, X., Li, J., Huang, X., Ma, J., Lou, W.: New publicly verifiable databases with efficient updates. IEEE Trans. Dependable Sec. Comput. 12(5), 546–556 (2015)
7. Chen, X., Li, J., Weng, J., Ma, J., Lou, W.: Verifiable computation over large database with incremental updates. IEEE Trans. Comput. 65(10), 3184–3195 (2016)
8. Curtmola, R., Garay, J.A., Kamara, S., Ostrovsky, R.: Searchable symmetric encryption: improved definitions and efficient constructions. In: Proceedings of the 13th ACM Conference on Computer and Communications Security, CCS 2006, Alexandria, VA, USA, 30 October–3 November 2006, pp. 79–88 (2006)
9. Gajek, S.: Dynamic symmetric searchable encryption from constrained functional encryption. In: Sako, K. (ed.) CT-RSA 2016. LNCS, vol. 9610, pp. 75–89. Springer, Cham (2016). doi:10.1007/978-3-319-29485-8_5
10. Goh, E.: Secure indexes. IACR Cryptology ePrint Archive 2003:216 (2003)
11. Golle, P., Staddon, J., Waters, B.: Secure conjunctive keyword search over encrypted data. In: Jakobsson, M., Yung, M., Zhou, J. (eds.) ACNS 2004. LNCS, vol. 3089, pp. 31–45. Springer, Heidelberg (2004). doi:10.1007/978-3-540-24852-1_3
12. Kamara, S., Papamanthou, C., Roeder, T.: Dynamic searchable symmetric encryption. In: The ACM Conference on Computer and Communications Security, CCS 2012, Raleigh, NC, USA, 16–18 October 2012, pp. 965–976 (2012)
13. Kermanshahi, S.K., Liu, J.K., Steinfeld, R.: Multi-user cloud-based secure keyword search. In: Pieprzyk, J., Suriadi, S. (eds.) ACISP 2017. LNCS, vol. 10342, pp. 227–247. Springer, Cham (2017). doi:10.1007/978-3-319-60055-0_12
14. Liu, J.K., Liang, K., Susilo, W., Liu, J., Xiang, Y.: Two-factor data security protection mechanism for cloud storage system. IEEE Trans. Comput. 65(6), 1992–2004 (2016)
15. Nishide, T., Yoneyama, K., Ohta, K.: Attribute-based encryption with partially hidden encryptor-specified access structures. In: Bellovin, S.M., Gennaro, R., Keromytis, A., Yung, M. (eds.) ACNS 2008. LNCS, vol. 5037, pp. 111–129. Springer, Heidelberg (2008). doi:10.1007/978-3-540-68914-0_7
16. Ryu, E., Takagi, T.: Efficcient conjunctive keyword-searchable encryption. In: 21st International Conference on Advanced Information Networking and Applications (AINA 2007), Workshops Proceedings, 21–23 May 2007, Niagara Falls, Canada, vol. 1, pp. 409–414 (2007)
17. Song, D.X., Wagner, D., Perrig, A.: Practical techniques for searches on encrypted data. In: IEEE S & P 2000, Berkeley, California, USA, 14–17 May 2000, pp. 44–55 (2000)
18. Stefanov, E., Papamanthou, C., Shi, E.: Practical dynamic searchable encryption with small leakage. In: 21st Annual Network and Distributed System Security Symposium, NDSS 2014, San Diego, California, USA, 23–26 February 2014 (2014)
19. Sun, S.-F., Liu, J.K., Sakzad, A., Steinfeld, R., Yuen, T.H.: An efficient non-interactive multi-client searchable encryption with support for boolean queries. In: Askoxylakis, I., Ioannidis, S., Katsikas, S., Meadows, C. (eds.) ESORICS 2016. LNCS, vol. 9878, pp. 154–172. Springer, Cham (2016). doi:10.1007/978-3-319-45744-4_8

38   Y. Wang et al.

20. Wang, J., Chen, X., Huang, X., You, I., Xiang, Y.: Verifiable auditing for out-sourced database in cloud computing. IEEE Trans. Comput. **64**(11), 3293–3303 (2015)
21. Wang, J., Ma, H., Tang, Q., Li, J., Zhu, H., Ma, S., Chen, X.: Efficient verifiable fuzzy keyword search over encrypted data in cloud computing. Comput. Sci. Inf. Syst. **10**(2), 667–684 (2013)
22. Wang, P., Wang, H., Pieprzyk, J.: Keyword field-free conjunctive keyword searches on encrypted data and extension for dynamic groups. In: Franklin, M.K., Hui, L.C.K., Wong, D.S. (eds.) CANS 2008. LNCS, vol. 5339, pp. 178–195. Springer, Heidelberg (2008). doi:10.1007/978-3-540-89641-8_13
23. Wang, S., Liang, K., Liu, J.K., Chen, J., Yu, J., Xie, W.: Attribute-based data sharing scheme revisited in cloud computing. IEEE Trans. Inf. Forensics Secur. **11**(8), 1661–1673 (2016)
24. Wang, Y., Wang, J., Chen, X.: Secure searchable encryption: a survey. J. Commun. Inf. Netw. **1**(4), 52–65 (2016)
25. Zhang, Y., Chen, X., Li, J., Wong, D.S., Li, H., You, I.: Ensuring attribute privacy protection and fast decryption for outsourced data security in mobile cloud computing. Inf. Sci. **379**, 42–61 (2017)
26. Zuo, C., Macindoe, J., Yang, S., Steinfeld, R., Liu, J.K.: Trusted boolean search on cloud using searchable symmetric encryption. In: IEEE Trustcom 2016, pp. 113–120. IEEE (2016)

An Efficient Key-Policy Attribute-Based Searchable Encryption in Prime-Order Groups

Ru Meng[1]([✉]), Yanwei Zhou[1], Jianting Ning[2], Kaitai Liang[3], Jinguang Han[3], and Willy Susilo[4]

[1] School of Computer Science, Shaanxi Normal University, Xi'an, China
{mengru,zyw}@snnu.edu.cn
[2] Department of Computer Science,
National University of Singapore, Singapore, Singapore
ningjt@comp.nus.edu.sg
[3] Department of Computer Science, University of Surrey, Guildford, UK
ktliang88@gmail.com, jghan22@gmail.com
[4] School of Computing and Information Technology,
Institute of Cybersecurity and Cryptology, University of Wollongong,
Wollongong, Australia
wsusilo@uow.edu.au

Abstract. Public key encryption with keyword search (PEKS) is a promising cryptographic mechanism to enable secure search over encrypted data in cloud. The mechanism allows a semi-trusted cloud server to return related encrypted contents without knowing *what the query is* and *what the corresponding contents are*. It has been combined with attribute based encryption (ABE) to support more expressiveness in search. Most of the existing searchable ABE schemes, however, are restricted to heavy complexity. In particular, the size of ciphertext and pairing cost in the test phase are both linear in the size of the keyword set, say $O(n)$, where n is the number of keyword. This limitation hinders the scalability of searchable ABE in practice. To address this long-lasting open problem, this paper proposes a new key-policy attribute-based search encryption (KP-ABSE) scheme. Our construction can be regarded as a *novel* combination of fast decryption, anonymous-like encryption, and KP-ABE technologies. As of independent interest, the scheme is built in asymmetric bilinear groups. The scheme is further proved secure under the asymmetric decisional DBDH, decisional q-BDHE and decisional linear assumptions in the standard model. Compared with existing KP-ABSE schemes, our new scheme achieves the following properties: (1) flexible access structure for search - any monotonic access structure, (2) *constant* ciphertext size, (3) *constant* pairing operations in the test phase.

Keywords: Key-policy attribute-based encryption · Searchable encryption · Prime-order groups · Efficiency

© Springer International Publishing AG 2017
T. Okamoto et al. (Eds.): ProvSec 2017, LNCS 10592, pp. 39–56, 2017.
https://doi.org/10.1007/978-3-319-68637-0_3

1   Introduction

The proliferation of cloud computing has attracted many attentions from academic and industrial communities since it provides powerful computing capability and considerable storage space. It can reduce Internet users' local data management and maintenance cost significantly. Users can access cloud services whenever and wherever once they are authorized by service providers. Due to its merits, companies and individuals are willing to store their data in a remote cloud. Since users will lose their control on data after outsourcing their data to the cloud, they concern that the data may be illegally accessed by the cloud server administrator and network attackers. Considering the confidentiality of the outsourced data, users often encrypt it first, and then store the ciphertext to cloud servers. However, it is difficult to search an "exact" file among encrypted data stored in cloud.

In 2000, Song et al. [45] first proposed the definition of searchable encryption (SE). In [45], a data owner is allowed to encrypt both files and the corresponding keywords, and store the ciphertexts to cloud. When searching for a file with keywords W, the data user generates a trapdoor using his/her secret key and further sends the trapdoor to the server. After receiving the trapdoor, the server searches out the encrypted file where the keywords W matches, and returns the search result to the user. Finally, the user can use the secret key to decrypt the ciphertext and obtain the file. In 2004, Boneh et al. [8] introduced the concept of public-key encryption with keyword search (PEKS), and constructed a concrete PEKS scheme based on bilinear groups with prime order. In 2006, Khader [25] proposed an identity-based PEKS derived from identity-based encryption (IBE). In 2007, Abdalla et al. [1] presented a generic construction of PEKS by using anonymous IBE, and discussed the consistency in PEKS schemes.

Previous PEKS schemes can only support simple query and the size of ciphertexts and trapdoor (search token) is super-polynomial in the number of keywords. In practice, fine-grained access control is required. In 2013, Lai et al. [28] proposed an expressive searchable encryption scheme based on KP-ABE scheme. This scheme supports any monotonic formula, for example, ("sender : Bob AND priority : urgent OR subject : recruitment"). However, the trapdoor can leak the information of keywords, namely the test algorithm can detect whether the encrypted data contains some keywords in trapdoor. In 2014, Lv et al. [38] proposed an expressive and secure asymmetric searchable encryption (ESASE) scheme, which was based on an asymmetric bilinear group with composite order and supports non-monotonic query. Nevertheless, the scheme only disclosed whether the keywords in the trapdoor are primed or not. In 2016, Cui et al. [14] proposed an efficient and expressive keyword searchable encryption scheme constructed in a bilinear group with prime order. The scheme is selectively secure in the standard model. It supports keyword search policies in terms of conjunctive, disjunctive and any monotonic Boolean formula. However, it brings some critical issue to search efficiency. In most existing expressive searchable encryption schemes derived from ABE, both the size of ciphertext and the search cost are linear in the number of keywords. Specifically, in the test (search) algorithm, it usually requires one pairing operation for a single keyword (embedded in a given ciphertext). Hence, the existing expressive searchable encryption schemes built on top of ABE are not efficient and scalable.

Attrapadung *et al.* [2] and Hohenberger *et al.* [24] presented KP-ABE schemes with constant-size ciphertext and fast decryption, respectively. In 2014, Lai *et al.* [27] proposed a new KP-ABE with constant-size ciphertext and fast decryption, which is adaptability secure in the standard model. KP-ABE schemes do not consider the privacy issue of attributes associated with ciphertext. However, searchable encryption requests that ciphertext should not reveal any information about keywords except that a valid trapdoor is provided.In this paper, we propose a new efficient key-policy attribute-based searchable encryption (KP-ABSE) scheme which is derived from an asymmetric bilinear group with prime order. In this scheme, the privacy of keyword in both ciphertext and trapdoor are addressed. Moreover, both the size of ciphertext and the computation cost of the test algorithm are constant. Compared with expressive searchable encryption based on bilinear groups with prime order, our work is more efficient.

1.1 Technical Roadmap

Protecting Privacy of Keywords in Ciphertext. (1) We use anonymity from the asymmetric technique [15] to encrypt keywords in group $\mathbb{G}$; while trapdoors are generated in group $\hat{\mathbb{G}}$ to prevent cloud servers, and adversaries from raising keyword guess attacks using pairing operations [5]. As claimed in [15], asymmetric bilinear groups provide good properties, including compact representation of group elements, a flexible choice of elliptic curve implementation [18] and strong security [20]. (2) We use the linear splitting technique [9] to split the random exponent used to hide keywords into two parts. As a result, adversaries cannot obtain any information about keywords even if they acquire the ciphertext and public parameters. Secret keys are randomized in the test algorithm.

Protecting Privacy of Keywords in Access Structure. We divide each keyword into two parts: the keyword name and the keyword value [26]. In practice, keyword values are more sensitive than keyword names. If the set of attributes associated with a users private key does not satisfy the access structure associated with a ciphertext, attribute values in the access structure are hidden, while other information, such as attribute names, about the access structure is public. Suppose that the access structure in personal health database is (illness = diabetes) OR (gender = male) OR (department = medical) OR (affiliation= city hospital) where illness, gender, department and affiliation are keyword names and diabetes, male, medical and city hospital are keyword values. The keyword names contains less sensitive information and can be released, while keyword values are very sensitive and should be kept secret. Hence, in our scheme, we mainly consider to protect the privacy of keyword values. PKES is subject to the offline keywords dictionary guessing attacks since anyone who knows the trapdoor and public parameters can conclude the value embedded in the trapdoor by executing exhaustive search. To prevent the above attacks, the designated technique [43] is used. The idea is that trapdoors are encrypted under the public key of the cloud server such that adversaries cannot acquire any information about keywords without knowing the secret key. Therefore, trapdoors can be transferred in public channels.

1.2   Contributions

We propose a new key-policy attribute-based search encryption scheme (KP-ABSE) which is derived from KP-ABE in asymmetric bilinear group with prime order. The proposed scheme has the following good properties: (1) It is expressive and supports any monotonic access structure; (2) It has constant-size ciphertext and supports fast decryption; (3) The number of pairing operations needed in the test algorithm is constant. Therefore, it reduces the computation cost on cloud server side as well as communication cost between the data users and cloud. One disadvantage of our scheme is that the size of trapdoors is $\mathcal{O}(n \cdot \ell)$, where n is the number of attributes in the system and ℓ is the number of leaf nodes in the access structure. Note that we will regard this as an open problem of our research work. However, depending on applications, one should take into consideration if the increase of trapdoor size is worthy.

1.3   Related Work

Attribute-Based Encryption. To implement fine-grained access control on sensitive data, Sahai and Water [44] introduced the definition of attribute-based encryption (ABE). ABE schemes can be classified into two types: key-policy ABE (KP-ABE) [21] and ciphertext-policy ABE (CP-ABE) [4]. In a KP-ABE scheme [21], secret keys are associated with access structures; while ciphertexts are labeled with sets of attributes. A user can decrypt a ciphertext if and only if the access structure associated with his secret key can be satisfied by the attributes labeled in ciphertexts. On the contrary, in a CP-ABE scheme [4], secret keys are labeled with sets of attributes; while ciphertexts are associated with access structures.

Goyal *et al.* [21] proposed a KP-ABE scheme which supports any monotonic access structure. Later, Ostrovsky *et al.* [41] presented a KP-ABE system which supports non-monotonic access structures. Lewko *et al.* [29] proposed the first fully secure KP-ABE scheme supporting any monotonic access structure. Chase *et al.* [10,11] considered multi-authority KP-ABE schemes. The first CP-ABE was proposed by Bethencourt *et al.* [4] and was proven to be secure in the generic group model. Later, Cheung and Newport [12] presented a CP-ABE scheme which is secure in the standard model; while, it can only support restricted access structures, for example AND gate. Lewko *et al.* [30] considered multi-authority CP-ABE schemes to reduce the trust on central authority. Some ABE variants and applications can be seen in [32,33,39,40,46].

Attribute-Based Encryption with Fast Decryption. In KP-ABE schemes, both the size of the ciphertext and the decryption cost are linear with the number of required attributes. To reduce the size of ciphertext and decryption cost, some new KP-ABE were presented [2,27,44]. Meanwhile, in CP-ABE scenario, the size of ciphertext and decryption cost were also considered. Emura *et al.* [16] proposed a CP-ABE scheme with constant-size ciphertext which can only supports restricted access structures, such as AND gate. Herranz *et al.* [23] described a CP-ABE scheme with constant-size ciphertext which supports threshold access structures. Hohenberger [24] proposed a KP-ABE with fast decryption. In [24], the decryption cost is constant, instead of linear with the number of required attributes. In 2014, Lai *et al.* [27] proposed a KP-ABE with constant-size ciphertext and fast decryption.

Keyword search over Encrypted Data. Boneh *et al.* [8] initiated the research on PEKS and gave a specific construction which only supports equality queries. Abdalla *et al.* [1] addressed the consistency in PEKS schemes, and analyzed the relationship between PEKS and anonymous IBE. To guarantee the correctness of the searching results, verifiable keyword search schemes have been proposed [3,17,42]. In these schemes, each keyword is represented as the root of one polynomial. It is easy to check whether a keyword is included by evaluating the polynomial on the keyword and verify whether the output is zero or not. Zheng *et al.* [48] proposed a novel PEKS called verifiable attribute-based keyword search (VABKS). This allows legitimate data users to outsource the (often costly) search operations to cloud servers and verify whether cloud servers have faithfully executed the search operations. Some variants of ABE searchable encryption have been proposed in [34–37].

1.4 Organization

The rest of this paper is organized as follows. In Sect. 2, we briefly review definitions and models used in this paper. Section 3 describes the preliminaries used throughout this paper and notions of KP-ABSE. In Sect. 4, a concrete KP-ABSE scheme is presented. We compare our work with other related works in Sect. 5. Section 6 concludes the paper.

2   System Definitions

2.1 System Algorithms

A key-policy attribute-based search encryption (KP-ABSE) system includes four parties, namely, data owner, cloud server, Trusted Key Generator (TKG), and data user.

Definition 1. *A KP-ABSE system consists of the following algorithms* [14]:

1. *$Setup(1^\lambda) \rightarrow (pars, msk)$: intaking a security parameter λ, the TKG runs the setup algorithm to construct the public parameters pars, and the master secret key msk. The pars is published, while the msk is kept secret.*

2. $sKeyGen(pars) \rightarrow (pk_s, sk_s)$: *intaking pars, the TKG runs the server key generation algorithm to construct the public key pk_s and the private key sk_s for the cloud server.*

3. $Encrypt(pars, \boldsymbol{W}) \rightarrow CT$: *intaking pars, and a set of keywords $\boldsymbol{W}$, a data owner runs the encryption algorithm to output a ciphertext CT.*

4. $Trapdoor(pars, msk, pk_s, \mathbb{A}) \rightarrow T_{\mathbb{M}}$: *intaking pars, msk, pk_s and an access structure $\mathbb{A}$ (corresponding to some keyword set), the TKG runs the trapdoor generation algorithm to construct a trapdoor $T_{\mathbb{M}}$, and further sends $T_{\mathbb{M}}$ to the cloud server.*

5. $Test(pars, sk_s, CT, T_{\mathbb{M}}) \rightarrow 0/1$: *Intaking pars, sk_s, CT and $T_{\mathbb{M}}$, the cloud server runs the test algorithm. It outputs 1 if the keyword set embedded in CT matches the access structure in $T_{\mathbb{M}}$, and 0 otherwise.*

Correctness: A key-policy attribute-based search encryption is correct if

$$
\Pr\left[Test(pars, sk_s, CT, T_{\mathbb{M}}) \rightarrow 1 \,\middle|\, \begin{array}{l} Setup(1^{\lambda}) \rightarrow (pars, msk); \\ Encrypt(pars, \mathbf{W}) \rightarrow CT; \\ sKeyGen(pars) \rightarrow (pk_s, sk_s); \\ Trapdoor(pars, msk, pk_s, \mathbb{A}) \rightarrow T_{\mathbb{M}} \end{array} \right] = 1.
$$

2.2 System Workflow

The architecture of our system workflow is shown in Fig. 1, which is composed of four entities: *a trusted key generator (TKG)* who publishes the system parameter and holds a master private key and is responsible for trapdoor generation for the system. We may regard the TKG as trusted device(s), like TPM. A user may make use of this device in some untrusted computers (like those in library or public area) to generate a token for further search. But the device may not have sufficient knowledge about positive or negative cases (on access control rules). Because it may not be allowed to access, say the access control list.

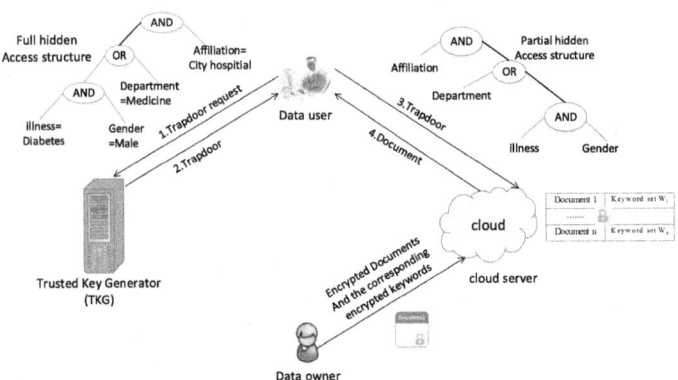

Fig. 1. System workflow

data owners who outsource encrypted data to a public cloud, *data users* who are privileged to search and access encrypted data, and *a cloud server* who executes the keyword search operations for data users. To enable the cloud server to search over ciphertexts, the data owners append every encrypted document with encrypted keywords. A data user issues a trapdoor request by sending a keyword access structure to the TKG which generates and returns a trapdoor corresponding to the access structure. After obtaining a trapdoor, the data user sends the trapdoor and the corresponding partial hidden access structure (i.e., the access structure without keyword values) to the designated cloud server. The latter performs the testing operations between each ciphertext and the trapdoor using its private key, and forwards the matching ciphertexts to the data user.

2.3 Adversary Models

In this paper, we assume that data owner, data user and the cloud server are semi-trusted, while the TKG is fully trusted. However, for a data user, he/she may choose to guess the keyword set embedded into a given ciphertext without the help of the server. For a "curious" server, it may curiously guess the keyword set in the ciphertext of which the corresponding search trapdoor is not given; it may also guess the keyword information from a given search trapdoor. Therefore, we define the following three security models.

Indistinguishability Against Chosen Keyword-Set Attacks (IND-CKA). This security model focuses on the privacy of the keyword set associated with a given ciphertext. There are two kinds of adversaries in this model, one is outside-attacker, and the other is the cloud server itself. Below, we define two security games by constructing interactions between a challenger $\mathcal{B}$ and an adversary $\mathcal{A}$.

IND-CKA Security for Outsider. This security game between $\mathcal{A}_1$ and $\mathcal{B}$ is used to show that a system outsider, without the help of the cloud server, cannot tell if a given ciphertext contains some specified keyword set (here the outsider is allowed to commit to two known keyword sets at the outset of the game).

Definition 2. *A KP-ABSE scheme is $IND\text{-}CKA^{\mathcal{A}_1}$ secure if no PPT adversary $\mathcal{A}_1$ can win the game below with non-negligible advantage* [14].

1. **Init.** $\mathcal{A}_1$ *commits to two equal length challenge keyword sets* W_0^*, W_1^*.
2. **Setup.** $\mathcal{B}$ *runs* $Setup(1^\lambda)$, *and further sends pars to* $\mathcal{A}_1$. *It runs* $sKeyGen(pars)$ *and next returns* pk_s *to* $\mathcal{A}_1$.
3. **Phase 1.** $\mathcal{A}_1$ *issues search trapdoor queries to* $\mathcal{B}$ *by submitting* $(\mathbb{M}_1, \rho_1, \{W_{\rho_1(i)}\}), ..., (\mathbb{M}_{q_1}, \rho_{q_1}, \{W_{\rho_{q_1}(i)}\})$. $\mathcal{B}$ *returns the corresponding trapdoors to* $\mathcal{A}_1$ *by running the algorithm Trapdoor.*
4. **Challenge.** $\mathcal{B}$ *returns the challenge ciphertext* $CT^* = Encrypt(pars, W_\beta^*)$ *to* $\mathcal{A}_1$, *where* $\beta \in_R \{0, 1\}$. *Note that the challenge ciphertext cannot match any trapdoor constructed in Phase 1 (namely, both of the challenge keyword sets cannot match the given trapdoors).*

5. **Phase 2.** $\mathcal{A}_1$ *continues making queries as in Phase 1, by issuing* $(\mathbb{M}_{q_1+1},$ $\rho_{q_1+1}, \{W_{\rho_{q_1+1}(i)}\}), ..., (\mathbb{M}_q, \rho_q, \{W_{\rho_q(i)}\})$, *with a restriction that the queries cannot match the given challenge keyword sets.*
6. **Guess.** $\mathcal{A}_1$ *outputs a guess bit* $\beta' \in \{0,1\}$. *If* $\beta = \beta'$, $\mathcal{A}_1$ *wins.*

The advantage of $\mathcal{A}_1$ *is defined as* $Adv_{\mathcal{A}_1}(1^\lambda) = |Pr[\beta' = \beta] - \frac{1}{2}|$.

IND-CKA Security for the Cloud Server. This security game between $\mathcal{A}_2$ and $\mathcal{B}$ is used to show that the cloud server, without a valid search trapdoor, cannot tell if a given ciphertext contains some specified keyword set (here the cloud server is allowed to commit to two "known" keyword sets in advance).

Definition 3. *A KP-ABSE scheme is* $IND\text{-}CKA^{\mathcal{A}_2}$ *secure if no PPT adversary* $\mathcal{A}_2$ *can win the game below with non-negligible advantage* [14].

1. **Init.** $\mathcal{A}_2$ *commits to two equal length challenge keyword sets* $\boldsymbol{W}_0^*, \boldsymbol{W}_1^*$.
2. **Setup.** $\mathcal{B}$ *runs* $Setup(1^\lambda)$ *to send pars to* $\mathcal{A}_2$. *It further runs* $sKeyGen(pars)$ *to return* pk_s, sk_s *to* $\mathcal{A}_2$.
3. **Phase 1.** $\mathcal{A}_2$ *issues search trapdoor queries to* $\mathcal{B}$ *by submitting* $(\mathbb{M}_1, \rho_1,$ $\{W_{\rho_1(i)}\}), ..., (\mathbb{M}_{q_1}, \rho_{q_1}, \{W_{\rho_{q_1}(i)}\})$. *For each query* $(\mathbb{M}_j, \rho_j, \{W_{\rho_j(i)}\})$, $j \in$ $[1, q_1]$, $\mathcal{B}$ *returns the corresponding trapdoor* $T_{\mathbb{M}_j}$ *to* $\mathcal{A}_2$ *by running the algorithm* $Trapdoor$.
4. **Challenge.** $\mathcal{B}$ *randomly chooses* $\beta \in \{0,1\}$ *and returns the challenge ciphertext* $CT^* = Encrypt(pars, \boldsymbol{W}_\beta^*)$ *to* $\mathcal{A}_2$ *with a restriction that the challenge ciphertext cannot match any trapdoor given in Phase 1.*
5. **Phase 2.** $\mathcal{A}_2$ *continues making queries by issuing* $(\mathbb{M}_{q_1+1}, \rho_{q_1+1},$ $\{W_{\rho_{q_1+1}(i)}\}), ..., (\mathbb{M}_q, \rho_q, \{W_{\rho_q(i)}\})$, *with a restriction that the queries cannot match the given challenge keyword sets.*
6. **Guess.** $\mathcal{A}_2$ *outputs a guess bit* $\beta' \in \{0,1\}$. *If* $\beta = \beta'$, $\mathcal{A}_2$ *wins.*

The advantage of $\mathcal{A}_2$ *is defined as* $Adv_{\mathcal{A}_2}(1^\lambda) = |Pr[\beta' = \beta] - \frac{1}{2}|$.
For $\mathcal{A} \in \{\mathcal{A}_1, \mathcal{A}_2\}$, *an KP-ABSE system is selectively IND-CKA secure if the advantage function referring to the security* $Game_{\Pi,\mathcal{A}}^{(IND)}$, $Adv_{\Pi,\mathcal{A}}^{(IND)}(\lambda) = Pr[\beta \neq \beta'] - \frac{1}{2}$ *is negligible in the security parameter* λ *for any probabilistic polynomial time adversary algorithm* $\mathcal{A}$.

3 Preliminaries

3.1 Bilinear Maps

Let $\mathbb{G}$, $\hat{\mathbb{G}}$ and $\mathbb{G}_T$ be all multiplicative groups of prime order $p \in \Theta(2^\lambda)$, respectively generated by $g, \hat{g}$ and $e : \mathbb{G} \times \hat{\mathbb{G}} \to \mathbb{G}_T$ is an efficient bilinear map with the following properties: (1) *Bilinearity*: for all $a, b \in_R \mathbb{Z}_p$, $e(g^a, \hat{g}^b) = e(g, \hat{g})^{ab}$; (2) *Non-degeneracy*: $e(g, \hat{g}) \neq 1_{\mathbb{G}_T}$, where $1_{\mathbb{G}_T}$ is the unit of $\mathbb{G}_T$; (3) *Computability*: for all $g \in \mathbb{G}$ and $\hat{g} \in \hat{\mathbb{G}}$, $e(g, \hat{g})$ can be computed efficiently.

3.2   Complexity Assumptions

Definition 4. Asymmetric Decisional Bilinear Diffie-Hellman (DBDH) Assumption *[47] is that all Probabilistic Polynomial Time (PPT) algorithm $\mathcal{A}$ have an advantage negligible in λ of distinguishing $e(g, \hat{g})^{abc} \in \mathbb{G}_T$ from a random element in $\mathbb{G}_T$ by given the vector $y = (g, g^a, g^c, \hat{g}, \hat{g}^a, \hat{g}^b)$. The advantage of $\mathcal{A}$ is defined as $|Pr[\mathcal{A}(y, e(g, \hat{g})^{abc}) = 1] - Pr[\mathcal{A}(y, Z) = 1]|$, where the probability is over the randomly chosen $g \leftarrow \mathbb{G}, \hat{g} \leftarrow \hat{\mathbb{G}}$, a, b, c, and the random bits consumed by $\mathcal{A}$.*

Definition 5. Asymmetric Decisional q-Bilinear Diffie-Hellman Exponent (q-BDHE) Assumption *[6] is that all PPT algorithms $\mathcal{A}$ have an advantage negligible in λ of distinguishing $e(g, \hat{g})^{a^{q+1}b} \in \mathbb{G}_T$ from a random element in $\mathbb{G}_T$ by given the vector*

$$y = g, g^b, g^a, g^{a^2}, ..., g^{a^q}, g^{a^{q+2}}, \hat{g}, \hat{g}^a, \hat{g}^{a^2}, ..., \hat{g}^{a^q}, \hat{g}^{a^{q+2}} ..., \hat{g}^{a^{2q}}, T$$

The advantage of $\mathcal{A}$ is defined as $|Pr[\mathcal{A}(y, e(g, \hat{g})^{a^{q+1}b}) = 1] - Pr[\mathcal{A}(y, T) = 1]|$, where the probability is over the randomly chosen a, b, and the generator $g, \hat{g}$, and the random bits consumed by $\mathcal{A}$.

Definition 6. Asymmetric Decisional Linear Assumption *[7] is that all PPT algorithms $\mathcal{A}$ have an advantage negligible in λ of distinguishing $Z = g^{x_3+x_4} \in \mathbb{G}$ from a random element in $\mathbb{G}$ by given the vector $y = \{g, g^{x_1}, g^{x_2}, g^{x_1 x_3}, g^{x_2 x_4}, \hat{g}, g^{\hat{x}_1}, g^{\hat{x}_2}\}$. The advantage of $\mathcal{A}$ is defined as $|Pr[\mathcal{A}(y, g^{x_3+x_4} = 1] - Pr[\mathcal{A}(y, Z) = 1]|$, where the probability is over the randomly chosen $x_1, x_2, x_3, x_4 \in \mathbb{Z}_p$, and the random bits consumed by $\mathcal{A}$. We remark that the elements $\hat{g}, g^{\hat{x}_1}, g^{\hat{x}_2}$ were not explicitly included in Boenh's et al. original formulation.*

3.3   Building Blocks

Definition 7. Access Structure *[31]. Let $\{P_1, ..., P_n\}$ be a set of parties. A collection $\mathbb{A} \subseteq 2^{\{P_1, ..., P_n\}}$ is monotone if $\forall B, C: B \in \mathbb{A}$ and $B \subseteq C$, then $C \in \mathbb{A}$. An access structure (respectively, monotone access structure) is a collection (respectively, monotone collection) $\mathbb{A}$ of non-empty subsets of $\{P_1, ..., P_n\}$, i.e., $\mathbb{A} \subseteq 2^{\{P_1, ..., P_n\}} \setminus \{\}$. The set in $\mathbb{A}$ are called the authorized sets, and the sets not in $\mathbb{A}$ are called the unauthorized sets.*

Note in our setting keywords will play the role of parties and we only consider the monotone access structures, and the negation of a keyword is regarded as a separate keyword.

Definition 8. Linear Secret-Sharing Schemes (LSSS) *[31]. A secret sharing scheme Π over a set of parties P is called linear (over $\mathbb{Z}_p$) if*

1. The shares for each party form a vector over $\mathbb{Z}_p$.

2. *There exists a matrix* $\mathbb{M}$ *called the share-generating matrix for* Π. *The matrix* $\mathbb{M}$ *has* l *rows and* n *columns. For all* $i = 1, ..., l$, *the* i*th row of* $\mathbb{M}$ *is labeled by a party* $\rho(i)$ (ρ *is a function from* $\{1, ..., l\}$ *to* P)*. When we consider the column vector* $v = (\alpha, r_2, ..., r_n)$, *where* $\alpha \in \mathbb{Z}_p$ *is the secret to be shared and* $r_2, ..., r_n \in \mathbb{Z}_p$ *are randomly chosen, then* $\mathbb{M}v$ *is the vector of* l *shares of the secret* α *according to* Π. *The share* $(\mathbb{M}v)_i$ *belongs to party* $\rho(i)$.

The linear reconstruction property: let Π be an LSSS for access structure $\mathbb{A}$, W denote an authorized set, and define $I \subseteq \{1, ..., l\}$ as $I = \{i | \rho(i) \in W\}$. The vector $(1, 0, ..., 0)$ is in the span of rows of $\mathbb{M}$ indexed by I, and there exist constants $\{\omega_i \in \mathbb{Z}_p\}_{i \in I}$ such that, for any valid shares $\{\lambda_i\}$ of a secret α according to Π, we have $\sum_{i \in I} \omega_i \lambda_i = \alpha$. These constants $\{\omega_i\}$ can be found in time polynomial in the size of share-generating matrix $\mathbb{M}$. But for unauthorized sets of rows I, the target vector is not in the span of the rows of the set I. Moreover, there will exists a vector ω, such that $\omega \cdot (1, 0, ..., 0) = -1$ and $\omega \cdot \mathbb{M}_i = 0$ for all $i \in I$.

Definition 9. *Target Collision Resistant Hash Function [13].* *A TCR hash function* H *guarantees that given a random element* x *which is from the valid domain of* H, *a PPT adversary* A *cannot find* $y \neq x$ *such that* $H(x) = H(y)$. *We let* $Adv_{H,A}^{TCR} = Pr[(x, y) \leftarrow \mathcal{A}(1^k) : H(x) = H(y), x \neq y, x, y \in DH]$ *be the advantage of* A *in successfully finding collisions from a TCR hash function* H, *where* DH *is the valid input domain of* H, k *is the security parameter. If a hash function is chosen from a TCR hash function family,* $Adv_{H,A}^{TCR}$ *is negligible.*

4   A New KP-ABSE

4.1   Construction

- **Setup**$(1^\lambda) \rightarrow (pars, msk)$. The setup algorithm takes as input a security parameter 1^λ. It chooses bilinear groups $\mathbb{G}, \hat{\mathbb{G}}$ of prime order p with generators $g, \hat{g}$, respectively. It symmetrically random chooses $u, h, \delta \in \mathbb{G}$, $\hat{u}, \hat{h}, \hat{\delta} \in \hat{\mathbb{G}}$ and $\alpha, d_1, d_2, d_3, d_4 \in \mathbb{Z}_p^*$. It then sets $g_1 = g^{d_1}, g_2 = g^{d_2}, g_3 = g^{d_3}, g_4 = g^{d_4}$. It also chooses a collision-resistant hash function H that maps group elements in $\mathbb{G}_T$ to group elements in $\mathbb{G}$. The public parameters $pars$ and the master secret key msk are given by

$$pars = (H, g, u, h, \delta, \hat{u}, g_1, g_2, g_3, g_4, e(g, \hat{g})^\alpha),$$

$$msk = (\alpha, \hat{g}, \hat{h}, \hat{\delta}, d_1, d_2, d_3, d_4).$$

- **sKeyGen**$(pars) \rightarrow (pk_s, sk_s)$. The algorithm takes as input the public parameter $pars$. It randomly chooses $\kappa \in \mathbb{Z}_p^*$ and outputs the public and private key pair $(pk_s, sk_s) = (g^\kappa, \kappa)$ for the cloud server.
- **Trapdoor**$(pars, pk_s, msk, \mathbb{A} = (\mathbb{M}, \rho, \mathcal{T})) \rightarrow T_{\mathbb{M}, \rho}$. The algorithm takes as input the public parameter $pars$, the server public key pk_s, the master private key msk and an LSSS access structure $(\mathbb{M}, \rho, \mathcal{T})$, where $\mathbb{M}$ is $l \times n$

share-generating matrix, ρ is a map from each row of $\mathbb{M}$ to an attribute name, $\mathcal{T} = (z_{\rho(1)}, ..., z_{\rho(l)})$ and $z_{\rho(i)}$ is the value of keyword name $\rho(i)$ specified by the access formula. It randomly chooses a vector $\boldsymbol{v} = (\alpha, y_2, ..., y_n) \in \mathbb{Z}_p^n$, and computes $\lambda_i = \boldsymbol{v} \cdot \mathbb{M}_i$ for each $i = [l]$. Let Q_i denote the set $[n] \setminus \{\rho(i)\}$ for each $i \in [l]$. For each row $\mathbb{M}_i$ of $\mathbb{M}$, it chooses random $r, r', t_{1,1}, t_{1,2}, ..., t_{l,1}, t_{l,2} \in \mathbb{Z}_p$, computes $D = g^r, \hat{D} = \hat{g}^{r'}$, and outputs the trapdoor as $T_{\mathbb{M},\rho} = ((\mathbb{M}, \rho), D, \hat{D}, \{D_i, R_i, T_{i,1}, T_{i,2}, T_{i,3}, T_{i,4}, \{Q_{i,j}, Q'_{i,j}, Q''_{i,j}, Q'''_{i,j}\}_{j \in Q_i}\}_{i \in [l]})$

$$D_i = \hat{g}^{\lambda_i} \hat{\delta}^{d_1 d_2 t_{i,1} + d_3 d_4 t_{i,2}}, R_i = H(e(pk_s, \hat{D})^r) \cdot \hat{g}^{d_1 d_2 t_{i,1} + d_3 d_4 t_{i,2}},$$

$$T_{i,1} = (\hat{u}^{z_{\rho(i)}} \hat{h})^{-d_2 t_{i,1}}, Q_{i,j} = (\hat{u}^{z_j})^{-d_2 t_{i,1}};$$

$$T_{i,2} = (\hat{u}^{z_{\rho(i)}} \hat{h})^{-d_1 t_{i,1}}, Q'_{i,j} = (\hat{u}^{z_j})^{-d_1 t_{i,1}};$$

$$T_{i,3} = (\hat{u}^{z_{\rho(i)}} \hat{h})^{-d_4 t_{i,2}}, Q''_{i,j} = (\hat{u}^{z_j})^{-d_4 t_{i,2}};$$

$$T_{i,4} = (\hat{u}^{z_{\rho(i)}} \hat{h})^{-d_3 t_{i,2}}, Q'''_{i,j} = (\hat{u}^{z_j})^{-d_3 t_{i,2}}.$$

- **Encrypt**$(pars, \boldsymbol{W} = (\mathrm{w}_1, ..., \mathrm{w}_n)) \to CT$. The algorithm takes as input the public parameter $pars$ and a keyword set $\boldsymbol{W}$ (each keyword is denoted as keyword name and keyword value, i is the generic keyword name and w_i is the corresponding keyword value), where $\mathrm{w}_1, ..., \mathrm{w}_n \in \mathbb{Z}_p$ are the values of $\boldsymbol{W}$. It chooses random $\mu, s, s_1, s_2 \in \mathbb{Z}_p$, and outputs a ciphertext $CT = (C, C', C'', E_1, E_2, E_3, E_4)$ as

$$C = e(g, \hat{g})^{\alpha \mu}, C' = g^{\mu}, C'' = \delta^{-\mu} (h \prod_{i=1}^{n} u^{\mathrm{w}_i})^s$$

$$E_1 = g_1^{s-s_1}, E_2 = g_2^{s_1}, E_3 = g_3^{s-s_2}, E_4 = g_4^{s_2}.$$

- **Test**$(pars, sk_s, CT, T_{\mathbb{M},\rho})$. The algorithm takes as input the public parameter $pars$, the server private key sk_s, a ciphertext $CT = (C, C', C'', E_1, E_2, E_3, E_4)$ on a keyword set $\boldsymbol{W}$ and a trapdoor $T_{\mathbb{M},\rho}$ associated with an access structure $\mathbb{A} = (\mathbb{M}, \rho, \mathcal{T})$. If the keyword set $\boldsymbol{W}$ does not satisfy $\mathbb{A}$, output $\bot$. Otherwise, if the keyword set $\boldsymbol{W}$ satisfies $\mathbb{A}$, the test algorithm first finds $\mathcal{I} \subseteq [1, l]$ and constants $\{\omega_i\}_{i \in \mathcal{I}} \in \mathbb{Z}_p$ such that $\sum_{i \in \mathcal{I}} \omega_i \mathbb{M}_i = (1, 0, ..., 0)$ and $\mathrm{w}_{\rho(i)} = \mathrm{z}_{\rho(i)}$ for $\forall i \in \mathcal{I}$. The algorithm then does as follows:

(1) Pre-processing step on the private key
Let Q_i denote the set $[n] \setminus \{\rho(i)\}$ for each $i \in \mathcal{I}$. Note that if $j \in Q_i$, then $j \neq \rho(i)$. Since for each $i \in \mathcal{I}$, $\mathrm{w}_{\rho(i)} = \mathrm{z}_{\rho(i)}$, then we have

$$\hat{T}_{i,1} = T_{i,1} \prod_{j \in Q_i} Q_{i,j}^{\mathrm{w}_j} = (\hat{h} \prod_{j=1}^{n} \hat{u}^{\mathrm{w}_j})^{-d_2 t_{i,1}},$$

$$\hat{T}_{i,2} = T_{i,2} \prod_{j \in Q_i} (Q'_{i,j})^{\mathrm{w}_j} = (\hat{h} \prod_{j=1}^{n} \hat{u}^{\mathrm{w}_j})^{-d_1 t_{i,1}},$$

$$\hat{T}_{i,3} = T_{i,3} \prod_{j \in Q_i} (Q''_{i,j})^{w_j} = (\hat{h} \prod_{j=1}^{n} \hat{u}^{w_j})^{-d_4 t_{i,2}},$$

$$\hat{T}_{i,4} = T_{i,4} \prod_{j \in Q_i} (Q'''_{i,j})^{w_j} = (\hat{h} \prod_{j=1}^{n} \hat{u}^{w_j})^{-d_3 t_{i,2}},$$

(2) $I_{\mathbb{M},\rho}$ is a set of minimum subsets satisfied $(\mathbb{M}, \rho)$, it then checks whether there is an $\mathcal{I} \in I_{\mathbb{M},\rho}$ statisfying

$$e(C', \prod_{i \in \mathcal{I}} D_i^{\omega_i}) e(C'', \prod_{i \in \mathcal{I}} (\frac{R_i}{H_2(e(D, \hat{D})^\kappa)})^{\omega_i}) e(E_1, \prod_{i \in \mathcal{I}} (\hat{T}_{i,1})^{\omega_i}) e(E_2, \prod_{i \in \mathcal{I}} (\hat{T}_{i,2})^{\omega_i})$$

$$\cdot e(E_3, \prod_{i \in \mathcal{I}} (\hat{T}_{i,3})^{\omega_i}) e(E_4, \prod_{i \in \mathcal{I}} (\hat{T}_{i,4})^{\omega_i})$$

$$= e(g^\mu, \prod_{i \in \mathcal{I}} (\hat{g}^{\lambda_i} \hat{\delta}^{d_1 d_2 t_{i,1} + d_3 d_4 t_{i,2}})^{\omega_i}) \cdot e(\delta^{-\mu}(h \prod_{i=1}^{n} u^{w_i})^s, \prod_{i \in \mathcal{I}} (\hat{g}^{d_1 d_2 t_{i,1} + d_3 d_4 t_{i,2}})^{\omega_i})$$

$$e(g_1^{s-s_1}, (\hat{h} \prod_{j=1}^{n} \hat{u}^{w_j})^{-d_2 t_{i,1} w_i}) e(g_2^{s_1}, (\hat{h} \prod_{j=1}^{n} \hat{u}^{w_j})^{-d_1 t_{i,1} w_i})$$

$$\cdot e(g_3^{s-s_2}, (\hat{h} \prod_{j=1}^{n} \hat{u}^{w_j})^{-d_4 t_{i,2} w_i}) e(g_4^{s_2}, (\hat{h} \prod_{j=1}^{n} \hat{u}^{w_j})^{-d_3 t_{i,2} w_i})$$

$$= e(g^\mu, \prod_{i \in \mathcal{I}} \hat{g}^{\lambda_i \omega_i}) e(g^\mu, \prod_{i \in \mathcal{I}} (\hat{\delta}^{d_1 d_2 t_{i,1} + d_3 d_4 t_{i,2}})^{\omega_i})$$

$$\cdot e(\delta^{-\mu}, \prod_{i \in \mathcal{I}} (\hat{g}^{d_1 d_2 t_{i,1} + d_3 d_4 t_{i,2}})^{\omega_i}) e((h \prod_{i=1}^{n} u^{w_i})^s, \prod_{i \in \mathcal{I}} \hat{g}^{(d_1 d_2 t_{i,1} + d_3 d_4 t_{i,2})\omega_i})$$

$$e(g^{s d_1}, (\hat{h} \prod_{j=1}^{n} \hat{u}^{w_j})^{-d_2 t_{i,1} w_i}) e(g^{-d_1 s_1}, (\hat{h} \prod_{j=1}^{n} \hat{u}^{w_j})^{-d_2 t_{i,1} w_i}) e(g^{d_2 s_1}, (\hat{h} \prod_{j=1}^{n} \hat{u}^{w_j})^{-d_1 t_{i,1} w_i})$$

$$e(g^{s d_3}, (\hat{h} \prod_{j=1}^{n} \hat{u}^{w_j})^{-d_4 t_{i,2} w_i}) e(g^{-d_3 s_2}, (\hat{h} \prod_{j=1}^{n} \hat{u}^{w_j})^{-d_4 t_{i,2} w_i}) e(g^{d_4 s_2}, (\hat{h} \prod_{j=1}^{n} \hat{u}^{w_j})^{-d_3 t_{i,2} w_i})$$

$$= e(g, \hat{g})^{\alpha \mu} = C$$

4.2   Security Proof

Theorem 1. Under the asymmetric decisional DBDH assumption, the asymmetric decisional q-BDHE assumption and the asymmetric decisional linear assumption, our scheme is selectively indistinguishable against chosen keyword-set attacks (selectively IND-CKA).

Proof. The proof is divided into two parts, depending on the role of the adversary. In the first part, the adversary is assumed to be an outside attacker, and in the second part, the adversary is assumed to be the cloud sever who performs search operations. The proof details will be given in the full version of the paper due to space limit.

5   Comparison

To specifically highlight the contributions of our research work, we compare our scheme with three related works, namely [14,28,48]. Lai *et al.* [28] is an expressive searchable encryption protocol built in composite order group, while [14,48] are expressive searchable encryption schemes with prime order group. Below, we compare the above schemes in terms of communication cost, computation cost, features and security. In [48], S is the number of the data user's attributes, and N is the number of attributes that are involved in the data owner's access control policy. Let $|par|$, $|msk|$, $|T_{M,\rho}|$, $|M|$ be the size of the public parameter, the master private key, the trapdoor and the access structure, respectively. We let $|\mathbb{G}|$, $|\hat{\mathbb{G}}|$, and $|\mathbb{G}_T|$ denote the size of the element in $\mathbb{G}, \hat{\mathbb{G}}, \mathbb{G}_T$, respectively. Let l be the number of keywords in an access structure, n be the maximum number of keywords in the system, and m be the size of a keyword set associated with a ciphertext. Denote E as an exponentiation operation, P as a pairing operation, x_1 as the number of elements in $I_{M,\rho} = \{\mathcal{I}_1, ..., \mathcal{I}_{x_1}\}$, x_2 as $|\mathcal{I}_1| + \cdots + |\mathcal{I}_{x_1}|$.

Table 1. Storage and communication overhead comparison

	Public parameter	Master private key	Trapdoor	Ciphertext	Bilinear group
[28]	$n + 5$	$n + 4$	$2l + |M|$	$m + 2$	Composite
[48]	5	3	$N + 3$	$S + 3$	Prime
[14]	9	5	$6l + |M|$	$5m + 2$	Prime
Ours	10	8	$(4n + 2)l + |M|$	7	Asymmetric prime

From Table 1, it can be seen that only [28] is built on composite order group, suffering from the heaviest communication cost (with linear cost in all metrics), while others are in prime order group. According to [22], prime order group have clear advantage in the parameter size over composite order group pairing-friendly elliptic curves. Although being constructed in prime order group, [14,48] come at $O(S)$ and $O(m)$ price in ciphertext storage/communication. However, ours only requires constant value in the same metric. The reason behind the constant cost (in our construction) relies on the "aggregation" of ciphertext components, aggregating keyword set as a whole (much like some technique used in hierarchical IBE). We note that the size of trapdoor in our scheme is bound at $O(nl)$. This seems as a trade-off between reducing the cost in ciphertext and (meanwhile) enlarging the size of trapdoor. However, we here state that increasing the size of trapdoor does bring efficiency in test phase. We will discuss this in the next paragraph.

Table 2 shows that our scheme only requires constant pairing cost $(7P)$ in test phase, while others are restricted to linear pairing cost. In the same metric, the exponentiation cost of our scheme maintains the same magnitude as that of others. Except [48], pairing computation exists in the encryption phase of all other schemes. Compared to [28] (with composite order group), our scheme may enjoy around 50 times faster in pairings (if [28] equips a 1024-bit composite order elliptic curve) [19]. The decryption techniques used in [14,48] drag down the efficiency of decryption. This is so because the pairings mainly depend on the size of attribute set, in particular, an attribute needs one pairing computation.

Table 2. Computation cost comparison

	Trapdoor	Enc	Test
[28]	$4lE$	$2(m+1)E+P$	$\leq 2x_2P + x_2E$
[48]	$(2N+2)E$	$(S+4)E$	$(2S+2)P + SE_T$
[14]	$(16l+1)E$	$(7m+2)E+P$	$\leq (6x_2+1)P + (x_2+1)E$
Ours	$(15l+1)E$	$(n+6)E+P$	$\leq 7P + (x_2+1)E$

However, we employ "fast decryption" technology and auxiliary components $Q_{i,j}$ into our construction, so that the test algorithm are free of linear cost, namely, the efficiency of the test algorithm is not restricted to the size of attribute set.

We show the feature and security comparison in Table 3. We use KGA to denote keyword guessing attacks. It is clear to see that our scheme supports any monotonic assess structure while others only provide AND and OR level of expressiveness. Enjoying more expressiveness, our scheme maintains the same security level with Cui et al.'s scheme [14]. Zheng et al. [48] opted to use an authenticated private channel to eliminate the keyword guessing attacks. However, it may not be scalable in practice. To enable publicly trapdoor delivery, [14] and our schemes slightly degrade the keyword privacy level to only allow a designated server to launch KGA. We state that our scheme is the first of its type, in the literature, to provide security and expressiveness simultaneously without significantly jeopardizing the efficiency. It is worthy of mentioning that the generation/computation cost of trapdoor (in our scheme) can be further off-loaded to the a trusted party holding the master private key (because of our sophisticated construction technique), so that system user can enjoy lighter computation complexity.

Table 3. Property and security comparison

	Expressiveness	Security	Trapdoor delivery
[28]	AND, OR	Adaptive chosen keyword attacks in standard model	Public channel
[48]	AND, OR	Selective security against chosen-keyword attack in ROM	Authenticated private channel
[14]	Any monotonic access structure	Selective indistinguishability against chosen keyword set attack in standard model	Public channel
Ours	Any monotonic access structure	Selective indistinguishability against chosen keyword set attack in standard model	Public channel

6   Conclusions

Attribute-based keyword search has attracted many attentions since it can support secure search over encrypted data with expressive access structure. Nevertheless, the size of ciphertexts but also the pairing cost (incurred in the test phase) are linear in the number of keyword. That is the main drawback of the most of the existing searchable encryption systems with ABE. To tackle the above opened problem, we propose a new KP-ABES scheme with outstanding features, namely expressive access structures, constant size ciphertext, and constant pairing cost (in search). There are some interesting open problems brought by this research work as well, for example, how to reduce the size of search trapdoor, and how to renew/provoke attribute.

Acknowledgements. The authors would like to thank the anonymous reviewers for their valuable comments and suggestions to improve the quality of the paper. This work is supported by the National Natural Science Foundation of China (61572303), the Summit of the Six Top Talents Program of Jiangsu Province (Grant No. 2015-DZXX-020). The National Research Foundation, Prime Minister Office, Singapore under its Corporate Laboratory@University Scheme, National University of Singapore, and Singapore Telecommunications Ltd.

References

1. Abdalla, M., Bellare, M., Catalano, D., Kiltz, E., Kohno, T., Lange, T., Malone-Lee, J., Neven, G., Paillier, P., Shi, H.: Searchable encryption revisited: consistency properties, relation to anonymous IBE, and extensions. J. Cryptol. **21**(3), 350–391 (2008)
2. Attrapadung, N., Libert, B., de Panafieu, E.: Expressive key-policy attribute-based encryption with constant-size ciphertexts. In: Catalano, D., Fazio, N., Gennaro, R., Nicolosi, A. (eds.) PKC 2011. LNCS, vol. 6571, pp. 90–108. Springer, Heidelberg (2011). doi:10.1007/978-3-642-19379-8_6
3. Benabbas, S., Gennaro, R., Vahlis, Y.: Verifiable delegation of computation over large datasets. In: Rogaway, P. (ed.) CRYPTO 2011. LNCS, vol. 6841, pp. 111–131. Springer, Heidelberg (2011). doi:10.1007/978-3-642-22792-9_7
4. Bethencourt, J., Sahai, A., Waters, B.: Ciphertext-policy attribute-based encryption. In: S&P 2007, pp. 321–334. IEEE Computer Society (2007)
5. Boneh, D., Boyen, X.: Efficient selective identity-based encryption without random oracles. J. Cryptol. **24**(4), 659–693 (2011)
6. Boneh, D., Boyen, X., Goh, E.-J.: Hierarchical identity based encryption with constant size ciphertext. In: Cramer, R. (ed.) EUROCRYPT 2005. LNCS, vol. 3494, pp. 440–456. Springer, Heidelberg (2005). doi:10.1007/11426639_26
7. Boneh, D., Boyen, X., Shacham, H.: Short group signatures. In: Franklin, M. (ed.) CRYPTO 2004. LNCS, vol. 3152, pp. 41–55. Springer, Heidelberg (2004). doi:10.1007/978-3-540-28628-8_3
8. Boneh, D., Di Crescenzo, G., Ostrovsky, R., Persiano, G.: Public key encryption with keyword search. In: Cachin, C., Camenisch, J.L. (eds.) EUROCRYPT 2004. LNCS, vol. 3027, pp. 506–522. Springer, Heidelberg (2004). doi:10.1007/978-3-540-24676-3_30

9. Boyen, X., Waters, B.: Anonymous hierarchical identity-based encryption (without random oracles). In: Dwork, C. (ed.) CRYPTO 2006. LNCS, vol. 4117, pp. 290–307. Springer, Heidelberg (2006). doi:10.1007/11818175_17

10. Chase, M.: Multi-authority attribute based encryption. In: Vadhan, S.P. (ed.) TCC 2007. LNCS, vol. 4392, pp. 515–534. Springer, Heidelberg (2007). doi:10.1007/978-3-540-70936-7_28

11. Chase, M., Chow, S.S.M.: Improving privacy and security in multi-authority attribute-based encryption. In: CCS 2009, pp. 121–130. ACM (2009)

12. Cheung, L., Newport, C.C.: Provably secure ciphertext policy ABE. In: CCS 2007, pp. 456–465. ACM (2007)

13. Cramer, R., Shoup, V.: Design and analysis of practical public-key encryption schemes secure against adaptive chosen ciphertext attack. SIAM J. Comput. **33**(1), 167–226 (2004)

14. Cui, H., Wan, Z., Deng, R., Wang, G., Li, Y.: Efficient and expressive keyword search over encrypted data in the cloud. IEEE Trans. Dependable Secure Comput. **PP**(99), 1 (2016)

15. Ducas, L.: Anonymity from asymmetry: new constructions for anonymous HIBE. In: Pieprzyk, J. (ed.) CT-RSA 2010. LNCS, vol. 5985, pp. 148–164. Springer, Heidelberg (2010). doi:10.1007/978-3-642-11925-5_11

16. Emura, K., Miyaji, A., Nomura, A., Omote, K., Soshi, M.: A ciphertext-policy attribute-based encryption scheme with constant ciphertext length. In: Bao, F., Li, H., Wang, G. (eds.) ISPEC 2009. LNCS, vol. 5451, pp. 13–23. Springer, Heidelberg (2009). doi:10.1007/978-3-642-00843-6_2

17. Fiore, D., Gennaro, R.: Publicly verifiable delegation of large polynomials and matrix computations, with applications. In: CCS 2012, pp. 501–512. ACM (2012)

18. Freeman, D., Scott, M., Teske, E.: A taxonomy of pairing-friendly elliptic curves. J. Cryptol. **23**(2), 224–280 (2010)

19. Freeman, D.M.: Converting pairing-based cryptosystems from composite-order groups to prime-order groups. In: Gilbert, H. (ed.) EUROCRYPT 2010. LNCS, vol. 6110, pp. 44–61. Springer, Heidelberg (2010). doi:10.1007/978-3-642-13190-5_3

20. Galbraith, S.D., Paterson, K.G., Smart, N.P.: Pairings for cryptographers. Discrete Appl. Math. **156**(16), 3113–3121 (2008)

21. Goyal, V., Pandey, O., Sahai, A., Waters, B.: Attribute-based encryption for fine-grained access control of encrypted data. In: CCS 2006, pp. 89–98. ACM (2006)

22. Guillevic, A.: Comparing the pairing efficiency over composite-order and prime-order elliptic curves. In: Jacobson, M., Locasto, M., Mohassel, P., Safavi-Naini, R. (eds.) ACNS 2013. LNCS, vol. 7954, pp. 357–372. Springer, Heidelberg (2013). doi:10.1007/978-3-642-38980-1_22

23. Herranz, J., Laguillaumie, F., Ràfols, C.: Constant size ciphertexts in threshold attribute-based encryption. In: Nguyen, P.Q., Pointcheval, D. (eds.) PKC 2010. LNCS, vol. 6056, pp. 19–34. Springer, Heidelberg (2010). doi:10.1007/978-3-642-13013-7_2

24. Hohenberger, S., Waters, B.: Attribute-based encryption with fast decryption. In: Kurosawa, K., Hanaoka, G. (eds.) PKC 2013. LNCS, vol. 7778, pp. 162–179. Springer, Heidelberg (2013). doi:10.1007/978-3-642-36362-7_11

25. Khader, D.: Public key encryption with keyword search based on K-resilient IBE. In: Gavrilova, M., Gervasi, O., Kumar, V., Tan, C.J.K., Taniar, D., Laganá, A., Mun, Y., Choo, H. (eds.) ICCSA 2006. LNCS, vol. 3982, pp. 298–308. Springer, Heidelberg (2006). doi:10.1007/11751595_33

26. Lai, J., Deng, R.H., Li, Y.: Expressive CP-ABE with partially hidden access structures. In: ASIACCS 2012, pp. 18–19. ACM (2012)

27. Lai, J., Deng, R.H., Li, Y., Weng, J.: Fully secure key-policy attribute-based encryption with constant-size ciphertexts and fast decryption. In: ASIACCS 2014, pp. 239–248. ACM (2014)
28. Lai, J., Zhou, X., Deng, R.H., Li, Y., Chen, K.: Expressive search on encrypted data. In: ASIACCS 2013, pp. 243–252. ACM (2013)
29. Lewko, A., Okamoto, T., Sahai, A., Takashima, K., Waters, B.: Fully secure functional encryption: attribute-based encryption and (hierarchical) inner product encryption. In: Gilbert, H. (ed.) EUROCRYPT 2010. LNCS, vol. 6110, pp. 62–91. Springer, Heidelberg (2010). doi:10.1007/978-3-642-13190-5_4
30. Lewko, A., Waters, B.: Decentralizing attribute-based encryption. In: Paterson, K.G. (ed.) EUROCRYPT 2011. LNCS, vol. 6632, pp. 568–588. Springer, Heidelberg (2011). doi:10.1007/978-3-642-20465-4_31
31. Lewko, A., Waters, B.: New proof methods for attribute-based encryption: achieving full security through selective techniques. In: Safavi-Naini, R., Canetti, R. (eds.) CRYPTO 2012. LNCS, vol. 7417, pp. 180–198. Springer, Heidelberg (2012). doi:10.1007/978-3-642-32009-5_12
32. Li, X., Liang, K., Liu, Z., Wong, D.S.: Attribute-based encryption: traitor tracing, revocation and fully security on prime order groups. In: CLOSER 2017, pp. 281–292. SciTePress (2017)
33. Li, Y., Liang, K., Su, C., Wu, W.: DABEHR: decentralized attribute-based electronic health record system with constant-size storage complexity. In: Au, M.H.A., Castiglione, A., Choo, K.-K.R., Palmieri, F., Li, K.-C. (eds.) GPC 2017. LNCS, vol. 10232, pp. 611–626. Springer, Cham (2017). doi:10.1007/978-3-319-57186-7_44
34. Liang, K., Huang, X., Guo, F., Liu, J.K.: Privacy-preserving and regular language search over encrypted cloud data. IEEE Trans. Inf. Forensics Secur. 11(10), 2365–2376 (2016)
35. Liang, K., Su, C., Chen, J., Liu, J.K.: Efficient multi-function data sharing and searching mechanism for cloud-based encrypted data. In: ASIACCS 2016, pp. 83–94. ACM (2016)
36. Liang, K., Susilo, W.: Searchable attribute-based mechanism with efficient data sharing for secure cloud storage. IEEE Trans. Inf. Forensics Secur. 10(9), 1981–1992 (2015)
37. Liu, J.K., Au, M.H., Susilo, W., Liang, K., Lu, R., Srinivasan, B.: Secure sharing and searching for real-time video data in mobile cloud. IEEE Netw. 29(2), 46–50 (2015)
38. Lv, Z., Hong, C., Zhang, M., Feng, D.: Expressive and secure searchable encryption in the public key setting. In: Chow, S.S.M., Camenisch, J., Hui, L.C.K., Yiu, S.M. (eds.) ISC 2014. LNCS, vol. 8783, pp. 364–376. Springer, Cham (2014). doi:10.1007/978-3-319-13257-0_21
39. Ning, J., Cao, Z., Dong, X., Wei, L.: Traceable and revocable CP-ABE with shorter ciphertexts. Sci. China Inf. Sci. 59(11), 119102:1–119102:3 (2016)
40. Ning, J., Dong, X., Cao, Z., Wei, L., Lin, X.: White-box traceable ciphertext-policy attribute-based encryption supporting flexible attributes. IEEE Trans. Inf. Forensics Secur. 10(6), 1274–1288 (2015)
41. Ostrovsky, R., Sahai, A., Waters, B.: Attribute-based encryption with non-monotonic access structures. In: CCS 2007, pp. 195–203. ACM (2007)
42. Papamanthou, C., Shi, E., Tamassia, R.: Signatures of correct computation. In: Sahai, A. (ed.) TCC 2013. LNCS, vol. 7785, pp. 222–242. Springer, Heidelberg (2013). doi:10.1007/978-3-642-36594-2_13
43. Rhee, H.S., Park, J.H., Susilo, W., Lee, D.H.: Improved searchable public key encryption with designated tester. In: ASIACCS 2009, pp. 376–379. ACM (2009)

44. Sahai, A., Waters, B.: Fuzzy identity-based encryption. In: Cramer, R. (ed.) EURO-CRYPT 2005. LNCS, vol. 3494, pp. 457–473. Springer, Heidelberg (2005). doi:10.1007/11426639_27
45. Song, D.X., Wagner, D., Perrig, A.: Practical techniques for searches on encrypted data. In: S&P 2000, pp. 44–55. IEEE Computer Society (2000)
46. Wang, S., Liang, K., Liu, J.K., Chen, J., Jianping, Y., Xie, W.: Attribute-based data sharing scheme revisited in cloud computing. IEEE Trans. Inf. Forensics Secur. $11(8)$, 1661–1673 (2016)
47. Waters, B.: Efficient identity-based encryption without random oracles. In: Cramer, R. (ed.) EUROCRYPT 2005. LNCS, vol. 3494, pp. 114–127. Springer, Heidelberg (2005). doi:10.1007/11426639_7
48. Zheng, Q., Shouhuai, X., Giuseppe Ateniese, V.: VABKS: verifiable attribute-based keyword search over outsourced encrypted data. In: INFOCOM 2014, pp. 522–530. IEEE (2014)

Secure Multi-label Classification over Encrypted Data in Cloud

Yang Liu[1], Xingxin Li[1], Youwen Zhu[1,2(✉)], Jian Wang[1], and Zhe Liu[1]

[1] College of Computer Science and Technology,
Nanjing University of Aeronautics and Astronautics, Nanjing 211106, China
{liuyang005,lixingxin,zhuyw}@nuaa.edu.cn
[2] Guangxi Key Laboratory of Trusted Software,
Guilin University of Electronic Technology, Guilin 541004, China

Abstract. In multi-label (ML) learning, each training instance is associated with a set of labels to present its multiple semantic information, and the task is to predict the associated labels for each unclassified instance. Nowadays, many multi-label learning approaches have been proposed, unfortunately, all of the existing approaches did not consider the issue of protecting the privacy information. In this paper, we propose a scheme for secure multi-label classification over encrypted data in cloud. Our scheme can outsource the multi-label classification task to the cloud servers which dramatically reduce the storage and computation burden of data owner and data users. Based on the theoretical proof, our scheme can protect the privacy information of data owner and data users, the cloud servers can not learn anything useful about the input data and output multi-label classification results. Additionally, we evaluate our computation complexity and communication overheads in detail.

Keywords: Multi-label learning · Cloud security · Privacy · Classification

1 Introduction

In traditional supervised learning, each instance is only associated with one label in a set of candidate labels. However, in many real-world applications, one instance is usually associated with multiple labels simultaneously. For example, in text categorization, a document may belong to multiple topics like *economy* and *environment*; in gene function prediction, a gene may belong to several functional classes like *energy* and *transcription*. Thus, multi-label learning has been developed fast for these kinds of applications. In the multi-label learning, each instance is associated with a set of labels, and the task is to predict the associated label set for unclassified instances.

Nowadays, many approaches have been proposed for multi-label classification problems, such as multi-label text categorization algorithms [13,18,20], multi-label decision trees algorithms [3], multi-label kernel methods [1,4], multi-label lazy learning algorithm [24], multi-label neural networks [25]. In these traditional

T. Okamoto et al. (Eds.): ProvSec 2017, LNCS 10592, pp. 57–73, 2017.
https://doi.org/10.1007/978-3-319-68637-0_4

multi-label learning, the training instances and test instances is owned by just one party. That is, the training instances owner uses his own data to learn out a multi-label classification model, and then classify his own test instances. With the flourishing development of cloud computing, now the data owner can provide his multi-label classification model as a service to any consumers who want to classify their unclassified instances. Then for the data owner, the training dataset and classification task can be outsourced to the cloud servers which can ease his burden of storage and computation; for the consumers, they don't need to build a multi-label classification model by themselves, which will be very difficult and expensive for the individuals and small organizations who just have a small number of training instances and limited computing power. However, this will bring the risk of privacy leaking for both data owner and consumers. On the one hand, the data owner's multi-label training instances dataset and classification model are his precious treasure, he would be reluctant to release to them the cloud servers and consumers; on the other hand, the consumers' unclassified instances and the classification results may contain sensitive information, such as personal gene sequence and physical condition, they do not want any information about these to be known to the data owner and cloud servers. Several secure schemes [10,17,22] have been proposed for the privacy-preserving classification problem. Nonetheless, these existing approaches just consider one-label classification, and are not suitable for multi-label classification.

In this paper, we investigate the secure multi-label classification over encrypted data in cloud and propose a secure scheme for the privacy leaking problem. Our scheme is based on the famous multi-label lazy learning approach ML-kNN [24]. We use Paillier cryptosystem to encrypt the training instances dataset of data owner and the unclassified instances of consumers. The data owner outsources his encrypted data and the multi-label classification task to the cloud servers. The consumers submit their encrypted unclassified instances to the cloud servers for classifying. The cloud servers perform computation on the ciphertext in the classification process, they can not learn anything useful about the dataset of the data owner and unclassified instances of the consumers. Additionally, only the consumers can obtain their multi-label classification results.

Our main contributions in this paper can be summarized as follows.

- For the first time, we formalize the problem of secure multi-label classification, and propose a secure k-nearest neighbor based multi-label classification scheme, which can correctly complete multi-label classification and preserve the privacy of both data owner and consumers with practical efficiency.
- We formally prove the security of our scheme, which shows our proposed approaches can securely preserve the input instance and output classification results of each consumer, and guarantee the security of the data owner's training dataset and classification model.

The remainder of the paper is organized as follows. In Sect. 2 introduce preliminaries and definitions. In Sect. 3, we introduce the models and design goal. In Sect. 4, we present our secure scheme in details. Then, we theoretically prove the security of our scheme, and evaluate the computation and communication cost in Sect. 5. In Sect. 6, we review the related work. At last, we conclude the paper in Sect. 7.

2 Preliminaries and Problem Definition

2.1 Multi-label Learning

Let $\mathcal{X} = \mathbb{R}^d$ denote the d-dimensional feature domain of instances and $\mathcal{Y} = \{y_1, y_2, ..., y_q\}$ be the label domain which is composed of q possible labels. The multi-label classification problem can be formulated as follows. Given a multi-label classification training set $T = \{(\boldsymbol{x}_1, \boldsymbol{Y}_1), (\boldsymbol{x}_2, \boldsymbol{Y}_2), ..., (\boldsymbol{x}_m, \boldsymbol{Y}_m)\}$ which includes m training instances, where $\boldsymbol{x}_i = (x_{i1}, x_{i2}, ..., x_{id}) \in \mathcal{X}$ is the i-th instance, $\boldsymbol{Y}_i \subseteq \mathcal{Y}$ is a subset of labels which is associated with the instance $\boldsymbol{x}_i$. The goal of multi-label learning system is to build a multi-label classifier $h : \mathcal{X} \to 2^{\mathcal{Y}}$, which optimizes some pre-defined criterion or specific evaluation metric, and can assign label set $h(\boldsymbol{x}) \subseteq \mathcal{Y}$ to unclassified instances.

As for classical classification problems, most algorithms associate the multi-label classifier h with a real-valued function $f : \mathcal{X} \times \mathcal{Y} \to \mathbb{R}$, where $f(\boldsymbol{x}, y)$ corresponds to the probability that instance $\boldsymbol{x}$ is associated with label y. Given a instance $\boldsymbol{x}$ and its associated label set $\boldsymbol{Y}$, a successful learning system is assumed to produce the function $f(.,.)$ that tends to assign larger values to labels in $\boldsymbol{Y}$ than those labels not in $\boldsymbol{Y}$. i.e., $f(\boldsymbol{x}, y_1) > f(\boldsymbol{x}, y_2)$ for any $y_1 \in \boldsymbol{Y}$ and $y_2 \notin \boldsymbol{Y}$. Generally, the multi-label classifier $h(\cdot)$ can be derived from the function $f(\cdot, \cdot)$ as:

$$h(\boldsymbol{x}) = \{y \mid f(\boldsymbol{x}, y) > t(\boldsymbol{x}), y \in \boldsymbol{Y}\} \tag{1}$$

where $t(\boldsymbol{x})$ is a threshold function which is usually set to be the zero constant function.

2.2 Paillier Cryptosystem

The Paillier cryptosystem is an additive homomorphic and probabilistic asymmetric encryption scheme [14]. The encryption function $E_{pk}(.,.)$ of Paillier cryptosystem is defined as:

$$E_{pk}(m, r) = g^m \times r^N mod N^2 \tag{2}$$

where $m \in \mathbb{Z}_N$ is the plaintext message for encryption, N is a product of two large primes p and q, g generates a subgroup of order N, r is a random number in $\mathbb{Z}_N$. The public key pk for encryption is (N, g), and the secret key sk for decryption is (p, q). Given $a, b \in \mathbb{Z}_N$, the Paillier encryption scheme exhibits the following properties:

- **Homomorphic Addition:**

$$E_{pk}(a + b) = E_{pk}(a) * E_{pk}(b) \bmod N^2;$$

- **Homomorphic Multiplication:**

$$E_{pk}(a * b) = E_{pk}(a)^b \bmod N^2;$$

- **Semantic Security:** The Paillier cryptosystem is semantically secure [8], i.e., given a set of ciphertexts, an adversary cannot deduce any information about the plaintext.

We will use Paillier cryptosystem to encrypt data in our scheme. As a probabilistic encryption, Paillier cryptosystem also has the self-blinding property, that is, $E_{pk}(m, r_1) * r_2^N = E_{pk}(m, r_1 r_2)$ and $m = D_{sk}(E_{pk}(m, r_1)) = D_{sk}(E_{pk}(m, r_1) * r_2^N)$ for any $r_1, r_2 \in \mathbb{Z}_N$.

For simplicity, we also use $E_{pk}(m)$ to denote the encrypted result of m while it is no need to emphasize the random parameter r.

2.3   Secure Computing Protocol

In our scheme we need to perform secure computation on encrypted data, suppose that there are two semi-honest parties P_1 and P_2, and the secret key sk of Paillier cryptosystem is known only to P_2, and pk is public, we will use several secure computing protocols as following.

- **Secure Multiplication (SM) Protocol:** As shown in Protocol 1, this protocol considers that P_1 has the $(E_{pk}(a), E_{pk}(b))$ and P_2 has sk. By three steps of the protocol, it can output $E_{pk}(a * b)$ to P_1, where a and b are not known to P_1 and P_2. During this process, no information about a and b will be revealed to P_1 and P_2, and the output $E_{pk}(a * b)$ is known only to P_1.

Protocol 1. $\mathrm{SM}(E_{pk}(a), E_{pk}(b)) \rightarrow E_{pk}(a * b)$

Input: P_1 has the $(E_{pk}(a), E_{pk}(b))$, P_2 has sk
Output: $E_{pk}(a * b)$ known only to P_1
    1: P_1:
    (a). Pick two random numbers $r_a, r_b \in \mathbb{Z}_N$
    (b). $a' \leftarrow E_{pk}(a) * E_{pk}(r_a)$
    (c). $b' \leftarrow E_{pk}(b) * E_{pk}(r_b)$; send a', b' to P_2
    2: P_2:
    (a). Receive a', b' from P_1
    (b). $h_a \leftarrow D_{sk}(a')$; $h_b \leftarrow D_{sk}(b')$
    (c). $h \leftarrow h_a * h_b \bmod N$
    (d). $h' \leftarrow E_{pk}(h)$; send h' to P_1
    3: P_1:
    (a). Receive h' from P_2
    (b). $s \leftarrow h' * E_{pk}(a)^{N - r_b}$
    (c). $s' \leftarrow s * E_{pk}(b)^{N - r_a}$
    (d). $E_{pk}(a * b) \leftarrow s' * E_{pk}(r_a * r_b)^{N-1}$

- **Secure k-Nearest Neighbors Protocol** (SkNN): This protocol is proposed in literature [5]. P_1 has a encrypted training instances dataset $T = \{E_{pk}(\boldsymbol{x}_1), ..., E_{pk}(\boldsymbol{x}_m)\}$ and a encrypted test instance $\boldsymbol{t}' = E_{pk}(\boldsymbol{t})$, this protocol outputs a k-nearest neighbors vector $N_{\boldsymbol{t}'} = (n_1, ..., n_m)$, where $n_i = E_{pk}(1)$ if $\boldsymbol{x}_i$ belongs to kNN of instance $\boldsymbol{t}'$ in T, otherwise $n_i = E_{pk}(0)$. P_1 and P_2 can not learn any useful information about T, $\boldsymbol{t}'$ and $N_{\boldsymbol{t}'}$.
- **Secure Minimum Protocol** (SMIN): This protocol is proposed in literature [5]. It supposes that P_1 has two encrypted values $E_{pk}(X)$ and $E_{pk}(Y)$, then P_1 obtains the output $\varGamma = E_{pk}(1)$ if $X \geqslant Y$, otherwise $\varGamma = E_{pk}(0)$. Neither P_1 nor P_2 know the comparison result hidden in the output ciphertext $\varGamma$.

2.4   ML-kNN

ML-kNN [24] is adapted from the famous k-nearest neighbors algorithm. It assigns unclassified instance's associated label set according to the associated label sets of its k-nearest neighbors. Suppose that $T = \{(\boldsymbol{x}_1, \boldsymbol{Y}_1), (\boldsymbol{x}_2, \boldsymbol{Y}_2), ..., (\boldsymbol{x}_m, \boldsymbol{Y}_m)\}$ is the multi-label training dataset, where $\boldsymbol{x}_i \in \mathbb{R}^d$, each instance $\boldsymbol{x}_i$ is associated with a set of labels $Y_i \subseteq \mathcal{Y}$, where $\mathcal{Y} = \{y_1, y_2, ..., y_q\}$ is the label set. Let $\boldsymbol{y}_i = (y_{i1}, y_{i2}, ..., y_{iq})^T$ be the label vector of instance $\boldsymbol{x}_i$, and $y_{ij} = 1$ if $\boldsymbol{x}_i$ is associated with label y_j, otherwise $y_{ij} = 0$.

Let $N_{\boldsymbol{x}_i} = (N_{i1}, N_{i2}, ..., N_{im})^T$ denote the kNN vector of $\boldsymbol{x}_i$, and $N_{ij} = 1$ if instance $\boldsymbol{x}_j$ belongs to the k-nearest neighbors of $\boldsymbol{x}_i$, otherwise $N_{ij} = 0$. Let H_1^l denote the event that instance $\boldsymbol{x}$ is associated with label l, H_0^l denote the event that instance $\boldsymbol{x}$ is not associated with label l, $E_j^l (j \in \{0, 1, .., k\})$ denote the event that there are j neighbors are associated with label l among the k nearest neighbors $N_{\boldsymbol{x}}$, ML-kNN computes the prior probabilities as:

$$P(H_1^l) = \big(s + \textstyle\sum_{i=1}^{m} y_{il}\big)/(s * 2 + m)$$
$$P(H_0^l) = 1 - P(H_1^l) = \big(s + m - \textstyle\sum_{i=1}^{m} y_{il}\big)/(s * 2 + m) \tag{3}$$

where s is the smooth parameter.

Based on the label vector of each instance in $N_{\boldsymbol{x}_i}$, ML-kNN defines a *membership counting* vector as:

$$C_{\boldsymbol{x}_i}(l) = \sum_{a \in N_{\boldsymbol{x}_i}} \boldsymbol{y}_a(l), \, l \in \mathcal{Y} \tag{4}$$

where $C_{\boldsymbol{x}_i}(l)$ counts how many neighbors of instance $\boldsymbol{x}_i$ are associated with label l.

Then ML-kNN computes the posterior probabilities as:

$$P(E_j^l | H_1^l) = \big(s + c(j)\big)/\big(s * (k + 1) + \textstyle\sum_{p=0}^{k} c(p)\big)$$
$$P(E_j^l | H_0^l) = \big(s + c'(j)\big)/\big(s * (k + 1) + \textstyle\sum_{p=0}^{k} c'(p)\big) \tag{5}$$

where $c(j)$ counts the number of instances $\boldsymbol{x}_i$ in the training dataset T which are associated with label l and $C_{\boldsymbol{x}_i}(l) = j$, $c'(j)$ counts the number of instances $\boldsymbol{x}_i$ in the training dataset T which are not associated with label l and $C_{\boldsymbol{x}_i}(l) = j$.

Let t denote a test instance, the goal of ML-kNN is to output its label vector y_t. Firstly, ML-kNN will find instance t's kNN vector N_t . Then for each label $l \in \mathcal{Y}$, ML-kNN obtain $C_t(l)$ based on Eq. (4). Then the label vector y_t will be determined by the following maximum a posteriori principle:

$$y_t(l) = \operatorname*{argmax}_{b \in \{0,1\}} P(H_b^l) P(E_{C_t(l)}^l | H_b^l) \tag{6}$$

3   Models and Design Goal

3.1   System Model

There are four parties in our system: a data owner(denoted as DO), a data user(denoted as DU) and two cloud servers(denoted as CS_1 and CS_2). DO owns the multi-label training instance dataset $T = \{(\boldsymbol{x}_1, \boldsymbol{Y}_1), (\boldsymbol{x}_2, \boldsymbol{Y}_2), ..., (\boldsymbol{x}_m, \boldsymbol{Y}_m)\}$ which consist of m instances. DO produces a pair of key (pk, sk) using Paillier cryptosystem, where pk is the public key and sk is the secret key. Then DO encrypts the training instance dataset T into T' as: $T' = \{(\boldsymbol{x}_1', \boldsymbol{Y}_1'), (\boldsymbol{x}_2', \boldsymbol{Y}_2'), ..., (\boldsymbol{x}_m', \boldsymbol{Y}_m')\}$, where $\boldsymbol{x}_i' = (E_{pk}(x_{i1}), ..., E_{pk}(x_{id})), \boldsymbol{Y}_i' = (E_{pk}(y_{i1}), ..., E_{pk}(y_{iq}))(i \in \{1, ..., m\})$. Then DO submits the T' to CS_1, submits the sk to CS_2, and outsources the computation over the encrypted data to these two cloud servers. After that, DO does not need to do any further computation task. All the future computation will be completed by CS_1 and CS_2. Therefore our scheme does not require DO to be online for the classification.

Suppose DU wants to classify his unclassified instance t, he encrypts the instance t into $t' = E_{pk}(t) = (E_{pk}(t_1), ..., E_{pk}(t_d))$ using the pk of DO, then submits t' to CS_1. Then CS_1 and CS_2 will work together to obtain the multi-label classification results of instance t and return them to DU.

It should be noted that the employed PaillierPaillier cryptosystem can encrypt only the non-negative integers in its plaintext space. However, in real world applications, most multi-label instances are in real number field. In our scheme, before DO and DU encrypting their data, they should convert the multi-label instances into integer field through multiplying the instances by a multiple of ten. Then they encrypt their instances and submit the encrypted data to the cloud servers (Fig. 1).

3.2   Design Goal

To enable secure ML-kNN classification based on above system model, our proposed scheme should simultaneously achieve the following security and performance guarantees:

- **Dataset Privacy**: The contents of DO's dataset should not be revealed to cloud servers and DU during execution of the protocols.
- **User Privacy**: DO and cloud servers should not learn any useful information about each dimension of DU's unclassified instance t.

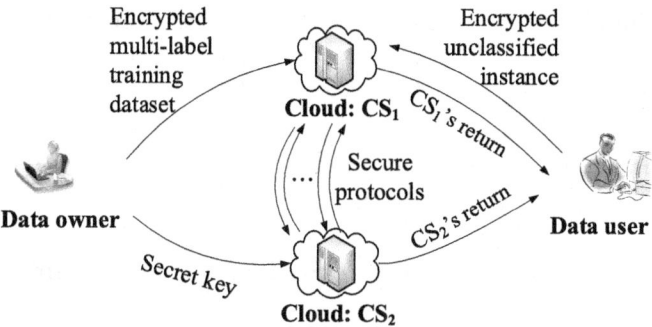

Fig. 1. System model

- **Result Privacy**: DO and cloud servers cannot obtain the content of final multi-label classification result. The output should be revealed only to DU.
- **Low computation overhead on DU and DO**: After outsourcing the encrypted dataset to cloud servers, DO does not need to do any further computation task. Besides, our protocols should incur low computation overhead on DU.

3.3 Threat Model

In this work, we assume all parties (DO, DU, cloud servers CS_1 and CS_2) are semi-honest (or honest-but-curious) [7], that is, each participant in our model will strictly follow the designed protocol, but try to infer more additional information about others input during the execution of the protocol. Besides, following previous works [5], we assume the two cloud servers CS_1 and CS_2 are non-colluding. This non-colluding assumption is practical and reasonable because the cloud servers need to maintain their reputation and take their own financial interests into account.

4 Our Proposed Scheme

As we mentioned in the Sect. 1, although a lot of multi-label learning algorithms have been proposed, all these algorithms didn't consider privacy-preserving problem. Additionally, the existing privacy-preserving classification approaches just consider one-label classification, and are not suitable for multi-label classification. In this section, we will introduce a privacy-preserving multi-label learning algorithm which is based on ML-kNN [24].

Specifically, our scheme consists of two stages:

- **Secure Training Stage: Build the multi-label classification model**
  In this stage, CS_1 and CS_2 will work together to build a multi-label classification model based on the encrypted dataset T', this stage will be performed just once, and the model can be used to classify any unclassified multi-label instance.

- **Secure Classifying Stage: Classify the Unclassified Instance**
  In this stage, CS_1 and CS_2 will use the multi-label classification model to classify the unclassified instance which is submitted by DU. The classification results will be known only to DU.

We will present the details of our secure training stage and secure classifying stage in Sects. 4.1 and 4.2, respectively.

4.1 Secure Training Stage: Build the Multi-label Classification Model

In the secure training stage, CS_1 and CS_2 will work together to build a multi-label classification model. The whole stage consists of four steps as shown in Protocol 3.

Protocol 2. Computing the prior probabilities $P(H_b^l)$

Input: CS_1 inputs the T'
Output: CS_1 obtains the prior probabilities
1: **for** $l \in \mathcal{Y}$ **do**
2:     CS_1 computes:

$$P(H_1^l)_a = E_{pk}\left(s + \sum_{i=1}^{m} y_{il}\right) = E_{pk}(s) * \prod_{i=1}^{m} E_{pk}(y_{il}) \bmod N^2$$
$$P(H_1^l)_b = P(H_0^l)_b = E_{pk}(s * 2 + m) = E_{pk}(s)^2 * E_{pk}(m) \bmod N^2$$
$$P(H_0^l)_a = E_{pk}\left(s + m - \sum_{i=1}^{m} y_{il}\right) = E_{pk}(s) * E_{pk}(m) * \prod_{i=1}^{m} E_{pk}(y_{il})^{N-1} \bmod N^2$$

where s is the smoothing parameter
3: **end for**

In the first step, as shown in Protocol 2, CS_1 has the encrypted dataset T', he will compute the prior probabilities $P(H_b^l)(b \in \{0,1\})$ for each label $l \in \mathcal{Y}$ as Eq. (3). Since the Paillier cryptosystem can encrypt only the non-negative integers and there will be float-point numbers in these prior probabilities, CS_1 encrypts the $P(H_1^l)$ and $P(H_0^l)(l \in \mathcal{Y})$ into two parts, respectively:

$$P(H_1^l)_a = E_{pk}\left(s + \sum_{i=1}^{m} y_{il}\right) = E_{pk}(s) * \prod_{i=1}^{m} E_{pk}(y_{il}) \bmod N^2$$
$$P(H_1^l)_b = P(H_0^l)_b = E_{pk}(s * 2 + m) = E_{pk}(s)^2 * E_{pk}(m) \bmod N^2 \quad (7)$$
$$P(H_0^l)_a = E_{pk}\left(s + m - \sum_{i=1}^{m} y_{il}\right) = E_{pk}(s) * E_{pk}(m) * \prod_{i=1}^{m} E_{pk}(y_{il})^{N-1} \bmod N^2$$

In the second step, CS_1 and CS_2 will use the SkNN protocol to find the kNN of each instance x' in dataset T' and obtain the kNN vector $N_{x'}$.

In the third step, CS_1 and CS_2 work together to compute the posterior probabilities $P(E_j^l|H_b^l)(l \in \mathcal{Y}, j \in \{0,1,...,k\})$ as Eq. (5). For each label $l \in \mathcal{Y}$, CS_1 defines $D(j) = E_{pk}(0), D'(j) = E_{pk}(0)(j \in \{0,1,...,k\})$. Then for each instance x'_i in T', CS_1 and CS_2 compute the $C_{x'_i}(l)$ using the Protocol 1 as:

$$C_{x'_i}(l) = \prod_{p=1}^{m} SM\left(N_{x'_i}(p), y'_p(l)\right) \bmod N^2 (l \in \mathcal{Y}) \quad (8)$$

Protocol 3. Secure Training Stage: Build the multi-label classification model

Input: CS_1 has the T', CS_2 has sk
Output: CS_1 obtains the multi-label classification model
1: **Step 1: Computing the prior probabilities**
2:   CS_1 computes the prior probabilities as shown in Protocol 2.
3: **Step 2: Computing the kNN**
4: **for** $i \in \{1, 2, ..., m\}$ **do**
5:    CS_1 and CS_2 use the SkNN protocol to find kNN of instance x_i' in T', obtain the kNN vector $N_{x_i'}$
6: **end for**
7: **Step 3: Computing the posterior probabilities** $P(E_j^l|H_b^l)$
8: **for** $l \in \mathcal{Y}$ **do**
9:    **for** $j \in \{0, 1, ..., k\}$ **do**
10:     CS_1 defines: $D(j) = E_{pk}(0), D'(j) = E_{pk}(0)$
11:    **end for**
12:    **for** $i \in \{1, 2, ..., m\}$ **do**
13:     CS_1 and CS_2 compute $C_{x_i'}(l) = \prod_{p=1}^{m} SM(N_{x_i'}(p), y_p'(l)) \bmod N^2$
14:     **for** $j \in \{0, 1, ..., k\}$ **do**
15:      CS_1 defines: $A(j) = Y_{il}', A'(j) = E_{pk}(1) * Y_{il}'^{N-1} \bmod N^2$
16:      CS_1 constructs a $(k+1)$-dimension vector $Q = (q_0, ..., q_k)$ as:

$$Q = \pi\big((C_{x_i'}(l) * E_{pk}(0)^{N-1} \bmod N^2), ..., (C_{x_i'}(l) * E_{pk}(k)^{N-1} \bmod N^2)\big),$$

      where π is a permutation function.
17:      CS_1 sends vector Q to CS_2
18:      CS_2 receives vector Q from CS_1 and decrypts it, then constructs a $(k+1)$-dimension vector $Q' = (q_0', ..., q_k')$, where $q_i' = E_{pk}(1)$ if $q(i) = E_{pk}(0)$, otherwise $q_i' = E_{pk}(0)(i \in \{0, ..., k\})$
19:      CS_2 sends vector Q' to CS_1
20:      CS_1 obtains $Q = \pi^{-1}(Q')$
21:      CS_1 computes: $D(j) = D(j) * SM(A(j), q(j)) \bmod N^2$
         $D'(j) = D'(j) * SM(A(j), q(j)) \bmod N^2$
22:     **end for**
23:    **end for**
24:    **for** $j \in \{0, 1, ..., k\}$ **do**
25:     CS_1 computes:

$$P(E_j^l|H_1^l)_a = E_{pk}(s) * D(j) \bmod N^2, P(E_j^l|H_1^l)_b = E_{pk}(s)^{k+1} * \prod_{p=0}^{k} D(p) \bmod N^2$$
$$P(E_j^l|H_0^l)_a = E_{pk}(s) * D'(j) \bmod N^2, P(E_j^l|H_0^l)_b = E_{pk}(s)^{k+1} * \prod_{p=0}^{k} D'(p) \bmod N^2$$
$$P_k^l(a) = P(H_1^l) * P(E_j^l|H_1^l)_a * P(H_0^l)_b * P(E_j^l|H_0^l)_b \bmod N^2$$
$$P_k^l(b) = P(H_1^l)_b * P(E_j^l|H_1^l)_b * P(H_0^l)_a * P(E_j^l|H_0^l)_a \bmod N^2$$

26:    **end for**
27: **end for**
28: **Step 4: Building the classification model**
29: **for** $l \in \mathcal{Y}$ **do**
30:    CS_1 defines a $(k+1)$-dimension vector $W_l = (w_{l0}, ..., w_{lk})$,
       where $w_{lj} = SMIN(P_j^l(a), P_j^l(b))(j \in \{0, 1, ..., k\})$
31: **end for**

After that, CS_1 defines $A(j) = Y'_{il}$, $A'(j) = E_{pk}(1) * Y'^{N-1}_{il} \bmod N^2$. Since the Y'_{il} just has two possible values: $Y'_{il} = E_{pk}(0)$ or $Y'_{il} = E_{pk}(1)$, then when $A(j) = E_{pk}(0)$, $A'(j) = E_{pk}(1)$, otherwise, $A(j) = E_{pk}(1)$, $A'(j) = E_{pk}(0)$. Now CS_1 and CS_2 need to add the $A(j)$ to $D(j)$, add $A'(j)$ to $D'(j)$ according to $C_{x'_i}(l)$, respectively. Since neither CS_1 nor CS_2 know the true value of $C_{x'_i}(l)$, CS_1 constructs a $(k+1)$-dimension vector $Q = (q_0, ..., q_k)$ as:

$$Q = \pi\big((C_{x'_i}(l) * E_{pk}(0)^{N-1} \bmod N^2), ..., (C_{x'_i}(l) * E_{pk}(k)^{N-1} \bmod N^2)\big) \quad (9)$$

where π is a permutation function.

Since $0 \leq D_{sk}\big(C_{x'_i}(l)\big) \leq k$, there will be one and only one $q_i = E_{pk}(0)(i \in \{0, ..., k\})$. Then CS_1 sends vector Q to CS_2. CS_2 receives vector Q and decrypts it, then constructs a $(k+1)$-dimension vector $Q' = (q'_0, ..., q'_k)$, where $q'_i = E_{pk}(1)$ if $q(i) = E_{pk}(0)$, otherwise $q'_i = E_{pk}(0)(i \in \{0, ..., k\})$. Obviously that there will be one and only one $q'_i = E_{pk}(1)$, all the other $q'_i = E_{pk}(0)(i \in \{0, ..., k\})$. Then CS_2 sends vector Q' back to CS_1, and CS_1 obtains $Q = \pi^{-1}(Q')$. Then CS_1 computes:

$$
\begin{aligned}
D(j) &= D(j) * SM\big(A(j), q(j)\big) \bmod N^2 \\
D'(j) &= D'(j) * SM\big(A(j), q(j)\big) \bmod N^2
\end{aligned}
\quad (10)
$$

Now CS_1 computes the posterior probabilities $P(E^l_j|H^l_b)(l \in \mathcal{Y}, j \in \{0, 1, ..., k\})$ as Eq. (5). Obviously, there will be float-point numbers as same as the prior probabilities. Then CS_1 also encrypts the posterior probabilities into two parts like the prior probabilities as flowing:

$$
\begin{aligned}
P(E^l_j|H^l_1)_a &= E_{pk}(s) * D(j) \bmod N^2 \\
P(E^l_j|H^l_1)_b &= E_{pk}(s)^{k+1} * \prod_{p=0}^{k} D(p) \bmod N^2 \\
P(E^l_j|H^l_0)_a &= E_{pk}(s) * D'(j) \bmod N^2 \\
P(E^l_j|H^l_0)_b &= E_{pk}(s)^{k+1} * \prod_{p=0}^{k} D'(p) \bmod N^2
\end{aligned}
\quad (11)
$$

Since in ML-kNN [24], the final multi-label classification results of instance t are decided based on Eq. (6), then for $j \in \{0, 1, ..., k\}$, CS_1 can compute:

$$
\begin{aligned}
P^l_j(a) &= P(H^l_1)_a * P(E^l_j|H^l_1)_a * P(H^l_0)_b * P(E^l_j|H^l_0)_b \bmod N^2 \\
P^l_j(b) &= P(H^l_1)_b * P(E^l_j|H^l_1)_b * P(H^l_0)_a * P(E^l_j|H^l_0)_a \bmod N^2
\end{aligned}
\quad (12)
$$

In the forth step, CS_1 will compare the $P^l_j(a)$ and $P^l_j(b)$ to build the final multi-label classification model. Specifically, CS_1 constructs a $(k+1)$-dimension vector as: $W_l = (w_{l0}, ..., w_{lk})$, where $w_{lj} = SMIN\big(P^l_j(a), P^l_j(b)\big)(l \in \mathcal{Y}, j \in \{0, 1, ..., k\})$. Then the W_l is the encrypted classification result of label l for different $C_t(l) \in \{0, ..., k\}$.

4.2   Secure Classifying Stage: Classify the Unclassified Instance

Suppose that DU has encrypted the instance t into t' using the pk of DO and submitted t' to CS_1.

Protocol 4. Secure Classifying Stage: Classify the Unclassified Instance

Input: CS_1 has the encrypted dataset $\boldsymbol{T'}$, vector $W_l(l \in \mathcal{Y})$ and encrypted unclassified instance $\boldsymbol{t'}$ which is submitted by DU , CS_2 has sk

Output: DU obtains the multi-label classification result of instance $\boldsymbol{t'}$

1: CS_1 and CS_2 find the kNN of instance $\boldsymbol{t'}$ in dataset $\boldsymbol{T'}$ using the SkNN protocol, obtain kNN vector $N_{\boldsymbol{t'}}$

2: **for** $l \in \mathcal{Y}$ **do**

3:    CS_1 and CS_2 computes:

$$C_{\boldsymbol{t'}}(l) = \prod_{p=1}^{m} SM\big(N_{\boldsymbol{t'}}(p), \boldsymbol{y}_p'(l)\big) \bmod N^2$$

4:    CS_1 constructs a $(k+1)$-dimension vector $Q = (q_0, ..., q_k)$ as:
$Q = \pi\big((C_{\boldsymbol{t'}}(l) * E_{pk}(0)^{N-1} \bmod N^2), ..., (C_{\boldsymbol{t'}}(l) * E_{pk}(k)^{N-1} \bmod N^2)\big)$,
where π is a permutation function.

5:    CS_1 sends vector Q to CS_2

6:    CS_2 receives vector Q from CS_1 and decrypts it

7:    CS_2 constructs a $(k+1)$-dimension vector $Q' = (q_0', ..., q_k')$, where $q_i' = E_{pk}(1)$ if $q(i) = E_{pk}(0)$, otherwise $q_i' = E_{pk}(0)(i \in \{0, ..., k\})$

8:    CS_2 sends vector Q' to CS_1

9:    CS_1 obtains $Q = \pi^{-1}(Q')$

10:    CS_1 computes:

$$R_{\boldsymbol{t'}}(l) = \prod_{j=0}^{k} SM\big(q_j, W_l(j)\big) \bmod N^2$$

11:    CS_1 generates a non-zero random integer α, computes:

$$R_{\boldsymbol{t'}}'(l) = E_{pk}(\alpha) * R_{\boldsymbol{t'}}(l) \bmod N^2$$

12:    CS_1 sends $R_{\boldsymbol{t'}}'(l)$ to CS_2, sends α to DU

13:    CS_2 receives $R_{\boldsymbol{t'}}'(l)$ from CS_1 and decrypts it, sends the $D_{sk}\big(R_{\boldsymbol{t'}}'(l)\big)$ to DU

14:    DU computes $\boldsymbol{\Phi} = D_{sk}\big(R_{\boldsymbol{t'}}'(l)\big) - \alpha$:
   if $\boldsymbol{\Phi} = 1$: instance $\boldsymbol{t}$ is associated with label l
   if $\boldsymbol{\Phi} = 0$: instance $\boldsymbol{t}$ is not associated with label l

15: **end for**

Firstly, CS_1 and CS_2 will find the kNN of instance $\boldsymbol{t'}$ in dataset $\boldsymbol{T'}$ using the SkNN protocol, obtain kNN vector $N_{\boldsymbol{t'}}$. Then for each label $l \in \mathcal{Y}$, CS_1 and CS_2 compute:

$$C_{\boldsymbol{t'}}(l) = \prod_{p=1}^{m} SM\big(N_{\boldsymbol{t'}}(p), \boldsymbol{y}_p'(l)\big) \bmod N^2 \tag{13}$$

After that, CS_1 and CS_2 need to find the corresponding classified result for label l according to the $C_{\boldsymbol{t'}}(l)$. Since neither CS_1 nor CS_2 know the true value of $C_{\boldsymbol{t'}}(l)$, CS_1 constructs a $(k+1)$-dimension vector $Q = (q_0, ..., q_k)$ as:

$$Q = \pi\big((C_{\boldsymbol{t'}}(l) * E_{pk}(0)^{N-1} \bmod N^2), ..., (C_{\boldsymbol{t'}}(l) * E_{pk}(k)^{N-1} \bmod N^2)\big) \tag{14}$$

where π is a permutation function.

Then CS_1 sends vector Q to CS_2. CS_2 receives vector Q from CS_1 and decrypts it, constructs a $(k+1)$-dimension vector $Q' = (q_0', ..., q_k')$, where $q_i' = E_{pk}(1)$ if $q(i) = E_{pk}(0)$, otherwise $q_i' = E_{pk}(0)(i \in \{0, ..., k\})$. Then CS_2

sends vector Q' back to CS_1. CS_1 obtains $Q = \pi^{-1}(Q')$, computes:

$$R_{t'}(l) = \prod_{j=0}^{k} SM(q_j, W_l(j)) \bmod N^2 \tag{15}$$

$R_{t'}(l)$ is the encrypted classified result for label l of instance t'.

For protecting the real classified result from CS_2, CS_1 generates a non-zero random integer α and computes $R'_{t'}(l) = E_{pk}(\alpha) * R_{t'}(l) \bmod N^2$. Then CS_1 sends $R'_{t'}(l)$ to CS_2, sends α to DU. CS_2 receives $R'_{t'}(l)$ from CS_1 and decrypts it, sends the $D_{sk}(R'_{t'}(l))$ to DU.

Finally, DU computes $\boldsymbol{\Phi} = D_{sk}(R'_{t'}(l)) - \alpha$, then if $\boldsymbol{\Phi} = 1$, instance t is associated with label l; if $\boldsymbol{\Phi} = 0$, instance t is not associated with label l.

5   Evaluation

In this section, we prove the security of our scheme, and then analyze our cost in computation and communication.

5.1   Security Analysis

A formal security definition under semi-honest model can be described as follows [7]:

Definition 1. Let $f(x, y)$ be a functionality, and $f_1(x, y)$ (resp. $f_2(x, y)$) denote the first (resp. second) element of $f(x, y)$. Let Π be a two-party protocol for computing $f(x, y)$. The view of the first (resp. second) party during an execution of Π on (x, y), denoted $VIEW_1(x, y)$ (resp. $VIEW_2(x, y)$), is $(x, r, m_1, \cdots, m_t)$ (resp. $(y, r, m_1, \cdots, m_t)$), where x (resp. y) represents the input of the first (resp. second) party, r represents the randomness and m_i represents the i-th message it has received. We say that protocol Π privately computes function f, i.e. Π is secure against semi-honest adversaries, if there exists probabilistic polynomial-time algorithms S_1 and S_2, such that

$$(S_1(x, f_1(x, y)) \stackrel{c}{\equiv} (VIEW_1(x, y)) \tag{16}$$

$$(S_2(y, f_2(x, y)) \stackrel{c}{\equiv} (VIEW_2(x, y)) \tag{17}$$

where $\stackrel{c}{\equiv}$ represents computational indistinguishability.

With the above security definition, we now prove the security of proposed ML-kNN classification scheme. Note that the secure computing protocols (SM, SkNN, SMIN) have been proved secure in previous works, thus the proof of those protocols is omitted. We skip details and give sketches of the proof of the following theorems due to space limitation.

Theorem 1. *Our secure training stage, namely Protocol 3, is provably secure under semi-honest model. Cloud servers cannot learn any useful information about the dataset $\boldsymbol{T}$ and ML-kNN classification model.*

Proof (Sketch). In our secure training stage, CS_1 can access the encrypted dataset T' and the messages received from are all encrypted values. Thus the view of CS_1 is $VIEW_1 = (e_1, e_2, \cdots, e_\alpha)$, where e_i are all ciphertexts and α is the number of encrypted values that CS_1 can access. We use a simulator S_1 to simulate client's view and then we can obtain $S_1 = (r_1, r_2, \cdots, r_\alpha)$, where r_i are all random numbers. Since Paillier cryptosystem is a semantically secure encryption scheme, S_1 is computationally indistinguishable from $VIEW_1$.

Besides, the view of CS_2 is $VIEW_2 = (D_{sk}(Q))$ where $D_{sk}(Q)$ is a binary vector. Similarly, we can construct a simulator S_2, each element of which is randomly chosen from $\{0, 1\}$. It is clearly that $VIEW_2$ and S_2 are computationally indistinguishable because of π is a permutation function.

Based on the above analysis, we can claim that our training stage is secure under semi-honest model. Cloud servers cannot learn any useful information about the dataset T and ML-kNN classification model.

Theorem 2. *Our secure classifying stage, namely Protocol 4, is secure. No information about ML-kNN classification model, DU's query and the classification results are disclosed to cloud servers.*

Proof (Sketch). In classifying stage, CS_1's view is $VIEW_1 = (t', C_{t'}(l), Q, Q', R_{t'}(l))$ and CS_2's view is $VIEW_2 = (D_{sk}(Q), R'_{t'}(l))$. Note that the messages CS_1 obtains are all encrypted values and all values CS_1 receives are random numbers, we can easily construct the simulators S_1 and S_2 which is computationally indistinguishable from $VIEW_1$ and $VIEW_2$, respectively. Thus, Our Classifying Stage is secure under semi-honest model. No information about ML-kNN classification model, DU's query and the classification results are disclosed to cloud servers.

5.2   Computation and Communication Complexity

In this section, we will analyze our computation cost and communication overheads, respectively.

Computation Complexity. There are four steps in secure training stage. In step 1, as shown in Protocol 2, the computation complexity is bounded by $O(qm)$ exponentiations, where q is the number of label in label set and m is the number of instance in training dataset. There are $O(m)$ instantiations of SkNN protocol in Step 2. Note that the computation complexity of the SkNN protocol proposed in [5] is bounded by $O(md + k)$ encryptions, decryptions and exponentiations. Thus the total computation complexity of Step 2 is bounded by $O(m^2 d + km)$ encryptions, decryptions and exponentiations. In step 3, it needs $O(qmk)$ instantiations of SM protocol, complexity of which is bounded by $O(1)$ encryptions, decryptions and exponentiations. The total computation complexity of Step 3 is bounded by $O(qmk(m+k))$ encryptions, decryptions and exponentiations. Besides, the computation complexity of Step 4 is bounded by $O(qk)$ instantiations of SMIN protocol. Considering the SMIN protocol proposed in [5], the computation complexity of Step 4 is bounded by $O(qk\sigma)$, where σ is the bit length of each attribute in training dataset.

The computation complexity of secure classifying stage is bounded by $O(1)$ instantiations of SkNN protocol and $O(q(m+k))$ instantiations of SM protocol. Considering the computation complexity of the SkNN protocol and SM protocol is bounded by $O(md+k)$ and $O(1)$ encryptions, decryptions and exponentiations, the total computation complexity is bounded by $O(md+q(m+k))$ encryptions, decryptions and exponentiations.

Communication Complexity. Suppose the size of ciphertext of employed Paillier cryptosystem is $\mathcal{K}$. In secure classifying stage, firstly, the SkNN protocol needs to be done 1 time to find the kNN of instance t' which communication complexity is bounded by $O(mk\mathcal{K})$ bits. While computing $C_{t'}(l)$, SM protocol needs to be done qm times which communication complexity is bounded by $O(\mathcal{K})$ bits. After that, CS_1 sends q $(k+1)$-dimensional vectors to CS_2, then CS_2 returns q $(k+1)$-dimensional vectors back to CS_1, since all the data transferred between two clouds are in encrypted form, the communication complexity is bounded by $O(qk\mathcal{K})$ bits. Therefore, the communication complexity for classifying one unclassified instance is bounded by $O(\mathcal{K}(mk+qm+qk))$ bits.

6 Related Work

We simple review the related work as follows.

Multi-label classification. Multi-label classification methods can be divided into two main categories: problem transformation and algorithm adaptation. Problem transformation methods tackle multi-label learning problem by transforming it into other well-established learning scenarios. Representative algorithms include first-order approaches Binary Relevance [1], high-order approach Classifier Chains [15] which transform the task of multi-label learning into the task of binary classification, second-order approach Calibrated Label Ranking [16] which transforms the task of multi-label learning into the task of label ranking, and high-order approach Random k-labelsets [19] which transforms the task of multi-label learning into the task of multi-class classification. Algorithm adaptation methods tackle multi-label learning problem by adapting popular learning techniques to deal with multi-label data directly. Representative algorithms include AdaBoost.MH and AdaBoost.MR [18] are two multi-label extensions of the AdaBoost algorithm [6], ML-C4.5 [3] is an adaptation of the popular C4.5 algorithm, BP-MLL [25] is derived from the back-propagation algorithm of neural networks, Multi-label k-nearest neighbor (ML-kNN) [24] which our scheme is based on is adapted from the famous k-nearest neighbors algorithm.

Data mining over encrypted data in cloud. With the prosperous development of cloud computing, many works have been done for privacy-preserving data mining (PPDM) in clouds. Zhang et al. [23] explored how to enable secure image search in the data outsourcing environment. Wang et al. [21] considered the problem of secure and private outsourcing of shape-based feature extraction and proposed two approaches with different levels of security by using homomorphic encryption and the garbled circuit protocol. Li et al. [11] proposed a secure scheme for naïve Bayesian classification over encrypted data which can outsource the entire computation task of naïve Bayesian classification to cloud. Hu et al. [9] proposed an privacy-preserving computation outsourcing protocol for the prevailing scale-invariant feature transform (SIFT) over massive encrypted image data. In [26,27], Zhu et al. considered secure k-NN query over encrypted data in cloud. Li et al. [12] put forward an efficient hybrid method to compare encrypted numbers in cloud. Cheng et al. [2] gave a survey for securely analyzing large-scale data from Internet of Things in a quantum world. Although many works about PPDM have been developed, the domain of secure multi-label classification is still blank.

7   Conclusions

In this paper, we proposed a scheme for secure multi-label classification over encrypted data in cloud. Our scheme can handle the multi-label classification task by the cloud servers, then can dramatically reduce the storage and computation burden of data owner and data users. Besides, Our scheme can protect the privacy information of data owner and data users, the cloud servers can not learn anything useful about the input data and output multi-label classification results. At last, we proved the security and evaluated the complexity of our scheme.

Acknowledgments. This work is partly supported by the National Key Research and Development Program of China (No. 2017YFB0802300), the Natural Science Foundation of China (No. 61602240), the Natural Science Foundation of Jiangsu Province of China (No. BK20150760), the Research Fund of Guangxi Key Laboratory of Trusted Software (No. kx201611), and the Foundation of Graduate Innovation Center in NUAA (No. kfjj20161605).

References

1. Boutell, M.R., Luo, J., Shen, X., Brown, C.M.: Learning multi-label scene classification. Pattern Recognit. **37**(9), 1757–1771 (2004)
2. Cheng, C., Lu, R., Petzoldt, A., Takagi, T.: Securing the internet of things in a quantum world. IEEE Commun. Mag. **55**(2), 116–120 (2017)
3. Clare, A., King, R.D.: Knowledge discovery in multi-label phenotype data. In: De Raedt, L., Siebes, A. (eds.) PKDD 2001. LNCS, vol. 2168, pp. 42–53. Springer, Heidelberg (2001). doi:10.1007/3-540-44794-6_4
4. Elisseeff, A.E., Weston, J.: A kernel method for multi-labelled classification. Adv. Neural Inf. Process. Syst. **14**, 681–687 (2002)
5. Elmehdwi, Y., Samanthula, B.K., Jiang, W.: Secure k-nearest neighbor query over encrypted data in outsourced environments. In: 2014 IEEE 30th International Conference on Data Engineering (ICDE), pp. 664–675. IEEE (2014)

6. Freund, Y., Schapire, R., Abe, N.: A short introduction to boosting. J. Jpn. Soc. Artif. Intell. **14**, 771–780 (1999)
7. Goldreich, O.: Foundations of Cryptography II: Basic Applications. Cambridge University Press, New York (2004)
8. Goldwasser, S., Micali, S., Rackoff, C.: The knowledge complexity of interactive proof-systems. SIAM J. Comput. **18**(1), 186–208 (1989)
9. Hu, S., Qian, W., Wang, J., Zhan, Q., Ren, K.: Securing SIFT: privacy-preserving outsourcing computation of feature extractions over encrypted image data. IEEE Trans. Image Process. **25**(7), 3411–3425 (2016)
10. Kantarcoglu, M., Vaidya, J.: Privacy preserving naive bayes classifier for horizontally partitioned data. In: IEEE ICDM Workshop on Privacy Preserving Data Mining, pp. 3–9 (2003)
11. Li, X., Zhu, Y., Wang, J.: Secure naïve bayesian classification over encrypted data in cloud. In: Chen, L., Han, J. (eds.) ProvSec 2016. LNCS, vol. 10005, pp. 130–150. Springer, Cham (2016). doi:10.1007/978-3-319-47422-9_8
12. Li, X., Zhu, Y., Wang, J.: Efficient encrypted data comparison through a hybrid method. J. Inf. Sci. Eng. **33**(4), 953–964 (2017)
13. Mccallum, A.K.: Multi-label text classication with a mixture model trained by EM. In: AAAI Workshop on Text Learning, pp. 1–7 (1999)
14. Paillier, P.: Public-key cryptosystems based on composite degree residuosity classes. In: Stern, J. (ed.) EUROCRYPT 1999. LNCS, vol. 1592, pp. 223–238. Springer, Heidelberg (1999). doi:10.1007/3-540-48910-X_16
15. Read, J., Pfahringer, B., Holmes, G., Frank, E.: Classifier chains for multi-label classification. Mach. Learn. **85**(3), 333–359 (2011)
16. Rnkranz, J., Llermeier, E., Menc, L., Eneldo, A., Brinker, K.: Multilabel classification via calibrated label ranking. Mach. Learn. **73**(2), 133–153 (2008)
17. Samanthula, B.K., Elmehdwi, Y., Jiang, W.: k-Nearest neighbor classification over semantically secure encrypted relational data. IEEE Trans. Knowl. Data Eng. **27**(5), 1261–1273 (2015)
18. Schapire, R.E., Singer, Y.: Boostexter: a boosting-based system for text categorization. Mach. Learn. **39**(2), 135–168 (2000)
19. Tsoumakas, G., Vlahavas, I.: Random k-labelsets: an ensemble method for multilabel classification. In: Kok, J.N., Koronacki, J., Mantaras, R.L., Matwin, S., Mladenič, D., Skowron, A. (eds.) ECML 2007. LNCS, vol. 4701, pp. 406–417. Springer, Heidelberg (2007). doi:10.1007/978-3-540-74958-5_38
20. Ueda, N.: Parametric mixture models for multi-labeled text. In: Advances in Neural Information Processing Systems, pp. 721–728 (2002)
21. Wang, S., Nassar, M., Atallah, M., Malluhi, Q.: Secure and private outsourcing of shape-based feature extraction. In: Qing, S., Zhou, J., Liu, D. (eds.) ICICS 2013. LNCS, vol. 8233, pp. 90–99. Springer, Cham (2013). doi:10.1007/978-3-319-02726-5_7
22. Yi, X., Zhang, Y.: Privacy-preserving naive bayes classification on distributed data via semi-trusted mixers. Inf. Syst. **34**(3), 371–380 (2009)
23. Zhang, L., Jung, T., Liu, C., Ding, X., Li, X.Y., Liu, Y.: POP: privacy-preserving outsourced photo sharing and searching for mobile devices. In: IEEE International Conference on Distributed Computing Systems, pp. 308–317 (2015)
24. Zhang, M.-L., Zhou, Z.-H.: A k-nearest neighbor based algorithm for multi-label classification. In: IEEE International Conference on Granular Computing, vol. 2, pp. 718–721 (2005)

25. Zhang, M.-L., Zhou, Z.-H.: Multilabel neural networks with applications to functional genomics and text categorization. IEEE Trans. Knowl. Data Eng. **18**(10), 1338–1351 (2006)
26. Zhou, L., Zhu, Y., Castiglione, A.: Efficient k-NN query over encrypted data in cloud with limited key-disclosure and offline data owner. Comput. Secur. **69**, 84–96 (2017)
27. Zhu, Y., Huang, Z., Takagi, T.: Secure and controllable k-NN query over encrypted cloud data with key confidentiality. J. Parallel Distrib. Comput. **89**, 1–12 (2016)

A Secure Cloud Backup System
with Deduplication and Assured Deletion

Junzuo Lai[1,2], Jie Xiong[1], Chuansheng Wang[1(✉)], Guangzheng Wu[1],
and Yanling Li[1]

[1] Department of Computer Science, Jinan University, Guangzhou, China
laijunzuo@gmail.com, chueng0828@126.com
[2] State Key Laboratory of Cryptology, Beijing, China

Abstract. Cloud backup has been widely used in recent years. Over time, if the stored content is not under control, there will be a lot of redundant data stored in the cloud. When a user issues a delete instruction, the cloud service provider may not actually destroy the data, so that the user's data is exposed to the risk of being compromised. In order to avoid storing duplicate data and prevent deleted data from being recovered, we design a cloud backup system that can solve the two problems. No matter how large the files, each client only keeps one key. Through the experimental evaluation, we verify that our scheme is valid and our local overhead is greatly saved.

Keywords: Cloud storage · Shared data · Assured deletion · Data deduplication

1 Introduction

Cloud storage is a new concept that extends and develops from cloud computing. Many individuals and enterprises willing to outsource their data backup services to the cloud service provider (CSP). Although it's attractive, how to provide secure backup has become a concern. When the user deleted the cloud data, can we ensure that the data in the future will not be recovered? And the data on the cloud is not directly managed by users, can they ensure that data can not be accessed by unauthorized persons?

A direct way is to encrypt the data before uploading it. If the client deletes the data, he only deletes the corresponding key. However, when the stored data is large, a lot of problem have arisen. Client needs to manage a large number of keys, when the key size is comparable to the data item size, the outsourcing become meaningless. In order to get rid of the large local storage, we introduce a third-party server to manage keys. However, if the third-party collides with an adversary, the user's privacy will be exposed. So we consider reducing the number of keys, let each key to encrypt multiple files, but it can not support fine-grained assured deletion. Because cloud can't assuredly delete particular backup version or files, while other versions that share the common deleted data

© Springer International Publishing AG 2017
T. Okamoto et al. (Eds.): ProvSec 2017, LNCS 10592, pp. 74–83, 2017.
https://doi.org/10.1007/978-3-319-68637-0_5

should remain unaffected. In cloud backup, if the same file appears in multiple versions, then it's natural to store only one copy of the file and have the other versions refer to the file copy.

We present a secure cloud backup system that supports both deduplication and assured deletion. The client can only keep one key compared to the previous solution. Our highlight is that we have greatly saved our local expenses, decrease the users overhead and delete the specific files on the cloud without affecting shared data. The rest of the paper is organized as follows: Sect. 2 provides the necessary background. Section 3 gives some preliminaries such as system model, problem statement, and security definition, and Sect. 4 gives a concrete function design of our scheme. Section 5 presents the experimental results and analysis. Section 6 concludes and presents future work.

2   Background and Related Work

Deduplication. Douceur et al. [3] proposed the concept of convergent encryption (CE), which calculate the hash value of the data as a key to encrypt it. It achieves the same data file can generate the same ciphertext. After that, Bellare et al. [2] gave a general description of convergence encryption, and proposed message-locked encryption (MLE). However, these schemes can't resist the violent attack on keys. Thus, Bellare et al. [1] proposed a server-assisted MLE scheme (DupLESS), it introduces a trusted key server and uses its private key to generate a convergence key. It solves the problem that the plain space is vulnerable under the critical violent attack. Li et al. [5] proposed a key outsourcing storage scheme (DeKey) that supports block level deduplication. Li et al. [6] proposed two secure systems, namely SecCloud and SecCloud plus, aiming at achieving both data integrity and deduplication.

As an important means of protect data security, the ciphertext deduplication technique mainly focuses on the research of convergent encryption method, that is, using the same key to encrypt the same data.

Assured Deletion. Data stored in the cloud can't be directly controlled by the user. Assured deletion is to ensure that data can't be recover after being deleted. Perlman et al. [9] proposed a time-based file assured deletion method that deleted data permanently accessible after a scheduled time of arrival. The solution outsources the burden of key management to a minimum trusted third party. However the scheme can't achieve fine-grained deletion. Tangs [13] policy-based system (FADE) was designed for assured deletion in a cloud storage system that each file associates a DK with a file access policy, and each access policy associates a CK. The DK encrypts the file, and the CK encrypts the DK. When a policy is revoked, the policy's corresponding CK is destroyed by the key manager. But keys are managed by a third party easy to cause single-point failure.

Tang et al. [14] made improvements to FADE, they increases the number of the key manager which operation is based on the Shamir (k, n) threshold secret sharing scheme [12]. Rahumed et al. design a system called FadeVersion [10], which combines policy-based deletion with version control. Unfortunately, the above scheme require third party to manage the key. So, Mo et al. [8] proposed a fine-grained assured deletion involving only the client and the cloud. In this scheme, users only keep a small number of keys no matter how much data to store. Even if the adversary compromised the client or cloud in the future, the deleted data can't be recovered. Recently, Habib et al. [4] proposed Simplified File Assured Deletion (SFADE), it removed completely the dependency on key escrow system. Reardon et al. [11] focused on secure data deletion. Luo et al. [7] proposed a novel method to surely delete data in the cloud by overwriting.

3   Preliminaries

3.1   Assumptions and Problem Statement

Our assumption model shows in Fig. 1. The client divides the file into fix-size data block at first and encrypts file objects for uploading the cloud. After the backup, the client can download the data from the cloud, and calculates the key corresponding to the file object based on the key tree. In the end, it should decrypt the ciphertext data and assemble the decrypted data into original files.

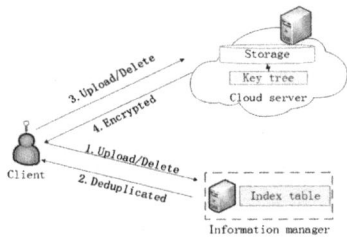

Fig. 1. Outline of proposed model.

In our model, the information manager stores the index table which records the file object related informations, include the file ID, tag t, file name, storage time, etc. Also, it responsible for the client requests to add, delete or update the file information, it also feeds back the relevant query results to the client. Besides, it'll compare the index table in the information manager according to the tag t of the file object. The result of the comparison is returned by the information manager to the client. For the CSP, when the user store files in the cloud, we assume that the cloud will store the key tree and encrypted files data. In order to construct the key tree, the cloud generates each node key modulators randomly to prepare for data encryption. The cloud also performs the insertion, deletion and update internal nodes or leaf modulators in the key tree and returns the relevant modulation information or ciphertext data to the client if necessary.

Based on the above assumption, file should be deleted after a specified retention period has passed. However, cloud storage does not provide the option of assured deletion. We focus on the problem which guarantees that the data deleted from a cloud system will be permanently inaccessible. Before uploading the data, our goal is to implement the removal of redundant data. Also, we want to require client only keep one key also can achieve the functions described above. The security goal is the adversary in the polynomial time, can not compromise the key we want to protected and the deleted files can not be recovered.

3.2   Security Definition

Client security. Our scheme encrypts the data first before storing in the cloud. After cryptographic operations, client is also perfectly deleted the secret key, This is the first one we should guarantee. Because if client becomes malicious and retains the key after upload operation, that the user wants to save their privacy better become meaningless. Moreover, if the client at this time is compromised by attacker, the key is leaked, security can not be guaranteed.

Adversary ability. We assume that an attacker can obtain a copy of any encrypted data. First, we suppose the encryption operation is secure, that means it is computationally infeasible to decrypt the data without the decryption key. For the hash function used by the key modulation function F in our scheme, it must be an collision-resistant hash function. That is polynomially infeasible to find two hash inputs could produce the same output or find a hash input to produce a special output. That is, suppose an arbitrary leaf node k, after the master key change and the modulator adjustment algorithm are executed after the $MT(k)$, even if the new master key is leaked in the future, the data key k is irreversible in the polynomial time. So, the attacker will not be able to recover the deleted file. At the same time, we agree that even an adversary obtains information about key and files in any physical medium or other media, data objects should be irrecoverable to an adversary who has unlimited use of the provided interface.

CSP security. We support anonymity against honest-but-curious CSP, because it needs to ensure the normal execution of the commands, and it may be observes and collects some of the relevant information, but it still does not know the master key. Note though, If the cloud and information manager collude with each other, a very small amount of privacy is revealed. When the attacker accesses to ciphertext from the CSP and gets less information from the information manager, the attacker can only guess the relationship between ciphertext and documents. Because the attacker has no decryption key, it is impossible to restore the plaintext content, but some privacy is revealed. So in our scheme, we assume that they will not collude with each other.

4   System Function Construction

In Fig. 1, we explain in detail the three functions: deduplication, data uploading and data deleting. We explain the the main idea of "key modulation". Each data key k is determined by a master key K and a unique modulator subset M_k, it's calculated by a one-way function $k = F(K, M_k)$. The M_k is an ordered list of modulators, represented as $<x_1, x_2, ..., x_l>$. The key hash chain is defined:

$$F(K, M_k) = H(...H(H(K \oplus x_1) \oplus x_2)... \oplus x_l), \tag{1}$$

Where $\oplus$ is the XOR operator, and H is a one-way hash function with collision-resistant. The master key is stored on the client, and modulators are stored in the cloud. To remove k, the client permanently removes K and selects a new master key K'. For all other data keys k', $k' = F(K', M'_{k'}) = F(K, M_{k'})$. Where $M_{k'}$ is a subset of modulators for k' before k is deleted, $M'_{k'}$ is a subset of modulators for k' after k is deleted. After removing the key k, we don't change any modulator in M_k, even if the adversary gains the new master key K' in the future, the key k can not be recovered after K is permanently deleted.

4.1 Deduplication

Before backing up, we divide the backup data file F into many file objects O_i, and set a maximum size threshold for each file object. If the size of the file is below this threshold, it can be treated as a single file object, otherwise we divide it. Let $H(\cdot)$ be an collision-resistant hash function, $f_{k^*}(\cdot)$ denotes a pseudo-random function (PRF). We first do hash operations for each file object O_i, $H(O) \rightarrow h$, then calculate tag t of each hash value $f_{k^*}(h) \rightarrow t$, then compare t. If the tag t of two data objects is equal, one is deleted, the other will be recorded into the information manager index table.

4.2 Uploading

We use $\{m\}_k$ as the notation for symmetric-key encrypting m with k. When the data is uploaded for the first time, the cloud randomly generates a key tree. As shown in Fig. 2(a). It's a complete binary tree, each internal node has two sub-nodes, each leaf node representing a data key. The client assigns a randomly generated leaf modulation for each leaf node, and assigns link modulator for each link. Note that each modulator is randomly generated and different from each other. Each leaf node encodes a data key. Let $P(k)$ represents the path from the root node to the node k. The cloud will send M_k to the client if the client need a certain key k. Then the client compute the data key by $k = F(K, M_k)$. Client uses the key k_i to encrypt the file object O_i and upload to the cloud. Each file object carries an ID identifier for the query, which is stored in the index table.

In Fig. 2(a), each leaf node is assigned a leaf modulator, such as x_4, where each link is assigned a link modulator, such as x_1, x_2, x_3. We represent M_k as $<x_1, x_2, x_3, x_4>$. When uploading a new backup file F' next time, the first thing is to remove the duplicate data. If there exits same data, the file object will be not uploaded, if it differ from the previous, the new ID' will be stored in the information manager and the relationship between F' and ID' will be recorded. At last the client will send a request to the cloud to insert a new leaf node in the key tree. Suppose that we want insert a new node at the position g, as shown in

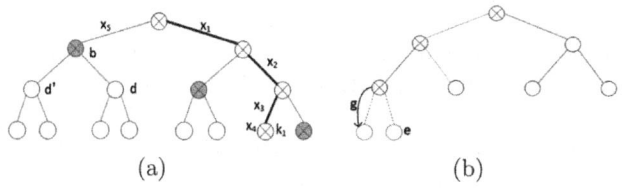

Fig. 2. (a) A modulation tree. (b) Add a new key e to the tree.

Fig. 2(b). The cloud sends the path $P(g)$ from the root to node g to the client. Let M_g^- be M_g without the last modulator x_g. The client replaces node g with a new internal node h, then sets g and a new leaf e serve as the children of h. Assigning the randomly generated modulator to the new leaf e and the link (h, g), link (h, e). Assigning a new leaf modulator to node g as follow:

$$x_g' = F(K, M_g^-) \oplus F(K, M_g^- + <x_{h,g}>) \oplus x_g. \tag{2}$$

The $x_{h,g}$ is the link modulator on (h, g), and x_g is the node modulator with g. Next, the client computes the new data key encoded by the new leaf e, i.e., $k' = F(K, M_g^- + <x_{h,e}, x_e>)$. This key is used to encrypt the new file object O'. The client sends the encrypted new file object $\{O'\}_{k'}$ and the modulator for (h, g), (h, e), g, e to the cloud. The cloud updates the modulation tree, stores the ciphertext After the above adjustment, we can guarantee that the data key encoded by the g node will not change before or after the insertion of the node.

4.3 Deleting

The main idea of the deletion is to build an index table that maintains the file storage location and data sharing informations. Before deleting, we access the index table first, and check whether the data to be deleted are shared. We delete the data on the cloud based on the location information. When the data to be deleted is not shared by other files, the corresponding information in the index table and the backup in the cloud should be deleted. In another case, it only deletes the data in the index table, so it will not affect other shared files. Next we explain how the system removes a file and can't recover it in the future.

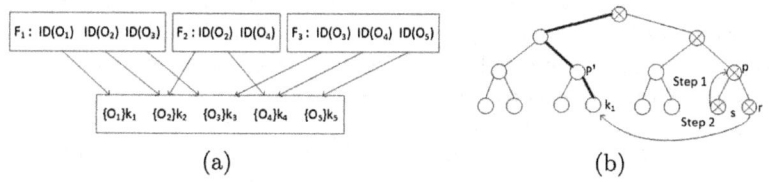

Fig. 3. (a) Illustration of deduplication and assured deletion. (b) Balancing the tree after k_1 is deleted.

Suppose the client wants to delete F_1. Figure 3(a) shows O_1 in file F_1 are not shared in other files. The cloud finds the encrypted item in its storage and the associated leaf node k_1 in the modulation tree. It searches the information about k_1 that consisting of nodes on the path from the root to leaf k_1 and the siblings nodes. The collection of sibling nodes is denoted B, as illustrated by Fig. 2(a). The $MT(k_1)$ is composed of nodes with cross inside and B is composed of shaded nodes. The cloud sends $MT(k_1)$ to the client to updates the master key K to K', but doesn't change any link modulator in the $MT(k)$. Let $P(b)$ be the path from root to node b, where and M_b be the list of link modulator along $P(b)$. In Fig. 3(a), $M_b = <x_5>$. First, the client calculates:

$$\delta(b) = F(K, M_b) \oplus F(K', M_b). \tag{3}$$

The client send $\{\delta(b)|b \in B\}$ to the cloud, for each internal node b belonging to the set B, the cloud adjusts the modulators on its child links, (b, d) and (b, d'):

$$\begin{aligned} x_{b,d} &:= x_{b,d} \oplus \delta(b) \\ x_{b,d'} &:= x_{b,d'} \oplus \delta(b), \end{aligned} \tag{4}$$

where ":=" is the assignment operator, $x_{b,d}$ is the link modulator on (b, d), and $x_{b,d'}$ is the link modulator on (b, d'). When b as a leaf node, the server adjusts the leaf modulator: where x_b is the leaf modulator of node b.

$$x_b := x_b \oplus \delta(b), \tag{5}$$

Balanced Adjustment Algorithm. In order to keep the worst case performance at $O(logn)$, we should complete the key tree back to a complete binary tree after we delete a certain key. See Fig. 3(b), we let r be the last leaf node of the last layer of the key tree. After we delete node k_1, we move r to the position of node k_1. The cloud sends the path $P(r)$ which from root node to the r node, with the sibling node s to the client. Let p be the parent of s and r. The balanced algorithm is divided into two steps: First, the client calculates a new leaf modulator for node s, as follows:

$$x'_s = F(K', M_p) \oplus H(F(K, M_p) \oplus x_{p,s} \oplus x_s) \tag{6}$$

where x_s is the leaf modulator of node s before adjustment, $x_{p,s}$ is a modulator on the link (p, s). The client sends x'_s to the cloud, cloud removes r and replaces the p node with s, and assigns the new leaf modulator x'_s to s node.

Second, inserting node r at the position of node k_1. Let p' be the parent of the node k_1 in $MT(k_1)$, and M'_p be the list of modulators of $P(p)$. The client selects a link modulator randomly for the link (p', r). The client computes a new leaf modulator for node r as follows:

$$x'_r = F(K, M_p + <x_{p,r}>) \oplus F(K', M_{p'} + <x_{p',r}>) \oplus x_r, \tag{7}$$

where $x_{p,r}$ is the link modulator on (p, r). Then the client will send $x_{p',r}$ and x'_r to the cloud server. After adjusting the balance algorithm, we can ensure that the reconstructed tree becomes a complete binary tree.

5   Experiments and Analysis

In this chapter, we have carried out a simulation experiment on our system, and realized the four functions. Finally, we have compared the system with other similar systems and analyzed the results.

Due to the limitations of the experimental equipment, we have only completed the simulation experiment at local host. We implement cloud storage servers and client both on local computer. Both client and cloud have the following parameters: 4 GB RAM, Microsoft Windows 7 system, the system type is 64 bit. We use the Java as the programming tool, and the development platform is eclipse.

Performance Comparison. In this paper, we compare our cloud backup system with the literature [10,15] taking into account local storage overhead, communication/computing overhead, deduplication, as shown in Table 1.

Table 1. Comparison of three schemes

Scheme	Deduplication	Assured deletion	Loc.overhead	Com.overhead
ADEC [15]	$Enc_{k_i}(C_i); Enc_{s_i}(V_i)$	overwrite s_k	$O(n)$	$O(1)$
FadeVersion [10]	$H(O) \rightarrow h$	delete s_k	$O(n)$	$O(1)$
Our scheme	$f_{k^*}(h) \rightarrow t$	delete k_i, $K \rightarrow K'$	$O(1)$	$O(\log n)$

From the Table 1, the ADEC [15] uses the k_i to encrypt the data block C_i, and the s_i to encrypt the V_i that the V_i is composed of data block. It's safe, but it adds to the burden of computation. In FadeVersion [10], they use the hash which input is a certain file object. The scheme compare the output of hash value to achieve deduplication. In our scheme, we first generate the hash value of data object, then generate tag t through a PRF. It can better guarantee the unpredictability of t, and the security is also stronger. In terms of assured deletion, the ADEC [15] overwrite s_k, it can only perform deletion from the beginning of the version history, it has some limitations. However, our scheme perform deletion to delete k_i, and change the master key K to K', all data keys remain unchanged except for the delete key k_i. Our scheme can greatly reduce the user's local storage cost, which have more advantageous than the literature [10,15]. and our scheme can save local storage space without the use of third-party key managers and achieve fine-grained assured deletions. For different sizes of documents we do the file test analysis when we create a file, download a file and delete a file.

We also tests the performance of assured deletion, and calculates the time taken to delete a block under different data volumes. For three operations, we have done experiments respectively. The relationship between the size of the file and the time they spend is shown in Fig. 4. In Fig. 4(a), where the x-axis shows

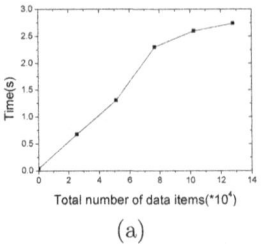
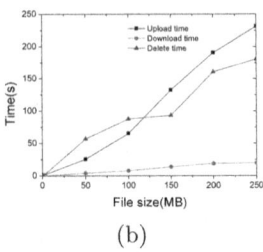

(a)   (b)

Fig. 4. The time spent on file operations

the file size scale, and the y-axis shows the average client computational time in three cases. Figure 4(b) shows the delete operation average computational time in total number of data items, we can see the computation overheads increase logarithmically with respect to the number of data items.

6   Conclusion and Future Work

In this paper, we presents a scheme has the ability to remove duplicate data and fine-grained assured deletion with the client only keeps one key. The scheme introduces the information manager to store and maintain the storage information. It reduces the network transmission costs and save storage space effectively. At the same time, the program also uses the collision-resistant hash function and the key modulation algorithm. Without using a third-party management keys, the user can delete a specific file in the cloud, and the deleted data can never be recovered. How to improve the performance of the cloud backup system while ensuring the security, it's our further study in the future. Due to the limited experimental conditions, we only realizes the simulation experiment, and can not accurately reflect the use of the system in the real network environment. In the near future, we'll complete experiments in a real network environment.

Acknowledgment. We are grateful to the anonymous reviewers for their helpful comments. The work of Junzuo Lai was supported by National Natural Science Foundation of China (No. 61572235), Guangdong Natural Science Funds for Distinguished Young Scholar (No. 2015A030306045), and Pearl River S&T Nova Program of Guangzhou.

References

1. Bellare, M., Keelveedhi, S., Ristenpart, T.: Dupless: server-aided encryption for deduplicated storage. IACR Cryptology ePrint Archive 2013, 429 (2013)
2. Bellare, M., Keelveedhi, S., Ristenpart, T.: Message-locked encryption and secure deduplication. In: Johansson, T., Nguyen, P.Q. (eds.) EUROCRYPT 2013. LNCS, vol. 7881, pp. 296–312. Springer, Heidelberg (2013). doi:10.1007/978-3-642-38348-9_18

3. Douceur, J.R., Adya, A., Bolosky, W.J., Simon, P., Theimer, M.: Reclaiming space from duplicate files in a serverless distributed file system. In: Proceedings of the 22nd International Conference on Distributed Computing Systems, pp. 617–624. IEEE (2002)
4. Habib, A.B., Khanam, T., Palit, R.: Simplified file assured deletion (sfade) - a user friendly overlay approach for data security in cloud storage system. In: International Conference on Advances in Computing, Communications and Informatics, pp. 1640–1644 (2013)
5. Li, J., Chen, X., Li, M., Li, J., Lee, P.P., Lou, W.: Secure deduplication with efficient and reliable convergent key management. IEEE Trans. Parallel Distrib. Syst. **25**(6), 1615–1625 (2014)
6. Li, J., Li, J., Xie, D., Cai, Z.: Secure auditing and deduplicating data in cloud. IEEE Trans. Comput. **65**(8), 2386–2396 (2016)
7. Luo, Y., Xu, M., Fu, S., Wang, D.: Enabling assured deletion in the cloud storage by overwriting. In: Proceedings of the 4th ACM International Workshop on Security in Cloud Computing. pp. 17–23. ACM (2016)
8. Mo, Z., Qiao, Y., Chen, S.: Two-party fine-grained assured deletion of outsourced data in cloud systems. In: 2014 IEEE 34th International Conference on Distributed Computing Systems (ICDCS), pp. 308–317. IEEE (2014)
9. Perlman, R.: File system design with assured delete. In: Third IEEE International Security in Storage Workshop, SISW 2005, p. 6. IEEE (2005)
10. Rahumed, A., Chen, H.C., Tang, Y., Lee, P.P., Lui, J.C.: A secure cloud backup system with assured deletion and version control. In: 2011 40th International Conference on Parallel Processing Workshops (ICPPW), pp. 160–167. IEEE (2011)
11. Reardon, J., Basin, D., Capkun, S.: On secure data deletion. IEEE Secur. Priv. **12**(3), 37–44 (2014)
12. Shamir, A.: How to share a secret. Commun. ACM **22**(11), 612–613 (1979)
13. Tang, Y., Lee, P.P.C., Lui, J.C.S., Perlman, R.: FADE: secure overlay cloud storage with file assured deletion. In: Jajodia, S., Zhou, J. (eds.) SecureComm 2010. LNICST, vol. 50, pp. 380–397. Springer, Heidelberg (2010). doi:10.1007/978-3-642-16161-2_22
14. Tang, Y., Lee, P.P., Lui, J.C., Perlman, R.: Secure overlay cloud storage with access control and assured deletion. IEEE Trans. Dependable Secure Comput. **9**(6), 903–916 (2012)
15. Tezuka, S., Uda, R., Okada, K.: Adec: assured deletion and verifiable version control for cloud storage. In: 2012 IEEE 26th International Conference on Advanced Information Networking and Applications (AINA), pp. 23–30. IEEE (2012)

Digital Signature and Authentication

Practical and Robust Secure Logging from Fault-Tolerant Sequential Aggregate Signatures

Gunnar Hartung$^{(\boxtimes)}$, Björn Kaidel$^{(\boxtimes)}$, Alexander Koch$^{(\boxtimes)}$, Jessica Koch$^{(\boxtimes)}$, and Dominik Hartmann

Karlsruhe Institute of Technology (KIT), Karlsruhe, Germany
{gunnar.hartung,bjoern.kaidel,alexander.koch,jessica.koch}@kit.edu,
dominik.hartman@student.kit.edu

Abstract. Keeping correct and informative log files is crucial for system maintenance, security and forensics. Cryptographic logging schemes offer integrity checks that protect a log file even in the case where an attacker has broken into the system.

A relatively recent feature of these schemes is resistance against truncations, i.e. the deletion and/or replacement of the end of the log file. This is especially relevant as system intruders are typically interested in manipulating the later log entries that point towards their attack. However, there are not many schemes that are resistant against truncating the log file. Those that are have at least one of the following disadvantages: They are memory intensive (they store at least one signature per log entry), or fragile (i.e. a single error in the log renders the signature invalid and useless in determining where the error occurred).

We obtain a publicly-verifiable secure logging scheme that is simultaneously robust, space-efficient and truncation secure with provable security under simple assumptions. Our generic construction uses forward-secure signatures, in a plain and a sequential aggregate variant, where the latter is additionally fault-tolerant, as recently formalized by Hartung et al. [9]. Fault-tolerant schemes can cope with a number of manipulated log entries (bounded a priori) and offer strong robustness guarantees while still retaining space efficiency. Our implementation and the accompanying performance measurements confirm the practicality of our scheme.

Keywords: Sequential Aggregate Signatures · Fault-Tolerance · Secure Logging · Truncation-Security · Forward-Security

G. Hartung—The project underlying this report was supported by the German Federal Ministry of Education and Research under Grant No. 01|S15035A. The responsibility for the contents of this publication lies with the author.
A. Koch, J. Koch and D. Hartmann—This work was supported by the German Federal Ministry of Education and Research within the framework of the project KASTEL_IoE in the Competence Center for Applied Security Technology (KASTEL).

© Springer International Publishing AG 2017
T. Okamoto et al. (Eds.): ProvSec 2017, LNCS 10592, pp. 87–106, 2017.
https://doi.org/10.1007/978-3-319-68637-0_6

1   Introduction

Log files are an indispensable source of information for administrators investigating incidents in a computer system. They provide fine-grained information on actions and events that happened within the system, such as business transactions, errors, or security violations. Attackers frequently modify log files to cover their traces, so being able to distinguish real and faked information is crucial.

Therefore, the need to detect modifications to log files is widely recognized among computer security professionals, and much effort has been devoted to finding solutions that unveil such modifications (see below). Cryptographic solutions must be resilient to attackers that gain full control of the log server which holds the secret key. Thus, a secure logging scheme must stay secure *even if the attacker obtains the secret key* at some point in time, and must continue to enable the discovery of illicit log changes which occurred before the secret key was stolen by the attacker. This protects old log entries from unnoticed modification.

As this is impossible with standard authentication schemes, Anderson [1] (later formalized in [2], as remarked in [6]) proposed *forward-secure* schemes. These schemes assume that time is divided into intervals, called *epochs*, and use distinct secret keys for all epochs. For efficiency, we require that the secret key for an epoch t is computed from the secret key of the previous epoch $t-1$, and that there is a *single* verification key. By securely erasing secret keys when they expire, one ensures that an attacker cannot forge signatures for previous epochs.

Detecting *log truncations* is a surprisingly hard problem, because any authentication information computed by the log server can only authenticate past entries, and so there is nothing that authenticates the end of such a chain. Ma and Tsudik [22] were the first to present a mechanism to detect truncations of log files. Their solution is based on forward-secure *sequential aggregate signatures*. These signature schemes allow to "integrate" a signature for a new message into an already existing signature, which still has the size of a single signature, but authenticates all aggregated messages simultaneously.

The core property of their solution lies in the fact that for specific (sequential) aggregate signature schemes (such as [4]), removing a message from a given aggregate signature is intractable under standard assumptions. Ma and Tsudik [22] use this property by keeping only a single signature for the entire log file, which is an aggregate of the signatures for each individual message. The hardness of removing an individual signature then guarantees that no attacker can remove *any* message from the log file without notice, as in truncation attacks.

Problems with Existing Solutions. The approach by [22] is fragile, i.e. a single erroneous log entry renders the signature invalid, without any information on where the error is located. In a following investigation, distinguishing between real and faked information is no longer possible.

Only two solutions proposed so far are robust and truncation-secure at the same time, namely the second immutable scheme in [22], and the scheme of

Hartung [8]. However, this robustness property is "bought" by falling back to single signatures for each log entry, resulting in a very large log signature that is linear in the log size. Moreover, the truncation security of the former scheme is only argued informally, lacking a rigorous proof.

Our Solution. We propose a solution that overcomes these problems. The theoretical part of this paper formalizes a well-motivated security notion for secure logging and provides a provably-secure generic construction combining the fault-tolerance approach of [9] with the non-robust construction of [22], and add a single forward-secure signature on the log length for truncation security. This results in a scheme that is publicly-verifiable (as defined in [10]), and simultaneously features short signatures, robustness and truncation resistance.

We employ a recent technique from [9] to construct so-called *fault-tolerant* aggregate signatures, port this technique to the world of *sequential* aggregate signatures, and wed it with forward-security required for securing log files, which might be of independent interest. This is because *sequential* aggregate signatures are easier to obtain, often more efficient than ordinary aggregate signatures, and fully sufficient to realize secure log files with short signatures.

The technique from [9] also features so-called selective verification: To verify a single log entry, one can use the signature's redundancy to call the verification routine on a smaller set, instead of the whole log file, see [9, Sect. 4.2]. (Space-inefficient logs using single signatures have this feature trivially.)

Our approach is provably secure and uses a tight security reduction. For this, we define a security model for the logging scenario that captures truncation attacks as well as a wide range of other manipulations. This distinguishes our work from previous publications [20,23] where truncation security is only argued for informally and it is not part of the security model.

We provide a secure logging scheme that can run on a stand-alone server without any interaction with another party. Our system does not require public ledgers (e.g. blockchains) or any other third party that needs to vouch for the integrity of the log file. However, our scheme can easily be combined with such techniques, and thus can be re-used as a building block for future schemes.

Contribution. In our work, we

- discuss why the notion of fault-tolerance from [9] is not applicable to the case of *sequential* aggregate signatures, give an alternative definition that also captures addition or removal of messages, adapt the generic construction of fault-tolerant aggregate signatures from [9] to the sequential aggregate case, prove its security, and prove its fault-tolerance w.r.t. our new definition,
- give a realistic and strong security notion for secure logging (similar to [8]) that also captures truncation attacks,
- give a generic construction of a publicly-verifiable robust secure logging scheme, which is space efficient and has a tight security reduction,
- present benchmark results based on a prototypical implementation of our scheme for multiple sets of parameters.

Related Work. Forward-secure signatures were first introduced by Bellare and Miner [2]. Many subsequent works followed, for example by Krawczyk [15] and Itkis and Reyzin [13]. Based on these works, Ma and Tsudik [20,21] first considered forward security for sequential aggregate signatures.

Schneier and Kelsey [24] presented a logging scheme based on forward-secure MACs. Their scheme includes encryption of log entries to preserve confidentiality. Crosby and Wallach [7] presented a log scheme which allows for secure deletion of log entries without sacrificing the verifiability of the whole log. Their scheme relies on frequent interactions between a log server and several auditors. PillarBox [5] is a logging system focusing on additional properties such as confidentiality of log entries and logging rules. They assume forward-secure MACs as a tool, and use interaction to obtain truncation security. The only works that consider truncation security in a non-interactive setting are [10,22] and [8], where only the latter takes a formal approach. The SALVE scheme in [8] additionally supports the secure generation of log excerpts which can be verified w.r.t. completeness for the excerpt criterion and w.r.t. correctness, without revealing log entries not in the excerpt. This scheme, [10] and the robust variants in [22] achieve robustness by recording one signature per message. In this paper, we obtain robustness without storing a signature for each log entry (saving storage space and potentially transmission bandwidth), while treating truncation security in a rigorous and formal manner.

2   Preliminaries

We define $[n] := \{1, \ldots, n\}$. For vectors/tuples v, $v[i]$ denotes its i-th entry. If M is a matrix, $\text{rows}(M)$ and $\text{cols}(M)$ denote its number of rows and columns. $M[i, j]$ is the entry in the i-th row and j-th column of M.

The *security parameter* is denoted by $\kappa \in \mathbb{N}$. A probabilistic algorithm $\mathcal{A}$ is probabilistic polynomial time (PPT) if its running time is polynomial in κ. All algorithms are implicitly given 1^κ as input, even when not stated explicitly.

For $m_1, m_2 \in \{0,1\}^*$, $m_1 \,\|\, m_2$ denotes the *concatenation* of m_1 and m_2. For technical reasons, we assume that m_1 and m_2 can be uniquely derived from $m_1 \,\|\, m_2$. We use the same symbol for the concatenation of sequences, i.e. let $n, n' \in \mathbb{N}$ and $C = (c_1, \ldots, c_n)$ and $C' = (c'_1, \ldots, c'_{n'})$ be two sequences, then $C \,\|\, C' := (c_1, \ldots, c_n, c'_1, \ldots, c'_{n'})$. If C' is a sequence with only one element c', we abbreviate this as $C \,\|\, c'$. If $C = (c_1, \ldots, c_n)$, then $|C| = n$.

2.1   Aggregate Signatures

Aggregate signature schemes were introduced by Boneh et al. [4]. Aggregate signatures can "combine" signatures from different signers on different messages into one single signature of equal size, authenticating all messages at once.

In their scheme, a signature is a single element of a group with a bilinear map. The aggregate of several signatures is their product in the group. Therefore, aggregation is very flexible: signatures can be aggregated in any order, and aggregated signatures can be aggregated further.

Sequential aggregate signatures [19] do not support this fully flexible aggregation: Messages are added to an aggregate one-by-one, each message by its signer. Signing and aggregation may be a single, inseparable process, i.e. once created, signatures cannot in general be combined further. While not as flexible, they are still useful in a wide range of applications, such as certificate chains, secure routing, version control systems, and securing log files [22].

Claims and Claim Sequences. A *claim* $c = (\mathsf{pk}, i, m)$ is a triple of a public key pk, an epoch number $i \in \mathbb{N}_0$, and a message m. It conveys the meaning that the owner of pk has signed the message m during epoch i.[1]

A *claim sequence* is a finite sequence of claims. The *empty signature* λ is a signature valid for only the empty claim sequence (). Let $C = (c_1, \ldots, c_n)$ be a claim sequence and $b \in \{0,1\}^*$ with $|b| \geq n$ a bit sequence specifying a selection of indices. Then $C[b]$ is the subsequence of C containing the elements c_j $(1 \leq j \leq n)$ where $b[j] = 1$. If $\mathcal{M}$ is a matrix with only 1 and 0 entries, then $C[\mathcal{M}_i]$ is the subsequence containing all c_j, where $\mathcal{M}[i,j] = 1$, for $i \in [\text{rows}(\mathcal{M})]$.

2.2 Forward-Secure Signatures

A forward-secure signature scheme [2] uses a distinct secret keys for signing in each time interval (epoch). Throughout this paper we assume w.l.o.g. that the current epoch number can be efficiently derived from the current secret key.

Definition 1. *A* forward-secure signature *(FSS)* scheme is a tuple of PPT algorithms $\mathsf{FS} = (\mathsf{KeyGen}, \mathsf{Update}, \mathsf{Sign}, \mathsf{Verify})$, where

- $\mathsf{KeyGen}(1^\kappa, 1^T)$ *takes as input the security parameter κ and an a priori upper bound T on the number of epochs. It outputs a key pair $(\mathsf{pk}, \mathsf{sk}_0)$, where sk_0 is the secret key for the first epoch.*
- $\mathsf{Update}(\mathsf{sk}_t)$ *takes as input the secret key sk_t of period t. If $t \geq T-1$ its output is not defined. If $t < T-1$ it computes the secret key sk_{t+1} for the following period $t+1$. It then securely erases the old secret key sk_t.*
- $\mathsf{Sign}(\mathsf{sk}_t, m)$ *takes as input a secret key sk_t and a message $m \in \{0,1\}^*$ and outputs a signature σ for claim (pk, t, m), where t is the epoch of sk_t.*
- $\mathsf{Verify}((\mathsf{pk}, t, m), \sigma)$ *outputs 1 if σ is a valid signature for the message m in epoch t under public key pk, and 0 otherwise.*

A FSS scheme is *correct* if any regularly signed message is valid, i.e. if for all epoch bounds $T = \text{poly}(\kappa)$, all indices $t \in \{0, \ldots, T-1\}$ and all messages $m \in \{0,1\}^*$, it holds that $\mathsf{Verify}((\mathsf{pk}, t, m), \mathsf{Sign}(\mathsf{sk}_t, m)) = 1$, where $(\mathsf{pk}, \mathsf{sk}_0) \leftarrow \mathsf{KeyGen}(1^\kappa, 1^T)$ and $\mathsf{sk}_{t+1} = \mathsf{Update}(\mathsf{sk}_t)$ for $t = \{0, \ldots, T-2\}$.

---

[1] The terms "claim" and "claim sequence" are borrowed from [9]. However, we have added an epoch index i to each claim, because we are considering forward security in this work.

Security Notion for Forward-Secure Signatures. The security experiment for forward-secure signatures consists of four phases and is based on [2]. The general idea is that an adversary should not be able to forge a signature for any earlier epoch, even if he knows the secret key of the current epoch.

- *Setup Phase.* The challenger $\mathcal{C}$ generates a key pair $(\text{pk}^*, \text{sk}_0^*) \leftarrow$ KeyGen$(1^\kappa, 1^T)$ (where T is the maximal number of epochs) and gives the public key pk^* and T to the adversary. It sets $t := 0$.
- *Query Phase.* The adversary $\mathcal{A}$ has access to an Update and a Sign oracle. When $\mathcal{A}$ calls the Update oracle, $\mathcal{C}$ computes $\text{sk}_{t+1}^* := \text{Update}(\text{sk}_t^*)$, sets $t := t + 1$, and returns "ok". $\mathcal{A}$ may only make $T - 1$ Update queries. $\mathcal{A}$ may (adaptively) issue signature queries to the Sign oracle for messages $m \in \{0,1\}^*$. For these queries, the challenger responds with a signature $\sigma \leftarrow \text{Sign}(\text{sk}_t^*, m)$.
- *Break In Phase.* $\mathcal{A}$ may send a *break in* request to obtain the current secret key. $\mathcal{C}$ sets $t_{\text{BreakIn}} := t$ and sends sk_t to $\mathcal{A}$. Afterwards, $\mathcal{A}$ is denied any further access to his oracles. We set $t_{\text{BreakIn}} := \infty$ if $\mathcal{A}$ does not break in.
- *Forgery Phase.* Finally, $\mathcal{A}$ outputs a claim (pk^*, t^*, m^*) and a corresponding signature σ^*.

The adversary *wins* the experiment iff σ^* is a valid signature for claim (pk^*, t^*, m^*), and it is *non-trivial*, which means that m^* was not queried to the Sign oracle during period t^*, and $t^* < t_{\text{BreakIn}}$.

A FSS scheme is *forward-secure existentially unforgeable under chosen message attacks* (FS-EUF-CMA-secure) if for each $T = \text{poly}(\kappa)$ any PPT adversary $\mathcal{A}$ wins the above experiment with a probability that is at most negligible in κ.

2.3 Forward-Secure Sequential Aggregate Signatures

The following definition is the forward-secure sequential aggregate signature definition in [20], which is based on [2,19].

Definition 2. *A* forward-secure sequential aggregate signature *(FS-SAS) scheme is a tuple of four PPT algorithms* AS = (KeyGen, Update, AggSign, Verify), *where*

- KeyGen$(1^\kappa, 1^T)$ *takes as input the security parameter κ and an a priori upper bound T on the number of epochs. It generates and outputs a key pair (pk, sk_0), where sk_0 is the initial secret key for the first epoch.*
- Update(sk_t) *takes as input the secret key sk_t of period t. If $t \geq T - 1$ the output of* Update *is not defined. If $t < T - 1$ it computes the secret key sk_{t+1} for the following period $t + 1$. It then securely erases the old secret key sk_t.*
- AggSign$(\text{sk}_t, C_{i-1}, \sigma_{i-1}, m_i)$ *takes as input a secret key sk_t for an epoch t, a claim sequence C_{i-1}, a corresponding signature σ_{i-1} and a message m_i. It outputs a signature σ_i for the new claim sequence $C_i := C_{i-1} \| (\text{pk}, t, m_i)$.*
- Verify(C, σ) *takes as input a claim sequence C and a signature σ and outputs 1 if σ is valid for C, and 0 otherwise.*

Informally, a signature is regular if it was generated with the correct use of the algorithms of a FS-SAS scheme. Formally, let C_i be a claim sequence and σ_i a signature. We say that σ_i is *regular* for C_i iff either $C_i = ()$ and $\sigma_i = \lambda$, or $C_i = C_{i-1} \,\|\, (\mathsf{pk}, t, m_i)$ and $\sigma_i \leftarrow \mathsf{AggSign}(\mathsf{sk}_t, C_{i-1}, \sigma_{i-1}, m_i)$ where σ_{i-1} is a regular signature for C_{i-1}, m_i is an arbitrary message, $(\mathsf{pk}, \mathsf{sk}_0)$ is a key pair output by $\mathsf{KeyGen}(1^\kappa, 1^T)$, and $\mathsf{sk}_{t+1} = \mathsf{Update}(\mathsf{sk}_t)$, for $t \in \{0, \dots, T-1\}$.

A FS-SAS scheme is *correct* if for all bounds on the number of epochs $T = \mathrm{poly}(\kappa)$, any signature σ which is regular for C is also valid for C.

Security Notion for FS-SAS Schemes. The security experiment for forward-secure sequential aggregate signatures in [20] consists of four phases and combines the experiments of forward-security [2] and sequential aggregate signatures [19].

- *Setup Phase.* The challenger generates a key pair $(\mathsf{pk}^*, \mathsf{sk}_0^*) \leftarrow \mathsf{KeyGen}(1^\kappa, 1^T)$, where T is the maximal number of time periods and gives the public key pk^* and T to the adversary. It sets $t := 0$.
- *Query Phase.* Here, the adversary $\mathcal{A}$ has access to an Update and an $\mathsf{AggSign}$ oracle. When $\mathcal{A}$ calls the Update oracle, the challenger computes $\mathsf{sk}_{t+1}^* := \mathsf{Update}(\mathsf{sk}_t^*)$, sets $t := t+1$, and returns "ok". $\mathcal{A}$ is not allowed to make more than $T-1$ queries to this oracle. The $\mathsf{AggSign}$ oracle takes as input a claim sequence C_{i-1}, a corresponding signature σ_{i-1} and a message m_i. It responds with $\sigma_i \leftarrow \mathsf{AggSign}(\mathsf{sk}_t^*, C_{i-1}, \sigma_{i-1}, m_i)$, where sk_t^* is the secret key for the current period t.
- *Break In Phase.* The adversary may send a *break in* request to obtain the current secret key. In this case, the experiment sets $t_{\mathsf{BreakIn}} := t$ and sends the current secret key sk_t for period t to $\mathcal{A}$. After $\mathcal{A}$ has broken in, he is denied any further access to his oracles. We set $t_{\mathsf{BreakIn}} := \infty$ if $\mathcal{A}$ does not break in.
- *Forgery Phase.* Finally, $\mathcal{A}$ outputs a claim sequence C^* and a corresponding signature σ^*.

The adversary *wins* the experiment iff σ^* is a valid signature for C^*, and C^* is *non-trivial*, i.e., C^* contains a claim $(\mathsf{pk}^*, t^*, m^*)$ for which $t^* < t_{\mathsf{BreakIn}}$ and $\mathcal{A}$ did not query m^* at its $\mathsf{AggSign}$ oracle during epoch t^*. A FS-SAS scheme is *forward-secure sequential aggregate signature existentially unforgeable under chosen message attacks* (FS-SAS-EUF-CMA-secure) if for each $T = T(\kappa) \in \mathrm{poly}(\kappa)$ all PPT adversaries $\mathcal{A}$ win the above experiment only with a probability that is negligible in κ.[2]

2.4 Cover-Free Families

Cover-free families [14] are a combinatorial structure that allows us to achieve fault-tolerance in our constructions, as in [9]. Let $\mathcal{S}$ be a finite set, $\mathcal{B}$ be a set of

---

[2] This security notion is slightly weaker with respect to the non-triviality of forgeries than the one for sequential aggregate signatures by Lysyanskaya et al. [19]. There, they allow for all messages in C^* to be already queried before, but in different order. However, our notion additionally considers forward security.

subsets (or *blocks*) of $\mathcal{S}$ and $d \in \mathbb{N}$. The pair $\mathcal{F} = (\mathcal{S}, \mathcal{B})$ is a *d-cover-free family* if for any d blocks $B_1, \ldots, B_d \in \mathcal{B}$ and any distinct $B \in \mathcal{B} \setminus \{B_1, \ldots, B_d\}$, we have that $B \not\subseteq B_1 \cup \cdots \cup B_d$, i.e. no block is covered by the union of any other d blocks of $\mathcal{B}$. $\mathcal{F}$ is a *cover-free family (CFF)* if it is d-cover-free for a $d \geq 1$.

A CFF with a linear order $\leq$ on $\mathcal{B}$ is called *ordered*. To simplify the presentation, we also assume an order on $\mathcal{S}$ and usually identify $\mathcal{S}$ with $[r]$, for $r = |\mathcal{S}|$ in this case. The *incidence matrix* $\mathcal{M}$ of an ordered CFF is defined via

$$\mathcal{M}[i, j] = \begin{cases} 1, & \text{if } i \in B_j, \\ 0, & \text{otherwise,} \end{cases}$$

for $i \in [r] = \mathcal{S}$, $\mathcal{B} = \{B_1 \leq \cdots \leq B_m\}$ and $j \in [m]$.

We denote the i-th row of $\mathcal{M}$ by $\mathcal{M}_i \in \{0, 1\}^m$. In this way, the rows of the matrix represent the elements of $\mathcal{S}$ and the columns represent the elements of $\mathcal{B}$.

3   Fault-Tolerant Forward-Secure Sequential Aggregate Signatures

In this section we define the syntax of forward-secure (multi-key) sequential aggregate signatures (SAS) with fault tolerance, discuss why the definition of fault-tolerance from [9] is not applicable in our case, and give an alternative definition. We then present a security notion that captures the forward-security property and is compatible with fault-tolerant sequential aggregate signatures, give a construction of such a scheme, and prove its fault-tolerance and its security.

Definition 3. *A key-evolving SAS scheme with list-verification Σ is a tuple of four PPT algorithms $\Sigma = (\mathsf{KeyGen}, \mathsf{Update}, \mathsf{AggSign}, \mathsf{Verify})$, where:*

- $\mathsf{KeyGen}(1^\kappa, 1^T)$ *takes as input the security parameter κ and an upper bound T on the number of epochs. It outputs a key pair $(\mathsf{pk}, \mathsf{sk}_0)$, where sk_0 is the secret key for the first epoch.*
- $\mathsf{Update}(\mathsf{sk}_t)$ *takes as input the secret key sk_t of period t. If $t \geq T - 1$ the output of Update is not defined. If $t < T - 1$ it computes the secret key sk_{t+1} for period $t + 1$ and securely erases the old key sk_t irrecoverably.*
- $\mathsf{AggSign}(\mathsf{sk}_t, C_{i-1}, \sigma_{i-1}, m_i)$ *takes as input a secret key sk_t for an epoch t, a claim sequence C_{i-1}, a corresponding signature σ_{i-1} and a message m_i. It outputs a signature σ_i for the new claim sequence $C_i := C_{i-1} \| (\mathsf{pk}, t, m_i)$.*
- $\mathsf{Verify}(C, \sigma)$ *takes as input a claim sequence C of length $n \in \mathbb{N}_0$ and a signature σ for C and outputs a sequence V (also of length n) of claims and error symbols $\bot$. We require that for each $i \in [n]$, either $V[i] = C[i]$ or $V[i] = \bot$. (In other words, V can be obtained from C by replacing claims with $\bot$.) Claims output by Verify are taken to be valid.*

Let C_i be a claim sequence and τ_i be a signature. We say that τ_i is *regular* for C_i iff either $C_i = ()$ and $\tau_i = \lambda$, or $C_i = C_{i-1} \| (\mathsf{pk}, t, m_i)$ and $\tau_i \leftarrow \mathsf{AggSign}(\mathsf{sk}_t, C_{i-1}, \tau_{i-1}, m_i)$ where τ_{i-1} is a regular signature for C_{i-1},

m_i is an arbitrary bit string, $t \in \{0, \ldots, T-1\}$, $T = T(\kappa) \in \mathrm{poly}(\kappa)$, and sk_t is the t-times updated version of some secret key sk_0 such that $(\mathsf{pk}, \mathsf{sk}_0)$ is a key-pair output by $\mathsf{KeyGen}(1^\kappa, 1^T)$. We say that a SAS scheme with list verification is *correct*, if it is *0-fault-tolerant*, as defined in the next section.

3.1   Fault Tolerance of FS-SAS Schemes

Let $C = (c_1, \ldots, c_n), C' = (c'_1, \ldots, c'_{n'})$ be claim sequences. We say that C and C' *differ on* ℓ *positions* ($0 \le \ell \le \min(n, n')$) iff $c_i \ne c'_i$ for ℓ indices $1 \le i \le \min(n, n')$ and $c_i = c'_i$ for the rest. Moreover, we say that C' *contains* d *errors* with respect to C iff they differ on ℓ positions and $d = |n - n'| + \ell$.

A key-evolving SAS scheme Σ with list verification is *tolerant against* d *errors*, if for all claim sequences C, C', such that C' contains at most d errors with respect to C and for all signatures τ that are regular for C, we have

$$V[i] = c_i \quad \text{for all } 1 \le i \le \min(n, n') \text{ where } c_i = c'_i,$$

where $V \leftarrow \Sigma.\mathsf{Verify}(C', \tau)$. In other words, Verify outputs *at least* all claims c_i from C that C' did not modify. (It may also output claims where $C[i] \ne C'[i]$, but our security proof will show that such events are extremely rare or trivial.)

A *d-fault-tolerant key-evolving SAS scheme* is an SAS scheme with list verification that is tolerant against d errors. A scheme is *fault-tolerant*, if it is d-fault-tolerant for some $d > 0$.

On the Definition of Fault-Tolerance. In [9] a *multiset* of claim–signature pairs (c_i, τ_i) is said to contain d errors if d signatures τ_i are not regular for their respective claim c_i. This definition is not applicable to *sequential* aggregate signatures due to the lack of individual signatures τ_i. A natural approach that comes to mind is to define the number of errors via "intermediate" claim sequences $C_i = (c_1, \ldots, c_i)$ and their respective signatures τ_i. (This might not even be well-defined, but let us ignore this problem for the moment.) Following this approach, one might say that a claim sequence C contains d errors iff d of the signatures τ_i are not regular outputs of $\mathsf{AggSign}(\mathsf{sk}_t, C_{i-1}, \tau_{i-1}, m_i)$.

This approach fails, however, as it does not distinguish between signatures τ_i, which are partially damaged but sufficiently intact to authenticate some of the claims, and signatures that are completely destroyed. For example, consider the claim sequence $C = (c_1, \ldots, c_n)$ and the signatures $\tau_1, \ldots, \tau_n$, where all τ_i for $1 \le i < n$ are regular for the respective intermediate claim sequence C_i, but τ_n is completely random. Then there was only one irregular step, and hence only one error with regard to this definition, but $\mathsf{Verify}(C, \tau_n)$ will output $(\perp, \ldots, \perp)$.

An alternative way to look at this is to observe that [9] implicitly assumes that the aggregation is correct, while errors only occur during signing. In the sequential aggregate case these two operations are inseparable in general, and we cannot assume that the aggregation did not introduce additional errors.

We therefore restrict our attention to specific changes to the claim sequence C: replacements of individual claims as well as addition or removal of claims at the end of the sequence. These changes closely model our secure-logging scenario, as they capture events where an attacker edits log entries after breaking in, or removes tail-end log messages. (Note that addition or removal of claims is not considered in [9].)

3.2 Security Notion

Let $\mathsf{AS} = (\mathsf{KeyGen}, \mathsf{Update}, \mathsf{AggSign}, \mathsf{Verify})$ be a key-evolving SAS scheme with list verification, $\mathcal{A}$ be a PPT algorithm, $\kappa \in \mathbb{N}$ a security parameter, and T be the number of epochs. The security experiment for a forward-secure SAS scheme with list verification is identical to that of forward-secure SAS schemes described in Sect. 2.3. The adversary $\mathcal{A}$ *wins* the experiment iff $\mathsf{Verify}(C^*, \tau^*)$ contains a claim c^* such that $c^* = (\mathsf{pk}^*, t^*, m^*)$ for some $m^* \in \{0, 1\}^*$ and $t^* < t_{\mathsf{BreakIn}}$, and c^* is *non-trivial* in the sense that m^* was not given as an input to the $\mathsf{AggSign}$ oracle during epoch t^*.

A key-evolving SAS scheme with list verification is called *forward-secure sequential aggregate signature existentially unforgeable under chosen message attacks* (FS-SAS-EUF-CMA-secure) if for all $T = T(\kappa) \in \mathrm{poly}(\kappa)$, the probability of each PPT adversary $\mathcal{A}$ to win the above experiment is negligible in κ.

We say that a key-evolving SAS scheme with list verification is *single-key* FS-SAS-EUF-CMA-secure, if the above holds for all PPT adversaries $\mathcal{A}$ that never output claim sequences (to the signature oracle or as the forgery C^*) that contain a claim $c = (\mathsf{pk}, t, m)$ for a public key $\mathsf{pk} \neq \mathsf{pk}^*$. Clearly, a FS-SAS-EUF-CMA-secure scheme is also single-key FS-SAS-EUF-CMA-secure.

3.3 Generic Construction

We claim that the generic construction of [9] preserves the forward-security property of the underlying signature scheme. We use it to convert a forward-secure SAS scheme FSSAS to a fault-tolerant forward-secure SAS scheme.

Let FSSAS be a forward-secure SAS scheme, $\mathcal{F}$ a d-cover-free family ($d \in \mathbb{N}_0$), and $\mathcal{M}$ its incidence matrix. A signature in the new scheme is a vector of signatures of FSSAS. The algorithms of our scheme are as follows:

- KeyGen and Update are identical to the respective algorithms of FSSAS.
- $\mathsf{AggSign}(\mathsf{sk}_t, C_{j-1}, \tau_{j-1}, m_j)$ takes as input a secret key sk_t, a claim sequence $C_{j-1} = (c_1, \ldots, c_{j-1})$, its corresponding signature τ_{j-1} and a message m_j to sign. The sequential aggregate signature is updated component-wise, according to the entries of $\mathcal{M}$. More precisely, we set

$$\tau_j[i] \leftarrow \mathsf{FSSAS.AggSign}(\mathsf{sk}_t, C_{j-1}[\mathcal{M}_i], \tau_{j-1}[i], m_j),$$

where $\mathcal{M}[i, j] = 1$, and let $\tau_j[i] := \tau_{j-1}[i]$ otherwise ($i \in [\mathrm{rows}(\mathcal{M})]$). Here, $C_0 := ()$ and $\tau_0[i] := \lambda$ for each i. The output is τ_j.

– Verify(C, τ) takes as input a claim sequence C of length $n \in \mathbb{N}_0$ and an aggregate signature τ for C. We compute a bit vector $b \in \{0,1\}^n$ that specifies for each claim if it can safely be considered valid. For this, let $v|_\ell$ denote the vector v, truncated to the first ℓ elements. We initialize b to 0^n, and iterate over all entries $\tau[i]$ of τ, letting $b \leftarrow b \vee \mathcal{M}_i|_n$ if FSSAS.Verify$(C[\mathcal{M}_i], \tau[i]) = 1$ in each iteration. (Here, $\vee$ denotes the bitwise logical OR of two bitstrings.) Finally, we build the output sequence V component-wise, by letting

$$V[j] = \begin{cases} C[j], & \text{if } b[j] = 1, \\ \bot, & \text{otherwise,} \end{cases} \qquad \text{for all } j \in [n].$$

Theorem 1. *Let Σ be the key-evolving SAS scheme with list verification defined above. If Σ is based on a d-CFF $\mathcal{F} = (\mathcal{S}, \mathcal{B})$, then it is tolerant against d errors.*

Theorem 2. *Let FSSAS be a key-evolving SAS scheme, $\mathcal{F}$ be a cover-free family with incidence matrix $\mathcal{M}$, and Σ be the scheme from Sect. 3.3. If there exists a PPT algorithm $\mathcal{A}$ that breaks the security of Σ with success probability $\varepsilon_\mathcal{A}$, then there exists an attacker $\mathcal{B}$ that breaks the FS-SAS-EUF-CMA-security of FSSAS with success probability $\varepsilon_\mathcal{B} \geq \varepsilon_\mathcal{A}$.*

Due to space constraints, we only give proof sketches here. The complete proofs can be found in the full version. For fault-tolerance, observe that each message m_j is redundantly aggregated into several of the signatures $\tau[i]$, namely those where $\mathcal{M}[i, j] = 1$. If errors occur on at most d positions, verification of a certain subset of all rows will fail. However, this subset cannot cover the rows for any correct message due to the cover-freeness of $\mathcal{F}$. Thus, each correct message can be verified from at least one row, and will therefore be output by our scheme.

For the security, note that our scheme essentially outputs the union of all messages that are contained in valid rows. Thus, to break the security, the attacker must create a signature where the target claim c^* is contained in at least one valid row, which constitutes a successful attack on the underlying scheme FSSAS.

4   Robust Secure Logging

In this section we introduce the notion of robust logging schemes and give a generic construction based on a plain forward-secure signature scheme, and a fault-tolerant forward-secure SAS scheme.

The syntax is as in FT-FS-SAS schemes, except that the key update algorithm may write to the log, and an additional error detection algorithm VerifyLog allows for fine-grained feedback on problems a log signature may have. This gives precise and reliable information on which parts of the log file are still trustworthy.

Definition 4. *A logging scheme with list verification $\Lambda = $ (KeyGen, Append, Update, ValidEntries, VerifyLog) is a tuple of five PPT algorithms, where*

– *KeyGen$(1^\kappa, 1^T)$ takes as input the security parameter κ and an a priori upper bound T on the number of epochs. It outputs a key pair (pk, sk$_0$), where sk$_0$ is the secret key for the first epoch.*

- Append($\mathsf{sk}_t, C_{i-1}, \sigma_{i-1}, m_i$) *takes as input a secret key* sk_t *for epoch* t, *a claim sequence* C_{i-1}, *a corresponding signature* σ_{i-1} *and a message* m_i. *It outputs a signature* σ_i *for the new claim sequence* $C_i := C_{i-1} \| (\mathsf{pk}, t, m_i)$, *thereby adding* m_i *to the log. (For efficiency, the public key is written just once into the log file in the single-key setting, instead of adding it to each log entry.)*
- Update(sk_t, C, σ) *takes as input the secret key* sk_t *of period* t. *If* $t \geq T - 1$ *the output is undefined. If* $t < T - 1$ *it computes the secret key* sk_{t+1} *for period* $t + 1$ *and securely erases the old key* sk_t. *The arguments* C *(a claim sequence) and* σ *(a signature) may be modified, e.g. to add epoch markers [3].*
- ValidEntries(C, σ) *takes as input a claim sequence* C *of length* $n \in \mathbb{N}_0$ *and a signature* σ *for* C *and outputs a sequence* V *(also of length* n*) of claims and error symbols* $\bot$. *We require that for each* $i \in [n]$, *either* $V[i] = C[i]$ *or* $V[i] = \bot$. *(I.e.,* V *can be obtained from* C *by replacing claims with* $\bot$.) *Claims output by* Verify *are taken to be valid.*
- VerifyLog(C, σ) *outputs either* $\emptyset$, *if the signature is without errors, or a subset of a set of error symbols* $\mathcal{E}$, *otherwise. We set* $\mathcal{E} := \{\bot_{\mathrm{sig}}, \bot_{\mathrm{len}}, \bot_{\mathrm{em}}\}$, *with the interpretation that* $\bot_{\mathrm{sig}} \in$ VerifyLog(C, σ) *iff the signature is not valid, i.e.* ValidEntries(C, τ) $\neq C$. *Moreover, if* $\bot_{\mathrm{len}} \in$ VerifyLog(C, σ), *the signature may have been truncated. Finally,* $\bot_{\mathrm{em}} \in$ VerifyLog(C, σ) *if some problem with epoch markers has been detected.*

Fault-tolerance is defined analogously to Sect. 3.1, substituting Append for AggSign, and ValidEntries for Verify. A logging scheme with list verification is *robust* if it is fault-tolerant and we have that regular log files are error-free (i.e. VerifyLog(C, σ) $= \emptyset$) and error-free log files are valid (i.e. ValidEntries(C, τ) $= C$). Note that, if the signature is valid in the sense that all claims are returned by ValidEntries, it is still possible that an attacker might have truncated the log. In this case an error symbol returned by VerifyLog points towards this possibility.

The security notion for logging schemes is similar to the FS-EUF-CMA notion for FT-FS-SAS schemes, but models the real world setting of secure logging more closely: The log server maintains a state which the adversary influences only through his oracles. In more detail, a log append oracle appends an entry to the internal log file, and an adversary can never again add messages to any earlier state of the log file. Moreover, the internal signatures remain hidden from him by default, as these usually stay on the server.

To strengthen the notion, we introduce an additional oracle returning the current signature, which models a public verification of the log file by a third party. To exclude trivial attacks, we explicitly disallow an adversary to truncate the log file to a state he has gotten a signature for. However, he may try to use these signatures to, e.g., truncate the log file to a different previous state.

At the end of the experiment, the attacker outputs a forgery. We require error-freeness (VerifyLog(C^*, σ^*) $= \emptyset$), as otherwise the adversary might use a combination of introducing faults and truncating the claim sequence to obtain a valid signature (verification of the forged signature and claim sequence outputs the full forged claim sequence) that violates other anti-truncation mechanisms.

Definition 5. *For a log scheme with list verification* $\Lambda = ($KeyGen, Append, Update, ValidEntries, VerifyLog$)$*, a PPT adversary* $\mathcal{A}$*, the number of epochs* T *and the security parameter* $\kappa \in \mathbb{N}_0$*, the security experiment* $FS\text{-}EUF\text{-}CLMA^3$- $Exp_{\Lambda,\mathcal{A},T}(\kappa)$ *is defined as follows:*

Setup Phase. *The experiment generates a key pair* $(\mathsf{pk}, \mathsf{sk}_0) \leftarrow$ KeyGen$(1^\kappa, 1^T)$*, the log file* $C_0 := ()$ *and signature* $\sigma_0 := \lambda$*. It initializes the epoch counter* $t := 0$*, and starts* $\mathcal{A}$ *with inputs* pk*,* T*.*

Query Phase. $\mathcal{A}$ *may adaptively issue queries to the following oracles:*

LogAppend Oracle. *The experiment appends the specified message* m *to the log and updates the signature via* $\sigma_i \leftarrow$ Append$(\mathsf{sk}_t, C_{i-1}, \sigma_{i-1}, m)$*, where* σ_{i-1} *denotes the previous signature, and returns "ok".*

NextEpoch Oracle. *The oracle updates the secret key, the log and its signature via* Update$(\mathsf{sk}_t, C_{i-1}, \sigma_{i-1})$*, increments the epoch counter* $t := t+1$ *and returns "ok". It may be queried at most* $T-1$ *times.*

GetSignature Oracle. *Whenever* $\mathcal{A}$ *calls the* GetSignature *oracle, the challenger responds with the current signature* σ_i *of the log.*

Break In Phase. *The adversary may break in to obtain the current secret key* sk_t*. If* $\mathcal{A}$ *does, the experiment sets* $t_{\mathsf{BreakIn}} := t$*. Otherwise, let* $t_{\mathsf{BreakIn}} := \infty$*.*

Forgery Phase. $\mathcal{A}$ *outputs a log file* C^**, and a forged signature* σ^* *for* C^**.*

We say that $\mathcal{A}$ *wins the experiment, iff the following conditions hold.*

– *The signature* σ^* *is error-free, i.e.* VerifyLog$(C^*, \sigma^*) = \emptyset$*. (This implies that the signature is valid.)*
– *The signature is non-trivial as defined next. Let* C' *be the subsequence of* C^* *that is obtained by deleting all claims* $c = ($pk$, t, m)$ *from* C^**, where* $t \geq t_{\mathsf{BreakIn}}$*.* $\mathcal{A}$*'s forgery is non-trivial, iff* $|C'| \neq 0$ *and* C' *does not equal the content of the log file during any* GetSignature *query.*

A logging scheme with list verification Λ *is said to be* FS-EUF-CLMA-*secure, iff for all* $T = T(\kappa) \in \text{poly}(\kappa)$ *and all probabilistic polynomial time attackers* $\mathcal{A}$ *the probability for* $\mathcal{A}$ *winning the above experiment is negligible in* κ*.*

4.1   Generic Construction

We give a generic construction of a simultaneously secure and robust log scheme $\Lambda = ($KeyGen, Append, Update, ValidEntries, VerifyLog$)$. Let AS be a key-evolving SAS scheme with list verification and FS a key-evolving signature scheme.

– KeyGen$(1^\kappa, 1^T)$ creates key pairs of the underlying schemes AS and FS as $(\mathsf{pk}_{\mathsf{AS}}, \mathsf{sk}_{\mathsf{AS}}) \leftarrow$ AS. KeyGen$(1^\kappa, 1^T)$, $(\mathsf{pk}_{\mathsf{FS}}, \mathsf{sk}_{\mathsf{FS}}) \leftarrow$ FS. KeyGen$(1^\kappa, 1^T)$ and returns $\mathsf{pk} = (\mathsf{pk}_{\mathsf{AS}}, \mathsf{pk}_{\mathsf{FS}})$ and $\mathsf{sk}_0 = (\mathsf{sk}_{\mathsf{AS}}, \mathsf{sk}_{\mathsf{FS}})$.

---

[3] *forward-secure existentially unforgeable under chosen log message attacks.*

– Append$(\mathsf{sk}_t, C_{i-1}, \tau_{i-1}, m_i)$ takes as input a secret key $\mathsf{sk}_t = (\mathsf{sk}_{\mathsf{AS}}, \mathsf{sk}_{\mathsf{FS}})$ for period t, a claim sequence $C_{i-1} = (c_1, \ldots, c_{i-1})$, its corresponding signature $\tau_{i-1} = (\sigma_{i-1}, s_{i-1})$ and a message m_i to sign. Both signature components are obtained from the signature algorithms of AS and FS via

$$\sigma_i \leftarrow \mathsf{AS.AggSign}(\mathsf{sk}_{\mathsf{AS}}, C_{i-1}, \sigma_{i-1}, m_i \,\|\, i), \text{ and}$$
$$s_i \leftarrow \mathsf{FS.Sign}(\mathsf{sk}_{\mathsf{FS}}, i).$$

Append securely erases the old length signature s_{i-1} so that it cannot be used in case of a later break in. The resulting signature $\tau_i = (\sigma_i, s_i)$ is returned.
– Update$(\mathsf{sk}_t, C_{i-1}, \tau_{i-1})$ takes as input the secret key $\mathsf{sk}_t = (\mathsf{sk}_{\mathsf{AS}}, \mathsf{sk}_{\mathsf{FS}})$, a claim sequence C_{i-1} and a corresponding signature τ_{i-1}, and appends an epoch marker to the log file that is valid for the current epoch t, via

$$\tau_i \leftarrow \mathsf{Append}(\mathsf{sk}_t, C_{i-1}, \tau_{i-1}, m_i),$$

where $m_i = \texttt{"End of epoch:"} \,\|\, t$. It then updates the components of sk_t via $\mathsf{sk}'_{\mathsf{AS}} \leftarrow \mathsf{AS.Update}(\mathsf{sk}_{\mathsf{AS}})$ and $\mathsf{sk}'_{\mathsf{FS}} \leftarrow \mathsf{FS.Update}(\mathsf{sk}_{\mathsf{FS}})$. (These algorithms erase the old keys securely.) The new secret key is $\mathsf{sk}_{t+1} = (\mathsf{sk}'_{\mathsf{AS}}, \mathsf{sk}'_{\mathsf{FS}})$, the new claim sequence is $C_i = C_{i-1} \,\|\, (\mathsf{pk}, t, m_i)$, and the new signature is τ_i.
– ValidEntries(C, τ) takes as input a claim sequence C and a signature $\tau = (\sigma, s)$ for C. It outputs $\mathsf{AS.Verify}(C', \sigma)$, where C' is the claim sequence generated from C by appending the message number i to m_i for all claims in C.
– VerifyLog(C, τ) takes as input a claim sequence C and a signature $\tau = (\sigma, s)$ for C. It maintains an error set E initialized to $\emptyset$. Firstly, it verifies the FS signature s using $b = \mathsf{FS.Verify}((\mathsf{pk}_{\mathsf{FS}}, t, |C|), s)$. If $b = 0$, it adds $\perp_{\mathrm{len}}$ to E. Then it proceeds with checking the epoch markers: For all claims $c_i = (\mathsf{pk}, t_i, m_i)$ and $c_{i+1} = (\mathsf{pk}, t_{i+1}, m_{i+1})$ in C, where $t_{i+1} \neq t_i$, consider two cases. If $t_{i+1} \neq t_i + 1$ then output $\perp_{\mathrm{em}}$, else check if $m_i = \texttt{"End of epoch:"} \,\|\, t_i$, otherwise output $\perp_{\mathrm{em}}$. Finally, it checks whether the signature is valid, i.e. ValidEntries$(C, \tau) = C$, and adds $\perp_{\mathrm{sig}}$ to E, if this is not the case. It outputs the set of errors E.

The log scheme Λ described above is d-fault-tolerant, if the underlying FT-FS-SAS scheme AS is d-fault-tolerant. We omit the proof due to space restrictions.

Theorem 3. *Our log scheme with list verification Λ is FS-EUF-CLMA-secure, if AS is FS-SAS-EUF-CMA-secure and FS is FS-EUF-CMA-secure. More precisely, for any PPT adversary $\mathcal{A}$ who breaks the FS-EUF-CLMA-security with success probability $\varepsilon_{\mathcal{A}}$, there exists a PPT adversary $\mathcal{B}$ who either breaks the FS-SAS-EUF-CMA-security of AS or the FS-EUF-CMA-security of FS with success probability at least $\varepsilon_{\mathcal{B}}^{\mathsf{AS}} \geq \frac{\varepsilon_{\mathcal{A}}}{2}$ and $\varepsilon_{\mathcal{B}}^{\mathsf{FS}} \geq \frac{\varepsilon_{\mathcal{A}}}{2}$, respectively.*

Let us first give some overview and intuition about the proof. To win the security experiment, an attacker $\mathcal{A}$ must either truncate the log file to a state he has not seen the signature for, or create a valid signature for a log file modified w.r.t. an epoch before his break-in. If $\mathcal{A}$ truncates the log file without detection, he must create a new signature s for the length of the log file, which violates the security of FS. If $\mathcal{A}$ forges a signature for log file modified w.r.t. a previous epoch, then $\mathcal{A}$ has broken the security of AS. Since we assume that both base schemes are secure, our resulting construction must be secure, too.

Proof. A FS-EUF-CLMA-adversary $\mathcal{A}$ can adaptively query the three oracles *LogAppend, GetSignature* and *NextEpoch* before he may break in, and then outputs a forgery (C^*, τ^*), where $\tau^* = (\sigma^*, s^*)$. As any signatures appended after the break in are trivial to produce, let C'^* be the claim sequence after deleting all claims (pk, t, m) of C^*, where $t \geq t_{\text{BreakIn}}$. Let C^{exp} be the internal claim sequence of the experiment, after $\mathcal{A}$ did his last *GetSignature* query in a period $t < t_{\text{BreakIn}}$. We consider two different events:

- E_1 occurs, if (C^*, τ^*) is error-free, non-trivial and C'^* is not a prefix of C^{exp}.
- E_2 occurs, if (C^*, τ^*) is error-free, non-trivial and C'^* is a prefix of C^{exp}.

We have $\varepsilon_{\mathcal{A}} \leq \Pr[E_1] + \Pr[E_2]$ and thus $\Pr[E_1] \geq \frac{\varepsilon_{\mathcal{A}}}{2}$ or $\Pr[E_2] \geq \frac{\varepsilon_{\mathcal{A}}}{2}$. Please note that in the following paragraphs sk_{AS}^i, sk_{FS}^i denote the secret keys of period i for the respective schemes.

Attack on the FS-SAS-EUF-CMA-security of AS. First we construct a FS-SAS-EUF-CMA-adversary $\mathcal{B}$ on AS, who uses a successful FS-EUF-CLMA-adversary $\mathcal{A}$ and has to simulate the FS-EUF-CLMA-security experiment for $\mathcal{A}$. The challenger in the FS-SAS-EUF-CMA-security experiment generates a key pair $(pk_{AS}, sk_{AS}^0) \leftarrow AS.\,KeyGen(1^\kappa, 1^T)$ and sends pk_{AS} and the maximal number of epochs T to $\mathcal{B}$. $\mathcal{B}$ uses FS to generate a key pair $(pk_{FS}, sk_{FS}^0) \leftarrow$ FS.$\,KeyGen(1^\kappa, 1^T)$, s.t. $pk := (pk_{AS}, pk_{FS})$ and $sk_0 := (sk_{AS}^0, sk_{FS}^0)$ for the current period 0. $\mathcal{B}$ forwards pk and T to $\mathcal{A}$. $\mathcal{B}$ initializes the log and signature it maintains towards $\mathcal{A}$ as $C_0 := ()$, $\sigma_0 := \lambda$ and sets $i := 0$, $t := 0$ and $\mathcal{L}_{FS} := \{sk_{FS}^0\}$.

We describe how $\mathcal{B}$ simulates the three oracles and the break in phase for $\mathcal{A}$:

LogAppend Oracle. $\mathcal{A}$ sends $\mathcal{B}$ a query m_i. $\mathcal{B}$ sets $C_i := C_{i-1} \,\|\, (pk_{AS}, t, m_i \,\|\, i)$ for the current period t. $\mathcal{B}$ sends an AggSign query $m_i \,\|\, i$ with claim sequence C_{i-1} and signature σ_{i-1} to his challenger who responds with a signature σ_i. Finally, it sets $i := i+1$ and sends $\mathcal{A}$ the string "ok".

NextEpoch Oracle. When $\mathcal{A}$ sends a *NextEpoch* query, $\mathcal{B}$ stops if $t \geq T-1$ and outputs $\bot$, otherwise $\mathcal{B}$ sets $m_i := $ "End of epoch:"$\,\|\, t$ and $C_i := C_{i-1} \,\|\, (pk_{AS}, t, m_i \,\|\, i)$. $\mathcal{B}$ obtains the signature σ_i for C_i from his AS.AggSign oracle the same way as before. $\mathcal{B}$ sends an *Update* query to the challenger, who computes $sk_{AS}^{t+1} := $ AS.$\,Update(sk_{AS}^t)$. $\mathcal{B}$ computes $sk_{FS}^{t+1} := $ FS.$\,Update(sk_{FS}^t)$ by its own. $\mathcal{B}$ sets $i := i+1$, $t := t+1$ and $\mathcal{L}_{FS} := \mathcal{L}_{FS} \cup \{sk_{FS}^{t+1}\}$ and returns "ok".

GetSignature Oracle. When $\mathcal{A}$ calls the *GetSignature* oracle, $\mathcal{B}$ determines the length i of the current claim sequence C_i and the period t_{last} of the last claim in C_i, which is either the current period t or $t-1$ (since an epoch switch always adds an end-of-epoch claim). $\mathcal{B}$ gets $sk_{FS}^{t_{\text{last}}}$ from $\mathcal{L}_{FS}$ and computes $s_i \leftarrow$ FS.Sign$(sk_{FS}^{t_{\text{last}}}, i)$. The new signature for C_i is now $\tau_i = (\sigma_i, s_i)$ and $\mathcal{B}$ sends τ_i to $\mathcal{A}$.

Break In Phase. When $\mathcal{A}$ breaks in, $\mathcal{B}$ sets $t_{\mathsf{BreakIn}} := t$ and sends his challenger also a *break in* request. $\mathcal{B}$ gets the current secret key $\mathsf{sk}_{\mathsf{AS}}^t$ and sends $\mathcal{A}$ the current secret key $\mathsf{sk}_t = (\mathsf{sk}_{\mathsf{AS}}^t, \mathsf{sk}_{\mathsf{FS}}^t)$.

If event E_1 occurs, then $\mathcal{A}$ sends $\mathcal{B}$ an *error-free* and *non-trivial* signature $\tau^* = (\sigma^*, s^*)$ for a claim sequence C^*, where C'^* is not a prefix of C^{exp}. Since τ^* is non-trivial, $i' := |C'^*| \neq 0$. In this case, there exists an index $j' \in [i']$, s.t. the claim $c_{j'}^* = (\mathsf{pk}, t_{j'}^*, m_{j'}^*) \neq c_{j'}^{\mathsf{exp}}$ and $t_{j'} < t_{\mathsf{BreakIn}}$. Let C' be the claim sequence that is generated by appending the message index i to m_i in each of the claims from C^*. Since $\mathcal{A}$'s forgery is valid, (C', σ^*) is also a valid forgery for $\mathcal{B}$'s challenger and it is non-trivial, because the claim $(\mathsf{pk}, t_{j'}^*, m_{j'}^* \| j')$ is fresh[4]. So $\mathcal{B}$ can forward this and therefore has success probability $\varepsilon_{\mathcal{B}}^{\mathsf{AS}} \geq \Pr[E_1]$.

Attack on the FS-EUF-CMA-security of FS. Next, we construct a FS-EUF-CMA-adversary $\mathcal{B}$ on FS, who uses a successful FS-EUF-CLMA-adversary $\mathcal{A}$ and has to simulate the FS-EUF-CLMA-security experiment for $\mathcal{A}$. The challenger in the FS-EUF-CMA-security experiment generates a key pair $(\mathsf{pk}_{\mathsf{FS}}, \mathsf{sk}_{\mathsf{FS}}^0) \leftarrow \mathsf{FS.KeyGen}(1^\kappa, 1^T)$ and sends $\mathsf{pk}_{\mathsf{FS}}$ and the maximal number of epochs T to $\mathcal{B}$. $\mathcal{B}$ uses the AS-scheme and generates a key pair $(\mathsf{pk}_{\mathsf{AS}}, \mathsf{sk}_{\mathsf{AS}}^0) \leftarrow \mathsf{AS.KeyGen}(1^\kappa, 1^T)$ and forwards $\mathsf{pk} = (\mathsf{pk}_{\mathsf{AS}}, \mathsf{pk}_{\mathsf{FS}})$ and T to $\mathcal{A}$. $\mathcal{B}$ initializes the log and signature it maintains towards $\mathcal{A}$ as $C_0 := ()$, $\sigma_0 := \lambda$ and sets $i := 0, t := 0, t' := 0$. We describe how $\mathcal{B}$ simulates the three oracles and the break in phase for $\mathcal{A}$:

LogAppend Oracle. $\mathcal{A}$ sends $\mathcal{B}$ a query m_i. $\mathcal{B}$ sets $C_i := C_{i-1} \| (\mathsf{pk}_{\mathsf{AS}}, t, m_i \| i)$ for the current period t and $\sigma_i \leftarrow \mathsf{AS.AggSign}(\mathsf{sk}_{\mathsf{AS}}, C_{i-1}, \sigma_{i-1}, m_i \| i)$. Then $\mathcal{B}$ sets $i := i + 1$ and sends $\mathcal{A}$ the string "ok".

NextEpoch Oracle. When $\mathcal{A}$ sends a *NextEpoch* query, $\mathcal{B}$ stops if $t \geq T - 1$ and outputs $\bot$, otherwise $\mathcal{B}$ sets $m_i :=$ "End of epoch:" $\| t$ and $C_i := C_{i-1} \| (\mathsf{pk}_{\mathsf{AS}}, t, m_i)$, and computes σ_i in the same way as before. $\mathcal{B}$ computes $\mathsf{sk}_{\mathsf{AS}}^{t+1} := \mathsf{AS.Update}(\mathsf{sk}_{\mathsf{AS}}^t)$ by its own, sets $i := i + 1, t := t + 1$ and returns "ok".

GetSignature Oracle. When $\mathcal{A}$ calls the *GetSignature* oracle $\mathcal{B}$ determines the length i of the current claim sequence C_i and the period t_{last} of the last claim in C_i (t_{last} is either t or $t-1$). If $t_{\mathsf{last}} - t' := d \neq 0$, then $\mathcal{B}$ sends d *Update* queries to his challenger, who computes $\mathsf{sk}_{\mathsf{FS}}^{t_{\mathsf{last}}}$ via updating the current $\mathsf{sk}_{\mathsf{FS}}^{t'}$ d times. Then $\mathcal{B}$ sends a query $m = i$ to his challenger, who responds with $s_i \leftarrow \mathsf{FS.Sign}(\mathsf{sk}_{\mathsf{FS}}^{t_{\mathsf{last}}}, i)$. The new signature for C_i is now $\tau_i = (\sigma_i, s_i)$ and $\mathcal{B}$ sends τ_i to $\mathcal{A}$. $\mathcal{B}$ sets $t' := t$ and if $t - t_{\mathsf{last}} = 1$, sends one more *Update* query.

Break In Phase. When $\mathcal{A}$ sends his *break in* request, $\mathcal{B}$ sets $t_{\mathsf{BreakIn}} := t$. If $t - t' := d \neq 0$, then $\mathcal{B}$ sends d *Update* queries to his challenger and then sends also a *break in* request. $\mathcal{B}$ gets the current secret key $\mathsf{sk}_{\mathsf{FS}}^t$ and sends $\mathcal{A}$ the current secret key $\mathsf{sk}_t = (\mathsf{sk}_{\mathsf{AS}}^t, \mathsf{sk}_{\mathsf{FS}}^t)$.

---

[4] Remember that we assume that m and i can be uniquely derived from $m \| i$, which implies that the claims $c_{j'}^*$ and $c_{j'}^{\mathsf{exp}}$ also differ after concatenating j' to their messages. Since j' is also only used once, the claim $c_{j'}^*$ cannot become equal to any other claim of C^{exp} after this concatenation, either.

If event E_2 occurs, then $\mathcal{A}$ sends $\mathcal{B}$ an *error-free* and *non-trivial* signature $\tau^* = (\sigma^*, s^*)$ for a claim sequence C^*, where C'^* is a prefix of C^{exp}. Let $|C^*| =: i^*$, $|C'^*| =: i'$, $|C^{\mathrm{exp}}| =: i^{\mathrm{exp}}$. Thus, s^* is a valid signature for i^*. We show that $i^* < i^{\mathrm{exp}}$ and i^* was not queried to $\mathcal{B}$'s challenger during the experiment before.

If $i^* \geq i^{\mathrm{exp}}$, then $i' > i^{\mathrm{exp}}$ is not possible, since C'^* is a prefix of C^{exp}. $i' < i^{\mathrm{exp}}$ is possible neither, since the claim $c_{i'}^*$ must then be $(\mathsf{pk}, t_{i'}, m_{i'} =$ "End of epoch:" $\| t_{i'})$ (since all claims where $t \geq t_{\mathsf{BreakIn}}$ were deleted, the last claim of C'^* must be a claim for an epoch marker – this follows from the error-freeness of τ^*) for $t_{i'} = t_{\mathsf{BreakIn}} - 1$. Because C'^* is a prefix of C^{exp} this is also a claim in C^{exp}. Since C^{exp} also contains no claims for any $t \geq t_{\mathsf{BreakIn}}$, this also has to be the last claim in C^{exp}. Therefore $|C'^*|$ must be equal to $|C^{\mathrm{exp}}|$. Thus, $i' = i^{\mathrm{exp}}$ and $C'^* = C^{\mathrm{exp}}$, but in this case, τ^* is not a non-trivial signature, because $\mathcal{A}$ queried his *GetSignature* oracle for $C'^* = C^{\mathrm{exp}}$ per definition.

So, we have $i^* < i^{\mathrm{exp}}$ and therefore $C^* = C'^*$ since C^* contains no claims with $t \geq t_{\mathsf{BreakIn}}$ in this case. So, C^* is also a prefix of C^{exp}. Because τ^* is an error-free and non-trivial signature, $\mathcal{A}$ has never queried the *GetSignature* oracle when the internal state of the log was equal to C^*. Thus, $\mathcal{B}$ has never queried his FS.Sign oracle for i^*, so s^* is a fresh and valid signature of i^* under $\mathsf{sk}_{t_{i^*}}$, with $t_{i^*} < t_{\mathsf{BreakIn}}$. Thus, $\mathcal{B}$ forwards a valid forgery (i^*, s^*) to his challenger with success probability $\varepsilon_{\mathcal{B}}^{\mathsf{FS}} \geq \Pr[E_2]$. In total, we have $\varepsilon_{\mathcal{B}}^{\mathsf{AS}} \geq \frac{\varepsilon_{\mathcal{A}}}{2}$ or $\varepsilon_{\mathcal{B}}^{\mathsf{FS}} \geq \frac{\varepsilon_{\mathcal{A}}}{2}$. $\square$

5   Implementation and Performance Results

We implemented our generic construction from Sect. 4.1 and conducted various benchmarks. Our scheme uses the BGLS-FS-SAS scheme [20,23] and the BM-FSS scheme [2]. Our results are shown in Table 1. Details of our implementation and benchmarks are provided in Appendix A.

Methodology. For our experiments, we defined several sets of processes. Each process was repeated three times. The averages and standard deviations shown in Table 1 have therefore been computed from a sample of size 3.

For the first set of processes, we called the KeyGen algorithm with the given parameter T and measured its total run-time. In the second set, we created a random key for T epochs, and then measured the run-time of updating the key T times, without computing any signatures. Table 1 shows the average run-time per invocation of Update.

The third process consisted of creating a key-pair valid for n epochs, and then calling the AggSign algorithm n times, switching epochs every ℓ messages. For each epoch switch, we created and signed an epoch marker first, and then updated the secret key. The process also included signing the current counter value with a forward-secure digital signature scheme and updating that scheme. The time shown in Table 1 is the total time of all signing and updating operations, divided by the number of messages, so it represents the average time needed for adding a single log entry to the log file. The standard deviation was computed over the average signing time in each run.

Table 1. Runtimes of our robust secure logging schemes based on the BGLS-FS-SAS from [20]. See the methodology section for an explanation of this table and the full version for more data.

Algorithm	Parameter	ℓ	avg [ms]	STD [ms]
KeyGen	$T = 10\,000$		38\,053	241
Update	$T = 10\,000$		18.6	0.033
AggSign + Update	$n =$ 1000 1000 1000	10 100 1000	67.5 60.4 59.7	0.014 0.048 0.019
Verify	$n =$ 1000 1000 1000	10 100 1000	271 227 22.5	2.05 1.87 0.15

The measurements in the last set of processes were obtained by calling Verify after a completion of a process from the third set. The time given in Table 1 is an average of the run-time of three executions divided by the number of messages that were verified. Hence, it represents the average verification time per message. The standard deviation was computed over the run-times of an individual execution divided by n. We did not consider invalid signatures in our experiments.

6   Conclusion

We give a simple solution to the problem of space-efficient logging, while still retaining robustness *and* truncation security for a properly formalized security notion of secure logging and achieve provable security. Combining a fault-tolerant forward-secure sequential aggregate signature with a forward-secure signature on the current log length elegantly solved these problems in combination. For this we modified the notion of fault-tolerance from [9] (which is based on cover-free families to introduce redundancy), to fit the more restricted setting of sequential aggregate signatures, allowing for more efficient implementations due to less requirements than in the case of general aggregation. Finally, we evaluated the performance of a prototype implementation of our space-efficient and truncation-resistant robust secure logging scheme.

A   Implementation Details

This section gives details about our implementation of the scheme from Sect. 4.1. Our implementation is written in C++11, and will be made available under a free software license. For the BM-FSS scheme, we chose a modulus size of 1024 bits, roughly equivalent to a security level of 80 bit. The BGLS scheme was instantiated using elliptic curve groups 160 bits, and the base field had 1024 bits.

We used an instantiation of the cover-free family based on polynomials, described in [16]. For a CFF supporting $n = 100$, 1000, and 10000 messages, we chose the field size $q = 5$, 11, and 23, respectively, and fixed the polynomial degree at $k = 2$. This led to $d = 2, 5$ and 11, respectively. (The resulting CFFs were slightly larger than required: They supported 125, 1331, and 12167 messages, respectively.) Whenever a hash function was needed, we used SHA-256. We used a constant string of 200 bytes for all messages.

Our experiments were conducted on a laptop computer with an Intel Core i5-2430M CPU [12] with a clock rate of 2.4 GHz. (Our implementation is not parallelized and therefore did not make use of the additional processor cores.) The processor has private (per-core) caches of 128 KB (Level 1) and 512 KB (Level 2), and a shared Level 3 Cache of 3072 KB [11, Sect. 1.1] The system was equipped with 5.7 GiB of RAM and running a 64-bit version desktop version of the Fedora 23 GNU/Linux operating system, equipped with Linux Kernel version 4.4.9-300. All code was compiled with the GNU C Compiler (version 5.3.1) and optimization level set to -O2. We used Shoups NTL library [25] (version 9.4.0) for the implementation of the BM-FSS scheme and the PBC library [18] (version 0.5.14) for the implementation of the BGLS-FS-SAS scheme.

References

1. Anderson, R.: Invited lecture. In: 4th ACM Computer and Communications Security (1997)
2. Bellare, M., Miner, S.K.: A forward-secure digital signature scheme. In: Wiener, M. (ed.) CRYPTO 1999. LNCS, vol. 1666, pp. 431–448. Springer, Heidelberg (1999). doi:10.1007/3-540-48405-1_28
3. Bellare, M., Yee, B.: Forward integrity for secure audit logs. Technical report, Computer Science and Engineering Department, University of California at San Diego (1997)
4. Boneh, D., Gentry, C., Lynn, B., Shacham, H.: Aggregate and verifiably encrypted signatures from bilinear maps. In: Biham, E. (ed.) EUROCRYPT 2003. LNCS, vol. 2656, pp. 416–432. Springer, Heidelberg (2003). doi:10.1007/3-540-39200-9_26
5. Bowers, K.D., Hart, C., Juels, A., Triandopoulos, N.: PillarBox: combating next-generation malware with fast forward-secure logging. In: Stavrou, A., Bos, H., Portokalidis, G. (eds.) RAID 2014. LNCS, vol. 8688, pp. 46–67. Springer, Cham (2014). doi:10.1007/978-3-319-11379-1_3
6. Boyen, X., Shacham, H., Shen, E., Waters, B.: Forward-secure signatures with untrusted update. In: Juels, A., Wright, R.N., di Vimercati, S.D.C. (eds.) CCS 2006, pp. 191–200. ACM (2006). doi:10.1145/1180405.1180430
7. Crosby, S.A., Wallach, D.S.: Efficient data structures for tamper- evident logging. In: Monrose, F. (ed.) USENIX 2009, pp. 317–334. USENIX Association (2009). http://www.usenix.org/events/sec09/tech/full_papers/crosby.pdf
8. Hartung, G.: Secure audit logs with verifiable excerpts. In: Sako, K. (ed.) CT-RSA 2016. LNCS, vol. 9610, pp. 183–199. Springer, Cham (2016). doi:10.1007/978-3-319-29485-8_11
9. Hartung, G., Kaidel, B., Koch, A., Koch, J., Rupp, A.: Fault-tolerant aggregate signatures. In: Cheng, C.-M., Chung, K.-M., Persiano, G., Yang, B.-Y. (eds.) PKC 2016. LNCS, vol. 9614, pp. 331–356. Springer, Heidelberg (2016). doi:10.1007/978-3-662-49384-7_13

10. Holt, J.E.: Logcrypt: forward security and public verification for secure audit logs In: Buyya, R., Ma, T., Safavi-Naini, R., Steketee, C., Susilo, W. (eds.) AusGrid 2006 and AISW 2006. CRPIT, vol. 54, pp. 203–211. Australian Computer Society (2006). doi:10.1145/1151828.1151852

11. Intel Corporation: 2nd Generation Intel Core Mobile Processor Datasheet, vol. 1, September 2012. https://www-ssl.intel.com/content/www/us/en/processors/core/2nd-gen-core-family-mobile-vol-1-datasheet.html. Accessed 29 May 2017

12. Intel Corporation: Intel Core i5–2430M Processor Specification. https://ark.intel.com/products/53450/Intel-Core-i5-2430M-Processor-3M-Cache-up-to-3_00-GHz. Accessed 29 May 2017

13. Itkis, G., Reyzin, L.: Forward-secure signatures with optimal signing and verifying. In: Kilian, J. (ed.) CRYPTO 2001. LNCS, vol. 2139, pp. 332–354. Springer, Heidelberg (2001). doi:10.1007/3-540-44647-8_20

14. Kautz, W.H., Singleton, R.C.: Nonrandom binary superimposed codes. IEEE Trans. Inf. Theor. **10**(4), 363–377 (1964). doi:10.1109/TIT.1964.1053689

15. Krawczyk, H.: Simple forward-secure signatures from any signature scheme. In: Gritzalis, D., Jajodia, S., Samarati, P. (eds.) CCS 2000, pp. 108–115. ACM (2000). doi:10.1145/352600.352617

16. Kumar, R., Rajagopalan, S., Sahai, A.: Coding constructions for blacklisting problems without computational assumptions. In: Wiener, M. (ed.) CRYPTO 1999. LNCS, vol. 1666, pp. 609–623. Springer, Heidelberg (1999). doi:10.1007/3-540-48405-1_38

17. Lu, S., Ostrovsky, R., Sahai, A., Shacham, H., Waters, B.: Sequential aggregate signatures, multisignatures, and verifiably encrypted signatures without random oracles. J. Crypt. **26**(2), 340–373 (2013). doi:10.1007/s00145-012-9126-5

18. Lynn, B.: The pairing-based crypto library. https://crypto.stanford.edu/pbc/. Accessed 29 May 2017

19. Lysyanskaya, A., Micali, S., Reyzin, L., Shacham, H.: Sequential aggregate signatures from trapdoor permutations. In: Cachin, C., Camenisch, J.L. (eds.) EURO-CRYPT 2004. LNCS, vol. 3027, pp. 74–90. Springer, Heidelberg (2004). doi:10.1007/978-3-540-24676-3_5

20. Ma, D.: Practical forward secure sequential aggregate signatures. In: Abe, M., Gligor, V.D. (eds.) ASIACCS 2008, pp. 341–352. ACM (2008). doi:10.1145/1368310.1368361

21. Ma, D., Tsudik, G.: A new approach to secure logging. In: Atluri, V. (ed.) DBSec 2008. LNCS, vol. 5094, pp. 48–63. Springer, Heidelberg (2008). doi:10.1007/978-3-540-70567-3_4

22. Ma, D., Tsudik, G.: A new approach to secure logging. ACM Trans. Storage (TOS) **5**(1) (2009). doi:10.1145/1502777.1502779

23. Ma, D., Tsudik. G.: Extended abstract: forward-secure sequential aggregate authentication. In: S&P 2007, pp. 86–91. IEEE Computer Society (2007). doi:10.1109/SP.2007.18

24. Schneier, B., Kelsey, J.: Cryptographic support for secure logs on untrusted machines. In: Rubin, A.D. (ed.) Proceedings of USENIX. USENIX Association (1998). https://www.usenix.org/conference/7th-usenix-security-symposium/cryptographic-support-securelogs-untrusted-machines

25. Shoup, V.: NTL: a library for doing number theory. http://shoup.net/ntl/. Accessed 29 May 2017

Verifiably Encrypted Group Signatures

Zhen Wang[1,2], Xiling Luo[1,2], and Qianhong Wu[1(✉)]

[1] School of Electronic and Information Engineering,
Beihang University, Beijing, China
`qianhong.wu@buaa.edu.cn`
[2] Beijing Key Laboratory for Network-Based Cooperative Air Traffic Management,
Beijing, China

Abstract. Recently, verifiably encrypted signatures (VESs) have been widely used in fair exchange, however most of them do not provide a method to protect the anonymity of the signer, leading to privacy leakage in fair exchange. Verifiably Encrypted Group Signature (VEGS) overcomes drawbacks of VES, which allows a verifier to check its validity without decryption. And VEGS does not reveal the identity of the signer, thus protecting the privacy of the signer. In VEGS systems, a signer generates a group signature with his private key, then encrypts it with the adjudicator's public key and outputs a VEGS. A verifier can check whether a VEGS is valid. The group manager reveals the identity of the VEGS if necessary. The adjudicator can extract the original group signature from the VEGS with his private key. In this paper, we propose the first concrete VEGS scheme according to our model. We define several security properties which are essential to VEGS schemes and we prove that our scheme is secure in the standard model. Additionally, we discuss some relevant issues about our scheme.

Keywords: Verifiably Encrypted Group Signature · Verifiably Encrypted Signature · Group signature · Security properties

1 Introduction

With the development of the Internet, fair exchange has been applied to online transaction. In fair exchange, two involved parties exchange goods with each other fairly. However, most existing protocols can not protect the privacy of the exchange parties. Suppose one person wants to exchange a file with company B on behalf of company A, however, he may not want to expose his identity. This leads to a big challenge to achieve fair exchange protocols since most of them use verifiably encrypted signature (VES), which exposes the identities of the two parties in the transaction.

VES is an encrypted signature and its validity can be checked without decryption. As stated in [17,20], a VES scheme consists of a signature scheme and an encryption scheme. Boneh et al. first proposed a VES scheme [6], which is constructed by aggregate signatures. Lu et al. [17], Nishimaki and Xagawa [18] independently proposed their VES schemes, which are both secure in the standard

© Springer International Publishing AG 2017
T. Okamoto et al. (Eds.): ProvSec 2017, LNCS 10592, pp. 107–126, 2017.
https://doi.org/10.1007/978-3-319-68637-0_7

model. However, the private key size is rather large. Besides, the scheme of Nishi-maki and Xagawa is based on Waters' dual signature scheme, leading to a large size of the signature. Rückert and Schröder [20] proposed a VES scheme based on a short signature scheme [4], which is efficient due to the short verification key. However, most existing VES schemes are based on Public Key Infrastructure (PKI), leading to high cost in the authentication and management of the public keys. Using identity-based cryptosystems, the above problem can be solved. Gu et al. [16] proposed an identity-based VES scheme with random oracles. However, their scheme was proved to be insecure [21]. Then Zhang et al. [22] proposed an identity-based VES scheme in the standard model. However, their scheme is a weak version of identity-based VES [15]. Besides, all above schemes can not pro-tect the anonymity of the signer, thus we have to use another technique called group signature.

Group signature was first introduced by Chaum and Heyst [11], which allows an authentic user generates a signature on behave of a group and hides his iden-tity from others. In their paper, they gave the basic ideas about group signature and presented four group signature schemes. However, they did not give spe-cific security definitions. Then several related works were presented [2,3,5,13]. However, all of them are too inefficient or provably secure with random ora-cles. Then Bellare et al. [9] first formalized the security definitions of the group signature and presented a group signature scheme which is secure in the stan-dard model. Ateniese et al. [1] also proposed a group signature which is secure without random oracles. However, all above schemes use Zero-Knowledge (ZK) proof technique which is inefficient. Later, Boyen and Waters [10] constructed a group signature scheme without ZK proof technique and their scheme is provably secure in the standard model.

Motivated by above works, we first formalized a new concept called verifiably encrypted group signature (VEGS), which is derived from verifiably encrypted signature (VES) and group signature. As a consequence, VEGS has similar prop-erties with both VES and group signature. VEGS can be checked without decryp-tion and protect the signer's anonymity. Besides, if there exists dispute, a trusted parties can trace the identity of the signer. Thus VEGS can be used to construct fair exchange protocols which hide the identity of the parties in the transaction.

For example, if Alice wishes to exchange signature on a file with company B on behalf of company A and she does not want to expose her identity, she can use a VEGS to complete the exchange instead of an original signature. Alice first sends a VEGS to company B. Then a staff of company B (known as Bob) checks whether the VEGS is valid. If the VEGS is valid, Bob generates a group signature and sends it to company A. Then Alice checks whether the group signature is valid. If it is valid, Alice sends her group signature to company B. If Alice does not sends her group signature to B, B sends the VEGS together with Bob's group signature to the adjudicator. If both of them are valid, the adjudicator recovers the original group signature of Alice and returns it to company B. The exchange reveals nothing about identities of Alice and Bob due to the anonymity of the group signature and VEGS. If someone denies that he generates the VEGS or group signature, the group manager can trace the identity of the signer. Besides, VEGS has useful applications such as online data exchange and online contact signing. And the special properties make it appealing to explore the potential in VEGS.

1.1 Our Contributions

We formalize a new concept of verifiably encrypted group signature (VEGS), which combines verifiably encrypted signature (VES) and group signature. VEGSs are encrypted group signatures which can be used to protect the anonymity of the signers. And VEGSs allow us to check their validity without decryption. In VEGS, the group master key and group tracing key are generated by the group master and the group manager keeps the group tracing key. A user generates a group signature with his private key, then encrypts it with the adjudicator's public key, and obtains a VEGS. A verifier checks whether the VEGS is valid. The group manager can open the VEGS and trace the identity of the signer if necessary. The adjudicator can extract the original group signature from the VEGS with his private key.

We define the security properties required in VEGS schemes, i.e., full-anonymity, full-traceability, unforgeability, opacity and extractability. Full-anonymity describes that no one can reveal the identity of the signer except the group manager. Full-traceability means that any valid VEGS can be traced to a valid identity by the group manager. Unforgeability guarantees that no one can forge a VEGS without a signing key. Opacity means that no one can extract a valid group signature from a VEGS without the adjudicator's private key. Extractability guarantees that if a VEGS is valid, then the original group signature can be extracted by the adjudicator.

We propose the first concrete VEGS scheme by employing Boyen-Waters group signature scheme [10] and the ElGamal encryption scheme [14]. Then we prove our VEGS scheme is secure in the standard model. Finally, we discuss the extensions of our VEGS scheme.

1.2 Outline

We organize the rest of the paper as follows. In Sect. 2 we give the relevant notions. In Sect. 3 we present definition of VEGS scheme and security definitions. In Sect. 4 we propose our concrete VEGS scheme, then we prove our scheme is secure in the standard model. In Sect. 5 we discuss the extensions of our VEGS scheme. Finally, we conclude in Sect. 6.

2   Preliminaries

In this section, we briefly review the bilinear maps and complexity assumptions that are essential in our construction.

2.1 Bilinear Maps

In our paper, we use composite order bilinear groups as stated in [7]. Let $\mathbb{G}$ and $\mathbb{G}_T$ be finite cyclic groups of order n, g be a generator of $\mathbb{G}$, and $n = pq$ has two large prime factors (p and q). A map $e : \mathbb{G} \times \mathbb{G} \to \mathbb{G}_T$ can be called an efficient bilinear map if it satisfies the following properties:

- *Bilinear*: For $\forall a, b \in \mathbb{Z}_n$, we have $e(g^a, g^b) = e(g, g)^{ab}$. Clearly, the bilinearity implies that for $\forall g_1, g_2, g_3 \in \mathbb{G}$, we have $e(g_1, g_3)e(g_2, g_3) = e(g_1 g_2, g_3)$.
- *Non-degeneracy*: $e(g, g) \neq 1$. In other words, the element $e(g, g)$ is a generator of $\mathbb{G}_T$.
- e is efficiently computable.

2.2 Complexity Assumptions

The security of our VEGS scheme is based on subgroup decision assumption, CDH assumption and aggregate extraction assumption. The subgroup decision assumption is based on the hardness of factoring [7], and aggregate extraction assumption is a variant of CDH assumption, thus all assumptions employed in our scheme are basic assumptions. We briefly review them below.

Subgroup Decision problem: Let $\mathbb{G}$ and $\mathbb{G}_T$ be finite cyclic groups of order $n = pq$, $\mathbb{G}_p$ and $\mathbb{G}_q$ be subgroups of $\mathbb{G}$ of order p and q, e be a bilinear map $e : \mathbb{G} \times \mathbb{G} \to \mathbb{G}_T$. Choose $w \in \mathbb{G}$ randomly, decide whether $w \in \mathbb{G}_q$.

The subgroup decision assumption is as follows.

Definition 1. *The (t, ϵ)-subgroup decision assumption holds if no adversary runs at most t time and has at least ϵ advantage in solving the subgroup decision problem.*

CDH problem: Given g, g^a, g^b, compute g^{ab}.

If the probability that adversary $\mathcal{B}$ solves the CDH problem is at least ϵ, then we have
$$Pr[\mathcal{B}(g, g^a, g^b) = g^{ab}] \geq \epsilon,$$

Then CDH assumption is as follows.

Definition 2. *The (t, ϵ)-CDH assumption holds if no adversary runs at most t time and has at least ϵ advantage in solving the CDH problem on $\mathbb{G}$.*

The aggregate extraction problem: Given $\mathbb{G}$, $\mathbb{G}_p$, $\mathbb{G}_q$, $n = pq$, p, q, g, g^a, g^b, g^δ, g^ζ and $g^{ab+\delta\zeta}$, compute g^{ab}.

If the probability that adversary $\mathcal{B}$ solves the aggregate extraction problem is at least ϵ, then we have

$$Pr[\mathcal{B}(g, g^a, g^b, g^\delta, g^\zeta, g^{ab+\delta\zeta}) = g^{ab}] \geq \epsilon,$$

Then aggregate extraction assumption is as follows.

Definition 3. *The (t, ϵ)-aggregate extraction assumption holds if no adversary runs at most t time and has at least ϵ advantage in solving the aggregate extraction problem on $\mathbb{G}$.*

3   Modelling VEGS

3.1   Definition of VEGS Scheme

VEGS works as follows. A group master sets up the system and distributes the keys of users. A group manager keeps the group tracing key, which can be used to reveal a user's identity from the VEGS. Group members first register in the system with their identities and obtain their signing keys. Then they generate group signatures with the signing keys, encrypt them with the adjudicator's public key and finally obtain VEGSs. A verifier can check whether the VEGS is valid without decrypting it. The adjudicator can reveal the original group signature from the VEGS with his private key.

A VEGS scheme consists of following algorithms: Setup, AKG, Enroll, Sign, Verify, VESign, VEVerify, Open, Adj.

Setup: Setup takes as input security parameter 1^λ, and outputs public parameters param for verification, a master key MK for enrollment of users, and a tracing key TK for revealing the identity from the VEGS.

AKG: AKG takes as input security parameter 1^λ, and outputs a pair of keys (SK_T, PK_T) for the adjudicator.

Enroll: Enroll takes as input a user's identity $\mathfrak{u}$, and the master key MK, outputs signing key $sk_\mathfrak{u}$ for a group member.

Sign: Sign takes as input a message $\mathfrak{m}$, the signing key $sk_\mathfrak{u}$, and outputs a group signature σ.

Verify: Verify takes as input a message $\mathfrak{m}$, a group signature σ and the public parameters param, outputs a bit $b \in \{0, 1\}$. If $b = 0$, the group signature is invalid. Otherwise, it is valid.

VESign: VESign takes as input a message $\mathfrak{m}$, a signing key $sk_\mathfrak{u}$ and the adjudicator's public key PK_T, outputs a VEGS ω.

VEVerify: VEVerify takes as input a message $\mathfrak{m}$, a VEGS ω, and public parameters param, outputs a bit $b \in \{0, 1\}$. If $b = 0$, the VEGS is invalid. Otherwise, it is valid.

Open: Open takes as input the tracing key TK, a VEGS ω, and outputs the identity $\mathfrak{u}$ of the signer.

Adj: Adj takes as input a VEGS ω, the adjudicator's private key SK_T, output the original group signature σ.

A VEGS scheme VEGS = (Setup, AKG, Enroll, Sign, Verify, VESign, VEVerify, Open, Adj) is correct if for all (param, MK, TK) $\leftarrow$ Setup(1^λ), $(SK, PK) \leftarrow$ AKG(1^λ), $\mathfrak{u}$, $sk_\mathfrak{u} \leftarrow$ Enroll(MK, $\mathfrak{u}$), $\mathfrak{m}$, and $\omega \leftarrow$ VESign($\mathfrak{m}, sk_\mathfrak{u}, PK_T$), it always holds that VEVerify($\mathfrak{m}$, VESign($\mathfrak{m}, sk_\mathfrak{u}, PK_T$), PK_T, param) = 1 and Verify($\mathfrak{m}$, Adj(VESign($\mathfrak{m}, sk_\mathfrak{u}, PK_T$), SK_T), param, $\mathfrak{u}$) = 1.

3.2   Security Definitions

Security is significant for VEGS schemes. Informally, a VEGS scheme is secure if it satisfies the following properties, i.e., anonymity, traceability, unforgeability, opacity and extractability. Briefly, anonymity means that given a valid VEGS, no one can extract the identity of the signer except the group manager who keeps the group tracing key. And traceability describes the property that the group manager can open any valid VEGS and reveal the identity of the signer. In our paper, we give stronger notions about anonymity and traceability called full-anonymity and full-traceability [9]. We define the new properties under stronger attack, which means that the adversary has the access to the private key oracle, the group signing oracle and VESign oracle. And for the attack of the full-traceability, we can even give the tracing key to the adversary. Unforgeability describes the property that no one can forge a VEGS without a signing key. And opacity means that no one can extract a valid group signature from a VEGS without the adjudicator's private key. Finally, extractability is also a necessary property and it guarantees that the valid group signature can be extracted from the valid VEGS. Formally, we define these properties by the following games.

Definition 4. *Full-anonymity is defined by the game* $\mathsf{Game}_{Anoy}(\lambda)$. *The involved parties in the game are a challenger and an adversary* $\mathcal{A}$.

- **Setup.** The challenger sets up the system, generates the system parameters and sends the public parameters to $\mathcal{A}$.
- **Query.** $\mathcal{A}$ submits an identity u to the challenger and asks for a private key, the challenger runs Enroll and returns the signing key sk_{u} to $\mathcal{A}$. $\mathcal{A}$ can query at most q_1 times for signing keys. $\mathcal{A}$ submits an identity u, a message $\mathfrak{m}$ to the challenger and asks for a group signature or VEGS, the challenger runs Sign or VESign and returns a group signature σ or a VEGS ω. $\mathcal{A}$ can query at most q_2 times for group signatures and q_3 times for VEGSs. If $\mathcal{A}$ submits a message $\mathfrak{m}$, a VEGS ω to the challenger, and asks for arbitration, the challenger first checks whether ω is valid, if it is not, then the challenger returns $\bot$. Otherwise, the challenger runs Adj and returns a group signature σ. $\mathcal{A}$ can query at most q_4 times for adjudication.
- **Challenge.** $\mathcal{A}$ randomly chooses two identities u_1, u_2 which have the same length, a message $\mathfrak{m}^*$ and sends them to the challenger. The challenger random picks a bit $b \in \{0,1\}$, generates a private key of u_b, and returns a VEGS $\omega_b \leftarrow \mathsf{VESign}(\mathfrak{m}^*, sk_{\mathsf{u}_b}, PK_T)$ to $\mathcal{A}$.
- **Guess.** Finally, $\mathcal{A}$ outputs a bit $b' \in \{0,1\}$ as a guess of b.

Define the probability that $\mathcal{A}$ wins in the above game as

$$Adv_{\mathcal{A}}^{Anon} = |Pr[b' = b] - \frac{1}{2}|.$$

A VEGS scheme is fully-anonymous if for every probability polynomial time (PPT) adversary $\mathcal{A}$, the probability that $\mathcal{A}$ wins in the above game is negligible. In fact, since we use the "selective-identity,adaptive-message" attack [10] in the above game, we call it CPA (chosen-plaintext attack)-ID model.

Definition 5. *Full-traceability is defined by the game* $\mathsf{Game}_{Trac}(\lambda)$ *which is played by a challenger and an adversary* $\mathcal{A}$.

– **Setup.** The challenger sets up the system, generates the system parameters and sends the public parameters to $\mathcal{A}$. In this step, $\mathcal{A}$ can also get the group tracing key.
– **Query.** In this step, $\mathcal{A}$ does the same thing as he does in $\mathsf{Game}_{Anoy}(\lambda)$.
– **Forge.** Finally, $\mathcal{A}$ outputs a pair $(\mathfrak{m}^*, \omega^*)$. The challenger first checks whether the VEGS is valid. If it is invalid, the challenger returns $\bot$. Otherwise, the challenger runs Open and obtains an identity $\mathfrak{u}^*$. If $\mathfrak{u}^* \in \mathcal{U}$ (we assume $\mathcal{U}$ is a set of all queried identities), then the challenger returns $\bot$. If $\mathfrak{u}^* \notin \mathcal{U}$ and $\mathcal{A}$ has not queried a private key of identity $\mathfrak{u}^*$, a group signature or VEGS on $(\mathfrak{u}^*, \mathfrak{m}^*)$, then $\mathcal{A}$ wins in the game.

A VEGS scheme is said to be fully-traceable if for every PPT adversary $\mathcal{A}$, the probability that $\mathcal{A}$ wins in the above game is negligible.

One may find that our definition of full-traceability simply implies unforgeability, thus we do not give more details about unforgeability. And we deduce that a fully-traceable VEGS scheme must be unforgetable.

Definition 6. *Opacity is defined by the game* $\mathsf{Game}_{Opac}(\lambda)$ *which is played by a challenger and an adversary $\mathcal{A}$.*

– **Setup.** The challenger sets up the system, generates the system parameters and sends the public parameters to $\mathcal{A}$.
– **Query.** In this step, $\mathcal{A}$ does the same thing as he does in $\mathsf{Game}_{Anoy}(\lambda)$.
– **Forge.** Finally, $\mathcal{A}$ outputs a pair $(\mathfrak{m}^*, \sigma^*)$. The challenger first checks whether the group signature σ^* is valid. If it is invalid, then the challenger returns $\bot$. If σ^* is valid and $\mathcal{A}$ has not queried a private key of identity $\mathfrak{u}^*$, a group signature on $(\mathfrak{u}^*, \mathfrak{m}^*)$, then $\mathcal{A}$ wins in the game.

A VEGS scheme is said to be opaque if for every PPT adversary $\mathcal{A}$, the probability that $\mathcal{A}$ wins in the above game is negligible.

Definition 7. *Extractability is defined by the game* $\mathsf{Game}_{Extr}(\lambda)$ *which is played by a challenger and an adversary $\mathcal{A}$.*

– **Setup.** The challenger sets up the system, generates the system parameters and sends the public parameters to $\mathcal{A}$.
– **Query.** In this step, $\mathcal{A}$ does the same thing as he does in $\mathsf{Game}_{Anoy}(\lambda)$.
– **Forge.** Finally, $\mathcal{A}$ submits a tuple $(\mathfrak{m}^*, \omega^*, \mathbf{param}^*)$ to the challenger.
– **Extract.** The challenger runs Adj and gets a group signature σ^*. If $\mathsf{VEVerify}(\mathfrak{m}^*, \omega^*, PK_T, \mathbf{param}^*) = 1$ and $\mathsf{Verify}(\mathfrak{m}^*, \sigma^*, \mathbf{param}^*) = 0$, then $\mathcal{A}$ wins in the game.

A VEGS scheme is extractable if for every PPT adversary $\mathcal{A}$, the probability that $\mathcal{A}$ wins in the above game is negligible.

4 VEGS Scheme

In this section, we present our VEGS scheme, which is based on Boyen-Waters group signature scheme [10] and ElGamal encryption scheme [14]. The VEGS scheme consists of following algorithms, Setup, Enroll, Sign, Verify, VESign, VEVerify, Open, Adj.

4.1 Construction of VEGS Scheme

Setup: Take as input a security parameter 1^λ, and setup the system as follows. Let $\mathbb{G}$ and $\mathbb{G}_T$ be finite cyclic groups of order $n = pq$, $\mathbb{G}_p$ and $\mathbb{G}_q$ be subgroups of $\mathbb{G}$ of order p and q, e be a bilinear map $e : \mathbb{G} \times \mathbb{G} \to \mathbb{G}_T$. Choose generators $g \in \mathbb{G}$ and $h \in \mathbb{G}_q$, a secret value $\alpha_1 \in \mathbb{Z}_n$ at random. Besides, choose random $g_2, u', u_1, ..., u_{n_u}, m', m_1, ..., m_{n_m} \in \mathbb{G}$, and set $g_1 = g^{\alpha_1}$, the master key $\mathsf{MK} = g_2^{\alpha_1}$, the group tracing key $\mathsf{TK} = q$. And the public parameters are $\mathsf{param} = (g, h, g_1, g_2, u', u_1, ...u_{n_u}, m', m_1, ..., m_{n_m})$.

AKG: Choose a secret value $\alpha_T \in \mathbb{Z}_n$, and set the adjudicator's keys as $(SK_T, PK_T) = (\alpha_T, g^{\alpha_T})$.

Enroll: Let $\mathfrak{u} = (k_1^u \cdots k_{n_u}^u)$ $(k_i^u \in \{0, 1\})$ be an identity of a group member, then his signing key is generated as follows. Choose $r_u \in \mathbb{Z}_n$ randomly, and compute,

$$ sk_{\mathfrak{u}} = d_{\mathfrak{u}} = (d_1, d_2, d_3) = \left(g_2^{\alpha_1} \left(u' \prod_{i=1}^{n_u} u_i^{k_i^u} \right)^{r_u}, g^{r_u}, h^{r_u} \right). $$

Sign: Suppose a user of identity $\mathfrak{u} = (k_1^u \cdots k_{n_u}^u)$ wishes to generate a group signature on message $\mathfrak{m} = (k_1^m \cdots k_{n_m}^m)$, then he does as follows. First, choose $r_u', r_m, t_1, ..., t_{n_u} \in \mathbb{Z}_n$, and set $t = \sum_{i=1}^{n_u} t_i$. Then compute,

$$ \sigma_1 = g_2^{\alpha_1} \left(u' \prod_{i=1}^{n_u} u_i^{k_i^u} \right)^{r_u + r_u'} \left(m' \prod_{j=1}^{n_m} m_j^{k_j^m} \right)^{r_m} h^{(r_u + r_u')t}, $$

$$ \sigma_2 = g^{r_u + r_u'}, $$

$$ \sigma_3 = g^{r_m}, $$

$$ \sigma_4 = h^t, $$

$$ \sigma_5 = \sigma_2^t = g^{(r_u + r_u')t}, $$

$$ c_i = u_i^{k_i^u} \cdot h^{t_i}, $$

$$ \pi_i = (u_i^{2k_i^u - 1} \cdot h^{t_i})^{t_i}, $$

$$ \sigma = (\sigma_1, \sigma_2, \sigma_3, \sigma_4, \sigma_5, c_1, ..., c_{n_u}, \pi_1, ..., \pi_{n_u}). $$

For simplicity, let $c = u' \prod_{i=1}^{n_u} c_i$ and $M = m' \prod_{j=1}^{n_m} m_j^{k_j^m}$, then we have $\sigma_1 = g_2^{\alpha_1} c^{r_u + r_u'} M^{r_m}$.

Verify: If a verifier wishes to check whether a group signature σ is valid, he first computes $c = u' \prod_{i=1}^{n_u} c_i$, then checks whether the following equations hold.

$$ \forall i = 1, ..., k : e(c_i, u_i^{-1} c_i) \stackrel{?}{=} e(h, \pi_i). $$

If all of them hold, then check whether the following equations hold.

$$ e(\sigma_1, g) \stackrel{?}{=} e(g_2, g_1) e(c, \sigma_2) e(M, \sigma_3). $$

$$e(\sigma_2, \sigma_4) \overset{?}{=} e(\sigma_5, h).$$

If the equations hold, then the group signature $\sigma = (\sigma_1, \sigma_2, \sigma_3, \sigma_4, \sigma_5, c_1, ..., c_{n_u}, \pi_1, ..., \pi_{n_u})$ is valid.

VESign: To create a VEGS of identity $u = (k_1^u \cdots k_{n_u}^u)$ on message $m = (k_1^m \cdots k_{n_m}^m)$, the signer first generates a group signature σ, then chooses a random $s \in \mathbb{Z}_n$, and computes,

$$\omega_1 = (PK_T)^s \cdot \sigma_1 = (PK_T)^s g_2^{\alpha_1} \left(u' \prod_{i=1}^{n_u} u_i^{k_i^u} \right)^{r_u + r_u'} \left(m' \prod_{j=1}^{n_m} m_j^{k_j^m} \right)^{r_m} h^{(r_u + r_u')t},$$

$$\omega_2 = g^s,$$

$$\omega_3 = \sigma_2 = g^{r_u + r_u'},$$

$$\omega_4 = \sigma_3 = g^{r_m},$$

$$\omega_5 = \sigma_4 = h^t,$$

$$\omega_6 = \sigma_5 = g^{(r_u + r_u')t},$$

$$\omega = (\omega_1, \omega_2, \omega_3, \omega_4, \omega_5, \omega_6, c_1, ..., c_{n_u}, \pi_1, ..., \pi_{n_u}).$$

In fact, we only encrypt σ_1, because the other part of the group signature is independent with the message m and identity u.

VEVerify: To verify if a VEGS is valid, a verifier checks whether the following equations hold.

$$\forall i = 1, ..., k : e(c_i, u_i^{-1} c_i) \overset{?}{=} e(h, \pi_i),$$

$$e(\omega_1, g) \overset{?}{=} e(PK_T, \omega_2) e(g_2, g_1) e(c, \omega_3) e(M, \omega_4),$$

$$e(\omega_3, \omega_5) \overset{?}{=} e(\omega_6, h).$$

where $c = u' \prod_{i=1}^{n_u} c_i$ and $M = m' \prod_{j=1}^{n_m} m_j^{k_j^m}$. If all equations hold, then the VEGS is valid. Otherwise, it is invalid.

Open: The group manager recovers the signer's identity from the VEGS as follows if necessary. For each $i = 1, ..., n_u$, if $(c_i)^q = g^0$, the group manager sets $k_i^u = 0$. Otherwise, he sets $k_i^u = 1$. Finally, the group manager outputs the signer's identity, $u = (k_1^u \cdots k_{n_u}^u)$.

Adj: Take as input a VEGS ω, the adjudicator's private key SK_T, output the original group signature as follows.

$$\sigma_1 = \frac{\omega_1}{\omega_2^{\alpha_T}} = g_2^{\alpha_1}\left(u'\prod_{i=1}^{n_u}u_i^{k_i^u}\right)^{r_u+r_u'}\left(m'\prod_{j=1}^{n_m}m_j^{k_j^m}\right)^{r_m}h^{(r_u+r_u')t},$$

$$\sigma_2 = \omega_3 = g^{r_u+r_u'},$$

$$\sigma_3 = \omega_4 = g^{r_m},$$

$$\sigma_4 = \omega_5 = h^t,$$

$$\sigma_5 = \omega_6 = g^{(r_u+r_u')t},$$

$$\sigma = (\sigma_1, \sigma_2, \sigma_3, \sigma_4, \sigma_5, c_1, ..., c_{n_u}, \pi_1, ..., \pi_{n_u}).$$

The correctness of our scheme is quite explicit and we will not prove it.

4.2   Security

Our VEGS scheme is secure in the standard model, which means that our scheme satisfies all properties described in Subsect. 3.2, we now prove it.

Theorem 1. *Our VEGS scheme is fully-anonymous (under CPA-ID attack) if the subgroup decision assumption holds.*

We do not prove it because the similar proof is given in [10].

Theorem 2. *Our VEGS scheme is fully-traceable if the underlying signature scheme is unforgeable.*

Proof. Suppose an adversary $\mathcal{A}$ breaks full-traceability of our VEGS scheme with advantage at least ϵ, then there exists an adversary $\mathcal{B}$ which can break the unforgeability of the underlying identity-based signature scheme [10] (also called two-level signature scheme) with the same advantage. $\mathcal{B}$ and $\mathcal{A}$ play the game $\mathsf{Game}_{Trac}(\lambda)$, $\mathcal{B}$ interacts with $\mathcal{A}$ and acts as a simulator. At the same time, $\mathcal{B}$ also plays a signature game called unforgeable game and tries to break the unforgeability of the underlying signature scheme. To complete the simulation, we assume that $\mathcal{B}$ plays the unforgeable game in $\mathbb{G}_p$, while he plays game $\mathsf{Game}_{Trac}(\lambda)$ in $\mathbb{G}$. We show how to construct $\mathcal{B}$.

– **Setup.** $\mathcal{B}$ gets the parameters of the signature scheme from his challenger, $\mathbf{param}_{\mathbb{G}_p} = (\tilde{g}, \tilde{g}_1 = \tilde{g}^\alpha, \tilde{g}_2, \tilde{u}', \tilde{u}_1, ..., \tilde{u}_{n_u}, \tilde{m}', \tilde{m}_1, ..., \tilde{m}_{n_m}) \in \mathbb{G}_p^{n_u+n_m+3}$. Then $\mathcal{B}$ chooses $(\hat{g}, \hat{g}_1 = \hat{g}^\beta, \hat{g}_2, h, \hat{u}', \hat{u}_1, ..., \hat{u}_{n_u}, \hat{m}', \hat{m}_1, ..., \hat{m}_{n_m}) \in \mathbb{G}_q^{n_u+n_m+4}$ randomly, and sets the public parameters as,

$$\mathbf{param}_{\mathbb{G}} = (g = \tilde{g}\hat{g}, g_1 = \tilde{g}_1\hat{g}_1, g_2 = \tilde{g}_2\hat{g}_2, h, u' = \tilde{u}'\hat{u}', u_1 = \tilde{u}_1\hat{u}_1, ..., u_{n_u} = \tilde{u}_{n_u}\hat{u}_{n_u},$$
$$m' = \tilde{m}'\hat{m}', m_1 = \tilde{m}_1\hat{m}_1, ..., m_{n_m} = \tilde{m}_{n_m}\hat{m}_{n_m}).$$

Besides, $\mathcal{B}$ chooses a random value $\alpha_T \in \mathbb{Z}_n$ and sets the adjudicator's private key as $(SK_T, PK_T) = (\alpha_T, g^{\alpha_T})$. Then $\mathcal{B}$ sends $\mathbf{param}_{\mathbb{G}}$, PK_T and the tracing key $\mathsf{TK} = q$ to $\mathcal{A}$. The parameters are distributed identically to what $\mathcal{A}$ expects.

– **Query.** In this step, $\mathcal{A}$ can make queries for private keys, group signatures and VEGSs. When $\mathcal{A}$ asks for a signing key of identity $\mathfrak{u} = (k_1^u \cdots k_{n_u}^u)$, $\mathcal{B}$ also asks his challenger for the user's (with the identity $\mathfrak{u}$) signing key. Then $\mathcal{B}$ receives the signing key of the underlying signature scheme, $\tilde{sk}_\mathfrak{u} = \tilde{d}_\mathfrak{u} = (\tilde{d}_1, \tilde{d}_2) = (\tilde{g}_2^\alpha (\tilde{u}' \prod_{i=1}^{n_u} \tilde{u}_i^{k_i^u})^{\tilde{r}_u}, \tilde{g}^{\tilde{r}_u})$. Then $\mathcal{B}$ chooses $\hat{r}_u \in \mathbb{Z}_q$ and computes,

$$sk_\mathfrak{u} = d_\mathfrak{u} = (d_1, d_2, d_3) = \left(\tilde{d}_1 \hat{g}_2^\beta \left(\hat{u}' \prod_{i=1}^{n_u} \hat{u}_i^{k_i^u}\right)^{\hat{r}_u}, \tilde{d}_2 \hat{g}^{\hat{r}_u}, h^{\hat{r}_u}\right).$$

It is obvious that the private keys generated by $\mathcal{B}$ have the same distribution with the real ones. If $\mathcal{A}$ asks for a group signature of identity $\mathfrak{u} = (k_1^u \cdots k_{n_u}^u)$ on message $\mathfrak{m} = (k_1^m \cdots k_{n_m}^m)$, $\mathcal{B}$ also submits the same identity $\mathfrak{u}$, the same message $\mathfrak{m}$ to his challenger and asks for an identity-based signature. Then $\mathcal{B}$ will obtain a signature,

$$\tilde{\sigma} = (\tilde{\sigma}_1, \tilde{\sigma}_2, \tilde{\sigma}_3) = \left(\tilde{g}_2^\alpha \left(\tilde{u}' \prod_{i=1}^{n_u} \tilde{u}_i^{k_i^u}\right)^{\tilde{r}_u+\tilde{r}_u'} \left(\tilde{m}' \prod_{j=1}^{n_m} \tilde{m}_j^{k_j^m}\right)^{\tilde{r}_m}, \tilde{g}^{\tilde{r}_u+\tilde{r}_u'}, \tilde{g}^{\tilde{r}_m}\right).$$

Next $\mathcal{B}$ chooses $t_1, ..., t_{n_u} \in \mathbb{Z}_n$, $r_u, r_m \in \mathbb{Z}_q$ at random and computes,

$$t = \sum_{i=1}^{n_u} t_i, c_i = u_i^{k_i^u} h^{t_i}, \pi_i = (u_i^{2k_i^u-1} h^{t_i})^{t_i},$$

$$\sigma_1 = \tilde{\sigma}_1 \hat{g}_2^\beta \left(\hat{u}' \prod_{i=1}^{n_u} \hat{u}_i^{k_i^u}\right)^{r_u} \left(\hat{m}' \prod_{j=1}^{n_m} \hat{m}_j^{k_j^m}\right)^{r_m} h^{r_u t},$$

$$\sigma_2 = \tilde{\sigma}_2 \hat{g}^{r_u}, \sigma_3 = \tilde{\sigma}_3 \hat{g}^{r_m}, \sigma_4 = h^t, \sigma_5 = (\tilde{\sigma}_2 \hat{g}^{r_u})^t$$
$$\sigma = (\sigma_1, \sigma_2, \sigma_3, \sigma_4, \sigma_5, c_1, ..., c_{n_u}, \pi_1, ..., \pi_{n_u}).$$

The distribution of the group signature is the same as the real one. If $\mathcal{A}$ submits an identity $\mathfrak{u} = (k_1^u \cdots k_{n_u}^u)$, a message $\mathfrak{m} = (k_1^m \cdots k_{n_m}^m)$ and asks for a VEGS. $\mathcal{B}$ first generates a group signature according to the above steps. Then $\mathcal{B}$ chooses $s \in \mathbb{Z}_n$ and computes,

$$\omega = (\omega_1, \omega_2, \omega_3, \omega_4, \omega_5, \omega_6, c_1, ..., c_{n_u}, \pi_1, ..., \pi_{n_u})$$
$$= ((PK_T)^s \sigma_1, g^s, \sigma_2, \sigma_3, \sigma_4, \sigma_5, c_1, ..., c_{n_u}, \pi_1, ..., \pi_{n_u}).$$

The distribution of the VEGS is the same as the real one. Besides, $\mathcal{A}$ can also submit a VEGS ω, and a message $\mathfrak{m}$ to $\mathcal{B}$ for adjudication. $\mathcal{B}$ first checks whether the VEGS is valid. If it is invalid, then $\mathcal{B}$ responses with an empty symbol $\perp$. Otherwise, $\mathcal{B}$ runs Adj and returns the valid group signature σ to $\mathcal{A}$.

– **Forge.** Finally, $\mathcal{A}$ outputs a pair $(\mathfrak{m}^*, \omega^*)$. $\mathcal{B}$ first checks whether the VEGS is valid. If it is invalid, then the challenger returns 0. Otherwise, $\mathcal{B}$ runs Open and obtains an identity $\mathfrak{u}^*$. If $\mathcal{A}$ has not queried a private key of identity $\mathfrak{u}^*$, a group signature or VEGS on $(\mathfrak{u}^*, \mathfrak{m}^*)$, then $\mathcal{A}$ successfully forges a valid VEGS.

And $\mathcal{B}$ can also forge a valid identity-based signature. $\mathcal{B}$ first decrypts the VEGS, and obtains a valid group signature,

$$
\sigma_1^* = \frac{\omega_1^*}{\omega_2^{*\alpha_T}} = g_2^{\alpha_1} \left(u' \prod_{i=1}^{n_u} u_i^{k_i^u} \right)^{r_u + r_u'} \left(m' \prod_{j=1}^{n_m} m_j^{k_j^m} \right)^{r_m} h^{(r_u + r_u')t},
$$

$$
\sigma_2^* = \omega_3^* = g^{r_u + r_u'},
$$

$$
\sigma_3^* = \omega_4^* = g^{r_m},
$$

$$
\sigma_4^* = \omega_5^* = h^t,
$$

$$
\sigma_5^* = \omega_6^* = g^{(r_u + r_u')t},
$$

$$
\sigma^* = (\sigma_1^*, \sigma_2^*, \sigma_3^*, \sigma_4^*, \sigma_5^*, c_1, ..., c_{n_u}, \pi_1, ..., \pi_{n_u}).
$$

Let $\gamma \in \mathbb{Z}_n$ be an integer and $\gamma \equiv 0 \pmod{q}$, $\gamma \equiv 1 \pmod{p}$ hold, then we have

$$
e(\sigma_1^{*\gamma}, \tilde{g}) = e(\tilde{g}_2, \tilde{g}_1) e \left(\tilde{u}' \prod_{j=1}^{n_u} \tilde{u}_j^{k_i^u}, \sigma_2^{*\gamma} \right) e \left(\tilde{m}' \prod_{j=1}^{n_m} \tilde{m}_j^{k_j^m}, \sigma_3^{*\gamma} \right).
$$

Thus $\mathcal{B}$ submits a tuple $(\mathfrak{u}^*, \mathfrak{m}^*, (\sigma_1^{*\gamma}, \sigma_2^{*\gamma}, \sigma_3^{*\gamma}))$ to his challenger. Since the signature has not been queried, $\mathcal{B}$ forges a valid identity-based signature $\sigma = (\sigma_1^{*\gamma}, \sigma_2^{*\gamma}, \sigma_3^{*\gamma})$. Therefore, if $\mathcal{A}$ breaks full-traceability of our VEGS scheme, then $\mathcal{B}$ also breaks the underlying identity-based signature scheme with the same advantage. Since the underlying identity-based signature scheme is unforgeable [10], our VEGS scheme satisfies full-traceability.

Theorem 3. *Our VEGS scheme is opaque if the aggregate extraction assumption holds on $\mathbb{G}$.*

Proof. Suppose an adversary $\mathcal{A}$ breaks opacity of our VEGS scheme with advantage at least ϵ, then there exists an adversary $\mathcal{B}$ that solves the aggregate extraction problem with a non-negligible probability. $\mathcal{B}$ and $\mathcal{A}$ play the game $\mathsf{Game}_{Opac}(\lambda)$, $\mathcal{B}$ simulates a challenger for $\mathcal{A}$ and tries to solve the given aggregate extraction problem on $\mathbb{G}$ (Given $\mathbb{G}, \mathbb{G}_p, \mathbb{G}_q, n = pq, p, q, g, g^a, g^b, g^\delta, g^\zeta, g^{ab+\delta\zeta}$, compute g^{ab}). We show how to construct $\mathcal{B}$.

-   **Setup.** Let $\mathbb{G}$ and $\mathbb{G}_T$ be finite cyclic groups of order $n = pq$, $\mathbb{G}_p$ and $\mathbb{G}_q$ be subgroups of $\mathbb{G}$ of order p and q, g be a generator of $\mathbb{G}$, e be a bilinear map $e : \mathbb{G} \times \mathbb{G} \to \mathbb{G}_T$. $\mathcal{B}$ generates the system parameters as follows. $\mathcal{B}$ chooses $u', u_1, ..., u_{n_u}, m', m_1, ..., m_{n_m} \in \mathbb{G}$ at random, and sets $g_1 = g^a$, $g_2 = g^b$, $PK_T = g^\delta$. Besides, choose a generator $h \in \mathbb{G}_q$. We assume $h = g^\eta$ and η is known to $\mathcal{B}$. Then $\mathcal{B}$ sends the public parameters $\mathbf{param} = (g, h, g_1, g_2, u', u_1, ...u_{n_u}, m', m_1, ..., m_{n_m})$ and the adjudicator's public key $PK_T = g^\delta$ to $\mathcal{A}$. The distribution of the parameters are the same as the real ones. Although $\mathcal{B}$ does not know $\mathsf{MK} = g_2^a$ and $SK_T = \delta$, we can still complete the simulation by playing some tricks. $\mathcal{B}$ first sets $l_u = 2(q_1 + q_2 + q_3)$ and $l_m = 2(q_2 + q_3)$ ($\mathcal{A}$ can query at most q_1 times for private keys, q_2 times for group signatures and q_3 times for VEGSs), and chooses x', z', n_u-length vector $X = (x_i)$ and n_m-length vector $Z = (z_j)$ at random, where x' and x_i are random values in $\{0, ..., l_u\}$, z' and z_j are random values in $\{0, ..., l_m\}$. Besides, $\mathcal{B}$ picks y', w', n_u-length vector $Y = (y_i)$ and n_m-length vector $W = (w_j)$, where y', y_i, w' and w_j are random elements in $\mathbb{Z}_n$. Next $\mathcal{B}$ sets $u' = g_2^{-l_u k_1 + x'} g^{y'}$, $u_i = g_2^{x_i} g^{y_i}$, $m' = g_2^{-l_m k_2 + z'} g^{w'}$, $m_j = g_2^{z_j} g^{w_j}$, where $0 \leq k_1 \leq n_u$ and $0 \leq k_2 \leq n_m$. Then define the following functions,

$$F_1(\mathfrak{u}) = -l_u k_1 + x' + \sum_{i=1}^{n_u} x_i k_i^u, \quad K_1(\mathfrak{u}) = y' + \sum_{i=1}^{n_u} y_i k_i^u$$

$$F_2(\mathfrak{m}) = -l_m k_2 + z' + \sum_{j=1}^{n_m} z_j k_j^m, \quad K_2(\mathfrak{m}) = w' + \sum_{j=1}^{n_m} w_j k_j^m$$

And we have

$$u' \prod_{i=1}^{n_u} u_i^{k_i^u} = g_2^{F_1(\mathfrak{u})} g^{K_1(\mathfrak{u})}$$

$$m' \prod_{j=1}^{n_m} m_j^{k_j^m} = g_2^{F_2(\mathfrak{m})} g^{K_2(\mathfrak{m})}$$

- **Query.** Private key queries: If $\mathcal{A}$ submits an identity $\mathfrak{u} = (k_1^u \cdots k_{n_u}^u)$ to $\mathcal{B}$ and asks for a signing key, $\mathcal{B}$ randomly chooses $r_u \in \mathbb{Z}_n$, and computes,

$$d_{\mathfrak{u}} = (d_1, d_2) = \left(g_1^{\frac{-K_1(\mathfrak{u})}{F_1(\mathfrak{u})}} \left(u' \prod_{i=1}^{n_u} u_i^{k_i^u} \right)^{r_u}, g_1^{\frac{-1}{F_1(\mathfrak{u})}} g^{r_u} \right).$$

Writing $\bar{r}_u = r_u - \frac{a}{F_1(\mathfrak{u})}$, then we have

$$d_1 = g_1^{\frac{-K_1(\mathfrak{u})}{F_1(\mathfrak{u})}} \left(u' \prod_{i=1}^{n_u} u_i^{k_i^u} \right)^{r_u}$$

$$= g_1^{\frac{-K_1(\mathfrak{u})}{F_1(\mathfrak{u})}} \left(g_2^{F_1(\mathfrak{u}} g^{K_1(\mathfrak{u})} \right)^{r_u}$$

$$= g_2^a (g_2^{F_1(\mathfrak{u})} g^{K_1(\mathfrak{u})})^{-\frac{a}{F_1(\mathfrak{u})}} (g_2^{F_1(\mathfrak{u})} g^{K_1(\mathfrak{u})})^{r_u}$$

$$= g_2^a \left(u' \prod_{i=1}^{n_u} u_i^{k_i^u} \right)^{r_u - \frac{a}{F_1(\mathfrak{u})}}$$

$$= g_2^a \left(u' \prod_{i=1}^{n_u} u_i^{k_i^u} \right)^{\bar{r}_u},$$

$$d_2 = g_1^{-\frac{1}{F_1(\mathfrak{u})}} g^{r_u} = g^{r_u - \frac{a}{F_1(\mathfrak{u})}}$$

$$= g^{\bar{r}_u}$$

$$d_3 = g_1^{-\frac{\eta}{F_1(\mathfrak{u})}} h^{r_u}$$

$$= h^{\bar{r}_u}$$

Therefore the private keys generated by $\mathcal{B}$ are indistinguishable from the real ones. Then $\mathcal{B}$ sends $d_{\mathfrak{u}} = (d_1, d_2, d_3)$ to $\mathcal{A}$.

Group signature queries: If $\mathcal{A}$ submits an identity $\mathfrak{u} = (k_1^u \cdots k_{n_u}^u)$, a message $\mathfrak{m} = (k_1^m \cdots k_{n_m}^m)$ to $\mathcal{B}$ and requests a group signature, $\mathcal{B}$ answers as follows. $\mathcal{B}$ chooses $r_u, r_u', r_m, t_1, ..., t_{n_u} \in \mathbb{Z}_n$ at random, sets $t = \sum_{i=1}^{n_u} t_i$, $c_i = u_i^{k_i^u} h^{t_i}$, $\pi_i = (u_i^{2k_i^u - 1} h^{t_i})^{t_i}$, and computes,

$$
\sigma_1 = g_1^{\frac{-K_2(\mathfrak{m}_\ell)}{F_2(\mathfrak{m}_\ell)}} \left(u' \prod_{i=1}^{n_u} u_i^{k_i^u} \right)^{r_u} \left(u' \prod_{i=1}^{n_u} u_i^{k_i^u} \right)^{r_u'} \left(m' \prod_{j=1}^{n_m} m_j^{k_j^m} \right)^{r_m} h^{(r_u + r_u')t}
$$

$$
= g_2^a \left(u' \prod_{i=1}^{n_u} u_i^{k_i^u} \right)^{r_u + r_u'} \left(m' \prod_{j=1}^{n_m} m_j^{k_j^m} \right)^{\bar{r}_m} h^{(r_u + r_u')t},
$$

$$
\sigma_2 = g^{r_u} g^{r_u'} = g^{r_u + r_u'},
$$

$$
\sigma_3 = g_1^{\frac{-1}{F_2(\mathfrak{m})}} g^{r_m} = g^{\bar{r}_m},
$$

$$
\sigma_4 = h^t,
$$

$$
\sigma_5 = g^{(r_u + r_u')t},
$$

$$
\sigma = (\sigma_1, \sigma_2, \sigma_3, \sigma_4, \sigma_5, c_1, ...c_{n_u}, \pi_1, ..., \pi_{n_u}),
$$

where $\bar{r}_m = r_m - \frac{a}{F_2(\mathfrak{m}_\ell)}$. The distribution of the group signature is the same as the real one.

VEGS queries: When $\mathcal{A}$ submits an identity $\mathfrak{u} = (k_1^u \cdots k_{n_u}^u)$, a message $\mathfrak{m} = (k_1^m \cdots k_{n_m}^m)$ to $\mathcal{B}$ and requests a VEGS, $\mathcal{B}$ can use a list $QueryList$ to response. $\mathcal{B}$ initializes list $QueryList := \emptyset$ and chooses random index $\ell^* \in \{1, ..., q_3\}$ to guess from which VEGS $\mathcal{A}$ selects and outputs the extraction. And $\mathcal{A}$ has not queried for a signing key at $\mathfrak{u}_{\ell^*}$ or group signature at $(\mathfrak{u}_{\ell^*}, \mathfrak{m}_{\ell^*})$. If $\ell \neq \ell^*$, $\mathcal{B}$ first generates a group signature $\sigma_\ell = (\sigma_{1,\ell}, \sigma_{2,\ell}, \sigma_{3,\ell}, \sigma_{4,\ell}, \sigma_{5,\ell}, c_1, ...c_{n_u}, \pi_1, ..., \pi_{n_u})$ as he does in group signature queries. Next $\mathcal{B}$ chooses $s \in \mathbb{Z}_n$ at random and computes,

$$
\omega_{1,\ell} = (PK_T)^s \sigma_{1,\ell} = (PK_T)^s g_2^a \left(u' \prod_{i=1}^{n_u} u_i^{k_i^u} \right)^{r_u + r_u'} \left(m' \prod_{j=1}^{n_m} m_j^{k_j^m} \right)^{\bar{r}_m} h^{(r_u + r_u')t},
$$

$$
\omega_{2,\ell} = g^s, \omega_{3,\ell} = \sigma_{2,\ell} = g^{r_u + r_u'}, \omega_{4,\ell} = \sigma_{3,\ell} = g^{\bar{r}_m}
$$

$$
\omega_{5,\ell} = \sigma_{4,\ell} = h^t, \omega_{6,\ell} = \sigma_{5,\ell} = g^{(r_u + r_u')t}
$$

$$
\omega_\ell = (\omega_{1,\ell}, \omega_{2,\ell}, \omega_{3,\ell}, \omega_{4,\ell}, c_1, ...c_{n_u}, \pi_1, ..., \pi_{n_u})
$$

$\mathcal{B}$ sends ω_ℓ to $\mathcal{A}$ and stores the tuple $(\mathfrak{u}_\ell, \mathfrak{m}_\ell, \sigma_\ell, \omega_\ell)$ in $QueryList$. If $\ell = \ell^*$, then $\mathcal{B}$ will embed the instance. $\mathcal{B}$ randomly chooses $r_u, r_u', r_m, t_1, ..., t_{n_u} \in \mathbb{Z}_n$ and sets,

$$\omega_{1,\ell^*} = g^{ab+\delta\zeta}\left(u'\prod_{i=1}^{n_u}u_i^{k_i^u}\right)^{r_u+r_u'}\left(m'\prod_{j=1}^{n_m}m_j^{k_j^m}\right)^{r_m}h^{(r_u+r_u')t}$$

$$= (g^\delta)^\zeta g_2^a\left(u'\prod_{i=1}^{n_u}u_i^{k_i^u}\right)^{r_u+r_u'}\left(m'\prod_{j=1}^{n_m}m_j^{k_j^m}\right)^{r_m}h^{(r_u+r_u')t}$$

$$\omega_{2,\ell^*}=g^\zeta, \omega_{3,\ell^*}=g^{r_u+r_u'}, \omega_{4,\ell^*}=g^{r_m}, \omega_{5,\ell^*}=h^t, \omega_{6,\ell^*}=g^{(r_u+r_u')t}$$

$$c_i = u_i^{k_i^u}h^{t_i}, \pi_i = (u_i^{2k_i^u-1}h^{t_i})^{t_i}$$

$$\omega_{\ell^*} = (\omega_{1,\ell^*},\omega_{2,\ell^*},\omega_{3,\ell^*},\omega_{4,\ell^*},\omega_{5,\ell^*},\omega_{6,\ell^*},c_1,...c_{n_u},\pi_1,...,\pi_{n_u}).$$

$\mathcal{B}$ sends ω_{ℓ^*} to $\mathcal{A}$ and stores the tuple $(u_{\ell^*},m_{\ell^*},\sigma_{\ell^*},\omega_{\ell^*})$ in $QueryList$. If one of $F_1(u_\ell)=0$, $F_2(m_\ell)=0$, $F_1(u_{\ell^*})\neq 0$, $F_2(m_{\ell^*})\neq 0$ holds, $\mathcal{B}$ stops the game (If one of them holds, $\mathcal{B}$ can not solve his problem). We denote this event by S_1. Otherwise, the distribution of the VEGSs are the same with the real ones.

Adjudication queries: In this phase, $\mathcal{A}$ is not allowed to make a query on $(m_{\ell^*},\omega_{\ell^*})$. When $\mathcal{A}$ submits a message $m_{\ell'} = (k_1^m\cdots k_{n_m}^m)$, a VEGS $\omega_{\ell'}$ to $\mathcal{B}$ and requests a group signature, $\mathcal{B}$ does as follows. $\mathcal{B}$ first checks whether the VEGS is valid. If it is invalid, $\mathcal{B}$ returns $\perp$. Otherwise, $\mathcal{B}$ checks whether the pair $(m_{\ell'},\omega_{\ell'})$ exists in the list $QueryList$, if it is not in $QueryList$, then the VEGS is invalid and $\mathcal{B}$ returns $\perp$ (If the VEGS is valid, then $\mathcal{A}$ forges a valid VEGS, and this contradicts the unforgeability of our VEGS scheme). If the tuple is in the list $QueryList$, and $\ell'=\ell$, then $\mathcal{B}$ finds out the tuple $(u_\ell,m_\ell,\sigma_\ell,\omega_\ell)$, and returns σ_ℓ to $\mathcal{A}$. The above simulation is perfect if $\mathcal{B}$ has not aborted.

- **Forge.** Finally, $\mathcal{A}$ outputs a valid signature $\sigma_{\ell^*} = (\sigma_{1,\ell^*},\sigma_{2,\ell^*},\sigma_{3,\ell^*},\sigma_{4,\ell^*},\sigma_{5,\ell^*},c_1,...,c_{n_u},\pi_1,...,\pi_{n_u})$ (on message m_{ℓ^*}) of identity u_{ℓ^*} with a non-negligible probability ϵ. That means $\mathcal{B}$ correctly guesses from which VEGS $\mathcal{A}$ extracts the group signature, and we denote this event by S_2.

Then $\mathcal{B}$ solves his problem by computing,

$$g^{ab} = \frac{\sigma_{1,\ell^*}}{(\sigma_{2,\ell^*})^{K_1(u_{\ell^*})}(\sigma_{3,\ell^*})^{K_2(m_{\ell^*})}\sigma_{5,\ell^*}^\eta}$$

The probability that $\mathcal{B}$ wins in the above game is as follows.

$$Pr[S_1\wedge S_2]=Pr[S_1]Pr[S_2].$$

The probability that $\mathcal{B}$ correctly guesses the index ℓ^* is $1/q_3$. Since we use the proof techniques in [19], we deduce that $Pr[S_1]\geq 1/(16(q_1+q_2+q_3)(q_2+q_3)(n_u+1)(n_m+1))$. Thus we have

$$Pr[S_1\wedge S_2]\geq\frac{1}{16(q_1+q_2+q_3)(q_2+q_3)(n_u+1)(n_m+1)}\cdot\frac{1}{q_3}$$

$$=\frac{1}{16q_3(q_1+q_2+q_3)(q_2+q_3)(n_u+1)(n_m+1)}$$

and the probability that $\mathcal{B}$ solves the aggregate extraction problem is at least $\epsilon/(16q_3(q_1 + q_2 + q_3)(q_2 + q_3)(n_u + 1)(n_m + 1))$, which is non-negligible.

Theorem 4. *Our VEGS scheme is extractable.*

Proof. The challenger plays the game $\mathsf{Game}_{Extr}(\lambda)$ with an adversary $\mathcal{A}$ as follows.

- **Setup.** $\mathcal{B}$ runs Setup and AKG and generates system parameters of VEGS scheme, and sends the public parameters $(\mathbf{param}, PK_T)$ to $\mathcal{A}$.
- **Query.** In this phase, the challenger runs algorithms Enroll, Sign, VESign and Adj to response $\mathcal{A}$.
- **Forge.** Finally, $\mathcal{A}$ submits a tuple $(\mathbf{m}^*, \omega^*, \mathbf{param}^*)$ to the challenger.
- **Extract.** If the given VEGS $\omega^* = (\omega_1^*, \omega_2^*, \omega_3^*, \omega_4^*, \omega_5^*, \omega_6^*, c_1, ...c_{n_u}, \pi_1, ..., \pi_{n_u})$ passes the check, then we can obtain a valid identity $\mathbf{u} = (k_1^u \cdots k_{n_u}^u)$. Besides, we have

$$e(\omega_1^*, g) = e(PK_T, \omega_2^*)e(g_2, g_1)e\,(c, \omega_3^*)\,e\,(M, \omega_4^*)\,,$$

$$e(\omega_3^*, \omega_5^*) = e(\omega_6^*, h).$$

Then a group signature can be extracted by computing,

$$\sigma_1^* = \frac{\omega_1^*}{\omega_2^{*\alpha_T}}, \sigma_2^* = \omega_3^*, \sigma_3^* = \omega_4^*, \sigma_4^* = \omega_5^*, \sigma_5^* = \omega_6^*$$

$$\sigma^* = (\sigma_1^*, \sigma_2^*, \sigma_3^*, \sigma_4^*, \sigma_5^*, c_1, ...c_{n_u}, \pi_1, ..., \pi_{n_u}).$$

and we have

$$e(\sigma_0^*, g) = e\left(\frac{\omega_1^*}{\omega_2^{*\alpha_T}}, g\right)$$
$$= e(\omega_1^*, g)e(\omega_2^{*\alpha_T}, g)^{-1}$$
$$= e(PK_T, \omega_2^*)e(g_2, g_1)e\,(c, \omega_3^*)\,e\,(M, \omega_4^*)\,e(\omega_2^*, g^{\alpha_T})^{-1}$$
$$= e(g_2, g_1)e\,(c, \sigma_2^*)\,e\,(M, \sigma_3^*)\,.$$
$$e(\omega_3^*, \omega_5^*) = e(\sigma_2^*, \sigma_4^*) = e(\sigma_5^*, h) = e(\omega_6^*, h).$$

It implies that if $\mathsf{VEVerify}(\mathbf{m}^*, \omega^*, PK_T, \mathbf{param}^*) = 1$ holds, then Verify $(\mathbf{m}^*, \sigma^*, \mathbf{param}^*) = 1$ always holds as well. Thus our VEGS scheme is extractable.

5   Extensions

In this section, we will discuss some extensions about our scheme.

5.1 Other Properties

In above paper, we discussed main properties of VEGS according to the security requirements of VES and group signature. In fact, there are other crucial properties for VEGS, we will give more details in this subsection.

Exculpability, first proposed by Chaum and Heystis [11], is also significant to group signature schemes. And we extend it to VEGS schemes. A VEGS scheme satisfies exculpability if on one can create VEGSs on behalf of other honest group members. Consider a malicious user who wishes to forge a VEGS on behalf other users. If he is not the group master, then he will not succeed to generate a valid VEGS if the VEGS scheme satisfies unforgeability. Then we consider the case that the malicious user is the group master. Ateniese et al. [1] pointed that Boyen-Waters group signature scheme does not satisfy (strong) exculpability because the group master generates and distributes users' secret keys, however their scheme can achieve exculpability by changing some settings to the group master. In their scheme, the group master is an ephemeral entity and the master key is destroyed once the group is set up. To achieve the exculpability of our VEGS scheme, we can construct the group master in the same way. Therefore, no one can create a valid VEGS on behalf of other users.

Coalition resistance means that if a group of signers collude together to generate a valid VEGS, then it must be traceable. Coalition resistance emphasizes the fact that it allows attacks by a coalition of group members. However, coalition resistance can still be obtained from full-traceability [9]. Therefore, we deduce that fully-traceable VEGS schemes are also coalition resistant.

Unlinkability requires that on one can determine whether two different VEGS are generated by the same group member except the group manager. Given two different VEGSs, if one (except the group manager) wishes to check whether they are created by the same user, he has to recover the identity of the signer. Then he breaks the anonymity of the VEGS if he succeeds with a non-negligible probability. It implies the anonymity immediately. Thus we can deduce that fully-anonymous VEGS schemes also satisfy unlinkability.

5.2 Batch Verification

To improve efficiency of our VEGS scheme, some measures can be taken. One method is to perform fast batch verification [10,12]. The generic definition of batch verification was given by Bellare et al. [8], then Camenisch et al. [12] instantiates it to the case of signatures from many signers and aggregate signatures. We can also use their method to simplify the verification of our VEGS scheme. Suppose a verifier wish to check if a VEGS is valid, and the different things he need to do is that he chooses $\theta_1, ..., \theta_{n_u} \in \mathbb{Z}_n$, then tests,

$$\prod_{i=1}^{n_u} e(c_i^{\theta_i}, u_i^{-1} c_i) e(h^{-\theta_i}, \pi_i) \stackrel{?}{=} 1.$$

Since we batch the pairs into a multi-pairing, which is similar to multi-exponentiation algorithm, we can reduce the cost of the pairing computations.

As stated in [10], to get better efficiency, some pre-computations and extra storage are also required.

5.3 Dynamic Groups

The above VEGS scheme is called a static VEGS scheme since we do not consider the case where users join and leave after the group is set up. To achieve dynamic groups where users can both join and leave the group, we need to add some modifications to the VEGS scheme. When a user is allowed to join the group, the group master distributes the user's private key with the group master key. When a user leaves the group, it is very different for the discussion of leave operation. The group master needs to publish the recovered signing keys, then he generates a new group master key and distributes each user's private key. And what calls for attention is that the revocation information is published on public channel while the signing keys are transferred in secret channel. The above method can also be used in the cases where multiple users are revoked.

Besides, someone may find that the group master in the dynamic VEGS is not an ephemeral entity, it involves in the scheme when users join or leave the group. Therefore the weakness of our VEGS scheme is that it can not achieve dynamic groups and exculpability simultaneously. However we believe it will be solved in the future works.

6 Conclusion

In this paper, we formalized the concept of VEGS which is derived from VES and group signature. Then we presented the first VEGS scheme based on Boyen-Waters group signature scheme and ElGamal encryption scheme. We defined the security properties which are necessary for VEGS schemes, i.e., anonymity, traceability, unforgeability, opacity and extractability. Then we proved our VEGS scheme is secure in the standard model according to the definitions. Additionally, we discussed the extentions of our VEGS scheme. The results showed that our VEGS scheme has many applications. However, there still exists a few open problems (e.g., achieving dynamic groups and exculpability simultaneously, using prime order groups), which will motivate more works on VEGS.

Acknowledgment. This paper is supported by Collaborative Innovation Center Of Geospatial Technology (No. ZF102T1701), by Beijing Municipal Science and Technology Project (No. D161100005816001), and by the Natural Science Foundation of China through projects 61672083.

References

1. Ateniese, G., Camenisch, J., Hohenberger, S., Medeiros, B.D.: Practical group signatures without random oracles. In: Theory and Application of Cryptographic Techniques (2005)
2. Ateniese, G., Camenisch, J., Joye, M., Tsudik, G.: A practical and provably secure coalition-resistant group signature scheme. In: Bellare, M. (ed.) CRYPTO 2000. LNCS, vol. 1880, pp. 255–270. Springer, Heidelberg (2000). doi:10.1007/3-540-44598-6_16
3. Ateniese, G., Song, D., Tsudik, G.: Quasi-efficient revocation of group signatures. In: Blaze, M. (ed.) FC 2002. LNCS, vol. 2357, pp. 183–197. Springer, Heidelberg (2003). doi:10.1007/3-540-36504-4_14
4. Boneh, D., Boyen, X.: Short signatures without random oracles and the SDH assumption in bilinear groups. J. Cryptol. **21**(2), 149–177 (2008)
5. Boneh, D., Boyen, X., Shacham, H.: Short group signatures. In: Franklin, M. (ed.) CRYPTO 2004. LNCS, vol. 3152, pp. 41–55. Springer, Heidelberg (2004). doi:10.1007/978-3-540-28628-8_3
6. Boneh, D., Gentry, C., Lynn, B., Shacham, H.: Aggregate and verifiably encrypted signatures from bilinear maps. In: Biham, E. (ed.) EUROCRYPT 2003. LNCS, vol. 2656, pp. 416–432. Springer, Heidelberg (2003). doi:10.1007/3-540-39200-9_26
7. Boneh, D., Goh, E.-J., Nissim, K.: Evaluating 2-DNF formulas on ciphertexts. In: Kilian, J. (ed.) TCC 2005. LNCS, vol. 3378, pp. 325–341. Springer, Heidelberg (2005). doi:10.1007/978-3-540-30576-7_18
8. Bellare, M., Garay, J.A., Rabin, T.: Fast batch verification for modular exponentiation and digital signatures. In: Nyberg, K. (ed.) EUROCRYPT 1998. LNCS, vol. 1403, pp. 236–250. Springer, Heidelberg (1998). doi:10.1007/BFb0054130
9. Bellare, M., Micciancio, D., Warinschi, B.: Foundations of group signatures: formal definitions, simplified requirements, and a construction based on general assumptions. In: Biham, E. (ed.) EUROCRYPT 2003. LNCS, vol. 2656, pp. 614–629. Springer, Heidelberg (2003). doi:10.1007/3-540-39200-9_38
10. Boyen, X., Waters, B.: Compact group signatures without random oracles. In: Vaudenay, S. (ed.) EUROCRYPT 2006. LNCS, vol. 4004, pp. 427–444. Springer, Heidelberg (2006). doi:10.1007/11761679_26
11. Chaum, D., van Heyst, E.: Group signatures. In: Davies, D.W. (ed.) EUROCRYPT 1991. LNCS, vol. 547, pp. 257–265. Springer, Heidelberg (1991). doi:10.1007/3-540-46416-6_22
12. Camenisch, J., Hohenberger, S., Pedersen, M.Ø.: Batch verification of short signatures. In: Naor, M. (ed.) EUROCRYPT 2007. LNCS, vol. 4515, pp. 246–263. Springer, Heidelberg (2007). doi:10.1007/978-3-540-72540-4_14
13. Camenisch, J., Lysyanskaya, A.: Dynamic accumulators and application to efficient revocation of anonymous credentials. In: Yung, M. (ed.) CRYPTO 2002. LNCS, vol. 2442, pp. 61–76. Springer, Heidelberg (2002). doi:10.1007/3-540-45708-9_5
14. ElGamal, T.: A public key cryptosystem and a signature scheme based on discrete logarithms. In: Blakley, G.R., Chaum, D. (eds.) CRYPTO 1984. LNCS, vol. 196, pp. 10–18. Springer, Heidelberg (1985). doi:10.1007/3-540-39568-7_2
15. Galindo, D., Herranz, J., Kiltz, E.: On the generic construction of identity-based signatures with additional properties. In: Lai, X., Chen, K. (eds.) ASIACRYPT 2006. LNCS, vol. 4284, pp. 178–193. Springer, Heidelberg (2006). doi:10.1007/11935230_12

16. Gu, C., Zhu, Y.F.: An ID-based verifiable encrypted signature scheme based on Hess's scheme. In: Feng, D., Lin, D., Yung, M. (eds.) CISC 2005. LNCS, vol. 3822, pp. 42–52. Springer, Heidelberg (2005). doi:10.1007/11599548_4

17. Lu, S., Lynn, B., Ostrovsky, R., Sahai, A., Shacham, H., Waters, B.: Sequential aggregate signatures, multisignatures, and verifiably encrypted signatures without random oracles. J. Cryptol. **26**(2), 340–373 (2013)

18. Nishimaki, R., Xagawa, K.: Verifiably encrypted signatures with short keys based on the decisional linear problem and obfuscation for encrypted VES. Des. Codes Crypt. **77**(1), 61–98 (2015)

19. Paterson, K.G., Schuldt, J.C.N.: Efficient identity-based signatures secure in the standard model. In: Batten, L.M., Safavi-Naini, R. (eds.) ACISP 2006. LNCS, vol. 4058, pp. 207–222. Springer, Heidelberg (2006). doi:10.1007/11780656_18

20. Rückert, M., Schröder, D.: Security of verifiably encrypted signatures and a construction without random oracles. In: Shacham, H., Waters, B. (eds.) Pairing 2009. LNCS, vol. 5671, pp. 17–34. Springer, Heidelberg (2009). doi:10.1007/978-3-642-03298-1_2

21. Zhang, Z.F.: Cryptanalysis of an identity-based verifiably encrypted signature scheme. Chin. J. Comput. **29**(9), 1688–1693 (2006)

22. Zhang, L., Wu, Q.H., Qin, B.: Identity-based verifiably encrypted signatures without random oracles. In: Pieprzyk, J., Zhang, F. (eds.) ProvSec 2009. LNCS, vol. 5848, pp. 76–89. Springer, Heidelberg (2009). doi:10.1007/978-3-642-04642-1_8

Deniable Ring Authentication
Based on Projective Hash Functions

Shengke Zeng[1,2(✉)], Yi Mu[2], Guomin Yang[2], and Mingxing He[1]

[1] School of Computer and Software Engineering, Xihua University,
Chengdu 610039, China
`zengshengke@gmail.com`
[2] School of Computing and Information Technology,
Institute of Cybersecurity and Cryptology, University of Wollongong,
Wollongong, NSW 2522, Australia

Abstract. Deniable authentication allows the participants to deny an authentication process as there is no any evidence that it ever took place. It is quite suitable for the privacy-preserving scenario. Combining with the ring signature property, the deniable authentication can reach the source hiding. In other words, the receiver is only convinced that a member in a group is authenticating a message without knowing which one. It is also deniable, that is the receiver cannot convince anyone else that this message was indeed authenticated. We present a deniable ring authentication based on the projective hash function. With this building block the underlying (encryption) scheme is not required to be CCA secure, which results in a more *realistic* deniable authentication protocol.

Keywords: Deniable ring authentication · Privacy-preserving communication · Projective hash function · NIWI proof

1 Introduction

Authentication is the most important security primitive in the communication. When communicating with others in the Internet-based service, it is necessary for us to make sure the legitimate of our counterpart with authentication protocol. The trivial way to authenticate the communication partner is to share a common secret. If the party A shows the right secret to the party B, then B is convinced that A is the right person he will communicate with as this secret is only known to them. Obviously, the main task for this scenario is to share this secret. Therefore, the pre-step of authentication is to run a key agreement protocol [8]. An alternative method for message authentication is by a digital signature. The sender authentication to message m is the sender's signature. The unforgeability of this signature algorithm ensures the soundness of authentication. In such a public key scenario, it is not necessary for anyone to share secrets. The corresponding public key can be utilized for signature verification. In a digital signature scheme, the non-repudiation property holds. In

T. Okamoto et al. (Eds.): ProvSec 2017, LNCS 10592, pp. 127–143, 2017.
https://doi.org/10.1007/978-3-319-68637-0_8

other words, the output signature is bound to a party upon the unforgeability of the signature scheme. Although this property is useful for the contract signing or non-repudiated transactions, it is not suitable for the privacy protection.

Privacy-preserving authentication is necessary if the participants want to protect their privacy during the authentication. Suppose Alice wants to obtain a kind of service from server S. The server S should make sure that Alice is the legitimate user, thus the authentication with S is required. On the other hand, Alice does not want to leak this authentication transcript as it may expose her privacy, i.e., her identity, her position, or the service. In this situation, Alice may want to speak privately to S. Therefore, the public verification of digital signature schemes is not suitable for the authentication, which is required to protect user privacy.

How to keep the authentication transcript private? Server S may show it to anyone else since S has the transcript. The intuitive method is to make the authentication transcript to be simulatable. In other words, the communication transcript is not bound to some party if it can be generated by anybody without the secret. Obviously, the digital signatures with non-repudiation is not simulatable without the secret; otherwise it violates the unforgeability. Let us go back to the first scenario. Since party A and B share a common secret, the transcript of the sender A also can be produced by the receiver B. Therefore, this communication transcript is not bound to A and A can deny it.

Following the simulation paradigm, the notion of deniable authentication was formalized by Dwork, Naor and Sahai [11]. The authentication flows occur between the sender A and the receiver B. Upon the common input message m, A and B perform the authentication protocol interactively. Finally, the receiver B is convinced that the sender A authenticates the message m; however, B cannot convince anyone else that the authentication process occurred. This is termed as the deniable authentication.

1.1   Related Work

Deniable authentication was proposed by Dolev *et al.* [9] and then formalized by Dwork *et al.* [11]. In their work, the solution for deniable authentication is based on CCA-secure encryption. The receiver B uses the public key of the sender A to encrypt a message m and a random value t. m is also known to A. If A can extract the right t from the ciphertext, B is convinced that A is indeed authenticating m as only A can decrypt the ciphertext correctly. Their deniability can be proven via a black-box simulation. In order to make sure the simulation is smooth, a challenge-response is required. Their method is that, instead of returning t directly, A just gives the commitment/encryption of t. Upon the receipt of $C(t)$, B reveals t. This is the key step for the simulation. In this way, the simulator can extract the right t without A's secret key. Thus, the deniability is achieved. It can be viewed as *full* deniability. That means anyone can run this simulator to produce the "fake" transcript and it is indistinguishable from the real one. The simulation in [11] requires a rewinding step which prevents the perfect simulation in the current environment. Dwork *et al.* handled this problem by using the *timing* assumption [11]. It limits the number of executions which would be performed by the adversary.

The unforgeability of Dwork *et al.*'s deniable authentication relies on the CCA2 of the underlying encryption scheme. Most of proposed deniable authentications follow such CCA-based paradigm. For example, Naor [16] followed the CCA-paradigm to achieve the black-box simulation deniability in the ring authentication by rewinding steps. Dowsley [10] reduced the communication rounds of Naor's by using the broadcast encryption. Di Raimondo *et al.* [19] showed that if the underlying encryption scheme is plaintext-awareness, the deniability of the authentication can be reached without rewinding steps. Zeng *et al.* [22] followed Raimondo's idea to present a deniable ring authentication based on PA-secure multi-receiver encryption.

For the *full* (even concurrent) deniability, there are some other approaches with stronger assumptions. Jiang *et al.* [15] resorted to the public random oracles [17] to propose a deniable key exchange. The simulation depends on the witness extraction by pRO, the rewinding steps are not necessary. Yao *et al.* [20,21] proposed deniable Internet Key exchanges based on the knowledge of exponent assumption [7]. By the KEA assumption, the witness can be extracted and then the transcripts can be perfectly simulated. Another way to simulate the transcript is to apply the timed commitment/encryption [4]. The idea is that the receiver uses *moderate* commitment/encryption to commit the challenge value r. If the sender can send back the correct r within time T, the receiver accepts this authentication. The simulator can obtain the value r after T as this timed commitment/encryption can be forced decommitted/decrypt beyond time T. Jiang [14] presented a timed encryption scheme and applied it to build a concurrently deniable key exchange.

These approaches either are based on CCA-paradigm (even PA) encryptions or rely on stronger assumptions. Di Raimondo *et al.* [18] pointed out that deniable authentications can be constructed out of different primitives. In order to reduce the secure requirements of the underlying building blocks, Di Raimondo *et al.* presented two constructions without using CCA encryptions. One is based on multi-trapdoor commitment [12], the another one builds on *projective hash functions* [6].

1.2 Contribution

We focus on the fully deniable authentication with source hiding. That is the sender is even anonymous to the receiver during the deniable authentication. It is suitable for the privacy-enhanced environment. With the challenge-response sub-protocol, our protocol satisfies the black-box simulation. The simulator without any secrets produces an indistinguishable transcript such that our protocol satisfies the *full* deniability. Our motivation is to construct secure communication protocol with looser security requirements for the underlying schemes, which is more realistic. We do not adopt encryptions to a MAC key to construct authentication, where soundness requires the underlying schemes must be CCA such as [10, 16, 22].

We observe that the specific properties of the projective hash function [6] can be used to build authentication. Thus, our construction is based on *projection* and *smoothness* of projective hash function to realize authentication other than CCA encryptions to a secret MAC key. Factually, the construction of underlying projective hash function is not necessary to be CCA secure. Differing with the encryption-paradigm based deniable ring authentications, our construction has shorter transcripts. Indeed, in the encryption-paradigm based deniable ring authentications [16,22], the receiver should encrypt the MAC key for N times and sends N ciphertexts in each round to reach the sender anonymity. However, our protocol just needs to send constant-size transcripts in the first three rounds.

1.3   Organization

This paper is organized as follows. In Sect. 2 we introduce the building blocks of our protocols. In Sect. 3 we formalize the security model for deniable ring authentication. We present the generic construction of deniable ring authentication protocol based on projective hash function and NIWI proof in Sect. 4. Then we analyze the security and the performance of our protocol in Sects. 5 and 6 respectively. We conclude this paper in Sect. 7. Finally, we give an instantiation of our construction in the Appendix A.

2   Tools

In this section, we introduce the underlying tools which are used to build the deniable ring authentication. Traditional deniable authentication protocols are built on the encryption to a MAC key. Dwork *et al.* proved that the soundness of such authentication is based on CCA2 secure encryption. Di Raimondo *et al.* showed that the deniable authentication can be constructed by other primitives other than encryption, such as the non-malleable commitment scheme and the projective hash function. Such constructions can improve the efficiency and the requirement of CCA property is not necessary. Following Di Raimondo's idea, we make use of the properties of projective hash function to present our deniable ring authentication in addition to using a commitment scheme and non-interactive witness indistinguishable proof (NIWI) to obtain the source hiding. Therefore, we introduce these building blocks in this section.

2.1   Projective Hash Functions

Projective hash functions were introduced by Cramer and Shoup [6] and later formalized by Benhamouda *et al.* [3]. The properties of projective hash functions can be used to design the authenticated key exchange protocols [2,3], public key encryption with keyword search [5], and non-interactive commitments [1]. We first review the original definition of projective hash functions.

Definition. Define a domain $\mathcal{X}$ and an NP language $\mathcal{L}$ with $\mathcal{L} \subset \mathcal{X}$. The projective hash function is over $\mathcal{L}$. For a word $c \in \mathcal{L}$, the value of this function can be calculated by either a secret hashing key $\mathtt{hk}$ or a public projection key $\mathtt{hp}$ with a witness ω of the fact that $c \in \mathcal{L}$. Specifically, a projective hash function over $\mathcal{L} \subset \mathcal{X}$ is defined as follows.

- HashKG($\mathcal{L}$): generates a secret hashing key $\mathtt{hk}$ for the NP language $\mathcal{L}$;
- ProjKG($\mathtt{hk}, \mathcal{L}$): generates a projection key $\mathtt{hp}$ from the hashing key $\mathtt{hk}$;
- Hash($\mathtt{hk}, \mathcal{L}, c$): outputs the value of this hash function from the hashing key $\mathtt{hk}$, for the word c;
- ProjHash($\mathtt{hp}, \mathcal{L}, c, \omega$): outputs the value of this hash function from the projection key $\mathtt{hp}$, the witness ω, for the word $c \in \mathcal{L}$.

Projection. We say this hash function family is *projective* if Hash ($\mathtt{hk}$, $\mathcal{L}, c$) = ProjHash ($\mathtt{hp}, \mathcal{L}, c, \omega$). That means the value of the hash function can be computed even without knowing the secret hashing key $\mathtt{hk}$.

Smoothness. This projective hash function is smooth if $c \notin \mathcal{L}$, then Hash($\mathtt{hk}, \mathcal{L}, c$) is statistically indistinguishable from a random value. That means it gives no information about the hash value of any point out of $\mathcal{L}$.

In order to apply the projective hash function to the secure authentication, we have to embed the message to projective hash function in case of forgeability. Therefore, we make a slight change of it. We let $\mathcal{Y}$ be an arbitrary set and the projective hash function maps $\mathcal{X} \times \mathcal{Y}$ to another set. In our scenario, the set $\mathcal{Y}$ can be viewed as the message space $\mathcal{M}$.

2.2 Commitment Scheme

In this paper, we use a commitment scheme to hide the sensitive value such that the sender is anonymous to the receiver during the authentication. We require the commitment scheme has two properties: perfect hiding and binding. The perfect hiding states that even an unbounded adversary cannot obtain the committed value from the commitment. In other words, the committed value can be switched to another values by using a trapdoor. In contrast, the binding states that the committed value is fixed and cannot be modified without the trapdoor. In order to give an NIWI proof for the commitment, the hiding key and the commitment key are required to be indistinguishable.

2.3 Non-interactive Witness Indistinguishable Proofs

Informally, the NIWI proof system states that given two different witnesses for the statement, the generated proof reveals no information about which witness is used to construct this proof. This non-interactive proof system enables the prover P to convince the verifier V the truth of a statement. Let R be a computable relation, if $(x, w) \in \mathrm{R}$, where x is the statement and w is the witness. We let $\mathcal{L}$ be an NP language consisting of statements in R. An NIWI proof system (P, V) for $\mathcal{L}$ should be complete, sound and witness indistinguishable.

- **Completeness.** If one knows the witness for a statement, the proof can be constructed certainly. For any common reference string crs, $V_{\mathrm{crs}}(x, P_{\mathrm{crs}}(x, w)) = 1$ holds always.
- **Soundness.** If one does not have this witness, it is impossible for him to construct a valid proof. For any adversary $\mathcal{A}$, it holds that $\Pr[V_{\mathrm{crs}}(x, \pi) = 1 : (x, \pi) \leftarrow \mathcal{A}(\mathrm{crs})] = 0$
- **Witness Indistinguishability.** It means that the proof does not reveal which witness is used. Formally:

$$\Pr[(x, w_0, w_1) \leftarrow \mathcal{A}; \pi \leftarrow P_{crs}(x, w_0) : \mathcal{A}_{crs}(\pi) = 1 \wedge (x, w_0), (x, w_1) \in \mathrm{R}]$$
$$\approx \Pr[(x, w_0, w_1) \leftarrow \mathcal{A}; \pi \leftarrow P_{crs}(x, w_1) : \mathcal{A}_{crs}(\pi) = 1 \wedge (x, w_0), (x, w_1) \in \mathrm{R}]$$

3 Deniable Ring Authentication

3.1 Syntax

In this section, we formalize the notion of deniable ring authentication, which is a deniable authentication with sender anonymity to the receiver. In order to understand it well, we first introduce the syntax of deniable authentication. Then, we extend this notion to deniable ring authentication.

Deniable Authentication. We assume the sender has published its public key and it is not necessary for the receiver to publish the public key. The sender engages with the receiver to authenticate a message m in an interactive protocol. In the end of the protocol execution, the receiver accepts or rejects the sender's authentication to m. On the other hand, both the sender and the receiver can deny the involvement of this conservation.

Extension for Deniable Ring Authentication. Although the sender can deny its authentication as the conversation transcript does not leave any evidence in the deniable authentication, the receiver knows the sender. If the sender wants to seek privacy-enhanced protection, namely, it wishes even to be anonymous to the receiver, the deniable ring authentication is necessary. The same to the ring signature, deniable ring authentication includes a group of participants to meet the sender's anonymity. The goal for the actual sender S is to be anonymous to the receiver R although each one in this group reveals its secret. The sender S can randomly choose some participants, say $P_1, P_2, \ldots$ to form a set $\mathcal{R}$. We assume all the public keys in $\mathcal{R}$ can be accessed by R. S executes the deniable ring authentication protocol with R interactively by using $\mathcal{R}$. Finally, R accepts or rejects this authentication to m. Since this authentication transcript leaves no information, all the participants in $\mathcal{R}$ can deny that this authentication has ever occurred. Besides that, the probability that receiver's decision on the actual sender is no more the $1/N$, where N is the size of $\mathcal{R}$.

3.2 Security Model

We formalize the security model for the deniable ring authentication. The security model consists of following four properties: *completeness, soundness(unforgeability), deniability* and *anonymity.*

Completeness. If the sender S with a group of participants engages the receiver R to execute the deniable ring authentication protocol $\lambda_{\mathcal{DRA}}$ for a given message m and a random chosen ring $\mathcal{R}$ (this is a collection of the public keys of all the participants other than the receiver R) honestly, then R accepts this authentication to m with overwhelming probability.

Remark 1. After the execution of $\lambda_{\mathcal{DRA}}$, the receiver R is convinced that one member (cannot decide which one) in $\mathcal{R}$ authenticates m if S and R follow this protocol $\lambda_{\mathcal{DRA}}$.

Soundness (Unforgeability). Consider an adversary $\mathcal{A}$ trying to forge an authentication. It may corrupt the participants and have access to the authentication oracle which returns the authentication transcript. The soundness means that $\mathcal{A}$ without the corresponding secret cannot forge a new authentication transcript which would be accepted by the receiver. Formally, the soundness of $\lambda_{\mathcal{DRA}}$ can be described in the following game Ω between a challenger $\mathcal{C}$ and an adversary $\mathcal{A}$.

Setup. $\mathcal{C}$ runs Setup to generate ν key pairs $(PK_i, SK_i)_{i=1}^{\nu}$. $\mathcal{A}$ is given the public keys $\mathcal{PK} = \{PK_1, \ldots, PK_\nu\}$. After that, $\mathcal{A}$ outputs a corrupted set $\mathcal{D} \subseteq \{1, \ldots, \nu\}$, for which $\mathcal{A}$ is given $\{SK_i | i \in \mathcal{D}\}$.

Authentication Query. $\mathcal{A}$ can issue authentication queries as she wishes. She chooses a message m, a ring $\mathcal{R} = \{PK_{j1}, \ldots, PK_{jN}\}$ for each authentication query, where $N > 1$ and $PK_i \in \mathcal{R}$. Consequently, $\mathcal{C}$ returns the corresponding authentication transcript tr for $\mathcal{A}$ by using SK_i.

   Finally, $\mathcal{A}$ generates a forgery $(m^*, tr^*, \mathcal{R}^*)$ where $\mathcal{R}^* \cap \mathcal{D} = \emptyset$. $\mathcal{A}$ is said success if the R accepts tr^* w.r.t. $(m^*, \mathcal{R}^*)$ and $(m^*, \mathcal{R}^*)$ was not queried to authentication oracle. We use $\mathsf{Succ}_{\mathcal{DRA}}^{sd}(\mathcal{A}, \Omega)$ to denote the success event of $\mathcal{A}$.

Definition 1. *Let $\lambda_{\mathcal{DRA}}$ be a deniable authentication protocol. $\lambda_{\mathcal{DRA}}$ is sound (unforgeable) if for any polynomial time adversary $\mathcal{A}$, $\Pr[\mathsf{Succ}_{\mathcal{DRA}}^{sd}(\mathcal{A}, \Omega)]$ is negligible.*

Deniability. We use the *simulation* paradigm to formalize this notion in $\lambda_{\mathcal{DRA}}$. We first consider the simulation game Ω^{sim} between $\mathcal{A}$ and a simulator $\mathcal{S}$.

Setup. A trusted party runs Setup to generate ν key pairs $(PK_i, SK_i)_{i=1}^{\nu}$. $\mathcal{A}$ is given the public keys $\mathcal{PK} = \{PK_1, \ldots, PK_\nu\}$. After that, $\mathcal{A}$ outputs a corrupted set $\mathcal{D} \subseteq \{1, \ldots, \nu\}$, for which $\mathcal{A}$ is given $\{SK_i | i \in \mathcal{D}\}$. Finally, $\mathcal{PK}$ and $\{SK_i | i \in \mathcal{D}\}$ are also given to $\mathcal{S}$.

Authentication Query. $\mathcal{A}$ can issue authentication queries as she wishes. She chooses a message m, a ring $\mathcal{R} = \{PK_{j1}, \ldots, PK_{jN}\}$ for each authentication query, where $N > 1$. Upon this query, $\mathcal{S}$ returns the corresponding authentication transcript tr for $\mathcal{A}$ using $\mathcal{PK}$ and the corrupted keys $\{SK_i | i \in \mathcal{D}\}$.

   In the end, $\mathcal{A}$ outputs his view $\mathsf{view}_{\mathcal{DRA}}(\mathcal{A}, \Omega^{sim})$.

We then consider the real game Ω^{rea} where $\mathcal{S}$ is provided with $\{PK_i, SK_i\}_{i=1}^{\nu}$ and follows the real deniable ring authentication protocol to execute the authentication oracle. At the end of the game Ω^{rea}, $\mathcal{A}$ outputs its view $\mathsf{view}_{\mathcal{DRA}}(\mathcal{A}, \Omega^{rea})$. The deniability requires that $\mathcal{A}$'s view in Ω^{sim} and Ω^{rea} is indistinguishable.

Definition 2. *Let $\lambda_{\mathcal{DRA}}$ be a deniable authentication protocol. $\lambda_{\mathcal{DRA}}$ is* deniable *if for any polynomial time adversary $\mathcal{A}$, there exists a polynomial time simulator $\mathcal{S}$, such that $\mathsf{view}_{\mathcal{DRA}}(\mathcal{A}, \Omega^{sim}) \approx \mathsf{view}_{\mathcal{DRA}}(\mathcal{A}, \Omega^{rea})$.*

Anonymity. This property means that the identity of the sender S is anonymous to the receiver R, which is incomparable with deniability. The fact that the primitive is deniable does not imply that it enjoys anonymity. Indeed, both S and R can deny their participation to the conservation. However, they know each other in the execution of this protocol. Obviously, the property of anonymity is w.r.t. the relationship between the sender S and the receiver R. We formalize the anonymity property below between a challenger $\mathcal{C}$ and an adversary $\mathcal{A}$.

Setup. $\mathcal{C}$ runs Setup to generate ν key pairs $(PK_i, SK_i)_{i=1}^{\nu}$. $\mathcal{A}$ is given the public keys $\mathcal{PK} = \{PK_1, \ldots, PK_\nu\}$. After that, $\mathcal{A}$ outputs a corrupted set $\mathcal{D} \subseteq \{1, \ldots, \nu\}$, for which $\mathcal{A}$ is given $\{SK_i | i \in \mathcal{D}\}$.

Authentication Query. $\mathcal{A}$ can issue authentication queries as it wishes. $\mathcal{A}$ chooses a message m, a ring $\mathcal{R} = \{PK_{j1}, \ldots, PK_{jN}\}$ for each authentication query, where $N > 1$, $PK_i \in \mathcal{R}$ and $\mathcal{R} \subseteq \mathcal{PK}$. Upon this query, $\mathcal{C}$ returns the corresponding authentication transcript tr w.r.t. $(m, \mathcal{R})$ for $\mathcal{A}$ using SK_i.

Anonymity Test. $\mathcal{A}$ can issue this query once with a message m, a ring $\mathcal{R} = \{PK_i | i \in \mathcal{D}\}$ and any two public keys $PK_{i0}, PK_{i1} \in \mathcal{R}$. Consequently, $\mathcal{C}$ takes $b \leftarrow \{0, 1\}$, executes $\lambda_{\mathcal{DRA}}$ to produce the transcript tr with SK_{ib} and returns tr to $\mathcal{A}$.

Finally, $\mathcal{A}$ guesses a bit b' for b. $\mathcal{A}$ is said success if $b' = b$. We use $\mathsf{Succ}_{\mathcal{DRA}}^{anon}(\mathcal{A}, \Omega)$ to denote the success event of $\mathcal{A}$.

Definition 3. *Let $\lambda_{\mathcal{DRA}}$ be a deniable ring authentication protocol. $\lambda_{\mathcal{DRA}}$ is* anonymous *if for any polynomial time adversary $\mathcal{A}$, $\Pr[\mathsf{Succ}_{\mathcal{DRA}}^{anon}(\mathcal{A}, \Omega)] = \frac{1}{2} + negl(\kappa)$ (where κ is the security parameter) is negligible.*

4   Generic Construction

In this section, we give a generic construction of authentication protocol with deniability based on projective hash function. In order to realize the source hiding, we employ the NIWI proof to convince the receiver that the committed value is indeed the output of one $\mathsf{Hash}(\mathsf{hk}_i, \mathcal{L}, c)$ calculated by hk_i without revealing which one. The instantiation of this construction is given in the Appendix A.

4.1 Deniable Ring Authentication Protocol $\lambda_{\mathcal{DRA}}$

The main technical tools are projective hash function and NIWI proof. The formal description is as follows.

For each participant P_i in the system, it obtains the key pair (SK_i, PK_i) by invoking the hashing key generation algorithm HashKG($\mathcal{L}$) and the projection key generation algorithm ProjKG($\text{hk}, \mathcal{L}$) respectively. Specially, the public key of P_i is $PK_i = \text{hp}_i$ and the private key of P_i is $SK_i = \text{hk}_i$. All the public keys can be accessed by anyone.

The sender S authenticates a message $m \in \mathcal{M}$ to the receiver R. S wishes to deny its involvement after executing the authentication. In addition, S also hopes to be anonymous to R during this conversation. S chooses a number of public keys from $\mathcal{PK}$ including its public key PK_S to form set $\mathcal{R}$. That is $\mathcal{R} = \{PK_1, \cdots, PK_S, \cdots, PK_N\}$, where N is the size of the set $\mathcal{R}$. Upon the receipts of $\mathcal{R}$ from S, R begins to interact with S to execute the authentication.

Setup. This algorithm is done by the system. Take $\text{crs} \leftarrow \{0,1\}^{l(\kappa)}$ as the common reference string, where $l(\kappa)$ is polynomial in the security parameter κ.

Key Generation. This algorithm is done by each participant P_i itself. Upon the input of common reference string crs, the hashing key hk and the projection key hp are generated. The private/public keypair of each P_i is $(SK_i, PK_i) = (\text{hk}_i, \text{hp}_i)$.

Deniable Ring Authentication Protocol $\lambda_{\mathcal{DRA}}$.

1. With crs, the set $\mathcal{R} = \{PK_1, \cdots, PK_N\}$, message $m \leftarrow \mathcal{M}$ and NP language $\mathcal{L}$. R picks a word $c \in \mathcal{L}$ with the witness ω, sends $flow_1 = (m, c)$ to the set $\mathcal{R}$.
2. Upon the receipt of (m, c) from R, S first computes the hash value by using the private hashing key hk and the word c, then hides this hash value by a secure commitment scheme COM regarding to Sect. 2.2. Suppose the sender S is the participant P_I, S does as follow:
   - compute $\sigma_I = \text{Hash}(\text{hk}_I, \mathcal{L}, c; m)$ with the word c, the message m and its private key $SK_I = \text{hk}_I$;
   - choose r_I randomly, compute $C_I = \text{COM}(\sigma_I; r_I)$;
   - send $flow_2 = C_I$ to the receiver R.
3. Upon the receipt of the commitment C_I, R reveals ω and sends $flow_3 = \omega$ to the set $\mathcal{R}$.
4. Upon the receipt of ω, S first checks that the value ω is indeed the witness for $c \in \mathcal{L}$:
   - check $\text{ProjHash}(\text{hp}_i, \mathcal{L}, c, \omega; m) \overset{?}{=} \sigma_I$ for $i = I$;
     If this equation holds, S is sure that it can deny successfully later. The following work for S is to convince R that σ_I in the commitment C_I is indeed consistent with one σ_i calculated by R without revealing which σ_i. Thus, S does as follows:
   - compute $\sigma_i = \text{ProjHash}(\text{hp}_i, \mathcal{L}, c, \omega; m)$ for $1 \leq i \leq N$;

- let $\mathcal{L}'$ be an NP language:

$$\mathcal{L}' \triangleq \{(\{\sigma_i\}_{i=1}^N, C_I) \mid \exists \sigma_I \in \{\sigma_i\}_{i=1}^N, \text{ s.t. } C_I = \text{COM}(\sigma_I; r_I)\}$$

let $S_{\text{crs}}(x; (\sigma_I, r_I))$ be an NIWI proof for $x \in \mathcal{L}'$ with witness (σ_I, r_I) under the common reference string crs. Compute $\pi = S_{\text{crs}}((\{\sigma_i\}_{i=1}^N, C_I); (\sigma_I, r_I))$;
- send $flow_4 = \pi$ to the receiver R.

Finally, R computes $\sigma_i = \text{ProjHash}(\text{hp}_i, \mathcal{L}, c, \omega; m)$ for $1 \le i \le N$ and accepts this authentication if $R_{\text{crs}}(\{\sigma_i\}_{i=1}^N, C_I, \pi) = 1$, where $R_{\text{crs}}(\cdot)$ is the verification algorithm for $S_{\text{crs}}(\cdot)$.

Remark 2. The receiver R uses each public key hp_i in $\mathcal{R}$ to calculate the hash values $\{\sigma_i\}_{i=1}^N$. Someone returns one σ_i, which implies he knows the corresponding private key hk_i due to the smoothness of projective hash function, otherwise there exists a distinguisher who can decide the word c belongs to an NP language $\mathcal{L}$ or not. The authentication completes. However, the returned σ_i leaks S's identity, i.e., R can check this σ_i using the corresponding public key hp_i and the witness ω. For S's privacy (source hiding), the returned σ_i must be hidden in the commitment. However, R cannot check the committed σ_i if he cannot open this commitment. Our strategy is to use the NIWI proof for S to convince R that the committed value in C_I indeed equals to exactly one σ_i without opening the commitment. The anonymity follows the perfect hiding of the commitment and the witness indistinguishability of NIWI proof.

5   Security

We analyze the security of protocol $\lambda_{\mathcal{DRA}}$ with the properties of *soundness*, *deniability* and *anonymity* according to the security model in Sect. 3.2.

5.1   Soundness (Unforgeability)

Our deniable ring authentication $\lambda_{\mathcal{DRA}}$ is sound (against forgeability), which means that for $(m, \mathcal{R}, c \in \mathcal{L})$, a member who does not belong to the set $\mathcal{R}$, can not forge an authentication transcript w.r.t. $(m, \mathcal{R}, c \in \mathcal{L})$. Indeed, the adversary has two sides to trick the receiver. The one is to forge an accepted σ_I such that σ_I is exactly one σ_i. However it is impossible due to the smoothness of projective hash function. The another one is to commit a fake value then trick the receiver to accept the NIWI proof π for a forged C_I. However, it does not happen if the commitment scheme is perfect binding and the NIWI proof system is sound.

Theorem 1. *Assume that $\mathcal{L}$ is a hard NP language and the projective hash function over $\mathcal{L}$ is smooth, the commitment scheme COM is with perfect binding and the NIWI proof system is sound, then the deniable ring authentication protocol $\lambda_{\mathcal{DRA}}$ achieves the soundness (unforgeability).*

Proof. Let $\mathcal{A}$ be a probabilistic polynomial time adversary against the soundness of $\lambda_{\mathcal{DRA}}$ and Ω be the soundness game as the definitions in Sect. 3.2. We construct an adversary $\mathcal{A}'$ that, given a word c^*, is able to decide if $c^* \in \mathcal{L}$ or not.

$\mathcal{A}'$ maintains the Setup algorithm of $\lambda_{\mathcal{DRA}}$ to generate ν key pairs $(PK_i, SK_i)_{i=1}^{\nu}$. $\mathcal{A}'$ gives $\mathcal{A}$ the public keys $\mathcal{PK} = \{PK_1, \cdots, PK_\nu\}$ and the corrupted keys $\{SK_i | i \in \mathcal{D}\}$ where $\mathcal{D}$ is a corrupted set as $\mathcal{A}$ asks.

When $\mathcal{A}$ queries an authentication transcript on message m and a set $\mathcal{R} = \{PK_{j1}, \cdots, PK_{jN}\} \subseteq \mathcal{PK}$, $\mathcal{A}'$ chooses a word c for an language $\mathcal{L}$ and prepares $flow_1 = (m, c)$. Since the private keys $\{SK_i\}_{i=1}^{\nu}$ are known to $\mathcal{A}'$, it uses SK_I (where $PK_I \in \mathcal{R}$) to generate $flow_2 = COM(\sigma_I; r_I)$ with randomly chosen r_I. Then $\mathcal{A}'$ queries to its challenger on the witness for $c \in \mathcal{L}$. Upon the receipt of witness ω from challenger, $\mathcal{A}'$ shows $flow_3 = \omega$. Finally, $\mathcal{A}'$ uses the NIWI witness (σ_I, r_I) to produce the NIWI proof π normally. $\mathcal{A}'$'s authentication simulation for $\mathcal{A}$ is perfect.

Finally, $\mathcal{A}$ challenges a forgery on $(m^*, \mathcal{R}^*)$. $\mathcal{A}$ cannot corrupt set $\mathcal{R}^*$ and $(m^*, \mathcal{R}^*)$ was not queried to authentication oracle. $\mathcal{A}$ actives $\mathcal{A}'$ with incoming $(m^*, \mathcal{R}^*)$. $\mathcal{A}'$ uses the given word c^* as the $flow_1$. $\mathcal{A}'$ chooses a random value $\hat{\omega}$ as $flow_3$. This a gap with the real execution. However, $\mathcal{A}$ cannot find the difference unless it can get a correct σ_I such that $\sigma_I = \text{Hash}(\text{hk}_I, \mathcal{L}, c^*; m)$ for $I \in \mathcal{R}^*$ and check $\sigma_I \neq \text{ProjHash}(\text{hp}_I, \mathcal{L}, c^*, \hat{\omega}; m)$. We claim if $\mathcal{A}$ gets such σ_I and aborts it then $\mathcal{A}'$ makes a successful decision that $c^* \in \mathcal{L}$ with non-negligible probability. Since if $c^* \notin \mathcal{L}$, the output of hash value $\text{Hash}(\text{hk}_I, \mathcal{L}, c^*; m)$ is totally random due to the smoothness of the projective hash function. $\mathcal{A}$ can only guess the correct value in this case, which is negligible for $\mathcal{A}$. If this challenge for forgery proceeds, it implies that $\mathcal{A}$ cannot obtain a correct σ_I to find that $\hat{\omega}$ is not consistent with the real witness. Thus $\mathcal{A}$ has to commit a fake hash value in C_I and tries to produces an NIWI proof π for language $\mathcal{L}' = \{(\{\sigma_i\}_{i=1}^{N}, C_I) \mid \exists \sigma_I \in \{\sigma_i\}_{i=1}^{N}, \text{s.t. } C_I = COM(\hat{\sigma}; r_I)\}$. $\mathcal{A}'$ computes σ_i by using the given word c^* and the private keys $SK_i = \text{hk}_i$ for $1 \leq i \leq N$ where $N = |\mathcal{R}^*|$. $\mathcal{A}'$ verifies the validity of π by the common input $(\{\sigma_i\}_{i=1}^{N}, C_I)$. Due to the perfect binding of $COM(\cdot)$, this verification would fail as it conflicts the soundness of the NIWI proof system. Thus, $\Pr[\text{Succ}_{\mathcal{DRA}}^{sd}(\mathcal{A}, \Omega)]$ is negligible. $\square$

5.2 Deniability

We follow the simulation paradigm to show the protocol $\lambda_{\mathcal{DRA}}$ satisfies the deniability. The deniability states that an adversary $\mathcal{A}$ interacts with a simulator $\mathcal{S}$ in the real game Ω^{rea} and the simulation game Ω^{sim}, respectively, however the two views $\text{view}_{\mathcal{DRA}}(\mathcal{A}, \Omega^{rea})$ and $\text{view}_{\mathcal{DRA}}(\mathcal{A}, \Omega^{sim})$ are indistinguishable.

In the real game Ω^{rea}, the simulator $\mathcal{S}$ is provided with $\{PK_i, SK_i\}_{i=1}^{\nu}$. With these secrets, $\mathcal{S}$ follows the real deniable ring authentication protocol $\lambda_{\mathcal{DRA}}$ perfectly to interact with $\mathcal{A}$.

In the simulation game Ω^{sim}, the simulator $\mathcal{S}$ is provided with $\{PK_i\}_{i=1}^{\nu}$ and the corrupted set $\mathcal{D}$. When $(m, \mathcal{R})$ is queried to **Authentication Query**, if $PK_i \in \mathcal{R} \land i \in \mathcal{D}$ for some i, the simulation proceeds normally and $\mathcal{A}$'s view equals the real one. Otherwise, $\mathcal{S}$ simulates the authentication transcript without any secrets. $\mathcal{S}$'s simulation works by the rewinding. That is, after getting $flow_1 = (m, c)$ from the receiver, $\mathcal{S}$ commits to a random value to calculate C_I. Once receiving ω which is revealed by the receiver, $\mathcal{S}$ rewinds the receiver and replaces the correct commitment to ω. The following simulation by $\mathcal{S}$ is normal as it does not need the secret anymore. With the witness ω for the language $\mathcal{L}$, the simulated transcript is statistically indistinguishable from the real one. Therefore, $\text{view}_{\mathcal{DRA}}(\mathcal{A}, \Omega^{rea}) = \text{view}_{\mathcal{DRA}}(\mathcal{A}, \Omega^{sim})$ and the deniability follows.

5.3 Anonymity

The deniability just ensures both the sender S and the receiver R to deny the involvement of the conversation. However, R knows the identity of S during the authentication. The property of anonymity can make sure that S is even anonymous to R during the execution of the authentication protocol. Our anonymity follows that the receiver cannot obtain σ_I from the sender, otherwise the receiver can decide who is taking participate in this conversation by checking that $\sigma_I \stackrel{?}{=}$ ProjHash($\text{hp}_i, \mathcal{L}, c, \omega; m$) for $i = 1, 2, \cdots, I$.

Theorem 2. *Assume that the commitment scheme COM is with perfect hiding and NIWI proof system is witness indistinguishable, then deniable ring authentication protocol $\lambda_{\mathcal{DRA}}$ achieves the anonymity.*

Proof. Let $\mathcal{A}$ be a probabilistic polynomial time adversary against the anonymity of $\lambda_{\mathcal{DRA}}$ and Ω be the anonymity game as the definitions in Sect. 3.2. Let $\mathcal{C}$ be the challenger of $\mathcal{A}$. $\mathcal{C}$ maintains the Setup algorithm to generate key pairs $(PK_i, SK_i)_{i=1}^{\nu}$. $\mathcal{A}$ is given the public key set $\mathcal{PK}$ and a corrupted set $\mathcal{D}$ as it asks.

When $\mathcal{A}$ makes authentication queries, the oracle run by $\mathcal{C}$ returns the corresponding transcripts normally.

When $\mathcal{A}$ challenges the anonymity, it outputs a message m^*, a word c^*, $\mathcal{R}^* = \{PK_i | i \in \mathcal{D}\}$ and any two public keys PK_{i0}, PK_{i1} from $\mathcal{R}^*$. $\mathcal{C}$ takes $b \leftarrow \{0, 1\}$ and generates $\sigma_{ib} = \text{Hash}(\text{hk}_{ib}, \mathcal{L}, c^*; m^*)$. $\mathcal{C}$ randomly chooses r_b to compute $C^* = COM(\sigma_{ib}; r_b)$. Finally, $\mathcal{C}$ produces an NIWI proof $\pi^* = \mathcal{C}_{\text{crs}}(\{\sigma_i\}_{i=1}^{N}, C^*; (\sigma_{ib}, r_b))$. However, for the challenge transcript (C^*, π^*), $\mathcal{A}$ has no obvious advantage to guess the right b. The reason is that COM is a commitment scheme with perfect hiding. The commitment C^* can be rewritten as $C^* = COM(\sigma_{i(1-b)}; r_{1-b})$ with the trapdoor. π^* is an NIWI proof with witness indistinguishability such that $\pi^* = \mathcal{C}_{\text{crs}}(\{\sigma_i\}_{i=1}^{N}, C^*; (\sigma_{i(b-1)}, r_{b-1}))$ is also an accepted proof. Therefore, $\Pr[\text{Succ}_{\mathcal{DRA}}^{anon}(\mathcal{A}, \Omega)] = \frac{1}{2} + negl(\kappa)$. $\square$

6 Performance

6.1 Comparison in Performance

We compare the protocol $\lambda_{\mathcal{DRA}}$ to those related deniable ring authentications such as Naor's scheme [16], Dowsley's scheme [10] and Zeng's scheme [22].

Note that there are also some non-interactive deniable ring authentication protocols which are efficient. However, the deniability of these schemes does not follow the zero-knowledge, hence only achieve the weak deniability. They are beyond the scope of this comparison. We compare these schemes according to the sides of computation and communication.

Computation. Review Naor's scheme first. In this proposal, the receiver R encrypts the message m concatenated with a random value r with N public keys respectively. It contains N encryptions in this step. If the encryption is implemented with Diffie-Hellman based scheme, $\mathcal{O}(N)$ exponentiations are required. Then the sender S decrypts one ciphertext to get r and executes N encryptions again. In the final step, S and R should verify N encryptions, respectively.

Dowsley's scheme uses the broadcast encryption as the building block to present the deniable ring authentication. The symmetric key K is encrypted under the broadcast encryption first, then an one-time symmetric key encryption is used to encrypt the message under K. Due to the property of broadcast encryption, it just requires $\mathcal{O}(1)$ exponentiation to perform in this step. Then S should execute 2 pairings to check the consistency of the encrypted messages, 2 pairings to decrypt, 1 symmetric decryption, $\mathcal{O}(1)$ exponentiation broadcast encryption and 1 symmetric encryption. Finally, both S and R perform $\mathcal{O}(1)$ exponentiation broadcast re-encryption.

Zeng's scheme was built on the multi-receiver encryption. R uses it to encrypt the authentication key k. In this step, it requires $\mathcal{O}(N)$ exponentiations and 1 pairing. Then S performs $\mathcal{O}(N)$ pairings to check the consistency of the N ciphertexts and to get k to complete the authentication.

Our protocol $\lambda_{\mathcal{DRA}}$ can be implemented by employing a smooth projective hash function under the DDH assumption, see the Appendix A. In this case, the receiver R needs $\mathcal{O}(1)$ computation cost to choose the word $c \in \mathcal{L}$ in the first round. Then $\mathcal{O}(1)$ computation cost is required for S to compute the hash value and the commitment in the next round. In the third round, R just needs to show the witness and hence no computation is required in this round. Finally, S and R perform a non-interactive witness indistinguishable proof. This can be instantiated by the Groth-Sahai NIWI proof system [13] with asymmetric bilinear map, see the Appendix A. In this case, it requires $\mathcal{O}(N)$ computation for S and R respectively to execute an NIWI proof. Note that, σ_i can be pre-computed by R in advance.

Communication. Naor's scheme needs to send N ciphertexts or random bits in *each* round. This is the major burden. Moreover, it requires 6 rounds to realize deniable ring authentication in the presence of big brother, which means all the private keys are revealed, inefficient.

Due to the broadcast encryption, the communication cost of Dowsley's scheme is ideal as it is just the constant communication size. Moreover, the broadcast encryption is verifiable, it does not need 2 more rounds (compared to Naor's scheme) to realize anonymity in the presence of big brother. However, broadcast encryption requires to generate the members' private keys by the third party. Therefore, sending out the private keys to the members is the extra cost. It requires the high-level secure channel, which is the underlying expense.

Zeng's scheme is only 2 rounds as it does not need the receiver to reveal the witness which is used to simulate. However, it is based on the Diffie-Hellman Knowledge assumption to reach the deniability, which is a strong assumption.

Our protocol $\lambda_{\mathcal{DRA}}$ follows the black-box simulation, thus it has 4 communication rounds. Unlike Naor's scheme, the communication size in the first three rounds is just constant. Only in the last round, it needs to send $\mathcal{O}(N)$ size message to complete the NIWI proof. The anonymity holds even each member reveals its private key due to the witness-indistinguishability of NIWI proof, hence it also remains anonymity in the presence of big brother with 4 rounds.

6.2   Security Requirement

For the construction of the deniable ring authentication protocol $\lambda_{\mathcal{DRA}}$, we hope the security requirement of the building block is minimum. Therefore, it is significant to seek a weaker form for the underlying building blocks for the practical reason. As we know, most deniable ring authentications are built on the encryption paradigm, which encrypts a MAC key to authenticate messages. The soundness of such constructions requires the underlying encryptions are CCA secure at least. For example, Naor's scheme [16] and Dowsley's scheme [10] require the underlying encryption schemes are CCA2 secure, and in Zeng's scheme [22] the underlying multi-receiver encryption is even plaintext-aware.

Our deniable ring authentication protocol $\lambda_{\mathcal{DRA}}$ is built on the specific properties (*projection* and *smoothness*) of projective hash function other than encryption paradigm. In other words, the soundness of protocol $\lambda_{\mathcal{DRA}}$ just depends on the smoothness of projective hash function, the perfect binding of commitment and soundness of NIWI proofs. Factually, the underlying building block is not necessarily CCA secure.

7   Conclusion

We present a new construction of deniable authentication with source hiding based on the projective hash function. Differing from the encryption paradigm schemes, our protocol does not require the underlying scheme to satisfy CCA secure. Our source-hiding property is achieved through a ring scheme. However, it does not require sending $\mathcal{O}(N)$ size message in each round. The instantiation of our scheme (in the Appendix A) can be realized under the standard assumptions.

Acknowledgments. This work is supported by the National Natural Science Foundation of China (61402376, U1433130), the Open Research Subject of Key Laboratory of Digital Space Security (szjj2014-078) and the Ministry of Education "chunhui plan" (Z2016150).

A   Instantiation of Protocol $\lambda_{\mathcal{DRA}}$

Setup. Choose two safe primes p, q and compute $n = pq$. Let $\mathbb{G}, \mathbb{H}, \mathbb{G}_{\mathbb{H}}$ be three multiplicative cyclic groups of order n that are associated to a non-degenerate bilinear pairing $\hat{e} : \mathbb{G} \times \mathbb{H} \rightarrow \mathbb{G}_{\mathbb{H}}$. Let g_1 and h_1 be the generators of $\mathbb{G}$ and $\mathbb{H}$, respectively. Choose $\mu_1, \mu_2, \mu_3 \leftarrow \mathbb{Z}_n$ and set $\eta = g_1^{\mu_1}$, $g_2 = g_1^{\mu_2}$, $h_2 = h_1^{\mu_3}$. Choose a collision-free hash function $H : \{0, 1\}^* \rightarrow \mathbb{Z}_n$. The common reference string $\mathrm{crs} = (n, \mathbb{G}, \mathbb{H}, \mathbb{G}_{\mathbb{H}}, \hat{e}, g_1, \eta, g_2, h_1, h_2, H)$ is the output of the algorithm **Setup**.

Key Generation. Choose $x_i, y_i \leftarrow \mathbb{Z}_n$, set $SK_i = \mathrm{hk}_i = (x_i, y_i)$, $PK_i = \mathrm{hp}_i = g_1^{x_i} \eta^{y_i}$. All the public keys $PK_1, PK_2, \cdots, PK_\nu$ are accessible by anyone.

Deniable Ring Authentication Protocol $\lambda_{\mathcal{DRA}}$.

1. With the set $\mathcal{R} = \{PK_1, \cdots, PK_N\}$ and message $m \leftarrow \mathcal{M}$, R picks a word $c \in \mathcal{L}$ with the witness $\omega \leftarrow \mathbb{Z}_n$, such that the language $\mathcal{L} = \{c | \exists \omega, c = (c_1, c_2) = (g_1^\omega, \eta^\omega)\}$. R sends $flow_1 = (m, c)$ to the set $\mathcal{R}$.
2. Upon the receipt of (m, c) from R, S computes as follows. Suppose the sender S is the participant P_I.
   - compute $\sigma_I = \mathrm{Hash}(\mathrm{hk}_I, \mathcal{L}, c; m) = (g_1^{\omega H(m)})^{x_I} (\eta^{\omega H(m)})^{y_I}$;
   - choose $r_I \leftarrow \mathbb{Z}_n$ randomly, compute $C_I = \mathrm{COM}(\sigma_I; r_I) = \sigma_I \cdot g_2^{r_I}$;
   - send $flow_2 = C_I$ to the receiver R.
3. Upon the receipt of the commitment C_I, R reveals the witness ω and sends $flow_3 = \omega$ to the set $\mathcal{R}$.
4. Upon the receipt of ω, S first checks that the value ω is indeed the witness for $c \in \mathcal{L}$:
   - check $\mathrm{ProjHash}(\mathrm{hp}_i, \mathcal{L}, c, \omega; m) \overset{?}{=} \sigma_I$ for $i = I$.
     If this equation holds, the following work for S is to prove for R that σ_I in the commitment C_I is indeed consistent with one σ_i calculated by R without revealing which σ_i. Thus, S does as follow:
   - for $i \neq I$, choose $t_i \leftarrow \mathbb{Z}_n$, compute $G_i = g_2^{t_i}$, $H_i = h_2^{t_i}$, $\pi_i^G = (g_1^{-1} g_2^{t_i})^{t_i}$ and $\theta_i^H = (h_1^{-1} h_2^{t_i})^{t_i}$;
   - for $i = I$, compute $t_I = -\sum_{i \neq I} t_i$, $G_I = g_1 g_2^{t_I}$, $H_I = h_1 h_2^{t_I}$, $\pi_I^G = (g_1 g_2^{t_I})^{t_I}$, $\theta_I^H = (h_1 h_2^{t_I})^{t_I}$;
   - for $1 \leq i \leq N$, compute $\sigma_i = \mathrm{ProjHash}(\mathrm{hp}_i, \mathcal{L}, c, \omega; m) = (g_1^{x_i} \eta^{y_i})^{H(m)\omega}$ and $\pi = g_1^{t_I} \cdot \prod_{i=1}^N (\sigma_i g_2^{t_i})^{t_i}$, $\theta = h_1^{t_I - r_I}$;
   - send $flow_4 = (\{G_i, H_i, \pi_i^G, \theta_i^H\}_{i=1}^N, \pi, \theta)$ to the receiver R.

Finally, R computes $\sigma_i = \mathrm{ProjHash}(\mathrm{hp}_i, \mathcal{L}, c, \omega; m) = (g_1^{x_i} \eta^{y_i})^{H(m)\omega}$ for $1 \leq i \leq N$ and accepts this authentication to m if

- $\hat{e}(G_i, H_i h_1^{-1}) \cdot \hat{e}(G_i g_1^{-1}, H_i) = \hat{e}(\pi_i^G, h_2) \cdot \hat{e}(g_2, \theta_i^H)$ for $1 \leq i \leq N$;
- $\prod_{i=1}^N G_i = g_1$;
- $\prod_{i=1}^N H_i = h_1$;
- $\prod_{i=1}^N \hat{e}(\sigma_i G_i, H_i) = \hat{e}(C_I g_1, h_1) \cdot \hat{e}(\pi, h_2) \cdot \hat{e}(g_2, \theta)$.

Due to the space limitation, the details on the security arguments of this instantiation will be given in the full version of this paper.

References

1. Abdalla, M., Benhamouda, F., Blazy, O., Chevalier, C., Pointcheval, D.: SPHF-friendly non-interactive commitments. In: Sako, K., Sarkar, P. (eds.) ASIACRYPT 2013. LNCS, vol. 8269, pp. 214–234. Springer, Heidelberg (2013). doi:10.1007/978-3-642-42033-7_12

2. Abdalla, M., Benhamouda, F., Pointcheval, D.: Public-key encryption indistinguishable under plaintext-checkable attacks. IET Inf. Secur. **10**(6), 288–303 (2016)

3. Benhamouda, F., Blazy, O., Chevalier, C., Pointcheval, D., Vergnaud, D.: New techniques for SPHFs and efficient one-round pake protocols. In: Canetti, R., Garay, J.A. (eds.) CRYPTO 2013. LNCS, vol. 8042, pp. 449–475. Springer, Heidelberg (2013). doi:10.1007/978-3-642-40041-4_25

4. Boneh, D., Naor, M.: Timed commitments. In: Bellare, M. (ed.) CRYPTO 2000. LNCS, vol. 1880, pp. 236–254. Springer, Heidelberg (2000). doi:10.1007/3-540-44598-6_15

5. Chen, R., Mu, Y., Yang, G., Guo, F., Wang, X.: Dual-server public-key encryption with keyword search for secure cloud storage. IEEE Trans. Inf. Forensics Secur. **11**(4), 789–798 (2016)

6. Cramer, R., Shoup, V.: Universal hash proofs and a paradigm for adaptive chosen ciphertext secure public-key encryption. In: Knudsen, L.R. (ed.) EUROCRYPT 2002. LNCS, vol. 2332, pp. 45–64. Springer, Heidelberg (2002). doi:10.1007/3-540-46035-7_4

7. Damgård, I.: Towards practical public key systems secure against chosen ciphertext attacks. In: Feigenbaum, J. (ed.) CRYPTO 1991. LNCS, vol. 576, pp. 445–456. Springer, Heidelberg (1992). doi:10.1007/3-540-46766-1_36

8. Diffie, W., Hellman, M.E.: New directions in cryptography. IEEE Trans. Inf. Theor. **22**(6), 644–654 (1976)

9. Dolev, D., Dwork, C., Naor, M.: Nonmalleable cryptography. SIAM J. Comput. **30**(2), 391–437 (2000)

10. Dowsley, R., Hanaoka, G., Imai, H., Nascimento, A.C.A.: Round-optimal deniable ring authentication in the presence of big brother. In: Chung, Y., Yung, M. (eds.) WISA 2010. LNCS, vol. 6513, pp. 307–321. Springer, Heidelberg (2011). doi:10.1007/978-3-642-17955-6_23

11. Dwork, C., Naor, M., Sahai, A.: Concurrent zero-knowledge. J. ACM **51**(6), 851–898 (2004)

12. Gennaro, R.: Multi-trapdoor commitments and their applications to proofs of knowledge secure under concurrent man-in-the-middle attacks. In: Franklin, M. (ed.) CRYPTO 2004. LNCS, vol. 3152, pp. 220–236. Springer, Heidelberg (2004). doi:10.1007/978-3-540-28628-8_14

13. Groth, J., Sahai, A.: Efficient non-interactive proof systems for bilinear groups. In: Smart, N. (ed.) EUROCRYPT 2008. LNCS, vol. 4965, pp. 415–432. Springer, Heidelberg (2008). doi:10.1007/978-3-540-78967-3_24

14. Jiang, S.: Timed encryption with application to deniable key exchange. Theor. Comput. Sci. **560**, 172–189 (2014)

15. Jiang, S., Safavi-Naini, R.: An efficient deniable key exchange protocol (Extended Abstract). In: Tsudik, G. (ed.) FC 2008. LNCS, vol. 5143, pp. 47–52. Springer, Heidelberg (2008). doi:10.1007/978-3-540-85230-8_4

16. Naor, M.: Deniable ring authentication. In: Yung, M. (ed.) CRYPTO 2002. LNCS, vol. 2442, pp. 481–498. Springer, Heidelberg (2002). doi:10.1007/3-540-45708-9_31

17. Pass, R.: On deniability in the common reference string and random oracle model. In: Boneh, D. (ed.) CRYPTO 2003. LNCS, vol. 2729, pp. 316–337. Springer, Heidelberg (2003). doi:10.1007/978-3-540-45146-4_19
18. Raimondo, M.D., Gennaro, R.: New approaches for deniable authentication. J. Cryptology **22**(4), 572–615 (2009)
19. Raimondo, M.D., Gennaro, R., Krawczyk, H.: Deniable authentication and key exchange. In: Proceedings of the 13th ACM Conference on Computer and Communications Security, CCS 2006, Alexandria, VA, USA, October 30–3 November 2006, pp. 400–409. ACM (2006)
20. Yao, A.C., Zhao, Y.: OAKE: a new family of implicitly authenticated diffie-hellman protocols. In: 2013 ACM SIGSAC Conference on Computer and Communications Security, CCS 2013, Berlin, Germany, 4–8 November 2013, pp. 1113–1128. ACM (2013)
21. Yao, A.C., Zhao, Y.: Privacy-preserving authenticated key-exchange over internet. IEEE Trans. Inf. Forensics Secur. **9**(1), 125–140 (2014)
22. Zeng, S., Chen, Y., Tan, S., He, M.: Concurrently deniable ring authentication and its application to LBS in vanets. Peer-to-Peer Netw. Appl. **10**(4), 844–856 (2017)

Authenticated Encryption and Key Exchange

INT-RUP Security of Checksum-Based Authenticated Encryption

Ping Zhang[1]([✉]), Peng Wang[2], Honggang Hu[1]([✉]), Changsong Cheng[3],
and Wenke Kuai[4]

[1] Key Laboratory of Electromagnetic Space Information, CAS,
University of Science and Technology of China, Hefei 230027, China
zgp@mail.ustc.edu.cn, hghu2005@ustc.edu.cn
[2] State Key Laboratory of Information Security,
Institute of Information Engineering, CAS, Beijing 100049, China
wp@is.ac.cn
[3] Network Security Research and Development Center,
The Third Research Institute of Ministry of Public Security,
Shanghai 200031, China
[4] Information and Communication Branch,
State Grid Anhui Electric Power Company, Hefei 230061, China
1037789458@qq.com

Abstract. Offset codebook mode (OCB) provides neither integrity under releasing unverified plaintext (INT-RUP) nor nonce-misuse resistance. The tag of OCB is generated by encrypting a plaintext checksum, which is vulnerable in the INT-RUP security model. This paper focuses on the weakness of the checksum processing in OCB. We describe a new type of structure, called plaintext and ciphertext checksum (PCC), which is a generalization of the plaintext checksum, and prove that all authenticated encryption schemes with PCC are insecure in the INT-RUP security model. Then, we fix the weakness of PCC and present another new type of structure, called intermediate checksum (IC), to generate the authentication tag. To settle the INT-RUP security of OCB in the nonce-misuse setting, we provide a modified OCB scheme based on IC, called OCB-IC. OCB-IC is proven INT-RUP secure up to the birthday bound in the nonce-misuse setting if the underlying tweakable blockcipher is a secure mixed tweakable pseudorandom permutation (MTPRP). Finally, we present some discussions about OCB-IC.

Keywords: Authenticated Encryption · INT-RUP · Nonce-misuse · Checksum · Tweakable Blockcipher

1 Introduction

Authenticated encryption (AE) is a cryptographic scheme, which provides privacy and authenticity concurrently. In classical security models, a conventional AE scheme consists of an encryption algorithm and a decryption algorithm. The

© Springer International Publishing AG 2017
T. Okamoto et al. (Eds.): ProvSec 2017, LNCS 10592, pp. 147–166, 2017.
https://doi.org/10.1007/978-3-319-68637-0_9

decryption algorithm includes two phases: plaintext computing and integrity verification. The plaintext corresponding to the ciphertext is released only if the tag is successfully verified. However, in some special settings, it is desirable to release unverified plaintext before verification. This case occurs when lightweight environments and low-end devices, such as smart cards, have not enough memory to store the entire plaintext, or when the decrypted plaintext needs to be processed in real time. What's more, releasing unverified plaintext improves the efficiency of certain applications. For example, the decryption algorithm of Encrypt-then-MAC composition [6] has two stages: the first stage verifies the MAC, and the second stage decrypts the ciphertext and obtains the corresponding plaintext. If this AE scheme is secure against the release of unverified plaintext, then a single stage (the second stage) would be sufficient for the decryption algorithm. Moreover, even if the attacker can not observe the unverified plaintext directly, it could find some certain properties of the plaintext by side channel attacks, such as [8,26]. As shown by Paterson and AlFardan [2,21] for TLS and DTLS, it is very difficult to prevent an attacker from learning the cause of decryption failures.

The issue of releasing unverified plaintext has lead to in-depth discussions in the CAESAR competition. For several AE schemes, such as IACBC [16], IAPM [16], OCB1 [25], OCB2 [23], OCB3 [17], vOCB [22], TAE [18,19], COPA [3], AEGIS [27], and ALE [7], the unverified plaintext obtained in the plaintext computing stage cannot be released. Note that releasing unverified plaintext does not imply omitting verification. Verification is essential to prevent incorrect plaintexts from being accepted. In this paper, we consider the security in this scenario where the attacker can observe the unverified plaintext, or any information relating to it, before the verification algorithm is completed. Andreeva et al. addressed the issue of releasing unverified plaintext, and formalized it as the RUP setting. In their paper [4], they provided two new notions called PA (Plaintext Awareness) and INT-RUP (Integrity under Releasing Unverified Plaintext). In the RUP setting, an adversary can obtain the unverified plaintexts resulting from decryption queries. On the one hand, for privacy, they proposed using both IND-CPA and PA. At the heart of PA notion is a plaintext extractor. The plaintext extractor is a stateful algorithm with the goal of mimicking the decryption oracle in order to fool the adversary. It cannot make encryption nor decryption queries, and does not know the secret key. An AE scheme achieves PA if it is infeasible to distinguish the decryption oracle from the plaintext extractor. On the other hand, an AE scheme is INT-RUP secure if an adversary can not generate a fresh valid ciphertext-tag pair given the additional power of access to an unverified decryption oracle, after the encryption oracle. There exist some related works about the security of AE schemes in the RUP setting, such as [9,10,28].

Problem Statement. The nonce-respecting AE schemes (such as OCB [17,23, 25], GCM [11], CCM [12], mCCM [14], OKH [1]) require that all nonces used in the encryption queries are distinct, while the nonce-misuse resistant AE schemes (such as COPA [3], McOE-G [13]) do not. The privacy and integrity of OCB are insecure in the nonce-misuse and RUP settings. For OCB, Andreeva et al. [4] also showed how to construct a forgery in the INT-RUP security model. The tag of OCB is generated by encrypting a XOR-sum of the plaintext blocks (plaintext checksum), which results in attacks in the RUP setting. As the plaintext and ciphertext blocks can be obtained by the adversary in the RUP setting, the adversary can forge the same checksum by changing some plaintext or ciphertext blocks. In their paper [4], they left fixing OCB to be INT-RUP in an efficient way as an open problem.

Our Contributions. This paper mainly considers the INT-RUP security of OCB in the nonce-misuse setting. We focus on the weakness of the checksum processing in OCB. The checksum of OCB is generated by the XOR-sum of the plaintext blocks, which is vulnerable in the INT-RUP security model. Then we describe a new type of structure, called plaintext and ciphertext checksum (PCC), which is a generalization of the plaintext checksum. It is very easy for an adversary to forge the same checksum by changing some plaintext or ciphertext blocks. Therefore, all authenticated encryption schemes, if their tag is generated by encrypting the XOR-sum of the plaintext and ciphertext blocks, are insecure in the INT-RUP security model. If an adversary $\mathcal{A}$ makes one encryption query, p decryption queries, and one forgery attempt, each consisting of l blocks of n bits, then the adversary makes a successful forgery with high probability (at least $1 - 2^{n-ld}$) by solving a system of linear equations in $GF(2)$ with n equations and $ld \geq n$ unknowns, where $d = \lceil \log_2 p \rceil$.

To fix the weakness of PCC, we provide another new type of structure, called intermediate checksum (IC), to generate the authentication tag. In the AE schemes with IC, the internal states in the encryption algorithm are hidden from adversaries, and the intermediate checksum obtained by the XOR-sum of internal states is again encrypted once or many times before being output, which guarantees no information leakage, except the collisions of the last block encryptions for authentication. Based on the IC structure, we propose a modified OCB scheme with IC, called OCB-IC, to settle the INT-RUP security of OCB in the nonce-misuse setting. OCB-IC inherits the advantages of OCB. We prove that OCB-IC is INT-RUP secure up to the birthday bound of $n/2$-bit security in the nonce-misuse setting if the underlying tweakable blockcipher (TBC) is a secure mixed tweakable pseudorandom permutation (MTPRP), where n is the block-size of the underlying TBC. In this paper, we do not settle the problem of privacy in the RUP setting. OCB-IC is PA insecure.

For each plaintext block of OCB-IC, the underlying TBC is invoked twice. Therefore, the rate of OCB-IC is $1/2$. Compared with OCB (rate $= 1$), the efficiency of OCB-IC is about half of it, but OCB-IC provides INT-RUP security. In other words, OCB-IC compromises the efficiency of the software and hardware implementations to achieve INT-RUP security. Compared with CCM [12], the efficiency of OCB-IC is better as CCM is a two-pass AE scheme. The related results are shown in Table 1. OCB-IC is a TBC-based one-pass parallelizable AE scheme. If this underlying TBC is instantiated by an AES and the XEX* construction, we will obtain a blockcipher-based provably secure instance, which is presented in Appendix.

Table 1. Comparison of properties among CCM [12], OCB [17,23,25], and OCB-IC.

Scheme	Rate	Structure type	INT-RUP	References
CCM	1/2	Two-pass	$\checkmark$	[4,12]
OCB	1	PCC (One-pass)	×	[4,17,23,25]
OCB-IC	1/2	IC (One-pass)	$\checkmark$	This Paper

In [9], Chakraborti et al. left it as an interesting open problem to find a property that makes "rate-1/2" AE schemes INT-RUP secure. Our works find a new structure IC, which will provide a new direction for settling the security of "rate < 1" AE schemes in the RUP setting. We believe that one can further extend it for any "rate < 1".

Organizations of This Paper. Notations and some preliminaries are presented in Sect. 2. In Sect. 3, we describe the INT-RUP security model of AE. In Sect. 4, we provide our main works. Finally, this paper ends up with a conclusion in Sect. 5.

2   Preliminaries

Notations. Let ϵ denote the empty string, and $\{0,1\}^*$ denote the set containing all finite bit strings (including ϵ). Let n be an integer, and $(\{0,1\}^n)^+$ be the set of all strings whose lengths are positive multiples of n bits. For a finite string x, $|x|$ stands for its length. For two finite strings x and y, let $x\|y$ or xy denote the concatenation of them. If X is a set, then $x \xleftarrow{\$} X$ is a value randomly chosen from X, and $|X|$ stands for the number of elements in X. Let $\varnothing$ be the empty set whose cardinality is 0. Let $\lceil \cdot \rceil$ be the operation that rounds up to an integer. Denote $Pr[\mathbf{A}|\mathbf{B}]$ as the conditional probability of event $\mathbf{A}$ given event $\mathbf{B}$.

Finite Field. Given a basis, the finite field $GF(2^n)$ can be viewed as the set $\{0,1\}^n$. For an n-bit string $a = a_{n-1} \cdots a_1 a_0 \in \{0,1\}^n$, we can define a polynomial $a(x) \in \mathbb{Z}[x]$ by $a(x) = a_{n-1}x^{n-1} + \cdots + a_1 x + a_0 \in GF(2^n)$. Hence, any integer between 0 and $2^n - 1$ can also be viewed as a polynomial with binary coefficients of degree at most $n-1$. The addition in the field $GF(2^n)$ is the addition of polynomials over $GF(2)$. We denote this operation by bitwise XOR, such as $a \oplus b$, where $a, b \in GF(2^n)$. To define multiplication in the field $GF(2^n)$, we need an irreducible polynomial $f(x)$ of degree n over $GF(2)$. The multiplication of two elements $A, B \in GF(2^n)$ is defined as the polynomial multiplication over $GF(2)$ reduced modulo $f(x)$, that is $A(x)B(x) \bmod f(x)$. We use point doubling (multiply $a \in \{0,1\}^n$ by 2) and XOR operations to compute the multiplication in actual operation, such as $3a = 2a \oplus a$.

Block Ciphers and Tweakable Blockciphers. A block cipher $E : \mathcal{K} \times \{0,1\}^n \to \{0,1\}^n$ is a function that inputs a key $K \in \mathcal{K}$ and a plaintext

$P \in \{0,1\}^n$, and produces a ciphertext $C = E(K,P)$, where $\mathcal{K}$ is a finite nonempty set and $n \geq 1$ is a number. For any $K \in \mathcal{K}$, $E_K(\cdot) = E(K,\cdot)$ is a permutation over $\{0,1\}^n$ and its inverse is $D_K = E_K^{-1}$. A tweakable blockcipher (TBC) $\widetilde{E} : \mathcal{K} \times \mathcal{T} \times \{0,1\}^n \to \{0,1\}^n$ is a function that takes a key $K \in \mathcal{K}$, a tweak $T \in \mathcal{T}$, and a plaintext $P \in \{0,1\}^n$ as inputs, and produces a ciphertext $C = E(K,T,P)$, where $\mathcal{K}$ and n are defined as above, and $\mathcal{T}$ is a finite nonempty set. For any $K \in \mathcal{K}$, $T \in \mathcal{T}$, $\widetilde{E}_K^T(\cdot) = \widetilde{E}_K(T,\cdot) = \widetilde{E}(K,T,\cdot)$ is a permutation over $\{0,1\}^n$ and its inverse is $\widetilde{D}_K = \widetilde{E}_K^{-1}$. Here n is called the blocksize, $\mathcal{K}$ is called the key space, $\mathcal{T}$ is called the tweak space.

Let $Perm(n)$ be the set of all permutations on n bits. Let $Perm(\mathcal{T},n)$ be the set of all mappings from $\mathcal{T}$ to permutations on n bits. Then $\pi \xleftarrow{\$} Perm(n)$ stands for a permutation randomly chosen from $Perm(n)$, and $\widetilde{\pi} \xleftarrow{\$} Perm(\mathcal{T},n)$ stands for a random permutation $\widetilde{\pi}(T,\cdot) = \widetilde{\pi}^T(\cdot)$ on $\{0,1\}^n$ for each $T \in \mathcal{T}$.

An adversary is a probabilistic algorithm with access to certain oracles. Let $\mathcal{A}^O \Rightarrow 1$ be the event that an adversary $\mathcal{A}$ outputs 1 after interacting with the oracle O. Suppose that $E : \mathcal{K} \times \{0,1\}^n \to \{0,1\}^n$ is a block cipher, and $\widetilde{E} : \mathcal{K} \times \mathcal{T} \times \{0,1\}^n \to \{0,1\}^n$ is a TBC.

(1) Let $\mathcal{A}$ be an adversary with access to an encryption oracle, $K \xleftarrow{\$} \mathcal{K}, \pi \xleftarrow{\$} Perm(n)$, and $\widetilde{\pi} \xleftarrow{\$} Perm(\mathcal{T},n)$, then the advantages of $\mathcal{A}$ against E and $\widetilde{E}$ are respectively defined as

$$Adv_E^{prp}(\mathcal{A}) = Pr[\mathcal{A}^{E_K(\cdot)} \Rightarrow 1] - Pr[\mathcal{A}^{\pi(\cdot)} \Rightarrow 1],$$
$$Adv_{\widetilde{E}}^{\widetilde{prp}}(\mathcal{A}) = Pr[\mathcal{A}^{\widetilde{E}_K(\cdot,\cdot)} \Rightarrow 1] - Pr[\mathcal{A}^{\widetilde{\pi}(\cdot,\cdot)} \Rightarrow 1],$$

where the probabilities are taken over the random coins used by the oracles and also over internal coins of $\mathcal{A}$, if any.

(2) Let $\mathcal{A}$ be an adversary with access to both encryption and decryption oracles, $K \xleftarrow{\$} \mathcal{K}, \pi \xleftarrow{\$} Perm(n)$, and $\widetilde{\pi} \xleftarrow{\$} Perm(\mathcal{T},n)$, then the advantages of $\mathcal{A}$ against E and $\widetilde{E}$ are respectively defined as

$$Adv_E^{sprp}(\mathcal{A}) = Pr[\mathcal{A}^{E_K^\pm(\cdot)} \Rightarrow 1] - Pr[\mathcal{A}^{\pi^\pm(\cdot)} \Rightarrow 1],$$
$$Adv_{\widetilde{E}}^{\widetilde{sprp}}(\mathcal{A}) = Pr[\mathcal{A}^{\widetilde{E}_K^\pm(\cdot,\cdot)} \Rightarrow 1] - Pr[\mathcal{A}^{\widetilde{\pi}^\pm(\cdot,\cdot)} \Rightarrow 1],$$

where the probabilities are taken over the random coins used by the oracles and also over internal coins of $\mathcal{A}$, if any.

If $Adv_E^{prp}(\mathcal{A})$ or $Adv_E^{sprp}(\mathcal{A})$ is negligible, the underlying block cipher E_K is a secure pseudorandom permutation (PRP) or strong PRP (SPRP). If $Adv_{\widetilde{E}}^{\widetilde{prp}}(\mathcal{A})$ or $Adv_{\widetilde{E}}^{\widetilde{sprp}}(\mathcal{A})$ is negligible, the underlying TBC $\widetilde{E}_K$ is a secure tweakable PRP (TPRP) or strong TPRP (STPRP). If the resources used by adversaries are at most R, we define the maximum advantage as $Adv(R) = max_{\mathcal{A}} Adv(\mathcal{A})$, where the resources include the running time t, the total of oracle queries q, the maximum block-length l, and the totally number of invoking the underlying primitive in all queries (the query complexity) σ.

Constructions of Blockcipher-based TBCs. Given a block cipher $E : \mathcal{K} \times \{0,1\}^n \rightarrow \{0,1\}^n$ and a secret mask Δ, let $\mathcal{T} = \{0,1\}^n \times \mathcal{I} \times \mathcal{J}$ be a tweak space, $\mathcal{I}$ be a set of tuples of large integers, and $\mathcal{J}$ be a set of tuples of small integers, we obtain a TBC $\widetilde{E} : \mathcal{K} \times \mathcal{T} \times \{0,1\}^n \rightarrow \{0,1\}^n$ by the XEX* construction:

$$\widetilde{E}_K^{N,i,j}(x) = E_K(x \oplus \Delta) \text{ and } \widetilde{E}_K^{N,i',j'}(x) = E_K(x \oplus \Delta') \oplus \Delta'$$

where $(N,i,j) \in \mathcal{T}_0$, $(N,i',j') \in \mathcal{T}_1$, $\mathcal{T}_0 \cap \mathcal{T}_1 = \varnothing$, $\mathcal{T}_0 \cup \mathcal{T}_1 = \mathcal{T}$, and $\Delta = 2^i 3^j L$, $\Delta' = 2^{i'} 3^{j'} L$, $L = E_K(N)$.

Let $\mathcal{A}$ be an adversary which makes an encryption query for tweaks from $\mathcal{T}_0$ and makes encryption and decryption queries for tweaks from $\mathcal{T}_1$. Let $K \xleftarrow{\$} \mathcal{K}$, $\widetilde{\pi} \xleftarrow{\$} Perm(\mathcal{T}_0, n)$, and $\widetilde{\pi}^{\pm 1} \xleftarrow{\$} Perm(\mathcal{T}_1, n)$. Then the advantage of $\mathcal{A}$ against $\widetilde{E} = XEX^*[E, 2^{\mathcal{I}} 3^{\mathcal{J}}]$ is defined as

$$Adv_{\widetilde{E}}^{\widetilde{mprp}}(\mathcal{A}) = Pr[\mathcal{A}^{\widetilde{E}_K(\cdot), \widetilde{E}_K^{\pm 1}(\cdot, \cdot)} \Rightarrow 1] - Pr[\mathcal{A}^{\widetilde{\pi}(\cdot), \widetilde{\pi}^{\pm 1}(\cdot, \cdot)} \Rightarrow 1],$$

where the probabilities are taken over the random coins used by the oracles and also over internal coins of $\mathcal{A}$, if any. If the advantage $Adv_{\widetilde{E}}^{\widetilde{mprp}}(\mathcal{A})$ is negligible, the underlying TBC $\widetilde{E}_K$ is a secure mixed tweakable pseudorandom permutation (MTPRP). The definition of MTPRP matches TPRP if $(\mathcal{T}_0, \mathcal{T}_1) = (\mathcal{T}, \varnothing)$ and STPRP if $(\mathcal{T}_0, \mathcal{T}_1) = (\varnothing, \mathcal{T})$. We rewrite Theorem 3 in [23], rename some notations, and obtain the following lemma.

Lemma 1 (Security of XEX*). *Fix a block cipher $E : \mathcal{K} \times \{0,1\}^n \rightarrow \{0,1\}^n$ and a tweakable blockcipher $\widetilde{E} : \mathcal{K} \times \mathcal{T} \times \{0,1\}^n \rightarrow \{0,1\}^n$, where $\mathcal{T} = \{0,1\}^n \times \mathcal{I} \times \mathcal{J}$ is a tweak space, $\mathcal{I}$ is a set of tuples of large integers, and $\mathcal{J}$ is a set of tuples of small integers. Assume $2^i 3^j \neq 1$ for all $(i,j) \in \mathcal{I} \times \mathcal{J}$. Let $\widetilde{E} = XEX^*[E, 2^{\mathcal{I}} 3^{\mathcal{J}}]$, one has*

$$Adv_{\widetilde{E}}^{\widetilde{mprp}}(t, q) \leq Adv_E^{sprp}(t', 2q) + 9.5q^2/2^n,$$

where $t' = t + 2cn(q+1)$ for some absolute constant c.

Authenticated Encryption (AE). A conventional AE with associated data scheme Π consists of an encryption algorithm and a decryption algorithm [24]. In order to consider the security of Π in the RUP setting, we must separate the decryption algorithm from the verification algorithm so that the decryption algorithm always releases plaintext [4]. A separated AE scheme is a triplet $\Pi = (\mathcal{E}, \mathcal{D}, \mathcal{V})$ — an encryption algorithm $\mathcal{E} : \mathcal{K} \times \mathcal{N} \times \mathcal{H} \times \mathcal{P} \rightarrow \mathcal{C} \times \mathcal{T}$, a decryption algorithm $\mathcal{D} : \mathcal{K} \times \mathcal{N} \times \mathcal{H} \times \mathcal{C} \times \mathcal{T} \rightarrow \mathcal{P}$, and a verification algorithm $\mathcal{V} : \mathcal{K} \times \mathcal{N} \times \mathcal{H} \times \mathcal{C} \times \mathcal{T} \rightarrow \top / \bot$, where we write

$$(C, T) \leftarrow \mathcal{E}_K(N, A, P),$$
$$P \leftarrow \mathcal{D}_K(N, A, C, T),$$
$$\top / \bot \leftarrow \mathcal{V}_K(N, A, C, T),$$

where $K \in \mathcal{K}$ is a key, $\mathcal{K} = \{0,1\}^k$, $k \geq 1$, $N \in \mathcal{N}$ is a nonce, $\mathcal{N} \subseteq \{0,1\}^n$, $n \geq 1$, $A \in \mathcal{H}$ is an associated data, $\mathcal{H} \subseteq \{0,1\}^*$, $P \in \mathcal{P}$ is a plaintext, $\mathcal{P} \subseteq \{0,1\}^*$, $C \in \mathcal{C}$ is a ciphertext, $\mathcal{C} \subseteq \{0,1\}^*$, and $T \in \mathcal{T}$ is a tag, $\mathcal{T} \subseteq \{0,1\}^*$. The symbols $\top$ and $\bot$ indicate the success and failure of the verification oracle, respectively. $\mathcal{E}_K(N, A, P) = (C, T)$ if and only if (iff) $\mathcal{D}_K(N, A, C, T) = P$ and $\mathcal{V}_K(N, A, C, T) = \top$. If there is no associated data A, we may omit it. A secure AE scheme returns $\bot$ if it receives an error (C, T) pair.

3   INT-RUP Security Model of Authenticated Encryption

Let $\Pi = (\mathcal{E}_K, \mathcal{D}_K, \mathcal{V}_K)$ be an AE scheme. Let $\mathcal{A}$ be an adversary which makes at most q_e queries to the encryption oracle $\mathcal{E}_K(\cdot)$, at most q_d queries to the decryption oracle $\mathcal{D}_K(\cdot)$, and at most q_v queries to the verification oracle $\mathcal{V}_K(\cdot)$. Firstly, $\mathcal{A}$ queries (N^i, A^i, P^i) to the encryption oracle $\mathcal{E}_K(\cdot)$ and receives $(C^i, T^i) = \mathcal{E}_K(N^i, A^i, P^i)$, where $1 \leq i \leq q_e$. Then, $\mathcal{A}$ has access to the decryption oracle $\mathcal{D}_K(\cdot)$ and obtains unverified plaintexts $P^{*j} = \mathcal{D}_K(N^{*j}, A^{*j}, C^{*j}, T^{*j})$, where $1 \leq j \leq q_d$. Without loss of generality, we assume that the adversary doesn't make redundant queries[1]. Note that $(N^{*j}, A^{*j}, C^{*j}, T^{*j}) \neq (N^i, A^i, C^i, T^i)$, where $1 \leq i \leq q_e$ and $1 \leq j \leq q_d$. Finally, $\mathcal{A}$ forges a challenge ciphertext $(N', A', C', T') \neq (N^i, A^i, C^i, T^i)$, where $1 \leq i \leq q_e$, to the verification oracle $\mathcal{V}_K(\cdot)$.

The forgery attempt succeeds if $\mathcal{V}_K(N', A', C', T') = \top$, failure otherwise. Then the INT-RUP-advantage of $\mathcal{A}$ against $\Pi = (\mathcal{E}_K, D_K, \mathcal{V}_K)$ is defined as

$$Adv_{\Pi}^{int-rup}(\mathcal{A}) = Pr[\mathcal{A}^{\mathcal{E}_K, \mathcal{D}_K, \mathcal{V}_K} \; forges].$$

4   INT-RUP Security of Checksum-Based Authenticated Encryption Schemes

4.1   INT-RUP Analysis of Authenticated Encryption with PCC

For all AE schemes, if their checksum is generated by the XOR-sum of the plaintext blocks, they are insecure in the RUP setting, such as IAPM [16], OCB [25], COPA [3], and OPP [15].

We describe a new type of structure, called plaintext and ciphertext checksum (PCC), which is a generalization of the plaintext checksum, and prove that all AE schemes with PCC are insecure in the INT-RUP security model. PCC is the XOR-sum of the plaintext and ciphertext blocks, including the XOR-sum of the whole plaintext or ciphertext blocks, the XOR-sum of the whole plaintext and ciphertext blocks, and the XOR-sum of the parts of plaintext and ciphertext

---

[1] It includes the following cases: (i) it doesn't repeat prior queries for each oracle, (ii) the adversary does not ask the decryption oracle $\mathcal{D}_K(Y)$ or the verification oracle $\mathcal{V}_K(Y)$ after receiving Y in response to an encryption query $\mathcal{E}_K(X)$, and (iii) the adversary does not ask the encryption oracle $\mathcal{E}_K(X)$ after receiving X in response to a decryption query $\mathcal{D}_K(Y)$.

blocks. INT-RUP is a strong security notion, which gives the adversary the ability to make decryption queries and observe the unverified plaintexts. The adversary can forge the same checksum by changing some plaintext or ciphertext blocks. Therefore the tag generated by plaintext and ciphertext checksum is vulnerable against integrity security in the RUP setting. The strategy of the attack comes from [4]. We present an improved version in Theorem 1.

Let $\Pi = (\mathcal{E}_K, \mathcal{D}_K, \mathcal{V}_K)$ be an AE mode with PCC. Assume that the authentication tag $T \leftarrow f(checksum)$, where f is a deterministic function, $checksum = \sum_{i=1}^{l}(P_i z_i^1 \oplus C_i z_i^2), z_i^1, z_i^2 \in \{0,1\}$, and l is the block-length of the plaintext or the ciphertext. There are three cases for PCC as follows: (1) If $z_i^1 = 0, z_i^2 = 1$ for all $1 \leq i \leq l$, then the tag is generated from the XOR-sum of the whole ciphertext blocks; (2) if $z_i^1 = 1, z_i^2 = 0$ for all $1 \leq i \leq l$, then the tag is generated from the XOR-sum of the whole plaintext blocks; (3) if $z_i^1 = 1$ for $i \in I$ and $z_j^2 = 1$ for $j \in J$, where the sets I and J are subsets of a set $\{1, \cdots, l\}$, and $I \cup J \neq \varnothing$, then the tag is generated from the XOR-sum of the plaintext and ciphertext blocks. For example, I and J may be a partial of a set $\{1, \cdots, l\}$, such as odd/even partial. If I or J is an empty set, this case is reduced to case (1) or case (2). Note that I and J are empty sets, which is not allowed.

Theorem 1. *For the above scheme* $\Pi = (\mathcal{E}_K, \mathcal{D}_K, \mathcal{V}_K)$, *for all* $ld \geq n$, *there exists an adversary* $\mathcal{A}$ *such that*

$$Adv_{\Pi}^{int-rup}(\mathcal{A}) \geq 1 - 2^{n-ld},$$

where $\mathcal{A}$ *makes one encryption query,* $2 \leq p \leq 2^d$ *decryption queries, and one forgery attempt, each consisting of* l *blocks of* n *bits. Then, the adversary solves a system of linear equations in* $GF(2)$ *with* n *equations and* ld *unknowns.*

Proof. In the INT-RUP security model, we assume that the adversary $\mathcal{A}$ firstly makes one encryption query and receives $(C, T) = \mathcal{E}_K(N, A, P)$, where $P = P_1 P_2 \cdots P_l$. Then $\mathcal{A}$ makes at most p decryption queries with the same nonce-associated data pair and obtains the corresponding unverified plaintexts $P^j = D_K(N, A, C^j, T^j)$ where $0 \leq j \leq p - 1, C^j = C_1^j C_2^j \cdots C_l^j$. Finally, $\mathcal{A}$ forges a new ciphertext $C' = C_1^{x_1} C_2^{x_2} \cdots C_l^{x_l}$ such that the new tag is equal to T, where $x_1, x_2, \cdots, x_l \in GF(p)$. If the forgery succeeds, the adversary needs to find $x_1, x_2, \cdots, x_l \in GF(p)$ such that

$$checksum = \sum_{i=1}^{l}(P_i z_i^1 \oplus C_i z_i^2) = \sum_{i=1}^{l}(P_i^{x_i} z_i^1 \oplus C_i^{x_i} z_i^2), \tag{1}$$

where $z_i^1, z_i^2 \in \{0, 1\}$ for all i.

Equation (1) can be converted into a system of linear equations in $GF(p)$ with n equations and l unknowns, one for every bit j:

$$checksum[j] = \sum_{i=1}^{l}(P_i^{x_i}[j]z_i^1 \oplus C_i^{x_i}[j]z_i^2), \qquad 0 \leq j \leq n - 1, \tag{2}$$

where $X[j]$ selects j-th bit of X, with $j = 0$ corresponding to the least significant bit, and $z_i^1, z_i^2 \in \{0, 1\}$ for all i.

The system of linear equations in $GF(p)$ with n equations and l unknowns is equivalent to a system of linear equations in $GF(2)$ with n equations and ld unknowns, where $d = \lceil \log_2 p \rceil$. The operation of this process is as follows.

Let $[x_i]_d = x_{i1}x_{i2} \cdots x_{id}$ be the d-bit binary representation of x_i, $[p-1]_d = p_1p_2 \cdots p_d$ be the d-bit binary representation of $p - 1$, then $C_i^{x_i} = C_i^0(x_{i1} \oplus 1)(x_{i2} \oplus 1) \cdots (x_{id} \oplus 1) \oplus C_i^1(x_{i1} \oplus 1)(x_{i2} \oplus 1) \cdots x_{id} \oplus \cdots \oplus C_i^{p-1}(x_{i1} \oplus p_1 \oplus 1)(x_{i2} \oplus p_2 \oplus 1) \cdots (x_{id} \oplus p_d \oplus 1)$, where $x_{i1}x_{i2} \cdots x_{id} = [s]_d$ corresponds to selecting $C_i^s, 0 \le s \le p - 1$.

It follows that, Eq. (2) can be converted into the following equation:

$$checksum[j] = \sum_{i=1}^{l} \{ [P_i^0[j](x_{i1} \oplus 1)(x_{i2} \oplus 1) \cdots (x_{id} \oplus 1) \oplus \cdots$$
$$\oplus P_i^{p-1}[j](x_{i1} \oplus p_1 \oplus 1)(x_{i2} \oplus p_2 \oplus 1) \cdots (x_{id} \oplus p_d \oplus 1)]z_i^1 \oplus$$
$$[C_i^0[j](x_{i1} \oplus 1)(x_{i2} \oplus 1) \cdots (x_{id} \oplus 1) \oplus \cdots$$
$$\oplus C_i^{p-1}[j](x_{i1} \oplus p_1 \oplus 1)(x_{i2} \oplus p_2 \oplus 1) \cdots (x_{id} \oplus p_d \oplus 1)]z_i^2 \},$$

where $0 \le j \le n - 1, p_1p_2 \cdots p_d = [p-1]_d, z_i^1, z_i^2 \in \{0, 1\}$ for all i.

The adversary needs to find $x_{11}, x_{12}, \cdots, x_{ld} \in GF(2)$ such that the above n equations are established. For a system of linear equations in $GF(2)$ with n equations and $ld \ge n$ unknowns, we can find a solution by using Gaussian elimination and the probability that this system of equations has a solution is $1 - 2^{n-ld}$ [5]. That is to say, the adversary can forge an output (N, A, C', T) with $C' \ne C$.

4.2   OCB with Intermediate Checksum: OCB-IC

In this section, we fix the weakness of PCC and provide another new type of structure, called IC, to generate the checksum. The internal states in the encryption algorithm are hidden from adversaries and the intermediate checksum obtained by the XOR-sum of internal states is again encrypted once or many times, which guarantees no information leakage, except the collision before the last block encryptions for authentication in the same nonce. The tag is generated by the PMAC1 algorithm [23] of either the plaintext or the ciphertext. Moreover, the decryption algorithm and the verification algorithm share parts of computing resources. Based on the IC structure, we propose a modified scheme called OCB-IC to settle the INT-RUP security of OCB in the nonce-misuse setting.

OCB-IC$[\widetilde{E}]$ is parameterized by a tweakable blockcipher $\widetilde{E} : \mathcal{K} \times \mathcal{T} \times \{0,1\}^n \to \{0,1\}^n$, where $\mathcal{T} = \{0,1\}^n \times \mathcal{I} \times \mathcal{J}$ is a tweak space, $\mathcal{I}$ is a set of tuples of large integers, and $\mathcal{J}$ is a set of tuples of small integers. We require tweaks to increase monotonically and perform the "special" operation ($j \in \mathcal{J}$ gets incremented and $i \in \mathcal{I}$ keeps the same) from the penultimate block to the final block, which makes tweaks' update highly efficient. For OCB-IC, the cost of the generating tag is minimal (as OCB-IC only invokes the underlying TBC twice). We assume that the plaintext length is a positive multiple of block-size n. The length of associated data is arbitrary.

The overview of OCB-IC$[\widetilde{E}]$ is depicted in Fig. 1. OCB-IC$[\widetilde{E}]$ is made up of three algorithms — an encryption algorithm $\mathcal{E}_K$, a decryption algorithm $\mathcal{D}_K$, and a verification algorithm $\mathcal{V}_K$. The detailed description of OCB-IC$[\widetilde{E}]$ is shown in Fig. 2.

We analyze and obtain the following theorems for the information theoretic security of OCB-IC$[\widetilde{E}]$. If the underlying tweakable blockcipher $\widetilde{E}$ is a secure MTPRP, OCB-IC$[\widetilde{E}]$ is proven INT-RUP secure in the nonce-misuse setting.

Theorem 2 (INT-RUP Security of OCB-IC with an Ideal TBC). *For OCB-IC$[\widetilde{E}]$, we replace tweakable blockciphers $\widetilde{E}_K$ with tweakable random permutations $\widetilde{\pi} \xleftarrow{\$} Perm(\mathcal{T}, n)$ to obtain OCB-IC$[\widetilde{\pi}]$, where $\mathcal{T} = \{0,1\}^n \times \mathcal{I} \times \mathcal{J}$ is a tweak space, $\mathcal{I}$ is a set of tuples of large integers, and $\mathcal{J}$ is a set of tuples of small integers. Let $\mathcal{A}$ be a nonce-misusing adversary. Let q_v be the number of forgery queries. Then we have*

$$Adv_{OCB-IC[\widetilde{\pi}]}^{int-rup}(\mathcal{A}) \leq (\sigma + q)^2/2^n + q_v q/2^n.$$

Proof. We assume that $\mathcal{A}$ is an adversary with access to the encryption oracle $\mathcal{E}[\widetilde{\pi}](\cdot)$, the decryption oracle $\mathcal{D}[\widetilde{\pi}](\cdot)$, and the verification oracle $\mathcal{V}[\widetilde{\pi}](\cdot)$. Firstly, the adversary $\mathcal{A}$ makes q encryption queries (N^i, A^i, P^i) and receives $(C^i, T^i) = \mathcal{E}[\widetilde{\pi}](N^i, A^i, P^i)$, where $1 \leq i \leq q$. Then, the adversary $\mathcal{A}$ has access to the decryption oracle $\mathcal{D}[\widetilde{\pi}](\cdot)$ and obtains the unverified plaintext $P^{*j} = \mathcal{D}[\widetilde{\pi}](N^{*j}, A^{*j}, C^{*j}, T^{*j})$, where $1 \leq j \leq q_d$. Note that $(N^{*j}, A^{*j}, C^{*j}, T^{*j}) \neq (N^i, A^i, C^i, T^i)$, where $1 \leq i \leq q$ and $1 \leq j \leq q_d$.

Finally, $\mathcal{A}$ forges a challenge ciphertext $(N', A', C', T') \neq (N^i, A^i, C^i, T^i)$ to the verification oracle $\mathcal{V}[\widetilde{\pi}](\cdot)$, where $C' = C_1' C_2' \cdots C_{l'}'$, $C^i = C_1^i C_2^i \cdots C_{l^i}^i$, and $1 \leq i \leq q$.

Let $\Gamma = \{(N^i, A^i, P^i, C^i, T^i)\}_{i=1}^q \cup \{(N^{*j}, A^{*j}, P^{*j}, C^{*j}, T^{*j})\}_{j=1}^{q_d}$ be the transcript (input-output pairs of OCB-IC) obtained by the encryption queries and decryption queries. Γ can be seen as a random variable, then the INT-RUP-advantage of $\mathcal{A}$ is

$$Adv_{OCB-IC[\widetilde{\pi}]}^{int-rup}(\mathcal{A}) = Pr[\mathcal{A}^{\mathcal{E}[\widetilde{\pi}], \mathcal{D}[\widetilde{\pi}], \mathcal{V}[\widetilde{\pi}]} \ forges]$$
$$\leq max_{\gamma \in \Gamma} Pr_{\mathcal{A}}[(N', A', C', T') \ is \ valid | \Gamma = \gamma].$$

Given an associated data A, we handle it by the PMAC1 algorithm and denote $Auth = PMAC1(A)$. Let **A** be an event that a collision of $Auth$ occurs for two different associated data. Let **T** be an event that a collision of the tag T occurs for two different plaintexts in the encryption oracle. Denote an event **E** as an union of events **A** and **T**, and $\mathbf{E} = \mathbf{A} \vee \mathbf{T}$. Let **F** be an event that the verification oracle $\mathcal{V}[\widetilde{\pi}](\cdot)$ returns $\top$ other than $\bot$. Then $Pr_{\mathcal{A}}[(N', A', C', T') \ is \ valid | \Gamma = \gamma] = Pr[\mathcal{A}^{OCB-IC[\widetilde{\pi}]} \ sets \ \mathbf{F} | \Gamma = \gamma]$ ($Pr[\mathbf{F}]$ for short). By the total probability formula, we can obtain

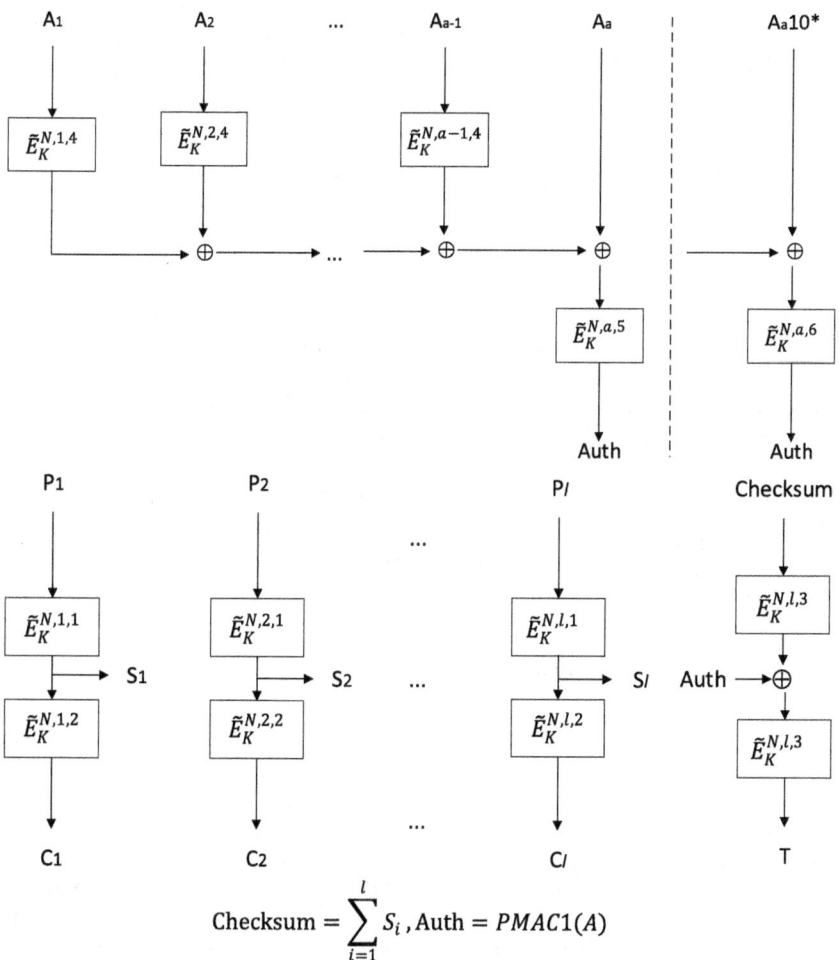

$$\text{Checksum} = \sum_{i=1}^{l} S_i\,, \text{Auth} = PMAC1(A)$$

Fig. 1. Illustrating OCB-IC$[\widetilde{E}]$ with a tweakable blockcipher $\widetilde{E} : \mathcal{K} \times \mathcal{T} \times \{0,1\}^n \to \{0,1\}^n$, where $\mathcal{T} = \{0,1\}^n \times \mathcal{I} \times \mathcal{J}$ is a tweak space, $\mathcal{I}$ is a set of tuples of large integers, and $\mathcal{J}$ is a set of tuples of small integers, e.g., $\mathcal{I} = \{0,1,2,\cdots,2^n-1\}, \mathcal{J} = \{0,1,2,\cdots,10\}$. **Top row**: the authentication of associated data A: $Auth = PMAC1(A)$. If the length of associated data $|A|$ is not a positive multiple of n bits, padding 10^* to A such that $|A10^*|$ is a positive multiple of n bits. The authentication of associated data is achieved by a PMAC1 algorithm [23]. If there is no associated data, then we set $Auth = 0$. **Bottom row**: the encryption and authentication of the plaintext P. The length of the plaintext P is a positive multiple of n bits. The plaintext P is encrypted twice to produce the ciphertext C and the value of intermediate states is used to generate the checksum. If $Auth$ is simply xored with the encrypted Checksum to obtain the tag, we can get the difference of $Auth$ which can be easily used to obtain a forging attack. Therefore the tag is generated by applying two encryptions for Checksum and $Auth$.

/*AD Processing*/ **Algorithm** $Auth(A)$ $//PMAC1_K^N(A)$ Partition A into $A_1\|\cdots\|A_a$ $|A_i| = n, 1 \le i \le a-1, 0 < |A_a| \le n$ for $i = 1$ to $a-1$ $\quad S_i \leftarrow \widetilde{E}_K^{N,i,4}(A_i)$ if $|A_a| = n$ $\quad \Sigma' \leftarrow S_1 \oplus S_2 \oplus \cdots \oplus S_{a-1} \oplus A_a$ $\quad Auth = \widetilde{E}_K^{N,a,5}(\Sigma')$ else $\quad \Sigma' \leftarrow S_1 \oplus S_2 \oplus \cdots \oplus S_{a-1} \oplus A_a 10^*$ $\quad Auth = \widetilde{E}_K^{N,a,6}(\Sigma')$ return $Auth$	/*Decryption Algorithm*/ **Algorithm** $OCB - IC.\mathcal{D}_K^N(A, C\|T)$: Partition C into $C_1\|\cdots\|C_l$, $|C_i| = n, 1 \le i \le l$ for $i = 1$ to l $\quad S_i \leftarrow (\widetilde{E}_K^{N,i,2})^{-1}(C_i)$ $\quad P_i \leftarrow (\widetilde{E}_K^{N,i,1})^{-1}(S_i)$ $P \leftarrow P_1 P_2 \cdots P_l$ return P
/*Encryption Algorithm*/ **Algorithm** $OCB - IC.\mathcal{E}_K^N(A, P)$: Partition P into $P_1\|\cdots\|P_l$, $|P_i| = n, 1 \le i \le l$ for $i = 1$ to l $\quad S_i \leftarrow \widetilde{E}_K^{N,i,1}(P_i)$ $\quad C_i \leftarrow \widetilde{E}_K^{N,i,2}(S_i)$ $C \leftarrow C_1 C_2 \cdots C_l$ $\Sigma \leftarrow S_1 \oplus S_2 \oplus \cdots \oplus S_l$ $T = \widetilde{E}_K^{N,l,3}(\widetilde{E}_K^{N,l,3}(\Sigma) \oplus Auth(A))$ return $C\|T$	/*Verification Algorithm*/ **Algorithm** $OCB - IC.\mathcal{V}_K^N(A, C\|T)$: Partition C into $C_1\|\cdots\|C_l$, $|C_i| = n, 1 \le i \le l$ for $i = 1$ to l $\quad S_i \leftarrow (\widetilde{E}_K^{N,i,2})^{-1}(C_i)$ $\Sigma \leftarrow S_1 \oplus S_2 \oplus \cdots \oplus S_l$ $T' = \widetilde{E}_K^{N,l,3}(\widetilde{E}_K^{N,l,3}(\Sigma) \oplus Auth(A))$ if $T' = T$, return $\top$, else return $\bot$

Fig. 2. OCB-IC[$\widetilde{E}$] with a tweakable blockcipher $\widetilde{E} : \mathcal{K} \times \mathcal{T} \times \{0,1\}^n \to \{0,1\}^n$, where $\mathcal{T} = \{0,1\}^n \times \mathcal{I} \times \mathcal{J}$ is a tweak space, $\mathcal{I}$ is a set of tuples of large integers, and $\mathcal{J}$ is a set of tuples of small integers, e.g., $\mathcal{I} = \{0, 1, 2, \cdots, 2^n - 1\}, \mathcal{J} = \{0, 1, 2, \cdots, 10\}$. The encryption algorithm $\mathcal{E}_K$ includes the encryption of the plaintext blocks, the authentications of associated data and the plaintext. The authentications of associated data and the plaintext are achieved by PMAC1 algorithm. If there is no associated data, then we set $Auth = 0$. The decryption algorithm $\mathcal{D}_K$ is straightforward similar to the encryption algorithm except no authentication of the tag at the end of the decryption process. The verification algorithm $\mathcal{V}_K$ outputs $\top$ if the new tag generated by the associated data-ciphertext pair is equal to the original tag, $\bot$ otherwise.

$$Pr[\mathbf{F}] = Pr[\mathbf{F}|\neg\mathbf{E}]Pr[\neg\mathbf{E}] + Pr[\mathbf{F}|\mathbf{E}]Pr[\mathbf{E}]$$
$$\le Pr[\mathbf{F}|\neg\mathbf{E}] + Pr[\mathbf{E}].$$

Claim 1. $Pr[\mathbf{E}] \le \sigma^2/2^n + q^2/2^n \le (\sigma + q)^2/2^n$.

Proof. The authentications of associated data and the plaintext are achieved by the PMAC1 algorithm. The function $PMAC1[\widetilde{\pi}] : \{0,1\}^* \to \{0,1\}^n$ is indistinguishable from a random function $R : \{0,1\}^* \to \{0,1\}^n$ and their distinguishing advantage is at most $\sigma^2/2^n$, where σ is the query complexity. We replace the PMAC1 algorithm with the random function R, then, in this case, the probability of the event $\mathbf{A}$ is just equal to a collision probability of R plus the probability of R hitting 0, which is at most $q(q-1)/2^{n+1} + q/2^n$, and the probability of the event $\mathbf{T}$ is just equal to a collision probability of R, which is at most $q(q-1)/2^{n+1}$. Therefore, the probability of the event $\mathbf{E}$ is

$$
\begin{aligned}
Pr[\mathbf{E}] &= Pr[\mathbf{A} \vee \mathbf{T}] \\
&\leq Pr[\mathbf{A}] + Pr[\mathbf{T}] \\
&\leq \sigma^2/2^n + q(q-1)/2^{n+1} + q/2^n + q(q-1)/2^{n+1} \\
&\leq \sigma^2/2^n + q^2/2^n.
\end{aligned}
$$

Claim 2. $Pr[\mathbf{F}|\neg\mathbf{E}] \leq q_v q/2^n$.

Proof. To derive the probability that $\mathcal{A}^{OCB-IC[\bar{\pi}]}$ sets $\mathbf{F}$ under the condition $\neg\mathbf{E}$: $Pr[\mathbf{F}|\neg\mathbf{E}]$, we analyze some cases as follows.

Case 1: T' is new, i.e., $T' \notin \{T^1, \cdots, T^q\}$. In this case, $\mathcal{A}$ already knows all the tags after the encryption oracle and with this knowledge it is trying to guess the image of another point. The probability of guessing this correctly is at most $1/(2^n - q)$, which is its success probability of $\mathcal{A}$.

Case 2: T' is old, i.e., $T' \in \{T^1, \cdots, T^q\}$. As all nonces can be repeated in all queries (nonce-misusing), we divide the set of nonce $\mathcal{N}$ used in the encryption oracle into two sets $\mathcal{N}_1$ and $\mathcal{N}_2$. The set $\mathcal{N}_1$ only contains a repeatable element N_0. i.e. $\mathcal{N} = \mathcal{N}_1 \bigcup \mathcal{N}_2$, $\mathcal{N}_1 = \{N_0\}$, $\mathcal{N}_2 = \mathcal{N}\backslash\mathcal{N}_1$. Similarity, we divide the set of block-length $\mathcal{L}$ used in the encryption oracle into two sets $\mathcal{L}_1$ and $\mathcal{L}_2$. The set $\mathcal{L}_1$ only contains a repeatable element l_0. i.e. $\mathcal{L} = \mathcal{L}_1 \bigcup \mathcal{L}_2$, $\mathcal{L}_1 = \{l_0\}$, $\mathcal{L}_2 = \mathcal{L}\backslash\mathcal{L}_1$. We divide the set of associated data $\mathcal{H}$ used in the encryption oracle into two sets $\mathcal{H}_1$ and $\mathcal{H}_2$. The set $\mathcal{H}_1$ only contains a repeatable element A_0. i.e. $\mathcal{H} = \mathcal{H}_1 \bigcup \mathcal{H}_2$, $\mathcal{H}_1 = \{A_0\}$, $\mathcal{H}_2 = \mathcal{H}\backslash\mathcal{H}_1$. We do a further case analysis as follows.

Case 2-1: If $N' \notin \mathcal{N}$, the finalization tweak $(N', l', 3)$ is new. The adversary tries to forge using a new nonce. The image of a single point under a random permutation is uniform, so the generated tag is an independent and uniform random value. Thus, the probability that the adversary can guess the correct value is $1/2^n$.

Case 2-2: If $N' \in \mathcal{N}_1$, $l' \notin \mathcal{L}$, the finalization tweak $(N', l', 3)$ is new. The adversary tries to forge using a new block-size. The image of a single point under a random permutation is uniform, so the generated tag is an independent and uniform random value. Thus, the probability that the adversary can guess the correct value is $1/2^n$.

Case 2-3: If $N' \in \mathcal{N}_1$, $l' \in \mathcal{L}_1$, the finalization tweak $(N', l', 3)$ in this case is the same with the forgery attempt.

1. If $A' \notin \mathcal{H}$, then it means that it yields a fresh random value by $PMAC1(A')$. Let $\mathbf{T}$ be the event that a collision of the tag T occurs for the forgery and encryption oracles. Let $\mathbf{A}$ be the event that a collision of $Auth$ occurs for

the forgery and encryption oracles. If C' is old, the probability of successful forgery is at most $q/2^n$. If C' is new, let $\mathbf{S}$ be the event that a collision of $\sum_i S_i$ occurs for the forgery and encryption oracles. $\mathbf{A}$ and $\mathbf{S}$ are independent events, and $Pr[\mathbf{A}] = Pr[\mathbf{S}] = 1/2^n$.

By the formula of total probability, we can obtain

$$
\begin{aligned}
Pr[\mathbf{T}] &= Pr[\mathbf{T} \wedge \mathbf{A} \wedge \mathbf{S}] + Pr[\mathbf{T} \wedge (\overline{\mathbf{A}} \vee \overline{\mathbf{S}})] \\
&= Pr[\mathbf{T}|\mathbf{A} \wedge \mathbf{S}]Pr[\mathbf{A} \wedge \mathbf{S}] + Pr[\mathbf{T}|\overline{\mathbf{A}} \vee \overline{\mathbf{S}}]Pr[\overline{\mathbf{A}} \vee \overline{\mathbf{S}}] \\
&\leq q/2^n - q/2^{2n+1} \\
&\leq q/2^{n+1}.
\end{aligned}
$$

2. If $A' \in \mathcal{H}_1$, the authentication of associated data A' is the same with A_0 from many nonce-associated data-ciphertext-tag pairs in the encryption oracle, where only the ciphertexts are distinct. The rest is similar to the PMAC1 processing of the ciphertext blocks. The probability of successful forgery is at most $q/2^n$.

Summarizing all cases, we have

$$
Pr[\mathbf{F}|\neg\mathbf{E}] \leq max\{1/(2^n - q), q/2^n, q/2^{n+1}, q/2^n\} \leq q/2^n
$$

for a single forgery query, where $q \geq 2$.

If the adversary $\mathcal{A}$ makes q_v forgery queries, then it is easy to obtain the probability $Pr[\mathbf{F}|\neg\mathbf{E}] \leq q_v \cdot q/2^n$.

By Claims 1 and 2, the INT-advantage of $\mathcal{A}$, after $q \geq 2$ encryption queries, q_d decryption queries, and q_v forgery queries, is

$$
Adv_{OCB-IC[\widetilde{\pi}]}^{int-rup}(\mathcal{A}) \leq (\sigma + q)^2/2^n + q_v q/2^n.
$$

Theorem 3 (INT-RUP Security of OCB-IC with a TBC). *Let $\widetilde{E} : \mathcal{K} \times \mathcal{T} \times \{0,1\}^n \to \{0,1\}^n$ be a tweakable blockcipher. Fix $n \geq 1$, $\mathcal{T} = \{0,1\}^n \times \mathcal{I} \times \mathcal{J}$ is a tweak space, $\mathcal{I}$ is a set of tuples of large integers, and $\mathcal{J}$ is a set of tuples of small integers, let $\mathcal{A}$ be a nonce-misusing adversary. Then we have*

$$
Adv_{OCB-IC[\widetilde{E}]}^{int-rup}(t, \sigma) \leq Adv_{\widetilde{E}}^{\widetilde{mprp}}(t', 2\sigma) + (\sigma + q)^2/2^n + q_v q/2^n,
$$

where $t' = t + cn\sigma$ for some absolute constant c.

4.3   Discussions

Properties of OCB-IC. OCB-IC is a "rate-$\frac{1}{2}$" one-pass parallelizable AE scheme. It is proven INT-RUP secure up to birthday bound in the nonce-misuse setting if the underlying TBC is a secure MTPRP. OCB-IC just settles the problems of integrity in the RUP and nonce-misuse settings, while the problems of privacy in the RUP and nonce-misuse settings still exist. It cannot achieve PA security. OCB-IC balances the security and the efficiency. The number of the underlying primitive invocations of OCB-IC is about twice than that of OCB [17,23,25]. Therefore, the efficiency of OCB-IC is about half of OCB. Compared with CCM [12], the efficiency of OCB-IC is better because CCM is a two-pass AE scheme. Comparisons among CCM, OCB, and OCB-IC are shown in Table 1. OCB-IC can be seen as a special instantiation of the generic B1 scheme of [20] in which one applies a PRF to the message as well as encrypting it with a secure nonce-based encryption scheme. OCB-IC is designed in terms of a TBC. If this TBC can be instantiated by using AES and the XEX* construction, we can obtain a provably secure instance, which is presented in Appendix.

Processing of Arbitrary Length Messages. When the length of the message is not a positive multiple of the blocksize n, our scheme requires to be extended. We can utilize an encryption of stream ciphers for the last incomplete block, which retains the mainly structure of OCB [17,23,25]. For simplicity, here we utilize a padding function *pad* such that the length of the message is a positive multiple of the blocksize n. Given an arbitrary length message $M \in \{0,1\}^*$, it needs to be padded to the plaintext $P = pad(M) = M10^{n-1-(|M| \bmod n)}$ before the encryption algorithm. Meanwhile, after the decryption algorithm, we use a corresponding un-padding function *unpad*, which removes the 10^* in P, to obtain the original message $M = unpad(P)$.

5   Conclusion

OCB [17,23,25] is insecure in the nonce-misuse and RUP settings. This paper mainly considers the INT-RUP security of OCB in the nonce-misuse setting. We focus on the weakness of the checksum processing in OCB. The tag of OCB is generated by encrypting a plaintext checksum, which is vulnerable against integrity security in the RUP setting. We describe a new type of structure PCC, which is a generalization of the plaintext checksum, and prove that all AE schemes with PCC are insecure in the INT-RUP security model. To fix the weakness of PCC, we provide another new type of structure IC to generate the checksum and propose a modified scheme called OCB-IC to settle the INT-RUP security of OCB in the nonce-misuse setting. OCB-IC is a TBC-based AE scheme. It retains the mainly structure of OCB and inherits its advantages. We prove that OCB-IC is INT-RUP secure up to the birthday bound in the nonce-misuse setting if the underlying tweakable blockcipher is a secure MTPRP. In this paper, we do not settle the problem of privacy in the RUP setting. OCB-IC is not PA secure. We leave it as an open problem to settle the PA security of OCB-IC in an efficient way.

Compared with OCB, OCB-IC invokes the underlying TBC twice for each plaintext block and provides INT-RUP security, i.e., OCB-IC compromises the efficiency of the software and hardware implementations to achieve INT-RUP security. Our works support works of Chakraborti et al. [9] and find a new structure IC, which will provide a new direction for settling the security of "rate < 1" AE schemes in the RUP setting.

Acknowledgments. We would like to express our sincere thanks to the editors and the anonymous reviewers for the valuable comments and suggestions. This work was supported by National Natural Science Foundation of China (Grant Nos. 61522210, 61632013, and 61271271), 100 Talents Program of Chinese Academy of Sciences, and Fundamental Research Funds for the Central Universities in China (Grant No. WK2101020005).

Appendix: Blockcipher-based OCB-IC

To realize OCB-IC with a tweakable blockcipher $\widetilde{E} : \mathcal{K} \times \mathcal{T} \times \{0,1\}^n \to \{0,1\}^n$, where $\mathcal{T} = \{0,1\}^n \times \mathcal{I} \times \mathcal{J}$ is a tweak space, $\mathcal{I}$ is a set of tuples of large integers, and $\mathcal{J}$ is a set of tuples of small integers, we use a conventional block cipher $E : \mathcal{K} \times \{0,1\}^n \to \{0,1\}^n$ to instantiate OCB-IC$[\widetilde{E}]$ by the XEX* construction $\widetilde{E} = XEX^*[E, 2^{\mathcal{I}}3^{\mathcal{J}}]$. Overloading the notation, we rewrite this scheme as OCB-IC[E].

The overview of OCB-IC[E] is depicted in Fig. 3. OCB-IC[E] is made up of three algorithms, an encryption algorithm $\mathcal{E}_K$, a decryption algorithm $\mathcal{D}_K$, and a verification algorithm $\mathcal{V}_K$. The detailed description of OCB-IC[E] is shown in Fig. 4. If the underlying block cipher E is a secure strong pseudorandom permutation (SPRP), OCB-IC[E] is proven INT-RUP security up to the birthday bound in the nonce-misuse setting.

Theorem 4 (INT-RUP Security of OCB-IC with a Block Cipher). *Fix a block cipher $E : \mathcal{K} \times \{0,1\}^n \to \{0,1\}^n$ and a tweakable blockcipher $\widetilde{E} : \mathcal{K} \times \mathcal{T} \times \{0,1\}^n \to \{0,1\}^n$, where $\mathcal{T} = \{0,1\}^n \times \mathcal{I} \times \mathcal{J}$ is a tweak space, $\mathcal{I}$ is a set of tuples of large integers, and $\mathcal{J}$ is a set of tuples of small integers. Assume $2^i 3^j \neq 1$ for all $(i,j) \in \mathcal{I} \times \mathcal{J}$. Let $\widetilde{E} = XEX^*[E, 2^{\mathcal{I}}3^{\mathcal{J}}]$, $\mathcal{A}$ be a nonce-misusing adversary, then we have*

$$Adv_{OCB-IC[E]}^{int-rup}(\mathcal{A}) \leq Adv_E^{sprp}(\mathcal{B}) + 39(\sigma+q)^2/2^n + q_v q/2^n,$$

where a new adversary $\mathcal{B}$ has an additional running time equal to the time needed to process the queries from $\mathcal{A}$.

Proof Sketch: We introduce dummy masks $\{2L, 2^2 L, \cdots, 2^l \cdot L, 2^l \cdot 3L\}$ to rewrite OCB-IC[E] in terms of the XEX* construction, where $L = E_K(N)$. By Lemma 1, OCB-IC[E] can be replaced with OCB-IC$[\widetilde{E}]$. Such a replacement costs us

$$\frac{9.5(2\sigma+2q)^2}{2^n} + Adv_E^{sprp}(t', 2 \cdot 2(\sigma+q)) = \frac{38(\sigma+q)^2}{2^n} + Adv_E^{sprp}(t', 4(\sigma+q)).$$

Therefore, combining with Theorem 3, we can easily obtain the bound of INT-RUP on OCB-IC[E].

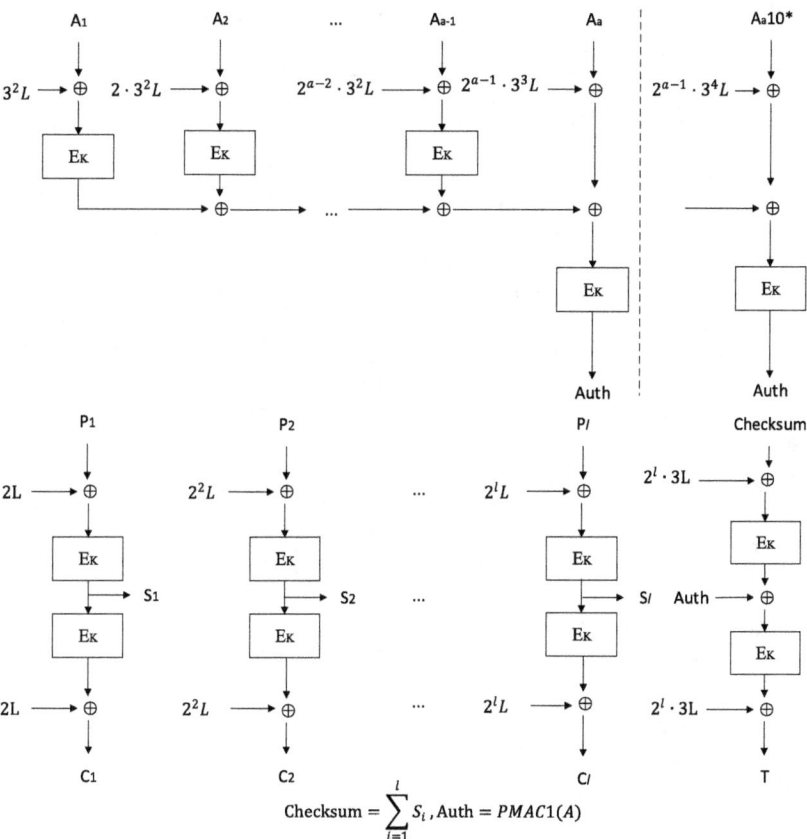

Fig. 3. OCB-IC[E] with a block cipher $E : \mathcal{K} \times \{0,1\}^n \to \{0,1\}^n$. This coincides with OCB-IC[$\widetilde{E}$], where $\widetilde{E} = XEX^*[E, 2^{\mathcal{I}}3^{\mathcal{J}}]$, $\mathcal{I}$ is a set of tuples of large integers, and $\mathcal{J}$ is a set of tuples of small integers, e.g., $\mathcal{I} = \{0, 1, 2, \cdots, 2^n - 1\}$, and $\mathcal{J} = \{0, 1, \cdots, 10\}$. **Top row**: the authentication of associated data A: $Auth = PMAC1(A)$. If the length of associated data $|A|$ is not a positive multiple of n bits, padding 10^* to A so as to $|A10^*|$ is a positive multiple of n bits. The authentication of associated data is achieved by PMAC1 algorithm (XE construction). If there is no associated data, then we set $Auth = 0$. **Bottom row**: the encryption and authentication of the plaintext P (XEX construction). The plaintext is encrypted twice to produce the ciphertext and the XOR-sum of intermediate states is used to generate the tag. We require that the length of the plaintext P is a positive multiple of n bits in OCB-IC[E]. Given an arbitrary-length message $M \in \{0,1\}^*$, it needs to be padded to the plaintext $P = pad(M) = M10^{n-1-(|M| \bmod n)}$ before the encryption algorithm in OCB-IC[E]. Meanwhile, we obtain the message after the decryption algorithm by the unpadding function $unpad(P) = M$.

| /*AD Processing*/
Algorithm $Auth(A)$ //$PMAC_K^N(A)$

Partition A into $A_1\|\cdots\|A_a$
$\|A_i\| = n, 1 \le i \le a-1, 0 < \|A_a\| \le n$
$L = E_K(N)$
for $i = 1$ to $a-1$
    $S_i \leftarrow E_K(A_i \oplus 2^{i-1}3^2L)$
if $\|A_a\| = n$
    $\Sigma' \leftarrow S_1 \oplus S_2 \oplus \cdots \oplus S_{a-1} \oplus A_a$
    $Auth = E_K(\Sigma' \oplus 2^{a-1}3^3L)$
else
    $\Sigma' \leftarrow S_1 \oplus S_2 \oplus \cdots \oplus S_{a-1} \oplus A_a10^*$
    $Auth = E_K(\Sigma' \oplus 2^{a-1}3^4L)$
return Auth

/*Encryption Algorithm*/
Algorithm $OCB-IC.\mathcal{E}_K^N(A,P)$:

Partition P into $P_1\|\cdots\|P_l$,
$\|P_i\| = n, 1 \le i \le l$
$L = E_K(N)$
for $i = 1$ to l
    $S_i \leftarrow E_K(P_i \oplus 2^iL)$
    $C_i \leftarrow E_K(S_i) \oplus 2^iL$
$C \leftarrow C_1C_2\cdots C_l$
$\Sigma \leftarrow S_1 \oplus S_2 \oplus \cdots \oplus S_l$
$T_A = E_K(\Sigma \oplus 2^l \cdot 3L) \oplus Auth(A)$
$T = E_K(T_A) \oplus 2^l \cdot 3L$
return $C\|T$ | /*Decryption Algorithm*/
Algorithm $OCB-IC.\mathcal{D}_K^N(A,C\|T)$:

Partition C into $C_1\|\cdots\|C_l$,
$\|C_i\| = n, 1 \le i \le l$
$L = E_K(N)$
for $i = 1$ to l
    $S_i \leftarrow E_K^{-1}(C_i \oplus 2^iL)$
    $P_i \leftarrow E_K^{-1}(S_i) \oplus 2^iL$
$P \leftarrow P_1P_2\cdots P_l$
return P

/*Verification Algorithm*/
Algorithm $OCB-IC.\mathcal{V}_K^N(A,C\|T)$:

Partition C into $C_1\|\cdots\|C_l$,
$\|C_i\| = n, 1 \le i \le l$
$L = E_K(N)$
for $i = 1$ to l
    $S_i \leftarrow E_K^{-1}(C_i \oplus 2^iL)$
$\Sigma \leftarrow S_1 \oplus S_2 \oplus \cdots \oplus S_l$
$T_A = E_K(\Sigma \oplus 2^l \cdot 3L) \oplus Auth(A)$
$T' = E_K(T_A) \oplus 2^l \cdot 3L$
if $T' = T$, return $\top$
else return $\bot$ |

Fig. 4. OCB-IC[E] with a block cipher $E : \mathcal{K} \times \{0,1\}^n \to \{0,1\}^n$. This coincides with OCB-IC[$\widetilde{E}$], where $\widetilde{E} = XEX^*[E, 2^{\mathcal{I}}3^{\mathcal{J}}]$, $\mathcal{I}$ is a set of tuples of large integers, and $\mathcal{J}$ is a set of tuples of small integers, e.g., $\mathcal{I} = \{0,1,2,\cdots,2^n-1\}$, and $\mathcal{J} = \{0,1,\cdots,10\}$. The encryption algorithm $\mathcal{E}_K$ includes the encryption of the plaintext blocks, the authentications of associated data and the plaintext. The decryption algorithm $\mathcal{D}_K$ is straightforward similar to the encryption algorithm except no authentication of the tag at the end of the decryption process. The verification algorithm $\mathcal{V}_K$ outputs $\top$ if the new tag generated by the nonce-associated data-ciphertext pair is equal to the original tag, $\bot$ otherwise.

References

1. Alomair, B.: Authenticated encryption: how reordering can impact performance. In: Bao, F., Samarati, P., Zhou, J. (eds.) ACNS 2012. LNCS, vol. 7341, pp. 84–99. Springer, Heidelberg (2012). doi:10.1007/978-3-642-31284-7_6
2. AlFardan, N.J., Paterson, K.G.: Lucky thirteen: breaking the TLS and DTLS record protocols. In: IEEE Symposium on Security and Privacy, pp. 526–540. IEEE Computer Society (2013)

3. Andreeva, E., Bogdanov, A., Luykx, A., Mennink, B., Tischhauser, E., Yasuda, K.: Parallelizable and authenticated online ciphers. In: Sako, K., Sarkar, P. (eds.) ASIACRYPT 2013. LNCS, vol. 8269, pp. 424–443. Springer, Heidelberg (2013). doi:10.1007/978-3-642-42033-7_22

4. Andreeva, E., Bogdanov, A., Luykx, A., Mennink, B., Mouha, N., Yasuda, K.: How to securely release unverified plaintext in authenticated encryption. In: Sarkar, P., Iwata, T. (eds.) ASIACRYPT 2014. LNCS, vol. 8873, pp. 105–125. Springer, Heidelberg (2014). doi:10.1007/978-3-662-45611-8_6

5. Bellare, M., Micciancio, D.: A new paradigm for collision-free hashing: incrementality at reduced cost. In: Fumy, W. (ed.) EUROCRYPT 1997. LNCS, vol. 1233, pp. 163–192. Springer, Heidelberg (1997). doi:10.1007/3-540-69053-0_13

6. Bellare, M., Namprempre, C.: Authenticated encryption: relations among notions and analysis of the generic composition paradigm. In: Okamoto, T. (ed.) ASIACRYPT 2000. LNCS, vol. 1976, pp. 531–545. Springer, Heidelberg (2000). doi:10.1007/3-540-44448-3_41

7. Bogdanov, A., Mendel, F., Regazzoni, F., Rijmen, V., Tischhauser, E.: ALE: AES-based lightweight authenticated encryption. In: Moriai, S. (ed.) FSE 2013. LNCS, vol. 8424, pp. 447–466. Springer, Heidelberg (2014). doi:10.1007/978-3-662-43933-3_23

8. Canvel, B., Hiltgen, A.P., Vaudenay, S., Vuagnoux, M.: Password interception in a SSL/TLS channel. In: Boneh, D. (ed.) CRYPTO 2003. LNCS, vol. 2729, pp. 583–599. Springer, Heidelberg (2003). doi:10.1007/978-3-540-45146-4_34

9. Chakraborti, A., Datta, N., Nandi, M.: INT-RUP analysis of block-cipher based authenticated encryption schemes. In: Sako, K. (ed.) CT-RSA 2016. LNCS, vol. 9610, pp. 39–54. Springer, Cham (2016). doi:10.1007/978-3-319-29485-8_3

10. Datta, N., Luykx, A., Mennink, B., et al.: Understanding RUP integrity of COLM. IACR Trans. Symmetric Cryptol. **2017**(2), 143–161 (2017)

11. Dworkin, M.J.: Recommendation for block cipher modes of operation: Galois/Counter mode (GCM) and GMAC. NIST SP 800–38D (2007)

12. Dworkin, M.J.: Recommendation for block cipher modes of operation: The CCM mode for authentication and confidentiality. NIST SP 800–38C (2004)

13. Fleischmann, E., Forler, C., Lucks, S.: McOE: a family of almost foolproof on-line authenticated encryption schemes. In: Canteaut, A. (ed.) FSE 2012. LNCS, vol. 7549, pp. 196–215. Springer, Heidelberg (2012). doi:10.1007/978-3-642-34047-5_12

14. Fouque, P.-A., Martinet, G., Valette, F., Zimmer, S.: On the security of the CCM encryption mode and of a slight variant. In: Bellovin, S.M., Gennaro, R., Keromytis, A., Yung, M. (eds.) ACNS 2008. LNCS, vol. 5037, pp. 411–428. Springer, Heidelberg (2008). doi:10.1007/978-3-540-68914-0_25

15. Granger, R., Jovanovic, P., Mennink, B., Neves, S.: Improved masking for tweakable blockciphers with applications to authenticated encryption. In: Fischlin, M., Coron, J.-S. (eds.) EUROCRYPT 2016. LNCS, vol. 9665, pp. 263–293. Springer, Heidelberg (2016). doi:10.1007/978-3-662-49890-3_11

16. Jutla, C.S.: Encryption modes with almost free message integrity. In: Pfitzmann, B. (ed.) EUROCRYPT 2001. LNCS, vol. 2045, pp. 529–544. Springer, Heidelberg (2001). doi:10.1007/3-540-44987-6_32

17. Krovetz, T., Rogaway, P.: The software performance of authenticated-encryption modes. In: Joux, A. (ed.) FSE 2011. LNCS, vol. 6733, pp. 306–327. Springer, Heidelberg (2011). doi:10.1007/978-3-642-21702-9_18

18. Liskov, M., Rivest, R.L., Wagner, D.: Tweakable block ciphers. In: Yung, M. (ed.) CRYPTO 2002. LNCS, vol. 2442, pp. 31–46. Springer, Heidelberg (2002). doi:10.1007/3-540-45708-9_3

19. Liskov, M., Rivest, R., Wagner, D.: Tweakable block ciphers. J. Cryptol. **24**(3), 588–613 (2011)
20. Namprempre, C., Rogaway, P., Shrimpton, T.: Reconsidering generic composition. In: Nguyen, P.Q., Oswald, E. (eds.) EUROCRYPT 2014. LNCS, vol. 8441, pp. 257–274. Springer, Heidelberg (2014). doi:10.1007/978-3-642-55220-5_15
21. Paterson, K.G., AlFardan, N.J.: Plaintext-recovery attacks against datagram TLS. In: NDSS 2012. The Internet Society (2012)
22. Reyhanitabar, R., Vaudenay, S., Vizár, D.: Authenticated encryption with variable stretch. In: Cheon, J.H., Takagi, T. (eds.) ASIACRYPT 2016. LNCS, vol. 10031, pp. 396–425. Springer, Heidelberg (2016). doi:10.1007/978-3-662-53887-6_15
23. Rogaway, P.: Efficient instantiations of tweakable blockciphers and refinements to modes OCB and PMAC. In: Lee, P.J. (ed.) ASIACRYPT 2004. LNCS, vol. 3329, pp. 16–31. Springer, Heidelberg (2004). doi:10.1007/978-3-540-30539-2_2
24. Rogaway, P.: Authenticated-encryption with associated-data. In: Atluri, V. (ed.) ACM-CCS 2002, pp. 98–107. ACM (2002)
25. Rogaway, P., Bellare, M., Black, J., Krovetz, T.: OCB: a block-cipher mode of operation for efficient authenticated encryption. In: Reiter, M.K., Samarati, P. (eds.) ACM-CCS 2001, pp. 196–205. ACM (2001)
26. Vaudenay, S.: Security flaws induced by CBC padding — applications to SSL, IPSEC, WTLS. In: Knudsen, L.R. (ed.) EUROCRYPT 2002. LNCS, vol. 2332, pp. 534–545. Springer, Heidelberg (2002). doi:10.1007/3-540-46035-7_35
27. Wu, H., Preneel, B.: AEGIS: a fast authenticated encryption algorithm. In: Lange, T., Lauter, K., Lisoněk, P. (eds.) SAC 2013. LNCS, vol. 8282, pp. 185–201. Springer, Heidelberg (2014). doi:10.1007/978-3-662-43414-7_10
28. Zhang, J., Wu, W.: Security of online AE schemes in RUP setting. In: Foresti, S., Persiano, G. (eds.) CANS 2016. LNCS, vol. 10052, pp. 319–334. Springer, Cham (2016). doi:10.1007/978-3-319-48965-0_19

Leakage-Resilient Non-interactive Key Exchange in the Continuous-Memory Leakage Setting

Suvradip Chakraborty[1($\boxtimes$)], Janaka Alawatugoda[2], and C. Pandu Rangan[1]

[1] Department of Computer Science and Engineering,
Indian Institute of Technology Madras, Chennai 600036, Tamil Nadu, India
{suvradip,rangan}@cse.iitm.ac.in
[2] Department of Computer Engineering, University of Peradeniya,
Peradeniya 20400, Sri Lanka
janaka@ce.pdn.ac.lk

Abstract. Recently, Chakraborty et al. (Cryptoeprint:2017:441) showed a novel approach of constructing several leakage-resilient cryptographic primitives by introducing a new primitive called *leakage-resilient non-interactive key exchange* (LR-NIKE). Their construction of LR-NIKE was only in the *bounded-memory leakage* model, and they left open the construction of LR-NIKE in continuous-memory leakage model. In this paper we address that open problem. Moreover, we extend the continuous-memory leakage model by addressing more realistic after-the-fact leakage. The main ingredients of our construction are a leakage-resilient storage scheme and a refreshing protocol (Dziembowski and Faust, Asiacrypt 2011) and a (standard) chameleon hash function (CHF), equipped with an additional property of *oblivious sampling*, which we introduce. We observe that the present constructions of CHF already satisfies our new notion. Further, our protocol can be used as a building block to construct leakage-resilient public-key encryption schemes, interactive key exchange and low-latency key exchange protocols in the continuous-memory leakage model, following the approach of Chakraborty et al. (Cryptoeprint:2017:441).

Keywords: Leakage-resilient · Key exchange protocols · After-the-fact leakage · Continuous-memory leakage

1 Introduction and Related Work

Leakage-resilient cryptography has emerged as a main research area in the field of cryptography during the last decade. The main goal of leakage-resilient cryptography is to analyze the consequences of side-channels (like power traces [28], EM emission [24], timing differences [7] etc.) on the security of the existing cryptosystems and providing secure and robust constructions of them that provably resist side-channel attacks. In order to realistically model side-channel attacks, many leakage models have been proposed like the only computation leaks information (OCLI) model [29], bounded-memory leakage model [1], continuous-memory leakage model [6,13], auxiliary input model [14] etc. All these models

© Springer International Publishing AG 2017
T. Okamoto et al. (Eds.): ProvSec 2017, LNCS 10592, pp. 167–187, 2017.
https://doi.org/10.1007/978-3-319-68637-0_10

have been extensively studied in the literature and many constructions of cryptographic primitives like stream ciphers [19,32], pseudo-random generators and functions (PRG/PRF) [16,31,32], public-key encryption (PKE) [6,13,26,30], signature schemes [20,25], authenticated key exchange (AKE) protocols [4,10,11], identity-based encryption (IBE) schemes [6,12,35] have been presented.

In this paper, we study the leakage resiliency of a rather unexplored yet fundamentally interesting primitive of Non-interactive Key Exchange (NIKE) in the *continuous-memory leakage* (CML) model [6,13]. In the CML model there is no bound on the amount of leakage an adversary may obtain throughout the lifetime of the cryptosystem (as opposed to bounded-memory leakage model). In particular, in the CML model the entire memory can leak (as opposed to OCL model where only parts of memory is allowed to leak at a time) and the total amount of leakage can even be *unbounded*. Clearly, without any other additional mechanism/assumption it is not possible to guarantee security for any primitive in the CML model, as otherwise the adversary may leak the entire secret key from memory. To deal with this, there is a provision of secret key update or refreshing. In particular, the time is partitioned into discrete epochs, and at the end of each time epoch the secret key is refreshed, keeping the public key unchanged. The *only* restriction is that the adversary is allowed to obtain a bounded information (leakage) from the memory/secret state in each epoch, but overall he can obtain unbounded leakage. Information leakage may happen during the secret key update process as well, and such leakage potentially depends on the randomness used for the update procedure.

Non-interactive Key Exchange (NIKE) is an important yet largely unexplored primitive until recently [9,21]. NIKE allows two (or more) parties to establish a shared key among themselves without any interaction, provided the public keys are pre-distributed. NIKE is very useful in any band-width-critical, power-critical, resource-critical systems, such as embedded devices, wireless and sensor networks, where the communication complexity should be minimum. The first rigorous study of NIKE was formulated by Freire et al. [21], who gave formal security models for NIKE and provably secure constructions of NIKE schemes in those models. However, as shown by Chakraborty et al. [9], this construction is completely *insecure*, even if the adversary obtains a single bit of leakage from the secret key of a party. Chakraborty et al. [9] then formulated appropriate leakage security model for NIKE and gave secure constructions of NIKE in the *bounded-memory leakage* (BML) setting. They demonstrated the fundamental importance of leakage-resilient NIKE (LR-NIKE) by constructing efficient PKE, AKE and low-latency key exchange (LLKE) protocols in the BML model, thus providing an unified umbrella for constructing these primitives generically from LR-NIKE. However, in the BML model, the total amount of leakage obtained by the adversary from the secret key of a party is *bounded* up to some fraction of the secret key size, which may not be a realistic assumption always. In particular, it does not capture side-channel attacks like power analysis or EM emission analysis attacks, where the adversary may obtain huge amount of power traces or EM radiation. However, they can be appropriately captured by the CML model, where the total leakage amount is unbounded. In fact, Chakraborty et al. [9] left open the construction of NIKE in the CML model.

Our Contribution. We solve the open problem posed by Chakraborty et al. [9] of constructing LR-NIKE in the continuous-memory leakage (CML) model. Further, we enhance their security model by addressing *after-the-fact* leakage.

Extending to after-the-fact leakage: We strengthen the security model of Chakraborty et al. [9] by considering *after-the-fact* leakage. In key exchange security models the adversary issues a *test* query to a chosen session and asks for the challenge. The challenge to the adversary is to distinguish the session key of the chosen session, usually called the *test session*, from a random session key [5,8,27]. After-the-fact leakage in the context of authenticated (interactive) key exchange is the leakage which happens after the test session is established [3], whereas after-the-fact leakage in the context of non-interactive key exchange is the leakage which happens after the test query is issued [9] (since there is no concept of a session in NIKE). It has been discussed in previous works [4,23] that achieving security against after-the-fact leakage in its most general form is impossible. This problem was alleviated in the context of PKE [23] and AKE [4] by considering the *split-state* leakage model. In the split-state model, the secret key is split into several disjoint parts and each of them is stored in separate memory locations. The adversary may obtain arbitrary leakage from each of parts, except that the leakage from all of these parts happens *independently*. Under this additional restriction it is possible to circumvent the impossibility result for after-the-fact leakage in case of PKE and AKE protocols [4,23].

Leakage-resilient NIKE construction: We consider a 2-split-state model (the secret key is split into two parts) and show that it is possible to construct after-the-fact leakage-resilient NIKE in the CML model. Our construction is inspired by the approach of Chakraborty et al. [9]. The construction of Chakraborty et al. [9] tolerates (bounded) leakage by using a (bounded) leakage-resilient chameleon hash function (CHF) and introducing a new technique, what they call leakage-resilient twisted PRF (LRT) trick. However, their construction is not secure against continuous-memory leakage, unless there is some way to update the PRF keys. We overcome this problem by using a new approach, i.e., by using the leakage-resilient storage (LRS) and its refreshing protocol [18], and a standard CHF, equipped with an additional property of oblivious sampling of the hashing key, which we introduce. We observe that the CHF construction of Döttling and Garg [17] already satisfies this notion. The LRS and refreshing protocols were also used in previous constructions of (interactive) leakage-resilient AKE protocols [4] to tolerate continuous leakage from the secret key. A direct consequence of our work is the construction of PKE, AKE and LLKE schemes in the CML model from our LR-NIKE in the CML model, following the generic transformation of Chakraborty et al. [9]. However, the leakage rate[1] tolerated by our LR-NIKE protocol in the CML model is not optimal (i.e., not $1 - o(1)$).

---

[1] Leakage rate is defined as the ratio of the amount of leakage to the size of the secret.

2   Preliminaries

2.1   Notations

We denote the security parameter by κ, which is implicitly taken as input by all the algorithms. For an integer $n \in \mathbb{N}$, where $\mathbb{N}$ denotes the set of natural numbers, we use the notation $[n]$ to denote the set $[n] \stackrel{\text{def}}{=} \{1, \ldots, n\}$. For a randomized function f, we write $f(x; r)$ to denote the unique output of f on input x with random coins r. We write $f(x)$ to denote a random variable for the output of $f(x; r)$, over the random coins r. For a set S, we let U_S denote the uniform distribution over S. For an integer $r \in \mathbb{N}$, let U_r denote the uniform distribution over $\{0, 1\}^r$, the bit strings of length r. For a distribution or random variable X, we denote by $x \leftarrow X$ the action of sampling an element x according to X. For a set S, we write $s \stackrel{\$}{\leftarrow} S$ to denote sampling s uniformly at random from the S. For two ensembles $\mathcal{X} = \{\mathcal{X}_\kappa\}_{\kappa \in \mathbb{N}}$ and $\mathcal{Y} = \{\mathcal{Y}_\kappa\}_{\kappa \in \mathbb{N}}$, we write $\mathcal{X} \approx_\epsilon \mathcal{Y}$ (statistical indistinguishability), meaning that every unbounded distinguisher has $\epsilon(\kappa)$ advantage in distinguishing $\mathcal{X}$ and $\mathcal{Y}$. Let $\mathbb{G}$ be a group of prime order p such that $\log_2(p) \geq \kappa$. Let g be a generator of $\mathbb{G}$, then for a (column/row) vector $A = (A_1, \cdots, A_n) \in \mathbb{Z}_p^n$, we denote by g^A the vector $C = (g^{A_1}, \cdots, g^{A_n})$. Furthermore, for a vector $B = (B_1, \cdots, B_n) \in \mathbb{Z}_p^n$, we denote by C^B the group element $X = \prod_{i=1}^n g^{A_i B_i} = g^{\sum_{i=1}^n A_i B_i}$.

2.2   Basics of Information Theory

Definition 1 (Min-entropy). The *min-entropy* of a random variable X, denoted as $\mathrm{H}_\infty(X)$ is defined as $\mathrm{H}_\infty(X) \stackrel{\text{def}}{=} -\log(\max_x \Pr[X = x])$.

This is a standard notion of entropy used in cryptography, since it measures the worst-case predictability of X.

Definition 2 (Average conditional min-entropy). The *average-conditional min-entropy* of a random variable X conditioned on a (possibly) correlated variable Z, denoted as $\mathrm{H}_\infty(X|Z)$ is defined as

$$\mathrm{H}_\infty(X|Z) = -\log\big(\mathbb{E}_{z \leftarrow Z}[\max_x \Pr[X = x|Z = z]]\big) = -\log\big(\mathbb{E}_{z \leftarrow Z}[2^{\mathrm{H}_\infty(X|Z=z)}]\big).$$

This measures the worst-case predictability of X *emphby an adversary that may observe a correlated variable* Z.

The following bound on average min-entropy was proved in Dodis et al. [15].

Lemma 1 [15]. *For any random variable X, Y and Z, if Y takes on values in $\{0,1\}^\ell$, then*

$$\widetilde{\mathrm{H}}_\infty(X|Y, Z) \geq \widetilde{\mathrm{H}}_\infty(X|Z) - \ell \quad \text{and} \quad \widetilde{\mathrm{H}}_\infty(X|Y) \geq \widetilde{\mathrm{H}}_\infty(X) - \ell.$$

2.3   Leakage-Resilient Storage (LRS)

We review the definitions of leakage-resilient storage according to Dziembowski and Faust [18]. The idea is to *split* the storage of elements into two parts using a randomized encoding function. As long as leakages from each of its two parts are bounded and independent of each other, no adversary can learn any useful information about the encoded element.

Definition 3 (Dziembowski-Faust leakage-resilient storage scheme). *For any $m, n \in \mathbb{N}$, the storage scheme $\Lambda_{\mathbb{Z}_q^*}^{n,m} = (\mathsf{Encode}_{\mathbb{Z}_q^*}^{n,m}, \mathsf{Decode}_{\mathbb{Z}_q^*}^{n,m})$ efficiently stores elements $s \in (\mathbb{Z}_q^*)^m$ where:*

- $\mathsf{Encode}_{\mathbb{Z}_q^*}^{n,m}(s) : s_L \xleftarrow{\$} (\mathbb{Z}_q^*)^n \backslash \{(0^n)\}$, *then* $s_R \leftarrow (\mathbb{Z}_q^*)^{n \times m}$ *such that* $s_L \cdot s_R = s$ *and outputs* (s_L, s_R).
- $\mathsf{Decode}_{\mathbb{Z}_q^*}^{n,m}(s_L, s_R) : $ *outputs* $s_L \cdot s_R$.

In the model we expect an adversary to see the results of a leakage function applied to s_L and s_R. This may happen each time computation occurs.

Definition 4 (λ-limited adversary). *If the amount of leakage obtained by the adversary from each of s_L and s_R is limited to $\lambda = (\lambda_1, \lambda_2)$ bits in total respectively, the adversary is known as a λ-limited adversary.*

Definition 5 (($\lambda_\Lambda, \epsilon_1$)-secure leakage-resilient storage scheme). *We say $\Lambda = (\mathsf{Encode}, \mathsf{Decode})$ is ($\lambda_\Lambda, \epsilon_1$)-secure leakage-resilient, if for any $s_0, s_1 \xleftarrow{\$} (\mathbb{Z}_q^*)^m$ and any λ_Λ-limited adversary $\mathcal{C}$, the leakage from $\mathsf{Encode}(s_0) = (s_{0L}, s_{0R})$ and $\mathsf{Encode}(s_1) = (s_{1L}, s_{1R})$ are statistically ϵ_1-close. For an adversary-chosen leakage function $\mathbf{f} = (f_1, f_2)$, and a secret s such that $\mathsf{Encode}(s) = (s_L, s_R)$, the leakage is denoted as $\big(f_1(s_L), f_2(s_R)\big)$.*

Lemma 2 [18]. *Suppose that $m < n/20$. Then $\Lambda_{\mathbb{Z}_q^*}^{n,m} = (\mathsf{Encode}_{\mathbb{Z}_q^*}^{n,m}, \mathsf{Decode}_{\mathbb{Z}_q^*}^{n,m})$ is (λ, ϵ)-secure for some ϵ and $\lambda = (0.3 \cdot n \log q, 0.3 \cdot n \log q)$.*

The encoding function can be used to design different leakage resilient schemes with bounded leakage. The next step is to define how to *refresh* the encoding so that a continuous leakage is also possible to defend against.

Definition 6 (Refreshing of leakage-resilient storage). *Let $(L', R') \leftarrow \mathsf{Refresh}_{\mathbb{Z}_q^*}^{n,m}(L, R)$ be a refreshing protocol that works as follows:*

- *Input :* (L, R) *such that* $L \in (\mathbb{Z}_q^*)^n$ *and* $R \in (\mathbb{Z}_q^*)^{n \times m}$.
- *Refreshing R :*
  1. $A \xleftarrow{\$} (\mathbb{Z}_q^*)^n \backslash \{(0^n)\}$ *and* $B \leftarrow$ *non-singular* $(\mathbb{Z}_q^*)^{n \times m}$ *s.t.* $A \cdot B = (0^m)$.
  2. $M \leftarrow$ *non-singular* $(\mathbb{Z}_q^*)^{n \times n}$ *such that* $L \cdot M = A$.
  3. $X \leftarrow M \cdot B$ *and* $R' \leftarrow R + X$.
- *Refreshing L :*
  1. $\tilde{A} \xleftarrow{\$} (\mathbb{Z}_q^*)^n \backslash \{(0^n)\}$ *and* $\tilde{B} \leftarrow$ *non-singular* $(\mathbb{Z}_q^*)^{n \times m}$ *s.t.* $\tilde{A} \cdot \tilde{B} = (0^m)$.

2. $\tilde{M} \leftarrow$ non-singular $(\mathbb{Z}_q^*)^{n \times n}$ s.t. $\tilde{M} \cdot R' = \tilde{B}$.

3. $Y \leftarrow \tilde{A} \cdot \tilde{M}$ and $L' \leftarrow L + Y$.

- Output : (L', R')

Let Λ = (Encode, Decode) be a $(\lambda_\Lambda, \epsilon_1)$-secure leakage-resilient storage scheme and Refresh be a refreshing protocol. We consider the following experiment Exp, which runs Refresh for ℓ rounds and lets the adversary obtain leakage in each round. For refreshing protocol Refresh, a $\lambda_{\mathsf{Refresh}}$-limited adversary $\mathcal{B}$, $\ell \in \mathbb{N}$ and $s \xleftarrow{\$} (\mathbb{Z}_q^*)^m$, we denote the following experiment by $\mathsf{Exp}_{(\mathsf{Refresh}, \Lambda)}(\mathcal{B}, s, \ell)$:

1. For a secret s, the initial encoding is generated as $(s_L^0, s_R^0) \leftarrow \mathsf{Encode}(s)$.
2. For $j = 1$ to ℓ run $\mathcal{B}$ against the jth round of the refreshing protocol.
3. Return whatever $\mathcal{B}$ outputs.

We require that the adversary $\mathcal{B}$ outputs a single bit $b \in \{0, 1\}$ upon performing the experiment Exp using $s \xleftarrow{\$} \{s_0, s_1\} \in (\mathbb{Z}_q^*)^m$. Now we define leakage-resilient security of a refreshing protocol.

Definition 7 (($\ell, \lambda_{\mathsf{Refresh}}, \epsilon_2$)-secure leakage-resilient refreshing Protocol). *For a $(\lambda_\Lambda, \epsilon_1)$-secure leakage-resilient storage scheme Λ = (Encode, Decode) with message space $(\mathbb{Z}_q^*)^m$, Refresh is $(\ell, \lambda_{\mathsf{Refresh}}, \epsilon_2)$-secure leakage-resilient, if for every $\lambda_{\mathsf{Refresh}}$-limited adversary $\mathcal{B}$ and any two secrets $s_0, s_1 \in (\mathbb{Z}_q^*)^m$, the statistical distance between $\mathsf{Exp}_{(\mathsf{Refresh}, \Lambda)}(\mathcal{B}, s_0, \ell)$ and $\mathsf{Exp}_{(\mathsf{Refresh}, \Lambda)}(\mathcal{B}, s_1, \ell)$ is bounded by ϵ_2.*

Theorem 1 [18]. *Let $m/3 \leq n, n \geq 16$ and $\ell \in \mathbb{N}$. Let n, m and $\mathbb{Z}_q^*$ be such that $\Lambda_{\mathbb{Z}_q^*}^{n,m}$ is (λ, ϵ)-secure leakage-resilient storage scheme (Definitions 3 and 5). Then the refreshing protocol $\mathsf{Refresh}_{\mathbb{Z}_q^*}^{n,m}$ (Definition 6) is a $(\ell, \lambda/2, \epsilon')$-secure leakage-resilient refreshing protocol for $\Lambda_{\mathbb{Z}_q^*}^{n,m}$ (Definition 7) with $\epsilon' = 2\ell q (3q^m \epsilon + m q^{-n-1})$.*

2.4 Decisional Bilinear Diffie-Hellman Assumption over Type-2 Pairing Groups (DBDH-2 Problem)

We recall the DBDH-2 problem according to Galindo [22]. Let $\mathcal{G}_2$ be a *type 2 pairing parameter generation* algorithm. It takes as input the security parameter 1^κ and outputs $gk = (\mathbb{G}_1, \mathbb{G}_2, \mathbb{G}_T, g_1, g_2, p, e, \psi)$ such that p is a prime, $(\mathbb{G}_1, \mathbb{G}_2, \mathbb{G}_T)$ are description of multiplicative cyclic groups of same order p, g_1, g_2 are generators of $\mathbb{G}_1$ and $\mathbb{G}_2$ respectively, $e : \mathbb{G}_1 \times \mathbb{G}_2 \to \mathbb{G}_T$ is a non-degenerate efficiently computable bilinear map, and ψ is an efficiently computable isomorphism $\psi : \mathbb{G}_2 \to \mathbb{G}_1$, and that $g_1 = \psi(g_2)$. We say that the DBDH-2 assumption holds for type-2 pairings if the advantage of the adversary $\mathcal{A}_{\mathsf{DBDH-2}}$ denoted by $\mathsf{Adv}_{\mathcal{A}_{\mathsf{DBDH-2}}, \mathcal{G}_2}^{\mathsf{dbdh-2}}(\kappa)$ is negligible, where

$$\mathsf{Adv}_{\mathcal{A}_{\mathsf{DBDH-2}}, \mathcal{G}_2}^{\mathsf{dbdh-2}}(\kappa) = |\Pr[\mathcal{A}(g_2, g_2^a, g_2^b, g_1^c, e(g_1, g_2)^{abc}) = 1]$$
$$- Pr[\mathcal{A}(g_2, g_2^a, g_2^b, g_1^c, e(g_1, g_2)^z) = 1]|.$$

where the probability is taken over the random choices of the algorithm $\mathcal{G}_2$ and the internal coin tosses of the algorithm $\mathcal{A}$.

3   Chameleon Hash Functions with Oblivious Sampling

Informally, a chameleon hash function (CHF) is a (keyed) collision-resistant hash function for which the knowledge of a trapdoor (corresponding to the hashing key) enables efficient collision finding. Without knowing the trapdoor it is hard to find any collision. For our case, we require the property that the hashing key can be sampled *obliviously*, without the knowledge of the trapdoor. The security guarantee is that the both these modes of generating the hashing key are computationally indistinguishable. More formally, CHF consists of four PPT algorithms (Cham.KeyGen$_0$, Cham.KeyGen$_1$, Cham.Eval, Cham.TCF).

1. Cham.KeyGen$_0$(1^κ): The key generation algorithm takes as input 1^κ and output the hashing key along with a trapdoor (hk, ck) respectively. The public key hk defines a chameleon hash function, denoted ChamH$_{hk}$(.,.).
2. Cham.KeyGen$_1$(1^κ): The oblivious key generation algorithm takes as input 1^κ, and outputs the hashing key hk only.
3. Cham.Eval(hk, m, r): The hash function evaluation algorithm that takes as input hk, a message $m \in \mathcal{D}$, and a randomizer $r \in \mathcal{R}_{cham}$ and outputs a hash value $h = $ ChamH$_{hk}(m, r)$.
4. Cham.TCF(ck, $(m, r), m'$): The trapdoor collision finder algorithm takes as the trapdoor ck, a message-randomizer pair (m, r), an additional message m', and outputs a value $r' \in \mathcal{R}_{cham}$ such that ChamH$_{hk}(m, r) = $ ChamH$_{hk}(m', r')$.

Our chameleon hash functions must satisfy the usual properties like correctness, reversibility, random trapdoor collision, and additionally *indistinguishability of hashing key generation*.

- **Reversibility:** *The reversibility property is satisfied if* $r' = $ Cham.TCF (ck, $(m, r), m'$) *is equivalent to* $r = $ Cham.TCF(ck, $(m', r'), m$).
- **Correctness:** *The correctness property is satisfied if for message pair* (m, m'), *and a randomizer* r, *if we compute* (hk, ck) $\leftarrow$ Cham.KeyGen$_0$(1^κ), *and* $r' = $ Cham.TCF(ck, $(m, r), m'$), *we have that* ChamH$_{hk}(m, r) = $ ChamH$_{hk}(m', r')$.
- **Random Trapdoor Collisions:** *The random trapdoor collision property is satisfied if for a trapdoor* ck, *an arbitrary message pair* (m, m'), *and a randomizer* r, $r' = $ Cham.TCF(ck, $(m, r), m'$) *has uniform probability distribution on the randomness space* $\mathcal{R}_{cham}$.
- **Indistinguishability of hashing key generation:** *The two ensembles* {hk : (hk, ck) $\leftarrow$ Cham.KeyGen$_0$(1^κ)}$_{k \in \mathbb{N}}$ *and* {hk : hk $\leftarrow$ Cham.KeyGen$_1$(1^κ)}$_{k \in \mathbb{N}}$ *are computationally indistinguishable.*

$\mathcal{A}$ wins if it outputs (m, r) and (m', r') such that $(m, r) \neq (m', r')$ and ChamH$_{hk}(m, r) = $ ChamH$_{hk}(m', r')$.

We observe that the chameleon hash construction of Döttling and Garg [17] supports oblivious sampling.

Construction of CHF with Oblivious Sampling. In this section, we show that the chameleon hash function construction of Döttling and Garg [17] already admits the property of oblivious sampling that we want for our construction of CLR-NIKE. The construction is as follows:

1. Cham.KeyGen$_0$(1^κ): Let $\mathbb{G}$ be a cyclic group of prime order $p,$, with g as a generator. The key generation algorithm does the following:
    - Sample $2n$ random elements $\{(z_{1,0}, z_{1,1}), \cdots, (z_{n,0}, z_{n,1})\} \xleftarrow{\$} \mathbb{Z}_p^{2n}$.
    - Compute $g_{j,0} = g^{z_{j,0}}$, $g_{j,1} = g^{z_{j,1}}$ $\quad \forall j \in [n]$

    Set hk $= (g, \{g_{j,0}, g_{j,1}\}_{j \in [n]})$, and ck $= \{z_{j,0}, z_{j,1}\}_{j \in [n]}$.
2. Cham.KeyGen$_1$(1^κ): Sample $2n$ random group elements
    $\{(g_{1,0}, g_{1,1}), \cdots, g_{n,0}, g_{n,1})\} \xleftarrow{\$} \mathbb{G}^{2n}$. Set hk $= (g, \{g_{j,0}, g_{j,1}\}_{j \in [n]})$, and ck $\leftarrow \perp$.
3. Cham.Eval(hk, m, r): Here, $m \in \{0,1\}^n$ and $r \xleftarrow{\$} \mathbb{Z}_p$. Compute the hash value as: ChamH$_{\text{hk}}(m, r) = g^r \prod_{j \in [n]} g_{j,m_j}$, m_j denotes the jth bit of m.
4. Cham.TCF(ck, $(m, r), m'$): Parse ck as ck $= \{z_{j,0}, z_{j,1}\}_{j \in [n]}$. Let $m' = (m'_1, \cdots, m'_n)$. Output $r' = r + (z_{1,m_1} + \cdots + z_{n,m_n}) - (z_{1,m'_1} + \cdots + z_{n,m'_n})$. Observe that, ChamH$_{\text{hk}}(m, r) = g^r \prod_{j \in [n]} g_{j,m_j} = g^{r'} \prod_{j \in [n]} g_{j,m'_j} = $ ChamH$_{\text{hk}}(m', r')$.

As pointed out in Döttling and Garg [17], it is easy to show that the above chameleon hash function is collision resistant based on the hardness of the discrete-log problem.

The correctness, reversibility properties are straightforward to see. The value r' is also random over $\mathbb{Z}_p$, since the values r, $\{z_{j,0}, z_{j,1}\}_{j \in [n]}$ are also sampled randomly from $\mathbb{Z}_p$, hence satisfying the random trapdoor collision property as well. The indistinguishability of hashing key generation also follows in a straightforward manner by observing that the way the hashing key hk is sampled does not matter. The output of both Cham.KeyGen$_0$ and Cham.KeyGen$_1$ are actually identically distributed—a tuple of $(2n + 1)$ random group elements.

4 Leakage-Resilient NIKE in Continuous-Memory Leakage Model

In this section, we give the definition of continuous leakage-resilient non-interactive key exchange (CLR-NIKE) adapted from [9], with the addition of a key refreshing algorithm NIKErefresh. The adversary is *not* allowed to register the same public key more than once. When we write pk_U, we mean that pk_U is associated with the user with identifier $U \in \mathcal{IDS}$, where $\mathcal{IDS}$ denotes the identity space. In the leakage-free scenario, this setting was also considered in the work of Freire et al. [21], which they called the Simplified(S)-NIKE. We denote by $\mathcal{PK}$, $\mathcal{SK}$ and $\mathcal{SHK}$ the space of public keys, secret keys and shared keys respectively. A CLR-NIKE scheme CLR-NIKE, consists of a tuple of algorithms (NIKEcommon_setup, NIKEgen, NIKEkey, NIKErefresh).

1. NIKEcommon_setup($1^{\kappa}, \lambda$): The Setup algorithm takes as input the security parameter κ and the overall leakage bound λ that can be tolerated by the NIKE scheme, and outputs a set of global parameters of the system denoted by *params*.

2. NIKEgen($1^{\kappa}, params$): The key generation algorithm is probabilistic and can be executed independently by all the users. It takes as input the security parameter κ and *params* and outputs a public/secret key pair $(pk, sk) \in \mathcal{PK} \times \mathcal{SK}$.

3. NIKEkey(pk_U, sk_V): The shared key generation algorithm takes the public key of user U, namely pk_U and the secret key of user V, namely sk_V, and outputs a shared key $shk_{UV} \in \mathcal{SHK}$ for the two keys or a failure symbol $\perp$ if $U = V$.

4. NIKErefresh(sk): The key-refresh algorithm takes the secret key sk of a user, and produces a fresh secret key sk' corresponding to pk. Each new signing key sk' produced by the key-refresh algorithm is functionally equivalent to the original key.

The *correctness* requirement states that for any two pairs (pk_U, sk_U) and (pk_V, sk_V), the shared keys computed by them should be identical.

4.1 CLR-CKS-heavy Security Model

The CLR-CKS-heavy model of Chakraborty et al. [9] can be viewed as a continuous leakage-resilient version of the CKS-heavy security model for NIKE given by Friere et al. [21]. The CLR-CKS-heavy model [9] addresses before-the-fact leakage setting.

Adversarial Powers. The CLR-CKS-heavy security model is stated in terms of a security game between a challenger $\mathcal{C}$ and an adversary $\mathcal{A}$. The adversary $\mathcal{A}$ is modeled as a probabilistic polynomial time (PPT) algorithm. We denote by $\Pi_{U,V}$ the protocol run between principal U, with intended principal V. Initially, the challenger $\mathcal{C}$ runs the NIKEcommon_setup algorithm to output the set of public parameters *params*, and gives *params* to $\mathcal{A}$. The challenger $\mathcal{C}$ also chooses a random bit b in the beginning of the security game and answers all the legitimate queries of $\mathcal{A}$ until $\mathcal{A}$ outputs a bit b'. $\mathcal{A}$ is allowed to ask the following queries:

1. RegisterHonest queries($1^{\kappa}, params$): This query allows the adversary to register honest parties in the system. The challenger runs the NIKEgen algorithm to generate a key pair (pk_U, sk_U) and records the tuple $(honest, pk_U, sk_U)$. It then returns the public key pk_U to $\mathcal{A}$. We refer to the parties registered via this query as *honest* parties.

2. RegisterCorrupt queries(pk_U): This query allows the adversary to register arbitrary corrupt parties in the system. Here, $\mathcal{A}$ supplies a public key pk_U. The challenger records the tuple $(corrupt, pk_U, \perp)$. We demand that all the public keys involved in this query are distinct from one another and from the honestly generated public keys from above. The parties registered via this query are referred to as *corrupt*.

3. Extract queries(pk_U): In this query the adversary $\mathcal{A}$ supplies the public key pk_U of a honest party. The challenger looks up the corresponding tuple $(honest, pk_U, sk_U)$ and returns the secret key sk_U to $\mathcal{A}$.

4. Reveal queries(pk_U, pk_V): This query can be categorized in to two types – HonestReveal queries and CorruptReveal queries. Here the adversary supplies a pair of public keys pk_U and pk_V. In the HonestReveal query, both pk_U and pk_V are honestly registered; whereas in CorruptReveal query, one of the public key is registered as honest while the other is registered as corrupt. The challenger runs the NIKEkey algorithm using the secret key of the honest party (in case of HonestReveal query using the secret key of any one of the parties) and the public key of the other party, and returns the result to $\mathcal{A}$.

5. Leakage queries: The adversary can ask continuous-memory leakage queries. The adversary $\mathcal{A}$ runs for arbitrarily many leakage rounds $j = 1, 2, \cdots$. For each round the challenger $\mathcal{C}$ initializes a list $\mathcal{L} := 0$. In each round j the adversary chooses a leakage-function $f_j : \{0,1\}^* \to \{0,1\}^*$. The challenger checks if $|\mathcal{L}| + |f_j(sk)| \leq \lambda$. If so, it returns $f_j(sk)$, and updates $|\mathcal{L}| = |\mathcal{L}| + |f_j(sk)|$. Else, the next-round secret key is sampled as $sk' \leftarrow$ NIKErefresh(sk), and the challenger sets $|\mathcal{L}| := 0$.

6. Test(pk_U, pk_V): Here $\mathcal{A}$ supplies two distinct public keys pk_U and pk_V, that were both registered as *honest*. If $pk_U = pk_V$, the challenger aborts and returns $\bot$. Otherwise, it uses the bit b to answer the query. If $b = 0$, the challenger runs the NIKEkey algorithm using the public key of one party say pk_U, and the private key of the other party sk_V and sends the result to $\mathcal{A}$. If $b = 1$, a random shared key is sampled from $\mathcal{SHK}$, and sends to $\mathcal{A}$.

Definition 8 (λ-CLR-CKS-heavy validity). *The* Test *query is said to be valid in the* CLR-CKS-heavy *model if:*

1. *The adversary $\mathcal{A}$ should not be allowed to ask* Extract(pk_U) *or* Extract(pk_V) *queries.*
2. *The adversary $\mathcal{A}$ should not be allowed to ask* HonestReveal(pk_U, pk_V) *or* HonestReveal(pk_V, pk_U) *queries.*
3. *The output length of the leakage queries queried by $\mathcal{A}$ to each party involved in the* Test *queries is at most λ per occurrence.*
4. *After the* Test *query $\Pi_{U,V}$ is activated, the leakage functions $f_j(sk_U)$ and $f_j(sk_V)$ may not be asked by the adversary.*

Security Game and Security Definition. The security game and security definition of the CLR-CKS-heavy model is defined as below:

Definition 9 (λ-CLR-CKS-heavy security game). *Security of a NIKE protocol in the generic (CLR-CKS-heavy model is defined the following security game, which is played by a PPT adversary $\mathcal{A}$ against the protocol challenger $\mathcal{C}$.*

- **Stage 1:** The challenger $\mathcal{C}$ runs LR $-$ NIKEcommon_setup algorithm to output the global parameters *params* and return it to $\mathcal{A}$.

- **Stage 2:** $\mathcal{A}$ may ask any number of RegisterHonest, RegisterCorrupt, Extract, HonestReveal, CorruptReveal, and Leakage queries.
- **Stage 3:** At any point of the game $\mathcal{A}$ may ask a Test query that is λ-CLR-CKS-heavy valid. The challenger chooses a random bit b to respond to this queries. If $b = 0$, the actual shared key between the respective pairs of parties involved in the corresponding test query is returned to $\mathcal{A}$. If $b = 1$, the challenger samples a random shared key from $\mathcal{SHK}$, records it for later and returns that to $\mathcal{A}$.
- **Stage 4:** $\mathcal{A}$ may continue asking RegisterHonest, RegisterCorrupt, Extract, HonestReveal, CorruptReveal, and Leakage queries provided the Test query is still valid.
- **Stage 5:** At some point $\mathcal{A}$ outputs the bit $b' \leftarrow \{0,1\}$ which is its guess of the value b. $\mathcal{A}$ wins *if $b' = b$.*

Let $Succ_\mathcal{A}$ denote the event that $\mathcal{A}$ wins the above security game (Definition 9).

Definition 10 (λ-CLR-CKS-heavy-security). *Let q_H, q_C, q_E, q_{HR}, and q_{CR} denote the number of* RegisterHonest, RegisterCorrupt, Extract, HonestReveal *queries, and* CorruptReveal *query respectively. A NIKE protocol π is said to be λ-CLR-CKS-heavy-secure if there is no PPT algorithm $\mathcal{A}$ that can win the λ-CLR-CKS-heavy security game with non-negligible advantage. The advantage of an adversary $\mathcal{A}$ is defined as:*

$$\mathsf{Adv}^{\mathrm{CLR\text{-}CKS\text{-}heavy}}_{\pi,\mathcal{A}}(\kappa, q_H, q_C, q_E, q_{HR}, q_{CR}) = |2\Pr(Succ_\mathcal{A}) - 1|.$$

Extending CLR-CKS-heavy Model Addressing After-the-Fact Leakage. The *validity* condition (Definition 8) of the CLR-CKS-heavy security model [9] *does not* allow the adversary to query leakage functions to either of the parties involved in the Test query *after* the Test query is issued. However, achieving after-the-fact leakage for NIKE in its most general form is *impossible*, since the adversary can ask challenge-dependent leakage queries and trivially win the game. So, for after-the-fact leakage to make sense, we must enforce some restriction on the leakage functions. This was done in the context of public-key encryption [23] and for (interactive) key exchange protocols [2–4] by requiring the secret key to be *split* into parts and allowing independent leakage from each of these parts; the so called *split-state* model. We can formulate similar security model for NIKE, by requiring that the secret key of the parties are split into parts and the adversary can obtain independent but arbitrary leakage from each of these parts.

A tuple of t adaptively chosen efficiently computable leakage functions $\mathbf{f} = (f_{1j}, f_{2j}, \ldots, f_{ij}, \ldots, f_{tj})$ are introduced; j indicates the jth leakage occurrence and the size t denotes that the secret key is split into t parts, which is *protocol-specific*. A tuple leakage parameter is defined as $\boldsymbol{\lambda} = (\lambda_1, \lambda_2, \ldots, \lambda_i, \ldots, \lambda_t)$ for each of the leakage function f_{ij}. The adversary is restricted to obtain at most λ_i amount of leakage from each ith key part independently: the adversary cannot use the output of f_{1j} as an input parameter to the f_{2j} and so on. This prevents the adversary from observing a connection between parts.

4.2 After-the-Fact CLR-CKS-Heavy-Secure NIKE Protocol: CLR-NIKE

Let $\mathcal{G}_2$ be a type 2 pairing parameter generation algorithm, which outputs $gk = (\mathbb{G}_1, \mathbb{G}_2, \mathbb{G}_T, g_1, g_2, p, e, \psi)$, ChamH $: \{0,1\}^* \times \mathcal{R}_{cham} \to \mathbb{Z}_p$ be a chameleon hash function supporting oblivious sampling of hashing keys. Let $\Lambda_{\mathbb{Z}_q^*}^{n,1} = (\mathsf{Encode}_{\mathbb{Z}_q^*}^{n,1}, \mathsf{Decode}_{\mathbb{Z}_q^*}^{n,1})$ be the LRS scheme which is used to encode secret keys and $\mathsf{Refresh}_{\mathbb{Z}_q^*}^{n,1}$ be the $(\ell, \boldsymbol{\lambda}, \epsilon)$-secure leakage-resilient refreshing protocol of $\Lambda_{\mathbb{Z}_q^*}^{n,1}$.

1. NIKEcommon_setup(1^κ): The set up algorithm comprises of the following:
   - Run $gk \leftarrow \mathcal{G}_2(1^\kappa)$, where $gk = (\mathbb{G}_1, \mathbb{G}_2, \mathbb{G}_T, g_1, g_2, p, e, \psi)$.
   - Sample $\alpha, \beta, \gamma, \delta \leftarrow \mathbb{G}_1$.
   - Run hk $\leftarrow$ Cham.KeyGen$_1(1^\kappa, \lambda)$ (Corresponds to oblivious sampling)
   Set $params := (gk, \alpha, \beta, \gamma, \delta, \mathsf{hk})$.
2. NIKEgen($1^\kappa, params$): A party with identifier ID_A (say) sets up its public-secret key pair as follows:
   - Sample $x_{A_L} \xleftarrow{\$} (\mathbb{Z}_p^*)^n \setminus \{(0^n)\}$, $x_{A_R} \xleftarrow{\$} (\mathbb{Z}_p^*)^{n \times 1} \setminus \{(0^{n \times 1})\}$ and $r_A' \xleftarrow{\$} \mathcal{R}_{cham}$.
   - Compute $Z_A' = g_2^{x_{A_L}}$, $Z_A = (Z_A')^{x_{A_R}}$ and $t_A \leftarrow \mathsf{ChamH}_{\mathsf{hk}}(Z_A || ID_A; r_A')$.
   - Compute $Y_A \leftarrow \alpha \beta^{t_A} \gamma^{t_A^2}$, $X_A' = Y_A^{x_{A_L}}$, and $X_A = (X_A')^{x_{A_R}}$
   Set $pk_A := (X_A, Z_A, r_A')$; $sk_A := (x_{A_L}, x_{A_R})$.
3. NIKEkey(pk_B, sk_A): Let us assume that party ID_A and ID_B with public-secret key pairs (pk_A, sk_A) and (pk_B, sk_B) respectively want to establish a shared key among them. We show the computation from the perspective of party ID_A. The computation at party ID_B's end follows identically.
   - Parse pk_B as (X_B, Z_B, r_B'); if $pk_A = pk_B$, return $\bot$.
   - Compute $t_B \leftarrow \mathsf{ChamH}_{\mathsf{hk}}(Z_B || ID_B; r_B')$.
   - Check if $e(X_B, g_2) \overset{?}{=} e(\alpha \beta^{t_B} \gamma^{t_B^2}, Z_B)$; if not, set the shared key $shk_{A,B} \leftarrow \bot$.
   - Compute $T_A' = \delta^{x_{A_L}}$, $T_A = (T_A')^{x_{A_R}}$.
   - Finally compute the shared key as $shk_{AB} \leftarrow e(T_A, Z_B)$.
4. NIKErefresh(sk_A): The refreshing algorithm takes the secret key $x_A = (x_{A_L}, x_{A_R})$ of a particular round and generates the next round secret key, $(x_{A_L}', x_{A_R}') \leftarrow \mathsf{Refresh}_{\mathbb{Z}_q^*}^{n,1}(x_{A_L}, x_{A_R})$. Details of the Refresh algorithm is in Sect. 2.3.

Correctness: We now show the correctness of the above NIKEkey algorithm, i.e., the shared key computed by both ID_A and ID_B are identical. We denote $x_{A_L} = (x_{A_L}^{(1)}, \cdots, x_{A_L}^{(n)})$ and $x_{A_R} = (x_{A_R}^{(1)}, \cdots, x_{A_R}^{(n)})$, and similarly, for x_{B_L} and x_{B_R} respectively.

$$e(T_A, Z_B) = e\left((T_A')^{x_{A_R}}, (Z_B')^{x_{B_R}}\right) = e\left(\prod_{k=1}^n \delta^{x_{A_L}^{(k)} x_{A_R}^{(k)}}, \prod_{k'=1}^n g^{x_{B_L}^{(k')} x_{B_R}^{(k')}}\right)$$

$$= e\left(\prod_{k=1}^n \delta^{x_{B_L}^{(k)} x_{B_R}^{(k)}}, \prod_{k'=1}^n g^{x_{A_L}^{(k')} x_{A_R}^{(k')}}\right) = e(T_B, Z_A).$$

Remark 1. In our leakage-resilient NIKE protocol, CLR-NIKE, the secret key of a party is x and it is encoded using the LRS scheme. After getting the encoded values x_L and x_R of x, the value x must be securely erased from memory. In practice, such a secure erasure may not be possible always and some traces of the secret key may be leaked to the adversary. In order to avoid such a vulnerability, we pick x_L and x_R at random and then use them as the encodings of x. In this way we refrain from using the secret key x directly. Note that, this approach is identical to first picking a random element $x \in \mathbb{Z}_p^*$ and then encoding it to obtain x_L and x_R. Since the value x is not available to the adversary, it can get only bounded and independent leakage (under split-state assumption) from x_L and x_R respectively. We can then use the security of the LRS scheme from to argue security of our NIKE protocol.

Theorem 2. *Let ChamH be a family of chameleon hash function with oblivious sampling, $\mathsf{Refresh}_{\mathbb{Z}_q^*}^{n,1}$ be a $(\ell, \lambda, \epsilon)$-secure leakage-resilient refreshing protocol of the leakage-resilient storage scheme $\Lambda_{\mathbb{Z}_q^*}^{n,1}$. Then the above NIKE protocol CLR-NIKE is λ-CLR-CKS-heavy-secure in the split-state model assuming the intractability of the DBDH-2 assumption with respect to the parameter generator $\mathcal{G}_2$. In particular, let $\mathcal{A}$ be an adversary against CLR-NIKE in the CLR-CKS-heavy security model making q_H number of RegisterHonest user queries. Then, using $\mathcal{A}$ as a black box we can construct an adversary $\mathcal{A}_{\mathsf{DBDH-2}}$ against the DBDH-2 problem such that:*

$$\mathsf{Adv}_{\mathsf{CLR\text{-}NIKE},\mathcal{A}}^{\mathsf{CLR\text{-}CKS\text{-}heavy}}(\kappa) \leq q_H^2 \left(2\epsilon + \mathsf{Adv}_{\mathcal{A},\mathsf{ChamH}}^{\mathsf{coll}}(\kappa) + \mathsf{Adv}_{\mathcal{A}_{\mathsf{DBDH-2}},\mathcal{G}_2}^{\mathsf{dbdh-2}}(\kappa) \right).$$

Proof. The proof of this theorem will proceed via the game hopping technique [34]: define a sequence of games and relate the adversary's advantage of distinguishing each game from the previous game to the advantage of breaking the security of one of the underlying cryptographic primitive. Let $\mathrm{Adv}_{Game_i}(\mathcal{A})$ denote the advantage of the adversary $\mathcal{A}$ in Game i.

Game 0: This is the original security game with adversary $\mathcal{A}_{\mathsf{DBDH-2}}$. When the Test query is asked, the Game 0 challenger chooses a random bit $b \xleftarrow{\$} \{0,1\}$. If $b = 0$, the real shared key is given to $\mathcal{A}$, otherwise a random value chosen from the shared key space is given. So, we have:

$$\mathrm{Adv}_{Game_0}(\mathcal{A}) = \mathsf{Adv}_{\mathsf{CLR\text{-}NIKE},\mathcal{A}}^{\mathsf{CLR\text{-}CKS\text{-}heavy}}(\kappa).$$

Game 1: Initially $\mathcal{A}_{\mathsf{DBDH-2}}$ chooses two identities $ID_A, ID_B \in [q_H]$, where q_H denotes the number of RegisterHonest queries made by $\mathcal{A}$. Effectively $\mathcal{A}_{\mathsf{DBDH-2}}$ is guessing that ID_A and ID_B to be honestly registered by $\mathcal{A}$ will be involved in the Test query later. When $\mathcal{A}$ makes its Test query on a pair of identities $\{ID_I, ID_J\}$, $\mathcal{A}_{\mathsf{DBDH-2}}$ checks if $\{ID_I, ID_J\} = \{ID_A, ID_B\}$. If so, it continues with the simulation and gives the result to $\mathcal{A}$; else it aborts the simulation.

$$\mathrm{Adv}_{Game_1}(\mathcal{A}) \geq \mathrm{Adv}_{Game_0}(\mathcal{A})/q_H^2.$$

Game 2: We construct an algorithm $\mathcal{B}$ against a leakage-resilient refreshing protocol challenger of $\mathsf{Refresh}_{\mathbb{Z}_q^*}^{n,1}$, using the adversary $\mathcal{A}$ as a subroutine. Hence, the goal of $\mathcal{B}$ is to properly simulate the view of $\mathcal{A}$, and at the same time break the security of the $\mathsf{Refresh}$ algorithm.

The $(\ell, \boldsymbol{\lambda}, \epsilon)$-$\mathsf{Refresh}_{\mathbb{Z}_q^*}^{n,1}$ refreshing protocol challenger chooses $(s_0, s_1) \leftarrow \mathbb{Z}_q^*$ and $(s_0', s_1') \leftarrow \mathbb{Z}_q^*$ and sends them to the algorithm $\mathcal{B}$. Further, the refreshing protocol challenger randomly chooses $s \leftarrow \{s_0, s_1\}$ and $s' \leftarrow \{s_0', s_1'\}$ and uses s and s' as the secrets to compute the leakage from encodings of s and s'. Let $\boldsymbol{\lambda} = (\lambda_1, \lambda_2)$ be the leakage bound and the refreshing protocol challenger continuously refresh the two encodings of the secrets s and s'.

When the algorithm $\mathcal{B}$ gets the challenge of (s_0, s_1) and (s_0', s_1') from the refreshing protocol challenger, $\mathcal{B}$ uses s_0 and s_0' as the secret keys of the parties ID_A and ID_B respectively and computes their corresponding public keys. For all other parties $\mathcal{B}$ sets secret/public key pairs by itself. Using the setup keys, $\mathcal{B}$ answers all the queries from $\mathcal{A}$ and simulates the view of challenger of protocol CLR-NIKE. $\mathcal{B}$ computes the leakage of secret keys by computing the adversarial leakage function $\mathbf{f} = (f_{1j}, f_{2j})$ on the corresponding secret key (encodings of secret key), except the secret key of the protocol principals ID_A and ID_B. In order to obtain the leakage of the secret keys of ID_A and ID_B, algorithm $\mathcal{B}$ queries the refreshing protocol challenger with the adversarial leakage function $\mathbf{f}$, and passes that leakage to $\mathcal{A}$.

If the secrets s and s' chosen by the refreshing protocol challenger are s_0 and s_0' respectively, the leakage of the secret key of ID_A and ID_B simulated by $\mathcal{B}$ (with the aid of the refreshing protocol challenger) is the real leakage. Then the simulation is identical to Game 1. Otherwise, the leakage of the secret keys of ID_A and ID_B simulated by $\mathcal{B}$ are leakages of random values. Then the simulation is identical to Game 2. Hence, by the $(\ell, \boldsymbol{\lambda}, \epsilon)$-$\mathsf{Refresh}_{\mathbb{Z}_q^*}^{n,1}$ security we get:

$$|\mathrm{Adv}_{Game_2}(\mathcal{A}) - \mathrm{Adv}_{Game_1}(\mathcal{A})| \leq 2\epsilon.$$

Game 3: In this game the challenger changes the way in which it answers RegisterCorrupt queries. In particular let, ID_A and ID_B be identities of two honest parties involved in the Test query with public keys (X_A, Z_A, r_A') and (X_B, Z_B, r_B') respectively. Let ID_D be the identity of the party with public key (X_D, Z_D, r_D') that is subject to a RegisterCorrupt query. If $t_D = \mathsf{ChamH}_{\mathsf{hk}}(Z_A || ID_A; r_A')$ or $t_D = \mathsf{ChamH}_{\mathsf{hk}}(Z_B || ID_B; r_B')$, the challenger aborts. Note that if the above happens, then the challenger has successfully found a collision of the chameleon hash function. By the difference lemma [33] we have:

$$|\mathrm{Adv}_{Game_3}(\mathcal{A}) - \mathrm{Adv}_{Game_2}(\mathcal{A})| \leq \mathsf{Adv}_{\mathcal{A},\mathsf{ChamH}}^{\mathrm{coll}}(\kappa).$$

Game 4: In this game the challenger samples the hashing key differently. In particular the challenger runs $(\mathsf{hk}, \mathsf{ck}) \leftarrow \mathsf{Cham}.\mathsf{KeyGen}_0(1^\kappa)$, instead of running $\mathsf{Cham}.\mathsf{KeyGen}_1$. It follows from the *indistinguishability of hashing key generation* property that Game 3 and Game 4 are computationally indistinguishable. Hence,

$$|\mathrm{Adv}_{Game_4}(\mathcal{A}) - \mathrm{Adv}_{Game_3}(\mathcal{A})| \leq negl(\kappa).$$

Game 5: In this game we construct an adversary $\mathcal{A}_{\mathsf{DBDH\text{-}2}}$ for the DBDH-2 problem using the adversary $\mathcal{A}$. The adversary $\mathcal{A}_{\mathsf{DBDH\text{-}2}}$ receives as input $(g_2, g_2^a, g_2^b, g_1^c, T)$, and its goal is to determine if $T = e(g_1, g_2)^{sbc}$ or a random element from $\mathbb{G}_T$, where g_1 and g_2 are generators of the group $\mathbb{G}_1$ and $\mathbb{G}_2$ respectively and a, b, c are random elements from $\mathbb{Z}_p$. We now describe how $\mathcal{A}_{\mathsf{DBDH\text{-}2}}$ sets up the environment for $\mathcal{A}$ and simulates all its queries properly.

$\mathcal{A}_{\mathsf{DBDH\text{-}2}}$ runs $\mathsf{Cham.KeyGen}(1^\kappa, \lambda)$ to obtain a key pair for a chameleon hash function, $(\mathsf{hk}, \mathsf{ck})$. It then chooses two messages $m_1, m_2 \leftarrow \{0,1\}^*$ and $r_1, r_2 \leftarrow \mathcal{R}_{cham}$, where $\mathcal{R}_{cham}$ is the randomness space of the chameleon hash function. $\mathcal{A}_{\mathsf{DBDH\text{-}2}}$ then computes the values $t_A = \mathsf{Cham.Eval}(m_1; r_1)$ and $t_B = \mathsf{Cham.Eval}(m_2; r_2)$.

Let us define a polynomial of degree 2 $p(t) = p_0 + p_1 t + p_2 t^2$ over $\mathbb{Z}_p$ such that t_A and t_B are the roots of $p(t)$, i.e., $p(t_A) = 0$ and $p(t_B) = 0$. Also, let $q(t) = q_0 + q_1 t + q_2 t^2$ be a random polynomial of degree 2 over $\mathbb{Z}_p$. $\mathcal{A}_{\mathsf{DBDH\text{-}2}}$ then sets $\alpha = (g_1^c)^{p_0} \cdot g_1^{q_0}$, $\beta = (g_1^c)^{p_1} \cdot g_1^{q_1}$, $\gamma = (g_1^c)^{p_2} \cdot g_1^{q_2}$ and $\delta = g_1^c$ (g_1^c was obtained as instance of the hard problem). Note that, since $p_i, q_i \overset{\$}{\leftarrow} \mathbb{Z}_p$ are randomly chosen, the values of α, β and γ are also random. Also note that $\alpha \beta^t \gamma^{t^2} = (g_1)^{p_1(t)} g_1^{q(t)}$. In particular $Y_A = g_1^{q(t_A)}$ and $Y_B = g_1^{q(t_B)}$ (since $p(t_A) = p(t_B) = 0$). $\mathcal{A}_{\mathsf{DBDH\text{-}2}}$ then simulates all the queries of $\mathcal{A}$ as follows:

- RegisterHonest: When $\mathcal{A}_{\mathsf{DBDH\text{-}2}}$ receives as input a RegisterHonest user query from $\mathcal{A}_{\mathsf{CLR\text{-}NIKE}}$ for a party with identity ID, it fist checks whether $ID \in \{ID_A, ID_B\}$. Depending upon the result it does the following:
  - If $ID \notin \{ID_A, ID_B\}$, $\mathcal{A}_{\mathsf{DBDH\text{-}2}}$ runs $\mathsf{NIKE.gen}$ to generate a pair of keys (pk, sk), and makes returns pk to $\mathcal{A}_{\mathsf{CLR\text{-}NIKE}}$.
  - If $ID \in \{ID_A, ID_B\}$, $\mathcal{A}_{\mathsf{DBDH\text{-}2}}$ does the following. Without loss of generality let $ID = ID_A$. Now, $\mathcal{A}_{\mathsf{DBDH\text{-}2}}$ uses the trapdoor ck of the chameleon hash to produce $r_A' \in \mathcal{R}_{cham}$ such that $\mathsf{Cham.Eval}(g_2^a \| ID_A; r_A') = \mathsf{Cham.Eval}(m_1; r_1)$. Note that, by the random trapdoor collision property of the chameleon hash function, r_A' is uniformly distributed over $\mathcal{R}_{cham}$ and also independent of r_1. Similarly when $ID = ID_B$, $\mathcal{A}_{\mathsf{DBDH\text{-}2}}$ uses the trapdoor ck to produce $r_B' \in \mathcal{R}_{cham}$ such that $\mathsf{Cham.Eval}(g_2^b \| ID_B; r_B') = \mathsf{Cham.Eval}(m_2; r_2)$. The value r_B' is also uniformly distributed over $\mathcal{R}_{cham}$ and also independent of r_2. $\mathcal{A}_{\mathsf{DBDH\text{-}2}}$ then sets:

$$pk_A = (\psi(g_2^a)^{q(t_A)}, g_2^a, r_A') \text{ and } pk_B = (\psi(g_2^b)^{q(t_B)}, g_2^B, r_B').$$

  Note that these are correct public keys since $p(t_A) = p(t_B) = 0$.
- RegisterCorrupt: Here $\mathcal{A}_{\mathsf{DBDH\text{-}2}}$ receives as input a public key pk and an identity string ID from $\mathcal{A}$. If $ID \in \{ID_A, ID_B\}$, $\mathcal{A}_{\mathsf{DBDH\text{-}2}}$ aborts as in the original attack game.
- HonestReveal: When $\mathcal{A}$ supplies identities of two honest parties, ID and ID' say, $\mathcal{A}_{\mathsf{DBDH\text{-}2}}$ checks if $\{ID, ID'\} = \{ID_A, ID_B\}$. If this happens, $\mathcal{A}_{\mathsf{DBDH\text{-}2}}$ aborts. Else, if $\{ID, ID'\} \cap \{ID_A, ID_B\} \leq 1$, there are three cases:

- $ID \cap \{ID_A, ID_B\} \neq \phi$ and $ID' \cap \{ID_A, ID_B\} = \phi$. In this case, the challenger $\mathcal{A}_{\text{DBDH-2}}$ runs NIKE.key$(pk_{ID}, sk_{ID'})$ to produce the shared key $shk_{ID,ID'}$. Note that $\mathcal{A}_{\text{DBDH-2}}$ can do this since it knows the secret key $sk_{ID'}$ of the party ID'. $\mathcal{A}_{\text{DBDH-2}}$ then gives $shk_{ID,ID'}$ to $\mathcal{A}$.
- $ID \cap \{ID_A, ID_B\} = \phi$ and $ID' \cap \{ID_A, ID_B\} \neq \phi$. In this case, the challenger $\mathcal{A}_{\text{DBDH-2}}$ runs NIKE.key$(pk_{ID'}, sk_{ID})$ to produce the shared key $shk_{ID,ID'}$. Note that $\mathcal{A}_{\text{DBDH-2}}$ can do this since it knows the secret key $sk_{ID'}$ of the party ID'. $\mathcal{A}_{\text{DBDH-2}}$ then gives $shk_{ID,ID'}$ to $\mathcal{A}$.
- $\{ID, ID'\} \cap \{ID_A, ID_B\} = \phi$. In this case, the challenger $\mathcal{A}_{\text{DBDH-2}}$ runs NIKE.key$(pk_{ID'}, sk_{ID})$ (it can use $sk_{ID'}$ also) to produce the shared key $shk_{ID,ID'}$. $\mathcal{A}_{\text{DBDH-2}}$ then gives $shk_{ID,ID'}$ to $\mathcal{A}$.

• CorruptReveal: When $\mathcal{A}_{\text{NIKE}}$ supplies two identities ID and ID' where ID was registered as corrupt and ID' was registered as honest, $\mathcal{A}_{\text{DBDH-2}}$ checks if $ID' \in \{ID_A, ID_B\}$. If $ID' \notin \{ID_A, ID_B\}$, $\mathcal{A}_{\text{DBDH-2}}$ runs NIKE.key$(pk_{ID}, sk_{ID'})$ to obtain $shk_{ID,ID'}$ and returns it to $\mathcal{A}_{\text{NIKE}}$. However, if $ID' \in \{ID_A, ID_B\}$, $\mathcal{A}_{\text{DBDH-2}}$ checks whether the public key $pk_{ID} = (X_{ID}, Z_{ID}, r'_{ID}, r_{ID})$ by checking the pairing. This makes sure that pk_{ID} is of the form (Y_{ID}^d, g_2^d, r'_D) for some $d \in \mathbb{Z}_p$, where $Y_D = (g_1^c)^{p(t_{ID})} g_1^{q(t_{ID})}$, and $r'_D \leftarrow \mathcal{R}_{cham}$. This means that $X_{ID} = (g_1^{cd})^{p(t_{ID})} g_1^{dq(t_{ID})}$. From this the value g_1^{cd} can be computed as:

$$g_1^{cd} = (X_{ID}/\psi(Z_{ID})^{q(t_{ID})})^{1/p(t_{ID})} \mod p.$$

Note that the value $1/p(t_{ID})$ is well defined since $p(t_{ID}) \neq 0 \mod p$. Also note that $t_{ID} \neq t_A, t_B$, since we have already eliminated the hash collisions. Assume w.l.o.g. that $ID' = ID_A$. So writing the public key of ID_A as (Y_A, Z_A, r'_A, r_A), the shared key between ID_A and ID is given by:

$$shk_{ID_A,ID} = e(g_1^{cd}, Z_A).$$

Leakage queries: The adversary may ask for leakage from the secret key of the parties ID_A and ID_B. Initially, the challenger initializes two lists $\mathcal{L}_1 := 0$ and $\mathcal{L}_2 := 0$. Let us suppose that the adversary specifies a tuple leakage function $\mathbf{f} = (f_{1j}, f_{2j})$ to a party (say ID_A) in the jth leakage occurrence. The challenger checks if $|\mathcal{L}_1| + |f_{1j}(x_{A_L})| \leq \lambda_1$ and $|\mathcal{L}_2| + |f_{2j}(x_{A_R})| \leq \lambda_2$. If so, it returns $f_{1j}(x_{A_L})$ and $f_{2j}(x_{A_R})$ respectively, updates $|\mathcal{L}_1| = |\mathcal{L}_1| + |f_{1j}(x_{A_L})|$, and $|\mathcal{L}_2| = |\mathcal{L}_2| + |f_{2j}(x_{A_R})|$. Else, refresh the secret key as $(x'_{A_L}, x'_{A_R}) \leftarrow$ Refresh$_{\mathbb{Z}_q^*}^{n,1}(x_{A_L}, x_{A_R})$, and the challenger resets $\mathcal{L}_1 := 0$ and $\mathcal{L}_2 := 0$.

• Test query: Here, $\mathcal{A}_{\text{DBDH-2}}$ returns T.

This completes the description of simulation by $\mathcal{A}_{\text{DBDH-2}}$. If $\mathcal{A}$ can distinguish between real and random key in Game 5, then it is equivalent to solving the DBDH-2 problem. To see this, note that for user ID_A we have $Z_A = g_2^a$ and $X_A = \psi(Z_A)^{q(t_A)}$, and for user ID_B we have $Z_B = g_2^b$ and $X_B = \psi(Z_B)^{q(t_B)}$. Hence, $shk_{ID_A,ID_B} = e((g_1^c)^b, Z_A) = e((g_1^c)^a, Z_B) = e(g_1, g_2)^{abc}$.

Since the simulation done by $\mathcal{A}_{\mathsf{DBDH-2}}$ is perfect, we have:

$$\mathrm{Adv}_{Game5}(\mathcal{A}) = \mathrm{Adv}_{Game4}(\mathcal{A}).$$

Game 6. In this game the challenger $\mathcal{A}_{\mathsf{DBDH-2}}$ chooses T randomly from the target group $\mathbb{G}_T$. Since T is now completely independent of the challenge bit, we have $\mathrm{Adv}_{Game5}(\mathcal{A}_{\mathsf{CLR-NIKE}}) = 0$. Game 5 and Game 6 are identical unless adversary $\mathcal{A}_{\mathsf{DBDH-2}}$ can distinguish $e(g_1, g_2)^{abc}$ from a random element. Hence,

$$|\mathrm{Adv}_{Game6}(\mathcal{A}) - \mathrm{Adv}_{Game5}(\mathcal{A})| \leq \mathsf{Adv}^{\mathrm{dbdh-2}}_{\mathcal{A}_{\mathsf{DBDH-2}}, \mathcal{G}_2}(\kappa).$$

By combining all the above expression from Game 0- Game 6 we have:

$$\mathsf{Adv}^{\mathrm{CLR-CKS-heavy}}_{\mathsf{CLR-NIKE}, \mathcal{A}}(\kappa) \leq q_H^2 \left(2\epsilon + \mathsf{Adv}^{\mathrm{coll}}_{\mathcal{A}, \mathsf{ChamH}}(\kappa) + \mathsf{Adv}^{\mathrm{dbdh-2}}_{\mathcal{A}_{\mathsf{DBDH-2}}, \mathcal{G}_2}(\kappa) \right). \qquad \square$$

Leakage Tolerance of Our CLR-NIKE Protocol. The order of the groups $\mathbb{G}_1$, $\mathbb{G}_2$ and $\mathbb{G}_T$ are p. Let $m = 1$ in the LRS scheme $\Lambda^{n,1}_{\mathbb{Z}_q^*}$. It is shown in Dziembowski and Faust [18] that, if $m < n/20$, then the leakage parameter for the LRS scheme is $\boldsymbol{\lambda}_\Lambda = (0.3n \log p, 0.3n \log p)$, where $\boldsymbol{\lambda}_\Lambda$ denotes the leakage tolerated by the LRS scheme. Let $n = 21$, then $\boldsymbol{\lambda}_\Lambda = (6.3 \log p, 6.3 \log p)$ bits. According to [18], if $m/3 \leq n$ and $n \geq 16$, the refreshing protocol $\mathsf{Refresh}^{n,1}_{\mathbb{Z}_p^*}$ of the LRS scheme $\Lambda^{n,1}_{\mathbb{Z}_p^*}$ is tolerant to (continuous) leakage up to $\boldsymbol{\lambda}_{\mathsf{Refresh}} = \boldsymbol{\lambda}_\Lambda / 2 = (3.15 \log p, 3.15 \log p)$ bits, per occurrence. When a secret key s (of size $\log p$ bits) of our protocol is encoded into two parts, the left part s_L will be $n \cdot \log p = 21 \log p$ bits and the right part s_R will be $n \cdot 1 \cdot \log p = 21 \log p$ bits. For a tuple leakage function $\mathbf{f} = (f_{1j}, f_{2j})$ (each leakage function $f_{(.)}$ for each of the two parts s_L and s_R), there exists a tuple leakage bound $\boldsymbol{\lambda} = (\lambda_1, \lambda_2)$ for each leakage function $f_{(.)}$, such that $\lambda_1 = \lambda_2 = 3.15 \log p$ bits, per occurrence, which is $\frac{3.15 \log p}{21 \log p} \times 100\% = 15\%$ of the size of a part. The overall leakage amount is unbounded since continuous leakage is allowed. So the leakage bound for our protocol is upper bounded by the leakage tolerated by the refreshing protocol $\mathsf{Refresh}^{n,1}_{\mathbb{Z}_p^*}$. Using the aforementioned primitives the leakage bound of our protocol is $3.15 \log p$ bits per occurrence.

5 Construction of Other Leakage-Resilient Primitives from CLR-NIKE

In this section, we briefly mention how to construct other continuous leakage-resilient (CLR) primitives from CLR-NIKE. Chakraborty et al. [9] showed generic constructions of leakage-resilient CCA-secure PKE, AKE, and low-latency key exchange (LLKE) protocols in the bounded memory leakage model, starting from a (bounded) leakage-resilient NIKE. We observe that their generic transformation goes through in a straightforward manner, if we replace the underlying bounded leakage-resilient primitives with their CLR counterparts. In particular, in the construction of leakage-resilient CCA-secure PKE of

Chakraborty et al. [9], if we replace the bounded leakage-resilient (BLR) NIKE with our CLR-CKS-secure-NIKE, we obtain CLR-CCA-secure PKE scheme tolerating after-the-fact leakage. The leakage rate of the PKE scheme will be same as the leakage rate of the underlying CLR-NIKE scheme. For our construction of CLR-AKE protocol, we need a CLR-CKS-heavy-secure NIKE and a CLR signature scheme. Informally, a CLR signature scheme achieves existential unforgeability against adaptive chosen message attacks, even when the adversary is given *continuous leakage* from the signing key. The CLR signature scheme can be instantiated with the constructions of Brakerski et al. [6] or Dodis et al. [13]. By instantiation with our CLR-NIKE protocol from Sect. 4.2 and the CLR signature scheme of Brakerski et al. [6] or Dodis et al. [13], we obtain CLR-AKE protocol secure against after-the-fact leakage. We point out that the AKE constructions of Alawatugoda et al. [3,4] are also secure against continuous after-the-fact leakage; however in the Only Computation Leaks (OCL) model, which is strictly weaker than the continuous memory leakage model we consider in this paper. The AKE construction of Chen et al. [11] is secure against after-the-fact memory leakage in non-split state model, however; in the bounded leakage model. Whereas, our AKE construction is secure in continuous after-the-fact memory leakage model, although in split-state model. Chakraborty et al. [9] also introduced leakage-resilient LLKE protocols and gave an appropriate security model in the bounded memory leakage model. Their model can be naturally extended to consider continuous after-the-fact memory leakage in split-state. The construction of CLR-LLKE can also be obtained by suitably replacing the underlying NIKE of Chakraborty et al. [9] with a CLR-CKS-heavy-secure NIKE and a CLR signature scheme. All of these can be instantiated similarly as mentioned above. We note that, that the CLR signature schemes of both Brakerski et al. [6] and Dodis et al. [13] achieve the optimal leakage rate of $1 - o(1)$. Hence, the leakage tolerated by our CLR-AKE and CLR-LLKE protocols per invocation are $\min(\lambda_{\text{CLR-NIKE}}, \lambda_{\text{sig}})$, where $\lambda_{\text{CLR-NIKE}}$ and λ_{sig} are the leakage bounds tolerated by the CLR-NIKE and the CLR signature schemes respectively between any two successive secret key (signing key) refreshes.

6   Conclusion and Future Works

In this paper we address the open problem of constructing a NIKE protocol in the continuous memory leakage (CML) model. Further, we also address after-the-fact leakage and show a secure construction of NIKE in split-state model. Our protocol cannot achieve the optimum leakage rate $1 - o(1)$ as the underlying storage scheme and its refreshing protocol do not support that. One interesting open problem will be constructing a leakage-resilient NIKE in the $1 - o(1)$-continuous-memory leakage model.

Acknowledgments. The work was initiated when the first and second authors were visiting IACR-SEAMS workshop on "Cryptography: Foundations and New Directions" at VAISM, Vietnam in the winter of 2016. The work is partially supported by Project No. CCE/CEP/22/VK&CP/CSE/14-15 on Information Security & Awareness (ISEA)

Phase-II by Ministry of Electronics & Information Technology, Government of India. Janaka Alawatugoda acknowledges the grant NRC 16-020 of National Research Council, Sri Lanka.

References

1. Akavia, A., Goldwasser, S., Vaikuntanathan, V.: Simultaneous hardcore bits and cryptography against memory attacks. In: Reingold, O. (ed.) TCC 2009. LNCS, vol. 5444, pp. 474–495. Springer, Heidelberg (2009). doi:10.1007/978-3-642-00457-5_28
2. Alawatugoda, J., Boyd, C., Stebila, D.: Continuous after-the-fact leakage-resilient key exchange. In: Susilo, W., Mu, Y. (eds.) ACISP 2014. LNCS, vol. 8544, pp. 258–273. Springer, Cham (2014). doi:10.1007/978-3-319-08344-5_17
3. Alawatugoda, J., Stebila, D., Boyd, C.: Modelling after-the-fact leakage for key exchange. In: Proceedings of the 9th ACM Symposium on Information, Computer and Communications Security, pp. 207–216. ACM (2014)
4. Alawatugoda, J., Stebila, D., Boyd, C.: Continuous after-the-fact leakage-resilient eCK-secure key exchange. In: Groth, J. (ed.) IMACC 2015. LNCS, vol. 9496, pp. 277–294. Springer, Cham (2015). doi:10.1007/978-3-319-27239-9_17
5. Bellare, M., Rogaway, P.: Entity authentication and key distribution. In: Stinson, D.R. (ed.) CRYPTO 1993. LNCS, vol. 773, pp. 232–249. Springer, Heidelberg (1994). doi:10.1007/3-540-48329-2_21
6. Brakerski, Z., Kalai, Y.T., Katz, J., Vaikuntanathan, V.: Overcoming the hole in the bucket: public-key cryptography resilient to continual memory leakage. IACR Cryptology ePrint Archive, Report 2010/278 (2010)
7. Brumley, D., Boneh, D.: Remote timing attacks are practical. In: USENIX Security Symposium, pp. 1–14 (2003)
8. Canetti, R., Krawczyk, H.: Analysis of key-exchange protocols and their use for building secure channels. In: Pfitzmann, B. (ed.) EUROCRYPT 2001. LNCS, vol. 2045, pp. 453–474. Springer, Heidelberg (2001). doi:10.1007/3-540-44987-6_28
9. Chakraborty, S., Janaka Alawatugoda, C., Rangan, P.: New approach to practical leakage-resilient public-key cryptography. Cryptology ePrint Archive, Report 2017/441 (2017). http://eprint.iacr.org/2017/441
10. Chakraborty, S., Paul, G., Rangan, C.P.: Efficient compilers for after-the-fact leakage: from CPA to CCA-2 secure PKE to AKE. In: Pieprzyk, J., Suriadi, S. (eds.) ACISP 2017. LNCS, vol. 10342, pp. 343–362. Springer, Cham (2017). doi:10.1007/978-3-319-60055-0_18
11. Chen, R., Mu, Y., Yang, G., Susilo, W., Guo, F.: Strongly leakage-resilient authenticated key exchange. In: Sako, K. (ed.) CT-RSA 2016. LNCS, vol. 9610, pp. 19–36. Springer, Cham (2016). doi:10.1007/978-3-319-29485-8_2
12. Chow, S.S.M., Dodis, Y., Rouselakis, Y., Waters, B.: Practical leakage-resilient identity-based encryption from simple assumptions. In: Proceedings of the 17th ACM Conference on Computer and Communications Security, pp. 152–161. ACM (2010)
13. Dodis, Y., Haralambiev, K., López-Alt, A., Wichs, D.: Cryptography against continuous memory attacks. In: 2010 51st Annual IEEE Symposium on Foundations of Computer Science (FOCS), pp. 511–520. IEEE (2010)
14. Dodis, Y., Kalai, Y.T., Lovett, S.: On cryptography with auxiliary input. In: STOC, pp. 621–630 (2009)

15. Dodis, Y., Ostrovsky, R., Reyzin, L., Smith, A.: Fuzzy extractors: How to generate strong keys from biometrics and other noisy data. SIAM J. Comput. **38**(1), 97–139 (2008)

16. Dodis, Y., Pietrzak, K.: Leakage-resilient pseudorandom functions and side-channel attacks on feistel networks. In: Rabin, T. (ed.) CRYPTO 2010. LNCS, vol. 6223, pp. 21–40. Springer, Heidelberg (2010). doi:10.1007/978-3-642-14623-7_2

17. Döttling, N., Garg, S.: Identity-based encryption from the diffie-hellman assumption. Cryptology ePrint Archive, Report 2017/543 (2017). http://eprint.iacr.org/2017/543

18. Dziembowski, S., Faust, S.: Leakage-resilient cryptography from the inner-product extractor. In: Lee, D.H., Wang, X. (eds.) ASIACRYPT 2011. LNCS, vol. 7073, pp. 702–721. Springer, Heidelberg (2011). doi:10.1007/978-3-642-25385-0_38

19. Dziembowski, S., Pietrzak, K.: Leakage-resilient cryptography. In: IEEE 49th Annual IEEE Symposium on Foundations of Computer Science, FOCS 2008, pp. 293–302. IEEE (2008)

20. Faonio, A., Nielsen, J.B., Venturi, D.: Mind your coins: fully leakage-resilient signatures with graceful degradation. In: Halldórsson, M.M., Iwama, K., Kobayashi, N., Speckmann, B. (eds.) ICALP 2015. LNCS, vol. 9134, pp. 456–468. Springer, Heidelberg (2015). doi:10.1007/978-3-662-47672-7_37

21. Freire, E.S.V., Hofheinz, D., Kiltz, E., Paterson, K.G.: Non-interactive key exchange. In: Kurosawa, K., Hanaoka, G. (eds.) PKC 2013. LNCS, vol. 7778, pp. 254–271. Springer, Heidelberg (2013). doi:10.1007/978-3-642-36362-7_17

22. Galindo, D.: Boneh-Franklin identity based encryption revisited. In: Caires, L., Italiano, G.F., Monteiro, L., Palamidessi, C., Yung, M. (eds.) ICALP 2005. LNCS, vol. 3580, pp. 791–802. Springer, Heidelberg (2005). doi:10.1007/11523468_64

23. Halevi, S., Lin, H.: After-the-fact leakage in public-key encryption. In: Ishai, Y. (ed.) TCC 2011. LNCS, vol. 6597, pp. 107–124. Springer, Heidelberg (2011). doi:10.1007/978-3-642-19571-6_8

24. Hutter, M., Mangard, S., Feldhofer, M.: Power and EM attacks on passive 13.56MHz RFID devices. In: CHES, pp. 320–333 (2007)

25. Katz, J., Vaikuntanathan, V.: Signature schemes with bounded leakage resilience. In: Matsui, M. (ed.) ASIACRYPT 2009. LNCS, vol. 5912, pp. 703–720. Springer, Heidelberg (2009). doi:10.1007/978-3-642-10366-7_41

26. Kiltz, E., Pietrzak, K.: Leakage resilient elgamal encryption. In: Abe, M. (ed.) ASIACRYPT 2010. LNCS, vol. 6477, pp. 595–612. Springer, Heidelberg (2010). doi:10.1007/978-3-642-17373-8_34

27. LaMacchia, B., Lauter, K., Mityagin, A.: Stronger security of authenticated key exchange. In: Susilo, W., Liu, J.K., Mu, Y. (eds.) ProvSec 2007. LNCS, vol. 4784, pp. 1–16. Springer, Heidelberg (2007). doi:10.1007/978-3-540-75670-5_1

28. Messerges, T.S., Dabbish, E.A., Sloan, R.H.: Examining smart-card security under the threat of power analysis attacks. IEEE Trans. Comput. **51**(5), 541–552 (2002)

29. Micali, S., Reyzin, L.: Physically observable cryptography (extended abstract). In: Naor, M. (ed.) TCC 2004. LNCS, vol. 2951, pp. 278–296. Springer, Heidelberg (2004). doi:10.1007/978-3-540-24638-1_16

30. Naor, M., Segev, G.: Public-key cryptosystems resilient to key leakage. In: Halevi, S. (ed.) CRYPTO 2009. LNCS, vol. 5677, pp. 18–35. Springer, Heidelberg (2009). doi:10.1007/978-3-642-03356-8_2

31. Petit, C., Standaert, F.-X., Pereira, O., Malkin, T.G., Yung, M.: A block cipher based pseudo random number generator secure against side-channel key recovery. In: Proceedings of the 2008 ACM Symposium on Information, Computer and Communications Security, pp. 56–65. ACM (2008)

32. Pietrzak, K.: A leakage-resilient mode of operation. In: Joux, A. (ed.) EURO-CRYPT 2009. LNCS, vol. 5479, pp. 462–482. Springer, Heidelberg (2009). doi:10.1007/978-3-642-01001-9_27
33. Shoup, V.: Oaep reconsidered. J. Cryptol. **15**(4), 223–249 (2002)
34. Shoup, V.: Sequences of games: a tool for taming complexity in security proofs. IACR Cryptology EPrint Archive, 2004:332 (2004)
35. Yuen, T.H., Chow, S.S.M., Zhang, Y., Yiu, S.M.: Identity-based encryption resilient to continual auxiliary leakage. In: Pointcheval, D., Johansson, T. (eds.) EURO-CRYPT 2012. LNCS, vol. 7237, pp. 117–134. Springer, Heidelberg (2012). doi:10.1007/978-3-642-29011-4_9

New Framework of Password-Based Authenticated Key Exchange from Only-One Lossy Encryption

Haiyang Xue[1,2(✉)], Bao Li[1,2,3], and Jingnan He[1,2]

[1] Data Assurance and Communication Security Research Center,
Institute of Information Engineering, Chinese Academy of Sciences, Beijing, China
[2] Science and Technology on Communication Security Laboratory, Chengdu, China
[3] University of Chinese Academy of Sciences, Beijing, China

Abstract. In this paper, we introduce a new framework of password-based key exchange (PAKE). Until now, most PAKEs are based on smooth projective hash function on secure encryption. Our PAKE does not rely on smooth projective hash function, and consists of a variate lossy encryption, called only-one lossy encryption, and indistinguishable plaintext checkable secure encryption. We also give construction of only-one lossy encryption based decisional Diffie Hellman (DDH) and learning with errors (LWE) assumptions. Although the instantiation based on DDH assumption does not improve efficiency of precious works, our framework provides more easier and elegant way to construct PAKE from LWE assumption.

Keywords: Password-based key exchange · Lossy encryption · DDH assumption · LWE assumption

1 Introduction

Password-based authenticated key exchange (PAKE) allows two users to mutually authenticate each other and agree on a high-entropy session key based on a shared low-entropy password. The challenge in designing such protocols is to prevent *off-line* dictionary attacks where an adversary exhaustively enumerates potential passwords, attempting to match the correct password. The secure goal of PAKE is to restrict the adversary's advantage to that of *online* dictionary attack. The seminal work in the area of PAKE was given by Bellovin and Merritt [4]. After that, Bellare et al. [6], and Boyko et al. [5] proposed formal security models for PAKE. Since then, a large number of constructions were presented in the random oracle model [1,5,6]. But the random oracle model is known to be not sound [8], we only consider standard model in this paper.

The first PAKE protocol to achieve security in standard model was given by Goldreich and Lindel [10]. There are several works to improve and simplify Goldreich and Lindel's scheme. Unfortunately, they are inefficient in terms of communication, computation and round complexity. Katz, Ostrovsky and Yung

© Springer International Publishing AG 2017
T. Okamoto et al. (Eds.): ProvSec 2017, LNCS 10592, pp. 188–198, 2017.
https://doi.org/10.1007/978-3-319-68637-0_11

[16] demonstrated the first efficient PAKE (KOY) under DDH assumption with common reference string(CRS). On the ground of concrete construction of KOY protocol, a framework of PAKE (GL-PAKE) was abstracted by Gennaro and Lindell [11]. GL-PAKE consists of two smooth projective hash functions [7] (SPHF) on chosen ciphertext secure(IND-CCA) encryption. Following the work of KOY, Jiang and Gong [14] improved and gave a PAKE with mutual authentication under DDH assumption. Groce and Katz [12] abstracted the prototol of Jiang and Gong's protocol and give a framework of PAKE (GK-PAKE) by using of SPHF on IND-CPA secure encryption and IND-CCA secure encryption. Recently, Abdalla, Benhamouda and Pointcheval [2] pointed out that the underlying IND-CCA secure encryption in GL-PAKE and GK-PAKE once can be replaced by indistinguishable plaintext checkable secure (IND-PCA) scheme.

Both the GL-PAKE and GK-PAKE frameworks are based on SPHF over secure encryption. It seems that SPHF over encryption scheme is inevitable. Although SPHF supports efficient constructions based on DDH, QR and DCR [19] assumptions. The reliance on SPHF leads to limitations on resulting protocols: firstly, all SPHF are based on decisional assumptions which are generally weaker than computational assumptions. Secondly, When based on lattice assumptions, SPHF is unnatural and it is also an open problem to construct concrete SPHF based on lattice assumptions [17], making the SPHF based PAKE unsuitable in a possible upcoming post quantum world. We also note Katz and Vaikuntanathan [17] proposed an *approximate* SPHF over LWE-based IND-CCA secure encryption, and gave a LWE based PAKE by modifying GL-PAKE. But the protocol is inefficient and is more like a existence result.

One exception (that does not rely on SPHF) is the framework given by Canetti et al. [9] (CDVW-PAKE) based on oblivious transfer protocol and IND-CCA secure encryption. The CDVW-PAKE has the advantage of basing on computational assumption. But, the oblivious transfer protocol needs more communications (it needs 1 out of $|D|$ oblivious transfer, and $|D|$ commitments from the sender, where $|D|$ is the size of password space and the size of real-world password space $|D|$ is generally large [23]), the instantiations of CDVW-PAKE generally needs more communications (the commitments contains at least $|D|$ random string). Precisely, the communications is a linear function of password space.[1]

Thus, a new framework of PAKE, that does not rely on SPHF, has less communication independent with password space, and is more fitable to lattice assumption, is needed. We give such framework in this paper and propose its instantiations based on DDH and LWE assumptions.

1.1   Our Contributions

We propose a new framework of PAKE based on a variant of lossy encryption and IND-PCA secure encryption in this paper. This framework has the following

---

[1] Even optimizing the protocol by parse the password into bits, the communications still depends on the password space.

benefits: it does not rely on SPHF, making it possible to instantiate the framework on lattice assumptions; the communications is independent of the password space, and generally less then that based on oblivious transfer.

The basic tool is a strong variant of tag-based lossy encryption. Lossy encryption was proposed by Bellare *et al.* [3] by extending meaningful/meaningless encryption in [15]. The public key has two indistinguishable modes: in the normal mode, the cryptosystem behaves normally, and in the *lossy* mode, the ciphertext statistically loses information of the message.

We extend the lossy encryption to tag-based one to fits the application of PAKE. The tag-based encryption, called only-one lossy encryption, has the following properties: (1) The lossy encryption has a hidden branch in public key. Given public key it is difficult to find this branch; (2) only when tag is equal to this branch the encryption is normal and decryptable, in the other case the encryption of any two messages is statistically indistinguishable; (3) With a trapdoor, there is an algorithm to decide whether a tag is equal to the hidden branch in public key. At a first look, the tag-based encryption looks like All-But-One technique but it has essential difference. Take the general All-But-One lossy trapdoor function in [21] as example, in the All-But-One technique, the "one" is lossy and secure to prove the security, the others is invertible to provide inversion functionality. But the Only-one lossy encryption is that the one is decryptable to provide the functionality and the others is lossy and statistically secure to provide security.

Based on only-one lossy encryption and IND-PCA secure encryption, we propose a framework of PAKE, and prove its security in standard model. After that, we also give two instantiations based on DDH assumption and learning with errors (LWE) assumption.

1.2 Related Works

Peikert et al. proposed the notion of dual mode cryptosystem [20] aimming at universal composable secure oblivious transfer. In the dual mode cryptosystem, it requires two setup algorithms, and in one mode, there should be a algorithm to generate decryption key for ciphertext on all tag. We do not require this in only-one lossy encryption.

Canetti et al. [9] propose a framework of based on oblivious transfer protocol and IND-CCA secure encryption. The CDVW-PAKE has the advantage of basing on computational assumption. But, the oblivious transfer needs more communications (it needs $|D|$ commitment, where $|D|$ is the size of password space), the instantiations of CDVW-PAKE generally needs more communications (at least needs commitments of $|D|$ randomness).

2 Preliminaries

In this section, we give some notions and recall the definition of lossy encryption and the BPR secure mode of PAKE.

2.1 Notations

If S is a set, we denote by $|S|$ the cardinality of S, and denote by $x \leftarrow S$ the process of sampling x uniformly from S. A function is *negligible* (negl) if for every $c > 0$ there exists a λ_c such that $f(\lambda) < 1/\lambda^c$ for all $\lambda > \lambda_c$. If A and B are distributions, $A =_s B$ means that the statistical distance between A and B is negligible.

For any $s > 0$, and $\mathbf{c} \in \mathbb{R}^n$ define the Gaussian function: $\forall \mathbf{x} \in \mathbb{R}^n$, $\rho_{s,\mathbf{c}} = exp(-\pi \|\mathbf{x} - \mathbf{c}\|^2/s^2)$. For any $\mathbf{c} \in \mathbb{R}$, real $s > 0$, and n-dimensional lattice Λ, define the discrete Guassian distribution over Λ as $\forall \mathbf{x} \in \Lambda, \mathcal{D}_{\Lambda,s,\mathbf{c}}(\mathbf{x}) = \frac{\rho_{s,\mathbf{c}}(\mathbf{x})}{\rho_{s,\mathbf{c}}(\Lambda)}$, where $\rho_{s,\mathbf{c}}(\Lambda) = \sum_{\mathbf{y} \in \Lambda} \rho_{s,\mathbf{c}}(\mathbf{y})$. we omit the parameter $\mathbf{c}$ when it is 0. For $\alpha \in \mathbb{R}^+$, Ψ_α is defined to be the distribution on $\mathbb{R}/\mathbb{Z}$ of a mormal variable with mean 0 and standard deviation $\alpha/\sqrt{2\pi}$, reduced modulo 1. Let $\bar{\Psi}_\alpha$ be the discrete distribution of the random variable $|q \cdot X| \mod q$ where X has distribution Ψ_α.

2.2 Encryption

For formal definition of lossy encryption please refer citeBellare2009a. We first recall the definition of IND-PCA security given by Abdalla et al. [2], then give the definition of witness extractable encryption. Any (labeled) public-key encryption scheme is defined by three algorithms:

- KeyGen(1^λ) generates a key pair: a public key pk and a secret key sk;
- Enc(pk, label, m, r) encrypts the message m under the key pk with label label, using the random coins r;
- Dec(sk, label, C) decrypts the ciphertext C, using the secret key sk, label label. For any key pairs (pk, sk), any label label, any random coin r and any message m, it holds that Dec$(sk, \text{label}, \text{Enc}(pk, \text{label}, m, r)) = m$ with overwhelming probability.

Definition 1 (IND-PCA Security [2]). *A (labeled) public-key encryption scheme (KeyGen, Enc, Dec) is said to be indistinguishable plaintext checkable (IND-PCA) secure if the advantage of any PPT adversary A in the following interaction is negligible in the security parameter:*

1. *KeyGen(1^λ) outputs (pk, sk), A is given pk by the challenger.*
2. *A may adaptively query the decryption check oracle DCheck(label, C, m), which answers whether the decryption of C under the label l is m.*
3. *At some point, A outputs a label label* and two messages m_0 and m_1, and receives a challenge ciphertext $c^* = $ Enc$(pk, \text{label}^*, m_b, r)$ for a uniformly chosen bit b.*
4. *A may continue to adaptively query the decryption check oracle DCheck(label, C, m) with (label, C, m) such that (label, C) ≠ (label*, C*).*
5. *Finally, A outputs a bit b'. The advantage of A is denoted as $|Pr[b' = 1|b = 0] - Pr[b' = 1|b = 1]|$.*

2.3   Password-Based Authenticated Key Exchange

As the space limits, we omit the secure definition of BPR model [6] with mutual authentication which is added by [12]. For more details, please refer [12].

3   Only-One Lossy Encryption

As a basic tool of PAKE, we first propose the definition of only-one lossy encryption. And as a preparation of PAKE, we also give the instantiations based on DDH and LWE assumptions.

Informally, in the only-one lossy encryption, there is a branch hided in public key; With a trapdoor, there is a algorithm to decide which tag is equal to this branch; But without the trapdoor the branch is secure; If tag is equal to this branch the encryption works as normal and can decrypted with security key; If tag is not equal to this branch, the ciphertext of any two message is statistically indistinguishable. The following is the formal definition.

Definition 2 (Only-one lossy encryption). *The only-one lossy encryption consists a tuple of probability polynomial time (PPT) algorithms (NormSamp, KeyGen, Enc, Dec, Decide).*

- *NormSamp(λ), given security parameters λ, outputs the public parameters pp, corresponding trapdoor td together with a normal branch b in tag space D.*
- *KeyGen(b), given the normal branch b, outputs (pk, sk) where pk is a public encryption key and sk is the corresponding decryption key on tag b.*
- *Enc(pk, tag, m, r), given public key, and tag tag$\in$ D, message $m \in \{0,1\}^l$ and randomness r, outputs a ciphertext c of m on tag tag.*
- *Dec(sk, c), given a decryption key, ciphertext c on tag b, outputs a message m in $\{0,1\}^l$.*
- *Decide(td, pk, tag), given the trapdoor td generated by NormSamp, public key with branch b and a tag tag, outputs 1 if tag = b, 0 otherwise.*

Those algorithms satisfy the following secure requirements:

Correctness. *For all $m \in \{0,1\}^l$ and pk with normal branch b,*

$$Dec(sk, Enc(pk, b, m)) = m.$$

Lossiness. *For any pk with normal branch b, any tag tag $\neq$ b, and any pair of message $m_0, m_1 \in \{0,1\}^l$, there is*

$$\{Enc(pk, tag, m_0, r)|r \leftarrow \mathcal{R}\} =_s \{Enc(pk, tag, m_1, r)|r \in \mathcal{R}\}$$

Normal Branch Hidding. *For any the two distinct branches (b, b^*) in tag space, the two ensembles $\{pk|(pk, sk) \leftarrow KeyGen(b)\}$ and $\{pk|(pk, sk) \leftarrow KeyGen(b^*)\}$ are computational indistinguishable.*

Note that the only-one lossy encryptions has some property similar with dual mode cryptosystem given by [20], but has main differences. As their aim is universal composable secure oblivious transfer, in the dual mode cryptosystem, it requires two setup algorithms, and in one mode, there should be a algorithm to generate decryption key for ciphertext on all tag. We do not require this in only-one lossy encryption. There is another difference, the branch space in dual mode cryptosystem is $\{0,1\}$, while in only-one lossy encryption the tag space is D.

In the following, we give the constructions based on DDH and LWE assumptions.

3.1   Only-One Lossy Encryption from DDH Assumption

Let $\mathbb{G}$ be a cyclic group of prime order p with a generator g. The DDH assumption is the following: for random generator $g, h \in \mathbb{G}$, and for independent $a, b, c \in Z_p$ the tuples (g, g^a, g^b, g^{ab}) abd (g, g^a, g^b, g^c) are computational indistinguishable. We now construct a only one lossy encryption scheme based on DDH assumption.

- NormSamp(λ), given security parameters λ, chooses $a \leftarrow Z_p$ and $b \leftarrow Z_p$, computes $h = g^a$. It outputs the public parameters $pp = (\mathbb{G}, g, h)$, corresponding trapdoor $td = a$ together with a normal branch b.
- KeyGen(b), given the normal branch b, chooses $r \leftarrow Z_p$, computes $g_1 = g^s, h_1 = h^s g^b$. It outputs $pk = (g_1, h_1)$ and $sk = s$.
- Enc, given public key (g_1, h_1), and tag tag$\in Z_p$ and message $m \in Z_p$, chooses $r_1, r_2 \leftarrow Z_p$. It computes $c_1 = g^{r_1} h^{r_2}, c_2 = g_1^{r_1}(h_1/g^{\mathsf{tag}})^{r_2} \cdot m$, outputs a ciphertext $c = (c_1, c_2)$.
- Dec, given a decryption key s, ciphertext $c = (c_1, c_2)$ on tag b, outputs a message m by computing c_2/c_1^s.
- Decide(td, pk, tag), given the trapdoor $td = a$, public key with branch b and a tag tag, outputs 1 if $h_1/g_1^a = g^{\mathsf{tag}}$, 0 otherwise.

Theorem 1. *The above scheme is a only one lossy encryption under the DDH assumption on* $\mathbb{G}$.

As the space limit, we omit the formal proof.

3.2   Only-One Lossy Encryption from LWE Assumption

We recall the definition of LWE assumption.

Definition 3 (Learning With Errors (LWE)). *Let* $m = m(n), q = q(n)$ *be integers, and* χ *be a distribution on* Z_q. *Let* $\boldsymbol{A} \leftarrow Z_q^{m \times n}$, $\boldsymbol{s} \leftarrow Z_q^n$, $\boldsymbol{e} \leftarrow \chi^m$, *then* $LWE(m, n, a, \chi)$ *problem is to find* $\boldsymbol{s}$, *given* $(\boldsymbol{A}, \boldsymbol{As} + \boldsymbol{e})$.

This is the search version of the LWE problem. Regev [22] proved the security of $LWE(m, n, q, \mathcal{D}_{Z,\alpha q})$ when $m = poly(n)$ and $\alpha q \geq 2\sqrt{n}$.

Definition 4 (Decisional Learning With Errors (DLWE)). *Let* $m = m(n), q = q(n)$ *be integers, and* χ *be a distribution on* Z_q. *Let* $\mathbf{A} \leftarrow Z_q^{m \times n}$, $\mathbf{s} \leftarrow Z_q^n$, $\mathbf{e} \leftarrow \chi^m$, *then* $DLWE(m, n, a, \chi)$ *problem is that given* $(\mathbf{A}, \mathbf{b})$, *decide whether* $\mathbf{b}$ *is distributed by* $\mathbf{As} + \mathbf{e}$ *or chosen uniformly at random from* $Z^n q$.

The hardness of DLWE can be reduced to the hardness of the search version of LWE [22].

We now present the constructions of a only-one lossy encryption. This only-one lossy encryption is a modified and weaker version of dual-mode encryption based on LWE assumption proposed by Peikert et al. [20], which is also a Regev-like scheme [22]. The scheme uses lslossy algorithm in [13] to decide the normal branch.

- NormSamp(λ): chooses a random matrix $\mathbf{A} \leftarrow Z_q^{n \times m}$ uniformly random together with a trapdoor $t = \mathbf{S}$ as described by Gentry et al. [13]. It chooses k random vectors $\mathbf{v}_1, \mathbf{v}_2, \cdots, \mathbf{v}_k \leftarrow Z_q^m$. It generates a normal branch $b \in \{1, \cdots, k\}$ and outputs $(\mathbf{A}, \mathbf{v}_1, \cdots, \mathbf{v}_k)$ as CRS, $\mathbf{S}$ as trapdoor, and b as normal branch.
- KeyGen(b): given the normal branch $b \in \{1, \cdots, k\}$, it chooses a random $\mathbf{s} \in Z_q^n$ and errors vector $\mathbf{x} \leftarrow \chi^m$. It computes and outputs $pk = \mathbf{s}^T \mathbf{A} + \mathbf{x} + \mathbf{v}_b$.
- Enc(pk, tag, m): given public key, and tag tag$\in \{1, \cdots, k\}$ and message $m \in \{0, 1\}$, it chooses a vector $\mathbf{e} \in Z^m$ according to $\mathcal{D}_{Z^m, r}$, where r is given in security analysis. It computes $\mathbf{u} = \mathbf{A}\mathbf{e}$ and $c = (pk - \mathbf{v}_{\text{tag}})^T \mathbf{e} + m \cdot \lfloor 2/q \rfloor$ and outputs ciphertext $\mathbf{u}, c$.
- Dec(sk, $\mathbf{u}$, c): given ciphertext $\mathbf{u}, c$, it computes $c - \mathbf{s}^T \mathbf{u}$ and outputs 0 if it is close to 0 than to $\lfloor q/2 \rfloor$, otherwise outputs 1.
- Decide($\mathbf{S}$, pk, tag): It computes $\mathbf{d} = pk - \mathbf{v}_{\text{tag}}$. Run lslossy algorithm in [13] with input $(\mathbf{S}, \mathbf{A}, \mathbf{d})$, if lslossy outputs "lossy", tag is not the normal branch of pk, else it is.

The proof of the above only-one lossy encryption is implied by Lemmas 6.2, 6.3 and 6.6 in [13], and we just give sketch proof. The correctness of the decryption algorithm is guaranteed by Lemma 1. The correctness of the Decide algorithm is implied by Lemma 3. For any tag$\neq b$, $pk - \mathbf{v}_{\text{tag}} = \mathbf{s}^T \mathbf{A} + \mathbf{x} + \mathbf{v}_b - \mathbf{v}_{\text{tag}}$. As both $\mathbf{v}_b$ and $\mathbf{v}_{\text{tag}}$ are independent and randomly chosen, $\mathbf{v}_b - \mathbf{v}_{\text{tag}}$ is randomly chosen, thus $\mathbf{s}^T \mathbf{A} + \mathbf{x} + \mathbf{v}_b - \mathbf{v}_{\text{tag}}$ is randomly chosen. Take $\mathbf{s}^T \mathbf{A} + \mathbf{x} + \mathbf{v}_b - \mathbf{v}_{\text{tag}}$ to be $\mathbf{p}$ in Lemma 2, we have the lossy property. At last, the normal branch hiding is implied by replacing $\mathbf{s}^T \mathbf{A} + \mathbf{x}$ with a random element.

4   New Framework of PAKE

We now present the new framework for PAKE from only-one lossy encryption and IND-PCA secure encryption scheme. In this construction, the following primitives are required: Let (NormSamp, KeyGen, Enc, Dec, Decide) be the only-one lossy encryption and $CENC = $ (CKeyGen, CEnc, CDec) be a lable-based IND-PCA secure encryption. (For more information of label-based IND-PCA

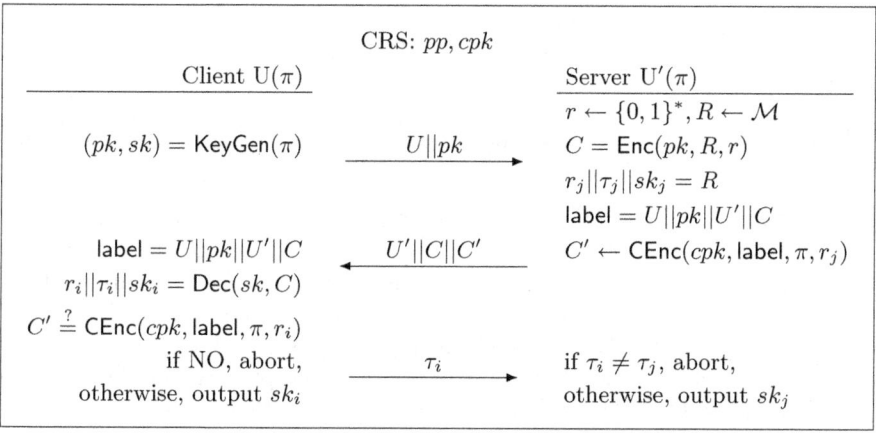

Fig. 1. New framework of PAKE

secure encryption, please refer [2]) Let the branch space of lossy encryption be equal to the password space and they both do not include 0. The protocol is displayed in Fig. 1.

Initialization: The CRS consists of public parameters pp generated by NormSamp, and the public keys cpk of IND-CPA secure encryption generated by CKeyGen.

Protocol execution. Figure 1 demonstrates the execution of the protocol.

Stage 1: When a client U (holds π) wants to authenticate to the server U' (holds π), it generate the public key pk of only-one lossy encryption from $(pk, sk) \leftarrow$ KeyGen(π), and sends $U\|pk$ to U'.

Stage 2: On receiving the message $U\|pk$, U' randomly chooses randomness r and a random message R in plaintext space $\mathcal{M}$, and computes ciphertext $C =$ Enc(pk, R, r) with randomness r. It parse R into three bit strings r_j, τ_j, sk_j. It sets label $= U\|pk\|U'\|C$, encrypts π as $C' \leftarrow$ CEnc(cpk, label, π, r_j) with randomness r_j. Then U' sends $U'\|C\|C'$ to U.

Stage 3: On receiving the message $U'\|C\|C'$, user U decrypt C using sk and decomposes massage as $r_i\|\tau_i\|sk_i \leftarrow$ Dec[sk, C]. It sets label $= (U\|pk\|U'\|C)$ and checks $C' \stackrel{?}{=}$ CEnc(cpk, label, π, r_i). If no, aborts else sends τ_i to U' and outputs sk_i which means that U' has successfully authenticated to U.

Stage 4: On receiving the message τ_i, U' checks that if $\tau_i = \tau_j$ or not. If $\tau_i \neq \tau_j$, U' aborts, otherwise U has successfully authenticated to U' and U' outputs sk_j.

If both parties are honest and there is no adversarial interference, then it guarantees that $r_i\|\tau_i\|sk_i = r_j\|\tau_j\|sk_j$. Both parties will accept and output the same session key.

Theorem 2. *If the underling encryption scheme are only-one lossy encryption and IND-PCA secure encryption scheme, the PAKE in Fig. 1 is secure in the BPR model.*

As the space limit, we omit the proof. Please refre the full paper for the formal proof.

Instantiations. We instantiate the framework in Sect. 3 based on DDH assumption and LWE assumption. Although, in case of DDH, we get a scheme with communication complexity of 8 group elements which has one more groups than the scheme in [12]. Our framework can be instantiated based on LWE assumption, which the GK-PAKE can not be instantiated based on lattice assumptions. Based on LWE assumption, the only-one lossy encryption is the one give in Sect. 3.2, and the IND-PCA secure encryption can be that is IND-CCA secure given by Gentry et al. [13] or that given by Micciancio and Peikert [18].

5   Conclusion

We give a framework of PAKE, which consists of only-one lossy encryption and IND-PCA secure encryption. Our framework can be instantiated from lattice assumptions. Only-one lossy encryption can be constructed based DDH and LWE assumptions. Although the instantiation of our framework based on DDH assumption does not improve efficiency of precious works, our framework provides more easier and elegant way to construct PAKE from lattice assumptions.

Acaknowledgement. Haiyang Xue is supported by the Foundation of Science and Technology on Communication Security Laboratory (9140C110206150C11049), National Natural Science Foundation of China (No. 61602473, 61502480, 61672019) and National Cryptography Development Fund MMJJ20170116. Bao Li is supported by the Foundation of Science and Technology on Communication Security Laboratory (9140C110206150C11049) and the National Natural Science Foundation of China (No. 61379137).

References

1. Abdalla, M., Pointcheval, D.: Simple password-based encrypted key exchange protocols. In: Menezes, A. (ed.) CT-RSA 2005. LNCS, vol. 3376, pp. 191–208. Springer, Heidelberg (2005). doi:10.1007/978-3-540-30574-3_14
2. Abdalla, M., Benhamouda, F., Pointcheval, D.: Public-key encryption indistinguishable under plaintext-checkable attacks. In: Katz, J. (ed.) PKC 2015. LNCS, vol. 9020, pp. 332–352. Springer, Heidelberg (2015). doi:10.1007/978-3-662-46447-2_15
3. Bellare, M., Hofheinz, D., Yilek, S.: Possibility and impossibility results for encryption and commitment secure under selective opening. In: Joux, A. (ed.) EUROCRYPT 2009. LNCS, vol. 5479, pp. 1–35. Springer, Heidelberg (2009). doi:10.1007/978-3-642-01001-9_1

4. Bellovin, M., Merritt, M.: Encrypted key exchange: Password-based protocols secure against dictionary attacks. In: 1992 IEEE Symposium on Security and Privacy, pp. 72–84 (1992)
5. Boyko, V., MacKenzie, P., Patel, S.: Provably secure password-authenticated key exchange using Diffie-Hellman. In: Preneel, B. (ed.) EUROCRYPT 2000. LNCS, vol. 1807, pp. 156–171. Springer, Heidelberg (2000). doi:10.1007/3-540-45539-6_12
6. Bellare, M., Pointcheval, D., Rogaway, P.: Authenticated key exchange secure against dictionary attacks. In: Preneel, B. (ed.) EUROCRYPT 2000. LNCS, vol. 1807, pp. 139–155. Springer, Heidelberg (2000). doi:10.1007/3-540-45539-6_11
7. Cramer, R., Shoup, V.: Universal hash proofs and a paradigm for adaptive chosen ciphertext secure public-key encryption. In: Knudsen, L.R. (ed.) EUROCRYPT 2002. LNCS, vol. 2332, pp. 45–64. Springer, Heidelberg (2002). doi:10.1007/3-540-46035-7_4
8. Canetti, R., Goldreich, O., Halevi, S.: The random oracle methodology, revisited. J. ACM 51(4), 557–594 (2004)
9. Canetti, R., Dachman-Soled, D., Vaikuntanathan, V., Wee, H.: Efficient password authenticated key exchange via oblivious transfer. In: Fischlin, M., Buchmann, J., Manulis, M. (eds.) PKC 2012. LNCS, vol. 7293, pp. 449–466. Springer, Heidelberg (2012). doi:10.1007/978-3-642-30057-8_27
10. Goldreich, O., Lindell, Y.: Session-key generation using human passwords only. In: Kilian, J. (ed.) CRYPTO 2001. LNCS, vol. 2139, pp. 408–432. Springer, Heidelberg (2001). doi:10.1007/3-540-44647-8_24
11. Gennaro, R., Lindell, Y.: A framework for password-based authenticated key exchange. In: Biham, E. (ed.) EUROCRYPT 2003. LNCS, vol. 2656, pp. 524–543. Springer, Heidelberg (2003). doi:10.1007/3-540-39200-9_33
12. Groce, A., Katz, J.: A new framework for efficient password-based authenticated key exchange. In: ACM Conference on Computer and Communications Security, pp. 516–525 (2010)
13. Gentry, C., Peikert, C., Vaikuntanathan, V.: Trapdoors for hard lattice and new cryptographic constructions. In: STOC, pp. 197–206 (2008)
14. Jiang, S., Gong, G.: Password based key exchange with mutual authentication. In: Handschuh, H., Hasan, M.A. (eds.) SAC 2004. LNCS, vol. 3357, pp. 267–279. Springer, Heidelberg (2004). doi:10.1007/978-3-540-30564-4_19
15. Kol, G., Naor, M.: Cryptography and game theory: designing protocols for exchanging information. In: Canetti, R. (ed.) TCC 2008. LNCS, vol. 4948, pp. 320–339. Springer, Heidelberg (2008). doi:10.1007/978-3-540-78524-8_18
16. Katz, J., Ostrovsky, R., Yung, M.: Efficient password-authenticated key exchange using human-memorable passwords. In: Pfitzmann, B. (ed.) EUROCRYPT 2001. LNCS, vol. 2045, pp. 475–494. Springer, Heidelberg (2001). doi:10.1007/3-540-44987-6_29
17. Katz, J., Vaikuntanathan, V.: Smooth projective hashing and password-based authenticated key exchange from lattices. In: Matsui, M. (ed.) ASIACRYPT 2009. LNCS, vol. 5912, pp. 636–652. Springer, Heidelberg (2009). doi:10.1007/978-3-642-10366-7_37
18. Micciancio, D., Peikert, C.: Trapdoors for lattices: simpler, tighter, faster, smaller. In: Pointcheval, D., Johansson, T. (eds.) EUROCRYPT 2012. LNCS, vol. 7237, pp. 700–718. Springer, Heidelberg (2012). doi:10.1007/978-3-642-29011-4_41
19. Paillier, P., Pointcheval, D.: Efficient public-key cryptosystems provably secure against active adversaries. In: Lam, K.-Y., Okamoto, E., Xing, C. (eds.) ASIACRYPT 1999. LNCS, vol. 1716, pp. 165–179. Springer, Heidelberg (1999). doi:10.1007/978-3-540-48000-6_14

20. Peikert, C., Vaikuntanathan, V., Waters, B.: A framework for efficient and composable oblivious transfer. In: Wagner, D. (ed.) CRYPTO 2008. LNCS, vol. 5157, pp. 554–571. Springer, Heidelberg (2008). doi:10.1007/978-3-540-85174-5_31
21. Peikert, C., Waters, B.: Lossy trapdoor functions and their applications. In: Ladner, R.E., Dwork, C. (eds) STOC 2008, pp. 187-196 (2008)
22. Rege, O.: On lattices, learning with errors, random linear codes, and cryptography. J. ACM **56**(6), 1–40 (2009)
23. Wang, D., Jian, G., Huang, X., Wang, P.: Zipfs law in passwords. ACM Trans. Info. Syst. Sec. **1**(1), 33 pages (2015). Article 1

Security Models

Impossibility of the Provable Security of the Schnorr Signature from the One-More DL Assumption in the Non-programmable Random Oracle Model

Masayuki Fukumitsu[1]([⊠]) and Shingo Hasegawa[2]

[1] Faculty of Information Media, Hokkaido Information University,
Nishi-Nopporo 59-2, Ebetsu, Hokkaido 069-8585, Japan
`fukumitsu@do-johodai.ac.jp`
[2] Graduate School of Information Sciences, Tohoku University,
41 Kawauchi, Aoba-ku, Sendai, Miyagi 980-8576, Japan
`hasegawa@cite.tohoku.ac.jp`

Abstract. The security of the Schnorr signature was widely discussed. In the random oracle model (ROM), it is provable from the DL assumption, whereas there is a negative circumstantial evidence in the standard model. Fleischhacker, Jager and Schröder showed that the tight security of the Schnorr signature is unprovable from a strong cryptographic assumption, such as the One-more DL (OM-DL) assumption and the computational and decisional Diffie-Hellman assumption, in the ROM via a generic reduction as long as the underlying cryptographic assumption holds. However, it remains open whether or not the impossibility of the provable security of the Schnorr signature from a strong assumption via a *non-tight* and reasonable reduction. In this paper, we show that the security of the Schnorr signature is unprovable from the OM-DL assumption in the non-programmable ROM as long as the OM-DL assumption holds. Our impossibility result is proven via a non-tight and non-restricted Turing reduction.

Keywords: Schnorr signature · Non-programmable random oracle model · Impossibility result · One-more DL assumption

1 Introduction

The Schnorr signature is one of the representative signature schemes. This signature scheme has a simple and efficient construction. Its security was discussed in several literatures. Pointcheval and Stern [20] showed that it is provable to be strongly existentially unforgeable against the chosen message attack (seuf-cma) in the random oracle model (ROM) from the discrete logarithm (DL) assumption. Subsequently, Abdalla et al. [1] expands their result to cover more signatures which can be obtained via the Fiat-Shamir transformation [9].

© Springer International Publishing AG 2017
T. Okamoto et al. (Eds.): ProvSec 2017, LNCS 10592, pp. 201–218, 2017.
https://doi.org/10.1007/978-3-319-68637-0_12

On the other hand, there is a negative circumstantial evidence for the provable security of the Schnorr signature in the *standard model*. More specifically, the Schnorr signature is unprovable to be secure from the DL assumption in the standard model via an algebraic reduction as long as the One-more DL (OM-DL) assumption holds [18]. The OM-DL assumption [3] is parameterized by a polynomial T and it intuitively states that any probabilistic polynomial-time (PPT) adversary $\mathcal{A}$ cannot find the DLs $(x_1, x_2, \ldots, x_T)$ of given T elements $(y_1, y_2, \ldots, y_T)$ in a group $\mathbb{G}$, even when $\mathcal{A}$ adaptively obtains at most $T - 1$ DLs of arbitrary elements. We occasionally call such an OM-DL assumption T-*OM-DL assumption* explicitly.

For the provable security of the Schnorr signature, the affirmative results were given in the ROM, whereas the impossibility result was given in the standard model. The ROM is different from the standard model in the two features. The one is that the hash value is a truly random string in the ROM, whereas it is a pseudorandom string in the standard model. The other is that the *programming technique* [20] is utilizable in the ROM, although it cannot be used in the standard model. The programming technique is a proof technique where a reduction $\mathcal{R}$, which is constructed in the security proof, simulates the random oracle by setting hash values itself. By this technique, the security of many cryptographic schemes e.g. [8,16] was proven in the ROM. In fact, the forking lemma [20] can be realized by this technique for security proofs of several cryptographic schemes including the Schnorr signature. However, it is known that such a programming property is strong [23]. On the theoretical cryptography, one of the interests is how one can relax the property of the ROM to prove the security of cryptographic schemes. For this purpose, intermediate security models between the ROM and the standard model were proposed. One of these is a *non-programmable ROM (NPROM)*. The concept of the NPROM was introduced by Nielson [17] in order to give an impossibility result on the existence of a non-interactive non-committing encryption. Their definition was given in the simulation-based security model. Subsequently, Fischlin et al. [11] formalized the NPROM for the game-based security proof, and discussed the security of a trapdoor-permutation-based key-encapsulation and a full-domain hash in the NPROM. In the NPROM, any parties of the security proof such as a reduction $\mathcal{R}$ and an adversary obtain hash values from the random oracle as well as the ROM, but $\mathcal{R}$ is prohibited to simulate it, namely it cannot set the hash values and we cannot use the programming technique.

The security of the Schnorr signature was also discussed in the NPROM. Fischlin and Fleischhacker [10] first gave a negative circumstantial evidence. They showed that the Schnorr signature is unprovable to be euf-cma from the DL assumption in the NPROM via a single-instance (SI) reduction as long as the OM-DL assumption holds. Subsequently, their impossibility result was extended in the several literatures [13,14,23]. In particular, Fukumitsu and Hasegawa [14] proved that the DL assumption is incompatible with the euf-cma security of the Schnorr signature in the NPROM via a sequentially multi-instance (SMI) reduction. In other words, the Schnorr signature may be unprovable to be euf-cma from the DL assumption in the NPROM as long as the DL assumption holds. The SMI reduction is a reduction such that it can invoke an adversary of the target cryptographic scheme polynomially many times, although it is prohibited to invoke the clones of the adversary concurrently.

However, it remains the possibility that it is provable from a cryptographic assumption which is stronger than the DL assumption, such as the OM-DL assumption and the computational and decisional Diffie-Hellman assumption [5]. This question was also discussed. As the affirmative result which is depicted in Table 1, Paillier and Vergnaud [18] showed that the Schnorr signature is provable to be unkeybreakable against the chosen-message attack (ukb-cma) from the OM-DL assumption in the standard model. Although it was proven via a tight reduction, the ukb-cma security is considered to be weak.

Table 1. The affirmative results on proving the security of the Schnorr signature

	Model	Security	Tightness	Underlying assumption
[1, 20]	ROM	seuf-cma		DL
[18]	Standard	ukb-cma	$\checkmark$	OM-DL

On the other hand, the negative circumstantial evidences were given in several literatures. Fleischhacker et al. [12] showed that the Schnorr signature is unprovable to be universally unforgeable against the key only attack (uuf-koa) from some cryptographic assumption, such as not only the DL assumption, but also the OM-DL assumption, in the ROM via a tight and generic reduction as long as the underlying cryptographic assumption holds. Recall that Paillier and Vergnaud [18] had also given such an impossibility result from the DL assumption via a tight and algebraic reduction. It should be noted that their impossibility result does not contradict to the affirmative results by [1,20]. This is because the results by [1,20] considered a non-tight reduction for the security proofs, whereas these impossibility results are only for *tight* reductions. In this sense, the result by [12] does not exclude the possibility that such a security can be proven via a non-tight reduction. Moreover, they only considered the strong constrained reduction, namely a generic reduction. The impossibility results mentioned above are collected in Table 2. Note that "only" in the Tightness column means that its impossibility excludes only a tight reduction. Eventually, it remains open whether or not the impossibility of the provable security of the Schnorr signature from a strong assumption in the NPROM via a non-tight and reasonable reduction.

1.1 Our Contributions

In this paper, we give an impossibility result on the provable security of the Schnorr signature from the OM-DL assumption in the NPROM via a Turing reduction. It is given by the following theorem.

Table 2. The impossibility results on proving the security of the Schnorr signature

	Model	Security	Tightness of reduction	Underlying assumption	Type of reduction	Assumptions on impossibility
[18]	ROM	uuf-cma	only	DL	algebraic	OM-DL assumption
[12]	ROM	uuf-koa	only	DL	generic	DL assumption
[12]	ROM	uuf-koa	only	OM-DL	generic	OM-DL assumption
[10]	NPROM	euf-cma		DL	SI	OM-DL assumption
[14]	NPROM	SMA [2]		DL	SMI	DL assumption
[ours]	**NPROM**	**suf-cma**		**OM-DL**	**Turing**	**OM-DL assumption**
[18]	Standard	uuf-cma		DL	algebraic	OM-DL assumption

Theorem 6 (Informal). *The Schnorr signature is unprovable to be selectively unforgeable against the chosen-message attack (suf-cma) from the OM-DL assumption in the NPROM via a Turing reduction as long as the OM-DL assumption holds.*

The intuition of the proof of the theorem is the following. Assume that a PPT Turing reduction algorithm $\mathcal{R}$ which solves the OM-DL problem by invoking any sf-cma forger $\mathcal{F}$ of the Schnorr signature exists. We shall construct a PPT *meta-reduction* algorithm [6] $\mathcal{M}$ which solves the OM-DL problem by running $\mathcal{R}$. This means that the OM-DL assumption is broken if there exists such a reduction $\mathcal{R}$. The theorem follows from the contraposition. In the construction of $\mathcal{M}$, we employ the technique introduced by Pass [19] and used by Zhang et al. [22].

In our theorem, we consider the *suf-cma* security [15]. The suf-cma security informally states that any PPT forger $\mathcal{F}$ cannot forge one m_{i*} of given N messages $(m_1, \ldots, m_N)$ even if $\mathcal{F}$ obtains polynomially many signatures from the signing oracle on messages other than the target message m_{i*}. It is known that suf-cma is weaker than euf-cma [15]. Putting together with Theorem 6, the impossibility of the ordinary euf-cma security also follows. Thus, our result states that the euf-cma security of the Schnorr signature is unprovable without the programming technique even from the OM-DL assumption as long as the OM-DL assumption holds. This means that the programming technique is required for us to prove the security of the Schnorr signature even from a strong cryptographic assumption. In other words, one should put forward a new technique or modify the Schnorr signature to prove its security in the NPROM or the standard model.

1.2 Related Works

Pass [19] gave an impossibility of the provable security on the Schnorr ID scheme [21] by which the Schnorr signature is derived via the Fiat-Shamir transformation. They showed that the Schnorr ID is unprovable to be secure against the impersonation under the active attack (imp-aa secure) from several interactive assumptions such as the OM-DL assumption. Note that the imp-aa security of the Schnorr ID was proven from the OM-DL assumption in [4]. This difference is induced by the parameter T of the OM-DL assumption. Bellare and Palacio [4] in fact considered the case where the parameter T is equivalent to the number of the access to the oracle in the imp-aa game, whereas Pass considered that T is asymptotically smaller than the number of the oracle access. It is known that the T_1-OM-DL assumption may be strictly weaker than the T_2-OM-DL assumption when $T_2 > T_1$ [7]. These imply that the Schnorr ID may be unprovable to be secure from the T-OM-DL assumption where the parameter T is strictly smaller than the number of the oracle access.

Although they focused on the provable security of the Schnorr ID, their result seems not to directly elucidate the question on the provable security of the Schnorr signature from the OM-DL assumption in the NPROM. This is because the relationship between the security of the Schnorr signature in the NPROM and the security of the Schnorr ID has not been known so far. Therefore, we address this question by directly observing the relationship between the security of the Schnorr signature and the OM-DL assumption.

2 Preliminaries

For any natural number n, let $\mathbb{Z}_n$ denote the residue ring $\mathbb{Z}/n\mathbb{Z}$. The notation $x \in_U X$ means that an element x is sampled uniformly at random from the finite set X. We denote by $x := y$ that x is defined or substituted as y. For any algorithm $\mathcal{A}$, we define by $y \leftarrow \mathcal{A}(x)$ that $\mathcal{A}$ takes x as input and then outputs y. When $\mathcal{A}$ is probabilistic, we write $y \leftarrow \mathcal{A}(x; r)$ to denote that $\mathcal{A}$ takes x as input with a randomness r and then outputs y, and $\mathcal{A}(x)$ is the random variable on input x, where the probability is taken over the internal coin flips of $\mathcal{A}$. A function ϵ is *negligible* if for any polynomial ν, there exists a natural number λ_0 such that for any $\lambda > \lambda_0$, $\epsilon(\lambda) < 1/\nu(\lambda)$.

2.1 Signature Scheme

A signature scheme Sig consists of a tuple (KGen, Sign, Ver) of three polynomial-time algorithms. KGen is a probabilistic polynomial-time (PPT) key generator which takes a security parameter 1^λ as input, and then outputs a *key pair* (sk, pk) of a secret key and a public key. Sign is a PPT signing algorithm which takes a key pair (sk, pk) and a message m as input, and then outputs a signature σ. Ver is a deterministic verification algorithm which takes a public key pk, a message m and a signature σ as input, and then outputs 1 if σ is a *valid* signature on the message m under the public key pk.

We now introduce the notions of the existential unforgeability against the chosen message attack (euf-cma) and the selective unforgeability against the chosen message attack (suf-cma). Let $\mathsf{Sig} := (\mathsf{KGen}, \mathsf{Sign}, \mathsf{Ver})$ be a signature scheme. The *ef-cma game* is defined in the following way: on a security parameter λ,

EF Init $\mathcal{F}$ is given a public key pk such that a challenger $\mathcal{C}$ generates $(sk, pk) \leftarrow \mathsf{KGen}(1^\lambda)$.

Signing Oracle When $\mathcal{F}$ hands an i-th message $\overline{m}_i$ to $\mathcal{C}$, $\mathcal{C}$ replies its signature $\overline{\sigma}_i \leftarrow \mathsf{Sign}(sk, pk, \overline{m}_i)$.

EF Challenge When $\mathcal{F}$ finally returns a pair (m^*, σ^*), $\mathcal{C}$ outputs 1 if $m^* \notin \{\overline{m}_i\}_i$ and $\mathsf{Ver}(pk, m^*, \sigma^*) = 1$.

Then $\mathcal{F}$ is said to *win the ef-cma game* if $\mathcal{C}$ outputs 1 in this game. In a similar manner, the *N-sf-cma game* is defined in the following way, where N is a polynomial in a security parameter λ: on a security parameter λ,

SF Init $\mathcal{F}$ is given a public key pk and a sequence $(m_1, m_2, \ldots, m_N)$ of N distinct messages such that a challenger $\mathcal{C}$ generates $(sk, pk) \leftarrow \mathsf{KGen}(1^\lambda)$ and samples $m_1, m_2, \ldots, m_N$ at random.

Signing Oracle It coincides with the one of the ef-cma game.

SF Challenge When $\mathcal{F}$ finally returns a pair (m_{i^*}, σ_{i^*}), $\mathcal{C}$ outputs 1 if $m_{i^*} \notin \{\overline{m}_i\}_i$ and $\mathsf{Ver}(pk, m_{i^*}, \sigma_{i^*}) = 1$.

Then $\mathcal{F}$ is said to *win the N-sf-cma game* if $\mathcal{C}$ outputs 1 in this game. Let goal $\in \{\mathrm{euf}, N\text{-suf}\}$. The signature scheme Sig is said to be *goal-cma* if for any PPT forger $\mathcal{F}$, $\mathcal{F}$ wins the corresponding game with negligible probability. The probability is taken over the internal coin flips of KGen and $\mathcal{F}$, and the choices of $m_1, m_2, \ldots, m_N$ only for the N-suf-cma. On the relationship between euf-cma and N-suf-cma, the following proposition holds.

Proposition 1 ([15]). Let Sig be a signature scheme, and let N be a polynomial in a security parameter λ. If Sig is euf-cma, then Sig is also N-suf-cma.

2.2 Cryptographic Assumption

We now introduce the One-more DL (OM-DL) assumption. We write GGen to denote a PPT group parameter generator which takes a security parameter λ as input, and then outputs a *group parameter* $(\mathbb{G}, p, g)$ of a group description $\mathbb{G}$ which is of prime order p with a generator g. For any group parameter $(\mathbb{G}, p, g) \leftarrow \mathsf{GGen}(1^\lambda)$ and any element $y \in \mathbb{G}$, an element $x \in \mathbb{Z}_p$ is said to be the *discrete logarithm (DL)* of y if it holds that $y = g^x$ in $\mathbb{G}$.

Let T be a polynomial in a security parameter λ. An algorithm $\mathcal{A}$ is said to *solve the T-OM-DL problem* if a challenger $\mathcal{C}$ outputs 1 in the *T-OM-DL game* that is defined in the following way: on a security parameter λ,

OM Init $\mathcal{A}$ is given a tuple $(\mathbb{G}, p, g, y_1, y_2, \ldots, y_T)$ such that $\mathcal{C}$ generates a group parameter $(\mathbb{G}, p, g) \leftarrow \mathsf{GGen}(1^\lambda)$, and then samples T distinct instances $y_1, \ldots, y_T \in_\mathsf{U} \mathbb{Z}_p$.

OM Oracle $\mathcal{A}$ is allowed to access the *DL oracle*. Namely, when $\mathcal{A}$ sends a t-th query $\overline{y}_t \in \mathbb{G}$, $\mathcal{A}$ receives the DL $\overline{x}_t \in \mathbb{Z}_p$ of $\overline{y}_t$.

OM Challenge When $\mathcal{A}$ eventually outputs a tuple $(x_1, x_2, \ldots, x_T)$, $\mathcal{C}$ outputs 1 if $\mathcal{A}$ made at most $T-1$ queries to the DL oracle in the **OM Oracle** phase, and for any $1 \le t \le T$, x_t is the DL of y_t.

The *T-OM-DL assumption holds* if for any PPT algorithm $\mathcal{A}$, $\mathcal{A}$ solves the T-OM-DL problem with negligible probability. The probability is taken over the internal coin flips of GGen and $\mathcal{A}$, and the choices of $y_1, \ldots, y_T$. Contrarily, the T-OM-DL assumption is said to be *tractable* if it does not hold.

3 Impossibility of Provable Security of Schnorr Signature from OM-DL Assumption in NPROM

In this section, we show the impossibility of proving that the Schnorr signature is N-suf-cma from the T-OM-DL assumption in the NPROM.

We now introduce the Schnorr signature [21].

$\mathsf{KGen}(1^\lambda)$ outputs a key pair (sk, pk) where $(\mathbb{G}, p, g) \leftarrow \mathsf{GGen}(1^\lambda)$, $sk \in_U \mathbb{Z}_p$, $y := g^{sk}$, and then $pk := (\mathbb{G}, p, g, y)$.

$\mathsf{Sign}(sk, pk, m)$ outputs a signature $\sigma := (\mathrm{cmt}, \mathrm{res})$ on the message m under the public key pk which is issued in the following way:
  (1) set $\mathrm{cmt} := g^{\mathrm{st}}$ by sampling $\mathrm{st} \in_U \mathbb{Z}_p$;
  (2) set $\mathrm{cha} := H_{pk}(\mathrm{cmt}, m)$, where $H_{pk} : \{0,1\}^* \to \mathbb{Z}_p$ is a hash function parametrized by pk; and
  (3) set $\mathrm{res} := \mathrm{st} + sk \cdot \mathrm{cha} \bmod p$.

$\mathsf{Ver}(pk, m, \sigma)$ outputs 1 if it holds that $\mathrm{cmt} = g^{\mathrm{res}} y^{-H_{pk}(\mathrm{cmt}, m)}$.

Let N and T be polynomials in a security parameter λ. We now explain the situation where *the Schnorr signature is provable to be N-suf-cma from the T-OM-DL assumption*. This is defined by the black-box reduction in a similar manner to e.g. [10,20]. This situation holds if there exist a non-negligible function ϵ and a PPT reduction algorithm $\mathcal{R}$ such that $\mathcal{R}$ solves the T-OM-DL problem with probability ϵ by invoking a forger $\mathcal{F}$ which wins the N-sf-cma game with non-negligible probability. Here, we restrict a reduction $\mathcal{R}$ to accessing the DL oracle at most $T-1$ times, since $\mathcal{R}$ aims to win the T-OM-DL game.

3.1 Case: Vanilla Reduction

For ease of the explanation, we first consider only the situation where $\mathcal{R}$ is vanilla, in a sense that the *vanilla reduction* $\mathcal{R}$ invokes a forger $\mathcal{F}$ only once and it is not allowed to rewind $\mathcal{F}$. In more detail, $\mathcal{R}$ can solve the T-OM-DL problem with non-negligible probability ϵ once $\mathcal{R}$ invokes an winning N-sf-cma forger $\mathcal{F}$. Here, $\mathcal{R}$ would play a role of a challenger in the N-sf-cma game.

The overview of $\mathcal{R}$ is depicted in Fig. 1. Let $(\mathbb{G}, p, g, y_1, y_2, \ldots, y_T)$ be a T-OM-DL instance given from a T-OM-DL challenger $\mathcal{C}$ to the reduction $\mathcal{R}$.

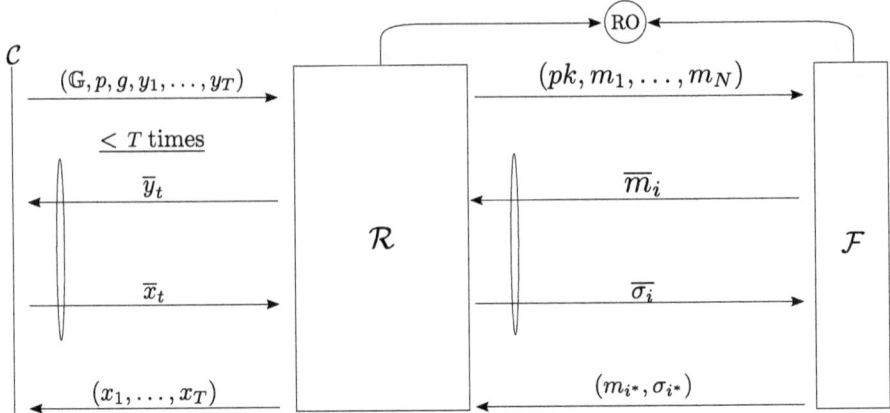

Fig. 1. Vanilla reduction $\mathcal{R}$

$\mathcal{R}$ aims to find a solution $(x_1, x_2, \ldots, x_T)$ of the instance $(\mathbb{G}, p, g, y_1, y_2, \ldots, y_T)$ in the following way. According to the **SF Init** phase of the N-sf-cma game, $\mathcal{R}$ would generate a tuple $(pk, m_1, m_2, \ldots, m_N)$ of a public key pk of the Schnorr signature and N distinct messages $m_1, m_2, \ldots, m_N$, and then invoke an winning N-sf-cma forger $\mathcal{F}$ on the tuple $(pk, m_1, m_2, \ldots, m_N)$. When $\mathcal{F}$ hands an i-th message $\overline{m}_i$ to $\mathcal{R}$ in the **Signing Oracle** phase, $\mathcal{R}$ should reply its signature $\overline{\sigma}_i$ under the public key pk. Note that $\mathcal{R}$ may fail to issue a valid signature of some $\overline{m}_i$, since it is a PPT algorithm. In this case, $\mathcal{F}$ is allowed to return $\perp$ as a final output. On the other hand, $\mathcal{F}$ returns a valid signature σ_{i^*} of the i^*-th message m_{i^*} with non-negligible probability for some index $1 \leq i^* \leq N$ if $\mathcal{F}$ receives all valid signatures in this phase. Finally, $\mathcal{R}$ finds a solution $(x_1, x_2, \ldots, x_T)$ of the instance $(\mathbb{G}, p, g, y_1, y_2, \ldots, y_T)$ with probability ϵ.

Here, the T-OM-DL adversary $\mathcal{R}$ can access the DL oracle at most $T - 1$ times. Namely, $\mathcal{R}$ would send a t-th instance $\overline{y}_t \in \mathbb{G}$ to receive its DL $\overline{x}_t \in \mathbb{Z}_p$.

In the *non-programmable random oracle model (NPROM)* [10], $\mathcal{R}$ and $\mathcal{F}$ should obtain hash values from the random oracle in a similar manner to the ordinary ROM. Then, $\mathcal{R}$ can observe all random oracle queries by $\mathcal{F}$, but it is not allowed to program these values.

Theorem 2. *Let $T < N$. Assume that the Schnorr signature is provable to be N-suf-cma from the T-OM-DL assumption in the NPROM via a vanilla reduction. Then, the T-OM-DL assumption is tractable.*

Proof (Sketch). Let $T < N$. Assume that the Schnorr signature is provable to be N-suf-cma from the T-OM-DL assumption in the NPROM via a vanilla reduction. Namely, there exist a non-negligible function ϵ and a PPT vanilla reduction $\mathcal{R}$ such that $\mathcal{R}$ solves the T-OM-DL problem with probability ϵ by invoking a forger $\mathcal{F}$ which wins the N-sf-cma game with non-negligible probability.

By invoking an winning N-sf-cma forger $\mathcal{F}$ once and accessing the DL oracle at most $T - 1$ times in the **OM Oracle** phase, $\mathcal{R}$ finds the solution $(x_1, \ldots, x_T)$

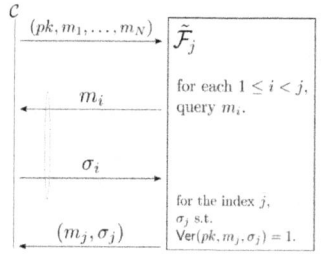

Algorithm: N-sf-cma forger $\tilde{\mathcal{F}}_j(pk, m_1, m_2, \ldots, m_N)$

(F-1) for each $1 \leq i < j$, hand the i-th message m_i,
and then obtain its signature σ_i. Once $\tilde{\mathcal{F}}_j$ finds
σ_i such that $\mathsf{Ver}(pk, m_i, \sigma_i) \neq 1$, then return $\bot$;
(F-2) find a valid signature σ_j of the j-th message m_j,
and then return (m_j, σ_j).

Fig. 2. N-sf-cma forger $\tilde{\mathcal{F}}_j$

of a given instance $(\mathbb{G}, p, g, y_1, \ldots, y_T)$ with probability ϵ. It suffices for finding
the solution $(x_1, \ldots, x_T)$ that a simulator of $\mathcal{F}$ is provided to $\mathcal{R}$. Hereafter, we
describe hypothetical N-sf-cma forgers $\tilde{\mathcal{F}}_j$ for $1 \leq j \leq N$. It should be noted that
$\mathcal{R}$ can solve the T-OM-DL problem if the hypothetical forger $\tilde{\mathcal{F}}_j$ for any index
$1 \leq j \leq N$ is provided for $\mathcal{R}$. We shall construct a meta-reduction algorithm $\mathcal{M}$
which solves the T-OM-DL problem with non-negligible probability by utilizing
$\mathcal{R}$ and simulating several forgers $\tilde{\mathcal{F}}_j$.

Hypothetical Forgers $\tilde{\mathcal{F}}_j$. We fix an index $1 \leq j \leq N$. A hypothetical forger
$\tilde{\mathcal{F}}_j$ is depicted in Fig. 2. On a tuple $(pk, m_1, \ldots, m_N)$, the hypothetical forger
$\tilde{\mathcal{F}}_j$ obtains a signature $\sigma_i := (\mathrm{cmt}_i, \mathrm{res}_i)$ of the i-th message m_i for each index
$1 \leq i < j$ in (F-1). As mentioned in the definition of $\mathcal{R}$, $\tilde{\mathcal{F}}_j$ is allowed to return
$\bot$ if it receives a non-valid signature of some handed message in the **Signing
Oracle** phase. Otherwise, $\tilde{\mathcal{F}}_j$ finds a signature $\sigma_j := (\mathrm{cmt}_j, \mathrm{res}_j)$ of the j-th
message m_j in (F-2). Note that $\tilde{\mathcal{F}}_j$ queries a pair (cmt_i, m_i) to the random
oracle for all $1 \leq i \leq j$, due to the verification in (F-1) and the finding the
challenge signature σ_j in (F-2). Since the N-sf-cma challenger $\mathcal{C}$ gives distinct
messages $m_1, \ldots, m_N$ to $\tilde{\mathcal{F}}_j$, we have $m_j \notin \{m_i\}_{1 \leq i < j}$. On the other hand, it
holds that $\mathsf{Ver}(pk, m_j, \sigma_j) = 1$. Thus $\tilde{\mathcal{F}}_j$ always wins the N-sf-cma game if it
receives a valid signature σ_i of m_i for all $1 \leq i < j$. It should be noted that
the process (F-2) is not required to be done in PPT here. We will construct a
meta-reduction $\mathcal{M}$ which simulates several forgers $\tilde{\mathcal{F}}_j$ for $\mathcal{R}$ in PPT.

Meta-Reduction $\mathcal{M}$. We depict in Fig. 3 a meta-reduction $\mathcal{M}$ which solves the
T-OM-DL problem with non-negligible probability by utilizing $\mathcal{R}$ with the simulation of several forgers $\tilde{\mathcal{F}}_j$. Note that the i-th slot means the period from
sending the i-th message m_i by $\tilde{\mathcal{F}}_N$ in (a) of (T-1) to receiving the hash value
of (cmt_i, m_i) in (b) of (T-1).

We now explain the idea of the meta-reduction $\mathcal{M}$. $\mathcal{M}$ aims to make $\mathcal{R}$
to solve the T-OM-DL problem. Recall that $\mathcal{R}$ can solve the T-OM-DL problem with non-negligible probability ϵ if some forger $\tilde{\mathcal{F}}_{i^*}$ is provided, where
$1 \leq i^* \leq N$. Therefore, $\mathcal{M}$ simulates the forger $\tilde{\mathcal{F}}_{i^*}$ for $\mathcal{R}$. In the simulation of
$\tilde{\mathcal{F}}_{i^*}$, $\mathcal{M}$ is required to find a signature σ_{i^*} of the challenge message m_{i^*} in PPT.

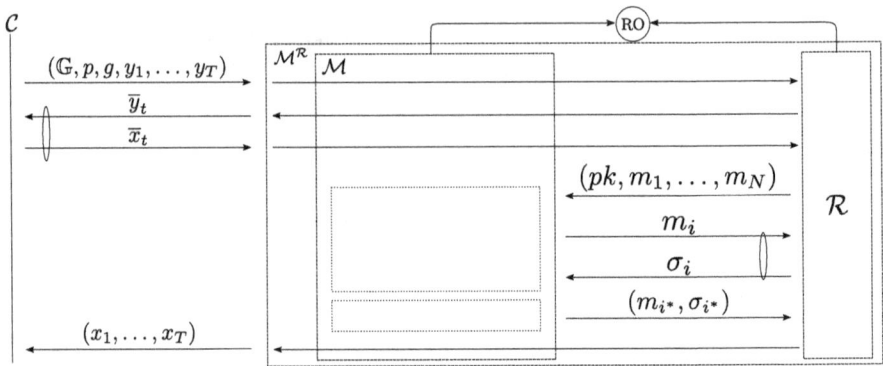

Algorithm: Meta-reduction $\mathcal{M}(\mathbb{G}, p, g, y_1, y_2, \dots, y_T)$

(M-1) sample random coins r, and then run $\mathcal{R}(\mathbb{G}, p, g, y_1, y_2, \dots, y_T; r)$. Hereafter, $\mathcal{M}$ records to List all inputs and outputs of $\mathcal{R}$, such as queries and responses in the **OM Oracle** phase, and interactions between $\mathcal{R}$ and $\mathcal{F}$.

(M-2) proceed in the following way according to an $\mathcal{R}$'s output:

    Access to DL oracle When $\mathcal{R}$ sends $\overline{y}_t \in \mathbb{G}$, forward it to the DL oracle, and reply its solution $\overline{x}_t$ to $\mathcal{R}$.

    Invocation of $\mathcal{F}$ Given $(pk, m_1, \dots, m_N)$ by $\mathcal{R}$, simulate $\tilde{\mathcal{F}}_N$ as follows:

        (T-1) for each $1 \leq i < N$,

            (a) hand the i-th message m_i to $\mathcal{R}$, and then receive its signature $\sigma_i := (\mathrm{cmt}_i, \mathrm{res}_i)$.

            (b) if $\mathsf{Ver}(pk, m_i, \sigma_i) \neq 1$, then return $\bot$, and then go to (M-4). During the verification, $\mathcal{M}$ queries (cmt_i, m_i) to the random oracle.

            (c) if $\mathcal{R}$ does not access the DL oracle during the i-th slot, set $i^* := i$, and then go to (M-3).

        (T-2) abort.

(M-3) rewind $\mathcal{R}(\mathbb{G}, p, g, y_1, y_2, \dots, y_T; r)$ in the following way. Here, $\mathcal{M}$ simulates $\tilde{\mathcal{F}}_{i^*}$ instead of $\tilde{\mathcal{F}}_N$.

    – Until just after obtaining the hash value of $(\mathrm{cmt}_{i^*-1}, m_{i^*-1})$, $\mathcal{M}$ runs in the same way as (M-1) and (M-2) except that it replies all of instances $\overline{y}_t$ sent from $\mathcal{R}$ by using List instead of the DL oracle.

    – For the i^*-th message m_{i^*}, $\mathcal{M}$ queries $(\mathrm{cmt}_{i^*}, m_{i^*})$ to the random oracle, and then returns the pair (m_{i^*}, σ_{i^*}) as an $\tilde{\mathcal{F}}_{i^*}$'s final output, where the signature σ_{i^*} has been obtained in (T-1).

(M-4) When $\mathcal{R}$ outputs a tuple $(x_1, x_2, \dots, x_T)$, output it and then halt.

Fig. 3. Meta-reduction $\mathcal{M}$

For the purpose of overcoming the difficulty, $\mathcal{M}$ utilizes the ability of $\mathcal{R}$. $\mathcal{R}$ should reply a valid signature σ_i for each message m_i queried by an N-sf-cma forger. In order to obtain the target signature σ_{i^*}, $\mathcal{M}$ first runs $\mathcal{R}$ with the simulation of $\tilde{\mathcal{F}}_N$ in (M-1) and (M-2). Then, $\mathcal{M}$ rewinds $\mathcal{R}$ in (M-3) when it has obtained a signature σ_{i_0} of some message m_{i_0} at some desirable point, namely

$\mathcal{R}$ does not queries to the DL oracle during the i_0-th slot. After the rewind, it simulates $\tilde{\mathcal{F}}_{i^*}$ for $i^* = i_0$. In this case, $\mathcal{M}$ merely returns the signature σ_{i^*} as the $\tilde{\mathcal{F}}_{i^*}$'s final output.

It should be noted that $\mathcal{R}$ has a possibility that it fails to reply a valid signature of some message handed by the forger. As mentioned in the situation of $\mathcal{R}$, an N-sf-cma forger is allowed to return $\bot$ in such a case. In (T-1), $\mathcal{M}$ behaves as the same as $\tilde{\mathcal{F}}_N$. Therefore, $\mathcal{M}$ correctly simulates $\tilde{\mathcal{F}}_N$ to $\mathcal{R}$ in this case. Hereafter, we consider the opposite case.

By the above observation, the following conditions are required for $\mathcal{M}$ to solve the T-OM-DL problem:

(Con-1) $\mathcal{M}$ does not abort in (T-2);
(Con-2) The number of the access to the DL oracle of $\mathcal{M}$ is at most $T - 1$; and
(Con-3) $\mathcal{M}$ correctly simulates $\tilde{\mathcal{F}}_{i^*}$ in (M-3) in the $\mathcal{R}$'s viewpoint.

Lemma 3. *The condition (Con-1) holds.*

Proof. This abortion occurs when for any index $1 \leq i < N$, $\mathcal{R}$ accesses the DL oracle during the i-th slot. In this case, the number of the access to the DL oracle of $\mathcal{R}$ is to be at least $N - 1$. However, this does not occur. This is because it holds that $T < N$ by the assumption and $\mathcal{R}$ is supposed to access the DL oracle at most $T - 1$ times. Namely, the access number to the DL oracle cannot exceed $T - 1 < N - 1$. Thus, $\mathcal{M}$ does not reach (T-2), and hence $\mathcal{M}$ does not abort. □

Lemma 3 implies that $\mathcal{M}$ does not abort in (M-2). It follows that either $\mathcal{R}$ fails to reply some signature, or there exists an index $1 \leq i_0 < N$ such that $\mathcal{M}$ obtains the valid signature σ_{i_0} without the DL oracle during the i_0-th slot. We now consider the case where $\mathcal{M}$ does not return $\bot$ in (M-2). Then the latter always holds. Therefore, the index i_0 is set as the challenge index i^* in (c) of (T-1), and hence $\mathcal{M}$ rewinds $\mathcal{R}$ with the simulation of $\tilde{\mathcal{F}}_{i^*}$. As in (M-3), $\mathcal{M}$ runs $\mathcal{R}$ in the same way as (M-1) and (M-2) until the point where $\mathcal{M}$ obtains the hash value of $(\mathrm{cmt}_{i^*-1}, m_{i^*-1})$ from the random oracle. This point is called the *forking point*.

Lemma 4. *The condition (Con-2) holds.*

Proof. As mentioned above, there exists an index $1 \leq i^* < N$ such that $\mathcal{M}$ obtains the valid signature σ_{i^*} without the DL oracle during the i^*-th slot. As in Fig. 3, $\mathcal{M}$ runs $\mathcal{R}$ in (M-1)–(M-2) and (M-3)–(M-4), respectively. Let $T_{1,\mathrm{before}}$ and $T_{1,\mathrm{after}}$ be the numbers of the access to the DL oracle by $\mathcal{R}$ before and after the forking point in (M-1)–(M-2), and let $T_{2,\mathrm{before}}$ and $T_{2,\mathrm{after}}$ be the numbers of the access to the DL oracle by $\mathcal{R}$ before and after the forking point in (M-3)–(M-4), respectively.

We now observe the number of the access to the DL oracle of $\mathcal{M}$. In (M-1)–(M-2), $\mathcal{M}$ forwards all DL oracle queries by $\mathcal{R}$. Since $\mathcal{R}$ does not query in the i^*-th slot, it holds that $T_{1,\mathrm{after}} = 0$. Hence $\mathcal{M}$ makes $T_{1,\mathrm{before}}$ queries to the DL oracle here. On the other hand, $\mathcal{M}$ makes no query before the forking point in

(M-3)–(M-4). This is because $\mathcal{M}$ replies all queries by using List without the DL oracle. After that, $\mathcal{M}$ forwards all DL oracle queries by $\mathcal{R}$. These imply that $\mathcal{M}$ makes $T_{2,\text{after}}$ queries to the DL oracle in (M-3)–(M-4). Totally, the number of the DL oracle accesses by $\mathcal{M}$ is $T_{1,\text{before}} + T_{2,\text{after}}$. It should be noted that the behaviors of $\mathcal{R}$ and $\mathcal{M}$ before the forking point in (M-1)–(M-2) and (M-3)–(M-4) are identical as described in (M-3). It follows that $T_{1,\text{before}} = T_{2,\text{before}}$. Therefore, the number of the DL oracle accesses by $\mathcal{M}$ is $T_{2,\text{before}} + T_{2,\text{after}}$. By the assumption of $\mathcal{R}$, that by $\mathcal{R}$ is at most $T - 1$. Thus, the number $T_{2,\text{before}} + T_{2,\text{after}}$ can be also bounded by $T - 1$.   □

Lemma 5. *The condition (Con-3) holds.*

Proof. We now show that $\mathcal{M}$ simulates the hypothetical forger $\tilde{\mathcal{F}}_{i^*}$ in (M-3). Again, running $\mathcal{R}$ in (M-3) is the same way as in (M-1) and (M-2) before the forking point. It follows that for each $1 \leq i < i^*$, $\mathcal{M}$ hands the i-th message m_i to $\mathcal{R}$, and then obtains its signature σ_i as in (T-1). Here, $\mathcal{M}$ makes query (cmt_i, m_i) to the random oracle. Thus, $\mathcal{M}$ behaves as in (F-1) of $\tilde{\mathcal{F}}_{i^*}$. Moreover, $\mathcal{M}$ queries $(\text{cmt}_{i^*}, m_{i^*})$ to the random oracle, and then returns the pair (m_{i^*}, σ_{i^*}) of the i^*-th message m_{i^*} and its signature σ_{i^*}. Since σ_{i^*} is a valid signature of the i^*-th message m_{i^*} as mentioned above, $\mathcal{M}$ also behaves as in (F-2) in the $\mathcal{R}$'s viewpoint. Thus, $\mathcal{M}$ simulates $\tilde{\mathcal{F}}_{i^*}$ correctly.   □

We now evaluate the running time of $\mathcal{M}$. $\mathcal{M}$ runs $\mathcal{R}$ twice. In (M-2) and (M-3), $\mathcal{M}$ just accesses the DL oracle at most $T - 1$ times by Lemma 4, hands at most $N - 1$ messages to $\mathcal{R}$, verifies the obtained signatures σ_i, and then queries to the random oracle polynomially many times. Therefore, it runs in polynomial time. Thus, $\mathcal{M}$ solves the T-OM-DL problem with non-negligible probability ϵ in PPT. Thus the T-OM-DL assumption is tractable.   □

3.2   Case: Turing Reduction

We next consider the situation where $\mathcal{R}$ is Turing reduction. In this situation, $\mathcal{R}$ is allowed to concurrently and adaptively invoke $\mathcal{F}$ at most I_i times and rewind it at most I_r times for some polynomials I_i and I_r, whereas a vanilla reduction $\mathcal{R}$ can invoke $\mathcal{F}$ only once and is prohibited to rewind it.

On a T-OM-DL instance $(\mathbb{G}, p, g, y_1, y_2, \ldots, y_T)$ to $\mathcal{R}$, $\mathcal{R}$ would execute the following processes:

Access to DL oracle When $\mathcal{R}$ sends a t-th instance $\overline{y}_t$ to the DL oracle, it receives its DL $\overline{x}_t$.

Invoke $\mathcal{F}$ When $\mathcal{R}$ invokes a k-th forger $\mathcal{F}^{(k)}$ on $(pk_k, m_{k,1}, m_{k,2}, \ldots, m_{k,N})$, $\mathcal{R}$ behaves as follows:
- If the k-th invocation $\mathcal{F}^{(k)}$ of $\mathcal{F}$ hands an i_k-th message $\overline{m}_{k,i_k}$ to $\mathcal{R}$, $\mathcal{R}$ should reply its valid signature $\overline{\sigma}_{k,i_k}$. As in the situation of a vanilla reduction, $\mathcal{F}^{(k)}$ can return $\bot$ once $\mathcal{R}$ fails to reply a valid signature of some message.

- If $\mathcal{R}$ has correctly replies all of signatures, $\mathcal{R}$ obtains a pair $\left(m_{k,i_k^*}, \sigma_{k,i_k^*}\right)$ of the i_k^*-th message m_{k,i_k^*} and its valid signature σ_{k,i_k^*} from $\mathcal{F}^{(k)}$.

Query to random oracle $\mathcal{R}$ queries some string to the random oracle to obtain its hash value.

Finally, $\mathcal{R}$ outputs the solution $(x_1, x_2, \ldots, x_T)$ of $(\mathbb{G}, p, g, y_1, y_2, \ldots, y_T)$.

The Turing reduction $\mathcal{R}$ may rewind $\mathcal{F}^{(k)}$ just after the following processes:

- $\mathcal{F}^{(k)}$ hands some message $\overline{m}_{k,i}$ to $\mathcal{R}$; and
- $\mathcal{F}^{(k)}$ queries to the random oracle. This is because $\mathcal{R}$ can observe the queries and the responses of $\mathcal{F}^{(k)}$ in the NPROM setting.

Theorem 6. *Let $T < N$. Assume that the Schnorr signature is provable to be N-suf-cma from the T-OM-DL assumption in the NPROM via a Turing reduction. Then, the T-OM-DL assumption is tractable.*

Proof (Sketch). This can be proven in the similar manner to Theorem 2. Let $T < N$. Assume that the Schnorr signature is provable to be N-suf-cma from the T-OM-DL assumption in the NPROM via a Turing reduction. Namely, there exist polynomials I_i and I_r, a non-negligible function ϵ and a PPT Turing reduction $\mathcal{R}$ such that $\mathcal{R}$ solves the T-OM-DL problem with probability ϵ by invoking a forger $\mathcal{F}$ which wins the N-sf-cma game with non-negligible probability. In the setting of the Turing reduction, $\mathcal{R}$ can concurrently invoke the N-sf-cma forger $\mathcal{F}$ at most I_i times. Moreover, $\mathcal{R}$ would rewind $\mathcal{F}$ during some k-th invocation $\mathcal{F}^{(k)}$ of $\mathcal{F}$, and the total number of the rewind by $\mathcal{R}$ is bonded by I_r. As well as Theorem 2, we aim to construct a PPT meta-reduction $\mathcal{M}$ which solves T-OM-DL problem with non-negligible probability by utilizing $\mathcal{R}$ with the simulation of the several hypothetical forgers $\tilde{\mathcal{F}}_j$.

The Turing reduction $\mathcal{R}$ Invokes Hypothetical Forgers $\tilde{\mathcal{F}}_j$ We consider the same hypothetical forgers $\tilde{\mathcal{F}}_j$ as Theorem 2, namely Fig. 2. For any $1 \le k \le I_i$ and any $1 \le j \le N$, we explicitly denote by $\tilde{\mathcal{F}}_j^{(k)}$ the hypothetical forger $\tilde{\mathcal{F}}_j$ which is invoked at k-th time, by $(pk_k, m_{k,1}, \ldots, m_{k,N})$ the tuple given to $\tilde{\mathcal{F}}_j^{(k)}$, and by $\sigma_{k,i_k} = (\mathrm{cmt}_{k,i_k}, \mathrm{res}_{k,i_k})$ the i_k-th signature of the message m_{k,i_k} under the public key pk_k, respectively.

$\mathcal{R}$ would rewind $\tilde{\mathcal{F}}_j^{(k)}$ at some points. It should be noted that the reduction $\mathcal{R}$ which invokes such forgers I_i times and rewinds these I_r times can be converted into the Turing reduction $\mathcal{R}'$ so that it invokes the forger $I := I_i + I_r$ without any rewind in the following way: Given an instance $(\mathbb{G}, p, g, y_1, y_2, \ldots, y_T)$, $\mathcal{R}'$ runs $\mathcal{R}(\mathbb{G}, p, g, y_1, y_2, \ldots, y_T)$. $\mathcal{R}'$ forwards any interactions among $\mathcal{R}$, the DL oracle, the random oracle and forgers. When $\mathcal{R}$ requests to rewind a k-th invocation $\tilde{\mathcal{F}}_j^{(k)}$ with some query at some point, $\mathcal{R}'$ starts a new invocation of $\tilde{\mathcal{F}}_j$ on $(pk_k, m_{k,1}, \ldots, m_{k,N})$ which is the same input to $\tilde{\mathcal{F}}_j^{(k)}$, and runs the new invocation in the same way as the k-th invocation just before the point where $\mathcal{R}$ rewinds $\tilde{\mathcal{F}}_j^{(k)}$. After that, $\mathcal{R}'$ forwards the $\mathcal{R}$'s query to the new invocation.

Since $\tilde{\mathcal{F}}_j$ is deterministic, the behaviors of the k-th invocation and the new invocation before the rewind are identical. Hence, $\mathcal{R}'$ perfectly emulates the rewind in the $\mathcal{R}$'s viewpoint. Therefore, we hereafter suppose that $\mathcal{R}$ invokes the forger I times without any rewind.

We also note that $\mathcal{R}$ can win the T-OM-DL game with probability ϵ even when different hypothetical forgers $\tilde{\mathcal{F}}_j$ are given for each invocation. This is because any forger $\tilde{\mathcal{F}}_j$ wins the N-sf-cma game, and $\mathcal{R}$ would appropriately behave if no matter what winning N-sf-cma forger is provided for each invocation.

Meta-Reduction $\mathcal{M}$. We depict in Fig. 4 the meta-reduction $\mathcal{M}$ in this case. In an analogous fashion to Theorem 2, the i_k-*th slot of* $\tilde{\mathcal{F}}_N^{(k)}$ is the period from handing the i_k-th message m_{k,i_k} by $\tilde{\mathcal{F}}_N^{(k)}$ to receiving the hash value of $(\mathrm{cmt}_{k,i_k}, m_{k,i_k})$ from the random oracle in (M-2). Any $\mathcal{F}_N^{(k)}$ is allowed to output $\perp$ if $\mathcal{R}$ fails to reply a valid signature of some message handed by $\mathcal{F}_N^{(k)}$. We only consider the case where $\mathcal{R}$ replies a valid signature for any message handed by the forger.

As well as the proof of Theorem 2, $\mathcal{M}$ can solve the T-OM-DL problem with non-negligible probability if the following conditions hold:

(Con-1) For any k-th invocation $\tilde{\mathcal{F}}_N^{(k)}$, $\mathcal{M}$ does not abort in (M-2);
(Con-2) The number of the access to the DL oracle of $\mathcal{M}$ is at most $T - 1$; and
(Con-3) For any k, $\mathcal{M}$ correctly simulates $\tilde{\mathcal{F}}_{i_k^*}^{(k)}$ in (M-3) in the $\mathcal{R}$'s viewpoint.

One can show that these conditions hold in a similar manner to Lemmas 3, 4 and 5.

Lemma 7. *The condition (Con-1) holds.*

Proof. We fix a k-th invocation $\tilde{\mathcal{F}}_N^{(k)}$ of $\tilde{\mathcal{F}}_N$. This abortion occurs when for any index $1 \leq i_k < N$, $\mathcal{R}$ accesses the DL oracle during the i_k-th slot of $\tilde{\mathcal{F}}_N^{(k)}$. In this case, the number of the access to the DL oracle of $\mathcal{R}$ is to be at least $N - 1$. However, this does not occurs due to the same reason as Lemma 3. $\qquad\square$

We fix an index $1 \leq k \leq I$. Lemma 7 implies that $\mathcal{M}$ does not abort in (M-2) on the k-th invocation $\tilde{\mathcal{F}}_N^{(k)}$. It follows that either $\mathcal{R}$ fails to reply some signature to $\tilde{\mathcal{F}}_N^{(k)}$, or there exists an index $1 \leq i_k' < N$ such that $\mathcal{M}$ obtains the valid signature $\sigma_{i_k'}$ without the DL oracle during the i_k'-th slot of $\tilde{\mathcal{F}}_N^{(k)}$. We now consider the case where $\mathcal{M}$ does not return $\perp$ in (M-2). Then the latter always holds. Therefore, the index i_k' is set as the challenge index i_k^*, and hence $\mathcal{M}$ rewinds $\mathcal{R}$ with the simulation of $\tilde{\mathcal{F}}_{i_k^*}^{(k)}$ in (M-3). As in Fig. 4, $\mathcal{M}$ runs $\mathcal{R}$ in the same way as (M-1) and (M-2) until $\mathcal{M}$ obtains the hash value of $(\mathrm{cmt}_{k,i_k^*-1}, m_{k,i_k^*-1})$. In the analogical manner to Theorem 2, this point is called the *forking point of the k-th invocation.*

Lemma 8. *The condition (Con-2) holds.*

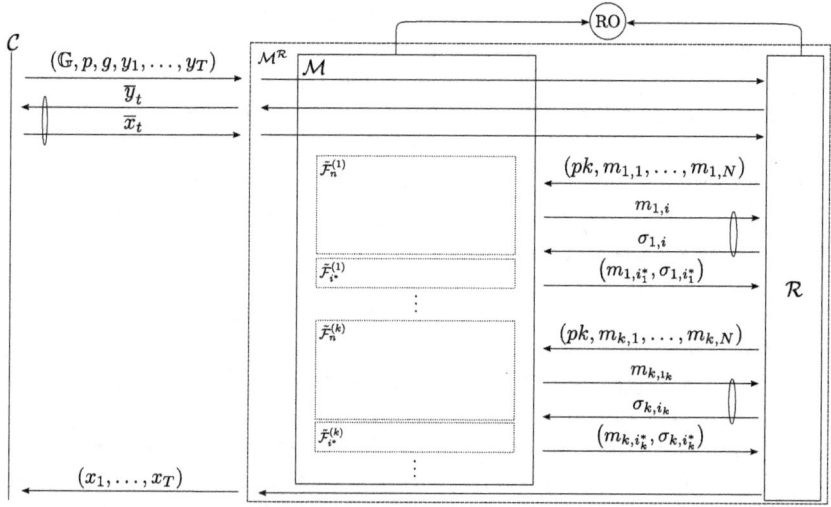

Algorithm: Meta-reduction $\mathcal{M}(\mathbb{G}, p, g, y_1, y_2, \ldots, y_T)$

(M-1) sample random coins r, and then run $\mathcal{R}(\mathbb{G}, p, g, y_1, y_2, \ldots, y_T; r)$. Hereafter, $\mathcal{M}$ records to List all inputs and outputs of $\mathcal{R}$, such as queries and responses in the **OM Oracle** phase, and interactions between $\mathcal{R}$ and $\mathcal{F}$.

(M-2) proceed in the following way according to an $\mathcal{R}$'s output:

Access to DL oracle with $\overline{y}_t \in \mathbb{G}$: forward it to the DL oracle, and reply its solution $\overline{x}_t$ to $\mathcal{R}$.

Invoking a k-th forger $\mathcal{F}^{(k)}$ on $(pk_k, m_{k,1}, m_{k,2}, \ldots, m_{k,N})$: start to simulate $\tilde{\mathcal{F}}_N$, and then hand the 1st message $m_{k,1}$ of $\tilde{\mathcal{F}}_N^{(k)}$ to $\mathcal{R}$.

Receiving a signature σ_{k,i_k} of the i_k-th message m_{k,i_k} handed by $\tilde{\mathcal{F}}_N^{(k)}$: query the i_k-th pair $(\text{cmt}_{k,i_k}, m_{k,i_k})$ to the random oracle.

Obtaining a hash value cha_{k,i_k} of the pair $(\text{cmt}_{k,i_k}, m_{k,i_k})$: check the following items sequentially:

- if $\text{Ver}(pk_k, m_{k,i_k}, \sigma_{k,i_k}) \neq 1$, then return $\perp$ as an $\mathcal{F}^{(k)}$'s final output.
- if $\mathcal{R}$ does not access the DL oracle during the i_k-th slot of $\tilde{\mathcal{F}}_N^{(k)}$, set $i_k^* := i_k$, and then go to (M-3).
- if $i_k + 1 = N$, then abort.
- Otherwise, hand the $(i_k + 1)$-th message m_{k,i_k+1} of $\tilde{\mathcal{F}}_N^{(k)}$ to $\mathcal{R}$.

(M-3) rewind $\mathcal{R}(\mathbb{G}, p, g, y_1, y_2, \ldots, y_T; r)$ in the following way. Here, $\mathcal{M}$ simulates $\tilde{\mathcal{F}}_{i_k^*}^{(k)}$ instead of $\tilde{\mathcal{F}}_N^{(k)}$.

- Until just after obtaining the hash value of $\left(\text{cmt}_{k,i_k^*-1}, m_{k,i_k^*-1}\right)$, $\mathcal{M}$ runs in the same way as (M-1) and (M-2) except that it replies all of instances $\overline{y}_t$ sent from $\mathcal{R}$ by using List instead of the DL oracle.

- For the i_k^*-th message m_{k,i_k^*}, query $\left(\text{cmt}_{k,i_k^*}, m_{k,i_k^*}\right)$ to the random oracle, and proceed to the following according to an $\mathcal{R}$'s output:

Obtaining a hash value cha_{k,i_k^*} of the challenge pair $\left(\text{cmt}_{k,i_k^*}, m_{k,i_k^*}\right)$: returns the pair $\left(m_{k,i_k^*}, \sigma_{k,i_k^*}\right)$ as an $\tilde{\mathcal{F}}_{i_k^*}^{(k)}$'s final output, where the signature σ_{k,i_k^*} has been obtained in (M-2).

(M-4) When $\mathcal{R}$ outputs a tuple $(x_1, x_2, \ldots, x_T)$, output it and then halt.

Fig. 4. Meta-reduction $\mathcal{M}$

Proof. We say that $\mathcal{R}$ accesses the DL oracle on the *k-th turn* if $\mathcal{R}$ accesses the DL oracle after the k-th invocation $\mathcal{F}^{(k)}$ makes a signing oracle query or a random oracle query. For each $1 \leq k \leq I$, let $T_{k,1,\text{before}}$ and $T_{k,1,\text{after}}$ be the numbers of the access to the DL oracle by $\mathcal{R}$ on the k-th turn before and after the forking point of $\tilde{\mathcal{F}}_N^{(k)}$ in (M-2), and let $T_{k,2,\text{before}}$ and $T_{k,2,\text{after}}$ be the numbers of the access to the DL oracle by $\mathcal{R}$ on the k-th turn before and after the forking point of $\tilde{\mathcal{F}}_{i_k^*}^{(k)}$ in (M-3), respectively. Let T_{others} be the number of the access to the DL oracle of $\mathcal{R}$ at the other points.

We now fix a k-th invocation, and focus on the number of the access to the DL oracle of $\mathcal{M}$ on the k-th turn. In (M-2), $\mathcal{M}$ forwards all DL queries by $\mathcal{R}$. Since $\mathcal{R}$ does not query to the DL oracle on *any* turn during the i_k^*-th slot of $\tilde{\mathcal{F}}_N^{(k)}$, it holds that $T_{k,1,\text{after}} = 0$. These imply that the number of the access to the DL oracle of $\mathcal{M}$ on the k-th turn in (M-2) is $T_{k,1,\text{before}}$. On the other hand, $\mathcal{M}$ makes no query to the DL oracle on *any* turn before the forking point of the k-th invocation in (M-3). This is because $\mathcal{M}$ responses any query by $\mathcal{R}$ with using List without the DL oracle. It follows that the number of the access to the DL oracle of $\mathcal{M}$ on the k-th turn in (M-3) is $T_{k,2,\text{after}}$. Therefore, the number of the access to the DL oracle of $\mathcal{M}$ on the k-th turn is $T_{k,1,\text{before}} + T_{k,2,\text{after}}$. In a similar manner to Lemma 4, the behaviors of $\mathcal{R}$ and $\mathcal{M}$ before the forking point of the k-th invocation in (M-2) and (M-3) are identical, and hence $T_{k,1,\text{before}} = T_{k,2,\text{before}}$. Thus the number of the access to the DL oracle of $\mathcal{M}$ on the k-th turn is $T_{k,2,\text{before}} + T_{k,2,\text{after}}$. This means that the number of the access of $\mathcal{M}$ in any k-th turn can be evaluated by that of $\mathcal{R}$ just in (M-3).

Totally, the number of the access to the DL oracle of $\mathcal{M}$ can be evaluated by $\sum_{k=1}^{I}(T_{k,2,\text{before}} + T_{k,2,\text{after}}) + T_{\text{others}}$. By the above observation, the number of the access to the DL oracle of $\mathcal{M}$ is the same as that of the single running of $\mathcal{R}$, although $\mathcal{M}$ runs $\mathcal{R}$ sometimes. Thus the number $\sum_{k=1}^{I}(T_{k,2,\text{before}} + T_{k,2,\text{after}}) + T_{\text{others}}$ of accessing the DL oracle by $\mathcal{M}$ is bounded by $T - 1$ since $\mathcal{R}$ is supposed to access the DL oracle at most $T - 1$. □

Lemma 9. *The condition (Con-3) holds.*

Proof. This lemma can be proven in the same way as Lemma 5. We fix an index $1 \leq k \leq I$. As mentioned above, $\mathcal{M}$ obtains the valid signature $\sigma_{i_k^*}$ of the i_k^*-th message $m_{i_k^*}$. We now show that $\mathcal{M}$ simulates the hypothetical forger $\tilde{\mathcal{F}}_{i_k^*}^{(k)}$ in (M-3). Recall that running $\mathcal{R}$ in (M-3) is the same way as in (M-1) and (M-2) before the forking point of the k-th invocation. It follows that for each $1 \leq i_k < i_k^*$, $\mathcal{M}$ hands the i_k-th message m_{k,i_k} to $\mathcal{R}$, and then obtains its signature σ_{k,i_k}. Here, $\mathcal{M}$ makes the query $(\text{cmt}_{k,i_k}, m_{k,i_k})$ to the random oracle. Thus, $\mathcal{M}$ behaves as in (F-1) of $\tilde{\mathcal{F}}_{i_k^*}^{(k)}$. Moreover, $\mathcal{M}$ queries $(\text{cmt}_{k,i_k^*}, m_{k,i_k^*})$ to the random oracle. After $\mathcal{M}$ has been received the hash value of $(\text{cmt}_{k,i_k^*}, m_{k,i_k^*})$, it returns the pair $(m_{k,i_k^*}, \sigma_{k,i_k^*})$ of the i_k^*-th message m_{k,i_k^*} and its signature σ_{k,i_k^*}. Since σ_{k,i_k^*} is a valid signature of the i_k^*-th message m_{k,i_k^*}, $\mathcal{M}$ also behaves as in (F-2) in the $\mathcal{R}$'s viewpoint. Thus, $\mathcal{M}$ simulates $\tilde{\mathcal{F}}_{i_k^*}^{(k)}$ correctly. □

We now evaluate the running time of $\mathcal{M}$. $\mathcal{M}$ runs $\mathcal{R}$ at most $I + 1$ times in (M-1) and (M-3). In (M-2) and (M-3), $\mathcal{M}$ just accesses the DL oracle at most $T - 1$ times by Lemma 8, hands at most $I(N - 1)$ messages to $\mathcal{R}$, verify the obtained signatures σ_i, and then queries to the random oracle polynomially many times. Therefore, it runs in polynomial time. Thus, $\mathcal{M}$ solves the T-OM-DL problem with non-negligible probability ϵ in PPT, and hence the T-OM-DL assumption is tractable. □

By Theorem 6 and Proposition 1, the following corollary holds.

Corollary 10. *Let $T < N$. Assume that the Schnorr signature is provable to be euf-cma in the NPROM from the T-OM-DL assumption via a Turing reduction. Then, the T-OM-DL assumption is tractable.*

Acknowledgment. We would like to thank anonymous reviewers for their valuable comments and suggestions. A part of this work is supported by JSPS KAKENHI Grant Number 15K16001.

References

1. Abdalla, M., An, J.H., Bellare, M., Namprempre, C.: From identification to signatures via the fiat-shamir transform: necessary and sufficient conditions for security and forward-security. IEEE Trans. Inf. Theor. **54**(8), 3631–3646 (2008)
2. Bader, C., Jager, T., Li, Y., Schäge, S.: On the impossibility of tight cryptographic reductions. In: Fischlin, M., Coron, J.-S. (eds.) EUROCRYPT 2016. LNCS, vol. 9666, pp. 273–304. Springer, Heidelberg (2016). doi:10.1007/978-3-662-49896-5_10
3. Bellare, M., Namprempre, C., Pointcheval, D., Semanko, M.: The one-more-RSA-inversion problems and the security of Chaum's blind signature scheme. J. Cryptol. **16**(3), 185–215 (2003)
4. Bellare, M., Palacio, A.: GQ and Schnorr identification schemes: proofs of security against impersonation under active and concurrent attacks. In: Yung, M. (ed.) CRYPTO 2002. LNCS, vol. 2442, pp. 162–177. Springer, Heidelberg (2002). doi:10.1007/3-540-45708-9_11
5. Boneh, D.: The decision Diffie-Hellman problem. In: Buhler, J.P. (ed.) ANTS 1998. LNCS, vol. 1423, pp. 48–63. Springer, Heidelberg (1998). doi:10.1007/BFb0054851
6. Boneh, D., Venkatesan, R.: Breaking RSA may not be equivalent to factoring. In: Nyberg, K. (ed.) EUROCRYPT 1998. LNCS, vol. 1403, pp. 59–71. Springer, Heidelberg (1998). doi:10.1007/BFb0054117
7. Bresson, E., Monnerat, J., Vergnaud, D.: Separation results on the "one-more" computational problems. In: Malkin, T. (ed.) CT-RSA 2008. LNCS, vol. 4964, pp. 71–87. Springer, Heidelberg (2008). doi:10.1007/978-3-540-79263-5_5
8. Coron, J.-S.: Optimal security proofs for PSS and other signature schemes. In: Knudsen, L.R. (ed.) EUROCRYPT 2002. LNCS, vol. 2332, pp. 272–287. Springer, Heidelberg (2002). doi:10.1007/3-540-46035-7_18
9. Fiat, A., Shamir, A.: How to prove yourself: practical solutions to identification and signature problems. In: Odlyzko, A.M. (ed.) CRYPTO 1986. LNCS, vol. 263, pp. 186–194. Springer, Heidelberg (1987). doi:10.1007/3-540-47721-7_12
10. Fischlin, M., Fleischhacker, N.: Limitations of the meta-reduction technique: the case of Schnorr signatures. In: Johansson, T., Nguyen, P.Q. (eds.) EUROCRYPT 2013. LNCS, vol. 7881, pp. 444–460. Springer, Heidelberg (2013). doi:10.1007/978-3-642-38348-9_27

11. Fischlin, M., Lehmann, A., Ristenpart, T., Shrimpton, T., Stam, M., Tessaro, S.: Random oracles with(out) programmability. In: Abe, M. (ed.) ASIACRYPT 2010. LNCS, vol. 6477, pp. 303–320. Springer, Heidelberg (2010). doi:10.1007/978-3-642-17373-8_18

12. Fleischhacker, N., Jager, T., Schröder, D.: On tight security proofs for Schnorr signatures. In: Sarkar, P., Iwata, T. (eds.) ASIACRYPT 2014. LNCS, vol. 8873, pp. 512–531. Springer, Heidelberg (2014). doi:10.1007/978-3-662-45611-8_27

13. Fukumitsu, M., Hasegawa, S.: Black-Box separations on Fiat-Shamir-type signatures in the non-programmable random oracle model. In: Lopez, J., Mitchell, C.J. (eds.) ISC 2015. LNCS, vol. 9290, pp. 3–20. Springer, Cham (2015). doi:10.1007/978-3-319-23318-5_1

14. Fukumitsu, M., Hasegawa, S.: Impossibility on the provable security of the Fiat-Shamir-type signatures in the non-programmable random oracle model. In: Bishop, M., Nascimento, A.C.A. (eds.) ISC 2016. LNCS, vol. 9866, pp. 389–407. Springer, Cham (2016). doi:10.1007/978-3-319-45871-7_23

15. Goldwasser, S., Micali, S., Rivest, R.L.: A digital signature scheme secure against adaptive chosen-message attacks. SIAM J. Comput. $17(2)$, 281–308 (1988)

16. Kakvi, S.A., Kiltz, E.: Optimal security proofs for full domain hash, revisited. In: Pointcheval, D., Johansson, T. (eds.) EUROCRYPT 2012. LNCS, vol. 7237, pp. 537–553. Springer, Heidelberg (2012). doi:10.1007/978-3-642-29011-4_32

17. Nielsen, J.B.: Separating random oracle proofs from complexity theoretic proofs: the non-committing encryption case. In: Yung, M. (ed.) CRYPTO 2002. LNCS, vol. 2442, pp. 111–126. Springer, Heidelberg (2002). doi:10.1007/3-540-45708-9_8

18. Paillier, P., Vergnaud, D.: Discrete-log-based signatures may not be equivalent to discrete log. In: Roy, B. (ed.) ASIACRYPT 2005. LNCS, vol. 3788, pp. 1–20. Springer, Heidelberg (2005). doi:10.1007/11593447_1

19. Pass, R.: Limits of provable security from standard assumptions. In: STOC 2011, pp. 109–118 (2011)

20. Pointcheval, D., Stern, J.: Security arguments for digital signatures and blind signatures. J. Cryptol. $13(3)$, 361–396 (2000)

21. Schnorr, C.: Efficient signature generation by smart cards. J. Cryptol. $4(3)$, 161–174 (1991)

22. Zhang, J., Zhang, Z., Chen, Y., Guo, Y., Zhang, Z.: Black-box separations for one-more (static) CDH and its generalization. In: Sarkar, P., Iwata, T. (eds.) ASIACRYPT 2014. LNCS, vol. 8874, pp. 366–385. Springer, Heidelberg (2014). doi:10.1007/978-3-662-45608-8_20

23. Zhang, Z., Chen, Y., Chow, S.S.M., Hanaoka, G., Cao, Z., Zhao, Y.: Black-box separations of hash-and-sign signatures in the non-programmable random oracle model. In: Au, M.-H., Miyaji, A. (eds.) ProvSec 2015. LNCS, vol. 9451, pp. 435–454. Springer, Cham (2015). doi:10.1007/978-3-319-26059-4_24

Bit Security of the Hyperelliptic Curves Diffie-Hellman Problem

Fangguo Zhang[1,2](✉)

[1] School of Data and Computer Science,
Sun Yat-sen University, Guangzhou 510006, China
isszhfg@mail.sysu.edu.cn
[2] Guangdong Provincial Key Laboratory of Information Security,
Sun Yat-sen University, Guangzhou 510006, China

Abstract. The Diffie-Hellman problem as a cryptographic primitive plays an important role in modern cryptology. The Bit Security or Hard-Core Bits of Diffie-Hellman problem in arbitrary finite cyclic group is a long-standing open problem in cryptography. Until now, only few groups have been studied. Hyperelliptic curve cryptography is an alternative to elliptic curve cryptography. Due to the recent cryptanalytic results that the best known algorithms to attack hyperelliptic curve cryptosystems of genus $g < 3$ are the generic methods and the recent implementation results that hyperelliptic curve cryptography in genus 2 has the potential to be competitive with its elliptic curve cryptography counterpart. In this paper, we generalize Boneh and Shparlinksi's method and result about elliptic curve to the case of Jacobians of hyperelliptic curves. We prove that the least significant bit of each coordinate of hyperelliptic curves Diffie-Hellman secret value in genus 2 is hard as the entire Diffie-Hellman value, and then we also show that any bit is hard as the entire Diffie-Hellman value. Finally, we extend our techniques and results to hyperelliptic curves of any genus.

Keywords: Hyperelliptic curves · Bit security · Diffie-Hellman problem

1 Introduction

The discrete logarithm problem (DLP) and Diffie-Hellman problem (DHP) are basic cryptographic primitives, they play an important role in modern cryptology. For example the Diffie-Hellman key exchange [14], the ElGamal encryption [16], the official U.S. Digital Signature Algorithm (DSA) [17], and the BLS short signature scheme [9], etc. Due to Pohlig and Hellman attack [37], it is restricted to groups of prime order p in this paper, where the DLP is the problem to compute $x \in \mathbb{Z}_p^*$ given (g, g^x), and the DHP or computational Diffie-Hellman problem (CDHP) is the problem to compute g^{ab} given (g, g^a, g^b), here $g \in G$ is a generator of group G. Maurer and Wolf [34,35] have proved that, for every cyclic group G with prime order p, there exists polynomial time algorithm that

© Springer International Publishing AG 2017
T. Okamoto et al. (Eds.): ProvSec 2017, LNCS 10592, pp. 219–235, 2017.
https://doi.org/10.1007/978-3-319-68637-0_13

reduces the computation of DLP in G to the computation of CDHP in G if we are able to find an elliptic curve, called *auxiliary elliptic curve*, over $\mathbb{F}_p$ with smooth order.

From many cryptographic applications, we know it is very important that partial information of the secret key is not computable or predictable with any significant advantage over a random guess. This is related to Bit Security or Hard-Core Bits problem. Informally speaking, the Bit Security or Hard-Core Bits for DLP can be described as follows: given (g, g^x), if an adversary can compute certain bits (or more generally, certain predicates) of x? Blum and Micali [6] introduced the concept of hard-core bits for one-way functions and showed the existence of a hard-core predicate for the discrete logarithm function in any group G.

However, for the case of the DHP no such result has been proven. Informally speaking, the Bit Security or Hard-Core Bits for DHP or CDHP can be described as follows: given (g, g^a, g^b), if an adversary can compute certain bits (or more generally, certain predicates) of $K = g^{ab}$? In another word, if the hardness of CDH bits and the entire CDH is same? This is a long-standing open problem in cryptography. Until now, only few groups have been studied: Boneh and Venkatesan [8] formulated the hidden number problem (HNP) and showed that in the multiplicative group of finite field $\mathbb{F}_p$ computing approximately $(\log p)^{1/2}$ of the bits of the Diffie-Hellman secret is as hard as computing the entire secret. This result is improved in [23]. Boneh and Shparlinksi in [7] achieved a breakthrough for the elliptic curve Diffie-Hellman problem. By using certain twists of the given curve they showed that predicting the least significant bit of the elliptic curve Diffie-Hellman secret in a family of curves is as hard as computing the entire secret. Alternatively, if one looks for a polynomial time reduction of the DHP to the problem of predicting partial information on the same short Weierstrass model, some results have been established using Gröbner bases [27]. Very recently, Shani [38] also studied the bit security of elliptic curve Diffie-Hellman problem defined over prime fields and extension fields. Fazio et al. modified Boneh and Shparlinski's idea and applied it to the case of finite fields $\mathbb{F}_{p^2}$, they proved the unpredictability of every single bit of one of the coordinates of the secret Diffie-Hellman value over finite fields $\mathbb{F}_{p^2}$. Wang et al. [39] generalised this work to extension fields $\mathbb{F}_{p^m}$, where m is polynomial in $\log p$. Li et al. [32] have studied the bit security of CDHP in LUC and XTR. Galbraith et al. [20] have studied the bit security of bilinear Diffie-Hellman problem in bilinear pairing group. About the DHP and its bit security, the Chap. 21 in Galbraith's book [19] is a good reference.

Hyperelliptic curves are a natural generalisation of elliptic curves, and Jacobians of hyperelliptic curves was suggested by Koblitz [30] that they also been considered for cryptographic applications. The main advantage of genus g over elliptic curve (genus 1) is that a much smaller base field (about g times fewer bits) with same security level. However, for large genus there are subexponential time attacks on the DLP [1]. For genus 2 curves, just as with their elliptic curve counterpart, the best known algorithms to solve the discrete logarithm in such groups are the generic attacks such as Pollard rho method [22]. The practical potential of genus 2 curves in public-key cryptography has recently been highlighted by the fast performance numbers presented. Especially, Gaudry [21] showed that scalar multiplication on the Kummer surface associated with the Jacobian of a genus 2 curve can be more efficient than scalar multiplication on the Jacobian itself. After that, many papers [5,10] showed that hyperelliptic curve cryptography in genus 2 has the potential to be competitive with its genus 1 elliptic curve cryptography counterpart.

Our Contributions. In this paper, we study the bit security of CDHP in Jacobian group of hyperelliptic curves. The contribution of the paper is as the following.

1. We firstly generalize Boneh and Shparlinksi's method to the case of Jacobians for genus 2 hyperelliptic curves. We prove that the least significant bit of any coordinate of hyperelliptic Diffie-Hellman value with genus 2 over finite fields is unpredictable.
2. We extend the least significant bit to every bit case, show that for genus 2 hyperelliptic curves, to compute any bit of any coordinate of Diffie-Hellman value is hard as for computing the entire Diffie-Hellman value.
3. We also generalize these results from genus 2 hyperelliptic curves to any genus hyperelliptic curves.

Organization. The rest of this paper is organized as follows. Section 2 introduces some mathematical preliminaries, including hyperelliptic curves and hyperelliptic curve Diffie-Hellman problem, twisting hyperelliptic curves and hidden number problem with chosen multiplier. Section 3 gives the main results and proofs about the unpredictability of least significant bit of hyperelliptic Diffie-Hellman value with genus 2. Section 4 extends the least significant bit to every bit case. Section 5 generalizes the results of hyperelliptic Diffie-Hellman value with genus 2 to the case of any genus hyperelliptic curves. Section 6 gives the conclusions.

2   Mathematical Preliminaries

2.1   Hyperelliptic Curves and Hyperelliptic Curve Diffie-Hellman Problem

We first introduce the definition and operations of hyperelliptic curves over finite field, more details can be found in references [4,19]. Let $\overline{\mathbb{K}}$ be the algebraic closure of the field $\mathbb{K}$. A hyperelliptic curve C of genus $g \geq 1$ over $\mathbb{K}$ is given by

$$C : y^2 + h(x)y = f(x) \tag{1}$$

where $f(x)$ is a monic polynomial of degree $2g+1$, $h(x)$ is a polynomial of degree at most g, and there are no solutions $(x, y) \in \overline{\mathbb{K}} \times \overline{\mathbb{K}}$ simultaneously satisfying the Eq. (1) and the partial derivative equations $2y + h(x) = 0$ and $h'(x)y - f'(x) = 0$.

Let $P = (x, y)$ be a finite point on hyperelliptic curve C, the opposite of P is defined as $-P = (x, -y - h(x))$.

A divisor on C is a finite formal sum $D = \Sigma_P m_P P$, where m_P are integers that are 0 for almost all P. The degree of D is defined by $\deg D = \Sigma_P m_P$. The set of all the divisors defined over $\mathbb{K}$ forms an abelian group with the set of divisors of degree 0 as its subgroup, that is $Div_C^0 \subset Div_C$. The function field of C over $\mathbb{K}$, denoted $\mathbb{K}(C)$, is the field of fraction of the polynomial ring $\mathbb{K}[C] = \mathbb{K}[x, y]/(y^2 + h(x)y - f(x))$. To every rational function $F \in \mathbb{K}(C)$, it can associate a divisor via the valuations at all points of the curve: $div(F) = \Sigma_{P \in C(\mathbb{K})} v_P(F)P$. These so called principal divisors are of degree zero and form a subgroup of Div_C^0. We denote the group of principal divisors as $Princ_C$. The Jacobian or the divisor class group of the curve C is given by $J_C = Div_C^0/Princ_C$.

From the work of Cantor [11] and Koblitz [30], the element $D = \Sigma m_i P_i - (\Sigma m_i)P_\infty$ (here $\Sigma m_i \leq g$, $P_i = (x_i, y_i)$, P_∞ is the point at infinity) of J_C has a Mumford representation, D can be only determined by two polynomials u and v in $\mathbb{K}[x]$, where $u(x) = \Pi(x - x_i)^{m_i}$, and u, v satisfy: 1) $\deg v < \deg u \leq g$; 2) $v(x_i) = y_i$, for all the i that made $m_i \neq 0$; 3) $v^2 + vh - f \equiv 0$ (mod u). In general we write $D = (u(x), v(x))$, it can be represented by 2g-tuple $(u_{g-1}, ..., u_1, u_0, v_{g-1}, ..., v_1, v_0)$.

We will focus on the most cryptographically common case of genus 2 curves, where C is an imaginary hyperelliptic curve over a large prime field $\mathbb{F}_p$. A hyperelliptic curve C over $\mathbb{F}_p$ with genus 2 is defined by

$$C : y^2 = x^5 + f_3 x^3 + f_2 x^2 + f_1 x + f_0 \tag{2}$$

In this case, any element $D = (u(x), v(x))$ of the Jacobian group $J_C(\mathbb{F}_p)$ will satisfy: $u(x)$ is monic, $\deg v < \deg u \leq 2$ and $u|v^2 - f$. When $\deg u = 0$, this is the zero element O; When $\deg u = 1$, this is the element of $(x - u_0, v_0)$, it is related to the degenerate divisor $D = P - P_\infty$ for some point P, we call the element with this form a degenerate element; The general case is $D = (u(x), v(x)) = (x^2 + u_1 x + u_0, v_1 x + v_0)$, we call the element with this form a general element. When we randomly choose an element D from $J_C(\mathbb{F}_p)$, D is a general element with the probability about $1 - \frac{1}{p}$. We also use (u_1, u_0, v_1, v_0) to represent a general element $D = (u(x), v(x))$.

Cantor's algorithm can perform addition and doubling operations in Jacobian group. In this paper, we will need the explicit formulas for the group operations. Harley [24] optimized Cantor's algorithm and obtained the first practical explicit formulas in genus 2, and then Lange [31] extended it and got significant improvements. The formulas were subsequently improved by Costello and Lauter [12] through a more direct geometric interpretation of the group law. Diao and Joye [13] presented an efficient unified addition formulae for hyperelliptic curve cryptography. Very recently, Hisil and Costello [26] combines several techniques to arrive at explicit formulas in Jacobian coordinates that are significantly faster than those in previous works. For the genus 2 curves over large prime field $\mathbb{F}_p$, let $D_1 = (u_{11}, u_{10}, v_{11}, v_{10})$ and $D_2 = (u_{21}, u_{20}, v_{21}, v_{20})$ be two general elements of the Jacobian group. Table 1 in Appendix A is the explicit affine formula for general point addition which derived from the results in [12, 26].

Let $D \in J_C(\mathbb{F}_p)$ be an element of prime order q. The DLP in $J_C(\mathbb{F}_p)$ is: given another element $D' \in < D >$, to determine the integer m such that $D' = mD$. We define the hyperelliptic curve Diffie-Hellman function as

$$DH_{J,D}(aD, bD) = abD$$

where a, b are in $\mathbb{Z}_q$. The hyperelliptic curve DHP is to compute $DH_{J,D}(D_1, D_2)$ given $(C, J_C(\mathbb{F}_p), D, D_1, D_2)$.

2.2   Twisting Hyperelliptic Curves

Let C be a curve with genus g defined over a field $\mathbb{K}$. A curve C' defined over $\mathbb{K}$ that is isomorphic to C over $\overline{\mathbb{K}}$, is called a twist of C.

For a hyperelliptic curve C of genus 2 over $\mathbb{F}_p$ given by the equation

$$C : \quad y^2 = x^5 + f_3 x^3 + f_2 x^2 + f_1 x + f_0$$

For any $\lambda \in \mathbb{F}_p^*$, we define $\phi_\lambda(C)$ to be a twist of C:

$$\phi_\lambda(C) : \quad y^2 = x^5 + \lambda^4 f_3 x^3 + \lambda^6 f_2 x^2 + \lambda^8 f_1 x + \lambda^{10} f_0$$

For any point $P = (x, y) \in C$, $\phi_\lambda(P) = (\lambda^2 x, \lambda^5 y) \in \phi_\lambda(C)$. This curve isomorphism can reduce an isomorphism between $J_C(\mathbb{F}_p)$ and $J_{\phi_\lambda(C)}(\mathbb{F}_p)$, we denote this group isomorphism as $\phi_\lambda^* : J_C(\mathbb{F}_p) \to J_{\phi_\lambda(C)}(\mathbb{F}_p)$.

The explicit formulas for ϕ_λ^* is:

$$\phi_\lambda^* : J_C(\mathbb{F}_p) \to J_{\phi_\lambda(C)}(\mathbb{F}_p)$$
$$O(= P_\infty - P_\infty) \to O'(= P'_\infty - P'_\infty)$$
$$(x_1, y_1) \to (\lambda^2 x_1, \lambda^5 y_1)$$
$$(u_1, u_0, v_1, v_0) \to (\lambda^2 u_1, \lambda^4 u_0, \lambda^3 v_1, \lambda^5 v_0)$$

Therefore, we have

$$DH_{\phi_\lambda^*(J), \phi_\lambda^*(D)}(\phi_\lambda^*(D_1), \phi_\lambda^*(D_2)) = \phi_\lambda^*(DH_{J,D}(D_1, D_2)).$$

In this paper, we are working with the family of curves $\{\phi_\lambda(C)\}_{\lambda \in \mathbb{F}_p^*}$ and their Jacobians $\{J_{\phi_\lambda(C)}(\mathbb{F}_p)\}_{\lambda \in \mathbb{F}_p^*}$ associated with a given curve C and its Jacobians $J_C(\mathbb{F}_p)$. Hence, if the hyperelliptic DHP is hard to compute in $J_C(\mathbb{F}_p)$, then it is also hard to compute for all $\{J_{\phi_\lambda(C)}(\mathbb{F}_p)\}_{\lambda \in \mathbb{F}_p^*}$.

2.3   HNP-CM Problem and HNP-CM^d Problems

The Hidden Number Problem with Chosen Multiplier (HNP-CM) is a variant of the Hidden Number Problem (HNP). It is firstly proposed by Boneh and Shparlinski [7].

We denote by LSB(z) the least significant bit of an integer $z > 0$.

Definition 1 (HNP-CM [7]). *Fix an $\varepsilon > 0$. Let p be a prime. For an $\alpha \in \mathbb{F}_p$ let $L : \mathbb{F}_p* \rightarrow \{0,1\}$ be a function satisfying*

$$Pr_{t \in \mathbb{F}_p*}[L(t) = LSB(\alpha \cdot t \mod p)] \geq \frac{1}{2} + \epsilon$$

The HNP-CM problem is: given an oracle for $L(t)$, find α in polynomial time. For small ϵ there might be multiple α satisfying the above condition. In this case the list-HNP-CM problem is to find the list of all such $\alpha \in F_p^*$. Due to Alexi et al. [3], there is an algorithm to solve the list-HNP-CM for any $\epsilon > 0$.

Theorem 1 *[7]. Let p be a $n-$ bit prime and let $\epsilon > 0$. Then, given ϵ, the list HNP-CM problem can be solved in expected polynomial time in n and $1/\epsilon$.*

Informally speaking, suppose one has an oracle $\mathcal{A}$ such that $\mathcal{A}(t) = \text{LSB}(\alpha \cdot t \mod p)$, then one can compute α using $O(\log_2(p))$ oracle queries.

The HNP-CM^d problem is a variant of HNP-CM problem, it is defined as follows:

Definition 2 (HNP-CM^d [7]). *Fix an $\varepsilon > 0$. Let p be a prime. For an $\alpha \in \mathbb{F}_p$ let $L : \mathbb{F}_p* \rightarrow \{0,1\}$ be a function satisfying*

$$Pr_{t \in \mathbb{F}_p*}[L^d(t) = LSB(\alpha^d \cdot t \mod p)] \geq \frac{1}{2} + \epsilon$$

The HNP-CM^d problem is: given an oracle for $L^d(t)$, find α in polynomial time. For small ϵ there might be multiple α satisfying the condition. In this case the list-HNP-CM^d problem is to find all such $\alpha \in F_p^*$. We will use it for $d = 2$, $d = 3$, $d = 4$ and $d = 5$ in this paper. About the HNP-CM^d problem, Boneh and Shparlinski gave the following theorem:

Theorem 2 *[7]. Fix an integer $d > 1$. Let p be a $n-$ bit prime and let $\epsilon > 0$. Then, given ϵ, the HNP-CM^d problem can be solved in expected polynomial time in $\log p$ and d/ϵ.*

3   Our Results for Least Significant Bit

For the degenerate element $(x - u_0, v_0)$, it can be represented by $(0, u_0, 0, v_0)$, therefore, it is a special case of general element. So we will only consider the general element case. For any general element $D = (u_1, u_0, v_1, v_0)$ of $J_C(\mathbb{F}_p)$, we use $u_1(D)$ to denote the u_1- coordinate of D, similarly for $u_0(D)$, $v_1(D)$ and $v_0(D)$. The main result for the least significant bit of hyperelliptic curve DHP is the following theorem.

Theorem 3. *Let p be a prime, and let C be a hyperelliptic curve with genus 2 over $\mathbb{F}_p$. Let $D \in J_C(\mathbb{F}_p)$ be an element of prime order. Given $(C, J_C(\mathbb{F}_p), D, aD, bD)$, if there is an efficient algorithm for predicting the least significant bit of any coordinate of abD, then there is an efficient algorithm for computing the DHP on $J_C(\mathbb{F}_p)$.*

Let $\mathcal{A}_{u_1}(C, J_C(\mathbb{F}_p), D, aD, bD)$ be an oracle that returns $\mathrm{LSB}(u_1(abD))$ where $D \in J_C(\mathbb{F}_p)$. Similarly, let $\mathcal{A}_{u_0}(C, J_C(\mathbb{F}_p), D, aD, bD)$ be an oracle that returns $\mathrm{LSB}(u_0(abD))$, $\mathcal{A}_{v_1}(C, J_C(\mathbb{F}_p), D, aD, bD)$ returns $\mathrm{LSB}(v_1(abD))$ and $\mathcal{A}_{v_0}(C, J_C(\mathbb{F}_p), D, aD, bD)$ returns $\mathrm{LSB}(v_0(abD))$, respectively. To prove the above theorem, we need the following lemmas.

Lemma 1. *Given $(C, J_C(\mathbb{F}_p), D, aD, bD)$, to compute any one coordinate of abD is hard as the entire abD.*

Proof. Let $aD = (u_{a,1}, u_{a,0}, v_{a,1}, v_{a,0})$ and $bD = (u_{b,1}, u_{b,0}, v_{b,1}, v_{b,0})$. Assume that $abD = (u_{ab,1}, u_{ab,0}, v_{ab,1}, v_{ab,0})$.

Now, we prove that computing u_1-coordinate of abD is hard as the entire abD. Similar method can be used to prove other coordinate cases.

Assume that there is an oracle $\mathcal{B}$ that given $(C, J_C(\mathbb{F}_p), D, aD, bD)$ and returns $u_1(abD)$, that is

$$\mathcal{B}(C, J_C(\mathbb{F}_p), D, aD, bD) = u_1(abD) = u_{ab,1}.$$

We rewrite $abD = (u_{ab,1}, \mathbf{u_{ab,0}}, \mathbf{v_{ab,1}}, \mathbf{v_{ab,0}})$, and by the oracle $\mathcal{B}$, $u_{ab,1}$ is already known. Now we show how to find out $\mathbf{u_{ab,0}}, \mathbf{v_{ab,1}}$ and $\mathbf{v_{ab,0}}$, therefore the entire abD.

From the Mumford representation of the element in Jacobian group of hyperelliptic curve with genus 2, for $abD = (u_{ab,1}, u_{ab,0}, v_{ab,1}, v_{ab,0}) = (x^2 + u_{ab,1}x + u_{ab,0}, v_{ab,1}x + v_{ab,0})$, we have

$$(v_{ab,1}x + v_{ab,0})^2 - (x^5 + f_3x^3 + f_2x^2 + f_1x + f_0) \equiv 0 \mod (x^2 + u_{ab,1}x + u_{ab,0}).$$

Replacing x^2 with $-(u_{ab,1}x + u_{ab,0})$ on the left side, we have

$$(v_{ab,1}x + v_{ab,0})^2 - (u_{ab,1}x + u_{ab,0})^2 x + f_3(u_{ab,1}x + u_{ab,0})x + f_2(u_{ab,1}x + u_{ab,0})$$
$$- f_1x - f_0 = 0.$$

Comparing the coefficients of x^i for $i = 1$ and 0, we get the following equations about $\mathbf{u_{ab,0}}, \mathbf{v_{ab,1}}, \mathbf{v_{ab,0}}$.

$$\mathbf{v_{ab,0}}^2 - \mathbf{v_{ab,1}^2}\mathbf{u_{ab,0}} + 2u_{ab,1}\mathbf{u_{ab,0}^2} + (f_2 - u_{ab,1}f_3 - u_{ab,1}^3)\mathbf{u_{ab,0}} - f_0 = 0 \quad (3)$$

$$2\mathbf{v_{ab,0}}\mathbf{v_{ab,1}} - \mathbf{u_{ab,0}^2} - u_{ab,1}\mathbf{v_{ab,1}^2} + (f_3 + 3u_{ab,1}^2)\mathbf{u_{ab,0}} + f_2u_{ab,1} - f_3u_{ab,1}^2 - u_{ab,1}^4 - f_1 = 0 \quad (4)$$

We now call $\mathcal{B}$ one more time as follows:

$$\mathcal{B}(C, J_C(\mathbb{F}_p), D, aD, bD + D) = u_1(abD + aD) = u_{ab+a,1}$$

From the explicit formula of general point addition in Jacobian group of hyperelliptic curve with genus 2, we know that $u_{ab+a,1}$ is also a function about $\mathbf{u_{ab,0}}, \mathbf{v_{ab,1}}, \mathbf{v_{ab,0}}$:

$$u_{ab+a,1} = u_{ab,1} - u_{a,1}$$
$$+ 2\frac{(\mathbf{v_{ab,0}} - v_{a,0})(u_{a,1}(u_{ab,1} - u_{a,1}) - (\mathbf{u_{ab,0}} - u_{a,0})) - u_{a,0}(u_{ab,1} - u_{a,1})(\mathbf{v_{ab,1}} - v_{a,1})}{(u_{ab,1} - u_{a,1})(\mathbf{v_{ab,0}} - v_{a,0}) - (\mathbf{u_{ab,0}} - u_{a,0})(\mathbf{v_{ab,1}} - v_{a,1})}$$
$$- \frac{((\mathbf{u_{ab,0}} - u_{a,0})(u_{a,1}(u_{ab,1} - u_{a,1}) - (\mathbf{u_{ab,0}} - u_{a,0})) - u_{a,0}(u_{ab,1} - u_{a,1})^2)^2}{((u_{ab,1} - u_{a,1})(\mathbf{v_{ab,0}} - v_{a,0}) - (\mathbf{u_{ab,0}} - u_{a,0})(\mathbf{v_{ab,1}} - v_{a,1}))^2}$$

This is:

$$((u_{ab,1} - u_{a,1})(\mathbf{v_{ab,0}} - v_{a,0}) - (\mathbf{u_{ab,0}} - u_{a,0})(\mathbf{v_{ab,1}} - v_{a,1}))^2(u_{ab+a,1}$$
$$- u_{ab,1} + u_{a,1} - 2((\mathbf{v_{ab,0}} - v_{a,0})(u_{a,1}(u_{ab,1} - u_{a,1}) - (\mathbf{u_{ab,0}} - u_{a,0})) - u_{a,0}(u_{ab,1}$$
$$- u_{a,1})(\mathbf{v_{ab,1}} - v_{a,1}))((u_{ab,1} - u_{a,1})(\mathbf{v_{ab,0}} - v_{a,0}) - (\mathbf{u_{ab,0}} - u_{a,0})(\mathbf{v_{ab,1}} - v_{a,1}))$$
$$+ ((\mathbf{u_{ab,0}} - u_{a,0})(u_{a,1}(u_{ab,1} - u_{a,1}) - (\mathbf{u_{ab,0}} - u_{a,0})) - u_{a,0}(u_{ab,1} - u_{a,1})^2)^2 = 0 \quad (5)$$

The Eqs. (3)–(5) form a 3-variates polynomial system. This multivariate polynomial system has total degree $3 \times 2 \times 4 = 24$. So, due to the Bézou Theorem, the number of the solution does not exceed 24. We solve this 3-variates polynomial system and obtain $u_{ab,0}, v_{ab,1}, v_{ab,0}$ of abD, so the entire abD.

A detailed Magma [33] implementation for such 3-variates polynomial system according to a genus 2 curve over $GF(2^{127} - 1)$ which used in [10] is provided in Appendix B.

According to our experiments, most cases we can obtain one solution, therefore the entire abD is obtained. However, sometimes, this 3-variates polynomial system will output more than one solutions. In this case, we can find the correct solution for abD up to at most 24 times testings.   □

When one of λ^2, λ^3, λ^4 and λ^5 is a permutation of $\mathbb{F}_p^*$, it is very easy to get v_i from LSB(v_i) or u_i from LSB(u_i) using HNP-CM directly. Therefore, we can have a very simple proof for Theorem 3. For example, when $p = 2 \mod 3$, we can show that "Predicting LSB$(v_1(abD))$ is hard as $v_1(abD)$": Assume that there is an efficient algorithm $\mathcal{A}_{v_1}$ for predicting the least significant bit of v_1-coordinate of abD, i.e., given $(C, J_C(\mathbb{F}_p), D, aD, bD)$,

$$\mathcal{A}_{v_1}(C, J_C(\mathbb{F}_p), D, aD, bD) = \text{LSB}(v_1(abD)).$$

Now, we choose a random number $\lambda \in \mathbb{F}_p^*$ and call the oracle

$$\mathcal{A}_{v_1}(\phi_\lambda(C), \phi_\lambda^*(J_C(F_p)), \phi_\lambda^*(D), \phi_\lambda^*(aD), \phi_\lambda^*(bD))$$

to get LSB$(v_1(\phi_\lambda^*(abD))) = \text{LSB}(\lambda^3 v_1(abD))$. Since $\gcd(3, p - 1) = 1$, it follows that cubing is a permutation of $\mathbb{F}_p^*$. This is an HNP-CM problem (here $t = \lambda^3$ and $\alpha = v_1(abD)$). So, in this case, we can get v_1 from LSB(v_1) using the solving algorithm of HNP-CM. Then combining this with Lemma 1, we can get the entire abD.

To prove the Theorem 3 in general case, similar to Boneh and Shparlinski's [7] approach on elliptic curve case, we will use the method of Alexi et al. [3] to deal with it. When λ^2, λ^3, λ^4 and λ^5 are all not permutation of $\mathbb{F}_p^*$, we can not get v_i from $\mathrm{LSB}(v_i)$ or u_i from $\mathrm{LSB}(u_i)$ using HNP-CM directly. We may only use some $\delta-$fraction of the $\lambda \in \mathbb{F}_p^*$. To simplify notation we henceforth denote $(\phi_\lambda(C), J_{\phi_\lambda(C)}(\mathbb{F}_p), \phi_\lambda(D), \phi_\lambda(aD), \phi_\lambda(bD))$ by $\overline{\phi_\lambda a D b D}$.

Lemma 2. *Let $\epsilon, \delta \in \{0,1\}$. Let p be a prime, and let C be a hyperelliptic curve with genus 2 over F_p. Let $D \in J_C(\mathbb{F}_p)$ be an element of prime order n. Suppose there is a $t-$time algorithm $\mathcal{A}_{u_1}$ such that*

$$|Pr_\lambda[\mathcal{A}_{u_1}(\overline{\phi_\lambda a D b D}) = LSB(\lambda^2 u_1(abD))] - \frac{1}{2}| > \epsilon$$

for at least a $\delta-$fraction of the $\lambda \in \mathbb{F}_p^*$.
Then there is an algorithm $\mathcal{B}$ for all $\lambda \in \mathbb{F}_p^*$ satisfying

$$Pr_\lambda[\mathcal{B}(\overline{\phi_\lambda a D b D}) = LSB(\lambda^2 u_1(abD))] > \frac{1}{2} + \frac{\epsilon\delta}{8}$$

is true with probability at least $\frac{\epsilon\delta}{8}$ over the choice of a, b in $[1, n-1]$.

Proof. This lemma is the hyperelliptic curve with genus 2 case of Lemmas 1 and 2 in Boneh and Shparlinski's [7] paper. Here we will give a sketch of the proof which mostly same as Boneh and Shparlinski's proof. For more details to see Boneh and Shparlinski's [7] original proof.

According to Boneh and Shparlinski's proof, the algorithm $\mathcal{B}$ can be constructed as follows:

Input: $C, J_C(\mathbb{F}_p), D, D_1, D_2$.
Output: $\mathcal{A}_{u_1}(C, J_C(\mathbb{F}_p), D, D_1, D_2)$.

1. Pick $u = (4/\epsilon\delta)^3$, choose a, b pairs from $[1, n-1]$ randomly and run $\mathcal{A}_{u_1}$ on all tuples $< C, J_C(\mathbb{F}_p), D, aD, bD >$;
2. Let v be the number of rums in which $\mathcal{A}_{u_1}$ correctly outputs $\mathrm{LSB}(u_1(abD))$;
3. If $v > u/2$ then $\mathcal{B}$ outputs $\mathcal{A}_{u_1}(C, J_C(\mathbb{F}_p), D, D_1, D_2)$;
4. Otherwise outputs the complement of $\mathcal{A}_{u_1}(C, J_C(\mathbb{F}_p), D, D_1, D_2)$.

As same as Boneh and Shparlinski's [7] discussion, for at least $\delta-$fraction of the $\lambda \in F_p^*$, we have

$$Pr_{a,b}[\mathcal{B}(\overline{\phi_\lambda a D b D}) = \mathrm{LSB}(\lambda^2 u_1(abD))] > \frac{1}{2} + \frac{\epsilon}{2}$$

and for the remaining $\lambda \in F_p^*$, we have:

$$Pr_{a,b}[\mathcal{B}(\overline{\phi_\lambda a D b D}) = \mathrm{LSB}(\lambda^2 u_1(abD))] > \frac{1}{2} - \frac{\epsilon\delta}{4}$$

Then using a standard counting argument, we have

$$Pr_\lambda[\mathcal{B}(\overline{\phi_\lambda aDbD}) = \mathrm{LSB}(\lambda^2 u_1(abD))] > \frac{1}{2} + \frac{\epsilon\delta}{8}$$

is true with probability at least $\frac{\epsilon\delta}{8}$ over the choice of a, b in $[1, n-1]$ for all $\lambda \in \mathbb{F}_p^*$. $\qquad\square$

Now, we give the proof of Theorem 3.

The proof of Theorem 3: Let p be a prime, and let C be a hyperelliptic curve with genus 2 over $\mathbb{F}_p$. Let $D \in J_C(\mathbb{F}_p)$ be an element of prime order. Suppose there is an efficient algorithm $\mathcal{A}$ for predicting the LSB of any coordinate of abD given $(C, J_C(\mathbb{F}_p), D, aD, bD)$, formally, we assume that there is an expected t−time algorithm $\mathcal{A}$ such that

$$|Pr_\lambda[\mathcal{A}_{u_1}(\overline{\phi_\lambda aDbD}) = \mathrm{LSB}(\lambda^2 u_1(abD))] - \frac{1}{2}| > \epsilon$$

for at least a δ−fraction of the $\lambda \in \mathbb{F}_p^*$.

To use the above Lemma 2, we first randomize the hyperelliptic curve DHP $(C, J_C(\mathbb{F}_p), D, aD, bD)$ by computing $D' = a_0aD$ and $D'' = b_0bD$ for random $a_0, b_0 \in [1, n-1]$. Then applying Lemma 2, there is an algorithm $\mathcal{B}$ for all $\lambda \in \mathbb{F}_p^*$ satisfying

$$Pr_\lambda[\mathcal{B}(\phi_\lambda(C), J_{\phi_\lambda(C)}(\mathbb{F}_p), \phi_\lambda(D), \phi_\lambda(D'), \phi_\lambda(D'')) = \mathrm{LSB}(\lambda^2 u_1(a_0b_0abD))]$$
$$> \frac{1}{2} + \frac{\epsilon\delta}{8}$$

is true with probability at least $\frac{\epsilon\delta}{8}$ over the choice of a_0, b_0 in $[1, n-1]$. Define

$$L^2(\lambda) = \mathcal{B}(\phi_\lambda(C), J_{\phi_\lambda(C)}(\mathbb{F}_p), \phi_\lambda(D), \phi_\lambda(D'), \phi_\lambda(D'')).$$

From the knowledge of probability theory, when we repeat choosing a_0, b_0 in $[1, n-1]$ randomly $\lceil \frac{8}{\epsilon\delta} \rceil$ times, then there is at least one time we have

$$Pr_\lambda[L^2(\lambda) = \mathrm{LSB}(\lambda^2 u_1(a_0b_0abD))] > \frac{1}{2} + \frac{\epsilon\delta}{8}$$

with probability $1 - (1 - \frac{\epsilon\delta}{8})^{\lceil \frac{8}{\epsilon\delta} \rceil}$. This is an $HNP - CM^2$ problem where $u_1(a_0b_0abD)$ is the hidden number. Therefore, we can use the solving algorithm of Theorem 2 for all $\lceil \frac{8}{\epsilon\delta} \rceil$ cases to find a list of candidates $\{(a_i, b_i), u_1(a_ib_iabD)\}$ for i from 1 to $\lceil \frac{8}{\epsilon\delta} \rceil$.

For any candidates, applying Lemma 1, we can get a candidate value a_ib_iabD. There is at least one correct a_ib_iabD with probability $1 - (1 - \frac{\epsilon\delta}{8})^{\lceil \frac{8}{\epsilon\delta} \rceil}$, and then using $((a_ib_i)^{-1} \bmod n)a_ib_iabD$, we obtain the entire abD. $\qquad\square$

4   Extention to Any Bit

For any $z = \sum_{i=0}^{n} z_i 2^i$, $bit_i(z)$ denotes the i-th bit of the binary representation of z, so $\mathrm{LSB}(z) = bit_0(z)$. In this section, we will show that if the hyperelliptic curve Diffie-hellman problem is hard, then not only the least significant bit, but also every bit (i.e., $bit_i(z)$) of the hyperelliptic curve Diffie-hellman value is unpredictable.

We have two approaches to achieve this goal.

One approach is from LSB-HNP-CM to bit_i-NHP-CM. As generalized by Håstad and Näslund [25] and Kiltz [29], HNP-CM can also be defined for every bit of z, and the related theorems also hold, i.e., Fix an $\varepsilon > 0$. Let p be a prime. For an $\alpha \in \mathbb{F}_p$ let $L : \mathbb{F}_p* \to \{0, 1\}$ be a function satisfying

$$\mathrm{Pr}_{t \in \mathbb{F}_p*}[L(t) = bit_i(\alpha \cdot t \mod p)] \geq \frac{1}{2} + \epsilon$$

The bit_i-NH problem is: given an oracle for $L(t)$, find α in polynomial time. As claimed in Theorem 5 of [29], for all odd primes p, the bit_i-NHP-CM is efficiently solvable for all bits. Therefore, similar to the discussion for LSB case, it is not hard to extend the results of LSB to the case of any i-th bit.

Another approach is AGS-list decoding method. The list decoding approach for hard-core predicates is developed by Akavia et al. [2] and extended by Morillo and Rafols [36]. A predicate will correspond to some error correcting code, predicting a predicate will correspond to access to a corrupted codeword, and the task of inverting one-way functions will correspond to the task of list decoding a corrupted codeword. The framework of AGS-list decoding method is as the following: Firstly, for given the one way function f, construct a codeword C_f, and such that the following properties hold for C_f: **Accessibility, Concentration** and **Recoverability**, then using Lemma 1 and Theorem 6 of [2], it can be proved that the predicate is hard-core. For the definitions of these properties, please refer to [2].

Following Akavia et al.'s framework, we can generalize the result of Fazio et al. in [18] for every bit of the elliptic curve DHP is hard-core to hyperelliptic curve DHP as follows:

Let p be a prime, and let C be a hyperelliptic curve with genus 2 over $\mathbb{F}_p$. Let $D \in J_C(\mathbb{F}_p)$ be an element of prime order. The $Q = abD$ is the Diffie-Hellman secret value of $(C, J_C(\mathbb{F}_p), D, aD, bD)$. For any $\lambda \in \mathbb{F}_p^*$, $\phi_\lambda(C)$ is the twist of C, $J_{\phi_\lambda(C)}(\mathbb{F}_p) = \phi_\lambda^*(J_C(\mathbb{F}_p))$. Let $bit_i : \mathbb{F}_p \to \{0, 1\}$ denote the $i - th$ bit predicate (In [18], they use $\{\pm 1\}$, it is just the convention that a 0 bit is encoded as -1). Consider the codeword:

$$C_Q : \mathbb{F}_p \to \{0, 1\} \text{ defined as } C_Q(\lambda) = bit_i(\lambda u_1(Q)).$$

Similar to the proof in [18] for elliptic curve case, it can be proven that the codeword C_Q satisfies the properties of **Accessibility, Concentration** and **Recoverability**. Here we omitted the proofs of these properties for the limited space. Using Theorem 6 and the learning algorithm of [2], it can be proved that this predicate is hard-core. For more detail, refer to [2,18].

From above discussion, we give the following claim without proof:

Claim 1. *Let p be a prime, and let C be a hyperelliptic curve with genus 2 over $\mathbb{F}_p$. Let $D \in J_C(\mathbb{F}_p)$ be an element of prime order. If there is an efficient algorithm for predicting the any bit of any coordinate of abD given $(C, J_C(\mathbb{F}_p), D, aD, bD)$, then there is an efficient algorithm for computing the DHP on $J_C(\mathbb{F}_p)$.*

5   Generalization to General Hyperelliptic Curves

Let $C : y^2 + h(x)y = f(x)$ be a hyperelliptic curve of genus $g \geq 1$ over $\mathbb{F}_q$, $J(C; \mathbb{F}_q)$ be the Jacobian of C defined over $\mathbb{F}_q$. Let $D = (u_{g-1}, ..., u_1, u_0, v_{g-1}, ..., v_1, v_0)$ be an element of $J(C; \mathbb{F}_q)$ with order n. Costello and Lauter [12] gave an explicit formulas for addition and doubling for any genus hyperelliptic Jacobian group. So, we can define the hyperelliptic DHP on any genus hyperelliptic Jacobian group as same as genus 2 case: given $C, J_C(\mathbb{F}_p), D, aD, bD$, to compute abD.

For a hyperelliptic curve with genus g over $\mathbb{F}_p$(Similar discussion can be applied to non-prime fields),

$$C : y^2 = x^{2g+1} + f_{2g-1}x^{2g-1} + f_{2g-2}x^{2g-2} + \cdots + f_1 x + f_0$$

Let C' be another hyperelliptic curves with genus g over $\mathbb{F}_p$ with equation:

$$C' : y^2 = x^{2g+1} + f'_{2g-1}x^{2g-1} + f'_{2g-2}x^{2g-2} + \cdots + f'_1 x + f'_0$$

We say that C is isomorphic to C' if there exists $\lambda \in \mathbb{F}_p$ such that $f'_i = \lambda^{4g+2-2i} f_i$ mod p. The isomorphisms that preserve hyperelliptic curves given by above equations are all of the form $(x, y) \rightarrow (\lambda^2 x, \lambda^{2g+1} y)$ for some $\lambda \in \mathbb{F}_p^*$.

We define $\phi_\lambda : (x, y) \rightarrow (\lambda^2 x, \lambda^{2g+1} y)$, then $C' = \phi_\lambda(C)$ is a twist of C. This curves isomorphism can reduce an isomorphism between $J_C(\mathbb{F}_p)$ and $J_{C'}(\mathbb{F}_p)$, we denote this group isomorphism as $\phi_\lambda^* : J_C(\mathbb{F}_p) \rightarrow J_{\phi_\lambda(C)}(\mathbb{F}_p)$. Now, we can define the explicit formulas for ϕ_λ^* as follows: $\phi_\lambda^*(O) = O'$, $\phi_\lambda^*(x_1, y_1) = (\lambda^2 x_1, \lambda^{2g+1} y_1)$,

$$
\begin{aligned}
&\phi_\lambda^*(u(x), v(x)) \\
&= \phi_\lambda^*(u_{g-1}, ..., u_1, u_0, v_{g-1}, ..., v_1, v_0) \\
&= \phi_\lambda^*(P_1 + P_2 + ... + P_g - gP_\infty) \\
&\quad (here\ P_i = (x_i, y_i),\ v(x_i) = y_i) \\
&= \phi_\lambda^*((x_1, y_1) + (x_2, y_2) + ... + (x_g, y_g) - gP_\infty) \\
&= (\lambda^2 x_1, \lambda^{2g+1} y_1) + (\lambda^2 x_2, \lambda^{2g+1} y_2) + ... + (\lambda^2 x_g, \lambda^{2g+1} y_g) - gP'_\infty) \\
&= (\prod_{i=1}^{g}(x - \lambda^2 x_i), v'_{g-1} x^{g-1} + ... + v'_1 x + v'_0) \\
&\quad (here\ v'(\lambda^2 x_i) = \lambda^{2g+1} y_i) \\
&= (\lambda^2 u_{g-1}, ..., \lambda^{2(g-1)} u_1, \lambda^{2g} u_0, \lambda^3 v_{g-1}, ..., \lambda^{2g-1} v_1, \lambda^{2g+1} v_0)
\end{aligned}
$$

Therefore, we have $DH_{\phi_\lambda^*(J),\phi_\lambda^*(D)}(\phi_\lambda^*(D_1),\phi_\lambda^*(D_2)) = \phi_\lambda^*(DH_{J,D}(D_1,D_2))$. So if the hyperelliptic DHP is hard to compute in $J_C(\mathbb{F}_p)$, then it is also hard to compute for all $\{J_{\phi_\lambda(C)}(\mathbb{F}_p)\}_{\lambda\in\mathbb{F}_p^*}$. Similar to the case of $g = 2$, we can use HNP-CM^d to study the bit security of hyperelliptic curve DHP with any genus.

Using Costello and Lauters explicit formulas for addition and doubling for any genus hyperelliptic Jacobian group, Lemma 1 can extend to hyperelliptic curve with any genus, and using twisted hyperelliptic curves with any genus, Lemma 2 is also true for any genus hyperelliptic curves. Therefore, we have the following claim:

Claim 2. *Let p be a prime, and let C be a hyperelliptic curve with genus g over $\mathbb{F}_p$. Let $D \in J_C(\mathbb{F}_p)$ be an element of prime order. Given $(C, J_C(\mathbb{F}_p), D, aD, bD)$, if there is an efficient algorithm for predicting any one bit of any coordinate of abD, then there is an efficient algorithm for computing the DHP on $J_C(\mathbb{F}_p)$.*

6   Conclusions and Further Works

Hyperelliptic curve cryptography is an alternative to elliptic curve cryptography. Due to the recent many research work on genus 2 hyperelliptic curve cryptography, especially for their cryptanalysis and fast implementation, that hyperelliptic curve cryptography in genus 2 has the potential to be competitive with its elliptic curve cryptography counterpart. In this paper, we studied the bit security of hyperelliptic Curves DHP, we show that the least significant bit of each coordinate of hyperelliptic Curves Diffie-Hellman secret value K in genus 2 is hard-core, and then we show that any bit is hard-core. Finally, we extend our techniques and results to any genus hyperelliptic curves.

There are some further works at this topic. Similar to elliptic curve case, we can also define a function whose domain is a subgroup of $J_C(\mathbb{F}_p)$, such as hyperelliptic pairing. When we consider the one-way function defined over the Jacobian of hyperelliptic curve, we call such function "hyperelliptic curve based one-way function", following the approach of Duc and Jetchev [15] for elliptic curve case, it seems that all the bits of hyperelliptic curve based one way functions are hard to compute too.

Jetchev and Venkatesan [28] studied the bits security of elliptic curve Diffie-Hellman secret keys using elliptic curves isogeny theory. The hyperelliptic Jacobians also have explicit isogenies, there are some research work on them. An natural question is if we can study the bits security of hyperelliptic curve Diffie-Hellman secret keys using hyperelliptic curves isogeny theory. It seems this can also be done.

Acknowledgements. This work is supported by the National Natural Science Foundation of China (No. 61379154 and 61672550). Part of this work was done during the author was visiting the UbiSeC lab at University at Buffalo, State University of New York.

A Appendix: Explicit Formula for Addition in Genus 2

B Appendix: Magma Program

```
p:=2^127-1; K := GF(p);
P<x> := PolynomialRing(GF(p));
f3:= 34744234758245218589390329770704207149;
f2:= 132713617209345335075125059444256188021;
f1:= 90907655901711006083734360528442376758;
f0:= 66679866221737283378235608571799992816;
C := HyperellipticCurve(x^5+f3*x^3+f2*x^2+f1*x+f0);
J := Jacobian(C); D:=Random(J);
n:=289480223093290488481692399956590251384511779730915513741
    01475732892580332259;
a:=Random(1,n); b:=Random(1,n);
A:=a*D; B:=b*D;
C:=a*B; M:=(b+1)*A;
ua1:=Coefficient(A[1], 1); ua0:=Coefficient(A[1], 0);
va1:=Coefficient(A[2], 1); va0:=Coefficient(A[2], 0);
uab1:=Coefficient(C[1], 1);
uaba1:=Coefficient(M[1], 1);


P3<x,y,z> := PolynomialRing(K, 3);
g1:=z^2-y^2*x+2*uab1*x^2+(f2-uab1*f3-uab1^3)*x-f0;
g2:=2*z*y-x^2-uab1*y^2+(f3 +3*uab1^2)*x+f2*uab1-f3*uab1^2-uab1^4-f1;
g3:=((uab1-ua1) *(z-va0) - (x- ua0)* (y-va1))^2*(uaba1- uab1+ua1)
-2*((z-va0)*(ua1*(uab1-ua1)- (x- ua0)) - ua0*(uab1-ua1)*(y-va1))
*((uab1-ua1)*(z-va0) - (x- ua0)* (y-va1))+((x- ua0)* (ua1*(uab1-ua1)
 - (x- ua0))- ua0*(uab1-ua1)^2 )^2;


I := ideal<P3 | g1, g2, g3>;

v := Variety(I, K);

v;
```

Table 1. Addition in genus 2

Input: $D_1 = (u_{11}, u_{10}, v_{11}, v_{10}), D_2 = (u_{21}, u_{20}, v_{21}, v_{20}))$
Output: $D_3 = D_1 + D_2 = (u_{31}, u_{30}, v_{31}, v_{30})$

Step	Expression
1	$A = (v_{10} - v_{20})(u_{21}(u_{11} - u_{21}) - (u_{10} - u_{20})) - u_{20}(u_{11} - u_{21})(v_{11} - v_{21})$ $B = (u_{10} - u_{20})(u_{21}(u_{11} - u_{21}) - (u_{10} - u_{20})) - u_{20}(u_{11} - u_{21})^2$ $C = (u_{11} - u_{21})(v_{10} - v_{20}) - (u_{10} - u_{20})(v_{11} - v_{21})$
2	$u_{31} = (u_{11} - u_{21}) + 2\frac{A}{C} - \frac{B^2}{C^2}$ $u_{30} = (u_{11} - u_{21})\frac{A}{C} + \frac{A^2}{C^2} + (u_{11} + u_{21})\frac{B^2}{C^2} - (v_{11} + v_{21})\frac{B}{C}$ $v_{31} = (u_{10} - u_{30})\frac{C}{B} - u_{31}(u_{11} - u_{31})\frac{C}{B} + (u_{11} - u_{31})\frac{A}{B} - v_{11}$ $v_{30} = (u_{10} - u_{30})\frac{A}{B} - u_{30}(u_{11} - u_{31})\frac{C}{B} - v_{10}$
3	$Output : (u_{31}, u_{30}, v_{31}, v_{30})$

References

1. Adleman, L.M., DeMarrais, J., Huang, M.-D.: A subexponential algorithm for discrete logarithms over the rational subgroup of the Jacobians of large genus hyperelliptic curves over finite fields. In: Adleman, L.M., Huang, M.-D. (eds.) ANTS 1994. LNCS, vol. 877, pp. 28–40. Springer, Heidelberg (1994). doi:10.1007/3-540-58691-1_39
2. Akavia, A., Goldwasser, S., Safra, S.: Proving hard-core predicates using list decoding. In: FOCS 2003, pp. 146–157. IEEE Computer Society (2003)
3. Alexi, W., Chor, B., Goldreich, O., Schnorr, C.: RSA and Rabin functions: certain parts are as hard as the whole. SIAM J. Comput. **17**, 194–209 (1988)
4. Avanzi, R., Cohen, H., Doche, C., Frey, G., Lange, T., Nguyen, K., Vercauteren, F.: Handbook of Elliptic and Hyperelliptic Cryptography. Chapman and Hall/CRC, Boca Raton (2006)
5. Bernstein, D.J., Chuengsatiansup, C., Lange, T., Schwabe, P.: Kummer strikes back: new DH speed records. In: Sarkar, P., Iwata, T. (eds.) ASIACRYPT 2014. LNCS, vol. 8873, pp. 317–337. Springer, Heidelberg (2014). doi:10.1007/978-3-662-45611-8_17
6. Blum, M., Micali, S.: How to generate cryptographically strong sequences of pseudo-random bits. SIAM J. Comput. **13**(4), 850–864 (1984)
7. Boneh, D., Shparlinski, I.E.: On the unpredictability of bits of the elliptic curve Diffie-Hellman scheme. In: Kilian, J. (ed.) CRYPTO 2001. LNCS, vol. 2139, pp. 201–212. Springer, Heidelberg (2001). doi:10.1007/3-540-44647-8_12
8. Boneh, D., Venkatesan, R.: Hardness of computing the most significant bits of secret keys in diffie-hellman and related schemes. In: Koblitz, N. (ed.) CRYPTO 1996. LNCS, vol. 1109, pp. 129–142. Springer, Heidelberg (1996). doi:10.1007/3-540-68697-5_11
9. Boneh, D., Lynn, B., Shacham, H.: Short signatures from the weil pairing. In: Boyd, C. (ed.) ASIACRYPT 2001. LNCS, vol. 2248, pp. 514–532. Springer, Heidelberg (2001). doi:10.1007/3-540-45682-1_30
10. Bos, J.W., Costello, C., Hisil, H., Lauter, K.: Fast cryptography in genus 2. In: Johansson, T., Nguyen, P.Q. (eds.) EUROCRYPT 2013. LNCS, vol. 7881, pp. 194–210. Springer, Heidelberg (2013). doi:10.1007/978-3-642-38348-9_12
11. Cantor, D.G.: Computing in the Jacobian of a hyperelliptic curve. Math. Comput. **48**, 95–101 (1987)
12. Costello, C., Lauter, K.: Group law computations on Jacobians of hyperelliptic curves. In: Miri, A., Vaudenay, S. (eds.) SAC 2011. LNCS, vol. 7118, pp. 92–117. Springer, Heidelberg (2012). doi:10.1007/978-3-642-28496-0_6
13. Diao, O., Joye, M.: Unified addition formulæ for hyperelliptic curve cryptosystems. In: The 3rd International Conference on Symbolic Computation and Cryptography (SCC 2012), pp. 45–50 (2012)
14. Diffie, W., Hellman, M.: New directions in cryptography. IEEE Trans. Inf. Theor. **22**, 644–654 (1976)
15. Duc, A., Jetchev, D.: Hardness of computing individual bits for one-way functions on elliptic curves. In: Safavi-Naini, R., Canetti, R. (eds.) CRYPTO 2012. LNCS, vol. 7417, pp. 832–849. Springer, Heidelberg (2012). doi:10.1007/978-3-642-32009-5_48
16. ElGamal, T.: A public-key cryptosystem and a signature scheme based on discrete logarithms. IEEE Trans. Inf. Theor. **31**, 469–472 (1985)

17. FIPS 186–2, Digital signature standard, Federal Information Processing Standards Publication 186–2, February 2000
18. Fazio, N., Gennaro, R., Perera, I.M., Skeith III, W.E.: Hard-core predicates for a Diffie-Hellman problem over finite fields. In: Canetti, R., Garay, J.A. (eds.) CRYPTO 2013. LNCS, vol. 8043, pp. 148–165. Springer, Heidelberg (2013). doi:10.1007/978-3-642-40084-1_9
19. Galbraith, S.D.: Mathematics of Public Key Cryptography. Cambridge University Press, Cambridge (2012)
20. Galbraith, S.D., Hopkins, H.J., Shparlinski, I.E.: Secure bilinear Diffie-Hellman bits. In: Wang, H., Pieprzyk, J., Varadharajan, V. (eds.) ACISP 2004. LNCS, vol. 3108, pp. 370–378. Springer, Heidelberg (2004). doi:10.1007/978-3-540-27800-9_32
21. Gaudry, P.: Fast genus 2 arithmetic based on theta functions. J. Math. Crypt. JMC **1**(3), 243–265 (2007)
22. Gaudry, P., Thomé, E., Thériault, N., Diem, C.: A double large prime variation for small genus hyperelliptic index calculus. Math. Comput. **76**(257), 475–492 (2007)
23. González Vasco, M.I., Näslund, M., Shparlinski, I.E.: New results on the hardness of Diffie-Hellman bits. In: Bao, F., Deng, R., Zhou, J. (eds.) PKC 2004. LNCS, vol. 2947, pp. 159–172. Springer, Heidelberg (2004). doi:10.1007/978-3-540-24632-9_12
24. Harley, R.: Fast arithmetic on genus 2 curves. For C source code and further explanations. http://cristal.inria.fr/~harley/hyper
25. Håstad, J., Näslund, M.: The security of all RSA and discrete log bits. J. ACM **51**(2), 187–230 (2004)
26. Hisil, H., Costello, C.: Jacobian coordinates on genus 2 curves. In: Sarkar, P., Iwata, T. (eds.) ASIACRYPT 2014. LNCS, vol. 8873, pp. 338–357. Springer, Heidelberg (2014). doi:10.1007/978-3-662-45611-8_18
27. Jao, D., Jetchev, D., Venkatesan, R.: On the bits of elliptic curve Diffie-Hellman keys. In: Srinathan, K., Rangan, C.P., Yung, M. (eds.) INDOCRYPT 2007. LNCS, vol. 4859, pp. 33–47. Springer, Heidelberg (2007). doi:10.1007/978-3-540-77026-8_4
28. Jetchev, D., Venkatesan, R.: Bits security of the elliptic curve Diffie–Hellman secret keys. In: Wagner, D. (ed.) CRYPTO 2008. LNCS, vol. 5157, pp. 75–92. Springer, Heidelberg (2008). doi:10.1007/978-3-540-85174-5_5
29. Kiltz, E.: A primitive for proving the security of every bit and about universal hash functions and hard core bits. In: Freivalds, R. (ed.) FCT 2001. LNCS, vol. 2138, pp. 388–391. Springer, Heidelberg (2001). doi:10.1007/3-540-44669-9_39
30. Koblitz, N.: Hyperelliptic cryptography. J. Crypt. **1**, 139–150 (1989)
31. Lange, T.: Formulae for arithmetic on genus 2 hyperelliptic curves. Appl. Algebra Eng. Commun. Comput. **15**(5), 295–328 (2005)
32. Li, W.-C.W., Näslund, M., Shparlinski, I.E.: Hidden number problem with the trace and bit security of XTR and LUC. In: Yung, M. (ed.) CRYPTO 2002. LNCS, vol. 2442, pp. 433–448. Springer, Heidelberg (2002). doi:10.1007/3-540-45708-9_28
33. MAGMA Computational Algebra System. http://magma.maths.usyd.edu.au/magma/
34. Maurer, U.M.: Towards the equivalence of breaking the Diffie-Hellman protocol and computing discrete logarithms. In: Desmedt, Y.G. (ed.) CRYPTO 1994. LNCS, vol. 839, pp. 271–281. Springer, Heidelberg (1994). doi:10.1007/3-540-48658-5_26
35. Maurer, U.M., Wolf, S.: The relationship between breaking the Diffie-Hellman protocol and computing discrete logarithms. SIAM J. Comput. **28**(5), 1689–1721 (1999)
36. Morillo, P., Ràfols, C.: The security of all bits using list decoding. In: Jarecki, S., Tsudik, G. (eds.) PKC 2009. LNCS, vol. 5443, pp. 15–33. Springer, Heidelberg (2009). doi:10.1007/978-3-642-00468-1_2

37. Pohlig, S.C., Hellman, M.E.: An improved algorithm for computing logarithms over GF(p) and its cryptographic significance. IEEE Trans. Inf. Theor. **24**, 106–110 (1978)
38. Shani, B.: On the bit security of elliptic curve Diffie–Hellman. In: Fehr, S. (ed.) PKC 2017. LNCS, vol. 10174, pp. 361–387. Springer, Heidelberg (2017). doi:10.1007/978-3-662-54365-8_15
39. Wang, M., Zhan, T., Zhang, H.: Bit security of the CDH problems over finite fields. In: Dunkelman, O., Keliher, L. (eds.) SAC 2015. LNCS, vol. 9566, pp. 441–461. Springer, Cham (2016). doi:10.1007/978-3-319-31301-6_25

Natural sd-RCCA Secure
Public-Key Encryptions

Yuan Chen[1(✉)], Qingkuan Dong[1], and Qiqi Lai[2(✉)]

[1] State Key Laboratory of Integrated Services Networks,
Xidian University, Xi'an 710071, People's Republic of China
yuanchen@xidian.edu.cn, qkdong@mail.xidian.edu.cn
[2] School of Computer Science, Shaanxi Normal University,
Xi'an 710119, People's Republic of China
laiqq@snnu.edu.cn

Abstract. Replayable CCA (RCCA) security is a reasonable relaxation of CCA security for public-key encryptions. Pd-RCCA and sd-RCCA security are two variants of it according to a "replaying" can be detected publicly or secretly. Existing "natural" RCCA schemes satisfy pd-RCCA security, while those satisfying only sd-RCCA security are left as open. We present such schemes via KEM+DEM hybrid paradigm. Sd-RCCA secure DEMs are sufficient for this purpose. It is known that an RCCA secure DEM can be achieved by combining a passive secure DEM with a regular (but not a strong) secure message authentication code (MAC), where forgeries for old messages might be possible. Unfortunately, most practical MACs are deterministic, which makes the two notions equivalent. However, the recently proposed probabilistic MACs activate this paradigm. We formalize the related notions and the paradigm, then show natural examples of regular secure probabilistic MACs under the DDH assumption, based on which natural instances of sd-RCCA secure schemes are given.

Keywords: sd-RCCA security · Probabilistic MAC · Hybrid encryption · Public-key encryption

1 Introduction

Replayable CCA (RCCA) security is a relaxed variant of CCA security for Public-Key Encryptions (PKE). It is proved to be sufficient for several cryptographic tasks [1–3], and is believed to be sufficient for almost all the uses of CCA-secure encryptions [4,5]. In addition, it makes it possible to consider secure rerandomizable encryptions [6,7].

In the definition of RCCA security, the decryption oracle answers 'test' whenever a queried ciphertext decrypts to one of the questioned messages m_0 or m_1. This allows an adversary to modify a challenge ciphertext to another if the underlying plaintext is unchanged. Then by requiring such modification can be detected, RCCA security is strengthened. According to such detection can be

© Springer International Publishing AG 2017
T. Okamoto et al. (Eds.): ProvSec 2017, LNCS 10592, pp. 236–250, 2017.
https://doi.org/10.1007/978-3-319-68637-0_14

done given only the public key or even the secret key, two stronger variants of RCCA security are introduced in [1], i.e., publicly detectable RCCA (pd-RCCA) and secretly detectable RCCA (sd-RCCA) security.

It is known that CCA $\Rightarrow$ pd-RCCA $\Rightarrow$ sd-RCCA $\Rightarrow$ RCCA and all the implications are strict. The two leftmost are shown in [1], and the rightmost is shown in [7]. Nevertheless, almost all existing RCCA secure schemes satisfy the stronger pd-RCCA security, such as the schemes adding arbitrary padding to ciphertexts in the encryption while discarding it in the decryption, those allowing for more than one representation of ciphertexts, and even a recently proposed very natural LWE based schemes [8]. "Natural" RCCA secure schemes only satisfying the weaker sd-RCCA security are left as open in [1]. We will show such schemes in this paper. We simply denote sd-RCCA but not pd-RCCA security as sd-RCCA security later.

There is already a line to construct sd-RCCA secure schemes, which is related to rerandomizability. In fact, a publicly rerandomizable RCCA scheme could be sd-RCCA secure but never be pd-RCCA [1]. One of the two somewhat artificial counterexamples showing the gap between pd-RCCA and sd-RCCA security are given in this way. However, it seems difficult to build a natural such scheme. We follow another line in this paper, which simply follows the popular KEM+DEM hybrid paradigm [9].

In the paradigm, KEM uses asymmetric techniques to encrypt a key, which is then used as the key by a symmetric cipher DEM to encrypt the message. It is well known that the combination of a CCA secure KEM with a (one-time) CCA secure DEM yield a CCA secure PKE. For RCCA security, similar result holds. For our purpose, we can relax one of the KEM and DEM to be sd-RCCA secure. In fact, sd-RCCA secure KEMs seem as difficult to be built as PKEs, so we seek for sd-RCCA secure DEMs.

We note that it has already been pointed out in [1] that an RCCA secure DEM can be achieved by combining a passive secure DEM with a regular (but not strong) secure message authentication code (MAC), since for a regular MAC it is possible to forge a new MAC value for an old message. Now, if for such MACs the validity of the forgery can be verified only secretly, then we obtain the desired DEMs. However, almost all practical MACs are deterministic, for which regular and strong security are equivalent, then we should find such natural MAC schemes from multi-value or probabilistic ones. Existing multi-value MACs are just conceptual or unnatural [10], so we turn to probabilistic MACs.

Probabilistic MACs have been recently proven to be useful and can be constructed efficiently from some standard hardness assumptions [11,12]. Some schemes in [11] appear to meet our requirements. One may think that probabilistic MACs are overkilled since only one-time security for MACs is required, and information-theoretically secure ones exist. However, we are focus on such a stage that if the MAC in a CCA secure scheme is slightly weakened, then it might be naturally degenerated to a sd-RCCA secure one. This is the main reason why we deem our paradigm as "natural". Another reason is that when instantiating some hybrid encryptions with proper probabilistic MACs, we obtain sd-RCCA secure PKEs with very "natural" number theoretic operations as those in CCA secure ones.

In Sects. 2 and 3, we formalize the related notions and results mentioned above. In Sect. 4, we show two natural examples of MAC schemes as desired. The first one follows the construction from hash proof systems (HPS) in [11], which is instantiated directly with a universal$_2$ HPS by Cramer and Shoup [13], without the variant used in [11]. The second one comes directly from [11], which is the (so-called) full secure variant of the key-homomorphic weak PRF based construction when instantiated by a DDH-based example. From these MAC schemes, we further instantiate two natural PKE schemes as desired.

1.1 Further Discussions and Related Notions

Building RCCA secure schemes more efficient than CCA secure ones is another open problem left in [1]. Although a MAC scheme satisfying our requirement and more efficient than existing strong secure MAC schemes seems helpful, our schemes fail for that purpose. The reason is informally given in Sect. 5.2.

Detectability is studied in isolation in [14], where a notion called DCCA security is defined when danger can be detected publicly. Pd-RCCA is a natural case for DCCA security, but generally sd-RCCA is not. However, our schemes are obviously DCCA secure, thus show an overlap between sd-RCCA and DCCA security.

2 Preliminaries

2.1 RCCA Security for PKE

Definition 1 (PKE). *A public-key encryption scheme consists of three algorithms. Probabilistic PKE.Gen that on input the security parameter k, generates public and private-keys (pk, sk), pk defines the message space $\mathcal{M}$. Probabilistic PKE.Enc encrypts a message $m \in \mathcal{M}$ into a ciphertext c by using pk. PKE.Dec decrypts cf by using sk, outputs either $m \in \mathcal{M}$ or a special symbol $\perp \notin \mathcal{M}$. Correctness is required, i.e., for all (pk, sk) generated by PKE.Gen, and $m \in \mathcal{M}$, $PKE.Dec_{sk}(PKE.Enc_{pk}(m)) = m$.*

Definition 2 (RCCA security for PKEs). *We say a PKE scheme $\mathcal{PKE} = (PKE.Gen, PKE.Enc, PKE.Dec)$ is RCCA secure if for every probabilistic polynomial-time oracle machine (PPT) $\mathcal{A}_E$ that plays the following game, its advantage $Adv_{\Pi,\mathcal{A}_E}^{rcca}(k) = |Pr[\tilde{b} = b] - \frac{1}{2}|$ is negligible in k.*
    [RGAME.PKE]
    Step 1. $(pk, sk) \leftarrow PKE.Gen(1^k)$
    Step 2. $(m_0, m_1, v) \leftarrow \mathcal{A}_E^{\mathcal{O}}(pk)$
    Step 3. $b \leftarrow \{0, 1\}$, $c \leftarrow PKE.Enc_{pk}(m_b)$.
    Step 4. $\tilde{b} \leftarrow \mathcal{A}_E^{\mathcal{O}}(v, c)$
    By $\mathcal{O}$, we denote $PKE.Dec_{sk}(\cdot)$, except that in step 4 $\mathcal{O}$ returns 'test' for any ciphertext decrypts to m_0 or m_1.

In RCCA secure schemes, a "replay" of plaintexts by modifying the ciphertext is allowed. Publicly-detectable (pd) and secretly-detectable (sd) RCCA security are defined according to whether the "replay" can be detected given pk or sk. The definitions are related to a notion of compatible relations. We now give the definitions in [1].

Definition 3 (Compatible relations for PKEs). *Let* $\mathcal{PKE} = (PKE.Gen, PKE.Enc, PKE.Dec)$ *be a PKE. Then for* $\mathcal{PKE}$*, we say a family of binary relations* $\equiv$ *on ciphertext pairs is compatible, if for any* (pk, sk) *of* $\mathcal{PKE}$*, we have:*

1. *For any ciphertexts* c, c'*, if* $c \equiv c'$*, then* $PKE.Dec_{sk}(c) = PKE.Dec_{sk}(c')$*.*
2. *For any* $m \in \mathcal{M}$*, if* c *and* c' *are two independent encryptions of* m*, then* $\Pr[c \equiv c']$ *is negligible in* k*.*

Given c *and* c'*, if* $\equiv$ *can be computed efficiently with the sole knowledge of* pk*, then we say* $\equiv$ *is publicly computable, and rewrite it as* $\equiv_{pk}$*, if the computation needs also the knowledge of* sk*, then we say* $\equiv$ *is secretly computable, and rewrite it as* $\equiv_{sk}$*.*

Definition 4 (pd-RCCA/sd-RCCA security for PKEs). *We say* $\mathcal{PKE}$ *is pd-RCCA secure if there exists a publicly computable compatible relation* $\equiv_{pk}$*, such that* $\mathcal{PKE}$ *is secure according to the above definition of RCCA security with the modification that* $\mathcal{O}$ *returns test for any* c' *with* $c' \equiv_{pk} c$*. Denote the game as* **pd-RGAME.PKE**. *We say* $\mathcal{PKE}$ *is sd-RCCA secure if the above holds for a secretly computable* $\equiv_{sk}$*. Denote the game as* **sd-RGAME.PKE**.

For any pd/sd-RCCA secure scheme, $c \equiv c$, otherwise the scheme cannot be pd/sd-RCCA secure. It is shown in [1] that "CCA $\Rightarrow$ pd-RCCA $\Rightarrow$ sd-RCCA $\Rightarrow$ RCCA".

REMARK: Since we are interested in RCCA secure schemes which are not CCA secure, the compatible relation $\equiv$ showing the pd- or sd-RCCA security must not be the equality relation: $c' \equiv c$ if $c' = c$. Therefore, we address that for such $\equiv$, publicly or secretly computable, it must be satisfied that it is easy to find a $c' \neq c$, such that $c' \equiv c$. That is, there exists a PPT machine, when given pk, c as inputs, it outputs a $c' \neq c$, such that $c' \equiv c$ with non-negligible probability. Otherwise, pd-RCCA or sd-RCCA secure schemes are trivially CCA secure.

2.2 KEM+DEM and Related Security Notions

Definition 5 (KEM). *A key encapsulation mechanism (KEM) consists of three algorithms. Probabilistic* **KEM.Gen** *that on input* 1^k *outputs a public/private key pair* (pk, sk)*,* pk *defines the key space* $\mathcal{K}_K$*. Probabilistic encapsulation algorithm* **KEM.Enc** *that on input* 1^k *and a public key* pk*, outputs a pair* (dk, ψ)*, where* $dk \in \mathcal{K}_K$ *is a key and* ψ *is its ciphertext. Decapsulation algorithm* **KEM.Dec**, *on input* sk *and* ψ*, outputs either a key* $dk \in \mathcal{K}_K$ *or the special symbol* $\perp$*. Correctness is required, i.e., for all* (pk, sk) *generated by* **KEM.Gen**, *and all* $(dk, \psi) \leftarrow$ **KEM.Enc**$_{pk}(1^k)$*,* **KEM.Dec**$_{sk}(\psi) = dk$*.*

Definition 6 (CCA for KEMs). *We say a KEM* $\mathcal{KEM}$ = (*KEM.Gen,*
KEM.Enc, KEM.Dec) is CCA secure if for every PPT $\mathcal{A}_E$ *that plays the following*
game, its advantage $Adv^{cca}_{\Pi,\mathcal{A}_K}(k) = |Pr[\tilde{\delta} = \delta] - \frac{1}{2}|$ *is negligible in* k.
  [GAME.KEM]
  Step 1. $(pk, sk) \leftarrow$ *KEM.Gen*(1^k)
  Step 2. $(dk_1, \psi) \leftarrow$ *KEM.Enc*$_{pk}(1^k)$, $dk_0 \leftarrow \mathcal{K}_K$, $\delta \leftarrow \{0, 1\}$.
  Step 3. $\tilde{\delta} \leftarrow \mathcal{A}^{\mathcal{O}}_K(pk, \psi, dk_\delta)$
  $\mathcal{O}$ *denotes KEM.Dec*$_{sk}(\cdot)$. *In Step 3,* $\mathcal{A}_K$ *is restricted not to ask* ψ *to* $\mathcal{O}$.

Definition 7 (DEM). *A data encapsulation mechanism (DEM) is a one-time*
symmetric-key encryption, consists of two algorithms. DEM.Enc that takes as
input 1^k, *a key* dk *and a message* $m \in \mathcal{M}$ *(*$\mathcal{M}$ *is usually assumed to be*
$\{0, 1\}^*$*), outputs a ciphertext* χ. *DEM.Dec that takes as input a* dk *and a cipher-*
text χ, *outputs a message* m *or the special symbol* $\perp$. *For our purpose, we*
allow DEM.Enc to be probabilistic. Correctness is required, i.e., for all $m \in \mathcal{M}$,
DEM.Dec$_{dk}$(*DEM.Enc*$_{dk}(m)) = m$.

Definition 8 (OT/CCA/RCCA security for DEMs). *We say a DEM*
$\mathcal{DEM}$ = (*DEM.Enc, DEM.Dec) is OT/CCA/RCCA secure if for every PPT* $\mathcal{A}_D$
that plays the following game, its advantage $Adv^{ot/cca/rcca}_{\Pi,\mathcal{A}_D}(k) = |Pr[\tilde{b} = b] - \frac{1}{2}|$
is negligible in k.
  [GAME.DEM]
  Step 1. $(m_0, m_1, v) \leftarrow \mathcal{A}_D(1^k)$
  Step 2. $dk \leftarrow \mathcal{K}_D$, $b \leftarrow \{0, 1\}$, $\chi \leftarrow$ *DEM.Enc*$_{dk}(m_b)$.
  Step 3. $\tilde{b} \leftarrow \mathcal{A}^{\mathcal{O}}_D(v, \chi)$
  For the OT security, $\mathcal{O}$ *is null. For the CCA security,* $\mathcal{O}$ *is DEM.Dec*$_{dk}(\cdot)$,
  and in Step 3 $\mathcal{A}_D$ *is restricted not to ask* χ *to* $\mathcal{O}$. *For the RCCA security, all is*
  the same except that in step 3 $\mathcal{O}$ *returns 'test' for any ciphertext that decrypts*
  to m_0 *or* m_1.

To define pd-RCCA and sd-RCCA security for DEMs, we should first define
compatible relations for them. We note that the second requirement in the definitions of compatible relations for PKEs is not necessary now. Although our
DEMs are randomized, it seems impossible for an adversary to generate random
encryptions for both m_0 and m_1 since we only require one-time security, thus
the attack mentioned for PKEs doesn't work for DEMs. Due to this, we define
compatible relations for DEMs without this requirement, which are simpler but
sufficient for our purpose.

Definition 9 (compatible relations for DEMs). *Let* $\mathcal{DEM}$ = (*DEM.Enc,*
DEM.Dec) be a DEM scheme. For $\mathcal{DEM}$, *we say a family of binary relations*
$\equiv$ *on ciphertext pairs is compatible, if for any* dk *of* $\mathcal{DEM}$ *and any ciphertexts*
c, c', *if* $c \equiv c'$, *then DEM.Dec*$_{dk}(c) =$ *DEM.Dec*$_{dk}(c')$.
  Given c *and* c', *if* $\equiv$ *can be computed efficiently without the knowledge of* dk,
then we say $\equiv$ *is publicly computable, if the computation needs the knowledge of*
dk, *then we say* $\equiv$ *is secretly computable, and rewrite it as* $\equiv_{dk}$.

Definition 10 (pd-RCCA/sd-RCCA for DEMs). *We say $\mathcal{DEM}$ is pd-RCCA secure if there exists a publicly computable compatible relation $\equiv$, such that $\mathcal{DEM}$ is secure according to the definition of RCCA security with the modification that $\mathcal{O}$ returns test for any c' with $c \equiv c'$. Denote the game as pd-RGAME.DEM. We say $\mathcal{DEM}$ is sd-RCCA secure if the above holds for a secretly computable $\equiv_{dk}$. Denote the game as sd-RGAME.DEM.*

KEM+DEM hybrid paradigm works as follows, and it is well known that if $\mathcal{KEM}$ and $\mathcal{DEM}$ are IND-CCA secure then the following $\mathcal{HPKE}$ is IND-CCA secure (as a public-key encryption) [9].

HPKE.Enc$_{pk}(m)$	HPKE.Dec$_{sk}(c)$
$(dk, \psi) \leftarrow$ KEM.Enc$_{pk}()$	$(\psi, \chi) \leftarrow c$
$\chi \leftarrow$ DEM.Enc$_{dk}(m)$	$dk \leftarrow$ KEM.Dec$_{sk}(\psi)$
Output $c = (\psi, \chi)$	$m \leftarrow$ DEM.Dec$_{dk}(\chi)$
	Output m

3 Sd-RCCA Secure Hybrid Public-Key Encryptions from Sd-RCCA Secure DEMs

It's easy to see that sd-RCCA secure KEMs lead to sd-RCCA secure hybrid encryptions, but such KEMs are almost as hard to be achieved as for PKEs. So, we seek for the other way. It can be proved that sd-RCCA security for DEMs is also sufficient.

Theorem 1. *If $\mathcal{KEM}$ is CCA-secure and $\mathcal{DEM}$ is sd-RCCA secure (but not pd-RCCA secure), then the hybrid scheme $\mathcal{HPKE}$ (as a PKE) by following KEM+DEM paradigm is sd-RCCA secure (but not pd-RCCA secure). In particular, for every $\mathcal{H}$, there exist $\mathcal{A}_K$ and $\mathcal{A}_D$ with*

$$Adv_{\mathcal{HPKE},\mathcal{H}}^{\text{sd-rcca}}(k) \leq 2Adv_{\mathcal{KEM},\mathcal{A}_K}^{\text{cca}}(k) + Adv_{\mathcal{DEM},\mathcal{A}_D}^{\text{sd-rcca}}(k). \tag{1}$$

*Proof (*PROOF*).* We first prove the sd-RCCA security of $\mathcal{HPKE}$ from the security of $\mathcal{KEM}$ and $\mathcal{DEM}$.

Let $\equiv_{dk}$ be a compatible relation for $\mathcal{DEM}$, we define a compatible relation for $\mathcal{HPKE}$ as follows: $(\psi, \chi) \equiv_{pk,sk} (\psi', \chi')$ if $\psi = \psi'$ and $\chi \equiv_{dk} \chi$ where $dk = $ KEM.Dec$_{sk}(\psi) = $ KEM.Dec$_{sk}(\psi')$. It is straightforward to verify $\equiv_{pk,sk}$ is compatible for $\mathcal{HPKE}$ as long as $\equiv_{dk}$ is compatible for $\mathcal{DEM}$.

Now, let $\mathcal{H}$ be an adversary playing sd-RGAME.PKE. Let (ψ^*, χ^*) be the challenge ciphertext, dk^* is the encapsulated key in ψ^*. We modify the game by using a random key dk^+ in place of dk^* in both the encryption and decryption oracle, i.e., dk^+ is used to form the challenge ciphertext, and a decryption oracle query is replied by using dk^+ whenever dk^* should be used. Call this game sd-RGAME.PKE'. Let F and F' be events that $\tilde{b} = b$ in sd-RGAME.PKE and sd-RGAME.PKE', respectively. Then we claim that $|\Pr[F] - \Pr[F']| = 2Adv_{\mathcal{KEM}}^{\text{cca}}(k)$, which is shown by constructing $\mathcal{A}_K$ that attacks the underlying KEM scheme by using $\mathcal{H}$.

$\mathcal{A}_K$ asks to obtain the challenge (pk, dk_δ, ψ^*) in GAME.KEM, then sends pk to $\mathcal{H}$. After $\mathcal{H}$ chooses its m_0 and m_1, $\mathcal{A}_K$ randomly chooses $b \in \{0, 1\}$, computes $\chi^* = $ DEM.Enc$_{dk_\delta}(m_b)$, and sends (ψ^*, χ^*) to $\mathcal{H}$.

$\mathcal{A}_K$ answers $\mathcal{H}$'s decryption query (ψ, χ) as follows:

– If $\psi = \psi^*$ and so that $\chi \neq \chi^*$, then
  • If $\chi \equiv_{dk_\delta} \chi^*$ then $\mathcal{A}_K$ returns 'test' (note that $\mathcal{A}_K$ knows dk_δ).
  • Else $\mathcal{A}_K$ uses dk_δ to decrypt χ, and returns the result to $\mathcal{H}$.
– If $\psi \neq \psi^*$, then $\mathcal{A}_K$ just forwards ψ to its own decryption oracle KEM.Dec$_{sk}(\cdot)$.
  • If $\perp$ is returned, then $\mathcal{A}_K$ returns $\perp$ to $\mathcal{H}$.
  • If dk is returned, then $\mathcal{A}_K$ uses this dk to decrypt χ, and returns the result to $\mathcal{H}$.

This perfectly simulates the decryption oracle for $\mathcal{H}$. When $\mathcal{H}$ outputs $\tilde{b}$, $\mathcal{A}_K$ checks whether or not $\tilde{b} = b$, if so it outputs $\tilde{\delta} = 1$, else outputs $\tilde{\delta} = 0$. Now, we have $\Pr[\tilde{b} = b | \delta = 1] = \Pr[F]|$, and $\Pr[\tilde{b} = b | \delta = 0] = \Pr[F']$. Then it is easy to see $|\Pr[F] - \Pr[F']| = 2Adv_{\mathcal{KEM},\mathcal{A}_K}^{cca}(k)$.

Next we argue that $\mathcal{H}$ in sd-RGAME.PKE′ in fact conducts an attack against the sd-RCCA security of DEM, i.e. $|\Pr[F'] - \frac{1}{2}| = Adv_{\mathcal{DEM},\mathcal{A}_D}^{sd-rcca}(k)$, where $\mathcal{A}_D$ is constructed as follows. $\mathcal{A}_D$ first runs PKE.Gen to generate (pk, sk), then sends pk to $\mathcal{H}$. After $\mathcal{H}$ chooses its (m_0, m_1), $\mathcal{A}_D$ gives them to its own encryption oracle and gets χ^*. Then $\mathcal{A}_D$ runs KEM.Enc to generate (dk^*, ψ^*), and gives (ψ^*, χ^*) to $\mathcal{H}$. It should be noticed that now the key dk^+ used in encryption oracle of GAME.DEM is chosen randomly from $\mathcal{K}_D$, so is independent of dk^*.

$\mathcal{A}_D$ answers $\mathcal{H}$'s decryption query (ψ, χ) as follows:

– If $\psi = \psi^*$ and so that $\chi \neq \chi^*$, then $\mathcal{A}_D$ forwards χ to its own decryption oracle, and returns the result to $\mathcal{H}$.
– If $\psi \neq \psi^*$, then $\mathcal{A}_D$ uses sk to decrypt ψ.
  • If the result is $\perp$, then $\mathcal{A}_D$ returns $\perp$ to $\mathcal{H}$.
  • If dk is returned, then $\mathcal{A}_D$ uses this dk to decrypt χ, and returns the result to $\mathcal{H}$.

When $\mathcal{H}$ outputs $\tilde{b}$, $\mathcal{A}_D$ outputs $\tilde{b}$, too. $\mathcal{A}_D$ perfectly simulates sd-RGAME.PKE′, and $\mathcal{A}_D$ wins if $\mathcal{H}$ does. So, $|\Pr[F'] - \frac{1}{2}| = Adv_{\mathcal{DEM},\mathcal{A}_D}^{sd-rcca}(k)$.

Finally, we have:

$$Adv_{\mathcal{HPKE},\mathcal{H}}^{sd-rcca}(k) - Adv_{\mathcal{DEM},\mathcal{A}_D}^{sd-rcca}(k) = |\Pr[F] - \frac{1}{2}| - |\Pr[F'] - \frac{1}{2}|$$
$$\leq |\Pr[F] - \Pr[F']|$$
$$= 2Adv_{\mathcal{KEM},\mathcal{A}_K}^{cca}(k).$$

Then (1) follows immediately.

It remains to show $\mathcal{HPKE}$ is not pd-RCCA secure.

Since $\mathcal{DEM}$ is sd–RCCA secure but not pd-RCCA secure, there exists a compatible relation showing the sd-RCCA security, which is secretly but not publicly computable, let $\equiv_{dk}$ be the compatible relation. We claim that if χ satisfies $\chi \equiv_{dk} \chi^*$, then for any publicly computable compatible relation $\equiv_{pk}$, we must have $(\psi^*, \chi) \not\equiv_{pk} (\psi^*, \chi^*)$. If this is admitted, then the decryption of (ψ^*, χ) is m_b and the decryption oracle will not return 'test', so $\mathcal{HPKE}$ is not pd-RCCA secure.

We now prove our claim. Intuitively, $\chi \equiv_{dk} \chi^*$ cannot be publicly computed, but when given ψ^* this $\equiv_{dk}$ can be publicly computed, then ψ^* must reveal the information of dk^*, which contradicts with the CCA security of $\mathcal{KEM}$.

More formally, if there exist some publicly computable $\equiv_{pk}$, such that $(\psi^*, \chi) \equiv_{pk} (\psi^*, \chi^*)$, then we construct a CCA adversary $\mathcal{A}$ against $\mathcal{KEM}$ as follows: given (pk, ψ, dk_δ), $\mathcal{A}$ uses dk_δ to generate two DEM ciphertexts χ and χ' with $\chi \equiv_{dk} \chi'$, then checks whether or not $(\psi, \chi) \equiv_{pk} (\psi, \chi')$, if so output 1, else output 0.

Since $\chi \equiv_{dk} \chi^*$ cannot be publicly computed, if ψ^* encapsulates a dk independent of dk_δ, then except for a negligible probability, we have $(\psi, \chi) \not\equiv_{pk} (\psi, \chi^*)$. Then it is easy to see $\Pr[\mathcal{A} = \delta]$ is almost 1.

4 Sd-RCCA Secure DEMs from Regular Secure and Secretly Detectable MACs

It has already been pointed out that RCCA secure SKEs can be given by the "encrypt-then-authenticate" paradigm by using a regular but not necessarily strong secure MAC. For sd-RCCA secure DEMs, we follow the same paradigm. However, the underlying MAC needs to be regular secure (but not strong one-time secure), and the validity of a successful forge can be verified only secretly (but not publicly). We now formalize these notions for MACs.

4.1 MAC and Related Security Notions

Definition 11 (MAC). *MAC is a pair of algorithms (MAC.Sign, MAC.Ver). A key space $\mathcal{K}_M$ is defined by security parameter k. MAC.Sign takes a key $mk \in \mathcal{K}_M$ and a message $m \in 0, 1^*$ as inputs, and outputs a string σ. MAC.Ver takes a triple (mk, m, σ) as input and outputs a decision of whether or not (m, σ) is valid with respect to mk.*

Since we will use randomized MACs to achieve sd-RCCA secure DEMs, MAC.Sign is allowed to be probabilistic, but MAC.Ver is still deterministic. For probabilistic MACs, a proper security notion should allow an adversary to make MAC.Sign$(mk, \cdot)$ and MAC.Ver$(mk, \cdot)$ queries [15]. However, for our setting we need only one-time security, i.e., only once access to MAC sign is permitted. In fact, the weaker notion without access to MAC.Ver$(mk, \cdot)$ is sufficient.

Definition 12 (regular/strong security for MACs). *We say a MAC $\mathcal{MAC} = (MAC.Sign, MAC.Ver)$ is secure against one-time chosen message attack, or shorten as regular one-time secure, if for every PPT oracle machine $\mathcal{F}$ that* *plays the following game, the probability that the game output 1 (i.e., the advantage of $\mathcal{F}$, denoted as $Adv_{MAC,\mathcal{F}}^{forge}(k)$) is negligible in k.*

[GAME.MAC].
Step1. $m \leftarrow \mathcal{F}(1^k)$
Step2. $mk \leftarrow \mathcal{K}_M$, $\sigma \leftarrow MAC.Sign_{mk}(m)$
Step3. $(m', \sigma') \leftarrow \mathcal{F}(\sigma)$
Step4. If $m' \neq m$ and $MAC.Ver_{mk}(m', \sigma') = 1$ then output 1 else output 0
Strong one time security is defined all the same except that $m' \neq m$ is replaced
with $(m', \sigma') \neq (m, \sigma)$ in step 4.

For deterministic MACs, the two definitions are equivalent. However, for a regular randomized MACs, it might be possible to efficiently generate another valid MAC value σ' for m, which is not allowed for a strong secure one. For such forgery, we distinguish two cases:

Definition 13. (Publicly/secretly detectable forgery). *Let $\mathcal{MAC}$ be a regular secure (but not strong one-time secure) MAC and (m', σ') be a forgery output by an adversary when given (m, σ) with $m' = m$. Then we say $\mathcal{MAC}$ is publicly-detectable if given (m, σ, σ'), the validity of σ' can be verified efficiently without the knowledge of mk, else we say $\mathcal{MAC}$ is secretly-detectable.*

4.2 Sd-RCCA Secure DEMs from the "encrypt-then-authenticate" Paradigm

One can obtain an sd-RCCA secure DEM easily by following the "encrypt-then-authenticate" paradigm from a regular MAC and a one-time secure DEM, and it is well known that the latter can be just a one-time pad. We now formalize the paradigm.

Theorem 2. *Let $\mathcal{DEM}^{ot}$ be a one-time secure (deterministic) DEM, $\mathcal{MAC}$ be a MAC which is regular secure (but not strong one-time secure), and is secretly-detectable (but not publicly-detectable), then the following DEM $\mathcal{DEM}^{sd-rcca}$ is sd-RCCA secure (but not pd-RCCA secure). In particular, the sd-detectable compatible relation $\equiv_e$ should be $\chi = (c, \sigma) \equiv_e \chi' = (c', \sigma')$ if and only if $c = c'$, $\sigma \neq \sigma'$ and both $MAC.Ver_{mk}(c, \sigma) = 1$ and $MAC.Ver_{mk}(c', \sigma') = 1$.*

$DEM.Enc_{dk,mk}(m)$	$DEM.Dec_{dk,mk}(\chi)$
$c \leftarrow DEM.Enc_{dk}(m)$	parse χ as $c\|\sigma$
$\sigma \leftarrow MAC.Sign_{mk}(c)$	If $MAC.Ver_{mk}(c, \sigma) = 1$ then
Output $\chi = (c\|\sigma)$	$m \leftarrow DEM.Dec_{dk}(c)$
	Else output $\perp$ EndIf
	Output m.

Proof. The compatibility of $\equiv_e$ is obvious. We first prove the sd-RCCA security.

Let $\mathcal{A}_D$ be an adversary playing sd-RGAME.DEM, we construct a passive adversary $\mathcal{B}$ against $\mathcal{DEM}^{ot}$ by using $\mathcal{A}_D$ as follows:

$\mathcal{B}$ forwards 1^k to $\mathcal{A}_D$. Given (m_0, m_1) from $\mathcal{A}_D$, $\mathcal{B}$ requests (m_0, m_1) to the encryption oracle of GAME.DEM to obtain c^*. Then $\mathcal{B}$ randomly chooses mk from $\mathcal{K}_M$, computes $\sigma^* = MAC.Sign_{mk}(c^*)$, sends $\chi^* = (c^*, \sigma^*)$ to $\mathcal{A}_D$.

For a decryption query $\chi = (c, \sigma)$ from $\mathcal{A}_D$, if $c = c^*$, then $\mathcal{B}$ checks if $MAC.Ver_{mk}(c^*, \sigma) = 1$ by using mk, if so, it returns 'test', for all other cases $\mathcal{B}$ just returns $\perp$.

Finally, when $\mathcal{A}_D$ outputs $\tilde{b}$, $\mathcal{B}$ outputs $\tilde{b}$, too.

The simulation is correct unless $MAC.Ver(c, \sigma) = 1$ for some $c \neq c^*$. Let Forge denote this event, we have $\Pr[\text{Forge}] \leq q_D \cdot Adv_{\mathcal{MAC}, \mathcal{A}_D}^{\text{forge}}$.

It remains to show $\mathcal{DEM}^{sd-rcca}$ is not pd-RCCA secure. Assume that there exist a publicly computable relation such that $\mathcal{DEM}$ is pd-RCCA secure, let $\equiv$ be the relation. Since the underlying $\mathcal{MAC}$ is secretly but not publicly detectable, it is possible to forge a new and valid σ' efficiently for c, but the validity of (c, σ') cannot be verified publicly. However, we note that it must be the case that $(c, \sigma') \equiv (c, \sigma)$, else the decryption of (c, σ') is m, thus $\mathcal{DEM}^{sd-rcca}$ cannot be pd-RCCA secure for this $\equiv$. Since $\equiv$ is a publicly computable relation, this means that the validity of σ' can be verified publicly, which leads to a contradict.

4.3   Achieving Sd-RCCA Security from Regular MACs by Other Paradigms

There are also some other methods using MACs to achieve CCA secure hybrid encryptions, such as a CCCA secure KEM plus an authenticated encryption (which is shortened as AE and can be built from a passively secure DEM and a MAC) [16], a CCA secure Tag-KEM (which can be constructed by a LCCA secure KEM and a MAC) plus a passively secure DEM [17], an RCCA secure KEM plus a CCA secure Tag-DEM (which can be constructed by an OT secure DEM and a MAC) [18], and so on. Instantiating the MAC underlying these constructions with a regular one-time secure (but not strongone-time secure), secretly-detectable (but not publicly-detectable) one will also yield sd-RCCA secure hybrid encryptions.

In Sect. 5, we also instantiate a scheme for the CCCA secure KEM plus AE paradigm, so we formalized the paradigm here without the formal definition for the CCCA security for KEMs, which follows directly from [16].

Definition 14 (AE). *An authenticated encryption scheme is a one-time symmetric-key encryption, consists of two algorithms. AE.Enc that takes as input 1^k, a key dk and a message $m \in \mathcal{M}$, outputs a ciphertext χ. AE.Dec that takes as input a dk and a ciphertext χ, outputs a message m or the special symbol $\perp$. For our purpose, we allow AE.Enc to be probabilistic. Correctness is required, i.e., for all $m \in \mathcal{M}$, AE.Dec$_{dk}$(AE.Enc$_{dk}$(m)) = m.*

Definition 15 (OT/ROT security for AE). *The one-time(OT) security of AE captures privacy and authenticity simultaneously, which is defined by the following game, where $\mathcal{O}$ is a decrypt-or-reject oracle, which returns AE.Dec$_{dk}$(ψ)*

if $b = 1$, else always returns $\perp$. In Step 3, $\mathcal{A}_A$ is allowed only one query to $\mathcal{O}$, which is restricted not to be χ.

[GAME.AE]
Step 1. $(m_0, m_1, v) \leftarrow \mathcal{A}_A(1^k)$
Step 2. $dk \leftarrow \mathcal{K}_D$, $b \leftarrow \{0, 1\}$, $\chi \leftarrow$ AE.Enc$_{dk}(m_b)$.
Step 3. $\tilde{b} \leftarrow \mathcal{A}_A^{\mathcal{O}}(v, \chi)$
Replayable one-time security (ROT) of AEs is defined similarly except that in step 3 $\mathcal{O}$ returns 'test' for any ciphertext that decrypts to m_0 or m_1.

The compatible relations for AEs are defined almost the same as for DEMs, then pd-ROT and sd-ROT security for AEs follow immediately.

Theorem 3. *If $\mathcal{KEM}$ is CCCA-secure and $\mathcal{AE}$ is sd- but not pd-ROT secure, then the hybrid scheme $\mathcal{HPKE}$ by following KEM+DEM paradigm with the DEM substituted by an AE is sd- but not pd-RCCA secure (as a PKE).*

The proof for sd-RCCA security is rather similar as in [16], and the proof for not pd-RCCA security is almost the same as for Theorem 1, so we do not show anymore.

For sd- but not pd-ROT secure AEs, we can still follow the "encrypt-then-authenticate" paradigm.

Theorem 4. *Let $\mathcal{DEM}^{ot}$ be a one-time secure (deterministic) DEM, $\mathcal{MAC}$ be a MAC which is regular (but not strong) one-time secure, and is secretly-detectable (but not publicly-detectable), then the AE defined the same as in Theorem 2 is sd-RCCA secure (but not pd-RCCA secure).*

The proof is also almost the same as for Theorem 2.

5   Instantiations

5.1   Instantiations of Regular but Not Strong, Secretly but Not Publicly Detectable MACs

There are some motivations for probabilistic MACs as pointed in [11]. And such MACs give rise to natural regular but not strong MACs. For example, the constructions from labeled hash proof systems (HPS) when instantiate it directly with the universal$_2$ HPS by Cramer and Shoup [13], the DDH-based constructions achieving full security from key-homomorphic weak-PRFs, and the second LPN-based construction. We only briefly sketch the two DDH-based ones here without the tedious descriptions of HPS and key-homomorphic weak-PRFs.

Firstly, consider the probabilistic MAC constructions from labeled hash proof systems (HPS) in [11]. When instantiating it directly with the universal$_2$ HPS by Cramer and Shoup [13] without the modification done in [11], we obtain a regular but not strong MAC.

Let $\mathbb{G}$ be a group of prime-order p and let g_1, g_2 be two independent generators of $\mathbb{G}$. Define $\mathcal{M} = \mathbb{Z}_p$, then

- Gen(1^k): Pick $mk = (x_1, x_2, y_1, y_2)$ randomly in $\mathbb{Z}_p^4$.
- MAC.Sign$_{mk}(m)$: Pick r randomly in $\mathbb{Z}_p$, let $C = (u, v) = (g_1^r, g_2^r)$ and $K = u^{x_1 m + y_1} v^{x_2 m + y_2}$, then output $\sigma = (C, K)$.
- MAC.Ver$_{mk}(m, \sigma)$: Parse σ as $((u, v), K)$ and output accept iff $K = u^{x_1 m + y_1} v^{x_2 m + y_2}$.

Theorem 5. *The above MAC scheme is regular but not strong one-time secure and secretly-detectable but not publicly-detectable under the DDH assumption on G.*

Proof. The regular security is directly from [11]. Since given a mac value $\sigma = (C, K) = ((u, v), K)$ of m, one can generate another valid mac value σ' of m by randomly chooses a $r' \in \mathbb{Z}_p$ then let $\sigma' = ((u^{r'}, v^{r'}), K^{r'})$. The validity is obvious, in fact, σ' is the mac value of m under the randomness rr'. Thus, the scheme is not strongly secure.

The validity of σ' cannot be verified publicly given (m, σ, σ'). In fact, since a valid (m, σ') pair has the same distribution as (m, σ), if there is an algorithm $\mathcal{A}$ which can publicly verify the validity of σ' given (m, σ, σ'), then it can distinguish whether or not (m, σ') has the same distribution as (m, σ). Thus, we can construct an efficient DDH and random tuple distinguisher $\mathcal{D}$: given (g_1, g_2, g_3, g_4), let $g = g_1$, then randomly choose $(x_1, x_2, y_1, y_2) \in \mathbb{Z}_p^4$ and $m \in \mathbb{Z}_p$, let $u = g_1^r, v = g_2^r, K = u^{x_1 m + y_1} v^{x_2 m + y_2}$, $u' = g_3^r, v' = g_4^r, K' = u'^{x_1 m + y_1} v'^{x_2 m + y_2}$, and $\sigma = ((u, v), K), \sigma' = ((u', v'), K')$, run $\mathcal{A}$ on (m, σ, σ'). If σ' is valid, then output 1 to indicate DDH tuple, else output 0. It is obvious that if $\mathcal{A}$ wins then $\mathcal{D}$ wins, too.

It is interesting to note that a HPS is naturally a KEM, but the malleability of the HPS cannot yield RCCA security for the KEM, for example, in σ', the encapsulate key is not K anymore. However, when the HPS is used as a MAC, σ' is still a valid mac value of m.

Secondly, consider the DDH-based constructions achieving full security from key-homomorphic weak-PRFs. Let $\mathbb{G}$ be a group of prime-order p and let g be a generator of $\mathbb{G}$. Define $\mathcal{M} = \{0, 1\}^k$, then

- Gen(1^k): Pick $mk = (x, x_1', x_2', ..., x_k')$ randomly in $\mathbb{Z}_p^{k+1}$.
- MAC.Sign$_{mk}(m)$: Pick r randomly in $\mathbb{Z}_p$, let $u = g^r$ and $w = u^{x + \sum x_i' m_i}$, then output $\sigma = (u, w)$.
- MAC.Ver$_{mk}(m, \sigma)$: Parse σ as (u, w) and output accept iff $w = u^{x + \sum x_i' m_i}$.

Theorem 6. *The above MAC scheme is regular but not strong one-time secure and secretly-detectable but not publicly-detectable under the DDH assumption on G.*

Proof. The regular security is directly from [11]. Since given a mac value $\sigma = (u, w)$ of m, one can generate another valid mac value σ' of m by randomly chooses a $r' \in \mathbb{Z}_p$ then let $\sigma' = ((u^{r'}, w^{r'}))$. The validity is obvious, in fact, σ' is the mac value of m under the randomness rr'. Thus, the scheme is not strongly secure.

The validity of σ' cannot be verified publicly given (m, σ, σ'). In fact, since a valid (m, σ') pair has the same distribution as (m, σ), if there is an algorithm $\mathcal{A}$ which can publicly verify the validity of σ' given (m, σ, σ'), then it can distinguish whether or not (m, σ') has the same distribution as (m, σ). Thus, we can construct an efficient DDH and random tuple distinguisher: given $(g_1, g_2 = g_1^x, g_3 = g_1^r, g_4)$, randomly choose $(x_1', x_2', ..., x_k') \in \mathbb{Z}_p^k$ and $m \in \{0, 1\}^k$, then it should be noted that $\sigma = (g_1, g_2 g_1^{\sum x_i' m_i})$ is a valid mac value of m under the key $mk = (x, x_1', x_2', ..., x_k')$. Let $\sigma' = (g_3, g_4 g_3^{\sum x_i' m_i})$, run $\mathcal{A}$ on (m, σ, σ'). If σ' is valid, then output 1 to indicate DDH tuple, else output 0.

5.2   Instantiations of sd-RCCA Secure Hybrid Encryptions

Firstly, we instantiate the refined Cramer-Shoup hybrid scheme in [19] with the first MAC scheme in the last section to obtain our first sd-RCCA secure scheme. Let $\mathbb{G}$ be a group of prime-order p and let g_1, g_2 be two independent generators of $\mathbb{G}$, TCR be a target collision resistant hash functions, and KDF be a key derivation function with proper domain and range. Define $\mathcal{M} = \mathbb{Z}_p$, then

- $\mathsf{Gen}(1^k)$: Pick $x_1, x_2, y_1, y_2, z_1, z_2$ randomly in $\mathbb{Z}_p^6$, let $pk = (c, d, h) = (g_1^{x_1} g_2^{x_2}, g_1^{y_1} g_2^{y_2}, g_1^{z_1} g_2^{z_2})$, $sk = (x_1, x_2, y_1, y_2, z_1, z_2)$, output (pk, sk).
- $\mathsf{HPKE.Enc}_{pk}(m)$: Pick r, r' randomly in $\mathbb{Z}_p$, let $u = g_1^r$, $v = g_2^r$ and $\alpha = TCR(u, v)$, then let $w = (c^\alpha d)^r$, $K = h^r$ and $(dk, mk) = KDF(K)$, where $mk = (x_1', x_2', y_1', y_2')$, then let $e = dk + m$, $u' = g_1^{r'}$, $v' = g_2^{r'}$, and $w' = (u'^{x_1' e + y_1'} v'^{x_2' e + y_2'})^{r'}$, output $C = (u, v, w, e, u', v', w')$.
- $\mathsf{HPKE.Dec}_{sk}(C)$: Parse C as (u, v, w, e, u', v', w'), let $\alpha = TCR(u, v)$, $K = h^r$ and $(dk, mk) = KDF(K)$, parse mk as (x_1', x_2', y_1', y_2'), output $m' = e - dk$ if and only if $w = u^{x_1 \alpha + y_1} v^{x_2 \alpha + y_2}$ and $w' = u'^{x_1' e + y_1'} v'^{x_2' e + y_2'}$.

For the naturalness, we note that HPSs are natural components for PKEs. In addition, if $mk = (x_1', x_2', y_1', y_2')$ is not derived from K, but added in the sk, thus $(c', d') = (g_1^{x_1'} g_2^{x_2'}, g_1^{y_1'} g_2^{y_2'})$ must be added in pk, then the resulting scheme might be more natural as a PKE. However, the scheme is not secure any more, since the knowledge of r' allows one to generate the MAC value for any messages publicly. Our scheme provides a natural way to solve this problem, and can reduce the size of the public-key. Another way to solve this is letting $r' = r$. However, this will directly results in CCA security, and is not suitable for our purpose. The original CCA secure Cramer-Shoup can be seen as such an scheme, and which further integrates w and w' by letting $\alpha = TCR(u, v, e)$. This also somewhat explains the difficulty to build an RCCA secure PKE more efficient than existing CCA secure ones. The similar thing also happens to our second scheme.

Secondly, we instantiate a hybrid scheme by using the CCCA-secure KEM in [16] with an authenticated encryption, where the second DDH-based MAC presented above is used. Let $\mathbb{G}$ be a group of prime-order p and let g be a generator of $\mathbb{G}$, TCR be a target collision resistant hash functions, and KDF be a key derivation function with proper domain and range. Define $\mathcal{M} = \{0,1\}^k$, then

- $\mathsf{Gen}(1^k)$: Pick x, y, z randomly in $\mathbb{Z}_p^3$, let $pk = (c, d, h) = (g^x, g^y, g^z)$, $sk = (x, y, z)$, output (pk, sk).
- $\mathsf{HPKE.Enc}_{pk}(m)$: Pick r, r' randomly in $\mathbb{Z}_p$, let $u = g^r$, $w = (c^\alpha d)^r$ where $\alpha = TCR(u)$, then let $K = h^r$ and $(dk, mk) = KDF(K)$, where $mk = (x', x_1', x_2', ..., x_k')$, then let $e = dk \oplus m$, $u' = g^{r'}$, and $w' = u'^{x + \sum x_i' e_i}$, output $C = (u, w, e, u', w')$. (what if $w = (c^\alpha d)^r u'^{x + \sum x_i' e_i}$)
- $\mathsf{HPKE.Dec}_{sk}(C)$: Parse C as (u, w, e, u', w') and let $\alpha = TCR(u)$, $K = h^r$ and $(dk, mk) = KDF(K)$, parse mk as $(x', x_1', x_2', ..., x_k')$, output $m' = e \oplus dk$ if and only if $w = u^{x\alpha + y}$ and $w' = u'^{x' + \sum x_i' e_i}$.

Our sd-RCCA secure schemes are less efficient than existing CCA secure ones. In fact, in an efficient CCA secure hybrid encryption scheme, it is often the case that the KEM ciphertext is deterministically related to the encapsulation key, which makes it impossible to achieve RCCA security. However, regular MACs more efficient than strong ones still bring us a light.

6 Conclusion

We introduce regular (but not strong) probabilistic MACs into KEM+DEM style hybrid paradigm to construct sd-RCCA secure public-key encryptions. We show two examples of such MACs under the DDH assumption based on the work in [11]. Instantiating proper DDH-based hybrid encryptions with these MACs, we obtain "natural" instances of sd-RCCA secure ones. This solves an open problem left in [1].

Acknowledgment. This work is supported by the National Natural Science Foundations of China (Nos. 61402353, 61373172) and the Fundamental Research Funds for the Central Universities (No. GK201603084).

References

1. Canetti, R., Krawczyk, H., Nielsen, J.B.: Relaxing chosen-ciphertext security. In: Boneh, D. (ed.) CRYPTO 2003. LNCS, vol. 2729, pp. 565–582. Springer, Heidelberg (2003). doi:10.1007/978-3-540-45146-4_33
2. Maurer, U., Rüedlinger, A., Tackmann, B.: Confidentiality and integrity: a constructive perspective. In: Cramer, R. (ed.) TCC 2012. LNCS, vol. 7194, pp. 209–229. Springer, Heidelberg (2012). doi:10.1007/978-3-642-28914-9_12
3. Coretti, S., Maurer, U., Tackmann, B.: Constructing confidential channels from authenticated channels—public-key encryption revisited. In: Sako, K., Sarkar, P. (eds.) ASIACRYPT 2013. LNCS, vol. 8269, pp. 134–153. Springer, Heidelberg (2013). doi:10.1007/978-3-642-42033-7_8
4. An, J.H., Dodis, Y., Rabin, T.: On the security of joint signature and encryption. In: Knudsen, L.R. (ed.) EUROCRYPT 2002. LNCS, vol. 2332, pp. 83–107. Springer, Heidelberg (2002). doi:10.1007/3-540-46035-7_6

5. Shoup, V.: ISO 18033-2: an emerging standard for public-key encryption. Final Committee Draft, December 2004
6. Groth, J.: Rerandomizable and replayable adaptive chosen ciphertext attack secure cryptosystems. In: Naor, M. (ed.) TCC 2004. LNCS, vol. 2951, pp. 152–170. Springer, Heidelberg (2004). doi:10.1007/978-3-540-24638-1_9
7. Prabhakaran, M., Rosulek, M.: Rerandomizable RCCA encryption. In: Menezes, A. (ed.) CRYPTO 2007. LNCS, vol. 4622, pp. 517–534. Springer, Heidelberg (2007). doi:10.1007/978-3-540-74143-5_29
8. El Bansarkhani, R., Dagdelen, Ö., Buchmann, J.: Augmented learning with errors: the untapped potential of the error term. Cryptology ePrint Archive, Report 2014/733
9. Cramer, R., Shoup, V.: Design and analysis of practical public-key encryption schemes secure against adaptive chosen ciphertext attack. SIAM J. Comput. 33(1), 167–226 (2003)
10. Krawczyk, H.: The order of encryption and authentication for protecting communications (or: How secure is SSL?). In: Kilian, J. (ed.) CRYPTO 2001. LNCS, vol. 2139, pp. 310–331. Springer, Heidelberg (2001). doi:10.1007/3-540-44647-8_19
11. Dodis, Y., Kiltz, E., Pietrzak, K., Wichs, D.: Message authentication, revisited. In: Pointcheval, D., Johansson, T. (eds.) EUROCRYPT 2012. LNCS, vol. 7237, pp. 355–374. Springer, Heidelberg (2012). doi:10.1007/978-3-642-29011-4_22
12. Alwen, J., Hirt, M., Maurer, U., Patra, A., Raykov, P.: Key-indistinguishable message authentication codes. In: Abdalla, M., De Prisco, R. (eds.) SCN 2014. LNCS, vol. 8642, pp. 476–493. Springer, Cham (2014). doi:10.1007/978-3-319-10879-7_27
13. Cramer, R., Shoup, V.: Universal hash proofs and a paradigm for adaptive chosen ciphertext secure public-key encryption. In: Knudsen, L.R. (ed.) EUROCRYPT 2002. LNCS, vol. 2332, pp. 45–64. Springer, Heidelberg (2002). doi:10.1007/3-540-46035-7_4
14. Hohenberger, S., Lewko, A., Waters, B.: Detecting dangerous queries: a new approach for chosen ciphertext security. In: Pointcheval, D., Johansson, T. (eds.) EUROCRYPT 2012. LNCS, vol. 7237, pp. 663–681. Springer, Heidelberg (2012). doi:10.1007/978-3-642-29011-4_39
15. Bellare, M., Goldreich, O., Mityagin, A.: The power of verification queries in message authentication and authenticated encryption. IACR Cryptology ePrint Archive, 2004, 309
16. Hofheinz, D., Kiltz, E.: Secure hybrid encryption from weakened key encapsulation. In: Menezes, A. (ed.) CRYPTO 2007. LNCS, vol. 4622, pp. 553–571. Springer, Heidelberg (2007). doi:10.1007/978-3-540-74143-5_31
17. Abe, M., Gennaro, R., Kurosawa, K.: Tag-KEM/DEM: a new framework for hybrid encryption. J. Cryptology 21(1), 97–130 (2008)
18. Chen, Y., Dong, Q.: RCCA security for KEM+DEM style hybrid encryptions and a general hybrid paradigm from RCCA-secure KEMs to CCA-secure encryptions. Secur. Commun. Netw. 7(8), 1219–1231 (2014)
19. Shoup, V.: Using hash functions as a hedge against chosen ciphertext attack. In: Preneel, B. (ed.) EUROCRYPT 2000. LNCS, vol. 1807, pp. 275–288. Springer, Heidelberg (2000). doi:10.1007/3-540-45539-6_19

Long-Term Secure Time-Stamping
Using Preimage-Aware Hash Functions
(Short Version)

Ahto Buldas[1,2], Matthias Geihs[3(✉)], and Johannes Buchmann[3]

[1] Tallinn University of Technology, Tallinn, Estonia
[2] Cybernetica AS, Tallinn, Estonia
[3] Darmstadt University of Technology, Darmstadt, Germany
`mgeihs@cdc.informatik.tu-darmstadt.de`

Abstract. The lifetime of commonly used digital signature schemes is limited because their security is based on computational assumptions that potentially break in the future. In 1993, Bayer et al. suggested that the lifetime of a digital signature can be prolonged by time-stamping the signature together with the signed document. Based on this idea, various long-term timestamp schemes have been proposed and standardized that repeatedly renew the protection with new timestamps. In order to minimize the risk of a design failure affecting the security of these schemes, it is indispensable to formally analyze their security. However, many of the proposed schemes have not been subject to a formal security analysis yet. In this paper, we address this issue by formally describing and analyzing a long-term timestamp scheme that uses hash trees for timestamp renewal. Our analysis shows that the security level of the described scheme degrades cubic over time, which suggests that in practice the scheme should be instantiated with a certain security margin.

Keywords: Long-term security · Timestamps · Preimage aware hash functions

1 Introduction

1.1 Motivation

More and more information is generated and stored in digital form. In many cases it is important to ensure the integrity of this information. For example, in the case of electronic health records, it is indispensable that unintentional changes to the health records can be detected. Most commonly, integrity of such sensitive information is protected using digital signature schemes. However, most digital signature schemes used today provide security only for a limited time period.

This work has been co-funded by the DFG as part of project S6 within the CRC 1119 CROSSING. The full version can be found on the IACR ePrint Archive [2].

© Springer International Publishing AG 2017
T. Okamoto et al. (Eds.): ProvSec 2017, LNCS 10592, pp. 251–260, 2017.
https://doi.org/10.1007/978-3-319-68637-0_15

Their security is based on computational assumptions, i.e., security holds only as long as the computational resources of an attacker are insufficient to solve a certain computational problem. The widely used RSA digital signature scheme [10], for example, is broken if prime factors of large integers can be computed. Using current computer technology, this seems to be infeasible, however, it has been shown that quantum computers can factor large integers efficiently.

To mitigate the security risk, Bayer et al. [1] in 1993 proposed a method for prolonging the validity of a digital signature beyond the validity of the corresponding digital signature scheme. Their idea was to timestamp the signature together with the signed document. This proves that the signature for the document was known when the corresponding signature scheme was considered secure, and hence, the signature must be genuine. Because the security of timestamps also relies on computational assumptions, timestamps must be renewed, as well, by obtaining new timestamps.

To understand the security of long-term integrity protection using timestamp renewal, a security model must be provided for such a scheme. However, formal security analysis of long-term timestamp schemes has not received much attention until recently. In [7], Geihs et al. analyze the security of long-term timestamp schemes that use signature-based timestamp services. Their analysis is done in the random oracle model and shows that the security level of the analyzed long-term timestamp scheme degrades gradually over time. An alternative method for time-stamping uses Merkle Hash Trees [1,9] instead of digital signatures and relies on the availability of a trusted public repository. The security of long-term timestamp schemes based on this time-stamping method, however, has not been studied yet.

1.2   Contribution

In this work we analyze the security of a long-term timestamp scheme based on the ideas of Bayer et al. [1] in a setting where timestamps are generated using Merkle Hash Trees. We present a new security notion called *extractable time-stamping* for such timestamp schemes in the ideal primitive model [6]. Extractable time-stamping engages important aspects of existing security notions for short-term timestamp schemes [4] and is naturally suitable for analyzing the security of long-term timestamp schemes. We prove a bound on the security level of the hash-based long-term timestamp scheme and reveal that security degrades cubic over time. We also provide a framework for estimating the security loss over time in a practical scenario. Such a framework is valuable for engineers who design systems that for long-term integrity protection of digital information.

2   Extractable Time-Stamping

In the following we formally define extractable time-stamping for short-term timestamp schemes (i.e., timestamp schemes without renewal). We first start with a description of a typical hash-based timestamp scheme based on the ideas of Bayer, Haber, and Stornetta [1,8]. Then, we propose an extraction-based security definition for this scheme. The security definition engages important aspects of existing security notions for timestamp schemes [4] and will be useful for analyzing the security of long-term timestamp schemes later in Sect. 3. We also prove a bound on the security of the described timestamp scheme in terms of the security of the used hash function.

2.1   Scheme Description

We describe a hash-based timestamp scheme based on the ideas of Bayer, Haber, and Stornetta [1,8]. The scheme is instantiated with a hash function H and a set of allowed hash chain shapes $\mathcal{S}$. It uses a trusted repository Rep with the following functionality. If Rep receives a hash value r at time t, it stores r associated with t so that later everybody can verify that r was received at time t.

The time-stamping procedure is divided into rounds. During each round, a timestamp server receives a set of bitstrings $\{x_1, \dots, x_n\}$ from clients $C_1, \dots, C_n$. At the end of each round it runs algorithm Stamp to generate timestamps for these bitstrings and returns the timestamps to the clients. Algorithm Verify is used to verify timestamps.

Stamp: On input of bitstrings $x_1, \dots, x_n$ ($n \leq |\mathcal{S}|$), a hash tree [9] is computed from leafs $x_1, \dots, x_n$ with shape described by $\mathcal{S}$. Let r be the root of that hash tree and c_i be the hash chain corresponding to the path from leaf x_i to the root r. The timestamp server publishes the root hash r at the repository Rep and for $i \in \{1, \dots, n\}$, sends c_i as the response to request x_i. Hash chain c_i is also called a *timestamp* for bitstring x_i.

Verify: On input x, hash chain c, and hash value r published at the repository, it is checked that c has allowed shape (i.e., shape$(c) \in \mathcal{S}$), and c is a hash chain from x to r (i.e., $x \overset{c}{\rightsquigarrow} r$). The algorithm outputs 1 if these conditions hold, otherwise the algorithm outputs 0.

2.2   Security Definition

We present an extraction-based security notion for the timestamp scheme described above. Informally, extractability of a timestamp scheme TS means that if a root hash r is published at the repository at time t and later someone comes up with a bitstring x and a hash chain c such that TS.Verify$(x, c, r) = 1$, then x must have been known at time t (i.e., x is extracted when r is published). Our notion of extractable time-stamping is reminiscent of PrA hash functions [6] and knowledge-binding commitments [4]. Formally, we define extractable time-stamping in Definition 1 in the ideal primitive model [6], where there exists an ideal primitive P (e.g., a random oracle) for which all calls are recorded in an advice string adv.

Algorithm 1. The extractable time-stamping experiment $\mathbf{Exp}_{P,\mathsf{TS}}^{\mathrm{ExTs}}(\mathcal{A},\mathcal{E})$.

$(x,c,r) \leftarrow \mathcal{A}^{\mathsf{P,Rep}}$;
if TS.Verify$(x,c,r) = 1$, $r \in \mathsf{R}$, and
$x \notin \mathsf{L}[r]$ then
$\quad\mid$ return 1;
else
$\quad\mid$ return 0;

oracle P(m):
$z \leftarrow P(m)$;
adv $\leftarrow$ adv$\|(m,z)$;
return z;

oracle Rep(r):
$X \leftarrow \mathcal{E}(\mathrm{adv}, r)$;
$\mathsf{R} \leftarrow \mathsf{R} \cup \{r\}$;
$\mathsf{L}[r] \leftarrow X$;
return X;

Definition 1 (Extractable Time-Stamping). *Let* $\epsilon : \mathbb{N}^3 \to [0,1]$. *A timestamp scheme* TS^P *using ideal primitive* P *is* ϵ-*secure* extractable *(ExTs) if for all integers* $p_\mathcal{E}$, $p_\mathcal{A}$, *and* $q_\mathcal{E}$, *there is a* $p_\mathcal{E}$-*step extractor* $\mathcal{E}$, *such that for every* $p_\mathcal{A}$-*step adversary* $\mathcal{A}$ *that makes at most* q *calls to* Rep,

$$\mathbf{Adv}_{P,\mathsf{TS}}^{\mathrm{ExTs}}(\mathcal{A},\mathcal{E}) = \Pr\left[\mathbf{Exp}_{P,\mathsf{TS}}^{\mathrm{ExTs}}(\mathcal{A},\mathcal{E}) = 1\right] \leq \epsilon(p_\mathcal{E}, p_\mathcal{A}, q) .$$

2.3 Security Analysis

We analyze the security of the timestamp described in Sect. 2.1. For this, we first recall some useful properties of hash chain shapes from [3].

Definition 2. *We say that a timestamp scheme associated with allowed shapes* $\mathcal{S}$ *is* N-*bounded if* $|\mathcal{S}| \leq N$.

Definition 3. *An* N-*bounded timestamp scheme is said to be* shape-compact, *if the length of allowed hash chains does not exceed* $2\log_2 N$.

We now proof a bound on the security of the hash-based timestamp scheme from Sect. 2.1 when instantiated as N-bounded and shape compact.

Theorem 1. *The timestamp scheme from Sect. 2.1 instantiated as* N-*bounded and shape compact and with an* ϵ-*secure* PrA *hash function* H^P *is* ϵ'-*secure extractable with*

$$\epsilon'(p_\mathcal{E}, p_\mathcal{A}, q) = \epsilon\left(\frac{\alpha \cdot p_\mathcal{E}}{2N}, \beta \cdot (p_\mathcal{A} + 2Nq), 2Nq\right) ,$$

for some small constants α *and* β.

A proof of Theorem 1 can be found in the full paper [2].

3 Extractable Long-Term Time-Stamping

We now turn to formally analyzing the security of long-term timestamp schemes. These schemes allow to renew protection so that cryptographic primitives that are about to break can be replaced. Again, we start with a description of a typical long-term timestamp scheme construction following the ideas of Bayer, Haber, and Stornetta [1]. Then, we describe our extraction-based security model for long-term time-stamping. Finally, we use this model to obtain a bound on the security level of the described scheme.

3.1 Scheme Description

We describe a long-term timestamp scheme based on the ideas of Bayer, Haber, and Stornetta [1]. The scheme uses several short-term timestamp schemes for protection renewal. We use $\mathcal{TS} = \{TS_i\}_i$ to denote the set of short-term timestamp schemes available for usage over time. We denote for each timestamp scheme $TS_i \in \mathcal{TS}$ by t_i^s the associated start time, which defines when the scheme becomes available for usage, and by t_i^b the associated breakage time, which defines when timestamps for this scheme are not considered valid anymore. We also assume the existence of a repository Rep that is used for publishing root hash values.

The long-term timestamp scheme is defined by algorithm $Stamp$ for creating an initial timestamp, algorithm $Renew$ for renewing a timestamp, and algorithm $Verify$ for verifying a timestamp.

$Stamp$: This algorithm gets as input a timestamp scheme identifier i and a sequence of bitstrings $x_1, \ldots, x_n$. It creates timestamps for the bitstrings using scheme TS_i by computing $(r, c_1, \ldots, c_n) \leftarrow TS_i.Stamp(x_1, \ldots, x_n)$. Afterwards, the root hash r is published together with identifier i at the repository Rep. Let t be the time when (r, i) is published. For $j \in \{1, \ldots, n\}$, the algorithm responds to request x_j with long-term timestamp $T_j = [(i, c_j, r, t)]$.

$Renew$: This algorithm gets as input a timestamp scheme identifier i' and a sequence of bitstrings with timestamps $(x_1, T_1), \ldots, (x_n, T_n)$. The algorithm renews the timestamps using scheme $TS_{i'}$ as follows. First, it computes new timestamps $(r', c'_1, \ldots, c'_n) \leftarrow TS_{i'}.Stamp(x_1\|T_1, \ldots, x_n\|T_n)$ for the bitstrings and their long-term timestamps. Then, it publishes the root hash r' together with the timestamp scheme identifier i' at the repository Rep. Let t' be the time when (r', i') is published. For $j \in \{1, \ldots, n\}$, the algorithm sends (i', c'_j, r', t') as the response to request (x_j, T_j). The client receiving (i', c'_j, r', t') updates its long-term timestamp T_j by appending (i', c'_j, r', t').

$Verify$: This algorithm takes as input a bitstring x, a long-term timestamp $T = (C_1\|\ldots\|C_n)$, where $C_j = (i_j, c_j, r_j, t_j)$, a time t, a reference R to the trusted repository Rep, and a set of admissible timestamp schemes $\mathcal{TS} = \{TS_i\}_i$. For $j \in \{1, \ldots, n\}$, it is verified that $TS_{i_j}.Verify((x\|C_1\|\ldots\|C_{j-1}), c_j, r_j) = 1$, $(i_j, r_j) \in R[t_j]$, and $t_{i_j}^b > t_{j+1}$ (i.e., it is checked that each timestamp has been renewed correctly and when the previous timestamp was still valid). The algorithm outputs 1 if these conditions hold, otherwise it outputs 0.

3.2 Adversary Model

We now describe fundamentals for analyzing the security of long-lived systems. Commonly used security models for short-lived systems consider a fixed adversary that is allowed to perform a certain amount of computation before it halts. However, this model is not adequate for long-lived systems, where the computational power of an adversary may change over time.

Model of Real Time. To realize a suitable adversary model for long-lived systems we must be able to set in relation real time with other events happening in the system (e.g., the arise of a new computational technology). Therefore, we must specify a formalism the captures the notion of real time.

In recent literature, various approaches to modeling real time have been considered. Schwenk [11] and Geihs et al. [7] model real time by defining a global clock that advances whenever the adversary performs work. Another model of real time has been proposed by Canetti et al. [5] working in a computational framework that supports concurrency. They define a global clock as a distinguished process running concurrently to all other processes and ticking at a defined rate.

For our work we consider a sequential model of computation and follow the time formalism used by Schwenk [11] and Geihs et al. [7]. That is, we use a global clock Clock that holds a state time, initialized to 0. We allow the adversary to advance time by calling $\text{Clock}(t)$ as an oracle and if $t > \text{time}$, the clock is set to $\text{time} = t$ (Algorithm 2). We remark that by advancing time the adversary will burn computation power and trigger events in its environment.

Model of Computation. We consider adversaries $\mathcal{A}^{\text{Clock}}$ associated with a global clock Clock. We bound the computational power of adversary $\mathcal{A}$ with respect to the time defined by Clock. For $\rho : \mathbb{N} \to \mathbb{N}$, we say $\mathcal{A}$ is ρ-*step-bounded* if at any time t, it performed less than $\rho(t)$ computation steps. We say $\mathcal{A}$ is ρ-*call-bounded* if at any time t, it performed less than $\rho(t)$ oracle calls.

We model progression in computational technology by defining an adversary $\mathcal{A}^{\text{Clock}}$ as a sequence $(\mathcal{A}_0^{\text{Clock}}, \mathcal{A}_1^{\text{Clock}}, \mathcal{A}_2^{\text{Clock}}, \dots)$ of machines such that $\mathcal{A}_t \in \mathcal{M}_t$, where $\mathcal{M}_t$ represents the class of computing machines available at time t (i.e., $\mathcal{M}_t$ reflects the computational technology available at time t). Executing $\mathcal{A}^{\text{Clock}}$ at $\text{time} = t$ means executing the component $\mathcal{A}_t^{\text{Clock}}$. The adversary $\mathcal{A}_t^{\text{Clock}}$ then runs until it calls $\text{Clock}(t')$ after which the control is given to $\mathcal{A}_{t'}^{\text{Clock}}$. Here, $\mathcal{A}_{t'}^{\text{Clock}}$ gets access to the internal state of $\mathcal{A}_t^{\text{Clock}}$. An extractors $\mathcal{E}$ is also defined as a sequence $(\mathcal{E}_0, \mathcal{E}_1, \mathcal{E}_2, \dots)$ such that $\mathcal{E}_t \in \mathcal{M}_t$, but the components do not have access to the clock-oracle. Calling an extractor $\mathcal{E}$ at $\text{time} = t$ means calling $\mathcal{E}_t$.

3.3   Security Definition

We define the security of extractable long-term time-stamping using an experiment $\mathbf{Exp}^{\text{ExLTs}}$ (Algorithm 2). Similar to the definition of extractable (short-term) time-stamping, the security definition for extractable long-term time-stamping is given in the ideal primitive model [6]. Additionally, a global clock Clock as described in Sect. 3.2.

The experiment $\mathbf{Exp}^{\text{ExLTs}}$ considers an adversary $\mathcal{A}$ and an extractor $\mathcal{E}$. The adversary $\mathcal{A}$ may publish root hash values r at the repository Rep at any time by calling $\text{Rep}(r)$. When Rep is called with root hash r at time t, it records r associated with t in a global table R and also calls the extractor $\mathcal{E}$ with input adv and r. The extractor $\mathcal{E}$ extracts a set of bitstrings X and stores them associated with time t in a table L. A long-term timestamp scheme is considered secure if there exists an extractor such that for any possible adversary, whenever the adversary outputs a long-term timestamp T valid for bitstring x and time t (i.e., $\mathsf{Verify}(x, c, t, \mathsf{R}) = 1$), the extractor extracts x at time t (i.e., $x \in \mathsf{L}[t]$).

Definition 4 (Extractable Long-Term Time-Stamping). *Let $\mathcal{M}$ describe the available machines classes and $\mathcal{TS}$ describe the available timestamp schemes. Let $\epsilon : \mathbb{N}^4 \to [0, 1]$. A long-term timestamp scheme LTS^P, which uses an ideal primitive P, is ϵ-secure extractable (for $\mathcal{M}$ and $\mathcal{TS}$) if for all bounds $\rho_\mathcal{E}$, ρ_A, and q, there is a $\rho_\mathcal{E}$-bounded extractor $\mathcal{E} \in \mathcal{M}$, such that for every ρ_A-step-bounded and q-call-bounded adversary $\mathcal{A} \in \mathcal{M}$, and for every time t:*

$$\mathbf{Adv}_{P,\mathsf{LTS},\mathcal{TS}}^{\mathrm{ExLTs}}(\mathcal{A}, \mathcal{E}, t) = \Pr\left[\mathbf{Exp}_{P,\mathsf{LTS},\mathcal{TS}}^{\mathrm{ExLTs}}(\mathcal{A}, \mathcal{E}, t) = 1\right] \leq \epsilon(\rho_\mathcal{E}, \rho_A, q, t) \ .$$

Algorithm 2. The extractable long-term time-stamping experiment $\mathbf{Exp}_{P,\mathsf{LTS},\mathcal{TS}}^{\mathrm{ExLTs}}(\mathcal{A}, \mathcal{E}, t^*)$.

$(x, T, t) \leftarrow \mathcal{A}^{\mathsf{Clock},\mathsf{P},\mathsf{Rep}}$;
if $\mathsf{LTS.Verify}(x, T, t, \mathsf{R}, \mathcal{TS}) = 1$, $x \notin \mathsf{L}[t]$, $\mathtt{time} \leq t^*$ **then**
 | **return** 1;
else
 | **return** 0;

---

oracle $\mathtt{Clock}(t)$:	oracle $\mathsf{P}(m)$:	oracle $\mathsf{Rep}(r)$:
if $t > \mathtt{time}$ **then**	$z \leftarrow P(m)$;	$X \leftarrow \mathcal{E}(\mathsf{adv}, r)$;
	$\mathtt{time} \leftarrow t$;	$\mathsf{adv} \leftarrow \mathsf{adv}\|\|(m, z)$;	$t \leftarrow \mathtt{time}$;
	return z;	$\mathsf{R}[t] \leftarrow \mathsf{R}[t]\|\|r$;
		$\mathsf{L}[t] \leftarrow \mathsf{L}[t]\|\|X$;
		return X;

3.4   Security Analysis

Before we analyze the security of the long-term timestamp scheme described in Sect. 3.1, we adapt the notion of (short-term) extractable time-stamping from Sect. 2 to the setting where different classes of computing machines are considered.

Definition 5 (Extractable Time-Stamping (for Machine Classes)). *Let $\mathcal{M}_\mathcal{E}$ and $\mathcal{M}_A$ be classes of machines and $\epsilon : \mathbb{N}^3 \to [0, 1]$. We say a non-renewable timestamp scheme TS is ϵ-secure extractable for adversaries of $\mathcal{M}_A$ and extractors of $\mathcal{M}_\mathcal{E}$ if for all integers $\rho_\mathcal{E}$, ρ_A, and $q_\mathcal{E}$, there exists a $\rho_\mathcal{E}$-step extractor $\mathcal{E} \in \mathcal{M}_\mathcal{E}$, such that for every ρ_A-step adversary $\mathcal{A} \in \mathcal{M}_A$ that makes at most q calls to Rep:*

$$\mathbf{Adv}_{P,\mathsf{TS}}^{\mathrm{ExTs}}(\mathcal{A}, \mathcal{E}) \leq \epsilon(\rho_\mathcal{E}, \rho_A, q) \ .$$

We now prove a bound on the security level of the long-term timestamp scheme described in Sect. 3.1 in terms of the security level of the available (short-term) timestamp schemes.

Theorem 2. *Let $\mathcal{M}$ describe the available computing machine classes and $\mathcal{TS} = \{\mathsf{TS}_i^P\}_i$ describe the available timestamp schemes, which use an ideal primitive P. If for every i, TS_i^P is ϵ_i-secure extractable for adversaries of $\mathcal{M}_{t_i^b}$ and extractors of $\mathcal{M}_{t_i^s}$, then the long-term timestamp scheme described in Sect. 3.1 is ϵ-secure extractable with*

$$\epsilon(\rho_{\mathcal{E}}, \rho_{\mathcal{A}}, q, t) = \sum_{i \in \{i: t_i^b \leq t\}} \epsilon_i \left(\alpha \cdot \rho_{\mathcal{E}}(t_i^b), \beta \cdot \left(\rho_{\mathcal{A}}(t_i^b) + q(t_i^b)\rho_{\mathcal{E}}(t_i^b) \right), q(t_i^b) \right) ,$$

for some small constants α and β.

We refer the reader to the full paper [2] for a proof of Theorem 2.

4   Evaluation

We evaluate which protection level the long-term timestamp scheme described in Sect. 3.1 provides in a practical scenario. For our evaluation we consider a scenario where data is protected over a time period of Y years. The security level of the long-term timestamp scheme is evaluated in terms of the security level of the hash functions that are used to instantiate the available (short-term) timestamp schemes. Here, we assume that all used hash functions have the same security level during their validity period.

4.1   Scenario

We assume that $\mathcal{TS} = \{\mathsf{TS}_i\}_i$ is the set of available (short-term) timestamp schemes, and for each i we denote by H_i the hash function used by TS_i. We assume that the PrA-security of a hash function derives from the ratio of the adversary power p_A and the extractor power $p_{\mathcal{E}}$, and is influenced by the number of repository calls q and a base security level δ. Concretely, we assume that each hash function H_i is ϵ-secure PrA until its breakage time t_i^b with $\epsilon(p_{\mathcal{E}}, p_A, q) = \frac{p_A}{p_{\mathcal{E}}} q\delta$. Furthermore, we assume that each (short-term) timestamp scheme TS_i is N-bounded and shape compact, which means that each timestamp round up to N timestamps are generated. For our practical security analysis we neglect the constants α and β derived in Theorems 1 and 2 as we expect them to be close to 1 in most cases.

By Theorem 1 we obtain that each short-term timestamp scheme TS_i is ϵ'-secure extractable until time t_i^b with

$$\epsilon'(p_{\mathcal{E}}, p_A, q) \leq \epsilon \left(\frac{p_{\mathcal{E}}}{2N}, p_A + 2Nq, 2Nq \right) = \frac{p_A + 2Nq}{p_{\mathcal{E}}} (2N)^2 q\delta .$$

Furthermore, using Theorem 2 we obtain that the long-term timestamp scheme is ϵ''-secure long-term extractable with

$$\epsilon''(\rho_\mathcal{E}, \rho_\mathcal{A}, q, t) \leq \sum_{i \in I_t} \left(\frac{\rho_\mathcal{A}(t_i^b)}{\rho_\mathcal{E}(t_i^b)} + \left(\frac{2N}{\rho_\mathcal{E}(t_i^b)} + 1 \right) q(t_i^b) \right) (2N)^2 q(t_i^b) \delta .$$

Now we assume that the adversary and the extractor have the same computation power and observe that any reasonable extractor $\mathcal{E}$ should extract at least $2N$ bitstrings before the breakage time of a scheme (i.e., $\frac{\rho_\mathcal{A}(t)}{\rho_\mathcal{E}(t)} = 1$, $\rho_\mathcal{E}(t_i^b) \geq 2N$). Let time t denote the number of years that the experiment is running and assume that each year a maximum of L new timestamp schemes become available, and at most R root hashes are published at the repository, i.e., $|I_t| = |\{i : t_i^b \leq t\}| \leq tL$ and $q(t) \leq tR$. We obtain the following bound on the security level of the long-term timestamp scheme:

$$\epsilon''(\rho_\mathcal{E}, \rho_B, q, t) \leq 12t^3 (NR)^2 L\delta .$$

4.2   Results

Assuming $L = 10$, $N = 2^{32}$, $R = 365$, and $-\log_2(\delta) = 192$, we show in Fig. 1 the degradation of the security level $-\log_2(\epsilon'')$ of the analyzed long-term timestamp scheme over time. The graph shows that the security level degrades from 104 to 84 over a time period of 100 years. We stress that this degradation takes place even though the security level for all the used hash functions is at least 192 in the corresponding validity period.

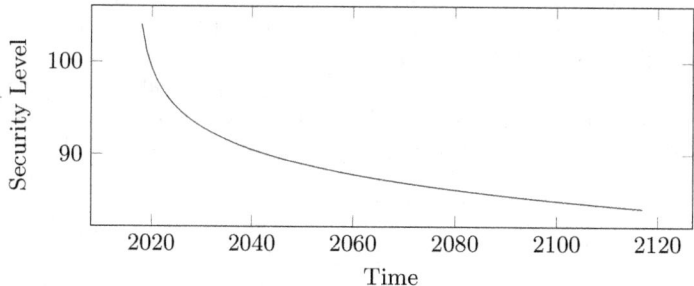

Fig. 1. The degradation of the security level of long-term time-stamping over time.

5   Conclusions and Future Work

We have formally analyzed the security of a long-term timestamp scheme based on the ideas of Bayer et al. [1] and shown that the security level of that scheme degrades cubic over time, even if the security level of the used cryptographic primitives is held constant. This shows that long-lived systems need to be designed using a certain security margin. The techniques provided in our security analysis can be used to analyze other long-lived cryptographic systems.

For future work it would be interesting to see whether the security bound proved by us can be improved, thereby reducing the security loss over time. It would also be interesting to establish a security model for long-term time-stamping in the standard model (i.e., without using ideal primitives).

References

1. Bayer, D., Haber, S., Stornetta, W.S.: Improving the efficiency and reliability of digital time-stamping. In: Capocelli, R., De Santis, A., Vaccaro, U. (eds.) Sequences II: Methods in Communication, Security, and Computer Science, pp. 329–334. Springer, New York (1993). doi:10.1007/978-1-4613-9323-8_24

2. Buldas, A., Geihs, M., Buchmann, J.: Long-term secure time-stamping using preimage-aware hash functions. Cryptology ePrint Archive, Report 2017/754 (2017). http://eprint.iacr.org/2017/754

3. Buldas, A., Laanoja, R.: Security proofs for hash tree time-stamping using hash functions with small output size. In: Boyd, C., Simpson, L. (eds.) ACISP 2013. LNCS, vol. 7959, pp. 235–250. Springer, Heidelberg (2013). doi:10.1007/978-3-642-39059-3_16

4. Buldas, A., Laur, S.: Knowledge-binding commitments with applications in time-stamping. In: Okamoto, T., Wang, X. (eds.) PKC 2007. LNCS, vol. 4450, pp. 150–165. Springer, Heidelberg (2007). doi:10.1007/978-3-540-71677-8_11

5. Canetti, R., Cheung, L., Kaynar, D., Lynch, N., Pereira, O.: Modeling computational security in long-lived systems. In: van Breugal, F., Chechik, M. (eds.) CONCUR 2008. LNCS, vol. 5201, pp. 114–130. Springer, Heidelberg (2008). doi:10.1007/978-3-540-85361-9_12

6. Dodis, Y., Ristenpart, T., Shrimpton, T.: Salvaging merkle-damgård for practical applications. In: Joux, A. (ed.) EUROCRYPT 2009. LNCS, vol. 5479, pp. 371–388. Springer, Heidelberg (2009). doi:10.1007/978-3-642-01001-9_22

7. Geihs, M., Demirel, D., Buchmann, J.A.: A security analysis of techniques for long-term integrity protection. In: 14th Annual Conference on Privacy, Security and Trust, PST 2016, Auckland, New Zealand, 12–14 December 2016, pp. 449–456 (2016)

8. Haber, S., Stornetta, W.S.: How to time-stamp a digital document. In: Menezes, A.J., Vanstone, S.A. (eds.) CRYPTO 1990. LNCS, vol. 537, pp. 437–455. Springer, Heidelberg (1991). doi:10.1007/3-540-38424-3_32

9. Merkle, R.C.: A Certified Digital Signature. In: Brassard, G. (ed.) CRYPTO 1989. LNCS, vol. 435, pp. 218–238. Springer, New York (1990). doi:10.1007/0-387-34805-0_21

10. Rivest, R.L., Shamir, A., Adleman, L.M.: A method for obtaining digital signatures and public-key cryptosystems. Commun. ACM **21**(2), 120–126 (1978)

11. Schwenk, J.: Modelling time for authenticated key exchange protocols. In: Kutyłowski, M., Vaidya, J. (eds.) ESORICS 2014. LNCS, vol. 8713, pp. 277–294. Springer, Cham (2014). doi:10.1007/978-3-319-11212-1_16

On the Hardness of Sparsely Learning Parity with Noise

Hanlin Liu, Di Yan, Yu Yu$^{(\boxtimes)}$, and Shuoyao Zhao

Shanghai JiaoTong University, Shanghai, China
{hans1024,yandi821,Zhao_sy2016}@sjtu.edu.cn, yuyu@yuyu.hk

Abstract. Learning Parity with Noise (LPN) represents the average-case analogue of the NP-Complete problem "decoding random linear codes", and it has been extensively studied in learning theory and cryptography with applications to quantum-resistant cryptographic schemes. In this paper, we study a sparse variant of the LPN whose public matrix consists of sparse vectors (or alternatively each element of the matrix follows the Bernoulli distribution), of which the variant considered by Benny, Boaz and Avi (STOC 2010) falls into a (extreme) special case. We show a win-win argument that at least one of the following is true: (1) either the hardness of sparse LPN is implied by that of the standard LPN under the same noise rate; (2) there exist new black-box constructions of public-key encryption (PKE) schemes and oblivious transfer (OT) protocols from the standard LPN.

1 Introduction

LEARNING PARITY WITH NOISE. The Learning Parity with Noise (LPN) problem is a well-known problem in cryptography and learning theory. The computational version of LPN problem with parameters $n \in \mathbb{N}$ (length of binary secret vector), $0 < \mu < 1/2$ (noise rate), $q = \mathsf{poly}(n)$ (the number of query) postulates that it is computationally infeasible to recover the binary secret vector $x \leftarrow \{0,1\}^n$ given $(A, A \cdot x + e)$, where A is a random $q \times n$ binary matrix, $e \leftarrow \mathcal{B}_\mu^q$, $\mathcal{B}_\mu$ denotes the Bernoulli distribution with parameter μ (i.e., $\Pr[\mathcal{B}_\mu = 1] = \mu$ and $\Pr[\mathcal{B}_\mu = 0] = 1 - \mu$), '·' denotes matrix vector multiplication over $\mathbf{GF}(2)$ and '+' denotes bitwise addition over $\mathbf{GF}(2)$. The decisional version of LPN simply assumes that $(A, A \cdot x + e)$ is pseudorandom (i.e., computationally indistinguishable from uniform randomness) given A. While seemingly stronger, the decisional version is known to be polynomially equivalent to its computational counterpart [3,8,14].

HARDNESS OF LPN. The computational LPN problem is an average-case analogue of "decoding random linear codes" [6], which is a well-known NP-complete problem. Feldman et al. [11] show that any efficient algorithm for LPN would imply efficient learners for important function classes such as 2-DNF formulas, juntas, and any function with a sparse Fourier spectrum. When $\mu = O(1)$ is a constant (less than 1/2 and independent of the secret size n), the best known

© Springer International Publishing AG 2017
T. Okamoto et al. (Eds.): ProvSec 2017, LNCS 10592, pp. 261–267, 2017.
https://doi.org/10.1007/978-3-319-68637-0_16

LPN solvers [9,16] require the time complexity and the number of training samples both $2^{O(n/\log n)}$. If the number of training samples $q = \mathsf{poly}(n)$, the time complexity (of the best known algorithm) goes up to $2^{O(n/\log n)}$ [17]. The time complexity goes up to $2^{O(n)}$ given only $q = O(n)$ queries [18]. Under low noise rate $\mu = n^{-c}$ ($0 < c < 1$), the security of LPN is less well understood: on the one hand, for $q = n + O(1)$ we can already do an efficient distinguishing attacks using time complexity $2^{O(n^{1-c})}$; on the other hand, for (even super-)polynomial q the best known attacks [5,7,10,15,21] are not asymptotically better, i.e., still at the order of $2^{\Theta(n^{1-c})}$. LPN can be used to build public-key encryption (PKE) schemes and oblivious transfer (OT) protocols under low noise rate $\mu = O(1\sqrt{n})$ [1] or assuming subexponential hardness [22]. We mention that LPN does not succumb to known quantum algorithms, which makes it a promising candidate for "post-quantum cryptography". Furthermore, LPN also enjoys simplicity and is more suitable for weak-power devices (e.g., RFID tags) than other quantum-secure candidates such as LWE [20].

SPARSE LEARNING PARITY WITH NOISE. We study the hardness of the Sparse Learning Parity with Noise (SLPN) problem, which is a variant of LPN by letting the public matrix A follow the Bernoulli distribution $\mathcal{B}_\mu^{q \times n}$, or equivalently (not exactly the same though), the rows of A be independently sampled from uniform distribution of length n and Hamming weight μn. Note that the variant considered in [2], referred to as the 3LIN problem, falls into a special case for $\mu = 3/n$, and it is conjectured that the 3LIN resist sub-exponential time algorithms who are restricted to $O(n^{1.4})$ samples. Compared with standard LPN, sparse LPN significantly reduces the amount of public randomness needed.

OUR CONTRIBUTIONS. In this paper, we show that under the standard LPN assumption, at least one of the following is true:

1. either sparse LPN is hard;
2. or CPA secure public-key encryption schemes and oblivious transfer (OT) protocols are implied.

Note that we impose no noise rate or additional sub-exponential hardness about the LPN, and thus the second result is unlikely to be true (otherwise it will be a breakthrough). Therefore, we prove the hardness of the sparse LPN problem via an unconventional reduction from standard LPN. The main proof technique is borrowed from the work of Barak et al. [4], i.e., any efficient algorithm that falsifies the first statement (sparse LPN is hard) can be used to construct CPA secure PKE and OT in a black-box manner.

2   Preliminaries

We denote the binary logarithm by $\log(\cdot)$. For a binary string $\mathbf{x}$ we use $|\mathbf{x}|$ to denote its Hamming weight, i.e., the number of 1's in $\mathbf{x}$. $\mathbf{x} \xleftarrow{\$} \mathcal{X}$ refers to drawing an element $\mathbf{x}$ from set $\mathcal{X}$ uniformly at random, and $\mathbf{x} \xleftarrow{\$} X$ denotes drawing an element $\mathbf{x}$ according to distribution X. $\mathcal{B}_\mu$ refers to the Bernoulli distribution with parameter μ, i.e., $\Pr[x = 1] = \mu$ and $\Pr[x = 0] = 1 - \mu$, and $\mathcal{B}_\mu^q$ denotes its q-fold repetition. U_n refers to a uniform random distribution over $\mathbb{Z}_2^n$. A function $f(\cdot)$ is negligible if for any positive constant c $f(n) < n^{-c}$ holds for all sufficiently large n's, and $f(\cdot)$ is noticeable if there exists positive constant c such that that $f(n) \geq n^{-c}$ for all sufficiently large n's.

We give below the definitions for decisional versions of the LPN and its variants. Decisional versions are more handy for cryptographic applications and they imply (and are equivalent to in case of the standard LPN) their computational counterparts.

Definition 1 (Standard LPN). *The (decisional) $\mathbf{LPN}_{n,\mu,q}$ problem is hard if for every probabilistic polynomial-time (PPT) distinguisher $\mathbf{D}$, we have*

$$\left| \Pr_{\mathbf{A,s,e}}[\mathbf{D}(\mathbf{A}, \mathbf{A} \cdot \mathbf{s} \oplus \mathbf{e}) = 1] - \Pr_{\mathbf{A},\mathbf{U}_q}[\mathbf{D}(\mathbf{A}, \mathbf{U}_q) = 1] \right| = \mathsf{negl}(n),$$

where $\mathbf{A} \xleftarrow{\$} \mathbb{Z}_2^{q \times n}$, $\mathbf{s} \xleftarrow{\$} \mathbb{Z}_2^n$, $\mathbf{e} \leftarrow \mathcal{B}_\mu^q$ and $\mathbf{U}_q$ is a uniform distribution over $\mathbb{Z}_2^q$.

Definition 2 (Knapsack LPN). *The (decisional) knapsack LPN problem, denoted by $\mathbf{Knapsack\text{-}LPN}_{n,\mu,q}$, is hard if for every PPT distinguisher $\mathbf{D}$, we have*

$$\left| \Pr_{\mathbf{C,b}}[\mathbf{D}(\mathbf{C}, \mathbf{b}^\mathsf{T} \cdot \mathbf{C}) = 1] - \Pr_{\mathbf{C},\mathbf{U}_q}[\mathbf{D}(\mathbf{C}, \mathbf{U}_q) = 1] \right| = \mathsf{negl}(n),$$

where $\mathbf{C} \xleftarrow{\$} \mathbb{Z}_2^{(n+q) \times q}$, $\mathbf{b} \leftarrow \mathcal{B}_\mu^{n+q}$ and $\mathbf{U}_q$ is a uniform distribution over $\mathbb{Z}_2^q$.

Definition 3 (Sparse LPN). *The (decisional) sparse LPN problem, denoted by $\mathbf{S\text{-}LPN}_{n,\mu,q}$, is hard if for every PPT distinguisher $\mathbf{D}$, we have*

$$\left| \Pr_{\mathbf{A,s,e}}[\mathbf{D}(\mathbf{A}, \mathbf{A} \cdot \mathbf{s} \oplus \mathbf{e}) = 1] - \Pr_{\mathbf{A},\mathbf{U_q}}[\mathbf{D}(\mathbf{A}, \mathbf{U_q}) = 1] \right| = \mathsf{negl}(n),$$

where $\mathbf{A} \leftarrow \mathcal{B}_\mu^{q \times n}$, $\mathbf{s} \xleftarrow{\$} \mathbb{Z}_2^n$, $\mathbf{e} \leftarrow \mathcal{B}_\mu^q$ and $\mathbf{U}_q$ is a uniform distribution over $\mathbb{Z}_2^q$.

Theorem 1 (LPN implies knapsack LPN [19]). *The $\mathbf{LPN}_{n,\mu,n+q}$ problem is hard implies that the $\mathbf{Knapsack\text{-}LPN}_{n,\mu,q}$ problem is hard.*

3   Hardness of the Sparse LPN Problem

In this section, we show that the sparse LPN problem is most likely hard. Otherwise (if the sparse LPN can be refuted by an efficient algorithm), then it leads to more surprising results that PKE and OT can be constructed in a black-box manner from standard LPN, which is unlikely especially for noise rate $\mu = \omega(1)/\sqrt{n}$.

We aim to prove the main result, which we stated as Hypothesis 1 below.

Hypothesis 1 (Hardness of (decisional) Sparse LPN). *The decisional LPN problem for secret size* $2n$*, noise rate* μ *and sample complexity* q*, i.e.,* $\textbf{\textit{S-LPN}}_{2n,\mu,q}$ *is hard.*

Theorem 2. *Assume that for* $q \geq 2n$ *the* $\textbf{\textit{LPN}}_{n,\mu,q}$ *problem is hard, then at least one of the following is true:*

1. *either Hypothesis 1 is true, namely,* $\textbf{\textit{S-LPN}}_{2n,\mu,q}$ *is hard;*
2. *or CPA secure public-key encryption schemes and oblivious transfer (OT) protocols are implied.*

Proof. Assume for contradiction that Hypothesis 1 does not hold, then there exists a polynomial-time $\mathbf{D}$ that distinguishes the following distributions with non-negligible probability, i.e., there exists a polynomial $p(\cdot)$ such that the following holds for infinitely many n's

$$\Pr_{\mathbf{B},\mathbf{x},\mathbf{e}}[\mathbf{D}(\mathbf{B}, \mathbf{B}\cdot\mathbf{x}\oplus\mathbf{e}) = 1] - \Pr_{\mathbf{B},\mathbf{U_q}}[\mathbf{D}(\mathbf{B}, \mathbf{U_q}) = 1] \geq 1/p(n) ,$$

where $\mathbf{B} \leftarrow \mathcal{B}_\mu^{q\times 2n}$, $\mathbf{x} \xleftarrow{\$} \mathbb{Z}_2^{2n}$ and $\mathbf{e} \leftarrow \mathcal{B}_\mu^q$. Then, it implies a two-pass (single-bit) key agreement protocol (which is equivalent to public-key encryption), as depicted in Fig. 1. We have by Theorem 1 that $\mathbf{LPN}_{n,\mu,q}$ ($q \geq 2n$) implies $\mathbf{Knapsack\text{-}LPN}_{n,\mu,n}$, namely, a q-fold hybrid argument of knapsack LPN states that $(\mathbf{C}, \mathbf{B}\cdot\mathbf{C})$ is computationally indistinguishable to $(\mathbf{C}, \mathbf{U}_{q\times n})$. Informally, this means that $\mathbf{A} = \mathbf{B}\cdot\mathbf{C}$ looks like a uniform $q \times n$ matrix to any PPT adversary. It follows that the security of the protocol can be guaranteed due to the $\mathbf{LPN}_{n,\mu,q}$ assumption, i.e., $(\mathbf{A}, \mathbf{As}+\mathbf{e})$ is computationally indistinguishable

Alice		Bob
$\mathbf{B} \leftarrow \mathcal{B}_\mu^{q\times 2n}$		$\mathbf{s} \xleftarrow{\$} \mathbb{Z}_2^n$
$\mathbf{C} \xleftarrow{\$} \mathbb{Z}_2^{2n\times n}$	$\xrightarrow{\mathbf{A}=\mathbf{B}\cdot\mathbf{C}}$	$\mathbf{e} \leftarrow \mathcal{B}_\mu^q$
		$m \xleftarrow{\$} \{0,1\}$
		if $m = 1$ then $r := \mathbf{BCs}\oplus\mathbf{e}$
	$\xleftarrow{r}$	else if $m = 0$ then $r \xleftarrow{\$} \mathbb{Z}_2^q$
$m' \leftarrow \mathbf{D}(\mathbf{B}, r)$		

Fig. 1. A two-pass bit agreement protocol that enables Bob to send a single bit to Alice securely (against passive adversaries) with noticeable correctness, which is based on any efficient distinguisher D that constitutes a counterexample to Hypothesis 1.

to $(\mathbf{A}, \mathbf{U}_q)$. Meanwhile, Alice is able to decrypt m with at least noticeable probability.

$$
\begin{aligned}
\Pr[m' = m] &= \underbrace{\Pr[m = 1]}_{1/2} \cdot \Pr[m' = 1 | m = 1] + \underbrace{\Pr[m = 0]}_{1/2} \cdot \underbrace{\Pr[m' = 0 | m = 0]}_{1 - \Pr[m'=1|m=0]} \\
&= 1/2 + (\Pr[m' = 1 | m = 1] - \Pr[m' = 1 | m = 0])/2 \\
&= 1/2 + \frac{\Pr_{\mathbf{B},\mathbf{s},\mathbf{e}}[\mathsf{D}(\mathbf{B}, \mathbf{B} \cdot \mathbf{s} \oplus \mathbf{e}) = 1] - \Pr_{\mathbf{B},\mathbf{U}_q}[\mathsf{D}(\mathbf{B}, \mathbf{U}_q) = 1]}{2} \\
&\geq 1/2 + \frac{1}{2p(n)},
\end{aligned}
$$

where $\mathbf{x} = \mathbf{C}\mathbf{s}$ is a uniform distribution over $\mathbb{Z}_2^n$. Using parallel repetition and privacy amplification, it is known [12,13] that any protocol which achieves bit-agreement with noticeable correlation can be turned into a full-fledged key-agreement protocol (without increasing the number of rounds), which further implies a CPA secure public-key encryption. Furthermore, note that the two-round key agreement protocol can be easily adapted to an OT protocol. That is, if Alice replaces $\mathbf{A} = \mathbf{B}\mathbf{C}$ with a uniformly random $\mathbf{A} \xleftarrow{\$} \mathbb{Z}_2^{q \times n}$, then the information about m is statistically hidden (and not decryptable by Alice). This yields a 2-round oblivious transfer protocol secure against honest-but-curious receiver: imagine Alice has a choice bit $b \in \{0, 1\}$, she then sets $pk_b := \mathbf{B}\mathbf{C}$ and $pk_{1-b} \xleftarrow{\$} \mathbb{Z}_2^{q \times n}$ and sends pk_0 and pk_1 to Bob. Bob, who holds two bits σ_0 and σ_1, uses the bit agreement protocol to encrypt σ_0 and σ_1 under pk_0 and pk_1, respectively. Alice can then recover σ_b but gets no information about σ_{1-b}.

4   Conclusion

We present non-trivial evidence that the sparse LPN should be hard as long as the standard LPN under the same noise rate is hard, and otherwise it leads to more surprising (and perhaps breakthrough for certain parameters) results that public-key encryptions and oblivious transfer protocols can be based on standard LPN at any noise rate and without resorting to subexponential hardness assumptions.

References

1. Alekhnovich, M.: More on average case vs approximation complexity. Comput. Complex. **20**, 755–786 (2011)
2. Applebaum, B., Barak, B., Wigderson, A.: Public-key cryptography from different assumptions. In: Proceedings of the 42nd ACM Symposium on Theory of Computing, STOC 2010, Cambridge, Massachusetts, USA, 5–8 June 2010, pp. 171–180 (2010)
3. Applebaum, B., Ishai, Y., Kushilevitz, E.: Cryptography with constant input locality. J. Cryptol. **22**(4), 429–469 (2009)

4. Barak, B., Dodis, Y., Krawczyk, H., Pereira, O., Pietrzak, K., Standaert, F.-X., Yu, Y.: Leftover hash lemma, revisited. In: Rogaway, P. (ed.) CRYPTO 2011. LNCS, vol. 6841, pp. 1–20. Springer, Heidelberg (2011). doi:10.1007/978-3-642-22792-9_1

5. Becker, A., Joux, A., May, A., Meurer, A.: Decoding random binary linear codes in $2^{n/20}$: how $1 + 1 = 0$ improves information set decoding. In: Pointcheval, D., Johansson, T. (eds.) EUROCRYPT 2012. LNCS, vol. 7237, pp. 520–536. Springer, Heidelberg (2012). doi:10.1007/978-3-642-29011-4_31

6. Berlekamp, E.R., McEliece, R.J., van Tilborg, H.C.A.: On the inherent intractability of certain coding problems (corresp.). IEEE Trans. Inf. Theor. **24**(3), 384–386 (1978)

7. Bernstein, D.J., Lange, T., Peters, C.: Smaller decoding exponents: ball-collision decoding. In: Rogaway, P. (ed.) CRYPTO 2011. LNCS, vol. 6841, pp. 743–760. Springer, Heidelberg (2011). doi:10.1007/978-3-642-22792-9_42

8. Blum, A., Furst, M., Kearns, M., Lipton, R.J.: Cryptographic primitives based on hard learning problems. In: Stinson, D.R. (ed.) CRYPTO 1993. LNCS, vol. 773, pp. 278–291. Springer, Heidelberg (1994). doi:10.1007/3-540-48329-2_24

9. Blum, A., Kalai, A., Wasserman, H.: Noise-tolerant learning, the parity problem, and the statistical query model. J. ACM **50**(4), 506–519 (2003)

10. Canteaut, A., Chabaud, F.: A new algorithm for finding minimum-weight words in a linear code: Application to mceliece's cryptosystem and to narrow-sense BCH codes of length 511. IEEE Trans. Inf. Theor. **44**(1), 367–378 (1998)

11. Feldman, V., Gopalan, P., Khot, S., Ponnuswami, A.K.: New results for learning noisy parities and halfspaces. In: 47th Annual IEEE Symposium on Foundations of Computer Science (FOCS 2006), 21–24 October 2006, Berkeley, California, USA, Proceedings, pp. 563–574 (2006)

12. Holenstein, T.: Key agreement from weak bit agreement. In: STOC, pp. 664–673 (2005)

13. Holenstein, T.: Strengthening Key Agreement using Hard-Core Sets. PhD thesis, ETH Zurich, Zurich, Switzerland (2006)

14. Katz, J., Shin, J.S., Smith, A.D.: Parallel and concurrent security of the HB and hb+ protocols. J. Cryptol. **23**(3), 402–421 (2010)

15. Kirchner, P.: Improved generalized birthday attack. IACR Cryptology ePrint Archive 2011:377 (2011)

16. Levieil, É., Fouque, P.-A.: An improved LPN algorithm. In: De Prisco, R., Yung, M. (eds.) SCN 2006. LNCS, vol. 4116, pp. 348–359. Springer, Heidelberg (2006). doi:10.1007/11832072_24

17. Lyubashevsky, V.: The parity problem in the presence of noise, decoding random linear codes, and the subset sum problem. In: Chekuri, C., Jansen, K., Rolim, J.D.P., Trevisan, L. (eds.) APPROX/RANDOM -2005. LNCS, vol. 3624, pp. 378–389. Springer, Heidelberg (2005). doi:10.1007/11538462_32

18. May, A., Meurer, A., Thomae, E.: Decoding random linear codes in $\tilde{\mathcal{O}}(2^{0.054n})$. In: Advances in Cryptology - ASIACRYPT 2011–17th International Conference on the Theory and Application of Cryptology and Information Security, Seoul, South Korea, December 4–8, 2011, Proceedings, pp. 107–124 (2011)

19. Micciancio, D., Mol, P.: Pseudorandom knapsacks and the sample complexity of LWE search-to-decision reductions. In: Rogaway, P. (ed.) CRYPTO 2011. LNCS, vol. 6841, pp. 465–484. Springer, Heidelberg (2011). doi:10.1007/978-3-642-22792-9_26

20. Regev, O.: On lattices, learning with errors, random linear codes, and cryptography. J. ACM **56**(6), 34:1–34:40 (2009)

21. Stern, J.: A method for finding codewords of small weight. In: Cohen, G., Wolf-mann, J. (eds.) Coding Theory 1988. LNCS, vol. 388, pp. 106–113. Springer, Heidelberg (1989). doi:10.1007/BFb0019850
22. Yu, Y., Zhang, J.: Cryptography with auxiliary input and trapdoor from constant-noise LPN. In: Robshaw, M., Katz, J. (eds.) CRYPTO 2016. LNCS, vol. 9814, pp. 214–243. Springer, Heidelberg (2016). doi:10.1007/978-3-662-53018-4_9

Lattice and Post-quantum Cryptography

Provable Secure Post-Quantum Signature Scheme Based on Isomorphism of Polynomials in Quantum Random Oracle Model

Bagus Santoso$^{1(\boxtimes)}$ and Chunhua Su^2

^{1} Department of Computer and Network Engineering,
University of Electro-Communications, Chofu, Japan
santoso.bagus@uec.ac.jp
^{2} Division of Computer Science, University of Aizu, Aizuwakamatsu, Japan
chsu@u-aizu.ac.jp

Abstract. Since a quantum adversary is supposed to be able to perform hash computation with superposition of the quantum bits, it is natural that in random oracle model, the reduction algorithm for security proof should allow the quantum adversary to query random oracle in superposition of quantum bits. However, due to physical nature of quantum states, any observation on a superposition of quantum bits will be noticed by quantum adversaries. Hence, to simulate the true random oracle, the reduction algorithm has to answer the queries without observing their content. This makes the classical reduction algorithms fail to properly perform rewinding and random oracle programming against quantum adversaries and it has been shown recently that several signature schemes generated by Fiat-Shamir transformation might be insecure against quantum adversaries although they have been proven secure in classical setting against classical adversaries.

In this paper, we propose a method to construct reduction algorithm without rewinding of quantum adversary and such that the random oracle programming is unnoticeable by the quantum adversary except with negligible probability. We show the feasibility of our method by applying it on signature scheme generated via Fiat-Shamir transformation of an identification scheme whose security is based on the decisional problem of isomorphism of polynomials with two secrets.

Keywords: Isomorphism of polynomials · Quantum random oracle model · Fiat-Shamir transformation

1 Introduction

It has been known that quantum computers can break all current standard public key cryptographic schemes which are relying their security on the hardness of factoring integers and discrete logarithm problem. Due to the recent advance in quantum computing, there are immediate demands to find new alternative cryptographic schemes which can resist attackers who may use quantum computers.

© Springer International Publishing AG 2017
T. Okamoto et al. (Eds.): ProvSec 2017, LNCS 10592, pp. 271–284, 2017.
https://doi.org/10.1007/978-3-319-68637-0_17

Such schemes are widely called as *post-quantum* cryptographic schemes. A number of *post-quantum* identification schemes and their corresponding signature schemes from Fiat-Shamir transformation have been proposed [6,10,13]. However, the security of these schemes are proven against only classical adversaries, not quantum adversaries.

Meanwhile, recently, there have been several works point out that several security proofs which are assuming classical adversaries might not work if we replace the classical adversaries with quantum adversaries [2,7]. The main cause of this is the capability of a quantum computer to store an exponential number of values in a polynomial number of *qubits*, which is an analogue of bits in classical computers, and the fact that one single computational operation on a polynomial number of qubits applies to all exponential number of values represented by those qubits.

Evaluation of hash values by quantum adversary. We give an illustration as follows. A polynomial time classical adversary may only be able to evaluate a polynomial number of hash values by computing the hash function on each variable one by one, but a quantum adversary is capable to evaluate an exponential number of hash values by applying hash function on one variable consisting of polynomial number of qubits. For a security proof with random oracle, a single execution or evaluation of hash value via a hash function is represented by a single query to random oracle. Thus, in order to represent evaluation of exponential numbers of evaluation of hash values by a quantum adversary, we require that the random oracle is able to receive the query in the form of a quantum state which is a superposition of exponential number of values, and returns the query also in a quantum state representing the superposition of the evaluation of hash function applied to each values. A quantum adversary thus may "hide" which hash value that it actually uses to perform the "attack" among exponential number of hash values which are superpositioned in a single quantum state.

Difficulties and the impossible result on constructing security proof against quantum adversary. This becomes a big problem when we are trying to prove security of a signature scheme which is obtained by Fiat-Shamir transformation. It is a common knowledge that the ordinary way to prove the security of such signature scheme is by applying the rewinding technique which requires the reduction algorithm to rewind the adversary at least twice to obtain two distinct forged signatures which are corresponding to different hash values returned by random oracle which are actually the answer of the same query. As described in [2,7], the classical rewinding is difficult to apply in the quantum setting. The classical rewinding technique requires us to know which hash value is used for the forgery so that we can rewind the adversary back to the point when it sent the query so that the reduction algorithm can answer the query with a value different from the first one. However, a quantum adversary may "hide" which hash value that it actually uses to perform the forgery among exponential number of hash values which are superpositioned in a single quantum state, and thus it is hard to determine which stage we need to rewind to.

Another problem with quantum adversary is the measurement of a quantum state. The only way to determine which value which is will be used among exponential number of values superpositioned in a quantum state, we need to perform a measurement. And once we did a measurement of a quantum state, the quantum state can not restored to its original state and it has been shown that quantum state cloning is not possible [15]. Thus, though we might think to try to avoid rewinding using the technique of "online extraction" from Fischlin [8], we can not use this technique in direct manner, since Fischlin's technique requires us to observe (measure) the queries and the corresponding answers to the random oracle. Without measurement, we only see the superposition of exponential number of queries and answers, but if we measure any query to random oracle which is in the form of a quantum state, then we might end up in disturbing the quantum state to an extent that the quantum adversary will notice it.

Finally, [7] Dagdelen et al. even proved that it is *impossible* to construct a security proof for a signature schemes which is generated from an identification scheme via Fiat-Shamir transformation if the commitment phase of the identification scheme is independent from the witness of the public keys.

Main idea. Our basic idea is to utilize the technique to prove the security of signature schemes generated from a special kind of identification scheme which is invented by Goh et al. [9] and generalized in [1]. In brief, the scope of applicability of this technique is signature schemes which are generated from identification schemes (three passes identification scheme with commitment, challenge, and response) via Fiat-Shamir transformation where we can use a certain kind of decisional hard problem as the base to prove the security (soundness).

We apply our basic idea by using the *decisional version* of the isomorphism of polynomials as the basic hard problem. This decisional problem generally says that distinguishing between problem instances with solution (*legitimate* instance) and problem instances without solution (*non-legitimate* instance) is hard. We construct the identification scheme such that (1) the instance of decisional isomorphism of polynomials can be embedded on the public key and (2) only legitimate instances allow multiple accepting transcripts with multiple challenges for each commitment, while any non-legitimate instance only allow one accepting transcript per commitment. An adversary is expected to succeed when the instance used in public key is legitimate and is expected to fail when the instance used in public key is non-legitimate. Thus, without extracting any witness of the problem, we can use adversary as distinguisher. By this, we can bypass the issue of rewinding. The only left problem is how to do the "programming" of random oracle (for keeping consistency with the simulated signing oracle) in the presence of quantum adversary. Fortunately, this issue has been resolved by Dagdelen et al. [7] by estimating the probability of quantum adversary noticing the programming of random oracle.

Isomorphism of Polynomials in Brief. The problem of Isomorphism of Polynomials (IP) is a member of the family of computational problems in multivariate cryptography. It is described informally as follows. Let $\mathbf{F} = (f_1, \ldots, f_m)$ and $\mathbf{G} = (g_1, \ldots, g_m)$ be two sets of $m \geq 1$ non-linear polynomials in $\mathbb{K}[x_1, \ldots x_n]$, where $\mathbb{K}$ is a field. Precisely, the IP problem is a computational problem of finding any invertible mappings S and T such that $\mathbf{G} = T \circ \mathbf{F} \circ S$ holds. When T is restricted to be an identical mapping, the IP problem is called as Isomorphism of Polynomials with one secret (IP1S) and the general IP problem is often called as Isomorphism of Polynomials with two secrets (IP2S). Based on the most recent result in [5], it is estimated that a wide class of instances of IP2S problem for $m > 2$ is still hard in average case with complexity of $O(n^5 q^{n/2})$ with $m = n$. Since IP2S problem does not posses periodic structure like Factoring or Discrete Logarithm Problem which can be exploited by quantum algorithm for solving Factoring and Discrete Logarithm Problem, it is believed that IP2S still retain its hardness even against quantum computers. In this paper, we use the decisional version of IP2S problem, where given sets of non-linear polynomials $\mathbf{F}$ and $\mathbf{G}$, we are only required to output one bit indicating whether $\mathbf{F}$ and $\mathbf{G}$ is isomorphic or not.

Why our idea does not contradict the impossibility result of [7]. It is should be noted that our technique can be applied even to signature schemes generated from identification schemes via Fiat-Shamir transformation, where the commitment is independent from the witness. At first glance, this seems contradict to the impossibility result of Dagdelen et al. [7] which says that it is impossible to construct security proof (in the form of reduction algorithm) for such signature schemes. However, a more detailed look into the result of Dagdelen et al. [7] reveals that their work is *implicitly* assume that the reduction algorithm must *extract* the witness from the adversary. Our technique does not contradict their result since our reduction algorithm *does not* extract the witness from the adversary.

2   Preliminaries

Complexity related Notations. A non-negative function μ is called *negligible* if there exists a positive $\lambda \in \mathbb{N}$ such that for any $c > 0$, $\lambda' > \lambda$, $\mu(\lambda') < \lambda^{-c}$ holds. A non-negative function μ is called *non-negligible* if it is not negligible. Let $\lambda \in \mathbb{N}$ denote the general security parameter for the rest of this paper. Unless noted otherwise, in this paper, all polynomials are positive integer polynomials in λ. We say that a value x is polynomial if x is related to λ such that x can be represented by some polynomial in λ. A *classical* algorithm is an algorithm which proceeds just like the classical Turing Machine, and a *quantum* algorithm is an algorithm which proceeds just like the quantum Turing Machine. An algorithm (whether classical or quantum) is said to compute a task *efficiently* if it completes the task within polynomial time with non-negligible probability. A random selection of element x from a set $\mathbb{S}$ according to uniform distribution is denoted by $x \leftarrow_\$ \mathbb{S}$.

Algebraic Notations. We denote by $\mathbb{F}_q$, a finite field with q elements. Throughout this paper, we assume that we are always able to efficiently pick random element of $\mathbb{F}_q$. The general linear group consisting all non-singular square matrices of dimension n over finite field $\mathbb{F}_q$ is denoted by $GL_n(\mathbb{F}_q)$ and the group of all square matrices of dimension n over finite field $\mathbb{F}_q$ is denoted by $\mathcal{M}_n(\mathbb{F}_q)$.[1]

Definition 1 (IDENTIFICATION (ID) SCHEME). *An identification scheme ID is a tuple of algorithms* $(\mathsf{Setup}_{id}, \mathsf{KGen}_{id}, \mathsf{P}, \mathsf{V})$ *defined as follows.* Setup_{id} *is a setup parameter generator, which takes input security parameter* λ *and outputs setup parameter* **param**. KGen_{id} *is a key-generation algorithm which takes input setup parameter* **param**, *and outputs a public key and a secret key* $(\mathsf{pk}, \mathsf{sk})$. *A pair of algorithms* (P, V) *denotes an interactive protocol consisting of a prover* P *and a verifier* V, *where a common input is* (**param**, pk) *and an auxiliary input of* P *is* sk. *After interactions,* V *outputs a bit as a verification result to indicate whether it accepts* P *or not. A tuple of strings* tr' *is said to be an accepting transcript if there exist a communication transcript* tr *such that* $\mathsf{tr} = \mathsf{tr}'$ *from* (P, V) *where* V *accepts* P.

Definition 2 (SIGNATURE SCHEME). *A signature scheme is a tuple of algorithms* $(\mathsf{Setup}_{sig}, \mathsf{KGen}_{sig}, \mathsf{Sign}, \mathsf{SVer})$ *defined as follows.* Setup_{sig} *is a setup parameter generator, which takes input security parameter* λ *and input setup parameter* **param**. Setup_{sig} *is a key-generation algorithm which takes input setup parameter* **param**, *and outputs a public key and a secret key* $(\mathsf{pk}, \mathsf{sk})$. *The signing algorithm* Sign *takes input the secret key* sk *and message* m, *and generates the signature* σ. *The verification algorithm* SVer *takes input the public key* pk, *the message* m, *and the signature* σ *and returns a bit* $b \in \{0, 1\}$ *such that* $b = 1$ *if and only if* σ *is a valid signature of the message* m. *The basic requirement for a well-defined signature scheme is that for all message* m *and* $(\mathsf{pk}, \mathsf{sk})$ *generated by* Setup_{sig}, $\mathsf{SVer}(\mathsf{pk}, m, \mathsf{Sign}(\mathsf{sk}, m)) = 1$.

The following game is representing an attack scenario towards a signature scheme. The game is between an adversary A *and a challenger* $\mathcal{C}_{sig}$. *First,* $\mathcal{C}_{sig}$ *runs the* Setup_{sig} *and* KGen_{sig} *to obtain* (pk, sk). *Upon receiving* pk *as input from* $\mathcal{C}_{sig}$, A *is allowed to make queries to* $\mathcal{C}_{sig}$, *i.e., signature queries to obtain signature of some message and hash queries to obtain the hash value (in random oracle model). At the end,* A *outputs a message-signature pair of forgery candidate* (m, σ). *The challenger* $\mathcal{C}_{sig}$ *outputs* $b \in \{0, 1\}$ *such that* $b = 1$ *if and only if* A *never asked for a signature of* m *and* $\mathsf{SVer}(pk, m, \sigma) = 1$ *holds. The adversary* A *is said to* win *the game if* A *outputs* (m, σ) *such that* $\mathcal{C}_{sig}$ *outputs* $b = 1$. *We said that the signature scheme is* existentially unforgeable under chosen message attacks *(EUF-CMA) against classical (resp. quantum) adversaries if the probability of any classical (resp. quantum) adversary* A *to win the above game is negligible. In the case of* A *being a quantum adversary,* A *is allowed to send hash query in the form of superposition of quantum states.*[2]

---

[1] We will describe more detail about the quantum algorithm in the following sections.

[2] As same as in [3,7], regardless whether A is classical or quantum adversary, it is only allowed to send the signature queries in classical form (not superposition of quantum states).

Definition 3 (MULTIVARIATE QUADRATIC (MQ) FAMILY). *A Multivariate Quadratic (MQ) family, denoted by the notation $\mathcal{MQ}(n, m, \mathbb{F}_q)$, is a family of functions $\mathbf{F}(x)$, which is defined as follows.*

$$\mathbf{F}(x) = \left\{ (f_1(x), \ldots, f_m(x)) \middle| \begin{array}{l} f_k(x) = \sum_{i,j} a_{k,i,j} x_i x_j + \sum_i b_{k,i} x_i, \\ a_{k,i,j} . b_{k,i} \in \mathbb{F}_q \ for \ k \in [1, m] \end{array} \right\}, \quad (1)$$

where $x = (x_1, \ldots, x_n)$. For the simplicity, constant terms are omitted without any security loss. Any $\mathbf{F} \in \mathcal{MQ}(n, m, \mathbb{F}_q)$ is called an MQ function.

Definition 4 (Isomorphism of Polynomials with Two Secrets (IP2S) Problem). *An isomorphism of polynomials with two secrets (IP2S) problem related to $\mathcal{MQ}(n, m, \mathbb{F}_q)$ is defined as follows.*

Given: $\mathbf{F}, \mathbf{G} \leftarrow\!\!\$ \ \mathcal{MQ}(n, m, \mathbb{F}_q)$.
Output: $S \in GL_n(\mathbb{F}_q)$ and $T \in GL_m(\mathbb{F}_q)$ such that $\mathbf{G} = T \circ \mathbf{F} \circ S$ holds, or output $\perp$ if there are no such matrices S and T.

An algorithm is said to solve *IP2S problem related to $\mathcal{MQ}(n, m, \mathbb{F}_q)$ if it efficiently solves the above problem. An IP2S problem related to $\mathcal{MQ}(n, m, \mathbb{F}_q)$ is* classical-hard (resp. quantum-hard) *if there is no classical (resp. quantum) algorithm solves it efficiently.*

Remark 1. IP2S problem was initially described with S and T being invertible affine transforms [11,12]. Note that an invertible affine transform A can be represented by a pair of matrices (A_0, A_1) where A_0 is an invertible matrix, and $A(x) = A_0 x + A_1$. Faugère and Perret introduce IP2S in the form as described in Definition 4 as *Polynomial Linear Equivalence (PLE)* problem. In [4], it has been shown that PLE and IP2S are equivalent when IP2S is homogeneous, i.e., $\mathbf{F} \in \mathcal{MQ}(n, m, \mathbb{F}_q)$ such that for any $k \in [1, m]$, $i \in [1, n]$: $b_{k,i} = 0$. Unless noted otherwise, in order to simplify the argument on the security, for the rest of the paper, we assume that any $\mathbf{F} \in \mathcal{MQ}(n, m, \mathbb{F}_q)$ which is used to define IP2S and its variants is always *homogeneous*. We also assume that n, m, q are polynomial.

Remark 2. The IP2S is actually a special case of a more general problem called *Morphism of Polynomials (with two secrets)* (MP). MP problem is similar to IP2S, with differences on the domain of S and T, i.e., S and T can be taken from any affine mappings (including non-invertible maps, not only invertible ones). In [12], Patarin et al. have proven that MP is NP-hard by showing that one can polynomially reduce an NP-hard problem, the Tensor Rank problem, into MP. Although IP2S has been shown to be not NP-hard, the hardness of specific instances of IP2S[3] in average cases seems to be exponential, since the current best algorithm to solve it is with complexity of $O(n^5 2^{n/2})$ [5].

Definition 5. (Decisional Isomorphism of Polynomials with Two Secrets (DIP2S) Problem). *A decisional isomorphism of polynomials with two secrets (DIP2S) problem related to $\mathcal{MQ}(n, m, \mathbb{F}_q)$ is the decisional version of IP2S problem, which only requires one bit value for output.*

---

[3] When limited $\mathbf{F}$ to a certain class called *homogeneous* polynomials.

Given: F, G $\leftarrow^\$ \mathcal{MQ}(n, m, \mathbb{F}_q)$,
Output: $b \in \{0, 1\}$, *where* $b = 1$ *if there exist* $S \in GL_n(\mathbb{F}_q)$ *and* $T \in GL_m(\mathbb{F}_q)$ *such that* **G** $= T \circ$ **F** $\circ S$ *holds, and* $b = 0$ *if there are no such matrices.*

An algorithm is said to solve *DIP2S problem related to* $\mathcal{MQ}(n, m, \mathbb{F}_q)$ *if it solves the above problem efficiently. A DIP2S problem related to* $\mathcal{MQ}(n, m, \mathbb{F}_q)$ *is* classical-hard (resp. quantum-hard) *if there is no classical (resp. quantum) algorithm efficiently solves it.*

In this paper, we will use the model of quantum computation developed in [3, 7] with the same notations. Readers are advised to look into [3, 7] for a more detailed explanation on description and notations related to the quantum computation and quantum random oracle. Here we only describe several notations and concepts which we use directly in this paper.

Quantum Computation. A single quantum system Q is associated with a Hilbert space $\mathcal{H}$, where a quantum state in the system is represented as vector $|\varphi\rangle \in \mathcal{H}$ with Euclidean norm $\||\varphi\rangle\| = \sqrt{\langle\varphi|\varphi\rangle} = 1$, where $\langle\cdot|\cdot\rangle$ denotes the inner product. The joint or composite quantum state of two quantum systems Q_1 and Q_2 over Hilbert spaces $\mathcal{H}_1$ and $\mathcal{H}_2$, respectively, is represented through the tensor product $\mathcal{H}_1 \otimes \mathcal{H}_2$. The product quantum state of $|\varphi_1\rangle \in \mathcal{H}_1$ and $|\varphi_2\rangle \in \mathcal{H}_2$ is denoted by $|\varphi_1\rangle|\varphi_2\rangle = |\varphi_1\rangle \otimes |\varphi_2\rangle$ or simply $|\varphi_1, \varphi_2\rangle$. An n-qubit system is associated in the joint quantum system of n two-dimensional Hilbert spaces. W.l.o.g., unless noted otherwise, we always assume that any quantum state $|\varphi\rangle$ is pure and represented in orthonormal standard computational basis $|x\rangle = |x_1, \ldots, x_n\rangle$ for $x = x_1 \cdots x_n \in \{0, 1\}^n$, such that $|\varphi\rangle = \sum_{x \in \{0,1\}^n} \alpha_x |x\rangle$, where α_x are complex *amplitudes* satisfying $\sum_{x \in \{0,1\}^n} |\alpha_x|^2 = 1$.

We assume that a quantum algorithm is actually a sequence of transformation sequences, where each transformation sequence is composed out of a quantum operation on quantum systems for input, output, oracle calls, and work space (of sufficiently many qubits). A quantum operations on a quantum system is described by a unitary transformation. And to measure polynomial running time, we assume that each unitary transformation is approximated (to sufficient precision) by members of a set of universal quantum gates, where at most polynomially many gates are used. To simplify the discussion in this paper, we assume that a quantum algorithm will always use projective measurement when extracting information from the quantum states, although main results in this paper will still hold without this assumption. We recall the following lemma.

Lemma 1. *Let* $|\varphi\rangle = \sum_{x \in \{0,1\}^n} \alpha_x |x\rangle$ *be a quantum state. The probability that one obtains* $x \in \{0, 1\}^n$ *from the projective measurement of* $|\varphi\rangle$ *is* $|\alpha_x|^2$.

Quantum Random Oracle Model (QROM). The quantum random oracle $\mathcal{O}$ is associated with a random function H with a given domain and range. A quantum random oracle $\mathcal{O}$ can evaluate H on the input in superposition. Thus, one can evaluate the hash function in parallel for many inputs simultaneously by sending query to the quantum random oracle $\mathcal{O}$ in the form $\sum \alpha_x |x\rangle$, and then obtaining $\sum \alpha_x |H(x)\rangle$ as the answer. Here we state the following lemma which is the result of combining several lemmas in [7].

Lemma 2. *Let* A *be a quantum algorithm with oracle access to* $\mathcal{O}$ *and let* $|\varphi\rangle = \sum_{x \in \{0,1\}^n} \alpha_x |x\rangle$ *be a query to* $\mathcal{O}$ *such that there exists* $x \in \{0,1\}^n$ *with* $|\alpha_x|^2 \leq \varepsilon$. *If we modify* $\mathcal{O}$ *into oracle* $\mathcal{O}'$ *such that the answer to the query* $|\varphi\rangle$ *is modified the quantum state which corresponds to the oracle answer to* $|x\rangle$ *is sampled independently, then the statistical distance between the measurement of the answer from* $\mathcal{O}$ *and* $\mathcal{O}'$ *is at most* $4\sqrt{\varepsilon}$.

3   Signature Scheme Based on IP2S

In this section we show the construction of our proposed signature scheme. Basically our signature scheme is based on the parallel version of identification scheme proposed by Santoso [14] which is transformed into signature scheme via Fiat-Shamir transform.

3.1   Basic Identification Scheme

Setup Parameter Generator and Key Generator. The setup parameter generator $\mathsf{Setup}_{\mathrm{id}}$ takes input security parameter λ and generate a setup parameter **param** $= (n, m, q)$, where n, m, q are polynomials. The key generator $\mathsf{KGen}_{\mathrm{id}}$ selects randomly an MQ function $\mathbf{F} \in \mathcal{MQ}(n, m, \mathbb{F}_q)$, and two matrices $S \in GL_n(\mathbb{F}_q), T \in GL_m(\mathbb{F}_q)$. Then, $\mathsf{KGen}_{\mathrm{id}}$ computes another MQ function $\mathbf{G} = T \circ \mathbf{F} \circ S$. Finally, $\mathcal{K}_{\mathrm{gen}}$ sets the public key $\mathsf{pk} = (\mathbf{G}, \mathbf{F})$ and secret key $\mathsf{sk} = (T, S)$.

Interactive Protocol. Next we describe the interactive protocol (P, V) that enables any prover P to identify himself to a verifier V. A complete round of the interactive protocol of the proposed ID scheme is performed as follows.

Step 1 (Commitment). P picks randomly matrices $L_1, \ldots, L_\ell \in GL_m(\mathbb{F}_q)$ and $R_1, \ldots, R_\ell \in GL_n(\mathbb{F}_q)$, and sends the *commitment* $\mathbf{Y} = (\mathbf{Y}_1, \ldots, \mathbf{Y}_\ell)$ to verifier V, where for $i = [1, \ell]$, $\mathbf{Y}_i = L_i \circ \mathbf{G} \circ R_i$ holds.
Step 2 (Challenge). Upon receiving the commitment $\mathbf{Y}$ from prover P, verifier V picks randomly the *challenge* string $b = b_1 \cdots b_\ell \in \{0, 1\}^\ell$.
Step 3 (Response). Receiving the challenge string $b = b_1 \cdots b_\ell$ from verifier V, prover P performs the followings for each $i \in [1, \ell]$.
 – if $b_i = 0$, P sets $Z_{i,0} = L_i$ and $Z_{i,1} = R_i$,
 – if $b_i = 1$, P sets $Z_{i,0} = L_i T$ and $Z_{i,1} = SR_i$.
 – P sets $Z_i = (Z_{i,0}, Z_{i,1})$
 – P sends the *response* $Z = (Z_1, \ldots, Z_\ell)$ to verifier V.
Step 4 (Verification). Receiving the response $Z = (Z_1, \ldots, Z_\ell)$, where $Z_i = (Z_{i,0}, Z_{i,1}) \in \mathcal{M}_m(\mathbb{F}_q) \times \mathcal{M}_n(\mathbb{F}_q)$ from prover P, the verifier V performs the followings for each $i \in [1, \ell]$.

– Check whether $Z_{i,0} \in GL_m(\mathbb{F}_q)$, $Z_{i,1} \in GL_n(\mathbb{F}_q)$ holds,
– if $b_i = 0$, check whether $\mathbf{Y}_i = Z_{i,0} \circ \mathbf{G} \circ Z_{i,1}$ holds,
– if $b_i = 1$, check whether $\mathbf{Y}_i = Z_{i,0} \circ \mathbf{F} \circ Z_{i,1}$ holds.

Verifier V accepts P by outputting single bit '1' if the result of all checking described above give positive results. Otherwise, V rejects P by outputting single bit '0'.

The following theorem states that if we know the challenge chosen by the verifier before hand, we can simulate the responses of true prover and also the commitments of the prover. This property is well-known as *special honest verifier zero-knowledge* in literatures.

Theorem 1 (Special Honest Verifier Zero Knowledge). *There exists a polynomial time algorithm M such that on inputs $\mathbf{F}, \mathbf{G} \in \mathcal{MQ}(n, m, \mathbb{F}_q)$ where $\mathbf{G} = T \circ \mathbf{F} \circ S$ for some $(T, S) \in GL_m(\mathbb{F}_q) \times GL_n(\mathbb{F}_q)$, the algorithm M, given $b = b_1 \cdots b_\ell \in \{0,1\}^\ell$, outputs an accepting transcript $(\mathbf{Y}, b, Z)$ which is indistinguishable from the accepting transcript produced by a true interaction between an honest prover P and an honest verifier V with the same inputs $\mathbf{F}, \mathbf{G}$.*

Proof. We show the construction of the algorithm M. On inputs $\mathbf{F}, \mathbf{G} \in \mathcal{MQ}(n, m, \mathbb{F}_q)$, given $b = b_1 \cdots b_\ell \in \{0,1\}^\ell$, M proceeds follows.

Step 1. Choose randomly $Z = (Z_1, \ldots, Z_\ell)$ from $(GL_m(\mathbb{F}_q) \times GL_n(\mathbb{F}_q))^\ell$, where $Z_i = (Z_{i,0}, Z_{i,1}) \in GL_m(\mathbb{F}_q) \times GL_n(\mathbb{F}_q)$ for $i \in [1, \ell]$.
Step 2. Compute $\mathbf{Y} = (\mathbf{Y}_1, \ldots, \mathbf{Y}_\ell)$ such that for $i \in [1, \ell]$, $\mathbf{Y}_i = Z_{i,0} \circ \mathbf{G} \circ Z_{i,1}$ if $b_i = 0$ and $\mathbf{Y}_i = Z_{i,0} \circ \mathbf{F} \circ Z_{i,1}$ if $b_i = 1$.
Steo 3. Output $(\mathbf{Y}, b, Z)$.

Note that in a true interaction between a real prover P and a real honest verifier V, for $i \in [1, \ell]$, (L_i, R_i) is randomly chosen from $GL_m(\mathbb{F}_q) \times GL_n(\mathbb{F}_q)$ in the commitment step. Thus, for $i \in [1, \ell]$, (L_iT, SR_i) is also randomly distributed over $GL_m(\mathbb{F}_q) \times GL_n(\mathbb{F}_q)$, where (T, S) satisfies $\mathbf{G} = T \circ \mathbf{F} \circ S$. On the other hand, notice that in the procedure of M described above that $(Z_{i,0}, Z_{i,1})$ are randomly picked from $GL_m(\mathbb{F}_q) \times GL_n(\mathbb{F}_q)$. As a result, we can conclude that the distribution of $(Z_{i,0}, Z_{i,1})$ is the same as the distribution of (L_i, R_i) when $b_i = 0$ and (L_iT, SR_i) when $b_i = 1$, where (L_i, R_i) and/or (L_iT, SR_i) are produced by true interaction between P and V. By this, it is easy to see that the distribution of $\mathbf{Y}$ computed by M and $\mathbf{Y}$ produced by a real prover P in commitment step. This completes the proof of Theorem 1.   □

Theorem 2. *If the interactive protocol (P, V) is executed with $\mathrm{pk} = (\mathbf{F}, \mathbf{G})$ such that there is no pair $(T, S) \in GL_m(\mathbb{F}_q) \times GL_n(\mathbb{F}_q)$ satisfying $\mathbf{G} = T \circ \mathbf{F} \circ S$, then for each commitment $\mathbf{Y} \in (\mathcal{MQ}(n, m, \mathbb{F}_q))^\ell$, there only one possible $b \in \{0,1\}^\ell$, such that there exists $Z \in (GL_m(\mathbb{F}_q) \times GL_n(\mathbb{F}_q))^\ell$ where $(\mathbf{Y}, b, Z)$ is an accepting transcript.*

Proof. We prove the above theorem by contradiction. Suppose that we have two possible challenges, $b, b' \in \{0,1\}^\ell$, where $b \neq b'$, such that both $(\mathbf{Y}, b, Z)$ and

$(\mathbf{Y}, b', Z')$ are accepting transcripts. However it easy to see that from accepting transcripts $(\mathbf{Y}, b, Z)$ and $(\mathbf{Y}, b', Z')$, we can compute $(T, S) \in GL_m(\mathbb{F}_q) \times GL_n(\mathbb{F}_q)$ such that $\mathbf{G} = T \circ \mathbf{F} \circ S$ holds. This contradicts the assumption and thus completes the proof of above theorem.   □

From the above theorem, we can easily derive the following corollary.

Corollary 1. *If the interactive protocol* (P, V) *is executed with* $\mathsf{pk} = (\mathbf{F}, \mathbf{G})$ *such that there is no pair* $(T, S) \in GL_m(\mathbb{F}_q) \times GL_n(\mathbb{F}_q)$ *satisfying* $\mathbf{G} = T \circ \mathbf{F} \circ S$, *then there is no one is accepted by an honest verifier except with probability* $1/2^\ell$.

3.2   Construction of Signature Scheme

The construction of the signature scheme from the above identification scheme (Sect. 3.1) follows the standard Fiat-Shamir transform.

Parameter Setup and Key Generation: The setup parameter generator $\mathsf{Setup}_{\mathrm{sig}}$ and key generator $\mathsf{KGen}_{\mathrm{sig}}$ of signature scheme are the same as setup parameter generator $\mathsf{Setup}_{\mathrm{id}}$ and key generator $\mathsf{KGen}_{\mathrm{id}}$ from identification scheme respectively, i.e., $\mathsf{Setup}_{\mathrm{sig}} = \mathsf{Setup}_{\mathrm{id}}$, $\mathsf{KGen}_{\mathrm{sig}} = \mathsf{KGen}_{\mathrm{id}}$. Thus, here we have the public key $\mathsf{pk} = (\mathbf{G}, \mathbf{F})$ and secret key $\mathsf{sk} = (T, S)$ such that $\mathbf{G} = T \circ \mathbf{F} \circ S$.

Signing: Given input a message m, the signing algorithm computes $\mathbf{Y}_1, \ldots, \mathbf{Y}_\ell$ with the same method as the prover in the commitment step of identification scheme. Then it computes $b = b_1 \cdots b_\ell = H(m, \mathbf{Y}_1, \ldots, \mathbf{Y}_\ell)$ where $H : \{0,1\}^* \to \{0,1\}^\ell$ is a hash-function. Then it computes $(Z_1, \ldots, Z_\ell)$ in the same way the prover in the identification scheme does in the response step. It finally outputs $\sigma = (b, Z_1, \ldots, Z_\ell)$ as the signature of m.

Verification: Given input a message-signature pair (m, σ), where $\sigma = (b, Z_1, \ldots, Z_\ell)$, $Z_i = (Z_{i,0}, Z_{i,1})$ for $i \in [1, \ell]$, the verification algorithm computes $\mathbf{Y}_i = Z_{i,0} \circ \mathbf{G} \circ Z_{i,1}$ if $b_i = 0$ and $\mathbf{Y}_i = Z_{i,0} \circ \mathbf{F} \circ Z_{i,1}$ if $b_i = 1$ for $i \in [1, \ell]$. It outputs 1 (valid) if $b = H(m, \mathbf{Y}_1, \ldots, \mathbf{Y}_\ell)$ holds and $(Z_{i,0}, Z_{i,1}) \in GL_m(\mathbb{F}_q) \times GL_n(\mathbb{F}_q)$ holds for $i \in [1, \ell]$, and outputs 0 (invalid) otherwise.

3.3   Security of Signature Scheme

First, we will state the following theorem which represents the security of our signature scheme.

Theorem 3. *If DIP2S is quantum-hard then the signature scheme described in Sect. 3.2 is existential unforgeability under chosen message attacks against quantum adversaries.*

We will prove the Theorem 3 using contradiction. We show that a quantum adversary A who wins the game associated to existential unforgeability under chosen message attacks with non-negligible probability can be used to solve the Decisional IP2S problem with non-negligible probability.

Proof (Outline). Here we describe the outline of the proof. At the heart of the proof is an algorithm B which is given access to the quantum adversary A. The procedure of B is described as follows.

- Given $\mathbf{F}, \mathbf{G} \in \mathcal{MQ}(n, m, \mathbb{F}_q)$ as inputs, B simulates the key generation algorithm of the signature scheme ($\mathsf{Setup}_{\mathrm{sig}}$) by forwarding $\mathbf{F}, \mathbf{G}$ as public keys to the adversary A.
- In order to answer a signature query on a message m, B randomly chooses $b \in \{0, 1\}^\ell$, and then uses the simulator in the special honest verifier zero-knowledge proof to construct $(\mathbf{Y}, Z)$ which satisfies the condition to pass the verification at identification scheme. B returns $\sigma = (b, \mathbf{Y})$ as the signature of m. Also, B modifies (programs) the random oracle at point $(m, \mathbf{Y})$ with b such that any query to random oracle afterwards will always be consistent with this value.
- Assuming that A can not: (1) distinguish between the signatures constructed by B and those from true signer, and (2) detect the programming of random oracle done by B, A will output the forgery: with <u>non-negligible probability</u> if $\mathbf{F}$ and $\mathbf{G}$ are *isomorphic*, and with <u>probability $1/2^\ell$</u> if $\mathbf{F}$ and $\mathbf{G}$ are *not isomorphic*.[4]
- Algorithm B outputs 1 if A outputs forgery, and outputs 0 if A does not output forgery,

Since the distribution of the outputs of B depends on whether $\mathbf{F}$ and $\mathbf{G}$ are isomorphic, it is easy to see that we can directly use B to distinguish between the case when there exists $(T, S) \in GL_m(\mathbb{F}_q) \times GL_n(\mathbb{F}_q)$ such that $\mathbf{G} = T \circ \mathbf{F} \circ S$ and the case when there no such $(T, S) \in GL_m(\mathbb{F}_q) \times GL_n(\mathbb{F}_q)$ exists, and then to solve the Decisional IP2S problem.

A quick look in to the above construction reveals that the critical issue which determines whether B will work as expected is the probability that A notices the simulation of signer and the programming of random oracle. If we can guarantee that this probability is negligible, then B is guaranteed to work as expected, and we can use B to solve Decisional IP2S problem. By borrowing the special honest verifier zero-knowledge property of the underlying identification scheme and the lemmas about the maximum statistical distance between two programmed random oracle model, we prove that the probability that A is able to notice simulation of signer and the programming of random oracle is negligible. This completes the outline of the proof.   □

Remark 3. One can see a similarity between the line of our security proof and the security proof of signature schemes from lossy identification schemes shown in [1]. However, in this paper, the success probability of the adversary A constructing a forgery when $\mathbf{F}$ and $\mathbf{G}$ are not isomorphic can not be derived by the same method as in [1]. The technique used in [1] requires the rewinding of A, but we can not rewind A here since we assume that A is a quantum adversary. Hence,

---

[4] By adapting Theorem 2 and Corollary 1, we can see that this clearly holds. See Remark 3 for a more detailed explanation.

actually here we adapt Theorem 2 into the signature scheme, and use the fact that for each valid $\mathbf{Y}$ in the signing process, there is only one valid sequence $b \in \{0,1\}^{\ell}$ which can lead to a valid signature, where $b = H(m, \mathbf{Y})$, in the case when $\mathbf{F}$ and $\mathbf{G}$ is not isomorphic. And since the output H is supposed to be completely random in random oracle model, it is easy to see that the probability that the valid sequence matches with the output of random oracle is no more than $1/2^{\ell}$.

Next, we show that the probability that A is able to notice simulation of signer and the programming of random oracle is negligible.

Claim 1. Assume that A does not notice the programming of random oracle by B. If the identification scheme associated with the signature scheme described in Sect. 3.2 satisfies special honest verifier zero-knowledge, then the probability that A can distinguish between the signatures from B and ones from true signer is negligible.

Proof. Since the signature produced by B is created by the simulator of the special honest verifier zero-knowledge, then the statement that A can distinguish those signatures with the ones from true signer with non-negligible probability will automatically contradict the existence of simulator which proves that underlying identification scheme satisfies special honest verifier zero-knowledge.

What remains now is to show that the probability that A can notice the programming of the random oracle is negligible. Now let us look into the interaction between A and random oracle in more detail. Let assume that adversary A sends a signing query m and B proceeds to modify one basis (or state) which represents the answer to random oracle query $(m, \mathbf{Y})$ within the quantum state $|\varphi\rangle$, where $|\varphi\rangle$ is the answer from the random oracle, and $\mathbf{Y}$ is the randomness in the signature of m, as describe in Sect. 3.2.

This modification will be noticed by A if A has ever evaluated $H(m, \mathbf{Y})$ before hand. According to the definition of quantum random oracle in Sect. 2, the probability of evaluating $H(m, \mathbf{Y})$ is the same as the probability to get $x' = (m, \mathbf{Y})$ from the measurement of a quantum query $|\varphi\rangle$. Thus, the probability that A has ever evaluated $H(m, \mathbf{Y})$ before hand depends on the magnitude of $|\alpha_{x'}|$ in each query to random oracle. Let q_H be the maximum number of queries to random oracle and q_S be the maximum number of queries to signing oracle. The probability that $|\alpha_{x'}|^2 > 2^{-\gamma n}$ in any of q_H queries to random oracle is at most $q_H 2^{-(1-\gamma)n}$.

We still need to find the upper bound that A notice the programming from the distribution difference of measurements of the answers from the random oracle and signing oracle when $|\alpha_{x'}|^2 \leq 2^{-\gamma n}$ in any queries. From Lemma 2, we can see that the statistical distance between the measurement of an answer from unmodified and an answer modified oracles corresponding to the same x' is upper bounded by $4\sqrt{2^{-(1-\gamma)n}}$. Since we have a total $(q_H + q_S)$ queries, the total probability that A notices the modification is upper bounded by $q_H 2^{-(1-\gamma)n} + 4(q_H + q_S)\sqrt{2^{-(1-\gamma)n}}$. Taking $\gamma = 1/2$, this value becomes negligible, and thus completes our argument that the probability that A is able to notice simulation of signer and the programming of random oracle is negligible. This completes the proof of the above claim. □

4   Conclusion

We have shown the first concrete construction of a signature scheme via Fiat-Shamir transform based on Isomorphism of Polynomials and proven its security under existential forgery attack by quantum adversaries. Inside the security proof, we used programmable random oracle and allowed quantum adversaries to send queries to and receive answers from random oracle in superposition of quantum bits in order to capture the ability of quantum adversaries to perform hash calculation with superpositioned quantum bits. We provided the upper bound of the probability that a quantum adversary notices the programming of the random oracle and the simulation of the signature oracle. We successfully avoided the rewinding of the quantum adversary and the extraction of witness by using the decisional version of the underlying hard problem, i.e., Isomorphism of Polynomials with Two Secrets (IP2S) in the same manner as Abdalla et al. [1].

We believed that our security proof technique can be extended to other post-quantum signature schemes which are constructed via Fiat-Shamir transform. We plan to investigate the applicability of our technique to other schemes and then construct an abstraction of our security proof technique in the similar manner to Abdalla et al. [1].

References

1. Abdalla, M., Fouque, P.A., Lyubashevsky, V., Tibouchi, M.: Tightly secure signatures from lossy identification schemes. J. Cryptol. **29**(3), 597–631 (2016)
2. Ambainis, A., Rosmanis, A., Unruh, D.: Quantum attacks on classical proof systems: The hardness of quantum rewinding. In: FOCS, pp. 474–483. IEEE Computer Society (2014)
3. Boneh, D., Dagdelen, Ö., Fischlin, M., Lehmann, A., Schaffner, C., Zhandry, M.: Random oracles in a quantum world. In: Lee, D.H., Wang, X. (eds.) ASIACRYPT 2011. LNCS, vol. 7073, pp. 41–69. Springer, Heidelberg (2011). doi:10.1007/978-3-642-25385-0_3
4. Bouillaguet, C., Faugre, J.C., Fouque, P.A., Perret, L.: Isomorphism of polynomials: New results (2010–2012). http://citeseerx.ist.psu.edu/viewdoc/summary?doi=10.1.1.156.9570
5. Bouillaguet, C., Fouque, P.-A., Véber, A.: Graph-theoretic algorithms for the "Isomorphism of Polynomials" problem. In: Johansson, T., Nguyen, P.Q. (eds.) EUROCRYPT 2013. LNCS, vol. 7881, pp. 211–227. Springer, Heidelberg (2013). doi:10.1007/978-3-642-38348-9_13
6. Cayrel, P.-L., Véron, P., El Yousfi Alaoui, S.M.: A zero-knowledge identification scheme based on the q-ary syndrome decoding problem. In: Biryukov, A., Gong, G., Stinson, D.R. (eds.) SAC 2010. LNCS, vol. 6544, pp. 171–186. Springer, Heidelberg (2011). doi:10.1007/978-3-642-19574-7_12

7. Dagdelen, Ö., Fischlin, M., Gagliardoni, T.: The fiat–shamir transformation in a quantum world. In: Sako, K., Sarkar, P. (eds.) ASIACRYPT 2013. LNCS, vol. 8270, pp. 62–81. Springer, Heidelberg (2013). doi:10.1007/978-3-642-42045-0_4

8. Fischlin, M.: Communication-efficient non-interactive proofs of knowledge with online extractors. In: Shoup, V. (ed.) CRYPTO 2005. LNCS, vol. 3621, pp. 152–168. Springer, Heidelberg (2005). doi:10.1007/11535218_10

9. Goh, E.J., Jarecki, S., Katz, J., Wang, N.: Efficient signature schemes with tight reductions to the diffie-hellman problems. J. Cryptol. **20**(4), 493–514 (2007)

10. Lyubashevsky, V.: Fiat-shamir with aborts: applications to lattice and factoring-based signatures. In: Matsui, M. (ed.) ASIACRYPT 2009. LNCS, vol. 5912, pp. 598–616. Springer, Heidelberg (2009). doi:10.1007/978-3-642-10366-7_35

11. Patarin, J.: Hidden Fields Equations (HFE) and Isomorphisms of Polynomials (IP): two new families of asymmetric algorithms. In: Maurer, U. (ed.) EURO-CRYPT 1996. LNCS, vol. 1070, pp. 33–48. Springer, Heidelberg (1996). doi:10.1007/3-540-68339-9_4

12. Patarin, J., Goubin, L., Courtois, N.: Improved algorithms for isomorphisms of polynomials. In: Nyberg, K. (ed.) EUROCRYPT 1998. LNCS, vol. 1403, pp. 184–200. Springer, Heidelberg (1998). doi:10.1007/BFb0054126

13. Sakumoto, K., Shirai, T., Hiwatari, H.: Public-key identification schemes based on multivariate quadratic polynomials. In: Rogaway, P. (ed.) CRYPTO 2011. LNCS, vol. 6841, pp. 706–723. Springer, Heidelberg (2011). doi:10.1007/978-3-642-22792-9_40

14. Santoso, B.: Refining identification scheme based on isomorphism of polynomials with two secrets: A new theoretical and practical analysis. In: Proceedings of the 3rd ACM International Workshop on ASIA Public-Key Cryptography, AsiaPKC 2016, New York, NY, USA, pp. 31–38. ACM (2016)

15. Wootters, W.K., Zurek, W.H.: A single quantum cannot be cloned. Nature **299**, 802 (1982)

Bootstrapping Fully Homomorphic Encryption with Ring Plaintexts Within Polynomial Noise

Long Chen[1,2] and Zhenfeng Zhang[1,2(✉)]

[1] Trusted Computing and Information Assurance Laboratory, Institute of Software, Chinese Academy of Sciences, Beijing, China
{chenlong,zfzhang}@tca.iscas.ac.cn
[2] University of Chinese Academy of Sciences, Beijing, China

Abstract. Despite a great deal of progress in resent years, efficiency of fully homomorphic encryption (FHE) is still a major concern. Specifically, the bootstrapping procedure is the most costly part of a FHE scheme. FHE schemes with ring element plaintexts, such as the ring-LWE based BGV scheme, are the most efficient ones, since they can not only encrypt a ring element instead of a single bit in one ciphertext, but also support CRT-based ciphertext packing techniques. Thanks to homomorphic operations in a SIMD fashion (Single Instruction Multiple Data), the ring-LWE BGV scheme can achieve a nearly optimal homomorphic evaluation. However, the BGV scheme, as implemented in HElib, can only bootstrap within super-polynomial noise so far. Note that such a noise rate for a ring-LWE based scheme is less safe and more costly, because one has to choose larger dimensions to ensure security. On the other hand, existing polynomial noise bootstrapping techniques can only be applied to FHE schemes with bit plaintexts. In this paper, we provide a polynomial noise bootstrapping method for the BGV scheme with ring plaintexts. Specifically, our bootstrapping method allows users to choose any plaintext modulus $p > 1$ and any modulus polynomial $\Phi(X)$ for the BGV scheme. Our bootstrapping method incurs only polynomial error $O(n^3) \cdot B$ for lattice dimension n and noise bound B comparing to $(B \cdot poly(n))^{\tilde{O}(\log(n))}$ for previous best methods. Concretely, to achieve 70 bit security, the dimension of the lattice that we use is no more than 2^{12}, while previous methods in HElib need about 2^{14} to 2^{16}.

Keywords: Fully homomorphic encryption · Bootstrap · Ring plaintext

1 Introduction

Fully homomorphic encryption (FHE) is a holy grail of cryptography. FHE [25] supports arbitrarily computation on encrypted data, even by parties that do not have the secret decryption key. In recent years, many FHE schemes have been proposed based on various assumptions such as ideal lattice (or ring-LWE) [9,25,28,40], GACD [14,17,18,42], and standard-LWE [5,7,8,30]. Most of homomorphic encryption schemes introduce "noise" in the ciphertexts, and the "noise"

© Springer International Publishing AG 2017
T. Okamoto et al. (Eds.): ProvSec 2017, LNCS 10592, pp. 285–304, 2017.
https://doi.org/10.1007/978-3-319-68637-0_18

accumulates during the homomorphic operations. To address this problem, Gentry [25] proposed a bootstrapping technique to convert a somewhat homomorphic encryption (SWHE) scheme to a FHE scheme. Generally, a bootstrapping technique is using an encrypted secret key to decrypt ciphertexts homomorphically. The bootstrapping procedure is computationally very expensive, and influences both of the efficiency and security of a FHE scheme.

Currently, the ring-LWE based BGV scheme, proposed by Brakerski, Gentry and Vaikuntanathan [7], is one of the most efficient SWHE schemes. Since it can encrypt a ring element instead of a single bit in one ciphertext, the ring-LWE based BGV scheme has advantages in aspects of the ciphertext/plaintext ratio and the complexity of homomorphic operations comparing with another widely studied standard assumptions based SWHE scheme named the GSW scheme [30]. More importantly, the ring-LWE based BGV scheme naturally supports a ciphertext-packing technique based on polynomial-CRT (Chinese Remainder Theorem) [41], which allows packing a number of plaintext elements into independent "slots" in the plaintext space and performing SIMD style (Single Instruction Multiple Data) operations. By this technique, Gentry et al. [28] showed the batched BGV scheme[1] can achieve a nearly optimal homomorphic evaluation (up to poly-logarithmic factors). Due to its efficiency, the batched BGV scheme has been reported to be open source implemented by [19, 29, 31, 32]. Other FHE schemes which support the ciphertext-packing technique based on CRT include [14, 21], but the hardness assumptions of these schemes, unlike the commonly used learning with errors (LWE) assumption [39] or its ring-based analogue [35], are not currently supported by a worst-case hardness theorem. Besides, two other packed ciphertexts techniques have been proposed [6, 33] so far, both of which are based on kinds of matrix operation skills rather than the algebra structure for the rings. However, these two batched SWHE schemes [6, 33] can not compare with the batched BGV scheme in aspects of the ciphertext expansion rate, the complexity for homomorphic operations and the overhead. In short, the ring-LWE based BGV scheme is one of the most practical candidates for SWHE considering security and efficiency.

Several bootstrapping techniques have been proposed for the ring-LWE based BGV scheme, such as [3, 27, 32, 37], but none of them can incur polynomial noise in the security parameter λ. Specifically, in [27], Gentry et al. provide a better bootstrapping technique for special choice $q = p^t \pm a$ for some t and a small value of a. Following their work, Alperin-Sheriff and Peikert [3] uses the ring/field switching technique [26] to improve the above bootstrapping procedure to be performed in quasilinear time. This method is implemented in [32], with efficient runtime, for the case of characteristic-p plaintext spaces with $p > 2$. Generally, the bootstrap procedure of [27] need homomorphically extract certain bits(digits) of the plaintexts. The homomorphic (non-linear) bit(digit)-extraction procedure is recursively computed by each bit(digit), so the calculation circuit at least has

---

[1] We notice that in the original paper of the BGV FHE scheme (also, the GSW FHE scheme later on), the authors did provide methods for bootstrapping their SWHE scheme. For convenience, in this paper we call the BGV scheme (GSW scheme) when we refer to the SWHE scheme in their original paper.

$O(\log q)$ levels. Then the noise/modulus rate grows at least $n^{O(\log n)}$ times for the whole bootstrapping procedure, where n is the dimension of the lattice. These bootstrapping methods can reduce the required approximation factor of underlying hard problem to $n^{O(\log n)}$. Very recently, Albrecht [1] shows the actual conceret security of LWE instances used in HElib is far more less than what they are originally promised. Another work for bootstrapping BGV ciphertexts belongs to Orsini, van de Pol and Smart [37]. Their technique takes advantage of a representation of the group $\mathbb{Z}_q^+$ over the finite field $\mathbb{F}_p$, followed by polynomial interpolation of the reduction $\mod p$ map over the coefficients of the algebraic group. The depth of the circuit that they need is $O(\log n)$. Asymmetrically, the required approximation factor of underlying hard problem is also $n^{O(\log n)}$. Generally, since the noises for the BGV ciphertexts grow quadratically ($B \to B^2 \cdot poly(n)$) with every multiplication (before "refreshing"), the noise accumulation for bootstrapping can not be polynomial when the decryption circuits have polynomial multiplication levels.

Different with the above bootstrapping methods for the batched BGV scheme, [4,10] present bootstrapping techniques for the GSW scheme [30] proposed by Gentry, Sahai and Waters, whose runtime and associated approximation factor are both small polynomials. Following their ideas, Ducas and Micciancio [22] provides a bootstrapping method and associated implementation that allow to perform the entire computation in less than a second, which is optimized by [15,16] recently. The main technique of their approaches [4,10,15,22] is that the decryption circuit is evaluated by the GSW scheme, the noise growth in the homomorphic multiplication operation of which is asymmetric and "quasi-additive" [30]. However, different with packed ciphertexts FHE schemes, the above schemes [4,15,22,30] only encrypt bits as plaintexts, so the overhead of evaluating bounded circuits is at least $O(\lambda)$. Based on this reason, the batched BGV scheme [32] still has much better amortized per-bit timing.

Why Bootstrapping with Polynomial Noise is Important? The primarily concern is the security. It is widely believed [38] that the hardness of the LWE problem (and the ring LWE problem as well) depends on the largest-ratio between the modulus and the noise bound. The less noise accumulates during the bootstrapping, the smaller the largest-ratio could be. According to the experimental results given by Chen and Nguyen [13], the underlying lattice problems with such approximation factors need very large dimensions to make sure enough security, even if they are still hard. Secondarily, the polynomial noise accumulation makes it possible to use a much smaller dimension lattice to achieve the same security level. Therefore, the efficiency of the whole scheme can be improved.

1.1 Our Contributions

In this paper, we provide an efficient bootstrapping method for the ring LWE based batched BGV scheme in [28] with polynomial noise accumulation. Specifically, we bootstrap the packed BGV ciphertexts within only $\tilde{O}(n^2 \cdot q_0)$ times noise in the refresh key, in dimension n and the level-0 modulus $q_0 = \Theta(n)$, orders better than the existing best result for the BGV scheme in HElib [32]. As a consequence, the approximation factor of the underlying lattice problems is $\tilde{O}(n^{6.5})$ respectively, if we allow one homomorphic multiplication before bootstrapping and choose reasonable parameters. Concretely, to achieve 70 bit security, the dimension of the lattices that we use are no more than 2^{12}, while previous methods in HElib need about 2^{14} to 2^{16}.

Furthermore, our recryption procedure cost $\tilde{O}(n^2)$ homomorphic operations for $\Theta(n)$ bits. So the computation complexity for bootstrapping is $\tilde{O}(n^3)$. Additionally, our SWHE scheme can evaluate a $O(\log n)$ levels circuit before bootstrapping for proper parameters. Therefore, the SWHE scheme can evaluate at most $O(n^3)$ gates without bootstrapping. We show that for particular parameters, our FHE scheme can achieve *polylog* overhead for per gate in some optimal cases.

Our bootstrapping method allow users to choose any integer $p > 1$ as the plaintext modulus. Moreover, one is allowed to choose any cyclotomic polynomial $\Phi(X)$ (with large enough degree) as the modulus polynomial, and not restricted to the popular power-of-two cyclotomic polynomials $X^{2^k} + 1$. There are several reasons to consider arbitrary cyclotomic rings besides power-of-two ones. The most obvious, practical reason is that powers of two are sparsely distributed, and the desired concrete security level for an application may call for a ring dimension much smaller than the next-largest power of two. So restricting to powers of two could lead to key sizes and runtimes that are at least twice as large as necessary. A more fundamental reason is to implement SIMD operations on "packed" ciphertexts, the cyclotomics should have requisite algebraic properties. For example, in homomorphic evaluation of AES [29], plaintext slots need to hold elements of F_{2^8}. A final important reason is diversification of security assumptions, since a series of works [11,12,23,24] show that certain choices of rings lead to weak instances of the ring-LWE problem.

1.2 Main Techniques

Our main idea is to evaluate the decryption circuit of the ring LWE based BGV scheme with GSW scheme, since the GSW scheme has a quasi-additive noise accumulation. But unfortunately, the ring-LWE based GSW scheme in [30] *can only encrypts a single bit as plaintext*. The reason is that the noise term in the multiplication of GSW ciphertexts $\mathbf{C}_{mult} := \mathbf{C}_1 \odot \mathbf{C}_2$ is $\mathbf{e}_{mult} := \bar{\mathbf{C}}_1 \mathbf{e}_2 + \mu_2 \mathbf{e}_1$, where μ_1, μ_2 are the corresponding plaintexts, $\bar{\mathbf{C}}_1$ is a matrix with small coefficients and $\Phi[X]$ is a cyclotomic polynomial. The canonical embedding norm $\|\mu_2 \mathbf{e}_1\|_\infty^{can}$ can be as large as $\|\mu_2\|_1 \cdot \|\mathbf{e}_1\|_\infty^{can}$.

Obviously, directly applying existing bootstrapping methods will not work, since the GSW scheme can not support the general homomorphic multiplication gate for ring elements. Fortunately, we observe that the GSW scheme with ring plaintexts can homomorphically evaluate *the quasi-boolean AND gate*. The two inputs of a quasi-boolean AND gate are restricted to $a, b \in \{0, 1\} \subseteq R_p$ and the output is $a \cdot b \in \{0, 1\} \subseteq R_p$, where $\cdot$ is just the multiplication in R_p. In fact, if the plaintext belongs to $\{0, 1\} \subseteq R_p$, the "quasi-additive" noise growth property for ring GSW can still apply.

A greater obstacle is to efficiently express the decryption function of the BGV scheme as a circuit with R_p-addition gates, R_p-scale multiplication gates and quasi-boolean AND gates. This task is more difficult than that in [4], since the decryption function for the ring LWE based BGV scheme need to compute polynomial arithmetic modulo $\Phi_m(X)$. Unlike the special case where the order m of the cyclotomic is a power of two, in general the cyclotomic polynomial $\Phi_m(X)$ can be quite "irregular" and dense, with large coefficients. For example, $\Phi_{3 \cdot 5 \cdot 7 \cdot 11 \cdot 13}[X]$ has coefficients up to ± 552. Therefore, the generic algorithms for modular operation are rather complex and hard to implement. To deal with this problem, we invent a subroutine named *degree decomposition*. Using this subroutine and bit decomposition, we convert the decryption function of BGV scheme to $Dec\,(\mathbf{c}, \mathbf{s}) = \sum_{i \text{ s.t. } \bar{c}_i = 1} \bar{s}_i \mod q \mod p$, where $\bar{c}_i \in \{0, 1\}$ are bits derived from the ciphertext $\mathbf{c}$, and $\bar{s}_i \in R_q = \mathbb{Z}_q / \Phi_m(X)$ are ring elements derived from the secret key $\mathbf{s}$. Then for decryption, we just need to compute addition of polynomials $\bar{s}_i$. For bootstrapping, the evaluation key is encryptions of each coefficient of $\bar{s}_i$. Consequently, we just have to compute the homomorphic modular$-q$ addition and successfully avoid to evaluate polynomial modulo $\Phi_m(X)$.

Note that the bootstrapping methods in [15, 22] need to use power-of-two cyclotomic polynomials and do not fit the batched BGV scheme. So our bootstrapping method is inspired by [4]. The detailed analysis of the homomorphic evaluation of these three type gates by the ring GSW scheme with ring elements is provided in Sect. 3. The description of our decryption circuit and the bootstrapping procedure is in Sect. 4.

1.3 Related Works

Despite the previously introduced related works, we also notice that [33] provides a packed ciphertexts variant of LWE based GSW scheme and an optimized bootstrapping prodecue. In fact, the noise/modulus rate grows $O(\sqrt{n}\lambda)$ times for their bootstrapping procedure, where n is the dimension of the lattice and the security parameter is λ. So the approximate factor for the underlying lattice problem is $O(n^{1.5}\lambda)$.

However, the LWE based batched GSW SWHE scheme can not match the ring-LWE based batched BGV SWHE scheme in efficiency, because the ciphertext expansion of the batched GSW scheme is $\tilde{O}(n^2 \log q)$ and the computation cost for one homomorphic multiplication is larger than $\tilde{O}(n^{2.3})$. Furthermore, the security of the public key SWHE scheme in [33] requires the circular security with respect to some particular functions, which is different with all previous SWHE constructions.

2   Preliminaries

In this paper, we use bold lower case letters to denote vectors and bold upper case letters to denote matrices. $\phi(\cdot)$ denote the Euler's function. For matrix

$\mathbf{A}$, we use $\mathbf{A}_{(i)}$ to denote the ith column vector of $\mathbf{A}$, and $\mathbf{A}_{(i,j)}$ to denote the ith column jth row entry of $\mathbf{A}$. For vector $\mathbf{a}$, $\mathbf{a}_{(i)}$ denotes the ith entry of $\mathbf{a}$. All vectors are expressed as columns. For a n-degree polynomial a, we write $a = a^{(0)} + a^{(1)}X + a^{(2)}X^2 + \ldots + a^{(n-1)}X^{n-1}$, where $a^{(j)}$ denote the each coefficient. $\|\cdot\|_\infty$ denotes l_∞ norm and $\|\cdot\|_1$ denotes l_1 norm. Define the canonical embedding norm $\|a\|_\infty^{can} = \|\sigma(a)\|_\infty, a \in R$, where σ is the canonical embedding. Particularly,

$$\|a\|_\infty \le c_m \cdot \|a\|_\infty^{can}, \tag{1}$$

where c_m is the ring constant. For canonical embedding norm, see [20] for details.

2.1 Ring-LWE

We now recall the ring-LWE probability distribution and (decisional) computational problem. Let K be the mth cyclotomic number field having dimension $n = \phi(m)$ and $R = \mathcal{O}_K$ be its ring of integers which embeds as a lattice. $R^\vee \subset K$ is the dual fractional ideal of R. See [35,36] for a more general form.

Definition 1 *(ring-LWE)[35,36]. For an $s \in R_q^\vee$ and a distribution χ over the field tensor product $K_\mathbb{R} = K \otimes_\mathbb{Q} \mathbb{R}$, a sample from the ring-LWE distribution $A_{s,\chi}$ over $R_q \times K_\mathbb{R}/qR^\vee$ is generated by choosing $a \leftarrow R_q$ uniformly at random, choosing $e \leftarrow \chi$, and outputting $(a, b = a \cdot s + e)$.*

The decision version of the ring-LWE problem, denoted R-DLWE$_{q,\chi}$, is to distinguish with non-negligible advantage between independent samples from $A_{s,\chi}$, where s is uniformly chosen from $R_q^\vee$ once and for all, and the same number of uniformly random and independent samples from $R_q \times K_\mathbb{R}/qR^\vee$.

On the computational complexity, the theorem below capture reductions from ideal lattice GapSVP (GapSIVP) to ring-LWE for certain parameters. We state the result in terms of (l_∞ norm) B-bounded distributions.

Definition 2 (B-bounded distribution). *A distribution ensemble $\{\chi_n\}_{n \in \mathbb{N}}$, supported over $K_\mathbb{R}$, is called (l_∞ norm) B-bounded if*

$$\Pr_{e \leftarrow \chi_n}[\|e\|_\infty > B] = negl(n).$$

Theorem 1 [35,36]. *Let R be the mth cyclotomic ring, having dimension $n = \phi(m)$. Let $q = q(n)$, $q = 1 \bmod m$ be a $poly(n)-$bounded integer, and $B = \omega(\sqrt{n \log n})$. There is a $poly(n)-$time quantum reduction from $n^{\omega(1)}q/B$-approximate SIVP (or SVP) on ideal lattices in R to solving R-DLWE$_{q,\chi}$ where χ is a distribution bounded by B with overwhelming probability.*

2.2 Useful Subroutines

Let $R = \mathbb{Z}[X]/f(X)$, where $f(X)$ is a t-degree polynomial, and $R_q = R/qR$. We define two subroutines called DegDecomp and PowerofDeg as follows. For $\mathbf{u} = (u_1, u_2, \ldots, u_d) \in R_q^d$ and $\mathbf{v} = (v_1, v_2, \ldots, v_d) \in R_q^d$,

$$\mathsf{DegDecomp}(\mathbf{u}) = \left(u_1^{(0)}, u_1^{(1)}, \ldots, u_1^{(t-1)}, \ldots, u_d^{(0)}, u_d^{(1)}, \ldots, u_d^{(t-1)} \right) \in \mathbb{Z}_q^{dt}$$

$$\text{PowerofDeg}(\mathbf{v}) = (v_1, v_1 X \bmod f(X), \ldots, v_1 X^{t-1} \bmod f(X),$$
$$\ldots, v_d, v_d X \bmod f(X), \ldots, v_d X^{t-1} \bmod f(X)) \in R_q^{dt}.$$

Obviously, $\langle \text{DegDecomp}(\mathbf{u}), \text{PowerofDeg}(\mathbf{v}) \rangle \bmod q = \langle \mathbf{u}, \mathbf{v} \rangle \bmod f(X) \bmod q$. Interestingly, to compute the left inner product, one do not need modulo polynomial $f(X)$ operation.

The bit decomposition technique is first introduced in [8] and widely used in most of FHE schemes. We describe these subroutines as follows.

- BitDecomp($\mathbf{v} \in R_q^d$): Decompose each coefficient of $\mathbf{v}$ into its bit representation. Namely, write $\mathbf{v} = \sum_{j=0}^{\lfloor \log q \rfloor} 2^j \cdot \mathbf{u}_j$ with all $\mathbf{u}_j \in R_2^d$, and output $(\mathbf{u}_0, \mathbf{u}_1, \ldots, \mathbf{u}_{\lceil \log q \rceil - 1}) \in R_2^{d \cdot \lceil \log q \rceil}$.
- Powersof2($\mathbf{v} \in R_q^d$): Let

$$\mathbf{w}_j = 2^j \mathbf{v} \ (\bmod q, f(x)) \in R_q^d, \, j = 0, \ldots, \lceil \log q \rceil$$

and output $(\mathbf{w}_0, \mathbf{w}_1, \ldots, \mathbf{w}_{\lfloor \log q \rfloor - 1}) \in R_q^{d \cdot \lceil \log q \rceil}$.

Obviously, $\langle \text{BitDecomp}(\mathbf{u}), \text{Powerof2}(\mathbf{v}) \rangle = \langle \mathbf{u}, \mathbf{v} \rangle$.

2.3 Symmetric Group and $\mathbb{Z}_q$-Embedding

Let S_r denote the symmetric group of order r, which can be represented by the multiplicative group r-by-r permutation matrices $P_\pi = [e_{\pi(1)} e_{\pi(2)} \cdots e_{\pi(r)}]$ for $\pi \in S_r$, where $e_i \in \{0, 1\}^r$ is the ith standard basis vector. The additive cyclic group $(\mathbb{Z}_r, +)$ embeds into the symmetric group S_r via the injective homomorphism that sends the generator $1 \in \mathbb{Z}_r$ to the "cyclic shift" permutation $\pi \in S_r$, defined as $\pi(i) = i + 1$ for $1 \leq i < r$ and $\pi(r) = 1$. Notice such permutation matrices can be simplified as its first column vector in $\{0, 1\}^r$, and multiplied in only $O(r^2)$ operations, since we only need to multiply one matrix by the first column of the other.

Suppose that $q = r_1 r_2 \cdots r_t$, where the r_i are pairwise coprime. By the Chinese Remainder Theorem, the ring $\mathbb{Z}_q$ is isomorphic to the direct product of rings $\mathbb{Z}_{r_1} \times \mathbb{Z}_{r_2} \times \cdots \mathbb{Z}_{r_t}$ as well. Combining this with the group embeddings of $(\mathbb{Z}_{r_i}, +)$ into S_{r_i}, we have an (efficient) group embedding from $(\mathbb{Z}_q, +)$ into $S_{r_1} \times S_{r_2} \times \cdots \times S_{r_t}$, where we denote as Ψ. Furthermore, let $\varphi_i : \mathbb{Z}_q \to \{0, 1\}^{r_i}$ be one of the homomorphisms which is from an element in $\mathbb{Z}_q$ to the cyclic permutation that corresponds to an element in $\mathbb{Z}_{r_i}$, i.e., φ_i restricts the image of Ψ on one of the symmetric group S_{r_i}.

2.4 The Batched BGV SWHE Scheme

The ring-LWE based batched BGV SWHE scheme [7,28] is defined over ring $R := \mathbb{Z}[X]/\Phi_m[X]$, where $\Phi_m(X)$ is the mth cyclotomic polynomial [34]. R_p the localisation of R at p. The aggregated plaintext space of the batched BGV cryptosystem is R_p for a prime integer p coprime to m. Specifically, the BGV scheme is parameterized by a sequence of decreasing moduli $q_L \gg q_{L-1} \gg \cdots \gg q_0$, and an "$l$th level ciphertext" in the scheme is $\mathbf{c} = (c_0, c_1) \in R_{q_l}^2$. Secret keys are elements $z \in R$ with "small" coefficients. A level-l ciphertext $\mathbf{c}$ encrypts a plaintext element $\mu \in R_p$ with respect to $\mathbf{s} = (1, -z)$ if we have $[\langle \mathbf{s}, \mathbf{c} \rangle]_{q_l} = [c_0 - z \cdot c_1]_{q_l} = \mu + p \cdot e$ (in R) for some "small" noise term $p \cdot \|e\| \ll q_l$. After each homomorphic operation, modulus q_l at level l is switched to q_{l-1} at level $l - 1$ by an algorithm ModulusSwitch. Also, the respective key is switched by an algorithm KeySwitch. When it comes to level 0, no more homomorphic operation can be performed unless the bootstrapping procedure is proceeded.

The most important optimization for the ring-LWE based BGV scheme is batching. The polynomial $\Phi_m(X)$ modulo p factors into $k^{(R)}$ irreducible polynomials, i.e., $\Phi_m(X) \equiv \prod_{i=1}^{k^{(R)}} F_i(X) (\bmod\, p)$. Each $F_i(X)$ has degree $d^{(R)} = \phi(m)/k^{(R)}$, where $d^{(R)}$ is the multiplicative order of p in $\mathbb{Z}_m^*$. In the batched BGV scheme, each of these $k^{(R)}$ factors corresponds to a "plaintext slot". By the Chinese Remainder Theorem, addition and multiplication correspond to SIMD operations on the slots, which allows us to process $k^{(R)}$ input values at once.

In [28], Gentry et al. proved that we can use the batched BGV SWHE scheme to implement shallow arithmetic circuit with low overhead, on the condition that bootstrapping is not needed. Specifically, we have the following lemma.

Lemma 1 ([28]). *For security parameter λ, any t-gate, depth-L arithmetic circuit of average width $\Omega(\lambda)$ over underlying plaintext space $\mathbb{F}_p$ can be evaluated homomorphically by the batched BGV scheme in time $t \cdot \tilde{O}(L) \cdot polylog(\lambda)$.*

3   GSW Scheme with Ring Plaintexts

In this section we provide a variant of symmetric GSW scheme which encrypts a ring element $\mu \in \mathbb{Z}_p[X]/\Phi_m(X)$ as plaintext, different with the original ring-LWE based GSW scheme in [30] which can only encrypt a single bit. A ciphertext of our scheme can be easily transformed back to a BGV ciphertext with same μ as the aggregated plaintext. This scheme can support three type homomorphic gates: the homomorphic R_p-addition, the homomorphic R_p-multiplication and the homomorphic quasi-boolean AND operation. Also, for convenience to transform back to BGV ciphertexts, we put the plaintexts at low bits, different with that in the original GSW scheme in [30].

3.1   The Scheme Description

Our scheme is parameterized by an integer m (that defines the cyclotomic polynomial Φ_m and $\phi(m) = n$), the integer p (that defines the plaintext space $\mathbb{Z}_p[X]/\Phi_m$) and a modulus $Q(= poly(n) \gg p)$. For simplicity of the analysis, we will assume that $Q = 2^\tau$ for some integer τ.[2] We use ring $R = \mathbb{Z}[X]/\Phi_m$ and $R_Q = R/QR$.

---

[2] Actually, we can set $Q = \kappa^\tau$ for some integer τ and small integer κ which is coprime with p. The choice of κ causes a compromise between noise accumulation and efficiency.

RGSW.Keygen(1^n): Randomly sample $z \in R_Q$, then we define the secret key as a vector $\mathbf{s} = (1, -z)^T \in R_Q^2$.

RGSW.Enc(μ, $\mathbf{s}$): For inputs $\mu \in \mathbb{Z}_p[X]/\Phi_m$ and $z \in R_Q$, pick $\mathbf{a} \in R_Q^{2\tau}$ uniformly at random, and $\mathbf{e} \in R^{2\tau} \simeq \mathbb{Z}^{2\tau\phi(m)}$ with a distribution $\chi^{2\tau\phi(m)}$, where χ is a B-bounded discrete subgaussian distribution, and output

$$\text{RGSW.Enc}(\mu)_{\mathbf{s}} = \mathbf{C} = [\mathbf{a}z + p\mathbf{e}, \mathbf{a}] + \mu\mathbf{G} \in R_Q^{2\tau \times 2},$$

where $\mathbf{G} = (\mathbf{I}, 2\mathbf{I}, \dots, 2^{\tau-1}\mathbf{I})^T \in R_Q^{2\tau \times 2}$. Notice that $\mathbf{C} \cdot \mathbf{s} = p\mathbf{e} + \mu\mathbf{Gs} \in R_Q^{2\tau}$.

RGSW.Dec($\mathbf{C}$, $\mathbf{s}$): Let $\mathbf{c}$ be the first row of $\mathbf{C}$, and output $\mu = \langle \mathbf{c}, \mathbf{s} \rangle_Q \mod p$.

RGSW.HomAdd($\mathbf{C}_1$, $\mathbf{C}_2$): Addition of two ciphertext matrices is just standard addition in $\mathbb{Z}_Q[X]/\Phi_m(X)$.

RGSW.ScalMult(u, $\mathbf{C}$): Homomorphic multiplying the ciphertext $\mathbf{C}$ with ring element $u \in \mathbb{Z}_Q[X]/\Phi_m$ for each coefficient less than p can performed as $u \cdot \mathbf{C}$.

RGSW.QBAND($\mathbf{C}_1$, $\mathbf{C}_2$): On input two ciphertexts $\mathbf{C}_1, \mathbf{C}_2 \in R_Q^{2\tau \times 2}$ which the plaintexts corresponding to belongs to $\{0,1\} \subseteq R_p$, first computes the bit decomposition of $\mathbf{C}_1 = \sum_{i=1}^{\tau} 2^{i-1}\mathbf{D}_i$ (where each $\mathbf{D}_i \in R_Q^{2\tau \times 2}$ has entries with coefficients in $\{0,1\}$), and then the result can be represented as

$$\mathbf{C}_1 \odot \mathbf{C}_2 := [\mathbf{D}_1, \mathbf{D}_2, \dots \mathbf{D}_\tau] \cdot \mathbf{C}_2. \tag{2}$$

The computation in Eq. (2) can be accelerated using FFT/NTT as [22]. Also we let $\mathbf{C}_1 \odot \mathbf{C}_2 \odot \mathbf{C}_3$ denote the homomorphic quasi-boolean AND between $\mathbf{C}_1 \odot \mathbf{C}_2$ and $\mathbf{C}_3$, and so on.

3.2   Analysis

Security of the above scheme follows the fact that a fresh ciphertext is just $\mu\mathbf{G}$ plus a matrix of 2τ independent ring-LWE$_{q,\chi}$ samples under secret key z, which is pseudorandom and hence hides the $\mu\mathbf{G}$ term. So the IND-CPA security follows immediately from the assumed hardness of ring-DLWE$_{q,\chi}$ problem.

Definition 3. *We say that a ciphertext $\mathbf{C}$ encrypts a plaintext μ with noise matrix $\mathbf{e}$ if $\mathbf{C}$ is an encryption of $\mu \in \mathbb{Z}_p[X]/\Phi_m$ and $p\mathbf{e} = \mathbf{Cs} - \mu\mathbf{Gs} \pmod{Q}$. For convenience, we say $\mu\mathbf{G}$ is the ciphertext that encrypts μ with noise zero.*

Correctness of the decryption algorithm of our scheme directly follows the following lemma.

Lemma 2. *If a ciphertext $\mathbf{C}$ encrypts a plaintext $\mu \in \mathbb{Z}_Q[X]/\Phi_m$ with noise $\mathbf{e}$ such that $\| \mathbf{e} \|_\infty < \lfloor Q/2p \rfloor$, then $Dec_{sk}(\mathbf{C}) = \mu$.*

Proof. Remember that $\mathbf{s} = (1, -z)^T \in R_Q^2$, and we have

$$\mathbf{Cs} = [\mathbf{a}z + p\mathbf{e}, \mathbf{a}]\,\mathbf{s} + \mu\mathbf{Gs} = p\mathbf{e} + \mu\mathbf{Gs}.$$

Then the first entry of $\mathbf{Cs}$ is $u = p\mathbf{e}_{(1)} + \mu \mod Q$. Since $\| \mathbf{e} \|_\infty < \lfloor Q/2p \rfloor$, we have $|p\mathbf{e}_{(1)}| < \lfloor Q/2 \rfloor$, then $u \mod p = \mu$.   □

Noise growth by the evaluation of the homomorphic operation can be analysed by the following lemma.

Lemma 3. *Let* $\mathbf{s} \in R_Q^2$ *be a secret key. Let* $\mathbf{C}_1, \mathbf{C}_2 \in R_Q^{2\tau \times 2}$ *be ciphertexts that encrypt* $\mu_1, \mu_2 \in \mathbb{Z}_p[X]/\Phi_m$ *with noise vectors* $\mathbf{e}_1, \mathbf{e}_2 \in R^{2\tau} \simeq \mathbb{Z}^{2\tau\phi(m)}$, *respectively. Let* $\mathbf{C}_{add} := \mathbf{C}_1 + \mathbf{C}_2$, $\mathbf{C}_{scal} := \mu_1 \cdot \mathbf{C}_2$ *and* $\mathbf{C}_{QBAND} := \mathbf{C}_1 \odot \mathbf{C}_2$. *Then, we have* $\mathbf{C}_{add}\mathbf{s} = p\mathbf{e}_{add} + (\mu_1 + \mu_2)\mathbf{Gs}$, $\mathbf{C}_{scal}\mathbf{s} = p\mathbf{e}_{scal} + (\mu_1\mu_2)\mathbf{Gs}$ *and* $\mathbf{C}_{QBAND}\mathbf{s} = p\mathbf{e}_{QBAND} + (\mu_1\mu_2)\mathbf{Gs}$, *where* $\mathbf{e}_{add} := \mathbf{e}_1 + \mathbf{e}_2$, $\mathbf{e}_{QBAND} := \overline{\mathbf{C}}_1\mathbf{e}_2 + \mu_2\mathbf{e}_1$ *and* $\mathbf{e}_{scal} := \mu_1\mathbf{e}_2$ *for* $\overline{\mathbf{C}}_1 := [\mathbf{D}_1, \mathbf{D}_2, \ldots \mathbf{D}_\tau]$. *In particular,* $\|\mathbf{e}_{scal}\|_\infty^{can} \leq \|\mu_1\|_1 \cdot \|\mathbf{e}_2\|_\infty^{can}$ *and* $\|\mathbf{e}_{QBAND}\|_\infty^{can} \leq \tilde{O}(\phi(m))\|\mathbf{e}_2\|_\infty^{can} + \|\mathbf{e}_1\|_\infty^{can}$.

Proof. We can immediately prove the statements for $\mathbf{C}_{add}$.

For $\mathbf{C}_{scal}$, we have

$$\mathbf{C}_{scal}\mathbf{s} = \mu_1 \cdot \mathbf{C}_2\mathbf{s} = \mu_1 \cdot (p\mathbf{e}_2 + \mu_2\mathbf{Gs}) = p\mu_1\mathbf{e}_2 + \mu_1\mu_2\mathbf{Gs}.$$

So the bound of canonical norm for $\mathbf{e}_{mult}$ is obvious.

Remind that $\mathbf{C}_1 = \sum_{i=1}^\tau 2^{i-1}\mathbf{D}_i$, so $\overline{\mathbf{C}}_1 \cdot \mathbf{G} = \mathbf{C}_1$. For $\mathbf{C}_{QBAND}$, we have

$$\begin{aligned}
\mathbf{C}_{QBAND}\mathbf{s} &= \overline{\mathbf{C}}_1 \cdot \mathbf{C}_2\mathbf{s} \\
&= \overline{\mathbf{C}}_1 \cdot (p\mathbf{e}_2 + \mu_2\mathbf{Gs}) \\
&= p\overline{\mathbf{C}}_1 \cdot \mathbf{e}_2 + \mu_2\mathbf{C}_1\mathbf{s} \\
&= p(\overline{\mathbf{C}}_1 \cdot \mathbf{e}_2 + \mu_2\mathbf{e}_1) + (\mu_1\mu_2)\mathbf{Gs}.
\end{aligned}$$

Each $\mathbf{D}_i \in R_Q^{2\tau \times 2}$ consists of entries in R_Q with coefficients in $\{0, 1\}$. So the canonical norms of these entries are bounded by $\phi(m)$. Then we have

$$\|\mathbf{e}_{QBAND}\|_\infty^{can} \leq \phi(m) \cdot 2\tau\|\mathbf{e}_2\|_\infty^{can} + \|\mu_2\|_1\|\mathbf{e}_1\|_\infty^{can} \leq \tilde{O}(\phi(m))\|\mathbf{e}_2\|_\infty^{can} + \|\mathbf{e}_1\|_\infty^{can}.$$

$\square$

From the above lemma we can see that the noise accumulation for homomorphic quasi-boolean AND gate is quasi-additive. Since $\odot$ is defined to be left associative, we can analyze the behavior of the noise terms under a series of homomorphic quasi-boolean AND operations as follows.

Corollary 1. *Suppose* $\mathbf{C}_i$ *for* $i \in [h]$ *are ciphertexts with noise vectors* $\mathbf{e}_i$, *which the plaintexts corresponding to belongs to* $\{0, 1\} \subseteq R_p$. *The canonical norm of each entry in the fresh noise vectors is bounded by* B. *Then the canonical norm of each entry of the noise vector in*

$$\mathbf{C} \leftarrow \mathbf{G} \odot \underset{i \in [h]}{\odot} \mathbf{C}_i = (((\mathbf{G} \odot \mathbf{C}_1) \odot \mathbf{C}_2) \cdots) \odot \mathbf{C}_h$$

is bounded by $\tilde{O}(\phi(m)) \cdot h \cdot B$.

Computation Complexity of the three homomorphic gates is analysed by the following lemma.

Lemma 4. *The three types homomorphic gates, i.e., RGSW.HomAdd, RGSW. QBAND, and RGSW.ScalMult, can be computed in time $\tilde{O}(n)$.*

Proof. Each ciphertext in RGSW scheme belongs to $R_Q^{2\tau \times 2}$, so there are $4 \cdot \tau$ ring elements for one ciphertext, for $\tau = \log Q = O(\log n)$. In addition, the computation complexity of addition and the scalar multiplication for elements in R_Q is $O(\phi(m)) = O(n)$. The complexity of multiplication for ring elements by FFT is $O(n \log n)$. Generally, the complexity for the homomorphic quasi-boolean AND gate is no more than $\tilde{O}(n)$. □

3.3 Ciphertexts Transformation from GSW to BGV

Note that our Ring-GSW ciphertext is $\mathbf{C} = [\mathbf{a}z + p\mathbf{e}, \mathbf{a}] + \mu \mathbf{G} \in R_Q^{2\tau \times 2}$, so the first row vector $\mathbf{c} = [a_1 z + pe_1 + \mu, a_1] \in R_Q^2$ is a BGV ciphertext under the secret key $\mathbf{s} = (1, -z)$.[3] Then by applying key-switching and modulus-switching we get a logical BGV ciphertexts encrypted the same aggregated plaintext μ.

Trans$(\mathbf{C} \in R_Q^{2\tau \times 2})$: Output the first row vector of $\mathbf{C}$ as $\mathbf{c} = \mathbf{C}_{(1)}^T \in R_Q^2$.

4 Our Bootstrapping Method

In this section, we present our bootstrapping technique in detail. There are different kinds of circuits to evaluate the decryption function of the BGV scheme, but it seems that few of them can be constructed by only three types of gates above. The finally chosen decryption circuit is similar to the one in [4]. At high level our ciphertexts refreshing algorithm consists of three steps. Firstly, we homomorphically evaluate the decryption circuit of the BGV scheme and output a GSW refreshed ciphertext that encrypts the same plaintext. Secondly, we transform it back to a BGV ciphertext. Thirdly, we switch the secret key back to the original one. In the following, we denote the BGV scheme (the GSW scheme) encryption of aggregated plaintext μ under secrete key $\mathbf{s}$ as $\mathsf{BGV.Enc_s}(\mu)$ ($\mathsf{RGSW.Enc_s}(\mu)$, respectively). Also, we denote the ciphertext space of the GSW scheme as $\mathcal{C}$.

4.1 The Blueprint for Bootstrapping

As the discussion in [4], the decryption function for LWE based FHE schemes can be written as the "rounded inner product" though bit decomposition. Similarly, we observe that, for the batched BGV scheme, the ciphertext is $\mathbf{c} = (c_0, c_1) \in R_q^2$,

---

[3] Actually, the distribution of z is different with that in BGV scheme, but this do not influence the key switching algorithm.

the secret key is $\mathbf{s} = (1, -z) \in R_q^2$, the plaintext is $\mu \in R_p$, and the decryption function[4] is

$$\mathbf{Dec}(\mathbf{c}, \mathbf{s}) = (c_0 - c_1 \cdot z) \bmod q, \Phi(X) \bmod p = \mu. \tag{3}$$

Using the two subroutines described in Sect. 2.2, we can express the above function as

$$\mathbf{Dec}(\mathbf{c}, \mathbf{s}) = \langle \hat{\mathbf{c}}, \hat{\mathbf{s}} \rangle \bmod q \bmod p = \left(\sum_{i \text{ s.t. } \bar{c}_i = 1} \bar{s}_i \bmod q \right) \bmod p = \mu, \tag{4}$$

for $\hat{\mathbf{c}} = \mathsf{DegDecomp}(\mathbf{c})$, $\hat{\mathbf{s}} = \mathsf{PowerofDeg}(\mathbf{s})$, $\bar{\mathbf{c}} = \mathsf{BitDecomp}(\hat{\mathbf{c}}) \in \{0, 1\}^{2n\beta}$, $\bar{\mathbf{s}} = \mathsf{Powerof2}(\hat{\mathbf{s}}) \in R_q^{2n\beta}$, $\beta = \lceil \log q \rceil + 1$ and $\mu \in R_p$. To explain our bootstrapping procedure, we adopt the notion from [37], i.e., the decryption procedure can be performed using two maps: rep and red.

- *The representation map* rep describes a representation of an element in R_q by elements in the symmetric groups, which we will detail later on. Let $\oplus$ denote the computation between the images of rep, i.e.,

$$\mathsf{rep}(a) \oplus \mathsf{rep}(b) = \mathsf{rep}(a + b) \text{ for } a, b \in R_q. \tag{5}$$

- *The reduction map* red takes an image $\mathsf{rep}(a)$ for $a \in R_q$ and maps it to R_p, which satisfies that

$$\mathsf{red}(\mathsf{rep}(a)) = a \bmod p \tag{6}$$

So (4) can be write as

$$\mathbf{Dec}(\mathbf{c}, \mathbf{s}) = \mathsf{red}\left(\bigoplus_{i \text{ s.t. } \bar{c}_i = 1} \mathsf{rep}(\bar{s}_i) \right) = \mu. \tag{7}$$

To fulfill homomorphic decryption, an image $\mathsf{rep}(a)$ for $a \in R_q$ can be encrypted by the described GSW scheme with ring plaintexts. Moreover, the operation $\oplus$ can be homomorphically evaluated over GSW ciphertexts, i.e., we have

$$\mathsf{RGSW.Enc}(\mathsf{rep}(a)) \oplus \mathsf{RGSW.Enc}(\mathsf{rep}(b)) = \mathsf{RGSW.Enc}(\mathsf{rep}(a) \oplus \mathsf{rep}(b)) \tag{8}$$

for $a, b \in R_q$. Also, the red map can be homomorphically evaluated on GSW encryptions. Namely, we homomorphically compute

$$\mathsf{red}(\mathsf{RGSW.Enc}(\mathsf{rep}(a))) = \mathsf{RGSW.Enc}(\mathsf{red}(\mathsf{rep}(a))) \text{ for } a \in R_p. \tag{9}$$

---

[4] Without loss of generality, one can always use modulus switching to gain level-0 BGV ciphertexts before bootstrapping. So for simplicity, we write q_l as q and omit all the level tag l.

Generally, the decryption function (7) can be homomorphically evaluated as

$$\mathsf{Eval}\left(\mathbf{Dec}, \mathbf{c}, \{\mathsf{RGSW.Enc}(\mathsf{rep}(\bar{s}_i))\}_{i=0,\ldots,2\phi(m)\lceil\log q\rceil}\right)$$

$$= \mathsf{red}\left(\bigoplus_{i \text{ s.t. } \bar{c}_i=1} \mathsf{RGSW.Enc}\left(\mathsf{rep}(\bar{s}_i)\right)\right)$$

$$= \mathsf{red}\left(\mathsf{RGSW.Enc}\left(\bigoplus_{i \text{ s.t. } \bar{c}_i=1} \mathsf{rep}(\bar{s}_i)\right)\right)$$

$$= \mathsf{RGSW.Enc}\left(\mathsf{red}\left(\bigoplus_{i \text{ s.t. } \bar{c}_i=1} \mathsf{rep}(\bar{s}_i)\right)\right)$$

$$= \mathsf{RGSW.Enc}\left(\left(\sum_{i \text{ s.t. } \bar{c}_i=1} \bar{s}_i \mod q\right) \mod p\right)$$

$$= \mathsf{RGSW.Enc}(\mu).$$

After that, scheme transformation from GSW ciphertexts to BGV ciphertexts and key-switching will complete the bootstrapping procedure. The blueprint of our bootstrapping algorithm can be formalized by the Algorithm 1.

Algorithm 1. The Efficient Bootstrap Algorithm
___
Input:

   The level-0 batched BGV scheme ciphertext $\mathbf{c} = \mathsf{BGV.Enc}_{\mathbf{s}_0}(\mu)$ under secret key $\mathbf{s}_0$, where $\bar{\mathbf{s}} = \mathsf{Powerof2}(\mathsf{PowerofDeg}(\mathbf{s}_0))$ and $\bar{\mathbf{c}} = \mathsf{BitDecomp}(\mathsf{DegDecomp}(\mathbf{c}))$;
   The refresh key $\mathcal{K} = \{K_i = \mathsf{RGSW.Enc}_{\mathbf{s}'}(\mathsf{rep}(\bar{s}_i)), i = 1, \ldots, 2\phi(m)\lceil\log q\rceil\}$;
   The key-switching information $\tau_{\mathbf{s}' \to \mathbf{s}_L}$.

Output:

   A level-L batched BGV scheme ciphertext $\mathbf{c}^*$ encrypted μ under key $\mathbf{s}_L$.

1: Compute the function

$$D = \bigoplus_{i \text{ s.t. } \bar{c}_i=1} K_i,$$

   // Here $\bar{c}_i$ denote the ith entry of $\bar{\mathbf{c}}$.

2: $\mathbf{C} = \mathsf{HomRed}(D)$
   // Homomorphically evaluate the map *red* under GSW scheme with ring plaintexts with input D,

3: $\tilde{\mathbf{c}} = \mathsf{Trans}(\mathbf{C})$
   // Using scheme transformation algorithm we transform Ring-GSW ciphertext $\mathbf{C}$ under secret key $\mathbf{s}'$ back to BGV ciphertext $\tilde{\mathbf{c}}$ under secret key $\mathbf{s}'$.

4: $\mathbf{c}^* = \mathsf{SwitchKey}(\tilde{\mathbf{c}}, \tau_{\mathbf{s}' \to \mathbf{s}_L})$
   // Using key-switching information $\tau_{\mathbf{s}' \to \mathbf{s}_L}$ to transform ciphertext $\tilde{\mathbf{c}}$ back to level-L BGV ciphertext $\mathbf{c}^*$ under key $\mathbf{s}_L$

4.2   The Representation Map rep

For simplicity, we always assume that $q_0 = q = r_1 r_2 \cdots r_t$ and all r_i are pairwise coprime before bootstrapping. This always can be satisfied by modulus switching. Note that the secret key consists of elements in $R_q = \mathbb{Z}_q[X]/\Phi_m[X]$ and each ring element $a \in R_q$ has $\phi(m)$ coefficients in $\mathbb{Z}_q$. As described in Sect. 2.3, by Chinese Remainder Theorem, there is a group embedding Ψ from $\mathbb{Z}_q$ into the direct product of symmetric groups $S_{r_1} \times S_{r_2} \times \ldots S_{r_t}$. rep consists of n such group embeddings for each coefficient of a ring element, and $\widehat{\text{rep}}_j$ denote the one from jth coefficient. That is

$$\text{rep}(a) = \left(\widehat{\text{rep}}_1(a), \widehat{\text{rep}}_2(a), \ldots, \widehat{\text{rep}}_{\phi(m)}(a) \right).$$

Hence, each $\widehat{\text{rep}}_j(a)$ is represented as t binary vectors $\varphi_i(a^{(j)}) \in \{0,1\}^{r_i}, i = 1, \ldots, t$. The operation $\oplus$ is corresponding to the permutation matrix multiplications in each symmetric group S_{r_i} in parallel.

Since $\text{rep}(a)$ finally consists of $t \cdot \phi(m)$ binary vectors, we can encrypt it by encrypting each entry of the vectors. Moreover, since the operation $\oplus$ is corresponding to binary matrix multiplications, it can be always homomorphically computed by quasi-boolean AND gates and addition gates.

Lemma 5. *Let a, a_1, a_2 to be arbitrary elements in R_q and the representation map rep is defined as above. Let $r = \max_{1 \leq i \leq t} r_i$. Then $\text{rep}(a)$ can be encrypted as less than $t \cdot \phi(m) \cdot r$ GSW ciphertexts. The encryption of $\text{rep}(a_1) \oplus \text{rep}(a_2)$ can be homomorphically computed from the encryption of $\text{rep}(a_1)$ and $\text{rep}(a_2)$ within $O(t \cdot r^3 \cdot \phi(m))$ homomorphic operations, and the noise growth is less than $O(\phi(m) \cdot r) \cdot B^{can}$ where B^{can} is the bound of the canonical norm of noise in the input ciphertexts.*

4.3   The Reduction Map red

Our reduction map red is constructed similarly to [4] except that we work on the ring elements instead of integers and the modulus of our plaintext space is $p \geq 2$.

Specifically, we first define the map $\widehat{\text{red}}_j$ from a direct product of symmetric groups $S_{r_1} \times S_{r_2} \times \ldots S_{r_t}$ to $\mathbb{Z}_p$ as testing whether the input equals to $\widehat{\text{rep}}_j(v)$ for all v such that $v \mod p = \kappa$, multiplying each test results by corresponding κ and then summing them up. The $\widehat{\text{red}}_j$ can be expressed as

$$\widehat{\text{red}}_j(g) = \sum_{\kappa=1}^{p-1} \kappa \sum_{v \in \mathbb{Z}_q \, s.t. \, v \bmod p = \kappa} [g = \widehat{\text{rep}}_j(v)],$$

where each equality test $[g = \widehat{\text{rep}}_j(v)]$ return 0 for false and 1 for true. Since each g is expressed by t indicator vectors, the test of whether g equals $\widehat{\text{rep}}_j$ can be performed by selecting the appropriate entries of each indicator vector and then

---

Algorithm 2. The red Map Algorithm

Input: A element $\mathsf{rep}(x)$ which is represented as $t \cdot \phi(m)$ vectors $\varphi_i(x_{(j)}) \in \{0,1\}^{r_i}, i = 1, \ldots, t; j = 1, \ldots, \phi(m)$ corresponding to x in R_q,
Output: $y \in R_p$ which $y = x \mod p$.
1: for $j = 1$ to $\phi(m)$
2:     for $v = -\lfloor q/2 \rfloor + 1$ to $\lfloor q/2 \rfloor$
3:         for $i = 1$ to t
4:             select the $v_i (= v \mod r_i)$th element in $\varphi_i (x_{(j)})$ as $a_i \in \{0,1\}$
5:             $a \leftarrow a \cdot a_i \in \{0,1\}$
6:         end for
7:         $y_{(j)} \leftarrow y_{(j)} + \kappa * a \in \mathbb{Z}_p$ where $\kappa = v \mod p$
8:     end for
9: end for
10: Output $y \in R_p$ of which the jth coefficient is $y_{(j)} \in \mathbb{Z}_p$

---

multiplying them together. So composing all the maps $\widehat{\mathsf{red}}_j$ for $j = 1, \ldots \phi(m)$ together, the red map can be computed by Algorithm 2.

Define $\mathbf{C}_{i,j} \in \mathcal{C}^{r_i}$ as the ith ciphertext vector corresponding to the jth coefficient of the polynomial $\mathsf{rep}(x)$. To evaluate Algorithm 2 homomorphically, we propose Algorithm 3.

Algorithm 3. The HomRed Algorithm

Input: Ring GSW ciphertext vectors $\mathbf{C}_{i,j} \in \mathcal{C}^{r_i}, i = 1, \ldots, t; j = 1, \ldots, \phi(m)$ that encrypt $t \cdot \phi(m)$ vectors $\varphi_i(x_{(j)}) \in \{0,1\}^{r_i}, i = 1, \ldots, t; j = 1, \ldots, \phi(m)$ which represent $\mathsf{rep}(x)$
Output: d encrypts $y \in R_p$ as the original plaintext, where $y = x \mod p$.
1: for $j = 1$ to $\phi(m)$
2:     Put d_j as the ciphertext that encrypts all zero vector with noise noise
3:     for integer $v = -\lfloor q/2 \rfloor + 1$ to $\lfloor q/2 \rfloor$
4:         $c \leftarrow \mathbf{G}$
5:         for $i = 1$ to t
6:             select the $v_i (= v \mod r_i)$th element of $\mathbf{C}_{i,j}$ as c_i
7:             $c \leftarrow c \odot c_i$
8:         end for
9:         $d_j \leftarrow d_j + \kappa \cdot c \in \mathbb{Z}_p$ where integer $\kappa = v \mod p$
10:     end for
11:     $d \leftarrow x^j \cdot d_j$
12: end for
13: Output ciphertext d

Lemma 6. *Let a be a ring element in R_q. Given the encryption of $\mathsf{rep}(a)$ as above, the HomRed algorithm can successfully output a GSW ciphertext which plaintext is just $a \mod p$. Moreover, the number of the homomorphic operations is no more than $O(\phi(m) \cdot q \cdot t)$ and the noise growth is less than $O(\phi(m) \cdot p \cdot q \cdot t)$.*

4.4   Bootstrapping Within Polynomial Noise

To bootstrap, the evaluation key is the encryption of the rep image of each element of secret key vector $\bar{s} \in R_{q_0}^d$ under the GSW scheme with secret key s' and modulus Q. Particularly, to apply the symmetric embedding, we set the level-0 modulus q_0 to be a product of different small prime integers, the size of which are $O(1)$. Since the operation $\oplus$ of red image and red map can both be produced homomorphically, the Algorithm 1 can correctly output the bootstrapped ciphertext. Importantly, the output of the BGV scheme ciphertext is with modulus Q, and $Q = q_L \gg q_0$ is the level-L modulus. Generally, we have the following theorem.

Theorem 2 (Main Theorem). *Given the evaluation key which is defined as above, we can bootstrap batched BGV HE scheme within $\tilde{O}(n^2 \cdot q_0)$ times of noise in the evaluation key.*

Proof. Since the permutation matrices are always binary, the step 1 of the Algorithm 1 is always evaluated by homomorphic quasi-boolean AND gates and addition gates. If the canonical norm of noise in ciphertexts of the refresh key are bounded by B^{can}, according to Lemma 5, the noise in the result of step 1 of the Algorithm 1 is bounded by $\tilde{O}(n) \cdot B^{can}$. Similarly, according to Lemma 6, we compute ciphertexts encrypting elements in $\{0, 1\} \subset R_p$ in Algorithm 3 until we get d_j's and we then only perform scalar multiplication and homomorphic addition on d_j. Moreover, the canonical norm of x^j is 1. If the canonical norms of noises in input ciphertexts in Algorithm 3 are bounded by $\tilde{B}^{can}$, the canonical norms of noises in the result ciphertexts in step 2 are bounded by $\tilde{O}(nq \log q) \cdot \tilde{B}^{can}$. Also we notice that scheme transformation and key switching procedure only increase noise by a constant factor. So totally we bootstrap in $\tilde{O}(n^2 \cdot q)$ times noise. According to the relations of l_∞ and canonical norm as Eq. (1), the l_∞ norm of noise in refreshed ciphertexts $B_{refresh}$ satisfies $B_{refresh} = \tilde{O}\left(n^2 \cdot q\right) B^{can}$. $\square$

Asymptotic Parameters. For the worst case, to make decryption algorithm at 0-Level function well, we need to make sure that

$$\tilde{O}\left(B_{refresh}^{L+1}\right) \leq \frac{Q}{2p}. \tag{10}$$

Therefore $Q = \tilde{O}(n^2 \cdot q \cdot B^{can})^{L+1}$ satisfies the above inequality. Here L can be any positive constant integer that be chosen at first and independent on dimension n and security parameter λ. For instance, we can set $q = \Theta(n)$ and $B^{can} = \omega\left(\sqrt{n \log n}\right)$. For $L = 1$, $Q = \tilde{O}(n^7)$ suffices. Since the l_∞ bound B on fresh noise satisfies $B \leq c_m \cdot B^{can}$, we can estimate B as the same asymptotic level as B^{can}. According to Theorem 1, the security of our scheme can be relied on the hardness of $GapSVP_{\tilde{O}(n^{6.5})}$ for idea lattice.

4.5   Computation Complexity

Computation complexity for the above bootstrapping method is analysed by the following theorem.

Theorem 3. *The computation complexity of bootstrapping procedure described in Algorithm 1 is no more than $\tilde{O}(n^3)$.*

Proof. The step 1 in the Algorithm 1 uses at most $\phi(m) \cdot \lceil \log q \rceil$ operations $\oplus$. As it is explained in Lemma 5, each $\oplus$ operations cost $O(t \cdot r^3 \cdot \phi(m))$ basic homomorphic operations. Next, the step 2 in the Algorithm 1 uses $O(\phi(m) \cdot p \cdot q \cdot t)$ operations. r and t have sizes of $O(1)$ and $O(\log n)$. Totally, the number of homomorphic operations for ring GSW scheme is no more than $\tilde{O}(n^2)$. Moreover, according to Lemma 4, the complexity of each GSW scheme homomorphic gate is $\tilde{O}(n)$. The complexity of scheme transformation and key switching for batched BGV scheme are both $\tilde{O}(n)$. In the end, the computation complexity of bootstrapping procedure described in Algorithm 1 is no more than $\tilde{O}(n^3)$.   □

Overhead. In [28], Gentry et al. proved that one can use the batched BGV SWHE scheme to implement any (wide enough) bounded level arithmetic circuit within polylog overhead. When the depth of the circuit is beyond what we can handle, the bootstrapping is inevitable. In optimal cases, we can evaluate $O(n^3)$ gates in $3 \log n$ levels with the batched BGV SWHE scheme in time $\tilde{O}(n^3)$ according to Lemma 1, and then, bootstrap using our method within time $\tilde{O}(n^3)$. So the per-gate overhead is polylog in these cases, which is asymmetrically optimal as same as the scheme in [28].

5   Parameter Calculation

The literature [35] gives us a straightforward reduction from the worst-case lattice problems to the security of our FHE scheme. However, the worst-case connection can not provide hints on definite security for any concrete choice of parameters. Therefore, one has to take into account experiments on the hardness of lattice problems.

Our parameter estimation approach directly follows [1,2] and uses the LWE estimator https://bitbucket.org/malb/lwe-estimator/src. Specifically, we provide example parameters as follows. We set the canonical norm bound for fresh noise vector as $B = 6 \cdot \sigma = 19.2$. Then, we set $p = 3$, $q_0 = 5 \cdot 7 \cdot 11 \cdot 13 = 5005 \approx 2^{12}$. Also, we set $Q = 2^\tau$, $L = 1$. The Eq. (10) can be formalized as

$$(4 \cdot n^2 \cdot q \cdot \log q \cdot p \cdot \tau \cdot B)^{L+1} \le \frac{Q}{2p}.$$

Table 1. Example Parameters. k denotes the number of slots.

Security	m	n	q_L	p	k
70	2323	2200	2^{109}	3	3
80	2867	2760	2^{110}	3	12
100	4325	3440	2^{111}	3	4

We obtain a concrete set of example parameters in Table 1. Remind that k denotes the number of slots in the plaintext, and $Q = q_L$ is the modulus of the GSW scheme, as well as the level L modulus of the BGV scheme.

Acknowledgements. We would like to thank the anonymous reviewers for their valuable comments. The work is supported by the National Natural Science Foundation of China (No.U1536205), the National Key Research and Development Program of China (No.2017YFB0802005,2017YFB0802504) and the National Basic Research Program of China (No.2013CB338003).

References

1. Albrecht, M.R.: On dual lattice attacks against small-secret LWE and parameter choices in HElib and SEAL. In: Coron, J.-S., Nielsen, J.B. (eds.) EUROCRYPT 2017. LNCS, vol. 10211, pp. 103–129. Springer, Cham (2017). doi:10.1007/978-3-319-56614-6_4
2. Albrecht, M.R., Player, R., Scott, S.: On the concrete hardness of learning with errors. J. Math. Cryptol. **9**(3), 169–203 (2015). http://www.degruyter.com/view/j/jmc.2015.9.issue-3/jmc-2015-0016/jmc-2015-0016.xml
3. Alperin-Sheriff, J., Peikert, C.: Practical bootstrapping in quasilinear time. In: Canetti, R., Garay, J.A. (eds.) CRYPTO 2013. LNCS, vol. 8042, pp. 1–20. Springer, Heidelberg (2013). doi:10.1007/978-3-642-40041-4_1
4. Alperin-Sheriff, J., Peikert, C.: Faster bootstrapping with polynomial error. In: Garay, J.A., Gennaro, R. (eds.) CRYPTO 2014. LNCS, vol. 8616, pp. 297–314. Springer, Heidelberg (2014). doi:10.1007/978-3-662-44371-2_17
5. Brakerski, Z.: Fully homomorphic encryption without modulus switching from classical GapSVP. In: Safavi-Naini, R., Canetti, R. (eds.) CRYPTO 2012. LNCS, vol. 7417, pp. 868–886. Springer, Heidelberg (2012). doi:10.1007/978-3-642-32009-5_50
6. Brakerski, Z., Gentry, C., Halevi, S.: Packed ciphertexts in LWE-based homomorphic encryption. In: Kurosawa, K., Hanaoka, G. (eds.) PKC 2013. LNCS, vol. 7778, pp. 1–13. Springer, Heidelberg (2013). doi:10.1007/978-3-642-36362-7_1
7. Brakerski, Z., Gentry, C., Vaikuntanathan, V.: (Leveled) fully homomorphic encryption without bootstrapping. In: Proceedings of the 3rd Innovations in Theoretical Computer Science Conference, pp. 309–325. ACM (2012)
8. Brakerski, Z., Vaikuntanathan, V.: Efficient fully homomorphic encryption from (standard) LWE. In: Annual Symposium on Foundations of Computer Science, 2011(2), pp. 97–106 (2011)
9. Brakerski, Z., Vaikuntanathan, V.: Fully homomorphic encryption from ring-LWE and security for key dependent messages. In: Rogaway, P. (ed.) CRYPTO 2011. LNCS, vol. 6841, pp. 505–524. Springer, Heidelberg (2011). doi:10.1007/978-3-642-22792-9_29
10. Brakerski, Z., Vaikuntanathan, V.: Lattice-based FHE as secure as PKE. In: Proceedings of the 5th Conference on Innovations in Theoretical Computer Science, pp. 1–12. ACM (2014)
11. Chen, H., Lauter, K.E., Stange, K.E.: Attacks on search RLWE. IACR Cryptology ePrint Archive 2015, 971 (2015). http://eprint.iacr.org/2015/971
12. Chen, H., Lauter, K.E., Stange, K.E.: Vulnerable galois RLWE families and improved attacks. IACR Cryptology ePrint Archive 2016, 193 (2016). http://eprint.iacr.org/2016/193

13. Chen, Y., Nguyen, P.Q.: BKZ 2.0: better lattice security estimates. In: Lee, D.H., Wang, X. (eds.) ASIACRYPT 2011. LNCS, vol. 7073, pp. 1–20. Springer, Heidelberg (2011). doi:10.1007/978-3-642-25385-0_1

14. Cheon, J.H., Coron, J.-S., Kim, J., Lee, M.S., Lepoint, T., Tibouchi, M., Yun, A.: Batch fully homomorphic encryption over the integers. In: Johansson, T., Nguyen, P.Q. (eds.) EUROCRYPT 2013. LNCS, vol. 7881, pp. 315–335. Springer, Heidelberg (2013). doi:10.1007/978-3-642-38348-9_20

15. Chillotti, I., Gama, N., Georgieva, M., Izabachène, M.: Faster fully homomorphic encryption: Bootstrapping in less than 0.1 seconds. In: Advances in Cryptology - ASIACRYPT 2016–22nd International Conference on the Theory and Application of Cryptology and Information Security, Hanoi, Vietnam, December 4–8, 2016, Proceedings, Part I, pp. 3–33 (2016). https://doi.org/10.1007/978-3-662-53887-6_1

16. Chillotti, I., Gama, N., Georgieva, M., Izabachène, M.: Improving TFHE: faster packed homomorphic operations and efficient circuit bootstrapping. IACR Cryptology ePrint Archive 2017, 430 (2017). http://eprint.iacr.org/2017/430

17. Coron, J.-S., Mandal, A., Naccache, D., Tibouchi, M.: Fully homomorphic encryption over the integers with shorter public keys. In: Rogaway, P. (ed.) CRYPTO 2011. LNCS, vol. 6841, pp. 487–504. Springer, Heidelberg (2011). doi:10.1007/978-3-642-22792-9_28

18. Coron, J.-S., Naccache, D., Tibouchi, M.: Public key compression and modulus switching for fully homomorphic encryption over the integers. In: Pointcheval, D., Johansson, T. (eds.) EUROCRYPT 2012. LNCS, vol. 7237, pp. 446–464. Springer, Heidelberg (2012). doi:10.1007/978-3-642-29011-4_27

19. Crockett, E., Peikert, C.: Λoλ: Functional lattice cryptography. In: Proceedings of the 2016 ACM SIGSAC Conference on Computer and Communications Security, 2016, pp. 993–1005 (2016). http://doi.acm.org/10.1145/2976749.2978402

20. Damgård, I., Pastro, V., Smart, N., Zakarias, S.: Multiparty computation from somewhat homomorphic encryption. In: Safavi-Naini, R., Canetti, R. (eds.) CRYPTO 2012. LNCS, vol. 7417, pp. 643–662. Springer, Heidelberg (2012). doi:10.1007/978-3-642-32009-5_38

21. Doröz, Y., Hu, Y., Sunar, B.: Homomorphic AES evaluation using the modified scheme. Des. Codes Crypt. 80(2), 333–358 (2016). http://dx.doi.org/10.1007/s10623-015-0095-1

22. Ducas, L., Micciancio, D.: FHEW: bootstrapping homomorphic encryption in less than a second. In: Oswald, E., Fischlin, M. (eds.) EUROCRYPT 2015. LNCS, vol. 9056, pp. 617–640. Springer, Heidelberg (2015). doi:10.1007/978-3-662-46800-5_24

23. Eisenträger, K., Hallgren, S., Lauter, K.: Weak instances of PLWE. In: Joux, A., Youssef, A. (eds.) SAC 2014. LNCS, vol. 8781, pp. 183–194. Springer, Cham (2014). doi:10.1007/978-3-319-13051-4_11

24. Elias, Y., Lauter, K.E., Ozman, E., Stange, K.E.: Provably weak instances of Ring-LWE. In: Gennaro, R., Robshaw, M. (eds.) CRYPTO 2015. LNCS, vol. 9215, pp. 63–92. Springer, Heidelberg (2015). doi:10.1007/978-3-662-47989-6_4

25. Gentry, C.: Fully homomorphic encryption using ideal lattices. In: STOC, vol. 9, pp. 169–178 (2009)

26. Gentry, C., Halevi, S., Peikert, C., Smart, N.P.: Field switching in BGV-style homomorphic encryption. J. Comput. Secur. 21(5), 663–684 (2013)

27. Gentry, C., Halevi, S., Smart, N.P.: Better bootstrapping in fully homomorphic encryption. In: Fischlin, M., Buchmann, J., Manulis, M. (eds.) PKC 2012. LNCS, vol. 7293, pp. 1–16. Springer, Heidelberg (2012). doi:10.1007/978-3-642-30057-8_1

28. Gentry, C., Halevi, S., Smart, N.P.: Fully homomorphic encryption with polylog overhead. In: Pointcheval, D., Johansson, T. (eds.) EUROCRYPT 2012. LNCS, vol. 7237, pp. 465–482. Springer, Heidelberg (2012). doi:10.1007/978-3-642-29011-4_28

29. Gentry, C., Halevi, S., Smart, N.P.: Homomorphic evaluation of the AES circuit. In: Safavi-Naini, R., Canetti, R. (eds.) CRYPTO 2012. LNCS, vol. 7417, pp. 850–867. Springer, Heidelberg (2012). doi:10.1007/978-3-642-32009-5_49

30. Gentry, C., Sahai, A., Waters, B.: Homomorphic encryption from learning with errors: conceptually-simpler, asymptotically-faster, attribute-based. In: Canetti, R., Garay, J.A. (eds.) CRYPTO 2013. LNCS, vol. 8042, pp. 75–92. Springer, Heidelberg (2013). doi:10.1007/978-3-642-40041-4_5

31. Halevi, S., Shoup, V.: Algorithms in HElib. In: Garay, J.A., Gennaro, R. (eds.) CRYPTO 2014. LNCS, vol. 8616, pp. 554–571. Springer, Heidelberg (2014). doi:10.1007/978-3-662-44371-2_31

32. Halevi, S., Shoup, V.: Bootstrapping for HElib. In: Oswald, E., Fischlin, M. (eds.) EUROCRYPT 2015. LNCS, vol. 9056, pp. 641–670. Springer, Heidelberg (2015). doi:10.1007/978-3-662-46800-5_25

33. Hiromasa, R., Abe, M., Okamoto, T.: Packing messages and optimizing bootstrapping in GSW-FHE. In: Katz, J. (ed.) PKC 2015. LNCS, vol. 9020, pp. 699–715. Springer, Heidelberg (2015). doi:10.1007/978-3-662-46447-2_31

34. Lin, D.: Introduction to Algebra and Finite Fields. Higher Education Press, Beijing (2006)

35. Lyubashevsky, V., Peikert, C., Regev, O.: On ideal lattices and learning with errors over rings. J. ACM (JACM) **60**(6), 43 (2013)

36. Lyubashevsky, V., Peikert, C., Regev, O.: A toolkit for ring-LWE cryptography. In: Johansson, T., Nguyen, P.Q. (eds.) EUROCRYPT 2013. LNCS, vol. 7881, pp. 35–54. Springer, Heidelberg (2013). doi:10.1007/978-3-642-38348-9_3

37. Orsini, E., van de Pol, J., Smart, N.P.: Bootstrapping BGV Ciphertexts with a Wider Choice of p and q. In: Katz, J. (ed.) PKC 2015. LNCS, vol. 9020, pp. 673–698. Springer, Heidelberg (2015). doi:10.1007/978-3-662-46447-2_30

38. van de Pol, J., Smart, N.P.: Estimating key sizes for high dimensional lattice-based systems. In: Stam, M. (ed.) IMACC 2013. LNCS, vol. 8308, pp. 290–303. Springer, Heidelberg (2013). doi:10.1007/978-3-642-45239-0_17

39. Regev, O.: On lattices, learning with errors, random linear codes, and cryptography. J. ACM (JACM) **56**(6), 34 (2009)

40. Smart, N.P., Vercauteren, F.: Fully homomorphic encryption with relatively small key and ciphertext sizes. In: Nguyen, P.Q., Pointcheval, D. (eds.) PKC 2010. LNCS, vol. 6056, pp. 420–443. Springer, Heidelberg (2010). doi:10.1007/978-3-642-13013-7_25

41. Smart, N.P., Vercauteren, F.: Fully homomorphic SIMD operations. Des. Codes Crypt. **71**(1), 57–81 (2014)

42. van Dijk, M., Gentry, C., Halevi, S., Vaikuntanathan, V.: Fully homomorphic encryption over the integers. In: Gilbert, H. (ed.) EUROCRYPT 2010. LNCS, vol. 6110, pp. 24–43. Springer, Heidelberg (2010). doi:10.1007/978-3-642-13190-5_2

Revocable Predicate Encryption from Lattices

San Ling, Khoa Nguyen, Huaxiong Wang, and Juanyang Zhang$^{(\boxtimes)}$

Division of Mathematical Sciences, School of Physical and Mathematical Sciences,
Nanyang Technological University, Singapore, Singapore
{lingsan,khoantt,hxwang,zh0078ng}@ntu.edu.sg

Abstract. Predicate encryption, formalized by Katz, Sahai, and Waters (EUROCRYPT 2008), is an attractive branch of public-key encryption, which provides fine-grained and role-based access to encrypted data. As for many multi-user cryptosystems, an efficient revocation mechanism is necessary and imperative in the context of predicate encryption, in order to address scenarios when users misbehave or their private keys are compromised. The formal model of revocable predicate encryption was introduced by Nieto, Manulis and Sun (ACISP 2012), who suggest the strong, full-hiding security notion, demanding that the ciphertexts do not leak any information about the encrypted data, the attribute and the revocation information associated with it.

In this work, we introduce the first construction of lattice-based revocable predicate encryption. Our scheme satisfies the full-hiding security notion (in a selective manner) in the standard model, based on the hardness of the Learning With Errors (LWE) problem. In terms of asymptotic efficiency, the scheme is somewhat comparable to the pairing-based instantiation put forward by Nieto, Manulis and Sun. Furthermore, better efficiency could be easily achieved in the random oracle model.

1 Introduction

The notion of predicate encryption (PE), formalized by Katz et al. [19], is an emerging paradigm of public-key encryption, which provides fine-grained and role-based access to encrypted data. In a PE scheme, the user's private key, issued by an authority, is associated with a predicate f, while a ciphertext is bound to an attribute a. The system then ensures that the user can decrypt the ciphertext if and only if $f(a) = 1$. PE can be viewed as a generalization of attribute-based encryption (ABE) [17,40]. Whereas the latter reveals the attribute bound to each ciphertext, the former preserves the privacy of not only the encrypted data but also the attribute. These powerful properties of PE yield numerous potential applications (see, e.g., [10,19,46]).

As for many multi-user cryptosystems, an efficient revocation mechanism is necessary and imperative in the PE setting. When some users misbehave or when their private keys are compromised, the users should be revoked from the system and should no longer be able to decrypt the ciphertext. In the ABE setting, Boldyreval et al. [8] suggested a revocation mechanism based on a time-based key

© Springer International Publishing AG 2017
T. Okamoto et al. (Eds.): ProvSec 2017, LNCS 10592, pp. 305–326, 2017.
https://doi.org/10.1007/978-3-319-68637-0_19

update procedure. In their model, a ciphertext is not only bound to an attribute but also to a time period. The key authority, who possesses the up-to-date list of revoked users, have to publish an update key at each time period so that only non-revoked users can update their private keys to decrypt ciphertexts bound to the same time slot. This mechanism is known as indirect revocation, since the revocation information is not controlled by the message sender, but by the authority. A naïve solution for indirect revocation, first mentioned by Boneh and Franklin [9], consists of broadcasting user-specific update keys to all non-revoked users. However, this simple solution is inefficient, because the periodic workload of the authority is $O(N - r)$, where N is the number of users in the system and r is the number of revoked users at the given time period. Boldyreval et al. [8] adopted the classic subset-cover framework due to Naor et al. [28], which employs binary trees to handle user revocation, and reduced the size of update keys to $O\left(r \log \frac{N}{r}\right)$. Concrete pairing-based instantiations of revocable ABE following Boldyreval et al.'s approach were proposed in [5, 39]. This approach, however, admits several limitations, since it requires the key authority to stay online regularly, and the non-revoked users to download updated system information periodically.

To eliminate the burden caused by the key update phase, Attrapadung and Imai [5] suggested the direct revocation mechanism for ABE, in which the revocation information can be controlled by the message sender. Each ciphertext is now bound to an attribute a as well as the current revocation list RL. Meanwhile, each private key associated with a predicate f is assigned a unique index I. The decryption procedure is successful if and only if $f(a) = 1$ and $I \notin$ RL. In this direct revocation model, the authority only can stay off-line after issuing private keys for users, and non-revoked users do not have to update their keys. Despite of the clear efficiency advantages for both the key authority and users, this approach requires that senders possess the current revocation list and perform encryptions based on it. The setting that the message sender should possess the revocation information might be inconvenient in certain scenarios, but it is well-suited in cases such information is naturally known to the sender. For instance, in Pay-TV systems [17], the TV program distributor should own the list of revoked users.

In [30,31], Nieto, Manulis and Sun (NMS) adapted the Attrapadung-Imai direct revocation mechanism into the context of PE, and formalized the notion of revocable predicated encryption (RPE). As discussed in [30,31], involved privacy challenges may rise when one plugs the revocation problem into the PE setting. In particular, Nieto, Manulis and Sun consider two security notions: attribute-hiding and full-hiding. The former means that the ciphertext only preserves privacy of attribute (and of the encrypted data) as in ordinary PE. The latter is a very strong notion which additionally guarantees that the revocation information is not leaked by the ciphertext. This requirement is suitable for applications where it is necessary for the sender to hide the list of revoked users. Nieto, Manulis and Sun pointed out that a generic construction of full-hiding RPE can be obtained by a combination of a PE scheme and an anonymous broadcasting scheme, but it is inefficient since the size of the ciphertexts is linearly dependent on the maximal number of users N. Then they proposed a more efficient paring-based instantiation of full-hiding RPE for inner-product predicates, which relies on the PE schemes by Okamoto and Takashima [33] and Lewko et al. [21], as well as the subset-cover framework [28].

In this work, inspired by the potentials of PE and the advantages of the direct revocation mechanism, we consider full-hiding RPE in the context of lattice-based cryptography, and aim to design the first such scheme from lattice assumptions. Lattice-based cryptography, pioneered by the seminal works by Regev [38] and Gentry et al. [15], has been one of the most exciting research areas in the last decade. Lattices provide several advantages over conventional number-theoretic cryptography, such as conjectured resistance against quantum adversaries and faster arithmetic operations. In the scope of lattice-based revocation schemes, there have been several proposals [11, 12, 29, 47], but they only consider the setting of identity-based encryption (IBE). To the best of our knowledge, the problem of constructing lattice-based RPE schemes has not been addressed so far.

OUR RESULTS AND TECHNIQUES. We introduce the first construction of RPE from lattices. Our scheme satisfies the full-hiding security notion [30, 31] (in a selective manner) in the standard model, based on the hardness of the Learning With Errors (LWE) problem [38]. The scheme inherits the main advantage of the direct revocation mechanism: the authority does not have to be online after the key generation phase, and key updating is not needed. Let N be the maximum expected number of private keys in the system and let r be the number of revoked keys. Then, the efficiency of our scheme is comparable to that of the pairing-based RPE scheme from [30, 31], in the following sense: the size of public parameters is $O(N)$; the size of the private key is $O(\log N)$, and the ciphertext has size $O\left(r \log \frac{N}{r}\right)$ which is ranged between $O(1)$ (when no key is revoked) and $O\left(\frac{N}{2}\right)$ (in the worst case when every second key is revoked).

At a high level, we adopt the approach suggested by Nieto, Manulis and Sun in their pairing-based instantiation [30, 31], for which we introduce several modifications. Recall that, in [30, 31], to obtain a full-hiding RPE, the authors apply the tree-based revocation technique from [28] to two layers of PE [21, 33], in the following manner: the main PE layer deals with predicate vector $\overrightarrow{x}$ and attribute vector $\overrightarrow{y}$, while an additional layer is introduced to handle the index I of the private key (encoded as a "predicate") and the revocation list RL (encoded as an "attribute"). Thanks to the attribute-hiding property of the second PE layer, RL is kept hidden. It is worth noting that Nieto, Manulis and Sun managed to prove the full-hiding security by exploiting the dual system encryption techniques [49] underlying the PE blocks. Their security proof fairly relies on the fact that the simulator is able to compute at least one private key for all predicates, including those for which the challenge attributes satisfy.

To adapt the approach from [30, 31] into the lattice setting, we employ as the main PE layer the scheme for inner-product predicates put forward by Agrawal, Freeman and Vaikuntanathan [2] and subsequently improved by Xagawa [50].

However, we were not able to find a suitable lattice-based ingredient to be used as the second PE layer, so that it interacts smoothly and securely with the main layer (which might due to the fact that there has not been a lattice analogue of the dual system encryption techniques). Instead, we use a variant of Agrawal et al.'s anonymous IBE [1] to realize the second layer as follows. We first consider a binary tree with N leaves, where N is the maximum expected number of private keys. We then associate each node θ in the binary tree with an "identifier" $\mathbf{D}_\theta$. Then, for each $I \in [N]$, we equip the private key indexed by I with "decryption keys" corresponding to all identifiers in the tree path from I to the root. When generating a ciphertext with respect to revocation list RL, the sender aims to the identifiers $\mathbf{D}_{\theta'}$'s, for all θ' belonging to the cover set determined by RL. Thanks to the anonymity of the scheme, RL is kept hidden. Furthermore, the correctness of the tree-based revocation technique from [28] ensures that the ciphertext is decryptable using the private key indexed by I if and only if $I \notin$ RL.

To combine the AFV PE layer with the above anonymous IBE layer, we rely on a splitting technique that can be seen as a secret sharing mechanism and that was used in previous lattice-based revocation schemes [11, 29, 47]. To this end, for each $I \in [N]$, we split a public matrix $\mathbf{U}$ into two random parts: (i) $\mathbf{U}_I$ which is associated with the main PE layer; (ii) $\mathbf{U} - \mathbf{U}_I$ that is linked with the second layer.

The efficiency of our RPE can be improved in the random oracle model, where instead of storing all the matrices $\mathbf{D}_\theta$'s in the public parameters, we simply obtain them as outputs of a random oracle.

OTHER RELATED WORKS. The subset-cover framework, proposed by Naor et al. [28] in the context of broadcast encryption, is arguably the most well-known revocation technique for multi-user systems. It uses a binary tree, each leaf of which is designated to each user. Non-revoked users are partitioned into disjoint subsets, and are assigned keys according to the Complete Subtree (CS) method or the Subset Difference (SD) method. This framework was first considered in the IBE setting by Boldyreva et al. [8]. Subsequently, several identity-based instantiations from pairings [8, 24] and from lattices [11, 12, 29, 47] were proposed, providing various improvements. Seo and Emura [42] suggested a strong security notion for revocable IBE, that takes into account the threat of decryption key exposure attacks. There have been several constructions satisfying this strong notion, which operate in the subset-cover framework, e.g., [41–45, 48]. The framework also found applications in the context of revocable group signatures [22, 23], revocable ABE [5, 8, 39] and revocable PE [20, 30, 31].

Predicate encryption for inner-product predicates was introduced by Katz et al. [19]. In such a scheme, attribute a and predicate f are expressed as vectors $\overrightarrow{x}$ and $\overrightarrow{y}$ respectively, and we say $f(a) = 1$ if and only if $\langle \overrightarrow{x}, \overrightarrow{y} \rangle = 0$ (hereafter, $\langle \overrightarrow{x}, \overrightarrow{y} \rangle$ denotes the inner product of vector $\overrightarrow{x}$ and vector $\overrightarrow{y}$). Katz, Sahai, and Waters also demonstrated the expressiveness of inner-product predicates: they can be used to encode several other predicates, such as equalities, hidden vector predicate, polynomial evaluation and CNF/DNF formulae. Following the work of [19], a number of pairing-based predicate encryption schemes [6, 21, 32–35] for inner products have been proposed. In the lattice-based world, Agrawal et al. [2] proposed the first such scheme, and Xagawa [50] suggested an improved variant.

Organization. The rest of this paper is organized as follows. In Sect. 2, we recall some background on lattice-based cryptography, revocable predicate encryption and the Complete Subtree method. Our main construction is described and analyzed in Sect. 3. Finally, we discuss possible extensions of our scheme and some open questions in Sect. 4.

2 Preliminaries

NOTATIONS. The acronym PPT stands for "probabilistic polynomial-time". We often write $x \hookleftarrow \chi$ to indicate that we sample x from probability distribution χ. If Ω is a finite set, the notation $x \xleftarrow{\$} \Omega$ means that x is chosen uniformly at random from Ω. Meanwhile, if x is an output of PPT algorithm $\mathcal{A}$, then we write $x \leftarrow \mathcal{A}$.

We use bold upper-case letters (e.g., $\mathbf{A}, \mathbf{B}$) to denote matrices and use bold lower-case letters (e.g., $\mathbf{x}, \mathbf{y}$) to denote column vectors. In addition, we user over-arrows to denote predicate and attribute vectors as $\overrightarrow{x}, \overrightarrow{y}$. For two matrices $\mathbf{A} \in \mathbb{R}^{n \times m}$ and $\mathbf{B} \in \mathbb{R}^{n \times k}$, we denote by $[\mathbf{A} \mid \mathbf{B}] \in \mathbb{R}^{n \times (m+k)}$ the column-concatenation of $\mathbf{A}$ and $\mathbf{B}$. For a vector $\mathbf{x} \in \mathbb{Z}^n$, $||\mathbf{x}||$ denotes the Euclidean norm of $\mathbf{x}$. We use $\widetilde{\mathbf{A}}$ to denote the Gram-Schmidt orthogonalization of matrix $\mathbf{A}$, and $||\mathbf{A}||$ to denote the Euclidean norm of the longest column in $\mathbf{A}$. If n is a positive integer, $[n]$ denotes the set $\{1, .., n\}$. For $c \in \mathbb{R}$, let $\lfloor c \rceil = \lceil c - 1/2 \rceil$ denote the integer closest to c.

2.1 Background on Lattices

Integer lattices. An m-dimensional lattice Λ is a discrete subgroup of $\mathbb{R}^m$. A full-rank matrix $\mathbf{B} \in \mathbb{R}^{m \times m}$ is a basis of Λ if $\Lambda = \{\mathbf{y} \in \mathbb{R}^m : \exists \mathbf{s} \in \mathbb{Z}^m, \mathbf{y} = \mathbf{B} \cdot \mathbf{s}\}$. We are interested in integer lattices, i.e., when $\Lambda \subseteq \mathbb{Z}^m$. For any integer $q \geq 2$ and any $\mathbf{A} \in \mathbb{Z}_q^{n \times m}$, define the q-ary lattice: $\Lambda_q^\perp(\mathbf{A}) = \{\mathbf{r} \in \mathbb{Z}^m : \mathbf{A} \cdot \mathbf{r} = \mathbf{0} \bmod q\} \subseteq \mathbb{Z}^m$. For any $\mathbf{u}$ in the image of $\mathbf{A}$, define the coset $\Lambda_q^{\mathbf{u}}(\mathbf{A}) = \{\mathbf{r} \in \mathbb{Z}^m : \mathbf{A} \cdot \mathbf{r} = \mathbf{u} \bmod q\}$.

A fundamental tool in lattice-based cryptography is an algorithm that generates a matrix $\mathbf{A}$ statistically close to uniform over $\mathbb{Z}_q^{n \times m}$ together with a short basis $\mathbf{T_A}$ of $\Lambda_q^\perp(\mathbf{A})$.

Lemma 1 [3,4,26]. *Let $n \geq 1, q \geq 2$ and $m \geq 2n \log q$ be integers. There exists a PPT algorithm $\mathsf{TrapGen}(n, q, m)$ that outputs a pair $(\mathbf{A}, \mathbf{T_A})$ such that $\mathbf{A}$ is statistically close to uniform over $\mathbb{Z}_q^{n \times m}$ and $\mathbf{T_A} \in \mathbb{Z}^{m \times m}$ is a basis for $\Lambda_q^\perp(\mathbf{A})$, satisfying $||\widetilde{\mathbf{T_A}}|| \leq O(\sqrt{n \log q})$ and $||\mathbf{T_A}|| \leq O(n \log q)$. with all but negligible probability in n.*

Micciancio and Peikert [26] consider a structured matrix $\mathbf{G}$, called the *primitive matrix*, which admits a publicly known short basis.

Lemma 2 [26]. *Let $n \geq 1, q \geq 2$ be integers and let $m \geq n\lceil \log q \rceil$. There exists a full-rank matrix $\mathbf{G} \in \mathbb{Z}_q^{n \times m}$ such that the lattice $\Lambda_q^\perp(\mathbf{G})$ has a known basis $\mathbf{T_G} \in \mathbb{Z}^{m \times m}$ with $\|\widetilde{\mathbf{T_G}}\| \leq \sqrt{5}$. Furthermore, there exists a deterministic polynomial-time algorithm $\mathbf{G}^{-1}$ which takes the input $\mathbf{U} \in \mathbb{Z}_q^{n \times m}$ and outputs $\mathbf{X} = \mathbf{G}^{-1}(\mathbf{U})$ such that $\mathbf{X} \in \{0,1\}^{m \times m}$ and $\mathbf{GX} = \mathbf{U}$.*

Discrete Gaussians. Let $\Lambda \subseteq \mathbb{Z}^m$ be a lattice. For any vector $\mathbf{c} \in \mathbb{R}^m$ and parameter $s > 0$, define $\rho_{s,\mathbf{c}}(\mathbf{r}) = \exp(-\pi \frac{\|\mathbf{r} - \mathbf{c}\|^2}{s^2})$ and $\rho_{s,\mathbf{c}}(\Lambda) = \sum_{\mathbf{r} \in \Lambda} \rho_{s,\mathbf{c}}(\mathbf{r})$ The discrete Gaussian distribution over Λ with $\mathbf{c}$ and s is $\forall \mathbf{r} \in \Lambda, \mathcal{D}_{\Lambda,s,\mathbf{c}}(\mathbf{r}) = \frac{\rho_{s,\mathbf{c}}(\mathbf{r})}{\rho_{s,\mathbf{c}}(\Lambda)}$. If $\mathbf{c} = \mathbf{0}$, for simplicity, we often use the notations ρ_s and $\mathcal{D}_{\Lambda,s}$.

Gentry et al. [15] showed how to sample from discrete Gaussians over lattices that have sufficiently short bases.

Lemma 3 [15]. *There exists a PPT algorithm $\mathsf{SampleGaussian}(\mathbf{B}, s, \mathbf{c})$ that, given a basis $\mathbf{B}$ of an m-dimensional lattice Λ, a Gaussian parameter $s \geq \|\widetilde{\mathbf{B}}\| \cdot \omega(\sqrt{\log m})$, and a center $\mathbf{c} \in \mathbb{R}^m$, outputs a sample from a distribution that is statistically close to $\mathcal{D}_{\Lambda,s,\mathbf{c}}$.*

We also need the following lemma for proving the correctness and security of the construction in Sect. 3. The lemma is obtained based on known facts from [15, Lemma 5.2], [27] and [13, Lemma 5],

Lemma 4. *Let $n \geq 1, q \geq 2$, $m \geq 2n \log q$ and $k \geq 1$ be integers. Let $\mathbf{F}$ be a full-rank matrix in $\mathbb{Z}_q^{n \times m}$ and $\mathbf{T_F}$ be a basis of $\Lambda_q^\perp(\mathbf{F})$. Assume that $s \geq \|\widetilde{\mathbf{T_F}}\| \cdot \omega(\sqrt{\log n})$. Then, for $\mathbf{Z} \hookleftarrow (\mathcal{D}_{\mathbb{Z}^m,s})^k$, the distribution of $\mathbf{FZ} \bmod q$ is statistically close to the uniform distribution over $\mathbb{Z}_q^{n \times k}$.*

In particular, Lemma 4 holds when $\mathbf{F}$ is a uniformly random matrix in $\mathbb{Z}_q^{n \times m}$ (see [15, Lemma 5.1] or when $\mathbf{F}$ is the matrix $\mathbf{G} \in \mathbb{Z}_q^{n \times m}$ in Lemma 2.

Sampling algorithms. It was shown in [1,26] how to efficiently sample short vectors from specific lattices. Looking ahead, we will use algorithm $\mathsf{SampleLeft}$ to sample keys in the RPE scheme of Sect. 3, while algorithm $\mathsf{SampleRight}$ will be employed to generate keys in the security proof.

$\mathsf{SampleLeft}(\mathbf{A}, \mathbf{M}, \mathbf{T_A}, \mathbf{u}, s)$: On input a rank n matrix $\mathbf{A} \in \mathbb{Z}_q^{n \times m}$, a matrix $\mathbf{M} \in \mathbb{Z}_q^{n \times m_1}$, a trapdoor $\mathbf{T_A}$ of $\Lambda_q^\perp(\mathbf{A})$, a vector $\mathbf{u} \in \mathbb{Z}_q^n$, and a Gaussian parameter $s \geq \|\widetilde{\mathbf{T_A}}\| \cdot \omega(\sqrt{\log(m + m_1)})$, it outputs a vector $\mathbf{z} \in \mathbb{Z}^{(m+m_1)}$, which is sampled from a distribution statistically close to $\mathcal{D}_{\Lambda_q^\mathbf{u}(\mathbf{F}),s}$. Here we define $\mathbf{F} = [\mathbf{A}|\mathbf{M}] \in \mathbb{Z}_q^{n \times (m+m_1)}$.

$\mathsf{SampleRight}(\mathbf{A}, \mathbf{R}, t, \mathbf{G}, \mathbf{T_G}, \mathbf{u}, s)$: On input matrices $\mathbf{A} \in \mathbb{Z}_q^{n \times m}, \mathbf{R} \in \mathbb{Z}^{m \times m}$, a scalar $t \in \mathbb{Z}_q \backslash \{0\}$, the primitive matrix $\mathbf{G} \in \mathbb{Z}_q^{n \times m}$ together with trapdoor $\mathbf{T_G}$ of $\Lambda_q^\perp(\mathbf{G})$, a vector $\mathbf{u} \in \mathbb{Z}_q^n$, and a Gaussian parameter $s \geq \|\widetilde{\mathbf{T_B}}\| \cdot \|\mathbf{R}\| \cdot \omega(\sqrt{\log m})$, it outputs a vector $\mathbf{z} \in \mathbb{Z}^{2m}$, which is sampled from a distribution statistically close to $\mathcal{D}_{\Lambda_q^\mathbf{u}(\mathbf{F}),s}$. Here we define $\mathbf{F} = [\mathbf{A}|\mathbf{AR} + t\mathbf{G}] \in \mathbb{Z}_q^{n \times 2m}$.

The above sampling algorithms are easily extended to the case where instead of taking a vector $\mathbf{u} \in \mathbb{Z}_q^n$ as input, one takes a matrix $\mathbf{U} \in \mathbb{Z}_q^{n \times k}$, for some $k \geq 1$. In this case, the output is a matrix $\mathbf{Z} \in \mathbb{Z}^{2m \times k}$.

We will also need a variant of left over hash lemma from [1].

Lemma 5. *Suppose that* $m > (n+1) \log q + \omega(\log n)$ *and* $q > 2$ *is a prime. Choose* $\mathbf{A} \xleftarrow{\$} \mathbb{Z}_q^{n \times m}$, $\mathbf{B} \xleftarrow{\$} \mathbb{Z}_q^{n \times \kappa}$ *and* $\mathbf{R} \xleftarrow{\$} \{-1, 1\}^{m \times \kappa}$ *where* $\kappa = \kappa(n)$ *is polynomial in* n. *Then for any vector* $\mathbf{v} \in \mathbb{Z}_q^m$, *the distribution of* $(\mathbf{A}, \mathbf{AR}, \mathbf{R}^\top \mathbf{v})$ *is statistically close to the distribution of* $(\mathbf{A}, \mathbf{B}, \mathbf{R}^\top \mathbf{v})$.

Learning With Errors. We now recall the Learning With Errors (LWE) problem [38], as well as its hardness.

Definition 1 (LWE). *Let* $n, m \geq 1, q \geq 2$, *and let* χ *be a probability distribution on* $\mathbb{Z}$. *For* $\mathbf{s} \in \mathbb{Z}_q^n$, *let* $\mathbf{A}_{\mathbf{s}, \chi}$ *be the distribution obtained by sampling* $\mathbf{a} \xleftarrow{\$} \mathbb{Z}_q^n$ *and* $e \hookleftarrow \chi$, *and outputting the pair* $(\mathbf{a}, \mathbf{a}^\top \mathbf{s} + e) \in \mathbb{Z}_q^n \times \mathbb{Z}_q$. *The* (n, q, χ)-LWE *problem asks to distinguish* m *samples chosen according to* $\mathbf{A}_{\mathbf{s}, \chi}$ *(for* $\mathbf{s} \xleftarrow{\$} \mathbb{Z}_q^n$) *and* m *samples chosen according to the uniform distribution over* $\mathbb{Z}_q^n \times \mathbb{Z}_q$.

If q is a prime power and $B \geq \sqrt{n} \cdot \omega(\log n)$, then there exists an efficient sampleable B-bounded distribution χ (i.e., χ outputs samples with norm at most B with overwhelming probability) such that (n, q, χ)-LWE is as least as hard as worst-case lattice problem SIVP with approximate factor $O(nq/B)$ (see [25,26, 36,38]).

2.2 The Agrawal-Freeman-Vaikuntanathan Predicate Encryption Scheme

Next, we recall the LWE-based predicate encryption, proposed by Agrawal, Freeman and Vaikuntanathan (AFV) [2]. The scheme is for inner-product predicates, where an attribute is expressed as a vector $\overrightarrow{y} \in \mathbb{Z}_q^\ell$ (for some integers q and ℓ) and a predicate $f_{\overrightarrow{x}}$ is associated with a vector $\overrightarrow{x} \in \mathbb{Z}_q^\ell$. We say that $f_{\overrightarrow{x}}(\overrightarrow{y}) = 1$ if $\langle \overrightarrow{x}, \overrightarrow{y} \rangle = 0$, and $f_{\overrightarrow{x}}(\overrightarrow{y}) = 0$ otherwise. The set $\mathbb{A} = \mathbb{Z}_q^\ell$ is called the attribute space, while the set $\mathbb{P} = \{f_{\overrightarrow{x}} \mid \overrightarrow{x} \in \mathbb{Z}_q^\ell\}$ is called the predicate space.

In the AFV scheme, the key authority possesses a short basis $\mathbf{T_A}$ for a public lattice $\Lambda_q^\perp(\mathbf{A})$, outputted by the TrapGen algorithm. Each predicate $f_{\overrightarrow{x}} \in \mathbb{P}$ is associated with a super-lattice of $\Lambda_q^\perp(\mathbf{A})$, a short vector of which can be efficiently computed using the trapdoor $\mathbf{T_A}$. Such a short vector allows to decrypt a Dual-Regev ciphertext [15] bound to an attribute vector $\overrightarrow{y} \in \mathbb{A}$ satisfying $f_{\overrightarrow{x}}(\overrightarrow{y}) = 1$. In order to improve efficiency, Xagawa [50] suggested an enhanced variant that employs the primitive matrix $\mathbf{G}$. In the below, we will describe the AFV scheme with Xagawa's improvement. The scheme works with appropriately chosen parameters n, q, m, s and LWE error distribution χ.

Setup: Generate $(\mathbf{A}, \mathbf{T_A}) \leftarrow \mathsf{TrapGen}(n, q, m)$. Pick $\mathbf{u} \xleftarrow{\$} \mathbb{Z}_q^n$ and for each $i \in [\ell]$, sample $\mathbf{A}_i \xleftarrow{\$} \mathbb{Z}_q^{n \times m}$. Output $\mathsf{pp} = (\mathbf{A}, \{\mathbf{A}_i\}_{i \in [\ell]}, \mathbf{u})$ and $\mathsf{msk} = \mathbf{T_A}$.

KeyGen: For vector $\overrightarrow{x} = (x_1, \ldots, x_\ell) \in \mathbb{Z}_q^\ell$, set $\mathbf{A}_{\overrightarrow{x}} = \sum_{i=1}^{\ell} \mathbf{A}_i \mathbf{G}^{-1}(x_i \cdot \mathbf{G}) \in \mathbb{Z}_q^{n \times m}$
and output the key $\mathsf{sk}_{\overrightarrow{x}} = \mathbf{r} \in \mathbb{Z}^{2m}$ using $\mathbf{r} \leftarrow \mathsf{SampleLeft}\,(\mathbf{A}, \mathbf{A}_{\overrightarrow{x}}, \mathbf{T_A}, \mathbf{u}, s)$.
Enc: To encrypt message $M \in \{0,1\}$ under vector $\overrightarrow{y} = (\overrightarrow{y}_1, \ldots, \overrightarrow{y}_\ell) \in \mathbb{Z}_q^\ell$,
choose $\mathbf{s} \xleftarrow{\$} \mathbb{Z}_q^n$, $\mathbf{e} \hookleftarrow \chi^m$, $e \hookleftarrow \chi$, and $\mathbf{R}_i \xleftarrow{\$} \{-1,1\}^{m \times m}$ for each $i \in [\ell]$, then
output $\mathsf{ct} = (c', \mathbf{c}_0, \{\mathbf{c}_i\}_{i \in [\ell]})$, where:

$$c' = \mathbf{u}^\top \mathbf{s} + e + M \cdot \lfloor \frac{q}{2} \rfloor \in \mathbb{Z}_q,$$

$$\mathbf{c}_0 = \mathbf{A}^\top \mathbf{s} + \mathbf{e} \in \mathbb{Z}_q^m,$$

$$\forall i \in [\ell]: \quad \mathbf{c}_i = (\mathbf{A}_i + y_i \cdot \mathbf{G})^\top \mathbf{s} + \mathbf{R}_i^\top \mathbf{e} \in \mathbb{Z}_q^m.$$

Dec: Set $\mathbf{c}_{\overrightarrow{x}} = \sum_{i=1}^{\ell} \left(\mathbf{G}^{-1}(x_i \cdot \mathbf{G}) \right)^\top \mathbf{c}_i \in \mathbb{Z}_q^m$. Then compute $z = c' - \mathbf{r}^\top [\mathbf{c}_0 \mid \mathbf{c}_{\overrightarrow{x}}] \in \mathbb{Z}_q$ and output $\lfloor \frac{2}{q} \cdot z \rceil \in \{0,1\}$.

Agrawal, Freeman and Vaikuntanathan showed that, under the (n, q, χ)-LWE assumption, their PE scheme satisfies the weak attribute-hiding security notion defined by Katz et al. [19], in a selective attribute setting. Xagawa [50] proved that the same assertion holds for his improved scheme variant. In Sect. 3, the scheme will be used as a building block for our lattice-based instantiation of revocable predicate encryption.

2.3   Revocable Predicate Encryption

Now, we recall the definition of RPE from [5,30,31], and its full-hiding security notion suggested by Nieto et al. [30,31].

Definition 2. *A revocable predicate encryption scheme consists of four algorithms* (Setup, KeyGen, Enc, Dec) *and has an associated predicate space* $\mathbb{P}$, *an attribute space* $\mathbb{A}$, *an index space* $\mathcal{I}$ *and a message space* $\mathcal{M}$.

Setup(1^λ) *takes as input a security parameter* λ. *It outputs a state information* ST, *a set of public parameters* pp *and a master secret key* msk. *We assume* pp *to be an implicit input of all other algorithms.*
KeyGen$(msk, ST, \overrightarrow{x}, I)$ *takes as input the master secret key* msk, *the state* ST, *a predicate vector* $\overrightarrow{x}$ *corresponding to a predicate* $f_{\overrightarrow{x}} \in \mathbb{P}$ *and an index* $I \in \mathcal{I}$. *It outputs an updated state* ST *and a private key* $\mathsf{sk}_{\overrightarrow{x}, I}$.
Enc$(\overrightarrow{y}, RL, M)$ *takes as input an attribute vector* $\overrightarrow{y} \in \mathbb{A}$, *a revocation list* $RL \subseteq \mathcal{I}$, *and a message* $M \in \mathcal{M}$. *It outputs a ciphertext* ct.
Dec$(ct, \mathsf{sk}_{\overrightarrow{x}, I})$ *takes as input a ciphertext* ct *and a private key* $\mathsf{sk}_{\overrightarrow{x}, I}$. *It outputs a message* M *or the distinguished symbol* $\perp$.

Correctness. The correctness requirement demands that, for all pp and msk generated by Setup (1^λ), all $f_{\overrightarrow{x}} \in \mathbb{P}$, $\overrightarrow{y} \in \mathbb{A}$, $I \in \mathcal{I}$, all state information ST, all $\mathsf{sk}_{\overrightarrow{x}, I} \leftarrow$ KeyGen(msk, ST, $\overrightarrow{x}, I$) and ct $\leftarrow$ Enc($\overrightarrow{y}$, RL, M), if $I \notin$ RL then:

1. If $f_{\overrightarrow{x}}(\overrightarrow{y}) = 1$ then $\mathsf{Dec}\left(\mathsf{ct}, \mathsf{sk}_{\overrightarrow{x}, I}\right) = M$.
2. If $f_{\overrightarrow{x}}(\overrightarrow{y}) = 0$ then $\mathsf{Dec}\left(\mathsf{ct}, \mathsf{sk}_{\overrightarrow{x}, I}\right) = \perp$ with all but negligible probability.

Full-Hiding Security. In [30,31], Nieto, Manulis and Sun introduced the notion of full-hiding security against chosen plaintext attacks for RPE, which demands that ciphertexts do not leak any information about the plaintexts, the attributes, nor the revoked indexes. This notion can be defined in the strong, adaptive manner, or in the relaxed, selective sense where the adversary is required to announce the challenge attribute vectors $\overrightarrow{y}^{(0)}, \overrightarrow{y}^{(1)}$ and revocation lists $\mathsf{RL}^{(0)}, \mathsf{RL}^{(1)}$ before seeing public parameters. In this work, we consider the latter.

Definition 3. *An RPE scheme is selectively full hiding against chosen plaintext attacks if any PPT adversary $\mathcal{A}$ has negligible advantage in the following game:*

1. *$\mathcal{A}$ announces the attribute vectors $\overrightarrow{y}^{(0)}, \overrightarrow{y}^{(1)}$, revocation lists $\mathsf{RL}^{(0)}, \mathsf{RL}^{(1)}$.*
2. *$\mathsf{Setup}\left(1^{\lambda}\right)$ is run to generate a state information ST, a set of public parameters pp and a master secret key msk. Then $\mathcal{A}$ is given pp.*
3. *$\mathcal{A}$ may make queries for private keys. For a query of a predicate vector and an index in the form $(\overrightarrow{x}, I)$, $\mathcal{A}$ is given $\mathsf{sk}_{\overrightarrow{x}, I} \leftarrow \mathsf{KeyGen}(\mathsf{msk}, \mathsf{ST}, \overrightarrow{x}, I)$, subject to one of the following restrictions:*
    - *$f_{\overrightarrow{x}}(\overrightarrow{y}^{(0)}) = f_{\overrightarrow{x}}(\overrightarrow{y}^{(1)}) = 0$;*
    - *$f_{\overrightarrow{x}}(\overrightarrow{y}^{(0)}) = f_{\overrightarrow{x}}(\overrightarrow{y}^{(1)}) = 1$ and $I \in \mathsf{RL}^{(0)} \cap \mathsf{RL}^{(1)}$;*
    - *$f_{\overrightarrow{x}}(\overrightarrow{y}^{(0)}) = 1 \wedge f_{\overrightarrow{x}}(\overrightarrow{y}^{(1)}) = 0$ and $I \in \mathsf{RL}^{(0)}$;*
    - *$f_{\overrightarrow{x}}(\overrightarrow{y}^{(0)}) = 0 \wedge f_{\overrightarrow{x}}(\overrightarrow{y}^{(1)}) = 1$ and $I \in \mathsf{RL}^{(1)}$.*
4. *$\mathcal{A}$ outputs two challenge plaintexts $M^{(0)}, M^{(1)}$. A uniformly random bit b is chosen, and $\mathcal{A}$ is given the ciphertext $\mathsf{ct}^* \leftarrow \mathsf{Enc}(\overrightarrow{y}^{(b)}, \mathsf{RL}^{(b)}, M^{(b)})$.*
5. *The adversary may continue to make additional queries for private keys, subject to the same restrictions as before.*
6. *$\mathcal{A}$ outputs a bit b' and succeeds if $b' = b$. The advantage of $\mathcal{A}$ in the game is defined as: $\mathsf{Adv}_{\mathcal{A}}^{\mathsf{sFH}}(\lambda) = \left| \Pr\left[b' = b\right] - \frac{1}{2} \right|$.*

Remark 1. In the above game, the restrictions for private-key queries are to prevent the adversary to trivially win the game by decrypting the challenge ciphertext ct^*. For the same reason, it is necessary to assume that the two ciphertexts $\mathsf{Enc}(\overrightarrow{y}^{(0)}, \mathsf{RL}^{(0)}, M^{(0)})$ and $\mathsf{Enc}(\overrightarrow{y}^{(1)}, \mathsf{RL}^{(1)}, M^{(1)})$ have the same size.

2.4 The Complete Subtree Method

The complete subtree (CS) method, introduced by Naor et al. [28], has been widely used in revocation systems. It makes use of a node selection algorithm (called $\mathsf{KUNodes}$). In the algorithm, we build a complete binary tree BT and use the following notation: If θ is a non-leaf node, then θ_{ℓ} and θ_r denote the left and right child of θ, respectively. Whenever ν is a leaf node, the set $\mathsf{Path}(\nu)$ stands for the collection of nodes on the path from ν to the root (including ν and the root). The $\mathsf{KUNodes}$ algorithm takes as input the binary tree BT and a revocation list RL, and outputs a set of nodes Y which is the smallest subset of nodes that contains an ancestor of all the leaf nodes corresponding to non-revoked indexes. It is known [28] that the set Y generated by KUNodes(BT, RL) has a size at most $r \log \frac{N}{r}$, where r is the number of indexes in RL. The detailed description of algorithm KUNodes is given below.

> KUNodes(BT, RL)
>
> $X, Y \leftarrow \emptyset; \forall \nu \in$ RL : add Path(ν) to X
>
> $\forall \theta \in X$: if $\theta_\ell \notin X$, then add θ_ℓ to Y; if $\theta_r \notin X$, then add θ_r to Y
>
> If $Y = \emptyset$, then add root to Y; Return Y

In Sect. 3, we will employ the CS method to realize user revocation.

3 Our Lattice-Based RPE Scheme

This section presents our construction of lattice-based RPE scheme for inner-product predicates. As we briefly discussed in Sect. 1, the scheme employs two encryption layers: the AFV PE scheme [2,50] and a variant of Agrawal et al.'s anonymous IBE scheme [1]. Revocation is realized using the CS method and a splitting technique that can be seen as a secret sharing mechanism and that was used in previous lattice-based revocation schemes [11,29,47].

Before describing our scheme in detail, let us discuss a small issue in existing PE schemes [2,13,16,50] from lattices. Recall that the correctness of PE requires in particular that if $f_{\overrightarrow{x}}(\overrightarrow{y}) = 0$ then the decryption algorithm with private key $\mathsf{sk}_{\overrightarrow{x}}$ must fail with all but negligible probability when applying to a ciphertext associated with $\overrightarrow{y}$. However, in the LWE-based public-key encryption schemes used in the above constructions, the decryption algorithm does not fail: it outputs a random element in the plaintext space $\mathcal{M}$. To overcome this issue and enforce correctness, the following idea was suggested and implemented in [2,13,16,50], assuming that the scheme can be modified to work with plaintext space $\mathcal{M}'$, such that $|\mathcal{M}|/|\mathcal{M}'| = \mathsf{negl}(\lambda)$, where λ is the security parameter. Then, to encrypt an element of $\mathcal{M}$, one encodes it to an element of $\mathcal{M}'$ and proceeds with the encoding. Since the probability that a random element in $\mathcal{M}'$ is a proper encoding is negligible, the correctness of the scheme is ensured.

Our scheme operates with plaintext space $\mathcal{M} = \{0, 1\}$. Following the idea discussed above, let us define the encoding function $\mathsf{encode} : \mathcal{M} \to \{0, 1\}^k$ for $k = \omega(\log \lambda)$, such that for each $b \in \mathcal{M}$, we have $\mathsf{encode}(b) = (b, 0, \dots, 0) \in \{0, 1\}^k$ - the binary vector that has b as the first coordinate and 0 elsewhere. This encoding technique has the desirable property, as we have $2/2^k = 2^{-\omega(\log \lambda)} = \mathsf{negl}(\lambda)$.

3.1 Description of the Scheme

Our scheme works with security parameter λ and global parameters N, ℓ, n, q, m, k, $\mathbf{G}, s, B, \chi$ specified below.

◇ $N = \mathsf{poly}(\lambda)$: the maximum expected number of users;
◇ $\ell = \mathsf{poly}(\lambda)$: the length of predicate and attribute vectors;
◇ Lattice parameter $n = O(\lambda)$, prime modulus $q = \widetilde{O}(\ell^2 n^4)$, dimensions $m = \lceil 2n \log q \rceil$ and $k = \omega(\log \lambda)$;
◇ The primitive matrix $\mathbf{G}$ with public trapdoor $\mathbf{T_G}$ (see Lemma 2);
◇ Gaussian parameter $s = \widetilde{O}(\ell\sqrt{m})$; Norm bound $B = \widetilde{O}(\sqrt{m})$ and B-bounded distribution χ.

The attribute space is set as $\mathbb{A} = \mathbb{Z}_q^\ell$. Each $\overrightarrow{x} \in \mathbb{A}$ is associated with predicate $f_{\overrightarrow{x}} : \mathbb{A} \rightarrow \{0, 1\}$, where for all $\overrightarrow{y} \in \mathbb{A}$, we have: $f_{\overrightarrow{x}}(\overrightarrow{y}) = 1$ if and only if $\langle \overrightarrow{x}, \overrightarrow{y} \rangle = 0$. The predicate space is then defined as $\mathbb{P} = \{f_{\overrightarrow{x}} \mid \overrightarrow{x} \in \mathbb{A}\}$. The scheme works with index space $\mathcal{I} = [N]$.

We now provide the detailed description of the scheme.

$\mathsf{Setup}(1^\lambda)$: On input security parameter λ, this algorithm works as following:

1. Run the algorithm $\mathsf{TrapGen}(n, q, m)$ to generate a matrix $\mathbf{A} \in \mathbb{Z}_q^{n \times m}$ together with a basis $\mathbf{T_A}$ for $\Lambda_q^\perp(\mathbf{A})$ such that $\|\widetilde{\mathbf{T_A}}\| \le O(\sqrt{n \log q})$.
2. Pick $\mathbf{U} \xleftarrow{\$} \mathbb{Z}_q^{n \times k}$.
3. Sample $\mathbf{A}_i \xleftarrow{\$} \mathbb{Z}_q^{n \times m}$, for each $i \in [\ell]$.
4. Build a binary tree BT with N leaf nodes. For each node $\theta \in \mathsf{BT}$, choose $\mathbf{D}_\theta \xleftarrow{\$} \mathbb{Z}_q^{n \times m}$, which will be viewed as the "identifier" of the node.
5. Initialize the state $\mathsf{ST} = \emptyset$, which records the assigned indexes so far.
6. Output ST, $\mathsf{pp} = (\mathbf{A}, \{\mathbf{A}_i\}_{i \in [\ell]}, \mathbf{U}, \mathsf{BT})$ and $\mathsf{msk} = \mathbf{T_A}$.

$\mathsf{KeyGen}(\mathsf{msk}, \mathsf{ST}, \overrightarrow{x}, I)$: On input the master key msk, state ST, a predicate vector $\overrightarrow{x} = (x_1, \ldots, x_\ell) \in \mathbb{Z}_q^\ell$ and an index $I \in [N]$, this algorithm performs the following steps:

1. If $I \in \mathsf{ST}$, then return $\bot$. Else, update the state $\mathsf{ST} \leftarrow \mathsf{ST} \cup \{I\}$.
2. Pick $\mathbf{U}_I \xleftarrow{\$} \mathbb{Z}_q^{n \times k}$.
3. Set $\mathbf{A}_{\overrightarrow{x}} = \sum\limits_{i=1}^{\ell} \mathbf{A}_i \mathbf{G}^{-1}(x_i \cdot \mathbf{G})$ and get $\mathbf{Z} \leftarrow \mathsf{SampleLeft}(\mathbf{A}, \mathbf{A}_{\overrightarrow{x}}, \mathbf{T_A}, \mathbf{U}_I, s)$. We note that $\mathbf{Z}$ is a matrix in $\mathbb{Z}^{2m \times k}$ satisfying $[\mathbf{A} \mid \mathbf{A}_{\overrightarrow{x}}] \cdot \mathbf{Z} = \mathbf{U}_I$.
4. For each $\theta \in \mathsf{Path}(I)$, sample $\mathbf{Z}_\theta \leftarrow \mathsf{SampleLeft}(\mathbf{A}, \mathbf{D}_\theta, \mathbf{T_A}, \mathbf{U} - \mathbf{U}_I, s)$. We remark that each $\mathbf{Z}_\theta$ is a matrix in $\mathbb{Z}^{2m \times k}$ satisfying $[\mathbf{A} \mid \mathbf{D}_\theta] \cdot \mathbf{Z}_\theta = \mathbf{U} - \mathbf{U}_I$.
5. Output the updated state ST and $\mathsf{sk}_{\overrightarrow{x}, I} = (I, \mathbf{Z}, \{\mathbf{Z}_\theta\}_{\theta \in \mathsf{Path}(I)})$.

$\mathsf{Enc}(\overrightarrow{y}, \mathsf{RL}, M)$: On input an attribute vector $\overrightarrow{y} = (y_1, \ldots, y_\ell) \in \mathbb{Z}_q^\ell$, a revocation list $\mathsf{RL} \subseteq [N]$ and a message $M \in \{0, 1\}$, this algorithm performs the following steps:

1. Sample $\mathbf{s} \xleftarrow{\$} \mathbb{Z}_q^n$, $\mathbf{e}' \hookleftarrow \chi^k$ and $\mathbf{e} \hookleftarrow \chi^m$.
2. Pick $\mathbf{R}_i, \mathbf{S}_\theta \xleftarrow{\$} \{-1, 1\}^{m \times m}$ for each $i \in [\ell]$ and $\theta \in \mathsf{KUNodes}(\mathsf{BT}, \mathsf{RL})$.

3. Output $\mathsf{ct} = \big(\mathbf{c}', \mathbf{c}_0, \{\mathbf{c}_i\}_{i\in[\ell]}, \{\widehat{\mathbf{c}}_\theta\}_{\theta\in\mathsf{KUNodes(BT,RL)}}\big)$, where:

$$\mathbf{c}' = \mathbf{U}^\top \mathbf{s} + \mathbf{e}' + \lfloor\tfrac{q}{2}\rfloor \cdot \mathsf{encode}(M) \in \mathbb{Z}_q^k,$$

$$\mathbf{c}_0 = \mathbf{A}^\top \mathbf{s} + \mathbf{e} \in \mathbb{Z}_q^m,$$

$$\forall i \in [\ell]: \quad \mathbf{c}_i = (\mathbf{A}_i + y_i \cdot \mathbf{G})^\top \mathbf{s} + \mathbf{R}_i^\top \mathbf{e} \in \mathbb{Z}_q^m,$$

$$\forall \theta \in \mathsf{KUNodes(BT, RL)}: \quad \widehat{\mathbf{c}}_\theta = \mathbf{D}_\theta^\top \mathbf{s} + \mathbf{S}_\theta^\top \mathbf{e} \in \mathbb{Z}_q^m.$$

$\mathsf{Dec}(\mathsf{ct}, \mathsf{sk}_{\overrightarrow{x},I})$: On input a ciphertext $\mathsf{ct} = \big(\mathbf{c}', \mathbf{c}_0, \{\mathbf{c}_i\}_{i\in[\ell]}, \{\widehat{\mathbf{c}}_{\theta'}\}_{\theta'}\big)$, where $\{\widehat{\mathbf{c}}_{\theta'}\}_{\theta'}$ denotes a collection of vectors in $\mathbb{Z}_q^m$, and a private key $\mathsf{sk}_{\overrightarrow{x},I} = \big(I, \mathbf{Z}, \{\mathbf{Z}_\theta\}_{\theta\in\mathsf{Path}(I)}\big)$, this algorithm proceeds as follows:

1. Compute $\mathbf{c}_{\overrightarrow{x}} = \sum_{i=1}^{\ell}\big(\mathbf{G}^{-1}(x_i \cdot \mathbf{G})\big)^\top \mathbf{c}_i \in \mathbb{Z}_q^m.$
2. For all pairs (θ, θ'), compute $\mathbf{d}_{\theta,\theta'} = \mathbf{c}' - \mathbf{Z}^\top [\mathbf{c}_0 \mid \mathbf{c}_{\overrightarrow{x}}] - \mathbf{Z}_\theta^\top [\mathbf{c}_0 \mid \widehat{\mathbf{c}}_{\theta'}] \in \mathbb{Z}_q^k.$
3. If there exists a pair (θ, θ') such that $\lfloor\tfrac{2}{q} \cdot \mathbf{d}_{\theta,\theta'}\rceil = \mathsf{encode}(M')$, for some $M' \in \{0,1\}$, then output M'. Otherwise, output $\perp$.

3.2   Correctness, Efficiency and Potential Implementation

Correctness. We will demonstrate that the scheme satisfies the correctness requirement with all but negligible probability. We proceed as in [2,13,50].

Suppose that $\mathsf{ct} = \big(\mathbf{c}', \mathbf{c}_0, \{\mathbf{c}_i\}_{i\in[\ell]}, \{\widehat{\mathbf{c}}_\theta\}_{\theta\in\mathsf{KUNodes(BT,RL)}}\big)$ is an honestly computed ciphertext of message $M \in \{0,1\}$, with respect to some $\overrightarrow{y} \in \mathcal{A}$ and some $\mathsf{RL} \subseteq [N]$. Let $\mathsf{sk}_{\overrightarrow{x},I} = \big(I, \mathbf{Z}, \{\mathbf{Z}_\theta\}_{\theta\in\mathsf{Path}(I)}\big)$ be a correctly generated private key, where $I \notin \mathsf{RL}$. We first observe that the following holds:

$$\mathbf{c}_{\overrightarrow{x}} = \sum_{i=1}^{\ell}\big(\mathbf{G}^{-1}(x_i \cdot \mathbf{G})\big)^\top \mathbf{c}_i = (\mathbf{A}_{\overrightarrow{x}} + \langle\overrightarrow{x},\overrightarrow{y}\rangle \cdot \mathbf{G})^\top \mathbf{s} + \sum_{i=1}^{\ell}\big(\mathbf{R}_i\mathbf{G}^{-1}(x_i \cdot \mathbf{G})\big)^\top \mathbf{e}.$$

By construction, since $I \notin \mathsf{RL}$, there exists (θ, θ') corresponding to the same node in BT with $[\mathbf{A} \mid \mathbf{A}_{\overrightarrow{x}}] \cdot \mathbf{Z} + [\mathbf{A} \mid \mathbf{D}_{\theta'}] \cdot \mathbf{Z}_\theta = \mathbf{U}$. We now consider two cases:

1. Suppose that $\langle\overrightarrow{x},\overrightarrow{y}\rangle = 0$. Then $\mathbf{c}_{\overrightarrow{x}} = (\mathbf{A}_{\overrightarrow{x}})^\top \mathbf{s} + \sum_{i=1}^{\ell}\big(\mathbf{R}_i\mathbf{G}^{-1}(x_i \cdot \mathbf{G})\big)^\top \mathbf{e}.$

For the pair (θ, θ') specified above, the following holds:

$$\begin{aligned}
\mathbf{d}_{\theta,\theta'} &= \mathbf{c}' - \mathbf{Z}^\top [\mathbf{c}_0 \mid \mathbf{c}_{\overrightarrow{x}}] - \mathbf{Z}_\theta^\top [\mathbf{c}_0 \mid \widehat{\mathbf{c}}_{\theta'}]\\
&= \mathbf{U}^\top \mathbf{s} + \mathbf{e}' + \lfloor\tfrac{q}{2}\rfloor \cdot \mathsf{encode}(M) - \mathbf{Z}^\top\left([\mathbf{A} \mid \mathbf{A}_{\overrightarrow{x}}]^\top \mathbf{s} + \begin{bmatrix}\mathbf{e}\\(\mathbf{R}_{\overrightarrow{x}})^\top\mathbf{e}\end{bmatrix}\right)\\
&\quad\quad - \mathbf{Z}_\theta^\top\left([\mathbf{A} \mid \mathbf{D}_{\theta'}]^\top \mathbf{s} + \begin{bmatrix}\mathbf{e}\\\mathbf{S}_{\theta'}^\top\mathbf{e}\end{bmatrix}\right)\\
&= \lfloor\tfrac{q}{2}\rfloor \cdot \mathsf{encode}(M) + \underbrace{\mathbf{e}' - \mathbf{Z}^\top\begin{bmatrix}\mathbf{e}\\(\mathbf{R}_{\overrightarrow{x}})^\top\mathbf{e}\end{bmatrix} - \mathbf{Z}_\theta^\top\begin{bmatrix}\mathbf{e}\\\mathbf{S}_{\theta'}^\top\mathbf{e}\end{bmatrix}}_{\text{error}},
\end{aligned}$$

where $\mathbf{R}_{\overrightarrow{x}} = \sum\limits_{i=1}^{\ell} \left(\mathbf{R}_i \mathbf{G}^{-1}(x_i \cdot \mathbf{G}) \right)$. As in [1,2,13,50], the above error term can be showed to be bounded by $s\ell m^2 B \cdot \omega(\log n) = \widetilde{O}(\ell^2 n^3)$, with all but negligible probability. In order for the decryption algorithm to recover $\mathsf{encode}(M)$, and subsequently the plaintext M, it is required that the error term is bounded by $q/5$, i.e., $\|\mathsf{error}\|_\infty < q/5$. This is guaranteed by our setting of modulus q, i.e., $q = \widetilde{O}\left(\ell^2 n^4 \right)$.

2. Suppose that $\langle \overrightarrow{x}, \overrightarrow{y} \rangle \neq 0$. In this case, we have: $\mathbf{c}_{\overrightarrow{x}} = \left(\mathbf{A}_{\overrightarrow{x}} + \langle \overrightarrow{x}, \overrightarrow{y} \rangle \cdot \mathbf{G} \right)^\top \mathbf{s} + \sum\limits_{i=1}^{\ell} \left(\mathbf{R}_i \mathbf{G}^{-1}(x_i \cdot \mathbf{G}) \right)^\top \mathbf{e}$. Then for each pair (θ, θ'), the following holds:

$$\mathbf{d}_{\theta, \theta'} = \mathbf{U}^\top \mathbf{s} + \mathbf{e}' + \lfloor \tfrac{q}{2} \rfloor \cdot \mathsf{encode}(M) - \mathbf{Z}^\top \left([\mathbf{A} \mid \mathbf{A}_{\overrightarrow{x}} + \langle \overrightarrow{x}, \overrightarrow{y} \rangle \cdot \mathbf{G}]^\top \mathbf{s} \right.$$
$$\left. + \begin{bmatrix} \mathbf{e} \\ (\mathbf{R}_{\overrightarrow{x}})^\top \mathbf{e} \end{bmatrix} \right) - \mathbf{Z}_\theta^\top \left([\mathbf{A} \mid \mathbf{D}_{\theta'}]^\top \mathbf{s} + \begin{bmatrix} \mathbf{e} \\ \mathbf{S}_{\theta'}^\top \mathbf{e} \end{bmatrix} \right)$$

Observe that the above contains the term $\mathbf{Z}^\top [\mathbf{0} \mid \langle \overrightarrow{x}, \overrightarrow{y} \rangle \cdot \mathbf{G}]^\top \mathbf{s}$ which can be written as $\langle \overrightarrow{x}, \overrightarrow{y} \rangle \cdot (\mathbf{G}\mathbf{Z}_2)^\top \mathbf{s} \in \mathbb{Z}_q^k$, where $\mathbf{Z}_2 \in \mathbb{Z}^{m \times k}$ is the bottom part of matrix $\mathbf{Z}$. By Lemma 4, we have that the distribution of $\mathbf{G}\mathbf{Z}_2 \in \mathbb{Z}_q^{n \times k}$ is statistically close to uniform. This implies that, vector $\mathbf{d}_{\theta, \theta'} \in \mathbb{Z}_q^k$, for each pair (θ, θ'), is indistinguishable from uniform. As a result, the probability that the last $k - 1$ coordinates of vector $\lfloor \tfrac{2}{q} \cdot \mathbf{d}_{\theta, \theta'} \rceil$ are all 0 is at most $2^{-(k-1)} = 2^{-\omega(\log \lambda)}$, which is negligible in λ. In other words, except for negligible probability, the decryption algorithm outputs $\perp$ since it does not obtain a proper encoding $\mathsf{encode}(M) \in \{0,1\}^k$, for $M \in \{0,1\}$.

Efficiency. The efficiency aspect of our RPE scheme is as follows:

- The bit-size of public parameters pp is $((\ell + 2N)nm + nk) \log q = \left(\widetilde{O}(\ell) + O(N) \right) \cdot \widetilde{O}\left(\lambda^2 \right)$.
- The private key $\mathsf{sk}_{\overrightarrow{x}, I}$ has bit-size $O(\log N) \cdot \widetilde{O}(\lambda)$.
- The bit-size of ciphertext ct is $\left(\widetilde{O}(\ell) + O(r \log \tfrac{N}{r}) \right) \cdot \widetilde{O}(\lambda)$.

The efficiency of our scheme is comparable to that of the pairing-based RPE scheme from [30,31], in the following sense: the size of public parameters is $O(N)$; the size of the private key is $O(\log N)$, and the ciphertext has size $O\left(r \log \tfrac{N}{r} \right)$ which is ranged between $O(1)$ (when no key is revoked) and $O\left(\tfrac{N}{2} \right)$ (in the worst case when every second key is revoked).

In Sect. 4, we will discuss a variant of our scheme in the random oracle model, which has shorter public parameters.

Potential Implementation. While the focus of this work is to provide the first provably secure construction of RPE from lattice assumptions, it would be desirable to back it up with practical implementations and to compare the implementation details with those of pairing-based counterparts. However, this would be a highly challenging task, due to two main reasons:

1. We are not aware of any concrete implementation of the two building blocks of our scheme, i.e., the AFV PE [2,50] and Agrawal et al.'s IBE [1].
2. In [30,31], Nieto, Manulis and Sun did not provide implementation details of their pairing-based RPE scheme.

Given these circumstances, we leave the implementation aspect of our scheme as a future investigation. Nevertheless, in the following, we will discuss the potential of such implementation, by analyzing the main cryptographic operations needed for implementing the scheme. Apart from simple operations such as samplings of uniformly random matrices and vectors whose entries are in $\mathbb{Z}_q$ or $\{-1,1\}$, as well as multiplication and addition operations over $\mathbb{Z}_q$, the algorithms of the scheme requires the following time-consuming tasks:

◇ Generation of a lattice trapdoor;
◇ Samplings of discrete Gaussian vectors over lattices;
◇ Samplings of LWE noise vectors.

We note that it is feasible to implement the listed above cryptographic tasks using the algorithms provided in [15,26], which were recently improved in [14,27]. Some implementation results of those cryptographic tasks were reported in [18], which may serve as a stepping stone of potential implementation of our scheme.

3.3   Security

In the following theorem, we prove that our scheme in Sect. 3 is selectively full hiding in the standard model, under the LWE assumption.

Theorem 1. *Our RPE scheme satisfies the selective full-hiding security defined in Definition 3, assuming hardness of the (n, q, χ)-LWE problem.*

Proof. We proceed via a series of games, similar to those in [2,13,16]. First, we define the auxiliary algorithms for generating simulated public parameters, private keys and ciphertexts, and then, we describe the games.

Auxiliary algorithms. We consider the following auxiliary algorithms.

Sim.Setup$(1^\lambda, \mathbf{A}, \mathbf{U}, \overrightarrow{y}^*, \mathsf{RL}^*)$: On input a security parameter λ, a matrix $\mathbf{A} \in \mathbb{Z}_q^{n \times m}$, $\mathbf{U} \in \mathbb{Z}_q^{n \times k}$, the challenge attribute vector $\overrightarrow{y}^* = (y_1^*, \ldots, y_\ell^*) \in \mathbb{Z}_q^\ell$ and revocation list $\mathsf{RL}^* \subseteq [N]$, this algorithm performs the following steps:

1. For each $i \in [\ell]$, choose $\mathbf{R}_i \xleftarrow{\$} \{-1,1\}^{m \times m}$ and set $\mathbf{A}_i = \mathbf{AR}_i - y_i^* \cdot \mathbf{G}$.
2. Build a binary tree BT and choose $\mathbf{S}_\theta \xleftarrow{\$} \{-1,1\}^{m \times m}$ for each $\theta \in \mathsf{BT}$. Set the identifier: $\mathbf{D}_\theta = \begin{cases} \mathbf{AS}_\theta, & \text{if } \theta \in \mathsf{KUNodes}(\mathsf{BT}, \mathsf{RL}^*), \\ \mathbf{AS}_\theta + \mathbf{G}, & \text{otherwise.} \end{cases}$
3. Initialize the state ST.
4. Output $\mathsf{ST}, \mathsf{pp} = (\mathbf{A}, \{\mathbf{A}_i\}_{i \in [\ell]}, \mathbf{U}, \mathsf{BT})$ and $\mathsf{msk}^* = (\{\mathbf{R}_i\}_{i \in [\ell]}, \{\mathbf{S}_\theta\}_{\theta \in \mathsf{BT}})$.

Sim.KeyGen$(\mathsf{msk}^*, \mathsf{ST}, \overrightarrow{x}, I, \overrightarrow{y}^*, \mathsf{RL}^*)$: This algorithm takes as input msk^*, state ST, a predicate vector $\overrightarrow{x} \in \mathbb{Z}_q^\ell$, an index $I \in [N]$, the challenge attribute vector $\overrightarrow{y}^* \in \mathbb{Z}_q^\ell$ and revocation list $\mathsf{RL}^* \subseteq [N]$, such that the following condition holds: If $\langle \overrightarrow{x}, \overrightarrow{y}^* \rangle = 0$ then $I \in \mathsf{RL}^*$. The algorithm returns $\perp$ if $I \in \mathsf{ST}$. Otherwise, it outputs the updated state $\mathsf{ST} \leftarrow \mathsf{ST} \cup \{I\}$ and private key $\mathsf{sk}_{\overrightarrow{x}, I} = (I, \mathbf{Z}, \{\mathbf{Z}_\theta\}_{\theta \in \mathsf{Path}(I)})$ computed based on $\langle \overrightarrow{x}, \overrightarrow{y}^* \rangle$ as follows.

1. **Case 1:** $\langle \overrightarrow{x}, \overrightarrow{y}^* \rangle \neq 0$.

   (a) If $I \notin \mathsf{RL}^*$, then there is exactly one node θ^* in the intersection $\mathsf{Path}(I) \cap \mathsf{KUNodes}(\mathsf{BT}, \mathsf{RL}^*)$.

   Using Lemma 3, sample $\mathbf{Z}_{\theta^*} \hookleftarrow (\mathcal{D}_{\mathbb{Z}^{2m}, s})^k$ and set $\mathbf{U}_I = \mathbf{U} - [\mathbf{A} \mid \mathbf{D}_{\theta^*}] \cdot \mathbf{Z}_{\theta^*}$. For each node $\theta \in \mathsf{Path}(I) \backslash \{\theta^*\}$, sample $\mathbf{Z}_\theta \leftarrow \mathsf{SampleRight}(\mathbf{A}, \mathbf{S}_\theta, 1, \mathbf{G}, \mathbf{T_G}, \mathbf{U} - \mathbf{U}_I, s)$. (See Sect. 2.1 for the description of algorithm $\mathsf{SampleRight}$.)

   (b) If $I \in \mathsf{RL}^*$, choose $\mathbf{U}_I \xleftarrow{\$} \mathbb{Z}_q^{n \times k}$. Then for each $\theta \in \mathsf{Path}(I)$, sample $\mathbf{Z}_\theta \leftarrow \mathsf{SampleRight}(\mathbf{A}, \mathbf{S}_\theta, 1, \mathbf{G}, \mathbf{T_G}, \mathbf{U} - \mathbf{U}_I, s)$.

   As $\mathbf{A}_{\overrightarrow{x}} = \sum\limits_{i=1}^{\ell} \mathbf{A}_i \mathbf{G}^{-1}(x_i \cdot \mathbf{G}) = \mathbf{A}\big(\sum\limits_{i=1}^{\ell} \mathbf{R}_i \mathbf{G}^{-1}(x_i \cdot \mathbf{G})\big) - \underbrace{\langle \overrightarrow{x}, \overrightarrow{y}^* \rangle}_{\neq 0} \cdot \mathbf{G}$,

   sample $\mathbf{Z} \leftarrow \mathsf{SampleRight}(\mathbf{A}, \sum\limits_{i=1}^{\ell} \mathbf{R}_i \mathbf{G}^{-1}(x_i \cdot \mathbf{G}), -\langle \overrightarrow{x}, \overrightarrow{y}^* \rangle, \mathbf{G}, \mathbf{T_G}, \mathbf{U}_I, s)$

   satisfying $[\mathbf{A} \mid \mathbf{A}_{\overrightarrow{x}}] \cdot \mathbf{Z} = \mathbf{U}_I$.

2. **Case 2:** $\langle \overrightarrow{x}, \overrightarrow{y}^* \rangle = 0$. In this case, the condition $I \in \mathsf{RL}^*$ implies that $\mathsf{Path}(I) \cap \mathsf{KUNodes}(\mathsf{BT}, \mathsf{RL}^*) = \emptyset$. Note that, here we do not have a trapdoor for the matrix $[\mathbf{A} \mid \mathbf{A}_{\overrightarrow{x}}]$, but we can instead compute $\mathbf{Z}$ and $\{\mathbf{Z}_\theta\}_{\theta \in \mathsf{Path}(I)}$ as follows. First, we sample $\mathbf{Z} \hookleftarrow (\mathcal{D}_{\mathbb{Z}^{2m}, s})^k$ and set $\mathbf{U}_I = [\mathbf{A} \mid \mathbf{A}_{\overrightarrow{x}}] \cdot \mathbf{Z}$. Then, for each $\theta \in \mathsf{Path}(I)$, we sample $\mathbf{Z}_\theta \leftarrow \mathsf{SampleRight}(\mathbf{A}, \mathbf{S}_\theta, 1, \mathbf{G}, \mathbf{T_G}, \mathbf{U} - \mathbf{U}_I, s)$.

Sim.Enc$(\mathsf{msk}^*, M, \mathbf{d}_0, \mathbf{d}')$: On input msk^*, a message $M \in \{0, 1\}$, and $\mathbf{d}_0 \in \mathbb{Z}_q^m$, $\mathbf{d}' \in \mathbb{Z}_q^k$, it outputs $\mathsf{ct} = (\mathbf{c}', \mathbf{c}_0, \{\mathbf{c}_i\}_{i \in [\ell]}, \{\mathbf{c}_\theta\}_{\theta \in \mathsf{KUNodes}(\mathsf{BT}, \mathsf{RL})})$, where:

$$\mathbf{c}' = \mathbf{d}' + \lfloor \tfrac{q}{2} \rfloor \cdot \mathsf{encode}(M) \in \mathbb{Z}_q^k,$$

$$\mathbf{c}_0 = \mathbf{d}_0 \in \mathbb{Z}_q^m,$$

$$\forall i \in [\ell]: \quad \mathbf{c}_i = \mathbf{R}_i^\top \mathbf{d}_0 \in \mathbb{Z}_q^m,$$

$$\forall \theta \in \mathsf{KUNodes}(\mathsf{BT}, \mathsf{RL}^*): \quad \widehat{\mathbf{c}}_\theta = \mathbf{S}_\theta^\top \mathbf{d}_0 \in \mathbb{Z}_q^m.$$

The series of games. Let $\mathcal{A}$ be the adversary in the selective full-hiding game of Definition 3. We consider the following series of games.

- $\mathsf{Game}_0^{(b)}$: This game is the real security game in Definition 3, where the chosen bit is $b \in \{0, 1\}$.
- $\mathsf{Game}_1^{(b)}$: This game is the same as $\mathsf{Game}_0^{(b)}$, except that algorithms $\mathsf{Setup}(1^\lambda)$ and $\mathsf{Enc}(\overrightarrow{y}^{(b)}, \mathsf{RL}^{(b)}, M^{(b)})$ are replaced by $\mathsf{Sim.Setup}(1^\lambda, \mathbf{A}, \mathbf{U}, \overrightarrow{y}^{(b)}, \mathsf{RL}^{(b)})$ and $\mathsf{Sim.Enc}(\mathsf{msk}^*, M^{(b)}, \mathbf{A}^\top \mathbf{s} + \mathbf{e}, \mathbf{U}^\top \mathbf{s} + \mathbf{e}')$, respectively, where $\mathbf{A} \xleftarrow{\$} \mathbb{Z}_q^{n \times m}$, $\mathbf{U} \xleftarrow{\$} \mathbb{Z}_q^n$, $\mathbf{s} \xleftarrow{\$} \mathbb{Z}_q^n$, $\mathbf{e} \hookleftarrow \chi^m$, and $\mathbf{e}' \hookleftarrow \chi^k$.

- $\mathsf{Game}_2^{(b)}$: It is the same as $\mathsf{Game}_1^{(b)}$, except that $\mathsf{KeyGen}\left(\mathsf{msk}, \mathsf{ST}, \overrightarrow{x}, I\right)$ is replaced by algorithm $\mathsf{Sim}.\mathsf{KeyGen}\left(\mathsf{msk}^*, \mathsf{ST}, \overrightarrow{x}, I, \overrightarrow{y}^{(b)}, \mathsf{RL}^{(b)}\right)$.
- $\mathsf{Game}_3^{(b)}$: It is the same as $\mathsf{Game}_2^{(b)}$, except that $\mathsf{Sim}.\mathsf{Enc}\left(\mathsf{msk}^*, M^{(b)}, \mathbf{d}_0, \mathbf{d}'\right)$ takes as inputs $\mathbf{d}_0 \xleftarrow{\$} \mathbb{Z}_q^m$ and $\mathbf{d}' \xleftarrow{\$} \mathbb{Z}_q^k$.
- Game_4: In this final game, we make the following changes:
  $\mathsf{Sim}.\mathsf{Setup}\left(1^\lambda, \mathbf{A}, \mathbf{U}, \overrightarrow{y}^{(b)}, \mathsf{RL}^{(b)}\right)$ is replaced by $\mathsf{Setup}(1^\lambda)$.
  $\mathsf{Sim}.\mathsf{KeyGen}(\mathsf{msk}^*, \mathsf{ST}, \overrightarrow{x}, I, \overrightarrow{y}^{(b)}, \mathsf{RL}^{(b)})$ is replaced by $\mathsf{KeyGen}\left(\mathsf{msk}, \mathsf{ST}, \overrightarrow{x}, I\right)$.

  Instead of computing $\mathbf{c}' = \mathbf{d}' + \lfloor \frac{q}{2} \rfloor \cdot \mathsf{encode}(M^{(b)}) \in \mathbb{Z}_q^k$, we sample $\mathbf{c}' \xleftarrow{\$} \mathbb{Z}_q^k$.

To prove Theorem 1, we will first demonstrate in the following lemmas that any two consecutive games in the above series are either statistically indistinguishable or computationally indistinguishable under the LWE assumption.

Lemma 6. $\mathcal{A}$'s view in $\mathsf{Game}_0^{(b)}$ is statistically close to the view in $\mathsf{Game}_1^{(b)}$.

Proof. We will show that the public parameters $\mathsf{pp} = \left(\mathbf{A}, \{\mathbf{A}_i\}_{i \in [\ell]}, \mathbf{U}, \mathsf{BT}\right)$ and ciphertext $\mathsf{ct} = \left(\mathbf{c}', \mathbf{c}_0, \{\mathbf{c}_i\}_{i \in [\ell]}, \{\widehat{\mathbf{c}}_\theta\}_{\theta \in \mathsf{KUNodes}(\mathsf{BT}, \mathsf{RL})}\right)$ produced by algorithms $\mathsf{Sim}.\mathsf{Setup}\left(1^\lambda, \mathbf{A}, \mathbf{U}, \overrightarrow{y}^{(b)}, \mathsf{RL}^{(b)}\right)$ and $\mathsf{Sim}.\mathsf{Enc}(\mathsf{msk}^*, M^{(b)}, \mathbf{A}^\top \mathbf{s} + \mathbf{e}, \mathbf{U}^\top \mathbf{s} + \mathbf{e}')$ in $\mathsf{Game}_1^{(b)}$ are statistically close to those by Setup and Enc respectively, in $\mathsf{Game}_0^{(b)}$.

Firstly, we observe that matrix $\mathbf{A}$ is truly uniform in $\mathsf{Game}_1^{(b)}$. In $\mathsf{Game}_0^{(b)}$, it is generated via algorithm $\mathsf{TrapGen}$, and is statistically close to uniform over $\mathbb{Z}_q^{n \times m}$ by Lemma 1. Furthermore, $\mathbf{U} \in \mathbb{Z}_q^{n \times k}$ is truly uniform in both games.

Let $\overrightarrow{y}^{(b)} = (y_1^{(b)}, \ldots, y_\ell^{(b)})$. For each $i \in [\ell]$ and each $\theta \in \mathsf{BT}$, the matrices $\mathbf{A}_i, \mathbf{D}_\theta \in \mathbb{Z}_q^{n \times m}$ are truly uniform in $\mathsf{Game}_0^{(b)}$, while in $\mathsf{Game}_1^{(b)}$, they are set as $\mathbf{A}_i = \mathbf{A}\mathbf{R}_i - y_i^{(b)} \cdot \mathbf{G}, \mathbf{D}_\theta = \mathbf{A}\mathbf{S}_\theta + \rho_\theta \cdot \mathbf{G}$, where $\mathbf{R}_i, \mathbf{S}_\theta \xleftarrow{\$} \{-1, 1\}^{m \times m}$ and $\rho_\theta \in \{0, 1\}$. Then, the ciphertext components $\mathbf{c}', \mathbf{c}_0, \{\mathbf{c}_i\}_{i \in [\ell]}$ and $\{\widehat{\mathbf{c}}_\theta\}_{\theta \in \mathsf{KUNodes}(\mathsf{BT}, \mathsf{RL})}$ in both games can be expressed as:

$$\begin{cases} \mathbf{c}' = \mathbf{U}^\top \mathbf{s} + \mathbf{e}' + \lfloor \frac{q}{2} \rfloor \cdot \mathsf{encode}(M^{(b)}) \in \mathbb{Z}_q^k, \\ \mathbf{c}_0 = \mathbf{A}^\top \mathbf{s} + \mathbf{e} \in \mathbb{Z}_q^m, \\ \mathbf{c}_i = (\mathbf{A}_i + y_i^{(b)} \cdot \mathbf{G})^\top \mathbf{s} + \mathbf{R}_i^\top \mathbf{e} = \mathbf{R}_i^\top (\mathbf{A}^\top \mathbf{s} + \mathbf{e}) \in \mathbb{Z}_q^m, \quad \forall i \in [\ell], \\ \widehat{\mathbf{c}}_\theta = \mathbf{D}_\theta^\top \mathbf{s} + \mathbf{S}_\theta^\top \mathbf{e} = \mathbf{S}_\theta^\top (\mathbf{A}^\top \mathbf{s} + \mathbf{e}) \in \mathbb{Z}_q^m, \quad \forall \theta \in \mathsf{KUNodes}(\mathsf{BT}, \mathsf{RL}^{(b)}), \end{cases}$$

where $\mathbf{s} \xleftarrow{\$} \mathbb{Z}_q^n$, $\mathbf{e}' \hookleftarrow \chi^k$ and $\mathbf{e} \hookleftarrow \chi^m$. By Lemma 5, the joint distributions of $\left(\mathbf{A}, \mathbf{A}\mathbf{R}_i - \overrightarrow{y}_i^{(b)} \cdot \mathbf{G}, \mathbf{R}_i^\top \mathbf{e}\right)$ and $\left(\mathbf{A}, \mathbf{A}_i, \mathbf{R}_i^\top \mathbf{e}\right)$, $\left(\mathbf{A}, \mathbf{A}\mathbf{S}_\theta + \rho_\theta \cdot \mathbf{G}, \mathbf{S}_\theta^\top \mathbf{e}\right)$ and $\left(\mathbf{A}, \mathbf{D}_\theta, \mathbf{S}_\theta^\top \mathbf{e}\right)$ as statistically indistinguishable. It implies that the distributions of $\left(\mathbf{A}, \{\mathbf{A}_i\}_{i \in [\ell]}, \mathbf{U}, \{\mathbf{D}_\theta\}_{\theta \in \mathsf{BT}}, \mathbf{c}', \mathbf{c}_0, \{\mathbf{c}_i\}_{i \in [\ell]}, \{\widehat{\mathbf{c}}_\theta\}_{\theta \in \mathsf{KUNodes}(\mathsf{BT}, \mathsf{RL})}\right)$ in $\mathsf{Game}_0^{(b)}$ and $\mathsf{Game}_1^{(b)}$ are statistically indistinguishable. This concludes the lemma. $\qquad\square$

Lemma 7. $\mathcal{A}$'s view in $\mathsf{Game}_1^{(b)}$ is statistically close to the view in $\mathsf{Game}_2^{(b)}$.

Proof. Recall that, from $\text{Game}_1^{(b)}$ to $\text{Game}_2^{(b)}$, we replace the real key generation algorithm KeyGen by Sim.KeyGen. Thus, we need to show that for all queries of the form $(\overrightarrow{x}, I)$ from $\mathcal{A}$, the private keys $\text{sk}_{\overrightarrow{x}, I} = \left(I, \mathbf{Z}, \{\mathbf{Z}_\theta\}_{\theta \in \text{Path}(I)}\right)$ outputted by Sim.KeyGen and KeyGen are statistically indistinguishable.

We first note that, in both cases, matrices $\mathbf{Z} \in \mathbb{Z}^{2m \times k}$, $\{\mathbf{Z}_\theta \in \mathbb{Z}^{2m \times k}\}_{\theta \in \text{Path}(I)}$ satisfy $[\mathbf{A} \mid \mathbf{A}_{\overrightarrow{x}}] \cdot \mathbf{Z} + [\mathbf{A} \mid \mathbf{D}_\theta] \cdot \mathbf{Z}_\theta = \mathbf{U}, \forall \theta \in \text{Path}(I)$. Next, we observe that, in KeyGen, the columns of these matrices are sampled via algorithm SampleLeft, while in Sim.KeyGen, they are either sampled via algorithm SampleRight or sampled from $\mathcal{D}_{\mathbb{Z}^m, s}$. The properties of these sampling algorithms (see Sect. 2) then guarantee that the two distributions are statistically indistinguishable.   □

Lemma 8. *Under the (n, q, χ)-LWE assumption, $\mathcal{A}$'s view in $\text{Game}_2^{(b)}$ is computationally indistinguishable from the view in $\text{Game}_3^{(b)}$.*

Proof. From $\text{Game}_2^{(b)}$ to $\text{Game}_3^{(b)}$, we change the inputs $\mathbf{d}_0, \mathbf{d}'$ to algorithm Sim.Enc from LWE instances to uniformly random vectors in $\mathbb{Z}_q^m$ and $\mathbb{Z}_q^k$, respectively. Suppose that $\mathcal{A}$ has non-negligible advantage in distinguishing $\text{Game}_2^{(b)}$ from $\text{Game}_3^{(b)}$. We use $\mathcal{A}$ to construct an LWE solver $\mathcal{B}$ as follows:

- $\mathcal{B}$ requests for $m + k$ LWE instances $\{(\mathbf{a}_j, v_j) \in \mathbb{Z}_q^n \times \mathbb{Z}_q\}_{j \in [m+k]}$.
- $\mathcal{B}$ forms the following matrices and vectors: $\mathbf{A} = [\mathbf{a}_1, \ldots, \mathbf{a}_m] \in \mathbb{Z}_q^{n \times m}$, $\mathbf{U} = [\mathbf{a}_{m+1}, \ldots, \mathbf{a}_{m+k}] \in \mathbb{Z}_q^{n \times k}$, $\mathbf{d}_0 = [v_1, \cdots, v_m]^\top \in \mathbb{Z}_q^m$, $\mathbf{d}' = [v_{m+1}, \cdots, v_{m+k}]^\top \in \mathbb{Z}_q^k$, and runs Sim.Setup$(1^\lambda, \mathbf{A}, \mathbf{U}, \overrightarrow{y}^{(b)}, \text{RL}^{(b)})$ as in $\text{Game}_2^{(b)}$.
- $\mathcal{B}$ answers the private key queries of the form $(\overrightarrow{x}, I)$, as in $\text{Game}_2^{(b)}$, by running algorithm Sim.KeyGen$(\text{msk}^*, \text{ST}, \overrightarrow{x}, I, \overrightarrow{y}^{(b)}, \text{RL}^{(b)})$.
- When receiving from $\mathcal{A}$ two messages $M^{(0)}, M^{(1)} \in \{0, 1\}$, $\mathcal{B}$ prepares a challenge ciphertext ct^* by running Sim.Enc$\left(\text{msk}^*, M^{(b)}, \mathbf{d}_0, \mathbf{d}'\right)$.
- Finally, after being allowed to make additional queries, $\mathcal{A}$ guesses whether it is interacting with $\text{Game}_2^{(b)}$ or $\text{Game}_3^{(b)}$. Then, $\mathcal{B}$ outputs $\mathcal{A}$'s guess as the answer to the LWE challenger.

Recall that by Definition 1, for each $j \in [m + k]$, either $v_j = \langle \mathbf{a}_j, \mathbf{s} \rangle + e_j$ for secret $\mathbf{s} \xleftarrow{\$} \mathbb{Z}_q^n$ and noise $e_j \hookleftarrow \chi$; or v_j is uniformly random in $\mathbb{Z}_q$. On the one hand, if $v_j = \langle \mathbf{a}_j, \mathbf{s} \rangle + e_j$, then the adversary $\mathcal{A}$'s view is as in $\text{Game}_2^{(b)}$. On the other hand, if v_j is uniformly random in $\mathbb{Z}_q$, then $\mathcal{A}$'s view is as in $\text{Game}_3^{(b)}$. Hence, algorithm $\mathcal{B}$ can solve the (n, q, χ)-LWE problem with non-negligible probability, assuming that the adversary $\mathcal{A}$ can distinguish $\text{Game}_2^{(b)}$ from $\text{Game}_3^{(b)}$ with non-negligible advantage. This concludes the lemma.   □

Lemma 9. *$\mathcal{A}$'s view in $\text{Game}_3^{(b)}$ is statistically close to the view in Game_4.*

Proof. Firstly, based on the same argument as in Lemma 6, we can deduce that the output of algorithm Sim.Setup$(1^\lambda, \mathbf{A}, \mathbf{U}, \overrightarrow{y}^{(b)}, \text{RL}^{(b)})$ in $\text{Game}_3^{(b)}$ is statistically close that of Setup(1^λ) in Game_4.

Secondly, based on the same argument as in Lemma 7, we can deduce that the output of algorithm $\mathsf{Sim.KeyGen}\big(\mathsf{msk}^*, \mathsf{ST}, \overrightarrow{x}, I, \overrightarrow{y}^{(b)}, \mathsf{RL}^{(b)}\big)$ in $\mathrm{Game}_3^{(b)}$ is statistically close to that of $\mathsf{KeyGen}\big(\mathsf{msk}, \mathsf{ST}, \overrightarrow{x}, I\big)$ in Game_4.

Finally, the shift from $\mathbf{c}' = \mathbf{d}' + \lfloor \frac{q}{2} \rfloor \cdot \mathsf{encode}(M^{(b)}) \in \mathbb{Z}_q^k$ to a uniformly random $\mathbf{c}' \in \mathbb{Z}_q^k$ is only a conceptual change, because vector $\mathbf{d}'$ in $\mathrm{Game}_3^{(b)}$ is uniformly random over $\mathbb{Z}_q^k$. $\qquad\Box$

The theorem now follows from the fact that the advantage of $\mathcal{A}$ in Game_4 is 0, since Game_4 no longer depends on the bit b. $\qquad\Box$

4   Extensions and Open Questions

In this section, we discuss several possible extensions of our lattice-based RPE scheme, as well as some questions that we left open.

4.1   Extensions

Multi-bit version. The scheme presented in Sect. 3 only allows to encrypt 1-bit messages. Using standard techniques for multi-bit LWE-based encryption, e.g., [1,15,37], we can achieve a τ-bit variant with small overhead, for any $\tau = \mathsf{poly}(\lambda)$. A notable change in this case is that we will employ a revised encoding function $\mathsf{encode}' : \{0,1\}^\tau \to \{0,1\}^{\tau+k}$, where for any $\mu \in \{0,1\}^\tau$, vector $\mathsf{encode}'(\mu)$ is obtained by appending $k = \omega(\log \lambda)$ entries 0 to vector μ.

Better efficiency in the random oracle model. The RPE scheme from Sect. 3 has relatively large public parameters pp, i.e., of bit-size $\big(\widetilde{O}(\ell) + O(N)\big) \cdot \widetilde{O}(\lambda^2)$, for which the dependence on N is due to the fact that we have to associate each node θ in the binary tree with a uniformly random matrix in $\mathbf{D}_\theta \in \mathbb{Z}_q^{n \times m}$, in order to obtain full-hiding security in the standard model. Fortunately, the size of pp can be reduced to $\widetilde{O}(\ell) \cdot \widetilde{O}(\lambda^2)$ (which is comparable to that of the underlying PE scheme [2,50]), if we work in the random oracle model [7]. The idea is as follows.

Let $\mathcal{H} : \{0,1\}^* \to \mathbb{Z}_q^{n \times m}$ be a random oracle. Then, in the scheme, for each node θ, we obtain uniformly random matrix $\mathbf{D}_\theta$ as $\mathbf{D}_\theta := \mathcal{H}(\mathbf{A}, \{\mathbf{A}_i\}_{i \in [\ell]}, \mathbf{U}, \theta)$. The rest of the scheme remains the same. In the security proof, we first simulate the generation of $\mathbf{D}_\theta$ as in the proof of Theorem 1. Then, it remains to program the random oracle such that $\mathcal{H}(\mathbf{A}, \{\mathbf{A}_i\}_{i \in [\ell]}, \mathbf{U}, \theta) := \mathbf{D}_\theta$. This modification allows us to make the size of pp independent of N.

4.2   Open Questions

We introduced the first revocable predicate encryption scheme based on the LWE assumption. While the pairing-based scheme from [30,31] achieved adaptive full-hiding security, our construction is only proven secure in the selective setting. Achieving the stronger notion of [30,31] seems to require that the underlying PE be adaptively secure. However, to the best of our knowledge, existing lattice-based PE schemes [2,13,16,50] only achieved selective security. We therefore view the problem of constructing adaptively secure lattice-based RPE as an interesting open question.

Finally, as shown in [19,50], some applications of PE for inner-product predicate over R^ℓ (in our scheme, $R = \mathbb{Z}_q$) require that R has exponentially large cardinality. Those include implementations of PE for CNF formulae [19] and hidden vector encryption [10]. However, for our scheme, this requires to set the modulus q to be exponential in λ. Hence, it would be desirable to achieve a lattice-based PE scheme supporting both revocation and exponentially large R, that demands only polynomial moduli. One possible approach towards tackling this question is to adapt the techniques introduced by Xagawa [50], where one works with $R = \mathrm{GF}(q^n)$ instead of $\mathbb{Z}_q$.

Acknowledgements. We thank the reviewers for helpful discussions and comments. The research was supported by the "Singapore Ministry of Education under Research Grant MOE2016-T2-2-014(S)". Huaxiong Wang was also supported by NTU under Tier 1 grant RG143/14.

References

1. Agrawal, S., Boneh, D., Boyen, X.: Efficient lattice (H)IBE in the standard model. In: Gilbert, H. (ed.) EUROCRYPT 2010. LNCS, vol. 6110, pp. 553–572. Springer, Heidelberg (2010). doi:10.1007/978-3-642-13190-5_28
2. Agrawal, S., Freeman, D.M., Vaikuntanathan, V.: Functional encryption for inner product predicates from learning with errors. In: Lee, D.H., Wang, X. (eds.) ASIACRYPT 2011. LNCS, vol. 7073, pp. 21–40. Springer, Heidelberg (2011). doi:10.1007/978-3-642-25385-0_2
3. Ajtai, M.: Generating hard instances of the short basis problem. In: Wiedermann, J., van Emde Boas, P., Nielsen, M. (eds.) ICALP 1999. LNCS, vol. 1644, pp. 1–9. Springer, Heidelberg (1999). doi:10.1007/3-540-48523-6_1
4. Alwen, J., Peikert, C.: Generating shorter bases for hard random lattices. Theory Comput. Syst. **48**(3), 535–553 (2011)
5. Attrapadung, N., Imai, H.: Attribute-based encryption supporting direct/indirect revocation modes. In: Parker, M.G. (ed.) IMACC 2009. LNCS, vol. 5921, pp. 278–300. Springer, Heidelberg (2009). doi:10.1007/978-3-642-10868-6_17
6. Attrapadung, N., Libert, B.: Functional encryption for inner product: achieving constant-size ciphertexts with adaptive security or support for negation. In: Nguyen, P.Q., Pointcheval, D. (eds.) PKC 2010. LNCS, vol. 6056, pp. 384–402. Springer, Heidelberg (2010). doi:10.1007/978-3-642-13013-7_23
7. Bellare, M., Rogaway, P.: Random oracles are practical: a paradigm for designing efficient protocols. In: CCS 1993, pp. 62–73. ACM (1993)
8. Boldyreva, A., Goyal, V., Kumar, V.: Identity-based encryption with efficient revocation. In: CCS 2008, pp. 417–426. ACM (2008)
9. Boneh, D., Franklin, M.: Identity-based encryption from the weil pairing. In: Kilian, J. (ed.) CRYPTO 2001. LNCS, vol. 2139, pp. 213–229. Springer, Heidelberg (2001). doi:10.1007/3-540-44647-8_13

10. Boneh, D., Waters, B.: Conjunctive, subset, and range queries on encrypted data. In: Vadhan, S.P. (ed.) TCC 2007. LNCS, vol. 4392, pp. 535–554. Springer, Heidelberg (2007). doi:10.1007/978-3-540-70936-7_29

11. Chen, J., Lim, H.W., Ling, S., Wang, H., Nguyen, K.: Revocable identity-based encryption from lattices. In: Susilo, W., Mu, Y., Seberry, J. (eds.) ACISP 2012. LNCS, vol. 7372, pp. 390–403. Springer, Heidelberg (2012). doi:10.1007/978-3-642-31448-3_29

12. Cheng, S., Zhang, J.: Adaptive-ID secure revocable identity-based encryption from lattices via subset difference method. In: Lopez, J., Wu, Y. (eds.) ISPEC 2015. LNCS, vol. 9065, pp. 283–297. Springer, Cham (2015). doi:10.1007/978-3-319-17533-1_20

13. Gay, R., Méaux, P., Wee, H.: Predicate encryption for multi-dimensional range queries from lattices. In: Katz, J. (ed.) PKC 2015. LNCS, vol. 9020, pp. 752–776. Springer, Heidelberg (2015). doi:10.1007/978-3-662-46447-2_34

14. Genise, N., Micciancio, D.: Faster gaussian sampling for trapdoor lattices with arbitrary modulus. IACR Cryptology ePrint Archive 2017:308 (2017)

15. Gentry, C., Peikert, C., Vaikuntanathan, V.: Trapdoors for hard lattices and new cryptographic constructions. In: STOC 2008, pp. 197–206. ACM (2008)

16. Gorbunov, S., Vaikuntanathan, V., Wee, H.: Predicate encryption for circuits from LWE. In: Gennaro, R., Robshaw, M. (eds.) CRYPTO 2015. LNCS, vol. 9216, pp. 503–523. Springer, Heidelberg (2015). doi:10.1007/978-3-662-48000-7_25

17. Goyal, V., Pandey, O., Sahai, A., Waters, B.: Attribute-based encryption for fine-grained access control of encrypted data. In: CCS 2006, pp. 89–98. ACM (2006)

18. Gur, K.D., Polyakov, Y., Rohloff, K., Ryan, G.W., Savas, E.: Implementation and evaluation of improved Gaussian sampling for lattice trapdoors. IACR Cryptology ePrint Archive, 2017:285 (2017)

19. Katz, J., Sahai, A., Waters, B.: Predicate encryption supporting disjunctions, polynomial equations, and inner products. In: Smart, N. (ed.) EUROCRYPT 2008. LNCS, vol. 4965, pp. 146–162. Springer, Heidelberg (2008). doi:10.1007/978-3-540-78967-3_9

20. Lee, K., Kim, I., Hwang, S.O.: Privacy preserving revocable predicate encryption revisited. Secur. Commun. Netw. **8**(3), 471–485 (2015)

21. Lewko, A., Okamoto, T., Sahai, A., Takashima, K., Waters, B.: Fully secure functional encryption: attribute-based encryption and (hierarchical) inner product encryption. In: Gilbert, H. (ed.) EUROCRYPT 2010. LNCS, vol. 6110, pp. 62–91. Springer, Heidelberg (2010). doi:10.1007/978-3-642-13190-5_4

22. Libert, B., Peters, T., Yung, M.: Group signatures with almost-for-free revocation. In: Safavi-Naini, R., Canetti, R. (eds.) CRYPTO 2012. LNCS, vol. 7417, pp. 571–589. Springer, Heidelberg (2012). doi:10.1007/978-3-642-32009-5_34

23. Libert, B., Peters, T., Yung, M.: Scalable group signatures with revocation. In: Pointcheval, D., Johansson, T. (eds.) EUROCRYPT 2012. LNCS, vol. 7237, pp. 609–627. Springer, Heidelberg (2012). doi:10.1007/978-3-642-29011-4_36

24. Libert, B., Vergnaud, D.: Adaptive-ID secure revocable identity-based encryption. In: Fischlin, M. (ed.) CT-RSA 2009. LNCS, vol. 5473, pp. 1–15. Springer, Heidelberg (2009). doi:10.1007/978-3-642-00862-7_1

25. Micciancio, D., Mol, P.: Pseudorandom knapsacks and the sample complexity of lwe search-to-decision reductions. In: Rogaway, P. (ed.) CRYPTO 2011. LNCS, vol. 6841, pp. 465–484. Springer, Heidelberg (2011). doi:10.1007/978-3-642-22792-9_26

26. Micciancio, D., Peikert, C.: Trapdoors for lattices: simpler, tighter, faster, smaller. In: Pointcheval, D., Johansson, T. (eds.) EUROCRYPT 2012. LNCS, vol. 7237, pp. 700–718. Springer, Heidelberg (2012). doi:10.1007/978-3-642-29011-4_41

27. Micciancio, D., Walter, M.: Gaussian sampling over the integers: efficient, generic, constant-time. IACR Cryptology ePrint Archive 2017:259 (2017)
28. Naor, D., Naor, M., Lotspiech, J.: Revocation and tracing schemes for stateless receivers. In: Kilian, J. (ed.) CRYPTO 2001. LNCS, vol. 2139, pp. 41–62. Springer, Heidelberg (2001). doi:10.1007/3-540-44647-8_3
29. Nguyen, K., Wang, H., Zhang, J.: Server-aided revocable identity-based encryption from lattices. In: Foresti, S., Persiano, G. (eds.) CANS 2016. LNCS, vol. 10052, pp. 107–123. Springer, Cham (2016). doi:10.1007/978-3-319-48965-0_7
30. González-Nieto, J.M., Manulis, M., Sun, D.: Fully private revocable predicate encryption. In: Susilo, W., Mu, Y., Seberry, J. (eds.) ACISP 2012. LNCS, vol. 7372, pp. 350–363. Springer, Heidelberg (2012). doi:10.1007/978-3-642-31448-3_26
31. González-Nieto, J.M., Manulis, M., Sun, D.: Fully private revocable predicate encryption. IACR Cryptology ePrint Archive 2012:403 (2012)
32. Okamoto, T., Takashima, K.: Hierarchical predicate encryption for inner-products. In: Matsui, M. (ed.) ASIACRYPT 2009. LNCS, vol. 5912, pp. 214–231. Springer, Heidelberg (2009). doi:10.1007/978-3-642-10366-7_13
33. Okamoto, T., Takashima, K.: Fully secure functional encryption with general relations from the decisional linear assumption. In: Rabin, T. (ed.) CRYPTO 2010. LNCS, vol. 6223, pp. 191–208. Springer, Heidelberg (2010). doi:10.1007/978-3-642-14623-7_11
34. Okamoto, T., Takashima, K.: Achieving short ciphertexts or short secret-keys for adaptively secure general inner-product encryption. In: Lin, D., Tsudik, G., Wang, X. (eds.) CANS 2011. LNCS, vol. 7092, pp. 138–159. Springer, Heidelberg (2011). doi:10.1007/978-3-642-25513-7_11
35. Okamoto, T., Takashima, K.: Adaptively attribute-hiding (hierarchical) inner product encryption. In: Pointcheval, D., Johansson, T. (eds.) EUROCRYPT 2012. LNCS, vol. 7237, pp. 591–608. Springer, Heidelberg (2012). doi:10.1007/978-3-642-29011-4_35
36. Peikert, C.: Public-key cryptosystems from the worst-case shortest vector problem: extended abstract. In: STOC 2009, pp. 333–342. ACM (2009)
37. Peikert, C., Vaikuntanathan, V., Waters, B.: A framework for efficient and composable oblivious transfer. In: Wagner, D. (ed.) CRYPTO 2008. LNCS, vol. 5157, pp. 554–571. Springer, Heidelberg (2008). doi:10.1007/978-3-540-85174-5_31
38. Regev, O.: On lattices, learning with errors, random linear codes, and cryptography. In: STOC 2005, pp. 84–93. ACM (2005)
39. Sahai, A., Seyalioglu, H., Waters, B.: Dynamic credentials and ciphertext delegation for attribute-based encryption. In: Safavi-Naini, R., Canetti, R. (eds.) CRYPTO 2012. LNCS, vol. 7417, pp. 199–217. Springer, Heidelberg (2012). doi:10.1007/978-3-642-32009-5_13
40. Sahai, A., Waters, B.: Fuzzy identity-based encryption. In: Cramer, R. (ed.) EUROCRYPT 2005. LNCS, vol. 3494, pp. 457–473. Springer, Heidelberg (2005). doi:10.1007/11426639_27
41. Seo, J.H., Emura, K.: Efficient delegation of key generation and revocation functionalities in identity-based encryption. In: Dawson, E. (ed.) CT-RSA 2013. LNCS, vol. 7779, pp. 343–358. Springer, Heidelberg (2013). doi:10.1007/978-3-642-36095-4_22
42. Seo, J.H., Emura, K.: Revocable identity-based encryption revisited: security model and construction. In: Kurosawa, K., Hanaoka, G. (eds.) PKC 2013. LNCS, vol. 7778, pp. 216–234. Springer, Heidelberg (2013). doi:10.1007/978-3-642-36362-7_14
43. Seo, J.H., Emura, K.: Revocable hierarchical identity-based encryption. Theor. Comput. Sci. 542, 44–62 (2014)

44. Seo, J.H., Emura, K.: Revocable identity-based cryptosystem revisited: security sodels and constructions. IEEE Trans. Inf. Forensics Secur. **9**(7), 1193–1205 (2014)
45. Seo, J.H., Emura, K.: Adaptive-ID secure revocable hierarchical identity-based encryption. In: Tanaka, K., Suga, Y. (eds.) IWSEC 2015. LNCS, vol. 9241, pp. 21–38. Springer, Cham (2015). doi:10.1007/978-3-319-22425-1_2
46. Shi, E., Bethencourt, J., Chan, H.T.-H., Song, D.X., Perrig, A.: Multi-dimensional range query over encrypted data. In: IEEE Symposium on Security and Privacy (S&P 2007), pp. 350–364. IEEE Computer Society (2007)
47. Takayasu, A., Watanabe, Y.: Lattice-based revocable identity-based encryption with bounded decryption key exposure resistance. In: Pieprzyk, J., Suriadi, S. (eds.) ACISP 2017. LNCS, vol. 10342, pp. 184–204. Springer, Cham (2017). doi:10.1007/978-3-319-60055-0_10
48. Watanabe, Y., Emura, K., Seo, J.H.: New revocable IBE in prime-order groups: adaptively secure, decryption key exposure resistant, and with short public parameters. In: Handschuh, H. (ed.) CT-RSA 2017. LNCS, vol. 10159, pp. 432–449. Springer, Cham (2017). doi:10.1007/978-3-319-52153-4_25
49. Waters, B.: Dual system encryption: realizing fully secure IBE and HIBE under simple assumptions. In: Halevi, S. (ed.) CRYPTO 2009. LNCS, vol. 5677, pp. 619–636. Springer, Heidelberg (2009). doi:10.1007/978-3-642-03356-8_36
50. Xagawa, K.: Improved (hierarchical) inner-product encryption from lattices. In: Kurosawa, K., Hanaoka, G. (eds.) PKC 2013. LNCS, vol. 7778, pp. 235–252. Springer, Heidelberg (2013). doi:10.1007/978-3-642-36362-7_15

Public Key Encryption and Signcryption

Provable Secure Constructions for Broadcast Encryption with Personalized Messages

Kamalesh Acharya[✉] and Ratna Dutta

Department of Mathematics, Indian Institute of Technology Kharagpur,
Kharagpur 721302, India
kamaleshiitkgp@gmail.com, ratna@maths.iitkgp.ernet.in

Abstract. Broadcast encryption is an efficient way to send the broadcast messages, but, it does not yield a productive way to send the personalized messages to individuals. A broadcast encryption with personalized messages (BEPM) skillfully sends the broadcast message to a group of users together with the personalized messages to individual users. This article identifies constructional flaws in the BEPM scheme of Xu et al. and designs three BEPM constructions, namely, BEPM-I, BEPM-II and BEPM-III. BEPM-I, BEPM-III are selectively secure. Unlike the existing similar works, these schemes eliminate the need of storing public key and secret key for transmitting personalized messages. We emphasize that BEPM-III employs multilinear maps and achieves logarithmic size public parameter with increasing computation cost. More positively, BEPM-II achieves adaptive security with the parameter size and computation cost as in the existing BEPM. All our constructions have constant communication cost and proven to be secure in the standard security model under reasonable assumptions in generic group model. Furthermore, our schemes are fully collision resistant and flexible for adding and removing of users from the broadcast system.

Keywords: Broadcast encryption · Personalized messages · Chosen plaintext attack · Adaptive security

1 Introduction

BEPM. Broadcast encryption with personalized messages (BEPM) is an interesting cryptographic primitive that aims to transmit not only the encrypted broadcast message to a set of recipients, but also the personalized messages to individual users. More precisely, BEPM enables a broadcaster to generate a public header for a group of users. The broadcaster also sets a session key and personalized keys to encrypt respectively a common message and personalized messages using symmetric key encryption. A subscriber uses its secret key issued by a trusted third party to recover both the session key and its personalized key.

BEPM overcomes the potential limitation of traditional broadcast encryption (BE) schemes in protecting user's privacy. Typically, a BE is one of the multi-recipient public key encryption that enables a broadcaster to broadcast an

© Springer International Publishing AG 2017
T. Okamoto et al. (Eds.): ProvSec 2017, LNCS 10592, pp. 329–348, 2017.
https://doi.org/10.1007/978-3-319-68637-0_20

encrypted message to a group of users in such a way that only the subscribed users are capable of recovering the message. The concept of broadcast encryption was formalised by Fiat and Noar [6] and followed by several works [1–5,7,10,12] due to its numerous applications, particularly in pay TV, radio broadcast, digital rights management and many more.

However, to ensure the user's privacy, one requires to encrypt personalized message and transmit them to each individual users. BE and other multi-recipient public key encryption schemes such as attribute-based encryption, functional encryption etc., where same encrypted messages is broadcasted for all the recipients are expensive in this regard. On the contrary, BEPM is a cost-efficient primitive that provides an efficient way to transmit encrypted personalized messages individually together with transmitting the encrypted common message.

Applications. BEPM has emerged as an object of fundamental interest for many real life applications where confidentiality must be assured not only for the encrypted common content, but also for the encrypted personalized messages for individual users. For instance, consider the following scenarios where BEPM is an appropriate choice.

- A manager of a software company wants to send business strategy, rules and regulations of the company as common message together with login id and password of the systems allocated for the employees. He can use a BEPM to transmit common message as broadcast message while login id, password of individual employees as personalized messages.
- Let an institute take the interview to select students. After the interview, the institute is willing to send the common selection notification to the selected participants as broadcast message and provides login id, password to individual candidates as personalized messages for their temporary registration through institute website using a BEPM.
- To inform the guardians about the governing body decision regarding the qualifying mark and performance analysis of the students in the annual examination, the head of the institute can use BEPM whereby the qualifying mark is broadcasted as common message and the performance of individual students is sent to the corresponding guardian as a personalized message.
- Suppose that a sports channel provides a subscription to users on monthly, half-yearly and yearly basis agreement. It may employ a BEPM to send the sports content as broadcast message to the subscribers and a reminder showing the expiry date of the current agreement and individual offer for next subscription as personalized message.

Designing efficient BEPM is not a trivial task. The efficiency of a BEPM is measured by its computation and communication overhead together with low storage for the public parameter and private key. Computation cost is measured by encryption and decryption overhead, while communication cost is measured by the number of bits in the ciphertext beyond what is needed for the description of recipient set (or revocation set) and payload for the symmetric key encryption of the message. Security is another crucial factor. Security of a BEPM scheme is analysed in selective, semi-static or adaptive security model. In selective security model, the adversary declares the challenge recipient set at the beginning of the game. The challenger sets the public key, secret key accordingly using this challenge recipient set. In semi-static security model, the adversary declares a recipient set G at the beginning of the security game similar to selective security. However, it declares a subset of G as the challenge set in the challenge phase. On the other hand, the challenge set in adaptive security model is chosen by the adversary in challenge generation phase only. Adaptive security is the strongest security model in broadcast encryption framework as introduced by Gentry et al. [7] in 2008.

Related Work. Kurosawa [9] proposed a multi-recipient scheme based on ElGamal scheme. Security of the scheme depends on the Decisional Diffie-Hellman (DDH) assumption. Hiwatari et al. [8] proposed schemes secure under the hardness of Hashed Decisional Diffie-Hellman (HDDH) problem. Each recipient receives a different encrypted message in these multi-recipient schemes and ciphertext size grows linearly to the maximum number of users supported by the system. These schemes are not efficient for sending the common broadcast message together with the personalized messages as it will additionally requires to transmit the encrypted common message. Consequently, the ciphertext size gets double. Yang [14] proposed a public key encryption using Chameleone hash in a multi-recipient set up where all the recipients receives the same encrypted message. This scheme is secure under a variant of the square Bilinear Decisional Diffie-Hellman (sqBDDH) assumption. It has ciphertext size linear to the number of subscribed users. Sending different personalized messages to different users using [14] is costly.

Ohtake et al. [11] addressed these issues and proposed the first BEPM using the BE scheme of Boneh et al. [4]. They additionally used a set of public key, secret key pairs for the personalized encryption. Security is proven in a weaker security model, namely the selective semantic security under the Decisional Bilinear Diffie-Hellman Exponent (DBDHE) assumption. The public parameter size of the scheme can be reduced further using the same security model and security assumption (see our first construction in Sect. 3). Xu et al. [13] attempted to reduce the public parameter size using multilinear maps which is unfortunately flawed (see Remark 4 in Sect. 5).

Our Contribution. In this paper, we present three constructions with concrete security analysis in the standard security model under reasonable assumptions. The first and third constructions are selectively secure and reduce the storage size while the second construction achieves adaptive security with the similar parameter size and computation cost as the existing BEPM scheme [11]. The communication costs are similar to that of [11] for all our designs. More precisely, we summarise below our contribution in this work:

- Our first construction is based on the BE scheme of Boneh et al. [4] and selectively secure under DBDHE assumption. In contrast to the previous BEPM construction [11], we have reduced the storage size by eliminating the need

of public key, secret key for transmitting personalized messages. Reduction of parameter size does not increase the computation cost.
- We propose another BEPM scheme with adaptive security employing the broadcast encryption of [4] under the hardness of the modified Decisional Bilinear Diffie-Hellman Exponent (mDBDHE) assumption which is a variant of the Oracle Decisional Bilinear Diffie-Hellman Exponent (ODBDHE) assumption secure in the generic group model. Achieving adaptive security does not blow up the parameter sizes and computation costs of the existing scheme [11].
- Our third construction is multilinear map based following Boneh et al. [5]. Use of multilinear maps reduces the public parameter size to logarithmic with the maximum number of users supported by the system at the expense of increases the computation cost. The scheme is selectively secure under the hardness of Decisional Hybrid Diffie-Hellman Exponent (DHDHE) assumption.

All of our constructions require constant communication cost.

Our first and third constructions are suitable for applications that require to minimize the total length of the header and public key such as DVD content protection where the public key needs to be embedded in the header to decrypt the header.

Like [11], all of our constructions are fully collision resistant. If the users outside the group of selected users collide, they will be unable to recover the broadcast message and the personalized messages. The broadcaster can efficiently add new users in the system as long as the number of selected users does not exceed the maximum number of users permissible in the system. In addition the broadcaster can efficiently revoke users from the system.

2   Preliminaries

Notation: Let $[m]$ denote integers from 1 to m and $[a, b]$ denote integers from a to b. We use the notation $x \in_R S$ to denote x is a random element of S and λ to represent bit size of prime integer p. Let $\epsilon : \mathbb{N} \to \mathbb{R}$ be a function, where $\mathbb{N}$ and $\mathbb{R}$ are the sets of natural and real number respectively. The function $\epsilon(\lambda)$ is said to be a *negligible function* if for every positive integer c, $\exists$ an integer N_c such that for every $\lambda > N_c$, $\epsilon(\lambda) \leq \frac{1}{\lambda^c}$.

2.1   Broadcast Encryption with Personalized Messages

The concept of *broadcast encryption with personalized messages* (BEPM) was proposed by Ohtake et al. [11] in 2010.

Syntax of BEPM: We formally describe below BEPM = (BEPM.Setup, BEPM.KeyGen, BEPM.Encrypt, BEPM.Decrypt) following the definition of Gentry et al. [7]. It consists of three probabilistic polynomial time (PPT) algorithms BEPM.Setup, BEPM.KeyGen, BEPM.Encrypt and a deterministic polynomial time algorithm BEPM.Decrypt:

$(\mathsf{PP}, \mathsf{MK}) \leftarrow \mathsf{BEPM.Setup}(N, \lambda)$: The PKGC takes as input the total number of users N that the system can accommodate and security parameter λ and constructs the public parameter PP and a master key MK. It makes PP public and keeps MK.

$(sk_i) \leftarrow \mathsf{BEPM.KeyGen}(\mathsf{PP}, \mathsf{MK}, i)$: Taking as input PP, MK and a subscribed user $i \in [N]$, the PKGC generates a secret key sk_i for user i and sends sk_i to i through a secure communication channel between them.

$(\mathsf{Hdr}, K, \{K_i\}_{i \in G}) \leftarrow \mathsf{BEPM.Encrypt}(G, \mathsf{PP})$: The broadcaster selects a group of users $G \subseteq [N]$ and produces a header Hdr, a session key K and personalized keys K_i for each subscribed users $i \in G$ using PP. It makes the header Hdr containing the subscribed user set G public and keeps secret the session key K and personalized keys $K_i, i \in G$.

$(K, K_i) \leftarrow \mathsf{BEPM.Decrypt}(\mathsf{PP}, sk_i, \mathsf{Hdr}, i)$: A subscribed user i with its secret key sk_i uses PP, Hdr for the subscribed user set G and outputs the session key K and its personalized key K_i.

Correctness: The scheme BEPM is said to be correct if the session key K can be retrieved from the header Hdr by any subscribed user i in G. Suppose $(\mathsf{PP}, \mathsf{MK}) \leftarrow \mathsf{BEPM.Setup}(N, \lambda)$, $(\mathsf{Hdr}, K, \{K_i\}_{i \in G}) \leftarrow \mathsf{BEPM.Encrypt}(G, \mathsf{PP})$. Then for every subscribed user $i \in G$,

$$\mathsf{BEPM.Decrypt}\Big(\mathsf{PP}, \mathsf{BEPM.KeyGen}(\mathsf{PP}, \mathsf{MK}, i), \mathsf{Hdr}, i\Big) = (K, K_i).$$

Remark 1. The BEPM described above is a key encapsulation mechanism. We can convert this into message encryption setting by exploiting a symmetric key encryption scheme as follows: Use the session key K generated in BEPM.Encrypt to create a symmetric key encryption of a message; the personalized keys $K_i, i \in G$ generated in BEPM.Encrypt to construct symmetric key encryption of the personalized messages and broadcast these encrypted messages along with the header Hdr. Decryption process recover K and $K_i, i \in G$, as in BEPM.Decrypt and uses these to get back the message and respective personalized message. This requires an additional computation and communication cost of computing and broadcasting of $|G|+1$ symmetric key encryption during BEPM.Encrypt and $|G|+1$ symmetric key decryption during BEPM.Decrypt.

2.2 Security Framework

- **Key Indistinguishability under Chosen Plaintext Attack (IND-CPA)**

Selective security of BEPM is defined as the following key indistinguishability game played between a challenger $\mathcal{C}$ and an adversary $\mathcal{A}$. We will define the security game following Gentry et al. [7].

Initialization: The adversary $\mathcal{A}$ selects a recipient set G and provides it to $\mathcal{C}$.

Setup: The challenger $\mathcal{C}$ generates $(\mathsf{PP}, \mathsf{MK}) \leftarrow \mathsf{BEPM.Setup}(N, \lambda)$. It keeps the master key MK secret and makes the public parameter PP public.

Query 1: The adversary $\mathcal{A}$ sends key generation queries for $i_1, \ldots, i_m \notin G$ to $\mathcal{C}$ and receives the secret key $sk_i \leftarrow \mathsf{BEPM.KeyGen}(\mathsf{PP}, \mathsf{MK}, i)$ for $i \notin \{i_1, \ldots, i_m\}$.

Challenge: The challenger $\mathcal{C}$ generates $(\mathsf{Hdr}^*, K, \{K_i\}_{i \in G}) \leftarrow \mathsf{BEPM.Encrypt}(G, \mathsf{PP})$. It picks $b \in_R \{0, 1\}$. If $b = 0$, $\mathcal{C}$ sends $(\mathsf{Hdr}^*, K, \{K_i\}_{i \in G})$ to $\mathcal{A}$; else if $b = 1$, $\mathcal{C}$ provides $(\mathsf{Hdr}^*, R, \{R_i\}_{i \in G})$ to $\mathcal{A}$, where $R, R_i, i \in G$ are random keys.

Query 2: This is similar to Query 1 phase.

Guess: The adversary $\mathcal{A}$ outputs a guess $b' \in \{0, 1\}$ of b and wins if $b' = b$.

Adversary's advantage in the above security game for a BEPM scheme X is defined as $Adv_{A,X}^{IND\text{-}CPA} = |Pr(b' = b) - \frac{1}{2}|$. The probability is taken over random bits used by $\mathcal{C}$ and $\mathcal{A}$.

Definition 1. *The* BEPM *scheme* X *is* (t, q, ϵ)-*secure if* $Adv_{A,X}^{IND\text{-}CPA} \leq \epsilon$ *for every PPT adversary* $\mathcal{A}$ *with running time at most* t *and making at most* q *key generation queries.*

For *adaptive security* there is no initialization phase and G is selected in the challenge phase. Query 1 phase does not have any restriction.

2.3   Complexity Assumptions

Definition 2 *(Bilinear Map).* *Let* $\mathbb{G}$ *and* $\mathbb{G}_1$ *be two multiplicative groups of prime order* p. *Let* g *be a generator of* $\mathbb{G}$. *A bilinear map* $e : \mathbb{G} \times \mathbb{G} \longrightarrow \mathbb{G}_1$ *is a function having the following properties:*

1. $e(u^a, v^b) = e(u, v)^{ab}$, $\forall\ u, v \in \mathbb{G}$ *and* $\forall\ a, b \in \mathbb{Z}_p$.
2. *The map is non-degenerate, i.e.,* $e(g, g)$ *is a generator of* $\mathbb{G}_1$.

The tuple $\mathbb{S} = (p, \mathbb{G}, \mathbb{G}_1, e)$ *is called a prime order bilinear group system.*

- *l-Decisional Bilinear Diffie-Hellman Exponent (l-DBDHE) Assumption* [4]

Input: $\langle Z = (\mathbb{S}, h, g, g^\alpha, \ldots, g^{\alpha^l}, g^{\alpha^{l+2}}, \ldots, g^{\alpha^{2l}}), K \rangle$, *where* $h \in_R \mathbb{G}, \alpha \in_R \mathbb{Z}_p, K$ *is either* $e(g, h)^{\alpha^{l+1}}$ *or a random element* $X \in \mathbb{G}_1$.
Output: 0 *if* $K = e(g, h)^{\alpha^{l+1}}$; 1 *otherwise.*

Definition 3. *The* (t, ϵ) l-DBDHE *assumption holds if for every PPT adversary* $\mathcal{A}$ *with running time at most* t, *the advantage of solving the above problem is at most* ϵ, *i.e.,* $Adv_{\mathcal{A}}^{l\text{-}DBDHE} = |Pr[\mathcal{A}(Z, K = e(g, h)^{\alpha^{l+1}}) = 0] - Pr[\mathcal{A}(Z, K = X) = 0]| \leq \epsilon$.

Definition 4 *(Asymmetric $\bar{v}$-linear map [5]).* *It considers group index as vector instead of integer and consists of the following two algorithms* $\mathsf{Asmul.Setup}, \mathsf{Asmul.e}_{\bar{v}_1, \bar{v}_2}(,)$

1. $\mathbb{S}' = (p, \{\mathbb{G}_{\bar{e}_i}\}_{i=0}^l, \{g_{\bar{e}_i}\}_{i=0}^l, e) \leftarrow$ Asmul.Setup$(\bar{v})$: *It takes as input $\bar{v}$, where $\bar{v} \in (\mathbb{Z}_p)^{l+1}$. Let $\bar{e}_i \in (\mathbb{Z}_p)^{l+1}$ for $i \in [0,l]$ be i-th standard basis with 1 at position i and 0 elsewhere. Let $\mathbb{G}_{\bar{e}_i}$ be the i-th source group, $\mathbb{G}_{\bar{v}}$ be the target group and $\mathbb{G}_{\bar{v}_i}$, $\bar{v}_i < \bar{v}$ (comparison holds componentwise) be the intermediate groups. Description of the source groups $\{\mathbb{G}_{\bar{e}_i}\}_{i=0}^l$ together with the generators $\{g_{\bar{e}_i}\}_{i=0}^l$ are published. It also outputs the multilinear map e.*

2. $g_{\bar{v}_1+\bar{v}_2}^{ab} \leftarrow$ Asmul.$e(g_{\bar{v}_1}^a, g_{\bar{v}_2}^b)$: *On input two elements $g = g_{\bar{v}_1}^a \in \mathbb{G}_{\bar{v}_1}$ and $h = g_{\bar{v}_2}^b \in \mathbb{G}_{\bar{v}_2}$ with $\bar{v}_1 + \bar{v}_2 \leq \bar{v}$, it outputs element of $\mathbb{G}_{\bar{v}_1+\bar{v}_2}$ as $e(g_{\bar{v}_1}^a, g_{\bar{v}_2}^b) = g_{\bar{v}_1+\bar{v}_2}^{ab}$.*

For multiple input, we write $e(g^{(1)}, g^{(2)}, \ldots, g^{(m)}) = e\left(g^{(1)}, e(g^{(2)}, \ldots, g^{(m)})\right)$, where $g^{(i)} \in \mathbb{G}_{\bar{v}_i}$. The tuple $\mathbb{S}' = (p, \{\mathbb{G}_{\bar{e}_i}\}_{i=0}^l, \{g_{\bar{e}_i}\}_{i=0}^l, e)$ is called a prime order multilinear group system.

- Decisional Hybrid Diffie-Hellman Exponent (DHDHE) Assumption [5]

Input: $\langle Z = (\mathbb{S}', \{X_i\}_{i=0}^n, V), K\rangle$, *where* $X_n = (g_{\bar{e}_n})^{\alpha^{2^n+1}}$, $X_i = (g_{\bar{e}_i})^{\alpha^{2^i}}$ *for* $i \in [0, n-1]$, $V = (g_{\bar{n}})^s$, K *is either* $(g_{2\bar{n}})^{s\alpha^{2^n}}$ *or a random* $X \in \mathbb{G}_{2\bar{n}}$, $\bar{n}$ *is vector of size $n+1$ with all 1, and $\alpha, s \in \mathbb{Z}_p$.*

Output: 0 *if* $K = (g_{2\bar{n}})^{s\alpha^{2^n}}$; 1 *otherwise.*

Definition 5. *The (t, ϵ)-DHDHE assumption holds if for every PPT adversary $\mathcal{A}$ with running time at most t, the advantage of solving the above described problem is at most ϵ, i.e.,*

$$Adv_{\mathcal{A}}^{\mathsf{DHDHE}} = |Pr[\mathcal{A}(Z, K = (g_{2\bar{n}})^{s\alpha^{2^n}}) = 0] - Pr[\mathcal{A}(Z, K = X) = 0]| \leq \epsilon.$$

- **Oracle Bilinear Diffie-Hellman Exponent (OBDHE) Problem [12]**

This is an extension of General Decisional Diffie-Hellman Exponent problem (GDDHE) [12], assuming that an extra resource $O_{g,e}^{x,y}$ takes restricted input (x, y) and output w such that $e(x, y) = e(g, w)$.

Let us consider a set of n variate polynomials $P = (p_1, \ldots, p_s), Q = (q_1, \ldots, q_s)$ with $p_1 = 1, q_1 = 1$ and a polynomial f where $\forall i, k; f, p_i, q_k \in \mathbb{F}_p[X_1, \ldots, X_n]$. Let $g^P = (g^{p_1}, \ldots, g^{p_s})$. The polynomial f depends on P, Q if there exists $a_{i,j}, b_i (1 \leq i, j \leq s) \in \mathbb{Z}_p$ such that $f = \sum_{1 \leq i,j \leq s} a_{i,j} p_i p_j + \sum_{1 \leq i,j \leq s} b_i q_i$. Otherwise, f is independent of P, Q.

The (P, Q, f)-Oracle Bilinear Diffie-Hellman Exponent $((P, Q, f)$-OBDHE) problem is defined as follows:

Definition 6. $((P, Q, f)$-OBDHE): *Given* $H(x_1, \ldots, x_n) = (g^{P(x_1, \ldots, x_n)}, g_1^{Q(x_1, \ldots, x_n)})$, *for random choices of $x_1, \cdots, x_n \in \mathbb{F}_p$, $T \in \mathbb{G}_1$, and access to the oracle $O_{g,e}^{x,y}$, decide whether $T = g_1^{f(x_1, \ldots, x_n)}$.*

Note that GDDHE problem is also of similar type, except that oracle access is not provided. Phan et al. [12] have proved that (P, Q, f)-OBDHE is intractable in generic group model, if f does not depend on $P\|P', Q$, where $\|$ denotes concatenation. If $x = g^{x_1}, y = g^{y_1}$, then $w = g^{x_1 y_1}$. Thus by providing access to the oracle, we are providing free multiplication in exponent. Let q' oracle queries be provided. Then $P' = (p'_1, p'_2, \ldots, p'_{q'})$.

- Modified Decisional Bilinear Diffie-Hellman Exponent (mDBDHE) Assumption

Input: $\langle Z = (\mathbb{S}, h, g, \{g^{\alpha^u}\}_{u \in [1,2l] \setminus \{l+1\}}, v, \{g^{\beta_u}\}_{u \in [l]}, O_{g,e}^{x,y}), K \rangle$, where $h, v \in_R \mathbb{G}, \alpha, \{\beta_u\}_{u \in [l]} \in_R \mathbb{Z}_p, K$ is either $e(g,h)^{\alpha^{l+1}}$ or a random element $X \in \mathbb{G}_1$, $O_{g,e}^{x,y}$ takes restricted input (x,y) and output w such that $e(x,y) = e(g,w)$. Let $C, S \subseteq [l]$ and $C \cap S = \phi$. Here x, y are restricted on the following inputs:

1. $x = g^{\alpha^i}$ or g^{β_i} for $i \in C$ and $y = v$.
2. $x = v \prod_{j \in S} g_{N+1-j}$ or g^{β_j} for $j \in S$ and $y = h$.

Output: 0 if $K = e(g,h)^{\alpha^{l+1}}$; 1 otherwise.

Definition 7. *The (t, ϵ) mDBDHE assumption holds if for every PPT adversary $\mathcal{A}$ with running time at most t, the advantage of solving the above problem is at most ϵ, i.e., $Adv_{\mathcal{A}}^{mDBDHE} = |Pr[\mathcal{A}(Z, K = e(g,h)^{\alpha^{l+1}}) = 0] - Pr[\mathcal{A}(Z, K = X) = 0]| \leq \epsilon$.*

Following [12], it is easy to verify that mDBDHE is an instance of (P, Q, f)-Oracle Bilinear Diffie-Hellman Exponent $((P, Q, f)$-OBDHE) problem. If we formulate mDBDHE problem as the (P, Q, f)-ODDHE problem then

$$P = (s, \{\alpha^u\}_{u \in [2l] \setminus \{l+1\}}, \gamma, \{\beta_u\}_{u \in [l]}),$$
$$P' = (\{\gamma \alpha^u\}_{u \in C}, \{\gamma \beta_u\}_{u \in C}, \{s \beta_u\}_{u \in S}, (\gamma + \sum_{j \in S} \alpha^{l+1-j})s),$$
$$Q = 1, \quad f = s\alpha^{l+1}.$$

To compute $f = s\alpha^{l+1}$, one of our multiplicands needs to be either s, $\{s\beta_u\}_{u \in S}$ or $(\gamma + \sum_{j \in S} \alpha^{l+1-j})s$ as there is factor s. Choosing s will not help because we do not have an α^{l+1}, similarly we can not choose $\{s\beta_u\}_{u \in S}$. To make f, one of our multiplicands is definitely $(\gamma + \sum_{u \in S} \alpha^{l+1-j})s$. The second multiplicand that can give us f is one from $\{\alpha^u\}_{u \in [2l] \setminus \{l+1\}}$. Multiplying these terms gives us terms of the form $\alpha^u(\gamma + \sum_{j \in S} \alpha^{l+1-j})s$, which includes $s\alpha^{l+1}$ if $u \in S$, but then we have to be able to produce the term $s\gamma \alpha^u$ for some $u \in S$ to be able to cancel it out.

To generate $s\gamma \alpha^u$, using only two multiplicands, we discuss the following possibilities:

- Again choose $\{\alpha^u\}$ and $(\gamma + \sum_{j \in S} \alpha^{l+1-j})s$, but this cancels out our desired term $s\alpha^{l+1}$ as well since we have to use the same u.
- Select s and $\gamma \alpha^u$ to get $s\gamma \alpha^u$ for some $u \in C$, but since $C \cap S = \phi$, we can not get $s\gamma \alpha^u$ for any $u \in S$.

- Take γ and $(\gamma + \sum_{u \in S} \alpha^{l+1-j})s$ to get $\gamma(\gamma + \sum_{u \in S} \alpha^{l+1-j})s$, which includes $s\gamma\alpha^u$ if $l + 1 - j \in S$, but then, we need to cancel $\gamma^2 s$ and the only way to get $\gamma^2 s$ is to use the same terms again which cancels our desired term $s\gamma\alpha^u$ as well.
- Select $\{\gamma\alpha^u\}_{u \in C}$ and $(\gamma + \sum_{j \in S} \alpha^{l+1-j})s$ to produce $(\gamma^2 s\alpha^u + s\gamma \sum_{u \in S} \alpha^{l+1-j+u})$, which contains $s\gamma\alpha^u$ if $l + 1 - j + u \in S$ but then, we need to cancel $s\gamma^2\alpha^u$ and the only way to get $s\gamma^2\alpha^u$ is to use the same terms again with the same u which cancels our desired term $s\gamma\alpha^u$ as well.

Hence f can not be expressed as a linear combination of $P||P', Q$. Therefore mDBDHE is cryptographically hard.

3   BEPM-I: BEPM with Selective Security

Our first construction BEPM-I is selectively secure and works as follows:

$(\mathsf{PP}, \mathsf{MK}) \leftarrow \mathsf{BEPM.Setup}(N, \lambda)$: Given the security parameter λ and the maximum number of users N supported by the system, the PKGC executes the following steps to generate the public parameter PP and a master key MK.

1. The PKGC chooses a prime order bilinear group system $\mathbb{S} = (p, \mathbb{G}, \mathbb{G}_1, e)$, where $\mathbb{G}, \mathbb{G}_1$ are groups of prime order p, g is generator of $\mathbb{G}$ and $e : \mathbb{G} \times \mathbb{G} \to \mathbb{G}_1$ is a bilinear mapping.
2. It selects $\alpha, \gamma \in_R \mathbb{Z}_p$ and sets $\mathsf{MK} = (\alpha, \gamma)$, $\mathsf{PP} = (\mathbb{S}, g, g_1, \ldots, g_N, g_{N+2}, \ldots, g_{2N}, v = g^\gamma)$, where $g_i = g^{\alpha^i}$ for $i \in [1, N] \cup [N + 2, 2N]$.
3. Finally, the PKGC keeps MK secret to itself and makes PP public.

$(sk_u) \leftarrow \mathsf{BEPM.KeyGen}(\mathsf{PP}, \mathsf{MK}, u)$: For each user $u \in [N]$, the PKGC extracts γ from MK and g_u from PP and generates a secret key as $sk_u = (g_u)^\gamma$. It sends sk_u to user u through a secure communication channel between them.

$(\mathsf{Hdr}, K, \{K_u\}_{u \in G}) \leftarrow \mathsf{BEPM.Encrypt}(G, \mathsf{PP})$: Using PP and a group of users $G \subseteq [N]$, the broadcaster does the following:

1. It chooses an integer $s \in_R \mathbb{Z}_p$.
2. It extracts $g, v, \{g_{N+1-j}\}_{j \in G}$ from PP, and computes C_1, C_2 as

$$C_1 = (v \prod_{j \in G} g_{N+1-j})^s = g^{s(\gamma + \sum_{j \in G} \alpha^{N+1-j})}, C_2 = g^s.$$

3. Using $g_N, g_1, v, \{g_u\}_{u \in G}$ available from PP, it sets a session key K and personalized keys $\{K_u\}_{u \in G}$ as

$$K = e(g_N, g_1)^s = e(g_{N+1}, g)^s, K_u = e(g_u, v)^s.$$

4. Finally, it publishes the header $\mathsf{Hdr} = (G, C_1, C_2)$ and keeps $K, \{K_u\}_{u \in G}$ secret to itself.

$(K, K_u) \leftarrow$ BEPM.Decrypt(PP, sk_u, Hdr, u): A subscribed user u with secret key $sk_u = g_u^\gamma$ uses the public parameter PP, the header Hdr $= (G, C_1, C_2)$, and recovers the session key K and its personalized key K_u by computing

$$K = \frac{e(g_u, C_1)}{e(sk_u \cdot \prod\limits_{j \in G, j \neq u} g_{N+1-j+u}, C_2)} = e(g_{N+1}, g)^s$$

$$K_u = e(sk_u, C_2) = e(g_u, v)^s.$$

Correctness: The correctness of BEPM.Decrypt algorithm follows from the argument below:

$$K = \frac{e(g_u, C_1)}{e\left(sk_u \cdot \prod\limits_{j \in G, j \neq u} g_{N+1-j+u}, C_2\right)} = \frac{e\left(g^{\alpha^u}, g^{s(\gamma + \sum\limits_{j \in G} \alpha^{N+1-j})}\right)}{e\left(g^{\{\alpha^u \gamma + \sum\limits_{j \in G, j \neq u} \alpha^{N+1-j+u}\}}, g^s\right)}$$

$$= \frac{e\left(g, g\right)^{s\alpha^u(\gamma + \sum\limits_{j \in G} \alpha^{N+1-j})}}{e\left(g, g\right)^{s\alpha^u(\gamma + \sum\limits_{j \in G, j \neq u} \alpha^{N+1-j})}} e(g, g)^{s\alpha^{N+1}} = e(g_{N+1}, g)^s$$

$$K_u = e(sk_u, C_2) = e(g_u{}^\gamma, g^s) = e(g_u, g^\gamma)^s = e(g_u, v)^s.$$

Performance Analysis

1. Storage: PP size is $(2N+1)|\mathbb{G}|$, SK size is $1|\mathbb{G}|$, where $|\mathbb{G}| =$ bit size of an element in $\mathbb{G}$.
2. Communication: Header size $= 2|\mathbb{G}|$.
3. Computation: Set up phase requires $2N$ exponentiations in $\mathbb{G}$, key generation needs 1 exponentiation in $\mathbb{G}$. Encryption phase requires 2 exponentiations in $\mathbb{G}$ and $|G| + 1$ exponentiation in $\mathbb{G}_1$. Here $|G| =$ number of users in the set G. Decryption phase requires 3 pairing and 1 inversion in $\mathbb{G}_1$.

A subset of a set of N users can be identified by N bits where i-th bit 1 indicates that i-th user is included and i-th bit 0 indicates it is not included. This information of subscribed user set is independent to any broadcast encryption. Thereby, we don't include indices of users in G in case of $|$Hdr$|$ computation as in other broadcast encryption schemes.

Remark 2. If a broadcaster wants involve a set of users S' with G, he needs to compute $C_1^* = (v \prod_{j \in S' \cup G} g_{n+1-j})^s$ and sets the additional personalized key accordingly. Now the broadcaster can do it efficiently by modifying C_1 as- $C_1^* = C_1(\prod_{j \in S'} g_{n+1-j})^s = (v \prod_{j \in G} g_{n+1-j})^s (\prod_{j \in S'} g_{n+1-j})^s = (v \prod_{j \in S' \cup G} g_{n+1-j})^s$. Similar technique is applicable to revoke a set of users $S' \subseteq G$ from G, only need to divide instead of multiply. Note that the broadcaster does not create personalized messages for revoked users, thereby corresponding personalized keys become inactive. This method is applicable for next two constructions BEPM-II, III also.

Remark 3. Using secret key of users outside G, PP, Hdr, it is not possible to recover session key K. If we formulate these values as an instance of (P,Q,f)-GDDHE problem then

$$P = (s, \{\alpha^u\}_{u \in [2N] \setminus \{N+1\}}, \gamma, \{\gamma \alpha^u\}_{u \in C}, (\gamma + \sum_{j \in S} \alpha^{N+1-j})s),$$

$$Q = 1, \; f = s\alpha^{N+1}.$$

A polynomial f depends on P, Q if there exists $a_{i,j}, b_i \in \mathbb{Z}_p$ such that $f = \sum_{1 \le i,j \le s} a_{i,j} p_i p_j + \sum_{1 \le i,j \le s} b_i q_i$. It is easy to follow that f can not be expressed as a linear combination of P, Q. (The explanation is similar to Sect. 2.3 which explain the hardness of modified Decisional Bilinear Diffie-Hellman Exponent problem). Therefore by (P, Q, f)-GDDHE assumption $K = e(g,g)^f = e(g_{N+1}, g)^s$ is not computable. Similarly, $f_1 = \alpha^u \gamma s, (u \in S)$ can not be expressed as a linear combination of P, Q, therefore personalized key $K_u = e(g,g)^{f_1} = e(g_u, v)^s$ is not computable. Therefore our scheme is fully collision resistance. Similar arguments are applicable for BEPM-II, BEPM-III.

Theorem 1 *(Key indistinguishability under CPA). Our proposed scheme BEPM-I described in Sect. 3 achieves selective IND-CPA security as per the key indistinguishability security model of Sect. 2.2 under N-DBDHE assumption.*

Proof. Assume that there is a PPT adversary $\mathcal{A}$ that breaks the selective IND-CPA security of our scheme BEPM-I with a non-negligible advantage. We construct a distinguisher $\mathcal{C}$ that attempts to solve the N-DBDHE problem using $\mathcal{A}$ as a subroutine. The distinguisher $\mathcal{C}$ takes as input an N-DBDHE instance $\langle Z, K \rangle$, where $Z = (\mathbb{S}, h, g, g_1, \ldots, g_N, g_{N+2}, \ldots, g_{2N})$, $\mathbb{S}$ is prime order bilinear group system, g is a generator of the group $\mathbb{G}$, $g_i = g^{\alpha^i}$ for $i \in [1, N] \cup [N+2, 2N]$, $h \in_R \mathbb{G}$, $\alpha \in \mathbb{Z}_p$, K is either $e(g,h)^{\alpha^{N+1}}$ or a random element of the target group $\mathbb{G}_1$. The distinguisher $\mathcal{C}$ attempts to output 0 if $K = e(g,h)^{\alpha^{N+1}}$; and 1 otherwise. Now $\mathcal{C}$ plays the role of a challenger in the security game and interacts with $\mathcal{A}$ as follows:

Initialization: The adversary $\mathcal{A}$ selects a target recipient set $G \subseteq [N]$ and declares it to $\mathcal{C}$.

Setup: The challenger $\mathcal{C}$ selects $r \in_R \mathbb{Z}_p$, computes $v = \dfrac{g^r}{\prod\limits_{j \in G} g_{N+1-j}}$ and sets the public parameter as PP $= (\mathbb{S}, g, g_1, \ldots, g_N, g_{N+2}, \ldots, g_{2N}, v)$. This corresponds to setting implicitly the master key MK as

$$\mathsf{MK} = (\alpha, \gamma = r - \sum_{j \in G} \alpha^{N+1-j}).$$

The challenger $\mathcal{C}$ hands over the public parameter PP to $\mathcal{A}$.

As $v = \dfrac{g^r}{\prod\limits_{j \in G} g_{N+1-j}} = \dfrac{g^r}{\prod\limits_{j \in G} g^{\alpha^{N+1-j}}} = g^{(r - \sum\limits_{j \in G} \alpha^{N+1-j})} = g^\gamma$, and $\gamma = r - \sum\limits_{j \in G} \alpha^{N+1-j}$, the distribution of v is the same as in the real scheme.

Query 1: The adversary $\mathcal{A}$ issues a series of key generation queries for users in $[N]\backslash G$ to $\mathcal{C}$. For a user $u \in [N]\backslash G$, the challenger $\mathcal{C}$ generates the secret key sk_u as $sk_u = \dfrac{g_u^r}{\prod\limits_{j \in G} g_{N+1-j+u}}$ and returns sk_u to $\mathcal{A}$. We note that the value of sk_u simulated by $\mathcal{C}$ is identical to that in the real scheme as

$$sk_u = \frac{g_u^r}{\prod\limits_{j \in G} g_{N+1-j+u}} = \frac{g^{r\alpha^u}}{\prod\limits_{j \in G} g^{\alpha^{N+1-j+u}}} = g^{\left(r\alpha^u - \sum\limits_{j \in G} \alpha^{N+1-j+u}\right)}$$

$$= g^{\alpha^u\left(r - \sum\limits_{j \in G} \alpha^{N+1-j}\right)} = g^{\gamma\alpha^u} = (g_u)^{\gamma}.$$

Challenge: The challenger $\mathcal{C}$ runs the following steps:

1. It sets $\mathsf{Hdr} = (G, h^r, h)$ where h is extracted from the given N-DBDHE instance $\langle Z, K \rangle$ and r is as selected by $\mathcal{C}$ in **Setup** phase. Let $h = g^s$ for some unknown integer $s \in \mathbb{Z}_p$.
2. For each $u \in G$, the challenger $\mathcal{C}$ sets $K_u, R_u \in \mathbb{G}_1$ as

$$K_u = e(g_u^r, h)e\left(\prod_{j \in G, j \neq u} g_{N+1-j+u}, h \right)^{-1} K^{-1},$$

$$R_u = e(g_u^r, h)e\left(\prod_{j \in G, j \neq u} g_{N+1-j+u}, h \right)^{-1} R^{-1},$$

where R is randomly selected by $\mathcal{C}$ from the target group $\mathbb{G}_1$ and K is extracted from the given N-DBDHE instance $\langle Z, K \rangle$.

3. The challenger $\mathcal{C}$ chooses a random $b \in \{0, 1\}$. If $b = 0$, $\mathcal{C}$ gives $(\mathsf{Hdr}, K, \{K_u\}_{u \in G})$ to $\mathcal{A}$; else if $b = 1$, $\mathcal{C}$ hands $(\mathsf{Hdr}, R, \{R_u\}_{u \in G})$ over to $\mathcal{A}$.

Observe that $\mathsf{Hdr} = (G, h^r, h) = (G, g^{rs}, g^s) = \left(G, g^{\left(\gamma + \sum\limits_{j \in G} \alpha^{N+1-j}\right)s}, g^s\right)$ has the same distribution as in the real construction from $\mathcal{A}$'s view.

Also see that if $K = e(g_{N+1}, h)$ then K_u has the distribution similar to the original protocol as

$$K_u = e(g_u^r, h)e\left(\prod_{j \in G, j \neq u} g_{N+1-j+u}, h \right)^{-1} K^{-1}$$

$$= e(g^{\alpha^u r}, h)e\left(g^{\sum\limits_{j \in G, j \neq u} \alpha^{N+1-j+u}}, h \right)^{-1} e(g_{N+1}, h)^{-1}$$

$$= e\left(g^{\alpha^u r} g^{-\sum\limits_{j \in G, j \neq u} \alpha^{N+1-j+u}}, h \right) e(g^{-\alpha^{N+1}}, h) = e\left(g^{\alpha^u r} g^{-\sum\limits_{j \in G} \alpha^{N+1-j+u}}, h \right)$$

$$= e\left(g^{\alpha^u\left(r - \sum\limits_{j \in G} \alpha^{N+1-j}\right)}, h \right) = e(g_u^{\gamma}, g^s) = e(g_u, g^{\gamma})^s = e(g_u, v)^s.$$

Query 2: This is similar to Query 1. The adversary $\mathcal{A}$ sends key generation queries for users $u \in [N]\backslash G$ and receives back the corresponding secret key sk_u simulated in the same manner by $\mathcal{C}$ as in Phase 1.

Guess: Finally, $\mathcal{A}$ outputs a guess $b' \in \{0, 1\}$ of b to $\mathcal{C}$. If $b' = b$, $\mathcal{C}$ outputs 0, indicating that $K = e(g, h)^{\alpha^{N+1}}$; otherwise, it outputs 1, indicating that K is random.

Therefore, if $\mathcal{A}$ has non-negligible advantage ε in correctly guessing b', then $\mathcal{C}$ solves N-DBDHE problem given to $\mathcal{C}$ with the same non-negligible advantage ε i.e., $Adv_{\mathcal{A},BEPM-I}^{\text{IND-CPA}} = Adv_{\mathcal{C}}^{\text{N-DBDHE}}$. Hence the theorem follows.

4   BEPM-II: BEPM with Adaptive Security

Our adaptively secure broadcast encryption with personalized messages scheme BEPM-II works as follows:

$(\text{PP}, \text{MK}) \leftarrow \text{BEPM.Setup}(N, \lambda)$: Given the security parameter λ and the maximum number of users N permissible in the system, the PKGC executes the following steps to generates the public parameter PP and a master key MK.

1. The PKGC chooses a prime order bilinear group system $\mathbb{S} = (p, \mathbb{G}, \mathbb{G}_1, e)$, where $\mathbb{G}, \mathbb{G}_1$ are groups of prime order p, g is a generator of $\mathbb{G}$ and $e : \mathbb{G} \times \mathbb{G} \to \mathbb{G}_1$ is a bilinear mapping.
2. It selects $\alpha, \gamma, \{\beta_i\}_{i\in[N]} \in_R \mathbb{Z}_p$ and sets $\text{MK} = (\alpha, \gamma)$, $\text{PP} = (\mathbb{S}, g, v = g^\gamma, \{g_i\}_{i\in[1,2N]\setminus\{N+1\}}, \{g^{\beta_u}\}_{u\in[N]})$, where $g_i = g^{\alpha^i}$.
3. Finally, the PKGC keeps MK secret to itself and makes PP public.

$(sk_u) \leftarrow \text{BEPM.KeyGen}(\text{PP}, \text{MK}, u)$: For each user $u \in [N]$, the PKGC extracts γ from MK and g_u, g^{β_u} from PP and generates a secret key $sk_u = (sk_{u_1}, sk_{u_2}) = ((g_u)^\gamma, (g^{\beta_u})^\gamma)$. It sends sk_u to user u through a secure communication channel between them.

$(\text{Hdr}, K, \{K_u\}_{u\in G}) \leftarrow \text{BEPM.Encrypt}(G, \text{PP})$: The broadcaster selects a group of users $G \subseteq [N]$ and does the following using PP:

1. It chooses an integer $s \in_R \mathbb{Z}_p$.
2. It extracts $g, v, \{g_{N+1-j}\}_{j\in G}$ from PP, and computes C_1, C_2 as

$$C_1 = (v \prod_{j\in G} g_{N+1-j})^s = g^{s\left(\gamma + \sum_{j\in G} \alpha^{N+1-j}\right)}, C_2 = g^s.$$

3. Using $g_N, g_1, v, \{g^{\beta_u}\}_{u\in G}$ available from PP, it sets a session key K and personalized keys $\{K_u\}_{u\in G}$ as

$$K = e(g_N, g_1)^s = e(g_{N+1}, g)^s, K_u = e(g^{\beta_u}, v)^s K.$$

4. Finally, the broadcaster publishes $\text{Hdr} = (G, C_1, C_2)$ and keeps K, $\{K_u\}_{u\in G}$ secret to itself.

$(K, K_u) \leftarrow \text{BEPM.Decrypt}(\text{PP}, sk_u, \text{Hdr}, u)$: A subscribed user u uses the public parameter PP, secret key $sk_u = (sk_{u_1}, sk_{u_2})$ where $sk_{u_1} = g_u^\gamma, sk_{u_2} = g^{\gamma\beta_u}$, the header $\text{Hdr} = (G, C_1, C_2)$, and recovers the session key K and its personalized key K_u by computing

$$K = \frac{e(g_u, C_1)}{e(sk_{u_1} \cdot \prod\limits_{j \in G, j \neq u} g_{N+1-j+u}, C_2)} = e(g_{N+1}, g)^s,$$

$$K_u = e(sk_{u_2}, C_2)K = e(g^{\beta_u \gamma}, g^s)K = e(g^{\beta_u}, g^s)K = e(g^{\beta_u}, v)^s K.$$

Performance Analysis

1. Storage: PP size is $(3N + 1)|\mathbb{G}|$, SK size is $2|\mathbb{G}|$, where $|\mathbb{G}| = $ bit size of an element in $\mathbb{G}$.
2. Communication: Header size $= 2|\mathbb{G}|$.
3. Computation: Set up phase requires $3N$ exponentiations in $\mathbb{G}$, key generation needs 2 exponentiations in $\mathbb{G}$. Encryption phase requires 2 exponentiation in $\mathbb{G}$ and $|G| + 1$ exponentiation in $\mathbb{G}_1$. Here $|G| = $ number of users in the set G. Decryption phase require 3 pairing and 1 inversion in $\mathbb{G}_1$.

Theorem 2 *(Key indistinguishability under CPA). Our proposed scheme BEPM-II described in Sect. 4 achieves adaptive IND-CPA security as per the key indistinguishability security model of Sect. 2.3 assuming the hardness of mDB-DHE assumption.*

Proof. Assume that there is a PPT adversary $\mathcal{A}$ that breaks the adaptive IND-CPA security of our proposed BEPM-II scheme with a non-negligible advantage. We construct a distinguisher $\mathcal{C}$ that attempts to solve the mDBDHE problem using $\mathcal{A}$ as a subroutine. The distinguisher $\mathcal{C}$ takes as input an mDBDHE instance $\langle Z, K \rangle$, where $Z = (\mathbb{S}, h, g, g_1, \ldots, g_N, g_{N+2}, \ldots, g_{2N}, v, \{g^{\beta_u}\}_{u \in [N]}, O_{g,e}^{x,y})$, $\mathbb{S}$ is prime order bilinear group system, $v, h \in_R \mathbb{G}$, g is a generator of the group $\mathbb{G}$, $\alpha, \{\beta_u\}_{u \in [N]} \in \mathbb{Z}_p$, $g_i = g^{\alpha^i}$ for $i \in [1, N] \cup [N + 2, 2N]$, $O_{g,e}^{x,y}$ takes restricted input (x, y) and outputs w such that $e(x, y) = e(g, w)$. Let $\bar{C}, \bar{S} \subseteq [N]$ and $\bar{C} \cap \bar{S} = \phi$. Here x, y are restricted on the following inputs:

1. $x = g^{\alpha^k}$ or g^{β_k} for $k \in \bar{C}$ and $y = v$.
2. $x = v \prod\limits_{j \in \bar{S}} g_{N+1-j}$ or g^{β_k} for $k \in \bar{S}$ and $y = h$.

K is either $e(g, h)^{\alpha^{N+1}}$ or a random element of the target group $\mathbb{G}_1$. In the security game, $\bar{C}$ will be used as the set of users corrupted by the adversary $\mathcal{A}$ i.e., the set of users for which key has been generated and $\bar{S}$ will be treated as the set of users G for which the challenge ciphertext has been generated. The distinguisher $\mathcal{C}$ attempts to output 0 if $K = e(g, h)^{\alpha^{N+1}}$; and 1 otherwise. Now $\mathcal{C}$ plays the role of a challenger in the security game and interacts with $\mathcal{A}$ as follows:

Setup: The challenger $\mathcal{C}$ uses $\langle Z, K \rangle$, and sets the public parameter PP as $\text{PP} = (\mathbb{S}, g, g_1, \ldots, g_N, g_{N+2}, \ldots, g_{2N}, v, \{g^{\beta_u}\}_{u \in [N]})$. This corresponds to setting implicitly the master key $\text{MK} = (\alpha, \gamma)$, considering $v = g^\gamma$ for some unknown $\gamma \in \mathbb{Z}_p$. The challenger $\mathcal{C}$ hands over the public parameter PP to $\mathcal{A}$.

Query 1: Receiving the key generation query from user u, the challenger $\mathcal{C}$ store u in a list of corrupted users $\bar{C}$, generates $sk_{u_1} = w_1, sk_{u_2} = w_2$ by running the oracles $O_{g,e}^{g_u,v}, O_{g,e}^{g^{\beta_u},v}$ and returns $sk_u = (sk_{u_1}, sk_{u_2})$ to $\mathcal{A}$. As $e(g_u, v = g^\gamma) = e(g, w_1) \Rightarrow w_1 = g_u^\gamma, e(g^{\beta_u}, v = g^\gamma) = e(g, w_2) \Rightarrow w_2 = g^{\gamma\beta_u}$, the value of sk_{u_1}, sk_{u_2} simulated by $\mathcal{C}$ are identical to that in the real scheme.

Challenge: The adversary $\mathcal{A}$ select a set of uncorrupted users $G \subseteq [N]$ with $G \cap \bar{C} = \phi$ on which it wants to be challenged. It sets $\bar{S} = G$ and sends G to $\mathcal{C}$. The challenger $\mathcal{C}$ executes the following steps:

1. It sets $C_2 = h$ where h is extracted from the given mDBDHE instance $\langle Z, K \rangle$. Let $h = g^s$ for some unknown integer $s \in \mathbb{Z}_p$.

2. It calculates $x = v \prod_{j \in G} g_{N+1-j}$, runs $O_{g,e}^{x,C_2}$ and sets the output as C_1.

   Notice that the value of C_1 simulated by $\mathcal{C}$ is identical to that in the real scheme as

   $$e\left(w = (v \prod_{j \in G} g_{N+1-j}), C_2\right) = e(g, C_1) \Rightarrow C_1 = (v \prod_{j \in G} g_{N+1-j})^s.$$

3. For each $u \in G$, the challenger $\mathcal{C}$ does the following:
   (a) $\mathcal{C}$ runs $O_{g,e}^{g^{\beta_u},h}$, to get $x = g^{s\beta_u}$.
       Observe that $e(g^{\beta_u}, h = g^s) = e(g, x) \Rightarrow x = g^{s\beta_u}$.
   (b) It computes $K_u, R_u \in \mathbb{G}_1$ as $K_u = e(g^{s\beta_u}, v)K, R_u = e(g^{s\beta_u}, v)R$ where R is randomly selected by $\mathcal{C}$ from the target group $\mathbb{G}_1$ and K is extracted from the given mDBDHE instance $\langle Z, K \rangle$.

4. It sets $\mathsf{Hdr} = (G, C_1, C_2)$.

5. The challenger $\mathcal{C}$ chooses a random $b \in \{0,1\}$. If $b = 0$, $\mathcal{C}$ gives $(\mathsf{Hdr}, K, \{K_u\}_{u \in G})$ to $\mathcal{A}$; else if $b = 1$, $\mathcal{C}$ returns $(\mathsf{Hdr}, R, \{R_u\}_{u \in G})$ to $\mathcal{A}$.

Observe that if $K = e(g_{N+1}, h)$ then K_u has the same distribution as in the original protocol since

$$K_u = e(g^{s\beta_u}, v)K = e(g^{s\beta_u}, g^\gamma)K = e(g^{\gamma\beta_u}, g^s)K = e(sk_{u_2}, C_2)K.$$

Query 2: Receiving the key generation query from user $u \notin G$, the challenger $\mathcal{C}$ replies as in Query 1.

Guess: Finally, $\mathcal{A}$ outputs a guess $b' \in \{0,1\}$ of b to $\mathcal{C}$. If $b' = b$, $\mathcal{C}$ outputs 0, indicating that $K = e(g, h)^{\alpha^{N+1}}$; otherwise, it outputs 1, indicating that K is random.

Therefore, if $\mathcal{A}$ has a non-negligible advantage in correctly guessing b', then $\mathcal{C}$ solves the mDBDHE problem given to $\mathcal{C}$ with the same non-negligible advantage i.e., $Adv_{\mathcal{A},BEPM-II}^{\mathsf{IND-CPA}} = Adv_{\mathcal{C}}^{\mathsf{mDBDHE}}$. Hence the theorem follows.

5   BEPM-III: BEPM from Multilinear Maps

We now describe our third construction which is a multilinear map based BEPM.

$(\mathsf{PP}, \mathsf{MK}) \leftarrow \mathsf{BEPM.Setup}(N, \lambda)$: Given the security parameter λ and maximum number of users $N = 2^n - 1$ supported by the system, the PKGC does the following:

1. It generates $\mathbb{S}' = (p, \{\mathbb{G}_{\bar{e}_i}\}_{i=0}^n, \{g_{\bar{e}_i}\}_{i=0}^n, e) \longleftarrow \mathsf{Asmul.Setup}(2\bar{n})$, where $\bar{n}$ is a vector of length $n+1$ having all 1, $\mathbb{G}_{\bar{e}_i}$ $(0 \le i \le n)$ is the i-th source group, $\mathbb{G}_{2\bar{n}}$ is the target group, $\mathbb{G}_{\bar{v}}$ $(\bar{v} < 2\bar{n})$ are intermediate groups and $g_{\bar{e}_i}$ is a generator of $\mathbb{G}_{\bar{e}_i}$.

2. The PKGC selects $\alpha, \gamma \in_R \mathbb{Z}_p$ and sets the master key $\mathsf{MK} = (\alpha, \gamma)$.

3. It computes $v = (g_{\bar{n}})^\gamma$, $X_n = (g_{\bar{e}_n})^{\alpha^{2^n+1}}$, and $X_i = (g_{\bar{e}_i})^{\alpha^{2^i}}$, where $i \in [0, n-1]$ and sets public parameter $\mathsf{PP} = (\mathbb{S}', \{X_i\}_{i=0}^n, v)$.

4. It keeps MK secret to itself and makes PP public.

Let us define $(X_i)^0 = g_{\bar{e}_i}, (X_i)^1 = g_{\bar{e}_i}{}^{\alpha^{2^i}}$. Then

$$(X_i)^{u_i} = (g_{\bar{e}_i})^{\alpha^{u_i 2^i}} = \begin{cases} (g_{\bar{e}_i})^{\alpha^{2^i}} & \text{if } u_i = 1 \\ g_{\bar{e}_i} & \text{if } u_i = 0 \end{cases}.$$

If $u = (u_0, u_1, \ldots, u_{n-1}, 0), u_i \in \{0,1\}$ is the binary representation of $u \in [N]$ i.e., $u = \sum_{i=0}^{n-1} u_i 2^i$, then using u, PP, one can compute $Z_u = g_{\bar{n}}^{\alpha^u}$ as

$$e\left((X_0)^{u_0}, (X_1)^{u_1}, \ldots, (X_{n-1})^{u_{n-1}}, g_{\bar{e}_n}\right)$$

$$= e\left((g_{\bar{e}_0})^{\alpha^{u_0 2^0}}, (g_{\bar{e}_1})^{\alpha^{u_1 2^1}}, (g_{\bar{e}_2})^{\alpha^{u_2 2^2}}, \ldots, (g_{\bar{e}_{n-1}})^{\alpha^{u_{n-1} 2^{n-1}}}, g_{\bar{e}_n}\right)$$

$$= e(g_{\bar{e}_0}, g_{\bar{e}_1}, g_{\bar{e}_2}, \ldots, g_{\bar{e}_n})^{\alpha^{\sum_{i=0}^{n-1} u_i 2^i}}$$

$$= e(g_{\bar{e}_0}, g_{\bar{e}_1}, g_{\bar{e}_2}, \ldots, g_{\bar{e}_n})^{\alpha^u} = g_{\bar{n}}^{\alpha^u} = Z_u. \tag{1}$$

Again, if $u' = u - (2^n + 1) = (u'_0, u'_1, u'_2, \ldots, u'_{n-1}, 0), u'_i \in \{0,1\}$ is binary representation of $u' \ge 0$, then using u', PP one can compute $Z_u = g_{\bar{n}}^{\alpha^u} = g_{\bar{n}}^{\alpha^{u'} + \alpha^{2^n+1}}, u \ge N+2$ as

$$e\left((X_0)^{u'_0}, (X_1)^{u'_1}, \ldots, (X_{n-1})^{u'_{n-1}}, g_{\bar{e}_n}{}^{\alpha^{2^n+1}}\right)$$

$$= e((g_{\bar{e}_0})^{\alpha^{u'_0 2^0}}, (g_{\bar{e}_1})^{\alpha^{u'_1 2^1}}, (g_{\bar{e}_2})^{\alpha^{u'_2 2^2}}, \ldots, (g_{\bar{e}_{n-1}})^{\alpha^{u'_{n-1} 2^{n-1}}}, g_{\bar{e}_n}{}^{\alpha^{2^n+1}})$$

$$= e(g_{\bar{e}_0}, g_{\bar{e}_1}, g_{\bar{e}_2}, \ldots, (g_{\bar{e}_n}))^{\alpha^{2^n+1}} \alpha^{\sum_{i=0}^{n-1} u'_i 2^i}$$

$$= e(g_{\bar{e}_0}, g_{\bar{e}_1}, g_{\bar{e}_2}, \ldots, g_{\bar{e}_n})^{\alpha^u} = (g_{\bar{n}})^{\alpha^u} = Z_u. \tag{2}$$

$(sk_u) \leftarrow \mathsf{BEPM.KeyGen}(\mathsf{PP}, \mathsf{MK}, u)$: For each user $u \in [N]$, the PKGC extracts γ from MK and computes Z_u using PP as in Eq. 1. It generates a secret key for user $u \in [N]$ as $sk_u = (Z_u)^\gamma$ and sends sk_u to user u through a secure communication channel between them.

$(\mathsf{Hdr}, K) \leftarrow \mathsf{BEPM.Encrypt}(G, \mathsf{PP})$: The broadcaster selects a group of users G, random integer $s \in \mathbb{Z}_p$ and does the following:

1. Using PP, the broadcaster computes

$$
\begin{aligned}
W' &= e(g_{\bar{e}_0}, g_{\bar{e}_1}, \ldots, g_{\bar{e}_{n-2}}, X_{n-1}, g_{\bar{e}_n}) \\
&= e(g_{\bar{e}_0}, g_{\bar{e}_1}, \ldots, g_{\bar{e}_{n-2}}, (g_{\bar{e}_{n-1}})^{\alpha^{2^{n-1}}}, g_{\bar{e}_n}) = (g_{\bar{n}})^{\alpha^{2^{n-1}}}, \\
W &= e(W', W') = (g_{2\bar{n}})^{\alpha^{2^n}}.
\end{aligned}
$$

2. It sets a session key K and personalized keys K_u as
$K = W^s = (g_{2\bar{n}})^{s\alpha^{2^n}} = (g_{2\bar{n}})^{s\alpha^{N+1}}, K_u = e(Z_u, v)^s.$

3. It generates C_1, C_2 as $C_1 = (v \prod_{j \in G} Z_{N+1-j})^s, C_2 = g_{\bar{n}}^s.$

4. Finally, it publishes the header $\mathsf{Hdr} = (G, C_1, C_2)$ and keeps $K, \{K_u\}_{u \in G}$ secret to itself.

$(K) \leftarrow \mathsf{BEPM.Decrypt}(\mathsf{PP}, sk_u, \mathsf{Hdr})$: A subscribed user u with secret key sk_u uses the public parameter PP, the header Hdr and recovers the session key K and its personalized key K_u as

$$
\begin{aligned}
K &= \frac{e(Z_u, C_1)}{e(sk_u \cdot \prod_{j \in G, j \neq u} Z_{N+1-j+u}, C_2)} = (g_{2\bar{n}})^{s\alpha^{N+1}}, \\
K_u &= e(sk_u, C_2) = e(Z_u, v)^s.
\end{aligned}
$$

Here C_1, C_2 are extracted from the header Hdr, Z_j's are computed using PP as in Eqs. 1 and 2.

Performance Analysis

1. Storage: PP size is $(\log_2(N+1)+2)|\mathbb{G}|$, SK size is $2|\mathbb{G}|$, where $|\mathbb{G}| =$ bit size of an element in $\mathbb{G}$.
2. Communication: Header size $= 2|\mathbb{G}|$.
3. Computation: Set up phase requires $\log_2(N+1)+2$ exponentiation in $\mathbb{G}$, key generation needs 1 exponentiations in $\mathbb{G}$ and 1 multilinear map. Encryption phase requires 2 exponentiation in $\mathbb{G}$, $|G|+2$ multilinear mapping and $|G|+1$ exponentiation in $\mathbb{G}_1$. Here $|G| =$ number of users in the set G. Decryption phase require $|G| + 2$ multilinear mapping and 1 inversion in $\mathbb{G}_1$.

Remark 4. In the scheme of Xu et al. [13] PP $= (\mathbb{S}', \{X_i\}_{i=0}^n, v, \{g_{\bar{n}}^{\beta_i}\}_{i=1}^n)$ where $\beta_i \in \mathbb{Z}_p$ and other components are as in Setup phase of BEPM-III. Broadcaster sets personalized key as $K_i = e(g_{\bar{n}}^{\beta_i}, v)^s$, where $s \in \mathbb{Z}_p$. Therefore it can not generate the personalized key for more than n users. Authors can generate $\{g_{\bar{n}}^{\beta_i}\}_{i=0}^N$ to fit the scheme for $N = 2^n - 1$ users, but then public parameter size will be linear to maximum number of users supported by the system and does not satisfy their claim that public parameter size is logarithmic to the maximum number of users supported by the system.

Theorem 3 *(Key indistinguishability under CPA). Our BEPM-III scheme described in Sect. 5 is selective IND-CPA secure under key indistinguishability security model of Sect. 2.2 under DHDHE assumption.*

Proof of Theorem 3 is similar to that of Theorem 1.

6   Efficiency

We compare our constructions with the existing BEPM scheme of Ohtake et al. [11] in Tables 1 and 2. We emphasize the following facts:

- Pubic parameter (PP) size for BEPM-I, II, III are $(2N + 1)|\mathbb{G}|, (3N + 1)|\mathbb{G}|, (\log(N + 1) + 2)|\mathbb{G}|$ respectively, whereas [11] has PP size $(3N + 2)|\mathbb{G}|$. Secret key size for BEPM-I, III is $1|\mathbb{G}|$ where as the secret key size of [11] is $2|\mathbb{G}|$. Here $|\mathbb{G}| =$ bit size of an element of $\mathbb{G}$.
- Similar to [11], header size is constant for all our constructions.
- Exponentiation in the setup phase (PP, MK generation) for BEPM-I, II, III are $2N + 1, 3N + 2, \log(N + 1) + 3$ in contrast to $3N + 1$ for [11]. BEPM-III additionally requires 1 multilinear map computation. All these computations are done once in offline.
- As for online computation, all the schemes require 2 exponentiations for encryption and 1 inversion in decryption, which are same as in [11]. BEPM-III is based on multilinear map and uses a total $2(|G| + 2)$ multilinear map for encryption and decryption.
- Our first and third constructions BEPM-I, BEPM-III achieve selective semantic security under N-DBDHE and DHDHE assumption respectively, while our second scheme BEPM-II is adaptively CPA secure under the hardness of mDBDHE problem. We achieve the adaptive security without blowing the parameter sizes, communication and computation cost.

Table 1. Comparative summaries of storage, communication bandwidth and security of BEPM schemes.

Scheme	|PP|	|SK|	|Hdr|	SM	Assumption
[11]	$(3N+2)\|\mathbb{G}\|$	$2\|\mathbb{G}\|$	$2\|\mathbb{G}\|$	Selective	N-DBDHE
BEPM-I	$(2N+1)\|\mathbb{G}\|$	$1\|\mathbb{G}\|$	$2\|\mathbb{G}\|$	Selective	N-DBDHE
BEPM-II	$(3N+1)\|\mathbb{G}\|$	$2\|\mathbb{G}\|$	$2\|\mathbb{G}\|$	Adaptive	mDBDHE
BEPM-III	$(\log(N + 1)+2)\|\mathbb{G}\|$	$1\|\mathbb{G}\|$	$2\|\mathbb{G}\|$	Selective	DHDHE

|PP| = public parameter size, |SK| = secret key size, |Hdr| = header size, SM= security model, N = total number of users, $|\mathbb{G}|$ = bit size of an element of $\mathbb{G}$, IND-CP(C)A=indistinguishability of ciphertext under chosen plaintext (ciphertext) attack, N-DBDHE = N-decisional bilinear diffie-hellman exponent, mDBDHE = modified decisional bilinear diffie-hellman exponent, DHDHE = decisional hybrid diffie-hellman exponent.

Table 2. Comparison of computation cost of parameter generation, encryption and decryption algorithm for BEPM schemes.

Scheme	PP	SK		Enc			Dec	
	#exp	#exp	#mlm	#exp	#mlm	#pr	#mlm	# inv
[11]	$3N+1$ in G	2in G	0	2 in G,$|G|+1$ in G_1	0	3	0	1 in G_1
BEPM-I	$2N$ in G	1 in G	0	2 in G,$|G|+1$ in G_1	0	3	0	1 in G_1
BEPM-II	$3N$ in G	2 in G	0	2 in G,$|G|+1$ in G_1	0	3	0	1 in G_1
BEPM-III	$\log(N+1)+2$ in G	1 in G	1	2 in G,$|G|+1$ in G_1	$|G|+2$	0	$|G|+2$	1 in G_1

PP = public parameter, SK = secret key, Enc = encryption, Dec = decryption, N = total number of users, #exp = number of exponentiations, #pr = number of pairings, #mlm = number of multilinear map, #inv = number of inversions, $|G|$ = number of users in the set G.

7   Conclusion

To send both broadcast and personalized messages efficiently, we have proposed three BEPM schemes. Our first and third constructions significantly reduce parameter sizes compared to BEPM of Ohtake al. [11] and achieve selective semantic security under N-DBDHE and DHDHE assumption respectively. The second scheme achieves adaptive security under mDBDHE assumption which is a variant of OBDHE assumption. We achieve constant communication cost for all of our constructions. Moreover, our schemes are fully collision resistant and able to include and exclude users efficiently.

References

1. Acharya, K., Dutta, R.: Secure and efficient construction of broadcast encryption with dealership. In: Chen, L., Han, J. (eds.) ProvSec 2016. LNCS, vol. 10005, pp. 277–295. Springer, Cham (2016). doi:10.1007/978-3-319-47422-9_16
2. Acharya, K., Dutta, R.: Adaptively secure broadcast encryption with dealership. In: Hong, S., Park, J.H. (eds.) ICISC 2016. LNCS, vol. 10157, pp. 161–177. Springer, Cham (2017). doi:10.1007/978-3-319-53177-9_8
3. Acharya, K., Dutta, R.: Adaptively secure recipient revocable broadcast encryption with constant size ciphertext. IACR Cryptology ePrint Archive, 2017:59 (2017)
4. Boneh, D., Gentry, C., Waters, B.: Collusion resistant broadcast encryption with short ciphertexts and private keys. In: Shoup, V. (ed.) CRYPTO 2005. LNCS, vol. 3621, pp. 258–275. Springer, Heidelberg (2005). doi:10.1007/11535218_16
5. Boneh, D., Waters, B., Zhandry, M.: Low overhead broadcast encryption from multilinear maps. In: Garay, J.A., Gennaro, R. (eds.) CRYPTO 2014. LNCS, vol. 8616, pp. 206–223. Springer, Heidelberg (2014). doi:10.1007/978-3-662-44371-2_12
6. Fiat, A., Naor, M.: Broadcast encryption. In: Stinson, D.R. (ed.) CRYPTO 1993. LNCS, vol. 773, pp. 480–491. Springer, Heidelberg (1994). doi:10.1007/3-540-48329-2_40
7. Gentry, C., Waters, B.: Adaptive security in broadcast encryption systems (with short ciphertexts). In: Joux, A. (ed.) EUROCRYPT 2009. LNCS, vol. 5479, pp. 171–188. Springer, Heidelberg (2009). doi:10.1007/978-3-642-01001-9_10
8. Hiwatari, H., Tanaka, K., Asano, T., Sakumoto, K.: Multi-recipient public-key encryption from simulators in security proofs. In: Boyd, C., González Nieto, J. (eds.) ACISP 2009. LNCS, vol. 5594, pp. 293–308. Springer, Heidelberg (2009). doi:10.1007/978-3-642-02620-1_21

9. Kurosawa, K.: Multi-recipient public-key encryption with shortened ciphertext. In: Naccache, D., Paillier, P. (eds.) PKC 2002. LNCS, vol. 2274, pp. 48–63. Springer, Heidelberg (2002). doi:10.1007/3-540-45664-3_4

10. Lewko, A., Sahai, A., Waters, B.: Revocation systems with very small private keys. In: IEEE Symposium on Security and Privacy (SP), pp. 273–285 (2010)

11. Ohtake, G., Hanaoka, G., Ogawa, K.: Efficient broadcast encryption with personalized messages. In: Heng, S.-H., Kurosawa, K. (eds.) ProvSec 2010. LNCS, vol. 6402, pp. 214–228. Springer, Heidelberg (2010). doi:10.1007/978-3-642-16280-0_15

12. Phan, D.H., Pointcheval, D., Shahandashti, S., Strefler, M.: Adaptive CCA broadcast encryption with constant-size secret keys and ciphertexts. Int. J. Inf. Secur. 12(4), 251–265 (2013)

13. Xu, K., Liao, Y., Qiao, L., Liu, Z., Yang, X.: An identity-based (IDB) broadcast encryption scheme with personalized messages (BEPM). PloS One 10(12), e0143975 (2015)

14. Yang, Z.: On constructing practical multi-recipient keyencapsulation with short ciphertext and public key. Secur. Commun. Netw. 8(18), 4191–4202 (2015)

Provably Secure Homomorphic Signcryption

Fatemeh Rezaeibagha[1]([⊠]), Yi Mu[1], Shiwei Zhang[1], and Xiaofen Wang[2,3]([⊠])

[1] School of Computing and Information Technology,
Institute of Cybersecurity and Cryptology, University of Wollongong,
Wollongong, Australia
{fr683,ymu,sz653}@uow.edu.au

[2] Department of Computer Science and Engineering, Center for Cyber Security,
University of Electronic Science and Technology of China,
Chengdu 611731, Sichuan, China
xfwang@uestc.edu.cn

[3] Guangxi Colleges and Universities Key Laboratory of Cloud Computing
and Complex Systems and Guangxi Key Laboratory of Trusted Software,
Guilin University of Electronic Technology, Guilin 541004, Gunagxi, China

Abstract. Signcryption has shown many useful applications, in particular for the environment where the computation and communication resources are constrained, for instance, for applications on lightweight devices. However, we notice that traditional signcryption schemes do not support homomorphic properties, which are very useful in many application scenarios. We also notice that the previous attempt of capturing the homomorphism in signcryption is not provably secure. In this paper, we propose a provably secure additive homomorphic signcryption. Our scheme offers the following two features: (1) Signing and encrypting are carried out in one go, unlike the traditional encryption and signature schemes which are computed separately. (2) We allow the collected signcrypted data items to be aggregated without requiring decryption. The second feature confirms the significance of the first feature in that the traditional signcryption cannot be applied due to lacking of the homomorphic property. Our scheme is the first provably secure signcryption that supports homomorphic property.

Keywords: Homomorphic signcryption · Data security · Provable security

1 Introduction

Encryption schemes have been commonly adopted to assure data confidentiality, which can protect the data against disclosure to unauthorized parties. To achieve data authentication, a signature scheme is usually required in addition to encryption. Usually, the data is digitally signed and then encrypted. Therefore, the additional computational resource is needed to handle both encryption and signature schemes. This has been seen to be an issue for lightweight devices such as wearable devices. Signcryption [19] provides a solution to the problem,

© Springer International Publishing AG 2017
T. Okamoto et al. (Eds.): ProvSec 2017, LNCS 10592, pp. 349–360, 2017.
https://doi.org/10.1007/978-3-319-68637-0_21

as it integrates signing and encrypting processes into one; therefore improves the computational efficiency.

In practice, the information could be obtained from multiple measurements, which might also be required to be transmitted from one site to another. These data items could be required to be aggregated in order to obtain the final result. The challenge is due to encrypted data, when we want to compute the encrypted data elements for addition or/and multiplication without decrypting them. This functionality is referred to as a homomorphic encryption. With homomorphic encryption, encrypted data elements can be aggregated for either additive operations or/and multiplicative operations. If a homomorphic encryption captures both additive and multiplicative operations, we call it fully homomorphic encryption. Homomorphic encryption has attracted a lot of attention (e.g., [2,4,8,9]). Although some progress has been made [6,13], fully homomorphic encryption [8] is still not computationally efficient for a practical use. Fortunately, it is sufficient for many applications to use homomorphic encryption (either fully additive or fully multiplicative), which can be efficiently constructed.

The homomorphic property will become infeasible if a signature is added to the encryption. This implies a challenge to construct a homomorphic signcryption. There is no any proper homomorphic signcryption scheme in the literature. Notice that Zhang et al. [18] introduced a homomorphic signcryption scheme, but its security was not properly proved, since the simulator cannot simulate the entire homomorphic signcryption; instead, the simulation for the encryption part was carried out separately without considering the signature verification. Actually, if the verification is considered, the adversary can differentiate which challenge message is encrypted by the challenger; therefore, it will not be semantically secure as claimed in their paper. In fact, it is indeed a challenge to achieve a provably secure homomorphic signcryption scheme mathematically.

The original signcryption scheme by Zheng [19] utilizes the symmetric-like encryption approach, which cannot adopt homomorphism in encryption with provable security. We move slightly away from original signcryption, by introducing a useful variant. The contribution of our work can be summarized as follows. We propose the first secure additive homomorphic signcryption scheme with provable security. The security analysis demonstrates that our scheme achieves the security against Chosen Plaintext Attack (IND-CPA) and Weak Unforgeability (WUF), under the Decisional Diffie-Hellman assumption and the Computational Diffie-Helman assumption, respectively.

The remaining of the paper is organized as follows. We describe the related work in Sect. 2. In Sect. 3, we present our system model and give the definitions of our scheme and security model. In Sect. 4, we present our scheme followed by the security proof of our scheme in Sect. 5. We conclude the paper in Sect. 6.

2   Related Work

In homomorphic encryption, the encryptions of different messages can be combined to conduct additive or/and multiplicative computations without revealing their original messages. In a fully homomorphic encryption, both additive and multiplicative operations can be carried out without decryption. The homomorphic encryption has been a useful method for designing secure computation protocols. In the work by Boneh et al. [3], the homomorphic properties of the current homomorphic public key systems are improved, in which given two ciphertexts, anyone can compute both addition and multiplication. Their scheme is commonly called the BGN homomorphic encryption. Although it is not yet a fully homomorphic encryption, it has many useful applications [1,16]. The underlying security of the BGN homomorphic encryption is based on a hardness assumption named Subgroup Decision Problem. Unfortunately, there is no any practical fully homomorphic encryption scheme yet. Therefore, the existing applications of fully homomorphic encryption in the literature are not practical.

With a natural thinking of homomorphism in digital signatures, Johnson et al. [11] proposed a homomorphic signature scheme, which unfortunately cannot work with any form of homomorphic encryption. Chan and Li [5] also proposed a BGN authentication scheme to convey the commitments on a message in order to provide statistically hiding and computationally binding properties under the subgroup decision problem. Notice that it is infeasible to construct a homomorphic signcryption scheme by combining a homomorphic encryption scheme and a homomorphic signature scheme.

There are many works in the literature which explored the applications of partial homomorphic encryption schemes such as Paillier's additive homomorphic encryption [14] and ElGamal encryption [7]. For example, Yi et al. [17] proposed a scheme that applied multi data servers with employing the Paillier and ElGamal cryptosystems in order to offer statistical analysis and also preserve patient privacy for wireless medical sensor devices. Han et al. [10] in another study illustrated a privacy-preserving aggregation scheme to support fault tolerance in order to aggregate health data in the cloud server. They also used the BGN cryptosystem by Boneh et al. [3], and proposed an aggregation protocol to compute the average.

The signcryption scheme by Zheng [19] is able to reduce the computational overhead of signature and encryption computation by combining them into a single algorithm. There are enormous applications of signcryption schemes which have been found in the literature. For example, in the studies proposed by Rao [15] and Liu et al. [12], attribute based signcryption schemes for secure sharing of health records and ensuring confidentiality and authenticity have been presented.

Despite of the usefulness of homomorphism in signcryption, it has not been explored thoroughly in research. As pointed out earlier, the homomorphic signcryption scheme due to Zhang et al. [18] can not be properly proved, as explained earlier. In this paper, we will investigate and explore this field of research. Fortunately, we are able to construct a provably secure scheme.

3   Definitions and Models

3.1   System Model

We define a general application scenario, where our scheme can be applied and its security model is defined. Our system consists of an honest-but-curious data server, a group of receivers and a group of users who signcrypt the messages. On top of these parties, there is a trusted server who sets up the entire system and is responsible for the management of cryptographic keys and user registration.

- Users: A user has the capacity of computing signcrytion with our proposed cryptographic method and sent the signcrypted data to the data server, who in turn aggregates these data without decryption and forwards it to the corresponding receiver.
- Receivers: In the case we considered in this work, a receiver can de-signcrypt the aggregated signcryption.
- Data Server: The data server is honest-but-curious, which means that the data server follows the correct procedure to aggregate the data items collected from users and is interested in the information, while it does not launch any active attack. We consider only one data server in the system; however, our method can be naturally applied to a distributed environment for multiple data servers. The data server can be located in different geographical locations.

We give an intuitive explanation of our scheme as follows. User data elements $(m_0, \cdots, m_n)$ are homomorphic-signcrypted as $(\mathsf{HSC}(m_0), \cdots, \mathsf{HSC}(m_n))$ and sent to the data server, who in turn computes the aggregated data items at a specific time. The integrated data $\mathsf{HSC}(m)$ is then sent to the receiver, who then decrypts and verifies the received message.

3.2   Complexity Assumptions

Definition 1 (Computational Diffie-Hellman (CDH) Assumption). *Let $\mathbb{G} = \langle g \rangle$ be a cyclic group of prime order p generated by a generator g. Given $g, g^a, g^b \in \mathbb{G}$ for randomly selected $a, b \in_R \mathbb{Z}_p$, there exists an algorithm $\mathcal{A}$ that computes g^{ab} with the advantage*

$$\mathsf{Adv}_{\mathcal{A}}^{\mathrm{CDH}} = \Pr\left[g^{ab} \leftarrow \mathcal{A}(\mathbb{G}, p, g, g^a, g^b) \,|\, a, b, \in_R \mathbb{Z}_p, \mathbb{G} = \langle g \rangle \right]. \quad (1)$$

The CDH assumption assumes that the advantage $\mathsf{Adv}_{\mathcal{A}}^{\mathrm{CDH}}$ is negligible for any probabilistic polynomial time (PPT) algorithm $\mathcal{A}$ under the security parameter 1^λ.

Definition 2 (Decisional Diffie-Hellman (DDH) Assumption). *Let $\mathbb{G} = \langle g \rangle$ and $a, b \in_R \mathbb{Z}_p$ as described in the CDH assumption. Given g, g^a, g^b, there exists an algorithm $\mathcal{A}$ that distinguishes g^{ab} with a random element $Z \in_R \mathbb{G}$ with the advantage*

$$\mathsf{Adv}_{\mathcal{A}}^{\mathrm{DDH}} = \left| \Pr\left[1 \leftarrow \mathcal{A}(\mathbb{G}, p, g, g^a, g^b, g^{ab}) \right] - \Pr\left[1 \leftarrow \mathcal{A}(\mathbb{G}, p, g, g^a, g^b, Z) \,|\, Z \in_R \mathbb{G} \right] \right|$$
$$(2)$$

The DDH assumption assumes that the advantage $\mathsf{Adv}_{\mathcal{A}}^{\mathrm{DDH}}$ is negligible for any PPT algorithm $\mathcal{A}$ under the security parameter 1^λ.

3.3 The Definition of Homomorphic Signcryption Scheme

Definition 3 (Homomorphic Signcryption). *A homomorphic signcryption (HSC) scheme consists of the following five algorithms:*

- params $\leftarrow$ Setup(1^λ). *Taking as input a security parameter 1^λ, it outputs the system public parameters* params.
- $(pk_s, sk_s) \leftarrow$ KeyGen$_s$(params). *Taking as input the system public parameters* params, *it outputs a pair of public key pk_s and secret key sk_s of a sender (patient).*
- $(pk_r, sk_r) \leftarrow$ KeyGen$_r$(params). *Taking as input the system public parameters* params, *it outputs a pair of public key pk_r and secret key sk_r of a receiver (doctor).*
- HSC(m) $\leftarrow$ Signcrypt(params, pk_r, sk_s, m). *Taking as input public parameters* params, *public key pk_r of doctor, private key sk_s of the patient, and a plaintext message m in the message space M, it outputs a homomorphic signcryption* HSC(m).
- $m \leftarrow$ De-Signcrypt(params, pk_s, sk_r, HSC(m)). *Taking as input public parameters* params, *a public key pk_s of the patient, a private key sk_r of doctor, and a ciphertext* HSC(m), *it outputs plaintext message m.*
- 0/1 $\leftarrow$ Verify(params, pk_s, sk_r, HSC(m), m'). *Taking as input public parameters* params, *a public key pk_s of the patient, a private key sk_r of doctor, a ciphertext* HSC(m), *and a message m', it outputs 1, if $m = m'$; otherwise, it outputs 0.*

Remark that the system public parameters params *is omitted if it is clear in the context. An HSC scheme is required to have ciphertext homomorphism as the following algorithm.*

- HSC(m) $\leftarrow$ IntSigncrypt(HSC(m_1), . . . , HSC(m_n)). *Taking as input* HSC(m_1), $\cdots$, HSC(m_n), *it outputs the integrated homomorphic sign-encryption* HSC(m), *where* m $= m_1 + \cdots + m_n$.

Definition 4 (Completeness). *An HSC scheme is complete if the following statement is always true.*

$\forall m \in M$, params $\leftarrow$ Setup(1^λ), $(pk_s, sk_s) \leftarrow$ KeyGen$_s$(params),

$(pk_r, sk_r) \leftarrow$ KeyGen$_r$(params),   HSC(m) $\leftarrow$ Signcrypt(params, pk_r, sk_s, m),

1 $\leftarrow$ Verify(params, pk_s, sk_r, HSC(m), De-Signcrypt(params, pk_s, sk_r, HSC(m))).

3.4 Security Model

Definition 5 (Confidentiality). *An HSC scheme is semantically secure against chosen plaintext attacks (IND-CPA) if no PPT adversary $\mathcal{A}$ wins the following game with non-negligible advantage with the security parameter λ.*

1. **Setup Phase.** The simulator $\mathcal{S}$ runs Setup to obtain system public parameters params. Then the simulator $\mathcal{S}$ runs the key generation algorithm KeyGen_r to obtain a public key and private key pair (pk_r, sk_r) for the receiver, it gives (pk_r, params) to the adversary $\mathcal{A}$.
2. **Challenge Phase.** $\mathcal{A}$ generates two plaintexts $m_0, m_1 \in M$ and a private key sk_s of the sender, and sends to $\mathcal{S}$. Then, $\mathcal{S}$ sets $\mathsf{HSC}(m_b) \leftarrow \mathsf{Signcrypt}(\mathsf{params}, pk_r, sk_s, m_b)$ for a random bit $b \leftarrow \{0,1\}$. It sends $\mathsf{HSC}(m_b)$ to $\mathcal{A}$.
3. **Guess Phase.** At the end of the game, $\mathcal{A}$ outputs a bit $b' \in \{0,1\}$ to $\mathcal{S}$ and wins the game if $b' = b$.

The adversary $\mathcal{A}$'s advantage in the above game is defined as

$$\mathsf{Adv}_{\mathcal{A}}^{\text{IND-CPA}} = \left| \Pr\left[b' = b \right] - \frac{1}{2} \right|.$$

Definition 6 (Weak Unforgeability). *An* HSC *scheme is weakly unforgeable if no PPT forger $\mathcal{F}$ has a non-negligible advantage in the following game:*

1. **Setup Phase.** The simulator $\mathcal{B}$ runs Setup, KeyGen_s and KeyGen_r to obtain two pairs of public key and private key (pk_s, sk_s) and (pk_r, sk_r). $\mathcal{B}$ gives $(pk_s, pk_r, \mathsf{params})$ to forger $\mathcal{F}$.
2. **Forgery Phase.** Finally, $\mathcal{F}$ returns a valid signature $\mathsf{HSC}(m^*)$

The forger $\mathcal{F}$'s advantage in the above game is defined as

$$\mathsf{Adv}_{\mathcal{F}}^{\text{WUF}} = \Pr\left[1 \leftarrow \mathsf{Verify}\left(\begin{array}{c} \mathsf{params}, pk_s, sk_r, \mathsf{HSC}(m^*), \\ \mathsf{De\text{-}Signcrypt}(\mathsf{params}, pk_s, sk_r, \mathsf{HSC}(m^*)) \end{array} \right) \right].$$

Note that the forger $\mathcal{F}$ is not allowed to perform Signcrypt *queries to simulator $\mathcal{B}$. The reason is that with the message, the forger $\mathcal{F}$ can forge a signcryption. However, it will not be a problem, provided the receiver is honest.*

4   Our Proposed Scheme

In this section, we propose our homomorphic signcryption scheme. An HSC scheme consists of the following algorithms.

- params $\leftarrow$ Setup(1^λ). Taking as input the security parameter 1^λ, it outputs system parameters params $= (p, g)$ where $\mathbb{G} = \langle g \rangle$ is a group of prime order p, generated by a generator g.
- $(pk_s, sk_s) \leftarrow \mathsf{KeyGen}_s(\mathsf{params})$. Taking as input params, the algorithm randomly selects a private key $sk_s = w \in_R \mathbb{Z}_p$, and computes the corresponding public key $pk_s = h = g^w$ for the sender (user).
- $(pk_r, sk_r) \leftarrow \mathsf{KeyGen}_r(\mathsf{params})$. Taking as input params, the algorithm randomly selects a private key $sk_r = (x_0, x_1, x_2) \in_R \mathbb{Z}_p^3$, and computes the correspond public key $pk_r = (y_0, y_1, y_2) = (g^{x_0}, g^{x_1}, g^{x_2})$ for the receiver.

- $\mathsf{HSC}(m) \leftarrow \mathsf{Signcrypt}(pk_r, sk_s, m)$. Taking as input public key pk_r of the receiver, secret key sk_s of the sender, and a plaintext message $m \in M = \{0,1\}^l$ for $l \leq n$ where $n = 32$, it computes

$$C_0 = g^t, \quad C_1 = g^m y_0^t, \quad C_2 = y_1^{wm} y_2^t,$$

where $t \in_R \mathbb{Z}_p$. It outputs $\mathsf{HSC}(m) = (C_0, C_1, C_2)$ as the homomorphic sign-encryption.

- $m \leftarrow \mathsf{De\text{-}Signcrypt}(params, pk_s, sk_r, \mathsf{HSC}(m))$. Given a homomorphic sign-encrypted message $\mathsf{HSC}(m)$, the public key $pk_s = h$ of the sender, the private key $sk_r = (x_0, x_1, x_2)$ of the receiver, the message is computed by

$$m' = \log_g \frac{C_1}{C_0^{x_0}}.$$

Then the algorithm runs the below Verify algorithm to verify the message m'. If it outputs 1, the message m' is accepted, and the algorithm outputs $m = m'$. Otherwise, the algorithm outputs $\perp$, which is an abort symbol. The correctness can be verified as

$$m = \log_g \frac{C_1}{C_0^{x_0}} = \log_g \frac{g^m y_0^t}{g^{tx_0}} = \log_g \frac{g^m g^{tx_0}}{g^{tx_0}} = \log_g g^m = m.$$

- $0/1 \leftarrow \mathsf{Verify}(params, pk_s, sk_r, \mathsf{HSC}(m), m')$. The verification algorithm outputs 1 if

$$C_2 = h^{x_1 m'} C_0^{x_2}.$$

Otherwise, the sign-encryption is rejected and it outputs 0. The correctness can be verified as

$$C_2 = h^{x_1 m} C_0^{x_2} = g^{w x_1 m} g^{t x_2} = y_1^{wm} y_2^t.$$

- $\mathsf{HSC(m)} \leftarrow \mathsf{IntSigncrypt}(\mathsf{HSC}(m_1), \ldots, \mathsf{HSC}(m_n))$. The algorithm parses the sign-encryption $\mathsf{HSC}(m_i)$ as $(C_{i,0}, C_{i,1}, C_{i,2})$ with randomness t_i. The algorithm integrates the sign-encryption by calculating

$$C_0 = \prod_{i=1}^n C_{i,0} = \prod_{i=1}^n g^{t_i} = g^{\sum_{i=1}^n t_i},$$

$$C_1 = \prod_{i=1}^n C_{i,1} = \prod_{i=1}^n g^{m_i} y_0^{t_i} = g^{\sum_{i=1}^n m_i} y_0^{\sum_{i=1}^n t_i},$$

$$C_2 = \prod_{i=1}^n C_{i,2} = \prod_{i=1}^n y_1^{wm_i} y_2^{t_i} = y_1^{w \sum_{i=1}^n m_i} y_2^{\sum_{i=1}^n t_i}.$$

Taking $\mathsf{m} = \sum_{i=1}^n m_i$ and $\mathsf{t} = \sum_{i=1}^n t_i$, the integrated sign-encryption $\mathsf{HSC(m)} = (C_0, C_1, C_2)$ has the same form of the original sign-encryption. Finally, the algorithm outputs $\mathsf{HSC(m)}$.

5   Security Analysis

Theorem 1. *If there exists a PPT algorithm $\mathcal{A}$ that can break the IND-CPA security of the HSC scheme with advantage $\mathsf{Adv}_{\mathcal{A}}^{\text{IND-CPA}}$, then there exists a PPT algorithm $\mathcal{B}$ that can solve the Decisional Diffie-Hellman (DDH) problem with advantage*

$$\mathsf{Adv}_{\mathcal{B}}^{\text{DDH}} \geq \frac{\mathsf{Adv}_{\mathcal{A}}^{\text{IND-CPA}}}{2}.$$

Proof. Suppose a PPT algorithm $\mathcal{S}$ that acts as the simulator of the system. We present a series of games (**Game 0**, **Game 1**, and **Game 2**) as follows.

– **Game 0**. This the original IND-CPA game for our HSC scheme.
   1. The simulator $\mathcal{S}$ runs Setup to obtain system public parameters params $= (p, g)$. Then $\mathcal{S}$ runs KeyGen_r to generate a receiver key pair $(sk_r, pk_r) = ((x_0, x_1, x_2), (y_0, y_1, y_2))$, and passes (pk_r, params) to the adversary $\mathcal{A}$.
   2. The adversary $\mathcal{A}$ generates two plaintexts $m_1, m_2 \in M$ and a sender private key $sk_s = w$. The simulator computes the sign-encryption $\text{HSC}(m_b) = (C_0, C_1, C_2)$ normally with a random bit $b \leftarrow \{0,1\}$ where

$$t \in_R \mathbb{Z}_p, \quad C_0 = g^t, \quad C_1 = g^{m_b} y_0^t, \quad C_2 = y_1^{wm_b} y_2^t.$$

   The simulator $\mathcal{S}$ sends $\text{HSC}(m_b)$ to the adversary $\mathcal{A}$.
   3. Finally, $\mathcal{A}$ outputs a bit $b' \in \{0,1\}$. If $b = b'$, $\mathcal{A}$ wins the game and $\mathcal{S}$ outputs 1. Otherwise $\mathcal{S}$ outputs 0.
– **Game 1**. This game is the same as **Game 0** except that the simulator replaces y_0^t with a random element $R_0 \in \mathbb{G}$ in computing C_1 in the step 2 as

$$t \in_R \mathbb{Z}_p, \quad \boxed{R_0 \in_R \mathbb{G}}, \quad C_0 = g^t, \quad C_1 = g^{m_b}\boxed{R_0}, \quad C_2 = y_1^{wm_b} y_2^t.$$

– **Game 2**. This game is the same as **Game 1** except that the simulator replaces y_2^t with a random element $R_1 \in \mathbb{G}$ in computing C_2 in the step 2 as

$$t \in_R \mathbb{Z}_p, \quad R_0, \boxed{R_1} \in_R \mathbb{G}, \quad C_0 = g^t, \quad C_1 = g^{m_b} R_0, \quad C_2 = y_1^{wm_b}\boxed{R_1}.$$

In the following, we analyse the three games presented above under the DDH assumption. Then, we construct a distinguisher algorithm $\mathcal{B}$ and estimate its probability in distinguishing differences among games. Let $\mathbf{E}_i$ be the event that $\mathcal{A}$ wins the **Game i** (i.e. $1 \leftarrow \mathcal{S}$) for $i = 1, 2, 3$. By Definition 5, the advantage of $\mathcal{A}$ winning the original game (**Game 0**) is

$$\mathsf{Adv}_{\mathcal{A}}^{\text{IND-CPA}} = \left| \Pr[\mathbf{E}_0] - \frac{1}{2} \right|. \tag{3}$$

Lemma 1. *If an adversary $\mathcal{A}$ can distinguish the difference between **Game 0** and **Game 1**, an algorithm $\mathcal{B}$ can be constructed to solve a DDH problem with the advantage*

$$\mathsf{Adv}_{\mathcal{B}}^{\text{DDH}} = |\Pr[\mathbf{E}_0] - \Pr[\mathbf{E}_1]|. \tag{4}$$

Proof. The algorithm $\mathcal{B}$ obtains a DDH instance (p, g, g^a, g^b, Z) from its challenger. The algorithm $\mathcal{B}$ proceeds the following game with the adversary $\mathcal{A}$ for our HSC scheme.

1. The algorithm $\mathcal{B}$ samples $x_1, x_2 \in_R \mathbb{Z}_p$, and computes

$$y_0 = g^b, \quad y_1 = g^{x_1}, \quad y_2 = g^{x_2}.$$

Then $\mathcal{B}$ packs $pk_r = (y_0, y_1, y_2)$ and $\mathsf{params} = (p, g)$, and sends them to the adversary $\mathcal{A}$.
2. The adversary $\mathcal{A}$ generates two plaintexts $m_1, m_2 \in M$ and a sender private key $sk_s = w$. The algorithm $\mathcal{B}$ computes the sign-encryption $\mathsf{HSC}(m_b) = (C_0, C_1, C_2)$ with a random bit $b \leftarrow \{0, 1\}$ where

$$C_0 = g^a, \quad C_1 = g^{m_b} Z, \quad C_2 = y_1^{wm_b}(g^a)^{x_2}.$$

Then $\mathcal{B}$ sends $\mathsf{HSC}(m_b)$ to the adversary $\mathcal{A}$.
3. Finally, $\mathcal{A}$ outputs a bit $b' \in \{0, 1\}$. If $b = b'$, $\mathcal{A}$ wins the game and $\mathcal{B}$ outputs 1. Otherwise, $\mathcal{B}$ outputs 0.

If $Z = g^{ab}$, the above game is exactly the same as the **Game 0**. Thus, we have

$$\Pr\left[1 \leftarrow \mathcal{B} \mid Z = g^{ab}\right] = \Pr[\mathbf{E}_0]. \tag{5}$$

Otherwise, $Z \in_R \mathbb{G}$ is a random element in $\mathbb{G}$, and the above game is exactly the same as the **Game 1**. Thus, we have

$$\Pr\left[1 \leftarrow \mathcal{B} \mid Z \in_R \mathbb{G}\right] = \Pr[\mathbf{E}_1]. \tag{6}$$

Therefore, by combining Eqs. (2), (5), and (6), we directly have Eq. (4) and complete the proof of this lemma.

Lemma 2. *If an adversary $\mathcal{A}$ can distinguish the difference between* **Game 1** *and* **Game 2**, *an algorithm $\mathcal{B}$ can be constructed to solve a DDH problem with the advantage*

$$\mathsf{Adv}_{\mathcal{B}}^{\mathrm{DDH}} = \left|\Pr[\mathbf{E}_1] - \Pr[\mathbf{E}_2]\right|. \tag{7}$$

Proof. The algorithm $\mathcal{B}$ obtains a DDH instance (p, g, g^a, g^b, Z) from its challenger. The algorithm $\mathcal{B}$ proceeds the following game with the adversary $\mathcal{A}$ for our HSC scheme.

1. The algorithm $\mathcal{B}$ samples $x_0, x_1 \in_R \mathbb{Z}_p$, and computes

$$y_0 = g^{x_0}, \quad y_1 = g^{x_1}, \quad y_2 = g^b.$$

Then $\mathcal{B}$ packs $pk_r = (y_0, y_1, y_2)$ and $\mathsf{params} = (p, g)$, and sends them to the adversary $\mathcal{A}$.

2. The adversary $\mathcal{A}$ generates two plaintexts $m_1, m_2 \in M$ and a sender private key $sk_s = w$. The algorithm $\mathcal{B}$ computes the sign-encryption $\mathsf{HSC}(m_b) = (C_0, C_1, C_2)$ with a random bit $b \leftarrow \{0, 1\}$ where

$$R_0 \in_R \mathbb{G}, \quad C_0 = g^a, \quad C_1 = g^{m_b} R_0, \quad C_2 = y_1^{wm_b} Z.$$

Then $\mathcal{B}$ sends $\mathsf{HSC}(m_b)$ to the adversary $\mathcal{A}$.
3. Finally, $\mathcal{A}$ outputs a bit $b' \in \{0, 1\}$. If $b = b'$, $\mathcal{A}$ wins the game and $\mathcal{B}$ outputs 1. Otherwise, $\mathcal{B}$ outputs 0.

If $Z = g^{ab}$, the above game is exactly the same as the **Game 1**. Thus, we have

$$\Pr\left[1 \leftarrow \mathcal{B} \mid Z = g^{ab}\right] = \Pr[\mathbf{E}_1]. \tag{8}$$

Otherwise, $Z \in_R \mathbb{G}$ is a random element in $\mathbb{G}$, and the above game is exactly the same as the **Game 2**. Thus, we have

$$\Pr\left[1 \leftarrow \mathcal{B} \mid Z \in_R \mathbb{G}\right] = \Pr[\mathbf{E}_2]. \tag{9}$$

Therefore, by combining Eqs. (2), (8), and (9), we directly have Eq. (7) and complete the proof of this lemma.

Lemma 3. *In **Game 2**, the adversary $\mathcal{A}$ has no advantage, i.e.*

$$\Pr[\mathbf{E}_2] = \frac{1}{2}. \tag{10}$$

Proof. In **Game 2**, the adversary is given the sign-encryption $\mathsf{HSC}(m_b) = (g^t, g^{m_b} R_0, y_1^{wm_b} R_1)$ where R_0 and R_1 are independent random elements, which work as one-time pads, rendering the bit b independent from adversary $\mathcal{A}$'s view. Therefore, the adversary $\mathcal{A}$ has no advantage of winning the game other than a random guess.

By combining Eqs. (3), (4), (7), and (10), we obtain

$$\mathsf{Adv}_{\mathcal{A}}^{\text{IND-CPA}} \leq 2 \cdot \mathsf{Adv}_{\mathcal{B}}^{\text{DDH}}.$$

Thus it completes the proof.

Since the DDH assumption states that $\mathsf{Adv}_{\mathcal{B}}^{\text{DDH}}$ is negligible, we have $\mathsf{Adv}_{\mathcal{A}}^{\text{IND-CPA}}$ is negligible for all PPT adversaries.

Theorem 2. *If there exists a PPT algorithm $\mathcal{A}$ that can break the weak unforgeability of the HSC scheme with advantage $\mathsf{Adv}_{\mathcal{A}}^{\text{WUF}}$, then there exists a PPT algorithm $\mathcal{B}$ that can solve the Computational Diffie-Hellman (CDH) problem with advantage*

$$\mathsf{Adv}_{\mathcal{B}}^{\text{CDH}} \geq \mathsf{Adv}_{\mathcal{A}}^{\text{WUF}}.$$

Proof. The algorithm $\mathcal{B}$ obtains a CDH instance (p, g, g^a, g^b) from its challenger. The algorithm $\mathcal{B}$ simulates the weak unforgeability game (Definition 6) for the adversary $\mathcal{A}$.

1. The algorithm $\mathcal{B}$ samples $x_0, x_2 \in_R \mathbb{Z}_p$, and computes

$$y_0 = g^{x_0}, \quad y_1 = g^b, \quad y_2 = g^{x_2}.$$

   Then $\mathcal{B}$ packs $pk_s = g^a$, $pk_r = (y_0, y_1, y_2)$, and $\mathsf{params} = (p, g)$. After that, $\mathcal{B}$ sends them to the adversary $\mathcal{A}$.
2. Ultimately, $\mathcal{A}$ outputs a valid homomorphic sign-encryption $\mathsf{HSC}(m^*) = (C_0^*, C_1^*, C_2^*)$ on arbitrary $m^* \in M$.

Finally, the algorithm $\mathcal{B}$ is able to compute g^{ab} by

$$g^{ab} = \left(\frac{C_2^*}{C_0^{*x_2}} \right)^{\left(\log_g \frac{C_1^*}{C_0^{*x_0}} \right)^{-1}}.$$

Therefore, we immediately obtain the theorem.

Since the CDH assumption states that $\mathsf{Adv}_{\mathcal{B}}^{\mathrm{CDH}}$ is negligible, we have $\mathsf{Adv}_{\mathcal{A}}^{\mathrm{WUF}}$ is negligible for all PPT adversaries.

6   Conclusion

Homomorphic signcryption is useful in many applications. However, it is a research challenge to accommodate the homomorphism feature in a traditional signcryption scheme. In this work, we proposed a variant of signcryption, which leads to a novel homomorphic signcryption scheme. We formally proved the security of our proposed scheme. Our work can be regarded as the first step toward provably secure homomorphic signcryption for broader applications.

Acknowledgement. We would like to thank the reviewers for constructive comments and Willy Susilo for the valuable discussions. The forth author was supported by the National Natural Science Foundation of China under Grants 61502086, the foundation from Guangxi Colleges and Universities Key Laboratory of Cloud Computing and Complex Systems (No. YF16202) and the foundation from Guangxi Key Laboratory of Trusted Software (No. PF16116X).

References

1. Bilogrevic, I., Jadliwala, M., Joneja, V., Kalkan, K., Hubaux, J., Aad, I.: Privacy-preserving optimal meeting location determination on mobile devices. IEEE Trans. Inf. Forensics Secur. **9**(7), 1141–1156 (2014)
2. Boneh, D., Gentry, C., Gorbunov, S., Halevi, S., Nikolaenko, V., Segev, G., Vaikuntanathan, V., Vinayagamurthy, D.: Fully key-homomorphic encryption, arithmetic circuit ABE and compact garbled circuits. In: Nguyen, P.Q., Oswald, E. (eds.) EUROCRYPT 2014. LNCS, vol. 8441, pp. 533–556. Springer, Heidelberg (2014). doi:10.1007/978-3-642-55220-5_30
3. Boneh, D., Goh, E.-J., Nissim, K.: Evaluating 2-DNF formulas on ciphertexts. In: Kilian, J. (ed.) TCC 2005. LNCS, vol. 3378, pp. 325–341. Springer, Heidelberg (2005). doi:10.1007/978-3-540-30576-7_18

4. Brakerski, Z., Gentry, C., Halevi, S.: Packed ciphertexts in LWE-based homomorphic encryption. In: Kurosawa, K., Hanaoka, G. (eds.) PKC 2013. LNCS, vol. 7778, pp. 1–13. Springer, Heidelberg (2013). doi:10.1007/978-3-642-36362-7_1

5. Chan, Y.-Y., Li, J.: BGN authentication and its extension to convey message commitments. In: Gavrilova, M., Gervasi, O., Kumar, V., Tan, C.J.K., Taniar, D., Laganá, A., Mun, Y., Choo, H. (eds.) ICCSA 2006. LNCS, vol. 3982, pp. 365–374. Springer, Heidelberg (2006). doi:10.1007/11751595_40

6. Cheon, J.H., Stehlé, D.: Fully homomophic encryption over the integers revisited. In: Oswald, E., Fischlin, M. (eds.) EUROCRYPT 2015. LNCS, vol. 9056, pp. 513–536. Springer, Heidelberg (2015). doi:10.1007/978-3-662-46800-5_20

7. ElGamal, T.: A public key cryptosystem and a signature scheme based on discrete logarithms. In: Blakley, G.R., Chaum, D. (eds.) CRYPTO 1984. LNCS, vol. 196, pp. 10–18. Springer, Heidelberg (1985). doi:10.1007/3-540-39568-7_2

8. Gentry, C.: Fully homomorphic encryption using ideal lattices. In: Proceedings of the 41st Annual ACM Symposium on Theory of Computing, STOC 2009, Bethesda, MD, USA, 31 May–2 June 2009, pp. 169–178. ACM (2009)

9. Gentry, C., Sahai, A., Waters, B.: Homomorphic encryption from learning with errors: conceptually-simpler, asymptotically-faster, attribute-based. In: Canetti, R., Garay, J.A. (eds.) CRYPTO 2013. LNCS, vol. 8042, pp. 75–92. Springer, Heidelberg (2013). doi:10.1007/978-3-642-40041-4_5

10. Han, S., Zhao, S., Li, Q., Ju, C., Zhou, W.: PPM-HDA: privacy-preserving and multifunctional health data aggregation with fault tolerance. IEEE Trans. Inf. Forensics Secur. 11(9), 1940–1955 (2016)

11. Johnson, R., Molnar, D., Song, D., Wagner, D.: Homomorphic signature schemes. In: Preneel, B. (ed.) CT-RSA 2002. LNCS, vol. 2271, pp. 244–262. Springer, Heidelberg (2002). doi:10.1007/3-540-45760-7_17

12. Liu, J., Huang, X., Liu, J.K.: Secure sharing of personal health records in cloud computing: Ciphertext-policy attribute-based signcryption. Future Gener. Comp. Syst. 52, 67–76 (2015)

13. Nuida, K., Kurosawa, K.: (Batch) Fully homomorphic encryption over integers for non-binary message spaces. In: Oswald, E., Fischlin, M. (eds.) EUROCRYPT 2015. LNCS, vol. 9056, pp. 537–555. Springer, Heidelberg (2015). doi:10.1007/978-3-662-46800-5_21

14. Paillier, P.: Public-key cryptosystems based on composite degree residuosity classes. In: Stern, J. (ed.) EUROCRYPT 1999. LNCS, vol. 1592, pp. 223–238. Springer, Heidelberg (1999). doi:10.1007/3-540-48910-X_16

15. Rao, Y.S.: A secure and efficient ciphertext-policy attribute-based signcryption for personal health records sharing in cloud computing. Future Gener. Comp. Syst. 67, 133–151 (2017)

16. Wang, X.: One-round secure fair meeting location determination based on homomorphic encryption. Inf. Sci. 372, 758–772 (2016)

17. Yi, X., Bouguettaya, A., Georgakopoulos, D., Song, A., Willemson, J.: Privacy protection for wireless medical sensor data. IEEE Trans. Dependable Sec. Comput. 13(3), 369–380 (2016)

18. Zhang, P., Yu, J., Liu, H.: A homomorphic signcryption scheme and its application in electronic voting. J. Shenzhen Univ. Sci. Eng. 28, 489–494 (2011)

19. Zheng, Y.: Digital signcryption or how to achieve cost(signature & encryption) ≪ cost(signature) + cost(encryption). In: Kaliski, B.S. (ed.) CRYPTO 1997. LNCS, vol. 1294, pp. 165–179. Springer, Heidelberg (1997). doi:10.1007/BFb0052234

Public-Key Encryption with Simulation-Based Sender Selective-Opening Security

Dali Zhu[1,2], Renjun Zhang[1,2], and Dingding Jia[2,3,4(✉)]

[1] Institute of Information Engineering, Chinese Academy of Sciences, Beijing, China
{zhudali,zhangrenjun}@iie.ac.cn
[2] School of Cyber Security, University of Chinese Academy of Sciences,
Beijing, China
[3] State Key Laboratory of Information Security,
Institute of Information Engineering, Chinese Academy of Sciences, Beijing, China
jiadingding@iie.ac.cn
[4] Data Assurance and Communication Security Research Center,
Chinese Academy of Sciences, Beijing, China

Abstract. We study public key encryptions (PKE) of simulation-based security against sender selective-opening (SIM-SSO) attacks, where the attacker can corrupt a subset of senders, learning the plaintexts together with the corresponding randomness. Concretely:

- We present a generic construction of SIM-SSO security under chosen plaintext attacks (SIM-SSO-CPA) by combining a lossy encryption given by Hemenway *et al.* (Asiacrypt 2011), along with a tailored compression algorithm. Our construction gives a simple and modular security analysis. We then present an instantiation based on the Matrix Diffie-Hellman Assumption.
- We show that the PKE construction from Boneh-Gentry-Hamburg scheme (FOCS 2007), and construction from a (public-key based) variant of Cocks' scheme (Peikert, Vaikuntanathan and Waters, Crypto 2008) are SIM-SSO-CPA secure. Even if these results may seem natural, not surprising at all, their SIM-SSO-CPA security have not been explicitly reported so far.
- We further show that two PKE constructions from homomorphic trapdoor commitments (Groth, Ostrovsky and Sahai, Crypto 2006, Eurocrypt 2006) are SIM-SSO-CPA secure.

Keywords: Sender Selective-Opening Security · Lossy encryption · Hash proof system

1 Introduction

Sender selective-opening (SSO) attacks consider scenarios that adversary may corrupt a part of senders. More formally, suppose a receiver receives a n tuple of

This work is Supported by the "Strategic Priority Program" of Chinese Academy of Sciences, Grant No. Y2W0012306, and the National Nature Science Foundation of China (No.61502484).

T. Okamoto et al. (Eds.): ProvSec 2017, LNCS 10592, pp. 361–380, 2017.
https://doi.org/10.1007/978-3-319-68637-0_22

ciphertexts $\boldsymbol{c} = (c[1], \ldots, c[n])$, each ciphertext $c[i] = \mathrm{Enc}_{pk}(m_i; r_i)$ is created by sender i with a fresh randomness r_i under pk. Now, given $\boldsymbol{c}$, the adversary can adaptively chooses a subset $\mathcal{I} \subseteq \{1, \ldots, n\}$ of ciphertexts to open, learning the messages $\{m_i\}_{i \in \mathcal{I}}$ and corresponding randomness $\{r_i\}_{i \in \mathcal{I}}$. The security requires privacy of the unopened messages preserved.

The study of sender-selective opening in PKE scenarios was initiated by Bellare, Hofheinz and Yilek [2]. They formulated the notions in two styles: indistinguishability-based selective-opening (IND-SSO) security and simulation-based selective-opening (SIM-SSO) security. Compared with the standard IND-CPA/CCA security, IND/SIM-SSO security is more complicated, for the reason that the opening of the randomness allows the adversary to check the correspondence between ciphertext and message. Relations among IND-SSO, SIM-SSO and standard security attract much attention such as in [1,3,14,20,24,25].

IND-SSO security is restricted to efficiently re-samplable plaintext distributions. SIM-SSO security does not suffer from such restrictions, but is the preferable notion of SSO security. In a nutshell, SIM-SSO security requires that the output of any adversary can be simulated by a simulator that sees only the opened messages. Unfortunately, SIM-SSO security is nonessential hard to achieve [1], because for many natural encryption schemes, there does not exist such simulator that satisfies the definition given in [2,11].

Known constructions of SIM-SSO secure encryption schemes either from lossy encryption [2,15,21–23] or from deniable encryption (as well as non-committing encryption) [7,13,30]. Lossy encryption has been shown to be a very useful tool in achieving SIM-SSO security. In [2], Bellare *et al.* proved that lossy encryption with efficient opening implies SIM-SSO-CPA security. However, it seems that the property of efficient openability is limited to the decisional composite residuosity (DCR) settings [32]. Hemenway *et al.* [21] proposed a general construction of lossy encryption from hash proof system, but it is not clear whether it supports efficient opening or not. This line of research continued in [35], Wee presented a new framework of Dual-mode cryptosystems via smooth projective hashing, but it also ignores the efficient opening property. The results in [21,35] are inspired by the work in [29]. Recently, Hofheinz *et al.* [23] proposed a SIM-SSO-CPA secure PKE scheme in the discrete-log setting, and further showed that lossy encryption scheme with efficient *weak* opening implies SIM-SSO-CPA security. In their construction, the key component is a hash function that is used to compress the space of ciphertexts.

Related Work. Several IND-SO-CCA secure schemes have been constructed by using lossy trapdoor functions [34], All-But-N lossy trapdoor functions [21], and All-But-Many lossy trapdoor functions [22]. Furthermore, known constructions of SIM-SSO-CCA secure schemes follow dedicated approaches [13,22,26,30]. Heuer *et al.* proved that the practical schemes RSA-OAEP and DHIES are SIM-SSO-CCA secure in the random oracle model. Selective opening security under receiver corruption were considered in [20,27,28].

1.1 Our Contribution

In this paper, firstly we present a generic construction for building SIM-SSO-CPA secure scheme from hash proof system, and then give an instantiation based on the Matrix Diffie-Hellman Assumption. Our construction is a combination of lossy encryption in [21] (note that the related schemes appeared in [29,35], namely, the two-message oblivious transfer protocol in [29], and the Dual-mode encryption scheme in [35]), and a tailored compression algorithm that compresses the space of ciphertexts. Then we prove that the PKE construction from Boneh-Gentry-Hamburg (BGH) scheme in [5], and the PKE construction from a (public-key based) variant of Cocks' scheme (short: Cocks' scheme) in [33] are SIM-SSO-CPA secure. We further prove that two PKE constructions from homomorphic trapdoor commitment in [16–18] are SIM-SSO-CPA secure. In the following there are some technique overviews.

The generic lossy encryption scheme in [21] is IND-SSO-CPA secure. To modify it to be SIM-SSO-CPA secure, one should seek an efficient algorithm Opener that will find correctly distributed random coins to open a lossy ciphertext to an arbitrary plaintext. But the property of efficient openability suffers from specific algebraic structure, but the lossy encryption in [21] does not have this structure (Note that in [21] secret keys play the role of random coins). Inspired by the ideas in [10,19,23], we observe that if the space of ciphertexts shrinks to a smaller one, then the number of random coins will increase. Then Opener can randomly guesses them one after another in a confined space, and checks whether these random coins meet the requirements. To do so, we tailor a compression algorithm that compresses the ciphertexts space to a logarithmic space of size L (L is at most $O(\log l)$ where l is the security parameter). We also require that the output of tailored compression algorithm statistically indistinguishable from random bits over $\{0,1\}^L$. These approaches assure that Opener algorithm runs in expected polynomial time, but the accurate running time depends on concrete settings. On the downside, our approach suffers from a small message space.

Besides, we prove that two PKE constructions from BGH scheme and Cocks' scheme are SIM-SSO-CPA secure. Both schemes have natural lossiness properties, and these properties have contained implicitly in the security proof. However, it is not our purpose to make them explicit. We concern about whether BGH scheme and Cocks' scheme support efficient opening or not. Since two schemes are based on factoring-related assumptions, with the knowledge of factorization of N such that $N = pq$, it is true that the efficient opening algorithms exists. Hence, we can convert BGH scheme and Cocks' scheme to lossy encryption with efficient opening (and thus SIM-SSO security) by setting p or q as the lossy secret key.

In [18], Groth et al. concluded that "parameter-switching" methodology [16, 17] in encryptions keys leads to lossy encryption. In fact, their (non-interactive) homomorphic trapdoor commitments can be converted into lossy encryption schemes. We show that the converted schemes support efficient weak opening. That is, when Opener opens a lossy ciphertext to an arbitrary plaintext, it needs an additional random coins.

One may notice that schemes in this paper can only achieve SIM-SSO-CPA security. An interesting open problem is to extend them to the chosen-ciphertext (CCA) setting to obtain SIM-SSO-CCA secure schemes. Besides, both of BGH scheme and Cocks' scheme are based on quadratic residuosity assumption, and the lossy encryption with efficient opening can be seen as a general framework that unifies two specific constructions. But how to extend their security to SIM-SSO-CCA security is also an open interesting problem.

Organization. The rest of our paper is organized as follows: in Sect. 2 we present some basic notions as well as several tools that are used in our paper; in Sect. 3 we describe our generic construction of SIM-SSO-CPA secure scheme, and provide an instantiation based on Matrix Diffie-Hellman Assumption; in Sect. 4 we prove that two PKE constructions from BGH scheme and Cocks' scheme are SIM-SSO-CPA secure; in Sect. 5 we prove that two PKE constructions from homomorphic trapdoor commitments are SIM-SSO-CPA secure.

2   Preliminaries

2.1   Notation

In this paper, we use $\mathbb{N}$ to represent the set of natural numbers, and $\mathbb{Z}$ represents the set of integers. We also use PPT to denote probability polynomial time for short. Let $[k]$ be the set of $\{1, \ldots, k\}$, $x \leftarrow S$ is used to denote picking an element x uniformly at random from S when S is a finite set, and to denote sampling an element according to S when S is a distribution. The statistical distance of two probability ensembles $\mathcal{X}$, $\mathcal{Y}$ is defined as $SD(\mathcal{X}, \mathcal{Y}) := \frac{1}{2}\Sigma_x |\Pr[\mathcal{X} = x] - \Pr[\mathcal{Y} = x]|$. If $SD(\mathcal{X}, \mathcal{Y})$ is negligible, we say that $\mathcal{X}$ and $\mathcal{Y}$ are statistical indistinguishability (abbr. $X \approx_s Y$). The length of a string x is denoted by $|x|$.

2.2   Public Key Encryption

A public key encryption (PKE) scheme consists of the following three PPT algorithms:

Keygen: the key generation algorithm that takes as input a security parameter 1^λ, and outputs a public/secret key pair $(pk, sk) \leftarrow \text{Keygen}(1^\lambda)$.

Enc: the encryption algorithm that takes as input the public key pk, a plaintext $m \in \mathcal{M}$, and outputs a ciphertext $c \leftarrow \text{Enc}(pk, m)$.

Dec: the decryption algorithm that takes the secret key sk, a ciphertext c as input, and outputs either a message $m \leftarrow \text{Dec}(sk, c) \in \mathcal{M}$ or a special $\perp$ to indicate that c is not a valid ciphertext.

Correctness. The PKE scheme satisfies correctness if $\text{Dec}(sk, c) = m$ with all but negligible probability whenever pk, sk is produced by $\text{Keygen}(1^\lambda)$ and c is produced by $\text{Enc}(pk, m)$.

2.3   Sender Selective-Opening Security

Following [2,3,13], we recall the definition of simulation-based sender selective-opening security against chosen plaintext attacks (SIM-SSO-CPA).

Definition 1 (SIM-SSO-CPA Security). *A PKE scheme* PKE = (Gen, Enc, Dec) *is SIM-SSO-CPA secure iff for every polynomially bound* $n = n(1^\lambda) > 0$, *every PPT relation R, and every stateful PPT adversary* $\mathcal{A}$, *there exists a stateful PPT simulator S such that*

$$\mathbf{Adv}^{\text{sim}-\text{sso}-\text{cpa}}_{\text{PKE},\mathcal{A},S,R}(1^\lambda) = |\Pr[\text{Exp}^{\text{real}}_{\text{PKE},\mathcal{A},R}(1^\lambda) = 1] - \Pr[\text{Exp}^{\text{ideal}}_{S,R}(1^\lambda) = 1]|$$

is negligible. The experiments $\text{Exp}^{\text{real}}_{\text{PKE},\mathcal{A},R}$ *and* $\text{Exp}^{\text{ideal}}_{S,R}$ *are defined as follows (Fig. 1):*

Experiment. $\text{Exp}^{\text{real}}_{\text{PKE},\mathcal{A}}(1^\lambda)$:
$(pk, sk) \leftarrow \text{Gen}(1^\lambda)$
$\text{dist} \leftarrow \mathcal{A}(pk)$
$(M_i)_{i \in [n]} \leftarrow \text{dist}$
$(R_i)_{i \in [n]} \leftarrow (\mathcal{R}_{\text{Enc}})_n$
$(C_i)_{i \in [n]} = \text{Enc}(pk, M_i; R_i)_{i \in [n]}$
$I \leftarrow \mathcal{A}(select, (C_i)_{i \in [n]})$
$out_\mathcal{A} \leftarrow \mathcal{A}(output, (M_i, R_i)_{i \in I})$
return $R(\text{dist}, (M_i)_{i \in [n]}, I, out_\mathcal{A})$

Experiment. $\text{Exp}^{\text{ideal}}_{S}(1^\lambda)$:
$\text{dist} \leftarrow S(1^\lambda)$
$(M_i)_{i \in [n]} \leftarrow \text{dist}$
$I \leftarrow S(select, (1^{|M_i|})_{i \in [n]})$
$out_S \leftarrow S(output, (M_i)_{i \in I})$
return $R(\text{dist}, (M_i)_{i \in [n]}, I, out_S)$

Fig. 1. The REAL-SIM-SSO-CPA and IDEAL-SIM-SSO-CPA experiment

2.4   Sender Selective-Opening Security from Lossy Encryption

Lossy Encryption with Efficient Opening. In [2], Bellare *et al.* defined lossy encryption, and proved that any lossy encryption scheme with efficient opening (short: LPKE, thus ciphertexts can be efficiently opened to arbitrary messages) is SIM-SSO-CPA secure. A LPKE consists of four algorithms (Gen, LGen, Enc, Dec) such that:

Gen(1^λ): The key generation algorithm that takes as input the security parameter 1^λ, and outputs a key pair (pk, sk) where pk is a real public key.

LGen(1^λ): The lossy key generation algorithm that takes as input the security parameter 1^λ, and outputs a key pair (pk, sk) where pk is a lossy public key.

Enc(pk, m): The encryption algorithm that takes as input a public key pk and a message m, where pk is either generated by Gen(1^λ) or by LGen(1^λ), and outputs a ciphertext c.

Dec(sk, c): The decryption algorithm that takes as input a ciphertext c and a secret sk, outputs either a message m if $c \leftarrow \text{Enc}(pk, m)$, or a special symbol $\perp$ to indicate that c is not a valid ciphertext.

LPKE should satisfy properties of correctness, indistinguishability, lossiness and efficient openability.

Correctness. For all $(pk, sk) \leftarrow \text{Gen}(1^\lambda)$, $c \leftarrow \text{Enc}(pk, m)$, it must be the case that $\text{Dec}(sk, c) = m$.

Indistinguishability. The first outputs of $\text{Gen}(1^\lambda)$ and $\text{LGen}(1^\lambda)$ can not be distinguished for any PPT adversary.

Lossiness. For any $(pk, sk) \leftarrow \text{LGen}(1^\lambda)$ and two distinct messages m_0, m_1, it holds that $\text{Enc}(pk, m_0) \approx_s \text{Enc}(pk, m_1)$. Thus, two distributions statistically close.

Efficient Openability. There exists an efficient algorithm Opener that, takes as input lossy keys sk and pk, message m, ciphertext $c \leftarrow \text{Enc}(pk, m; r)$, outputs random coins r' such that $\text{Enc}(pk, m; r') = c$.

Hofheinz, Jager and Rupp [23] defined lossy encryption with efficient *weak* opening (short: wLPKE) and proved that wLPKE is indeed SIM-SSO-CPA secure. The only difference between LPKE and wLPKE is that the Opener algorithm for wLPKE may receive an additional random coins that have been used to generate the ciphertext. More generally, the property of efficient weak openability is described as follows.

Efficient weak openability. There exists an efficient algorithm Opener that, takes as input lossy keys sk and pk, message m_0, the random coins r, ciphertext $c \leftarrow \text{Enc}(pk, m_0; r)$, and a message m_1, outputs random coins r' such that $\text{Enc}(pk, m_1; r') = c$.

3   SIM-SSO-CPA Secure PKE from Hash Proof System

In this section, we present a generic construction of SIM-SSO-CPA secure by combining a lossy encryption in [21](as well as the schemes in [29,35]), and a tailored compression algorithm that compresses the space of ciphertexts. We further give an instantiation based on the Matrix Diffie-Hellman Assumption. Before turning to the generic construction, we first recall the notions of hash proof system as introduced by Cramer and Shoup [9].

3.1   Hash Proof System

Smooth Projective Hashing. A smooth projective hash family consists of $(\Lambda, \mathcal{SK}, \mathcal{X}, \mathcal{L}, \mathcal{W}, \mathcal{Y}, \mathcal{PK}, \mu)$, where $\mathcal{X}, \mathcal{Y}, \mathcal{L}, \mathcal{W}, \mathcal{SK}, \mathcal{PK}$ are finite, non-empty sets, and $\mathcal{L} \subset \mathcal{X}$ is a language. Let $\Lambda : \mathcal{X} \to \mathcal{Y}$ be a collection of hash functions indexed by keys $sk \in \mathcal{SK}$ mapping from $\mathcal{X}$ to $\mathcal{Y}$. Also there exists an efficiently computable projection μ from $\mathcal{SK}$ to $\mathcal{PK}$. A hash family $\mathbf{H} = (\Lambda, \mathcal{SK}, \mathcal{X}, \mathcal{L}, \mathcal{W}, \mathcal{Y}, \mathcal{PK}, \mu)$ is projective if for all $sk \in \mathcal{SK}$, the action of Λ_{sk} on $\mathcal{L}$ is determined by $\mu(sk)$. A hash family $\mathbf{H} = (\Lambda, \mathcal{SK}, \mathcal{X}, \mathcal{L}, \mathcal{W}, \mathcal{Y}, \mathcal{PK}, \mu)$ is smoothness if for randomly chosen $sk \in \mathcal{SK}$, given $\mu(sk)$ and $x \in \mathcal{X} \setminus \mathcal{L}$, $\Lambda_{sk}(x)$ is statistically close to uniform distributions over $\mathcal{Y}$.

We also require that for $sk \in \mathcal{SK}$, it can be efficiently sampled sk' such that $\mu(sk) = \mu(sk')$, which will be used not in the actual scheme but in the security proof. In fact, all known hash proof systems have this property.

Subset Membership Assumption. We will consider two related subset membership assumptions pertaining to the non-empty set $\mathcal{X}$. The first assumption states that the uniform distributions over $\mathcal{L}$ and $\mathcal{X}$ are computationally indistinguishable, even given the public parameter. The second assumption requires that the uniform distributions over $\mathcal{L}$ and $\mathcal{X} \setminus \mathcal{L}$ are computationally indistinguishable, even knowing the public parameter. The two assumptions are equivalent when $\mathcal{L}$ is sparse in $\mathcal{X}$, i.e., $|\mathcal{L}|/|\mathcal{X}| = \mathrm{negl}(1^\lambda)$, since the distributions over $\mathcal{X}$ and $\mathcal{X} \setminus \mathcal{L}$ are then statistically indistinguishable.

Hash Proof System. Let $\mathbf{H} = (\Lambda, \mathcal{SK}, \mathcal{X}, \mathcal{L}, \mathcal{W}, \mathcal{Y}, \mathcal{PK}, \mu)$ be a projective hash family, and let $\Lambda[\mathcal{X}, \mathcal{L}, \mathcal{W}, \mathcal{R}]$ be any instance of a subset membership assumption, where $\mathcal{W}$ is the set of witness, and $\mathcal{R} \subset \mathcal{X} \times \mathcal{W}$ is a binary relation such that $x \in \mathcal{L}$ iff there exists a w satisfying $(x, w) \in \mathcal{R}$. A hash proof system provides efficient algorithm to randomly choose $sk \in \mathcal{SK}$ and $x \in \mathcal{X}$, efficient algorithm to compute $\mu(sk)$, and efficient algorithm (Priv, Pub) to compute $\Lambda_{sk}(x)$ for $x \in \mathcal{L}$ with witness w:

$$\Lambda_{sk}(x) = \mathrm{Priv}(sk, x) = \mathrm{Pub}(\mu(sk), x, w)$$

3.2 Generic Construction

Tailored Compression Algorithm. The study of instance compression was initiated by Harnik and Naor [19]. Inspired by the ideas in [10,19,31], we tailor a compression algorithm for the hash proof system. Roughly speaking, the tailored compression algorithm Z can shrink $\Lambda_{sk}(x)$ to a smaller bit string, and the output of Z statistically indistinguishable from random bits. Note that our definition is the generalization of the universal hash function that compress elements to bits in [23].

Definition 2 (Tailored Compression Algorithm for HPS). *Let $\mathbf{H} = (\Lambda, \mathcal{SK}, \mathcal{X}, \mathcal{L}, \mathcal{W}, \mathcal{Y}, \mathcal{PK}, \mu)$ be a smooth projective hash proof system. A tailored compression algorithm for HPS is a PPT algorithm Z such that for large enough l*

- *For any $\pi \in \mathcal{Y}$, the length L of $Z(\pi)$ is at most $O(\log l)$.*
- *Z outputs bits that uniformly distributed over $\{0,1\}^L$.*

Construction. Based on these building blocks, we can construct a generic lossy encryption with efficient weak opening with message space $\{0,1\}^{O(\log l)}$ (For simplicity, we stipulate that the length of $Z(\pi)$ is $O(\log l)$. Thus, only small message spaces are allowed.) The SIM-SSO-CPA secure scheme is described as follows.

Injective key generation: Samples an $x \in \mathcal{L}$, together with a corresponding witness w. Sets $pk = x$, $sk = w$.

Lossy key generation: Samples an $x \in \mathcal{X}$. Sets $pk = x$, $sk = \perp$.

Encryption: To encrypt a message $m \in \{0,1\}^{O(\log l)}$, chooses $sk \leftarrow \mathcal{SK}$, and returns the ciphertext $c = (c_1, c_2)$ as:

$$c_1 = \mu(sk), c_2 = Z(\Lambda_{sk}(x)) \oplus m.$$

Decryption: Given a ciphertext (c_1, c_2) and secret key $sk = w$, the algorithm first computes $\Lambda_{sk}(x)$, then returns $m = Z(\Lambda_{sk}(x)) \oplus c_2$.

3.3   Security Proof

The following theorem will be used in the security proof of the generic construction. The writing style of the proof in the rest of our paper refers to [2,23,35].

Theorem 1 ([2,23]). *The lossy encryption scheme with efficient opening (or efficient weak opening) is SIM-SSO-CPA secure.*

We prove that the construction in Sect. 3.2 satisfies the four properties of lossy encryption with efficient weak opening.

Theorem 2. *If H is a smooth projective HPS with the corresponding subset membership assumption hard, and the output of tailored compression algorithm Z statistically indistinguishable from uniform, then the generic construction yields a SIM-SSO-CPA secure scheme.*

Proof. **Correctness.** This is guaranteed by the projective property of the smooth projective hashing.

Indistinguishability. This follows immediately from the subset membership assumption.

Lossiness. In lossy mode, the lossy public key $x \leftarrow \mathcal{X}$, according to the smoothness property of HPS, $\Lambda_{sk}(x)$ is uniformly distributed over $\mathcal{Y}$ even given $\mu(sk)$ and x. Since the output of Z are statistically close to uniform, $Z(\Lambda_{sk}(x)) \oplus m$ will also be statistically close to uniform over $\{0,1\}^{O(\log l)}$ for any message m. Hence, lossiness follows readily.

Efficient weak openability. We note that in the generic setting, secret keys play the role of random coins. Consider the algorithm Opener, takes as input a lossy public key $x \leftarrow \mathcal{X}$, lossy secret key $sk \in \mathcal{SK}$, message $m' \in \{0,1\}^{O(\log l)}$, and ciphertext $c = (c_1, c_2) = (\mu(sk), Z(\Lambda_{sk}(x)) \oplus m)$ for some $m \in \{0,1\}^{O(\log l)}$, outputs sk' such that $\mu(sk') = c_1$ and $Z(\Lambda_{sk'}(x)) \oplus m' = c_2$. To do so, Opener samples sk' randomly and creates a set

$$\{sk' \in \mathcal{SK} : \mu(sk') = c_1 \wedge Z(\Lambda_{sk'}(x)) = m' \oplus c_2\}$$

We now analyze the behavior of the algorithm Opener. First, Opener can efficiently determine $\mu(sk') = c_1$. Second, Opener randomly guesses sk' one after another and check to see whether $Z(\Lambda_{sk'}(x)) = m' \oplus c_2$. As the output of Z is close to uniform, and the size of $Z(\Lambda_{sk'}(x))$ is at most $2^{O(\log l)}$, this will require about $O(l)$ steps. Also note that Opener algorithm runs in expected polynomial time, and has small probability of running for a long time.

3.4 Instantiation Based on Matrix Diffie-Hellman Assumption

Here, we describe one instantiation of the generic construction in Sect. 3.2. We then compare the efficency of this instantiation with the scheme in [23]. To instantiate our construction, we need to utilize a $\mathcal{D}_{l,k}$-Matrix Diffie-Hellman (short: $\mathcal{D}_{l,k}$-MDDH) Assumption, a $\mathcal{D}_{l,k}$-MDDH-based hash proof system in [12], and a universal hash function in [23] that maps group elements to bits.

Representing Elements in Groups. Let Gen be a PPT algorithm that takes as input 1^λ and outputs a description $\mathcal{G} = (\mathbb{G}, q, g)$, where $\mathbb{G}$ is a cyclic group with prime-order q, and g is the generator of $\mathbb{G}$. Following [12], we define $[a] = g^a \in \mathbb{G}$ as the implicit representation of a in $\mathbb{G}$. More generally, we also define such representations for matrix $\mathbf{A} = (a_{ij}) \in \mathbb{Z}_q^{n \times m}$ by:

$$[\mathbf{A}] = \begin{pmatrix} g^{a_{11}} & \cdots & g^{a_{1m}} \\ \vdots & \ddots & \vdots \\ g^{a_{n1}} & \cdots & g^{a_{nm}} \end{pmatrix} \in \mathbb{G}^{n \times m}$$

Matrix Diffie-Hellman Assumption. We recall the definition of the Matrix Diffie-Hellman Assumption as introduced in [12].

Definition 3 (Matrix Distribution). *Let $l, k \in \mathbb{N}$ such that $l > k$. The distribution $\mathcal{D}_{l,k}$ is called a matrix distribution if it outputs matrices in $\mathbb{Z}_q^{l \times k}$ of full rank k in probability polynomial time with all but negligible probability.*

Definition 4 ($\mathcal{D}_{l,k}$-Matrix Diffie-Hellman Assumption). *Let $\mathcal{D}_{l,k}$ be a matrix distribution. We say that the $\mathcal{D}_{l,k}$-Matrix Diffie-Hellman Assumption holds in $\mathbb{G}$ and relative to Gen if for all non-uniform polynomial time adversary $\mathcal{A}$, we have*

$$\mathbf{Adv}_{\mathcal{D}_{l,k}, \mathrm{Gen}}(\mathcal{A}) = |\Pr[\mathcal{A}(\mathcal{G}, [\mathbf{A}], [\mathbf{A}w]) = 1] - \Pr[\mathcal{A}(\mathcal{G}, [\mathbf{A}], [u]) = 1]|$$

is negligible, where the probability is taken over the output $\mathcal{G} = (\mathbb{G}, q, g) \leftarrow \mathrm{Gen}(1^\lambda)$, $\mathbf{A} \leftarrow \mathcal{D}_{l,k}$, $w \leftarrow \mathbb{Z}_q^k$, $u \leftarrow \mathbb{Z}_q^l$ and the coin tosses of adversary $\mathcal{A}$.

Instantiation. For instantiation, we need a hash function $H : G \rightarrow \{0,1\}$ to replace the tailored compression algorithm Z. The hash function H should satisfies the following property in [23]: for randomly choose $a \in G$, $H(a)$ is statistically indistinguishable from the uniform distribution over $\{0,1\}$; if a is a vector of group elements from G, then $H(a)$ is the component-wise application of the hash function, which outputs a bit vector of the same length as a. The details of the instantiation are given below.

Setup: Runs $(\mathbb{G}, q, g) \leftarrow \mathrm{Gen}(1^\lambda)$ and picks $\mathbf{A} \leftarrow \mathcal{D}_{l,k}$. Define the language

$$\mathcal{L} = \{[\mathbf{A}w] \in \mathbb{G}^l : w \in \mathbb{Z}_q^k\} \subset \mathcal{X}$$

The value $w \in \mathbb{Z}_q^k$ is a witness.

Injective key generation: Picks $w \leftarrow \mathbb{Z}_q^k$, and computes $[x] = [\mathbf{A}w]$. Let $pk = [x]$, $sk = w$.

Lossy key generation: Picks $u \leftarrow \mathbb{Z}_q^l$, and computes $[x] = [u]$. Let $pk = [x]$, $sk = \mathbf{A}$.

Encryption: On inputs a message $m \in \{0,1\}$, picks $k \leftarrow \mathbb{Z}_q^l$, then computes $c_1 = [k^{\mathrm{T}}\mathbf{A}]$, $c_2 = \mathrm{H}([k^{\mathrm{T}}x]) \oplus m$, and outputs ciphertext $c = (c_1, c_2)$.

Decryption: Given a ciphertext $c = (c_1, c_2)$, and $sk = w$, returns $m = \mathrm{H}([c_1 w]) \oplus c_2$.

Correctness follows readily from the projective property of $\mathcal{D}_{l,k}$-MDDH-based hash proof system in [12]. We put the concrete security proof in Appendix A, and present the property of efficient weak openability in the following.

Consider the algorithm Opener that takes as input a lossy public key $pk = (\mathcal{G}, [x])$ where $[x] = [u]$, a lossy secret key $\mathbf{A}$, the message m, random coins $k^{\mathrm{T}} \in \mathbb{Z}_q^l$, and ciphertext $c = (c_1, c_2) = ([k^{\mathrm{T}}\mathbf{A}], \mathrm{H}([k^{\mathrm{T}}x]) \oplus m)$. The outputs of Opener is random coins k'^{T} which is just a random vector in $\mathbb{Z}_q^l$. To this end, Opener samples $k'^{\mathrm{T}} \in \mathbb{Z}_q^l$ randomly subject to $k'^{\mathrm{T}}\mathbf{A} = k^{\mathrm{T}}\mathbf{A}$ until $\mathrm{H}([k'^{\mathrm{T}}x]) \oplus m' = c_2$.

As Opener knows secret key $\mathbf{A}$, this increases the dimension of the random coins space, and introduce the redundancy into the first equation $k'^{\mathrm{T}}\mathbf{A} = k^{\mathrm{T}}\mathbf{A}$. Thus, there are many different k' satisfying $k'^{\mathrm{T}}\mathbf{A} = k^{\mathrm{T}}\mathbf{A}$. Opener can randomly guesses k' one after another and checks whether the second equation $\mathrm{H}([k'^{\mathrm{T}}x]) \oplus m' = c_2$ is true. On average, it takes 2 such samplings until k' is found.

We emphasize that the opening algorithm needs to receive k as an additional input, hence our instantiation meets the notion of lossy encryption with efficient weak opening.

Comparison. In [23], Hofheinz *et al.* compared their scheme to other SSO-secure PKE schemes such as [2,13,21]. We tabulate the efficiency of our scheme, and only compare it to HJR16 scheme [23] (which we refer to as HJR scheme) in Fig. 2. The HJR scheme is more efficient, and the plaintext space scales better (indeed, only small message space are allowed). But HJR scheme has a large public key size, and the encryption and decryption procedures are computationally expensive (because it needs to define a matrix constructor). In our scheme, the size of public key and secret key is linear, and the encryption and decryption procedures are efficient, but the price is a rather small plaintext space. We conclude that both our scheme and HJR scheme is a feasibility result, and further improvements would be desirable.

Public-Key Encryption with Simulation-Based Sender 371

Scheme	Security	Assumption	$\lvert pk \rvert$	$\lvert sk \rvert$	$\lvert m \rvert$	$\lvert c \rvert - \lvert m \rvert$
HJR16 [23]	SIM-SSO-CPA	$\mathcal{D}_{l,k}$−MDDH	$(l \times k)\lvert G \rvert$	$(l-d) \times k$	$l-d$	$d \times \lvert G \rvert$
Ours	SIM-SSO-CPA	$\mathcal{D}_{l,k}$−MDDH	$l \times \lvert G \rvert$	k	1	$k \times \lvert G \rvert$

Fig. 2. Comparison of our scheme with HJR16 scheme in [23]. We use the same symbol as introduced in [23]. For a group G, $\lvert G \rvert$ denotes its size. For a matrix $\mathbf{A}$, d denotes the rank of $\mathbf{A}$. $\lvert m \rvert$ denotes the plaintext bitsize. $\lvert c \rvert - \lvert m \rvert$ denotes the ciphertext overhead.

4 SIM-SSO-CPA Secure Construction from Quadratic Residuosity

4.1 SIM-SSO-CPA Secure Construction from BGH Scheme

In this section, we show that the public-key scheme constructed from Boneh-Gentry-Hamburg (BGH) scheme [5] is SIM-SSO-CPA secure. Theorem 1 described in Sect. 3.3 will also be used in the security proof.

Quadratic Residuosity Assumption. Let $N = pq$ where p, q are two distinct safe primes, let $\left(\frac{x}{N}\right)$ denote the Jacobi symbol of $x \in \mathbb{Z}_N^*$, and let $J(N)$ be the set $\{x \in \mathbb{Z}_N^* : \left(\frac{x}{N}\right) = 1\}$. We denote by $QR(N)$ the subgroup of quadratic residues in $J(N)$. The quadratic residuosity assumption states that when the factorization of N is unknown, it is hard to distinguish random elements in $J(N) \setminus QR(N)$ from random elements in $QR(N)$.

Definition 5 (Quadratic Residuosity Assumption). *Let RSAGen be a PPT algorithm which, given a security parameter 1^λ, outputs two distinct primes p and q with their product $N = pq$. We say that the quadratic residuosity assumption holds for RSAGen if for all PPT distinguisher D, the function*

$$\lvert \Pr[\mathcal{D}(x, N) = 1 \vert x \leftarrow \mathbb{QR}_N] - \Pr[\mathcal{D}(x, N) = 1 \vert x \leftarrow \mathbb{J}(N) \setminus \mathbb{QR}(N)] \rvert$$

is negligible; where the probabilities are taken over $(N, p, q) \leftarrow RSAGen(1^\lambda)$ and sampling $x \in \mathbb{QR}_N$ and $x \in \mathbb{J}_N \setminus \mathbb{QR}_N$ uniformly at random.

IBE/PKE Compatible. Most of the concept of IBE/PKE compatible is copied from [5]. Let $\mathcal{Q}$ be a deterministic algorithm that takes as input (N, R, S) where $N \in \mathbb{Z}^+$ and $R, S \in \mathbb{Z}_N^*$, outputs two polynomials $f, g \in \mathbb{Z}_N^*[x]$. We say that $\mathcal{Q}$ is IBE/PKE compatible if $\mathcal{Q}$ satisfies the following two conditions:

- (Condition 1) If R and S are quadratic residues, then $f(r)g(s)$ is also a quadratic residue for all square roots r of R and s of S.
- (Condition 2) If R is a quadratic residue, then $f(r)f(-r)S$ is also a quadratic residue for all square roots r of R.

(Condition 1) will be used to decrypt ciphertexts, (Condition 2) is only used to prove security, and satisfies the conditions of the following lemma in [5].

Lemma 1. *Let $N = pq$ be an RSA modulus, $X \in QR(N)$, and $S \in J(N) \setminus QR(N)$. Let x be a value that is randomly chosen from the four square roots of X, and let f be a polynomial with the property that $f(x)f(-x)S$ is a quadratic residue. Then the Jacobi symbol $\left(\frac{f(x)}{N}\right)$ is uniformly distributed over $\{-1, +1\}$.*

Construction. Next we prove that the PKE scheme constructed from BGH satisfies the four properties of a lossy encryption scheme with efficient opening.

Let $RSAgen(1^\lambda)$ be an algorithm that generates two distinct primes p and q, and outputs p, q along with their product N. The SIM-SSO-CPA secure construction is described as follows.

$Gen(1^\lambda)$: generates $(N, p, q) \leftarrow RSAGen(1^\lambda)$. Chooses $v \in \mathbb{Z}_N^*$ uniformly at random, and computes $V = v^2$. Let $pk = (N, V)$, and $sk = v$.

$LGen(1^\lambda)$: generates $(N, p, q) \leftarrow RSAGen(1^\lambda)$. Chooses $V \in J(N) \setminus QR(N)$ uniformly at random. Let $pk = (N, V)$, and $sk = (p, q)$.

$Enc(N, pk, m)$: To encrypt a message $m \in \{-1, +1\}$, chooses $r \in \mathbb{Z}_N^*$ uniformly at random and sets $R = r^2$. Then computes:

$$(f, g) = \mathcal{Q}(N, R, V) \text{ and } c = m \cdot \left(\frac{f(r)}{N}\right)$$

Outputs the ciphertext (R, c).

$Dec(sk, c)$: Takes as input (R, c) and $sk = v$. Do:

$$(f, g) = \mathcal{Q}(N, R, V) \text{ and } m = c \cdot \left(\frac{g(v)}{N}\right)$$

Outputs m.

Theorem 3. *If the quadratic residuosity assumption holds for RSAGen, then the above construction is a lossy encryption scheme with efficient opening.*

Proof. **Correctness.** Given a real public key $pk = (N, V)$ where $V \in QR(N)$ as well as a ciphertext (R, c). The deterministic algorithm $\mathcal{Q}(N, R, V)$ outputs two polynomials f and g. Because both R and V is quadratic residues, (Condition 1) implies that

$$\left(\frac{f(r)}{N}\right) = \left(\frac{g(v)}{N}\right)$$

Given the secret key $sk = c$, the plaintext is decrypted by computing

$$c \cdot \left(\frac{g(v)}{N}\right) = m \cdot \left(\frac{f(r)}{N}\right)\left(\frac{g(v)}{N}\right) = m.$$

Indistinguishability. It immediately follows from the quadratic residuosity assumption.

Lossiness. The lossiness property has been contained in the security proof of the PKE scheme in [5], appendix B. In lossy mode, public keys are (N, V) where $V \in J(N) \setminus \mathrm{QR}(N)$. Consider the ciphertext (R, c), where $c = m \cdot \left(\frac{f(r)}{N} \right) \in \{-1, +1\}$, and $r^2 = R$ modulo N. According to Condition (2), $f(r)f(-r)V$ is a quadratic residue for all square roots of R. Then Lemma 1 shows that $\left(\frac{f(r)}{N} \right)$ is uniformly distributed over $\{-1, +1\}$, hence $m \cdot \left(\frac{f(r)}{N} \right)$ will also be uniformly random over $\{-1, +1\}$ for any plaintext m.

Efficient openability. To see this, consider the opening algorithm Opener which, takes as input a lossy secret key $sk = (p, q)$, lossy public key $pk = (N, V)$ where $V \in J(N) \setminus \mathrm{QR}(N)$, message m, and ciphertext (R, c), and outputs an r' such that $m \cdot \left(\frac{f(r')}{N} \right) = c$. Because the factorization of $N = pq$ is known, Opener can use p and q to efficiently compute the four square roots of R, and let r' be a randomly chosen from the four squares roots. The output of Opener is r', which is just a random elements in $\mathbb{Z}_N^*$.

4.2   SIM-SSO-CPA Secure Construction from Cocks' Scheme

Cocks [8] proposed an elegant IBE scheme based on the quadratic residuosity assumption modulo an RSA composite N. In [33], Peikert et al. defined a (public-key based) variant of Cocks' scheme. In this section, we prove that the public key scheme constructed from the version of Cocks' cryptosystem in [33] is SIM-SSO-CPA secure.

Construction. Let $RSAGen(1^\lambda)$ be an algorithm that generates two distinct primes p and q, and outputs p, q along with their product N. The SIM-SSO-CPA secure construction is described as follows.

$Gen(1^\lambda)$: Generates $(N, p, q) \leftarrow RSAGen(1^\lambda)$. Picks $r \in \mathbb{Z}_N^*$ uniformly at random, and let $y = r^2$. Let $pk = (N, y)$, $sk = r$. Outputs (pk, sk).

$LGen(1^\lambda)$: Generates $(N, p, q) \leftarrow RSAGen(1^\lambda)$. Picks $y \in J(N) \setminus \mathrm{QR}(N)$ uniformly at random. Let $pk = (N, y)$, $sk = (p, q)$. Outputs (pk, sk).

$Enc(pk, m)$: To encrypt a message $m \in \{-1, +1\}$, picks $s \leftarrow \mathbb{Z}_N^*$ such that $\left(\frac{s}{N} \right) = m$, outputs $c = s + y/s$.

$Dec(sk, c)$: Outputs the Jacobi symbol of $(c + 2 \cdot sk)$.

To prove the SIM-SSO-CPA security of the above construction, we recall a lemma that presented in [33].

Lemma 2. *Let $N = pq$ be the product of two distinct primes, let $y \in \mathbb{Z}_N^*$ and set $pk = (N, y)$. If $y \in J(N) \setminus \mathrm{QR}(N)$, then the ciphertext is statistically independent of the plaintext.*

Theorem 4. *If the quadratic residuosity assumption holds for RSAGen, then the above construction is a lossy encryption scheme with efficient opening.*

Proof. **Correctness.** The correctness of the scheme under real keys is guaranteed by the completeness of Cocks' cryptosystem.

Indistinguishability. This follows readily from the quadratic residuosity assumption.

Lossiness. In lossy mode, $y \in J(N) \setminus QR(N)$. Consider the ciphertext $c = s + y/s$, and the plaintext $m = \left(\frac{s}{N}\right)$, according to Lemma 2, the ciphertext c is statistically independent of the plaintext m.

Efficient openability. We say that the scheme is also efficiently openability, and the property implicitly contained in the proof of Lemma 2 in [33]. To see this, consider the algorithm Opener that on input a lossy secret key $sk = (p, q)$, lossy public key $pk = (N, y)$, plaintext m, ciphertext c. To claim c to any plaintext $m' \in \{-1, +1\}$, Opener has to find s' such that $s' + y/s' = s + y/s \mod N$ and $\left(\frac{s'}{N}\right) = m'$. Since Opener knows the factorization of N, it can efficiently compute four solutions of the equation $c = s + y/s \mod N$. Suppose s_0 is one of the solutions, then the other solutions are $(s_0 \mod p, y/s_0 \mod q)$, $(y/s_0 \mod p, s_0 \mod q)$, $(y/s_0 \mod p, y/s_0 \mod q)$. Let s' be a randomly chosen one of the four solutions, and the output of Opener is s', which is just a random element in $\mathbb{Z}_N^*$.

5   SIM-SSO-CPA Secure Construction from Homomorphic Trapdoor Commitment

The homomorphic trapdoor commitment in [16–18] consist of the following algorithms: Perfectly binding key generation, Perfectly hiding key generation, Commitment, Extraction, Trapdoor opening, Witness indistinguishability proof, Verification. The homomorphic trapdoor commitment can be converted into lossy encryption. That is, Perfectly binding key generation in homomorphic trapdoor commitment corresponds to Injective key generation in lossy encryption, Perfectly hiding key generation in homomorphic trapdoor commitment corresponds to Lossy key generation in lossy encryption, Commitment in homomorphic trapdoor commitment corresponds to Encryption in lossy encryption, Extraction in homomorphic trapdoor commitment corresponds to Decryption in lossy encryption, Trapdoor opening in homomorphic trapdoor commitment corresponds to Opening algorithm in lossy mode of the lossy encryption. Note that Trapdoor opening algorithm explicitly exists in homomorphic trapdoor commitment, but Opening algorithm is implicit in the lossy mode of the lossy encryption.

In this section, we prove that PKE constructions from the homomorphic trapdoor commitments only have the property of efficient weak openability, but still achieve SIM-SSO-CPA security. Theorem 1 in Sect. 3.3 will also be used for security proof.

5.1   SIM-SSO-CPA Secure Construction from Subgroup Decision Assumption

Let $\mathcal{G}$ be a PPT algorithm that takes as input security parameter 1^λ, outputs a tuple $(p, q, \mathbb{G}, \mathbb{G}_1, e, g)$ where p, q are distinct safe primes, $\mathbb{G}$ and $\mathbb{G}_1$ are cyclic groups with order $n = pq$, e is a bilinear map $e : \mathbb{G} \times \mathbb{G} \to \mathbb{G}_1$, g and $e(g,g)$ are the generators of $\mathbb{G}$ and $\mathbb{G}_1$, respectively. The definition of subgroup decision assumption is described as follows.

Definition 6. *We say that the generator $\mathcal{G}$ satisfies the subgroup decision assumption if for any PPT adversary $\mathcal{A}$, we have*

$$| \Pr[(p, q, \mathbb{G}, \mathbb{G}_1, e, g) \leftarrow \mathcal{G}(1^\lambda); n = pq; x \leftarrow \mathbb{Z}_n^*; h = g^x : \mathcal{A}(n, \mathbb{G}, \mathbb{G}_1, e, g, h) = 1]$$
$$- \Pr[(p, q, \mathbb{G}, \mathbb{G}_1, e, g) \leftarrow \mathcal{G}(1^\lambda); n = pq; x \leftarrow \mathbb{Z}_q^*; h = g^{px} : \mathcal{A}(n, \mathbb{G}, \mathbb{G}_1, e, g, h) = 1]|$$

is negligible.

Construction. Boneh-Goh-Nissim (BGN) scheme [6] is the main building block of the homomorphic trapdoor commitment scheme in [17,18], which based on the subgroup decision assumption. The SIM-SSO-CPA secure construction is described as follows.

$\text{Gen}(1^\lambda)$: Given a security parameter 1^λ, runs $\mathcal{G}(1^\lambda)$ to obtain a tuple $(p, q, \mathbb{G}, \mathbb{G}_1, e, g)$, let $n = pq$. Picks $x \leftarrow \mathbb{Z}_q^*$, sets $h = g^{px}$. The public key is $pk = (n, \mathbb{G}, \mathbb{G}_1, e, g, h)$, the secret key is $sk = q$.

$\text{LGen}(1^\lambda)$: Given a security parameter 1^λ, runs $\mathcal{G}(1^\lambda)$ to obtain a tuple $(p, q, \mathbb{G}, \mathbb{G}_1, e, g)$, let $n = pq$. Picks $x \leftarrow \mathbb{Z}_n^*$, sets $h = g^x$. The public key is $pk = (n, \mathbb{G}, \mathbb{G}_1, e, g, h)$, the secret key is $sk = x$.

$\text{Enc}(pk, m)$: To encrypt a message $m \in \{0, 1, 2, \ldots, T\}$ where T is a prime and $T < p$, picks $r \leftarrow \mathbb{Z}_n^*$, computes $c = g^m h^r$. Outputs c as the ciphertext.

$\text{Dec}(c, sk)$: To decrypt a ciphertext c, takes as input the secret key $sk = q$, computes $c^q = (g^m h^r)^q = (g^q)^m$, then uses Pollard's ρ algorithm to recover m.

We turn to proving SIM-SSO-CPA security of the above construction under subgroup decision assumption. The security has been embodied implicitly in the construction of homomorphic trapdoor commitment in [17].

Theorem 5. *The construction in Sect. 5.1 is a lossy encryption scheme with efficient weak opening assuming $\mathcal{G}$ satisfies the subgroup decision assumption.*

Proof. **Correctness.** Correctness of decryption follows from the completeness of the BGN cryptosystem.

Indistinguishability. The subgroup decision assumption implies that two kinds of keys are computational indistinguishability.

Lossiness. Given lossy public key $pk = (n, \mathbb{G}, \mathbb{G}_1, e, g, h)$ for $h = g^x$, where x is chosen uniformly from the set $\mathbb{Z}_n^*$. Because h has order n, so $h = g^x$ is uniformly random over $\mathbb{G}$. Now, for random $r \in \mathbb{Z}_n^*$, the ciphertext $c = g^m h^r = g^m (g^x)^r$ will also be uniformly distributed over $\mathbb{G}$.

Efficient weak openability. The scheme is efficiently weak openability. Consider the algorithm Opener that takes as input a lossy secret key $sk = x$, lossy public key $pk = (n, \mathbb{G}, \mathbb{G}_1, e, g, h)$ where $h = g^x$, plaintext m and m', random coins r, and ciphertext c such that $c = \text{Enc}(pk, m; r)$. To claim c to any plaintext m', Opener has to find r' such that $\text{Enc}(pk, m; r) = \text{Enc}(pk, m; r')$. Since Opener holds the secret key x, it can efficiently return $r' = r - \frac{(m'-m)}{x} \mod n$ which is just a random value in $\mathbb{Z}_n^*$.

Remarks. Note that the opening algorithm needs to receive an additional input, the random coins r that have been used to generate the ciphertext. So the construction meets the notion of weak opening. Also note that there is a gap in our proof. That is, we only succeed in proving weak opening. But this does not mean the above construction does not support a stronger opening algorithm.

5.2 SIM-SSO-CPA Secure Construction from Decisional Linear Assumption

Boneh, Boyen, and Shacham first proposed the decisional linear assumption [4]. Let $\mathcal{G}_{\text{DLIN}}$ be a PPT algorithm that takes as input security parameter 1^λ and outputs a tuple $(p, \mathbb{G}, g)$ where p is a prime, $\mathbb{G}$ is a cyclic group of order p, and g is a random generator of $\mathbb{G}$. The definition of decisional linear assumption is described as follows.

Definition 7 (Decisional Linear Assumption). *We say that the decisional linear assumption holds for the generator $\mathcal{G}_{\text{DLIN}}$ if for all PPT adversary $\mathcal{A}$ we have*

$$|\Pr[(p, \mathbb{G}, g) \leftarrow \mathcal{G}_{\text{DLIN}}(1^\lambda); x, y \leftarrow \mathbb{Z}_p^*; r, s \leftarrow \mathbb{Z}_p : \mathcal{A}(g, g^x, g^y, g^{xr}, g^{ys}, g^{r+s}) = 1]$$

$$- \Pr[(p, \mathbb{G}, g) \leftarrow \mathcal{G}_{\text{DLIN}}(1^\lambda); x, y \leftarrow \mathbb{Z}_p^*; r, s, d \leftarrow \mathbb{Z}_p : \mathcal{A}(g, g^x, g^y, g^{xr}, g^{ys}, g^d) = 1]|$$

is negligible.

Construction. Next we show that the PKE scheme constructed from homomorphic trapdoor commitment in [16,18] is a lossy encryption scheme with efficient weak opening, and this property has been contained implicitly in the construction of the original commitment scheme. Now, we present the SIM-SSO-CPA secure construction in the following.

$\text{Gen}(1^\lambda)$: Runs $(p, \mathbb{G}, g) \leftarrow \mathcal{G}_{\text{DLIN}}(1^\lambda)$, picks $x, y \leftarrow \mathbb{Z}_p^*$, sets $f = g^x$, $h = g^y$, picks $r_u, s_v \leftarrow \mathbb{Z}_p$, $z \leftarrow \mathbb{Z}_p^*$, and computes $(u, v, w) = (f^{r_u}, h^{s_v}, g^{r_u + s_v + z})$. Let $pk = (p, \mathbb{G}, g, f, h, u, v, w)$, $sk = (x, y, z)$.

$\text{LGen}(1^\lambda)$: Runs $(p, \mathbb{G}, g) \leftarrow \mathcal{G}_{\text{DLIN}}(1^\lambda)$, picks $x, y \leftarrow \mathbb{Z}_p^*$, let $f = g^x$, $h = g^y$, picks $r_u, s_v \leftarrow \mathbb{Z}_p$, and computes $(u, v, w) = (f^{r_u}, h^{s_v}, g^{r_u + s_v})$. Let $pk = (p, \mathbb{G}, g, f, h, u, v, w)$, $sk = (r_u, s_v)$.

$\text{Enc}(pk, m)$: On inputs pk and a message $m \in \{0, 1, 2, \ldots, T\}$ where T is a prime and $T < p$, picks $(r, s) \leftarrow \mathbb{Z}_p \times \mathbb{Z}_p$, and computes

$$c = (c_1, c_2, c_3) = (u^m f^r, v^m h^s, w^m g^{r+s})$$

$\text{Dec}(c, sk)$: On inputs the ciphertext $c = (c_1, c_2, c_3)$, and $sk = (x, y, z)$, computes $(g^z)^m = c_3 c_1^{-1/x} c_2^{-1/y}$, then recovers m by using Pollard's ρ method in the confined message space.

Theorem 6. *The above construction is a lossy encryption scheme with efficient weak opening assuming $\mathcal{G}_{\text{DLIN}}$ satisfies the decisional linear assumption.*

Proof. **Correctness.** Correctness of decryption follows from the completeness of *Extraction algorithm* from homomorphic trapdoor commitment.

Indistinguishability. Since real public keys $(u, v, w) = (f^{r_u}, h^{s_v}, g^{r_u + s_v + z})$ are not linear tuple, and lossy public key $(u, v, w) = (f^{r_u}, h^{s_v}, g^{r_u + s_v})$ are random linear tuple. Under the decision linear assumption, real public keys and lossy public keys are computational indistinguishability.

Lossiness. Given the lossy public key $pk = (f^{r_u}, h^{s_v}, g^{r_u + s_v})$, pk is a linear tuple, and pk is also the perfect hiding commitment key. Following the statistically hiding property of the homomorphic trapdoor commitment, the ciphertext $(u^m f^r, v^m h^s, w^m g^{r+s})$ hides m perfectly.

Efficient weak openability. To see this, consider the algorithm Opener that takes as input a lossy secret key (r_u, s_v), lossy public key $(f^{r_u}, h^{s_v}, g^{r_u + s_v})$, plaintexts m and m', random coins (r, s), ciphertext c such that $c = \mathrm{Enc}(pk, m; r, s)$. To claim c to any plaintext m', Opener has to find (r', s') such that satisfy $\mathrm{Enc}(pk, m; r, s) = \mathrm{Enc}(pk, m; r', s')$. Since Opener holds secret key $sk = (r_u, s_v)$, it can efficiently outputs $r' = r - (m' - m)r_u \bmod p$ and $s' = s - (m' - m)s_v \bmod p$, where r' and s' are random elements in $\mathbb{Z}_p$.

Remarks. Note that in the input of the opening algorithm, the random coins r and s are also necessary. Hence, the above construction meets the notion of weak opening. Also note that there is a gap in our proof, please see the Remarks in Sect. 5.1.

6   Conclusion

In this paper we study public key encryptions of simulation-based security against sender selective-opening attacks. In concrete, we present a generic construction that achieves SIM-SSO-CPA security from lossy encryption, and give an instantiation based on the Matrix Diffie-Hellman Assumption. In fact, our instantiation is inefficient, and a further improvement would be desirable.

We further prove that the PKE constructions from Boneh-Gentry-Hamburg scheme, Cocks' scheme and homomorphic trapdoor commitments are SIM-SSO-CPA secure. These schemes have natural lossiness property, but it is not our purpose to make them explicit. We focus on whether the efficient opening algorithm exists or not, and succeed in building PKE schemes that support efficient opening.

Acknowledgments. The authors would like to thank the anonymous reviewers for their invaluable comments and suggestions. The authors are also grateful to Xin Wang and Haiyang Hu for helpful discussions and advice.

A: Security Proof of the Instantiation in Sect. 3.4

We show that the instantiation satisfies the four properties of a lossy encryption scheme with efficient weak opening.

Proof. **Correctness.** This follows readily from the correctness of $\mathcal{D}_{l,k}$-MDDH-based hash proof system.

Indistinguishability. It is obvious that $(\mathcal{G}, [\mathbf{A}\boldsymbol{w}])$ and $(\mathcal{G}, [\boldsymbol{u}])$ are computationally indistinguishable under the $\mathcal{D}_{l,k}$-MDDH assumption.

Lossiness. Consider the lossy public key $[\boldsymbol{x}] = [\boldsymbol{u}]$ where $\boldsymbol{u} \leftarrow \mathbb{Z}_q^l$. According to the smoothness property of the $\mathcal{D}_{l,k}$-MDDH-based hash proof system, $[\boldsymbol{k}^{\mathrm{T}}\boldsymbol{u}]$ is statistically indistinguishable from a random element in $\mathbb{G}$. Since $\mathrm{H}([\boldsymbol{k}^{\mathrm{T}}\boldsymbol{u}])$ is statistically close to uniform distribution over $\{0,1\}$, hence $\mathrm{H}([\boldsymbol{k}^{\mathrm{T}}\boldsymbol{u}]) \oplus m$ will also be statistically close to uniform distribution over $\{0,1\}$ for any message m.

Efficient weak openability. Please read Sect. 3.2.

Remarks. Note that if we do not require the property of efficient weak openability, the compress function H is unnecessary. In this case, we need to make some changes of the construction. The Injective key generation algorithm and Lossy key generation algorithm will not change. It only needs to modify the encryption and decryption algorithm.

– **Encryption:** On input a message $m \in \mathbb{G}$, picks $\boldsymbol{k} \in \mathbb{Z}_q^l$, $\boldsymbol{c}_1 = [\boldsymbol{k}^{\mathrm{T}}\mathbf{A}]$, $\boldsymbol{c}_2 = [\boldsymbol{k}^{\mathrm{T}}\boldsymbol{x}] \cdot m$. Outputs ciphertext $c = (\boldsymbol{c}_1, \boldsymbol{c}_2)$.
– **Decryption:** Given ciphertext $c = (\boldsymbol{c}_1, \boldsymbol{c}_2)$, $sk = \boldsymbol{w}$. Outputs $m = (\boldsymbol{c}_2 \cdot m)/[\boldsymbol{c}_1 \cdot \boldsymbol{w}]$.

The modified construction is an instantiation of the generic lossy encryption in [21] (as well as the dual Cramer-Shoup scheme in [35], Sect. 2.2), and correctness can be easily verified. While $[\boldsymbol{x}] \in \mathcal{X}$, smoothness property shows that $[\boldsymbol{k}^{\mathrm{T}}\boldsymbol{x}]$ is completely undetermined. But without the compress function H, the space of random coins is large, so algorithm Opener needs to compute the set of all $\boldsymbol{k}^{\cdot} \in \mathbb{Z}_q^l$ such that $[\boldsymbol{k}'^{\mathrm{T}}\mathbf{A}] = [\boldsymbol{k}^{\mathrm{T}}\mathbf{A}]$ until $[\boldsymbol{k}'^{\mathrm{T}}\boldsymbol{x}] \cdot m' = [\boldsymbol{k}^{\mathrm{T}}\boldsymbol{x}] \cdot m$. Hence, Opener may not efficient. According to the result in [2], the modified scheme only achieves IND-SSO-CPA security.

References

1. Bellare, M., Dowsley, R., Waters, B., Yilek, S.: Standard security does not imply security against selective-opening. In: Pointcheval, D., Johansson, T. (eds.) EUROCRYPT 2012. LNCS, vol. 7237, pp. 645–662. Springer, Heidelberg (2012). doi:10.1007/978-3-642-29011-4_38
2. Bellare, M., Hofheinz, D., Yilek, S.: Possibility and impossibility results for encryption and commitment secure under selective opening. In: Joux, A. (ed.) EUROCRYPT 2009. LNCS, vol. 5479, pp. 1–35. Springer, Heidelberg (2009). doi:10.1007/978-3-642-01001-9_1
3. Böhl, F., Hofheinz, D., Kraschewski, D.: On definitions of selective opening security. In: Fischlin, M., Buchmann, J., Manulis, M. (eds.) PKC 2012. LNCS, vol. 7293, pp. 522–539. Springer, Heidelberg (2012). doi:10.1007/978-3-642-30057-8_31
4. Boneh, D., Boyen, X., Shacham, H.: Short group signatures. In: Franklin, M. (ed.) CRYPTO 2004. LNCS, vol. 3152, pp. 41–55. Springer, Heidelberg (2004). doi:10.1007/978-3-540-28628-8_3

5. Boneh, D., Gentry, C., Hamburg, M.: Space-efficient identity based encryption without pairings. In: 48th Annual IEEE Symposium on Foundations of Computer Science (FOCS 2007), pp. 647–657 (2007)

6. Boneh, D., Goh, E.-J., Nissim, K.: Evaluating 2-DNF formulas on ciphertexts. In: Kilian, J. (ed.) TCC 2005. LNCS, vol. 3378, pp. 325–341. Springer, Heidelberg (2005). doi:10.1007/978-3-540-30576-7_18

7. Canetti, R., Dwork, C., Naor, M., Ostrovsky, R.: Deniable encryption. In: Kaliski, B.S. (ed.) CRYPTO 1997. LNCS, vol. 1294, pp. 90–104. Springer, Heidelberg (1997). doi:10.1007/BFb0052229

8. Cocks, C.: An identity based encryption scheme based on quadratic residues. In: Honary, B. (ed.) Cryptography and Coding 2001. LNCS, vol. 2260, pp. 360–363. Springer, Heidelberg (2001). doi:10.1007/3-540-45325-3_32

9. Cramer, R., Shoup, V.: Universal hash proofs and a paradigm for adaptive chosen ciphertext secure public-key encryption. In: Knudsen, L.R. (ed.) EUROCRYPT 2002. LNCS, vol. 2332, pp. 45–64. Springer, Heidelberg (2002). doi:10.1007/3-540-46035-7_4

10. Deng, Y., Song, X., Yu, J., Chen, Y.: On instance compression, schnorr/guillouquisquater, and the security of classic protocols for unique witness relations. IACR Cryptol. ePrint Archive 2017, 390 (2017)

11. Dwork, C., Naor, M., Reingold, O., Stockmeyer, L.J.: Magic functions. In: 40th Annual Symposium on Foundations of Computer Science, FOCS 1999, pp. 523–534 (1999)

12. Escala, A., Herold, G., Kiltz, E., Ràfols, C., Villar, J.: An algebraic framework for Diffie-Hellman assumptions. In: Canetti, R., Garay, J.A. (eds.) CRYPTO 2013. LNCS, vol. 8043, pp. 129–147. Springer, Heidelberg (2013). doi:10.1007/978-3-642-40084-1_8

13. Fehr, S., Hofheinz, D., Kiltz, E., Wee, H.: Encryption schemes secure against chosen-ciphertext selective opening attacks. In: Gilbert, H. (ed.) EUROCRYPT 2010. LNCS, vol. 6110, pp. 381–402. Springer, Heidelberg (2010). doi:10.1007/978-3-642-13190-5_20

14. Fuchsbauer, G., Heuer, F., Kiltz, E., Pietrzak, K.: Standard security does imply security against selective opening for markov distributions. In: Kushilevitz, E., Malkin, T. (eds.) TCC 2016. LNCS, vol. 9562, pp. 282–305. Springer, Heidelberg (2016). doi:10.1007/978-3-662-49096-9_12

15. Fujisaki, E.: All-but-many encryption – a new framework for fully-equipped UC commitments. In: Sarkar, P., Iwata, T. (eds.) ASIACRYPT 2014. LNCS, vol. 8874, pp. 426–447. Springer, Heidelberg (2014). doi:10.1007/978-3-662-45608-8_23

16. Groth, J., Ostrovsky, R., Sahai, A.: Non-interactive zaps and new techniques for NIZK. In: Dwork, C. (ed.) CRYPTO 2006. LNCS, vol. 4117, pp. 97–111. Springer, Heidelberg (2006). doi:10.1007/11818175_6

17. Groth, J., Ostrovsky, R., Sahai, A.: Perfect non-interactive zero knowledge for NP. In: Vaudenay, S. (ed.) EUROCRYPT 2006. LNCS, vol. 4004, pp. 339–358. Springer, Heidelberg (2006). doi:10.1007/11761679_21

18. Groth, J., Ostrovsky, R., Sahai, A.: New techniques for noninteractive zero-knowledge. J. ACM 59(3), 11:1–11:35 (2012)

19. Harnik, D., Naor, M.: On the compressibility of NP instances and cryptographic applications. SIAM J. Comput. 39(5), 1667–1713 (2010)

20. Hazay, C., Patra, A., Warinschi, B.: Selective opening security for receivers. In: Iwata, T., Cheon, J.H. (eds.) ASIACRYPT 2015. LNCS, vol. 9452, pp. 443–469. Springer, Heidelberg (2015). doi:10.1007/978-3-662-48797-6_19

21. Hemenway, B., Libert, B., Ostrovsky, R., Vergnaud, D.: Lossy encryption: constructions from general assumptions and efficient selective opening chosen ciphertext security. In: Lee, D.H., Wang, X. (eds.) ASIACRYPT 2011. LNCS, vol. 7073, pp. 70–88. Springer, Heidelberg (2011). doi:10.1007/978-3-642-25385-0_4

22. Hofheinz, D.: All-but-many lossy trapdoor functions. In: Pointcheval, D., Johansson, T. (eds.) EUROCRYPT 2012. LNCS, vol. 7237, pp. 209–227. Springer, Heidelberg (2012). doi:10.1007/978-3-642-29011-4_14

23. Hofheinz, D., Jager, T., Rupp, A.: Public-key encryption with simulation-based selective-opening security and compact ciphertexts. In: Hirt, M., Smith, A. (eds.) TCC 2016. LNCS, vol. 9986, pp. 146–168. Springer, Heidelberg (2016). doi:10.1007/978-3-662-53644-5_6

24. Hofheinz, D., Rao, V., Wichs, D.: Standard security does not imply indistinguishability under selective opening. In: Hirt, M., Smith, A. (eds.) TCC 2016. LNCS, vol. 9986, pp. 121–145. Springer, Heidelberg (2016). doi:10.1007/978-3-662-53644-5_5

25. Hofheinz, D., Rupp, A.: Standard versus selective opening security: separation and equivalence results. In: Lindell, Y. (ed.) TCC 2014. LNCS, vol. 8349, pp. 591–615. Springer, Heidelberg (2014). doi:10.1007/978-3-642-54242-8_25

26. Huang, Z., Liu, S., Qin, B.: Sender-equivocable encryption schemes secure against chosen-ciphertext attacks revisited. In: Kurosawa, K., Hanaoka, G. (eds.) PKC 2013. LNCS, vol. 7778, pp. 369–385. Springer, Heidelberg (2013). doi:10.1007/978-3-642-36362-7_23

27. Jia, D., Lu, X., Li, B.: Receiver selective opening security from indistinguishability obfuscation. In: Dunkelman, O., Sanadhya, S.K. (eds.) INDOCRYPT 2016. LNCS, vol. 10095, pp. 393–410. Springer, Cham (2016). doi:10.1007/978-3-319-49890-4_22

28. Jia, D., Lu, X., Li, B.: Constructions secure against receiver selective opening and chosen ciphertext attacks. In: Handschuh, H. (ed.) CT-RSA 2017. LNCS, vol. 10159, pp. 417–431. Springer, Cham (2017). doi:10.1007/978-3-319-52153-4_24

29. Kalai, Y.T.: Smooth projective hashing and two-message oblivious transfer. In: Cramer, R. (ed.) EUROCRYPT 2005. LNCS, vol. 3494, pp. 78–95. Springer, Heidelberg (2005). doi:10.1007/11426639_5

30. Liu, S., Paterson, K.G.: Simulation-based selective opening CCA security for PKE from key encapsulation mechanisms. In: Katz, J. (ed.) PKC 2015. LNCS, vol. 9020, pp. 3–26. Springer, Heidelberg (2015). doi:10.1007/978-3-662-46447-2_1

31. Naor, M., Segev, G.: Public-key cryptosystems resilient to key leakage. In: Halevi, S. (ed.) CRYPTO 2009. LNCS, vol. 5677, pp. 18–35. Springer, Heidelberg (2009). doi:10.1007/978-3-642-03356-8_2

32. Paillier, P.: Public-key cryptosystems based on composite degree residuosity classes. In: Stern, J. (ed.) EUROCRYPT 1999. LNCS, vol. 1592, pp. 223–238. Springer, Heidelberg (1999). doi:10.1007/3-540-48910-X_16

33. Peikert, C., Vaikuntanathan, V., Waters, B.: A framework for efficient and composable oblivious transfer. In: Wagner, D. (ed.) CRYPTO 2008. LNCS, vol. 5157, pp. 554–571. Springer, Heidelberg (2008). doi:10.1007/978-3-540-85174-5_31

34. Peikert, C., Waters, B.: Lossy trapdoor functions and their applications. In: Proceedings of the 40th Annual ACM Symposium on Theory of Computing, pp. 187–196 (2008)

35. Wee, H.: KDM-security via homomorphic smooth projective hashing. In: Cheng, C.-M., Chung, K.-M., Persiano, G., Yang, B.-Y. (eds.) PKC 2016. LNCS, vol. 9615, pp. 159–179. Springer, Heidelberg (2016). doi:10.1007/978-3-662-49387-8_7

Homomorphic Secret Sharing from Paillier Encryption

Nelly Fazio[1], Rosario Gennaro[1], Tahereh Jafarikhah[2],
and William E. Skeith III[1(✉)]

[1] Graduate Center, The City College, CUNY, New York, NY, USA
{fazio,rosario,wes}@cs.ccny.cuny.edu
[2] The Graduate Center, CUNY, New York, NY, USA
jafarikhah@gmail.com

Abstract. A recent breakthrough by Boyle et al. [7] demonstrated secure function evaluation protocols for branching programs, where the communication complexity is sublinear in the size of the circuit (indeed just linear in the size of the inputs, and polynomial in the security parameter). Their result is based on the Decisional Diffie-Hellman assumption (DDH), using (variants of) the ElGamal cryptosystem. In this work, we extend their result to show a construction based on the circular security of the Paillier encryption scheme. We also offer a few optimizations to the scheme, including an alternative to the "Las Vegas"-style share conversion protocols of [7,9] which *directly* checks the correctness of the computation. This allows us to reduce the number of required repetitions to achieve a desired overall error bound by a constant fraction for typical cases, and for large programs, reduces the total computation cost.

Keywords: Homomorphic secret sharing · Function secret sharing · Paillier encryption · Secure function evaluation · Private information retrieval

1 Introduction

In this paper, following exciting recent results by Boyle et al. [7,9], we present new protocols for low-communication MPC. We extend the results in [7] (proven secure under the Decisional Diffie-Hellman Assumption) by showing that they can be based on the circular security of the Paillier encryption scheme [31]. Additionally, we describe a verification technique to directly check correctness of the actual computation, rather than the absence of a potential error as in [7]. This results in fewer repetitions of the overall computation for a given error bound.

R. Gennaro—supported by NSF Grant 1565403.

T. Okamoto et al. (Eds.): ProvSec 2017, LNCS 10592, pp. 381–399, 2017.
https://doi.org/10.1007/978-3-319-68637-0_23

1.1   Background and Motivation

Secure MultiParty Computation (MPC) has been a vital research area in Cryptography for the last 30 years. Since the early seminal works [4, 11, 20, 35, 36], we know that it is possible for two or more parties to compute a joint function of individual secret inputs. It is a very powerful tool, since most, if not all of the security problems can be solved in principle using a multiparty computation protocol. Those initial results established the feasibility of the solutions, and at the same time highlighted their complexity. The research of the last 30 years has been focused on inventing increasingly powerful MPC techniques to get more efficient solutions. One of the bottleneck parameters that immediately attracted researchers' attention was communication complexity: all the early results require communication between the parties which is at least as large as the size of the circuit representing the function being computed. Ideally one would like the parties to exchange just a few messages of limited size.

Most of the research on this issue focused on types of "homomorphic" encryption (resp. secret sharing) schemes, which allow the computation of a function to be carried out non-interactively directly on the encryption (resp. shares) of the secret inputs. For example *additively homomorphic encryption* [14, 16, 21, 28, 30, 31] allows the parties to publish encryptions of their inputs, and to compute any linear function without interaction (except for a final decryption step). Similarly this can be achieved by using *linear secret sharing* such as Shamir's [33]. These techniques were applied to the concept of *Private Information Retrieval (PIR)* [12, 13, 26] which allows the secure computation of a "selection" function (Party 1 holds n values $x_1, \ldots, x_n$, Party 2 holds an index i, the output is x_i) with communication which is sublinear in the size of the circuit.

General solutions for any function had to wait for the discovery by Gentry of *Fully Homomorphic Encryption (FHE)* [17] which enables the computation of arbitrary functions over encrypted input, breaking the circuit barrier in general. The drawback of FHE is that in spite of continuous progress, even the best implementations of FHE remain quite slow [18, 19, 29]. Additionally, the set of cryptographic assumptions underlying FHE remains limited to assumptions related to the complexity of lattice based problems, and do not include more classical assumptions such as factoring or discrete logarithm.

These observations motivated Boyle et al. to look for alternatives. In a very exciting recent result [7] they present a Homomorphic Secret Sharing scheme which allows the non-interactive computation of *Branching Programs* over the shares of the secret inputs. Further optimizations (as well as transporting some results to the generic group model for DDH-hard groups) are given by the same authors in [9]. Their scheme is orders of magnitude more efficient than FHE and its security is based on the DDH Assumption.

1.2   Our Results

We extend the results in [7,9] by showing that Homomorphic Secret Sharing for Branching Programs can be based on the (circular) security of the Paillier [31] encryption schemes.

While our protocols follow the same blueprint of the Homomorphic Secret Sharing in [7] our extensions were not immediate. Below we give an overview of the main technical problems and challenges we encountered, and the techniques used to overcome them.

1.3   Techniques

To begin, we give a very high-level review of the techniques used in [7]. We then outline where new techniques are needed for our work. Informally, the construction of [7] follows these steps:

1. The scheme uses the ElGamal encryption scheme modified to be additively homomorphic by placing the plaintext in the exponent. That is, encryptions of a message x look like $[\![x]\!] = (\alpha = g^r, \beta = h^r \cdot g^x)$, where $h = g^c$ is the public key. When messages are small, decryption is feasible by performing a discrete logarithm after the usual ElGamal decryption.
2. The scheme also uses, simple 2-out-of-2 additive sharing. Given $z \in Z_q$ where q is the order of the ElGamal group, we denote $\langle z \rangle = (z_1, z_2)$ such that $z_1 + z_2 = z \bmod q$, where each party P_i holds z_i.
3. Given $[\![x]\!] = (\alpha, \beta)$, $\langle y \rangle = (y_1, y_2)$ and $\langle cy \rangle = (w_1, w_2)$ each party P_i can now locally compute a share γ_i as $\gamma_i = \beta^{y_i} \cdot \alpha^{-w_i}$, such that $\gamma_1 \cdot \gamma_2 = g^{xy}$, i.e. a *multiplicative sharing* of g^{xy}. Note how this step effectively removes the randomness from the encryption of x, using the secret key c.
4. Finally, a clever technique is used to compute a *distributed discrete logarithm*, thus recovering an *additive* sharing of xy without the need for interaction. We point out that their procedure requires the multiplicative sharing to be in a *cyclic* group.

Abstracting out from the specifics, we can see that the scheme in [7] requires the following ingredients:

– An encryption scheme which is both *message* and *key homomorphic* over $\mathbb{Z}$ (or a finite quotient), i.e., a scheme that allows the transformation in step 3 above.
– A non-interactive method for transforming a multiplicative sharing of g^z into an additive sharing of z, where these two values "live" in the ciphertext and message space (respectively) of the encryption scheme.

Our Construction. We now address the challenge of adapting these techniques to make use of the Paillier cryptosystem [31]. Recall that Paillier is naturally additively homomorphic over the integers, which works in our favor here. Additionally, we can use a version of Paillier threshold decryption [15,24] to obtain the "key homomorphic" property which allows to perform Step 3.

Recall that a Paillier encryption of an integer x is of the form $g^x r^n \bmod n^2$, where n is an RSA modulus, $\mathrm{ord}(g) = n$, and $\mathrm{ord}(r^n) \mid \varphi(n)$. Since it is required that $(n, \varphi(n)) = 1$, we can use the Chinese Remainder Theorem to find an integer λ such that

$$\lambda \equiv \begin{cases} 1 & \bmod n \\ 0 & \bmod \varphi(n) \end{cases}.$$

Now if $\sigma = g^x r^n$ is an encryption of x, then by raising to the λ power we get: $\sigma^\lambda = (g^x r^n)^\lambda = g^x \bmod n^2$. While there are efficient procedures for completing the decryption (recovering x from g^x), note that we have already made substantial progress in obtaining the necessary ingredients for the [7] blueprint. Given an additive sharing $\langle \lambda y \rangle = (z_1, z_2)$ of λy (so that $z_1 + z_2 = \lambda y$), then $(\sigma^{z_1}, \sigma^{z_2})$ is a multiplicative sharing of g^{xy}, i.e.

$$\sigma^{z_1} \sigma^{z_2} = \sigma^{\lambda y} = g^{xy} \bmod n^2.$$

If xy is relatively small, we might hope to then perform the distributed discrete log protocol from [7], however there are a few complications. To begin, it is not entirely obvious that the distributed discrete log protocol would work in $\mathbb{Z}_{n^2}^\times$ which is not a cyclic group. For example, while certainly g^{xy} lives in $\langle g \rangle$, each party's shares do not – the shares sit in $\mathbb{Z}_{n^2}^\times$, and furthermore in different cosets of $\langle g \rangle$. Fortunately, we can modify the protocol in [7] (as well as most of the variants from [9], sans a few optimizations) to work for any finite group in a fairly straightforward way (see Sect. 3 for details).

The other main issue concerns the representation of our additive shares. In the original ElGamal-based scheme, additive shares of a value y satisfy $\sum y_i \equiv y \bmod q$, where q is the order of the group. Note that q is *public* in this case. Thus, each party can perform addition modulo q without knowledge of any secret values. In Paillier, however, we need to work with additive shares of values that work modulo $n\varphi(n)$, a value that must be kept secret. Therefore we do this sharing over the integers. Without a careful implementation this step can cause the size of the shares to grow exponentially, but we are able to avoid this problem. Details can be found in Sect. 4.

Verifying Computations. In [7,9], the authors describe "Las Vegas" style techniques to check for the *potential* risk of having incurred an incorrect computation during each step of the protocol. If the possibility of an error is never signaled, then the overall computation is considered correct. This method was then shown to provide efficiency improvements for several applications.

In this work, we describe a technique to *directly* check correctness which verifies the actual computation, rather than the absence of a potentially "risky" situation. This method of checking does not produce false negatives (erroneously reporting that the protocol failed), and allows us to reduce even further the number of required invocations for a desired overall error bound by a constant fraction. The price we pay for this (in addition to a negligible probability of a false positive), is some extra effort to compute the values used in the check. However, this effort depends linearly on the program size, whilst each repetition takes quadratic time in the program size. Hence, we achieve a savings in computation for large programs. Our verification method works both for the original ElGamal-based construction of [7] and for our Paillier-based construction, although the benefits are more pronounced for the latter. Details can be found in Sect. 5.

2   Preliminaries

2.1   Encryption

A public-key encryption system Π consists of three algorithms (KeyGen, Enc, Dec), where KeyGen is a key generation (randomized) algorithm that takes a security parameter k and outputs a public-secret key pair (PK, SK); Enc(PK, m) is the encryption (randomized) algorithm that on input a message m and the public key PK outputs a ciphertext c; and Dec(SK, c) decrypts ciphertext c with secret key SK. Obviously if (PK, SK) $\leftarrow$ KeyGen(1^k) and $c \leftarrow$ Enc(PK, m) then $m = $ Dec(SK, c).

Semantic Security. [21] says that no polynomial time adversary can distinguish between the encryption of two messages of its choice. For all PPT $\mathcal{A}$

$$Pr[b' = b : (\mathsf{PK}, \mathsf{SK}) \leftarrow \mathsf{KeyGen}(k), (m_0, m_1) \leftarrow \mathcal{A}(\mathsf{PK}),$$

$$b \leftarrow \{0, 1\}, b' \leftarrow \mathcal{A}^{\mathcal{O}_b}(\mathsf{PK})] \leq \frac{1}{2} + \nu(k)$$

where oracle $\mathcal{O}_b$ takes no input and outputs $c \leftarrow$ Enc(PK, m_b), and $\nu(k)$ is a negligible function.

Circular Security. A public-key encryption Π is circular secure if it remains secure even encrypting messages that depend on the secret keys in use. More precisely, if c with $length(c) = l(k)$ is the secret key of the public key encryption scheme Π which encrypts bits, there is a negligible function $\nu(k)$ that the following holds for all PPT $\mathcal{A}$:

$$Pr[b' = b : (\mathsf{PK}, \mathsf{SK}) \leftarrow \mathsf{KeyGen}(k), b \leftarrow \{0, 1\}, b' \leftarrow \mathcal{A}^{\mathcal{O}_b}(\mathsf{PK})] \leq \frac{1}{2} + \nu(k)$$

where oracle $\mathcal{O}$ takes no input and outputs $(D_1, D_2, \ldots, D_l)$ such that

$$\begin{cases} \forall i \in [l], D_i \leftarrow \mathsf{Enc}(\mathsf{PK}, 0) & \textit{if } b = 0 \\ \forall i \in [l], D_i \leftarrow \mathsf{Enc}(\mathsf{PK}, \mathsf{SK}^i) & \textit{if } b = 1 \end{cases}$$

in which SK^i is the i-th bit of SK. Later we will see that circular security plays an important role in the construction of our homomorphic secret sharing. We remark that circular security implies semantic security.

2.2   The Paillier Encryption Scheme

Let n be an RSA modulus, i.e. $n = pq$ where p, q are primes. A number z is said to be an n-th residue modulo n^2 if there exists a number $y \in \mathbb{Z}_{n^2}^\times$ such that $z = y^n$ mod n^2. We assume that there exists no polynomial time distinguisher for n-th residues $\bmod\, n^2$. We will refer to this hypothesis as the *Decisional Composite Residuosity Assumption* (DCRA).

More formally, we assume that there exists a randomized RSA key generation algorithm RSAGen that on input a security parameter 1^k selects two k-bit primes. Then we say that the DCRA holds (with respect to RSAGen) if for all PPT $\mathcal{A}$ there exists a negligible function $\nu(k)$, such that

$$Pr[b' = b : (p,q) \leftarrow \mathsf{RSAGen}(k), n = pq, b \leftarrow \{0,1\}, b' \leftarrow \mathcal{A}^{\mathcal{O}_b}(n)] \leq \frac{1}{2} + \nu(k)$$

where oracle $\mathcal{O}_b$ takes no input, selects y uniformly at random in $\mathbb{Z}_{n^2}^\times$ and outputs z such that $z = y$ if $b = 0$, and $z = y^n$ if $b = 1$.

The Paillier encryption scheme, whose security is based on DCRA is defined as follows (where we use the modified definition of the secret key λ from [16,24] used in their threshold variant of the scheme). The key generation algorithm $\mathsf{KeyGen}_{Paillier}(1^k)$ picks two k-bit prime numbers p and q such that $n = pq$ satisfies $(n, \varphi(n)) = 1$ (which will hold with high probability for such n), computes

$$\lambda = \begin{cases} 1 & \bmod\, n \\ 0 & \bmod\, \varphi(n) \end{cases} \tag{1}$$

and outputs $(\mathsf{PK}, \mathsf{SK})$ for $\mathsf{PK} = n$ and $\mathsf{SK} = \lambda$. Note that the existence of such a λ, as well as an efficient means of computing it, are given by the Chinese Remainder Theorem since $(n, \varphi(n)) = 1$. Note also that λ is unique in the range $[0, \ldots, n\varphi(n) - 1]$. The encryption algorithm for a message $x \in \mathbb{Z}_n$ is defined by

$$\mathsf{Enc}_{Paillier}(\mathsf{PK}, x) = (1 + n)^x \cdot r^n \bmod n^2$$

and the decryption algorithm for $\sigma < n^2$ is defined by

$$\mathsf{Dec}_{Paillier}(\mathsf{SK}, \sigma) = \frac{L(\sigma^\lambda \bmod n^2)}{L((1+n)^\lambda \bmod n^2)} \bmod n \ \text{ where } L(u) = \frac{u-1}{n}$$

Paillier is an additive homomorphic scheme; given only the public-key and $\sigma_i = \mathsf{Enc}_{Paillier}(x_i)$ then $\sigma_1 \cdot \sigma_2 \bmod n^2 = \mathsf{Enc}_{Paillier}(x_1 + x_2 \bmod n)$.

2.3   Homomorphic Secret Sharing

A 2-out-of-2 homomorphic secret sharing scheme (HSS) [7] deals with the scenario that a client wants to split a secret input $w \in \{0,1\}^n$ into shares (w_0, w_1), and sends each w_i to a different server. Each server holding a representation of a function f, can locally compute additive shares of $f(w)$.

A representation for a function is a program P (a collection of bit strings). For an input $w \in \{0,1\}^n$, the output of P is represented by $P(w)$. The symbol $\perp$ is used when the output of $P(w)$ is undefined. For simplicity we can consider the inputs and outputs of a function as binary strings. A HSS scheme consists of two algorithms: Share that splits the secret into two shares and Eval that evaluates a program P on two inputs such that the outputs are the additive shares of $P(w)$.

Definition 1. *A homomorphic secret sharing scheme with error bound δ for the collection of programs $\mathcal{P}$ consists of algorithms (Share, Eval) with the following properties:*

- Share$(1^k, w)$: *on the security parameter 1^k and $w \in \{0,1\}^n$ outputs (w_0, w_1).*
- Eval$(b \in \{0,1\}, w_b, P, \delta)$ *outputs y_b.*
- **Correctness:** *For every polynomial p there exists a negligible function ν such that for every k, w, P, δ in which $|P|, 1/\delta \le p(k)$*

$$Pr[y_0 + y_1 = P(w) : (w_0, w_1) \leftarrow Share(1^k, w),$$
$$y_b \leftarrow Eval(b, w_b, P, \delta), b \in \{0,1\}] \ge 1 - \delta - \nu(k)$$

- **Security:** *Each share computationally hides the secret input.*

We would like to apply a stronger version of HSS that allows homomorphic computation on encrypted inputs.

Definition 2. *A Distributed-Evaluation Homomorphic Encryption (DEHE) with error bound δ for a class of programs $\mathcal{P}$ consists of three algorithms (KeyGen, Enc, Eval) as follows:*

- $(PK, (e_0, e_1)) \leftarrow$ KeyGen(1^k): *It takes a security parameter 1^k and outputs a PK and a pair of evaluation keys (e_0, e_1).*
- $E_w := $ Enc(PK, w): *It encrypts a secret input bit w and output c.*
- Eval$_b := $ Eval$(b \in \{0,1\}, e_b, \mathbf{c} = (c_1, c_2, \ldots, c_n), P, \delta)$: *Outputs y_b as party b's share of output y.*
- **Correctness:** *For every polynomial p there exists a negligible function ν such that for every $k, w = (w^1, \ldots, w^n) \in \{0,1\}^n, P, \delta$ in which $|P|, 1/\delta \le p(k)$*

$$Pr[y_0 + y_1 = P(w) : (PK, (e_0, e_1)) \leftarrow KeyGen(1^k),$$
$$C \leftarrow (E_{w^1}, \ldots, E_{w^n}), y_b \leftarrow Eval_b] \ge 1 - \delta - \nu(k)$$

- **Security:** *Let D_b stand for the distribution obtained by applying the evaluation key e_b in this setting. The security of the DEHE scheme means that D_0 and D_1 are computationally indistinguishable.*

2.4   Restricted Multiplication Straight-Line Programs (RMS)

Our construction will provide non-interactive evaluation of some specific collection of programs called as restricted multiplication straight-line programs (RMS). The class of RMS programs with bound 1^M (where M is an upper bound for the size of a memory location) is an arbitrary sequence of the instructions as follow:

1. Load an input $x = (x^1, x^2, \ldots, x^n) \in \{0,1\}^n$ into memory: $y_j \leftarrow x^i$.
2. Add memory locations: $y_k \leftarrow y_i + y_j$.
3. Multiply a memory location by an input: $y_k \leftarrow x^i \cdot y_j$.
4. Output a memory location: $O_j \leftarrow y_j$.

Whenever the size of a memory value exceeds M, the program aborts and outputs $\perp$. We define the size of an RMS program as the number of its instructions. As pointed out in [7] RMS programs can be used to evaluate branching programs with constant overhead.

3   Share Conversion

Here we provide our first technical contribution: A generalization of the distributed discrete log and share conversion procedures from [7] which works in any finite group G, not just a cyclic group.

Consider the setting of two party computation, where one party holds x and the other party holds y such that $xy = g^b$ where g is an element of a group G (i.e. (x,y) is a multiplicative sharing relative to g of a small value b. Suppose that both parties have access to a random function $\phi : G \longrightarrow \{0, \ldots, k-1\}$ for $k \in \mathbb{N}$ (appropriate values for k will be determined shortly).

We will prove that if each party locally runs the procedure DDLog below (where the input a is set to the share held by each party and δ, M are parameters we will determine later) then at the end, the parties output values i, j such that $i - j = b$ with sufficiently high probability. In other words the procedure simultaneously computes the discrete log[1] of g^b and turns the multiplicative sharing into an additive one.

Algorithm 1. $\mathsf{DDLog}_{G,g}(a, \delta, M, \phi)$

1: $i = 0; h = a; T = 2M \ln(2/\delta)/\delta$
2: **while** $\phi(h) \neq 0$ **and** $i < T$ **do**
3:     $h = gh$
4:     $i = i + 1$
5: **end while**
6: **return** i

Let G be a finite group, and $g \in G$. Note that if two elements $x, y \in G$ have a product in $\langle g \rangle$, this is of course equivalent to saying that x and *the inverse* of y live in the same coset of $\langle g \rangle$, or put another way, x and y^{-1} differ by some number of "g-steps":

$$x = g^b y^{-1}. \tag{2}$$

---

[1] There is no contradiction here with the hardness of discrete log, since this works only for small values of b.

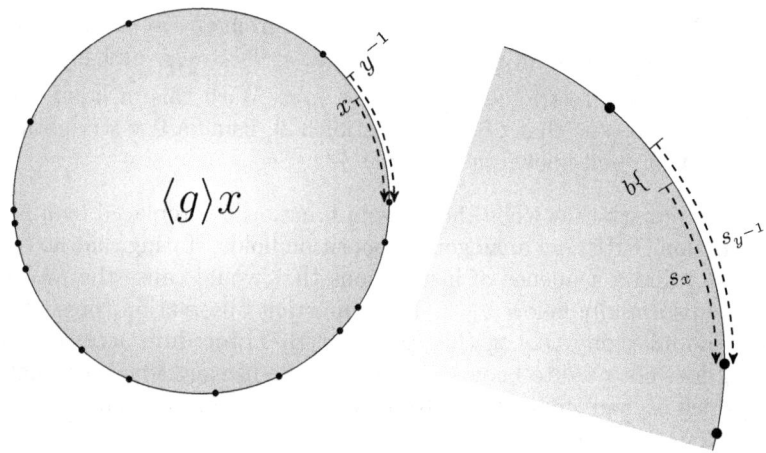

Fig. 1. Illustration of DDLog procedure on $xy = g^b$. Here, x, y are *multiplicative shares* of a small value b, which are inputs to DDLog. Both x and y^{-1} sit in the same coset $\langle g \rangle x$ of $\langle g \rangle$. The dots represent the elements of a random δ-sparse subset S in $\langle g \rangle x$. Note that (with good probability) the difference in the number of steps taken is $b = s_{y^{-1}} - s_x$, so that $(-s_x, s_{y^{-1}})$ is an additive sharing of b.

Define $S = \phi^{-1}(\{0\})$. Then the parties will be able to "synchronize" by counting g-steps to the next value in S, recovering an additive sharing of b. The parameter k can be used to balance the running time of the process with its success probability. The basic idea is depicted in Fig. 1. Note that the domain of ϕ must be the *entire group* G not just the particular coset where x, y^{-1} reside. Indeed, finding a useful representation of that coset (in order to instantiate ϕ) might be difficult.[2]

Fortunately this is not much of a complication – Eq. (2) combined with the fact that ϕ gives random labels to each element allows the same analysis to proceed for the restriction of ϕ to any coset. Indeed, Algorithm 1 is a proper generalization of the corresponding algorithm from [7] (where the group is cyclic $\langle g \rangle = G$ so there is only one coset), and a very similar argument suffices to show its correctness in our application. We provide a few details for completeness. Following the notation of [7], we set M to be an upper bound on the value being shared and T will be a "timeout" value.

Proposition 1 ([7, Propostion 3.2]). *Let G be any finite group, $g \in G$, $\delta > 0$, and $M \in \mathbb{N}$. If $M, T < \mathrm{ord}(g)$, then for any $x, y \in G$ such that $xy = g^b$ with $b < M$, we have*

$$\Pr_{\phi}\left[\mathsf{DDLog}(y^{-1}, \delta, M, \phi) - \mathsf{DDLog}(x, \delta, M, \phi) = b\right] \geq 1 - \delta$$

where ϕ is sampled uniformly from all functions from $G \longrightarrow \{0, \ldots, \lfloor 2M/\delta \rfloor\}$.

---

[2] For example in our DCRA-based construction, this would be equivalent to decryption.

Proof sketch: Modeling ϕ as a random function from $G \longrightarrow \{0, \ldots, \lfloor 2M/\delta \rfloor\}$, note that for any $a \in G$ we have $\Pr_{\phi \xleftarrow{\$} \mathcal{R}}[\phi(a) = 0] \approx \frac{\delta}{2M}$, and in particular the same is true of ϕ restricted to the coset $\langle g \rangle x$. With this in hand, the rest of the proof proceeds as that of [7, Propostion 3.2], using a few straightforward applications of the well known inequality $1 + x \leq e^x$.   □

Lastly, we remark that when the random function ϕ is replaced by a pseudo-random function (PRF), an analogous proposition holds, stating that no efficient adversary can find a sequence of instructions that would cause the probability to deviate substantially below $1 - \delta$. The important observation (present in [7]) is that by modularizing DDLog (in particular, this procedure accesses ϕ as an oracle, and does not need to know the seed), we can use any adversary that finds an input which is "bad" for a PRF ϕ to construct an adversary that distinguishes ϕ from random, thus breaking the security guarantee of the PRF.

4   Construction from **DCRA**

Using DDLog introduced in previous section as one of our sub-procedures, we will present an *HSS* scheme based on the circular security of Paillier's encryption which evaluates RMS programs (see Sect. 2.4). We make use of the following convenient notation, borrowed from [7]:

1. For input $x \in \mathbb{Z}_n$, $[\![x]\!]_\lambda$ is a Paillier encryption of x with respect to the secret key λ. That is, $[\![x]\!] := E(x) = \sigma = (1 + n)^x \cdot r^n \bmod n^2$ where $r \xleftarrow{\$} \mathbb{Z}_n^\times$, and λ is the unique integer in $[0, \ldots, n\varphi(n) - 1]$ satisfying Eq. (1). Note that $\sigma^\lambda = (1 + n)^x \in \mathbb{Z}_{n^2}^\times$ in this case.
2. $\langle y \rangle$ refers to *additive secret shares* of y, i.e., two values y_0, y_1 such that $y = y_0 + y_1$ *over the integers*.
3. Lastly, $\langle\!\langle y \rangle\!\rangle$ refers to *multiplicative secret shares* of $(1 + n)^y$ i.e., two values $h_0, h_1 \in \mathbb{Z}_{n^2}$ such that $h_0 \cdot h_1 = (1 + n)^y \bmod n^2$. These are intermediate values that arise during multiplication instructions, and will be converted back to $\langle y \rangle$ by the sub-routine DDLog.

Note that $[\![x]\!]_\lambda$ is a *global value* meaning that both parties receive the same value, in contrast to $\langle y \rangle$ and $\langle\!\langle y \rangle\!\rangle$, where each party has a different share. In the following we denote with $\lambda^{(i)}$ is the i-th bit of the binary representation of λ; that is, $\lambda = \sum_{i=0}^{\ell-1} 2^i \lambda^{(i)}$.

When evaluating an RMS program a dealer will share each input $x \in \mathbb{Z}_n$, in the following way $[\![x]\!]_\lambda$, $\{([\![x\lambda^{(i)}]\!]_\lambda\}_{i=0}^{\ell-1}, \langle x \rangle, \langle \lambda x \rangle$. Note that this will typically include encryptions of many bits of λ which is why we need the circular security assumption for Paillier.

Values y in memory locations will instead be stored as $\langle y \rangle, \langle \lambda y \rangle$. The original shares of all additive sharing are chosen randomly in $[-n^3, n^3]$ which result in a distribution that is statistically close to uniform for any shared value.

We first notice that additions are easily computed due to the homomorphic properties of Paillier's encryption and the additive secret sharing. One thing to note is that the size of the additive sharing increases by at most one bit after each addition since each player locally adds shares over the integers. This is not a major problem (since the size of the shares will still be polynomial by the end of the execution of the program). Furthermore, upon each multiplication step we will again have *small* additive shares for the product, as these shares are produced by DDLog (which outputs shares of *logarithmic* size in its polynomial running time). We discuss this further in what follows.

We now turn our attention to the computation of multiplication between an input x and a memory location value y. Since this value will be stored in a memory location (and so that it may be used again in subsequent multiplications) we need to compute $\langle xy \rangle$ and $\langle \lambda xy \rangle$.

The computation of $\langle xy \rangle$ uses $[\![x]\!]_\lambda$ and $\langle \lambda y \rangle$ via the following steps[3]

$$([\![x]\!]_\lambda, \langle \lambda y \rangle) \xrightarrow{\text{(a)}} \langle\!\langle xy \rangle\!\rangle \xrightarrow{\text{(b)}} \langle xy \rangle. \qquad (3)$$

A description of steps (a) and (b) follows:

(a) Let $z_1 + z_2 = \lambda y$ and $\sigma = [\![x]\!]_\lambda$. Then each player computes $\gamma_i = \sigma^{z_i} \bmod n^2$. Note that $\gamma_1 \cdot \gamma_2 = \sigma^{\lambda y} = (1+n)^{xy} \bmod n^2$. In other words $(\gamma_1, \gamma_2) = \langle\!\langle xy \rangle\!\rangle$. We denote with $(\gamma_1, \gamma_2) = \mathsf{MultShares}([\![x]\!]_\lambda, \langle \lambda y \rangle)$.

(b) Use the DDLog procedure on (γ_1, γ_2) with parameters δ, M (which will be specified by the RMS program being run on the shares) and random function ϕ. We denote with $\mathsf{ConvertShares}(\langle\!\langle xy \rangle\!\rangle, \delta, M, \phi)$ the pair

$$\langle xy \rangle = (-\mathsf{DDLog}(\gamma_1, \delta, M, \phi), \mathsf{DDLog}(\gamma_2^{-1}, \delta, M, \phi)).$$

Note that the first party negates the result of DDLog to maintain the invariant that the shares *add* to the shared value (DDLog output shares whose difference is the shared value), and that the second party must invert her share before invoking DDLog (see Fig. 1).

Then, to compute $\langle \lambda xy \rangle$ we use $\{([\![x \lambda^{(i)}]\!]_\lambda\}_{i=0}^{\ell-1}$ and $\langle \lambda y \rangle$ as follows

$$\left\{([\![x \lambda^{(i)}]\!]_\lambda, \langle \lambda y \rangle)\right\}_{i=0}^{\ell-1} \xrightarrow{\text{(c)}} \left\{\langle \lambda^{(i)} xy \rangle\right\}_{i=0}^{\ell-1} \xrightarrow{\text{(d)}} \langle \lambda xy \rangle. \qquad (4)$$

A description of steps (c) and (d) follows:

(c) ℓ invocations of step (a, b) above to compute each $\langle xy\lambda^{(i)} \rangle$.
(d) Each party will locally multiply the i-th share by the value 2^i and sum these shares together.

Note that if the shares in $\langle \lambda y \rangle$ are of size t at the beginning of this step, at the end they are of size at most $3t$ ($2t + \ell$ to be precise[4]). However these shares do

---

[3] Differently than in [7] we do not use $\langle y \rangle$ in the multiplication step – The additive sharing of y however needs to be stored so that we can compute the output at the end.

[4] $\ell \leq t$ since additive shares start of size ℓ and then they can grow as the result of addition operations.

not grow further since at the next step they are used "in the exponent", and the result of additive shares coming out of the DDLog procedure is always ℓ.

The following figures will present our homomorphic secret sharing scheme (Share, Eval).

Theorem 1. *Assuming that Paillier is circular secure, the scheme* (Share, Eval) *as described in Figs. 2 and 3 is a secure homomorphic secret sharing with error δ for the class of RMS programs.*

Homomorohic Secret Sharing Scheme-Share($1^k, x_1, \ldots, x_n$)

The inputs are security parameter 1^k and bits x_i for $i \in \{0, \ldots, n\}$.

- Sample k-bit prime numbers p, q, set $n = pq$ and $\varphi(n) = (p-1)(q-1)$.
- Compute $\lambda \in \mathbb{Z}_{n \cdot \varphi(n)}$ according to Equation 1. Let $\ell = \log(n^2)$.
- Sample a PRF $\phi : \mathbb{Z}_{n^2}^\times \longrightarrow \{0, \ldots, \lfloor 2M/\delta \rfloor\}$.
- For each input x_i sample the following;
  - $[\![x_i]\!]_\lambda$: A Paillier encryption of the integer x_i with public key n^2.
  - $\left[\!\!\left[\lambda^{(t)} x_i\right]\!\!\right]_\lambda$, $\forall t \in [l] := \{0, \ldots, l-1\}$: A Paillier encryption of the integer $\lambda^{(t)} x_i$ with public key n^2.
  - $\langle x_i \rangle \leftarrow$ AdditiveShare(x_i).
  - $\langle \lambda x_i \rangle \leftarrow$ AdditiveShare(λx_i) .
- Party b receives

$$\mathsf{Share}_b = \{\phi, ([\![x_i]\!]_\lambda, \{\left[\!\!\left[\lambda^{(t)} x_i\right]\!\!\right]_\lambda\}_{t \in [l]}, \langle x_i \rangle_b, \langle \lambda x_i \rangle_b)_{i \in [n]}\}.$$

Notation: The AdditiveShare operator on input x selects $\alpha \in [-n^3, n^3]$ uniformly at random and computes $\beta = x - \alpha$ over the integers. It sets $\langle x \rangle = (\alpha, \beta)$.

Fig. 2. Share for secret sharing an input x via the HSS scheme

The proof follows the same structure of the proof in [7] and we refer the reader to that proof. The only difference is that our additive sharings are *statistically* secure rather than *perfectly* secure as in [7]. This comes into play only in the proof of Lemma 3.11 in [7], specifically in the proof of the indistinguishability of Hybrid 0 versus Hybrid 1. In our simulation the shares of each player in Hybrid 1 are chosen uniformly at random in $[-n^3, n^3]$. For player P_1 this distribution is identical to the distribution in the real protocol (Hybrid 0). For player P_2 that's not the case, indeed the distribution of the shares of this player in the real protocol is uniform in $[-n^3 + x, n^3 + x]$ where x is the value being shared. It's not hard to see that the statistical distance between the two distributions is $\frac{2x}{2n^3}$ which is $O(\frac{1}{n})$ i.e. negligible in the worst case when $x = \lambda = O(n^2)$.

Homomorphic Share Evaluation of RMS Programs-$\mathsf{Eval}_{G,g}(b, \mathsf{Share}_b, P, \delta)$

Each party P_b runs on its secret share value Share_b, the RMS program P of size $\leq S$ with magnitude bound 1^M, error bound δ. Set $\delta' := \delta/((l+1)MS)$.

- Load inputs into memory:
  - $\langle y_j \rangle \leftarrow \langle x_i \rangle$.
  - $\langle \lambda y_j \rangle \leftarrow \langle \lambda x_i \rangle$.
  In which $\langle x_i \rangle$ and $\langle \lambda x_i \rangle$ are as in **Share**.
- Addition over memory values:
  - Compute $\langle y_k \rangle \leftarrow \langle y_i \rangle + \langle y_j \rangle$.
  - Compute $\langle \lambda y_k \rangle \leftarrow \langle \lambda y_i \rangle + \langle \lambda y_j \rangle$.
  Each party locally adds its shares over the integers.
- Multiplication of an input x_i and a memory value y_j:
  - For each $t \in [l]$,
    * Execute $\mathsf{MultShares}(\left[\!\left[\lambda^{(t)} x_i\right]\!\right]_\lambda, \langle \lambda y_j \rangle)$ and output $\langle\!\langle\!\langle \lambda^{(t)} x_i y_j \rangle\!\rangle\!\rangle$.
    * Run $\mathsf{ConvertShares}(\langle\!\langle\!\langle \lambda^{(t)} x_i y_j \rangle\!\rangle\!\rangle, \delta', M, \phi)$ and output $\langle \lambda^{(t)} x_i y_j \rangle$.
    * Set $\langle \lambda^{(t)} y_k \rangle \leftarrow \langle \lambda^{(t)} x_i y_j \rangle$.
  - Compute $\langle \lambda x_i y_j \rangle = \sum_{t \in [l]} 2^t \langle \lambda^{(t)} x_i y_j \rangle$.
  - Run $\mathsf{MultShares}([\![x_i]\!]_\lambda, \langle \lambda y_j \rangle)$ and output $\langle\!\langle x_i y_j \rangle\!\rangle$.
  - Execute $\mathsf{ConvertShares}(\langle\!\langle x_i y_j \rangle\!\rangle, \delta', M, \phi)$ and output $\langle x_i y_j \rangle$.
  - Set a new memory location k to value $y_k = x_i y_j$ by storing
    * Set $\langle \lambda y_k \rangle \leftarrow \langle \lambda x_i y_j \rangle$.
    * Set $\langle y_k \rangle \leftarrow \langle x_i y_j \rangle$.
- Output memory values:
  - If $b = 0$, set $\langle z \rangle \leftarrow \langle y_i \rangle$ otherwise let $\langle z \rangle$ be the additive inverse i.e., $\langle z \rangle \leftarrow -\langle y_i \rangle$.
  - Call the PRF ϕ on $(1+n)$ and shift the additive secret by its output meaning: $\langle z \rangle \leftarrow \langle z \rangle + \phi(1 + n)$.
  - $\langle O_j \rangle \leftarrow \langle z \rangle$.
  - Output $\langle O_j \rangle$.

Fig. 3. Procedures for performing homomorphic operations on secret shares

From Private to Public-Key. In the construction above, secret shares of an input x consisted of Paillier encryptions $[\![x]\!]_\lambda$, $\{[\![\lambda^{(i)} x]\!]_\lambda\}_{t \in [l]}$ and additive secret shares $\langle x \rangle, \langle \lambda x \rangle$. It is not immediately clear how one would generate those values without knowing the secret λ. However, by leveraging the homomorphic property of Paillier, we can generate these values for a secret sharing of x given only public key information which is independent of the input x. We can set up an initiative algorithm that samples a Paillier key pair (n, λ), encryptions of $\{[\![\lambda^i]\!]_\lambda\}_{t \in [l]}$, and evaluation key corresponding to additive secret shares of $\langle \lambda \rangle$. A user without any knowledge of the secret key can then compute $[\![x]\!]_\lambda$ and $\{[\![\lambda^i x]\!]_\lambda\}_{t \in [l]}$ using the public parameters and homomorphic property of the underlying encryption scheme. Values $\langle x \rangle$ and $\langle \lambda x \rangle$ can be computed by running Eval.

Optimizing the Generator. For protocols based on DDH, considerable practical performance improvements have been demonstrated in [9]. For example, by using the quadratic reciprocity theorem to choose pseudo-Mersenne primes p for which large prime order subgroups of $\mathbb{Z}_p^\times$ are generated by the integer 2, impressive speed-ups for DDLog are shown. Unfortunately, these techniques do not seem to transfer well to Paillier, as the analogous subgroups (for which 2 is a generator) would naturally be contained in the subgroup of n-th powers, rather than $\langle 1 + n \rangle$. While it might be the case that rejection sampling safe primes until $\langle 2 \rangle = \langle 1 + n \rangle$ is plausible,[5] and moreover such that the modulus n is close to a power of 2, it is not clear how this would affect security. However, we note that the "standard" generator $(1 + n)$ of the subgroup of order n actually admits a small optimization, which is as follows. Let h denote the share of one of the parties, which will be input into DDLog. First, write $h = an + b$, where $a, b < n$. Then notice that $h(1 + n) \equiv (a + b)n + b \bmod n^2$. Also, note that since the two inputs to corresponding DDLog invocations will be in the same coset of $\langle 1 + n \rangle$, the values b will also be identical for each share. So not only can we define the PRF ϕ to have domain $\mathbb{Z}_n$, more importantly we can substitute a multiplication (by $(1 + n) \bmod n^2$) with a simple *addition* of two values in $\mathbb{Z}_n$ (we only need to keep track of $(a + b) \bmod n$ for each step). Since performing the group multiplications was the most costly part of DDLog, this may yield considerable savings in computation.

5   Verifying Computations

The work of [7] mentions a "Las Vegas" style version of HSS in which one of the parties checks for the *potential* of the ConvertShares/DDLog procedure failing at each step. If there was never a chance of failure, then a special flag is set by this party to indicate that the results of the computation are guaranteed to be correct. This method was then shown to provide efficiency improvements for several applications. In particular, for *function secret sharing* applications (denoted "FSS" henceforth; see [6,8]) in which neither evaluator learns the output (e.g., PIR), this method can be used to reduce the number of parallel invocations required to attain a desired bound on the error probability of the protocol. In this section, we briefly describe a technique to *directly* check correctness which verifies the actual computation, rather than the absence of a potentially "risky" situation arising during DDLog. Since this method of checking does not produce false negatives (erroneously reporting that the protocol failed), we can reduce even further the number of required invocations for a desired overall error bound by a constant fraction. The price we pay for this (in addition to a negligible probability of a false positive), is some extra effort to compute the values used in the check. However, this effort depends *linearly* on the program size, whilst each repetition takes quadratic time in the program size. Hence, we achieve a savings in computation for large programs. We suspect this technique will be most useful in the case of Paillier-based

---

[5] At least the test is efficient if the factorization of the order of the group is known, as is the case if n was a product of safe primes.

constructions where some of the optimizations of [9] which reduce computation are not readily available. We nevertheless describe the method for both cases, as the ElGamal-based version has a simpler description.

The method works by constructing a sort of "hash" of the intermediate states of the computation in two ways – the states prescribed by multiplicative shares, and the states given by the additive shares after performing DDLog. We first consider the original case of ElGamal-encrypted inputs. Let $\mathbb{G}$ be a group of prime order q, and let $\langle g \rangle = \mathbb{G}$. Let m be the number of multiplication steps in the program being evaluated. Then we denote by $z_i = z_i^0 + z_i^1$ the exponents of the multiplicative sharing of the i-th multiplication step. That is, the players hold $g^{z_i^0}, g^{z_i^1}$. After running DDLog, the players will hold $\overline{z}_i^0, \overline{z}_i^1$, respectively. If the DDLog protocol was successful, it should be the case that $z_i = \overline{z}_i$ for $i = 0, \ldots, m-1$, where $\overline{z}_i = \overline{z}_i^0 + \overline{z}_i^1$. We now define polynomials $P, \overline{P} \in \mathbb{F}_q[X]$ for each of the two potential transcripts:

$$P(X) = \sum_{i=0}^{m-1} z_i X^i, \quad \overline{P}(X) = \sum_{i=0}^{m-1} \overline{z}_i X^i. \tag{5}$$

Note that each player ($j \in \{0,1\}$) can compute shares of these polynomials $P^j(X) = \sum z_i^j X^i$ and $\overline{P}^j(X) = \sum \overline{z}_i^j X^i$, so that $P = P^0 + P^1$ and $\overline{P} = \overline{P}^0 + \overline{P}^1$. Now consider the polynomial $(P - \overline{P}) \in \mathbb{F}_q[X]$. If DDLog succeeded at each multiplication step, then this polynomial is identically 0. On the other hand, if at any point DDLog failed, this polynomial will be non-zero, and of course will have degree at most $m-1$. Since q is prime, $(P - \overline{P})$ can have at most $m-1$ roots so that

$$\Pr_{\alpha \xleftarrow{\$} \mathbb{Z}_q} \left[(P - \overline{P})(\alpha) = 0 \right] \le \frac{m-1}{q} = \mathsf{negl}. \tag{6}$$

Thus, with high probability, $[(P - \overline{P})(\alpha) = 0] \iff$ [no errors occurred in DDLog]. For applications like PIR, this observation alone will suffice: we can modify the protocol to send a random α along with the query, and the servers will compute their shares of $(P_j - \overline{P}_j)(\alpha)$, which will be returned with the answers to the query. Note that the shares of $P(\alpha)$ must be computed in the exponent (which can nevertheless be done using Horner's rule), and the shares of $\overline{P}(\alpha)$ are computed directly in $\mathbb{Z}_q$. Hence the total additional cost is m exponentiations and m multiplications. We also mention a few optimizations. First, since each exponentiation will be to the same exponent α, we can pre-compute an addition chain for α and reuse this for all the exponentiations. Second, we note that it is not necessary to choose $\alpha \xleftarrow{\$} \mathbb{Z}_q$. We could for example choose $\alpha \xleftarrow{\$} \{1, \ldots, (m-1)2^{80}\}$ instead and still achieve the same effect as Eq. (6), meanwhile reducing the number of multiplications for exponentiations by a factor of two to four (for common choices of $\mathbb{G}$, as of this writing).

From Paillier Encryption. We can also adapt the above to work with Paillier. In this case, $(1 + n)$ will serve as our generator g, but since we now work in the larger, composite order group $\mathbb{Z}_{n^2}^{\times}$ (rather than $\langle g \rangle$), a few remarks are in order. First note that if $n = pq$ is an RSA modulus, then for $f \in \mathbb{Z}_n[X]$ with $\deg(f) = d$, f has at most d^2 roots. This follows at once from the Chinese Remainder Theorem: the roots $\alpha \in \mathbb{Z}_n$ of f are in bijective correspondence with the respective pairs of roots (α_p, α_q) of $f_p = (f \bmod p) \in \mathbb{Z}_p[X]$ and $f_q = (f \bmod q) \in \mathbb{Z}_q[X]$. Since $\deg(f_p), \deg(f_q) \leq d$ and since $\mathbb{Z}_p, \mathbb{Z}_q$ are fields, it follows that there can be at most d^2 roots of f in $\mathbb{Z}_n$, and thus the main point of (6) still holds (that is, $\Pr\left[(P - \overline{P})(\alpha) = 0\right] = \mathsf{negl}$).

We also remark on the importance of using Horner's rule in computing $(1 + n)^{P_j(\alpha)}$. Before, we were working in a cyclic group, and so the multiplicative shares were of the form $g^{P_j(\alpha)}$ for $j \in \{0, 1\}$. In this case, each player has a sequence of group elements γ_i^0, γ_i^1 such that $\gamma_i^0 \gamma_i^1 = (1 + n)^{z_i}$. Naturally we have

$$\left[\prod_{i=0}^{m-1} (\gamma_i^0)^{\alpha^i}\right] \left[\prod_{i=0}^{m-1} (\gamma_i^1)^{\alpha^i}\right] = (1 + n)^{P(\alpha)}$$

but at first glance, it seems that it might be somewhat expensive to raise the shares γ_i^j to the (large) exponents α^i: since the order of the group $(n\varphi(n))$ is *not public*, it might seem that this would take work proportional to the length of α^i, which is proportional to the multiplicative depth of the program. Fortunately using Horner's rule prevents us from having to compute or store α^i directly, and instead we can simply exponentiate by α repeatedly.[6] Lastly, since current values of n may be 2048 bits in length, choosing $\alpha \xleftarrow{\$} \{1, \ldots, (m-1)^2 \cdot 2^{80}\}$ will provide substantial savings. At this point, the protocol follows identically to the above version for ElGamal.

Applications. Applications of the above Las Vegas versions of ConvertShares include situations where it is unimportant to keep the intermediate states of the computation hidden from the receiver of the output. For example (as noted by [7]), using the scheme as an FSS to perform two-server PIR protocols. The benefit of this approach is that, for a target overall error bound, it further reduces the number of parallel repetitions of the protocol that must be performed to achieve it. Under the (generally wrong) assumption that the intermediate values of the computation are uniform in their domain, it is not hard to show that the probability of failure for a single round decreases by a factor of $\approx 1/2$. However, as noted this assumption is generally not true. What can be said, is that the smaller the intermediate values are (relative to their domain), the more of an advantage this method provides. For concreteness, an example: assuming half of the intermediate values are 0 and half are 1 (as would hold in expectation for the random case), then if the target error bound was 2^{-80} and the error for a single invocation *of the original* protocol was set to be $1/4$, then our protocol (assuming random intermediate values) would reduce this failure rate to $1/8$ and thus the required number of invocations would decrease from 40 to 27. Again,

---

[6] We note that naive polynomial evaluation could also be made reasonable by raising to $\alpha^i \bmod n$, since in any abelian group, if $\prod h_i \in H < G$ with $|H| = n$, then for any $k \in \mathbb{Z}$, $(\prod h_i)^k = (\prod h_i)^{k \bmod n} = \prod(h_i^{k \bmod n})$.

we note that while the computation cost increases, this increase is *linear* in the multiplicative depth of the program (and polynomial in a security parameter) which provides an advantage for large programs, especially for Paillier-based constructions where many of the speed-ups for DDLog from [9] do not seem available.

6 Conclusions and Future Work

We extend recent breakthrough results by Boyle et al. [7,9], which under the DDH Assumption, present homomorphic secret sharing and secure function evaluation protocols for branching programs with low communication complexity. We show how to construct similar protocols based on the circular security of the Paillier encryption scheme. In the process we extended their "distributed discrete log" procedures to work over any finite group, and in particular when the discrete log is being sought in a subgroup of unknown order. This technical contribution could be of independent interest and may lead to techniques for proving the security of such protocols under larger classes of computational assumptions.

Our result leaves several interesting open problems:

1. Analyze the circular security assumption on the Paillier encryption scheme and/or come up with alternative schemes with the same functionality that can be proven to be circular secure. This seems a non-trivial question, and as shown by [32], there is no chance for proving a "blanket" result for bit encryption, as there is no *black-box* reduction of circular security to semantic security. Indeed, there have been many results in the recent literature showing separations between the two notions under various assumptions [1,2,5,10,22, 25,27,34].
2. Construct Homomorphic Secret Sharing based on other assumptions. One interesting question here is if we can have HSS based *directly* on LWE which results in more efficient protocols than those based on FHE.
3. Extend the class of functions for which we can break the "circuit barrier" for communication complexity in secure MPC.
4. Explore further optimizations to the Paillier-based protocol. In particular, the work of [9] makes use of PKI for the setup phase, in place of performing general purpose MPC. Their technique seems to leverage heavily a sort of symmetry that is present in ElGamal, which is not shared by the Paillier encryption scheme: in particular, they make use of the fact that many different secret keys can exist for a single set of common parameters (the group $\mathbb{G}$ and generator g). With Paillier, the modulus n uniquely determines secret information, so it would seem new ideas are required.
5. Empirical data regarding implementations may also be of interest to have a better idea of at what point various trade-offs make sense (for example, making use of the verification process from Sect. 5 to reduce the number of repetitions vs trying to squash the degree using randomizing polynomials [3,23]).

References

1. Acar, T., Belenkiy, M., Bellare, M., Cash, D.: Cryptographic agility and its relation to circular encryption. In: Gilbert, H. (ed.) EUROCRYPT 2010. LNCS, vol. 6110, pp. 403–422. Springer, Heidelberg (2010). doi:10.1007/978-3-642-13190-5_21
2. Alamati, N., Peikert, C.: Three's compromised too: circular insecurity for any cycle length from (Ring-)LWE. In: Robshaw, M., Katz, J. (eds.) CRYPTO 2016. LNCS, vol. 9815, pp. 659–680. Springer, Heidelberg (2016). doi:10.1007/978-3-662-53008-5_23
3. Applebaum, B., Ishai, Y., Kushilevitz, E.: Computationally private randomizing polynomials and their applications. Comput. Complex. **15**(2), 115–162 (2006)
4. Ben-Or, M., Goldwasser, S., Wigderson, A.: Completeness theorems for non-cryptographic fault-tolerant distributed computation (extended abstract). In: STOC, pp. 1–10 (1988)
5. Bishop, A., Hohenberger, S., Waters, B.: New circular security counterexamples from decision linear and learning with errors. In: Iwata, T., Cheon, J.H. (eds.) ASIACRYPT 2015. LNCS, vol. 9453, pp. 776–800. Springer, Heidelberg (2015). doi:10.1007/978-3-662-48800-3_32
6. Boyle, E., Gilboa, N., Ishai, Y.: Function secret sharing. In: Oswald, E., Fischlin, M. (eds.) EUROCRYPT 2015. LNCS, vol. 9057, pp. 337–367. Springer, Heidelberg (2015). doi:10.1007/978-3-662-46803-6_12
7. Boyle, E., Gilboa, N., Ishai, Y.: Breaking the circuit size barrier for secure computation under DDH. In: Robshaw, M., Katz, J. (eds.) CRYPTO 2016. LNCS, vol. 9814, pp. 509–539. Springer, Heidelberg (2016). doi:10.1007/978-3-662-53018-4_19
8. Boyle, E., Gilboa, N., Ishai, Y.: Function secret sharing: improvements and extensions. In: Proceedings of the 2016 ACM SIGSAC Conference on Computer and Communications Security, pp. 1292–1303. ACM (2016)
9. Boyle, E., Gilboa, N., Ishai, Y.: Group-based secure computation: optimizing rounds, communication, and computation. In: Coron, J.-S., Nielsen, J.B. (eds.) EUROCRYPT 2017. LNCS, vol. 10211, pp. 163–193. Springer, Cham (2017). doi:10.1007/978-3-319-56614-6_6
10. Cash, D., Green, M., Hohenberger, S.: New definitions and separations for circular security. In: Fischlin, M., Buchmann, J., Manulis, M. (eds.) PKC 2012. LNCS, vol. 7293, pp. 540–557. Springer, Heidelberg (2012). doi:10.1007/978-3-642-30057-8_32
11. Chaum, D., Crépeau, C., Damgard, I.: Multiparty unconditionally secure protocols. In: Proceedings of the Twentieth Annual ACM symposium on Theory of Computing, pp. 11–19. ACM (1988)
12. Chor, B., Gilboa, N.: Computationally private information retrieval. In: Proceedings of the Twenty-Ninth Annual ACM symposium on Theory of Computing, pp. 304–313. ACM (1997)
13. Chor, B., Kushilevitz, E., Goldreich, O., Sudan, M.: Private information retrieval. J. ACM **45**(6), 965–981 (1998)
14. Cohen, J.D., Fischer, M.J.: A robust and verifiable cryptographically secure election scheme (extended abstract). In: 26th Annual Symposium on Foundations of Computer Science, Portland, Oregon, USA, pp. 372–382, 21–23 October 1985
15. Damgård, I., Jurik, M.: A length-flexible threshold cryptosystem with applications. In: Safavi-Naini, R., Seberry, J. (eds.) ACISP 2003. LNCS, vol. 2727, pp. 350–364. Springer, Heidelberg (2003). doi:10.1007/3-540-45067-X_30
16. Damgård, I., Jurik, M.: A generalisation, a simplification and some applications of Paillier's probabilistic public-key system. In: Kim, K. (ed.) PKC 2001. LNCS, vol. 1992, pp. 119–136. Springer, Heidelberg (2001). doi:10.1007/3-540-44586-2_9

17. Gentry, C.: Fully homomorphic encryption using ideal lattices. In: Proceedings of the 41st Annual ACM Symposium on Theory of Computing, STOC 2009, pp. 169–178. ACM, New York (2009)
18. Gentry, C., Halevi, S.: Implementing gentry's fully-homomorphic encryption scheme. Cryptology ePrint Archive, Report 2010/520 (2010)
19. Gentry, C., Halevi, S., Smart, N.P.: Fully homomorphic encryption with polylog overhead. In: Pointcheval, D., Johansson, T. (eds.) EUROCRYPT 2012. LNCS, vol. 7237, pp. 465–482. Springer, Heidelberg (2012). doi:10.1007/978-3-642-29011-4_28
20. Goldreich, O., Micali, S., Wigderson, A.: How to play any mental game or a completeness theorem for protocols with honest majority. In: STOC, pp. 218–229 (1987)
21. Goldwasser, S., Micali, S.: Probabilistic encryption. JCSS 28(2), 270–299 (1984)
22. Goyal, R., Koppula, V., Waters, B.: Separating IND-CPA and circular security for unbounded length key cycles. In: Fehr, S. (ed.) PKC 2017. LNCS, vol. 10174, pp. 232–246. Springer, Heidelberg (2017). doi:10.1007/978-3-662-54365-8_10
23. Ishai, Y., Kushilevitz, E.: Randomizing polynomials: a new representation with applications to round-efficient secure computation. In: Proceedings of the 41st Annual Symposium on Foundations of Computer Science, pp. 294–304. IEEE (2000)
24. Jurik, M.J.: Extensions to the Paillier cryptosystem with applications to cryptological protocols. In: BRICS (2003)
25. Koppula, V., Waters, B.: Circular security separations for arbitrary length cycles from LWE. In: Robshaw, M., Katz, J. (eds.) CRYPTO 2016. LNCS, vol. 9815, pp. 681–700. Springer, Heidelberg (2016). doi:10.1007/978-3-662-53008-5_24
26. Kushilevitz, E., Ostrovsky, R.: Replication is not needed: single database, computationally-private information retrieval. In: FOCS, pp. 364–373 (1997)
27. Marcedone, A., Orlandi, C.: Obfuscation ⇒ (IND-CPA security ⇏ circular security). In: Abdalla, M., De Prisco, R. (eds.) SCN 2014. LNCS, vol. 8642, pp. 77–90. Springer, Cham (2014). doi:10.1007/978-3-319-10879-7_5
28. Naccache, D., Stern, J.: A new public key cryptosystem based on higher residues. In: Proceedings of the 5th ACM Conference on Computer and Communications Security, pp. 59–66. ACM (1998)
29. Naehrig, M., Lauter, K., Vaikuntanathan, V.: Can homomorphic encryption be practical? In: Proceedings of the 3rd ACM Workshop on Cloud Computing Security Workshop, pp. 113–124. ACM (2011)
30. Okamoto, T., Uchiyama, S.: A new public-key cryptosystem as secure as factoring. In: Nyberg, K. (ed.) EUROCRYPT 1998. LNCS, vol. 1403, pp. 308–318. Springer, Heidelberg (1998). doi:10.1007/BFb0054135
31. Paillier, P.: Public-key cryptosystems based on composite degree residuosity classes. In: Stern, J. (ed.) EUROCRYPT 1999. LNCS, vol. 1592, pp. 223–238. Springer, Heidelberg (1999). doi:10.1007/3-540-48910-X_16
32. Rothblum, R.D.: On the circular security of bit-encryption. In: Sahai, A. (ed.) TCC 2013. LNCS, vol. 7785, pp. 579–598. Springer, Heidelberg (2013). doi:10.1007/978-3-642-36594-2_32
33. Shamir, A.: How to share a secret. Commun. ACM 22(11), 612–613 (1979)
34. Wichs, D., Zirdelis, G.: Obfuscating compute-and-compare programs under LWE. Technical report, Cryptology ePrint Archive, Report 2017/276 (2017). http://eprint.iacr.org/2017/276
35. Yao, A.C.C.: Protocols for secure computations (extended abstract). In: FOCS, pp. 160–164 (1982)
36. Yao, A.C.C.: How to generate and exchange secrets. In: 27th Annual Symposium on Foundations of Computer Science, pp. 162–167. IEEE (1986)

Fuzzy Public-Key Encryption
Based on Biometric Data

Hui Cui[1]([✉]), Man Ho Au[2], Baodong Qin[3], Robert H. Deng[4], and Xun Yi[1]

[1] School of Science, RMIT, Melbourne, Australia
hui.cui@rmit.edu.au
[2] Department of Computing, Hong Kong Polytechnic University,
Hong Kong, China
[3] National Engineering Laboratory for Wireless Security,
Xi'an University of Posts and Telecommunications, Xi'an, China
[4] School of Information Systems, Singapore Management University,
Singapore, Singapore

Abstract. Biometric data is an inherent representation of a human user, and it would be highly desirable to derive a private key of a public-key cryptographic scheme from a user's biometric input such that the user does not need to remember any password or carry any device to store the private key and is able to enjoy all benefits of the public-key cryptographic scheme. In this paper, we introduce a notion called fuzzy public-key encryption (FPKE), which is a public-key encryption (PKE) scheme that accepts a piece of fuzzy data (i.e., a noisy version of the original biometric data) as the private key to decrypt the ciphertext. Compared to the traditional PKE scheme where a private key is usually stored in a device (e.g., a USB token), an FPKE scheme does not need to use any device for the storage of the private key. We first define a formal security model for FPKE, and then give generic constructions of FPKE based on the cryptographic primitives of linear sketch and PKE with some special properties.

Keywords: Biometric input · Fuzzy data · Fuzzy public-key encryption

1 Introduction

In a traditional public-key encryption (PKE) scheme, each user has a pair of public and private keys. If a user, say Alice, is a privileged recipient of a ciphertext, i.e., the underlying message of this ciphertext is encrypted under the public key of Alice, Alice can decrypt the ciphertext using her private key. Since the leakage of the private key is fatal to any PKE scheme, it is crucial for all users to keep their private keys in secure manners. A widely accepted method is to store the private key in a physical device such as a smart card or a USB token, and ask the user to

---

B. Qin–State Key Laboratory of Cryptology, P.O.Box 5159, Beijing 100878, China.

© Springer International Publishing AG 2017
T. Okamoto et al. (Eds.): ProvSec 2017, LNCS 10592, pp. 400–409, 2017.
https://doi.org/10.1007/978-3-319-68637-0_24

memorize a password to activate the key [3]. However, it is inconvenient and challenging for users to always carry their hardware tokens (storing their private keys) and remember their passwords (for the key activation).

An ideal approach is to use the biometric data (e.g., fingerprints and irises [1]) as the private key since a piece of biometric data is unique to an individual, and thus it provides a convenient and secure way to link the private key and the user. There are already off the shelf sensors that can collect multiple biometric inputs from which enough entropy is able to be obtained at one time, and it is possible that in the near future longer strings will be generated from biometric inputs [9]. Unfortunately, biometric data is fuzzy (or noisy) and varies each time it is collected, and hence it cannot be directly used as a private key in a traditional PKE scheme. Seemingly, a fuzzy extractor [2] addresses this issue as it extracts a nearly uniform string from the biometric input and the extraction is error-tolerant as long as the biometric input remains sufficiently close to the original one, but it needs a piece of auxiliary data called a helper string in the extraction process, thereby still requiring a user to carry a device or rely on a remote equipment [9] to store the helper string[1]. To overcome the crux, Takahashi et al. [9] introduced the notion of fuzzy signature, which is a signature scheme that generates a signature using the biometric data as a signing key without requiring any helper string. In this paper, motivated by the results in [9], we propose a cryptographic primitive called fuzzy public-key encryption (FPKE) in which a user's biometric input is directly used as the private key to decrypt encrypted messages without any auxiliary information. During the rest of the paper, we will use the terms fuzzy data, noisy data, and biometric input (or data) interchangeably.

1.1 Challenges and Contributions

In a standard PKE scheme, the decryption algorithm takes the private key sk and a ciphertext CT as the input and outputs either a message M or a failure symbol $\perp$. In an FPKE scheme, however, the decryption algorithm takes a piece of fuzzy data x and a ciphertext CT as the input and outputs either a message M or a failure symbol $\perp$. It is worthy noting that FPKE is different from fuzzy identity-based encryption (FIBE) [8] in that the former treats the fuzzy data as the private key, while the latter uses the noisy data as the public key and the private key is derived from the measurement of the biometric data.

In brevity, an FPKE scheme consists of a key generation algorithm KeyGen that takes a piece of fuzzy data x as the input and outputs a public key pk, an encryption algorithm Encrypt that takes the public key pk and a message M as the input and outputs a ciphertext CT, and a decryption algorithm Decrypt that takes another piece of fuzzy data x' and a ciphertext CT as the input and outputs either a message M or a failure symbol $\perp$. Clearly, FPKE has an edge over PKE in that it does not require a device to store a user's private key.

With reference to [7,9], it is necessary for FPKE to be considered under a *fuzzy key setting* which is equipped with a mechanism of linear encoding and

---

[1] For details on the limitations of helper strings, please refer to [9].

error correction on the noisy data called *linear sketch* [7]. A fuzzy key setting
formalizes the setting over the type of the fuzzy data to be considered, e.g.,
the metric space which fuzzy data belongs to, the threshold which two sampled
fuzzy data are considered close or far with, the distribution which each piece of
fuzzy data is assumed to be chosen from, the fluctuation model of the fuzzy data,
and so on. A linear sketch scheme is associated with a fuzzy key setting and an
abelian group (e.g., $(\mathcal{K}, +)$, where $\mathcal{K}$ is the space for the element and $+$ denotes
the additive operation), and has two main algorithms, one called Sketch used to
generate a sketch c of an element $s \in \mathcal{K}$ using the fuzzy data item x and the
other named DiffRec used to output the difference $\triangle s = s - s'$ with the input
of two sketches c and c' (generated by the Sketch algorithm on inputs $s \in \mathcal{K}$, x
and $s' \in \mathcal{K}$, x', respectively). In this paper, the FPKE schemes are considered
under the fuzzy key setting and the linear sketch schemes defined in [7].

Another basic building block for an FPKE scheme is a traditional PKE
scheme but with two additional properties: key determinability and homomorphism. Key determinability means that the public key in the PKE scheme can be
derived from the private key via a deterministic algorithm, which can be satisfied
by many PKE schemes. Homomorphism is a bit more involved, which requires
that given a public key pk (corresponding to a private key sk), a shifted private
key $\triangle sk$, it is easy to output a public key pk' (corresponding to a private key
$sk' = sk + \triangle sk$). In addition, given a ciphertext CT on a message M targeted
for a public key pk, a shifted private key $\triangle sk$, it is easy to output a ciphertext
CT$'$ targeted for a public key pk' under the same message M.

Combining the linear sketch scheme and a PKE scheme with the additional
properties, we propose generic constructions for FPKE under the defined fuzzy
key setting. In summary, the contributions in this paper are twofold.

- We introduce a formal security definition for fuzzy public-key encryption
  (FPKE) under a specific fuzzy key setting.
- We present generic constructions of FPKE under a fuzzy key setting based
  on PKE schemes satisfying two additional properties and secure linear sketch
  schemes.

1.2   Related Work

Fuzzy Signature. Takahashi et al. [9] first introduced the notion of fuzzy signature, which is different from the standard signature in that it uses a piece
of fuzzy data (e.g., biometric data) as a private key but does not require any
auxiliary information (which is also called a helper string in a fuzzy extractor)
to generate signatures. However, in their generic construction, the fuzzy data is
assumed to be distributed uniformly, the public parameter is very large (proportional to the security parameter), and it requires bilinear groups, which adds
difficulties for the implementation in practice. Matsuda et al. [7] improved the
results in [9] by proposing another generic construction on fuzzy signature but
with relaxed requirements on the building blocks applied in [9], and gave a more
efficient fuzzy signature scheme.

Fuzzy Identity-Based Encryption. Sahai and Waters [8] put forth a notion called fuzzy identity-based encryption (FIBE), which is also known as attribute-based encryption (ABE), to enable encryption using biometric inputs as identities. Due to the error-tolerance property of the FIBE scheme, it allows the use of biometric inputs, which inherently have some noises each time they are sampled, in the encryption. Notice that FPKE is different from FIBE, because the former uses the noisy data as the private key, while the latter uses the fuzzy data as the public key and the private key is derived from the measurement of the biometric data.

1.3 Organization

The rest of this paper is organized as follows. In Sect. 2, we briefly describe the notations and definitions related to this work. In Sect. 3, we describe the system framework and security model of FPKE. In Sect. 4, we present generic constructions on FPKE, and analyze the security of them. Finally, we conclude this paper in Sect. 5.

2 Preliminaries

In this section, we briefly review the notations and some basic definitions that are to be used in this paper.

2.1 Basic Notations

Throughout this paper, all vectors are expressed in bold fonts such as $\mathbf{x}$, and the security parameter is denoted by λ.

Let $\mathbb{N}$, $\mathbb{Z}$ and $\mathbb{R}$ denote the sets of all natural numbers, all integers and all real numbers, respectively. If $n \in \mathbb{N}$, then $[n] := \{1, ..., n\}$. If $a \in \mathbb{R}$, then $\lfloor a \rceil$ means the integer that is the closest to a. In addition, if $\mathbf{a} = (a_1, a_2, ...)$, then $\lfloor \mathbf{a} \rceil := (\lfloor a_1 \rceil, \lfloor a_2 \rceil, ...)$.

Denote $x \leftarrow y$ as y is assigned to x. If S is a finite set, then $|S|$ denotes its size, and $x \leftarrow_R S$ denotes that x is uniformly chosen at random from S. If Φ is a distribution over some set, then $x \leftarrow_R \Phi$ denotes that x is chosen in terms of the distribution Φ. Assuming that $f : D \rightarrow R$ is a function and $y \in R$ is an element, then $f^{-1}(y)$ represents the set of pre-images of y under f, i.e., $f^{-1}(y) := \{x \in D | f(x) = y\}$. If x and y are bit-strings, then $|x|$ denotes the bit-length of x, and $(x||y)$ denotes the concatenation of x and y.

A function $f(\cdot) : \mathbb{N} \rightarrow [0, 1]$ is said to be negligible if for all positive polynomials $p(\cdot)$ and all sufficiently large λ, then $f(\lambda) < \frac{1}{p(\lambda)}$ holds.

2.2 Fuzzy Key Setting

We recall the formalization of the fuzzy key setting in [7,9] as follows. Formally, a fuzzy key setting $\mathcal{F}$ consists of $((d, X), t, \mathcal{X}, \Phi, \epsilon)$, of which (d, X) is the metric space with X (we assume that it constitutes an abelian group) being the space to which a fuzzy data item x belongs to and $d : X^2 \to \mathbb{R}$ being the corresponding distance function, $t \in \mathbb{R}$ is a threshold value determined by a security parameter λ, $\mathcal{X}$ is a distribution of fuzzy data over X, Φ is an error distribution, and $\epsilon \in [0,1]$ is an error parameter representing FRR. Notice that the false acceptance rate (FAR) and the false rejection rate (FRR) are determined based on the threshold value t. It is required that FAR $:= \Pr[x, x' \leftarrow_R \mathcal{X} : d(x, x') < t]$ is negligible in the security parameter λ. Also, for all pieces of fuzzy data $x \in X$, FRR $:= \Pr[e \leftarrow_R \Phi : d(x, x + e) \geq t] \leq \epsilon$.

3   Framework and Security Model

In this section, after presenting the framework of FPKE, we describe its security model in detail.

3.1   Framework

An FPKE scheme for a fuzzy key setting $\mathcal{F}$ is composed of the following four algorithms: a setup algorithm Setup, a key generation algorithm KeyGen, an encryption algorithm Encrypt and a decryption algorithm Decrypt.

- Setup(1^λ) $\to$ *par*. On input the security parameter λ, this algorithm outputs the public parameter *par*, which includes the fuzzy key setting $\mathcal{F} = ((d, X), t, \mathcal{X}, \Phi, \epsilon)$.
- KeyGen(*par*, x) $\to$ pk_f. On input the public parameter *par* and a fuzzy data item $x \in X$, this algorithm outputs a public key pk_f.
- Encrypt(*par*, pk_f, M) $\to$ CT. On input the public parameter *par*, the public key pk_f and a message M (in the message space), this algorithm outputs a ciphertext CT.
- Decrypt(*par*, pk_f, x, CT) $\to$ $M/\bot$. On input the pubic parameter *par*, the public key pk_f, a fuzzy data item $x' \in X$ and a ciphertext CT, this algorithm outputs a message M or a failure symbol $\bot$.

We say that an FPKE scheme with a fuzzy key setting $\mathcal{F}$ is correct, meaning that for all security parameters $\lambda \in \mathbb{N}$, all fuzzy data x, $x' \in X$ such that $d(x, x') < t$, all messages M in the message space, if *par* $\leftarrow$ Setup(1^λ), $pk_f \leftarrow$ KeyGen(*par*, x), CT $\leftarrow$ Encrypt(*par*, pk_f, M), we have that Decrypt(*par*, pk_f, x', CT) $= M$.

3.2   Security Model

Similar to the security definition of a PKE scheme, a secure FPKE scheme is required to be indistinguishable under the universal error model of a fuzzy key setting. An FPKE scheme under a fuzzy key setting $\mathcal{F}$ is said to be indistinguishable under chosen ciphertext attacks (IND-CCA secure) if for any probabilistic polynomial time (PPT) adversary $\mathcal{A}$, the advantage function

$$\mathbf{Adv}_{\mathrm{FPKE},\mathcal{A}}^{\mathrm{ind\text{-}cca}}(\lambda) = \Pr \left[b' = b \begin{array}{|l} par \leftarrow \mathrm{Setup}(1^\lambda) \\ x^* \leftarrow_R \mathcal{X}, \ b \leftarrow \{0,1\} \\ pk_f^* \leftarrow \mathrm{KeyGen}(par, x^*) \\ (M_0, M_1, state) \leftarrow \mathcal{A}^{\mathcal{O}_{\mathrm{Dec}(\cdot)}}(par, pk_f^*) \\ \mathrm{CT}^* \leftarrow \mathrm{Encrypt}(par, pk_f^*, M_b) \\ b' \leftarrow \mathcal{A}^{\mathcal{O}_{\mathrm{Dec}(\cdot)}}(par, pk_f^*, M_0, M_1, state, \mathrm{CT}^*) \end{array} \right] - 1/2$$

is negligible in the security parameter λ, where $|M_0| = |M_1|$, and $\mathcal{O}_{\mathrm{Dec}(\cdot)}$ is the decryption oracle which takes the public parameter par, the public key pk_f^*, a piece of fuzzy data x^* and a ciphertext CT as the input and outputs a message $M \leftarrow \mathrm{Decrypt}(par, pk_f^*, x^*, \mathrm{CT})$ with the restriction that for any query on a ciphertext CT to the $\mathcal{O}_{\mathrm{Dec}(\cdot)}$ oracle, CT should not be equal to CT^*.

4   Fuzzy Public-Key Encryption

In this section, we present generic constructions of FPKE, and analyze their security.

4.1   Public-Key Encryption

For the PKE scheme (e.g., [4]) to be used in this paper for the construction of an FPKE scheme, we define several additional properties as follows.

- Key Deterministic. It means that the key generation algorithm KeyGen first randomly chooses a private key sk_{pke} (from the space of private keys), and then computes the corresponding public key pk_{pke} (deterministically from sk_{pke}), which is known as Key Generation Process in [7]. Formally, a PKE scheme is key deterministic if the public parameter par_{pke} generated by the Setup algorithm specifies the space of private keys $\mathcal{K}_{pke}$, and there exists a deterministic algorithm KeyGen' such that the key generation algorithm KeyGen can be defined as KeyGen(par_{pke}) : $[sk_{pke} \leftarrow_R \mathcal{K}_{pke}; pk_{pke} \leftarrow$ KeyGen'(par_{pke}, sk_{pke}); Return (sk_{pke}, pk_{pke})].
- Homomorphic. A PKE scheme is homomorphic if it meets the following properties.
  - For the public parameter par_{pke} generated by the Setup algorithm, there is an abelian group ($\mathcal{K}_{pke}, +$) associated with the private key space $\mathcal{K}_{pke}$.
  - There exists a deterministic algorithm $M_{pk_{pke}}$ which takes the public parameter par_{pke} (output by the Setup algorithm), a public key pk_{pke} (created by the KeyGen algorithm) and a shift $\triangle sk \in \mathcal{K}_{pke}$ as the input, and outputs a shifted public key pk'_{pke}. Formally, for all par_{pke} output by the Setup algorithm, all $sk_{pke}, \triangle sk \in \mathcal{K}_{pke}$, it holds that KeyGen'($par_{pke}$, $sk_{pke} + \triangle sk$) = $M_{pk_{pke}}(par_{pke}$, KeyGen'(par_{pke}, sk_{pke}), $\triangle sk$).

- There exists a deterministic algorithm M_{en} which takes the public parameter par_{pke} (output by the Setup algorithm), a public key pk_{pke} (output by the KeyGen algorithm), a ciphertext CT and a shifted private key $\triangle sk \leftarrow \mathcal{K}_{pke}$ as the input, and outputs a shifted ciphertext CT'. Formally, for all $sk_{pke}, \triangle sk \in \mathcal{K}_{pke}$, the distributions $\{\text{CT}' \leftarrow \text{PKE.Encrypt}(par_{pke}, \text{KeyGen}'(par_{pke}, sk_{pke} + \triangle sk), M) : \text{CT}'\}$, and $\{\text{CT} \leftarrow \text{PKE.Encrypt}(par_{pke}, pk_{pke}, M); \text{CT}' \leftarrow M_{en}(par_{pke}, \triangle sk, \text{CT}) : \text{CT}'\}$ are identical. In addition, we require that for all public parameters par_{pke} (output by the PKE.Setup algorithm), all keys $sk_{pke}, \triangle sk \in \mathcal{K}_{pke}$, all ciphertext CT such that $\text{PKE.Decrypt}(par_{pke}, \text{CT}, pk_{pke}, sk_{pke}) = M$, it holds that $\text{PKE.Decrypt}(par_{pke}, \text{CT}', \text{KeyGen}'(par_{pke}, sk_{pke} + \triangle sk), sk_{pke} + \triangle sk) = M$, where $\text{CT}' \leftarrow M_{en}(par_{pke}, \triangle sk, \text{CT})$.

There exists PKE schemes, such as the ElGamal encryption scheme [4] and the tag-based encryption scheme [6], that meet the above requirements.

4.2   Generic Construction

Denote $\mathcal{F} = ((d, X), t, \mathcal{X}, \varPhi, \epsilon)$ as a fuzzy key setting. Let PKE = (PKE.Setup, PKE.KeyGen, PKE.Encrypt, PKE.Decrypt) be a selective-tag IND-CCA secure public-key encryption scheme with $\mathcal{K}$ being the space of private keys which is key deterministic and homomorphic. Assume that $\mathcal{S} = (\mathcal{S}.\text{Setup}, \mathcal{S}.\text{Sketch}, \mathcal{S}.\text{DiffRec})$ is a linear sketch scheme for the fuzzy key setting $\mathcal{F}$ (as defined in [7]), and Sig = (Sig.KeyGen, Sig.Sign, Sig.Verify) is a strong one-time signature scheme (as defined in [5]). A fuzzy public-key encryption scheme FPKE associated with the fuzzy key setting $\mathcal{F}$ is composed of the following algorithms.

- Setup. This algorithm takes the security parameter λ as the input. It first defines a fuzzy key setting $\mathcal{F} = ((d, X), t, \mathcal{X}, \varPhi, \epsilon)$. It then runs $par_{pke} \leftarrow_R \text{PKE.Setup}(1^\lambda)$, and $par_\mathcal{S} \leftarrow_R \mathcal{S}.\text{Setup}(\mathcal{K}, +)$. It outputs the public parameter $par = (par_{pke}, par_\mathcal{S}, \mathcal{F})$.
- KeyGen. This algorithm takes the public parameter par and a piece of fuzzy data $x \in X$ as the input. It parses $par = (par_{pke}, par_\mathcal{S})$, runs $sk \leftarrow_R \mathcal{K}$, $pk \leftarrow \text{PKE.KeyGen}'(par_{pke}, sk)$, $c \leftarrow_R \mathcal{S}.\text{Sketch}(par_\mathcal{S}, sk, x)$, and outputs the public key $pk_f = (pk, c)$.
- Encrypt. This algorithm takes the public parameter par, the public key pk_f and a message M as the input. It parses $par = (par_{pke}, par_\mathcal{S})$, $pk_f = (pk, c)$. Then it runs the Sign.KeyGen algorithm to generate a signing key ssk and a verification key svk, $\text{CT} \leftarrow_R \text{PKE.Encrypt}(par_{pke}, pk, svk, M)$, and the Sig.Sign algorithm on CT to create a signature σ using the signing key ssk. It outputs the ciphertext $\widetilde{\text{CT}} = (svk, \text{CT}, \sigma)$.
- Decrypt. This algorithm takes the public parameter par, the public key pk_f, the fuzzy data item $x' \in X$ and a ciphertext $\widetilde{\text{CT}}$ as the input. It parses $par = (par_{pke}, par_\mathcal{S})$, $pk_f = (pk, c)$, $\widetilde{\text{CT}} = (svk, \text{CT}, \sigma)$. If σ is a valid signature on CT under svk, it runs $sk' \leftarrow_R \mathcal{K}$, $pk' \leftarrow \text{PKE.KeyGen}'(par_{pke}, sk')$, $c' \leftarrow_R \mathcal{S}.\text{Sketch}(par_\mathcal{S}, sk', x')$, $\triangle sk \leftarrow \mathcal{S}.\text{DiffRec}(par_\mathcal{S}, c, c')$, $\text{PKE.Decrypt}(par_{pke}, M_{en}(par_{pke}, \triangle sk, \text{CT}), pk', sk') = M$, and outputs the message M.

Theorem 1. *Assuming that PKE with the key deterministic and homomorphic properties is selective-tag IND-CCA secure, Sig is strongly unforgeable, and $\mathcal{S}$ is a secure linear sketch scheme for a fuzzy key setting $\mathcal{F}$, then the above FPKE scheme for the fuzzy key setting $\mathcal{F}$ is IND-CCA secure.*

Proof. Assuming that there exists an adversary algorithm $\mathcal{A}$ that breaks the IND-CCA security of the FPKE scheme, then we can build an adversary algorithm $\mathcal{A}'$ that breaks the selective-tag IND-CCA security of the key deterministic and homomorphic PKE scheme, the strong unforgeability of the Sig scheme, or the security of the linear sketch scheme $\mathcal{S}$. Let $\mathcal{B}'$ be the challenger algorithm in the underlying PKE scheme.

- Setup. Algorithm $\mathcal{A}'$ creates a pair of signing and verification keys (ssk^*, svk^*) by running the Sig.KeyGen algorithm, and outputs svk^* as the target tag t^* to algorithm $\mathcal{B}'$. Algorithm $\mathcal{A}'$ is given the public parameter par_{pke} and a public key pk_{pke} generated by algorithm $\mathcal{B}'$. Algorithm $\mathcal{A}'$ defines a fuzzy key setting $\mathcal{F}$, and generates the public parameter $par_{\mathcal{S}}$. In addition, algorithm $\mathcal{A}'$ randomly chooses a sketch c' (note that due to the average-case indistinguishability (defined in [7]) of the linear sketch scheme $\mathcal{S}$, c' is indistinguishable to that generated following the original algorithm), computes $c \leftarrow \mathcal{S}.M_c(par_{\mathcal{S}}, c', \triangle sk, e)$ where $e \in X$ (this is making use of the linearity of the linear sketch scheme $\mathcal{S}$), and outputs a public key $pk_f = (pk, c)$ where $pk = M_{pk_{pke}}(par_{pke}, pk_{pke}, \triangle sk)$, $\triangle sk \in \mathcal{K}$ (this is because of the homomorphic property of the PKE scheme). Algorithm $\mathcal{A}'$ sends the public parameter $par = (par_{pke}, par_{\mathcal{S}}, \mathcal{F})$ and the pubic key pk_f to algorithm $\mathcal{A}$.
- Phase 1. Algorithm $\mathcal{A}$ adaptively issues queries on ciphertexts $\widetilde{CT}$ to the decryption oracle $\mathcal{O}_{\mathrm{Dec}(\cdot)}$. For each decryption query on a ciphertext $\widetilde{CT} = (svk, CT, \sigma)$, if σ is a valid signature on CT under the verification key svk, algorithm $\mathcal{A}'$ outputs a shifted CT' under the public key pk_{pke} but on the same message of CT as $CT' = M_{en}(par_{pke}, \triangle sk, CT)$. Notice that due to the homomorphic property of the PKE scheme, algorithm $\mathcal{A}'$ can easily output a shifted CT' for CT. Algorithm $\mathcal{A}'$ forwards CT' to algorithm $\mathcal{B}'$, and returns the result from algorithm $\mathcal{B}'$ to algorithm $\mathcal{A}$.
- Challenge. Algorithm $\mathcal{A}$ outputs two messages M_0^* and M_1^* of the same size. Algorithm $\mathcal{A}'$ forwards M_0^*, M_1^* to algorithm $\mathcal{B}'$ to obtain CT^* of the tag svk^*. After receiving CT^* on the message M_b^* for $b \in \{0, 1\}$ and the tag svk^* from algorithm $\mathcal{B}'$, algorithm $\mathcal{A}'$ runs the Sig.Sign algorithm to generate a signature σ^* on CT^*, and outputs $\widetilde{CT}^* = (svk^*, CT^*, \sigma^*)$ as the challenge ciphertext.
- Phase 2. Algorithm $\mathcal{A}$ continues issuing decryption queries on ciphertexts $\widetilde{CT}$ to algorithm $\mathcal{A}'$ with the constraint that $\widetilde{CT}$ does not equal the challenge ciphertext $\widetilde{CT}^*$. Algorithm $\mathcal{A}'$ responds as follows.
  1. $svk \neq svk^*$. In this case, algorithm $\mathcal{A}'$ responds as that in Phase 1.
  2. $svk = svk^*$, $(CT, \sigma) \neq (CT^*, \sigma^*)$. Due to the strong unforgeability of the Sig scheme, such queries have negligible probability to happen.
  3. $\widetilde{CT} = (svk^*, CT^*, \sigma^*)$. According to the security definition, these queries are not allowed.

- Guess. Algorithm $\mathcal{A}$ outputs a guess $b' \in \{0, 1\}$ for b. Algorithm $\mathcal{A}'$ forwards b' to algorithm $\mathcal{B}'$ who will output b' as the guess to the IND-CCA game of the PKE scheme.

To conclude, if algorithm $\mathcal{A}$ wins the IND-CCA security game of the FPKE scheme with non-negligible probability, then algorithm $\mathcal{A}'$ wins the IND-CCA security game of the key deterministic and homomorphic PKE scheme, or breaks the strong unforgeability of the Sig scheme or the security of the linear sketch scheme $\mathcal{S}$ with non-negligible probability.

Theorem 2. *Assuming that PKE with the key deterministic and homomorphic properties is IND-CCA secure, and $\mathcal{S}$ is a secure linear sketch scheme for a fuzzy key setting $\mathcal{F}$, then the above FPKE scheme removing the Sig scheme for the fuzzy key setting $\mathcal{F}$ is IND-CCA secure.*

Proof. The proof is similar to that of Theorem 1 except that (1) in the Challenge phase, algorithm $\mathcal{A}'$ directly forwards M_0^*, M_1^* to algorithm $\mathcal{B}'$ to obtain the challenge ciphertext $\widetilde{CT}^*$; and (2) in the Phase 2, the analysis of three cases will be removed.

5 Conclusions

Traditionally, in the scenario where messages are encrypted using a public-key encryption (PKE) scheme, to protect the privacy of a user's private key, the private key is stored in a physical device such as a USB token which is carried by the user. Nevertheless, it is not easy for a user to always keep a device with him/her. To address this issue, it has been suggested to use individually unique biometric data as the private key, but biometric data is fuzzy and changes each time it is collected, thereby becoming unsuitable for being directly used as a private key. In this paper, we introduced a notion of fuzzy public-key encryption (FPKE), in which a piece of biometric data can be used as the private key to decrypt ciphertexts while without requiring any auxiliary information. Compared to PKE, a salient advantage of FPKE is that it does not require a user to carry any device or memorize any password to use the private key. After describing the formal security definition of FPKE, we presented generic constructions of FPKE based on the cryptographic primitives of linear sketch and PKE with two additional properties, and formally analyzed the security of the proposed generic constructions of FPKE.

References

1. Connaughton, R., Bowyer, K.W., Flynn, P.J.: Fusion of face and iris biometrics. In: Handbook of Iris Recognition, pp. 219–237. Springer, Heidelberg (2007)
2. Dodis, Y., Ostrovsky, R., Reyzin, L., Smith, A.D.: Fuzzy extractors: how to generate strong keys from biometrics and other noisy data. SIAM J. Comput. **38**(1), 97–139 (2008)

3. Ellison, C., Schneier, B.: Ten risks of PKI: what you're not being told about public key infrastructure. Comput. Secur. J. **16**(1), 1–7 (2000)
4. Gamal, T.E.: A public key cryptosystem and a signature scheme based on discrete logarithms. IEEE Trans. Inf. Theor. **31**(4), 469–472 (1985)
5. Kiltz, E.: Chosen-ciphertext security from tag-based encryption. In: Halevi, S., Rabin, T. (eds.) TCC 2006. LNCS, vol. 3876, pp. 581–600. Springer, Heidelberg (2006). doi:10.1007/11681878_30
6. MacKenzie, P., Reiter, M.K., Yang, K.: Alternatives to non-malleability: definitions, constructions, and applications. In: Naor, M. (ed.) TCC 2004. LNCS, vol. 2951, pp. 171–190. Springer, Heidelberg (2004). doi:10.1007/978-3-540-24638-1_10
7. Matsuda, T., Takahashi, K., Murakami, T., Hanaoka, G.: Fuzzy signatures: relaxing requirements and a new construction. In: Manulis, M., Sadeghi, A.-R., Schneider, S. (eds.) ACNS 2016. LNCS, vol. 9696, pp. 97–116. Springer, Cham (2016). doi:10.1007/978-3-319-39555-5_6
8. Sahai, A., Waters, B.: Fuzzy identity-based encryption. In: Cramer, R. (ed.) EURO-CRYPT 2005. LNCS, vol. 3494, pp. 457–473. Springer, Heidelberg (2005). doi:10.1007/11426639_27
9. Takahashi, K., Matsuda, T., Murakami, T., Hanaoka, G., Nishigaki, M.: A signature scheme with a fuzzy private key. In: Malkin, T., Kolesnikov, V., Lewko, A.B., Polychronakis, M. (eds.) ACNS 2015. LNCS, vol. 9092, pp. 105–126. Springer, Cham (2015). doi:10.1007/978-3-319-28166-7_6

Proxy Re-encryption and Functional Encryption

An Efficient Certificateless Proxy Re-Encryption Scheme Without Pairing

S. Sharmila Deva Selvi, Arinjita Paul[(✉)], and Chandrasekaran Pandu Rangan

Theoretical Computer Science Lab, Department of Computer Science and Engineering, Indian Institute of Technology Madras, Chennai, India
{sharmila,arinjita,prangan}@cse.iitm.ac.in

Abstract. Proxy re-encryption (PRE) is a cryptographic primitive introduced by Blaze, Bleumer and Strauss [4] to provide delegation of decryption rights. PRE allows re-encryption of a ciphertext intended for Alice (delegator) to a ciphertext for Bob (delegatee) via a semi-honest proxy, who should not learn anything about the underlying message. In 2003, Al-Riyami and Patterson introduced the notion of certificateless public key cryptography which offers the advantage of identity-based cryptography without suffering from key escrow problem. The existing certificateless PRE (CLPRE) schemes rely on costly bilinear pairing operations. In ACM ASIA-CCS SCC 2015, Srinivasan *et al.* proposed the first construction of a certificateless PRE scheme without resorting to pairing in the random oracle model. In this work, we demonstrate a flaw in the CCA-security proof of their scheme. Also, we present the first construction of a CLPRE scheme without pairing which meets CCA security under the computational Diffie-Hellman hardness assumption in the random oracle model.

Keywords: Proxy re-encryption · Pairing-less · Public key · Certificateless · Unidirectional

1 Introduction

Due to segregation of data ownership and storage, security remains as one of the major concerns in public cloud scenario. In order to protect the stored data from illegal access and usage, users encrypt their data with their public keys before storing it in the cloud. To enable sharing of stored data, a naive approach would be that a user Alice shares her secret key with a legitimate user Bob. However, this would compromise the privacy of Alice. As a solution towards providing delegation of decryption rights, Blaze *et al.* [4] in 1998 proposed the concept

S. Sharmila Deva Selvi—Postdoctoral researcher supported by Project No. CCE/CEP/22/VK&CP/CSE/14-15 on Information Security & Awareness (ISEA) Phase-II by Ministry of Electronics & Information Technology, Government of India. A. Paul and C. Pandu Rangan—Work partially supported by Project No. CCE/CEP/22/VK&CP/CSE/14-15 on ISEA-Phase II.

© Springer International Publishing AG 2017
T. Okamoto et al. (Eds.): ProvSec 2017, LNCS 10592, pp. 413–433, 2017.
https://doi.org/10.1007/978-3-319-68637-0_25

of proxy re-encryption, which allows a proxy server with special information (re-encryption key) to translate a ciphertext for Alice into another ciphertext (with the same message) for Bob without learning any information about the underlying plaintext. Besides, this approach offloads the costly burden of secure data sharing from Alice to the resource-abundant proxy. As Alice delegates her decryption rights to Bob, Alice is termed as *delegator* and Bob as *delegatee*. Ever since, PRE has found a lot of applications such as encrypted email forwarding, distributed file systems, digital rights management (DRM) of Apple's iTunes, outsourced filtering of encrypted spam and content distribution [2,3].

Based on the direction of delegation, PRE schemes are classified into unidirectional and bidirectional schemes. In unidirectional schemes, a proxy can re-encrypt ciphertexts from Alice to Bob but not vice-versa, while in the bidirectional schemes, the proxy is allowed to re-encrypt ciphertexts in both directions. PRE schemes are also classified into single-hop and multihop schemes. In a single-hop scheme, a proxy cannot re-encrypt ciphertexts that have been re-encrypted once. In a multi-hop scheme, the proxy can further re-encrypt the re-encrypted ciphertexts. In this paper, we focus on single-hop unidirectional PRE schemes.

Several PRE constructions have been proposed in the literature, either in the Public Key Infrastructure (PKI) or identity based (IBE) setting. The schemes in the PKI setting entrusts a third party called the Certification Authority (CA) to assure the authenticity of a user's public key by digitally signing it and issuing Digital Certificates. However, the overhead involved in the revocation, storage and distribution of certificates has long been a concern, which makes public key cryptography inefficient. As a solution to the authenticity problem, Identity-based cryptography was introduced by Shamir in 1984 [9], which involves a trusted third party called the Private Key Generator (PKG) to generate secret keys of all users. Yet again, due to the unconditional trust placed on the PKG, identity based cryptography suffers from *key-escrow problem*. To avoid both certificate management problem in the PKI setting and key-escrow problem in the ID-based setting, certificateless cryptography was introduced in 2003 by Al-Riyami and Patterson [1]. Certificateless cryptography splits the task of key-generation of a user between a semi-trusted entity called Key Generation Center (KGC) and the user himself. This approach no longer relies on the use of certificates for key authenticity and hence does not suffer from certificate management problem. Also, the KGC does not have access to the secret keys of the users, which addresses the key-escrow problem inherent in IBE setting.

In this paper, we study proxy re-encryption in the light of certificateless public key cryptography. Consider the following scenario where Alice stores her encrypted data in the cloud, which provides services to billions of users. The number of cloud users being large, certificate management for public key authenticity is an overhead. This makes proxy re-encryption in PKI setting unfit for cloud services. On the other hand, a malicious PKG, entrusted with the power to generate user secret keys, can decrypt confidential data of the users due to which PRE in

IBE setting is highly impractical. Certificateless PRE affirmatively solves both the certificate management problem and key-escrow problem in the above scenario.

1.1 Related Work and Contribution

While several schemes achieving PRE have been proposed in the literature, a majority of these schemes are either in the PKI or IBE setting. In 2010, Sur *et al.* [11] introduced the notion of certificateless proxy re-encryption (CLPRE) and proposed a CCA secure CLPRE scheme in the random oracle model. However, in 2013, their scheme was shown to be vulnerable to chosen ciphertext attack by Zheng *et al.* [13]. In 2013, Guo *et al.* [6] proposed a CLPRE scheme in the random oracle model based on bilinear pairing which satisfies RCCA-security, a weaker notion of security. In 2014, Yang, Xu and Zhang [12] proposed a pairing-free CCA-secure CLPRE scheme in the random oracle model, which was shown to be vulnerable to chain collusion attack in [10]. In 2015, Srinivasan *et al.* [10] proposed the first CCA-secure unidirectional certificateless PRE scheme without pairing under the computational Diffie-Hellman assumption in the random oracle model. In this paper, we expose a critical weakness in the security proof of the scheme and provide a potential fix to make the scheme provably secure.

Another major contribution of this work is we propose an efficient pairing-free unidirectional single-hop certificateless proxy re-encryption scheme in the random oracle model. As stated, all the existing CLPRE schemes are vulnerable to attacks except for [6]. The CLPRE scheme due to Guo *et al.* [6] is based on bilinear pairing which is an expensive operation as compared to modular exponentiation operations in finite fields. Besides, their scheme [6] satisfies a weaker notion of security, namely RCCA-security and is based on *q-weak Decisional Bilinear Assumption*. Our scheme satisfies CCA security against both Type-I and Type-II adversaries and is based on a much standard assumption called the Computational Diffie Hellman (CDH) assumption.

2 Definition and Security Model

2.1 Definition

We describe the syntactical definition of unidirectional single-hop certificateless proxy re-encryption and its security notion adopted from [10]. A PRE scheme consists of the following algorithms:

- **Setup**(1^λ): A PPT algorithm run by the Key Generation Center (KGC), which takes the unary encoding of the security parameter λ as input and outputs the public parameters *params* and master secret key *msk*.
- **PartialKeyExtract**($msk, ID_i, params$): A PPT algorithm run by KGC which takes the master secret key *msk*, user identity ID_i and public parameters *params* as input, and outputs the partial public key and partial secret key pair (PPK_i, PSK_i).

- **UserKeyGen**($ID_i, params$): A PPT algorithm run by the user, which takes the identity ID_i of the user and the public parameters $params$ as input, and outputs the user generated secret key and public key pair (USK_i, UPK_i).
- **SetPrivateKey**($ID_i, PSK_i, USK_i, params$): A PPT algorithm run by the user, which takes as input the identity ID_i of the user, partial secret key PSK_i, user generated secret key USK_i and public parameters $params$, and outputs the full secret key SK_i of the user.
- **SetPublicKey**($ID_i, PPK_i, PSK_i, UPK_i, USK_i, params$): A PPT algorithm run by the user, which takes as input the the identity ID_i of the user, partial public key PPK_i, partial secret key PSK_i, user generated public key UPK_i, user generated secret key USK_i and public parameters $params$, and outputs the full public key PK_i of the user.
- **Re-KeyGen**($ID_i, ID_j, SK_i, PK_j, params$): A PPT algorithm run by the user (delegator) with identity ID_i which takes as input the identity ID_i of the delegator, identity ID_j of the delegatee, the full secret key SK_i of ID_i, full public key PK_j of ID_j and public parameters $params$, and outputs a re-encryption key $RK_{i \to j}$ or an error symbol $\perp$.
- **Encrypt**($ID_i, PK_i, m, params$): A PPT algorithm run by the sender which takes as input identity ID_i of receiver, full public key PK_i of ID_i, message $m \in \mathcal{M}$ and the public parameters $params$, and outputs the ciphertext C or an error symbol $\perp$. Note that C is termed as the first level ciphertext.
- **Re-Encrypt**($ID_i, ID_j, C, RK_{i \to j}, params$): A PPT algorithm run by the proxy which takes the identities ID_i, ID_j, a first level ciphertext C encrypted under identity ID_i, a re-encryption key $RK_{i \to j}$ and public parameters $params$ as input, and outputs a ciphertext D or an error symbol $\perp$. Note that D is termed as the second-level ciphertext.
- **Decrypt**($ID_i, SK_i, C, params$): A deterministic algorithm run by the receiver (delegator) which takes the identity ID_i, secret key SK_i of identity ID_i, first-level ciphertext C and public parameters $params$ as input, and outputs the message $m \in \mathcal{M}$ or an error symbol $\perp$.
- **Re-Decrypt** ($ID_j, SK_j, D, params$): A deterministic algorithm run by the receiver (delegatee) which takes the identity ID_j, secret key SK_j of identity ID_j, a second-level ciphertext D and public parameters $params$ as input, and outputs the message $m \in \mathcal{M}$ or an error symbol.

The consistency of a CLPRE scheme for any given public parameters $params$ and full public-private key pairs $\{(PK_i, SK_i), (PK_j, SK_j)\}$ is defined as follows:

1. Consistency between encryption and decryption; i.e.,

$$\mathbf{Decrypt}(ID_i, SK_i, C, params) = m, \ \forall m \in \mathcal{M},$$

where $C = \mathbf{Encrypt}(ID_i, PK_i, m, params)$.

2. Consistency between encryption, proxy re-encryption and decryption; i.e.,

$$\mathbf{Re\text{-}Decrypt}(ID_j, SK_j, D, params) = m, \ \forall m \in \mathcal{M},$$

where $D = \mathbf{Re\text{-}Encrypt}(ID_i, ID_j, C, RK_{i \to j}, params)$ and $C = \mathbf{Encrypt}(ID_i, PK_i, m, params)$.

2.2 Security Model

Due to the existence of two types of ciphertexts in a PRE scheme namely *first level* and *second level* ciphertexts, it is essential to prove the security for both levels. Again, there exists two types of adversaries specific to CLPRE: *Type-I* adversary and *Type-II* adversary. The Type I adversary models an attacker who can replace the public keys of the users by fake keys of its choice because of the absence of authenticating information for public keys [1]. However, the security proof demonstrates that the adversary cannot learn anything useful from this attack as it cannot derive the partial keys and in turn the full private keys needed for decryption without the cooperation of the KGC (who possesses the master secret key). The Type-II adversary models the semi-trusted KGC, who possesses the master secret key and tries to break the security of the system by eavesdropping or making decryption queries. Note that, the KGC is restrained from replacing the public keys of the users.

The security of a CLPRE scheme is modelled in the form of a security game between the two entities: the challenger $\mathcal{C}$ and the adversary $\mathcal{A}$. $\mathcal{A}$ can adaptively query the oracles as listed below which $\mathcal{C}$ answers and simulates an environment running CLPRE for $\mathcal{A}$. $\mathcal{C}$ maintains a list $P_{current}$ of the public keys to keep a track of the replaced public keys. $P_{current}$ consists of tuples of the form $\langle ID_i, PK_i, \hat{PK}_i \rangle$, where $\hat{PK}_i$ denotes the current value of the public key. To begin with, $\hat{PK}_i$ is assigned the value of the initial public key $\hat{PK}_i = PK_i$. $\mathcal{A}$ can make queries to the following oracles which are answered by $\mathcal{C}$:

- Public Key Extract($\mathcal{O}_{pe}(ID_i)$): Given an ID_i as input, compute the partial public key and secret key pair: $(PPK_i, PSK_i) = PartialKeyExtract(msk, ID_i, params)$, the user public key and secret key pair: $(USK_i, UPK_i) = UserKeyGen(ID_i, params)$, the full public key $PK_i = SetPublicKey(ID_i, PPK_i, PSK_i, UPK_i, USK_i, params)$. Return PK_i.
- Partial Key Extract($\mathcal{O}_{ppe}(ID_i)$): Given an ID_i as input, compute $(PPK_i, PSK_i) = PartialKeyExtract(msk, ID_i, params)$ and return (PPK_i, PSK_i).
- User Key Extract($\mathcal{O}_{ue}(ID_i)$): Given an ID_i as input, compute $(UPK_i, USK_i) = UserKeyGen(ID_i, params)$ and return (USK_i, UPK_i).
- Re-Key Generation($\mathcal{O}_{rk}(ID_i, ID_j)$): Compute $RK_{i \to j} = Re\text{-}KeyGen(ID_i, ID_j, SK_i, PK_j, params)$ and return $RK_{i \to j}$.
- Re-Encryption($\mathcal{O}_{re}(ID_i, ID_j, C)$): Given a first-level ciphertext C and two identities ID_i, ID_j as inputs, compute $RK_{i \to j} = Re\text{-}KeyGen(ID_i, ID_j, SK_i, PK_j, params)$ and compute the second level ciphertext as $D = Re\text{-}Encrypt(ID_i, ID_j, C, RK_{i \to j}, params)$.
- Decryption($\mathcal{O}_{dec}(ID_i, C)$): Given a first level ciphertext C encrypted under the public key of ID_i as input, compute the decryption of the ciphertext to obtain $m \in \mathcal{M}$. Return m or return $\perp$ if the ciphertext is invalid.
- Re-Decryption($\mathcal{O}_{redec}(ID_i, C)$): Given a second level ciphertext D re-encrypted under the public key ID_j as input, compute the decryption of the ciphertext to obtain $m \in \mathcal{M}$. Return m or return $\perp$ if the ciphertext is invalid.

– Public Key Replacement($\mathcal{O}_{rep}(ID_i, PK_i)$): Replace the value of the third component $\hat{PK}_i$ in the $PK_{current}$ list with the new value PK_i, provided PK_i is a valid public key.

Security Against Type-I Adversary $\mathcal{A}_I$

The Type-I adversary models an outside attacker without access to the master secret key, trying to learn some information about the underlying plaintext, given the ciphertext. We consider separate security models for the first level and second level ciphertexts against $\mathcal{A}_I$.

First Level Ciphertext Security: We consider the following security game where $\mathcal{A}_I$ interacts with the challenger $\mathcal{C}$ in following stages.

- Initialization: $\mathcal{C}$ runs $Setup(\lambda)$ to generate the public parameters $params$ and master secret key msk. It sends $params$ to $\mathcal{A}_I$ while keeping msk secret.
- Phase 1: The challenger $\mathcal{C}$ sets up the list of corrupt and honest users, initialises $\hat{PK}_i$ to PK_i for all users in the public key list $P_{current}$. $\mathcal{A}_I$ issues several queries to the above oracles simulated by $\mathcal{C}$, with the restriction that $\mathcal{A}_I$ cannot make partial key extract queries ($\mathcal{O}_{ppe}$) or user key extract queries ($\mathcal{O}_{ue}$) of the users whose public keys have been replaced as it is unreasonable to expect $\mathcal{C}$ to respond to such queries for public keys replaced by $\mathcal{A}_I$ [1].
- Challenge: $\mathcal{A}$ outputs two equal length messages m_0 and m_1 in $\mathcal{M}$ and the target identity ID_{ch}, with the following adversarial constraints:
  – ID_{ch} should not be a corrupt user.
  – $\mathcal{A}_I$ must not query the partial key extract oracle ($\mathcal{O}_{ppe}$) or user key extract oracle ($\mathcal{O}_{ue}$) of ID_{ch} at any point in time.
  – $\mathcal{A}_I$ must not query $\mathcal{O}_{rk}(ID_{ch}, ID_i)$, where ID_i is a corrupt user.
  – If $\mathcal{A}_I$ replaces the public key of ID_{ch}, it should not query the partial key extract oracle ($\mathcal{O}_{ppe}$) for ID_{ch}.
  On receiving $\{m_0, m_1\}$, $\mathcal{C}$ picks $\delta \in \{0,1\}$ at random and generates a challenge ciphertext $C^* = Encrypt(ID_{ch}, \hat{PK}_{ch}, m_\delta, params)$ and gives to $\mathcal{A}_I$.
- Phase 2: $\mathcal{A}_I$ issues the queries to the oracles similar to Phase 1, with the same adversarial constraint as mentioned in Phase 1 and the added constraints on the target identity ID_{ch} as mentioned in the Challenge phase. Additionally, there are other constraints as below:
  – $\mathcal{A}_I$ cannot query $\mathcal{O}_{dec}(ID_{ch}, C^*)$, for the same public key of ID_{ch} that was used to initially encrypt m_δ.
  – $\mathcal{A}_I$ cannot query the re-decryption oracle $\mathcal{O}_{redec}(ID_i, C)$ if (ID_i, C) is a challenge derivative[1].

---

[1] The definition of challenge derivative (ID_i, C) is adopted from [5] as stated below:
- Reflexitivity: (ID_i, C) is a challenge derivative of itself.
- Derivative by re-encryption: (ID_j, C') is a challenge derivative of (ID_i, C) if $C' \leftarrow \mathcal{O}_{re}(ID_i, ID_j, C)$.
- Derivative by re-encryption key: (ID_j, C') is a challenge derivative of (ID_i, C) if $RK_{i \to j} \leftarrow \mathcal{O}_{rk}(ID_i, ID_j)$ and $C' = Re - Encrypt(ID_i, ID_j, C, RK_{i \to j}, params)$.

- $\mathcal{A}_I$ cannot query $\mathcal{O}_{re}(ID_i, ID_j, C)$, if (ID_i, C) is a challenge derivative and ID_j is a corrupt user.
- $\mathcal{A}_I$ cannot query $\mathcal{O}_{rk}(ID_{ch}, ID_j)$, if ID_j is a corrupt user.
- Guess: $\mathcal{A}_I$ outputs its guess $\delta' \in \{0,1\}$.

We define the advantage of $\mathcal{A}_I$ in winning the game as:

$$Adv_{A_I, first}^{IND-CLPRE-CCA} = 2|Pr\lceil \delta' = \delta \rfloor - \frac{1}{2}|$$

where the probability is over the random coin tosses performed by $\mathcal{C}$ and $\mathcal{A}_I$. The scheme is said to be $(t, \epsilon) IND - CLPRE - CCA$ secure for the first level ciphertext against Type-I adversary $\mathcal{A}_I$ if for all t-time adversary $\mathcal{A}_I$ that makes q_{pe} queries to $\mathcal{O}_{pe}$, q_{ppe} queries to $\mathcal{O}_{ppe}$, q_{ue} queries to $\mathcal{O}_{ue}$, q_{re} queries to $\mathcal{O}_{re}$, q_{rk} queries to $\mathcal{O}_{rk}$, q_{dec} queries to $\mathcal{O}_{dec}$, q_{redec} queries to $\mathcal{O}_{redec}$ and q_{rep} queries to $\mathcal{O}_{rep}$, the advantage of $\mathcal{A}_I$ is $Adv_{A_I, first}^{IND-CLPRE-CCA} \leq \epsilon$.

Second Level Ciphertext Security: We consider the following security game for security of the second level ciphertext against Type-I adversary $\mathcal{A}_I$, where $\mathcal{A}_I$ interacts with the challenger $\mathcal{C}$ in following stages.

- Initialization: $\mathcal{C}$ runs $Setup(\lambda)$ to generate the public parameters $params$ and master secret key msk. It sends $params$ to $\mathcal{A}_I$ while keeping msk secret.
- Phase 1: The challenger $\mathcal{C}$ sets up the list of corrupt and honest users, initialises $\hat{PK}_i$ to PK_i for all users and updates the public key list $P_{current}$. $\mathcal{A}_I$ issues several queries to the above oracles simulated by $\mathcal{C}$ with the restriction that it cannot make partial key extract queries ($\mathcal{O}_{ppe}$) or user key extract queries ($\mathcal{O}_{ue}$) of the users whose public keys have already been replaced.
- Challenge: $\mathcal{A}_I$ outputs two messages m_0, m_1 in $\mathcal{M}$ where $|m_0| = |m_1|$, the target identity ID_{ch}, and the delegator's identity ID_{del} with the adversarial constraints as follows:
  - ID_{ch} should not be a corrupt user.
  - $\mathcal{A}_I$ must not query the partial key extract oracle ($\mathcal{O}_{ppe}$) or user key extract oracle ($\mathcal{O}_{ue}$) of ID_{ch} at any point in time.
  - If $\mathcal{A}_I$ replaces the public key of ID_{ch}, it should not query the partial key extract oracle ($\mathcal{O}_{ppe}$) for ID_{ch}.
  - $\mathcal{A}_I$ must not query $\mathcal{O}_{rk}(ID_{del}, ID_{ch})$.
  - $\mathcal{A}_I$ must not query $\mathcal{O}_{rk}(ID_{ch}, ID_i)$, where ID_i is a corrupt user.
  On receiving $\{m_0, m_1\}$, $\mathcal{C}$ picks $\delta \in \{0,1\}$ at random and generates a challenge ciphertext $D^* = Re - Encrypt(ID_{del}, ID_{ch}, Encrypt(ID_{ch}, \hat{PK}_{ch}, m_\delta, params), RK_{ID_{del} \to ID_{ch}}, params)$ and gives to $\mathcal{A}_I$.
- Phase 2: $\mathcal{A}_I$ issues the queries to the oracles similar to Phase 1, with the same adversarial constraint as mentioned in Phase 1 and constraints on the target identity ID_{ch} mentioned in the Challenge phase. Additionally, $\mathcal{A}_I$ cannot query $\mathcal{O}_{redec}(ID_{ch}, C^*)$, for the same public key of ID_{ch} that was used to initially encrypt m_δ.
- Guess: $\mathcal{A}_I$ outputs its guess $\delta' \in \{0,1\}$.

We define the advantage of $\mathcal{A}_I$ in winning the game as:

$$Adv_{\mathcal{A}_I,second}^{IND-CLPRE-CCA} = 2|Pr[\delta' = \delta] - \frac{1}{2}|$$

where the probability is over the random coin tosses performed by $\mathcal{C}$ and $\mathcal{A}_I$. The scheme is said to be $(t, \epsilon)IND-CLPRE-CCA$ secure for the second level ciphertext against Type-I adversary $\mathcal{A}_I$ if for all t-time adversary $\mathcal{A}_I$ that makes q_{pe} queries to $\mathcal{O}_{pe}$, q_{ppe} queries to $\mathcal{O}_{ppe}$, q_{ue} queries to $\mathcal{O}_{ue}$, q_{re} queries to $\mathcal{O}_{re}$, q_{rk} queries to $\mathcal{O}_{rk}$, q_{dec} queries to $\mathcal{O}_{dec}$, q_{redec} queries to $\mathcal{O}_{redec}$ and q_{rep} queries to $\mathcal{O}_{rep}$, the advantage of $\mathcal{A}_I$ is $Adv_{\mathcal{A}_I,second}^{IND-CLPRE-CCA} \leq \epsilon$.

Security Against Type-II Adversary $\mathcal{A}_{II}$

The Type-II adversary models an *honest-but-curious KGC* who has access to the master secret key msk, but is not allowed to replace the public keys of users. We consider separate security models for the first and second level ciphertexts.

First Level Ciphertext Security: We consider the following security game where $\mathcal{A}_{II}$ interacts with the challenger $\mathcal{C}$ as follows.

- Initialization: $\mathcal{C}$ runs $Setup(\lambda)$ to generate the public parameters $params$ and master secret key msk. It sends both $params$ and msk to $\mathcal{A}_{II}$.
- Phase 1: The challenger $\mathcal{C}$ maintains the list of honest and corrupt users and initialises $\hat{PK}_i$ to PK_i for all the users in the public key list $P_{current}$. $\mathcal{A}_{II}$ issues several queries to the above stated oracles simulated by $\mathcal{C}$ with the restriction that it cannot make partial key extract queries ($\mathcal{O}_{ppe}$) or user key extract queries ($\mathcal{O}_{ue}$) of the users whose public keys have been replaced.
- Challenge: $\mathcal{A}_{II}$ outputs two equal length messages $\{m_0, m_1\}$ in $\mathcal{M}$ and the target identity ID_{ch}, with the adversarial constraints as follows:
  - ID_{ch} should not be a corrupt user.
  - $\mathcal{A}_{II}$ must not replace the public key of ID_{ch}.
  - $\mathcal{A}_{II}$ must have not queried $\mathcal{O}_{rk}(ID_{ch}, ID_i)$, where ID_i is a corrupt user. On receiving $\{m_0, m_1\}$, $\mathcal{C}$ selects $\delta \in \{0,1\}$ at random, generates a challenge ciphertext $C^* = Encrypt(ID_{ch}, \hat{PK}_{ch}, m_\delta, params)$ and gives C^* to $\mathcal{A}_{II}$.
- Phase 2: $\mathcal{A}_{II}$ issues the queries to the oracles similar to Phase 1, with the same adversarial constraints as mentioned in Phase 1 and the constraints on the target identity ID_{ch} as mentioned in the Challenge phase. Additionally, there are other constraints as below:
  - $\mathcal{A}_{II}$ cannot query $\mathcal{O}_{dec}(ID_{ch}, C^*)$, for the same public key of ID_{ch} that was used to initially encrypt m_δ.
  - $\mathcal{A}_{II}$ cannot query the re-decryption oracle $\mathcal{O}_{redec}(ID, C)$ if (ID, C) is a challenge derivative.
  - $\mathcal{A}_{II}$ cannot query $\mathcal{O}_{re}(ID_i, ID_j, C)$, if (ID_i, C) is a challenge derivative and ID_j is a corrupt user.
  - $\mathcal{A}_{II}$ cannot query $\mathcal{O}_{rk}(ID_{ch}, ID_j)$, if ID_j is a corrupt user.
- Guess: $\mathcal{A}_{II}$ outputs its guess $\delta' \in \{0,1\}$.

We define the advantage of $\mathcal{A}_{II}$ in winning the game as:

$$Adv_{\mathcal{A}_{II},first}^{IND-CLPRE-CCA} = 2|Pr\lceil\delta' = \delta\rfloor - \frac{1}{2}|$$

where the probability is over the random coin tosses performed by $\mathcal{C}$ and $\mathcal{A}_{II}$. The scheme is said to be $(t,\epsilon)IND - CLPRE - CCA$ secure for the first level ciphertext against Type-II adversary $\mathcal{A}_{II}$ if for all t-time adversary $\mathcal{A}_{II}$ that makes q_{pe} queries to $\mathcal{O}_{pe}$, q_{ppe} queries to $\mathcal{O}_{ppe}$, q_{ue} queries to $\mathcal{O}_{ue}$, q_{re} queries to $\mathcal{O}_{re}$, q_{rk} queries to $\mathcal{O}_{rk}$, q_{dec} queries to $\mathcal{O}_{dec}$, q_{redec} queries to $\mathcal{O}_{redec}$ and q_{rep} queries to $\mathcal{O}_{rep}$, the advantage of $\mathcal{A}_{II}$ is $Adv_{\mathcal{A}_{II},first}^{IND-CLPRE-CCA} \leq \epsilon$.

Second Level Ciphertext Security: We consider the following security game where $\mathcal{A}_{II}$ interacts with the challenger $\mathcal{C}$ in the following stages.

- Initialization: $\mathcal{C}$ runs $Setup(\lambda)$ to generate the public parameters $params$ and master secret key msk. It sends both $params$ and msk to $\mathcal{A}_{II}$.
- Phase 1: The challenger $\mathcal{C}$ sets up the list of corrupt and honest users, initialises $\hat{PK}_i$ to PK_i for all the users and updates the public key list $P_{current}$. $\mathcal{A}_{II}$ issues several queries to the above stated oracles simulated by $\mathcal{C}$ with the restriction that it cannot make partial key extract queries ($\mathcal{O}_{ppe}$) or user key extract queries ($\mathcal{O}_{ue}$) of the users whose public keys have been replaced. Also, $\mathcal{A}_{II}$ cannot place queries to $\mathcal{O}_{ppe}$ as it already has access to msk and can generate the partial keys itself.
- Challenge: $\mathcal{A}_{II}$ outputs two messages m_0 and m_1 in $\mathcal{M}$ where $|m_0| = |m_1|$, the target identity ID_{ch}, and the delegator's identity ID_{del} with the adversarial constraints as follows:
  - ID_{ch} should not be a corrupt user.
  - $\mathcal{A}_{II}$ must not query the user key extract oracle ($\mathcal{O}_{ue}$) of ID_{ch}.
  - $\mathcal{A}_{II}$ must not replace the public key of ID_{ch}.
  - $\mathcal{A}_{II}$ must not query $\mathcal{O}_{rk}(ID_{del}, ID_{ch})$.
  - $\mathcal{A}_{II}$ must have not queried $\mathcal{O}_{rk}(ID_{ch}, ID_i)$, where ID_i is a corrupt user.
  On receiving $\{m_0, m_1\}$, $\mathcal{C}$ picks $\delta \in \{0,1\}$ at random and generates a challenge ciphertext $D^* = Re - Encrypt(ID_{del}, ID_{ch}, Encrypt(ID_{ch}, \hat{PK}_{ch}, m_\delta, params), RK_{ID_{del}\rightarrow ID_{ch}}, params)$ and gives to $\mathcal{A}_{II}$.
- Phase 2: $\mathcal{A}_{II}$ issues the queries to the oracles similar to Phase 1, with the same adversarial constraint as mentioned in Phase 1 and the added constraint on the target identity ID_{ch} as mentioned in the Challenge phase. Additionally, $\mathcal{A}_{II}$ cannot query $\mathcal{O}_{redec}(ID_{ch}, C^*)$, for the same public key of ID_{ch} that was used to initially encrypt m_δ.
- Guess: $\mathcal{A}_{II}$ outputs its guess $\delta' \in \{0,1\}$.

We define the advantage of $\mathcal{A}_{II}$ in winning the game as:

$$Adv_{\mathcal{A}_{II},second}^{IND-CLPRE-CCA} = 2|Pr\lceil\delta' = \delta\rfloor - \frac{1}{2}|$$

where the probability is over the random coin tosses performed by $\mathcal{C}$ and $\mathcal{A}_{II}$. The scheme is said to be $(t,\epsilon)IND - CLPRE - CCA$ secure for the second level ciphertext against Type-II adversary $\mathcal{A}_{II}$ if for all t-time adversary $\mathcal{A}_{II}$ that makes q_{pe} queries to $\mathcal{O}_{pe}$, q_{ppe} queries to $\mathcal{O}_{ppe}$, q_{ue} queries to $\mathcal{O}_{ue}$, q_{re} queries to $\mathcal{O}_{re}$, q_{rk} queries to $\mathcal{O}_{rk}$, q_{dec} queries to $\mathcal{O}_{dec}$, q_{redec} queries to $\mathcal{O}_{redec}$ and q_{rep} queries to $\mathcal{O}_{rep}$, the advantage of $\mathcal{A}_{II}$ is $Adv_{\mathcal{A}_{II}, second}^{IND-CLPRE-CCA} \leq \epsilon$.

Hardness Assumption

We state the computational hardness assumption we use to prove the security of our scheme. Let $\mathbb{G}$ be a cyclic group with a prime order q.

**Definition 1. *Computational Diffie-Hellman (CDH) assumption:* ** *The Computational Diffie-Hellman (CDH) assumption in $\mathbb{G}$ is, given elements $\{P, aP, bP\} \in \mathbb{G}$, there exists no PPT adversary which can compute $abP \in \mathbb{G}$ with a non-negligible advantage, where P is a generator of $\mathbb{G}$ and $a, b \in_R \mathbb{Z}_q^*$.*

3   Analysis of a Certificateless PRE Scheme by Srinivasan et al. [10]

3.1   Review of the Scheme

- **Setup(1^λ):**
  - Choose two large primes p and q such that $q|p-1$ and the security parameter λ defines the bit length of q. Let $\mathbb{G}$ be a subgroup of $\mathbb{Z}_p^*$ of order q and g is a generator of $\mathbb{G}$. Pick $x \in_R \mathbb{Z}_q^*$ and compute $y = g^x$.
  - Choose the following cryptographic hash functions:

$$H : \mathbb{G} \to \mathbb{Z}_q^*,$$
$$H_1 : \{0, 1\}^* \times \mathbb{G} \to \mathbb{Z}_q^*,$$
$$H_2 : \{0, 1\}^* \times \mathbb{G}^3 \to \mathbb{Z}_q^*,$$
$$H_3 : \mathbb{G} \to \{0, 1\}^{l_0+l_1},$$
$$H_4 : \{0, 1\}^{l_0} \times \{0, 1\}^{l_1} \to \mathbb{Z}_q^*,$$
$$H_5 : \mathbb{G}^2 \times \{0, 1\}^{l_0+l_1} \to \mathbb{Z}_q^*,$$
$$H_6 : \{0, 1\}^* \times \mathbb{G}^2 \to \mathbb{Z}_q^*$$

  Here $l_0 = \log q$ and l_1 is determined by the security parameter λ. The message space $\mathcal{M}$ is set to $\{0, 1\}^{l_0}$.
  - Return the public parameters $params = (p, q, \mathbb{G}, g, y, H, H_1, H_2, H_3, H_4, H_5, H_6)$. The master secret key is $msk = x$.
- **PartialKeyExtract$(msk, ID_i, params)$:**
  - Pick $s_1, s_2, s_3 \in_R \mathbb{Z}_q^*$ and compute $Q_1 = g^{s_1}$, $Q_2 = g^{s_2}$, $Q_3 = g^{s_3}$.
  - Compute $S_1 = s_1 + xH_1(ID_i, Q_1)$, $S_2 = s_2 + xH_1(ID_i, Q_2)$ and $S_3 = s_3 + xH_2(ID_i, Q_1, Q_2, Q_3)$.
  - Return the partial public key $PPK = (Q_1, Q_2, Q_3, S_3)$ and the partial secret key $PSK = (S_1, S_2)$.

- **UserKeyGen**$(ID_i, params)$:
  - Pick $z_1, z_2 \in_R \mathbb{Z}_q^*$ and compute (g^{z_1}, g^{z_2}).
  - Return $USK = (U_1, U_2) = (z_1, z_2)$ and $UPK = (P_1, P_2) = (g^{z_1}, g^{z_2})$.
- **SetPublicKey**$(ID_i, PPK, PSK, UPK, USK, params)$:
  - Pick $t_1, t_2 \in_R \mathbb{Z}_q^*$. Compute $T_1 = g^{t_1}$ and $T_2 = g^{t_2}$.
  - Compute $\mu_1 = t_1 + S_1 H_6(ID_i, P_1, T_1)$ and $\mu_2 = t_2 + S_2 H_6(ID_i, P_2, T_2)$.
  - Return the full public key $PK = (P_1, P_2, Q_1, Q_2, Q_3, S_3, T_1, T_2, \mu_1, \mu_2)$.
- **Public Verify**$(ID_i, PK, params)$:
  - Compute $R_1 = Q_1 \cdot y^{H_1(ID_i, Q_1)}$ and $R_2 = Q_2 \cdot y^{H_1(ID_i, Q_2)}$.
  - Check if $g^{\mu_1} \overset{?}{=} (T_1)(R_1)^{H_6(ID_i, P_1, T_1)}$, $g^{\mu_2} \overset{?}{=} (T_2)(R_2)^{H_6(ID_i, P_2, T_2)}$, $g^{S_3} \overset{?}{=} (Q_3)(y^{H_2(ID_i, Q_1, Q_2, Q_3)})$.
  - If all the above checks are satisfied, return $success$, else return $failure$.
- **SetPrivateKey**$(ID_i, PSK, USK, params)$:
  - Output the full secret key of the identity ID_i as $SK = (U_1, U_2, S_1, S_2)$.
- **Re-KeyGen**$(ID_i, ID_j, SK_i, PK_j, params)$:
  - Check the validity of the public key of ID_j by verifying if $Public\ Verify(ID_j, PK_j, params) = success$. If the check fails, return $\bot$.
  - Compute $R_{j,1} = Q_{j,1}(y^{H_1(ID_j, Q_{j,1})})$, $X_1 = P_{j,1}(R_{j,1}^{H(P_{j,1})})$.
  - Compute $X = P_{j,1}(P_{j,2})^{H(P_{j,1})}$ and $\alpha = H(X)$.
  - Select $h \in_R \{0,1\}^{l_0}$ and $\pi \in_R \{0,1\}^{l_1}$. Compute $v = H_4(h, \pi)$.
  - Compute $V = (X_1)^v$, $W = H_3(g^v) \oplus (h\|\pi)$.
  - Compute $rk = \dfrac{h}{U_{i,1} + H(P_{i,1})U_{i,2} + \alpha(S_{i,1} + H(R_{i,1})S_{i,2})}$.
  - Output the re-encryption key $RK_{i \to j} = (rk, V, W)$.
- **Encrypt**$(ID_i, PK_i, m, params)$:
  - Check the validity of the public key PK_i by verifying if $Public\ Verify(ID_i, PK_i, params) = success$. If the check fails, output $\bot$.
  - Compute $R_{i,1} = Q_{i,1}(y^{H_1(ID_i, Q_{i,1})})$, $R_{i,2} = Q_{i,2}(y^{H_1(ID_i, Q_{i,2})})$, $X = P_{i,1}(P_{i,2})^{H(P_{i,1})}$, $Y = R_{i,1}(R_{i,2})^{H(R_{i,1})}$, $\alpha = H(X)$ and set $Z = (X(Y)^\alpha)$.
  - Select $u \in_R \mathbb{Z}_q^*$ and $\omega \in_R \{0,1\}^{l_1}$. Compute $r = H_4(m, \omega)$.
  - Compute $D = (Z)^u$, $E = Z^r$, $F = H_3(g^r) \oplus (m\|\omega)$, $s = u + rH_5(D, E, F)$.
  - Return the ciphertext $C = (D, E, F, s)$ as the first level ciphertext.
- **Re-Encrypt**$(ID_i, ID_j, C, RK_{i \to j}, params)$:
  - Check validity of the ciphertext by computing Z as shown in $Encrypt(ID_i, PK_i, m, params)$ and performing the following checks.

$$(Z)^s \overset{?}{=} D \cdot E^{H_5(D, E, F)} \tag{1}$$

  If the check fails, return $\bot$.
  - Else, compute $E' = R^{rk}$.
  - Output $D = (E', F, V, W)$ as the second level ciphertext.
- **Decrypt**$(ID_i, SK_i, C, params)$:
  - Obtain the public key PK_i corresponding to ID_i. Check validity of the ciphertext by checking if Eq. 1 holds. If the check fails, output $\bot$.
  - Else, compute $R_{i,1} = Q_{i,1}(y^{H_1(ID_i, Q_{i,1})})$, $R_{i,2} = Q_{i,2}(y^{H_1(ID_i, Q_{i,2})})$, $X = P_{i,1}(P_{i,2})^{H(P_{i,1})}$, $Y = R_{i,1}(R_{i,2})^{H(R_{i,1})}$, $\alpha = H(X)$ and set $Z = (X(Y)^\alpha)$. Set $K = U_{i,1} + H(P_{i,1})U_{i,2} + \alpha(S_{i,1} + H(R_{i,1})S_{i,2})$.

- Compute $(m||\omega) = F \oplus H_3(E^{\frac{1}{k}})$. Output m if $E \stackrel{?}{=} (Z)^{H_4(m,\omega)}$ holds. Else, return $\perp$.
- **Re-Decrypt**$(ID_j, SK_j, D, params)$:
  - Compute $R_{j,1} = Q_{j,1}(y^{H_1(ID_j, Q_{j,1})})$, $X_1 = P_{j,1}(R_{j,1}^{H(P_{j,1})})$.
  - Compute $(h||\pi) = W \oplus H_3(V^{\frac{1}{U_{j,1}+H(P_{j,1})S_{j,1}}})$ and $(m||\omega) = F \oplus H_3(E'^{1/h})$.
  - Output m if $V \stackrel{?}{=} (X)_1^{H_4(h,\pi)}$, $E' \stackrel{?}{=} g^{h(H_4(m,\omega))}$. Else, return $\perp$.

3.2   Our Attack

In this section, we highlight the flaw in the security reduction of the CLPRE scheme due to Srinivasan et al. [10]. We demonstrate that the simulation of the random oracles does not comply with the real system due to which, the adversary can distinguish the simulation of the challenger from the real system. Note that the flaw is observed in the proof for both $Type-I$ and $Type-II$ adversary and we refer to both the two types of adversaries as $\mathcal{A}$ in general. Consider that the adversary constructs a first level dummy ciphertext $C_d = (D, E, F, s)$ in the following way under a public key PK_i. We use $Encrypt_{fake}$ to denote this technique to construct dummy ciphertexts.

- Compute Z using $Encrypt(ID_i, PK_i, m, params)$ algorithm.
- Select $u \in_R \mathbb{Z}_q^*$ and compute $D = (Z)^u$.
- Pick $r \in_R \mathbb{Z}_q^*$ and compute $E = (Z)^r$.
- Choose $F \in_R \{0,1\}^{l_0+l_1}$.
- Compute $s = u + rH_5(D, E, F) \mod q$.

Note that the computation of F and r in C_d using $Encrypt_{fake}$ violates the definition of the $Encrypt(ID_i, PK_i, m, params)$ algorithm. But C_d clears the ciphertext validity check of Eq. (1). The decryption algorithm $Decrypt(ID_i, SK_i, C_d, params)$ detects the ciphertext C_d as invalid and returns $\perp$. However, the $ReEncrypt(ID_i, ID_j, C_d, RK_{i \to j}, params)$ algorithm **accepts** C_d as a valid ciphertext. We use this knowledge to construct a distinguisher for the simulated environment from the real system described stepwise as follows:

1. After the *Challenge* phase, $\mathcal{A}$ generates a dummy ciphertext $C_1 = (D_1, E_1, F_1, s)$ under the target identity PK_{ch} using $Encrypt_{fake}$ as shown:
   - Compute Z_{ch} using $Encrypt(ID_i, PK_i, m, params)$ algorithm.
   - Select $u_1 \in_R \mathbb{Z}_q^*$ and compute $D_1 = (Z_{ch})^{u_1}$.
   - Pick $r_1 \in_R \mathbb{Z}_q^*$ and compute $E_1 = (Z_{ch})^{r_1}$.
   - Choose $F_1 \in_R \{0,1\}^{l_0+l_1}$.
   - Compute $s_1 = u_1 + r_1 H_5(D_1, E_1, F_1) \mod q$.
2. $\mathcal{A}$ generates another dummy ciphertext $C_2 = (D_2, E_2, F_2, s_2)$ in the same way described above considering random values $r_2 \in_R \mathbb{Z}_q^*$ and $F_2 \in_R \{0,1\}^{l_0+l_1}$.
3. $\mathcal{A}$ queries the re-encryption oracle $\mathcal{O}_{renc}(ID_{ch}, ID_j, C_1, RK_{ch \to j})$. As per $\mathcal{O}_{renc}$, $\mathcal{C}$ searches the H_4 list for a tuple of the form $(\langle m, \omega \rangle, r)$ such that $E_1 = (Z_{ch}^r)$. If no such tuple exists, $\mathcal{O}_{renc}$ outputs $\perp$. Note that, on an output $\perp$, $\mathcal{A}$ can distinguish between the simulation and

the real system, since C_1 is a valid ciphertext as per the definition of $ReEncrypt(ID_{ch}, ID_j, C, RK_{ch \to j}, params)$ algorithm and should produce a valid second level ciphertext D_1.

- If $\mathcal{O}_{renc}$ returns $\bot$, $\mathcal{A}$ aborts.
- Else, $\mathcal{O}_{renc}$ computes $D_1 = (E'_1, F_1, V_1, W_1)$ and outputs D_1.

4. Similarly, $\mathcal{A}$ queries the re-encryption oracle $\mathcal{O}_{renc}(ID_{ch}, ID_j, C_2, RK_{ch \to j})$. As per $\mathcal{O}_{renc}$, $\mathcal{C}$ searches the H_4 list for a tuple of the form $(\langle m, \omega \rangle, r)$ such that $E_2 = (Z^r_{ch})$. If no such tuple exists, $\mathcal{O}_{renc}$ outputs $\bot$. Note that, on an output $\bot$, $\mathcal{A}$ can distinguish between the simulation and the real system, since C_1 is a valid ciphertext as per the definition of $ReEncrypt(ID_{ch}, ID_j, C, RK_{ch \to j}, params)$ and should produce a valid second level ciphertext D_2.

- If $\mathcal{O}_{renc}$ returns $\bot$, $\mathcal{A}$ aborts.
- Else, $\mathcal{O}_{renc}$ computes $D_2 = (E'_2, F_2, V_2, W_2)$ and outputs D_2.

5. On receiving D_1 and D_2, $\mathcal{A}$ computes $T_1 = E'_1{}^{\frac{1}{r_1}}$ and $T_2 = E'_2{}^{\frac{1}{r_2}}$.

6. If $T_1 \stackrel{?}{=} T_2$ does not hold, $ReEncrypt(ID_{ch}, ID_j, C, RK_{ch \to j}, params) \neq \mathcal{O}_{renc}$, $\mathcal{A}$ learns it is not the real system and aborts. Else, if $T_1 \stackrel{?}{=} T_2$ holds, $\mathcal{A}$ cannot distinguish between the simulated environment and real system.

3.3   A Possible Fix

The flaw in the scheme can be fixed by modifying the encryption algorithm **Encrypt**$(ID_i, PK_i, m, params)$ with additional ciphertext validity checks in both **Re-Encrypt** and the **Decrypt**. The modified scheme is shown below.

- **Setup**(1^λ): The *Setup* algorithm remains the same as in [10] described in Sect. 3.1. Add another cryptographic hash function to the existing public parameters as defined:

$$\tilde{H} : \mathbb{G}^4 \times \{0,1\}^{l_0 + l_1} \to \mathbb{G}$$

Return public parameters $params = (p, q, \mathbb{G}, g, y, \tilde{H}, H, H_1, H_2, H_3, H_4, H_5, H_6)$ and the master secret key is $msk = x$, generated as described in Sect. 3.1.

- The **PartialKeyExtract, UserKeyGen, SetPublicKey, Public Verify, SetPrivateKey, Re-KeyGen** algorithms are the same as described in Sect. 3.1.

- **Encrypt**$(ID_i, PK_i, m, params)$:
  - Check the validity of the public key PK_i by verifying if **Public Verify**$(ID_i, PK_i) = success$. If the check fails, output $\bot$.
  - Compute $R_{i,1} = Q_{i,1}(y^{H_1(ID_i, Q_{i,1})})$, $R_{i,2} = Q_{i,2}(y^{H_1(ID_i, Q_{i,2})})$, $X = P_{i,1}(P_{i,2})^{H(P_{i,1})}$, $Y = R_{i,1}(R_{i,2})^{H(R_{i,1})}$, $\alpha = H(X)$ and set $Z = (X(Y)^\alpha)$.
  - Select $u \in_R \mathbb{Z}^*_q$ and $\omega \in_R \{0,1\}^{l_1}$. Compute $r = H_4(m, \omega)$.
  - Compute $D = (Z)^u$, $E = Z^r$.
  - Compute $\bar{D} = \tilde{H}(X, Y, D, E, F)^u$, $\bar{E} = \tilde{H}(X, Y, D, E, F)^r$.
  - Compute $F = H_3(g^r) \oplus (m \| \omega)$ and $s = u + rH_5(E, \bar{E}, F)$.
  - Return the ciphertext $C = (E, \bar{E}, F, s)$ as the first level ciphertext.

- **Re-Encrypt**$(ID_i, ID_j, C, RK_{i \to j}, params)$: On input of a re-encryption key $RK_{i \to j} = (RK_{i \to j}^{(1)}, V, W)$, a first level ciphertext $C = (E, \bar{E}, F, s)$ encrypted under PK_i, obtain a second level ciphertext D under PK_j as follows:
  - Compute $R_{i,1} = Q_{i,1}(y^{H_1(ID_i, Q_{i,1})})$, $R_{i,2} = Q_{i,2}(y^{H_1(ID_i, Q_{i,2})})$, $X = P_{i,1}(P_{i,2})^{H(P_{i,1})}$, $Y = R_{i,1}(R_{i,2})^{H(R_{i,1})}$, $\alpha = H(X)$ and set $Z = (X(Y)^\alpha)$.
  - Compute D and $\bar{D}$ as follows:

$$D = (Z)^s \cdot (E^{H_5(E, \bar{E}, F)})^{-1}$$
$$= Z^u \cdot Z^{r \cdot H_5(E, \bar{E}, F)} \cdot Z^{-r \cdot H_5(E, \bar{E}, F)}$$
$$= (Z)^u.$$

$$\bar{D} = \tilde{H}(X, Y, D, E, F)^s \cdot (\bar{E}^{H_5(E, \bar{E}, F)})^{-1}$$
$$= \tilde{H}(X, Y, D, E, F)^{u + r \cdot H_5(E, \bar{E}, F)} \cdot \tilde{H}(X, Y, D, E, F)^{-r \cdot H_5(E, \bar{E}, F)}$$
$$= \tilde{H}(X, Y, D, E, F)^u.$$

  - Check the validity of the ciphertext by performing the following checks.

$$(Z)^s \stackrel{?}{=} D \cdot E^{H_5(E, \bar{E}, F)} \tag{2}$$

$$\tilde{H}(X, Y, D, E, F)^s \stackrel{?}{=} \bar{D} \cdot \bar{E}^{H_5(E, \bar{E}, F)} \tag{3}$$

  If the check fails, return $\bot$.
  - Else, parse $RK_{i \to j}$ as (rk, V, W) compute $E' = R^{rk}$.
  - Output $D = (E', F, V, W)$ as the second level ciphertext.
- **Decrypt**$(ID_i, SK_i, C, params)$:
  - Obtain the public key PK_i corresponding to ID_i. Check if the ciphertext is well-formed by computing the values of D and $\bar{D}$ and checking if Eqs. 2 and 3 holds. If they do not hold, return $\bot$.
  - Else, compute $R_{i,1}, R_{i,2}, X, Y, \alpha, Z, K$ and retrieve m as described in the $Decrypt(ID_i, SK_i, C, params)$ algorithm in Sect. 3.1.
- **Re-Decrypt**$(ID_j, SK_j, D, params)$: Same as described in in Sect. 3.1.

4 Our Unidirectional CCA-secure CLPRE Scheme

4.1 Our Scheme

- **Setup**(1^λ): Given λ as the security parameter, choose a group $\mathbb{G}$ of prime order q. Let P be a generator of $\mathbb{G}$. Pick $s \in_R \mathbb{Z}_q^*$ and compute $P_{pub} = sP$. Choose cryptographic hash functions:

$$\tilde{H} : \{0,1\}^{l_{ID}} \times \mathbb{G}^2 \times \{0,1\}^{l_0 + l_1} \to \mathbb{G}$$
$$H_1 : \{0,1\}^{l_{ID}} \times \mathbb{G}^2 \to \mathbb{Z}_q^*$$
$$H_2 : \mathbb{Z}_q^* \times \mathbb{Z}_q^* \to \mathbb{Z}_q^*$$
$$H_3 : \mathbb{G} \to \mathbb{Z}_q^*$$
$$H_4 : \{0,1\}^{l_0} \times \{0,1\}^{l_1} \to \mathbb{Z}_q^*$$
$$H_5 : \mathbb{G}^2 \to \{0,1\}^{l_0 + l_1}$$
$$H_6 : \mathbb{G}^2 \times \{0,1\}^{l_0 + l_1} \to \mathbb{Z}_q^*$$

where $\{0,1\}^{l_0}$ is the size of the message space $\mathcal{M}$, l_1 is determined by the security parameter λ and $\{0,1\}^{l_{ID}}$ is the size of the identity of a user. Return the public parameters $params = (\mathbb{G}, q, P, P_{pub}, \tilde{H}, H_1, H_2, H_3, H_4, H_5, H_6)$ and master secret key $msk = s$.

- **PartialKeyExtract**$(msk, ID_i, params)$:
  - Choose $x_i, y_i \in_R \mathbb{Z}_q^*$.
  - Compute $X_i = x_i P$, $Y_i = y_i P$.
  - Compute $q_i = H_1(ID_i, X_i, Y_i)$.
  - Compute $d_i = (x_i + q_i s) \mod q$.
  - Return the Partial Public Key $PPK_i = (X_i, Y_i, d_i)$ and the Partial Private Key $PSK_i = y_i$.
- **UserKeyGen**$(ID_i, params)$:
  - Pick $z_i \in_R \mathbb{Z}_q^*$.
  - Compute $Z_i = z_i P$.
  - Return the user private key-public key pair $(USK_i, UPK_i) = (z_i, Z_i)$.
- **SetPrivateKey**$(ID_i, PSK_i, USK_i, params)$: Set the full secret key as $SK_i = \langle z_i, y_i \rangle$.
- **SetPublicKey**$(ID_i, PPK_i, PSK_i, UPK_i, USK_i, params)$: Set the full public key as $PK_i = \langle X_i, Y_i, Z_i, d_i \rangle$.
- **PublicVerify**$(ID_i, PK_i, params)$: We additionally provide public verifiability of the public keys of each user. This is done by the following check:

$$d_i P \stackrel{?}{=} X_i + H_1(ID_i, X_i, Y_i) \cdot Ppub \qquad (4)$$

If the check is satisfied, return *valid*, else return *invalid*.

Remark 1. Our public key verification algorithm $PublicVerify(ID_i, PK_i, params)$ ensures the validity of the public keys, since an adversary can replace the public keys with false keys of its choice.

- **Re-KeyGen**$(ID_i, ID_j, SK_i, PK_j, params)$:
  - Pick $\alpha_{ij}^{(1)}, \beta_{ij}^{(1)} \in_R \mathbb{Z}_q^*$.
  - Compute $\alpha_{ij}^{(2)}$ such that $\alpha_{ij}^{(1)} \cdot \alpha_{ij}^{(2)} = y_i \mod q$.
  - Compute $\beta_{ij}^{(2)}$ such that $\beta_{ij}^{(1)} \cdot \beta_{ij}^{(2)} = z_i \mod q$.
  - Compute $v_{ij} = H_2(\alpha_{ij}^{(2)} || \beta_{ij}^{(2)})$.
  - Compute $V_{ij} = v_{ij} \cdot Y_j$ and $W_{ij} = H_3(v_{ij}P) \oplus (\alpha_{ij}^{(2)} || \beta_{ij}^{(2)})$.
  - Return $RK_{i \to j} = (\alpha_{ij}^{(1)}, \beta_{ij}^{(1)}, V_{ij}, W_{ij})$.
- **Encrypt**$(ID_i, PK_i, m, params)$:
  - Check the validity of the public key of identity ID_i by checking if **PublicVerify**$(ID_i, PK_i, params)$=*valid*.
  - If *invalid*, return $\perp$.
  - Else, pick $\sigma \in_R \{0,1\}^{l_1}$, $u \in_R \mathbb{Z}_q^*$.
  - Compute $r = H_4(m, \sigma) \in \mathbb{Z}_q^*$.
  - Compute the ciphertext $C = (C_1, C_2, C_3, C_4)$ where:
    Compute $C_1 = rP \in \mathbb{G}$.

Compute $\overline{C}_1 = uP \in \mathbb{G}$.
Compute $C_2 = r\tilde{H}(ID_i, C_1, \overline{C}_1, C_3) \in \mathbb{G}$.
Compute $\overline{C}_2 = u\tilde{H}(ID_i, C_1, \overline{C}_1, C_3) \in \mathbb{G}$.
Compute $C_3 = H_5(rY_i, rZ_i) \oplus (m||\sigma) \in \{0,1\}^{l_0+l_1}$.
Compute $C_4 = u + rH_6(C_1, C_2, C_3) \in \mathbb{Z}_q^*$.
 – Return $C = (C_1, C_2, C_3, C_4)$.
- **Re-Encrypt**$(ID_i, ID_j, C, RK_{i \rightarrow j}, params)$: To verify that C is well-formed, compute $\overline{C}_1$ and $\overline{C}_2$ as given:

$$\overline{C}_1 = C_4 P - H_6(C_1, C_2, C_3) \cdot C_1$$
$$= uP + H_6(C_1, C_2, C_3)rP - H_6(C_1, C_2, C_3) \cdot C_1$$
$$= uP.$$
$$\overline{C}_2 = C_4 \cdot \tilde{H}(ID_i, C_1, \overline{C}_1, C_3) - H_6(C_1, C_2, C_3) \cdot C_2$$
$$= (u + rH_6(C_1, C_2, C_3))\tilde{H}(ID_i, C_1, \overline{C}_1, C_3) - H_6(C_1, C_2, C_3) \cdot C_2$$
$$= u\tilde{H}(ID_i, C_1, \overline{C}_1, C_3).$$

We verify if the ciphertext is well-formed by performing the following checks:

$$C_4 \cdot P \overset{?}{=} \overline{C}_1 + H_6(C_1, C_2, C_3) \cdot C_1 \tag{5}$$

$$C_4 \cdot \tilde{H}(ID_i, C_1, \overline{C}_1, C_3) \overset{?}{=} \overline{C}_2 + H_6(C_1, C_2, C_3) \cdot C_2 \tag{6}$$

If verification is successful, do the following computation:
 – Compute $D_1 = \alpha_{ij}^{(1)} \cdot C_1$.
 – Compute $D_2 = \beta_{ij}^{(1)} \cdot C_1$.
 – Return the re-encrypted ciphertext as $D = (D_1, D_2, D_3, D_4, D_5) = (D_1, D_2, C_3, V_{ij}, W_{ij})$.
- **Decrypt**$(ID_i, SK_i, C, params)$: Verify that C is a valid ciphertext by checking if Eqs. 5 and 6 holds. If satisfied, compute m using:

$$(m||\sigma) = C_3 \oplus H_5(y_i \cdot C_1, z_i \cdot C_1) \tag{7}$$

- **Re-Decrypt**$(ID_j, SK_j, D, params)$:
 – Compute $(\alpha_{ij}^{(2)}||\beta_{ij}^{(2)}) = W_{ij} \oplus H_3(\frac{1}{y_j}V_{ij})$.
 – Check if $V_{ij} \overset{?}{=} H_2(\alpha_{ij}^{(2)}||\beta_{ij}^{(2)}) \cdot Y_j$.
 – If satisfied, compute m as:

$$(m||\sigma) = C_3 \oplus H_5(\alpha_{ij}^{(2)} \cdot D_1, \beta_{ij}^{(2)} \cdot D_2) \tag{8}$$

4.2 Correctness

Due to space constraints, the correctness of our scheme appears in the full version of the paper [8].

4.3 Security Proof

First-level Ciphertext Security Against Type I Adversary

Theorem 1. *Our proposed scheme is CCA-secure against Type-I adversary for the first level ciphertext under the CDH assumption and the $EUF-CMA$ security of Schnorr signature scheme [7]. If a $(t,\epsilon)IND-CLPRE-CCA$ Type-I adversary $\mathcal{A}_I$ with an advantage ϵ breaks the IND-CLPRE-CCA security of the given scheme, $\mathcal{C}$ can solve the CDH problem with advantage ϵ' within time t' where:*

$$\epsilon' \geq \frac{1}{q_{H_5}}\left(\frac{(1-\omega)^{1+q_{rk}}\epsilon}{e(q_{ppe}+1)} - \frac{q_{H_4}}{2^{l_0+l_1}} - \frac{q_{H_6}}{2^{l_0+l_1}} - \frac{q_{\tilde{H}}}{2^{l_0+l_1}}\right.$$
$$\left. - q_{dec}\left(\frac{q_{H_5}/q}{1-(q_{H_4}/(2^{l_0+l_1}))} + \frac{q_{H_4}/(2^{l_0+l_1})}{1-(q_{H_5}/q)} + \frac{2}{q}\right)\right)$$

where ω is the advantage of an attacker against the EUF-CMA security game of the Schnorr signature scheme and e is the base of the natural logarithm. Time taken by $\mathcal{C}$ to solve the CDH problem is:

$$t' \leq t + (T_q)O(1) + (T_{\mathcal{O}})t_{exp}$$

where $T_q = q_{\tilde{H}} + q_{H_1} + q_{H_2} + q_{H_3} + q_{H_4} + q_{H_5} + q_{H_6}$, $T_{\mathcal{O}} = 4t_{pe} + 4t_{ppe} + 4t_{ue} + 2t_{rk} + 8t_{re} + 8t_{dec} + 6t_{redec}$. We denote the time taken for exponentiation operation in group $\mathbb{G}$ as t_{exp}.

Proof. Due to space constraints, the proof of the theorem is given in the full version of this paper [8].

Second-level Ciphertext Security Against Type I Adversary

Theorem 2. *Our proposed scheme is CCA-secure against Type-I adversary for the second level ciphertext under the CDH assumption and the $EUF-CMA$ security of the Schnorr signature scheme. If a $(t,\epsilon)IND-CLPRE-CCA$ Type-I adversary $\mathcal{A}_I$ with an advantage ϵ breaks the IND-CLPRE-CCA security of the given scheme, $\mathcal{C}$ can solve the CDH problem with advantage ϵ' within time t' where:*

$$\epsilon' \geq \frac{1}{q_{H_5}}\left(\frac{2(1-\omega)^{2+q_{rk}}\epsilon}{e(q_{ppe}+2)^2} - q_{dec}\left(\frac{q_{H_5}/q}{1-(q_{H_4}/(2^{l_0+l_1}))} + \frac{q_{H_4}/(2^{l_0+l_1})}{1-(q_{H_5}/q)} + \frac{2}{q}\right)\right)$$

where ω is the advantage of an attacker against the EUF-CMA security game of the Schnorr signature scheme and e is the base of the natural logarithm. Time taken by $\mathcal{C}$ to solve the CDH problem is:

$$t' \leq t + (T_q)O(1) + (T_\mathcal{O})t_{exp}$$

where $T_q = q_{\tilde{H}} + q_{H_1} + q_{H_2} + q_{H_3} + q_{H_4} + q_{H_5} + q_{H_6}$, $T_\mathcal{O} = 4t_{pe} + 4t_{ppe} + 4t_{ue} + 2t_{rk} + 8t_{re} + 8t_{dec} + 6t_{redec}$. We denote the time taken for exponentiation operation in group $\mathbb{G}$ as t_{exp}.

Proof. Due to space constraints, the proof of the theorem is given in the full version of this paper [8].

First-level Ciphertext Security Against Type II Adversary

Theorem 3. *Our proposed scheme is CCA-secure against Type-II adversary for the first level ciphertext under the CDH assumption and the $EUF - CMA$ security of the Schnorr signature scheme. If a $(t, \epsilon)IND-CLPRE-CCA$ Type-II adversary $\mathcal{A}_{II}$ with an advantage ϵ breaks the IND-CLPRE-CCA security of the given scheme, $\mathcal{C}$ can solve the CDH problem with advantage ϵ' within time t' where:*

$$\epsilon' \geq \frac{1}{q_{H_2}} \left(\frac{(1-\omega)^{1+q_{rk}}\epsilon}{e(q_{ppe} + q_{ue} + 1)} - \frac{q_{H_4}}{2^{l_0+l_1}} - \frac{q_{H_6}}{2^{l_0+l_1}} - \frac{q_{\tilde{H}}}{2^{l_0+l_1}} \right.$$
$$\left. - q_{dec}\left(\frac{q_{H_5}/q}{1 - (q_{H_4}/(2^{l_0+l_1}))} + \frac{q_{H_4}/(2^{l_0+l_1})}{1 - (q_{H_5}/q)} + \frac{2}{q} \right) \right)$$

where ω is the advantage of an attacker against the EUF-CMA security game of the Schnorr signature scheme and e is the base of the natural logarithm. Time taken by $\mathcal{C}$ to solve the CDH problem is:

$$t' \leq t + (T_q)O(1) + (T_\mathcal{O})t_{exp}$$

where $T_q = q_{\tilde{H}} + q_{H_1} + q_{H_2} + q_{H_3} + q_{H_4} + q_{H_5} + q_{H_6}$, $T_\mathcal{O} = 4t_{pe} + 4t_{ppe} + 4t_{ue} + 2t_{rk} + 8t_{re} + 8t_{dec} + 6t_{redec}$. We denote the time taken for exponentiation operation in group $\mathbb{G}$ as t_{exp}.

Proof. Due to space constraints, the proof of the theorem is given in the full version of this paper [8].

Second-level Ciphertext Security Against Type II Adversary

Theorem 4. *Our proposed scheme is CCA-secure against Type-II adversary for the second level ciphertext under the CDH assumption and the $EUF - CMA$ security of the Schnorr signature scheme. If a $(t, \epsilon)IND - CLPRE - CCA$ Type-II adversary $\mathcal{A}_{II}$ with an advantage ϵ breaks the IND-CLPRE-CCA security* *of the given scheme, $\mathcal{C}$ can solve the CDH problem with advantage ϵ' within time t' where:*

$$Pr[E_{H_5^*}] \geq \frac{2(1-\omega)^{2+q_{rk}}}{e(q_{ppe} + q_{ue} + 2)^2} - q_{dec}\left(\frac{q_{H_5}/q}{1 - (q_{H_4}/(2^{l_0+l_1}))} + \frac{q_{H_4}/(2^{l_0+l_1})}{1 - (q_{H_5}/q)} + \frac{2}{q}\right)$$

where ω is the advantage of an attacker against the EUF-CMA security game of the Schnorr signature scheme and e is the base of the natural logarithm. Time taken by $\mathcal{C}$ to solve the CDH problem is:

$$t' \leq t + (T_q)O(1) + (T_{\mathcal{O}})t_{exp}$$

where $T_q = q_{\tilde{H}} + q_{H_1} + q_{H_2} + q_{H_3} + q_{H_4} + q_{H_5} + q_{H_6}$, $T_{\mathcal{O}} = 4t_{pe} + 4t_{ppe} + 4t_{ue} + 2t_{rk} + 8t_{re} + 8t_{dec} + 6t_{redec}$. We denote the time taken for exponentiation operation in group $\mathbb{G}$ as t_{exp}.

Proof. Due to space constraints, the proof of the theorem is given in the full version of this paper [8].

5   Efficiency Comparison

We give a comparison of the efficiency of our proposed CLPRE scheme with the suggested fix to [10] as described in Sect. 3.3. In Table 1, we show the computational efficiency of our scheme and the modified scheme by comparing the time taken by the different algorithms in our protocols. Note that we use t_{exp} to denote the time required for exponentiation in a group. The comparison reveals that our scheme is more efficient than the existing scheme with our suggested fix.

Table 1. Efficiency comparison of the scheme [10] with the suggested fix with our CLPRE scheme indicates that our scheme is more efficient.

Scheme	Modified CLPRE scheme of Srinivasan *et al.* [10]	Our CLPRE scheme
Setup	t_{exp}	t_{exp}
PartialKeyExtract	$3t_{exp}$	$2t_{exp}$
UserKeyGen	$2t_{exp}$	t_{exp}
SetPublicKey	$2t_{exp}$	–
PublicVerify	$8t_{exp}$	$2t_{exp}$
Re-KeyGen	$5t_{exp}$	$2t_{exp}$
Encrypt	$10t_{exp}$	$4t_{exp}$
Re-Encrypt	$10t_{exp}$	$6t_{exp}$
Decrypt	$11t_{exp}$	$6t_{exp}$
Re-Decrypt	$6t_{exp}$	$4t_{exp}$

6   Conclusion

Although several CLPRE schemes have been proposed in the literature, to the best of our knowledge, only one scheme [6] has reported the certificateless property without any known attacks to the scheme. The scheme is based on costly bilinear pairing operation and satisfies a weaker notion of security, termed as RCCA security. Recently, Srinivasan *et al.* [10] proposed a CLPRE scheme without resorting to bilinear pairing in the random oracle model. However, we demonstrated that their security proof is flawed by presenting a concrete attack. We then presented a unidirectional CLPRE scheme which is pairing-free and satisfies CCA-security against both the Type-I and Type-II adversaries for the first and second level ciphertexts. We remark that a potential fix to [10] is also suggested in our paper but our proposed algorithm is more efficient as noted from our efficiency comparison. Our work affirmatively resolves the problems faced by PKI-based and IB-based PRE schemes by proposing an efficient pairing-free certificateless Proxy Re-encryption scheme.

References

1. Al-Riyami, S.S., Paterson, K.G.: Certificateless public key cryptography. In: Laih, C.-S. (ed.) ASIACRYPT 2003. LNCS, vol. 2894, pp. 452–473. Springer, Heidelberg (2003). doi:10.1007/978-3-540-40061-5_29
2. Ateniese, G., Fu, K., Green, M., Hohenberger, S.: Improved proxy re-encryption schemes with applications to secure distributed storage. In: IN NDSS (2005)
3. Ateniese, G., Kevin, F., Green, M., Hohenberger, S.: Improved proxy re-encryption schemes with applications to secure distributed storage. ACM Tran. Inf. Syst. Secur. (TISSEC) **9**(1), 1–30 (2006)
4. Blaze, M., Bleumer, G., Strauss, M.: Divertible protocols and atomic proxy cryptography. In: Nyberg, K. (ed.) EUROCRYPT 1998. LNCS, vol. 1403, pp. 127–144. Springer, Heidelberg (1998). doi:10.1007/BFb0054122
5. Chow, S.S.M., Weng, J., Yang, Y., Deng, R.H.: Efficient unidirectional proxy re-encryption. In: Bernstein, D.J., Lange, T. (eds.) AFRICACRYPT 2010. LNCS, vol. 6055, pp. 316–332. Springer, Heidelberg (2010). doi:10.1007/978-3-642-12678-9_19
6. Guo, H., Zhang, Z., Zhang, J., Chen, C.: Towards a secure certificateless proxy re-encryption scheme. In: Susilo, W., Reyhanitabar, R. (eds.) ProvSec 2013. LNCS, vol. 8209, pp. 330–346. Springer, Heidelberg (2013). doi:10.1007/978-3-642-41227-1_19
7. Schnorr, C.-P.: Efficient signature generation by smart cards. J. Cryptol. **4**(3), 161–174 (1991)
8. Sharmila Deva Selvi, S., Paul, A., Pandu Rangan, C.: An efficient certificateless proxy re-encryption scheme without pairing. Cryptology ePrint Archive, Report 2017/768 (2017). http://eprint.iacr.org/2017/768
9. Shamir, A.: Identity-based cryptosystems and signature schemes. In: Blakley, G.R., Chaum, D. (eds.) CRYPTO 1984. LNCS, vol. 196, pp. 47–53. Springer, Heidelberg (1985). doi:10.1007/3-540-39568-7_5
10. Srinivasan, A., Pandu Rangan, C.: Certificateless proxy re-encryption without pairing: revisited. In: Proceedings of the 3rd International Workshop on Security in Cloud Computing, SCC@ASIACCS 2015, Singapore, Republic of Singapore, 14 April 2015, pp. 41–52 (2015)

11. Sur, C., Jung, C.D., Park, Y., Rhee, K.H.: Chosen-ciphertext secure certificateless proxy re-encryption. In: De Decker, B., Schaumüller-Bichl, I. (eds.) CMS
2010. LNCS, vol. 6109, pp. 214–232. Springer, Heidelberg (2010). doi:10.1007/
978-3-642-13241-4_20
12. Yang, K., Xu, J., Zhang, Z.: Certificateless proxy re-encryption without pairings.
In: Lee, H.-S., Han, D.-G. (eds.) ICISC 2013. LNCS, vol. 8565, pp. 67–88. Springer,
Cham (2014). doi:10.1007/978-3-319-12160-4_5
13. Zheng, Y., Tang, S., Guan, C., Chen, M.-R.: Cryptanalysis of a certificateless
proxy re-encryption scheme. In: 2013 Fourth International Conference on Emerging
Intelligent Data and Web Technologies, Xi'an, Shaanxi, China, 9–11 September
2013, pp. 307–312 (2013)

Mergeable Functional Encryption

Vincenzo Iovino[1]([✉]) and Karol Żebrowski[2]

[1] University of Luxembourg, Luxembourg City, Luxembourg
vincenzo.iovino@uni.lu
[2] University of Warsaw, Warsaw, Poland
k.zebrowski@mimuw.edu.pl

Abstract. In this paper we put forward a new generalization of Functional Encryption (FE) that we call Mergeable FE (mFE). In a mFE system, given a ciphertext c_1 encrypting m_1 and a ciphertext c_2 encrypting m_2, it is possible to produce in an oblivious way a ciphertext encrypting the merged string $m_1||m_2$ under the security constraint that the new ciphertext does not leak more information about the original ciphertexts. For instance, let us suppose to have a token for a program (for inputs of variable length) P_x that, on input a string D representing a list of elements, checks if a given element x is in D, and suppose that c_1 (resp. c_2) encrypts a list D_1 (resp. D_2). Then the token evaluated on c_1 (resp. c_2) reveals if x is in list D_1 (resp. D_2) but the same token evaluated on c, the ciphertext resulting from the merge of c_1 and c_2, should only reveal if x is in D_1 or x is in D_2 but not in which of the two lists it is in.

This primitive is in some sense FE with the "best possible" homomorphic properties and, besides being interesting in itself, it offers wide applications. For instance, it has as special case multi-inputs FE (and thus indistinguishability obfuscation), but enables applications not possible with the latter.

Keywords: Functional Encryption · Obfuscation · Homomorphic cryptography

1 Introduction

Functional Encryption (FE) [5] is a sophisticated type of encryption that allows to finely control the amount of information that is revealed by a ciphertext. In a FE scheme, for any function f allowed by the system, the owner of the master secret key can compute a restricted key, called *token*, for f, that enables to compute $f(m)$ on a ciphertext encrypting m, and nothing else. In recent years, more expressive forms of FE were constructed in a series of works (see, e.g., [3,7,16,18]) culminating in the breakthrough of Garg *et al.* [10] who showed the first candidate construction of FE for all polynomial-size circuits from indistinguishability obfuscation. Another line of research investigated extensions and generalizations of FE such as multi-inputs FE [13], FE for randomized functionalities [14], FE in the private-key model [19] and in alternative models [4]. While these works

© Springer International Publishing AG 2017
T. Okamoto et al. (Eds.): ProvSec 2017, LNCS 10592, pp. 434–451, 2017.
https://doi.org/10.1007/978-3-319-68637-0_26

offer unique applications and pose new insights and challenges, we call for the need for a new and further generalization of FE not previously discussed in the literature.

We put forward the concept of mergeable FE (mFE) scheme. A mFE scheme is identical to a FE scheme but in addition it is endowed with a Merge algorithm that given two ciphertexts c_1 and c_2 encrypting respectively m_1 and m_2 can produce a ciphertext c encrypting $m_1||m_2$ where '$||$' represents the concatenation symbol, i.e., can *merge* the original ciphertexts, in an oblivious way without knowledge of the underlying plaintexts. As special case, a mFE also allows to *update* a ciphertext in an oblivious way. That is, having a ciphertext encrypting an unknown plaintext m, the system allows to produce a ciphertext c encrypting $m||m_2$ where m_2 is any plaintext. Notice that a mFE system represents in some sense a FE scheme with the best possible *homomorphic* properties. Indeed, it is easy to see that a FE scheme can not be in general fully homomorphic: for instance, the token for the function $f(\cdot)$ such that $f(x) = f(y)$ for some messages x, y but $f(g(x)) \neq f(g(y))$ for some function $g(\cdot)$, allows to distinguish whether a ciphertext c encrypts x or y by homomorphically evaluating the function $g(\cdot)$ on c. Instead, the restricted form of homomorphism allowed by mFE preserves and does *not* contradict its functional properties. Apart from being interesting in itself, the applications of mFE and the settings where it can be applied are vast and we will illustrate few of them.

Applications of mFE. The works of [13] introduced the concept of multi-inputs FE (MI-FE), a generalization of FE where a token corresponds to a multi-variate function that takes multiple ciphertexts as input. In these works, several settings were defined. mFE implies MI-FE[1]: to evaluate a multi-variate token on multiple ciphertexts it is sufficient to merge the ciphertexts. As special case, a mFE supporting a *single* merging operation implies 2-inputs MI-FE.

One of the most notable applications of FE is to searching over encrypted databases in a cloud computing setting. In this scenario, Alice, the manager of a company, can distribute a token for a function f to any of her employees who can use such tokens to perform queries over encrypted databases located in a cloud server. For instance, one database D_1 is produced by Bob and sent to the cloud server in an encrypted form under the public-key of Alice. Similarly, Eve produced her database D_2 and sent it to the cloud server in the same encrypted form. The two databases could contain information about products sold, respectively, by the companies of Bob and Eve and of interest for the company of Alice. Moreover, we assume that the cloud servers own a lot of computational power and space but are not trusted by Bob and Eve, i.e., Bob and Eve wish to leak as few information as possible to the servers. For simplicity, suppose that the databases are implemented as lists of elements, let us say $D_1 = (x_1||\ldots||x_n)$ and $D_2 = (y_1||\ldots||y_n)$. An employee of the company of Alice could be interested in searching whether a specific product x is in *one* of

---

[1] This holds for the public-key setting where the adversary is given the public-key that allows to encrypt messages corresponding to any dimension.

the two databases but he does not care in which one it is in. Thus, the employee sends to both servers a token for the function $f_x(D) \stackrel{\triangle}{=} 1$ iff the list D contains x.

The server evaluates the token on *both* encrypted databases one at time and then communicate to the employee whether the requested product x is or is not in the databases. Suppose that at some point there is a commercial agreement between the companies of Bob and Eve and as result of it they decide to merge their respective data without compromising the needs of the company of Alice and to keep on storing the merged encrypted data in the same cloud server. One solution could be to reveal to each other their data and re-encrypt anything under the public-key of Alice. However, this is not a valid solution as they wish to preserve the confidentiality of their own data. Another approach could be to store on the server just the concatenation of the previous ciphertexts. That is, if c_1 is the encryption of D_1 and c_2 is the encryption of D_2, then the new encrypted data could just consist of $c_1 || c_2$.

Anyway, recall that Bob and Eve wish to hide to the cloud server the contents of the new encrypted database. If the new encrypted database was just the concatenation of the encryptions of D_1 and D_2, then from a query for a product x, the server could figure out whether x was in the database of Alice or in the database of Bob by running the token separately on c_1 and c_2. Thus, this solution is not satisfactory. Another approach could to make Alice to create a *new* FE system and to ask the server to merge the two encrypted data under the *new* Alice's public-key. This solution incurs in a lot of problems as well. First of all, it requires a work from the Alice's side. Instead, Bob and Eve would like to merge their data without involving Alice's company (the employees of Alice are interested in searching whether a product is in *one* of the encrypted databases and *not* in which one it is in). That is, in the scenario we envision, Alice consents the companies with which she collaborates with to merge their own encrypted data without even informing her, i.e., in a *non-interactive* way. Furthermore, the size of the public-keys and parameters would grow (as the new system is based on the old one) and the main drawback is that Alice would have to re-compute and re-distribute *new* tokens to each employee. Instead, mFE offers a valid solution to this problem: if the databases are encrypted with a mFE system, then Bob and Eve can merge their own encrypted databases in an oblivious way hiding any information on the original databases to the server.

From mFE it is possible to derive CCA1-secure PKE with special homomorphic properties. Recall that FE (specifically, identity-based encryption) implies CCA1-secure public-key encryption (PKE) [8]. If the underlying FE scheme used in the construction of CCA1-secure PKE is in particular a mFE scheme, the resulting PKE scheme would be a CCA1-secure PKE scheme supporting merging operations.

We defer further applications to the full version.

The requirements of a mFE scheme. In view of the above and further applications we desire mFE systems to satisfy the following properties:

- The operation of merging two ciphertexts c_1 and c_2 can be performed having just the public-key of the system, c_1 and c_2.

- The size of the merged ciphertext should be proportional to the sum of the lengths of the old ciphertexts plus an *additive* factor polynomial in the security parameter. That is, suppose that c_1 has size m_1 and c_2 has size m_2 and let k be the security parameter. Then, the result of merging c_1 and c_2 must be a ciphertext of length $O(m_1 + m_2 + k)$. This is to rule out solutions where the ciphertext resulting from the merge has for instance length $k \cdot (|m_1| + \cdot |m_2|)$ that would bound the number of mergings to be logarithmic (or less) in the security parameter. We call this requirement *compactness*.
- The systems must be designed for the Turing Machine (TM) model of computation as the circuit model does not fit well with the mFE setting. In fact, circuits can compute over a fixed number of bits, and thus, even though the system allowed multiple merging operations, a token could be used only on ciphertexts resulting from a bounded number of merging operations.

Our solutions of Sect. 3 only support a single merging operation and are easily generalizable to bounded number of merging operation. In the full version we will discuss an heuristic construction supporting unbounded messages from new assumptions. Anyway, we stress that also a mFE supporting single merge is already sufficient for most of our applications like the implications of MI-FE, and all other applications when limited to a single operation.

We adopt as security definition an indistinguishability-based (IND) one. Recall that in the standard IND-Security game for FE an efficient adversary can output two challenge messages m_0 and m_1 and can ask any token for a function f that does not allow to distinguish the two messages, i.e., such that $f(m_0) = f(m_1)$. This is to avoid trivial attacks. In mFE this constraint is not sufficient. In fact, it could be that $f(m_0) = f(m_1)$ but $f(m||m_0) \neq f(m||m_1)$ allowing the adversary to distinguish by merging the challenge ciphertext with a ciphertext encrypting m. Notice that this situation is similar to the case of MI-FE. Therefore, we change the definition in the obvious way, by generalizing the above constraint to take in account any sequence of messages that "extends" the challenge messages (in poor words, to any message that has the challenge message as substring). More formally we also allow the challenge to be a pair of sequences (s_0, s_1) of merging operations with the same length and structure. Details are given in Sect. 2.1.

Overview of the construction. We assume that the reader is familiar with the construction of FE of Garg *et al.* [10]. Let us now sketch how to construct mFE scheme that supports a single merging operation. The technical details of our construction are tightly related with the need of proving its security so we will explain it step by step following an informal approach. Let us call ciphertexts of "first level" the ciphertexts encrypting directly messages and not resulting from merge operations. Suppose that in our scheme the ciphertexts of first level have the same form as in the Garg *et al.*'s scheme. Consider now the following implementation of the merge operation. To merge two ciphertexts (c_1, c_2, π_1) and (c_3, c_4, π_2), re-encrypt c_1 and c_3 under the first public-key to get Ct_1 and c_2 and c_4 under the second public-key to get Ct_2 adding a proof that Ct_1 and Ct_2 encrypt respectively strings $(c_1||c_3)$ and $(c_2||c_4)$ such that there exist proofs

π_1, π_2 of the fact that c_1 and c_2 encrypt the same message and c_3 and c_4 encrypt the same message with respect to some proof systems to be specified later. We call the $\mathcal{NP}$ language consisting of statements of such form L^2 to distinguish it from L^1, the language used for the ciphertexts of first level (consisting of pairs of ciphertexts that encrypt the same message). That is, the new ciphertext will be $(\mathsf{Encrypt}(\mathsf{Pk}_1, (c_1, c_3)), \mathsf{Enc}(\mathsf{Pk}_2, (c_2, c_4)), \pi)$, where π is a proof of the fact that Ct_1 and Ct_2 belong to L^2.

To simplify the construction, let us use the following tools. First of all, we employ (1) a non-interactive witness indistinguishable proof systems (NIWI) with statistical soundness [9] and (2) a statistically binding commitment scheme. In the public-key we put two CRSs of the NIWI system, one used to prove statements in L^1 and one for L^2, and a statistically binding commitment com. Actually for the needs of our reduction, the languages L^1 and L^2 are changed as follows. In the real scheme the NIWI is used to prove the following statement: "the pair of ciphertexts $(\mathsf{Ct}_1, \mathsf{Ct}_2)$ are well formed (as specified before) or com is a commitment to $(\mathsf{Ct}_1 || \mathsf{Ct}_2)$". Let us now sketch the security reduction. Recall that the adversary $\mathcal{A}$ selects as challenges two sequences ($s_0 = (m_1, m_2), s_1 = (m_3, m_4)$) of merging operations and let us denote by x_b^1 (resp. x_b^2) the *inner* string encrypted in the ciphertext *induced* by the sequence s_b with respect to the first (resp. second) public-key.

The definition is better explained by an example. For instance, with respect to the sequences s_0, x_0^1 is string $(\mathsf{Encrypt}(\mathsf{Pk}_1, m_1) || \mathsf{Encrypt}(\mathsf{Pk}_1, m_2))$. Furthermore, let use denote by $x_b^i[L]$ (resp. $x_b^i[R]$) the left part (resp. right part) of x_b^i, e.g., in the previous example $x_0^1[L] = \mathsf{Encrypt}(\mathsf{Pk}_1, m_1)$ and $x_0^1[R] = \mathsf{Encrypt}(\mathsf{Pk}_1, m_2)$. Note that the challenge ciphertext Ct consists of $(\mathsf{Ct}_1, \mathsf{Ct}_2, \pi)$ where, if for instance the challenge bit $b = 0$, Ct_1 encrypts x_0^1 and Ct_2 encrypts x_0^2 and π is a proof that $(\mathsf{Ct}_1, \mathsf{Ct}_2) \in L^2$ that is in turn relative to the two proofs π_1', π_2'. The latter proofs are such that (1) π_1' is a proof that $x_0^1[L]$ and $x_0^2[L]$ encrypt the same message (in the previous example m_1) and (2) π_2' is a proof that $x_0^1[R]$ and $x_0^2[R]$ encrypt the same message (in the previous example m_2). The security proof proceeds in a standard hybrid argument and is deferred to Sect. 3.1.

For simplicity we presented the construction for a *single* merging operation but it is straight-forward to extend it to a *bounded* number d of merging operations at cost of having parameters growing as d. In Sect. 3.2 we show how this construction can be also extended to support a bounded number of merging operations but for messages of *unbounded* length but for that we need *public-coin* diO instead of iO.

Related work. The primitive we introduce is novel yet it is related to the following cryptographic objects. mFE shares with homomorphic encryption (see [11]) the capability of "combining" different ciphertexts in an oblivious way but it extends homomorphic encryption with functional features. As discussed before, in some sense mFE achieves the best of possible homomorphism capabilities for FE. mFE shares with MI-FE [13] the capability of computing over *multiple* encrypted data and indeed mFE enables all the applications of MI-FE but the converse is not true.

In particular, MI-FE differs from mFE in an essential aspect. When two ciphertexts c_1 and c_2 are merged with mFE, it is not longer possible to recover the original information. Instead, while MI-FE allows to compute a function f over two ciphertexts c_1 and c_2 yet it is possible to swap c_2 with any other ciphertext c_3 to compute f over c_1 and c_3. We also remark that it is not known how to use MI-FE to re-encrypt so to imply mFE.

FE for randomized functionalities was studied by Goyal *et al.* [14] who presented two types of notions, one simulation-based and one indistinguishability-based. The simulation-based one can be defined only in limited settings due to known impossibility results [1,5], and moreover, to be useful in constructing mFE, simulation-based secure FE for randomized functionalities should be generalized to 2-inputs for which more severe impossibility results are known as it would imply VBB obfuscation. Instead, the indistinguishability-based notion is limited to statistically indistinguishable distributions, thus excluding the re-encryption functionality.

Target malleability introduced by Boneh *et al.* [6] restricts the set of homomorphic operations one can perform on encrypted data but does *not* offer functional features. Gentry *et al.* [12] construct an attribute-based encryption (ABE) scheme with fully homomorphic properties. In ABE the ciphertext is associated with a pair (m, x) where x is public and only m is hidden. The system of Gentry *et al.* allows homomorphic operations only on m, and thus is incomparable to ours.

2   Definitions

Functional Encryption. Functional encryption (FE) schemes are encryption schemes for which the owner of the master secret can compute restricted keys, called *tokens*, that allow to compute a *functionality* on the plaintext associated with a ciphertext. In this work we consider FE for Turing Machines (TMs) [17] and we assume that the reader is familiar with it. We assume a standard definition of FE scheme and its indistinguishability-based security as in [5].

2.1   Mergeable Functional Encryption

In this Section we will formally introduce the concept of mergeable functional encryption (mFE).

We first introduce our notation related to merging operations. To not overburden the discussion, we prefer to adopt a non too much formal style but expanding the definitions with concrete examples.

We denote the merge of string x_1 with string x_2 by $(x_1, x_2)^2$ and we call such string (x_1, x_2) a *sequence*. (We assume implicitly that the symbols '(',')' and ',' do not belong to the string alphabet and thus sequences can be parsed efficiently.

---

[2] Notice that the order is important, so the operation (x_1, x_2) is different from (x_2, x_1).

This can be formalized in standard ways but we over skip these details). Furthermore, we define a sequence of merging inductively in the obvious way. That is, a string in the message space is a sequence of merging operations and if s_1 and s_2 are sequences of merging operations, then (s_1, s_2) is a sequence of merging operations. For instance, the sequence $s = ((x_1, (x_2, x_3)), x_4)$ is the result of (1) merging x_2 with x_3 to get sequence s_1, then (2) merging x_1 with s_1 to get sequence s_2 and finally (3) s_2 with x_4 to get sequence s. Note that in this paper with a slight abuse of notation sometimes we use the notation $(x.y)$ and similar to denote both sequences of merging operations and lists of elements. We say that a sequence of merging operations s *splits over* the strings $(x_1, \ldots, x_n)$ if such variables appear in s in that order. For instance $(x_1, (x_2, (x_3, x_4)))$ splits over (x_1, x_2, x_3, x_4). We say that a sequence of merging operations s *ranges over* the set of strings M if the strings appearing in s belong to M. For instance $(x_1, (x_2, (x_3, x_2)))$ ranges over *any* set containing $\{x_1, x_2, x_3\}$. If s is a sequence we denote by $\mathsf{cat}(s)$ the concatenation of the strings which the sequence consists of. For instance if $s = ((x_1, (x_2, x_3)), x_4)$ then $\mathsf{cat}(s) = x_1 || x_2 || x_3 || x_4$.

We say that a sequence of merging operations s_1 splitting over the strings $(x_1, \ldots, x_n)$ has the same *structure* of a sequence of merging operations s_2 splitting over $(y_1, \ldots, y_m)$ if (1) $m = n$ and (2) if s_1' is the string obtained by replacing any string x_i in s_1 with $0^{|x_i|}$ and s_2' is the string obtained by replacing any string y_i in s_2 with $0^{|y_i|}$, then $s_1' = s_2'$. Note that this implies that for any i, $|x_i| = |y_i|$. For instance, $(010, (111, 001))$ does *not* have the same structure of $((010, 111), 001)$, $(010, (111, 001))$ does *not* have the same structure of $(010, (11, 001))$, but $(010, (11, 001))$ *does* have the same structure of $(111, (00, 110))$. That is, two sequences have the same structure if the sequence of parenthesis and commas correspond and any string has the same length. We say that $t(\cdot)$ is a function of merging operations if $t(\cdot)$ is a sequence of merging operations containing at least one special symbol $\star$ and if s is a sequence of merging operations then $t(s)$ is the result of replacing $\star$ with s in t. Furthermore, If $t(\cdot) = \star$ then $t(s) = s$ for any sequence of merging operations s. For instance, if $t(\cdot) = ((x_1, (x_2, *)), x_3)$ and $s = (x_3, x_4)$ then $t(s) = ((x_1, (x_2, (x_3, x_4))), x_3)$. We say that a function of merging operations $t(\cdot)$ *ranges over* the set of strings M if except the symbol $\star$ the strings appearing in t belong to M. For instance $t(\cdot) = (x_1, (\star, (x_3, x_2)))$ ranges over *any* set containing $\{x_1, x_2, x_3\}$. Finally, we stress that the strings in the sequence of merging operations we will consider will be both messages in the message space and ciphertexts. For instance, if c_1, c_2, c_3 and c_4 are ciphertexts, then $s = ((c_1, c_2), (c_3, c_4))$ is a sequence of merging operations on ciphertexts.

Definition 1 [mergeable Functional Encryption Scheme]. A *mergeable functional encryption* scheme mFE for functionality F is a tuple mFE = (Setup, KeyGen, Enc, Eval, Merge) of 5 algorithms with the following syntax:

1. Setup(1^λ) outputs *public* and *master secret* keys (Pk, Msk) for *security parameter* λ.
2. KeyGen(Msk, k), on input a master secret key Msk and *key* $k \in K$ outputs *token* Tok.

3. $\mathsf{Enc}(\mathsf{Pk}, m)$, on input public key Pk and *plaintext* $m \in M$ outputs *ciphertext* Ct: Furthermore, if s is a sequence of merging operations splitting over the strings $(x_1, \dots, x_n)$, with a slight abuse of notation, we denote by $\mathsf{Enc}(\mathsf{Pk}, s)$, the sequence s' that is equal to s except that for any $i \in [n]$, any occurrence of x_i is replaced by $\mathsf{Enc}(\mathsf{Pk}, x_i)$. For instance, $\mathsf{Enc}(\mathsf{Pk}, (x_1, (x_2, x_3))) = (c_1, (c_2, c_3))$ where c_1, c_2 and c_3 are respectively the encryptions of x_1, x_2 and x_3. (We stress that even if a sequence s contains two equal strings, e.g., $(x_1, (x_2, x_1))$, in the encryption of s any ciphertext is generated with *independent* randomness).
4. $\mathsf{Eval}(\mathsf{Pk}, \mathsf{Ct}, \mathsf{Tok})$ outputs $y \in \Sigma \cup \{\perp\}$.
5. $\mathsf{Merge}(1^\lambda, \mathsf{Pk}, \mathsf{Ct}_1, \mathsf{Ct}_2)$: if Ct_1 and Ct_2 are ciphertexts, the algorithm outputs a ciphertext Ct resulting from merging Ct_1 with Ct_2.

   With a slight abuse of notation, we also define Merge to take as input a sequence of merging operations on ciphertexts in the obvious way, described by the following example. Let $s_1 = (c_1, (c_2, c_3))$ be a sequence of merging operations on ciphertexts, then
   $$\mathsf{Merge}(1^\lambda, \mathsf{Pk}, s) \stackrel{\triangle}{=} \mathsf{Merge}(1^\lambda, \mathsf{Pk}, c_1, \mathsf{Merge}(1^\lambda, \mathsf{Pk}, c_2, c_3)).$$

In addition we make the following requirements:

- *Correctness*: For all $(\mathsf{Pk}, \mathsf{Msk}) \leftarrow \mathsf{Setup}(1^\lambda)$, all $k \in K$ and any sequence s splitting over strings $\in M$ such that $\mathsf{cat}(s) \in M$, for $\mathsf{Tok} \leftarrow \mathsf{KeyGen}(\mathsf{Msk}, k)$ and $\mathsf{Ct} \leftarrow \mathsf{Merge}(1^\lambda, \mathsf{Pk}, \mathsf{Enc}(\mathsf{Pk}, s))$, we have that $\mathsf{Eval}(\mathsf{Pk}, \mathsf{Ct}, \mathsf{Tok}) = F(k, \mathsf{cat}(s))$ whenever $F(k, \mathsf{cat}(s)) \neq \perp$, except with negligible probability in λ. (See [2] for a discussion about this condition.)
- *Compactness*: there exists a polynomial poly such that for all $(\mathsf{Pk}, \mathsf{Msk}) \leftarrow \mathsf{Setup}(1^\lambda)$, for any sequences s_1, s_2 splitting over strings $\in M$ such that $\mathsf{cat}(s_1), \mathsf{cat}(s_2) \in M$, for $\mathsf{Ct}_1 \leftarrow \mathsf{Merge}(1^\lambda, \mathsf{Pk}, \mathsf{Enc}(\mathsf{Pk}, s_1))$, $\mathsf{Ct}_2 \leftarrow \mathsf{Merge}(1^\lambda, \mathsf{Pk}, \mathsf{Enc}(\mathsf{Pk}, s_2))$, $\mathsf{Ct} \leftarrow \mathsf{Merge}(1^\lambda, \mathsf{Pk}, \mathsf{Ct}_1, \mathsf{Ct}_2)$, we have that $|\mathsf{Ct}| \in O(|\mathsf{Ct}_1| + |\mathsf{Ct}_2| + \mathsf{poly}(\lambda))$. Note that here sequences s_1, s_2 might be a single message.

Remark 2. Notice that the correctness requirement has as special case the correctness for traditional FE.

Indistinguishability-based security. The indistinguishability-based notion of security for mergeable functional encryption scheme $\mathsf{mFE} = (\mathsf{mFE.Setup}, \mathsf{mFE.KeyGen}, \mathsf{mFE.Enc}, \mathsf{mFE.Eval})$ for functionality F defined over (K, M) is formalized by means of the following game parametrized by a polynomial poly:
$\mathsf{mIND}_{\mathcal{A}}^{\mathsf{mFE}, \mathsf{poly}}$ between an adversary $\mathcal{A} = (\mathcal{A}_0, \mathcal{A}_1)$ and a *challenger* $\mathcal{C}$. Below, we present the definition for only one message; it is easy to see the definition extends naturally for multiple messages.

$\mathsf{mIND}_{\mathcal{A}}^{\mathsf{mFE,poly}}(1^\lambda)$

1. $\mathcal{C}$ generates $(\mathsf{Pk}, \mathsf{Msk}) \leftarrow \mathsf{mFE.Setup}(1^\lambda)$ and runs $\mathcal{A}_0$ on input Pk;
2. $\mathcal{A}_0$ submits queries for keys $k_i \in K$ for $i = 1, \ldots, q_1$ and, for each such query, $\mathcal{C}$ computes $\mathsf{Tok}_i = \mathsf{mFE.KeyGen}(\mathsf{Msk}, k_i)$ and sends it to $\mathcal{A}_0$. When $\mathcal{A}_0$ stops, it outputs two *challenge sequences of merging operations* s_0, s_1 and its internal state st.
3. $\mathcal{C}$ picks $b \in \{0, 1\}$ at random, computes the *challenge ciphertext* $\mathsf{Ct} = \mathsf{mFE.Merge}(\mathsf{Pk}, \mathsf{mFE.Encrypt}(\mathsf{Pk}, s_b))^a$ and sends Ct to $\mathcal{A}_1$ that resumes its computation from state st.
4. $\mathcal{A}_1$ submits queries for keys $k_i \in K$ for $i = q_1 + 1, \ldots, q$ and, for each such query, $\mathcal{C}$ computes $\mathsf{Tok}_i = \mathsf{mFE.KeyGen}(\mathsf{Msk}, k_i)$ and sends it to $\mathcal{A}_1$.
5. When $\mathcal{A}_1$ stops, it outputs b'.
6. **Output:** The challenger outputs 1 (i.e., the adversary wins the game) iff the following conditions are all satisfied:
   (a) $b = b'$.
   (b) s_0 and s_1 are sequences of strings over strings in $\mathcal{M}$ satisfying $|s_0| = |s_1|$.
   (c) for any function of merging operations $t(\cdot)$ of length $\leq \mathsf{poly}(\lambda)$ ranging over $\mathcal{M}$ it holds that: $F(k_i, t(s_0)) = F(k_i, t(s_1))$ for $i = 1 \ldots, q$.

---

^{a} We refer the reader to the definition of the procedure Merge for the use of this notation.

For any polynomial poly, the advantage of adversary $\mathcal{A}$ in the above game parametrized by poly is defined as

$$\mathsf{Adv}_{\mathcal{A}}^{\mathsf{mFE,mIND,poly}}(1^\lambda) = |\mathsf{Prob}[\mathsf{mIND}_{\mathcal{A}}^{\mathsf{mFE,poly}}(1^\lambda) = 1] - 1/2|.$$

Definition 3. We say that mFE is *indistinguishably secure* (IND-Secure, for short) for all probabilistic polynomial-time adversaries $\mathcal{A}$ there exists a polynomial poly such that the quantity $\mathsf{Adv}_{\mathcal{A}}^{\mathsf{mFE,mIND,poly}}(1^\lambda)$ is negligible in λ.

Definition 4 [Selective IND-Security]. The selective security game of mFE is similar to the above game except that the adversary has to declare the challenges at the beginning of the experiment. We say that a mFE scheme is selectively IND-Secure if any PPT adversaries has at most negligible advantage in such game.

We provided definitions for mFE supporting unbounded number of operations. It is straight-forward to adapt them to the case of mFE supporting one merging operation as needed in Sect. 3. Moreover, for mFE supporting one merging operation the compactness property is not required.

Building blocks. In our work we will indistinguishability obfuscation (iO) for Turing Machines [17], public-coin differing-inputs obfuscation (diO) [15], NIWI proof system [9] and other standard primitives.

3   Our mFE Scheme for One Merging Operation

Definition 5 [MFE scheme for one merging operation]. Let $\mathsf{NIWI}^i = (\mathsf{CRSGen}^i, \mathsf{Prove}^i, \mathsf{Verify}^i)$ for $i = 1, 2$ be two NIWI proof systems for some $\mathcal{NP}$-languages to be specified later, Com a (perfectly binding) commitment scheme, $\mathsf{E} = (\mathsf{E.Setup}, \mathsf{E.Encrypt}, \mathsf{E.Decrypt})$ a PKE scheme, and $i\mathcal{O}$ an iO for TMs with bounded inputs [17]. Let $n(\lambda)$ be a bound on the size of the messages that our mFE has to support and $m(\lambda)$ a bound on the size of ciphertexts of E that encrypt messages of length $n(\lambda)$. We define a mFE scheme $\mathsf{mFE}[\mathsf{NIWI}^1, \mathsf{NIWI}^2, \mathsf{Com}, \mathsf{E}] = (\mathsf{Setup}, \mathsf{KeyGen}, \mathsf{Enc}, \mathsf{Merge}, \mathsf{Eval})$ for functionality TM as follows.

- $\mathsf{Setup}(1^\lambda)$[3]: runs $(\mathsf{Pk}_1, \mathsf{Sk}_1) \leftarrow \mathsf{E.Setup}(1^\lambda)$, $(\mathsf{Pk}_2, \mathsf{Sk}_2) \leftarrow \mathsf{E.Setup}(1^\lambda)$, and $\mathsf{com} \leftarrow \mathsf{Com}(0^{2m(\lambda)})$, and sets $\mathsf{crs}^i \leftarrow \mathsf{CRSGen}^i(1^\lambda)^i$ for $i = 1, 2$. The procedure returns a pair $(\mathsf{Mpk}, \mathsf{Msk})$ where $\mathsf{Mpk} = (\mathsf{Pk}_1, \mathsf{Pk}_2, \mathsf{com}, \mathsf{crs}^1, \mathsf{crs}^2)$ and $\mathsf{Msk} = \mathsf{Sk}_1$.
- $\mathsf{Enc}(\mathsf{Pk}, m)$: on input $\mathsf{Pk} = (\mathsf{Pk}_1, \mathsf{Pk}_2, \mathsf{com}, \mathsf{crs}^1, \mathsf{crs}^2)$ and $m \in n(\lambda)$, the algorithm chooses randomness r_1 and r_2, and computes $\mathsf{Ct}_1 = \mathsf{E.Encrypt}(\mathsf{Pk}_1, m; r_1), \mathsf{Ct}_2 = \mathsf{E.Encrypt}(\mathsf{Pk}_2, m; r_2)$. Consider the following $\mathcal{NP}$-language[4]:
  $L^1 = \{(\mathsf{Ct}_1, \mathsf{Ct}_2) \in \{0, 1\}^{2m(\lambda)} : \exists m, r, r_1, r_2 : (\mathsf{Ct}_1 = \mathsf{E.Encrypt}(\mathsf{Pk}_1, m; r_1) \wedge \mathsf{Ct}_2 = \mathsf{E.Encrypt}(\mathsf{Pk}_2, m; r_2)) \vee \mathsf{com} = \mathsf{Com}(\mathsf{Ct}_1 \| \mathsf{Ct}_2; r)\}$.
  (Note that L^1 is relative to $\mathsf{com}, \mathsf{Pk}_1, \mathsf{Pk}_2$). The procedure outputs a ciphertext of first level $(1, \mathsf{Ct}_1, \mathsf{Ct}_2, \pi)$ where π is a proof of the fact that $(\mathsf{Ct}_1, \mathsf{Ct}_2) \in L^1$ computed with Prove^1 and crs^1 using as witness m, r_1, r_2.
- $\mathsf{KeyGen}(\mathsf{Msk}, M)$: on input Msk and a machine M, the algorithm outputs an iO of the following machine $T[M, \mathsf{Sk}_1, \mathsf{Pk}_1, \mathsf{Pk}_2, \mathsf{crs}^1, \mathsf{crs}^2, \mathsf{com}]$ as token.

Machine $T[M, \mathsf{Sk}_1, \mathsf{Pk}_1, \mathsf{Pk}_2, \mathsf{crs}^1, \mathsf{crs}^2, \mathsf{com}](l, \mathsf{Ct}_1, \mathsf{Ct}_2, \pi)$
1.   Pad with machine $T_2[M, \mathsf{Sk}_2, \mathsf{Pk}_1, \mathsf{Pk}_2, \mathsf{crs}^1, \mathsf{crs}^2, , \mathsf{com}]$
2.   if $l = 1$ then do
3.   If $\mathsf{Verify}^1(\mathsf{crs}^1, (\mathsf{Ct}_1, \mathsf{Ct}_2), \pi) = 0$ then return $\bot$
4.   set $m = \mathsf{E.Decrypt}(\mathsf{Sk}_1, \mathsf{Ct}_1)$ and return $M(m)$
5.   if $l = 2$ then do
6.   If $\mathsf{Verify}^2(\mathsf{crs}^2, (\mathsf{Ct}_1, \mathsf{Ct}_2), \pi) = 0$ then return $\bot$
7. $(c_1, c_2) = \mathsf{E.Decrypt}(\mathsf{Sk}_1, \mathsf{Ct}_1)$
8.   set $m_1 = \mathsf{E.Decrypt}(\mathsf{Sk}_1, c_1)$ and $m_2 = \mathsf{E.Decrypt}(\mathsf{Sk}_1, c_2)$
9.   return $M(m_1 \| m_2)$

---

[3] Formally, the procedure should also take as input the bound $m(\lambda)$ on the size of the messages (since it is used to generate the commitment) but for simplicity we omit such details.

[4] Formally we should define it as a family of languages indexed by the security parameter but henceforth for simplicity we omit this detail.

– Merge($\mathsf{Pk}, \mathsf{Ct}_1, \mathsf{Ct}_2$): Let $\mathsf{Ct}_1 = (c_1, c_2, \pi_1)$ and $\mathsf{Ct}_2 = (c_3, c_4, \pi_2)$. The procedure sets $\mathsf{Ct}'_1 = \mathsf{E.Encrypt}(PK_1, c_1||c_3)$ and $\mathsf{Ct}'_2 = \mathsf{E.Encrypt}(PK_2, c_2||c_4)$. Consider the following $\mathcal{NP}$-language L^2:
$L^2 = \{(\mathsf{Ct}_1, \mathsf{Ct}_2) \in \{0,1\}^{2m(\lambda)} : \exists c_1, c_2, c_3, c_4, \pi_1, \pi_2, r, r_1, r_2 : (\mathsf{Ct}'_1 = \mathsf{E.}$
$\mathsf{Encrypt}(\mathsf{Pk}_1, c_1||c_3; r_1) \wedge \mathsf{Ct}_2 = \mathsf{E.Encrypt}(\mathsf{Pk}_2, c_2||c_4; r_2) \wedge \mathsf{Verify}^1(\mathsf{crs}^1, c_1||$
$c_2) = 1 \wedge \mathsf{Verify}^1(\mathsf{crs}^1, c_3||c_4) = 1) \vee \mathsf{com} = \mathsf{Com}(\mathsf{Ct}_1||\mathsf{Ct}_2; r)\}$.
(Note that L^2 is relative to $\mathsf{com}, \mathsf{crs}^1, \mathsf{Pk}_1, \mathsf{Pk}_2$). The procedure computes a proof π of the fact that $(\mathsf{Ct}'_1, \mathsf{Ct}'_2) \in L^2$ using Prove^2 with crs^2 and witness $r_1, r_2, c_1, c_2, c_3, c_4, \pi_1, \pi_2$. The procedure outputs $(\mathsf{Ct}'_1, \mathsf{Ct}'_2, \pi)$.
– Eval($\mathsf{Pk}, \mathsf{Ct}, \mathsf{Tok}$): on input $\mathsf{Pk} = (\mathsf{Pk}_1, \mathsf{Pk}_2)$, $\mathsf{Ct} = (i, C_1, C_2, \pi)$ and $\mathsf{Tok} = i\mathcal{O}(T[M, \mathsf{Sk}_1, \mathsf{Pk}_1, \mathsf{Pk}_2, \mathsf{crs}, \mathsf{com}])$, returns the output $\mathsf{Tok}(\mathsf{Ct})$ (i.e., evaluates the obfuscated program on input Ct).

It is straight-forward to see that the scheme is correct.

3.1 Security Reduction

We assume that the reader is familiar with the overview presented in Sect. 1. We reduce the security of our mFE scheme to that of the underlying primitives via a series of hybrid experiments against a PPT adversary $\mathcal{A}$ attacking the selective IND-Security of mFE.

For simplicity we assume that the challenge sequences do *not* consist of single messages so that the challenge ciphertexts can not be of first level. However, it is easy to observe that in the latter case the reduction can be derived as special case of ours, but not to overburden the presentation we omit the details. Recall that the adversary $\mathcal{A}$ selects as challenges two sequences (s_0, s_1) of merging operations. We denote by x_b^1 (resp. x_b^2) the *inner* string encrypted in the ciphertext *induced* by the sequence s_b with respect to the first (resp. second) public-key. The definition is better explained by an example. For instance, if $s_0 = (m_1, m_2)$, then x_0^1 is the string $\mathsf{Encrypt}(\mathsf{Pk}_1, m_1)||\mathsf{Encrypt}(\mathsf{Pk}_1, m_2)$. Furthermore, we denote by $x_b^i[L]$ (resp. $x_b^i[R]$) the left part (resp. right part) of x_b^i, e.g., in the previous example $x_0^1[L] = \mathsf{Encrypt}(\mathsf{Pk}_1, m_1)$ and $x_0^1[R] = \mathsf{Encrypt}(\mathsf{Pk}_1, m_2)$. Note that in our construction the challenge ciphertext Ct with respect to the challenges (s_0, s_1) consist of $(\mathsf{Ct}_1, \mathsf{Ct}_2, \pi)$ where Ct_1 encrypts x_b^1 and Ct_2 encrypts x_b^2 and π is a proof that $(\mathsf{Ct}_1, \mathsf{Ct}_2) \in L^2$ that is in turn relative to (1) a NIWI proof π'_1 of the fact that $x_b^1[L]$ and $x_b^2[L]$ encrypt the same message and (2) a proof π'_2 of the fact that $x_b^1[R]$ and $x_b^2[R]$ encrypt the same message.

– H_0. This corresponds to the IND-Security game in which the chosen challenge sequence is s_0. Thus, the challenge ciphertext consists of $(\mathsf{Ct}_1, \mathsf{Ct}_2, \pi)$ where $(\mathsf{Ct}_1, \mathsf{Ct}_2)$ belong to L^2.
– H_1. This experiment is identical to H_0 except that the commitment com in the public-key is a commitment to $(\mathsf{Ct}_1, \mathsf{Ct}_2)$. Specifically, $\mathcal{A}$ selects its challenges $(s_0 = (m_1, m_2), s_1 = (m_3, m_4))$ and $x_0^1 = x_0^1[L]||x_0^1[R]$ and $x_0^2 = x_0^2[L]||x_0^2[R]$ are computed as described above along with (1) the NIWI proof π'_1 of the fact that $x_0^1[L]$ and $x_0^2[L]$ encrypt the same message (specifically

m_1) and (2) the NIWI proof π_2' of the fact that $x_0^1[R]$ and $x_0^2[R]$ encrypt the same message (specifically m_2). Then, the procedure Setup of mFE is run as in its definition except that com is set to be com $=$ Com$(($Ct$_1||$Ct$_2$)$; r$) for some fresh randomness r where Ct$_1$ is an encryption of x_0^1 and Ct$_2$ is an encryption of x_0^2. The rest of the experiment can be simulated by means of Msk and Pk generated by the procedure Setup. Indeed, note that in the challenge ciphertext Ct $=$ (Ct$_1$, Ct$_2$, π) the proof π is computed with respect to the proofs of "first level" π_1', π_2' and the randomness to encrypt x_0^1 in Ct$_1$ and x_0^2 in Ct$_2$.

Indistinguishability of H_1 from H_0. It is easy to see that the claim follows from the computational hiding property of com.

- H_2. This experiment is identical to H_1 except that the NIWI proof π in the challenge ciphertext Ct $=$ (Ct$_1||$Ct$_2$) is computed with respect to the randomness r used to generate com.

Indistinguishability of H_2 from H_1. It is easy to see that the claim follows from the witness indistinguishability property of NIWI observing that both the witness used in H_1 and the witness used in H_1 are valid witnesses of the fact that (Ct$_1$, Ct$_2$) $\in L^2$.

- H_3. This experiment is identical to H_2 except that Ct$_2$ is set to an encryption of x_1^2. The commitment com is still generated as com $=$ Com$(($Ct$_1||$Ct$_2$)$; r$) and the randomness r is still used as witness to compute the proof π in the challenge ciphertext Ct $=$ (Ct$_1$, Ct$_2$, π).

Indistinguishability of H_3 from H_2. It is easy to see that the claim follows from the IND-CPA security of E observing that Sk$_2$ is *never* needed to simulate the experiment.

- H_4. This experiment is identical to H_3 except that any token is changed to be the obfuscation of the following machine:

Machine $T_2[M, \mathsf{Sk}_2, \mathsf{Pk}_1, \mathsf{Pk}_2, \mathsf{crs}^1, \mathsf{crs}^2, \mathsf{com}](l, \mathsf{Ct}_1, \mathsf{Ct}_2, \pi)$
1. Pad with machine $T[M, \mathsf{Sk}_1, \mathsf{Pk}_1, \mathsf{Pk}_2, \mathsf{crs}^1, \mathsf{crs}^2, \mathsf{com}]$
2. if $l = 1$ then do
3.   If $\mathsf{Verify}^1(\mathsf{crs}^1, (\mathsf{Ct}_1, \mathsf{Ct}_2), \pi) = 0$ then return $\bot$
4.   set $m = \mathsf{E.Decrypt}(\mathsf{Sk}_2, \mathsf{Ct}_2)$ and return $M(m)$
5. if $l = 2$ then do
6.   If $\mathsf{Verify}^2(\mathsf{crs}^2, (\mathsf{Ct}_1, \mathsf{Ct}_2), \pi) = 0$ then return $\bot$
7. $(c_1, c_2) = \mathsf{E.Decrypt}(\mathsf{Sk}_2, \mathsf{Ct}_2)$
8.   set $m_1 = \mathsf{E.Decrypt}(\mathsf{Sk}_2, c_1)$ and $m_2 = \mathsf{E.Decrypt}(\mathsf{Sk}_2, c_2)$
9.   return $M(m_1||m_2)$

Indistinguishability of H_4 from H_3. For simplicity we can assume that $\mathcal{A}$ asks only one token query for the TM M computing the function f. The general case can be handled by a standard hybrid argument. By the statistical binding property of Com and by the correctness of E and by definition of $L^i, i = 1, 2$ and statistical soundness of NIWI, with all except negligible probability, there is exactly *one* pair of ciphertexts $(\mathsf{Ct}_1, \mathsf{Ct}_2)$ that encrypts different inner-messages, the challenge ciphertext, and by definition of the experiments, the message M_0 resulting from decrypting Ct_1 recursively using Sk_1 and the message M_1 resulting from decrypting Ct_2 recursively using Sk_2, are such that $f(M_0) = f(M_1)$ where f is the function associated with the token. Thus, we can invoke the security of $i\mathcal{O}$ to argue the indistinguishability of the two hybrids.

- H_5. This experiment is identical to H_4 except that Ct_1 is set to an encryption of x_1^1. The commitment com is still generated as $\mathsf{com} = \mathsf{Com}((\mathsf{Ct}_1||\mathsf{Ct}_2); r)$ and the randomness r is still used as witness to compute the proof π in the challenge ciphertext $\mathsf{Ct} = (\mathsf{Ct}_1, \mathsf{Ct}_2, \pi)$.
  Indistinguishability of H_5 from H_4. The indistinguishability of H_5 from H_4 is symmetrical to that of H_3 from H_2.

- H_6. This experiment is identical to H_5 except that any token is changed to be the obfuscation of the machine $T[M, \mathsf{Sk}_1, \mathsf{Pk}_1, \mathsf{Pk}_2, \mathsf{crs}^1, \mathsf{crs}^2, \mathsf{com}]$.
  Indistinguishability of H_6 from H_5. The indistinguishability of H_6 from H_5 is symmetrical to that of H_4 from H_3.

- H_7. This experiment is identical to H_6 except that the NIWI proof π in the challenge ciphertext $\mathsf{Ct} = (\mathsf{Ct}_1, \mathsf{Ct}_2)$ is computed with respect to the randomness r used to generate com.
  Indistinguishability of H_7 from H_6. The indistinguishability of H_7 from H_6 is symmetrical to that of H_2 from H_1.

- H_8. This experiment is identical to H_7 except that the commitment com in the public-key is a commitment to $0^{2m(\lambda)}$.
  Indistinguishability of H_8 from H_7. The indistinguishability of H_8 from H_7 is symmetrical to that of H_8 from H_7.

The indistinguishability of the above hybrid experiments implies the following theorem.

Theorem 6. If for $i = 1, 2$ $\mathsf{NIWI}^i = (\mathsf{CRSGen}^i, \mathsf{Prove}^i, \mathsf{Verify}^i)$ is a NIWI proof system for the $\mathcal{NP}$-language L^i, Com is a (perfectly binding) commitment scheme, $\mathsf{E} = (\mathsf{E.Setup}, \mathsf{E.Encrypt}, \mathsf{E.Decrypt})$ is a IND-CPA secure PKE scheme, and $i\mathcal{O}$ is an iO for TMs with bounded inputs, then the proposed scheme mFE is a selective IND-Secure mFE scheme for bounded messages supporting one merging operation. If in addition $i\mathcal{O}$ satisfies succinctness and input-specific running time, so mFE does.

3.2 Extension to Messages of Unbounded Length

To extend the above scheme to support messages of unbounded length we make the following changes, but first we would like to stress that, whereas in the case of bounded messages it is possible to concatenate strings of fixed length without a separator and indeed we often did this making use of the symbol '$||$', instead in the case of unbounded messages we would need to separate strings of variable length with a separator but with a slight abuse of notation we will continue to use the previous notation, i.e., we will write $z = x||y$ for strings $x, y \in \{0,1\}^\star$ assuming that it is possible to parse z in x and y.

1. We assume a public-coin differing-inputs obfuscation [15] (diO, in short) for TMs with unbounded inputs. This is necessary since the TM to be obfuscated have to read inputs of variable length.
2. We assume collision-resistant hash functions (CRHF, in short) $\mathsf{CRHF} = (\mathsf{Gen}, \mathsf{Hash})$ mapping strings from $\{0,1\}^\star$ to $\{0,1\}^\lambda$.
3. The Setup procedure of the mFE scheme is identical except that an hashing key hk is generated by $\mathsf{Gen}(1^\lambda)$, and com is a commitment to 0^λ.
4. The languages L^i are changed to the following languages L'^i.
   $L'^1 = \{(\mathsf{Ct}_1, \mathsf{Ct}_2) \in \{0,1\}^{2m(\lambda)} : \exists m, r, r_1, r_2 : (\mathsf{Ct}_1 = \mathsf{E}.\mathsf{Encrypt}(\mathsf{Pk}_1, m; r_1) \wedge \mathsf{Ct}_2 = \mathsf{E}.\mathsf{Encrypt}(\mathsf{Pk}_2, m; r_2)) \vee \mathsf{com} = \mathsf{Com}(\mathsf{Hash}(\mathsf{hk}, \mathsf{Ct}_1||\mathsf{Ct}_2); r)\}$.
   $L'^2 = \{(\mathsf{Ct}_1, \mathsf{Ct}_2) \in \{0,1\}^{2m(\lambda)} : \exists c_1, c_2, c_3, c_4, \pi_1, \pi_2, r, r_1, r_2 : (\mathsf{Ct}'_1 = \mathsf{E}.\mathsf{Encrypt}(\mathsf{Pk}_1, c_1||c_3; r_1) \wedge \mathsf{Ct}_2 = \mathsf{E}.\mathsf{Encrypt}(\mathsf{Pk}_2, c_2||c_4; r_2) \wedge \mathsf{Verify}^1(\mathsf{crs}^1, c_1||c_2) = 1 \wedge \mathsf{Verify}^1(\mathsf{crs}^1, c_3||c_4) = 1) \vee \mathsf{com} = \mathsf{Com}(\mathsf{Hash}(\mathsf{hk}, \mathsf{Ct}_1||\mathsf{Ct}_2); r)\}$.
   Note that L'^1 is relative to $\mathsf{com}, \mathsf{Pk}_1, \mathsf{Pk}_2, \mathsf{hk}$ and L'^2 is relative to $\mathsf{com}, \mathsf{crs}^1, \mathsf{Pk}_1, \mathsf{Pk}_2, \mathsf{hk}$ and the languages are still in $\mathcal{NP}$. As consequence, the NIWI proofs used in the modified scheme will be relative to the latter languages.
5. The machine $T[M, \mathsf{Sk}_1, \mathsf{Pk}_1, \mathsf{Pk}_2, \mathsf{crs}^1, \mathsf{crs}^2, \mathsf{com}]$ is changed to the machine $T'[M, \mathsf{Sk}_1, \mathsf{Pk}_1, \mathsf{Pk}_2, \mathsf{crs}^1, \mathsf{crs}^2, \mathsf{hk}, \mathsf{com}]$ with the obvious modification that the new machine verifies the proofs with respect to the new languages L'^i (and thus, implicitly using the hashing key hk).

Security reduction. We now show how a security reduction for the modified scheme supporting inputs of unbounded size. Such security reduction follows the lines of the security reduction of Sect. 3.1. Consider the following series of hybrid experiments against a PPT adversary $\mathcal{A}$ attacking the selective IND-Security of the modifed scheme.

- H'_0. Identical to H_0 except that com is a commitment to $\mathsf{Hash}(\mathsf{hk}, (\mathsf{Ct}_1, \mathsf{Ct}_2))$.
- H_1. This experiment is identical to H'_0 except that the commitment com in the public-key is a commitment to $\mathsf{Hash}(\mathsf{hk}, (\mathsf{Ct}_1, \mathsf{Ct}_2))$.

Claim 7 <u>Indistinguishability of H'_1 from H'_0.</u> Identical to the indistinguishability of H_1 from H_0.

- H'_2. This experiment is identical to H_1 except that the NIWI proof π in the challenge ciphertext $\mathsf{Ct} = (\mathsf{Ct}_1, \mathsf{Ct}_2)$ is computed with respect to the randomness r used to generate com.

Claim 8 <u>Indistinguishability of H'_2 from H'_1.</u> Identical to the indistinguishability of H_2 from H_1.

- H'_3. This experiment is identical to H'_2 except that Ct_2 is set to an encryption of x_1^2. The commitment com is still generated as $\mathsf{com} = \mathsf{Com}(\mathsf{Hash}(\mathsf{hk}, (\mathsf{Ct}_1, \mathsf{Ct}_2)); r)$ and the randomness r is still used as witness to compute the proof π in the challenge ciphertext $\mathsf{Ct} = (\mathsf{Ct}_1, \mathsf{Ct}_2, \pi)$.

Claim 9 <u>Indistinguishability of H_3' from H_2'</u>. Identical to the indistinguishability of H_3 from H_2.

- H_4'. This experiment is identical to H_3' except that any token is changed to be the obfuscation of the following machine:
  $T_2'[M, \mathsf{Sk}_2, \mathsf{Pk}_1, \mathsf{Pk}_2, \mathsf{crs}^1, \mathsf{crs}^2, \mathsf{hk}, \mathsf{com}]$ that is identical to
  $T_2[M, \mathsf{Sk}_2, \mathsf{Pk}_1, \mathsf{Pk}_2, \mathsf{crs}^1, \mathsf{crs}^2, \mathsf{hk}, \mathsf{com}]$ except that it verifies the proofs for the new languages L'^i.

Claim 10 <u>Indistinguishability of H_4 from H_3</u>. For simplicity we can assume that $\mathcal{A}$ asks only one token query for a TM M computing the function f. The general case can be handled by a standard hybrid argument. By the the correctness of E, by definition of $L^i, i = 1, 2$, and statistical soundness of NIWI, with all except negligible probability, the set of pairs of ciphertexts $S = \{(\mathsf{Ct}_1', \mathsf{Ct}_2')\}$ for which (1) there exists an associated valid (i.e., accepted by the verifier) NIWI proof of the fact that $\mathsf{Ct} \in L^2$ (or in the case of ciphertexts of first level, a proof of the fact that $\mathsf{Ct} \in L^1$) and (2) such that the message M_0 resulting from decrypting Ct_1 recursively using Sk_1 and the message M_1 resulting from decrypting Ct_2 recursively using Sk_2 satisfy $f(M_0) \neq f(M_1)$, have one of the following two forms:

1. $\forall \mathsf{Ct}' = (\mathsf{Ct}_1', \mathsf{Ct}_2') \in S$, $\mathsf{Hash}(\mathsf{hk}, \mathsf{Ct}') = \mathsf{Hash}(\mathsf{hk}, \mathsf{Ct})$ where $\mathsf{Ct} = (\mathsf{Ct}_1, \mathsf{Ct}_2)$ is the value committed in com.
2. Let $(\mathsf{Ct}_1', \mathsf{Ct}_2') \in S$ and $x_1 = (x_1[L], x_1[R])$ and $x_2 = (x_2[L], x_2[R])$ be the strings resulting from decrypting respectively Ct_1' with Sk_1 and Ct_2' with Sk_2. Then $\mathsf{Hash}(\mathsf{hk}, (x_1[L], x_2[L])) = \mathsf{Hash}(\mathsf{hk}, \mathsf{Ct})$ and $\mathsf{Hash}(\mathsf{hk}, (x_1[R], x_2[R])) = \mathsf{Hash}(\mathsf{hk}, \mathsf{Ct})$, where $\mathsf{Ct} = (\mathsf{Ct}_1, \mathsf{Ct}_2)$ is the value committed in com.

Furthermore, note that the set S does *not* contain the challenge ciphertext Ct committed in com. Consider now the following sampling algorithm Sampler. It takes as input a random string ρ and parses it as (hk, τ). The sampler runs the adversary $\mathcal{A}$ simulating to it the view in experiment H_4' until $\mathcal{A}$ asks the token query. Specifically, it uses the randomness hk for Hash and the randomness τ to generate the public-/secret- keys for E, for Com, and for the ciphertexts and the NIWI proofs. Then, it outputs the two (non-obfuscated) machines $T'[M, \mathsf{Sk}_1, \mathsf{Pk}_1, \mathsf{Pk}_2, \mathsf{crs}^1, \mathsf{crs}^2, \mathsf{hk}, \mathsf{com}]$ and $T_2'[M, \mathsf{Sk}_2, \mathsf{Pk}_1, \mathsf{Pk}_2, \mathsf{crs}^1, \mathsf{crs}^2, \mathsf{hk}, \mathsf{com}]$. Consider a distinguisher $\mathcal{D}$ that takes as input the randomness ρ and machine M' that is the obfuscation (with respect to di$\mathcal{O}$) of one of the two previous machines. $\mathcal{D}$ executes all steps of Sampler and continues the execution of $\mathcal{A}$ answering the token query sending M'. It is easy to see that if $\mathcal{A}$ has non-negligible advantage in distinguishing the two hybrids, so $\mathcal{D}$ does for the two machines. Thus, to prove the claim we have to show that Sampler is a public-coin differing-inputs sampler. Suppose towards a contradiction that there exists an adversary $\mathcal{B}$ that finds a differing-input to the pair of TMs sampled by Sampler. Then we build an algorithm $\mathcal{C}_{\mathsf{Hash}}$ that breaks the security of Hash. $\mathcal{C}_{\mathsf{Hash}}$ incorporates Sampler and $\mathcal{B}$. On input a random hashing key hk, the algorithm samples a uniform string τ and runs $\mathcal{B}$ and Sampler on

$\rho = (\mathsf{hk}, \tau)$. Let the output of Sampler be T', T_2' and let $\mathsf{Ct}' = (\mathsf{Ct}_1', \mathsf{Ct}_2')$ be the output of $\mathcal{B}$. Furthermore, let $\mathsf{Ct} = (\mathsf{Ct}_1, \mathsf{Ct}_2)$ be the challenge ciphertext committed in com that is computed by Sampler at the beginning of its execution. By the fact that the only distinguishing inputs for T' and T_2' are strings in S and by correctness of di$\mathcal{O}$ and by the above two facts, it holds that $\mathsf{Ct}' \neq \mathsf{Ct}$ and either (1) $\mathsf{Hash}(\mathsf{hk}, \mathsf{Ct}') = \mathsf{Hash}(\mathsf{hk}, \mathsf{Ct})$ or (2) $\mathsf{Hash}(\mathsf{hk}, (x_1'[L], x_2'[L])) = \mathsf{Hash}(\mathsf{hk}, \mathsf{Ct})$ and $\mathsf{Hash}(\mathsf{hk}, (x_1'[R], x_2'[R])) = \mathsf{Hash}(\mathsf{hk}, \mathsf{Ct})$, where $x_1' = (x_1'[L], x_1'[R])$ and $x_2' = (x_2'[L], x_2'[R])$ are the strings resulting from decrypting respectively Ct_1' with Sk_1 and Ct_2' with Sk_2. Observing that in the case (2) $\mathcal{C}_{\mathsf{Hash}}$ has the secret-keys $\mathsf{Sk}_1, \mathsf{Sk}_2$ to decrypt Ct_1 and Ct_2, we conclude that in both cases $\mathcal{C}_{\mathsf{Hash}}$ can find a collision for $\mathsf{Hash}(\mathsf{hk}, \mathsf{Ct})$ as desired.

– H_5'. This experiment is identical to H_4' except that Ct_1 is set to an encryption of x_1^1. The commitment com is still generated as com $=$ $\mathsf{Com}(\mathsf{Hash}(\mathsf{hk}, (\mathsf{Ct}_1, \mathsf{Ct}_2)); r)$ and the randomness r is still used as witness to compute the proof π in the challenge ciphertext $\mathsf{Ct} = (\mathsf{Ct}_1, \mathsf{Ct}_2, \pi)$.

Claim 11 Indistinguishability of H_5' from H_4'. The indistinguishability of H_5' from H_4' is symmetrical to that of H_3' from H_2'.

– H_6'. This experiment is identical to H_5' except that any token is changed to be the obfuscation of the machine $T'[M, \mathsf{Sk}_1, \mathsf{Pk}_1, \mathsf{Pk}_2, \mathsf{crs}^1, \mathsf{crs}^2, \mathsf{hk}, \mathsf{com}]$.

Claim 12 Indistinguishability of H_6' from H_5'. The indistinguishability of H_6' from H_5' is symmetrical to that of H_4' from H_3'.

– H_7'. This experiment is identical to H_6' except that the NIWI proof π in the challenge ciphertext $\mathsf{Ct} = (\mathsf{Ct}_1, \mathsf{Ct}_2)$ is computed with respect to the randomness r used to generate com.

Claim 13 Indistinguishability of H_7' from H_6'. The indistinguishability of H_7' from H_6' is symmetrical to that of H_2' from H_1'.

– H_8'. This experiment is identical to H_7' except that the commitment com in the public-key is a commitment to 0^λ.

Claim 14 Indistinguishability of H_8' from H_7'. The indistinguishability of H_8' from H_7' is symmetrical to that of H_8' from H_7'.

The indistinguishability of the above hybrid experiments implies the following theorem.

Theorem 15. If for $i = 1, 2$ NIWI^i $=$ $(\mathsf{CRSGen}^i, \mathsf{Prove}^i, \mathsf{Verify}^i)$ is a NIWI proof system for the $\mathcal{NP}$-language L^i, Com is a (perfectly binding) commitment scheme, E $=$ (E.Setup, E.Encrypt, E.Decrypt) is a IND-CPA secure PKE scheme, Hash is a CRHF, and di$\mathcal{O}$ is a public-coin differing-inputs obfuscator for TMs (with unbounded inputs), then the modified scheme is a selective IND-Secure mFE scheme for unbounded messages supporting one merging operation. If in addition i$\mathcal{O}$ satisfies succinctness and input-specific running time, so the mFE scheme does.

References

1. Agrawal, S., Gorbunov, S., Vaikuntanathan, V., Wee, H.: Functional encryption: new perspectives and lower bounds. In: Canetti, R., Garay, J.A. (eds.) CRYPTO 2013. LNCS, vol. 8043, pp. 500–518. Springer, Heidelberg (2013). doi:10.1007/978-3-642-40084-1_28

2. Bellare, M., O'Neill, A.: Semantically-secure functional encryption: possibility results, impossibility results and the quest for a general definition. In: Abdalla, M., Nita-Rotaru, C., Dahab, R. (eds.) CANS 2013. LNCS, vol. 8257, pp. 218–234. Springer, Cham (2013). doi:10.1007/978-3-319-02937-5_12

3. Boneh, D., Di Crescenzo, G., Ostrovsky, R., Persiano, G.: Public key encryption with keyword search. In: Cachin, C., Camenisch, J.L. (eds.) EUROCRYPT 2004. LNCS, vol. 3027, pp. 506–522. Springer, Heidelberg (2004). doi:10.1007/978-3-540-24676-3_30

4. Boneh, D., Raghunathan, A., Segev, G.: Function-private identity-based encryption: hiding the function in functional encryption. In: Canetti, R., Garay, J.A. (eds.) CRYPTO 2013. LNCS, vol. 8043, pp. 461–478. Springer, Heidelberg (2013). doi:10.1007/978-3-642-40084-1_26

5. Boneh, D., Sahai, A., Waters, B.: Functional encryption: definitions and challenges. In: Ishai, Y. (ed.) TCC 2011. LNCS, vol. 6597, pp. 253–273. Springer, Heidelberg (2011). doi:10.1007/978-3-642-19571-6_16

6. Boneh, D., Segev, G., Waters, B.: Targeted malleability: homomorphic encryption for restricted computations. In: Proceedings of the 3rd Innovations in Theoretical Computer Science Conference, pp. 350–366. ACM (2012)

7. Boneh, D., Waters, B.: Conjunctive, subset, and range queries on encrypted data. In: Vadhan, S.P. (ed.) TCC 2007. LNCS, vol. 4392, pp. 535–554. Springer, Heidelberg (2007). doi:10.1007/978-3-540-70936-7_29

8. Canetti, R., Halevi, S., Katz, J.: Chosen-ciphertext security from identity-based encryption. In: Cachin, C., Camenisch, J.L. (eds.) EUROCRYPT 2004. LNCS, vol. 3027, pp. 207–222. Springer, Heidelberg (2004). doi:10.1007/978-3-540-24676-3_13

9. Feige, U., Lapidot, D., Shamir, A.: Multiple non-interactive zero knowledge proofs based on a single random string (extended abstract). In: 31st Annual Symposium on Foundations of Computer Science (1990)

10. Garg, S., Gentry, C., Halevi, S., Raykova, M., Sahai, A., Waters, B.: Candidate indistinguishability obfuscation and functional encryption for all circuits. In: 54th Annual IEEE Symposium on Foundations of Computer Science, FOCS 2013, Berkeley, CA, USA, 26–29 October 2013, pp. 40–49. IEEE Computer Society (2013)

11. Gentry, C.: A fully homomorphic encryption scheme. Ph.D. Thesis, Stanford University (2009). crypto.stanford.edu/craig

12. Gentry, C., Sahai, A., Waters, B.: Homomorphic encryption from learning with errors: conceptually-simpler, asymptotically-faster, attribute-based. In: Canetti, R., Garay, J.A. (eds.) CRYPTO 2013. LNCS, vol. 8042, pp. 75–92. Springer, Heidelberg (2013). doi:10.1007/978-3-642-40041-4_5

13. Goldwasser, S., Gordon, S.D., Goyal, V., Jain, A., Katz, J., Liu, F.-H., Sahai, A., Shi, E., Zhou, H.-S.: Multi-input functional encryption. In: Nguyen, P.Q., Oswald, E. (eds.) EUROCRYPT 2014. LNCS, vol. 8441, pp. 578–602. Springer, Heidelberg (2014). doi:10.1007/978-3-642-55220-5_32

14. Goyal, V., Jain, A., Koppula, V., Sahai, A.: Functional encryption for randomized functionalities. In: Dodis, Y., Nielsen, J.B. (eds.) TCC 2015. LNCS, vol. 9015, pp. 325–351. Springer, Heidelberg (2015). doi:10.1007/978-3-662-46497-7_13

15. Ishai, Y., Pandey, O., Sahai, A.: Public-coin differing-inputs obfuscation and its applications. In: Dodis, Y., Nielsen, J.B. (eds.) TCC 2015. LNCS, vol. 9015, pp. 668–697. Springer, Heidelberg (2015). doi:10.1007/978-3-662-46497-7_26

16. Katz, J., Sahai, A., Waters, B.: Predicate encryption supporting disjunctions, polynomial equations, and inner products. In: Smart, N. (ed.) EUROCRYPT 2008. LNCS, vol. 4965, pp. 146–162. Springer, Heidelberg (2008). doi:10.1007/978-3-540-78967-3_9

17. Koppula, V., Lewko, A.B., Waters, B.: Indistinguishability obfuscation for turing machines with unbounded memory. Cryptology ePrint Archive, Report 2014/925 (2014). http://eprint.iacr.org/

18. Okamoto, T., Takashima, K.: Adaptively attribute-hiding (hierarchical) inner product encryption. In: Pointcheval, D., Johansson, T. (eds.) EUROCRYPT 2012. LNCS, vol. 7237, pp. 591–608. Springer, Heidelberg (2012). doi:10.1007/978-3-642-29011-4_35

19. Shen, E., Shi, E., Waters, B.: Predicate privacy in encryption systems. In: Reingold, O. (ed.) TCC 2009. LNCS, vol. 5444, pp. 457–473. Springer, Heidelberg (2009). doi:10.1007/978-3-642-00457-5_27

Protocols

Private Subgraph Matching Protocol

Zifeng Xu, Fucai Zhou$^{(\boxtimes)}$, Yuxi Li, Jian Xu, and Qiang Wang

Software College, Northeastern University, Shenyang, Liaoning, China
`fczhou@mail.neu.edu.cn`

Abstract. In many applications, information can be stored and managed using graph data structures, and there is a rich set of graph algorithms that can be used to solve different problems. The subgraph isomorphism problem is defined as, given two graphs G and H, whether G contains a subgraph that is isomorphic to H. The problem has been well studied for many years, and it can be used for many application areas, such as cheminformatics, pattern matching, data mining and image processing. In this paper, we present a private subgraph matching protocol, which solves a special case of the subgraph isomorphism problem. The protocol allows two parties, each holding a private graph, to jointly compute whether one graph is a subgraph of the other. During the protocol, each party learns no useful information about the graph of the other party. We prove that the protocol is secure in the semi-honest setting.

Keywords: Graph theory · Subgraph isomorphism problem · Multiparty computation · Homomorphic encryption

1 Introduction

In graph theory, the subgraph isomorphism problem is defined as, given two graphs G and H, determining whether there is a subgraph $G' \subseteq G$, such that G' is isomorphic to H [1]. The subgraph isomorphism problem have been extensively studied for many years, and several algorithms are proposed [1–7]. Since graph data structures have been widely used across various areas in industry, the problem can be used for solving many computational tasks in different applications, such as cheminformatics, computer vision and data mining.

Generally speaking, a graph consists of a set of vertices and a set of edges. The vertices are often used to represented entities, and the edges represent the relations between them. In a labeled graph, all the vertices are labeled with unique values. For directed and unweighted graphs, the edges are having orientations and no weight.

The subgraph matching problem a special case of the subgraph isomorphism problem. Formally speaking, a the subgraph matching problem between two labeled, directed and unweighted graphs, denoted as G and H, is defined as computing whether H is a subgraph of G, i.e. $H \subseteq G$. Let $H = (V_H, E_H)$ and $G = (V_G, E_G)$, where V and E are the sets of vertices and edges. $H \subseteq G$ is defined as $V_H \subseteq V_G$ and $E_H \subseteq E_G$.

© Springer International Publishing AG 2017
T. Okamoto et al. (Eds.): ProvSec 2017, LNCS 10592, pp. 455–470, 2017.
https://doi.org/10.1007/978-3-319-68637-0_27

The problem itself is trivial, and can be easily solved with straight forward solutions. However, no solution has been proposed in literature to solve the subgraph matching problem for two parties in a privacy-preserving manner.

1.1 Related Work

Graph data structure is widely used to store and manage data in the areas of chemistry, biology and biochemistry. A large number of algorithms based on subgraph isomorphism have been proposed to solve different problems [8–12]. Furthermore, many problems in pattern matching and recognition can be naturally converted into the subgraph isomorphism problem. Therefore, subgraph isomorphism is suitable for solving many problems in the area of computer vision [13, 14].

In the era of big data, the size of a single graph data and the size of a graph database have a rapid growth in recent years. Therefore, developing efficient subgraph isomorphism algorithms for large graph data and database is becoming an urgent task. As a result, several solutions that solves the subgraph isomorphism problem for large graphs and large graph databases have been proposed [15, 16]. In addition, several performance comparisons between the subgraph isomorphism algorithms for different types of graphs have been conducted [17, 18].

Furthermore, in the aspect of privacy protecting, various algorithms and protocols for different graph operations have been proposed [19–22]. However, as far as we can tell, the study of privacy-preserving subgraph isomorphism problems is still missing.

1.2 Our Contribution

In this paper, we propose a private subgraph matching protocol (PSM). The protocol solves the subgraph matching problem between two parties, a verifier and a prover, while protecting the privacies of the input graphs. At the end of the protocol, only the verifier learns the result.

We prove that the protocol is correct and zero-knowledge for both the verifier and the prover in the semi-honest setting. Furthermore, we analyse the leakage problem and the efficiency of our protocol.

2 Preliminaries

2.1 Paillier Cryptosystem

The Paillier cryptosystem is one of the most practical homomorphic encryption schemes, proposed by Paillier in 1999 [23]. Homomorphic encryption schemes allow the user to perform certain computation operations on the ciphertext space, such as addition and multiplication. The Paillier cryptosystem contains three algorithms, described as follows:

$(pk, sk) \leftarrow \text{KeyGen}(1^k)$: the key generation algorithm takes as input a security parameter k, and outputs a public key pk and a secret key sk.

$m^\oplus \leftarrow \mathrm{Enc}(pk, m)$: the encryption algorithm takes as inputs the public key pk and a plaintext m, and outputs the corresponding ciphertext $m^\oplus$.

$m \leftarrow \mathrm{Dec}(sk, m^\oplus)$: the decryption algorithm takes as inputs the secret key sk and a ciphertext $m^\oplus$, and outputs the corresponding plaintext m.

The Paillier cryptosystem supports homomorphic addition operation on the ciphertext space. For the rest of this paper, let $\oplus$ denotes the homomorphic addition operation. For any m_0 and m_1 chosen from the plaintext space, $\mathrm{Dec}(\mathrm{Enc}(m_0) \oplus \mathrm{Enc}(m_1)) = m_0 + m_1$ always holds.

In addition, the Paillier cryptosystem also supports homomorphic multiplication between a ciphertext and a plaintext. For the rest of this paper, let $\otimes$ denotes the homomorphic multiplication operation. For any m_0 and m_1 chosen from the plaintext space, $\mathrm{Dec}(\mathrm{Enc}(m_0) \otimes m_1) = m_0 \cdot m_1$ always holds.

The Paillier cryptosystem is proved to have semantic security against chosen-plaintext attacks, i.e. IND-CPA.

In our Private Subgraph Matching Protocol, we will use the Paillier cryptosystem to prevent from information leakage. For simplicity, we will use the notion $m^\oplus = \mathrm{Enc}(m)$ for the encryption algorithm and $m = \mathrm{Dec}(m^\oplus)$ for the decryption algorithm for the rest of the paper.

2.2 Private Subset Relation Protocol

Kissner and Song proposed several privacy-preserving set operations in 2005, and one of which is the private subset relation protocol [24]. Suppose there are two parties, *Alice* and *Bob*, each holding a private set, denoted as S_A and S_B, respectively. The protocol allows *Alice* and *Bob* to jointly compute whether S_A is a subset of S_B, in other words, whether S_B contains all the elements in S_A. The protocol is based on oblivious polynomial evaluation and an additive homomorphic encryption scheme, such as the Paillier cryptosystem. The protocol runs as follows:

1. *Bob* represents his set S_B as a polynomial $P(x) = \sum_{i=0}^{|S_B|} \alpha_i x^i$, where α_i is the coefficient for each term. $P(x)$ has the property that all the roots are exactly the elements in S_B. Then *Bob* encrypts all the coefficients using the Paillier cryptosystem, and sends them to *Alice*.

2. *Alice* obviously evaluates the polynomial using each elements in her set S_A as input, and obtains $|S_A|$ resulting ciphertexts. Then *Alice* homomorphically multiplies each ciphertext by a random number, and homomorphically compute the sum of all the resulting products. At last, *Alice* obtains a single ciphertext and sends it to *Bob*.

3. *Bob* decrypts the receiving ciphertext and checks whether the decrypted value is 0. A decryption of 0 will indicates that all the elements in S_A is also in S_A, i.e. $S_A \subseteq S_B$.

The construction of the protocol is efficient and straight forward. At the end of the protocol, *Bob* learns the subset relation result, and *Alice* learns the cardinality of S_B by counting the ciphertexts received from *Bob*. The protocol is secure under the semi-honest setting, which means no information is leaked during the protocol, beyond the subset relation result and the cardinality of S_B. However the protocol cannot deal with malicious *Alice*, since she can easily encrypts 0 from scratch and sends it to *Bob*.

In our private subgraph matching protocol, we will use the above protocol as a building block.

3   Model and Definition

We formally describe the private subgraph matching protocol (PSM). There are two parties that participates the protocol, a verifier and a prover. Each of the participates holds a private graph. The private graphs are directed, labeled and unweighted. The verifier wish to learn that whether the prover's graph is a subgraph of the verifier's graph. During the protocol, both of the parties wish to keep their graphs private. In other words, they do not want to leak any information about their graphs to the other party. At the end of the protocol, only the verifier learns the result.

Leakage. While achieving truly no information leakage is the ideal goal, our protocol leaks partial information about the graphs of the verifier and the prover. We define four information leakages that take place during the protocol, denoted as $\mathcal{L}_1$, $\mathcal{L}_2$, $\mathcal{L}_3$ and $\mathcal{L}_4$, respectively. Let $G_A = (V_A, E_A)$ and $G_B = (V_B, E_B)$ denote the graphs of the verifier and the prover, respectively. V_A and V_B are the vertex sets, and E_A and E_B are the edge sets. The degree of a vertex is defined as the number of neighbors of the vertex. Let $D(v)$ denotes the degree of the vertex v.

$\mathcal{L}_1$ is defined as the number of vertices of the verifier's graph, i.e. $\mathcal{L}_1 = |V_A|$. $\mathcal{L}_2$ is defined as the number of vertices with non-zero degree in the verifier's graph, i.e. $\mathcal{L}_2 = |\{v_a\}_{v_a \in V_A, D(v_a) \neq 0}|$. $\mathcal{L}_3$ is defined as the degree of each vertex of the verifier's graph, i.e. $\mathcal{L}_3 = \{D(v_a)\}_{v_a \in V_A}$. $\mathcal{L}_4$ is defined as the number of vertices with non-zero degree in the prover's graph, i.e. $\mathcal{L}_4 = |\{v_b\}_{v_b \in V_B, D(v_b) \neq 0}|$. We will discuss the leakage problem in more details in Sect. 5.2.

Threat Model. In our model, both of the verifier and the prover is considered as semi-honest or "honest-but-curious". Both of the parties will follow the protocol faithfully without forging any fake result. However they may try to learn or deduce any useful information about the graph of the other party by analysing the data they received during the protocol.

Definition 1 (Private Subgraph Matching Protocol). Two probabilistic polynomial time interactive Turing machines, a verifier and a prover, defines a private subgraph matching protocol if the following conditions hold:

Correctness: If both parties are honest, for any $G_A = (V_A, E_A)$ and any $G_B = (V_B, E_B)$, the private subgraph matching protocol computes whether $G_B \subseteq G_A$. At the end of the protocol, only the verifier learns the result.

Verifier Zero-knowledge: A semi-honest verifier learns no information about the prover's graph, beyond the result of the protocol and the pre-defined leakage $\mathcal{L}_4$.

Prover Zero-knowledge: A semi-honest prover learns no information about the verifier's graph, beyond the pre-defined leakages $\mathcal{L}_1$, $\mathcal{L}_2$ and $\mathcal{L}_3$.

4   Private Subgraph Matching Protocol

In this section, we describe the private subgraph matching protocol in details. First we introduce how the graphs are represented in the protocol, then we describe the detailed construction of the protocol.

4.1   Graph Representation

In our protocol, a graph is denoted as $G = (V, E)$, where V is the set of all vertices and E is the set of all edges. G is labeled, directed and unweighted, which means each vertex is labeled as a unique value, and the edges have orientations and no weight.

The vertex set is denotes as $V = \{v_1, ... v_m\}$, where $m = |V|$ is the number of vertices of graph G. Each v_i is labeled as an integer chosen from the domain $\mathbb{Z}_v$, where v being a positive integer. The edge set is denotes as $E = \{(v_i, v_j)\}$, where (v_i, v_j) represents an edge *from* vertex v_i *to* vertex v_j. E contains all the edges in graph G.

The neighbors or adjacent vertices of a vertex v is defined as the set of all vertices, such that there exists an edge *from* v *to* each of them in graph G. We denote the set of neighbors of a vertex v as $N(v)$.

The degree of a vertex v is defined as the number of neighbors of v, and in other words, number of edges *from* v. We denote the degree of a vertex v as $D(v)$, i.e. $D(v) = |N(v)|$.

Furthermore, the edges of graph G can also be represented as an adjacency list. The adjacency list has the form $\{v_i : N(v_i)\}_{v_i \in V, D(v_i) \neq 0}$. We denote the adjacency list of graph G as $A(G)$.

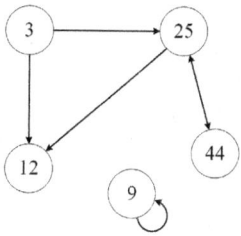

Fig. 1. Example graph

For example, we represent the graph illustrated in Fig. 1 as $G = (V, E)$, where V is the vertex set and E is the edge set. By the above definition,

$V = \{3, 25, 44, 9, 12\}$, and $E = \{(3, 25), (3, 12), (25, 12), (25, 44), (44, 25), (9, 9)\}$. The neighbors of vertice 25 is $N(25) = \{12, 44\}$. The degree of vertice 25 is $D(25) = |N(25)| = 2$. The adjacency list of G is

$$A(G) = \{3 : \{25, 12\},$$
$$25 : \{12, 44\},$$
$$44 : \{25\},$$
$$9 : \{9\}\}.$$

4.2   Protocol Construction

The participates of the private subgraph matching protocol are a verifier and a prover, denoted as P_A and P_B, respectively. Each of the participates holds a labeled, directed and unweighted graph, which is intended to be kept secret from the other participate. The graphs of the verifier and the prover are denoted as G_A and G_B, respectively. During the protocol, both of the verifier and the prover interactively compute whether G_B is a subgraph of G_A. At the end of the protocol, only the verifier learns the result.

The vertices and the edges of the input graphs are represented using the forms described in Sect. 4.1. The vertices of G_A and G_B are represented as $V_A = \{a_1, ..., a_m\}$ and $V_B = \{b_1, ..., b_n\}$, respectively. The edges of G_A and G_B are represented as $E_A = \{(a_i, a_j)\}$ and $E_B = \{(b_i, b_j)\}$, respectively.

During the protocol, the privacy of the input graphs is preserved by the Paillier cryptosystem, which is denoted as a tuple of algorithms, (KeyGen, Enc, Dec), as described in Sect. 2.1.

The protocol is described as follows:

Input: P_A holds $G_A = (V_A, E_A)$, and P_B holds $G_B = (V_B, E_B)$.
Output: P_A learns weather $G_B \subseteq G_A$.
Protocol:

Step 1: P_A runs the $(pk, sk) \leftarrow$ KeyGen(1^k) algorithm of the Paillier cryptosystem, and obtains a public key and a secret key. Then P_A sends pk to P_B.

As described in Sect. 4.1, each vertex of the input graphs are labeled as a value in $\mathbb{Z}_v$, where v is a positive integer. The public key of the Paillier cryptosystem contains a large number N, which specifies the plaintext domain as $\mathbb{Z}_N$. We require that N is large enough, such that an element drawn uniformly from $\mathbb{Z}_N$ will only has a negligible probability of representing an element in $\mathbb{Z}_v$. More details about the above condition are in [24].

Step 2

(a) P_A constructs a polynomial $P(x) = (x - a_1)...(x - a_m) = \sum_{i=0}^{m} \alpha_i x^i$ for all $a_i \in V_A$. $P(x)$ has the property that $P(x) = 0$ if and only if $x \in V_A$. Let $C = \{\alpha_0, ..., \alpha_m\}$ denotes the set of all the coefficients of $P(x)$.

(b) P_A uses the Paillier cryptosystem to encrypt all the elements in C, and obtains $C^\oplus = \{\text{Enc}(\alpha_0), ..., \text{Enc}(\alpha_m)\}$. Then P_A sends $C^\oplus$ to P_B.

Step 3

(a) Upon receiving $C^\oplus$, P_B uses the homomorphic property of the Paillier cryptosystem to homomorphically evaluate the polynomial $P(x)$, using all $b_i \in V_B$ as inputs. Then P_B homomorphically multiplies each evaluation result by a different non-zero random number γ. Let $\{r_1^\oplus, ..., r_n^\oplus\}$ denotes the set of results, where $r_i^\oplus = \text{Enc}(P(b_i)) \otimes \gamma$. Note that, $r_i^\oplus$ is a ciphertext under the Paillier cryptosystem.
(b) P_B homomorphically adds all $r_i^\oplus$ together to obtain a single ciphertext $r^\oplus = r_1^\oplus \oplus ... \oplus r_n^\oplus$. Then P_B sends $r^\oplus$ to P_A.

Step 4: P_A decrypts the received ciphertext, and obtains $r = \text{Dec}(r^\oplus)$. A decryption of zero will indicate that $V_B \subseteq V_A$, otherwise $V_B \nsubseteq V_A$. If $r = 0$, execute **Step 5.1**, otherwise execute **Step 5.2**. Note that, only one of **Step 5.1** and **Step 5.2** will be executed.

Step 5.1

(a) P_A constructs a set V_A' containing all the vertices $a_i \in V_A$ satisfying $N(a_i) \neq \emptyset$. Let $V_A' = \{a_1', ..., a_g'\}$. In other words, V_A' contains all the vertices in V_A that have a non-zero degree, and g is number of such vertices. Each $a_j' \in V_A'$ maps to a unique $a_i \in V_A$.
(b) P_A constructs a set of polynomial pairs $\{(F_1(x), G_1(y)), ..., (F_g(x), G_g(y))\}$, for each of the vertex $a_i' \in V_A'$. $F_i(x)$ is defined as $F_i(x) = (x - a_i')$. $G_i(y)$ is defined as $G_i(y) = \prod_{a_j \in N(a_i')}(y - a_j)$. $F_i(x)$ has the property that $F_i(x) = 0$ if and only if $x = a_i'$. $G_i(y)$ has the property that $G_i(y) = 0$ if and only if $y \in N(a_i')$. Then P_A rewrites $G_i(y)$ to the form $G_i(y) = \sum_{j=0}^{|N(a_i')|} \beta_{i,j} y^j$, where $\beta_{i,j}$ are coefficients of $G_i(y)$. Let $\beta_i = \{\beta_{i,0}, ..., \beta_{i,|N(a_i')|}\}$.
(c) P_A encrypts $-a_i'$ and β_i for $1 \leqslant i \leqslant g$ under the Paillier cryptosystem, and obtains $D_i^\oplus = \{\text{Enc}(-a_i'), \text{Enc}(\beta_{i,0}), ..., \text{Enc}(\beta_{i,|N(a_i')|})\}$, for $1 \leqslant i \leqslant g$. Then P_A sends $D_1^\oplus, ..., D_g^\oplus$ to P_B.

Step 5.2

(a) P_A constructs a set V_A' containing all the vertices $a_i \in V_A$ satisfying $N(a_i) \neq \emptyset$. Let $V_A' = \{a_1', ..., a_g'\}$. Then P_A constructs g sets, for each of $a_i' \in V_A'$. In each set, P_A generates $|N(a_i')| + 2$ random values. In other words, P_A constructs $D_1^\oplus, ..., D_g^\oplus$, where $D_i^\oplus = \{\gamma_0, ..., \gamma_{|N(a_i')|+2}\}$ and γ being random numbers. P_A sends $D_1^\oplus, ..., D_g^\oplus$ to P_B.
(b) Discard any data sent by P_B in later steps, and the protocol outputs $G_B \nsubseteq G_A$. In other words, **Step 7** will not be executed.

Step 6

(a) After receiving $D_1^\oplus, ..., D_g^\oplus$, P_B constructs a set V_B' in the same manner as V_A'. Let $V_B' = \{b_1', ..., b_h'\}$.
(b) For a certain $i \in [1, g]$ and a certain $j \in [1, h]$, P_B homomorphically evaluates the polynomial $F_i(b_j')$, and homomorphically multiplies the result by a non-zero random number γ. Then P_B homomorphically evaluates the polynomials $G_i(b_k)$, using all the vertices $b_k \in N(b_j')$ as inputs, and homomorphically multiplies each result by a non-zero random number γ. After that, P_B homomorphically adds all the previous results together to obtain a single ciphertext $r_{i,j}^\oplus$. P_B keeps doing the above computation for every $1 \leqslant i \leqslant g$ and every $1 \leqslant j \leqslant h$. In other words, P_B homomorphically computes

$$r_{i,j}^\oplus = (\text{Enc}(F_i(b_j')) \otimes \gamma) \oplus \sum_{b_k \in N(b_j')}^\oplus (\text{Enc}(G_i(b_k)) \otimes \gamma_k)$$

for $1 \leqslant i \leqslant g$ and $1 \leqslant j \leqslant h$, where γ are non-zero random numbers.
(c) P_B organizes all $r_{i,j}^\oplus$ into sets $\{r_{1,1}^\oplus, ..., r_{g,1}^\oplus\}, ..., \{r_{1,h}^\oplus, ..., r_{g,h}^\oplus\}$. In other words, P_B divided all $r_{i,j}^\oplus$ into h sets, and each set contains g ciphertexts. Then P_B send all the sets of ciphertexts to P_A.

Step 7: P_A decrypts all the received ciphertext, and checks the number of zeros in each set. If there is exact one zero in each set, the protocol outputs $G_B \subseteq G_A$, otherwise, outputs $G_B \nsubseteq G_A$.

5   Analysis

5.1   Security Analysis

In this section, we denote the verifier and the prover as P_A and P_B, respectively. Let $G_A = (V_A, E_A)$ be the graph of the verifier, and let $G_B = (V_B, E_B)$ be the graph of the prover. For simplicity, let g denotes the number of vertices with non-zero degree in G_A, and let h denotes the number of vertices with non-zero degree in G_B. $N(v)$ denotes the set of neighbors of vertex v.

Lemma 1 (Correctness). If both parties are honest, for any $G_A = (V_A, E_A)$ and any $G_B = (V_B, E_B)$, the private subgraph matching protocol computes whether $G_B \subseteq G_A$. At the end of the protocol, only the verifier learns the result.

Proof. In order to prove the correctness of the private subgraph matching protocol, we need to show that the protocol will output $G_B \subseteq G_A$ if both $V_B \subseteq V_A$ and $E_B \subseteq E_A$, otherwise, the protocol will output $G_B \nsubseteq G_A$.

Step 2–**Step 4** of the protocol are using the private subset relation protocol to compute whether $V_B \subseteq V_A$. If $V_B \nsubseteq V_A$, the protocol will always outputs $G_B \nsubseteq G_A$ in **Step 5.2**.

If $V_B \subseteq V_A$, **Step 5.1** will be executed. Let $V_A' = \{a_1', ..., a_g'\}$ be the set of vertices in V_A that satisfying $N(a_i) \neq \emptyset$ for $1 \leqslant i \leqslant g$. Let $V_B' = \{b_1', ..., b_h'\}$ be the set of vertices in V_B that satisfying $N(b_j) \neq \emptyset$ for $1 \leqslant j \leqslant h$.

We consider the edges of G_A and G_B as adjacency lists, denoted as $A(G_A)$ and $A(G_B)$, respectively, as described in Sect. 4.1. We denote $A(G_A)[i]$ as the i-th item in $A(G_A)$.

$A(G_A)[i]$ represents all the edges *from* the vertex a_i' in graph G_A. Therefore, $A(G_A)$ contains all the edges in E_A. Furthermore, we define that an item $A(G_B)[j]$ is a sub item of $A(G_A)[i]$, if $a_i' = b_j'$ and $N(b_j') \subseteq N(a_i')$. We denote the above operation as $A(G_B)[j] \subseteq A(G_A)[i]$. If all the items in $A(G_B)$ is a sub item of a certain item in $A(G_A)$, we say that $A(G_B)$ is a sub set of $A(G_A)$, denoted as $A(G_B) \subseteq A(G_A)$.

The meaning of $A(G_B)[j] \in A(G_A)$ is all the edges *from* b_j' in E_B are also in E_A. Therefore, the meaning of $A(G_B) \subseteq A(G_A)$ is all the edges in E_B are also in E_A, i.e. $E_B \subseteq E_A$.

In **Step 5.1**, for each $a_i' \in V_A'$, P_A constructs two polynomials $F_i(x)$ and $G_i(y)$. The root of $F_i(x)$ is a_i' and the roots of $G_i(y)$ are all the elements in $N(a_i')$. In **Step 6**, for each $b_j' \in V_B'$, P_B homomorphically computes $r_{i,j}^{\oplus} = (\text{Enc}(F_i(b_j')) \otimes \gamma) \oplus \sum_{b_k \in N(b_j')}^{\oplus} (\text{Enc}(G_i(b_k)) \otimes \gamma_k)$. The decryption of $r_{i,j}^{\oplus}$ will be 0 if and only if $A(G_B)[j] \in A(G_A)[i]$.

Therefore, in **Step 7**, P_A decrypts all the ciphertexts received. If there is exact one decryption of 0 in each $\{r_{1,1}^{\oplus}, ..., r_{g,1}^{\oplus}\}, ..., \{r_{1,h}^{\oplus}, ..., r_{g,h}^{\oplus}\}$, it indicates $A(G_B) \subseteq A(G_A)$, i.e. $E_B \subseteq E_A$, and the protocol outputs $G_B \subseteq G_A$. Otherwise, $A(G_B) \nsubseteq A(G_A)$, i.e. $E_B \nsubseteq E_A$, and the protocol outputs $G_B \nsubseteq G_A$. □

Lemma 2 (Verifier Zero-knowledge). A semi-honest verifier learns no information about the prover's graph, beyond the result of the protocol and the pre-defined leakage $\mathcal{L}_4$.

Proof. During the protocol, there are two parts where P_A receives information from P_B. The first part is during **Step 3**, where P_A receives a single ciphertext $r^{\oplus}$ under the Paillier cryptosystem. Upon decryption, a corresponding plaintext of 0 will indicate that V_B is a subset of V_A, which is a part of the final result of the protocol. Otherwise, the decryption will yields a random value. Since **Step 2**–**Step 4** essentially follows the private subset relation protocol, we skip the proof of $r^{\oplus}$ reveals no additional information about V_B, beyond whether $V_B \subseteq V_A$, and more details can be found in [24].

The second part is During **Step 6**, where P_A receives h sets, each containing g ciphertexts under the Paillier cryptosystem. By counting the number of sets received, P_A can learn the number of vertices with non-zero degree in G_B, which is the pre-defined leakage $\mathcal{L}_4$. By decrypting the sets of ciphertexts, the result plaintexts will indicate whether $E_B \subseteq E_A$, which is a part of the final result of the protocol.

Therefore, we can proof that the data P_A received during **Step 6** does not leak any additional information about G_B, if P_A cannot distinguish between the cases where P_B has different input graphs, given the knowledge of whether $G_B \subseteq G_A$ and $\mathcal{L}_4$. Consider the following experiment in the real model:

$\text{EXP}_{\mathcal{A}}^{\text{IND-CPA}}(1^k, \mathcal{L}_4):$

    $(pk, sk) \leftarrow \textbf{Step 1}(1^k)$

    $(G_0, G_1) \leftarrow \mathcal{A}$

    $b \xleftarrow{\$} \{0,1\}$

    $C^{\oplus} \leftarrow \textbf{Step 2}(V_A, pk)$

    $r^{\oplus} \leftarrow \textbf{Step 3}(C^{\oplus}, V_b, pk)$

    $V_b \subseteq V_A \leftarrow \textbf{Step 4}(r^{\oplus}, sk)$

    $D_1^{\oplus}, ..., D_g^{\oplus} \leftarrow \textbf{Step 5.1}(G_A, pk)$

    $\{r_{1,1}^{\oplus}, ..., r_{g,1}^{\oplus}\}, ..., \{r_{1,h}^{\oplus}, ..., r_{g,h}^{\oplus}\} \leftarrow \textbf{Step 6}(D_1^{\oplus}, ..., D_g^{\oplus}, G_b, pk)$

    $\hat{b} \leftarrow \mathcal{A}(\{r_{1,1}^{\oplus}, ..., r_{g,1}^{\oplus}\}, ..., \{r_{1,h}^{\oplus}, ..., r_{g,h}^{\oplus}\}, V_b \subseteq V_A, E_b \subseteq E_A \text{ or } E_b \nsubseteq E_A, \mathcal{L}_4)$

    if $\hat{b} = b$, output 1

    otherwise, output 0

In the above experiment, $\mathcal{A}$ is a probabilistic polynomial-time adversarial verifier with a private graph $G_A = (V_A, E_A)$. **Step 1**–**Step 6** are the steps of the protocol, and $\xleftarrow{\$}$ denotes randomly choosing.

First, $\mathcal{A}$ runs the **Step 1** of the protocol and obtains pk and sk. Then $\mathcal{A}$ choose two graphs $G_0 = (V_0, E_0)$ and $G_1 = (V_1, E_1)$, and sends them to a honest prover P_B. The vertices of the graphs are satisfying $V_0 \subseteq V_A$ and $V_1 \subseteq V_A$. The edges of the graphs are satisfying either $(E_0 \subseteq E_A, E_1 \subseteq E_A)$ or $(E_0 \nsubseteq E_A, E_1 \nsubseteq E_A)$. Furthermore, the number of vertices with non-zero degree of G_0 is the same with that of G_1.

P_B randomly picks a bit $b = \{0,1\}$, and chooses G_b to be his private graph. $\mathcal{A}$ and P_B then execute the rest of the protocol as normal until **Step 6**. At last, given the knowledge of the output of **Step 6**, $V_b \subseteq V_A$, $E_b \subseteq E_A$ or $E_b \nsubseteq E_A$ and $\mathcal{L}_4$, $\mathcal{A}$ guesses a bit $\hat{b}$. If $\hat{b} = b$, $\mathcal{A}$ wins the experiment. Otherwise, $\mathcal{A}$ loses. The advantage of $\mathcal{A}$ winning the above experiment is defined as $Adv_{\mathcal{A}} = \Pr[\text{EXP}_{\mathcal{A}}^{\text{IND-CPA}}(1^k, \mathcal{L}_4) = 1]$.

The output of **Step 6** is having the property that, if $E_b \subseteq E_A$, each set will contains exactly one 0 after decryption, and all other values are random numbers. If $E_b \nsubseteq E_A$, at least one of the sets contains non-zero random numbers only.

Due to the condition $(E_0 \subseteq E_A, E_1 \subseteq E_A)$ or $(E_0 \nsubseteq E_A, E_1 \nsubseteq E_A)$, the output of the **Step 6** will have the same property no matter which value b has, and the random numbers are indistinguishable for $\mathcal{A}$. As a result, $\{r_{1,1}^{\oplus}, ..., r_{g,1}^{\oplus}\}, ..., \{r_{1,h}^{\oplus}, ..., r_{g,h}^{\oplus}\}$ gives no additional information about the prover's graph, beyond the final result and $\mathcal{L}_4$. In other words, the advantages of $\mathcal{A}$ winning the above experiment will not be greater than a random guess, i.e. $Adv_{\mathcal{A}} = \Pr[\text{EXP}_{\mathcal{A}}^{\text{IND-CPA}}(1^k, \mathcal{L}_4) = 1] = |\frac{1}{2} + \epsilon|$, where ϵ is negligible.

At last, we construct a simulator $\mathcal{S}$ to simulate the view of the verifier in the ideal model. $\mathcal{S}$ is given the knowledge of $\mathcal{L}_4$. At **Step 3**, $\mathcal{S}$ sends a random value to P_A. At **Step 6**, $\mathcal{S}$ sends a random number of sets to P_A, each contain $\mathcal{L}_4$ random values. Due to the nature of the Paillier cryptosystem, P_A cannot distinguish between random values and the ciphertexts.

As a result, the view of the verifier in the ideal model will be indistinguishable from the view in the real model. In other words, $\text{View}_{P_A}^{\text{real}}[P_A, P_B(G_B))] \approx \text{View}_{P_A}^{\text{ideal}}[P_A, \mathcal{S}(\mathcal{L}_4)]$.

In conclusion, if both parties are honest, the verifier will not learn any information about the prover's graph, beyond the result of the protocol and the pre-defined leakage $\mathcal{L}_4$.   □

Lemma 3 (Prover Zero-knowledge). A semi-honest prover learns no information about the verifier's graph, beyond the pre-defined leakages $\mathcal{L}_1$, $\mathcal{L}_2$ and $\mathcal{L}_3$.

Proof. During the protocol, there are two parts where P_B receives information from P_A. The first part is during **Step 2**, where P_B receives a set of ciphertexts $C^{\oplus}$ under the Paillier cryptosystem. P_B can learn the information about $|V_A|$ by counting the ciphertexts received, which is the pre-defined leakage $\mathcal{L}_1$. Again, for the same reason, we skip the proof of $C^{\oplus}$ reveals no additional information about V_A beyond $|V_A|$, and more details can be found in [24].

The second part is During **Step 5.1** or **Step 5.2**. In the case where **Step 5.1** is executed, i.e. $V_B \subseteq V_A$, P_B receives g sets, $D_1^{\oplus}, ..., D_g^{\oplus}$, each containing $[3, |V_A| + 2]$ ciphertexts. By counting the number of sets received, P_B can learn the number of vertices with non-zero degree in G_A, which is the pre-defined leakage $\mathcal{L}_2$. By counting the number of elements in each set, P_B can learn the degree of each vertex in G_A, which is the pre-defined leakage $\mathcal{L}_3$. In addition, by counting number of ciphertexts in the largest set, $l = max(|D_i^{\oplus}|)_{1 \leqslant i \leqslant g}$, P_B can learn partial information about $|V_A|$, which is $|V_A|$ will be at least $l - 2$. However, we consider it as useless information, since P_B already learns $|V_A|$.

In the case where **Step 5.2** is executed, i.e. $V_B \not\subseteq V_A$, P_B receives g sets, $D_1^{\oplus}, ..., D_g^{\oplus}$, each containing $[3, |V_A| + 2]$ random values. Due to the nature of the Paillier cryptosystem, P_B cannot distinguish between ciphertexts and random values. Therefore, P_B cannot distinguish which step is executed. In other words, **Step 5.2** will not give more information to P_B than **Step 5.1**.

In order to prove that $D_1^{\oplus}, ..., D_g^{\oplus}$ does not reveal any additional information beyond $\mathcal{L}_2$ and $\mathcal{L}_3$, we need to show that P_B cannot distinguish between the cases where P_A has different input graphs, given the knowledge of $\mathcal{L}_1$, $\mathcal{L}_2$ and $\mathcal{L}_3$. Consider the following experiment in the real model:

$$\text{EXP}_{\mathcal{A}}^{\text{IND-CPA}}(1^k, \mathcal{L}_1, \mathcal{L}_2, \mathcal{L}_3):$$

$$(pk, sk) \leftarrow \textbf{Step 1}(1^k)$$

$$(G_0, G_1) \leftarrow \mathcal{A}$$

$$b \xleftarrow{\$} \{0, 1\}$$

$$C^{\oplus} \leftarrow \textbf{Step 2}(V_b, pk)$$

$$r^{\oplus} \leftarrow \textbf{Step 3}(C^{\oplus}, V_B, pk)$$

$$V_B \subseteq V_b \text{ or } V_B \nsubseteq V_b \leftarrow \textbf{Step 4}(r^{\oplus}, sk)$$

$$V_B \subseteq V_b:$$

$$\quad D_1^{\oplus}, ..., D_g^{\oplus} \leftarrow \textbf{Step 5.1}(G_b, pk)$$

$$V_B \nsubseteq V_b:$$

$$\quad D_1^{\oplus}, ..., D_g^{\oplus} \leftarrow \textbf{Step 5.2}(G_b, pk)$$

$$\hat{b} \leftarrow \mathcal{A}(D_1^{\oplus}, ..., D_g^{\oplus}, \mathcal{L}_1, \mathcal{L}_2, \mathcal{L}_3)$$

$$\text{if } \hat{b} = b, \text{ output } 1$$

$$\text{otherwise, output } 0$$

In the above experiment, $\mathcal{A}$ is a probabilistic polynomial-time adversarial prover with a private graph $G_B = (V_B, E_B)$. **Step 1**–**Step 5** are the steps of the protocol, and $\xleftarrow{\$}$ denotes randomly choosing.

First, a honest verifier P_A runs the **Step 1** of the protocol and obtains pk and sk. Then $\mathcal{A}$ choose two graphs $G_0 = (V_0, E_0)$ and $G_1 = (V_1, E_1)$, and sends them to P_A. The two graphs are satisfying the condition that the number of vertices of both graphs are the same, i.e. $|V_0| = |V_1|$. The number of vertices with non-zero degree of G_0 is the same with that of G_1. Let $V_0 = \{a_1, ..., a_m\}$ and $V_1 = \{b_1, ..., b_m\}$. The degree of each vertex in both graphs are the same, i.e. $D(a_i) = D(b_i)$ for $1 \leqslant i \leqslant m$.

After that, P_A randomly picks a bit $b = \{0, 1\}$, and and chooses G_b to be his private graph. $\mathcal{A}$ and P_A then execute the rest of the protocol as normal until **Step 5** (no matter which of **Step 5.1** and **Step 5.2** is executed). At last, given the knowledge of the outputs of **Step 5**, $\mathcal{L}_1$, $\mathcal{L}_2$ and $\mathcal{L}_3$, $\mathcal{A}$ guesses a bit $\hat{b}$. If $\hat{b} = b$, $\mathcal{A}$ wins the experiment. Otherwise, $\mathcal{A}$ loses. The advantage of $\mathcal{A}$ winning the above experiment is defined as $Adv_{\mathcal{A}} = \Pr[\text{EXP}_{\mathcal{A}}^{\text{IND-CPA}}(1^k, \mathcal{L}_1, \mathcal{L}_2, \mathcal{L}_3) = 1]$.

The outputs of **Step 5.1** are g sets of ciphertexts under the Paillier cryptosystem. Note that, no matter $b = 0$ or $b = 1$, the number of elements in each set will be fixed. Due to the nature of the Paillier cryptosystem, $\mathcal{A}$ cannot distinguish between two ciphertexts, given the knowledge of the corresponding plaintexts. Therefore, the outputs of **Step 5.1** give no information about the verifier's graph, beyond $\mathcal{L}_2$ and $\mathcal{L}_3$. In addition, $\mathcal{A}$ cannot distinguish which of **Step 5.1** and **Step 5.2** is executed, as explained before.

As a result, the advantages of $\mathcal{A}$ winning the above experiment will not be greater than a random guess, i.e. $Adv_{\mathcal{A}} = \Pr[\text{EXP}_{\mathcal{A}}^{\text{IND-CPA}}(1^k, \mathcal{L}_1, \mathcal{L}_2, \mathcal{L}_3) = 1] = |\frac{1}{2} + \epsilon|$, where ϵ is negligible.

At last, we construct a simulator $\mathcal{S}$ to simulate the view of the prover in the ideal model. $\mathcal{S}$ is given the knowledge of $\mathcal{L}_1$, $\mathcal{L}_2$ and $\mathcal{L}_3$. At **Step 2**, $\mathcal{S}$ sends a set of $\mathcal{L}_1 + 1$ random values to P_B. At **Step 5.2** (**Step 5.2** will always be executed at overwhelming probability), $\mathcal{S}$ sends $\mathcal{L}_2$ sets to P_B, each containing several random values. The number of random values in each set is determined by $\mathcal{L}_3$. Due to the nature of the Paillier cryptosystem, P_B cannot distinguish between random values and the ciphertexts.

As a result, the view of the prover in the ideal model will be indistinguishable from the view in the real model. In other words, $\text{View}_{P_B}^{\text{real}}[P_A(G_A), P_B)] \approx \text{View}_{P_B}^{\text{ideal}}[\mathcal{S}(\mathcal{L}_1, \mathcal{L}_2, \mathcal{L}_3), P_B]$.

In conclusion, if both parties are honest, the prover will not learn any information about the verifier's graph, beyond the pre-defined leakages $\mathcal{L}_1$, $\mathcal{L}_2$ and $\mathcal{L}_3$. □

5.2 Information Leakage

The security of the private subgraph matching protocol is mainly focused on protecting the privacies of the input graphs. Therefore preventing information from leakage is the first priority when designing the protocol. While truly no information leakage is the ideal goal, our protocol leaks partial information about the graphs. We define four information leakage, denoted as $\mathcal{L}_1$, $\mathcal{L}_2$, $\mathcal{L}_3$ and $\mathcal{L}_4$, respectively, as described in Sect. 3.

Commonly speaking, when considering labeled, directed and unweighted graph data, the most valuable information includes the labels of the vertices, the number of vertices, the edges between the vertices and the number of edges. The order of the values of such information may vary based on different applications.

In certain applications, the vertices give no useful information, while the information about the edges are consider valuable. For example, in a location based service, the paths of users traveling across the country are stored as graphs. The vertices of the graph represent all the cities within the country, and the edges represent how a certain user travels from city to city. In such scenario, the vertices is public information that can be acquired by anyone, while the edges should be kept secret, since the location information can be treated as sensitive data.

In our protocol, $\mathcal{L}_1$ is defined as the number of vertices of the verifier's graph. Since the verifier and the prover are jointly performing the protocol, it can be reasonable to assume that both of the parties know what does the graph of the other party represents, i.e. each of them has certain knowledge about the graph of the other party. In some applications, $\mathcal{L}_1$ can be a public information, which means leaking it will not affect preserving the privacy of the verifier's graph. However, in other applications, $\mathcal{L}_1$ may cause major information leakage.

There is an easy solution that can be applied to improve the situation, with the price of more computation costs. During **Step 2** of the protocol, P_A constructs the polynomial $P(x)$ as normal. Then he randomly chooses an irreducible polynomial $R(x)$ with degree d, and computes $P'(x) = P(x)R(x)$. The polynomial $P'(x)$ will have the same property as $P(x)$, and P_A uses $P'(x)$ instead in the later steps of the protocol. By using this solution, the prover can only learns the upper bond of the number of vertices in G_A, i.e. $|V_A| + d$.

$\mathcal{L}_2$ and $\mathcal{L}_4$ are defined as the number of vertices with non-zero degree in G_A and G_B, respectively. Normally speaking, $\mathcal{L}_2$ and $\mathcal{L}_4$ can be safely treated as unvalued information. In most circumstances, $\mathcal{L}_2$ and $\mathcal{L}_4$ contain very little information, and by acquiring them will not leads to more information leakage. Therefore, leaking $\mathcal{L}_2$ and $\mathcal{L}_4$ will be considered as acceptable in our protocol.

$\mathcal{L}_3$ is defined as the degree of each vertex of the verifier's graph. However, the prover will not have the knowledge of the labels of the vertices in G_A. Furthermore, in the cases where the vertices of the verifier's graph are public information, the prover will not have the knowledge of the mappings between the vertices and the elements in $\mathcal{L}_3$. In other words, even if the prover knows the degree of a certain vertex in G_A, he does not know which one. Therefore, we can also assume $\mathcal{L}_3$ is acceptable in our protocol.

5.3   Performance Analysis

In this section, we denote the graph of the verifier and the prover as $G_A = (V_A, E_A)$ and $G_B = (V_B, E_B)$, respectively. Let $|V_A| = m$ and $|V_B| = n$. Let the numbers of vertices with non-zero degree in G_A and G_B denoted as g and h, respectively.

The communication cost is measured in terms of ciphertexts being transmitted, and the computation cost is measured in terms of modular multiplications and exponentiations. Constructing k polynomials with degree d requires $O(kd)$ modular multiplications. Encrypting k plaintexts requires $O(k)$ modular exponentiations, and decrypting k ciphertexts requires $O(k)$ modular exponentiations. Obviously evaluating k polynomials with degree d requires $O(kd)$ modular exponentiations. Performing k homomorphic additions requires $O(k)$ modular multiplications, and performing k homomorphic multiplications requires $O(k)$ modular exponentiations.

Communication Cost: In **Step 2**, P_A sends m ciphertexts to P_B. In **Step 3**, P_B sends 1 ciphertext to P_A. In **Step 5.1** and **Step 5.2**, P_A sends $O(mg)$ ciphertexts to P_B in the worst case. In **Step 6**, P_B sends gh ciphertexts. As a result, the communication cost is $O(mg + gh)$ ciphertexts.

Communication Round: The communication round of our protocol is fixed, i.e. $O(1)$.

Verifier Computation Cost: In **Step 2**, P_A constructs 1 polynomial with degree m and encrypts $m + 1$ plaintexts. In **Step 4**, P_A decrypts 1 ciphertext. In **Step 5.1**, P_A constructs g polynomials with degree 1 and g polynomials with degree $O(m)$ in the worst case, and P_A encrypts $O(gm)$ plaintexts. In **Step 7**, P_A decrypts gh ciphertexts. As a result, the computation cost for the verifier is $O(mg + gh)$ modular exponentiations and $O(mg)$ modular multiplications.

Prover Computation Cost: In **Step 3**, P_B evaluates n polynomials with degree m, performs n homomorphic multiplications and n homomorphic additions.

In **Step 6**, P_B evaluates hg polynomials with degree 1 and $O(ng)$ polynomials with degree $O(m)$. P_B also performs $hg+O(ng)$ homomorphic multiplications and $O(ng)$ homomorphic additions. As a result, the computation cost for the prover is $O(mng)$ modular exponentiations and $O(ng)$ modular multiplications.

6 Conclusion

In this work, we proposed a private subgraph matching protocol. The two parties that participate the protocol are a verifier and a prover, and each of which holds a private graph. After jointly executing the protocol, the verifier learns whether the prover's graph is a subgraph of the verifier's graph. The protocol is based on the Paillier cryptosystem and oblivious polynomial evaluation, and we used a private subset relation protocol as a building block. We proved that our protocol is secure under the semi-honest setting, and we analysed the efficiency in terms of computation cost, communication cost and communication round. Further works may include further improving the leakage problem and reduce the computation costs.

Acknowledgements. This work was supported in part by the National Science and Technology Major Project under Grant No. 2013ZX03002006, the Liaoning Province Science and Technology Projects under Grant No. 2013217004, the Liaoning Province Doctor Startup Fund under Grant No. 20141012, the Fundamental Research Funds for the Central Universities under Grant Numbers N130317002, N151704002, the Shenyang Province Science and Technology Projects under Grant No. F14-231-1-08, and the National Natural Science Foundation of China under Grant Numbers 61272546, 61321491, 61402095, 61472184.

References

1. Ullmann, J.R.: An algorithm for subgraph isomorphism. J. ACM (JACM) **23**(1), 31–42 (1976)
2. Solnon, C.: All different-based filtering for subgraph isomorphism. Artif. Intell. **174**(12–13), 850–864 (2010)
3. Cordella, L.P., Foggia, P., Sansone, C., et al.: A (sub) graph isomorphism algorithm for matching large graphs. IEEE Trans. Pattern Anal. Mach. Intell. **26**(10), 1367–1372 (2004)
4. Messmer, B.T., Bunke, H.: A new algorithm for error-tolerant subgraph isomorphism detection. IEEE Trans. Pattern Anal. Mach. Intell. **20**(5), 493–504 (1998)
5. Eppstein, D.: Subgraph isomorphism in planar graphs and related problems. In: SODA 1995, pp. 632–640 (1995)
6. Shang, H., Zhang, Y., Lin, X., et al.: Taming verification hardness: an efficient algorithm for testing subgraph isomorphism. Proc. VLDB Endowment **1**(1), 364–375 (2008)
7. Messmer, B.T., Bunke, H.: Efficient subgraph isomorphism detection: a decomposition approach. IEEE Trans. Knowl. Data Eng. **12**(2), 307–323 (2000)
8. Raymond, J.W., Willett, P.: Maximum common subgraph isomorphism algorithms for the matching of chemical structures. J. Comput. Aided Mol. Des. **16**(7), 521–533 (2002)

9. Bonnici, V., Giugno, R., Pulvirenti, A., et al.: A subgraph isomorphism algorithm and its application to biochemical data. BMC Bioinform. **14**(7), S13 (2013)

10. Ehrlich, H.C., Rarey, M.: Maximum common subgraph isomorphism algorithms and their applications in molecular science: a review. Wiley Interdiscip. Rev. Comput. Mol. Sci. **1**(1), 68–79 (2011)

11. Koyutrk, M., Grama, A., Szpankowski, W.: An efficient algorithm for detecting frequent subgraphs in biological networks. Bioinformatics **20**(Suppl. 1), i200–i207 (2004)

12. Artymiuk, P.J., Grindley, H.M., Poirrette, A.R., et al.: Identification of beta-sheet motifs, of psi-loops, and of patterns of amino acid residues in three-dimensional protein structures using a subgraph-isomorphism algorithm. J. Chem. Inf. Comput. Sci. **34**(1), 54–62 (1994)

13. Wong, E.K.: Model matching in robot vision by subgraph isomorphism. Pattern Recogn. **25**(3), 287–303 (1992)

14. Llads, J., Mart, E., Villanueva, J.J.: Symbol recognition by error-tolerant subgraph matching between region adjacency graphs. IEEE Trans. Pattern Anal. Mach. Intell. **23**(10), 1137–1143 (2001)

15. Zhu, K., Zhang, Y., Lin, X., Zhu, G., Wang, W.: NOVA: a novel and efficient framework for finding subgraph isomorphism mappings in large graphs. In: Kitagawa, H., Ishikawa, Y., Li, Q., Watanabe, C. (eds.) DASFAA 2010. LNCS, vol. 5981, pp. 140–154. Springer, Heidelberg (2010). doi:10.1007/978-3-642-12026-8_13

16. Han, W.S., Lee, J., Lee, J.H.: Turbo ISO: towards ultrafast and robust subgraph isomorphism search in large graph databases. In: Proceedings of the 2013 ACM SIGMOD International Conference on Management of Data, pp. 337–348. ACM (2013)

17. Foggia, P., Sansone, C., Vento, M.: A performance comparison of five algorithms for graph isomorphism. In: Proceedings of the 3rd IAPR TC-15 Workshop on Graph-Based Representations in Pattern Recognition, pp. 188–199 (2001)

18. Lee, J., Han, W.S., Kasperovics, R., et al.: An in-depth comparison of subgraph isomorphism algorithms in graph databases. Proc. VLDB Endowment **6**(2), 133–144 (2012). VLDB Endowment

19. Brickell, J., Shmatikov, V.: Privacy-preserving graph algorithms in the semi-honest model. In: Roy, B. (ed.) ASIACRYPT 2005. LNCS, vol. 3788, pp. 236–252. Springer, Heidelberg (2005). doi:10.1007/11593447_13

20. Cao, N., Yang, Z., Wang, C., et al.: Privacy-preserving query over encrypted graph-structured data in cloud computing. In: 2011 31st International Conference on Distributed Computing Systems (ICDCS), pp. 393–402. IEEE (2011)

21. Meng, X., Kamara, S., Nissim, K., et al.: GRECS: graph encryption for approximate shortest distance queries. In: Proceedings of the 22nd ACM SIGSAC Conference on Computer and Communications Security, pp. 504–517. ACM (2015)

22. Chase, M., Kamara, S.: Structured encryption and controlled disclosure. In: Abe, M. (ed.) ASIACRYPT 2010. LNCS, vol. 6477, pp. 577–594. Springer, Heidelberg (2010). doi:10.1007/978-3-642-17373-8_33

23. Paillier, P.: Public-key cryptosystems based on composite degree residuosity classes. In: Stern, J. (ed.) EUROCRYPT 1999. LNCS, vol. 1592, pp. 223–238. Springer, Heidelberg (1999). doi:10.1007/3-540-48910-X_16

24. Kissner, L., Song, D.: Privacy-preserving set operations. In: Shoup, V. (ed.) CRYPTO 2005. LNCS, vol. 3621, pp. 241–257. Springer, Heidelberg (2005). doi:10.1007/11535218_15

A New Blockchain-Based Value-Added Tax System

Dimaz Ankaa Wijaya[1,2]([⊠]), Joseph K. Liu[1]([⊠]),
Dony Ariadi Suwarsono[3], and Peng Zhang[4]([⊠])

[1] Faculty of Information Technology, Monash University, Melbourne, Australia
{dimaz.wijaya,joseph.liu}@monash.edu
[2] Data61, CSIRO, Melbourne, Australia
[3] Directorate General of Taxes, Jakarta, Indonesia
dony.suwarsono@pajak.go.id
[4] College of Information Engineering, Shenzhen University, Shenzhen, China
zhangp@szu.edu.cn

Abstract. Value-Added Tax or VAT plays an important role in the Indonesian state revenue. Despite its importance, it requires a complex administration process to be done properly. The complexity of the tax administration creates loopholes that can be exploited by dishonest taxpayers to minimize the tax paid to the government. The current system does not prevent the dishonest taxpayers to forge tax invoices which bring tax loss for the government. We utilize the blockchain technology to create a novel approach of implementing the distributed ledger in taxation area. Our proposed protocol creates a transparent and secure VAT system as well as simplifies the process of administering the VAT. The system increases the tax compliance by reducing the risk of tax fraud and increasing the monitoring capability of the tax authority.

Keywords: Blockchain · Value-Added Tax · Tax credits

1 Introduction

In Indonesia, Value-Added Tax (VAT) was introduced in the 1983 tax reform to extend the tax base [1]. VAT is an indirect tax in which the tax is charged for every price increase. VAT contributes to 33.7% of the total inland revenue in 2017 Indonesian state budget [2]. VAT is an indirect tax; the tax is paid along the chain of business, but eventually the end user will be charged for the accumulated tax which is included in the final price of the goods or services purchased.

VAT provides a self-policing feature with tax credit mechanism. A tax invoice is a proof that the seller has collected the VAT from the buyer. The VAT paid by the buyer recovers a part of the tax previously paid by the seller to the previous seller. The tax due is calculated by subtracting the value of the tax invoice created and the tax invoices received. The tax due is paid at the end of VAT reporting period before submitting the tax return. Not every taxpayer can create a tax invoice; only those Taxable Person for VAT Purposes (TPVP) have permission to produce tax invoices.

© Springer International Publishing AG 2017
T. Okamoto et al. (Eds.): ProvSec 2017, LNCS 10592, pp. 471–486, 2017.
https://doi.org/10.1007/978-3-319-68637-0_28

In VAT, a seller creates a tax invoice for every taxable goods and services sold to a buyer. The buyer pays the price for the goods or services bought from the seller including the VAT. The tax invoice states that the seller has sold the goods or services to the buyer and the seller has received the VAT from the buyer [3–5]. The tax invoice received could then be used by the buyer to reduce her tax due because she has paid a part of her VAT to her seller. Before e-Faktur was developed, the tax invoices are paper-based documents and they must be kept well. e-Faktur was developed to help TPVP to create, manage, and organise the tax invoices that they no longer need to print the tax invoices. Every tax invoice record is kept in a centralised database managed by DGT. The seller only needs to create the tax invoice records and then upload the records to the server. The buyer imports the records to her e-Faktur account and they will be ready to be processed. e-Faktur helps the TPVPs in managing the tax invoices and in the same time helps DGT to collect the tax invoice records.

However, there are 2 problems related to the tax invoice fraud that are not covered by e-Faktur. First, e-Faktur does not prevent a dishonest TPVP to forge fictitious tax invoices which have no actual transaction. As creating tax invoices through the e-Faktur application is free, the dishonest TPVP creates tax invoices as much as she wants and sells the tax invoices to other dishonest TPVPs. In a sophisticated case, the tax invoice forgery could utilise layers of dishonest TPVPs in which they create fake transactions and send the forged tax invoices among themselves. By using such layering, it will be hard to determine all parties involved in the case if the paperworks are well-prepared by the dishonest TPVPs.

Second, the e-Faktur does not implement strict codification to determine the type of the goods or services mentioned in the tax invoices. Each TPVP is allowed to create their own codification. Therefore, as long as the tax invoice number and value match, redeeming the tax invoice will always succeed. The loose codification system could motivate a dishonest TPVP to forge tax invoices based on real transactions. The tax invoices originally must be given to the real buyers, but because of the loose codification system, the dishonest TPVP modifies and sells the tax invoices to other dishonest TPVPs.

We propose a new method to mitigate these problems. Our protocol reverses the process of managing the tax invoices. Any TPVP cannot create tax invoices to other TPVPs without first acquire valid tax credits. A TPVP needs to pay some money to get the tax credits, then they can create a tax invoice as a way to transfer the tax credits to another TPVP. By reversing the process, it is guaranteed that the tax credits in the system are representation of real tax money flowing through VAT system. The risk of the government suffers loss from tax invoice forgery is reduced since the tax is paid up front. By levying the VAT money to other parties, the motivation of a TPVP to act dishonestly is also reduced.

In order to enforce the new rules, we implement the blockchain technology in our protocol. The tax credits will be represented by tokens, and the tax invoices will be represented by transactions among the TPVPs. The blockchain technology helps the protocol to remain transparent for every participant and offers security of the transactions, in which it cannot be tampered once they are verified and validated by the authority. The blockchain also enables multiple parties to have a monitoring role in the system. Monitoring bodies will be able to audit the transactions while the end users are given a capability of tracking the tax they pay. We also implement a strict codification system based on an international standard. By using such standard, it is easier to analyse if there is any unusual transaction in the tax invoices.

2   Context

2.1   Bitcoin

Bitcoin was first introduced in 2008 as a new kind of virtual currency in a whitepaper written by Satoshi Nakamoto [6]. Bitcoin is different compared to fiat money or any existing electronic cash system since it does not employ any central authority to run the system. Instead, a peer-to-peer network is used to run the decentralized currency based on a consensus protocol. In Bitcoin, the consensus protocol is done by a concept called proof-of-work (PoW) which requires computing power, which is similar to Hashcash [7]. The PoW is also used to protect the information contained in the system from unauthorized tampering. By using the decentralized ledger, Bitcoin provides a mechanism to transfer value with accountability. Moreover, Bitcoin supports scripting language which can be used to develop various value transfer protocols.

2.2   Blockchain

Information inside the Bitcoin system is kept in a database structure called blockchain [8]. The blockchain is a type of decentralized database stored in multiple interconnected nodes through Internet. Each node keeps identical information without any master node controlling other nodes [9]. The transaction data are grouped in blocks. Each block is connected to a predecessor block by including its hash value into the next block's header data. In such system, new blocks are created by miners. The miners are participants providing the computing power. They compute a value which satisfies a certain requirement set by the network. The computing job is the PoW protecting the data from tampering.

2.3   Blockchain Case Studies

Multichain [10] is an open source blockchain project which can be deployed in a private environment. Multichain maintains compatibility with Bitcoin protocol, such as network protocol, transaction format, block format, and output script, including runtime parameter, JSON-RPC API, and most features in Bitcoin Developer Documentation [11]. In Multichain, each node is registered in a permission list and will be verified by other nodes against the list. If the condition is not satisfied, the node denies the connection request. Multichain also enables user to configure the behavior of the blockchain, e.g. target time, permission type, mining rewards, etc.

Everledger developed a blockchain-based system to track diamonds. The diamonds are numbered and recorded into the blockchain. For each diamond transaction involving these diamonds, the transaction records will be saved in the blockchain. Therefore, everyone buying these diamonds will be able to track the ownership history to determine whether these diamonds have any history of theft or involved in unethical activities [12]. Everledger utilizes the blockchain capability of securing the information and make the unauthorized data modification infeasible.

Bitnation is a blockchain project trying to provide governmental services by employing blockchain technology [12]. Although Bitnation does not have any real institution, its idea might become a breakthrough to run a government by taking advantages of modern technology. One of Bitnation's project collaborating with Estonian government is e-Resident. E-Residents can notarize official documents through the service provided to them.

Bitcoin can be used to store large amount of data as in asset management system extension protocol [13]. The protocol enables the users to store at most 520 bytes of data for each P2SH script, while the maximum data which can be stored in a transaction should be around 85 kB, since the maximum size of a transaction in Bitcoin is limited to 100 kB and the density of the data in the protocol is 85%.

2.4   Blockchain in Tax System

A report by PricewaterhouseCoopers describes the advantages of blockchain technology in taxation [14]. They concluded that blockchain technology could reduce VAT fraud by tracking where and when VAT has been paid. The blockchain-based tax system can also supply good quality data to authorities and regulators. Not mentioning the transparency of the data stored in the blockchain, multinational companies need to provide a consistent data set for tax authorities in different countries.

A study in VAT related to European Union (EU) intra-community trading shows that implementing blockchain in VAT system can reduce revenue loss between 50 to 60 billion Euro per year from missing trader intra-community (MTIC) fraud cases [15]. The blockchain solution is proposed to be utilized under the Digital Invoice Customs Exchange (DICE) which is a data sharing platform between several cooperating countries. The DICE is intended to replace the current system called The VAT Information Exchange System (VIES) which uses multiple centralized databases. A data exchange system is deployed to share information between the separated database systems maintained by different tax authorities. The distributed ledger will create a more integrated transaction data to be used by these tax authorities. The shared information is best used to mitigate risks from multinational transactions. The blockchain is not only fit for VAT; even the payroll tax can be implemented in a blockchain system [16].

2.5   Scope

In this paper, we limit our research scope to several parts of the VAT system, due to vast amount of regulations we need to adopt to our system. Our paper describes a method to identify taxpayers, transfer tax credits between taxpayers, and how to create tax invoices through blockchain technology. We assume that a private blockchain system already exists and this protocol works over that system. We also assume that the transaction fee is negligible since the closed system is maintained by a central authority which may receive funding from the government.

3 Preliminaries

3.1 Deterministic Address

Deterministic address is commonly used in Deterministic Wallet in Bitcoin environment to simplify the address storage in a wallet. By using deterministic addresses, a wallet only need to save a parent key and indexes. Those indexes are used to generate child keys (the addresses and the private keys altogether) by deriving them from the parent key and the indexes through a deterministic function [8, 17]. Hierarchical deterministic (HD) address is similar to deterministic address with additional feature of deriving child keys in the form of a tree [18]. Therefore, a child address derived from an index of a parent key can be further derived to create multiple child addresses.

3.2 Pay to Script Hash

Pay to Script Hash (P2SH) is one of the transaction methods available in Bitcoin system [19]. P2SH is a unique transaction in which to complete the transactions, users need to complete 2 phases. The first phase is the commit phase; in this phase, a user pays to a P2SH address generated from a P2SH script. The second phase is the redeem phase; in this phase, the receiver takes control by redeeming the transaction from the P2SH address to the destination address.

The P2SH is important in our proposed protocol, since the transaction related to tax invoice need to satisfy VAT regulations. Without the P2SH, a regular transaction will oversimplify the requirements and thus it may not fit the requirements.

3.3 Relative Lock-Time

Relative Lock-Time (RLT) is a type of Bitcoin transaction which utilizes time variable in the transaction, whether to lock the transaction or to use it inside a conditional procedure [20]. RLT does not mention a precise time in the future, but rather defines a relative time compared to the time the commit transaction is confirmed in the blockchain. RLT is defined as OP_CHECKSEQUENCEVERIFY (or also called as OP_CSV) which is a new definition of OP_NOP3 operation code.

3.4 Sequence Number

Sequence number (nSequence) in Bitcoin is 4 bytes information inside Bitcoin raw transaction to detect the version number of the transaction [21]. A transaction is considered as final if the nSequence shows the maximum number. After OP_CHECKSE-QUENCEVERIFY was deployed, nSequence has a new function of determining the earliest block to confirm. This new usage is active only if OP_CHECKSEQUENCE-VERIFY is activated.

3.5   Multisignature

Multisignature is a type of Bitcoin transaction which requires multiple digital signature to validate the transaction. The multisignature could be defined explicitly or could also be used inside a P2SH transaction. It is denoted as `m-of-n multisignature` with `m` is the minimum number of signature required to redeem the transaction and `n` is the number of possible signatures to validate the transaction. Multisignature requires multiple parties to agree upon a transaction before it is sent to the network. The agreement is proved by the digital signature provided by each party. In another word, the transaction cannot be validated without consent of minimum number of parties as determined by the multisignature. By employing multisignature, a dishonest action can be prevented by honest parties.

4   Our Proposed Solution

4.1   Overview

In our system, we define tokens called PAKO to represent the tax credits. PAKO works inside a system we define as Pajakoin. Pajakoin is a centralized blockchain system run by DGT. The overview of the system is described in Fig. 1.

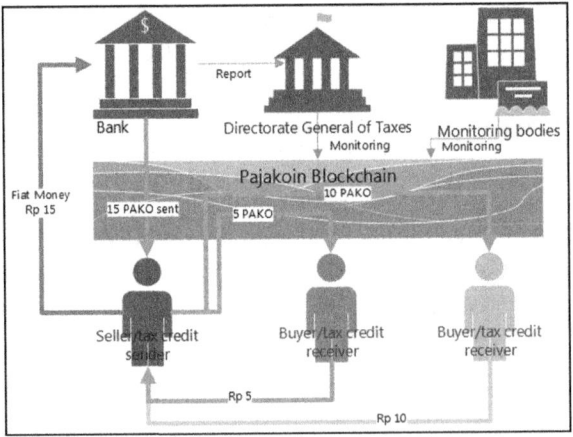

Fig. 1. Overview of Pajakoin system

The system works as follows. First, the TPVP needs to convert her fiat money into PAKO tokens. The process will be further explained later in Chap. 4.6. When the TPVP needs to create tax invoices, she creates PAKO transactions to transfer the PAKO to the buyers. The buyers pay the seller the same amount of money as the VAT they need to pay to the government. This mechanism is adapted from the VAT system. If later the buyers sell goods or services to others, they could then transfer the PAKO tokens to others.

The Pajakoin blockchain is a system limited to authorized participants only. DGT as the tax authority can closely monitor the PAKO transactions. Banks receive money from the TPVP and then create reports containing the amount of money received and the detail of PAKO buyers. These reports are sent to DGT which will be used to match the tax revenue and the PAKO transactions.

4.2   The System Participants

We define the participants of our proposed system as follows.

- DGT as the manager of the system will have a full control over the system.
- Banks as the agents selling PAKO to the taxpayers and collect the payment.
- Monitoring bodies as independent third parties (can be trusted government agencies) to monitor the system. The monitoring bodies will be able to audit the system through view permission.
- The taxpayers as the clients which are able to create transactions by using PAKO they purchased from the banks.

4.3   The Pajakoin Blockchain

We define a blockchain infrastructure very similar to Bitcoin blockchain in terms of its scripting language, but different in terms of how the blockchain works. We prefer a private (permissioned) blockchain over a public (permissionless) blockchain for security reasons. We adapt the user management from the Multichain system where the blockchain owner assigns authorizations to other users as follows: the blockchain will be managed by DGT, while banks, monitoring bodies, and the taxpayers will require a permission to view or create transactions in the blockchain. The banks will be allowed to view and create transactions. The monitoring bodies can only view the transactions without the ability to create any transaction. The TPVPs will be allowed to connect to the blockchain and create transactions. The limitation of their transactions lies on the P2SH script used in our proposed system.

The mining process through Proof of Work (PoW) and the transaction validation will be entirely done by DGT as the authority. Therefore, other participants do not need to provide any mining equipment. As the nodes are managed by multiple parties, they can detect if there is any block reorganisation in the system. Raw transactions created by the taxpayers or the banks can be sent directly to the nodes controlled by DGT. A transaction is considered as confirmed if it is included in a valid block. There is no need to wait for the block to have a certain depth since chain split is unlikely to happen in the closed system.

4.4   The Taxpayer's Identity

Every taxpayer is identified by her tax registration number. In Pajakoin system, the tax registration number is replaced by the Pajakoin address, which is similar to Bitcoin address. Each taxpayer has one or more unique Pajakoin addresses. They correspond to private keys in which only the respected taxpayer has the access to them. The private key is used to sign transactions related to the Pajakoin address. The taxpayer's Pajakoin addresses can only be used to receive PAKO if the taxpayer is the end user of the goods or services. The central authority lists all Pajakoin addresses owned by the taxpayers for administrative purposes. To identify these Pajakoin address, DGT can provide digital certificates for these taxpayers by signing the public keys. The digital certificates prove that DGT approves the usage of those Pajakoin addresses in the blockchain-based VAT system.

For TPVP, the taxpayer Pajakoin address is used to generate TPVP Pajakoin address. Unlike any regular taxpayer address, the TPVP can move her PAKO token from her TPVP Pajakoin address to other TPVPs as a representation of tax invoice creation. We separate the regular taxpayer and the TPVP. To mimic Taxable Person for VAT Purposes Registration Number (TPVPRN), we define a unique P2SH address as TPVP Pajakoin address which is shown in Fig. 2 below.

```
OP_IF

        2 (PUBKEY 1) (PUBKEY 2) 2 OP_CHECKMULTISIG

OP_ELSE

        (CSV VALUE) OP_NOP3 OP_DROP

        OP_DUP OP_HASH160 (PUBKEYHASH 2) OP_EQUALVERIFY OP_CHECKSIG

OP_ENDIF
```

Fig. 2. The P2SH script

PUBKEY 1 is owned by the TPVP, while **PUBKEY 2** and **PUBKEYHASH 2** are owned by DGT. The P2SH address from above script is the TPVP Pajakoin address uniquely generated for every TPVP. The TPVP Pajakoin address will always be unique for each TPVP because of the uniqueness of taxpayer's Pajakoin address as represented in PUBKEY 1. DGT generates PUBKEY 2 and PUBKEYHASH 2 by using HD address scheme, therefore DGT only needs a parent address to create child addresses for each associated TPVP Pajakoin address.

The **CSV VALUE** is used in the OP_CHECKSEQUENCEVERIFY operation. It is intended to "freeze" the PUBKEY 2's capability of redeeming the committed transaction. Once the predefined time expressed in the CSV VALUE has expired, then DGT must redeem the committed transaction by using a private key associated with the PUBKEY 2 and the PUBKEYHASH 2. Since the timeframe determined in VAT regulations is 3 months, we need to simplify this requirement to 90 days. The value is applied to every TPVP Pajakoin address.

4.5   The Bank's Address

We determine similar scheme as in Chap. 4.4 for the bank's address. This scheme is used to control the transactions created by the banks that they can only transfer the PAKO to existing addresses. Therefore, these transactions must be approved by DGT by employing `2-of-2 multisignature` which requires the bank's signature and DGT's signature, although it is not necessary to put a timelock in the scheme.

4.6 Acquiring and Selling PAKO

All PAKO tokens are created by DGT as the central authority in the system. The PAKO tokens are then distributed to the banks by sending the PAKO tokens to the banks' addresses. To make the protocol works, we need to slightly modify the VAT payment procedure. Instead of paying the tax due at the end of VAT tax period, the TPVPs are required to pay the VAT to acquire tax credits before they are transferred through tax invoices to other TPVPs. The VAT payment is described as PAKO acquisition, by buying PAKO from banks which have the authority to sell PAKO. The PAKO conversion rate is determined by DGT and the banks to make sure the amount of PAKO represents tax credits in real transactions.

The PAKO tokens bought from a bank are transferred to TPVP Pajakoin addresses owned by the people buying the PAKO. Only TPVPs are allowed buy PAKO tokens from the banks. A TPVP Pajakoin address has a limited time of 90 days to transfer the tokens as tax credits or redeem them to the banks to get their money back as tax overpayment. In this case, the redeem transactions need approval from DGT before execution in the form of digital signature provided by DGT.

4.7 Transferring PAKO

PAKO can only be transferred by the permission of DGT as the tax authority. Based on VAT regulations, there are several destinations of the PAKO transaction. The first one is transferring PAKO from a TPVP to other TPVPs in which the PAKO can be further transferred as tax credits. In this case, the sender needs to know the TPVP Pajakoin address of the receiver. The second one is transferring PAKO from a TPVP to non-TPVPs (or to regular taxpayer Pajakoin address) in which the PAKO cannot be further transferred as tax credits. In this case, the sender needs the receiver's taxpayer Pajakoin address. The third one, the PAKO is transferred to a coin-eater Pajakoin address, whenever TPVPs trade with non-taxpayers. This coin-eater Pajakoin address can be supplied by DGT for every TPVP.

Since our system relies heavily on P2SH protocol, it must also comply with the P2SH requirements, therefore there are 2 phases in a transaction: commit phase and redeem phase. But because the intermediary address used in the P2SH protocol is always the same, we only see a single transaction for each PAKO transfer, which is a transaction between TPVP addresses. The commit phase and the redeem phase are done in that single transaction.

There are 2 ways of redeeming the script. The first one, the receiver will be able to redeem the transaction with the approval from DGT, proved by digital signature provided by DGT to the TP to complete the transaction. DGT needs to check the transaction to make sure that the destination address is another TPVP Pajakoin address before approving it, therefore we make sure that the tax credits transfer is between TPVP Pajakoin addresses only. This way of redeeming the script requires a script as in Fig. 3 below.

```
0 (SIGNATURE 1) (SIGNATURE 2) 1 (P2SH SCRIPT)
```

Fig. 3. Redeem script by TPVP with the approval from DGT

The second way of redeeming the commit scheme is the act of DGT removing the expired tax credits from TPVP Pajakoin address. This mechanism is required so that the TP does not transfer tax credits beyond the determined timeframe; Indonesia VAT regulations determine 3 months of timeframe. Once the time expired, DGT shall redeem the transaction. The second redeem script is in Fig. 4. The **SIGNATURE 2** can only be created by DGT as the owner of **PUBKEY 2** mentioned in P2SH script in Fig. 2.

```
(SIGNATURE 2) (PUBKEY 2) 0 (P2SH SCRIPT)
```

Fig. 4. Redeem script by DGT

After the transaction is redeemed by any of these 2 different ways, then the transaction is considered final. The time count is reset to 90 days prior to token expiration.

4.8   Tax Invoice

The PAKO transaction can contain tax invoice information. There are 2 ways of embedding the data. The first choice is by utilizing the Null Data transaction which can contain up to 80 bytes of data. If the information is larger than 80 bytes, we use the second choice by utilizing a protocol proposed by Wijaya [13]. The protocol includes a hash-locked transaction (HLT) in the commit phase which will be revealed during the redeem phase.

We put the data into JSON format to save space and maximize the amount of data to be inserted. To determine the type of taxed goods or services, we use Harmonized Commodity Description and Coding System (also called Harmonized System or HS) which is a standardized codification of goods maintained by World Customs Organization Organisation Mondiale des Douanes (WCOOMD). The JSON data shall include goods or services codes, prices, tax base, and the VAT. The example of the data format is shown in Fig. 5.

The transaction needs to be sent from the seller's TPVP Pajakoin address to the buyer's TPVP Pajakoin address or taxpayer Pajakoin address, which is the same Pajakoin address where the PAKO is transferred. There is an intermediary P2SH address to accommodate the data storage. This information is then collected and analysed by DGT for tax compliance audit.

```
1 ▾ {
2 ▾   "taxables": [
3 ▾     {"taxable": {
4          "id": "520100",
5          "qty": "1",
6          "unit": "pc",
7          "value": "100000"
8        }
9      },
10 ▾    {"taxable": {
11         "id": "640319",
12         "qty": "1",
13         "unit": "pc",
14         "value": "50000"
15       }
16     }
17   ],
18   "total": 150000,
19   "taxbase": 135000,
20   "vat": 15000
21 }
```

Fig. 5. Tax invoice data format

4.9   VAT Periodic Tax Return

The PAKO transaction can contain tax invoice information. There are 2 ways of embedding the data. The first choice is by utilizing the Null Data transaction which can contain up to 80 bytes of data. If the information is larger than 80 bytes, we use the second choice by utilizing a protocol proposed by Wijaya [13]. The protocol includes a hash-locked transaction (HLT) in the commit phase which will be revealed during the redeem phase.

Although the Pajakoin mechanism has already covered VAT calculation contained in VAT periodic tax return through its token transactions, the VAT regulation requires every TPVP to submit VAT periodic tax return as mandatory. To comply the regulation, we propose a method to submit a report containing a compilation of transaction IDs. The sample is shown in Fig. 6. The identity of the TPVP is not explicitly defined in the report, but will be identified by the sender address of the report.

```
1 ▾ {
2    "version": "0",
3    "period": "201705",
4 ▾  "txid": [
5      "235cf6e9e0d3ad0f532ad2db5d49c46f79b539c02ef6b844a2ac009e9b7ebd21",
6      "8f1383275d70a8dbcd09d83ed72c00f310eec062e8616820debae5b1df832874",
7      "358fc25f33f065cf72ea0b23e40216d8bac8b61929d858edac12aa2ea8cd7bb2"
8    ]
9 }
```

Fig. 6. VAT periodic tax return data format

Since the VAT periodic tax return might require more than 80 bytes of space, then we use the same protocol as in tax invoice data storage from [13]. There is a slight difference in the destination Pajakoin address of the data storage transaction. Instead of sending the data to the buyer's Pajakoin address, we send the transaction to DGT's special Pajakoin address which is uniquely created to store every VAT periodic tax return for a specific TPVP. In other words, every TPVP may need to send the data to different Pajakoin address. To securely store the data, it may be encrypted by using a strong encryption method which is not discussed in the paper.

5 Security Evaluation

5.1 Cheating Model

We define several cheating models of the proposed protocol as follows. A dishonest taxpayer tries to create PAKO by herself to be used as tax credits. She could then sell the PAKO to other taxpayers or use it for her own need. We also define a model where a dishonest bank trying to embed new blocks containing fraudulent transactions into their controlled nodes.

We also define a dishonest bank trying to modify the sales report to DGT in order to minimise the tax money to be collected by the tax authority. With the assumption that DGT and monitoring bodies are always honest and the blockchain is negligible to modify, our scheme is secure if the probability of any participant tries to cheat is negligible.

5.2 Cheating Evaluation

We look into the possibility of a dishonest taxpayer creating PAKO by herself. Under the assumption that the blockchain is controlled in a centralised manner and no security vulnerability is found, the case is not possible. If, by any means, the taxpayer manages to create PAKO, then an audit can find such irregularity and the authority can take further actions to mitigate the problem. In the case where the bank tries to embed their own transactions by adding new blocks into their nodes, the system will evaluate the blocks against the blockchain managed by the trusted nodes. If the evaluation fails, then the blocks are rejected.

Sales report modification is also not possible if the banks do not modify the blockchain to comply the data. DGT or the monitoring bodies have the capability of auditing the total PAKO sold by each bank and thus makes the cheating model easy to identify.

6 Discussion

6.1 Centralized Blockchain

Deploying the Pajakoin in an open system such as Bitcoin will put the state revenue at stake, since there are motivations of the adversaries to disrupt the system by possible attacks such as 51% attack or Sybil attack. Therefore, Pajakoin is run in a closed system. Several actors including DGT, banks, and monitoring bodies maintain the blockchain by running one or more nodes. We have evaluated that the probability of any cheating participant to successfully launch an attack against the system is negligible.

6.2 Monitoring Mechanism

DGT as the Indonesian tax authority has been given a mandate to monitor as well as to enforce the tax regulations. Therefore, the major function of the monitoring is done by DGT. However regular taxpayers also can participate in the function. For DGT, an integrated data as proposed in our protocol enables further analysis. The information is interconnected and the probability of someone creating a fraudulent tax invoice without buying tax credits is negligible if the probability of unauthorized party creating tokens is negligible. The analysis flags suspicious transactions based on the patterns, considering the TPVP's field of business and the nature of the transaction.

For a non-TPVP taxpayer, the tokens received can be used to calculate the amount of tax paid to the government, which is currently a hard task to do, since there is no central system to record every taxed transaction. The tokens can be used as a mean to get discount as in loyalty program funded by the government. By providing this mechanism, the non-TPVP taxpayers are motivated to request for tax invoices, and in turn it reduces the probability of the tax invoices being shifted to unauthorized parties.

By employing the blockchain, the monitoring bodies can easily create audit projects. The blockchain mechanism ensures that the information inserted in the blocks can no longer be modified. If there is any block reorganization in the centralized blockchain, then the monitoring bodies can detect such occurrence and raise an enquiry to DGT to get an explanation why the event happens.

6.3 Supporting Databases

Blockchain is a protocol of communication which enables multiple users to share information securely. On top of blockchain there are databases and applications developed to add features and functions to be used by the end users. In order our system to work, DGT must maintain other databases to support the information contained inside the blockchain. The most important database is the taxpayer identity. This database connects the Pajakoin addresses to the respective taxpayers holding the private keys. The database enables the blockchain to remain pseudo-anonymous; without access to the database, determining the identity of the users requires effort. This characteristic is derived from Bitcoin's pseudo-anonymity model [6]. DGT must also maintain a database containing indexes for every deterministic address created for each TPVP for several purposes including signing token transactions and receiving VAT periodic tax returns.

6.4   Determining VAT Revenue

Since we are using token-based transaction in the proposed protocol, the final VAT revenue can be determined by calculating the number of tokens transferred to non-TPVP taxpayers and DGT special Pajakoin addresses. The money received from taxpayers buying PAKO tokens can still be refunded and therefore cannot be considered as final. Thus, this mechanism is easier compared to current system, where state revenue record and the tax reported in tax returns do still have discrepancies and therefore requires data consolidation.

6.5   Simplicity over Anonymity

We have decided to prioritize the simplicity of the design over anonymity. The address reuse is not recommended in the real world of Bitcoin system, but in our design, TPVP addresses and taxpayers' addresses as well as their associated public key pairs are reused to make the system easy to understand by people with different background. The addresses can be replaced, of course, but only in selected situations.

7   Conclusion

E-Faktur system was launched by DGT as an effort to simplify the administrative process of VAT, especially related to tax invoice. E-Faktur helps the TPVP to convert their paper-based administration to paperless. However, the system is unable to avoid the forged tax invoices being created by adversaries. The proposed protocol implements tax credits transfer in a blockchain system. The tax credits transfer ensures that there is no tax due to be paid at the end of the reporting period, since the tax due needs to be paid before a tax invoice is created. The proposed protocol reduces the risk of tax fraud by integrating the tax payment and the tax crediting system as well as simplifying the way the taxpayers submit the mandatory VAT reports. The proposed protocol enables tax authority to have more control over the tax crediting mechanism and therefore minimize fraud risks over it. The transaction data submitted by taxpayers by using the proposed protocol could then be used in further analysis to support more precise executive decisions regarding the tax.

8   Future Works

To emulate all regulations in VAT system, we might need a more flexible blockchain system. Since the Bitcoin-like blockchain has a limited operation code, smart contract could be a better option. For future works, we also need to work on a system which will reduce DGT's involvement in tax credits transfer and depend solely on the system and the script. For this purpose, we investigate the possibility of using smart contract system which has a greater flexibility in terms of writing scripts with more functions and features.

The blockchain type choice must also be revisited, since a blockchain system managed by a single central authority may not deliver the best impact in term of transparency and independency. We also need to investigate the effect of immediate VAT payment to the cashflow of the taxpayers. We could also consider to replace the PoW consensus with another mechanism to make the system more efficient.

Acknowledgement. This work was partially supported by Science & Technology Innovation Projects of Shenzhen, China (GJHZ20160226202520268, JCYJ20170302151321095).

References

1. Gillis, M.: Tax Reform and the Value Added Tax: Indonesia. World Tax Reform Case Studies of Developed and Developing Countries. ICEG, pp. 227–250 (1990)
2. Directorate General of Budget Ministry of Finance: Indonesian State Budget 2017 Information Book (2017)
3. Ministry of Finance Republic of Indonesia: Peraturan Menteri Keuangan Republik Indonesia Nomor 151/PMK.03/2013 Tentang Tata Cara Pembuatan dan Tata Cara Pembetulan atau Penggantian Faktur Pajak [Regulation of Ministry of Finance Republic of Indonesia Number 151/PMK.03/2013 about Procedures of Creating and Procedures of Correcting or Replacing Tax Invoice], M.o.F.R.o. Indonesia, Editor, Jakarta (2013)
4. Directorate General of Taxes Ministry of Finance: Peraturan Direktur Jenderal Pajak Nomor PER-16/PJ/2014 Tentang Tata Cara Pembuatan dan Pelaporan Faktur Pajak Berbentuk Elektronik [Regulation of Director General of Taxes Number PER-16/PJ/2014 About Procedures of Creating and Reporting Electronic Tax Invoice], D.G.o.T.M.o. Finance, Editor, Jakarta (2014)
5. Directorate General of Taxes Ministry of Finance: Peraturan Direktur Jenderal Pajak Nomor PER-17/PJ/2014 Tentang Perubahan Kedua Atas Peraturan Direktur Jenderal Pajak Nomor PER-24/PJ/2012 Tentang Bentuk, Ukuran, Tata Cara Pengisian Keterangan, Prosedur Pemberitahuan Dalam Rangka Pembuatan, Tata Cara Pembetulan atau Penggantian, dan Tata Cara Pembatalan Faktur Pajak [Regulation of Director General of Taxes Number PER-17/PJ/2014 About Second Amendment of Regulation of Director General of Taxes Number PER-24/PJ/2012 About Form, Size, Procedures for Filling in Information, Notice Procedure In Order of Making, Procedures for Repair or Replacement, and Procedures for Cancellation of Tax Invoice], D.G.o.T.M.o. Finance, Editor, Jakarta (2014)
6. Nakamoto, S.: Bitcoin: A peer-to-peer electronic cash system (2008)
7. Back, A.: Hashcash-a denial of service counter-measure (2002)
8. Franco, P.: Understanding Bitcoin: Cryptography, Engineering, and Economics. Wiley, New York (2015)
9. Bitcoin Wiki: Full node. 2014, 30 December 2015. https://en.bitcoin.it/wiki/Full_node. Accessed 27 Jan 2016
10. Greenspan, G.: MultiChain Private Blockchain—White Paper (2015)
11. Harding, D.A.: Bitcoin Developer Guide (2015). https://bitcoin.org/en/developer-guide. Accessed 12 Jan 2016
12. Mattila, J.: The Blockchain Phenomenon. In: The Blockchain Phenomenon. Berkeley Roundtable of the International Economy (2016)
13. Wijaya, D.A.: Extending asset management system functionality in bitcoin platform. In: 2016 International Conference on Computer, Control, Informatics and its Applications (IC3INA). IEEE (2016)

14. PricewaterhouseCoopers: How blockchain technology could improve the tax system (2016)
15. Ainsworth, R.T., Shact, A.: Blockchain (Distributed Ledger Technology) Solves VAT Fraud (2016)
16. Ainsworth, R.T., Viitasaari, V.: Payroll Tax & the Blockchain (2017)
17. Maxwell, G. Deterministic Wallets (2011). https://bitcointalk.org/index.php?topic=19137.0. Accessed 12 Sep 2015
18. Wuille, P.: Hierarchical Deterministic Wallets (2012). https://github.com/bitcoin/bips/blob/master/bip-0032.mediawiki. Accessed 29 Feb 2016
19. Andresen, G.: Pay to Script Hash (2012). https://github.com/bitcoin/bips/blob/master/bip-0016.mediawiki. Accessed 9 Jan 2016
20. Mark Friedenbach, B., Nicolas Dorier, K.: Relative lock-time using consensus-enforced sequence numbers (2016). https://github.com/bitcoin/bips/blob/master/bip-0068.mediawiki
21. Harding, D.A:. Sequence Number (Transactions) (2015). https://bitcoin.org/en/glossary/sequence-number. Accessed 12 Jan 2016

Verifiable Private Polynomial Evaluation

Xavier Bultel[1], Manik Lal Das[2], Hardik Gajera[2], David Gérault[1],
Matthieu Giraud[1(✉)], and Pascal Lafourcade[1]

[1] Université Clermont Auvergne, CNRS, LIMOS, Clermont-Ferrand, France
{xavier.bultel,david.gerault,matthieu.giraud,pascal.lafourcade}@uca.fr
[2] DA-IICT, Gandhinagar, India
maniklal@gmail.com, kidrah123@gmail.com

Abstract. Delegating the computation of a polynomial to a server in a verifiable way is challenging. An even more challenging problem is ensuring that this polynomial remains hidden to clients who are able to query such a server. In this paper, we formally define the notion of *Private Polynomial Evaluation* (PPE). Our main contribution is to design a rigorous security model along with relations between the different security properties. We define *polynomial protection* (PP), *proof unforgeability* (UNF), and *indistinguishability against chosen function attack* (IND-CFA), which formalizes the resistance of a PPE against attackers trying to guess which polynomial is used among two polynomials of their choice. As a second contribution, we give a cryptanalysis of two PPE schemes of the literature. Finally, we design a PPE scheme called PIPE and we prove that it is PP-, UNF- and IND-CFA-secure under the decisional Diffie-Hellman assumption in the random oracle model.

1 Introduction

Mathematical models are powerful tools that are used to make predictions about a system's behaviour. The idea is to collect a large set of data for a period of time and use it to build a function predicting the evolution of the system in the future. This topic has many applications, for instance, meteorology or economics. It can be used to predict the weather or the behaviour of stock exchange.

Consider a company that collects and stores a very large set of data, for example about the state of the soil, such as humidity, acidity, temperature and mineral content. Using it, it computes some function that predicts the state of the soil for next years. The clients are farmers who want to anticipate the state of the soil during the sowing periods to determine how much seeds to buy and when to plant them. The company gives its client access to the prediction function through a cloud server. A paying client can then interact with the server to evaluate the function on his own data. For economic reasons, the company does not want the clients to be able to recover the prediction function. Moreover, the clients do not trust the server: it might be corrupted to produce incorrect results. Hence, the server should provide a proof that its output is correct with regards to the secret prediction function. A similar scenario was studied in [GFLL15],

© Springer International Publishing AG 2017
T. Okamoto et al. (Eds.): ProvSec 2017, LNCS 10592, pp. 487–506, 2017.
https://doi.org/10.1007/978-3-319-68637-0_29

where a server receives medical data collected by sensors worn by the users, and provides the users with an evaluation of their health status. More precisely, the company defines a polynomial f which returns meaningful information, such as potential diseases. Then, it uploads this polynomial to the server, and sells to the end users the ability to query that function with their own medical data.

The underlying problem is how to delegate computations on a secret polynomial function to a server in a verifiable way. By *secret* we mean that no user should be able to retrieve the polynomial used by the server. By *verifiable* we mean that the server must be able to prove the correctness of its computation. To solve this problem, we propose the *Private Polynomial Evaluation* (PPE) primitive, which ensures that: (i) the polynomial f is protected as much as possible, and (ii) the user is able to verify the result given by the server.

Figure 1 illustrates a PPE scheme where x is the user data and $f(x)$ is the evaluation of the data by the function f of the company. Moreover, the proof π sent by the server and the verification key vk sent by the company allow the user to verify the correctness of the delegated computation.

Consider a company using a PPE scheme for prediction functions. An attacker wants to guess which prediction function is used by the company. Assume this attacker gains access to some of the data used to build the prediction function, for instance by corrupting a technician. Thus, the attacker can build several prediction functions by using different mathematical models and the collected data, and try to distinguish which of these functions is used by the company. Intuitively, in a secure PPE scheme, this task should be as hard as if the server only returned $f(x)$, and no additional information for verification. We formalise this notion and design a PPE scheme having this security property.

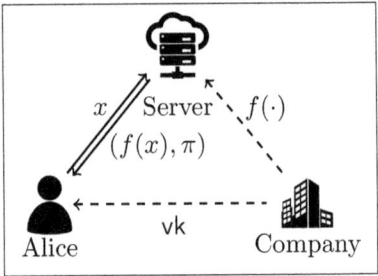

Fig. 1. Illustration of a PPE scheme.

Contributions

- We give a cryptanalysis of two PPE schemes, the first one presented by Guo *et al.* [GFLL15] and the second one presented by Gajera *et al.* [GND16]. Our attack allows an adversary to recover the secret polynomial in a single query.
- Our main contribution is to provide a formal definition and security framework for PPE schemes. We define two one-way notions, *Weak Polynomial Protection* (WPP) and *Polynomial Protection* (PP), stating that a user limited to k queries cannot recover the polynomial, where k is the degree of the polynomial. Additionally, we define IND-CFA which formalises the idea that no adversary can guess which of two polynomials of his choice is used. In essence, the proof of a correct computation should not reveal any information about the polynomial. We finally study the relations between these notions.

- We design PIPE (for Private IND-CFA Polynomial Evaluation), an efficient IND-CFA-secure PPE scheme. This scheme combines the Verifiable Secret Sharing introduced by Feldman [Fel87] and the ElGamal encryption scheme in order to achieve verifiability and IND-CFA security. We also formally prove its security under the DDH assumption in the random oracle model.

Related Works: Verifiable Computation (VC) refers to the cryptographic primitives where an untrusted server can prove the correctness of its output. It was introduced in [GGP10]. The aim of a such primitive is to allow a client with limited computational power to delegate difficult computations. Primitives where everyone can check the correctness of the computation are said to be *publicly verifiable* [PRV12]. This subject has led to a dense literature [PST13, CRR12, FG12, CKKC13, PHGR13]. In 2012, Canetti *et al.* [CRR12] proposed formal security models for VC. Fiore and Gennaro [FG12] propose a scheme for polynomial evaluations and matrix computations. Unlike our paper, these works consider that the polynomial used by the server is public.

To the best of our knowledge, four papers study how to hide the function used by the server [GFLL15, GND16, KZG10, NP99]. Kate *et al.* define a primitive called *commitment to polynomials* (CTP) [KZG10]. In this primitive, a user commits to a hidden polynomial f and reveals some points (x, y) together with a proof that $f(x) = y$. The user can open the commitment *a posteriori* to reveal the polynomial. CTP is close to PPE: the verification key in a PPE scheme can be viewed as a commitment in a CTP scheme, the main difference is that this verification key is computed by a trusted party (the company) and the points are evaluated by an untrusted party (the server). The authors formalise the hardness of guessing the polynomial knowing less than k points. In this model, the polynomial is randomly chosen, then they does not consider the case where the adversary tries to distinguish the committed polynomial between two chosen polynomials as in our IND-CFA model. Moreover, Kate *et al.* design two CTP schemes in [KZG10]. The first one is not IND-CFA since the commitment algorithm is deterministic. We prove that the second scheme is IND-CFA-secure in the extended version [BDG+17]. Moreover, we show that our scheme PIPE can be used as a CTP scheme, and we compare it to the scheme of Kate *et al.*. We show that our scheme solves an open problem described by Kate *et al.*: designing a scheme that is secure under a weaker assumption than t-SDDH.

Independently of Kate *et al.* [KZG10], Guo *et al.* [GFLL15] propose a scheme with similar security properties to delegate the computation of a secret health related function on the users' health record. The polynomials are explicitly assumed to have low coefficients and degree, which greatly reduces their randomness. However, the authors give neither security models nor proof. Later, Gajera *et al.* [GND16] show that any user can guess the polynomial using the Lagrange's interpolation on several points. They propose a scheme where the degree k is hidden and claim that it does not suffer from this kind of attack. We show that hiding the degree k is useless and that no scheme can be secure when user query more than k points to the server. Moreover, we give a cryptanalysis on these both schemes which requires only one query to the server. To the best of our knowledge, we present

the first security model for *Indistinguishability Against Chosen Function Attack*
(IND-CFA).

Finally, there has been lots of work done on a similar but slightly different topic,
Oblivious Polynomial Evaluation (OPE), introduced by Naor and Pinkas [NP99].
In OPE, there are two parties. One party A holds a polynomial f and another
party B holds an element x. The aim of OPE is that the party B receives $f(x)$
in such a way that A learns nothing about x and B learns nothing about f,
except $f(x)$. Researchers have studied OPE extensively and shown that it can be
used to solve various cryptographic problems, such as set membership, oblivious
keyword search, data entanglement, set-intersection and more [FIPR05,FNP04,
LP02]. Despite the similarities between OPE and PPE, they are different in nature.
In particular, OPE does not consider the verifiability of $f(x)$, whereas it is a crucial point in PPE. Additionally, in a PPE, the requirement that the server does not
learn anything about x is relaxed. In our scheme, the major contribution to computational cost is due to computation of the proof on server side and verification
of computation on user side. Since OPE doesn't consider verifying computation,
we feel that it would not be fair to compare the performances.

Outline: In the next section we recall the cryptographic notions used in this
paper. In Sect. 3, we show how to break schemes proposed by Guo *et al.* [GFLL15]
and by Gajera *et al.* [GND16]. In Sect. 4, we propose security models for PPE
schemes. Finally, in Sect. 5, we present our PPE scheme PIPE and we prove that it
is IND-CFA-secure before concluding.

2   Cryptographic Tools

We start by recalling the basic cryptographic assumptions used in this paper. In
the following, we denote by POLY(λ) the set of probabilistic polynomial time algorithms with respect to the security parameter λ.

Definition 1 (Discrete Logarithm assumption [DH76]). *Let p be a prime
number generated according to a security parameter $\lambda \in \mathbb{N}$. Let G be a multiplicative
group of order p, and $g \in G$ be a generator. The* discrete logarithm assumption (DL)
*in (G, p, g) states that there exists a negligible function ϵ such that for all $x \xleftarrow{\$} \mathbb{Z}_p^*$
and $\mathcal{A} \in$ POLY(λ): $Pr[x' \leftarrow \mathcal{A}(g^x) : x = x'] \leq \epsilon(\lambda)$*

Definition 2 (Decisional Diffie-Hellman assumption [Bon98]). *Let p be a
prime number generated according to a security parameter $\lambda \in \mathbb{N}$. Let G be a multiplicative group of order p, and $g \in G$ be a generator. The* Decisional Diffie-Hellman
*assumption (DDH) in (G, p, g) states that there exists a negligible function ϵ such
that for all $(x, y, z) \leftarrow (\mathbb{Z}_p^*)^3$ and $\mathcal{A} \in$ POLY(λ):*

$$|Pr[b \leftarrow \mathcal{A}(g^x, g^y, g^z) : b = 1] - Pr[b \leftarrow \mathcal{A}(g^x, g^y, g^{x \cdot y}) : b = 1]| \leq \epsilon(\lambda)$$

In the following, we recall definition and security requirements of public key cryptosystems.

Definition 3 (Public Key Encryption). *A Public Key Encryption (PKE) scheme is defined by three algorithms (* Gen, Enc, Dec *) as follows:*

Gen(λ): *It returns a public/private key pair (* pk, sk *).*
Enc$_{pk}$(m): *It returns the ciphertext c of the message m.*
Dec$_{sk}$(c): *It returns the plaintext m from the ciphertext c.*

A PKE scheme Π = (Gen, Enc, Dec) is *indistinguishable under chosen-plaintext attack* (IND-CPA) if for any probabilistic polynomial-time (PPT) adversary $\mathcal{A}$, the difference between $\frac{1}{2}$ and the probability that $\mathcal{A}$ wins the IND-CPA experiment presented in Fig. 2 is negligible in λ. The oracle Enc$_{pk}$(LR$_b$($\cdot,\cdot$)) takes (m_0, m_1) as input and returns Enc$_{pk}$(m_b). The standard definition of CPA experiment allows the adversary to call this oracle only one time. However, Bellare *et al.* [BBM00] prove that the two definitions of

$\mathsf{Exp}_{\Pi,\mathcal{A}}^{\mathsf{IND\text{-}CPA}}(\lambda)$:
$b \xleftarrow{\$} \{0,1\}$
$(\mathsf{pk},\mathsf{sk}) \leftarrow \mathsf{Gen}(\lambda)$;
$b' \leftarrow \mathcal{A}^{\mathsf{Enc_{pk}(LR_b(\cdot,\cdot))}}(\lambda,\mathsf{pk})$
return $(b = b')$

Fig. 2. IND-CPA experiment [BBM00].

CPA security are equivalent using a hybrid argument. For instance, the ElGamal encryption is IND-CPA.

Definition 4 (ElGamal Encryption [ElG85]). *The ElGamal PKE scheme is defined as follows:*

Gen(λ): *It returns* pk $= (G, p, g, h)$ *and* sk $= x$ *where G is a multiplicative group of prime order p, g is a generator of G, $h = g^x$ and x is uniform in $\mathbb{Z}_p^*$.*
Enc$_{pk}$(m): *It returns* $(c, d) = (g^r, h^r \cdot m)$ *where r is randomly chosen in $\mathbb{Z}_p^*$.*
Dec$_{sk}$((c, d)): *It returns* $m = d \cdot c^{-x}$.

A zero-knowledge proof (ZKP) allows a prover knowing a witness to convince a verifier that a statement s is in a given language without leaking any information except s. We recall the definition of a non-interactive ZKP.

Definition 5 (NIZKP [FS87]). *A non-interactive ZKP (NIZKP) for a language $\mathcal{L}$ is a couple of algorithms* (Prove, Verify) *such that:*

Prove(s, w): *It outputs a proof π that $s \in \mathcal{L}$ using the witness w.*
Verify(s, π): *It checks whether π is a valid proof that $s \in \mathcal{L}$ and outputs a bit.*

A NIZKP proof verifies the following properties:

Completeness: *For any statement $s \in \mathcal{L}$ and the corresponding witness w, we have that* Verify(s, Prove(s, w)) = 1.
Soundness: *There is no polynomial time adversary $\mathcal{A}$ such that $\mathcal{A}(\mathcal{L})$ outputs (s, π) such that* Verify(s, π) = 1 *and $s \notin \mathcal{L}$ with non-negligible probability.*

Zero-knowledge: *A proof* π *leaks no information, i.e. there exists a PPT algorithm* Sim *(called the* simulator*) such that outputs of* Prove(s, w) *and the outputs of* Sim(s) *follow the same probability distribution.*

We use the NIZKP given by Chaum and Pedersen [CP93] to prove the equality of two discrete logarithms. Let G be a multiplicative group, the language is the set of all statements $(g_1, h_1, g_2, h_2) \in G^4$ such that $\log_{g_1}(h_1) = \log_{g_2}(h_2) = x$.

Definition 6 (LogEq [CP93]). *Let G be a multiplicative group of prime order p and H be a hash function, $\mathcal{L}$ be the set of all $(g_1, h_1, g_2, h_2) \in G^4$ where $\log_{g_1}(h_1) = \log_{g_2}(h_2)$. We define the NIZKP* LogEq $=$ (Prove, Verify) *for $\mathcal{L}$ as follow:*

Prove$((g_1, h_1, g_2, h_2), w)$: *Using the witness* $w = \log_{g_1}(h_1)$, *it picks* $r \xleftarrow{\$} \mathbb{Z}_p^*$, *computes* $A = g_1^r$, $B = g_2^r$, $z = H(A, B)$ *and* $\omega = r + w \cdot z$. *It outputs* $\pi = (A, B, \omega)$.
Verify$((g_1, h_1, g_2, h_2), \pi)$: *Using* $\pi = (A, B, \omega)$, *it computes* $z = H(A, B)$. *If* $g_1^\omega = A \cdot h_1^z$ *and* $g_2^\omega = B \cdot h_2^z$ *then it outputs* 1, *else it outputs* 0.

LogEq *is unconditionally complete, sound and zero-knowledge in the ROM.*

We recall Lagrange's interpolation formula to find the single polynomial f of degree at most k from $k + 1$ points (x_i, y_i) such that $f(x_i) = y_i$.

Definition 7 (Lagrange's interpolation). *Let k be an integer and F be a field. For all $i \in \{0, \dots, k\}$, let $(x_i, y_i) \in F^2$ such that for all $i_1, i_2 \in \{0, \dots, k\}$, $x_{i_1} \neq x_{i_2}$. There exists one and only one polynomial f of degree at most k such that for all $i \in \{0, \dots, n\}$, $f(x_i) = y_i$. This polynomial is given by Lagrange's interpolation formula:*

$$f(x) = \sum_{i=0}^{k} \left(y_i \cdot \prod_{j=0, j \neq i}^{k} \frac{x - x_j}{x_i - x_j} \right).$$

In the following, we denote the set of polynomials with coefficients in the field F by $F[X]$ and we denote the set of all $f \in F[X]$ of degree k by $F[X]_k$.

3   Cryptanalysis of [GFLL15] and [GND16]

We start by presenting the inherent limitation of PPE schemes, then we explain how to break those presented by Guo *et al.* [GFLL15] and by Gajera *et al.* [GND16].

3.1   Inherent Limitation

In the scheme [GFLL15], the degree k of the polynomial f is public. Gajera *et al.* [GND16] use it to mount an attack: a user queries $k + 1$ points to guess the polynomial using Lagrange's interpolation. To fix this weakness, they propose a scheme where k is secret. However, any user can guess k and f after $k + 1$ interactions with the server. To do so, the attacker chooses an input x_0 and sends it to the server. He receives y_0 and computes the polynomial f_0 of degree 0 using Lagrange's interpolation on (x_0, y_0). Next, the attacker chooses a second and a different input x_1 and asks $y_1 = f(x_1)$ to the server. He computes the polynomial f_1 of degree 1 using Lagrange's interpolation on $\{(x_0, y_0), (x_1, y_1)\}$. By repeating this process until the interpolation gives the same polynomial $f_i = f_{i+1}$ for two consecutive iterations, he recovers the degree and the polynomial. This problem is an inherent limitation of PPE schemes and was already considered in the security model of Kate *et al.* [KZG10]. Thus, to preserve the protection of the polynomial, the server must refuse to evaluate more than k points for each client and we must assume that clients do not collude to collect more than k points.

3.2 Cryptanalysis of [GFLL15] and [GND16]

In addition to the protection of f, the scheme [GFLL15] requires that the user's data is encrypted for the server. More formally, the user uses an encryption algorithm to compute $x' = \mathsf{Enc}_k(x)$ and sends this cipher to the server which returns y'. Then, the user computes $y = \mathsf{Dec}_k(y')$ such that $y = f(x)$ where f is the secret polynomial. The encryption scheme is based on the discrete logarithm assumption. The decryption algorithm works in two steps: first the user computes a value h such that $h = g^{f(x)}$ where g is a generator of a multiplicative group of large prime order n, next he computes the discrete logarithm of h in base g using *Pollard's lambda method* [Pol78]. The authors assume that the size of $f(x)$ is reasonable: more formally, they define a set of possible inputs $\mathcal{X}$ and $M \in \mathbb{N}$ such that $\forall x \in \mathcal{X}, 0 \le f(x) < M$. The authors assume that the users can efficiently perform Pollard's lambda algorithm on any $h = g^y$ where $y < M$. Actually, for practical reasons, since $h = g^{f(x) \bmod n}$ and $\log_g(h) = f(x)$, we assume that $0 \le f(x) < n$ for any input x of reasonable size, *i.e.* $x \ll n$. Hence, the authors of [GFLL15] consider f as a positive polynomial in $\mathbb{Z}$ with sufficiently small coefficients.

It is easy to evaluate a small M' such that $M' > M$ by choosing M' such that Pollard's lambda algorithm on $g^{M'}$ is computable by a powerful server but is too slow for a practical application. For example, if Pollard's lambda algorithm takes less than one minute for the server but more than one hour for the user's computer, we can assume that $M' > M$ and attacks that are polynomial in M' are practical. To sum up, the user has the following tools:

- $M' \in \mathbb{N}$ such that $\forall x \in \mathcal{X}, 0 \le f(x) < M'$ and such that algorithms that require $p(M')$ operations (where p is a polynomial) are *easily computable*.
- A server which returns $y = f(x)$ for any input x. This server can be used at most k times where k is the degree of the polynomial.

Finally, note that the authors assume that $0 \le f(x)$ for any x and that $\mathcal{X} \subset \mathbb{N}$. We show that any user can guess the secret polynomial during his first interaction with the server. We first prove the following two properties.

Property 1. For any polynomial $f \in \mathbb{Z}[X]$ and any integers x and y, there exists $P \in \mathbb{Z}$ such that

$$f(x + y) = f(x) + y \cdot P.$$

Proof. Seen as a polynomial in y, $f(x+y) - f(x)$ has a root at $y = 0$. By the Factor Theorem y divide $f(x+y) - f(x)$. Hence, there exists $P \in \mathbb{Z}$ such that $f(x+y) - f(x) = y \cdot P$, i.e. $f(x+y) = f(x) + y \cdot P$.

Note that for any positive integers a and b such that $a < b$, we have $a \mod b = a$. Then, we can deduce the following property from Property 1.

Property 2. For any polynomial $f \in \mathbb{Z}[X]$ and any integers x and y such that $0 \le f(x) < y$ and $0 \le f(x+y)$, it holds that

$$f(x+y) \mod y = f(x).$$

Proof. From the previous property, we have $f(x+y) = f(x) + y \cdot P$, where P is an integer. Assume $P < 0$, we define $P' = -P > 0$, then $f(x+y) = f(x) - y \cdot P' \ge 0$. Hence we have $f(x) \ge y \cdot P' > f(x) \cdot P'$.

- If $0 < f(x)$ then we deduce $1 = f(x)/f(x) > P'$ and $1 > P'$.
- If $f(x) = 0$ then $0 \ge y \cdot P' > 0$.

In both cases, we obtain a contradiction. We conclude that $0 \le P$. Finally, we deduce $f(x+y) \mod y = f(x) + y \cdot P \mod y = f(x)$.

Our attack on [GFLL15] works as follows. The attacker chooses a vector of k integers $(x_1, x_2, \ldots, x_k) \in \mathbb{N}^k$ such that, for all $0 < i \le k$, $x_i' = \sum_{j=1}^{i} x_j$ where $x_i' \in \mathcal{X}$.

For the sake of clarity, we show to begin with the attack in the case where $\{1, \ldots, k\} \subset \mathcal{X}$. Thus the attacker chooses the vector $(x_1, x_2, \ldots, x_k) = (1, 1, \ldots, 1)$ and sends $x = k + M'$ to the server that returns the encryption of $y = f(x)$. Pollard's lambda algorithm complexity [Pol78] on M' is $O(M'^{1/2})$. We consider that $k \ll M'$ (for instance $k \approx 10$ as in [GFLL15]), thus $x < 2 \cdot M'$, the complexity of the decryption with Pollard's lambda algorithm is $O(f(2M')^{1/2}) \approx O(M'^{k/2})$. For all $1 \le i \le k$, the attacker computes $M_i' = k - i + M'$ and $y_i = y \mod M_i'$.

Since for all $a \in \mathcal{X}, M' > f(a)$, we have for all $1 \le i \le k$, $M_i' = k - i + M' \ge M' > f(a)$. Using Property 2 and since $i \in \mathcal{X}$, we deduce that

$$\begin{aligned}
y_i &= f(x) \mod M_i' \\
&= f(k + M') \mod M_i' \\
&= f(k - i + i + M') \mod M_i' \\
&= f(i + M_i') \mod M_i' = f(i).
\end{aligned}$$

Hence, the attacker obtains $k+1$ points from one single queried point and uses Lagrange's interpolation on $((1, y_1), (2, y_2), \ldots, (k, y_k), (x, y))$ to guess f. Then, the attacker can compute f with reasonable computation time.

Now, we show the generalized case for any set $\mathcal{X}$ where $|\mathcal{X}| \ge k$. To begin, the attacker chooses a vector of k integers $(x_1, \ldots, x_k)$ such that, for all $1 \le j \le k, x_j > 0$ and: $x_i' = \left(\sum_{j=1}^{i} x_j \right)$ where $x_i' \in \mathcal{X}$. Then the attacker sends the query

$x = \left(\sum_{i=1}^{k} x_i \right) + M'$ to the server such that $M' \in \mathbb{N}$ and for all $a \in \mathcal{X}$ we have $M' > f(a)$. After he sends the query to the server, the attacker receives the encryption of $y = f(x)$.

Pollard's lambda algorithm complexity [Pol78] on M' is $O(M'^{1/2})$. We consider that $k \ll M'$, $k \approx 10$ as in [GFLL15], thus $x < 2 \cdot M'$, the complexity of the decryption with Pollard's lambda algorithm is $O(f(2M')^{1/2}) \approx O(M'^{k/2})$.

With the $y = f(x)$ returned by the server, the attacker computes for all $1 \le i \le k$:

$$M'_i = \sum_{j=i+1}^{k} x_j + M'.$$

Then we define y_i for all $1 \le i \le k$ such that $y_i = y \mod M'_i$. Since for all $a \in \mathcal{X}, M' > f(a)$, we have for all $1 \le i \le k$ and for all $a \in \mathcal{X}$:

$$M'_i = \sum_{j=i+1}^{k} x_j + M' \ge M' > f(a) .$$

Using Properties 1 and 2 of Sect. 3 and since $x'_i \in \mathcal{X}$, we deduce:

$$y_i = f(x) \mod M'_i = f\left(\sum_{i=1}^{k} x_i + M' \right) \mod M'_i$$

$$= f\left(\sum_{j=i+1}^{k} x_j + \sum_{j=1}^{i} x_j + M' \right) \mod M'_i = f\left(\sum_{j=1}^{i} x_j + M'_i \right) \mod M'_i$$

$$= f\left(\sum_{j=1}^{i} x_j \right) = f(x'_i).$$

Finally, the attacker knows the k points of f: $(x'_i, f(x'_i))$ for $1 \le i \le k$, and also $(x, f(x))$. Hence, using Lagrange's interpolation, the attacker is able to retrieve the polynomial f.

It is possible to attack the scheme of Gajera *et al.* [GND16] in a similar way. Indeed, as in [GFLL15], the user knows a value M such that $\forall x \in \mathcal{X}, f(x) < M$. A simple countermeasure could be to not allow the user to evaluate inputs that are not in $\mathcal{X}$. Unfortunately, this is not possible in these two schemes since the user encrypts his data x. Hence, the server does not know whether $x \in \mathcal{X}$ or not.

4   Security Models

We revisit the formal security models for PPE schemes for two main reasons: (i) Kate *et al.* [KZG10] propose some models where the secret polynomial is randomly chosen. However, they present several practical applications where the polynomial is not actually random, and some information, such as bounds for $f(x)$ or candidates for f, can be inferred easily from the context. Their models are clearly not sufficient for analysing the security of this kind of applications. (ii) The schemes presented by Guo *et al.* [GFLL15] and Gajera *et al.* [GND16] consider polynomials that are not randomly chosen. The authors give neither security models nor security proofs. We show previously a practical attack on these two schemes where a user exploits some public information. To avoid such attacks, we need a model where public information does not give significant advantage.

Our goal is to design a model where the public parameters and the server's proofs of correctness give no advantage to an attacker. Ideally, we would like the attacker to have no more chances of guessing the polynomial than if he only had access to a server reliably returning polynomial evaluations with no proof of correctness. Our security model considers an attacker that tries to determine which polynomial is used by a PPE among two polynomials of his choice. This model is inspired by the IND-CPA model used in public key cryptography.

4.1   Formal Definition

In order to be able to define our security model, we first need to formally define a Private Polynomial Evaluation scheme.

Definition 8. *A* Private Polynomial Evaluation *(PPE) scheme is composed of four algorithms* (setup, init, compute, verif) *such that:*

setup(λ): *It returns a ring F and a public setup* pub.
init(pub, f): *It returns a server key* sk *and a verification key* vk *according to the polynomial $f \in F[X]$.*
compute(pub, vk, x, sk, f): *It returns y and a proof π that $y = f(x)$.*
verif(pub, vk, x, y, π): *It returns 1 if the proof π is "accepted" otherwise 0.*

4.2   Security Models

We start be redefining the notion of weak security presented in the literature. We then introduce the notion of chosen function attack and the natural notion of unforgeability. Proofs for Theorems 2, 3 and 4 are given in [BDG+17].

Polynomial Protection. We introduce the *Polynomial Protection* (PP) security. A PPE is PP-secure if no adversary can output a new point (not computed by the server) of the secret polynomial f with a better probability than by guessing. In this model, the polynomial is randomly chosen and the adversary cannot use the server more than k times, where k is the degree of f. This security model is similar to the *Hiding Model* [KZG10] except that the adversary chooses the points to be evaluated. We define the *Weak Polynomial Protection* (WPP) as the same model as PP except that the adversary has no access to the server.

$\mathbf{Exp}_{\Pi,\mathcal{A}}^{k\text{-}\mathsf{PP}}(\lambda)$:
$(\mathsf{pub}, F) \leftarrow \mathsf{setup}(\lambda)$;
$f \xleftarrow{\$} F[X]_k$;
$\Sigma \leftarrow \emptyset$;
$c \leftarrow 0$;
$(\mathsf{sk}, \mathsf{vk}) \leftarrow \mathsf{init}(\mathsf{pub}, f)$;
$(x_*, y_*) \leftarrow \mathcal{A}^{\mathsf{CO}_{\mathsf{PP}}(\cdot)}(\mathsf{pub}, \mathsf{vk}, F, k)$;
If $(x_*, y_*) \notin \Sigma$ and $f(x_*) = y_*$:
Then return 1;
Else return 0;

$\mathbf{Exp}_{\Pi,\mathcal{A}}^{\mathsf{UNF}}(\lambda)$:
$(\mathsf{pub}, F) \leftarrow \mathsf{setup}(\lambda)$;
$(f, \mathsf{st}) \leftarrow \mathcal{A}_1(\mathsf{pub}, F)$;
$(\mathsf{sk}, \mathsf{vk}) \leftarrow \mathsf{init}(\mathsf{pub}, f)$;
$(x_*, y_*, \pi_*) \leftarrow \mathcal{A}_2(\mathsf{pub}, \mathsf{sk}, \mathsf{vk}, F, f, \mathsf{st})$;
If $f(x_*) \neq y_*$ and $\mathsf{verif}(\mathsf{pub}, \mathsf{vk}, x_*, y_*, \pi_*)$:
Then return 1;
Else return 0;

$\mathbf{Exp}_{\Pi,\mathcal{A}}^{k\text{-}\mathsf{IND}\text{-}\mathsf{CFA}}(\lambda)$:
$b \xleftarrow{\$} \{0, 1\}^*$;
$(\mathsf{pub}, F) \leftarrow \mathsf{setup}(\lambda)$;
$(f_0, f_1, \mathsf{st}) \leftarrow \mathcal{A}_1(\mathsf{pub}, F, k)$;
$(\mathsf{sk}, \mathsf{vk}) \leftarrow \mathsf{init}(\mathsf{pub}, f_b)$;
$b_* \leftarrow \mathcal{A}_2^{\mathsf{CO}_{\mathsf{CFA}}(\cdot)}(\mathsf{pub}, \mathsf{vk}, F, k, \mathsf{st})$;
If $f_0 \notin F[X]_k$ or $f_1 \notin F[X]_k$:
Then return 0;
Else return $(b = b_*)$;

$\mathsf{CO}_{\mathsf{PP}}(x)$:
$(y, \pi) \leftarrow \mathsf{compute}(\mathsf{pub}, \mathsf{vk}, x, \mathsf{sk}, f)$;
$c \leftarrow c + 1$;
$\Sigma \leftarrow \Sigma \cup \{(x, y)\}$;
If $c = k + 1$:
Then return $\perp$;
Else return (y, π);

$\mathsf{CO}_{\mathsf{CFA}}(x)$:
$(y, \pi) \leftarrow \mathsf{compute}(\mathsf{pub}, \mathsf{vk}, x, \mathsf{sk}, f_b)$;
If $f_0(x) \neq f_1(x)$:
Then return $\perp$;
Else return (y, π);

Fig. 3. Security experiments and oracles definitions.

Definition 9 (PP and WPP). *Let Π be a PPE, $\mathcal{A}$ be a probabilistic polynomial time (PPT) adversary. $\forall k \in \mathbb{N}$, the k-Polynomial Protection (k-PP) experiment for $\mathcal{A}$ against Π denoted by $\mathsf{Exp}_{\Pi,\mathcal{A}}^{k\text{-}PP}(\lambda)$ is defined in Fig. 3, where $\mathcal{A}$ has access to the server oracle $\mathsf{CO}_{PP}(\cdot)$. We define the advantage of the adversary $\mathcal{A}$ against the k-PP experiment by:*

$$ADV_{\Pi,\mathcal{A}}^{k\text{-}PP}(\lambda) = Pr\left[1 \leftarrow Exp_{\Pi,\mathcal{A}}^{k\text{-}PP}(\lambda)\right].$$

A scheme Π is k-PP-secure if this advantage is negligible for any $\mathcal{A} \in \text{POLY}(\lambda)$.
We define the k-Weak Polynomial Protection (k-WPP) experiment as the k-PP experiment except that $\mathcal{A}$ does not have access to the oracle $\mathsf{CO}_{PP}(\cdot)$. In a similar way, we define the WPP advantage and security.

The only difference between PP and WPP is that the adversary has no access to the oracle in WPP, so PP security implies the WPP security.

Theorem 1. *For any Π and k, if Π is k-PP-secure then Π is k-WPP-secure.*

Chosen Function Attack. We define a model for *indistinguishability against chosen function attack.* In this model, the adversary chooses two polynomials

(f_0, f_1) and tries to guess the polynomial f_b used by the server, where $b \in \{0, 1\}$. The adversary has access to a server that evaluates and proves the correctness of $y = f_b(x)$ only if $f_0(x) = f_1(x)$. This is an inherent limitation: if the adversary can evaluate another point (x, y) such that $f_0(x) \neq f_1(x)$, then he can compare y with $f_0(x)$ and $f_1(x)$ and recover b. In practice, an adversary chooses (f_0, f_1) such that $f_0 \neq f_1$, but with k points (x_i, y_i) such that $f_0(x_i) = f_1(x_i)$. It allows the adversary to maximize his oracle calls in order to increase his chances of success. We remark that schemes [GFLL15, GND16] are not IND-CFA-secure: users know a value M and the set of inputs $\mathcal{X}$ such that $\forall x \in \mathcal{X}, f(x) < M$. An attacker may choose two polynomials f_0 and f_1 such that for a chosen a, $f_0(a) < M$ and $f_1(a) > M$. Since $\mathcal{X}$ is public, the attacker returns f_0 if and only if $a \in \mathcal{X}$.

Definition 10 (IND-CFA). *Let Π be a PPE, $\mathcal{A} = (\mathcal{A}_1, \mathcal{A}_2)$ be a two-party PPT adversary and k be an integer. The k-Indistinguishability against Chosen Function Attack (k-IND-CFA) experiment for $\mathcal{A}$ against Π is defined in Fig. 3, where $\mathcal{A}$ has access to the server oracle $\mathsf{CO}_{CFA}(\cdot)$. The advantage of the adversary $\mathcal{A}$ against the k-IND-CFA experiment is given by:*

$$\mathsf{Adv}_{\Pi, \mathcal{A}}^{k\text{-}IND\text{-}CFA}(\lambda) = \left| \frac{1}{2} - Pr\left[1 \leftarrow \mathsf{Exp}_{\Pi, \mathcal{A}}^{k\text{-}IND\text{-}CFA}(\lambda) \right] \right|.$$

A scheme Π is k-IND-CFA-secure if this advantage is negligible for any $\mathcal{A} \in$ POLY$(\lambda)^2$.

In Theorem 2, we prove that IND-CFA security implies WPP security: if there exists an adversary $\mathcal{A}$ against the WPP experiment who is able to *decrypt* a random polynomial from the public values, then we can use it to guess f_b in an IND-CFA experiment for any chosen polynomials (f_0, f_1). However, surprisingly, it is not true for the PP security

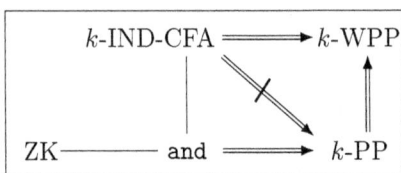

Fig. 4. Security relations.

(Theorem 3). The reason is that the oracle of the IND-CFA experiment has restriction, so it cannot be used to simulate the oracle of the PP experiment in a security reduction.

Theorem 2. *If Π is a k-IND-CFA-secure PPE, then it is k-WPP-secure.*

Theorem 3. *Let Π be a k-IND-CFA-secure PPE, it does not imply that Π is k-PP.*

However, we would like to have a simple and sufficient condition under which the IND-CFA security implies the PP security. For this, we define the *proof induced by a PPE* which is the proof algorithm used by the algorithm compute. We show that if this proof system is zero-knowledge, then the IND-CFA security implies the PP security.

Definition 11. *Let $\Pi = (\mathsf{setup}, \mathsf{init}, \mathsf{compute}, \mathsf{verif})$ be a PPE, the non-interactive proof inducted by Π, denoted $P_\Pi = (\mathsf{proof}_\Pi, \mathsf{ver}_\Pi)$ is defined as follows. For any $\lambda, k \in \mathbb{N}$, $(\mathsf{pub}, F) \leftarrow \mathsf{setup}(\lambda)$, $f \in F[X]_k$ and $(\mathsf{vk}, \mathsf{sk}) \leftarrow \mathsf{init}(\mathsf{pub}, f)$:*

proof$_\Pi$((pub, vk, x, y), (f, sk)): *returns π, where* $(y', \pi) \leftarrow$ compute(pub, vk, x, sk, f). ver$_\Pi$((pub, vk, x, y), π): *runs* $b \leftarrow$ verif(pub, vk, x, y, π) *and returns it.*

We say that Π is Zero-Knowledge *(ZK) if P_Π is Zero-Knowledge.*

Theorem 4. *Let Π be a ZK and k-IND-CFA-secure PPE, then Π is k-PP-secure.*

In Fig. 4, we recall all relations between our security properties.

Unforgeability. Finally, we define the unforgeability property for a PPE. A PPE is unforgeable when a dishonest server cannot produce a valid proof on the point (x, y) when $f(x) \neq y$. The secret polynomial f is chosen by the server.

Definition 12. *Let Π be a PPE, $\mathcal{A} = (\mathcal{A}_1, \mathcal{A}_2)$ be a two-party PPT adversary. The Unforgeability (UNF) experiment for $\mathcal{A}$ against Π is defined in Fig. 3. We define the advantage of the adversary $\mathcal{A}$ against the UNF experiment by:*

$$\mathsf{Adv}_{\Pi, \mathcal{A}}^{UNF}(\lambda) = Pr\left[1 \leftarrow \mathsf{Exp}_{\Pi, \mathcal{A}}^{UNF}(\lambda)\right].$$

A scheme Π is UNF-secure if this advantage is negligible for any $\mathcal{A} \in \text{POLY}(\lambda)^2$.

4.3   Security Against Collusion Attacks

To conclude, our security model implicitly prevents all non-inherent collusion attacks, because in our context the clients have no secret information. There are two kinds of collusion scenarios:

A client colludes with the server: If a client colludes with the server, then the server can obviously give him the secret polynomial. This limitation is inherent and cannot be prevented. On the other hand, all keys known by the clients are public and known to the server, the server has no advantage in colluding with a client. In particular, the collusion does not allow the server to forge fake validity proofs for others clients.

Several clients collude together: All clients have the same verification keys. Thus, a client gains no advantage by colluding with other clients, as long as the total number of known points is less than k after collusion. Obviously the inherent limitation of PPE still holds: if the collusion of clients learn more than k points, then they can guess the polynomial.

5   PIPE Description

We recall Feldman's Verifiable Secret Sharing (VSS) scheme and build a simple k-PP PPE that is not k-IND-CFA. We then propose some modifications based on the Feldman's VSS and the ElGamal scheme in order design our secure PPE scheme PIPE that is k-IND-CFA. We analyse its security and compare it with the scheme of Kate *et al.* [KZG10].

5.1   Feldman's Verifiable Secret Sharing

Feldman's VSS [Fel87] is based on Shamir's Secret Sharing [Sha79], where each
share is a point (x, y) of a secret polynomial f of degree k. Knowing more than k
shares, one can guess the polynomial f and can compute the secret $s = f(0)$. In
Feldman's VSS, there is a public value that allows anybody to check the validity
of a share. For any point (x, y), anybody can check if y is $f(x)$ or not. This scheme
works as follows. Let G be a multiplicative group of prime order p where DL is hard.
Let $f \in \mathbb{Z}_p^*[X]$ be the secret polynomial and $a_i \in F$ be a coefficient for all $0 \le i \le k$
such that

$$f(x) = \sum_{i=0}^{k} a_i \cdot x^i.$$

Let $g \in G$ be a generator of G. For all $i \in \{0, \ldots, k\}$, we set $h_i = g^{a_i}$. Values g and $\{h_i\}_{0 \le i \le k}$ are public, however, the coefficients a_i are hidden under DL
hypothesis. We remark that $f(x) = y$ if and only if $g^y = \prod_{i=0}^{k} h_i^{x^i}$ since

$$\prod_{i=0}^{k} h_i^{x^i} = \prod_{i=0}^{k} g^{a_i \cdot x^i} = g^{\sum_{i=0}^{k} a_i \cdot x^i} = g^{f(x)}.$$

Then, we can use it to check that (x, y) is a valid share.

5.2   Our Scheme: PIPE

Feldman's VSS can be used to design a PPE that is k-PP-secure: using the public values g and $\{h_i\}_{0 \le i \le k}$, any user can check that the point (x, y) computed by
the server is a point of f. However, in a practical use, the polynomial f is not randomly chosen in a large set. An IND-CFA attacker knows that $f = f_0$ or $f = f_1$
for two known polynomials (f_0, f_1), since he knows the coefficients $\{a_{0,i}\}_{0 \le i \le k}$ and
$\{a_{1,i}\}_{0 \le i \le k}$ of these two polynomials, he can compute the values $\{g^{a_{0,i}}\}_{0 \le i \le k}$ and
$\{g^{a_{1,i}}\}_{0 \le i \le k}$ and he can compare it with the public set $\{h_i\}_{0 \le i \le k}$.

   In order to construct our k-IND-CFA PPE, called PIPE, we give an ElGamal
key pair $(\mathsf{pk}, \mathsf{sk})$ to the server where $\mathsf{pk} = (G, p, g, h)$ and $h = g^{\mathsf{sk}}$ and we encrypt
all the h_i. Then for all $i \in \{0, \ldots, k\}$, the users do not know $h_i = g^{a_i}$ but know
the ElGamal ciphertext (c_i, d_i) such that $c_i = g^{r_i}$ and $d_i = h^{r_i} \cdot h_i$ where r_i is
randomly chosen. Since ElGamal is IND-CPA-secure, an attacker that chooses two
polynomials (f_0, f_1) cannot distinguish, for $0 \le i \le k$, if the ciphertext (c_i, d_i)
encrypts a coefficient of f_0 or of f_1. Thus, the attacks on the previous scheme are
no longer possible.

   Moreover, the user can check that $f(x) = y$ for a point (x, y) using the values
$\{(c_i, d_i)\}_{0 \le i \le k}$. We set $r(x) = \sum_{i=0}^{k} r_i \cdot x^i$. The user computes:

$$c = \prod_{i=0}^{k} c_i^{x^i} = \prod_{i=0}^{k} g^{r_i \cdot x^i} = g^{\sum_{i=0}^{k} r_i \cdot x^i} = g^{r(x)}.$$

On the other hand, he computes:

$$d' = \prod_{i=0}^{k} d_i^{x^i} = \left(\prod_{i=0}^{k} h^{r_i \cdot x^i}\right) \cdot \left(\prod_{i=0}^{k} g^{a_i \cdot x^i}\right) = h^{\sum_{i=0}^{k} r_i \cdot x^i} \cdot g^{\sum_{i=0}^{k} a_i \cdot x^i} = h^{r(x)} \cdot g^{f(x)}.$$

Finally, $(c, d') = (g^{r(x)}, h^{r(x)} \cdot g^{f(x)})$ is an ElGamal ciphertext of $g^{f(x)}$. Then, to convince the user that (x, y) is a valid point of f, the server proves that (c, d') is a ciphertext of g^y using a NIZKP of $\log_g(c) = \log_h(d'/g^y)$.

This leads us to the following formal definition of our scheme PIPE.

Definition 13. *Let* PIPE $=$ (setup, init, compute, verif) *be a PPE defined by:*

setup(λ): *Using the security parameter λ, it generates G a group of prime order p and a generator $g \in G$. It chooses a hash function* H $: \{0,1\}^* \to \mathbb{Z}_p^*$ *and it sets $F = \mathbb{Z}_p^*$. It sets* pub $= (G, p, g, H)$ *and returns* (pub, F).

init(pub, f): *We set $f(x) = \sum_{i=0}^{k} a_i \cdot x^i$. This algorithm picks* sk $\xleftarrow{\$} \mathbb{Z}_p^*$ *and computes* pk $= g^{\text{sk}}$. *For all $i \in \{0, \ldots, k\}$, it picks $r_i \xleftarrow{\$} \mathbb{Z}_p^*$ and computes $c_i = g^{r_i}$ and $d_i = $ pk$^{r_i} \cdot g^{a_i}$. Finally, it sets* vk $= (\{(c_i, d_i)\}_{0 \le i \le k}, $ pk$)$ *and returns* (vk, sk).

compute(pub, vk, x, sk, f): *Using* vk *which is equal to* $(\{(c_i, d_i)\}_{0 \le i \le k}, $ pk$)$, *this algorithm picks $\theta \xleftarrow{\$} \mathbb{Z}_p^*$ and computes*

$$c = \prod_{i=0}^{k} c_i^{x^i}, \quad \pi = (g^\theta, c^\theta, \theta + H(g^\theta, c^\theta) \cdot \text{sk}).$$

Finally, it returns $(f(x), \pi)$.

verif(pub, vk, x, y, π): *Using* vk $= (\{(c_i, d_i)\}_{0 \le i \le k}, $ pk$)$ *and* $\pi = (A, B, \omega)$, *this algorithm computes*

$$c = \prod_{i=0}^{k} c_i^{x^i}, \quad d = \frac{\left(\prod_{i=0}^{k} d_i^{x^i}\right)}{g^y}.$$

If $g^\omega = A \cdot $ pk$^{H(A,B)}$ and $c^\omega = B \cdot d^{H(A,B)}$, then the algorithm returns 1, else it returns 0.

5.3   Security

We prove the security of PIPE in our security model:

Lemma 1. *For any $k \in \mathbb{N}$,* PIPE *is k-IND-CFA-secure under the DDH assumption in the ROM.*

Lemma 2. PIPE *is unconditionally ZK-secure in the ROM.*

Lemma 3. PIPE *is unconditionally UNF-secure in the ROM.*

Proofs of Lemmas 1, 2 and 3 are presented in [BDG+17]. Using Lemmas 2 and 4 and Theorem 4, we have that PIPE is k-PP-secure. Hence, using Lemma 1 and Theorem 2, we deduce that PIPE is k-WPP-secure. Finally, we have the following theorem.

Theorem 5. *For any $k \in \mathbb{N}$, PIPE is is ZK, k-IND-CFA, k-PP, k-WPP and UNF-secure under the DDH assumption in the ROM.*

5.4   Comparison with PolyCommit$_{Ped}$

Kate *et al.* [KZG10] propose two CTP schemes that can be used as PPE schemes. Even if Kate *et al.* security model does not take into account IND-CFA security, we prove in [BDG+17] that one of these two schemes, called PolyCommit$_{Ped}$, is IND-CFA-secure. We recall the PolyCommit$_{Ped}$ scheme in Appendix A and we compare PIPE with this scheme in this section. Table 1 resumes this comparison.

The PIPE verification algorithm is in $\mathcal{O}(k)$ and the PolyCommit$_{Ped}$ one is in constant time. However, the PolyCommit$_{Ped}$ verification algorithm requires several pairing computations which are significantly costly in terms of computation time whereas PIPE only requires exponentiations and multiplication in a prime order group. Consequently, PIPE will be more efficient than PolyCommit$_{Ped}$ for sufficiently small polynomial degree k.

Table 1. Comparison of PIPE and PolyCommit$_{Ped}$.

	Setup size	Key size	Verif. cost	Pairing	Assumption	Security
PIPE	$\mathcal{O}(1)$	$\mathcal{O}(k)$	$\mathcal{O}(k)$	Paring free	DDH	IND-CFA
PolyCommit$_{Ped}$ [KZG10]	$\mathcal{O}(k)$	$\mathcal{O}(1)$	$\mathcal{O}(1)$	Pairing based	t-SDH	IND-CFA

The main advantage of PolyCommit$_{Ped}$ is that the verification key size is constant whereas the verification key size of PIPE is in $\mathcal{O}(k)$. However, the public setup size of PolyCommit$_{Ped}$ is in $\mathcal{O}(k)$ whereas the PIPE one is in constant. Since the client knows both the verification key and the public setup, PolyCommit$_{Ped}$ is advantageous only if each client has access to several polynomials simultaneously.

PIPE is secure under the DDH assumption whereas PolyCommit$_{Ped}$ is secure under the t-SDH assumption. Note that finding a scheme that is secure under a weaker assumption than t-SDH was an open problem mentioned by Kate *et al.* [KZG10]. Finally, note that the security PolyCommit$_{Ped}$ is proven in the standard model. A simple way to obtain a version of PIPE that is secure in the standard model is to use the interactive version of LogEq [CP93] instead of the non-interactive one in the algorithm. In return, it requires an interaction between the client and the server during the evaluation algorithm.

6   CFA Security for Commitments to Polynomials

Our scheme can be used as a *commitment to polynomials* scheme [KZG10] that is CFA-secure. We give an overview of a such scheme in Fig. 5. To commit a polynomial f, the committer computes $(\mathsf{vk}, \mathsf{sk}) \leftarrow \mathsf{init}(\mathsf{pub}, f)$ and returns the commitment vk to the user corresponding to the encryption of coefficients of the polynomial f. Then, the user sends his data to the committer (x_i in Fig. 5) and receives the results with correctness proof $((f(x_i), \mathsf{proof})$ in Fig. 5). To open the commitment, the committer reveals to the user the key vk together with f ($\mathsf{open}(\mathsf{vk}, f)$ in Fig. 5), then the user can open all the ElGamal ciphertexts of vk and check that they encrypt g^{a_i} where a_i are the coefficients of f.

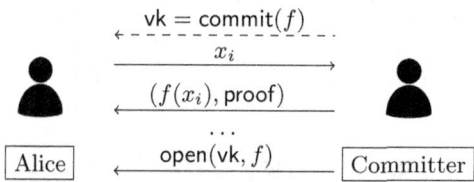

Fig. 5. PIPE scheme used as a commitment to polynomials scheme [KZG10].

7   Anonymous Private Polynomial Evaluation

In a practical scenario, the company does not allow anybody to interact freely with the computation server. The company distributes authentication keys to the clients, and the server uses a protocol to authenticate the client at the beginning of each interaction. It allows the server to verify that a client does not request to evaluate more than k points, where k is the degree of the polynomial. However, for a lot of applications, preserving the privacy of the clients is important. Guo *et al.* [GFLL15] propose an anonymous authentication mechanism for their scheme, which is broken and fixed by Gajera *et al.* [GND16].

We remark that anonymous authentication for PPE prevents the server from knowing how much points of the polynomial it gives to each client, leading to security issues. To solve this problem, we suggest that the server uses *k-times anonymous authentication* [TFS04]: this primitive allows a client to anonymously authenticate k times. If a client exceeds this limit, the server can identify him. Using such a scheme, the server can refuse to respond if the user requires more point evaluations than allowed, and the privacy of honest users is preserved.

8   Conclusion

In this paper, we gave a formal definition for a primitive called PPE. This primitive allows a company to delegate computations on a secret polynomial for users in a verifiable way. In essence, the user sends x and receives y from the server along with a proof of $y = f(x)$; even though he does not know the polynomial f. We proposed a security model of indistinguishability against chosen function attack (IND-CFA) and we built a PPE scheme called PIPE which is secure in this model. We proved that another scheme called PolyCommit$_{\mathsf{Ped}}$ [KZG10] is IND-CFA-secure, and we compared it with PIPE. Moreover, we exhibited a critical flaw in two papers which proposed schemes tackling the same problem. In the future, we aim at designing a scheme that is pairing free and that uses constant size verification keys. Another possible extension is to add practical privacy mechanism to protect the data sent by the users.

Acknowledgements. This research was conducted with the support of the FEDER program of 2014–2020, the region council of Auvergne-Rhône-Alpes, the support of the "Digital Trust" Chair from the University of Auvergne Foundation, the Indo-French Centre for the Promotion of Advanced Research (IFCPAR) and the Center Franco-Indien Pour La Promotion De La Recherche Avancée (CEFIPRA) through the project DST/CNRS 2015-03 under DST-INRIA-CNRS Targeted Programme.

A   PolyCommit$_{\mathsf{Ped}}$ Scheme [KZG10]

We recall the PolyCommit$_{\mathsf{Ped}}$ construction presented by Kate *et al.* [KZG10].

Definition 14. PolyCommit$_{\mathsf{Ped}}$ = (setup, init, compute, verif) *is a PPE scheme defined as follows:*

setup(λ): *Using the security parameter λ, it generates two groups $\mathbb{G}$ and $\mathbb{G}_T$ of prime order p (providing λ-bit security) such that there exists a symmetric bilinear pairing $e\colon \mathbb{G} \times \mathbb{G} \to \mathbb{G}_T$. Moreover, it chooses two generators g and h of $\mathbb{G}$ and picks $\alpha \leftarrow \mathbb{Z}_p^*$. It sets $F = \mathbb{Z}_p^*$, $\mathsf{pub} = (\mathbb{G}, \mathbb{G}_T, p, e, g, h, (g^\alpha, \ldots, g^{\alpha^k}), (h^\alpha, \ldots, h^{\alpha^k}))$ and returns (pub, F).*

init(pub, f): *Using $f(x) = \sum_{i=0}^{k} a_i \cdot x^i$, this algorithm chooses a random polynomial of degree k, $r(x) = \sum_{i=0}^{k} r_i \cdot x^i \in \mathbb{Z}_p[x]$ and sets $\mathsf{sk} = r(x)$. It computes $\mathcal{C} = \prod_{i=0}^{k}(g^{\alpha^i})^{a_i}(h^{\alpha^i})^{r_i} = g^{f(\alpha)}h^{r(\alpha)}$ and sets $\mathsf{vk} = \mathcal{C}$. Finally, it returns $(\mathsf{sk}, \mathsf{vk})$.*

compute($\mathsf{pub}, \mathsf{vk}, x_i, \mathsf{sk}, f$): *This algorithm computes $\psi_i(x) = (f(x) - f(x_i))/(x - x_i)$ and $\hat{\psi}_i(x) = (r(x) - r(x_i))/(x - x_i)$. Let $(\gamma_0, \ldots, \gamma_k)$ and $(\hat{\gamma}_0, \ldots, \hat{\gamma}_k)$ be such that $\psi_i(x) = \sum_{j=0}^{k} \gamma_j \cdot x^j$ and $\hat{\psi}_i(x) = \sum_{j=0}^{k} \hat{\gamma}_j \cdot x^j$. It computes $w_i = \prod_{j=0}^{k}(g^{\alpha^j})^{\gamma_j}(h^{\alpha^j})^{\hat{\gamma}_j} = g^{\psi_i(\alpha)}h^{\hat{\psi}_i(\alpha)}$. It sets $\pi = (x_i, r(x_i), w_i)$ and returns $(f(x_i), \pi)$.*

verif($\mathsf{pub}, \mathsf{vk}, x_i, f(x_i), \pi$): *If $e(\mathcal{C}, g)$ equals to $e(w_i, (g^\alpha)^{-x_i})e(g^{f(x_i)}h^{r(x_i)}, g)$, the algorithm outputs 1, else it outputs 0.*

References

[BBM00] Bellare, M., Boldyreva, A., Micali, S.: Public-key encryption in a multi-user setting: security proofs and improvements. In: Preneel, B. (ed.) EURO-CRYPT 2000. LNCS, vol. 1807, pp. 259–274. Springer, Heidelberg (2000). doi:10.1007/3-540-45539-6_18

[BDG+17] Bultel, X., Das, M.L., Gajera, H., Grault, D., Giraud, M., Lafourcade, P.:
          Verifiable private polynomial evaluation. Cryptology ePrint Archive, Report
          2017/756 (2017). http://eprint.iacr.org/2017/756
 [Bon98] Boneh, D.: The decision Diffie-Hellman problem. In: Buhler, J.P. (ed.) ANTS
          1998. LNCS, vol. 1423, pp. 48–63. Springer, Heidelberg (1998). doi:10.1007/
          BFb0054851
[CKKC13] Choi, S.G., Katz, J., Kumaresan, R., Cid, C.: Multi-client non-interactive
          verifiable computation. In: Sahai, A. (ed.) TCC 2013. LNCS, vol. 7785, pp.
          499–518. Springer, Heidelberg (2013). doi:10.1007/978-3-642-36594-2_28
  [CP93] Chaum, D., Pedersen, T.P.: Wallet databases with observers. In: Brickell,
          E.F. (ed.) CRYPTO 1992. LNCS, vol. 740, pp. 89–105. Springer, Heidelberg
          (1993). doi:10.1007/3-540-48071-4_7
 [CRR12] Canetti, R., Riva, B., Rothblum, G.N.: Two protocols for delegation of
          computation. In: Smith, A. (ed.) ICITS 2012. LNCS, vol. 7412, pp. 37–61.
          Springer, Heidelberg (2012). doi:10.1007/978-3-642-32284-6_3
  [DH76] Diffie, W., Hellman, M.E.: New directions in cryptography. IEEE Trans. Inf.
          Theor. **22**(6), 644–654 (1976)
 [ElG85] ElGamal, T.: A public key cryptosystem and a signature scheme based on
          discrete logarithms. IEEE Trans. Inf. Theor. **31**, 469–472 (1985)
 [Fel87] Feldman, P.: A practical scheme for non-interactive verifiable secret sharing.
          In: 28th FOCS, pp. 427–437. IEEE Computer Society Press, October 1987
 [FG12]   Fiore, D., Gennaro, R.: Publicly verifiable delegation of large polynomials
          and matrix computations, with applications. In: ACM CCS 2012. ACM Press
          (2012)
[FIPR05] Freedman, M.J., Ishai, Y., Pinkas, B., Reingold, O.: Keyword search
          and oblivious pseudorandom functions. In: Kilian, J. (ed.) TCC 2005.
          LNCS, vol. 3378, pp. 303–324. Springer, Heidelberg (2005). doi:10.1007/
          978-3-540-30576-7_17
 [FNP04] Freedman, M.J., Nissim, K., Pinkas, B.: Efficient private matching and
          set intersection. In: Cachin, C., Camenisch, J.L. (eds.) EUROCRYPT
          2004. LNCS, vol. 3027, pp. 1–19. Springer, Heidelberg (2004). doi:10.1007/
          978-3-540-24676-3_1
 [FS87]   Fiat, A., Shamir, A.: How to prove yourself: practical solutions to identi-
          fication and signature problems. In: Odlyzko, A.M. (ed.) CRYPTO 1986.
          LNCS, vol. 263, pp. 186–194. Springer, Heidelberg (1987). doi:10.1007/
          3-540-47721-7_12
[GFLL15] Guo, L., Fang, Y., Li, M., Li, P.: Verifiable privacy-preserving monitoring for
          cloud-assisted mHealth systems. In: INFOCOM. IEEE (2015)
 [GGP10] Gennaro, R., Gentry, C., Parno, B.: Non-interactive verifiable computing:
          outsourcing computation to untrusted workers. In: Rabin, T. (ed.) CRYPTO
          2010. LNCS, vol. 6223, pp. 465–482. Springer, Heidelberg (2010). doi:10.
          1007/978-3-642-14623-7_25
 [GND16] Gajera, H., Naik, S., Das, M.L.: On the security of "Verifiable Privacy-
          Preserving Monitoring for Cloud-Assisted mHealth Systems". In: Ray,
          I., Gaur, M.S., Conti, M., Sanghi, D., Kamakoti, V. (eds.) ICISS 2016.
          LNCS, vol. 10063, pp. 324–335. Springer, Cham (2016). doi:10.1007/
          978-3-319-49806-5_17
 [KZG10] Kate, A., Zaverucha, G.M., Goldberg, I.: Constant-size commitments to
          polynomials and their applications. In: Abe, M. (ed.) ASIACRYPT 2010.
          LNCS, vol. 6477, pp. 177–194. Springer, Heidelberg (2010). doi:10.1007/
          978-3-642-17373-8_11

[LP02] Lindell, Y., Pinkas, B.: Privacy preserving data mining. J. Crypt. **15**(3), 177–206 (2002)

[NP99] Naor, M., Pinkas, B.: Oblivious transfer and polynomial evaluation. In: Proceedings of the Thirty-First Annual ACM Symposium on Theory of Computing, STOC 1999, pp. 245–254. ACM, New York (1999)

[PHGR13] Parno, B., Howell, J., Gentry, C., Raykova, M.: Pinocchio: nearly practical verifiable computation. In: 2013 IEEE Symposium on Security and Privacy. IEEE (2013)

[Pol78] Pollard, J.M.: A Monte Carlo method for index computation (mod p). Math. Comput. **32**, 918–924 (1978). Springer

[PRV12] Parno, B., Raykova, M., Vaikuntanathan, V.: How to delegate and verify in public: verifiable computation from attribute-based encryption. In: Cramer, R. (ed.) TCC 2012. LNCS, vol. 7194, pp. 422–439. Springer, Heidelberg (2012). doi:10.1007/978-3-642-28914-9_24

[PST13] Papamanthou, C., Shi, E., Tamassia, R.: Signatures of correct computation. In: Sahai, A. (ed.) TCC 2013. LNCS, vol. 7785, pp. 222–242. Springer, Heidelberg (2013). doi:10.1007/978-3-642-36594-2_13

[Sha79] Shamir, A.: How to share a secret. Commun. Assoc. Comput. Mach. **22**(11), 612–613 (1979)

[TFS04] Teranishi, I., Furukawa, J., Sako, K.: k-times anonymous authentication (extended abstract). In: Lee, P.J. (ed.) ASIACRYPT 2004. LNCS, vol. 3329, pp. 308–322. Springer, Heidelberg (2004). doi:10.1007/978-3-540-30539-2_22

Author Index

Printed in the United States
By Bookmasters